Learning & Using
Study Skills

Learning & Using Study Skills

A Guide for Academic Success

Barbara L. Marrs

Phoenix Learning Resources, LLC

LEARNING & USING STUDY SKILLS

Revised Edition, Second Printing

Printed in the United States of America

Design and Production — Alice A Christ
    Personal Efficiency Program Inc., Sierra Vista, AZ
Cover Design — Phoenix Learning Resources
Cover Photos — istockphotos
Illustrations — George Saunders, Jr., Los Angeles, CA
Copyediting — Christle Tomita, La Habra, CA

Library of Congress Catalog No: 91-060376

Phoenix Learning Resources, LLC

910 Church Street • Honesdale, PA 18431
1-800-228-9345 • Fax: 570-253-3227 • www.phoenixlr.com

Item# 2875   ISBN 978-0-7915-2875-4

To my husband, Buck,
and to our children,
Terri, Robyn, and Sam

Preface to Students

Are study skills important? You bet they are! In fact, the College Board claims that study skills are the key to learning how to learn and are necessary for success in the five basic academic subjects of reading, writing, speaking and listening, mathematics, and reasoning.

This book was written to help you learn how to learn by focusing on the challenges that high school students typically have in study skills and by providing exercises for improving skills in the following 16 areas:

Time Management
Study Environment
Personal Aspects
Study-Reading
Listening for Notemaking
Exam Strategies
Writing Non-Fiction Assignments
Library Research
Learning How to Improve Your Math Skills
Memory for Learning
Efficient Reading for Speed and Comprehension
Vocabulary Development
Concentration While Learning
Health and Vision
Attitudes
Campus Involvement

Each chapter begins with a Scenario which expresses a school-related problem or situation common to high school students today. The Scenario is followed by Stimulus Questions which get you to think about the subject of the chapter. The next section is informational, providing answers to questions like the following: What is this skill? Why is it important? How do you do use this skill or improve in this skill?

Exercises are provided for practicing and applying the information presented in the chapter. Once you have finished the chapter, you have the opportunity to give your opinion of it with the section called "Your Turn to Talk Back."

You may use this book as a class text or as an individual program. You may begin at the beginning and work your way through the book, or you may be asked to complete only those chapters which address areas which have been identified as challenges for you. However you use the book, it will help you to improve your study skills and increase your success as a student.

Remember that the Internet has many websites and web pages that you can browse to learn more about learning skills. Ask your teacher to recommend some of these Internet materials. In addition, you can search the Internet for material on any of the 16 areas mentioned above by using the search box and filling in a word or a phrase, such as "time management," "memory," or "exam strategies" that describe the study skill that you are looking for.

Acknowledgments

I am grateful to:

Frank L. Christ for his inspiration, encouragement, and guidance on how to structure and organize the content. I also appreciate his generosity in letting me use his PLRS Learning Cycle and his Listening/Notemaking Record as well as content from "Six Steps to Better Management of Your Study Time" adapted by Dr. Richard Marrs.

Dr. Richard F. (Buck) Marrs for developing Exercise HV-3: Your Body's Warning Signs and Exercise HV-4: Breathing to Reduce Stress. As an educator psychologist his advice was most helpful. As my husband, he encouraged me throughout this project with his love, patience, and support.

Alice Christ for her sensitivity to the content and the students who would use this book, her artistry in designing the layout, her meticulous attention to details, and her delightful attitude and upbeat sense of humor.

CONTENTS

Chapter 1
Time Management

Chapter 1
Time Management

SCENARIO

Robyn has known for three weeks that her English paper is due on Monday, but she hasn't started it yet. She had planned to catch up by spending the whole weekend writing her paper. Then she was invited to the football game and the dance afterward on Friday night. "Oh well, I still have all day Saturday and Sunday to finish my paper," she thought. So she went to the game. An invitation to lunch with friends on Saturday cut into most of the day. Then a date to the movies that night was more than she could resist. Now, it is Sunday, and Robyn is overwhelmed by her assignment. She knows that there is no way that she can complete it by Monday.

Looking for sympathy, Robyn calls her friend, Stacy.

Robyn: Stacy, what are you going to do about your English paper? I haven't even started yet!

Stacy: Oh, I finished mine.

Robyn: When did you write it? You went to the football game and the dance on Friday, and you went out to lunch and to the movies on Saturday just like I did.

Stacy: I started it three weeks ago and spent a couple of hours each week working on it. I finished it on Thursday.

Robyn: I wish I had done that. I'll probably be up all night, and I still may not finish!

Which student do you identify with? What did Stacy do that Robyn failed to do? You're right if you said that Stacy *planned* ahead. Stacy *managed her time.*

STIMULUS QUESTIONS

1. Do you often feel that there are not enough hours in the day to do all that you need or want to do? Describe what happens when you feel this way.

_____

_____

_____

2. Are you frequently hurrying and scurrying to catch up? To arrive on time? To finish an assignment? What could you do to avoid hurrying to catch up?

_____

_____

_____

3. Do you procrastinate? That is, do you put off doing certain tasks until later only to find that later there isn't enough time to complete the task? Do you hear yourself say things like, "I'll do it tomorrow," or "I've waited this long, one more day won't make any difference?" Tell about the last time you procrastinated and what happened as a result.

_____

_____

_____

4. Think about and write down 3 things that you have been putting off—at school, at home, or at work.

■ _____

■ _____

■ _____

5.   Read over your list of 3 items. Could the delayed completion of these tasks have a harmful effect on you? Tell what you think may happen as a result of your procrastination on each of the 3 items you wrote down.

■ _____

_____

■ _____

_____

■ _____

_____

Look back over your responses to the stimulus questions. What conclusions can you draw about how you use your time? If you are not satisfied with how you spend your time, you are ready to learn the techniques for time management offered in this chapter.

LEARNING ABOUT TIME MANAGEMENT

What is Time Management?

Time Management is planning and monitoring the best way to spend your time so that your intended use of time matches your actual use of time. By following a plan for time management, you will be able to organize your tasks so that the most important ones get done on time. Through time management, you will be able to use time to your advantage; that is, you will avoid wasting time which will allow you to complete the things you must do and still have time for the things you want to do.

Why is Time Management Important?

Time Management is important because it helps you to focus on the things that need to be done and to schedule enough time to do them. By managing your time, you can work toward your goals and have time for both work and play. By learning how to manage your time, you can avoid wasting time. You can also reduce stress because you have time to do all of the things you need and want to do. By following a time management plan, you can resist the temptation to put off until later those important things which must be done today.

How to Do Time Management?

The basic rule of time management is to know what you have to do and plan enough time to do it. Before you can begin to manage your time, you need to decide what your priorities are. In other words, what is most important to you in your life at this time? After you identify your priorities, consider what it is that you hope to do in the near future. Is your goal to go to college, or do you plan to go to work after you complete high school? What are your needs? What do you need to do or to have to feel successful? By observing how you actually spend your time on a day-to-day basis, you can discover whether or not you are using your time in a way that will help you to reach your goals and fulfill your needs.

The following exercises are designed to teach you ways to manage yourself and your tasks so that you can use your time wisely. You will learn how to use a daily "To Do" list and a "Weekly Schedule" to set priorities, to avoid procrastination, to make time for school, homework and study, church and family, part-time work, after-school activities, and free time to use as you please.

EXERCISES

TM-1. Using the Daily "To Do" List

Without a doubt, one of the most useful time management tools is the simple "To Do" list. By making a "To Do" list for each day, you are creating a daily time plan to help you keep track of your time and your tasks.

Fill-out the "Things To Do Today" form (or, use a piece of notebook paper, a small memo pad, or a calendar). Be sure to list all of the things you need and want to do today. For example, an assignment that is due tomorrow must be done today, but a shopping trip could wait until another time. Completing the assignment is a higher priority (more important) than shopping.

THINGS TO DO TODAY	COMPLETED

TM-2. Ranking Your Tasks According to Priority

Go back over your list and place a number 1 to the left of your top priority tasks—those that *must* be done *today*. Then, go over your list again, and put a number 2 to the left of those things which *should* be done today, but which could be done tomorrow if you run out of time today. You are now ready to begin to follow your list. To get the most out of your day, complete the number 1 priority items first, then the number 2 items. Things that you cannot finish today can be carried over to tomorrow's list. Keep in mind that what may have been a number 2 priority today may be a number 1 tomorrow.

Just as smart business people think ahead and plan their "To Do" list the night before, you should find a few minutes each night to write out your "To Do" list for the next day. To keep what you need to accomplish fresh in your mind, review your list in the morning, perhaps as you eat breakfast. You, like a business person, can make the best use of your day by managing your time and your tasks and deciding your priorities.

TM-3. Deciding Your Priorities

Before you are ready to use a weekly time plan, you need to decide your priorities and evaluate your study needs. What do you really want: To prepare yourself for the current job market? To prepare for college? To make money? Or to have more play and leisure time?

You may be confusing yourself if your *intended time* does not match your *actual time*. *Intended time* is based on your goals, ambitions, or dreams. For example, you may intend to have a job in the future that provides you a style of living that requires much money. Your *actual time* spent is the time and energy you are actually spending right now to accomplish your intended dreams or goals.

---

1. Assess your *intentions* or *goals*
Identify what is most important in your life at this time by numbering in order of importance (1, 2, 3, 4, etc.) the activities in which you should be participating.

___ Prepare for college by studying   ___ Church activities

___ Sports activities   ___ Work/Money

___ Family activities   ___ Other

___ Leisure (play, TV, dating, Internet, etc.)   ___ Other

---

2. Assess your *actual time*
Look at the same list and number the items (1, 2, 3, 4, 5, etc.) according to the actual time you spend on each item. BE HONEST. For example, if you spend the most time on sports, label it #1.

___ Prepare for college by studying   ___ Church activities

___ Sports activities   ___ Work Money

___ Family activities   ___ Other

___ Leisure (play, TV, dating, etc.)   ___ Other

___ Surfing the Internet   ___ Other

Stress and confusion may be caused by your *actual time* not matching your *intentions* or *goals*. To release stress and eliminate any confusion, change your *actual time* to match your *intentions*. For example, give up some leisure time so that you can study more.

TM-4. Evaluating Your Study Needs

Now that you've decided your priorities, let's look at your courses and find out how easy or difficult they are going to be. Follow the directions to complete the "Evaluating Your Study Needs" chart on the next page.

1. List all your courses by title.

2. Write in your teachers' names.

3. Fill in their room location (building and office or room number) and conference period so that you can find them when you need help.

4. If you have graded quizzes, check the appropriate box. Record in the next column the number of major tests that you will have.

5. Check if class participation is graded. You are being graded if your teacher writes in a grade book during question periods.

6. Under "Written Assignments" and "Outside Reading," either write in "little," "some," or "much." Use abbreviations, if necessary. If you have no assignments, write "None."

7. Check (✓) if you have had some recent preparation for the course.

8. Under "Performance in Similar Course," record "superior," "average," or "could be improved."

9. After reviewing each course's requirements, your preparation, and past performance, write in the final box opposite each course title a YES or NO. For each YES answer in that last column, see your teacher for help or to find out where you can get help.

EVALUATING YOUR STUDY NEEDS

Class Title	Teacher	Room/ Office Location	Conf. Period	Quizzes	Tests	Class Participation	Written Assignments	Outside Reading	Course Preparation	Performance in Similar Course	Need for special Help

TM-5. Estimating Your Study Time

To help you determine how much study time you need, write down each of your classes and the grade you hope to receive in each. To challenge yourself, set your grade a little higher than you think you can easily reach. Spend a few minutes thinking about each class—how much reading, writing, homework and studying is necessary for you to receive the grade you desire. Then, estimate the amount of time you will need to spend each week for each class and write it on the following chart.

The general rule for college classes is that two hours of preparation and study are necessary for each hour of class.

ESTIMATING YOUR STUDY TIME

PERIOD	CLASS TITLE	DESIRED GRADE	TIME NEEDED

TM-6. Making Up a Schedule Based on Your Goals

Read all of these directions before you make up your weekly schedule (at the end of this exercise). Check off each direction as you complete it.

____ 1. Use the blocks in the left-hand side of the Weekly Schedule blank to write in time periods as suggested by your teacher.

____ 2. Record class and lab times in the appropriate day and period blocks.

____ 3. Record your travel times to and from campus.

____ 4. Record meal times if you have regular times for meals.

____ 5. Record all regularly scheduled personal activities such as clubs, employment, and athletics. Record any travel time to and from these activities as well.

____ 6. Record any special things that you do or need to do on a regular weekly basis.

____ 7. Study the diagram of the PLRS Learning Cycle, on the next page, before you add any more information to your schedule.

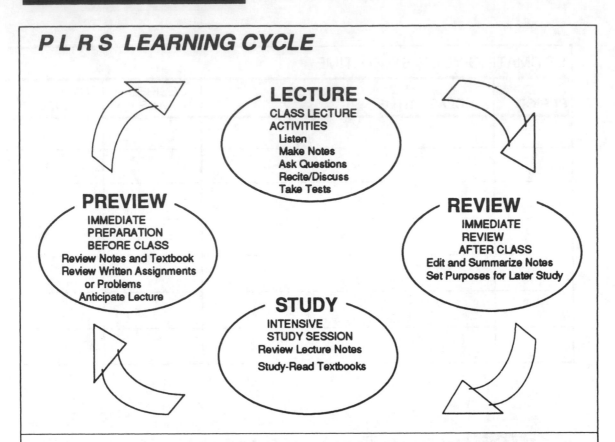

P L R S LEARNING CYCLE

PREVIEW 1 This preparation before class is similar to a warm-up before a physical activity. It develops a specific readiness for class as previous lecture notes and textbook study notes are reviewed. Written assignments and problems are proofread before being turned in.

LECTURE 2 Formal learning begins in the classroom where students and teachers engage in dialogue. Through efficient listening/notemaking techniques and by means of questions, frequent recitations, and lively discussion, learning takes place in a dynamic atmosphere.

REVIEW 3 This active response to classroom learning includes both recall and reorganization of the lecture and preparation for later intensive study. This review requires that lecture notes be edited and summarized and that any assignments be planned while its details are still fresh in the mind. The review following each course's final weekly class session can be expanded into a full review of all material covered in the past weeks (assignments and lectures).

STUDY 4 This intensive session normally occurs the night before the next class lecture. It begins with a brief review of the latest lecture notes. Then the textbook assignment is overviewed and mastered with a study-reading technique such as Survey-Question/Study-Read/Summarize-Test. Questions and personal reactions to the study-reading should be written down to be brought up for clarification and discussion in class.

By following the recommendations of the *PLRS LEARNING CYCLE*, you will increase dramatically the number of times you work at learning with little, if any, increase in your total study time. Some students will probably spend less time in the intensive study sessions because of the class previews and reviews. Cramming before major tests will be replaced by the weekly cumulative reviews that conclude each week's course work. *The key to efficient, effective learning lies in following the PLRS LEARNING CYCLE.*

___**8.** Whenever possible, schedule a preview time (5 to 30 minutes) some time before each class. During this preview, look over what you have studied the night before and review your notes from the previous day's class. On your schedule blank, use "P" to indicate this preview time.

___**9.** Whenever possible, schedule a review time (5 to 30 minutes) after your classes and before you begin to study any new material. Use this time to edit and summarize your notes. You could also look over any assignments that were given and begin to plan how you will do them. On your schedule blank, use "R" to indicate this review time. (Example: R/Chemistry)

___**10.** Schedule a weekly review for each course. Do it before Saturday, if possible. Actually, a good time is immediately after your last class on Friday. This weekly review gives you an opportunity to spread out all of the past week's notes along with the reading assignments for each class to see what you have accomplished in the past week during class and study time. You can also look ahead to plan next week by reading each course syllabus to determine how much reading you will need to do, what projects are due, and if any tests are scheduled.

___**11.** Schedule now your intensive study time for each class. Ordinarily, study the night before your next day's class. For example, since you have classes on Monday, Sunday night is a study night. When you schedule study time, be task-oriented rather than time-oriented. Think "blocks of time," not hours of study time. Start your study period with the courses you like the least or those that you are not doing well in. Try to study the same subjects at the same time each day. Although this seems to be a mechanical way of scheduling, you will find that such a routine can help you develop a pattern for efficient and effective study. On your schedule blank, use "S" to indicate this study time. (Example: S/Math)

___**12.** Keep open some late afternoon time for daily physical activity. Remember that the research indicates that regular exercise will not only give you a general sense of well-being, but can also reduce tension and help you face the pressures of a tough class, study, and work schedule.

___**13.** Label some blocks of time as OPEN TIME for emergencies.

___**14.** Save Friday night, all day Saturday, and some of Sunday for you to play, to relax, to do whatever you want to do. This is your reward for sticking to your schedule during the week.

___**15.** When you have completed filling out the Weekly Schedule blank, share it with a friend or take it to a teacher or counselor to have it reviewed.

WEEKLY SCHEDULE

Time Periods	SUN	MON	TUE	WED	THU	FRI	SAT

TM-7. Monitoring How Much You Study

Use the following exercise to check up on how much studying you are actually doing. It takes only a few minutes at the end of each day for seven consecutive days. Record honestly the amount of time you spend studying as well as time that you spend on time-wasting activities.

Directions:

1. List classes in the first column. Put the hardest or least liked first; the easiest and most liked last.

2. Record total number of class and lab hours (if any) for each course.

3. Under "Actual Study Time" are columns for seven consecutive days and a total. First label each column with abbreviations for weekdays starting with today. (ex: W Th F S S M T)

4. Each night before you go to bed, add up how much time you actually spent on each course reading, writing, reviewing, studying outside of your lecture and lab time and record that number in the appropriate column opposite course title. If you did nothing, put zero (0) in column for that day. Estimate 1/4, 1/3, 1/2 hours.

5. Do it every day for seven consecutive days

6. For each course, add across the number of study hours for all seven days and record in "Total" column. Next, add down each day's column to get total hours spent studying each day. Finally, add the total column to get number of hours you studied during the week for all courses. Enter that figure at bottom of "Total" column.

7. Record also on the "Time Wasting Activities" form below, your time wasters and the hours you spend on each daily. The one most high school students seem to spend lots of time doing, "watching TV," has already been listed. List some others on the lines below it. Add up at the end of each day the time you spend on each. At the end of seven days, add across and down for totals.

8. Show this worksheet to your teacher or counselor for comments and suggestions.

STUDY SCHEDULE WORKSHEET

CLASS TITLE	CLASS HOURS	ACTUAL STUDY TIME: ONE WEEK SEVEN CONSECUTIVE DAYS							TOTAL
TOTALS									

TIME WASTING ACTIVITIES

ACTIVITY	ACTUAL TIME WASTED: ONE WEEK SEVEN CONSECUTIVE DAYS							TOTAL
Watching TV								
Surfing the Web								
TOTALS								

TM-8. Revising Your Schedule - If Necessary

Directions: Use this extra form if you drop or add a class, change working hours, reschedule a class or lab, or make new personal commitments. As before, follow the directions in TM-6 as you revise your schedule.

WEEKLY SCHEDULE							

YOUR TURN TO TALK BACK

Look back over this chapter on time management and think for a few moments about the things you were asked to do. Answer the questions below on a separate sheet of paper and give it to your teacher.

■ What did you like about this chapter on time management?

■ What didn't you like about this chapter?

■ What did you learn about time management?

■ How will you put into practice what you learned about time management as a result of completing this chapter?

■ What Internet source did you find useful for this chapter?

Chapter 2
Study Environment

I spent hours studying, and I can't remember a thing!

Chapter 2
Study Environment

SCENARIO

Manny: I just don't get it. I spent hours in my room last night reading for the history test, and I can't remember a thing! I set myself up perfectly for a long night of studying. I had my favorite tunes blasting on the radio to drown out noise from my family, I had my pillows piled up on the bed so I could relax while I read. I was really organized; I mean I had my book, my notes, and my snacks right where I could reach them. I only left my room when I got a phone call. The book was so boring I just kept falling asleep, but every time I woke up, I started studying again. I really kept at it, but it was just a total waste of time. Today I couldn't remember one thing I studied last night!

Brian: Yeah, I know what you mean. I tried to study at the kitchen table, but it was useless. My sister sat across from me talking to her boyfriend on the phone for over an hour. The kids had the TV blasting so I kept losing my train of thought. Every time I looked at the refrigerator, I got hungry so I had to keep getting up to get another snack. No matter how hard I tried to study, I just couldn't seem to do it. It was a total waste of time.

STIMULUS QUESTIONS

1.   Like Manny and Brian, do you have trouble studying because there is too much noise or too many interruptions where you study? _____ Write down the things that bother you when you try to study.

   _____

   _____

   _____

2.   Do you have a regular place to study that you can call your own—where you can keep your study materials and supplies? Tell about the place where you usually study on the lines below.

   _____

   _____

   _____

3.   Are there too many things that attract your attention where you study so that you find it hard to pay attention to your study materials? _____ What do you find yourself thinking about or paying attention to when you try to study?

   _____

   _____

   _____

4.   Do you often fall asleep where you study? _____ If staying awake while you study is a problem for you, write down the reasons you think you have this problem.

   _____

   _____

   _____

5   Is the light where you study too bright or too dim so that you strain your eyes to read? _____ If there is a problem with the light where you read, what can you do to make it better?

_____

_____

_____

6.   Spend a few minutes thinking about the classes you are taking and the types of assignments you expect to have. Then, look over the list of items below and check off the ones you might need to keep in the place where you study. Be sure to write down any additional items you may need on the blank lines.

_____ index cards	_____ computer disks
_____ paper clips	_____ correction fluid
_____ pencils	_____ pencil sharpener
_____ erasers	_____ ruler
_____ ink pens	_____ straight-edge
_____ marking pens	_____ folders
_____ notebook paper	_____ notebook
_____ graph paper	_____ binder
_____ dictionary	_____ scissors
_____ hole punch	_____ printer paper and/or cartridges
_____ tape	_____ _____
_____ _____	_____ _____

Are the materials that you need to study or do homework readily at hand where you study? _____ What is missing?

_____

_____

_____

Now that you've done some thinking about where you study, read the questions below and the responses to each to see if the place where you study is a good environment for learning. As you continue to work your way through this chapter, you will learn how to improve your study environment.

LEARNING ABOUT GOOD STUDY ENVIRONMENT

What Is a Good Study Environment?

A good study environment should be a place where you have few to no interruptions. It should be a quiet place where you can think, read, and do your homework. There should be few things or people to distract you.

Whether you study at the library, at a friend's house, in your room, or under a tree, you should make sure that there is a good source of light. Light that is too bright or too dim causes eyestrain during study. Once your eyes feel tired, it is hard to go on studying.

The ideal place to study should have a table or a desk and a straight back chair. You will stay more alert and be able to study longer if you maintain good posture while studying. Students who relax too much (like Manny did on his bed) when trying to study often become drowsy and fall asleep. That is why it is better to study sitting at a table or desk instead of lying on a sofa or a bed when homework or studying must be done.

A good study environment should have all of the materials that you will need to complete your assignments, such as: textbooks, class notes, pens or pencils, paper, pencil sharpener, ruler, stapler, hole punch, dictionary, and any reference books you might need. If these things are not available where you study, be sure to plan ahead and take them with you. The best situation is when you can leave all of your study materials in one place where they will not be disturbed between study sessions. Time spent searching for supplies or running out to sharpen pencils takes away from your study time.

Why Is Having a Good Study Environment Important?

It is important to have a good study environment so that you can concentrate on your work and avoid wasting time like Manny and Brian did. You cannot learn anything unless you pay attention to it. If you are singing along with your favorite songs on the radio, answering the phone, getting up to get snacks, watching TV, talking with friends, or napping, you cannot be studying and learning at the same time. Finding a good place to do homework and to study will help you to learn and do more in less time—and, you will have more time left over to spend with friends and doing your favorite leisure time activities.

How Can You Create a Good Study Environment?

To create a good study environment for yourself, look for a place to study that is easy for you to get to, that is quiet, that has good light for reading, that has a table and chair, and that has as few things as possible to distract you from your work. Find out if the school or public library is open during the hours when you need to do your work. Look around to see if there is a quiet corner where you can study. If you prefer to study at home, is there a room away from family noise where you might work; for example, your bedroom, a den, the kitchen, the garage? A card table, a chair, a lamp, and a box of school supplies can turn any corner into a study area.

EXERCISES

SE-1. Evaluate Your Study Environment

List on the lines below the 3 places where you study most often.

1)_____ 2)_____ 3)_____

Read the following 14 statements and circle T or F to show whether each statement is true or false for each of your study places.

STUDY ENVIRONMENT	1	2	3
1. I am often interrupted by other people when I study here.	T F	T F	T F
2. I see many things here which remind me of other things besides studying.	T F	T F	T F
3. Music and sounds from TV often bother me when I study here.	T F	T F	T F
4. The phone often rings when I study here.	T F	T F	T F
5. I hear others "goofing off" when I study here.	T F	T F	T F
6. When I study here I usually take too many breaks.	T F	T F	T F
7. The distractions in this place especially bother me.	T F	T F	T F
8. I rarely study here at the same time each day.	T F	T F	T F
9. I have a hard time getting back to work after I take a break in this place.	T F	T F	T F

	T F	T F	T F
10. I talk to others when I study here.	T F	T F	T F
11. It is hard to study here because it is too warm (or too cold).	T F	T F	T F
12. The lighting and the furniture in this place are not very good for studying.	T F	T F	T F
13. I am distracted by members of the opposite sex in this place.	T F	T F	T F
14. This is not an enjoyable place for me to study.	T F	T F	T F
(Count your true and false responses for each column.) **TOTALS** (T)			
(F)			

The column with the most FALSE responses is the best place for you to study. The column with the most TRUE responses is the place where you are distracted the most.

Adapted from Nataupsky, Heulf, Bermudez. *The USAF Academy How-To-Study Program: A Handbook for Volunteer Counselors*, 2nd Edition. (FJSRL Technical Report 80-0016, July 1980) p. 37.

SE-2. Improving Your Study Environment

Look back over your written responses to the Stimulus Questions at the beginning of this chapter. Keeping what you wrote in mind, focus on the study environment that you determined was best for you in SE-1. Now, think about and write down how you can change the place you regularly study to make it a better environment for learning. If you weren't able to identify a good study environment, think about the places to study that are available to you. Then describe the best place you have to study and write down anything that you can do to make it a better learning environment.

The best place for me to study is _____

I can improve my learning environment by _____

_____

_____

_____

YOUR TURN TO TALK BACK

Think back on what you read and learned about creating a good study environment. Look back over the exercises you were asked to complete, and then respond to the questions below on a separate sheet of paper. Give your answers to your teacher.

■ What did you like about this chapter on study environment?

■ What didn't you like about this chapter?

■ What did you learn about creating a good study environment from this chapter?

■ What will you do about your study environment as a result of doing this chapter?

■ What Internet source did you find useful for this chapter?

Chapter 3
Personal Aspects

I just can't handle what's going on at home. I can't stay there and study!

Chapter 3
Personal Aspects

SCENARIO

Rob: Hey, Kevin, did you study for the biology test last night?

Kevin: No! I forgot all about it. My parents were fighting again last night. And, they were nagging me over and over about my grades. I just couldn't take it any more, so I went over to the Community Center and played basketball. I don't know how I am supposed to study when I don't have any peace and quiet at home. Sometimes I just feel like running away. Man, I know I'll fail that test. Then, my parents will really come down on me.

STIMULUS QUESTIONS:

1. What do you think will be on Kevin's mind when he takes his biology test?

   _____

   _____

2. Maybe you don't have the same problems that Kevin has, but are there other personal things like nagging parents, annoying brothers and sisters, girlfriends, or boyfriends that upset or concern you and keep you from doing your best at school? Write down your problems or concerns on the lines below.

   _____

   _____

   _____

3. Think about and write down the ways you think that personal problems interfere with learning.

   _____

   _____

   _____

4. Look back over the problems you wrote down. Think about how you try to solve your problems. For example, is there someone special like a best friend, your mom or dad, guardian, teacher or counselor you talk to about your problems? Write down how you go about getting help for solving your problems or coping with things that concern you. Be sure to include the people you see or the places you go for help. If you think that there is no place to go for help with your problems, simply write the word HELP in big letters on the lines below.

   _____

   _____

   _____

   By reading the questions and responses which follow, you will find out how personal aspects of life like problems, feelings, and conflicts affect you and your performance at school.

LEARNING ABOUT PERSONAL ASPECTS

What Are the Personal Aspects of Life That Can Interfere with Doing Your Best in School?

Do you ever worry about the way you look or the way you dress? Do you wonder if other people like you? Do you sometimes hate your hair? Your body? Your face? Do you often embarrass yourself? Does your skin break out? Are your friends pressuring you to do one thing while your parents demand that you do another? Are you sometimes confused about how you "fit in?" Are you having feelings that you've never had before? Do you sometimes feel like you are out of control?

If you've asked yourself these or similar questions, you are not alone. Most people have fears and concerns similar to those expressed in the questions raised in the paragraph above. It is normal for young people to be concerned with their appearance, popularity, dates, grades, money, peer pressure, friendships, and driving. The list goes on. As you can see, being a teenager or young adult can be highly stressful! Not only are teenagers dealing with all sorts of personal problems, they are dealing with constant change—physical as well as emotional. When too much change occurs at once, or if change is difficult to adjust to, a person may feel like he or she cannot handle things. This feeling may lead to low self-esteem or a poor self-concept. A lack of confidence increases these feelings. The less a person thinks of himself or herself, the harder it is to be succesful in life.

Any aspect of life that causes you to worry so that it takes up most of your time and energy will interfere with your school work. The trick for success in school is to learn to take care of your problems as soon as possible. When you face a problem that you can't handle yourself, then you need to use the resources around you. Get the best of your problems before they get the best of you.

Why Is It Important to Deal with the Personal Aspects of Going to School?

Too often when we fail to do something about our problems we become "stuck" in them. We can think of nothing else. Pretty soon our problems become too big to handle, and they overshadow everything else in our lives. To study and learn something, we have to pay attention to it. But it is difficult, if not impossible, to pay attention to something we are trying to study if we can only think of our problems. Therefore, to be successful in school, we must deal with the things that upset us by either resolving our problems or by learning how to cope with the things that we cannot change. A mind that is free from worry is free to learn.

How Can You Cope with Your Personal Problems or Challenges?

You can cope with your personal problems or challenges by following the three steps described below.

■ *First: Identify the problem.*

What is the problem? Exactly who or what is upsetting you? How do you feel about what is going on in your life? What do you want to happen or to change? What would make you happy? Who has control over the situation? Can you solve the problem by yourself, or do you need some help?

■ *Second: Take responsibility for the problem.*

Once you have figured out what the problem is you can begin to figure out what to do about it. Begin by taking responsibility for the problem. Looking to blame someone or something for your troubles is a waste of time. The act of blaming brings you no closer to a solution. Instead of wasting your physical and emotional energy placing blame, use your energy to collect all of the data that you can to help you understand the problem. As you collect more information, you will begin to see possible solutions to your problem.

■ *Third: Use your resources for solving the problem.*

Many resources are available to help you resolve or cope with your problems. You will then be able to think more clearly about what you should do.

Look to your family first. Many times your parents or guardians are the best ones to talk to because they may know you better than anyone else. A brother or a sister may also be helpful, especially if they have had a similar problem.

Sometimes talking to close friends can be very helpful. Even if they don't have any advice or alternatives for you, just being able to tell your problem to someone else helps you to focus on your problem. You have to know exactly what your problem is before you can begin to deal with it.

When friends or family cannot help, turn to an adult at school that you feel comfortable talking to. Many schools have counselors who are psychologists—people with special training and experience in assisting students solve their problems. If such counseling services are not available at your school, you should take advantage of the services in your community that specialize in teen counseling. Remember, you are not alone; there are many people who care about you and who are more than willing to assist you.

EXERCISES

PA-1. Keeping a Private Journal

Begin today to keep a private journal called "Notes to Myself" or some other title that pleases you. Use this journal to write about the things that happen each day and how you feel about them. Whatever feelings you have are OK. Feelings are a natural expression of your reaction to the people, things, and events in your life.

Don't worry about the way you write in your journal. Just let your ideas and feelings flow. Spelling, grammar, punctuation, and sentence structure are not important for this assignment because your journal is FOR YOUR EYES ONLY. The important thing to do is to WRITE—even if just a little— to get your feelings down on paper. Be sure to keep your journal in a safe place if you don't want someone else to read it.

By expressing your feelings on paper you will be releasing some of your stress. As you write, you will begin to focus more clearly on your problems and your feelings, and you will become more aware of what you want to do about your problems. Writing about the things that trouble you will help you to see them in a new way, a way that may help you decide what to do.

A spiral notebook or looseleaf notebook paper in a binder works very well for a journal. Set aside a special time each day to think back over the day and to write in your journal. Be sure to date each entry and to write in your journal in sequence. See the sample journal which follows.

Thursday

Life is the pits! Mandi is mad at me because I'm going to the prom with Ryan. How was I supposed to know she likes him? It's not my fault that he asked me instead of her! She says that if I don't back out of the date that she won't drive me to school any more. What am I supposed to do now? Ride my bicycle? No way! I'd die of total

○ embarrassment!!! Besides, my hair would be a mess by the time I'd get to school. Mandi is so mean! Sometimes I hate her.

Friday
Life is beautiful! I talked to Mom last night about my problem with Mandi. She said she will drive
○ me to school if I will help her with ironing and the cleaning on Saturday mornings. That's sure better than riding my bike!

Besides writing in a journal to help you cope with and work on your problems, you have people in your personal life who may be resources for assistance in solving your problems.

PA-2. Identifying and Using Personal Resources

We have listed some possible personal resources for you to use when you need to solve a problem. Put a check mark (✓) in front of each resource that you can use. Then, write the person's name on the line next to each resource you marked.

■ **Personal Resources**

___ mother or father _____

___ guardian or foster parent _____

___ brother or sister _____

___ best friend _____

___ minister, priest, or rabbi _____

___ boss _____

___ private counselor _____

___ family doctor _____

___ other _____

___ other _____

In addition to your personal resources, your school and community have services and people available to help you solve your problems.

PA-3. Identifying and Using School and Community Resources

Fill in the blanks on the form below. Ask your teacher and your school counselor to help you find the information you need.

■ School and Community Resources

My school counselor's name is:

_____

My school counselor is available at the following times:

_____

Another person at school I may discuss my problems with is:

_____

If your school has a "Stop-in" center where you may go for rap sessions or individual help, write the name of the center and the days and times it is open on the lines below:

_____

_____

The name of my local community center is:

_____

Call your community center and ask if counseling services or special peer counseling groups for teens are available. Write on the lines below what you find out.

_____

_____

Look in your phone book to see what community services are offered for teenagers in your area. Write the names and phone numbers for two such services in your area.

_____

_____

Remember, you do not have to face all of your troubles alone. Look to the personal, school, and community resources you have identified. Let them help you when you feel that you cannot cope by yourself.

YOUR TURN TO TALK BACK

If you would like to express your feelings about what you have learned in this chapter, please respond to the following questions. You may want to look back over the chapter first. When you have responded, turn your paper in to your teacher or counselor.

■ What did you like about this chapter called "Personal Aspects?"

■ What didn't you like about this chapter?

■ What did you learn about dealing with the personal aspects of going to school?

■ How will you put into practice what you learned from this chapter about problem solving?

■ What Internet source did you find useful for this chapter?

Chapter 4
Study-Reading

Shouldn't you be studying?

Chapter 4
Study-Reading

SCENARIO

Kim's television watching is interrupted by her mother.

Mom: Don't you have a history test tomorrow? Shouldn't you be studying?

Kim: Mom, I already did, and it didn't do any good. I spent two hours reading the chapter, and when I tried to recite the main ideas, I couldn't! It's all a blur. Reading the chapter was a total waste of time. I guess I'm just stupid!

Mom: You're not stupid, Kim. You just need some help with your studying. Bring your history book in here, and we'll read it section by section. As we complete each section, we'll see if we can pick out the main ideas. As we talk about the main ideas, you can write down some notes. My college roommate and I used to study like this, and it really helped.

STIMULUS QUESTIONS

1. Do you think Kim's mother's method of study-reading was helpful to Kim?_____

    Why, or why not?_____

    _____

2. Like Kim, have you ever spent time reading a chapter to discover afterwards that you didn't know what the chapter was about?

    _____

    _____

3. Think about how you usually read and study an assignment and describe what you do step-by-step on the lines which follow. Label each step "Step 1," "Step 2," and so on.

    _____

    _____

    _____

    _____

4. Do the steps you described in #3 give you the results you want?_____If you answered "yes," tell how those steps are successful for you. If you answered "no," tell how you think they need to be changed to give you the results you want.

    _____

    _____

    _____

    If you are not sure how to study-read your textbooks, or if you think that the way you study-read needs to be improved, then reading this chapter and completing the exercises will be most helpful to you. This chapter will tell you what study-reading is, why it is important to study-read, and how to do it.

LEARNING ABOUT STUDY-READING

What Is Study-Reading?

Study-reading is a method for reading nonfiction materials such as textbooks which helps you to concentrate and pay attention as you read so that you can:

- find the important information

- understand key points and concepts

- organize the information for learning

- relate new information to information you already know.

There are many different methods of study-reading. In this chapter you will be shown a method to practice and adapt to your own style of learning.

Why Is Study-Reading Important?

Without a study-reading method, chances are that you will remember very little of what you read. If you read your textbooks like you read novels and popular magazines, your rate of reading will be too fast to pick up the facts and important details that your teacher may expect you to learn.

Study-reading techniques help you to get the "big picture"—the general meaning—as well as to fill in the details or supporting information. Study-reading methods also help you keep your mind on what you are reading. If your mind is wandering or daydreaming, it is not on the material you are trying to read and learn. You will "draw a blank" at the end of the page and will have to reread. Study reading, if done correctly, saves you time because you pay attention to and learn the information the first time you read.

How Do You Study-Read?

Each subject you study requires special reading skills for the following reasons:

- the way the content is organized

- the difficulty of the vocabulary

- the length of the sentences

- the number of facts and details

- the types of things you are required to learn.

The first thing you should do in preparing to read an assignment in any of your textbooks is to know the following about your textbook:

- the parts of your textbook

    - preface
    - table of content
    - chapter introductions
    - summaries
    - study guides
    - glossary
    - index
    - appendices

- where each part is located in the book

- what the part is used for

- how the parts are organized into the total book

- how you can use each part for study-reading.

You can increase your study effectiveness by knowing what study aids are already included in your book. For example, if you run across a word or term you don't know, you can look it up in the glossary in your book. If the chapters in your books have introductions or summaries, you can read those first to get an idea of what the chapter is about. This will help you bring up information you already know about the subject as well as raise some questions.

By becoming familiar with the structure of a book or article before you begin to read, you will have an idea of how to read it. For example, if the chapters in the book are divided into sections for you with headings and sub-headings, you can easily decide how much to read at a time. If not, you will have to look over the material to see how you can logically divide it to get the most out of it as you read.

Be an active reader by making notes as you go along. If you are allowed to write in your books, use a highlighter to mark key words and phrases. *Always* read an entire paragraph before you mark any part of it or take notes on it. You cannot really determine what is most important until you have read the whole paragraph. Then, go back and highlight only the most important points. Students who mark their books as they read highlight too much information. Thus, they have extra information to go over when they review and study.

To take organized notes from your reading material, use the titles, subtitles, and headings provided for you in your book as headings in your notes. You can then jot down brief notes under each of your headings to remind you of the key points. Be sure to write down any words or definitions that are printed in bold letters. The special type such as ALL CAPITAL LETTERS, *italics*, and **boldface** used for some words and phrases shows you that the author thinks they are important and that you should pay special attention to them. If your book doesn't have subtitles or isn't broken into sections for you, you will have to work a little harder to identify main ideas as you read. Restate the main ideas in your own words and write them down. Summarize key points and concepts. Copy accurately any new terms and their definitions. The more accurate and complete your notes, the better study tool you will have. In Chapter 10, "Memory for Learning, " you will be shown how to write memory cards to master key points.

One of the best methods for study-reading textbooks that can be used in most classes is **SQ3R**. Each symbol in the name of this study-reading skill stands for a step the reader follows in using this method.

■ The steps of SQ3R are:

Survey. Read the title. Look over the whole chapter taking a quick *glance* at the *subtitles,* and *headings*. Read any *summaries*. This step should take about 5 to 10 minutes.

What will the survey step do for you? A quick survey will give you an overview (somewhat like a preview at the movies) of what will be covered in the assignment. This overview forms an outline for the information you will get from study-reading. By surveying the chapter, you can see how to divide it up for reading and studying. Surveying the assignment before you begin to read it can result in learning more in less time (increased reading speed and comprehension).

Question. Turn *titles, subtitles* and *headings* into *questions* which you will try to answer as you read. There are only 6 kinds of questions you can ask about anything. They are:

Who?	*Where?*	*Why?*	*What?*	*When?*	*How?*

Any other question is nothing more than a modified form of these 6 questions, such as:

What if?	*What about?*	*Why not?*	*How many?*	*How much?*

If you make a conscious effort to turn titles and headings into questions, your attention will be drawn to the material. For example, the title of this chapter is "Study-Reading." From this title, you might ask yourself, "What is study-reading?" "How will study-reading help me?" "Is it hard to study-read?" Now, you have a purpose for reading and a reason to pay attention to what you read—to find the answers to your questions. As you read to answer your questions, you will experience more interest in the material and deeper concentration than you would if you read the chapter "cold"— without questions.

Sometimes questions for discussion or study are provided for you at the back of the chapter. Always find and read these questions before you start to read the chapter. They are *clues* to the information that the author thinks is most significant. Let these *questions*, along with your own, *direct you in your reading* because they cover the most important ideas in the chapter. It may be helpful to copy these questions on a separate sheet of paper to remind you of what to look for as you read.

Read (R-1). Read with the definite *purpose* of making an active *search* for the *answers* to your questions or those that are provided in the text for you.

Recite (R-2). After you read a section under a heading, look away from the book and answer the questions you asked for that section. Answer either aloud or in writing. *Use your own words* to answer the questions. Support your answers with examples from the text. See if you can relate the information from the text to information you already know. If you can do all of this, then you know the material. If you cannot, then review the section again. Finally, if you didn't write out the answers to your questions, do it before you start another section. These notes will help you remember what you studied when you review them at a later time.

Review (R-3). After you have finished reading your assignment, begin to review it in sections. Pick a portion of the material you have chosen to study and look over your notes for an overall picture of the main points. Check your retention (how much you remember) by repeating step 4. Cover the main headings and recite the major points. Take only 5 to 10 minutes for this step.

The extra minutes you spend in using SQ3R will pay off when you discover that you won't need to reread your assignment to study it. The more you use SQ3R, the easier it will be for you to use it.

After you practice and use the SQ3R method, you will be able to adjust it to suit your own needs. Whether or not you continue to follow all of the steps of SQ3R, practice using the complete method until it becomes "natural" to you. You may wonder whether using this method will increase the amount of time it will take you to read your assignment. Until you learn how to use the method, it will take more time. But, once you learn and apply the method, it will save you time. The following exercises will guide you in practicing and learning the SQ3R method.

EXERCISES

SR-1. Naming the Steps of SQ3R

Each letter of the SQ3R method represents a symbol for the steps you should follow in using the method. Write the step for each letter below:

S _____

Q _____

R (1) _____

R (2) _____

R (3) _____

Check your answers by looking back at the SQ3R section of this chapter.

SR-2. Knowing the Steps of SQ3R

Define the steps of SQ3R. You may look back over the text for help if you need it.

STEP 1: **S = SURVEY**

List 3 things you do to survey a chapter:

■ _____

■ _____

■ _____

What is the purpose of surveying a chapter?

_____

_____

STEP 2: **Q = QUESTION**

Write down ways you can form questions from your reading assignment:

_____

_____

How does asking questions about the material you are reading help you learn the information?

_____

_____

_____

STEP 3: **R-1 = READ**

What should your purpose be as you read?

_____

_____

_____

STEP 4: **R-2 = RECITE**

To recite, you should:

_____

_____

_____

STEP 5: **R-3 = REVIEW**

Tell what you should do to review a chapter:

_____

_____

_____

_____

Check your answers against the Answer Key in Appendix A.

SR-3. Using the SQ3R Method

Your teacher will assign a chapter for you to read and study using the SQ3R method. Use this form as a guide to help you in applying SQ3R.

1. SURVEY the chapter. Write a brief statement or two telling what the chapter is about.

_____

_____

2. QUESTION. Write the questions you make from the titles, sub-titles, and headings here.

■_____

■_____

■_____

■_____
(Use another sheet of paper if necessary.)

3. READ the chapter searching for answers to your questions.

4. RECITE the answers to your questions as you find them and write them on the lines below.

Q 1:_____

Answer:_____

_____

Q 2:_____

Answer:_____

_____

Q 3:_____

Answer:_____

_____

Q 4:_____

Answer:_____

_____

(Use another sheet of paper if necessary.)

5. REVIEW each section of your chapter as you complete it. Write down the method of review you chose (recited out loud to yourself, talked it over with someone else, wrote a summary):

_____

_____

The SQ3R Method works very well for most nonfiction books. However, in a later chapter, a way of reading math assignments is described. (See Chapter 9, "Learning How to Improve Your Math Skills.")

YOUR TURN TO TALK BACK

Think about what you read and learned about study-reading in this chapter. Look back over the exercises you were asked to do, and then respond to the questions below. Give your responses to your teacher or counselor.

■ What did you like about this chapter on study-reading?

■ What didn't you like about this chapter?

■ What did you learn about study-reading from this chapter?

■ How will your study-reading habits change as a result of doing this chapter?

■ What Internet source did you find useful for this chapter?

Chapter 5
Listening for Notemaking

Before I know it, I'm not paying attention at all.

Chapter 5
Listening for Notemaking

SCENARIO

Mike: How are you doing in your biology class, Cheryl?

Cheryl: I'm really lost, Mike, because I can't keep up with the lecture and discussion. I try to listen and take notes, but while I'm busy writing something down, I miss other important information. I just can't listen and write notes at the same time! Once I get off track, I get confused and I have a terrible time listening. Before I know it, I'm not paying attention at all.

Mike: Maybe you are writing too much. I take notes during the lecture and discussion, too, but I don't try to write everything down. I listen first for things that sound important and then I just write down key words and phrases. If Mrs. Gonzales writes or draws something on the board, then I copy the whole thing. As soon after class as possible, I go back over my notes to make sure they make sense so that I can use them to study with later.

If something isn't clear, I just ask Sid because he gets straight "A's" in biology, and he can almost always answer any questions I have. If he can't, I try to catch Mrs. Gonzales before the next class and ask her.

Cheryl: Gee, that sounds like a lot of work.

Mike: Not really. Meet me after school at my locker and bring your notebook with you. We'll go over today's notes together. Maybe seeing how I make notes will help you.

Cheryl: Thanks, Mike. That would be great. See you at 3:00.

STIMULUS QUESTIONS

1. Which student do you most closely identify with in the scenario? _____

    Why?_____

    _____

    _____

2. Think about a personal situation where it would be helpful to take notes. Describe
    that situation here:

    _____

    _____

3. Do you take notes in all of your classes?_____

4. Are the notes you take helpful?_____

    Why or why not? _____

    _____

5. Do you think that you are a good listener?_____

6. How long can you remember most of what you hear in class?_____

    _____

7. Do you have a system or method for taking notes? _____

    _____

8. Does your mind often wander when you are trying to listen in class?_____

    Listening and notemaking are skills that can be combined to help you learn and
    remember what you see and hear in class. Both skills require hard work. They are
    active processes which require your full attention. While this chapter alone cannot
    make you an expert listener or notemaker, it can help you build upon the listening
    and notemaking skills you already have.

LEARNING ABOUT LISTENING AND NOTEMAKING

What Are Listening and Notemaking?

Listening and notemaking are skills that take practice and effort to learn. Listening is more than the ability to hear; it is *hearing with understanding*. Many students think that because they can hear, they also know how to listen. More than 45% of our waking hours each day are spent listening, yet few of us were ever taught how to listen.

Studies show that the average listener retains only half of what is said in a 10 minute oral presentation—no matter how carefully he or she thought they were listening. To increase the percentage of what we can remember when we receive information by listening, we need to take notes that will jog our memories at a later time.

Good notes should include the main ideas, overall concepts, and important facts or details in proper relationship to the main ideas. Notes should be brief, yet understandable. However, simply taking notes is not enough—we must learn to *make notes*. That is, we must learn to take the information we hear, read, experience, or observe and put it in our *own words* if we are to recall it later.

Why Is It Important to Learn How to Listen for Making Notes?

Since junior high and high school students spend about 55% of each day in school listening, the ability to listen well is not a skill that can be ignored. Instructions are not carried out, assignments are done incorrectly, mistakes are made, and misunderstandings happen when people don't know how to really listen. To be successful in school, you first need to hear the information that is being presented correctly, and then you need to make notes on the important points that you wish to remember.

Knowing what to do is much easier than actually being able to do it. For example, did you know that as you go through high school, you will spend approximately 4,000 hours in class? In college, you will spend another 2,500 hours listening to professors in various classes before you get your degree. To profit from these thousands of hours of listening without being bored, you will need to know how to listen in class as well as how to use a good system for making notes.

The benefits of having a good system for making notes are:

- you will learn more in class

- you will be involved with the information presented

- you will be less likely to become bored

- you will be able to pay attention better because your mind is actively involved with the subject matter

- your mind is less likely to wander when it is busy making notes

- class time will seem to pass more quickly because you will be busy listening for making notes

- your completed notes can be used as a study guide for your next quiz or test.

How Do You Listen and Make Notes Effectively?

You can be a better listener and notemaker in class if you follow the suggestions listed below.

1. **Prepare to listen**.
   Sometime before your classes, review your notes and any assignments so that you are ready for the new information you will get in the lecture.

2. **Have an open, positive attitude**.
   Decide that you will be open to new ideas and challenges and will listen for the main points being covered. Don't let your personal beliefs and prejudices keep you from listening to the speaker's message. If you are disagreeing with the speaker in your mind as you are listening, your mind is on your argument and not on listening to the speaker. You must fully receive the speaker's message before you evaluate or criticize it.

3. **Connect to what is being said**.
   Focus on how listening to this information will be helpful to you. Ask, "What can I learn or gain from listening to this?" Having a personal "stake" in the situation will help you be motivated to listen. In addition, connect this new information with the previous lecture and reading assignments you reviewed in suggestion 1.

4. **Listen actively**.
   Listen and watch for signals from the speaker that important points are about to be made. For example, when a speaker says, "In conclusion," "To sum up," or "Finally," you know that a major point is about to be made. Listen carefully and then write down main ideas and key points. Work to keep your attention on the message by constantly listening for what is coming next.

5. **Resist distractions**.
   Concentrate on the message being sent. (See Chapter 13, "Concentration While Learning" for some tips on concentrating.) Block out your personal and emotional problems for the time being by focusing on the speaker's words. Do your best to tune out other distractions such as outside noise.

6. **Attend as many classes as possible.**
If you must be absent from class, be sure to ask a friend to take notes for you. These notes will not be as effective as your own. *Remember, the most useful notes are those you make—in your own words.*

7. **Be prepared to take notes.**
Always take your notebook and pens or pencils to class with you. Ask to sit where you can easily see the speaker and any visual aids that may be used.

8. **Keep all of your notes in one notebook.**
Notes taken on stray slips of paper can lead to confusion. These notes are disorganized, easy to lose, and are very difficult to use for review and study.

9. **Keep your notes in order.**
To save time and to make review and studying easier, *always* put your NAME, CLASS, PERIOD, and the DATE at the top right-hand corner of each page. Keeping your notes dated and in order will make it easier for you to find a particular set of notes when you need them.

Use a separate notebook for each class. Or, if you prefer to keep all of your notes in one binder, separate the notes for each class with clearly marked dividers.

10. **Make your notes short and to the point.**
Don't take down every word you hear. *Make notes* by writing only key words and phrases, definitions, and repeated points. Summarize in your own words to make notes.

11. **Organize and edit your notes as soon as possible.**
Go back over your notes as soon after class as possible. Correct any errors, rewrite words that are hard to read and any statements that seem unclear. If you feel comfortable, share your notes with a classmate. Both of you will benefit as you compare your notes and make corrections and additions.

12. **Develop a personal notemaking shorthand.**
To speed up your ability to make notes, learn and use standard abbreviations and symbols as well as writing shortcuts of your own. For example, you might leave out the vowels and write "btn" for "between." Some other abbreviations that are helpful for notemaking are:

approximately	$\approx$		and	&
equal	=		continued	cont.
feet	ft.		not equal	$\neq$
greater than	>		inches	in.
ounces	oz.		less than	<
parallel	||		pounds	lbs.
with	w/		without	w/o

Whatever abbreviations you use, be sure to write them down in the front of your notebook for easy reference.

13. **Use a notemaking method**.

There are many methods or systems for making notes from lectures. Read the following selection about television and then look over each of the sample notemaking systems used to record the key information.

The Impact of Television: Good or Bad?

During television's 50 year existence in the U.S., its impact has been praised by those who adore TV and criticized by those who don't. Those who think TV has had a positive impact on our lives claim that it is the most profound development of modern times. It has changed the way we see ourselves and others. TV has expanded our international outlook. It brings the President of the United States and foreign leaders right into our homes. Television enriches our lives. It exposes us to new experiences, keeps us up on the latest news, educates and informs, entertains, and keeps us company. It even baby-sits our children. On the other hand, those who dislike TV refer to it as the "boob tube" and "idiot box." To them, watching TV is a waste of time, and in some cases, may be harmful. They claim that television has too much influence on our lives, especially where politics and elections are concerned. TV has been called a silly, inactive pastime that requires no thinking. Some claim that it is a mind altering experience loaded with hidden messages designed to make us think or act in particular ways. Critics of TV claim that it has created poor attention spans that affect learning skills in children. Although several studies have been done on the impact of TV in America, the data has been conflicting. Having grown up your entire life with television, what do you think?

The following samples of different methods of notemaking show how notes of the article you just read might look using the outlining, Cornell, a variation of the Cornell, graphic or pattern, and mapping methods.

The outlining method, shown below, is probably one with which you are already familiar.

SAMPLE 1: OUTLINING

Name:_____
Period._____
Date:_____

The Impact of Television: Good or Bad?

I. During TV's 50 years in U.S. its impact has been both praised and criticized.
   A. Positive impact of TV:
      1. most profound development of modern times
      2. changed way we see ourselves and others
         a. expanded international outlook
         b. President of U.S.
         c. foreign leaders
      3. enriches lives
         a. new experiences
         b. news
         c. educates and informs
         d. entertains
         e. keeps us company
         f. baby-sits

   B. Negative impact of TV:
      1. waste of time
      2. may be harmful
      3. too much influence on lives
         a. politics
         b. elections
      4. serious complaints:
         a. silly, inactive pastime
         b. requires no thinking
         c. mind altering
         d. sends hidden messages
         e. created poor attention spans
         f. affected learning skills in children

   C. No conclusive data from studies

Sample 2 shows how Cornell notes are made. This is a method for making notes that was developed at Cornell University so it is called the Cornell method. This method not only offers a way of taking organized notes, it provides a good study tool as well. By covering the right side of the paper, the items in the recall column can be used to test how well you remember what you wrote down.

SAMPLE 2: CORNELL METHOD

Name:_____

Period:_____

Date:_____

The Impact of Television: Good or Bad?

1. TV

During TV's 50 year existence in U.S., its impact has been praised by those who adore TV and criticized by those who don't.

2. Positive impact

Praised as most profound development of modern times. Changed way we see ourselves and others and expanded international outlook. TV enriches our lives: new experiences, news, educates, informs, entertains, keeps company, baby-sits.

3. Negative impact

Watching TV is a waste of time and may be harmful. Has too much influence on our lives, especially in politics and elections. Silly, inactive pastime, requires no thinking. Mind altering experience, loaded with hidden messages.Critics claim it creates poor attention span and affects children's learning.

4. Conclusions

Studies have shown conflicting data.

Sample 3 builds upon the Cornell method by adding details in "clusters" or groups under each key idea listed in the recall column.

SAMPLE 3: VARIATION OF CORNELL NOTES WITH RECALL COLUMN IN "CLUSTERS"

Name:_____
Period:_____
Date:_____

The Impact of Television: Good or Bad?

1. TV
- 50 yrs. in U.S.
- praised
- criticized

During TV's 50 year existence in the U.S., its impact has been praised by those who adore television and criticized by those who don't.

2. Positive Impact
- most profound development
- new outlook
- enriches lives

Praised as most profound development of modern times. Changed the way we see ourselves and others. Expanded international outlook. TV enriches lives: new experiences, news, educates, informs, entertains, keeps company, babysits.

3. Negative Impact
- wastes time
- harmful
- inactive
- mind altering
- hidden messages
- poor attention span
- hampers learning

Watching TV wastes time and may be harmful. Has too much influence on lives, especially in politics and elections. Silly, inactive pastime which requires no thinking. Mind altering experience, loaded with hidden messages to direct our thoughts and behavior. Critics claim it creates poor attention spans and affects children's learning skills.

4. Conclusions
- conflicting data

Studies show conflicting data.

The next three samples of notemaking methods are similar in that you make a visual picture or pattern out of the information as you create your notes. Those students who are visual learners—who remember best those things that they see rather than hear—often find that they can remember the contents of their notes better if they use the graphic or mapping methods.

SAMPLE 4: GRAPHIC, OR PATTERN, NOTES

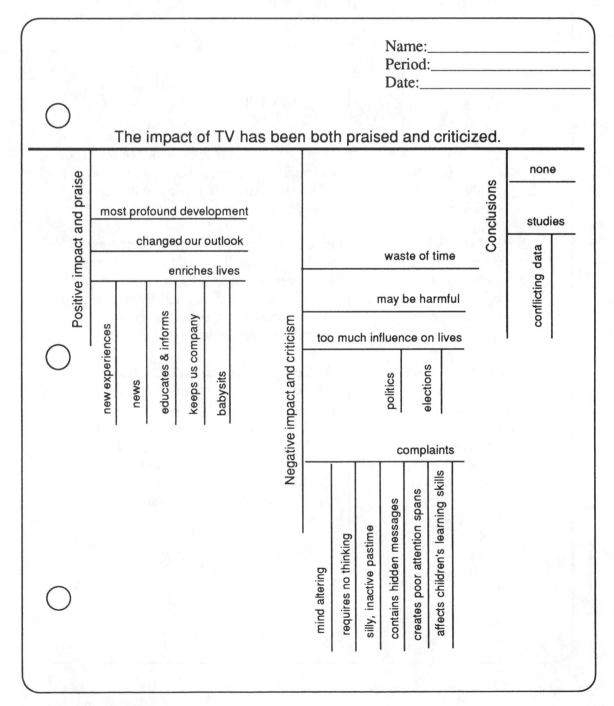

There are two commonly used mapping patterns: the Rake and the Sunbeam. The following figures will show you how we would make notes from the paragraph on the impact of television using both of these patterns.

SAMPLE 5: MAPPING: RAKE

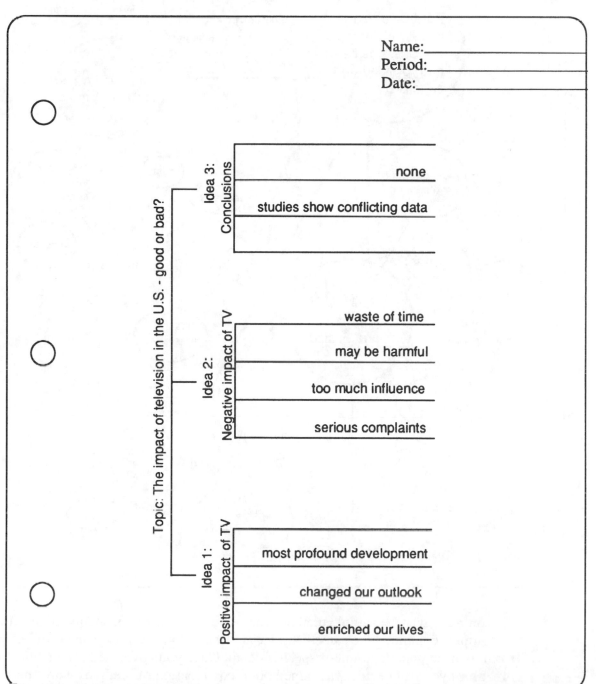

SAMPLE 5 (cont'd.): MAPPING: SUNBEAM

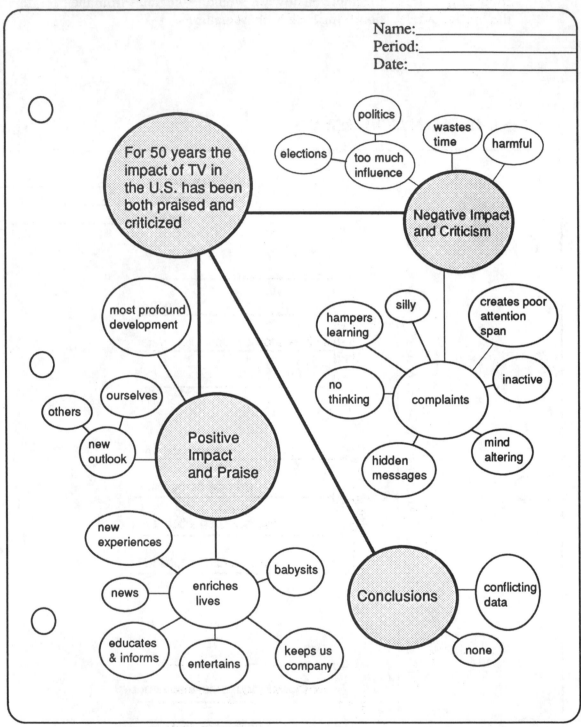

As you read over the sample methods for making notes, you probably noticed that all samples contained the same main ideas ideas and key points. They differed in form, wording, and amount of specific detail. Once you have used each method a few times you can decide which method or combination of methods works best for you.

EXERCISES

LN-1. Listening/Notemaking Record

Use the form below to evaluate one to four sets of notes from your classes. Your teacher may have you do four sets of notes from one class or two sets from two different classes.

Listening/Notemaking Record

Directions: Your teacher or counselor will give you specific instructions for completing this assignment. There is enough space provided on each form to analyze four sets of lecture notes.

Compare your notes against this checklist:	No.1 _____		No.2 _____		No.3 _____		No.4 _____	
1. Legibility of handwriting	Yes	No	Yes	No	Yes	No	Yes	No
2. Presence of irrelevant art work	Yes	No	Yes	No	Yes	No	Yes	No
3. Use of helpful diagrams and sketches	Much Some None		Much Some None		Much Some None		Much Some None	
4. Consistent format: phrases or sentences	Yes	No	Yes	No	Yes	No	Yes	No
5. Title and date of lecture near top of page	Yes	No	Yes	No	Yes	No	Yes	No
6. Subheadings or details indented	Yes	No	Yes	No	Yes	No	Yes	No
7. One main point per line	Yes	No	Yes	No	Yes	No	Yes	No
8. Use of abbreviations	Yes	No	Yes	No	Yes	No	Yes	No
	Clear	Obsure	Clear	Obscure	Clear	Obscure	Clear	Obscure
9. Brackets or other devices to indicate personal responses	Yes	No	Yes	No	Yes	No	Yes	No
10. Markings or numbers for emphasis	Yes	No	Yes	No	Yes	No	Yes	No
11. Writing notes on one side only	Yes	No	Yes	No	Yes	No	Yes	No
12. Completeness of notes	Yes	No	Yes	No	Yes	No	Yes	No
	Too Few Too Many		Too Few Too Many		Too Few Too Many		Too Few Too Many	
13. Accuracy of notemaking	Yes	No	Yes	No	Yes	No	Yes	No
14. Use of final summary after review and editing	Yes	No	Yes	No	Yes	No	Yes	No
15. Overall appearance: margins, spacing, etc.	Good Fair Poor		Good Fair Poor		Good Fair Poor		Good Fair Poor	

© Frank L. Christ 1985

LN-2. Finding the Best Notemaking Method for You

Look over the samples of the different methods for making notes in this chapter: outline, Cornell notes, variation of Cornell notes, graphic or pattern, and mapping (rake and sunbeam). Choose at least three of the notemaking methods and practice using each at least three times. Use the Notemaking Practice Record form to help you keep track of which method you use in what class as well as your reaction to using that method.

NOTEMAKING PRACTICE RECORD

Method 1: _____

    1st Trial-Class/Teacher/Period/Date _____

    Comments:_____

    _____

    _____

    2nd Trial-Class/Teacher/Period/Date _____

    Comments:_____

    _____

    _____

    3rd Trial-Class/Teacher/Period/Date_____

    Comments:_____

    _____

    _____

Method 2: _____

    1st Trial-Class/Teacher/Period/Date _____

    Comments: _____

    _____

    _____

    2nd Trial-Class/Teacher/Period/Date _____

    Comments: _____

    _____

    _____

3rd Trial-Class/Teacher/Period/Date _____

Comments: _____

_____

_____

Method 3: _____

1st Trial-Class/Teacher/Period/Date _____

Comments: _____

_____

_____

2nd Trial-Class/Teacher/Period/Date _____

Comments: _____

_____

_____

3rd Trial-Class/Teacher/Period/Date _____

Comments: _____

_____

_____

Now that you have experimented using the methods in different classes, you should have a good idea of which method works best for you when taking notes in a particular class.

YOUR TURN TO TALK BACK

Think about what you read and learned about listening and notemaking in this chapter. Look back over your responses to the exercises you were asked to complete and then respond to the questions below and give them to your teacher.

■ What did you like about this chapter on listening and notemaking?

■ What didn't you like about this chapter?

■ What did you learn about listening and notemaking from this chapter?

■ How will your listening and notemaking habits change as a result of doing this chapter?

■ What Internet source did you find useful for this chapter?

Chapter 6
Exam Strategies

Test Day Panic

Chapter 6
Exam Strategies

SCENARIO

The tardy bell is about to ring and students are rushing in to make last minute preparations for the big test that will be given in a few minutes.

Tammy: (*frantically*) I didn't study last night because I had a fight with my boyfriend. Tell me everything you know about what's going to be on the test!

Jason: Be quiet! I'm trying to read the rest of the chapter before we begin the test.

Alice: I can't remember a thing I studied!

Barry: I think I studied the wrong things!

Garret: (*yawning*): I stayed up all night studying. Now I'm so sleepy that I can hardly keep my eyes open. I didn't even take time to eat this morning. I feel awful! How am I going to be able to take the test?

Frank: (*Sitting quietly at his desk reading a comic book. Appears to be relaxed before the test because he has test taking skills.*)

STIMULUS QUESTIONS

1.   Which student in the scenario do you most closely identify with?

_____

       Tell why._____

_____

2.   Think about how you usually prepare to take a test. Describe your "exam strategy"—your plan for studying for and taking tests.

_____

_____

_____

3.   Look at the problems listed below that many students have before taking a test. Write next to each what you think could have been done to avoid the problem.

       overly tired _____

       nervous/scared_____

       unprepared _____

       lacking confidence _____

4.   Think about how you usually feel minutes before you take an exam. Write those feelings down and tell what you think are the reasons you feel this way.

_____

_____

_____

_____

       No matter what kind of a student you are, this chapter will help you face any exam and earn higher test scores. Read on to discover 6 strategies for preparing for exams and 6 strategies for taking exams. By reading about these strategies and doing the exercises which follow, you will learn the best way to study and review for tests. By paying attention to and practicing the techniques presented in this chapter, you will become "test-wise"—that is, you will know the tricks for taking true-false, completion, multiple-choice, and essay tests successfully.

LEARNING ABOUT EXAM STRATEGIES

What Are Exam Strategies?

The things you do to prepare for an exam and your plan for working your way through the exam are your exam strategies. To be a successful test taker, you need to plan your work and then work your plan. Your study plan begins the first day of the course and continues until you have completed your final exam.

Recommended exam strategies for test preparation are:

- Keep up with the work.
- Plan time for review.
- Find out about the test.
- Review the material.
- Test yourself.
- Be alert.

Strategies for taking the exam with success are:

- Read and interpret test directions correctly.
- Pace yourself for success.
- Never change an answer unless you are certain that the first answer is wrong.
- Answer the easiest questions first.
- Use one question to help you answer another.
- Know the techniques for taking different types of tests.

These strategies will be discussed in detail in this chapter.

Why Is It Important to Have and Follow Exam Strategies?

What you do before you take the test is as important as what you do during the test. Since a test puts you on the spot to prove what you know about a given subject, you need to face the challenge by coming to the test situation as well-prepared as possible. You should know the material, be rested, and if possible, be relaxed. A well-prepared, confident student has a head start on those students who don't follow a good study plan and therefore show up for the test in a state of panic.

Using exam strategies may add many points to your test scores because they help you learn the material and do your best on any type of exam.

How Do You Use Exam Strategies to Prepare for Tests?

You probably know students who spend a lot of time worrying and fussing about tests. Perhaps, you too, have wasted time and energy in the same way. But, there is no need to feel anxious about tests if you use the 6 exam strategies described below.

■ Keep up with the work.

Attend all classes, if possible. Keep up with the reading and assignments on a daily basis. Be sure that your class notes are complete. Copy notes from a classmate whenever you are absent. Always ask questions about information that is unclear or confusing to you. Get the information *right* before moving on to new material. Read over your notes after each class to make sure that they make sense and are readable. If not, correct your notes by discussing them with a classmate or with your teacher before the next class. For more efficient study, date your notes and keep them in order in a notebook. (For help with making good notes, see chapter 5, "Listening for Notemaking.") Take a few minutes as soon as possible after each class to summarize the most important points made in class. Also summarize key points from any reading assignments. When you are ready to study and review, these summaries will be most helpful and will save you time.

■ Plan time for review.

To do well on a test you should set aside a regular part of your study period for review. (Refer to Chapter 1, "Time Management" for help with making a study schedule.) The sooner you review your class notes and the notes from your reading assignments, the better your chances are for learning and remembering the information. Research has shown that students will remember material better if they review it soon after hearing or reading it.

Research also shows that more learning is achieved in less total time if students space their learning over a few days instead of trying to learn everything in one long study session.

How does the research apply to you? By reviewing your notes every day, even if just for a very short time, you will learn and remember the information better than if you try to learn it by studying all day or all night before a test like Garrett did in the scenario.

The method Garret used is called *cramming*. Cramming is when you try to learn a lot of new information in one study session. Cramming is a study method that seldom works because true learning does not occur. It may help you associate or relate to small parts of the material; however, don't expect to remember what you cram-studied for any length of time.

Regular, spaced review is a type of "rehearsing" the material. The more you "rehearse," the better you will learn the material and the easier it will be to recall. By reviewing notes from previous classes each time you study, you will be reinforcing or strengthening your recall of the information from those notes.

■ Find out about the test.

To improve your chances for doing well on a test, find out as much as possible about the test before you begin to study. Ask your teacher questions such as:

What type of test will it be? Essay? Multiple-choice? True-false? Other?

If the test will be an *essay* test, you will need to study for overall understanding. Pay more attention to concepts and general ideas and less attention to facts and details. If it will be an *objective* test (multiple-choice, true-false), study specific facts and details for recall and recognition.

What part of the textbook and class or lab notes will the test cover?
The answer to this question will help you to study the right things instead of the wrong things for the test. Valuable time will not be spent studying information that you will not be tested on.

What is the most important thing to study?
By having the teacher identify the most important things to study, you will know what to spend most of your study time on. In addition, your teacher will be giving lectures that will indicate what he or she thinks is important. (See the section, "Listen Actively" in Chapter 5, "Listening for Notemaking" for signals that tell the listener that key points are about to be made.) Spend your study time on the information that will be emphasized most.

How many questions will there be on the test?
Compare the number of items on the test to the amount of material to be covered on the test and that will give you an idea of how thoroughly your knowledge of the material will be tested.

How much time will be given to complete the test?
Knowing how much time you will have to answer all of the test items will tell you if you will need to recall quickly or if you will have more time to think.

May notes or the textbook be used during the test?
If you may use study aids such as your book or notes for the test, you will still need to study. You won't have to memorize details, but you will have to know your text and your notes well enough to quickly locate information that will help you answer the questions.

How will the test be graded?
If the test is an essay test, find out what factors besides content will influence your grade: neatness? writing in ink? skipping lines? spelling? punctuation? grammar?

If the test will be objective (true-false, multiple-choice, completion), find out if there is a penalty for guessing the answers to those items you aren't sure about.

If the test will be *graded on the number of right answers,* there is *no penalty for guessing*. For example, if there are 40 questions on the test and you answer 30 correctly, then your score is 30. Obviously, it would be a good idea to guess at the remaining 10 items to raise your score.

On an objective test *scored on the number of correct answers minus the number wrong—do not guess* . If you answer 30 out of 40 correctly on this test, your score will be 30. If you guess at the remaining 10 items, 1 point will be taken off your score for every item you guess incorrectly. In this case, guessing would lower your score.

■ **Review the material.**

The best ways to review information you are studying are to:

    1) talk about the material to yourself, using your own words;

    2) write a brief outline or summary of the material;

    3) get together with classmates and form a study group so that you can discuss the information with others. Be sure to keep your group small— no more than three or four students—so that there is less tendency to socialize.

These types of review will help you identify what you know about the material as well as what you don't know. Then you can concentrate on the information that is harder for you to learn. By using your own words to explain and summarize the information you make a personal connection to the material. Research shows that material that has personal meaning is more easily recalled than information that is not connected.

■ **Test yourself.**

Don't wait to be surprised! Sometime after your first study session, test yourself to see what you have learned. Try to put yourself in the teacher's shoes by predicting what questions will be asked on the test. Use your notes and reading materials to help you make sample test questions. Some clues as to what might be on the test can be found in the course outline, homework assignments, past quizzes and tests, discussion questions, and chapter summaries in your textbook. When you have written the types of questions you think will most likely be on your test, practice answering them. Then check your answers against your notes and text. If you do this in a study group, you will benefit from the other students' questions and you won't feel bored studying.

■ **Be alert.**

To help you feel more relaxed and confident as you go into the test situation, make sure you:

are rested. A good night's sleep the night before and some relaxation exercises prior to the test will help refresh your body and keep your mind alert. (See Chapter 14 "Health and Vision" and read the section on stress.)

are not hungry. A good meal will help calm your nerves and give you energy. Be careful not to overeat—it will make you sluggish.

allow yourself enough time to get to the test without rushing.

avoid last minute problems by having all of the supplies needed for the test (sharpened pencils, erasers, ink pens, paper).

reduce test anxiety naturally by doing stress reducing exercises such as deep breathing, stretching, or walking.

feel confident that you will do well.

Now that you know how to prepare for taking the test by studying and being ready, you need to know strategies for taking tests successfully.

How Do You Use Exam Strategies to Take Tests?

■ **Read and interpret test directions correctly.**

Directions are often overlooked, skipped, misread, and misunderstood. Don't botch the test by misunderstanding the directions! Never begin a test until you have looked over the entire exam and read the directions slowly and carefully.

Underline key words in the directions. Apply the directions to the first item on the test. Then *reread the directions* to see if you are responding correctly. Directions tell the WHAT, WHEN, WHERE, and HOW of answering test items.

■ **Pace yourself for success.**

Have you ever run out of time while taking a test? If so, you know how frustrating it can be, especially if you thought you knew the rest of the answers. To prevent this test-taking disaster from happening, pace yourself—make the best use of the time allotted for the test. Look at the amount of time you will have to complete the test and then look over the test to see how many questions it has. Set aside a few minutes for overviewing—looking over the entire test—and plan to save a few minutes for checking your work after you complete all items. Then, divide the remaining time by the number of items on the test. You can then figure out how much time to spend on each item. If some items are worth more points than others, you will want to spend more time on the more valuable questions.

Mark on your test or make a note on your answer sheet indicating where you need to be on the test by a certain time. Start at the beginning of the test and work your way through. Do not spend too much time on any one question. If you get "stuck" on an item, put a mark in the margin and move on. If you have time, you can go back and work on it after you have finished the rest of the test.

Be sure to watch the clock and pace yourself so you don't run out of time before you can complete all items.

■ **Never change an answer unless you are certain that the first answer is wrong.**

You have probably heard the expression "first impressions are usually right." In test-taking, research has shown that your first choice is usually the best. Trust your first impressions unless you are absolutely certain that they are wrong.

■ **Answer the easiest questions first.**

In the essay exam, a large part of your grade will depend on how thoroughly you answer each question. A well-written response to the easiest questions will help give you a solid base of points on which to build your total test score. Answering the easy ones first also gives you a feeling of confidence which helps carry you through the rest of the test.

■ **Use one question to help you answer another.**

Many times you will find that, upon reading the question the first time, you do not have an answer for the question. Do not worry. Many times your response to one question will trigger the answer to another. Sometimes the teacher will give away the answer to a question when asking another question on the test. This is perhaps the best reason for your previewing the entire test before doing any one item on the test.

■ **Know the techniques for taking different types of tests.**

Not all tests are alike. The most common types of tests are *objective* (true-false, fill-in-the-blank, matching, multiple-choice) and *subjective* (essay). Just as you vary your approach to reading different kinds of information, you need to vary your approach to taking different kinds of tests.

❑ **Objective tests.** Your success on the objective test will depend on your ability to pick, choose, or supply the correct answer. Besides knowing how the test will be graded (see "How will the test be graded?" in the section "How Do You Use Exam Strategies to Prepare for Tests?"), you should read the questions carefully, noting key words or phrases. These key words or phrases may give you clues as to how the question should be answered. Look at the following list of words that may trick you into making the wrong response.

all	except	none
always	may	not
best	must	seldom
every	never	sometimes

Example: The true-false statement "All hockey players are tough." is false even if one hockey player is not tough. The trick word in this statement is "all."

When a strong specific determining word such as "all" or "every" is used in a true-false test item, the statement is usually *false*. A true-false statement is false if *any part* of the statement is false. To be a better test taker, circle or underline these kinds of words on a test to help you avoid being tricked or confused.

Multiple-choice tests are often tricky because the questions usually have more than one satisfactory answer, but one is clearly better than the others. To avoid being tricked, *read all the answer choices before choosing your answer.*

❑ **Essay tests.** After you have studied for your essay type test, you will need to know how to take the test successfully. The following steps will help you improve your performance on essay type tests:

Step 1. Read over the entire test before you begin to answer any questions. This should take no more than a few minutes. While you overview the test, two things will happen: 1) your memory will be stimulated, and 2) you can plan how to use your exam time.

Step 2. Choose the essay question to answer first and reread the question underlining key words in the question.

Step 3. Begin writing by dumping on paper everything you can recall from your studying that seems relevant. Write down each idea or fact on a separate line. Do this rapidly. Do not judge your thoughts. Keep writing until you have nothing left to jot down. This activity helps you associate information you have to the subject asked about in the question.

Step 4. Look over your list of ideas and decide how you can organize them into categories. Start your organization process or analysis by reading the first line you wrote. Write an "A" in front of it. Then read through the rest of the list, line by line, and when you find similar ideas, put an "A" in front of them. When you are finished, find the next line that expresses a new idea. Label it "B." Go through the list and write a "B" next to all similar ideas. Continue this process through a "C" and possibly a "D" grouping. Look carefully at those items you didn't label. If they don't fit into one of your categories, cross them out.

Step 5. Next, decide the order of your categories and number them in order of importance. Your "C" list might be #1, your "A" list #2, and so on. You now have an outline to begin writing your essay answer.

Step 6. Begin writing your answer to the question by rephrasing the question in the sentence you write as the introduction to your essay answer. For example, if you are asked to list and explain four causes of the Civil War, you might begin your essay answer like this: "The four causes of the Civil War were 1) _____, 2)_____, 3)_____, and 4)_____." Then, select one of the causes and write a detailed explanation telling the origin of the cause and why it was an important reason for starting the war. Do the same with the remaining three causes.

Step 7. Write legibly—clearly and neatly. Write on every other line so that you have space to edit and make corrections when you proofread your answers.

Step 8. After you have completed these steps for all of the essay questions, use any time remaining to reread your answers for grammatical errors, sloppy spelling, and incomplete or unclear sentences. Make your changes neatly using a "$\wedge$" to insert a word or phrase and "XX's" to delete a letter, word, or phrase. Since you wrote on every other line, your changes will be very readable.

Try this method of writing essay exams before you actually take an essay exam. As you study your material, write out some questions that you think your teacher might ask on an exam. When you have completed your studying, put away your text and notes. Practice the upcoming exam by answering the questions you made up. Go through all eight steps as you answer each question. Grade by checking your answer against the text and your notes.

Complete the following exercises to sharpen your performance as a test taker.

EXERCISES

ES-1. Test Preparation Plan

Complete the Test Preparation Plan for one of your classes for which a test has been announced. Share your plan with your teacher when you have completely filled it out.

TEST PREPARATION PLAN

Class: _____

Date of test: _____ Day: _____ Period: _____

Type of test: (essay, true-false, multiple choice, matching, combination, other) _____

Number of test items:_____Time allotted for the test: _____

Number of points possible:_____ How test will be graded:_____

How much test grade counts in total class grade: _____

Content to be emphasized on the test: _____

_____

Material to be covered:

1) Textbook pages: _____

2) Class notes, assignments, or activities: _____

_____

3) Other: _____

_____

Study Plan:

Prepare your study plan by figuring out how many weeks or days remain until the test will be given. Then, look over the amount of material to be learned for the test. Divide the material into sections and give yourself deadlines for completing the reading and assignments. Be sure to allow time for reviewing by yourself as well as with classmates. Use the lines below to list your study activities and the dates by which they need to be completed.

Study Activity	Deadline for Completion

(Use additional paper if necessary.)

Preparation checklist:
_____ I have read all assignments.
_____ My classnotes are complete and in order.
_____ I have asked questions about material I didn't understand.
_____ I have reviewed all materials.
_____ I have made good use of study aids: outlines, summaries, etc.
_____ I have all the materials I will need for the test: pens, pencils, erasers, scratch
        paper, a watch, plus anything else the teacher said to bring.

ES-2. Two Minute Test on Following Directions

The following quiz is to test your skill in reading and following directions. Allow yourself just two minutes to complete the quiz. Set a timer or ask a friend to time you.

1. Read everything through carefully before you do anything.

2. Print your name in the upper left-hand corner of this page.

3. Write the date below your name in the upper left-hand corner.

4. Circle the number "4" at the beginning of this sentence.

5. After the date written just below your name, write your birth date.

6. Draw a line through this sentence.

7. Put an "X" in the upper right-hand corner of this page.

8. Punch a hole with your pencil through the number "8" at the beginning of this sentence.

9. Put a circle around your name in the upper left-hand corner of the page.

10. Now that you have read everything through carefully, do only only items 1 and 2.

HOW WELL DID YOU DO? Obviously, if you didn't read everything carefully before you began, you weren't following directions. If you did items 3 through 9, you "flunked" the test and you need to be more careful when reading and following directions.

ES-3. Recognizing the Key Words in Objective Test Items

Circle the word or words which may trick you into making the wrong response on the sample test items which follow.

> Example: If you are unclear about a test item, it is *never* better to guess.
> True or False?

The word "never" is in italics in the example because it is the word which tells you that the answer must be false because there may be instances when it is better to guess.

1. Every child must learn to read by the age of six if he or she is to do well in school.

2. For each statement below, circle the word which best completes the statement.

3. Answer yes or no: all opinions are based on fact.

4. Work rapidly to complete all of the multiple choice questions. There may be more than one correct answer.

5. It is not recommended that teenagers never abstain from the use of alcohol and drugs.

6. The following statements are either true or false. Rewrite the false ones so they are true.

7. All of the words listed below are descriptive words. Choose the word which is closest in meaning to "beautiful."

8. In your essay answer, explain the difference between fact and opinion.

Check your answers with the Answer Key in Appendix A.

ES-4. Knowing Key Words for Taking Essay Tests

Part 1 - Look up the definition for each word or phrase listed below and write its meaning on the line next to it.

1. analyze _____

_____

2. classify _____

_____

3. compare _____

_____

4. contrast _____

_____

5. compare and contrast _____

_____

6. criticize _____

_____

7. define _____

_____

8. demonstrate _____

_____

9. describe _____

_____

10. develop _____

_____

11. evaluate _____

_____

12. explain _____

_____

13. prove _____

_____

14. summarize _____

_____

15. trace _____

_____

Study your list of words and their meanings, then complete Part 2 of this exercise.

Part 2 —Match each word with its definition by writing the letter of the definition on the blank next to the word.

_____1. analyze   a. Explain each of the ideas/things to be compared and tell how they are alike.

_____2. classify   b. Enlarge on some idea or statement by explaining gradually.

_____3. compare   c. Give evidence, facts, or clear logical reasons to support what you say.

_____4. contrast   d. Present the main points or facts in a brief form.

_____5. criticize   e. Give the exact meaning in clear, concise terms.

_____6. define   f. Organize information/ideas into classes or categories.

_____7. demonstrate   g. Describe only how two or more ideas differ.

_____8. describe   h. Express your judgment about the value of the views or factors mentioned.

_____9. develop   i. Paint a word picture of something, list its characteristics, identifying or telling sequence.

_____10. evaluate   j. Tell the HOW, WHAT, and WHY of the material.

_____11. explain   k. In narrative form, tell the development, progress, or events from a given point of origin.

_____12. prove   l. Show the operation or function of some thing or concept by explaining it and giving examples.

_____13. summarize   m. Separate into various parts, then tell about the characteristics of each as it affects the whole.

_____14. trace   n. Tell the positive points and the negative points, then offer your opinion or conclusion.

Check your answers with the Answer Key in Appendix A.

YOUR TURN TO TALK BACK

Think about what you read and learned about using exam strategies. Look back over the exercises you were asked to complete and then respond to the questions below. When you have finished, give it to your teacher or counselor.

■ What did you like about this chapter on exam strategies?

■ What didn't you like about this chapter?

■ What did you learn about exam strategies from this chapter?

■ How will your exam strategies change as a result of doing this chapter?

■ What Internet source did you find useful for this chapter?

Chapter 7
Writing Non-Fiction Assignments

...next week we begin our research papers.

Chapter 7
Writing Non-Fiction Assignments

SCENARIO

Michelle: Hello, Kyoko? This is Michelle. Mrs. Casey asked me to call you since you have been absent from school this week and give you the assignments for our English class.

Kyoko: Oh, hi Michelle. It's really nice of you to call. I'm glad you have the assignments for me because I don't want to get behind. My cold is so bad that I will probably miss a few days next week, too.

Michelle: I'm sorry to hear you are feeling so awful. Anyway, here is what you have to do for English class. First, you have to write an autobiographical essay as described on page 142 in our English textbook. The paper has to be at least 3 pages long. The second assignment is to write a book report on *War of the Worlds*. Follow the same format we used for our last book report. Oh, I almost forgot; next week we begin our research papers.

Kyoko: Oh, my gosh! I think I'll be sick forever now. I hate to write. It takes me so long just to get started, and I have such a hard time trying to figure out what I want to say. Once I finally do complete a written assignment, I feel like it's not very good. Thanks for calling, Michelle, but I must admit that I felt much better before you called.

Michelle: I'm sorry. Get well soon. Bye.

STIMULUS QUESTIONS

1. Do you share any of Kyoko's feelings or problems when you have a written
    assignment to prepare?_____ Explain how you feel and what problems you
    have when writing a non-fiction assignment.

    _____

    _____

    _____

2. What do you do before you write a class assignment? Be honest; if you don't do
    anything, indicate that.

    _____

    _____

3. Of all the written assignments that you expect to have this year, which assignment
    do you think will give you the most trouble?

    _____

    Why?_____

    _____

4. Explain your feelings when your teacher tells you in the first week of class that
    you will have lots of written assignments for the semester.

    _____

    _____

5. Look at the list of writing assignments which follows. Add to it any written
    assignments that you expect to have which are not on the list. Then, rate them in
    order of difficulty for you by placing the #1 next to the most difficult, #2 next to
    the next hardest, and so on.

    _____book report   _____lab report

    _____personal essay/reaction   _____expository essay

    _____autobiography   _____research paper

    _____ journal   _____

Now that you've spent some time thinking about your feelings towards the different types of writing assignments you will be required to complete this year, you probably discovered that you have some negative feelings or fears about writing certain assignments. This chapter is designed to help you feel more confident about your writing as you learn some techniques for improving your skills in writing non-fiction assignments.

LEARNING ABOUT WRITING NON-FICTION ASSIGNMENTS

What Is Meant by Writing for Non-Fiction Assignments?

Writing for non-fiction assignments is organizing information based upon facts or actual events and recording it on paper. This type of writing passes on information gathered through research or experience. Non-fiction writing assignments usually follow a specific structure and must meet certain requirements. For example, a bibliography and footnotes will be required for a research paper, but would not be required for a lab report. Regardless of the type of assignment, the goal of the writer should always be the same: to write the message or information so clearly that there is no way that it can be misunderstood by the reader.

Why Is It Important to be Able to Write Assignments Skillfully?

When writing non-fiction assignments, you are showing what you know or have learned. To get full credit for what you know, your assignment must be written clearly or else your information will be lost in the muddled writing. The reader's impression of what you know will be formed by what you leave on the paper. To avoid being misjudged, it is extremely important to learn to skillfully complete all written assignments. Writing non-fiction assignments is a skill, a skill that can be learned.

As you learn to write assignments skillfully, you will be pushed into the world of information. You will be researching and processing new information and adding it to information you already have. Besides learning about something as you prepare your assignment, the type of assignment you write will prepare you to advance in your education or to perform well in the world of work. For example, the personal essays you write for class will prepare you to write the autobiographical essay which is required when you apply for college entrance or for certain jobs. The ability to write well gives you the power to communicate information to other people no matter where they are.

The best reason for learning to write assignments skillfully is to develop the skill of telling something clearly and accurately to someone who is not present. This skill will benefit you in school, on the job, and in your personal life. Failure to communicate clearly in writing can result in poor grades, embarrassment and costly mistakes on the job, and misunderstandings and hurt feelings in your personal life. Anything you do now to improve your writing skills will benefit you later on in life as well. Remember that writing is a lifelong challenge to communicate clearly to others.

How Can You Improve Your Writing Assignments?

You can improve your writing assignments by making sure that you *know exactly what it is that you want to communicate before you begin to write.* Once you know what you want to say, you need to say it as clearly as possible making sure that you have included all of the information that your readers will need and/or want to know. Many times what is perfectly clear in your mind does not come out the same way on paper. So, once the message is written, it needs to be read over carefully to make sure that the information is presented in an organized, accurate, and clear fashion that will not be misunderstood. Most writers, including professional writers, have someone else read their papers for clarity and errors in punctuation, grammar, and spelling.

As you answer the questions in the following self-check for successful writing, you will learn how to improve the quality of your writing assignments.

Self-Check for Writing Non-Fiction Assignments

■ **What is my purpose for writing?**

"Because this assignment is worth a lot of points and I will get a bad grade if I don't do it well" is a normal response to this question. To improve the quality of your assignments, you need to expand your understanding of your purpose for writing to include what it is that you want your readers to know or do when they are finished reading your assignment.

■ **What, exactly, is it that I want to say?**

If you don't know what it is that you are trying to say to your reader, your reader certainly won't know either. You must decide what it is that you want to communicate before you begin to write. *Good writing starts with good thinking.* You cannot write anything if you don't have anything to say.

■ **Who will be reading my assignment, and what does he/she expect?**

Smart writers will always consider who they are writing for. To be a smart writer, ask: "What does my reader want or need to know about the subject? How much or how little detail do I need to write for him or her? How does my reader feel about the subject matter?" For example, if you are writing an essay about the novel *To Kill A Mockingbird*, consider your English teacher's opinion of the book before you begin to write. That doesn't mean that you have to agree with your teacher's opinion, it just means that you should look for examples or reasons that support your opinion before you state it in your paper.

■ **Am I clearly and accurately communicating my message to the reader?**

To honestly answer this question, look for the following:

❑ vague or confusing words and phrases

> Example: *like because, way back when, we'll get to it later*

❑ illogical phrases

> Example: *same difference, past history*

❑ tired and overused expressions

> Example: *basically, like, really, Once upon a time...*

❑ slang words and expressions

> Example: *he goes* instead of *he says* or *he said*
> *rolls me* instead of *makes me laugh*
> *blood, bro*, or *homeboy* for *friend*

❑ wordy phrases

> Example: *not the same at all* when you mean *different*
> *in the event that* instead of *if*

❑ puffed up vocabulary, jargon, and wordy writing

> Example: *The alleged perpetrator of the crime exited the vehicle.*
> instead of *The suspect got out of the car.*

No one likes to wade through excess verbiage or fuzzy writing to find the point. State what you mean to say in clear, concise sentences composed of words you are familiar with. Also avoid using words only understood by your peer group.

■ **Do I have enough facts, reasons, or examples to provide specific information in my paper?**

Before you answer this question about your assignment, list on paper all of the thoughts and ideas you have about the topic. If you have none, then you need to research your topic so that you can present specific information in your paper.

■ **Is my message unified and well-developed?**

To find out if your message is unified, check to see that each paragraph has one main idea. Each main idea should relate to the topic of your paper. To discover whether or not your message is well-developed, check to see if you:

- ❑ introduced the main idea of your paper
- ❑ explained the main idea
- ❑ supported it with reasons, facts, and examples
- ❑ summarized and concluded the main idea.

■ **Are there any mistakes I need to correct before I turn in my assignment?**

Before turning in a written assignment of any type, always proofread it carefully, looking for and correcting:

- ❑ grammatical errors
- ❑ punctuation errors
- ❑ spelling errors
- ❑ typos
- ❑ incomplete sentences
- ❑ run-on sentences

■ **Does my paper look neat and clean?**

Remember, you will be judged both by the content and the way your paper looks. If your paper is wrinkled, messy, torn, stained, or hard to read, it will give the impression that the assignment was not very important to you. If the reader thinks that you didn't consider the assignment very important, he or she is likely to feel that little time, effort, or thought went into it. Make a good impression on your reader before he or she even begins to read your paper by making sure that it is neatly written or typed, clean, and wrinkle free.

EXERCISES

W-1. Writing Assignment Analysis

Using a recent writing assignment that was graded, analyze it by applying the self-check items below.

Title of the
assignment:_____**Grade:**_____

1. What was my purpose for writing this assignment?

_____

_____

2. What exactly was it I wanted to say?

_____

_____

_____

3. What did your teacher expect from you that you did not do in writing this assignment?

_____

_____

_____

4. Did I communicate clearly and accurately to my reader? Find any unclear sentences from your assignment and copy them on the lines which follow.

_____

_____

_____

_____

5. Rewrite any sentences you wrote for your response to #4. As you rewrite, be sure to replace slang words and expressions, wordy phrases, fuzzy or unclear phrases, or awkward sentence structure that makes your message confusing.

_____

_____

_____

_____

_____

_____

6. Did I check my paper for unity and make any necessary corrections?_____

7. Did I proofread for and correct:

_____ grammatical errors?
_____ punctuation errors?
_____ spelling mistakes?
_____ typos?
_____ incomplete sentences?
_____ run-on sentences?

8. Did my paper look professional?

_____ neatly written or typed?
_____ clean?
_____ free of wrinkles and tears?

W 2. Avoiding Wordy Phrases

Look at each wordy phrase and write a concise (shorter) phrase or word which expresses the same meaning.

WORDY PHRASE   **CONCISE PHRASE**

Ex. *as of yesterday*	*yesterday*
Ex. *in light of the fact that*	*because*

1. say it again   _____

2. gather together   _____

3. definitely different   _____

4. due to the fact that   _____

5. exactly identical   _____

6. the total sum   _____

7. in the event that   _____

8. at this point in time   _____

9. not the same at all   _____

10. not been the same since   _____

11. in most cases   _____

12. twenty years before 1980   _____

13. surrounded on all sides   _____

14. past history   _____

Check your answers with the Answer Key in Appendix A.

YOUR TURN TO TALK BACK

Think back on what you read and learned about writing non-fiction assignments in this chapter. Look back over the exercises you were asked to complete, and then respond to the questions below. Give your completed paper to your teacher or counselor.

- What did you like about this chapter about writing for non-fiction assignments?

- What didn't you like about this chapter?

- What did you learn about writing non-fiction assignments skillfully?

- How will you put into practice what you learned about writing non-fiction assignments from this chapter?

- What Internet source did you find useful for this chapter?

Chapter 8
Library Research

There are lots of books and articles here for the report, but you have to know how to locate them.

Chapter 8
Library and Internet Research

SCENARIO

Jake: Hey, Randy! I've been looking for information for my English class report, and I haven't found a thing! I don't know how I'm supposed to find anything in this library. It's just too confusing. Have you found anything yet?

Randy: Sure I have, Jake. There are lots of books and articles here for the report, but you have to know how to locate them. When I first tried to find materials here at the library, I didn't know how to begin. I wasted a lot of time and got really frustrated looking around on my own. Then I asked the librarian to help me. She showed me how to find library materials and to search the net for information. Whenever I do have trouble finding information, I just ask the librarian to help me.

STIMULUS QUESTIONS

1. Like Jake, do you ever feel "lost" in a library and have difficulty finding the information you need?

_____

2. Pretend you need to do research for a report on the migration habits of whales. Describe how you would find information about this topic.

_____

_____

_____

3. Once you have found a listing for the book, article, or report you want in the card or computer catalog, do you know how to find it in the library?_____ Whether your answer is YES or NO, tell how you would use the card catalog listing to find the information.

_____

_____

4. Do you know how to use an Internet search engine to find materials?

_____

5. Think about the types of materials that are kept in a library and attempt to list at least 6 here:

■_____   ■_____

■_____   ■_____

■_____   ■_____

Knowing your way around a library can save you hours of wasted time. Four important things to learn about your library which will speed up your research are: 1) the system of organization your library follows, 2) how to use the listings by author, subject matter, or title in the card catalog or on the computer. 3) how to use the *Reader's Guide to Periodical Literature* and 4) what reference materials are available both in the library and on the internet and how to use them as you do research.

LEARNING RESEARCH METHODS

What Is Research?

Research is the process used to collect ideas and information about any topic. It is using the library tools such as the card or computer catalog, CD-ROM, and the Internet to find books and articles about the subject you want to study. Your success at doing research will depend upon three things:

- your knowledge of the library's classification system

- your ability to use research tools, and

- your willingness to ask for help when you need it.

Why Is Research Important?

Research is important because it opens a door to knowledge. As the saying, goes "Knowledge is power." The more you know about a subject and the more accurate your information, the better prepared you are to draw a conclusion, make a decision, and take a particular course of action.

Research is not only a requirement for being successful in school, but it is an essential skill for success in various occupations. Even if you don't need to do research for your job as an adult, it will come in handy when you are looking for materials to read for pleasure, for information about favorite sport or hobby, for data on financial planning and investments, for learning ways to improve and maintain your home, for shopping tips, and so on.

How Is Research Done?

Research when done correctly, involves the following steps:

Step 1. Knowing where to find the information;

Step 2. Obtaining the information;

Step 3. Making sure the information is correct;

Step 4. Giving proper credit to your sources;

Step 5. Copy the information accurately.

Lets take the steps one-by-one and explore what is involved in each. For **Step 1, knowing where to find the information,** look in the card or computer catalog, CD-ROM, or the Internet for information on your topic. If the card catalog system is still in use, you will find books in the library by subject, title, and author. One sample card by subject follows.

STUDY SKILLS -- HIGH SCHOOL

LB
1632   Marrs, Barbara L. 1947-
M2   Learning & using study skills: a teenager's guide for academic success.
1991   Illustrations by George Saunders, Jr., Personal Efficiency Programs, Inc.,
        Sierra Vista, 1991.
          240 p. illus. 18 cm. $20.00
          Contents: Time Management.—Study Environment.—Personal Aspects.—Study
        Reading.—Listening for Notemaking.—Exam Strategies.—Writing Non-Fiction
        Assignments.—Library Research.—Learning How to Improve Your Math Skills.—
        Memory for Learning.—Efficient Reading for Speed & Comprehension.—Vocabulary
        Development.—Concentration While Learning.—Health and Vision.—Attitudes.—
        Campus Involvement.
          1. Study Skills—High School   I.Title. II. Title: A teenager's guide for
        academic success.

          LB1632.M290   XXX.XXXXX   XX-XXXXXX

The call number located in the upper left-hand corner of each card is the code to finding the book on the library shelves. Books are arranged numerically on the shelves according to the call number which is printed on the spine of each book. Since books on the same subject are arranged in the same area of the shelves, you might want to spend a few minutes looking at the surrounding books to see if any of them will also be helpful.

A sample search engine screen follows:

Step 2, obtaining the information, is pretty easy once you have the call number or have located an appropriate web page. If you have difficulty locating the material you need, be sure to ask the librarian to help you. When the information is in a book which cannot be checked out of the library, photocopy the pages a you need or take careful notes of the facts and details that you want to use for your assignment. With Internet information, print its web pages.

Step 3, making sure the information is correct, is an important step because the information is of no use if it is inaccurate. To help you decide if the information is likely to be correct, check on these two things:

- the date of publication
- the author's credentials (education and experience).

Ask yourself: "Is the publication date recent enough to include current research and information?" As a general rule, anything over ten years old is outdated.

Is the author a reliable source of information? To find out ask yourself: "What do I know about the author? Is he/she an expert on this topic? If you cannot tell, check to see what other works this author has had published, and look up the author in *Who's Who* or *Facts on File*. Or, if time is an issue, ask your teacher or the librarian.

To double-check the quality of the information in the book or article you have chosen, compare it to other books or articles written on the same subject. Does the information agree?

Whenever you use someone else's ideas in your reports or papers, you must complete **Step 4, giving proper credit to your sources.** To keep your sources straight while you research and to give accurate credit to your sources when you write your report or paper, make a bibliography card for each source as you use it. A bibliography card is usually a 3" x 5" index card. For books, it should include the following information:

- author's name, last name first
- title of the book (underlined)
- publisher
- place of publication
- date published, and
- call number in case you need to find the source again.

The sample bibliography card which follows illustrates how information should be written for a book.

LB 1632
.M2

Marrs, Barbara L.
Learning & Using Study Skills: A Teenager's Guide for
Academic Success
(Personal Efficiency Programs, Inc., Sierra Vista, AZ
1991).

For magazine and journal articles, include the following information on your bibliography card:

- author's name, last name first
- title of the article (in quotation marks)
- full title of the magazine or journal (underlined)
- date of the magazine or journal
- page numbers for the article, and
- call number (volume number).

LB 4230
.M3

Marrs, Barbara L.
"How Good Are Your Reading Skills?"
Chemical Engineering, (Feb., 1983), 185-188.

For Internet, listserv, and news group material, follow your teacher's recommendations for documenting Internet resources.

Step 5. Copy the information accurately once you have found the information you want to use. If you quote someone, be sure to quote them EXACTLY. When you repeat what someone said or wrote always enclose the statement in quotation marks ("—") and name the source you quoted. If you are summarizing or restating someone's ideas, you need not put quotation marks around them, but you do need to give credit to the person whose ideas you are using. Identifying your sources lends credibility (believability) to your paper or report and makes you sound like an expert.

For practice in applying the information you have read about in this chapter, complete the following exercises.

EXERCISES

LR-1. Preparing to Do Library Research

You will need to go to the library to complete these activities. Answer all questions completely.

1. Discover which classification system your library uses and identify it here:

   Dewey Decimal____Library of Congress____Other_____

2. Describe what CD-ROM databases are available in your library.

   _____

   _____

   _____

3. Do you have access to the Internet at the library? If not, is the Internet available at your public library or at home?

   _____

4. Pick a topic you have been assigned or choose a topic that interests you. Write your topic here:

   _____

5. Use six different sources, three from the library and three from the Internet, to search your topic and list them on the following bibliography cards. Be sure to include the call number for each book and the web address for each Internet source.

   ①

   Call No./Web Address _____

   Ref._____

   _____

   _____

   _____

② Call No./Web Address _____

Ref._____

_____

_____

_____

③ Call No./Web Address _____

Ref._____

_____

_____

_____

④ Call No./Web Address _____

Ref._____

_____

_____

_____

⑤

Call No./Web Address _____

Ref. _____

_____

_____

_____

⑥

Call No./Web Address _____

Ref. _____

_____

_____

_____

6. Find information about your topic in an encyclopedia and indicate what you found in the spaces provided:

Title of article: _____

Author: _____

Title of encyclopedia: _____

Volume: _____

Pages on which information appears: _____

7. Find the following reference books in your library and write the title of each on the spaces which follow. Give a brief description of the type of information contained in each book.

Book	Title	Description
almanac		
atlas		
dictionary		
thesaurus		

8. Define the following terms:

annual_____

_____

bibliography_____

_____

bimonthly_____

_____

copyright_____

_____

microfiche_____

_____

pamphlet_____

_____

periodicals_____

_____

primary source _____

_____

secondary source _____

_____

9. Find a newspaper issue for the day you were born. Fill out the blanks below:

Title of newspaper: _____

Publication date of newspaper: _____

Volume number of newspaper: _____

City where newspaper is located: _____

Title of major front-page news story: _____

_____

10. Write down the days and times your school library is open:

_____

11. Write down the name and location of your community library and the days and times it is open:

_____

_____

_____

12. Write the name and the web address of the three Internet search engines.

_____

_____

_____

Show this completed exercise to your teacher to see if you need more assistance or practice in doing library research.

YOUR TURN TO TALK BACK

Think about what you read and learned about library research. Look back over the exercises you were asked to complete and then respond to the questions below. Turn your completed responses in to your teacher or counselor.

■ What did you like about this chapter on library research?

■ What didn't you like about this chapter?

■ What did you learn about library research from this chapter?

■ How will your library research methods change as a result of doing this chapter?

■ What Internet source did you find useful for this chapter?

Chapter 9
Learning How to Improve Your Math Skills

Math tests aren't that bad if you take the time to learn the definitions, signs, formulas, and stuff like that.

Chapter 9
Learning How to Improve Your Math Skills

SCENARIO

Tracy: Jerome, do you want to come over tonight to study for tomorrow's math test?

Jerome: You bet I do, Tracy. Math tests scare me to death. I need all the help I can get!

Tracy: Oh, Jerome, math tests aren't that bad if you take the time to learn the definitions, signs, formulas, and stuff like that.

Jerome: It's not the equations that are so hard for me; it's the word problems. I can never figure out what I'm supposed to do. I guess I'm just not good at word problems.

Tracy: I agree that word problems are difficult, but I think they're kind of fun. The trick is to read them slowly and carefully—over and over if you have to—until you know what you must do to reach the solution. I learned some tips for reading word problems from the math teacher I had last year which I can show you tonight.

Jerome: Great! See you about seven o'clock.

STIMULUS QUESTIONS

1. Some students really like math and it seems easy for them. For other students, math is difficult and unpleasant. What do you think makes the difference?

    _____

    _____

    _____

2. How do you feel about your math class and doing math assignments?

    _____

    _____

3. Do you panic when you have to take a math test? _____

    Why or why not? _____

    _____

4. What do you think you could do to become a better student in math?

    _____

    _____

5. Talk to a friend or classmate who is doing well in math and ask him or her to tell you how he or she prepares for math tests. Write down the things that work for your friend that you think may be helpful to you.

    _____

    _____

    _____

Have you or any of your friends ever said "I hate math..." or "I just can't do math...?" Many times what are thought to be poor math skills is really a lack of knowing *how to learn* math. Sometimes *math anxiety*—fear of doing math— takes over and the student forgets the math skills he or she does have. Whether or not you suffer from math anxiety, you will find the information provided in this chapter helpful when you are working to solve math problems.

LEARNING ABOUT IMPROVING MATH SKILLS

What Are Math Skills?

To learn math you need to be an active listener, concentrate and pay attention, read carefully, follow directions, and think. You also have to work hard to learn the "language" of math: formulas, definitions, terms, signs, and theories. Practice and review are necessary until mastery is achieved. Failure to do any one of these can result in failure to correctly complete a math assignment or exam.

Math books put more demands on you as a reader than most types of materials. They contain explanations, definitions, signs, symbols, classifications, abbreviations, formulas, equations, charts, graphs, and problems—all of which you must be able to read and understand before you can solve the problems correctly. Reading math books successfully is a skill that can be learned with practice and patience.

Why Are Math skills Important?

Math skills are important because you will use them throughout your life both on the job and at home. For example, did you know that you use geometry when you play a game of pool? Algebra when you do financial planning? Weights and measurements when you cook? Percentages when you shop at a sale?

Some types of math problems you will be required to do in school may not directly transfer to your daily life; however, the mental discipline and reasoning skills it takes to correctly solve these problems will. Problem-solving is part of everyday life; the same skills it takes to solve math problems can be applied to solving other types of problems.

How Can You Improve Your Math Skills?

The best way to improve your math skills is to first pay attention in class. Listen to the teacher's explanation, think about it, react to it by asking questions, and then summarize the information by writing notes. Copy all sample problems and examples your teacher writes on the board. Double-check to be sure you copied them accurately and completely. *Always* ask the questions that occur to you. Other students may have the same question, too, even though they don't ask it out loud. Asking questions will help you and your teacher identify what you are confused about. If you are confused, chances are that other students are too. These suggestions, along with the ones listed below for reading and completing your math assignments, will help you improve your math skills—provided you follow them.

- **Be prepared when you go to class** by having your math book, paper, pencils, erasers, and any special equipment your teacher requires such as a compass, protractor, sliderule, or calculator.

■ **Read your math book deliberately**—slowly and carefully, making sure you understand each section before you move on to the next.

■ **Write down questions** that come up for you as you read your math book so that you can remember to ask them in class the next day.

■ **Ask your teacher to help you find an easier math book** to use as a reference if your math book is hard for you to read and understand.

■ **Take notes in class and as you read** your math book. Copy all formulas, theories, definitions, concepts, and examples correctly.

■ **Go over your class notes as soon as possible** after class to make sure that they are readable and complete, and that they make sense.

■ **Make memory cards**. In the next chapter, Chapter 10, "Memory for Learning," you will learn the method of using memory cards which can be used for mastering math definitions, formulas, rules, concepts, symbols and so on.

■ **Review your notes and memory cards** on a regular basis so that you can remember their contents.

■ **Overlearn math concepts, terms, and rules by repeating them** over and over and then reviewing them periodically.

■ **If you miss a class, see your teacher as soon as possible** to get the make up work and instructions.

■ **Get help from a friend, classmate, or family member** who does well in math when you have math homework or when you are studying for a math test.

■ **Do something about your math anxiety**. Talk to your math teacher about some ways that you can prepare for taking a math test that will reduce some of your fears about the test. If you feel that you need more help, see the school counselor for some suggestions and exercises for reducing stress.

In addition to following these suggestions for improving your math performance, use the following 7 problem-solving steps.

Step 1. Read the problem thoroughly, asking, "What is this all about?" If you are having trouble understanding the problem, read it out loud. Sometimes hearing the words as they are read helps to clear up misunderstandings. Also, be sure to check definitions and symbols and learn their meanings before you work on the problem.

Step 2. Re-read the problem, asking "What am I to find here?" Then, restate the problem in your own words to help you understand what is given and what must be done to solve the problem.

Step 3. Visualize the problem by using the facts given and drawing a diagram or a picture to help you understand the problem.

Step 4. Plan how you will solve the problem. Decide what process or formula you will use.

Step 5. Estimate the answer. Based upon the information given, guess at what you think a reasonable answer would be.

Step 6. Carry out the operations. Work the problem.

Step 7. Check your work. Compare your answer to your estimate, then check your results against the problem. This double-checking will minimize careless mistakes.

We have given you a number of suggestions and steps for improving your math skills. If you would like to remember these suggestions, read them several times aloud and copy them in your math notebook for easy reference. These suggestions can make a difference–if you use them. Begin by applying the suggestions to the exercises in this chapter and to your current math assignments.

EXERCISES

MS-1. Using the 7 Problem-Solving Steps

Choose a math problem from your current math book and use the 7 problem-solving steps listed in this chapter to solve the problem. Check off each step as you complete it.

Copy the problem completely and accurately here:

Step 1._____I read the problem thoroughly.

_____I read the problem out loud.

_____I learned the meanings of the definitions and symbols.

Step 2._____I reread the problem to make sure of what was asked for and what was given.

_____I restated the problem in my own words to make sure I understood it. The problem, in my own words, is written in the space below:

Step 3._____I drew a diagram or picture to help me visualize the problem.
My diagram or picture is in the space below:

Step 4._____I planned how to solve the problem. The process or formula I
used is written here:

Step 5._____I estimated the answer. My estimate is:

Step 6._____I carried out all operations. The problem is worked in the space which follows:

Step 7._____I checked my answer with my estimated answer.

_____I checked my answer against the problem.

_____I double-checked my work to minimize errors.

Now that you have had some practice applying the 7 problem-solving steps, continue to use them as you complete your math assignments.

YOUR TURN TO TALK BACK

Think about what you have read and learned about improving your math skills. Look back over the chapter and the exercises you were asked to complete and then respond to the questions below. Give your answers to your teacher or counselor.

- What did you like about this chapter on improving your math skills?

- What didn't you like about this chapter?

- What did you learn about improving your math skills?

- How will you improve your math skills as a result of doing this chapter?

- What Internet source did you find useful for this chapter?

Chapter 10
Memory for Learning

Chapter 10
Memory for Learning

SCENARIO

Theo: What a rotten day! I forgot everything I read as soon as I looked at the history test. I thought I knew that stuff, but my mind was a blank.

Kyle: I know what you mean. I remembered the teacher saying something about the causes of the Civil War, but I couldn't recall what he said. I knew that I had read something about the causes in our history book, too, but I forgot what I read. I have such a terrible memory! I'm sure that I'll get a lousy grade on that test.

Susan: Me, too. I read the book and took pretty good notes in class, but I forgot that the test was today, so I didn't study. I guessed at most of the answers.

STIMULUS QUESTIONS

1. Which student in the scenario has a memory problem similar to your own?

    _____

2. What are the hardest things for you to remember?

    _____

    _____

3. Why do you think it is difficult to remember the things you listed in your response to #2?

    _____

    _____

4. What are the easiest things for you to memorize?

    _____

    _____

5. Do you feel differently towards the things you listed in your response to #2 than you do towards the things you listed for #4?

    _____

    _____

6. Based upon your response to #5, what conclusions can you draw about how your feelings help you or hinder you when trying to memorize something?

    _____

    _____

7. How do you memorize biology or chemistry terms?

    _____

8. What do you do when your teacher says your assignment is to memorize 10 poems?

    _____

    _____

9. How do you *feel* about memorizing?

    _____

10. What do you think you could do to improve your memory?

    _____

    _____

Success in school is often measured by a student's ability to remember facts, definitions, concepts, statistics, and formulas on quizzes and tests. Many students who are good readers and good listeners have difficulty remembering what they read or heard in class because they don't know how to use and improve their memory skills.

How and why the memory works is a fascinating, yet puzzling subject. It is a subject too broad to be handled in a short chapter like this. This chapter will introduce you to memory techniques such as association and visualization, making and using memory cards, classification or grouping, and mnemonics.

LEARNING ABOUT MEMORY FOR LEARNING

What Is Memory for Learning?

Memory for learning is increasing your skill in remembering and retaining information. Like Kyle in the scenario, you may think that you have a poor memory. However, there is no such thing as a poor memory; there are only untrained memories. Using your memory for learning involves concentrating on and paying attention to the material you are trying to learn. The material must be understood before it can be learned. Once it is learned, it can be committed to memory. Through repetition, practice, and periodic review, information can be learned and remembered.

Why Is Memory for Learning Important?

How many times have you spent hours studying for an exam, only to forget everything when the test was in front of you? If you used a simple, effective method for learning and memorizing the information you study for tests, you would never face a test with a "blank" mind again. Since success in school is measured by how well you can recall facts, formulas, definitions, and concepts on quizzes and tests, having a method of memory for learning is very important. By improving your memory skills, you are preparing yourself for success in the classroom, on the job, and in all future learning experiences.

How Do We Memorize for Learning?

No one knows exactly how the memory works. Yet, out of years of experimentation and research have come some practical techniques and tips for improving memory and recalling information. The following 8 recommendations will assist you in improving your memory for learning.

1. *Be motivated to learn.*

You must want and intend to remember something to use your memory effectively. To motivate yourself to learn something, ask yourself why you need to learn it and what you will gain by learning it.

2. *Be interested in the information.*

The more you are interested in the information to be learned, the easier it will be to remember. The SQ3R method, presented in Chapter 4, "Study-Reading," is an excellent way to create an interest in new material.

3. *Pay attention to the material to be learned.*

You cannot learn anything unless you pay attention to it. Think of your mind as being elastic and snap it back when it stretches beyond the material. Keep your attention focused on long material by dividing it into smaller amounts and learning it a section at a time. Most textbooks are already divided for you with headings and subheadings to indicate the beginning of a new section.

4. *Select what to memorize.*

Before you begin to memorize information, you need to select what parts of the information you need or want to remember. It is impossible to remember everything. According to the Dutch scholar Erasmus, a good memory should be like a fisherman's net — that is, it should retain all of the big fishes but let the little ones escape. Selecting the "big fish" to learn, while letting the "little fish" go, is important. Because of the vast amount of information available in the world today, no one can remember everything, even in just one subject area. To memorize for learning, select only major concepts, important facts, and details.

5. *Organize the information by classifying or grouping.*

Once you have selected what it is you want to memorize, you need to organize the information. Material which is arranged or grouped according to a system, is more easily memorized and more readily recalled. The more consciously you organize information at the time you memorize it, the more easily you will find the information when you need it. One of the best ways to organize information for memorization is classification—putting things or ideas into groups of similar things or ideas. Some examples of classification are given in exercise M-1.

6. *Create associations for memorizing.*

Your chances of remembering something increase as you associate it with information that you already know or that is more readily recalled than the new information. Two effective methods for making associations are *visualization* and *mnemonics* (nee-mon-iks).

■ *Visualization* is simply seeing pictures in your mind that help you recall information. As you do exercise M-2, you will practice visualization as you associate items on a list with other items that you are asked to memorize.

■ *Mnemonics* is creating memory devices or tricks to help you remember new information. Two common types of memory devices are abbreviations and acronyms. Abbreviations are shortened forms for words, such as U.N. for United Nations. An acronym is a word formed from the first letter (or first few letters) of a series of words, such as **RADAR** for radio detecting and ranging.

You may be familiar with the following abbreviations and acronyms:

- ❑ **NOW**—National Organization for Women
- ❑ **ROY G. BIV**—for the color spectrum (red, orange, yellow, green, blue, indigo, violet)
- ❑ **FACE**—the musical notes on the spaces between the lines of the treble clef are f-a-c-e

Sometimes a silly sentence made from the first letter of each word you need to remember is helpful in remembering new information. Rhymes which contain the facts you are trying to learn can also be helpful.

For example, to learn a spelling rule, you may have been taught the rhyme: "I before E, except after C."

Or, to recall the date that Columbus discovered America, you may have been taught: "In 1492, Columbus sailed the ocean blue."

As you complete exercise M-3, you will be making up mnemonics of your own.

7. *Make and use memory cards.*

Memory cards are flash cards that you make to help you retain and recall what you have selected to learn. Use small index cards or small slips of paper to record key ideas, facts, formulas, and definitions. Put only one item per card. Put part of the information on one side of the card and the rest on the back as in the example which follows.

Two effective memory methods	*1. Visualization* *2. Mnemonics*
(side 1)	(side 2)

To study effectively with your memory cards, divide your cards for each class into groups of no more than 7. Shuffle the cards and begin quizzing yourself. Each time you respond correctly, put a "✓" at the top right-hand corner of the card. If you answer incorrectly, put an "X" on the card. This will let you see at a glance which cards need more study. Repeat until you know the information on the 7 cards before you select another group of cards to learn.

Always carry your cards with you so you can review them whenever you find yourself with a few moments to spare. Quickly review the cards you know and then spend your time on the cards you don't know.

8. *Review to retain.*

No matter what method of memorization you use when learning new material, you must review the information within the first 24 hours if you want to store that information in your long-term memory. Information which only makes it to the short-term memory is only retained for a brief time. For example, when you look up a number in the phone book, you will remember the number long enough to place the call. Unless you review the number, you most likely will forget it before you can dial it again at a later time. The phone number was only stored in the short-term memory long enough for you to dial the number right after you looked it up.

Research has shown that information that is not reviewed periodically is not transferred into the long-term memory and is easily forgotten. However, information that you review or repeat often, like phone numbers that you "know by heart," is recalled from memory whenever you want it because it has been transferred into the long-term memory.

To illustrate that we learn best by periodically reviewing, a study skills expert describes the "curve of forgetting" using two students as examples. The first student studied for one hour. Six weeks later, he remembered very little. The second student studied only 30 minutes on the first night. Then, he spaced his reviews of the material. He reviewed for 15 minutes the next day after his initial study period. One week after his first review, he reviewed again for 10 minutes. One month after his last review, he reviewed for only 5 minutes to recall what he learned during his first study session six weeks before. Although both students studied for an hour, the second one remembered almost everything for his test because he spaced his study/review of the material over a period of time to keep the information in his long-term memory.

EXERCISES

M-1. Classifying to Remember

Using the following list of activities, decide upon at least one form of classification which would allow you to break up the information into smaller portions of material.

Activity:

baseball, tennis, football, water polo, swimming, volleyball, cross-country, golf, track and field, soccer, wrestling

Classification by_____:

How did you do? There are a number of different classifications for the above activities. Compare your answer with the two examples in the Answer Key in Appendix A.

M-2. Creating Associations for Memorizing

Read the list below *one item at a time*. Then, cover the list and write down—in order—as many items as you can recall on a separate piece of paper.

1. giraffe	6. tire
2. carpet	7. umbrella
3. earrings	8. clown
4. curtains	9. pennies
5. pencil	10. bugle

Compare the list you wrote with the printed list. How many items did you recall? _____ Did you recall any in sequence?_____ If you are like most people, you recalled less than 50%. Your recall of these items will increase as you create associations with these words.

For purposes of this exercise, follow our images and associations for memorizing the list. Even though our associations are silly, do your best to picture them.

The first item on the list is giraffe. Begin your memorization by associating the "new data"—carpet to giraffe.

Picture a *giraffe* dancing on a bright red *carpet*. The giraffe is wearing huge round *earrings*. Your living room *curtains* are hanging from the earrings, flapping over the giraffe's feet. A *pencil* is between the giraffe's toes. As the giraffe dances, the pencil punctures a gigantic *tire*. The tire rolls over a huge, open purple *umbrella* attached to a *clown*. The clown is blowing *pennies* out of a *bugle*.

Now that you have made associations using our pictures, write down, in order, as many of the items as you can recall. Don't look back at the list or these associations until you have written down all of the items you remember.

1._____

2._____

3._____

4._____

5._____

6._____

7._____

8._____

9._____

10._____

Go back over the original list to check your recall. How many did you recall this time?_____ If you want to test your memory again, write the list *backwards*—in sequence. If your associations were strong enough you should have been able to recall the list just as well backwards as you did forwards.

Although this exercise in association may appear silly, the process of association is important. It is the key to memorization and can be applied to most types of data such as: names with people, dates with events, people with jobs or accomplishments, and words with definitions.

M-3. Using Mnemonics

Before you begin this exercise, look back at the examples of mnemonics in recommendation #6 of this chapter. Then, look at each of the following items listed below. Write an abbreviation or acronym for each on the line next to it.

1. United States Air Force_____

2. American Medical Association_____

3. Students Against Drunk Driving _____

4. The notes of the lines on the treble clef—E,G,B,D,F

_____

_____

5. The signs of the Zodiac: Aries, Taurus, Gemini, Cancer, Leo, Virgo, Libra, Scorpio, Sagittarius, Capricorn, Aquarius, Pisces

_____

_____

6. Choose something from one of your classes that you need to memorize. Write it here, and then make a mnemonic for it.

_____

_____

_____

_____

> Check your answers with the Answer Key in Appendix A to see examples of mnemonics for each of the items.

M-4. Using Memory Cards

Select 50 terms, definitions, or concepts to remember for any one of your classes. Make out memory cards for each item you want to remember. Use the cards for two weeks. At the end of the two weeks, report here how the cards worked for you.

_____

_____

_____

_____

YOUR TURN TO TALK BACK

Look back over this chapter on memory for learning and think for a few moments about the things you were asked to do. Then, answer the questions below and give them to your teacher or counselor.

■ What did you like about this chapter on memory for learning?

■ What didn't you like about this chapter?

■ What did you learn about memory for learning?

■ How will you put into practice what you learned about memory for learning as a result of doing this chapter?

■ What Internet source did you find useful for this chapter?

Chapter 11

Efficient Reading for
Speed and Comprehension

We're being bombarded by the information explosion!

Chapter 11
Efficient Reading for Speed and Comprehension

SCENARIO

Jennifer:	Terri, I just watched the most interesting show on TV about the information explosion and speed reading.
Terri:	What's the information explosion, Jennifer? I've never heard of it.
Jennifer:	It's how we're being bombarded with printed materials of all kinds. For example, thousands of new books are printed each year. Every time I go to the supermarket, I see four or five new magazines that I've never seen before. There's also e-mail, listservs, news groups, and zillions of web pages to read. Even my parents complain all the time that they can't keep up with the reading required for their jobs, much less read the local newspaper or a best seller that all their friends are talking about. They really feel overwhelmed.
Terri:	Gosh, I feel the same way. I hardly have time to read my schoolwork, much less the Danielle Steele novels I like so much. And, when I read a magazine or newspaper, I often don't understand what I'm reading. How are we supposed to keep up with all of this printed information?
Jennifer:	The TV program recommended some speed reading and comprehension techniques that President John F. Kennedy learned in a speed reading course to increase his reading speed from 300 words per minute to more than 1200 words per minute.
Terri:	That's fantastic! I wonder if we could do the same?

STIMULUS QUESTIONS

1. Do you think you read as fast as most teenagers? _____

2. How do you feel about reading books, magazines, and newspapers?

    _____

    _____

3. Do you read for your own enjoyment and personal interest?_____

    If you answered "Yes," write down some of the things you like to read.

    _____

    _____

4. Do you usually have trouble understanding what you read? _____

    Explain._____

    _____

5. Have you ever read a book that you wanted to read in one sitting?_____

In today's highly technological society, you will have more demands placed on you as a reader than your parents when they were your age. You will need to develop your reading and comprehension skills. The information and exercises in this chapter will help you build your skills of reading for speed and comprehension.

LEARNING ABOUT EFFICIENT READING FOR SPEED AND COMPREHENSION

What is Efficient Reading for Speed and Comprehension?

Reading for speed and comprehension is reading with a flexible rate that allows you to read as fast as you can while you still understand what you read. It is using various reading techniques, such as *surveying* or *previewing*, *skimming* and *scanning*, and *reading for main ideas,* to achieve your purpose for reading as quickly as possible. It is pushing beyond your normal reading rate to read faster and better.

Reading for speed and comprehension requires continual practice. This could include reading: at least one book a month, every issue of a news magazine, every issue of your favorite magazine, and the daily newspaper, in addition to all of your assigned schoolwork.

Why is Efficient Reading for Speed and Comprehension Important?

Here are at least three reasons why reading for speed and comprehension is important. 1) We learn in three ways: through experience, through listening, and through reading. Of these three, only reading can be speeded up to cope with an increasingly technological society. 2) In addition to reading for pleasure and self-improvement, most of the information that we need to live in our society is being printed. To complicate matters, the information is constantly changing to keep up with new technology. 3) Because of the changes in technology, job skills have changed from manual to mental. Reading for speed and comprehension is an essential tool for survival in today's world.

Reading for both speed and comprehension is the only way to read efficiently—to get the information you need in the shortest amount of time. If you read more slowly than you are able, you are wasting time. Reading too slowly can also decrease comprehension because attention is focused on small details instead of main ideas. By the time you finish reading, chances are you are bored and can't remember what you have read!

On the other hand, reading too rapidly can also cause a decrease in understanding because important ideas and key points are missed. It is important to adjust the rate to your speed of understanding so that you can maintain interest, get the key points and main ideas, and cover as much material in as little time as possible. Just to be able to function in the midst of the information explosion, you will need to develop the skills of reading for increased speed and comprehension.

How Can You Read for Increased Speed and Comprehension?

Here are some skills and techniques you can learn immediately for reading with increased speed and comprehension. The more you practice and apply the techniques, the greater your improvement will be. It takes drive and determination, as well as practice, to increase reading speed and comprehension skills.

1. Make time for personal reading.

Set aside time each day, perhaps before you go to sleep at night, for personal reading—novels, short stories, fashion or sports magazines—whatever you enjoy reading. You will be amazed at how much you can read by reading just a few minutes each day.

To illustrate how much reading you can complete by reading for a short period every day, read the following example reported by an expert in the field of reading. The average adult reader reads 250 to 300 words per minute (WPM). In just 15 minutes, this average reader, at 300 WPM, can read 4500 words. In one week, reading 15 minutes a day for 7 days, the average reader can read 31,500 words per week. That is 126,000 words per month, or 1,512,000 words in 12 months. That's about 20 books in just one year! Imagine, you can read approximately 20 books a year just by reading 15 minutes a day.

2. Overview everything you read.

Also called *surveying* or *previewing*, overviewing is looking over the reading material before you begin to read it. If you are going to read a book, read the title, preface, introduction, and back cover or jacket. For an article, read the title, introduction, and major and minor headings. Glance at all pictures and illustrations. For even more information from your overview of an article, read the first paragraph, the first sentence of every paragraph, and the last paragraph. Studies have shown that overviewing or previewing before you actually read can increase comprehension by as much as 30%! This happens because the overview often stimulates your interest and raises your curiosity about the book or article. It also helps bring to mind information you already know about the subject and raises questions about what you don't know. As you think about the subject and read to answer your questions, you will maintain better concentration and learn more from your reading. When you are reading to satisfy your curiosity, you will find that you can read faster and with greater comprehension because you are motivated to read.

Another advantage of overviewing is that sometimes you can get all of the information you need or want just from the overview process, and further reading is not necessary. It also helps you discover whether or not the book or article is interesting enough for you to read more closely, whether skimming and scanning will meet your needs, or whether you want to read it at all.

3. Skim and scan when reading.

To *skim*, you rapidly and selectively skip over words to identify main ideas. You skim when you look over a magazine article to see what it's about without reading the whole thing. To *scan*, you locate facts or details as quickly as possible. You scan when you look up a number in a phone book. Skimming and scanning are helpful tools when you are reading for specific information and you know ahead of time what you will be looking for as you read.

These tools can save you a great deal of time when you need to get information in a hurry. Skimming and scanning are also useful when you don't have time to thoroughly read a book or an article.

4. Use signal words and phrases when you read.

Being aware of signal words and phrases when you skim and scan will help you instantly decide which parts you need to read and which parts you can skip over. Signal words and phrases act like traffic signals when you read. They tell you when you should stop, slow down, or move ahead in your reading. Signal words and phrases are clues for what's coming next. They prepare you to guess at meaning or adjust to a change in direction in the author's train of thought.

The most common signal word is *and*. It connects ideas of equal importance. *And* also lets you know that more information is coming. Other words, such as *in addition*, *plus*, and *furthermore* also let you know that more information is to come.

On the other hand, words such as *finally, to sum up*, and *in conclusion*, signal that the end is near. By being alert to signal words, you can read more intelligently and more rapidly. Just as traffic signals tell you how to drive, signal words and phrases tell you how to read.

Look over the list of signal words and phrases in the Exercise section of this chapter. Skim over each until you feel certain that you can quickly identify signal words and phrases in your reading.

5. Read different materials at different rates.

As your purpose for reading varies, so should the *rate* at which you read each type of material. *The key to efficient reading is to learn when to read slowly and deliberately and when to read rapidly.*

Many readers have developed the habit of reading everything at the same rate. If it takes you the same amount of time to read 5 pages in a magazine as it does to read 5 pages in your science textbook, then you most likely have the habit of reading everything at the same rate. That means that you are reading too slowly for some materials and too quickly for others. The best test to determine if your rate of reading is right for the material is to stop periodically and ask yourself:

"What did I just read?" If you have no idea or only a fuzzy recollection, you are either reading so fast that you are missing important information or so slowly that your mind, which thinks much faster than you can read, is wandering off the subject. As a general rule, read slowly and carefully those materials which contain information and vocabulary that are new to you and that have many facts and details or difficult concepts. Save your faster rate of reading for subjects you are familiar with, for books or articles where you only need to get a general idea, and for materials that are not difficult or challenging to read.

6. Know your purpose for reading.

Knowing your purpose for reading something will help you decide how fast you can read it. Instead of opening a book or magazine and starting at the beginning and plodding your way through every word, decide ahead of time what you want to get from reading it. Then say, I will look at this, this, and this, but I will skip that because it doesn't relate to my purpose. You don't have to pay attention to everything just because it is there. Successful speed readers choose which parts to read and which parts to skip so that they pick up only the information they want.

7. Hold your book at the proper angle of sight.

Research has shown that you can increase your reading speed by 5% by holding or propping up your book at about a 90 degree angle, instead of laying the book flat on the table. The top of the book should be about the same distance from your eyes as the bottom of the book—about 14 to 20 inches. This position will make it possible for you to read with your neck in an upright position. By holding your head up instead of bending over the book, you will be able to read for longer periods of time because you will avoid neck and shoulder strain.

8. Pace with your finger or a card to increase reading speed.

Another way to read faster is *pacing*—quickly sweeping your index finger or a card across the lines of print, guiding your eyes along after it. This practice will help you break the habit of reading along at your usual comfortable rate.

9. Avoid moving your lips when you read.

The habit of lip-moving slows down your rate of reading to the rate of talking which is about 100 to 125 words per minute. Since the average high school student reads about 250 WPM, you can immediately increase your speed of reading by 100 to 150 WPM just by breaking the lip-moving habit.

How do you know if you move your lips when you read? Put a pencil between your lips before you begin to read silently. If it falls out as you read, then you have the habit of lip-moving. To break this habit, continue reading with a pencil between your lips. Each time it falls out, tell yourself that you will not move your lips as you read. This habit can usually be broken with conscious effort and practice.

10. Eliminate the habit of subvocalization.

The habit of subvocalization is similar to lip-moving except that the words are pronounced silently in the throat instead of with the lips. This habit slows down the reading rate to the rate of talking just as lip-moving does. To find out if you have the habit of subvocalization, place the tips of your fingers of one hand on the vocal chord area of your throat. Keep them there as you read silently.

If you feel vibrations as you read, you most likely have this habit. If you think you subvocalize when you read, practice reading with your fingertips placed on your vocal chords. Stop reading whenever you feel vibrations in your throat. Like lip-moving, this habit can usually be broken through conscious effort.

11. Don't regress or backtrack unnecessarily when you read.

Even the best readers occasionally go back to re-read a word, phrase, or sentence for better understanding. But when readers have the habit of unnecessarily re-reading words, phrases, or sentences, they are regressing. This habit is like taking a few steps backward for every step forward. Regressing really slows down reading rate. It can also lower comprehension because it makes reading a boring, drawn out task that is difficult to pay attention to.

To discover whether or not you have the habit of regressing, pick up a magazine or a newspaper article and a pen or pencil. As you read, trace a line under each line of print going from the left side of the paper to the right. If your eyes stop and back up, go back and make a second line under the word or phrase that you re-read. Each time you start reading again, be determined not to let yourself regress. With practice, this habit can be eliminated so that you only regress occasionally.

12. Read in phrases or thought units.

Beginning readers read one-word-at-a-time. As their reading skills progress, they read groups of words at a time. Efficient readers expand to reading in phrases and thought units. The following example shows what reading one-word-at-a-time is like:

> **An / efficient / reader / reads / groups / of / words / at / a / time.**

The same sentence, read in phrases, would be divided like this:

> **An efficient reader / reads groups / of words / at a time.**

In thought units, the sentence would be read:

> **An efficient reader / reads groups of words / at a time.**

By reading in phrases and thought units, you can increase your reading speed because you are reading more words at a time and making fewer stops along a line of print.

13. Give your full attention to the reading material.

Since the brain can only attend to one thing at a time, you will improve both your reading speed and comprehension by giving your full attention to your reading material. That means turning off the television if it distracts you from your reading. It also means staying off the phone when you are reading. For some students, it is not a problem to listen to music as they read. But, when the music is no longer in the background, and you find yourself singing along or thinking about the words, then your attention is on the music—not your reading.

14. Build your vocabulary.

One of the best ways to expand your literal comprehension is to build your vocabulary. Literal comprehension is that basic level of understanding we use to 1) recognize words and recall their meaning, and 2) identify main ideas and their supporting details. Whenever you look up a telephone number, read a recipe, or follow printed directions, you are using your literal comprehension skills. The reader who is rich in words will be wealthy with understanding. Chapter 12, "Vocabulary Development," offers many suggestions for building vocabulary.

15. Identify main ideas.

By developing the skill of rapidly locating main ideas in paragraphs, you will increase your comprehension, as well as your reading speed. The main idea is found in the topic sentence—the sentence around which the paragraph is written. The tricky part is to locate the topic sentence. While the topic sentence usually comes first in a paragraph, it may also occur in the middle or at the end as well. Sometimes the writer does not state the main idea in a topic sentence. Your challenge, as a reader, is to infer (make a good guess at) the main idea from the information the author does give you.

> Two key questions you can ask to help you find the topic and main idea of a paragraph are:
>
> ■ Who or what is the passage about? (Finding the answer to this question will provide the *topic* of the paragraph.)
>
> ■ What is being stated about the who or what identified in your response to question #1? (The answer to this question will be the *main idea* of the paragraph.)

16. Read with a pencil or marker.

If it is OK to write in your book, you can circle words you might want to look up or refer to later. Underline key points. Star a sentence that really catches your interest or that expresses a main idea. Make a note in the margin regarding some association you made with the information. Mark parallel lines next to whole sentences or paragraphs that you may want to re-read. Read each paragraph completely before you go back to mark or underline any part of it.

If it is not OK to write in your book, jot down brief notes or key words and phrases. Or, use stick-on notes to highlight sections of the article or book.

17. React and respond to what you read to increase comprehension.

Have you ever finished reading something only to ask "What was that all about?" If you couldn't answer your question, you had two problems: poor comprehension and no retention. When you do not understand or remember what you have read, reading is a waste of your valuable time. To understand and remember the ideas from your reading, you must react or respond to what you read. One of the most effective responses is to write a short summary of the main points. Other effective responses are:

- telling someone else about what you have read
- discussing what you have read with your study group
- talking about what you have read into a tape recorder
- marking and underlining your text after you have read each section
- making an outline
- repeating key points in an oral review
- taking notes on the reading
- making associations between the new information and information you already have learned.

The following exercises will provide you with some practice for improving your reading speed and comprehension. For even greater improvement, apply the techniques you learn from this chapter to your daily reading tasks.

EXERCISES

R-1. Using Techniques for Reading Improvement

Look back over the 17 techniques for reading improvement. Choose 5 to practice during the next three weeks. Keep a journal that will include the following information for each of the 5 techniques:

- date started
- technique practiced
- daily comments on using the technique
- date of end of practice, and
- concluding statements about how your reading skill has changed as a result of practicing the technique.

R-2. Using Signal Words and Phrases

Using the list of Signal Words and Phrases which appears on the next page as a guide, search for signal words and phrases in an article or chapter that your teacher has provided. Your teacher will tell you whether to circle the words and phrases or list them on a separate sheet of paper.

R-3. Reading in Thought Units

Go back to the first paragraph under the heading, "What is Efficient Reading for Speed and Comprehension?" Read the paragraph and break it into thought units by making slash (/) marks after each thought unit.

> After you have marked the paragraph, check it against the Answer Key in Appendix A. Change your marks to match ours. Then, practice reading the paragraph in thought units by focusing in one glance on all of the words between each slash mark.

For additional practice reading in phrases and thought units, select a newspaper or magazine article and mark it off in thought units. Then practice focusing on the thought units as you read. Practice this exercise several times a week for at least three weeks to improve your skill of reading in phrases and thought units.

SIGNAL WORDS AND PHRASES

To Show Addition or Another Idea
also
and
another
besides
but also
equally important
finally
first
in addition
next

To Show Summary or Repetition
as I have said
finally
in brief
in closing
in conclusion
in other words
in short
in summary
to conclude
to sum up

To Show Comparison
in like manner
in the same way
likewise
similarly

To Show Contrast or Change in Idea
although
anyway
but
even though
however
in contrast
instead
nevertheless
otherwise
yet

To Show a Specific Case
a few of these are
an example
especially
for example
for instance
in particular
let us consider
the following
you can see this in
the case of

To Show Purpose
all things considered
for this purpose
to this end
with this end in mind
with this object

To Show Place
above
across
adjacent to
below
beneath
beside
between
beyond
farther
here

To Show Amount
both
considerable
few
greater
less than
many
more than
under
several
some

To Show Time
afterward
at last
before
during
finally
immediately
later
often
soon
while

To Show Condition
because
if
since
which

To Show Result
as a result
because
consequently
for this reason
hence
so
then
therefore
thereupon
thus

To Strengthen a Point
basically
essentially
indeed
no doubt
typically
truly
undeniably
without a doubt
without any question

This is only a partial list of the signal words and phrases in each category. Look for these and similar signal words and phrases as you read.

R-4. Increasing Your Reading Speed

Did you know that you can increase your reading speed at the same time that you read a paperback novel? By using the steps for estimating reading rate listed below, you can practice building reading speed with any book that you will be reading over a period of time. To make your practice more fun, choose a book that you can easily comprehend and that is of high interest to you. Then, follow the steps below:

1. Select a sample for reading.

2. Determine the number of words in the sample.

    a. Count the number of words in 5 lines of print and divide by 5 to get the average number of words per line.

    b. Multiply the number of words per page by the number of pages in the selection to obtain the total word count.

    c. For best results, mark off your book into several 1,000 word passages.

3. Record your starting time or use a stopwatch.

4. Read your selection.

5. Record your ending time.

6. Divide the total number of words in the selection by reading time. (Carry the division to one decimal point for accuracy.)

    For example, if you read 1,000 words in 160 seconds, you would determine your rate in WPM like this:

$$
\begin{array}{r}
6.2 \\
\hline
160 \text{ seconds)}\overline{1{,}000.0 \text{ words}} \\
960.0 \\
\hline
40.0 \\
32.0 \\
\hline
8.0
\end{array}
$$

$$6.2 \times 60 = 372 \text{ WPM}$$

Keep a record of your rate in WPM so that you can monitor your progress. Repeat this exercise with five new 1,000 word passages from your book at least three times a week for one month.

YOUR TURN TO TALK BACK

Take a few moments to think about the things that were discussed about efficient reading for speed and comprehension in this chapter. Look over the exercises you were asked to complete. Then, respond to the questions below and give your answers to your teacher or counselor.

■ What did you like about this chapter on efficient reading for speed and comprehension?

■ What didn't you like about this chapter?

■ What did you learn about efficient reading for speed and comprehension?

■ How will you put into practice what you learned about efficient reading for speed and comprehension as a result of doing this chapter?

■ What Internet source did you find useful for this chapter?

Chapter 12
Vocabulary Development

I really didn't mean to say that.

Chapter 12
Vocabulary Development

SCENARIO

Buddy: How was your date with Felicia on Friday night, Kareem?

Kareem: I really messed it up! I thought I'd impress her by writing her a note complimenting her to show how I feel about her. I even put in some lines I heard in a romantic movie. I gave her the note Friday afternoon thinking that it would make her more excited about the date. I couldn't have been more wrong. When I got to her house Friday evening, she refused to go out with me.

Buddy: Why?

Kareem: It turns out that she didn't know what some of the words I wrote meant, so she looked them up in the dictionary. Apparently, I didn't know what they meant either, or I confused them with other words, because what I actually wrote her wasn't at all what I meant to say.

Buddy: What exactly did you say to her?

Kareem: I told her that her eyes made me think of *limpet* pools. She said that she didn't like being told that she had eyes which reminded me of clams! I later found out that I should have said *limpid* pools which means that they are like perfectly clear pools of water. I also wrote that her beauty left me *impassive*. The word I should have used was *impassioned* because I wanted to say that her beauty caused me to have strong feelings for her. The word I used instead means no feeling.

Buddy: That's terrible!

Kareem: I'm afraid the story gets worse. I also told her that her hair looked as soft to touch as *vermin*.

Buddy: That's disgusting! Didn't you know that vermin are things like flies, lice, and rats that carry disease?

Kareem: No, I thought I was telling her that her hair looked as soft as beautiful fur. The word I should have used was *ermine*. I feel so stupid and embarrassed that I will never be able to face Felicia again!

STIMULUS QUESTIONS

1. How do you feel when you learn than you have been misusing a word?

    _____

    _____

2. What do you think about other people when you hear them misuse or mispronounce a word?

    _____

    _____

3. What do you think someone would recommend as a good way to increase a person's vocabulary?

    _____

    _____

    _____

4. Some adults are saying that teens today have limited vocabularies because they watch too much television. Do you think that's true?

    _____

    Vocabulary will always be an important part of your personal and professional life. In this chapter, you will learn the four types of vocabularies and some ways to improve each.

LEARNING ABOUT VOCABULARY DEVELOPMENT

What is Vocabulary Development?

We don't really think about it, but we have more than one vocabulary. We have 4 vocabularies: speaking, listening, reading, and writing. We understand words we hear on radio or TV that we don't use when speaking or writing. Well-educated persons are equally at home with words they hear, speak, read, or write.

Vocabulary development is a lifelong task. As new technology is developed and our base of knowledge is expanded, new words come into being. These neologisms (new words), such as sitcom, modem, and yuppie, must be learned if we are to keep up with what's happening. As we go on to higher education or get new jobs, we are faced with new vocabulary. Each subject of study has its own specialized language as does each type of job, from laborers' jobs to executive positions. So, as we progress through life, all of our vocabularies need to constantly change. Learning new vocabulary is a constant challenge.

Why is Learning New Vocabulary Important?

Words are power. A broad knowledge of words, their meanings, and how they are used gives a person the power to communicate on both a personal and professional level. Learning new vocabulary can enrich your life in many ways: academically, socially, and professionally.

How Can You Improve Your Vocabulary?

Two good ways to improve your vocabulary are by using context clues (the other words in the sentence) and by analyzing the structure, or parts, of unfamiliar words.

■ In using the context to discover the meaning of an unfamiliar word, you see if the word is defined for you in the sentence or paragraph in which it is used. For example, if you didn't know the meaning of the word "neologism," you could figure it out from the words around it:

> Example: *Neologisms* are so confusing. As soon as I learn the *new words* or the *new meanings for established words,* they change again.

■ To discover meaning from examining word parts, you need to recognize and learn the meaning of various prefixes, root or base words, and suffixes. Studies have shown that you can learn to unlock the meaning of thousands of words just by learning a few word parts. Word parts are:

prefix—the group of letters before the root or base word which add to or change the meaning of the base word

> Example: *un* + changeable = not able to change

root or *base*—the basic word

> Example: un*change*able

suffix—the group of letters at the end of a word which add to or change its meaning

> Example: change*able* = ability to change

In addition to these two ways to improve your vocabulary, the following tips will also be helpful.

Tips for Improving Vocabulary

■ Keep a dictionary handy when you read so that you can look up new words. Most dictionaries give a lot of information about the word, such as: how to spell and pronounce the word, its history (where the word came from), what part of speech it is, its meanings, and examples of how it is used. The more you learn about a new word, the better your chances are of using and remembering it.

■ Each time you learn a new word, associate it with other words such as *synonyms* (words which mean the same thing) and *antonyms* (words which are opposite in meaning). A *thesaurus* is a good reference for finding synonyms.

■ Group words together into word families. For example, "vision," which means the power to see with the eye, would be grouped with "visit," which means to go see. By grouping words, you will increase your recall of what the word means.

■ Classify new words with words you already know. For example, the word "kidney" would be classified with "heart," "lungs," "stomach," and names of other organs.

■ Make *flash cards* for new words. Write the new word on one side of an index card. Write the definition on the other side. Copy the sentence from your reading that contains the new word under the definition on your card as an example of how the word is used. You now have a study card for reviewing new vocabulary.

■ To help you learn and remember a new word, use the word at least 3 times. First, write the word. Then, look up the word and write its definition. Copy the sentence from your reading that uses the word. Write a sentence of your own using the word correctly.

EXERCISES

V-1. Learning about Your Reading, Listening, Speaking, and Writing Vocabularies

As you complete Part A and Part B of this exercise, you should make a discovery about your different kinds of vocabularies.

Part A: Read at least 3 issues of one of your favorite magazines very carefully. Write down 10 words that you recognize the meaning of but that you think others may not know. Keep your list of words for later use.

Part B: Listen to a TV news show. Write down some words that you understand but that you think other students might not.

Look over the words you wrote down from the magazines and from the TV news show. Put a check by the words you use when speaking. Put a double check by those words you use in writing.

Then, fill-in the following blanks:

How many words from your two lists did you know by reading? _____

How many words did you recognize by listening? _____

How many words are in your speaking vocabulary? _____

How many words would you use when writing? _____

From doing this exercise, which vocabulary is your smallest? _____

Which is your largest vocabulary?_____

What conclusions can you draw about your speaking and listening vocabularies?

_____

_____

V-2. Ways Vocabulary Enriches Your Life

Read over the list of ways that vocabulary can enrich your life. Put a checkmark (✓) by each one you agree with.

_____1. having the tools to understand what you read or hear

_____2. expressing ideas and thoughts clearly and accurately

_____3. being able to follow the speeches of others

_____4. having the words to argue successfully

_____5. being able to influence and impress others with words

_____6. keeping up with new technology

_____7. getting a better job

_____8. broadening understanding of the world

_____9. increasing general and specific knowledge

_____10. avoiding embarrassment due to lack of understanding or misuse of words

_____11. getting information accurately

_____12. decreasing chances of being "conned" or fooled by others

_____13. eliminating possible learning problems or mistakes due to lack of understanding of terms or concepts

_____14. experiencing more creativity in expressing yourself.

V-3. Learning New Vocabulary with Flash Cards

Make flash cards for the unfamiliar words you come across while reading your textbooks. Also make cards for all assigned vocabulary words.

Turn your cards in to your teacher or counselor for credit.

YOUR TURN TO TALK BACK

Think about what you have read and learned about vocabulary development. Look back over the exercises you were asked to complete and then respond to the questions below. Give them to your teacher or counselor when you have finished.

■ What did you like about this chapter on vocabulary development?

■ What didn't you like about this chapter?

■ What did you learn about improving your vocabulary from this chapter?

■ How will your vocabulary improvement skills change as a result of completing this chapter?

■ What Internet source did you find useful for this chapter?

Chapter 13
Concentration While Learning

I never know what's going on in class.

Chapter 13
Concentration While Learning

SCENARIO

Maria: I never know what's going on in my English class because all I can do in there is stare at Jose. He is the cutest guy I've ever seen! How am I supposed to concentrate on some story when Jose is sitting right next to me?

Linda: I can't concentrate on my work in there either, but it isn't because of Jose. All I can think of in there is what I'm going to do after school with my friends.

Jahmal: I really try to pay attention in class, but by 6th period, I'm so hungry that all I can think of is food. Instead of concentrating on Shakespeare, I'm dreaming about cheeseburgers and fries.

Larry: Well, I'm having so many arguments with my parents lately about driving and what time I have to be home that I feel upset all of the time. I spend most of my class time thinking about how unfair my parents are. I try to listen and take notes, but I find myself thinking of arguments that I can use on my parents when I get home. Even in class when we read literature that I like, I think about my problems. I'd better get things settled with my parents soon so I can concentrate on my classes.

STIMULUS QUESTIONS

1. What are the things which keep you from concentrating in class?

    _____

    _____

2. Ask an older person, perhaps your mother, father, or guardian, how they are able to concentrate when they read or listen to a speech. Write down what solutions they have that you might consider using to help you concentrate.

    _____

    _____

    _____

3. Is it easier to concentrate more in some classes than in others? _____. Think about which classes you have problems concentrating in and the ones you don't. What do you think are some reasons that it is easier for you to concentrate in some classes more than in others?

    _____

    _____

    _____

Your ability to concentrate will vary from subject to subject just as your interest varies from one subject to the next. You probably realized in responding to the stimulus questions that it is easier to concentrate in the classes you like than in the ones you don't care for. You most likely realized that things like where the class takes place, who is in the class, what problems you are having, and your interests, all distract you from concentrating in the classroom. The same type of emotional and physical distractions can interfere with your concentration as you study at home. While this chapter cannot solve your problems, it can show you some ways to increase your power to concentrate while learning.

LEARNING ABOUT CONCENTRATION WHILE LEARNING

What Is Concentration While Learning?

Concentration while learning is focusing your thoughts, attention and efforts on the subject at hand. If you allow your mind to wander or to daydream, you cannot learn what you are attempting to learn. Concentration involves keen observation, focused attention, association, and visualization. To concentrate, you must observe what you are seeing, hearing, experiencing, or feeling. You must center or focus your attention on the information to be learned.

Why Is It Important to Concentrate While Learning?

The number one reason to concentrate while learning is that learning cannot take place unless you concentrate! A mind that is free to wander from the subject matter cannot attend to the material to be learned. If you have ever read an entire page or more only to discover that you have no idea what you just read, then you experienced reading without concentration. If you have ever sat through a speech or lecture and suddenly found yourself wondering what the speaker is talking about, you have not been concentrating while listening. Both experiences were a complete waste of your time because nothing was gained or learned.

Learning how to concentrate on the subject matter for your assignments will help you to learn more in less time. The chapters on "Listening for Notemaking" and "Study-Reading" describe how time and energy can be saved by paying attention and concentrating while reading and listening.

How Can You Increase Your Concentration While Learning?

Here are 5 suggestions for increasing your concentration while learning:

1. Be interested in the subject. If you are not naturally interested in the material, create an interest by asking questions about the material that will increase your curiosity about the subject. One way to focus your attention is to ask questions as you are reading or listening. Without having an interest in the subject, it is very hard to find the motivation to learn it.

2. Find your motivation for learning. Ask yourself, "Why do I need or want to learn this?" "What will I gain by learning this?" or, on the other hand, "What will I lose or what will happen if I don't learn it?" Knowing why you are learning something helps you to find the energy and desire to learn something.

3. Focus your attention. When your attention wavers, the learning process breaks down. You can only learn something if you pay attention to it. This is often very difficult to do, especially if you are not particularly interested in the subject matter you are expected to learn. (Once again, refer to Chapter #4, "Study-Reading," and Chapter #5, "Listening for Notemaking," for ways to focus your attention.)

4. Eliminate distractions. Keep distractions to a minimum whenever possible when you are trying to concentrate. A great deal of self-discipline is sometimes required to reduce distractions. For example, you may have to turn the volume down or change the station on your radio. You may even have to TURN OFF your music or the TV while you complete your learning tasks. Research has shown that when students listened to lively music when they read, the amount of information they understood and remembered decreased. Whenever you find yourself aware of the song on the radio or of something that is happening on the the television, your concentration on your studies is broken. Your mind is on the music or the program—not on your book.

Another major distraction for teenagers when doing homework at home is the telephone. If you spend more time talking on the telephone than you do completing your learning tasks, then extreme self-discipline is called for. You may actually have to unplug the phone or have a family member say that you are unavailable until your assignments have been completed. You may be surprised to discover that you will complete your homework in less time because you will not be interrupted, and then you will actually have more time to talk on the phone.

If physical or emotional problems are preventing you from concentrating, do your best to solve the problems as soon as possible so that you can get on with your learning tasks. For example, if you are hungry, stop and eat. If you are cold, put on something warmer. If you are angry or hurt, speak to the other party involved so that you can make up. If you have emotional or personal problems that you are unable to solve by yourself, make an appointment to see the school counselor right away.

When distractions in your learning environment interfere with your concentration, ask to move to another seat in the classroom, or whenever possible, move to another place to study. If you sit next to someone in class you like to talk to or who talks too much to you, ask to be moved—just so you can more easily pay attention. If you like to study with friends but discover that you get little done because you and your friends spend the time visiting, study alone. Whenever you can create a place to study where you can concentrate, you will have an easier time paying attention and learning. The fewer distractions you have to resist, the greater your chances of concentrating.

5. Visualize as you read or listen. Try to visualize or picture in your mind the things you are hearing or reading about. As you create pictures you will be increasing your chances of remembering new information because of associating it with your pictures. Research has shown that things which are seen are remembered longer than things which are read or heard. In your own experience, which can you remember better—a scene from a favorite movie or a passage from a favorite book?

EXERCISES

C-1. Improving Your Concentration in the Classroom

Think about your classes and pick one in which you have difficulty concentrating. Keep an index card or a small piece of paper on your desk. Put a "✓" on your card or paper each time you catch yourself daydreaming or letting your attention stray to something other than what your teacher is saying. If you are reading an assignment or working on a project in class, put a "✓" each time your mind wanders.

At the end of class, count the number of checks on your card or paper and write the total on the chart below. Since it takes at least 20 days to break a habit, continue keeping track of your concentration lapses for at least 20 school days.

Set a goal each day to get fewer checks than you did the day before. Once you are consciously aware that you are not concentrating, you can direct your attention back to the material to be learned.

Use the Concentration Chart below to summarize your improvement in concentration.

CONCENTRATION CHART			
MONDAY	Day 1 _____	Day 6 _____	Day 11 _____	Day 16 _____
TUESDAY	Day 2 _____	Day 7 _____	Day 12 _____	Day 17 _____
WEDNESDAY	Day 3 _____	Day 8 _____	Day 13 _____	Day 18 _____
THURSDAY	Day 4 _____	Day 9 _____	Day 14 _____	Day 19 _____
FRIDAY	Day 5 _____	Day 10 _____	Day 15 _____	Day 20 _____

C-2. What I Learned about Improving My Concentration

Use your Concentration Chart to help you answer the questions below.

1. Is it harder for you to concentrate on any particular day of the week than on the others?
   _____If YES, which day? _____

2. Was there any particular day each week when you had the least trouble concentrating?
   _____If YES, which day? _____

3. Indicate how much your concentration improved by writing the number of marks you got at the beginning of the exercise with the number you were getting at the end.

   _____

4. Was your improvement in concentration in class consistent or was it different from one day to the next?

   _____

5. Think back over the days when you recall having a hard time concentrating. What do you think was the problem?

   _____

6. If you can recall, what was different about the days when you had little trouble concentrating in class?

   _____

   _____

7. List the things you did when you caught yourself not concentrating to bring your concentration back to the subject at hand.

   _____

   _____

   _____

8. Discuss the results of this exercise with your teacher for more suggestions for improving your concentration during class.

YOUR TURN TO TALK BACK

Take a few moments to think about the things that were discussed about concentration while learning in this chapter. Also, glance over the tasks you were asked to complete. Then, respond to the questions below and give your answers to your teacher or counselor.

■ What did you like about this chapter on concentration while learning?

■ What didn't you like about this chapter?

■ What did you learn about concentration while learning?

■ How will you put into practice what you learned about concentration while learning as a result of doing this chapter?

■ What Internet source did you find useful for this chapter?

Chapter 14
Health and Vision

When I read, my eyes get tired and I get a headache.

Chapter 14
Health and Vision

SCENARIO

Ralph: Hey, Josh, did you finish the reading assignment for English class last night?

Josh: Oh, Ralph, I thought I'd never finish! It took me three hours to read it because I can only read for about twenty minutes before my eyes get tired. When I read longer, my eyes don't feel good, and I get a headache.

Ralph: I know what you mean, Josh. Before I got my new glasses, I used to get horrible headaches. I couldn't read anything that was written on the chalkboard. Sometimes my vision was blurred and I couldn't focus clearly on my book. Now, I don't have to squint to read the board, and I can easily focus on my book.

Josh: Maybe I need to get glasses. I'm going to talk to my parents about it tonight because these vision problems and headaches make it hard for me to do my schoolwork. Besides that, I can hardly see what's on television unless I sit right in front of it!

STIMULUS QUESTIONS

1.   Do you have a hard time staying awake in class? _____ If you do, tell why you think you are so tired/sleepy when you are in class.

_____

_____

2.   Do you frequently have difficulty concentrating on your studies because you can't stop worrying about someone or something? _____ If you answered YES, write down what it is that is worrying you.

_____

_____

3.   Do headaches or other physical problems bother you so much when you are in class that you find it hard to pay attention to what's being taught?_____ If you answered YES, describe the physical problem here:

_____

_____

4.   Do your eyes bother you when you are trying to read the chalkboard, your computer screen, or your textbook?_____ If you answered YES, describe the problem here:

_____

_____

5.   Are you so hungry in class that you find it hard to pay attention to your teacher and concentrate on your assignments?

_____

_____

6.   Do you have someone you can talk to about the things that concern or worry you?_____ If you answered YES, write down the people you can talk to —your support network—here:

_____

_____

If you answered NO, make an appointment today to see the school counselor. Everyone deserves and needs someone to talk over problems with.

Now that you have responded to the stimulus questions, you may have some idea of the health and/or vision problems that are keeping you from doing your best as a student. Hunger, exhaustion, physical pain or discomfort, vision problems, emotional problems, and stress all make reading, studying, and learning difficult, if not impossible. When the mind's attention is drawn elsewhere, it is not possible to concentrate on the material at hand. This chapter offers some information and exercises that will help you consider the importance of health and vision.

LEARNING ABOUT HEALTH AND VISION

What Are Good Health and Vision?

Good health means physical, mental, and emotional well-being. It is freedom from continual discomfort, pain, and disease so that you feel well enough to do the things you need and want to do.

Good vision is the ability to see shapes and images clearly. This ability to see well, to focus clearly, and to have the eyes work together when reading are important factors in being able to learn and study information from the printed page.

Why Is It Important to be Healthy and Have Good Vision?

Being healthy in body and mind helps us to get up in the morning and face the day with energy and a positive attitude. A healthy body and mind are free to explore and to learn, while the symptoms of poor health interfere with learning. Frequent absences from school, falling asleep in class, lack of energy to concentrate, and inability to pay attention due to pain or discomfort will cause problems and learning difficulties for any student.

Good vision, whether a natural asset or corrected by glasses or lenses, is an important factor in being a successful student. Good vision alone is not enough; good visual habits must also be practiced to allow for long periods of reading and studying. Poor vision and the use of poor visual habits can lead to:

- headaches
- tired eyes
- dislike for reading
- skipping lines or words while reading
- loosing place while reading
- slow reading
- confusing some letters and words with others
- restlessness, nervousness, irritability
- inattention and boredom.

As you can see, it pays to take good care of your eyes and maintain good vision.

How Can You Stay Healthy and Maintain Good Vision?

To have and maintain good vision, you should be conscious of how your eyes are working and feeling. For example, can you see and read the writing on the board in the classroom from where you sit? Do words blur together when you read your textbook? Do your eyes tire easily? Are your eyes frequently itchy, red or watery? These are the types of eye problems you should be aware of. Tell your parents, guardian, or the school nurse if you experience any of these. A regular examination by an eye care professional is desirable. If you wear glasses or contact lenses, be sure to wear them as directed to avoid eye strain or damage.

By this time, you undoubtedly have had health classes which have emphasized the importance of eating a well-balanced diet, getting enough sleep, and doing some kind of regular exercise. You most likely have had much information presented on the effects of stimulants and drugs on the mind and body. All of these things affect your health and general well-being. Another factor which affects overall health is stress. Stress, when allowed to go unchecked, can lead to physical, mental, and emotional problems. Reacting to stress is the body's way of warning that change must be made. Learn to listen to your body and to change those things which are causing stress or adapt to those things which cannot be changed.

Follow the recommendations below for a healthier you:

- eat regularly and well
- sleep regular hours
- exercise regularly
- avoid substance abuse (drugs and alcohol)
- practice stress-reducing techniques
- heed your body's warning signals.

To find out more about your health and vision and to learn some techniques for coping with stress, read and complete the activities which follow.

EXERCISES

HV-1. Checklist for Visual Health

Read carefully items #1 - #14 on the checklist below. Put a check mark (✓) in the column which most accurately describes how often you display the symptom described. You will need someone to help you with the remainder of the items on the checklist.

Visual Health Checklist	Frequently	Sometimes	Rarely
1. Headaches during or following reading			
2. Blurring of vision during visual tasks			
3. Burning or smarting eyes			
4. Excessive watering of eyes during reading			
5. Redness of eyes after visual tasks			
6. Losing place while reading			
7. Using finger or card to keep place			
8. Daydreaming/mind wandering when reading			
9. Returning to the line just read			
10. Avoiding visual tasks			
11. Becoming nervous during visual tasks			
12. Forgetting what was just read			
13. Regressing—re-reading words and phrases			
14. Extending book to arm's length or thrusting head back to read			

! *Before you complete this checklist, ask someone to observe you while you read. Have your observer read items #15 - #22 before you start to read so as to know what to look for. Read silently for at least 5 minutes so that your observer can see how often you display any of the behaviors described in items #15 - #22.*

	Frequently	Sometimes	Rarely
15. Blinking uncontrollably			
16. Frowning or squinting when reading			
17. Closing one eye while reading			
18. Moving head back and forth instead of eyes			
19. Holding head close to book or paper			
20. Moving lips while reading silently			
21. Reading with only one eye—lazy eye			
22. Cocking head to one side when reading.			

Look back over your checklist. If most of your checkmarks are in the "Frequently" column, talk to your parents or guardians about the possibility of needing a professional eye examination.

HV-2. Resting Your Eyes

Whether reading from printed material or a computer screen, your eyes will serve you better if you rest them regularly when you are reading and studying. One way to rest your eyes is to: stop reading every 30 minutes and close your eyes for at least 15 seconds. When you open your eyes, focus on a distant point—across the room or out the window. Shutting the eyes and then focusing on a distant point allows the short eye muscles that move the eyes during the reading process to relax and rest. You will be albe to read and study for several hours at a time if you do this exercise at least every 30 minutes.

Practice this exercise as you read your next assignment, keeping track of how long you read and the number of times that you stopped to do this exercise. When you have finished reading and doing this eye relaxation exercise, fill in the blanks in the statement below.

As I read_____.
                                     (book title)

beginning at _____and stopping at_____.
                    (time)   (time)

I stopped_____times and did my eye resting exercise.

HV-3. Your Body's Warning Signs

Stress is not a disease even though it can, if left unchecked, make you ill. The body is constantly sending out signals to keep you posted on your stress situation. This body and mind reporting system is like the reporting system built into an automobile. When something goes wrong with the engine, a dashboard light comes on or begins to flash, warning that something is wrong and needs to be tended to. The smart driver will see the light and take care of the problem. The uneducated driver will ignore the lights, figuring that they will go away.

Do you pay attention to the "warning lights" or signals in your body? To find out how stressed you are, complete this exercise by following these directions:

Read the following list of signs of stress. If the statement describes a symptom you have, place a "✓" under the TRUE column. If the statement does not apply to you, write a "✓" under the FALSE column. This is an exercise for your eyes only, so respond as honestly as you can.

SYMPTOM	TRUE	FALSE
1. I have experienced a general feeling of anxiety, irritability, or depression.	_____	_____
2. I often have a strong urge to cry or run and hide.	_____	_____
3. My throat and mouth often feel dry and parched.	_____	_____
4. I have trouble concentrating.	_____	_____
5. I have noticed my muscles trembling uncontrollably.	_____	_____
6. I have developed nervous tics (muscle spasms I can't control).	_____	_____
7. I often have cramping and diarrhea.	_____	_____
8. I have noticed a decrease/increase in appetite.	_____	_____
9. I just started to smoke, or I am smoking more.	_____	_____
10. I have increased my use of legal drugs.	_____	_____
11. I often have terrible headaches.	_____	_____
12. I have noticed increased or excessive sweating.	_____	_____

SYMPTOM	TRUE	FALSE
13. I am having frequent nightmares.	_____	_____
14. I have a tendency to be startled by small sounds.	_____	_____
15. I often feel "keyed up" or "wired."	_____	_____
16. I have trouble sleeping most nights.	_____	_____
17. I need to urinate more often than usual.	_____	_____
18. I seem to be accident prone.	_____	_____
19. I tire easily.	_____	_____
20. I have a tendency to stutter or experience other speech problems.	_____	_____

Look back over your responses to see how many of these symptoms you see in yourself. This chart is not meant to include all of the warning signs of stress. Neither is it meant to imply that these symptoms are the result only of stress. If you found yourself answering TRUE to these questions, you are noticing your warning signals—signals that something may be wrong and needs to be changed. If you are concerned about your responses to these questions, talk them over with your parents or guardian, or with the school nurse or counselor.

HV-4. Breathing to Reduce Stress

The following deep breathing exercise will help you give your body the oxygen it needs and, in so doing, help your body relax.

Step 1: Close your eyes.

Step 2: Place the palms of your hands on your diaphragm (the large muscle just below your rib cage).

Step 3: Keeping your eyes closed and your hands in place, take a deep breath through your mouth. Feel your muscles expand as the air enters your body.

Step 4: Slowly let the air out through your mouth. Feel your diaphragm contract and relax.

Step 5: Wait a few seconds before taking another breath, allowing your muscles to remain relaxed. Notice that you have little or no thought as you relax.

Step 6: Repeat the exercise three to five times. Your body will become more relaxed with each repetition. Notice how much better you feel the more relaxed you become.

HV-5. Creating a Healthier Me

To help you become a healthier person so that you will be able to do your best as a student, think carefully about any health and vision problems that you may have and fill-out the chart below.

Health/Vision Problem	What I Plan to Do about It & When
1.	
2.	
3.	
4.	
5.	

YOUR TURN TO TALK BACK

Think about what you read and learned in this chapter about health and vision. Look back over your responses to the exercises you were asked to complete and then respond to the questions below. Give your responses to your teacher or counselor.

■ What did you like about this chapter on health and vision?

■ What didn't you like about this chapter?

■ What did you learn about health and vision from this chapter?

■ How will your health and vision habits change as a result of doing this chapter?

■ What Internet source did you find useful for this chapter?

Chapter 15
Attitudes

Leave me alone, I'm not going to school today!

Chapter 15
Attitudes

SCENARIO

Ben: Hey, Sally! Where are you going? School is the other direction!

Sally: Leave me alone, Ben. I'm not going to school today—maybe never again.

Ben: Why not?

Sally: I just don't see any reason to go to school. None of my teachers like me, and I can't stand them. I don't like their classes either. All we ever do is read stupid stuff and answer dumb questions. No matter what I do, I get "D's" and "F's." What good is it doing me, anyway? I'd rather go to the mall. Hey, why don't you come with me?

Ben: Nah, I better not. Don't get me wrong; I don't like school any more than you do. In fact, I hate it. The teachers don't do their jobs because I never learn anything. You have to be smart for school to do you any good, and all of the other kids are smarter than me. I can't see how anything we do at school will help me later on in life, but my old man won't let me drive if I cut school.

Sally: Chicken!

STIMULUS QUESTIONS

1. Think about Sally's and Ben's remarks about school. What do you think their real problems with school are?

   _____

   _____

2. Do you think that going to school regularly is important? _____

   Why or why not?_____

   _____

   _____

   _____

3. Think about a time when you received a grade you were unhappy with. Whose fault was it, and why?

   _____

   _____

4. Look over your response to stimulus question #3. Did you take responsibility for your grade, or did you make excuses and blame someone else?

   _____

5. Read the following statements and put a checkmark by those which describe how you *often* feel.

   ____"Why should I do any work for a teacher I don't like?"
   ____"My teachers hate me."
   ____"I don't like my classes."
   ____"Going to school is a waste of time."
   ____"It is the teacher's job to make me learn."
   ____"The other kids are smarter than I am."
   ____"I only go to school because I have to."
   ____"We don't do anything in school that will help me in real life."
   ____"My classes are so boring that it's impossible to pay attention."
   ____"It doesn't matter how much or how little I study, I'm going to fail anyway."

6. Read again the statements that you checked, then as honestly as you can, describe your attitude toward school.

_____

_____

_____

Feeling good about who you are and what you can achieve strengthens your self-esteem, builds your self-confidence, and helps you perform in a more successful way.

By reading and working through this chapter, you will be able to examine your attitudes and identify how you can change them to achieve the goals you have in mind.

LEARNING ABOUT ATTITUDES

What Is Attitude?

Attitude is a mental set—a way of thinking—that affects behavior. Attitude is revealed by what people *do,* not by what they *say* they will do or by what they *intend* to do. Your thoughts, feelings, desires, goals, and relationships with others help to form your attitude. You talk to yourself and then act on your self-talk. For example, if you tell yourself that you are a nice, friendly person, you will begin to act that way. Soon others will see you that way, too.

Research shows that there is an ongoing and significant relationship between self-concept and academic achievement. No one is sure which comes first—a poor attitude or poor performance, but we know that attitude determines performance.

Why Is Attitude Important?

Having the attitude that you will do well puts you on the right track for success. When your personal expectations begin to stretch, and you believe you can meet those expectations, you can get rid of the thoughts and behaviors which limit your achievement. A true story about Flip Wilson, a popular comedian, illustrates how one's behavior and achievement can change by adopting an attitude of being a "winner."

Flip came from a large family that moved from town to town. His mother left them when Flip was only five years old. His father drank heavily and changed jobs often. Finally, they settled in a town where Flip met a teacher who changed his life. Flip's school records indicated that he was not a good student and that he lacked motivation. On his first day in class, however, the teacher announced that this new boy was one of the brightest students to ever enter her classroom and that she would like him to have a seat in the front row. Flip said that he worked extremely hard to prove to his classmates that this teacher was right. His change in attitude about himself was a turning point in his life.

Success breeds success. Each success allows you to upgrade your standards, behaviors, and self-image. If you see yourself as a winner, you will always try to succeed no matter what the odds. On the other hand, if you believe that you can't be successful as a student, chances are you won't be. A negative attitude is self-defeating. Adopt the attitude that goes with the image you want to project, and you will eventually live up to that image.

How Can You Develop A Positive Attitude?

You can change your attitude from a self-defeating or negative attitude to a positive attitude by taking the following steps:

1. Begin by changing your self-talk.

Tell yourself you can do better and then plan the behavior that will make your self-talk come true. For example, instead of telling yourself that you don't have a chance of passing your math test because your teacher asks trick questions, tell yourself that you will study hard enough so that you will pass no matter how tricky the questions are. Don't let anger or resentment help you form an attitude that will keep you from doing your best. Work to do your best no matter what the situation.

2. Make a personal decision and commitment to learn.

To learn something well, you have to want to learn it. Wanting to learn means that you are motivated to learn. It's easy to be motivated to learn things that really interest us like baseball statistics or titles of popular songs, but it is harder to learn math formulas unless we feel motivated to learn them. Without a firm decision and commitment that we will learn something, especially something which we may not find particularly interesting, chances are that we won't learn it.

3. Set realistic goals for yourself.

Since success leads to more success, set goals for yourself that you truly can reach within a reasonable amount of time. For example, if your overall grades are poor, don't set a goal of having an "A" average by the end of the quarter. Perhaps a goal of achieving a "B" average is more realistic. Once that goal is reached, then a new goal of getting even higher grades could be made.

4. Reward yourself when you reach your goals.

Plan a reward for yourself that you can look forward to as you work to reach your goal. Your reward will be an incentive for you to keep going, even when the going gets rough.

5. Take responsibility for your learning.

Sometimes you will have setbacks. Things will not go as you plan. Instead of making excuses and blaming others, take responsibility for what happened and learn from it. For instance, maybe you did study for your science test but found that you could answer very few questions. Instead of blaming the teacher for asking impossible questions, take the attitude that "I should have paid more attention in class and spent more time preparing for the test. I will do better next time."

Are you consciously aware of your attitude toward yourself? Your abilities? Your performance as a student? The exercises in this chapter are designed to help you become aware of some of your attitudes about yourself. These exercises will also help you focus on the attitudes you would like to change to become a more successful student.

EXERCISES

A-1. Things about Myself That Make Me Proud

Think about things you have done in your life that make you feel good about yourself and that give you a sense of pride. Write them on the lines below.

> **Example A:** I once helped a lost child find his mother in a grocery store.
>
> **Example B:** I have a natural talent for fixing things.

1._____

_____

2._____

_____

3._____

_____

Now, reflect on the things you wrote down, and consider what skills and/or abilities were involved in the accomplishments you listed. Write the skills or abilities for each on the lines below. If you have trouble thinking of the skills or abilities that you used, talk over the situation you wrote down with a parent, guardian, teacher, or friend.

> **Example A:** To help the lost child, I acted calmly and responsibly. I was kind to the child and tried to comfort him. I used good judgment by taking the child to a checkout stand where an announcement was made to locate the mother. The skills and abilities listed might be: compassion, calm and responsible behavior, and good judgment.
>
> **Example B:** To fix things, I first have to observe the problem, figure out what has to be done to correct the problem, and then correct the problem. The skills/abilities listed might be: observation, critical thinking, problem-solving, imagination, creativity, and using tools well.

1._____

_____

2._____

_____

3._____

_____

The purpose of this exercise was to help you focus on things which make you feel successful and which will help you to have a positive attitude about yourself. Whenever you feel like you aren't capable, think back over times when you did something which made you feel successful or proud.

A-2. The Attitude That Works

Imagine that you are in one of your hardest classes. Picture the best student in the class and the worst student in the class. Describe how the best student acts in class.

_____

_____

Describe how the worst student acts in class.

_____

_____

Sum up what you think the best student's attitude is toward the class and the teacher.

_____

_____

Sum up what you think the worst student's attitude is toward the class and the teacher.

_____

_____

Now, think about and express your attitude toward the class and the teacher.

_____

_____

_____

Compare your attitude with those of the best student and the worst student. Is yours closer to the best student's or the worst student's?_____
If your attitude is close to the best student's, you are probably on the right mental track in that class. If, on the other hand, your attitude is similar to the worst student's, you probably are not doing as well as you could in that class. Remember, a small change in attitude can result in big changes in behavior. Adopt the attitude that will work for you—that will help you to be more successful as a student.

A-3. Learning through the Experience of Another

Read a biography or an autobiography of a person whose attitudes towards himself or herself and towards life carried him or her to success in spite of odds and obstacles. Ask your teacher or librarian for suggestions (Possible subjects might be Robert Kennedy, Winston Churchill, Abraham Lincoln, Walt Disney, Lucille Ball, Bruce Jenner, Babe Ruth, Harriett Tubman, Betty Ford, and Martin Luther King.).

After you have read the book, either complete the questions below, or make an appointment with your teacher to discuss the book.

■ What is the title of the book?_____

■ Who is the author? _____

■ Who is the book about? _____

■ What is the main character best known for?

_____

_____

■ What obstacles or problems did the main character have to overcome to achieve what he or she wanted in life?

_____

■ Describe the main character's attitude toward life and what he or she wanted to accomplish.

_____

_____

_____

■ How did the main character's attitudes make a difference in his or her life?

_____

_____

_____

■ What "lessons" from this book can you apply to your own life?

_____

_____

_____

_____

_____

_____

_____

YOUR TURN TO TALK BACK

Think about what you read and learned about attitudes. Look back over your responses to the exercises you were asked to complete and then respond to the questions below. Give your paper to your teacher or counselor.

■ What did you like about this chapter on attitudes?

■ What didn't you like about this chapter?

■ What did you learn about attitudes from this chapter?

■ How will your attitudes change as a result of doing this chapter?

■ What Internet source did you find useful for this chapter?

Chapter 16
Campus Involvement

Why don't you get involved in some school activities?

Chapter 16
Campus Involvement

SCENARIO

Carla: Gee, Mom, I wish I didn't have to go to school. It's so boring. There's nothing fun to do.

Mom: Why don't you get involved in some school activities—clubs or sports, for example?

Carla: Other kids always seem to have things to do at school, but I don't. I don't really know anyone at school, so I don't even know who to ask about joining clubs. I just don't know how to get in. Besides, there probably isn't anything interesting to do.

Mom: Oh, don't give up so easily, Carla. I bet the school has some activity that you would be interested in. You've always loved to take pictures. Maybe they have a photography club at school. Let's call the school and find out.

Carla: That's a great idea, Mom. If there is photography club, I hope I can get in. I'd like to learn more about photography, and it would give me a chance to know other kids who are interested in it, too.

STIMULUS QUESTIONS

1.   Are you involved in school activities such as sports, clubs, student government, music or drama productions? _____ If your answer is YES, list your activities here:

_____

_____

      If your answer is NO, go to your school activities office and find out what activities the school has to offer. Name at least 1 activity that you would like to become involved in._____

2.   Look over the following list of campus resources. Put a check mark (✓) on the blank next to each of the resources that you know is available on your campus. Put a question mark (?) by those you are not sure of.

      _____ Library   _____ Learning Center
      _____ Counseling office   _____ School Psychologist
      _____ Career Counseling Center   _____ Student Store
      _____ Activities Office   _____ Computer Center
      _____ Tutoring Services   _____ Job Placement Office
      _____ Financial Aid Office   _____ Student Organizations
      _____ Health Center   _____ Other _____
      _____ Other _____   _____ Other _____

3.   Now, ask one of your teachers, counselors, or the school receptionist about the resources with a question mark. Then, list the ones that are available on your campus.

_____

_____

_____

      Becoming involved in an activity at school that interests you will make going to school a more enjoyable and rewarding experience. This chapter is designed to help you discover what resources are available to you on your school campus so that you can become involved in campus life.

LEARNING ABOUT CAMPUS INVOLVEMENT

What Does Campus Involvement Mean?

Campus involvement means more than going to school to attend classes. It means taking advantage of all of the activities that school has to offer beyond what is offered in the classroom. It is doing things, such as:

- performing in or working backstage on a school play

- practicing football or some other sport

- going to club meetings

- attending dances and sports events

- going on field trips

- working on the school paper or yearbook

- competing for your school in sports or academic events.

Why Is Campus Involvement Important?

Campus involvement is important because it helps students feel a sense of ownership and pride in their school. Along with these feelings comes a sense of belonging to a "family." When you get involved in extra activities on campus, school becomes more than a place to attend classes; it becomes a place to learn and practice skills outside of class. School can be a place to improve your athletic ability, your performance skills in speaking, singing, dancing, or acting, your writing skills, your artistic talents, your leadership and competitive skills, as well as be a place to develop your social skills. As you become more involved in school activities, your interest and motivation to become involved in campus life will increase.

How Can You Become Involved In Campus Life?

There are several steps you can take to become involved in campus life at your school.

Step 1. Find out what services, resources, and activities your school has to offer. Do this by asking your friends, classmates, teachers, and office staff. Read the school newspaper and take note of the daily announcements.

Step 2. Set a personal goal to become involved in a minimum of one activity each semester.

Step 3. Decide what activity, sport, or club you would like to participate in and find out how you can join.

Step 4. Join in! If you can talk a friend into joining the activity with you, it may make it easier or more comfortable for you at first. However, if you don't know someone who would like to join with you, go ahead and sign up by yourself. As you get involved in the new activity, you will make new friends who have interests in common with you. Once you have become involved in one activity, you will feel more confident about joining in other campus activities.

Many students go through school the hard way—alone. Teenagers, by nature, have many problems and need help more at this time in their lives than at any other time. But, because of ignorance of what help is available, or fear of asking for help, many teenagers face the trials of going to school, working out relationships, facing new challenges, and growing up by themselves. For some, going to school is a dreary experience; it is something they do only because they have to. For others, going to school is exciting and fun because they are motivated to be at school so they can join with their friends in various school activities. They also use many of the resources and services the school has to offer so that they can get all they can from going to school.

Your school and your community offer many services and activities to help support you during this exciting, yet often frustrating, time of your life. As you continue to read this chapter and complete the activities which follow, you will become aware of ways to increase your campus involvement by taking advantage of the many resources and activities available.

EXERCISES

H-1 Identifying Problems and Finding Solutions

The following is a list of problems that many teenagers have. Read over the list and put a check (✓) in the blank on the *left side* of any problems that you feel you would like some help with.

____Getting along with parents____	____Making friends____
____Making good grades____	____Being popular____
____Resisting peer pressure____	____Having enough money____
____Reading and studying____	____Understanding math____
____Using time well____	____Having fun____
____Getting a job____	____Taking tests well____
____Using the library____	____Writing papers____
____Being healthy____	____Looking good____
____Paying attention____	____Being motivated____
____Completing tasks____	____Picking a college____
____Finding a scholarship____	____Handling pressure____
____Other_____ ____	____Other _____ ____

To complete this exercise, you will be asked to put the problems you checked into the following groups: school, relationships, money, or other. You will be asked to identify the problems by placing the appropriate letter that indicates which group the problem belongs to on the line to the *right* of the problem: S = school, R = relationship, M = money, O = other. If you understand things better by seeing them in color, use some colored pencils or highlighters to color code problems of the same type.

Now, look over the problems you checked. Put the letter "*S*" by all of the problems you marked that relate to schoolwork and grades. Think about the resources that are on your campus, such as the library, learning center, or math tutoring room, where you might go for help in solving these problems. Write them here. (If you don't know where to go, your task is to find out. Begin by asking your teacher or counselor.)

Problem	Resource

Look again at the problems you checked and mark with the letter "*R*" all of the problems that have to do with relationships. List those problems here and indicate where you can go for help.

Problem	Resource

Now, write the letter "*M*" next to those problems that have to do with money and list them below along with the best place to go for help.

Problem	Resource

Mark the other problems you checked with an "*O*" and list them on the lines below as well as where you can go for help. Be sure to ask your teacher or counselor to direct you if cannot find the resource on your own.

Problem	Resource

CI-2. Knowing the School Personnel Who Can Help You

It is always easier to find help or to get information when we know the person who can give us what we need. This exercise is designed to help you discover the people on your school campus who are available to assist you while at school.

Name the person who has each of the following jobs at your school. Use the blank lines to list other people you find helpful.

Principal _____

Asst. Principal Curriculum & Instruction _____

Asst. Principal Guidance _____

Activities Director _____

Dean/Attendance _____

Dean/Discipline _____

Counselor/Psychologist _____

Guidance Counselors _____

Librarian _____

Career Resource Technician _____

R.O.P. or Job Counselor _____

Financial Secretary _____

Custodian_____

Other_____

_____

_____

CI-3. Getting Involved.

Refer back to Stimulus Question #1. In addition to what you listed there, what else would you like to get involved in at your school? Read the list of activities below. Put one "✓" next to those activities that you already participate in. Put two "✓✓'s" next to those you think you would like to join. As you make your choices, consider these three things:

- what you do well
- what you would like to do better
- what you would like to learn to do.

Sports:

_____Baseball	_____Swimming
_____Basketball	_____Softball
_____Cross-Country	_____Skiing
_____Golf	_____Tennis
_____Football	_____Track and Field
_____Field Hockey	_____Volleyball
_____Gymnastics	_____Water Polo
_____Soccer	_____Wrestling
_____(Other)_____	_____(Other)_____

Academic Clubs:

_____Academic Decathlon or Academic Competition Team
_____Debate Team
_____Honor Society
_____Language Clubs (French, German, Spanish, etc.)
_____Scholarship Clubs (History Club, Literature Club, etc.)
_____Model United Nations
_____Other _____

Career Clubs:

_____Computer Club
_____Future Business Leaders of America
_____Future Homemakers of America
_____Future Farmers of America
_____Negotiators and Future Lawyers
_____(Other)_____

Cultural and Service Clubs:

_____Innovations International   _____Key Club
_____Community Volunteers   _____Students Against Drunk Driving
_____(Other) _____   _____(Other) _____

Musical and Dramatic Arts Clubs:

_____Dance Club   _____Drama Club
_____Choral Club   _____Instrumental Groups
_____(Other) _____   _____(Other) _____

Literary Clubs and Activities:

_____Campus Newspaper   _____Yearbook
_____Photography Club   _____Creative Writing Club
_____Poetry Society   _____Other _____

Athletic Support Groups:

_____Cheerleaders   _____ Drill Team
_____Pep Club   _____ Flag Girls
_____(Other) _____   _____ (Other)_____

Student Government

_____Class Officer   _____Student Council
_____Room Representative   _____ (Other)_____

Once you have decided on what activities you would like to participate in, find out if the activity is offered at your school. If it isn't, talk to your campus activities director about starting a new club in your area of interest.

YOUR TURN TO TALK BACK

If you would like to express your feelings about what you have learned in this chapter, please respond to the following questions. (You may want to look back over the chapter first.) Give your paper to the teacher or counselor.

■ What did you like about this chapter on campus involvement?

■ What didn't you like about this chapter?

■ What did you learn about campus involvement at your school?

■ How will you become more involved with the resources available on your campus as a result of doing this chapter?

■ What Internet source did you find useful for this chapter?

Appendix A

Answer Key

ANSWER KEY

Chapter 4 —Study-Reading
SR-2. Knowing the Steps of SQ3R

Step 1: S=Survey
Any 3 of these answers:
read title,
look over the chapter,
glance at all subtitles and headings,
read any summaries,
divide the chapter into parts.

The purpose of surveying a chapter is to get a general idea
of its contents.

Step 2: Q=Question
Titles, sub-titles, and headings can be turned into questions using
WHO, WHAT, WHERE, WHEN, HOW, and WHY.

Asking questions about the material helps you learn it because the
questions give you a purpose for reading (to search for answers) and
they help you pay attention to what you are reading.

Step 3: R-1=Read
The purpose as you read is to find answers to the questions that you
have asked.

Step 4: R-2=Recite
To recite, you should look away from the book, and answer the
questions you asked supporting your answers with facts, details,
examples, or reasons.

Step 5: R-3= Review
To review, you should look over the chapter and your notes, check to
see how much you remember re-read any parts that are unclear.

Chapter 6 —Exam Strategies
ES 3. Recognizing the Key Words in Objective Test Items

1. every
2. best
3. all
4. may be more than one correct

5. not, never
6. either
7. closest in meaning
8. difference

Chapter 6 —Exam Strategies (cont'd.)

ES-4. Knowing Key Words for Taking Essay Tests—Part 2

1. m	6. e	10. n
2. f	7. l	11. j
3. a	8. i	12. c
4. g	9. b	13. d
5. h		14. k

Chapter 7 —Writing Non-Fiction Assignments

W-2. Avoiding Wordy Phrases

1. repeat	6. total or sum	10. changed
2. meet	7. if	11. usually or often
3. different	8. now or today	12. 1960
4. because	9. different	13. surrounded
5. identical		14. history

Chapter 10—Memory for Learning

M-1. Example 1: Classification by Sports Season

Fall	Winter	Spring
cross-country	basketball	baseball
football	soccer	swimming
	wrestling	golf
		track and field
		volleyball

Example 2: Classification by Team or Individual Sport

Team Sport	Individual Sport
baseball	cross-country
basketball	wrestling
football	golf
soccer	tennis
volleyball	track and field
	swimming

Chapter 10 — Memory for Learning (cont'd.)
M-3. Using Mnemonics

1. USAF
2. AMA
3. SADD
4. Every good boy does fine.
5. A tall girl called Lola Valentine liked selling sugar coated anchovy pizza.
6. Check with your teacher for #6.

Chapter 11— Efficient Reading for Speed and Comprehension
R-3. Reading in Thought Units

Compare the paragraph you marked with the one below:

Reading for speed and comprehension / is reading / with a flexible rate / that allows you / to read as fast as you can / while you still understand / what you read./ It is using / various reading techniques / such as *surveying* or *previewing*, / *skimming* and *scanning*, / and *reading for main ideas*, / to achieve your purpose / for reading / as quickly as possible./ It is pushing / beyond your normal reading rate / to read faster and better./

Table of Problem-Solving Strategies

Note for users of the five-volume edition:
Volume 1 (pp. 1–477) includes chapters 1–15
Volume 2 (pp. 478–599) includes chapters 16–19.
Volume 3 (pp. 600–785) includes chapters 20–25.
Volume 4 (pp. 786–1183) includes chapters 26–37.
Volume 5 (pp. 1140–1365) includes chapters 37–43.

Chapters 38–43 are not in the Standard Edition.

ActivPhysics OnLine™ Activities

www.masteringphysics.com

PHYSICS

FOR SCIENTISTS AND ENGINEERS SECOND EDITION

A STRATEGIC APPROACH

RANDALL D. KNIGHT

CALIFORNIA POLYTECHNIC STATE UNIVERSITY, SAN LUIS OBISPO

PEARSON

Addison
Wesley

San Francisco Boston New York
Cape Town Hong Kong London Madrid
Mexico City Montreal Munich Paris
Singapore Sydney Tokyo Toronto

Publisher:	Adam Black, Ph.D.
Development Manager:	Michael Gillespie
Development Editor:	Alice Houston, Ph.D.
Project Editor:	Martha Steele
Assistant Editor:	Grace Joo
Media Producer:	Deb Greco
Sr. Administrative Assistant:	Cathy Glenn
Director of Marketing:	Christy Lawrence
Executive Marketing Manager:	Scott Dustan
Sr. Market Development Manager:	Josh Frost
Market Development Associate:	Jessica Lyons
Managing Editor:	Corinne Benson
Sr. Production Supervisor:	Nancy Tabor
Production Service:	WestWords PMG
Illustrations:	Precision Graphics
Text Design:	Hespenheide Design
Cover Design:	Yvo Riezebos Design
Manufacturing Manager:	Evelyn Beaton
Manufacturing Buyers:	Carol Melville, Ginny Michaud
Photo Research:	Cypress Integrated Systems
Director, Image Resource Center:	Melinda Patelli
Manager, Rights and Permissions:	Zina Arabia
Image Permission Coordinator:	Michelina Viscusi
Cover Printer:	Phoenix Color Corporation
Text Printer and Binder:	Courier/Kendallville
Cover Image:	Composite illustration by Yvo Riezebos Design; photo of spring by Bill Frymire/Masterfile
Photo Credits:	See page C-1

Library of Congress Cataloging-in-Publication Data
Knight, Randall Dewey.
    Physics for scientists and engineers : a strategic approach / Randall D. Knight.--2nd ed.
      p. cm.
    ISBN-13: 978-0-8053-2736-6
    1. Physics--Textbooks. I. Title.
    QC23.2.K654 2007
    530--dc22

2007026996

ISBN-13: 978-0-321-51671-8
ISBN-10: 0-321-51671-0

PEARSON

Addison
Wesley

www.aw-bc.com

5 6 7 8 9 10—CRK—11

Brief Contents

About the Author

Randy Knight has taught introductory physics for over 25 years at Ohio State University and California Polytechnic University, where he is currently Professor of Physics. Professor Knight received a bachelor's degree in physics from Washington University in St. Louis and a Ph.D. in physics from the University of California, Berkeley. He was a post-doctoral fellow at the Harvard-Smithsonian Center for Astrophysics before joining the faculty at Ohio State University. It was at Ohio State that he began to learn about the research in physics education that, many years later, led to this book.

Professor Knight's research interests are in the field of lasers and spectroscopy, and he has published over 25 research papers. He also directs the environmental studies program at Cal Poly, where, in addition to introductory physics, he teaches classes on energy, oceanography, and environmental issues. When he's not in the classroom or in front of a computer, you can find Randy hiking, sea kayaking, playing the piano, or spending time with his wife Sally and their seven cats.

Preface to the Instructor

In 2003 we published *Physics for Scientists and Engineers: A Strategic Approach*. This was the first comprehensive introductory textbook built from the ground up on research into how students can more effectively learn physics. The development and testing that led to this book had been partially funded by the National Science Foundation. This first edition quickly became the most widely adopted new physics textbook in more than 30 years, meeting widespread critical acclaim from professors and students. In this second edition, we build on the research-proven instructional techniques introduced in the first edition and the extensive feedback from thousands of users to take student learning even further.

Objectives

My primary goals in writing *Physics for Scientists and Engineers: A Strategic Approach* have been:

- To produce a textbook that is more focused and coherent, less encyclopedic.
- To move key results from physics education research into the classroom in a way that allows instructors to use a range of teaching styles.
- To provide a balance of quantitative reasoning and conceptual understanding, with special attention to concepts known to cause student difficulties.
- To develop students' problem-solving skills in a systematic manner.
- To support an active-learning environment.

These goals and the rationale behind them are discussed at length in my small paperback book, *Five Easy Lessons: Strategies for Successful Physics Teaching* (Addison-Wesley, 2002). Please request a copy from your local Addison-Wesley sales representative if it is of interest to you (ISBN 0-8053-8702-1).

Textbook Organization

The 43-chapter extended edition (ISBN 0-321-51333-9/978-0-321-51333-5) of *Physics for Scientists and Engineers* is intended for a three-semester course. Most of the 37-chapter standard edition (ISBN 0-321-51661-3/978-0-321-51661-9), ending with relativity, can be covered in two semesters, although the judicious omission of a few chapters will avoid rushing through the material and give students more time to develop their knowledge and skills.

There's a growing sentiment that quantum physics is quickly becoming the province of engineers, not just scientists, and that even a two-semester course should include a reasonable introduction to quantum ideas. The *Instructor Guide* outlines a couple of routes through the book that allow most of the quantum physics chapters to be included in a two-semester course. I've written the book with the hope that an increasing number of instructors will choose one of these routes.

- **Extended edition,** with modern physics (ISBN 0-321-51333-9/978-0-321-51333-5): Chapters 1–43.
- **Standard edition** (ISBN 0-321-51661-3/978-0-321-51661-9): Chapters 1–37.
- **Volume 1** (ISBN 0-321-51662-1/978-0-321-51662-6) covers mechanics: Chapters 1–15.
- **Volume 2** (ISBN 0-321-51663-X/978-0-321-51663-3) covers thermodynamics: Chapters 16–19.
- **Volume 3** (ISBN 0-321-51664-8/978-0-321-51664-0) covers waves and optics: Chapters 20–25.
- **Volume 4** (ISBN 0-321-51665-6/978-0-321-51665-7) covers electricity and magnetism, plus relativity: Chapters 26–37.
- **Volume 5** (ISBN 0-321-51666-4/978-0-321-51666-4) covers relativity and quantum physics: Chapters 37–43.
- **Volumes 1–5** boxed set (ISBN 0-321-51637-0/978-0-321-51637-4).

The full textbook is divided into seven parts: Part I: *Newton's Laws*, Part II: *Conservation Laws*, Part III: *Applications of Newtonian Mechanics*, Part IV: *Thermodynamics*, Part V: *Waves and Optics*, Part VI: *Electricity and Magnetism*, and Part VII: *Relativity and Quantum Mechanics*. Although I recommend covering the parts in this order (see below), doing so is by no means essential. Each topic is self-contained, and Parts III–VI can be rearranged to suit an instructor's needs. To facilitate a reordering of topics, the full text is available in the five individual volumes listed in the margin.

Organization Rationale: Thermodynamics is placed before waves because it is a continuation of ideas from mechanics. The key idea in thermodynamics is energy, and moving from mechanics into thermodynamics allows the uninterrupted development of this important idea. Further, waves introduce students to functions of two variables, and the mathematics of waves is more akin to electricity and magnetism than to mechanics. Thus moving from waves to fields to quantum physics provides a gradual transition of ideas and skills.

The purpose of placing optics with waves is to provide a coherent presentation of wave physics, one of the two pillars of classical physics. Optics as it is presented in introductory physics makes no use of the properties of electromagnetic fields. There's little reason other than historical tradition to delay optics until after E&M. The documented difficulties that students have with optics are difficulties with waves, not difficulties with electricity and magnetism. However, the optics chapters are easily deferred until the end of Part VI for instructors who prefer that ordering of topics.

What's New in the Second Edition

This second edition reaffirms the goals and objectives of the first edition. At the same time, the extensive feedback we've received from scores of instructors has led to numerous changes and improvements to the text, the figures, and the end-of-chapter problems. These include:

- More streamlined presentations. We have shortened each chapter by one page, on average, by tightening the language and reducing superfluous material.
- Conceptual questions. By popular request, the end of each chapter now includes a section of conceptual questions similar to those in the *Student Workbook*.
- Pencil sketches. Each chapter contains several hand-drawn sketches in key worked examples to provide students with explicit examples of the types of drawings they should make in their own problem solving.
- New and revised end-of-chapter problems. Problems have been revised to incorporate the unprecedented use of data and feedback from more than 100,000 students working these problems in MasteringPhysics™. More than 20% of the end-of-chapter problems are new or significantly revised, including an increased number of problems requiring calculus.

Significant chapter and content changes include the following:

- Two-dimensional kinematics has been brought forward to Chapter 4, immediately following the chapter on vectors. This chapter also covers circular-motion kinematics in detail (rather than delaying circular-motion kinematics to the chapter on rotational dynamics) to give a more integrated understanding of kinematics.
- Newton's third law (Chapter 7) now immediately follows and is more closely linked to the chapter on dynamics in one dimension. Revised interaction diagrams are simpler to draw and conceptually more powerful.
- The mechanisms of heat transfer (conduction, convection, and radiation) have been included in Chapter 17 (Work, Heat, and the First Law of Thermodynamics).

- Spherical mirrors are now covered in Chapter 23 (Ray Optics), and the entirely new Chapter 24 (Optical Instruments) treats cameras, microscopes, telescopes, and vision. This is the only new chapter in the second edition.
- Dielectrics have been added to the section on capacitors in Chapter 30 (Potential and Field), and electric current (Chapter 31) now follows the presentation of electric potential.
- Some topics in Chapters 34 (Electromagnetic Induction) and 35 (Electromagnetic Fields and Waves) have been rearranged for a more logical presentation of ideas.
- Blackbody radiation and Wien's law have been added to Chapter 38 (The End of Classical Physics).

Pedagogical Features

Your Instructor's Professional Copy contains a 10-page illustrated overview of the pedagogical features in this second edition. The *Preface to the Student* demonstrates how these features are designed to help your students.

The Student Workbook

A key component of *Physics for Scientists and Engineers: A Strategic Approach* is the accompanying *Student Workbook*. The workbook bridges the gap between textbook and homework problems by providing students the opportunity to learn and practice skills prior to using those skills in quantitative end-of-chapter problems, much as a musician practices technique separately from performance pieces. The workbook exercises, which are keyed to each section of the textbook, focus on developing specific skills, ranging from identifying forces and drawing free-body diagrams to interpreting wave functions.

The workbook exercises, which are generally qualitative and/or graphical, draw heavily upon the physics education research literature. The exercises deal with issues known to cause student difficulties and employ techniques that have proven to be effective at overcoming those difficulties. The workbook exercises can be used in class as part of an active-learning teaching strategy, in recitation sections, or as assigned homework. More information about effective use of the *Student Workbook* can be found in the *Instructor Guide*.

Available versions: Extended (ISBN 0-321-51357-6/978-0-321-51357-1), Standard (ISBN 0-321-51642-7/978-0-321-51642-8), Volume 1 (ISBN 0-321-51626-5/978-0-321-51626-8), Volume 2 (ISBN 0-321-51627-3/978-0-321-51627-5), Volume 3 (ISBN 0-321-51628-1/978-0-321-51628-2), Volume 4 (ISBN 0-321-51629-X/978-0-321-51629-9), and Volume 5 (ISBN 0-321-51630-3/978-0-321-51630-5).

Instructor Supplements

- The **Instructor Guide for Physics for Scientists and Engineers** (ISBN 0-321-51636-2/978-0-321-51636-7) offers detailed comments and suggested teaching ideas for every chapter, an extensive review of what has been learned from physics education research, and guidelines for using active-learning techniques in your classroom.
- The **Instructor Solutions Manuals, Chapters 1–19** (ISBN 0-321-51621-4/978-0-321-51621-3) and **Chapters 20–43** (ISBN 0-321-51657-5/978-0-321-51657-2), written by the author and Professors Pawan Kahol (Missouri State University), Scott Nutter (Northern Kentucky University), and Larry Smith (Snow College), provide *complete* solutions to all the end-of-chapter problems. The solutions follow the four-step Model/Visualize/Solve/Assess

Field, Robert Glosser, and Charlie Hibbard for their contributions to the end-of-chapter problems; and to my colleague Matt Moelter for many valuable contributions and suggestions.

I especially want to thank my editor Adam Black, development editor Alice Houston, project editor Martha Steele, and all the other staff at Addison-Wesley for their enthusiasm and hard work on this project. Production supervisor Nancy Tabor, Jared Sterzer and the team at WestWords, Inc., and photo researcher Brian Donnelly get a good deal of the credit for making this complex project all come together. In addition to the reviewers and classroom testers listed below, who gave invaluable feedback, I am particularly grateful to Charlie Hibbard and Peter W. Murphy for their close scrutiny of every word and figure.

Finally, I am endlessly grateful to my wife Sally for her love, encouragement, and patience, and to our many cats (and especially to the memory of my faithful writing companion Spike) for their innate abilities to keep my keyboard and printer filled with cat fur and to always sit right in the middle of the carefully stacked page proofs.

Randy Knight, August 2007
rknight@calpoly.edu

Reviewers and Classroom Testers

Gary B. Adams, *Arizona State University*
Ed Adelson, *Ohio State University*
Kyle Altmann, *Elon University*
Wayne R. Anderson, *Sacramento City College*
James H. Andrews, *Youngstown State University*
Kevin Ankoviak, *Las Positas College*
David Balogh, *Fresno City College*
Dewayne Beery, *Buffalo State College*
Joseph Bellina, *Saint Mary's College*
James R. Benbrook, *University of Houston*
David Besson, *University of Kansas*
Randy Bohn, *University of Toledo*
Richard A. Bone, *Florida International University*
Gregory Boutis, *York College*
Art Braundmeier, *University of Southern Illinois, Edwardsville*
Carl Bromberg, *Michigan State University*
Meade Brooks, *Collin College*
Douglas Brown, *Cabrillo College*
Ronald Brown, *California Polytechnic State University, San Luis Obispo*
Mike Broyles, *Collin County Community College*
Debra Burris, *University of Central Arkansas*
James Carolan, *University of British Columbia*
Michael Chapman, *Georgia Tech University*
Norbert Chencinski, *College of Staten Island*
Kristi Concannon, *King's College*
Sean Cordry, *Northwestern College of Iowa*
Robert L. Corey, *South Dakota School of Mines*
Michael Crescimanno, *Youngstown State University*

Dennis Crossley, *University of Wisconsin–Sheboygan*
Wei Cui, *Purdue University*
Robert J. Culbertson, *Arizona State University*
Danielle Dalafave, *The College of New Jersey*
Purna C. Das, *Purdue University North Central*
Chad Davies, *Gordon College*
William DeGraffenreid, *California State University–Sacramento*
Dwain Desbien, *Estrella Mountain Community College*
John F. Devlin, *University of Michigan, Dearborn*
John DiBartolo, *Polytechnic University*
Alex Dickison, *Seminole Community College*
Chaden Djalali, *University of South Carolina*
Margaret Dobrowolska, *University of Notre Dame*
Sandra Doty, *Denison University*
Miles J. Dresser, *Washington State University*
Charlotte Elster, *Ohio University*
Robert J. Endorf, *University of Cincinnati*
Tilahun Eneyew, *Embry-Riddle Aeronautical University*
F. Paul Esposito, *University of Cincinnati*
John Evans, *Lee University*
Harold T. Evensen, *University of Wisconsin–Platteville*
Michael R. Falvo, *University of North Carolina*
Abbas Faridi, *Orange Coast College*
Nail Fazleev, *University of Texas–Arlington*
Stuart Field, *Colorado State University*
Daniel Finley, *University of New Mexico*
Jane D. Flood, *Muhlenberg College*
Michael Franklin, *Northwestern Michigan College*
Jonathan Friedman, *Amherst College*

Thomas Furtak, *Colorado School of Mines*
Alina Gabryszewska-Kukawa, *Delta State University*
Lev Gasparov, *University of North Florida*
Richard Gass, *University of Cincinnati*
J. David Gavenda, *University of Texas, Austin*
Stuart Gazes, *University of Chicago*
Katherine M. Gietzen, *Southwest Missouri State University*
Robert Glosser, *University of Texas, Dallas*
William Golightly, *University of California, Berkeley*
Paul Gresser, *University of Maryland*
C. Frank Griffin, *University of Akron*
John B. Gruber, *San Jose State University*
Stephen Haas, *University of Southern California*
John Hamilton, *University of Hawaii at Hilo*
Jason Harlow, *University of Toronto*
Randy Harris, *University of California, Davis*
Nathan Harshman, *American University*
J. E. Hasbun, *University of West Georgia*
Nicole Herbots, *Arizona State University*
Jim Hetrick, *University of Michigan–Dearborn*
Scott Hildreth, *Chabot College*
David Hobbs, *South Plains College*
Laurent Hodges, *Iowa State University*
Mark Hollabaugh, *Normandale Community College*
John L. Hubisz, *North Carolina State University*
Shane Hutson, *Vanderbilt University*
George Igo, *University of California, Los Angeles*
David C. Ingram, *Ohio University*
Bob Jacobsen, *University of California, Berkeley*
Rong-Sheng Jin, *Florida Institute of Technology*
Marty Johnston, *University of St. Thomas*
Stanley T. Jones, *University of Alabama*
Darrell Judge, *University of Southern California*
Pawan Kahol, *Missouri State University*
Teruki Kamon, *Texas A&M University*
Richard Karas, *California State University, San Marcos*
Deborah Katz, *U.S. Naval Academy*
Miron Kaufman, *Cleveland State University*
Katherine Keilty, *Kingwood College*
Roman Kezerashvili, *New York City College of Technology*
Peter Kjeer, *Bethany Lutheran College*
M. Kotlarchyk, *Rochester Institute of Technology*
Fred Krauss, *Delta College*
Cagliyan Kurdak, *University of Michigan*
Fred Kuttner, *University of California, Santa Cruz*
H. Sarma Lakkaraju, *San Jose State University*
Darrell R. Lamm, *Georgia Institute of Technology*
Robert LaMontagne, *Providence College*
Eric T. Lane, *University of Tennessee–Chattanooga*
Alessandra Lanzara, *University of California, Berkeley*
Lee H. LaRue, *Paris Junior College*
Sen-Ben Liao, *Massachusetts Institute of Technology*
Dean Livelybrooks, *University of Oregon*
Chun-Min Lo, *University of South Florida*
Olga Lobban, *Saint Mary's University*

Ramon Lopez, *Florida Institute of Technology*
Vaman M. Naik, *University of Michigan, Dearborn*
Kevin Mackay, *Grove City College*
Carl Maes, *University of Arizona*
Rizwan Mahmood, *Slippery Rock University*
Mani Manivannan, *Missouri State University*
Richard McCorkle, *University of Rhode Island*
James McDonald, *University of Hartford*
James McGuire, *Tulane University*
Stephen R. McNeil, *Brigham Young University–Idaho*
Theresa Moreau, *Amherst College*
Gary Morris, *Rice University*
Michael A. Morrison, *University of Oklahoma*
Richard Mowat, *North Carolina State University*
Eric Murray, *Georgia Institute of Technology*
Taha Mzoughi, *Mississippi State University*
Scott Nutter, *Northern Kentucky University*
Craig Ogilvie, *Iowa State University*
Benedict Y. Oh, *University of Wisconsin*
Martin Okafor, *Georgia Perimeter College*
Halina Opyrchal, *New Jersey Institute of Technology*
Yibin Pan, *University of Wisconsin-Madison*
Georgia Papaefthymiou, *Villanova University*
Peggy Perozzo, *Mary Baldwin College*
Brian K. Pickett, *Purdue University, Calumet*
Joe Pifer, *Rutgers University*
Dale Pleticha, *Gordon College*
Marie Plumb, *Jamestown Community College*
Robert Pompi, *SUNY-Binghamton*
David Potter, *Austin Community College–Rio Grande Campus*
Chandra Prayaga, *University of West Florida*
Didarul Qadir, *Central Michigan University*
Steve Quon, *Ventura College*
Michael Read, *College of the Siskiyous*
Lawrence Rees, *Brigham Young University*
Richard J. Reimann, *Boise State University*
Michael Rodman, *Spokane Falls Community College*
Sharon Rosell, *Central Washington University*
Anthony Russo, *Okaloosa-Walton Community College*
Freddie Salsbury, *Wake Forest University*
Otto F. Sankey, *Arizona State University*
Jeff Sanny, *Loyola Marymount University*
Rachel E. Scherr, *University of Maryland*
Carl Schneider, *U. S. Naval Academy*
Bruce Schumm, *University of California, Santa Cruz*
Bartlett M. Sheinberg, *Houston Community College*
Douglas Sherman, *San Jose State University*
Elizabeth H. Simmons, *Boston University*
Marlina Slamet, *Sacred Heart University*
Alan Slavin, *Trent College*
Larry Smith, *Snow College*
William S. Smith, *Boise State University*
Paul Sokol, *Pennsylvania State University*
LTC Bryndol Sones, *United States Military Academy*

Chris Sorensen, *Kansas State University*
Anna and Ivan Stern, *AW Tutor Center*
Gay B. Stewart, *University of Arkansas*
Michael Strauss, *University of Oklahoma*
Chin-Che Tin, *Auburn University*
Christos Valiotis, *Antelope Valley College*
Andrew Vanture, *Everett Community College*
Arthur Viescas, *Pennsylvania State University*
Ernst D. Von Meerwall, *University of Akron*
Chris Vuille, *Embry-Riddle Aeronautical University*
Jerry Wagner, *Rochester Institute of Technology*
Robert Webb, *Texas A&M University*

Zodiac Webster, *California State University, San Bernardino*
Robert Weidman, *Michigan Technical University*
Fred Weitfeldt, *Tulane University*
Jeff Allen Winger, *Mississippi State University*
Carey Witkov, *Broward Community College*
Ronald Zammit, *California Polytechnic State University, San Luis Obispo*
Darin T. Zimmerman, *Pennsylvania State University, Altoona*
Fredy Zypman, *Yeshiva University*

Preface to the Student

From Me to You

The most incomprehensible thing about the universe is that it is comprehensible.
   —Albert Einstein

The day I went into physics class it was death.
   —Sylvia Plath, *The Bell Jar*

Let's have a little chat before we start. A rather one-sided chat, admittedly, because you can't respond, but that's OK. I've talked with many of your fellow students over the years, so I have a pretty good idea of what's on your mind.

What's your reaction to taking physics? Fear and loathing? Uncertainty? Excitement? All of the above? Let's face it, physics has a bit of an image problem on campus. You've probably heard that it's difficult, maybe downright impossible unless you're an Einstein. Things that you've heard, your experiences in other science courses, and many other factors all color your *expectations* about what this course is going to be like.

It's true that there are many new ideas to be learned in physics and that the course, like college courses in general, is going to be much faster paced than science courses you had in high school. I think it's fair to say that it will be an *intense* course. But we can avoid many potential problems and difficulties if we can establish, here at the beginning, what this course is about and what is expected of you—and of me!

Just what is physics, anyway? Physics is a way of thinking about the physical aspects of nature. Physics is not better than art or biology or poetry or religion, which are also ways to think about nature; it's simply different. One of the things this course will emphasize is that physics is a human endeavor. The ideas presented in this book were not found in a cave or conveyed to us by aliens; they were discovered and developed by real people engaged in a struggle with real issues. I hope to convey to you something of the history and the process by which we have come to accept the principles that form the foundation of today's science and engineering.

You might be surprised to hear that physics is not about "facts." Oh, not that facts are unimportant, but physics is far more focused on discovering *relationships* that exist between facts and *patterns* that exist in nature than on learning facts for their own sake. As a consequence, there's not a lot of memorization when you study physics. Some—there are still definitions and equations to learn—but less than in many other courses. Our emphasis, instead, will be on thinking and reasoning. This is important to factor into your expectations for the course.

Perhaps most important of all, *physics is not math!* Physics is much broader. We're going to look for patterns and relationships in nature, develop the logic that relates different ideas, and search for the reasons *why* things happen as they do. In doing so, we're going to stress qualitative reasoning, pictorial and graphical reasoning, and reasoning by analogy. And yes, we will use math, but it's just one tool among many.

It will save you much frustration if you're aware of this physics–math distinction up front. Many of you, I know, want to find a formula and plug numbers into it—

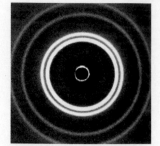

(a) X-ray diffraction pattern

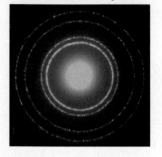

(b) Electron diffraction pattern

that is, to do a math problem. Maybe that worked in high school science courses, but it is *not* what this course expects of you. We'll certainly do many calculations, but the specific numbers are usually the last and least important step in the analysis.

Physics is about recognizing patterns. For example, the top photograph is an x-ray diffraction pattern showing how a focused beam of x rays spreads out after passing through a crystal. The bottom photograph shows what happens when a focused beam of electrons is shot through the same crystal. What does the obvious similarity in these two photographs tell us about the nature of light and the nature of matter?

As you study, you'll sometimes be baffled, puzzled, and confused. That's perfectly normal and to be expected. Making mistakes is OK too *if* you're willing to learn from the experience. No one is born knowing how to do physics any more than he or she is born knowing how to play the piano or shoot basketballs. The ability to do physics comes from practice, repetition, and struggling with the ideas until you "own" them and can apply them yourself in new situations. There's no way to make learning effortless, at least for anything worth learning, so expect to have some difficult moments ahead. But also expect to have some moments of excitement at the joy of discovery. There will be instants at which the pieces suddenly click into place and you *know* that you understand a powerful idea. There will be times when you'll surprise yourself by successfully working a difficult problem that you didn't think you could solve. My hope, as an author, is that the excitement and sense of adventure will far outweigh the difficulties and frustrations.

Getting the Most Out of Your Course

Many of you, I suspect, would like to know the "best" way to study for this course. There is no best way. People are different, and what works for one student is less effective for another. But I do want to stress that *reading the text* is vitally important. Class time will be used to clarify difficulties and to develop tools for using the knowledge, but your instructor will *not* use class time simply to repeat information in the text. The basic knowledge for this course is written down on these pages, and the *number-one expectation* is that you will read carefully and thoroughly to find and learn that knowledge.

Despite there being no best way to study, I will suggest *one* way that is successful for many students. It consists of the following four steps:

1. **Read each chapter *before* it is discussed in class.** I cannot stress too strongly how important this step is. Class attendance is much more effective if you are prepared. When you first read a chapter, focus on learning new vocabulary, definitions, and notation. There's a list of terms and notations at the end of each chapter. Learn them! You won't understand what's being discussed or how the ideas are being used if you don't know what the terms and symbols mean.

2. **Participate actively in class.** Take notes, ask and answer questions, and participate in discussion groups. There is ample scientific evidence that *active participation* is much more effective for learning science than passive listening.

3. **After class, go back for a careful re-reading of the chapter.** In your second reading, pay closer attention to the details and the worked examples. Look for the *logic* behind each example (I've highlighted this to make it clear), not just at what formula is being used. Do the *Student Workbook* exercises for each section as you finish your reading of it.

4. **Finally, apply what you have learned to the homework problems at the end of each chapter.** I strongly encourage you to form a study group with two or three classmates. There's good evidence that students who study regularly with a group do better than the rugged individualists who try to go it alone.

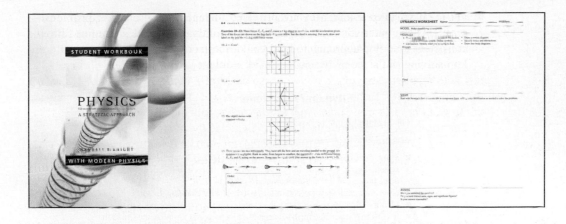

Did someone mention a workbook? The companion *Student Workbook* is a vital part of the course. Its questions and exercises ask you to reason *qualitatively,* to use graphical information, and to give explanations. It is through these exercises that you will learn what the concepts mean and will practice the reasoning skills appropriate to the chapter. You will then have acquired the baseline knowledge and confidence you need *before* turning to the end-of-chapter homework problems. In sports or in music, you would never think of performing before you practice, so why would you want to do so in physics? The workbook is where you practice and work on basic skills.

Many of you, I know, will be tempted to go straight to the homework problems and then thumb through the text looking for a formula that seems like it will work. That approach will not succeed in this course, and it's guaranteed to make you frustrated and discouraged. Very few homework problems are of the "plug and chug" variety where you simply put numbers into a formula. To work the homework problems successfully, you need a better study strategy—either the one outlined above or your own—that helps you learn the concepts and the relationships between the ideas.

A traditional guideline in college is to study two hours outside of class for every hour spent in class, and this text is designed with that expectation. Of course, two hours is an average. Some chapters are fairly straightforward and will go quickly. Others likely will require much more than two study hours per class hour.

Getting the Most Out of Your Textbook

Your textbook provides many features designed to help you learn the concepts of physics and solve problems more effectively.

- **TACTICS BOXES** give step-by-step procedures for particular skills, such as interpreting graphs or drawing special diagrams. Tactics Box steps are explicitly illustrated in subsequent worked examples, and these are often the starting point of a full *Problem-Solving Strategy*.

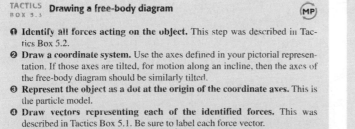

TACTICS
BOX 5.3   **Drawing a free-body diagram**   (MP)

❶ **Identify all forces acting on the object.** This step was described in Tactics Box 5.2.
❷ **Draw a coordinate system.** Use the axes defined in your pictorial representation. If those axes are tilted, for motion along an incline, then the axes of the free-body diagram should be similarly tilted.
❸ **Represent the object as a dot at the origin of the coordinate axes.** This is the particle model.
❹ **Draw vectors representing each of the identified forces.** This was described in Tactics Box 5.1. Be sure to label each force vector.
❺ **Draw and label the *net force* vector $\vec{F}_{net}$.** Draw this vector beside the diagram, not on the particle. Or, if appropriate, write $\vec{F}_{net} = \vec{0}$. Then check that $\vec{F}_{net}$ points in the same direction as the acceleration vector $\vec{a}$ on your motion diagram.

Exercises 24–29

TACTICS
BOX 33.3   **Evaluating line integrals**   (MP)

❶ If $\vec{B}$ is everywhere perpendicular to a line, the line integral of $\vec{B}$ is

$$\int_i^f \vec{B} \cdot d\vec{s} = 0$$

❷ If $\vec{B}$ is everywhere tangent to a line of length *l and* has the same magnitude B at every point, then

$$\int_i^f \vec{B} \cdot d\vec{s} = Bl$$

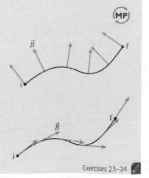

Exercises 23–24

■ **PROBLEM-SOLVING STRATEGIES** are provided for each broad class of problems—problems characteristic of a chapter or group of chapters. The strategies follow a consistent four-step approach to help you develop confidence and proficient problem-solving skills: MODEL, VISUALIZE, SOLVE, ASSESS.

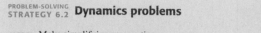

PROBLEM-SOLVING
STRATEGY 6.2 Dynamics problems (MP)

MODEL Make simplifying assumptions.

VISUALIZE Draw a **pictorial representation.**

■ Show important points in the motion with a sketch, establish a coordinate system, define symbols, and identify what the problem is trying to find. This is the process of translating words into symbols.
■ Use a motion diagram to determine the object s acceleration vector $\vec{a}$.
■ Identify all forces acting on the object and show them on a free-body diagram.
■ It s OK to go back and forth between these steps as you visualize the situation.

SOLVE The mathematical representation is based on Newton s second law:

$$\vec{F}_{net} = \sum_i \vec{F}_i = m\vec{a}$$

The vector sum of the forces is found directly from the free-body diagram. Depending on the problem, either

■ Solve for the acceleration, then use kinematics to find velocities and positions; or
■ Use kinematics to determine the acceleration, then solve for unknown forces.

ASSESS Check that your result has the correct units, is reasonable, and answers the question.

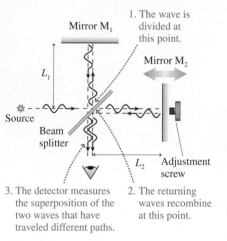

1. The wave is divided at this point.

Mirror M_1

Mirror M_2

L_1

Source

Beam splitter

L_2 Adjustment screw

3. The detector measures the superposition of the two waves that have traveled different paths.

2. The returning waves recombine at this point.

Annotated **FIGURE** showing the operation of the Michelson interferometer.

■ Worked **EXAMPLES** illustrate good problem-solving practices through the consistent use of the four-step problem-solving approach and, where appropriate, the Tactics Box steps. The worked examples are often very detailed and carefully lead you through the *reasoning* behind the solution as well as the numerical calculations. A careful study of the reasoning will help you apply the concepts and techniques to the new and novel problems you will encounter in homework assignments and on exams.

■ **NOTE ▶** paragraphs alert you to common mistakes and point out useful tips for tackling problems.

■ **STOP TO THINK** questions embedded in the chapter allow you to quickly assess whether you've understood the main idea of a section. A correct answer will give you confidence to move on to the next section. An incorrect answer will alert you to re-read the previous section.

■ Blue annotations on figures help you better understand what the figure is showing. They will help you to interpret graphs; translate between graphs, math, and pictures; grasp difficult concepts through a visual analogy; and develop many other important skills.

■ Pencil sketches provide practical examples of the figures you should draw yourself when solving a problem.

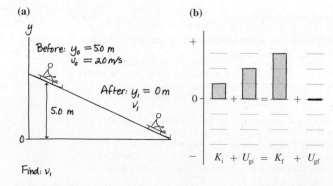

(a)

y

Before: $y_0 = 5.0$ m
$v_0 = 2.0$ m/s

After: $y_1 = 0$ m
v_1

5.0 m

Find: v_1

(b)

$K_i + U_{gi} = K_f + U_{gf}$

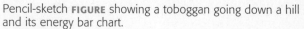

Pencil-sketch **FIGURE** showing a toboggan going down a hill and its energy bar chart.

- The learning goals and links that begin each chapter outline what to focus on in the chapter ahead and what you need to remember from previous chapters.
  - ▶ **Looking Ahead** lists key concepts and skills you will learn in the coming chapter.
  - ◀ **Looking Back** highlights important topics you should review from previous chapters.
- Schematic *Chapter Summaries* help you organize what you have learned into a hierarchy, from general principles (top) to applications (bottom). Side-by-side pictorial, graphical, textual, and mathematical representations are used to help you translate between these key representations.
- *Part Overviews and Summaries* provide a global framework for what you are learning. Each part begins with an overview of the chapters ahead and concludes with a broad summary to help you to connect the concepts presented in that set of chapters. KNOWLEDGE STRUCTURE tables in the Part Summaries, similar to the Chapter Summaries, help you to see the forest rather than just the trees.

Now that you know more about what is expected of you, what can you expect of me? That's a little trickier because the book is already written! Nonetheless, the book was prepared on the basis of what I think my students throughout the years have expected—and wanted—from their physics textbook. Further, I've listened to the extensive feedback I have received from thousands of students like you, and their instructors, who used the first edition of this book.

You should know that these course materials—the text and the workbook—are based on extensive research about how students learn physics and the challenges they face. The effectiveness of many of the exercises has been demonstrated through extensive class testing. I've written the book in an informal style that I hope you will find appealing and that will encourage you to do the reading. And, finally, I have endeavored to make clear not only that physics, as a technical body of knowledge, is relevant to your profession but also that physics is an exciting adventure of the human mind.

I hope you'll enjoy the time we're going to spend together.

Detailed Contents

Volume 1 contains chapters 1–15; Volume 2 contains chapters 16–19; Volume 3 contains chapters 20–25; Volume 4 contains chapters 26–37; Volume 5 contains chapters 37–43.

Part II   Conservation Laws

Part III   Applications of Newtonian Mechanics

OVERVIEW   Power Over Our Environment   339

Part VI Electricity and Magnetism

Part VII   Relativity and Quantum Physics

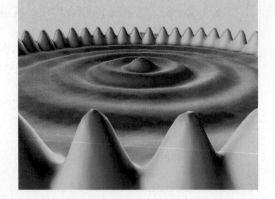

Introduction

Journey into Physics

Said Alice to the Cheshire cat,
"Cheshire-Puss, would you tell me, please, which way I ought to go from here?"
"That depends a good deal on where you want to go," said the Cat.
"I don't much care where—" said Alice.
"Then it doesn't matter which way you go," said the Cat.
　　—Lewis Carroll, *Alice in Wonderland*

Have you ever wondered about questions such as

Why is the sky blue?

Why is glass an insulator but metal a conductor?

What, really, is an atom?

These are the questions of which physics is made. Physicists try to understand the universe in which we live by observing the phenomena of nature—such as the sky being blue—and by looking for patterns and principles to explain these phenomena. Many of the discoveries made by physicists, from electromagnetic waves to nuclear energy, have forever altered the ways in which we live and think.

You are about to embark on a journey into the realm of physics. It is a journey in which you will learn about many physical phenomena and find the answers to questions such as the ones posed above. Along the way, you will also learn how to use physics to analyze and solve many practical problems.

As you proceed, you are going to see the methods by which physicists have come to understand the laws of nature. The ideas and theories of physics are not arbitrary; they are firmly grounded in experiments and measurements. By the time you finish this text, you will be able to recognize the *evidence* upon which our present knowledge of the universe is based.

Which Way Should We Go?

We are rather like Alice in Wonderland, here at the start of the journey, in that we must decide which way to go. Physics is an immense body of knowledge, and without specific goals it would not much matter which topics we study. But unlike Alice, we *do* have some particular destinations that we would like to visit.

The physics that provides the foundation for all of modern science and engineering can be divided into three broad categories:

- Particles and energy.
- Fields and waves.
- The atomic structure of matter.

A particle, in the sense that we'll use the term, is an idealization of a physical object. We will use particles to understand how objects move and how they interact with each other. One of the most important properties of a particle or a collection of particles is *energy*. We will study energy both for its value in understanding physical processes and because of its practical importance in a technological society.

A scanning tunneling microscope allows us to "see" the individual atoms on a surface. One of our goals is to understand how an image such as this is made.

Particles are discrete, localized objects. Although many phenomena can be understood in terms of particles and their interactions, the long-range interactions of gravity, electricity, and magnetism are best understood in terms of *fields,* such as the gravitational field and the electric field. Rather than being discrete, fields spread continuously through space. Much of the second half of this book will be focused on understanding fields and the interactions between fields and particles.

Certainly one of the most significant discoveries of the past 500 years is that matter consists of atoms. Atoms and their properties are described by quantum physics, but we cannot leap directly into that subject and expect that it would make any sense. To reach our destination, we are going to have to study many other topics along the way—rather like having to visit the Rocky Mountains if you want to drive from New York to San Francisco. All our knowledge of particles and fields will come into play as we end our journey by studying the atomic structure of matter.

The Route Ahead

Here at the beginning, we can survey the route ahead. Where will our journey take us? What scenic vistas will we view along the way?

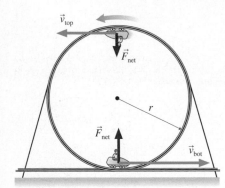

Parts I and II, *Newton's Laws* and *Conservation Laws,* form the basis of what is called *classical mechanics.* Classical mechanics is the study of motion. (It is called *classical* to distinguish it from the modern theory of motion at the atomic level, which is called *quantum mechanics.*) The first two parts of this textbook establish the basic language and concepts of motion. Part I will look at motion in terms of *particles* and *forces.* We will use these concepts to study the motion of everything from accelerating sprinters to orbiting satellites. Then, in Part II, we will introduce the ideas of *momentum* and *energy.* These concepts—especially energy—will give us a new perspective on motion and extend our ability to analyze motion.

Part III, *Applications of Newtonian Mechanics,* will pause to look at four important applications of classical mechanics: Newton's theory of gravity, rotational motion, oscillatory motion, and the motion of fluids. Only oscillatory motion is a prerequisite for later chapters. Your instructor may choose to cover some or all of the other chapters, depending upon the time available, but your study of Parts IV–VII will not be hampered if these chapters are omitted.

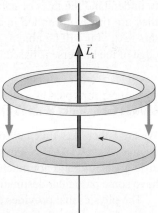

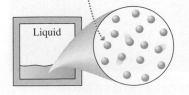

Atoms are held close together by weak molecular bonds, but they can slide around each other.

Part IV, *Thermodynamics,* extends the ideas of particles and energy to systems such as liquids and gases that contain vast numbers of particles. Here we will look for connections between the *microscopic* behavior of large numbers of atoms and the *macroscopic* properties of bulk matter. You will find that some of the properties of gases that you know from chemistry, such as the ideal gas law, turn out to be direct consequences of the underlying atomic structure of the gas. We will also expand the concept of energy and study how energy is transferred and utilized.

Waves are ubiquitous in nature, whether they be large-scale oscillations like ocean waves, the less obvious motions of sound waves, or the subtle undulations of light waves and matter waves that go to the heart of the atomic structure of matter. In **Part V,** *Waves and Optics,* we will emphasize the unity of wave physics and find that many diverse wave phenomena can be analyzed with the same concepts and mathematical language. It is here we will begin to accumulate evidence that the theory of classical mechanics is inadequate to explain the observed behavior of atoms, and we will end this section with some atomic puzzles that seem to defy understanding.

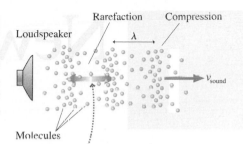

Individual molecules oscillate back and forth with displacement D. As they do so, the compressions propagate forward at speed v_{sound}. Because compressions are regions of higher pressure, a sound wave can be thought of as a pressure wave.

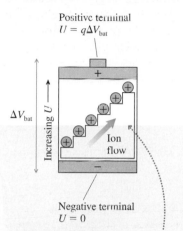

The charge escalator "lifts" charge from the negative side to the positive side. Charge q gains energy $\Delta U = q\Delta V_{bat}$.

Part VI, *Electricity and Magnetism,* is devoted to the *electromagnetic force,* one of the most important forces in nature. In essence, the electromagnetic force is the "glue" that holds atoms together. It is also the force that makes this the "electronic age." We'll begin this part of the journey with simple observations of static electricity. Bit by bit, we'll be led to the basic ideas behind electrical circuits, to magnetism, and eventually to the discovery of electromagnetic waves.

Part VII is *Relativity and Quantum Physics.* We'll start by exploring the strange world of Einstein's theory of *relativity,* a world in which space and time aren't quite what they appear to be. Then we will enter the microscopic domain of *atoms,* where the behaviors of light and matter are at complete odds with what our common sense tells us is possible. Although the mathematics of quantum theory quickly gets beyond the level of this text, and time will be running out, you will see that the quantum theory of atoms and nuclei explains many of the things that you learned simply as rules in chemistry.

We will not have visited all of physics on our travels. There just isn't time. Many exciting topics, ranging from quarks to black holes, will have to remain unexplored. But this particular journey need not be the last. As you finish this text, you will have the background and the experience to explore new topics further in more advanced courses or for yourself.

With that said, let us take the first step.

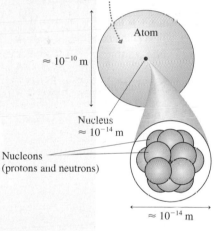

This picture of an atom would need to be 10 m in diameter if it were drawn to the same scale as the dot representing the nucleus.

1 Concepts of Motion

Motion takes many forms. Some are simple. Others, like this, are complex.

Socrates: *The nature of motion appears to be the question with which we begin.*

Plato, 375 BCE

The universe in which we live is one of change and motion. This motorcyclist was clearly in motion when the photograph was taken. In the course of a day you probably walk, run, bicycle, or drive your car, all forms of motion. The clock hands are moving inexorably forward as you read this text. The pages of this book may look quite still, but a microscopic view would reveal jostling atoms and whirling electrons. The stars look as permanent as anything, yet the astronomer's telescope reveals them to be ceaselessly moving within galaxies that rotate and orbit yet other galaxies.

Motion is a theme that will appear in one form or another throughout this entire book. Although we all have intuition about motion, based on our experiences, some of the important aspects of motion turn out to be rather subtle. So rather than jumping immediately into a lot of mathematics and calculations, this first chapter focuses on *visualizing* motion and becoming familiar with the *concepts* needed to describe a moving object. We will use mathematical ideas when needed, because they increase the precision of our thoughts, but we will defer actual calculations until Chapter 2. Our goal is to lay the foundations for understanding motion.

1.1 Motion Diagrams

The quest to understand motion dates to antiquity. The ancient Babylonians, Chinese, and Greeks were especially interested in the celestial motions of the night sky. The Greek philosopher and scientist Aristotle wrote extensively about the nature of moving objects. However, our modern understanding of motion did not begin until Galileo (1564–1642) first formulated the concepts of motion in mathematical terms.

FIGURE 1.1 Four basic types of motion.

Translational motion

Circular motion

Projectile motion

Rotational motion

FIGURE 1.2 Four frames from the movie of a car.

And it took Newton (1642–1727) and the invention of calculus to put the concepts of motion on a firm and rigorous footing.

As a starting point, let's define **motion** as the change of an object's position with time. Examples of motion are easy to list. Bicycles, baseballs, cars, airplanes, and rockets are all objects that move. The path along which an object moves, which might be a straight line or might be curved, is called the object's **trajectory.**

FIGURE 1.1 shows four basic types of motion that we will study in this book. Rotational motion is somewhat different from the other three in that rotation is a change of the object's *angular* position. We'll defer rotational motion until later and, for now, focus on motion along a line, circular motion, and projectile motion.

Making a Motion Diagram

An easy way to study motion is to make a movie of a moving object. A movie camera, as you probably know, takes photographs at a fixed rate, typically 30 photographs every second. Each separate photo is called a *frame,* and the frames are all lined up one after the other in a *filmstrip.* As an example, FIGURE 1.2 shows four frames from the movie of a car going past. Not surprisingly, the car is in a somewhat different position in each frame.

Suppose we cut the individual frames of the filmstrip apart, stack them on top of each other, and project the entire stack at once onto a screen for viewing. The

FIGURE 1.3 A motion diagram of the car shows all the frames simultaneously.

The same amount of time elapses between each image and the next.

result is shown in **FIGURE 1.3**. This composite photo, showing an object's position at several *equally spaced instants of time,* is called a **motion diagram.** As simple as motion diagrams seem, they will turn out to be a powerful tool for analyzing motion.

NOTE ▶ It's important to keep the camera in a *fixed position* as the object moves by. Don't "pan" it to track the moving object. ◀

Now let's take our camera out into the world and make a few motion diagrams. The following table shows how we can see important aspects of the motion in a motion diagram.

Examples of motion diagrams

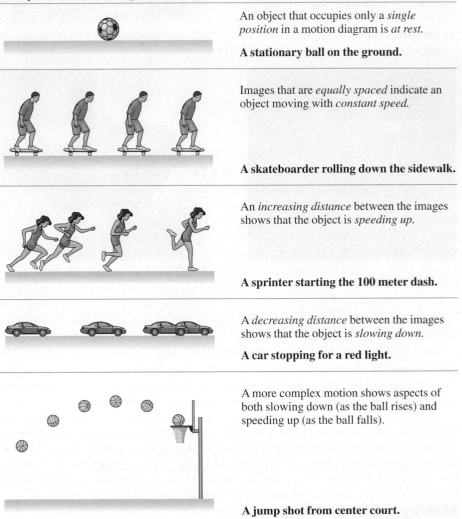

An object that occupies only a *single position* in a motion diagram is *at rest.*

A stationary ball on the ground.

Images that are *equally spaced* indicate an object moving with *constant speed.*

A skateboarder rolling down the sidewalk.

An *increasing distance* between the images shows that the object is *speeding up.*

A sprinter starting the 100 meter dash.

A *decreasing distance* between the images shows that the object is *slowing down.*

A car stopping for a red light.

A more complex motion shows aspects of both slowing down (as the ball rises) and speeding up (as the ball falls).

A jump shot from center court.

We have defined several concepts (at rest, constant speed, speeding up, and slowing down) in terms of how the moving object appears in a motion diagram. These are called **operational definitions,** meaning that the concepts are defined in terms of a particular procedure or operation performed by the investigator. For example, we could answer the question "Is the airplane speeding up?" by checking whether or not the images in the plane's motion diagram are getting farther apart. Many of the concepts in physics will be introduced as operational definitions. This reminds us that physics is an experimental science.

STOP TO THINK 1.1 Which car is going faster, A or B? Assume there are equal intervals of time between the frames of both movies.

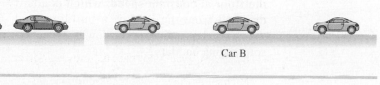

Car A   Car B

NOTE ► Each chapter will have several *Stop to Think* questions. These questions are designed to see if you've understood the basic ideas that have been presented. The answers are given at the end of the chapter, but you should make a serious effort to think about these questions before turning to the answers. If you answer correctly, and are sure of your answer rather than just guessing, you can proceed to the next section with confidence. But if you answer incorrectly, it would be wise to reread the preceding sections before proceeding onward. ◄

1.2 The Particle Model

For many objects, such as cars and rockets, the motion of the object *as a whole* is not influenced by the "details" of the object's size and shape. To describe the object's motion, all we really need to keep track of is the motion of a single point, such as a white dot painted on the side of the object.

If we restrict our attention to objects undergoing **translational motion,** which is the motion of an object along a trajectory, we can consider the object *as if* it were just a single point, without size or shape. We can also treat the object *as if* all of its mass were concentrated into this single point. An object that can be represented as a mass at a single point in space is called a **particle.** A particle has no size, no shape, and no distinction between top and bottom or between front and back.

If we treat an object as a particle, we can represent the object in each frame of a motion diagram as a simple dot rather than having to draw a full picture. **FIGURE 1.4** shows how much simpler motion diagrams appear when the object is represented as a particle. Note that the dots have been numbered 0, 1, 2, . . . to tell the sequence in which the frames were exposed.

Using the Particle Model

Treating an object as a particle is, of course, a simplification of reality. As we noted in the overview, such a simplification is called a *model*. Models allow us to focus on the important aspects of a phenomenon by excluding those aspects that play only a minor role. The **particle model** of motion is a simplification in which we treat a moving object as if all of its mass were concentrated at a single point.

The particle model is an excellent approximation of reality for the motion of cars, planes, rockets, and similar objects. People are somewhat more complex, because of moving arms and legs, but the motion of a person's body as a whole is still described reasonably well within the particle model. In later chapters, we'll find that the motion of more complex objects, which cannot be treated as a single particle, can often be analyzed as if the object were a collection of particles.

Not all motions can be reduced to the motion of a single point. Consider a rotating gear. The center of the gear doesn't move at all, and each tooth on the gear is moving in a different direction. Rotational motion is qualitatively different than translational motion, and we'll need to go beyond the particle model later when we study rotational motion.

FIGURE 1.4 Motion diagrams in which the object is represented as a particle.

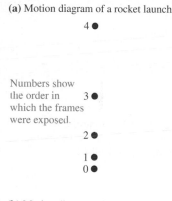

(a) Motion diagram of a rocket launch

4●

Numbers show the order in which the frames were exposed.   3●

2●

1●
0●

(b) Motion diagram of a car stopping

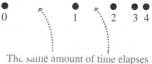

The same amount of time elapses between each image and the next.

A Word About Vectors and Notation

Before continuing, let's take a closer look at what a vector is. Vectors will be studied thoroughly in Chapter 3, so all we need for now is a little basic information. Some physical quantities, such as time, mass, and temperature, can be described completely by a single number with a unit. For example, the mass of an object is 6 kg and its temperature is 30°C. When a physical quantity is described by a single number (with a unit), we call it a **scalar quantity.** A scalar can be positive, negative, or zero.

Many other quantities, however, have a directional quality and cannot be described by a single number. To describe the motion of a car, for example, you must specify not only how fast it is moving, but also the *direction* in which it is moving. A **vector quantity** is a quantity having both a *size* (the "How far?" or "How fast?") and a *direction* (the "Which way?"). The size or length of a vector is called its *magnitude*. The magnitude of a vector can be positive or zero, but it cannot be negative.

When we want to represent a vector quantity with a symbol, we need somehow to indicate that the symbol is for a vector rather than for a scalar. We do this by drawing an arrow over the letter that represents the quantity. Thus $\vec{r}$ and $\vec{A}$ are symbols for vectors, whereas r and A, without the arrows, are symbols for scalars. In handwritten work you must draw arrows over all symbols that represent vectors. This may seem strange until you get used to it, but it is very important because we will often use both r and $\vec{r}$, or both A and $\vec{A}$, in the same problem, and they mean different things! Without the arrow, you will be using the same symbol with two different meanings and will likely end up making a mistake. Note that the arrow over the symbol always points to the right, regardless of which direction the actual vector points. Thus we write $\vec{r}$ or $\vec{A}$, never $\overleftarrow{r}$ or $\overleftarrow{A}$.

NOTE ► Some textbooks represent vectors with boldface type, such as **r** or **A**. This book will consistently display the vector arrow over vector symbols, just as you should do in handwritten work. ◄

Change in Position

Consider the following:

Sam is standing 50 feet (ft) east of the corner of 12th Street and Vine. He then walks northeast for 100 ft to a second point. What is Sam's change of position?

FIGURE 1.6 shows Sam's motion in terms of position vectors. Because we're free to place the origin of our coordinate system wherever we wish, we've placed it at the intersection. Sam's initial position is the vector $\vec{r}_0$ drawn from the origin to the point where he starts walking. Vector $\vec{r}_1$ is his position after he finishes walking. You can see that Sam has changed position, and a *change* of position is called a **displacement.** His displacement is the vector labeled $\Delta\vec{r}$. The Greek letter delta (Δ) is used in math and science to indicate the *change* in a quantity. Here it indicates a change in the position $\vec{r}$.

NOTE ► $\Delta\vec{r}$ is a *single* symbol. You cannot cancel out or remove the Δ in algebraic operations. ◄

FIGURE 1.6 Sam undergoes a displacement $\Delta\vec{r}$ from position $\vec{r}_0$ to position $\vec{r}_1$.

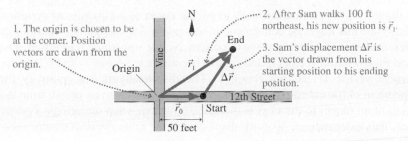

1. The origin is chosen to be at the corner. Position vectors are drawn from the origin.

2. After Sam walks 100 ft northeast, his new position is $\vec{r}_1$.

3. Sam's displacement $\Delta\vec{r}$ is the vector drawn from his starting position to his ending position.

N

End

Origin

$\vec{r}_1$

$\Delta\vec{r}$

Vine

12th Street

$\vec{r}_0$ Start

50 feet

STOP TO THINK 1.2   Three motion diagrams are shown. Which is a dust particle settling to the floor at constant speed, which is a ball dropped from the roof of a building, and which is a descending rocket slowing to make a soft landing on Mars?

(a) 0 ●
1 ●
2 ●
3 ●
4 ●

5 ●

(b) 0 ●

1 ●

2 ●

3 ●

4 ●

5 ●

(c) 0 ●

1 ●

2 ●

3 ●

4 ●

5 ●

1.3 Position and Time

As we look at a motion diagram, it would be useful to know *where* the object is (i.e., its *position*) and *when* the object was at that position (i.e., the *time*). These are easy measurements to make.

Position measurements can be made by laying a coordinate system grid over a motion diagram. You can then measure the (x, y) coordinates of each point in the motion diagram. Of course, the world does not come with a coordinate system attached. A coordinate system is an artificial grid that *you* place over a problem in order to analyze the motion. You place the origin of your coordinate system wherever you wish, and different observers of a moving object might all choose to use different origins. Likewise, you can choose the orientation of the *x*-axis and *y*-axis to be helpful for that particular problem. The conventional choice is for the *x*-axis to point to the right and the *y*-axis to point upward, but there is nothing sacred about this choice. We will soon have many occasions to tilt the axes at an angle.

Time, in a sense, is also a coordinate system, although you may never have thought of time this way. You can pick an arbitrary point in the motion and label it "$t = 0$ seconds." This is simply the instant you decide to start your clock or stopwatch, so it is the origin of your time coordinate. Different observers might choose to start their clocks at different moments. A movie frame labeled "$t = 4$ seconds" was taken 4 seconds after you started your clock.

We typically choose $t = 0$ to represent the "beginning" of a problem, but the object may have been moving before then. Those earlier instants would be measured as negative times, just as objects on the *x*-axis to the left of the origin have negative values of position. Negative numbers are not to be avoided; they simply locate an event in space or time *relative to an origin*.

To illustrate, **FIGURE 1.5a** shows an *xy*-coordinate system and time information superimposed over the motion diagram of a basketball. You can see that the ball's position is $(x_4, y_4) = (12$ m, 9 m$)$ at time $t_4 = 2.0$ s. Notice how we've used subscripts to indicate the time and the object's position in a specific frame of the motion diagram.

NOTE ► The first frame is labeled 0 to correspond with time $t = 0$. That is why the fifth frame is labeled 4. ◄

Another way to locate the ball is to draw an arrow from the origin to the point representing the ball. You can then specify the length and direction of the arrow. An arrow drawn from the origin to an object's position is called the **position vector** of the object, and it is given the symbol $\vec{r}$. **FIGURE 1.5b** shows the position vector $\vec{r}_4 = (15$ m, $37°)$.

The position vector $\vec{r}$ does not tell us anything different than the coordinates (x, y). It simply provides the information in an alternative form. Although you're more familiar with coordinates than with vectors, you will find that vectors are a useful way to describe many concepts in physics.

FIGURE 1.5 Position and time measurements made on the motion diagram of a basketball.

(a)

A coordinate system has been added to the motion diagram.

The ball's position in frame 4 can be specified with coordinates.

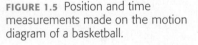
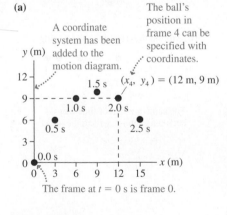

y (m)

12

9 · · · · · 1.5 s · $(x_4, y_4) = (12$ m, 9 m$)$

1.0 s   2.0 s

6   0.5 s   2.5 s

3

0   0.0 s
0   3   6   9   12   15 x (m)

The frame at $t = 0$ s is frame 0.

(b)

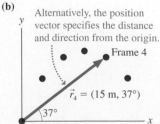

y

Alternatively, the position vector specifies the distance and direction from the origin.

Frame 4

$\vec{r}_4 = (15$ m, $37°)$

37° x

Displacement is a vector quantity; it requires both a length and a direction to describe it. Specifically, the displacement $\Delta\vec{r}$ is a vector drawn *from* a starting position *to* an ending position. Sam's displacement is written

$$\Delta\vec{r} = (100 \text{ ft, northeast})$$

where we've given both the length and the direction. The length, or magnitude, of a displacement vector is simply the straight-line distance between the starting and ending positions.

If you start 10 ft from a door and walk directly away from the door for 5 ft, you end up 15 ft from the door. The *procedure* by which you learn this is to *add* your change in position (5 ft) to your initial position (10 ft).

Similarly, we can answer the question "Where does Sam end up?" if we *add* his change in position (his displacement $\Delta\vec{r}$) to his initial position, the vector $\vec{r}_0$. Sam's final position in Figure 1.6, vector $\vec{r}_1$, can be seen as a combination of vector $\vec{r}_0$ *plus* vector $\Delta\vec{r}$. In fact, $\vec{r}_1$ is the *vector sum* of vectors $\vec{r}_0$ and $\Delta\vec{r}$. This is written

$$\vec{r}_1 = \vec{r}_0 + \Delta\vec{r} \tag{1.1}$$

Notice, however, that we are adding vector quantities, not numbers. Vector addition is a different process from "regular" addition. We'll explore vector addition more thoroughly in Chapter 3, but for now you can add two vectors $\vec{A}$ and $\vec{B}$ with the three-step procedure shown in Tactics Box 1.1.

TACTICS BOX 1.1   **Vector addition**   (MP)

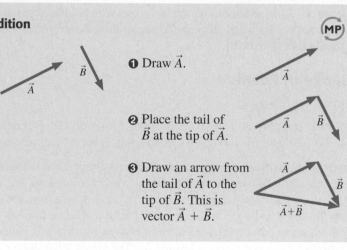

To add $\vec{B}$ to $\vec{A}$:

$\vec{A}$ $\vec{B}$

❶ Draw $\vec{A}$.

$\vec{A}$

❷ Place the tail of $\vec{B}$ at the tip of $\vec{A}$.

$\vec{A}$ $\vec{B}$

❸ Draw an arrow from the tail of $\vec{A}$ to the tip of $\vec{B}$. This is vector $\vec{A} + \vec{B}$.

$\vec{A}$ $\vec{B}$ $\vec{A}+\vec{B}$

If you examine Figure 1.6, you'll see that the steps of Tactics Box 1.1 are exactly how $\vec{r}_0$ and $\Delta\vec{r}$ are added to give $\vec{r}_1$.

NOTE ► A vector is not tied to a particular location on the page. You can move a vector around as long as you don't change its length or the direction it points. Vector $\vec{B}$ is not changed by sliding it to where its tail is at the tip of $\vec{A}$. ◄

In Figure 1.6, we chose *arbitrarily* to put the origin of the coordinate system at the corner. While this might be convenient, it certainly is not mandatory. **FIGURE 1.7** shows a different choice of where to place the origin. Notice something interesting. The initial and final position vectors $\vec{r}_0$ and $\vec{r}_1$ have become new vectors $\vec{r}_2$ and $\vec{r}_3$, but the displacement vector $\Delta\vec{r}$ has not changed! **The displacement is a quantity that is independent of the coordinate system.** In other words, the arrow drawn from the one position of an object to the next is the same no matter what coordinate system you choose. This independence gives the displacement $\Delta\vec{r}$ more *physical significance* than the position vectors themselves have.

FIGURE 1.7 Sam's displacement $\Delta\vec{r}$ is unchanged by using a different coordinate system.

The displacement vector is not affected by the choice of origin.

End

$\Delta\vec{r}$ $\vec{r}_3$

Start $\vec{r}_2$

50 feet   New origin

FIGURE 1.10
displacemen

(a) Rocket

(b) Car

EXAM
Alice
denly
ally b
and l

MOD

VISU
lem
until
equa
whe
sho

1.4 Velocity

It's no surprise that, during a given time interval, a speeding bullet travels farther than a speeding snail. To extend our study of motion so that we can compare the bullet to the snail, we need a way to measure how fast or how slowly an object moves.

One quantity that measures an object's fastness or slowness is its **average speed,** defined as the ratio

$$\text{average speed} = \frac{\text{distance traveled}}{\text{time interval spent traveling}} \tag{1.3}$$

If you drive 15 miles (mi) in 30 minutes ($\frac{1}{2}$ hour), your average speed is

$$\text{average speed} = \frac{15 \text{ mi}}{\frac{1}{2} \text{ hour}} = 30 \text{ mph} \tag{1.4}$$

Although the concept of speed is widely used in our day-to-day lives, it is not a sufficient basis for a science of motion. To see why, imagine you're trying to land a jet plane on an aircraft carrier. It matters a great deal to you whether the aircraft carrier is moving at 20 mph (miles per hour) to the north or 20 mph to the east. Simply knowing that the boat's speed is 20 mph is not enough information! The difficulty with speed is that it tells us nothing about the direction in which an object is moving.

It's the displacement $\Delta\vec{r}$, a vector quantity, that tells us not only the distance traveled by a moving object, but also the *direction* of motion. Consequently, a more useful ratio for an object undergoing a displacement $\Delta\vec{r}$ during the time interval Δt is the ratio $\Delta\vec{r}/\Delta t$. This ratio is a vector, because $\Delta\vec{r}$ is a vector, so it has both a magnitude and a direction. The size, or magnitude, of this ratio is very similar to the definition of speed: The ratio will be larger for a fast object than for a slow object. But in addition to measuring how fast an object moves, this ratio is a vector that points in the same direction as $\Delta\vec{r}$. That is, it points in the direction of motion.

It is convenient to give this ratio a name. We call it the **average velocity,** and it has the symbol $\vec{v}_{\text{avg}}$. **The average velocity of an object during the time interval Δt, in which the object undergoes a displacement $\Delta\vec{r}$, is the vector**

$$\vec{v}_{\text{avg}} = \frac{\Delta\vec{r}}{\Delta t} \tag{1.5}$$

An object's average velocity vector points in the same direction as the displacement vector $\Delta\vec{r}$. This is the direction of motion.

> **NOTE** ▶ In everyday language we do not make a distinction between speed and velocity, but in physics *the distinction is very important.* In particular, speed is simply "How fast," whereas velocity is "How fast, and in which direction." As we go along we will be giving other words more precise meaning in physics than they have in everyday language. ◀

As an example, **FIGURE 1.12a** shows two ships that start from the same position and move 5 miles in 15 minutes. Both ships have a speed of 20 mph, but their velocities are different. Because their displacements during Δt are $\Delta\vec{r}_A$ = (5 mi, north) and $\Delta\vec{r}_B$ = (5 mi, east), we can write their velocities as

$$\vec{v}_{\text{avg A}} = (20 \text{ mph, north})$$
$$\vec{v}_{\text{avg B}} = (20 \text{ mph, east}) \tag{1.6}$$

Notice how the velocity *vectors* in **FIGURE 1.12b** point in the direction of motion.

> **NOTE** ▶ Our goal in this chapter is to *visualize* motion with motion diagrams. Strictly speaking, the vector we have defined in Equation 1.5, and the vector we will show on motion diagrams, is the *average* velocity $\vec{v}_{\text{avg}}$. But to allow the motion diagram to be a useful tool, we will drop the subscript and refer to the average

The victory goes to the runner with the highest average speed.

FIGURE 1.12 The displacement vectors and velocities of ships A and B.

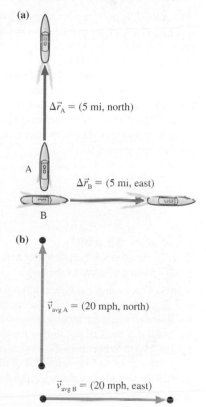

(a)

$\Delta\vec{r}_A$ = (5 mi, north)

A

$\Delta\vec{r}_B$ = (5 mi, east)

B

(b)

$\vec{v}_{\text{avg A}}$ = (20 mph, north)

$\vec{v}_{\text{avg B}}$ = (20 mph, east)

velocity as simply $\vec{v}$. Our definitions and symbols, which somewhat blur the distinction between average and instantaneous quantities, are adequate for visualization purposes, but they're not the final word on the subject. We will refine these definitions in Chapter 2, where our goal will be to develop the mathematics of motion. ◄

Motion Diagrams with Velocity Vectors

The velocity vector, as we've defined it, points in the same direction as the displacement $\Delta\vec{r}$, and the length of $\vec{v}$ is directly proportional to the length of $\Delta\vec{r}$. Consequently, the vectors connecting each dot of a motion diagram to the next, which we previously labeled as displacement vectors, could equally well be identified as velocity vectors.

This idea is illustrated in **FIGURE 1.13**, which shows four frames from the motion diagram of a tortoise racing a hare. The vectors connecting the dots are now labeled as velocity vectors $\vec{v}$. **The length of a velocity vector represents the average speed with which the object moves between the two points.** Longer velocity vectors indicate faster motion. You can see from the diagram that the hare moves faster than the tortoise.

Notice that the hare's velocity vectors do not change; each has the same length and direction. We say the hare is moving with *constant velocity*. The tortoise is also moving with its own constant velocity.

FIGURE 1.13 Motion diagram of the tortoise racing the hare.

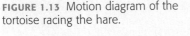
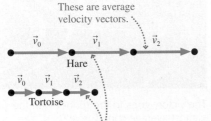

These are average velocity vectors.

The length of each arrow represents the average speed. The hare moves faster than the tortoise.

EXAMPLE 1.2 **Accelerating up a hill**

The light turns green and a car accelerates, starting from rest, up a 20° hill. Draw a motion diagram showing the car's velocity.

MODEL Use the particle model to represent the car as a dot.

VISUALIZE The car's motion takes place along a straight line, but the line is neither horizontal nor vertical. Because a motion diagram is made from frames of a movie, it will show the object moving with the correct orientation—in this case, at an angle of 20°. **FIGURE 1.14** shows several frames of the motion diagram, where we see the car speeding up. The car starts from rest, so the first arrow is drawn as short as possible and the first dot is labeled "Start." The displacement vectors have been drawn from each dot to the next, but then they have been identified and labeled as average velocity vectors $\vec{v}$.

FIGURE 1.14 Motion diagram of a car accelerating up a hill.

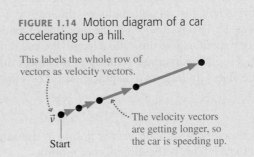

This labels the whole row of vectors as velocity vectors.

The velocity vectors are getting longer, so the car is speeding up.

Start

NOTE ▶ Rather than label every single vector, it's easier to give one label to the entire row of velocity vectors. You can see this in Figure 1.14. ◄

EXAMPLE 1.3 **It's a hit!**

Jake hits a ball at a 60° angle above horizontal. It is caught by Jim. Draw a motion diagram of the ball.

MODEL This example is typical of how many problems in science and engineering are worded. The problem does not give a clear statement of where the motion begins or ends. Are we interested in the motion of the ball just during the time it is in the air between Jake and Jim? What about the motion *as* Jake hits it (ball rapidly speeding up) or *as* Jim catches it (ball rapidly slowing down)? Should we include Jim dropping the ball after he catches it? The

point is that *you* will often be called on to make a *reasonable interpretation* of a problem statement. In this problem, the details of hitting and catching the ball are complex. The motion of the ball through the air is easier to describe, and it's a motion you might expect to learn about in a physics class. So our *interpretation* is that the motion diagram should start as the ball leaves Jake's bat (ball already moving) and should end the instant it touches Jim's hand (ball still moving). We will model the ball as a particle.

VISUALIZE With this interpretation in mind, **FIGURE 1.15** shows the motion diagram of the ball. Notice how, in contrast to the car of Figure 1.14, the ball is already moving as the motion diagram movie begins. As before, the average velocity vectors are found by connecting the dots with *straight* arrows. You can see that the average velocity vectors get shorter (ball slowing down), get longer (ball speeding up), and change direction. Each $\vec{v}$ is different, so this is *not* constant-velocity motion.

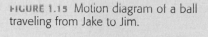

FIGURE 1.15 Motion diagram of a ball traveling from Jake to Jim.

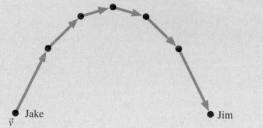

STOP TO THINK 1.3   A particle moves from position 1 to position 2 during the interval Δt. Which vector shows the particle's average velocity?

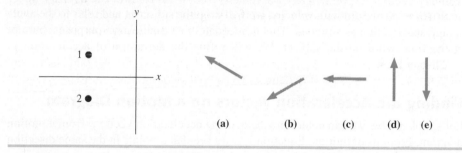

1.5 Linear Acceleration

The goal of this chapter is to find a set of concepts with which to describe motion. Position, time, and velocity are important concepts, and at first glance they might appear to be sufficient. But that is not the case. Sometimes an object's velocity is constant, as it was in Figure 1.13. More often, an object's velocity changes as it moves, as in Figures 1.14 and 1.15. We need one more motion concept, one that will describe a *change* in the velocity.

Because velocity is a vector, it can change in two possible ways:

1. The magnitude can change, indicating a change in speed; or
2. The direction can change, indicating that the object has changed direction.

We will concentrate for now on the first case, a change in speed. The car in Figure 1.14 was an example of a situation in which the magnitude of the velocity vector changed but not the direction. We'll return to the second case in Chapter 4.

How can we measure the change of velocity in a meaningful way? When we wanted to measure changes in position, the ratio $\Delta \vec{r}/\Delta t$ was useful. This ratio is the *rate of change of position*. By analogy, consider an object whose velocity changes from $\vec{v}_1$ to $\vec{v}_2$ during the time interval Δt. Just as $\Delta \vec{r} = \vec{r}_2 - \vec{r}_1$ is the change of position, the quantity $\Delta \vec{v} = \vec{v}_2 - \vec{v}_1$ is the change of velocity. The ratio $\Delta \vec{v}/\Delta t$ is then the *rate of change of velocity*. But what does it measure?

Consider two cars, a Volkswagen Beetle and a fancy Porsche. Let them start from rest, and measure their velocities after an elapsed time of 10 seconds. The Porsche, we can assume, will have a larger $\Delta \vec{v}$. Consequently, it will have the larger value of the ratio $\Delta \vec{v}/\Delta t$. Thus this ratio appears to measure how quickly the car speeds up. It has a large magnitude for objects that speed up quickly and a small magnitude for objects that speed up slowly. The ratio $\Delta \vec{v}/\Delta t$ is called the **average acceleration**, and

The Audi TT accelerates from 0 to 60 mph in 6 s.

its symbol is $\vec{a}_{avg}$. **The average acceleration of an object during the time interval Δt, in which the object's velocity changes by $\Delta \vec{v}$, is the vector**

$$\vec{a}_{avg} = \frac{\Delta \vec{v}}{\Delta t} \qquad (1.7)$$

An object's average acceleration vector points in the same direction as the vector $\Delta \vec{v}$. Note that acceleration, like position and velocity, is a vector. Both its magnitude and its direction are important pieces of information.

Acceleration is a fairly abstract concept. Position and time are our real hands-on measurements of an object, and they are easy to understand. You can "see" where the object is located and the time on the clock. Velocity is a bit more abstract, being a relationship between the change of position and the change of time. Motion diagrams help us visualize velocity as the vector arrows connecting one position of the object to the next. Acceleration is an even more abstract idea about changes in the velocity. Yet it is essential to develop a good intuition about acceleration because it will be a key concept for understanding why objects move as they do.

NOTE ▶ As we did with velocity, we will drop the subscript and refer to the average acceleration as simply $\vec{a}$. This is adequate for visualization purposes, but not the final word on the subject. We will refine the definition of acceleration in Chapter 2. ◀

Finding the Acceleration Vectors on a Motion Diagram

Let's look at how we can determine the average acceleration vector $\vec{a}$ from a motion diagram. From its definition, Equation 1.7, we see that $\vec{a}$ points in the same direction as $\Delta \vec{v}$, the change of velocity. This critical idea is the basis for a technique to find $\vec{a}$.

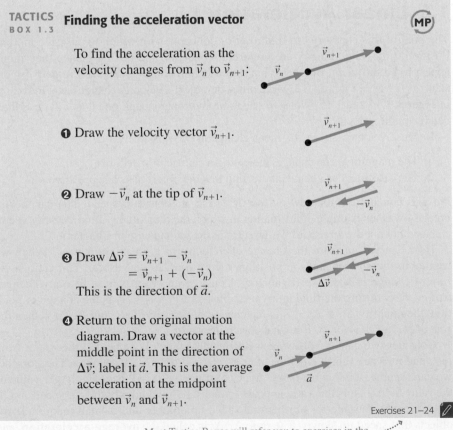

TACTICS BOX 1.3 Finding the acceleration vector

To find the acceleration as the velocity changes from $\vec{v}_n$ to $\vec{v}_{n+1}$:

❶ Draw the velocity vector $\vec{v}_{n+1}$.

❷ Draw $-\vec{v}_n$ at the tip of $\vec{v}_{n+1}$.

❸ Draw $\Delta \vec{v} = \vec{v}_{n+1} - \vec{v}_n$
   $= \vec{v}_{n+1} + (-\vec{v}_n)$
   This is the direction of $\vec{a}$.

❹ Return to the original motion diagram. Draw a vector at the middle point in the direction of $\Delta \vec{v}$; label it $\vec{a}$. This is the average acceleration at the midpoint between $\vec{v}_n$ and $\vec{v}_{n+1}$.

Exercises 21–24

Most Tactics Boxes will refer you to exercises in the
Student Workbook where you can practice the new skill.

Notice that the acceleration vector goes beside the dot, not beside the velocity vectors. This is because each acceleration vector is determined as the *difference* between the two velocity vectors on either side of a dot. The length of $\vec{a}$ does not have to be the exact length of $\Delta\vec{v}$; it is the direction of $\vec{a}$ that is most important.

The procedure of Tactics Box 1.3 can be repeated to find $\vec{a}$ at each point in the motion diagram. Note that we cannot determine $\vec{a}$ at the first and last points because we have only one velocity vector and can't find $\Delta\vec{v}$.

The Complete Motion Diagram

You've now seen several *Tactics Boxes* that help you achieve specific tasks. Tactics Boxes will appear in nearly every chapter in this book. We'll also, where appropriate, provide *Problem-Solving Strategies*. Problem solving will be discussed in more detail later in the chapter, but this is a good place for the first problem-solving strategy.

PROBLEM-SOLVING STRATEGY 1.1 Motion diagrams   (MP)

MODEL Represent the moving object as a particle. Make simplifying assumptions when interpreting the problem statement.

VISUALIZE A complete motion diagram consists of:

■ The position of the object in each frame of the film, shown as a dot. Use five or six dots to make the motion clear but without overcrowding the picture. More complex motions may need more dots.
■ The average velocity vectors, found by connecting each dot in the motion diagram to the next with a vector arrow. There is *one* velocity vector linking each *two* position dots. Label the row of velocity vectors $\vec{v}$.
■ The average acceleration vectors, found using Tactics Box 1.3. There is *one* acceleration vector linking each *two* velocity vectors. Each acceleration vector is drawn at the dot between the two velocity vectors it links. Use $\vec{0}$ to indicate a point at which the acceleration is zero. Label the row of acceleration vectors $\vec{a}$.

STOP TO THINK 1.4   A particle undergoes acceleration $\vec{a}$ while moving from point 1 to point 2. Which of the choices shows the velocity vector $\vec{v}_2$ as the particle moves away from point 2?

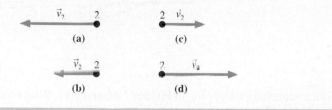

Examples of Motion Diagrams

Let's look at some examples of the full strategy for drawing motion diagrams.

EXAMPLE 1.4 The first astronauts land on Mars

A spaceship carrying the first astronauts to Mars descends safely to the surface. Draw a motion diagram for the last few seconds of the descent.

MODEL Represent the spaceship as a particle. It's reasonable to assume that its motion in the last few seconds is straight down. The problem ends as the spacecraft touches the surface.

VISUALIZE FIGURE 1.16 shows a complete motion diagram as the spaceship descends and slows, using its rockets, until it comes to rest on the surface. Notice how the dots get closer together as it slows. The inset shows how the acceleration vector $\vec{a}$ is determined at one point. All the other acceleration vectors will be similar, because for each pair of velocity vectors the earlier one is longer than the later one.

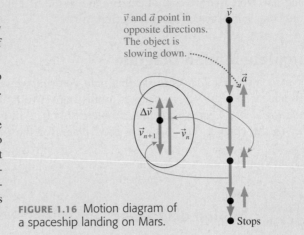

FIGURE 1.16 Motion diagram of a spaceship landing on Mars.

EXAMPLE 1.5 Skiing through the woods

A skier glides along smooth, horizontal snow at constant speed, then speeds up going down a hill. Draw the skier's motion diagram.

MODEL Represent the skier as a particle. It's reasonable to assume that the downhill slope is a straight line. Although the motion as a whole is not linear, we can treat the skier's motion as two separate linear motions.

VISUALIZE FIGURE 1.17 shows a complete motion diagram of the skier. The dots are equally spaced for the horizontal motion, indicating constant speed; then the dots get farther apart as the skier speeds up down the hill. The insets show how the average acceleration vector $\vec{a}$ is determined for the horizontal motion and along the slope. All the other acceleration vectors along the slope will be similar to the one shown because each velocity vector is longer than the preceding one. Notice that we've explicitly written $\vec{0}$ for the acceleration beside the dots where the velocity is constant. The acceleration at the point where the direction changes will be considered in Chapter 4.

FIGURE 1.17 Motion diagram of a skier.

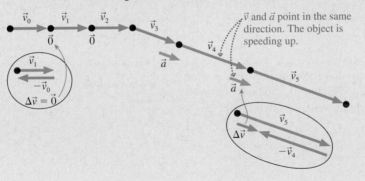

Notice something interesting in Figures 1.16 and 1.17. Where the object is speeding up, the acceleration and velocity vectors point in the *same direction*. Where the object is slowing down, the acceleration and velocity vectors point in *opposite directions*. These results are always true for motion in a straight line. **For motion along a line:**

- An object is speeding up if and only if $\vec{v}$ and $\vec{a}$ point in the same direction.
- An object is slowing down if and only if $\vec{v}$ and $\vec{a}$ point in opposite directions.
- An object's velocity is constant if and only if $\vec{a} = \vec{0}$.

NOTE ► In everyday language, we use the word *accelerate* to mean "speed up" and the word *decelerate* to mean "slow down." But speeding up and slowing down are both changes in the velocity and consequently, by our definition, *both* are accelerations. In physics, *acceleration* refers to changing the velocity, no matter what the change is, and not just to speeding up. ◄

EXAMPLE 1.6 Tossing a ball

Draw the motion diagram of a ball tossed straight up in the air.

MODEL This problem calls for some interpretation. Should we include the toss itself, or only the motion after the tosser releases the ball? Should we include the ball hitting the ground? It appears that this problem is really concerned with the ball's motion through the air. Consequently, we begin the motion diagram at the moment that the tosser releases the ball and end the diagram at the moment the ball hits the ground. We will consider neither the toss nor the impact. And, of course, we will represent the ball as a particle.

VISUALIZE We have a slight difficulty here because the ball retraces its route as it falls. A literal motion diagram would show the upward motion and downward motion on top of each other, leading to confusion. We can avoid this difficulty by horizontally separating the upward motion and downward motion diagrams. This will not affect our conclusions because it does not change any of the vectors. **FIGURE 1.18** shows the motion diagram drawn this way. Notice that the very top dot is shown twice—as the end point of the upward motion and the beginning point of the downward motion.

The ball slows down as it rises. You've learned that the acceleration vectors point opposite the velocity vectors for an object that is slowing down along a line, and they are shown accordingly. Similarly, $\vec{a}$ and $\vec{v}$ point in the same direction as the falling ball speeds up. Notice something interesting: The acceleration vectors point downward both while the ball is rising *and* while it is falling. Both "speeding up" and "slowing down" occur with the *same* acceleration vector. This is an important conclusion, one worth pausing to think about.

Now let's look at the top point on the ball's trajectory. The velocity vectors are pointing upward but getting shorter as the ball approaches the top. As the ball starts to fall, the velocity vectors are pointing downward and getting longer. There must be a moment—just an instant as $\vec{v}$ switches from pointing up to pointing down—when the velocity is zero. Indeed, the ball's velocity *is* zero for an instant at the precise top of the motion!

But what about the acceleration at the top? The inset shows how the average acceleration is determined from the last upward

FIGURE 1.18 Motion diagram of a ball tossed straight up in the air.

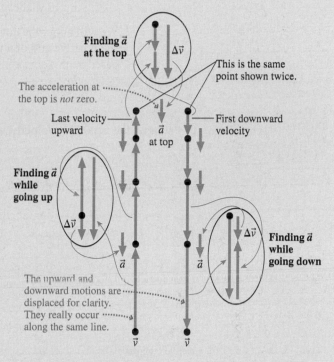

velocity before the top point and the first downward velocity. We find that the acceleration at the top is pointing downward, just as it does elsewhere in the motion.

Many people expect the acceleration to be zero at the highest point. But recall that the velocity at the top point *is* changing—from up to down. If the velocity is changing, there *must* be an acceleration. A downward-pointing acceleration vector is needed to turn the velocity vector from up to down. Another way to think about this is to note that zero acceleration would mean no change of velocity. When the ball reached zero velocity at the top, it would hang there and not fall if the acceleration were also zero!

1.6 Motion in One Dimension

As you've seen, an object's motion can be described in terms of three fundamental quantities: its position $\vec{r}$, velocity $\vec{v}$, and acceleration $\vec{a}$. These quantities are vectors, having a direction as well as a magnitude. But for motion in one dimension, the vectors are restricted to point only "forward" or "backward." Consequently, we can describe one-dimensional motion with the simpler quantities x, v_x, and a_x (or y, v_y, and a_y). However, we need to give each of these quantities an explicit *sign,* positive or negative, to indicate whether the position, velocity, or acceleration vector points forward or backward.

Determining the Signs of Position, Velocity, and Acceleration

1.1

Position, velocity, and acceleration are measured with respect to a coordinate system, a grid or axis that *you* impose on a problem to analyze the motion. We will find it convenient to use an *x*-axis to describe both horizontal motion and motion along an inclined plane. A *y*-axis will be used for vertical motion. A coordinate axis has two essential features:

1. An origin to define zero; and
2. An *x* or *y* label to indicate the positive end of the axis.

We will adopt the convention that **the positive end of an *x*-axis is to the right and the positive end of a *y*-axis is up.** The signs of position, velocity, and acceleration are based on this convention.

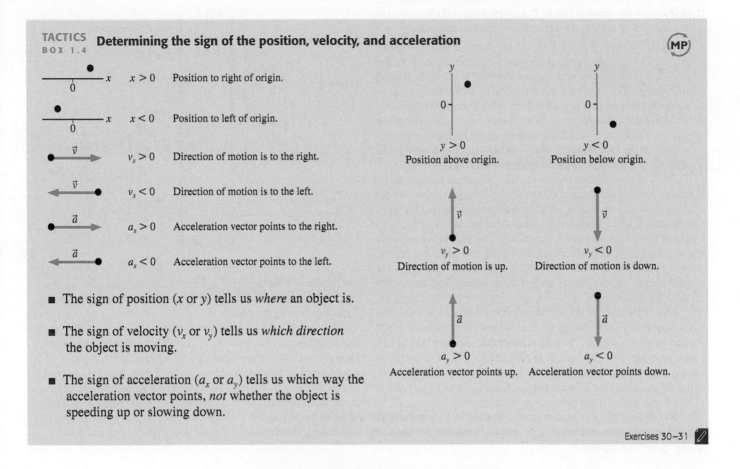

TACTICS BOX 1.4   Determining the sign of the position, velocity, and acceleration

$x > 0$ Position to right of origin.

$x < 0$ Position to left of origin.

$v_x > 0$ Direction of motion is to the right.

$v_x < 0$ Direction of motion is to the left.

$a_x > 0$ Acceleration vector points to the right.

$a_x < 0$ Acceleration vector points to the left.

- The sign of position (*x* or *y*) tells us *where* an object is.

- The sign of velocity (v_x or v_y) tells us *which direction* the object is moving.

- The sign of acceleration (a_x or a_y) tells us which way the acceleration vector points, *not* whether the object is speeding up or slowing down.

$y > 0$
Position above origin.

$y < 0$
Position below origin.

$v_y > 0$
Direction of motion is up.

$v_y < 0$
Direction of motion is down.

$a_y > 0$
Acceleration vector points up.

$a_y < 0$
Acceleration vector points down.

Exercises 30–31

Acceleration is where things get a bit tricky. A natural tendency is to think that a positive value of a_x or a_y describes an object that is speeding up while a negative value describes an object that is slowing down (decelerating). However, this interpretation *does not work.*

Acceleration was defined as $\vec{a}_{avg} = \Delta\vec{v}/\Delta t$. The direction of $\vec{a}$ can be determined by using a motion diagram to find the direction of $\Delta\vec{v}$. The one-dimensional acceleration a_x (or a_y) is then positive if the vector $\vec{a}$ points to the right (or up), negative if $\vec{a}$ points to the left (or down).

FIGURE 1.19 shows that this method for determining the sign of a does not conform to the simple idea of speeding up and slowing down. The object in Figure 1.19a has a positive acceleration ($a_x > 0$) not because it is speeding up but because the vector $\vec{a}$ points to the right. Compare this with the motion diagram of Figure 1.19b. Here the object is slowing down, but it still has a positive acceleration ($a_x > 0$) because $\vec{a}$ points to the right.

We found that an object is speeding up if $\vec{v}$ and $\vec{a}$ point in the same direction, slowing down if they point in opposite directions. For one-dimensional motion this rule becomes:

- An object is speeding up if and only if v_x and a_x have the same sign.
- An object is slowing down if and only if v_x and a_x have opposite signs.
- An object's velocity is constant if and only if $a_x = 0$.

Notice how the first two of these rules are at work in Figure 1.19.

Position-versus-Time Graphs

FIGURE 1.20 is a motion diagram, made at 1 frame per minute, of a student walking to school. You can see that she leaves home at a time we choose to call $t = 0$ min and makes steady progress for a while. Beginning at $t = 3$ min there is a period where the distance traveled during each time interval becomes less—perhaps she slowed down to speak with a friend. Then she picks up the pace, and the distances within each interval are longer.

FIGURE 1.20 The motion diagram of a student walking to school and a coordinate axis for making measurements.

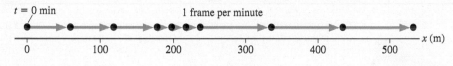

Figure 1.20 includes a coordinate axis, and you can see that every dot in a motion diagram occurs at a specific position. Table 1.1 shows the student's positions at different times as measured along this axis. For example, she is at position $x = 120$ m at $t = 2$ min.

The motion diagram is one way to represent the student's motion. Another is to make a graph of the measurements in Table 1.1. FIGURE 1.21a is a graph of x versus t for the student. The motion diagram tells us only where the student is at a few discrete points of time, so this graph of the data shows only points, no lines.

NOTE ▶ A graph of "a versus b" means that a is graphed on the vertical axis and b on the horizontal axis. Saying "graph a versus b" is really a shorthand way of saying "graph a as a function of b." ◀

However, common sense tells us the following. First, the student was *somewhere specific* at all times. That is, there was never a time when she failed to have a well-defined position, nor could she occupy two positions at one time. (As reasonable as this belief appears to be, it will be severely questioned and found not entirely accurate when we get to quantum physics!) Second, the student moved *continuously* through all intervening points of space. She could not go from $x = 100$ m to $x = 200$ m without passing through every point in between. It is thus quite reasonable to believe that her motion can be shown as a continuous line passing through the measured points, as shown in FIGURE 1.21b. A continuous line or curve showing an object's position as a function of time is called a **position-versus-time graph** or, sometimes, just a *position graph*.

FIGURE 1.19 One of these objects is speeding up, the other slowing down, but they both have a positive acceleration a_x.

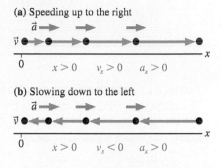

(a) Speeding up to the right

$x > 0$ $v_x > 0$ $a_x > 0$

(b) Slowing down to the left

$x > 0$ $v_x < 0$ $a_x > 0$

TABLE 1.1 Measured positions of a student walking to school

Time t (min)	Position x (m)
0	0
1	60
2	120
3	180
4	200
5	220
6	240
7	340
8	440
9	540

FIGURE 1.21 Position graphs of the student's motion.

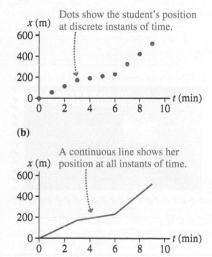

(a) Dots show the student's position at discrete instants of time.

(b) A continuous line shows her position at all instants of time.

NOTE ▶ A graph is *not* a "picture" of the motion. The student is walking along a straight line, but the graph itself is not a straight line. Further, we've graphed her position on the vertical axis even though her motion is horizontal. Graphs are *abstract representations* of motion. We will place significant emphasis on the process of interpreting graphs, and many of the exercises and problems will give you a chance to practice these skills. ◀

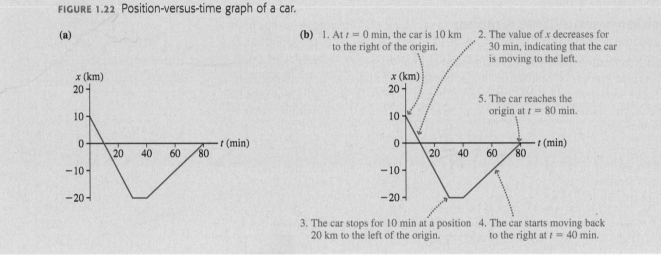

EXAMPLE 1.7 Interpreting a position graph
The graph in FIGURE 1.22a represents the motion of a car along a straight road. Describe the motion of the car.

MODEL Represent the car as a particle.

VISUALIZE As FIGURE 1.22b shows, the graph represents a car that travels to the left for 30 minutes, stops for 10 minutes, then travels back to the right for 40 minutes.

FIGURE 1.22 Position-versus-time graph of a car.

(a)

(b) 1. At $t = 0$ min, the car is 10 km to the right of the origin.

2. The value of x decreases for 30 min, indicating that the car is moving to the left.

5. The car reaches the origin at $t = 80$ min.

3. The car stops for 10 min at a position 20 km to the left of the origin.

4. The car starts moving back to the right at $t = 40$ min.

1.7 Solving Problems in Physics

Physics is not mathematics. Math problems are clearly stated, such as "What is $2 + 2$?" Physics is about the world around us, and to describe that world we must use language. Now, language is wonderful—we couldn't communicate without it—but language can sometimes be imprecise or ambiguous.

The challenge when reading a physics problem is to translate the words into symbols that can be manipulated, calculated, and graphed. **The translation from words to symbols is the heart of problem solving in physics.** This is the point where ambiguous words and phrases must be clarified, where the imprecise must be made precise, and where you arrive at an understanding of exactly what the question is asking.

Using Symbols

Symbols are a language that allows us to talk with precision about the relationships in a problem. As with any language, we all need to agree to use words or symbols in the same way if we want to communicate with each other. Many of the ways we use symbols in science and engineering are somewhat arbitrary, often reflecting historical roots. Nonetheless, practicing scientists and engineers have come to agree on how to use the language of symbols. Learning this language is part of learning physics.

The previous section began to introduce the symbols needed to describe motion along a line—the one-dimensional position, velocity, and acceleration of an object represented by the symbols x, v_x, and a_x (or y, v_y, and a_y if the motion is vertical). The vector nature of these quantities appears through their *signs:*

Richard Feynman, one of the greatest physicists of the 20th century, developed a new way to solve some difficult problems by representing complex ideas with special symbols and diagrams.

- v_x (or v_y) is positive if the velocity vector $\vec{v}$ points to the right (or up). It is negative if the velocity vector $\vec{v}$ points to the left (or down).
- a_x (or a_y) is positive if the acceleration vector $\vec{a}$ points to the right (or up). It is negative if the acceleration vector $\vec{a}$ points to the left (or down).

The appropriate sign for v is usually clear. Determining the sign of a is more difficult, and this is where a motion diagram can help.

We will use subscripts to designate a particular point in the problem. Scientists usually label the starting point of the problem with the subscript "0," not the subscript "1" that you might expect. When using subscripts, make sure that all symbols referring to the same point in the problem have the *same numerical subscript*. To have the one point in a problem characterized by position x_1 but velocity v_{2x} is guaranteed to lead to confusion!

Drawing Pictures

You may have been told that the first step in solving a physics problem is to "draw a picture," but perhaps you didn't know why, or what to draw. The purpose of drawing a picture is to aid you in the words-to-symbols translation. Complex problems have far more information than you can keep in your head at one time. Think of a picture as a "memory extension," helping you organize and keep track of vital information.

Although any picture is better than none, there really is a *method* for drawing pictures that will help you be a better problem solver. It is called the **pictorial representation** of the problem. We'll add other pictorial representations as we go along, but the following procedure is appropriate for motion problems.

TACTICS
BOX 1.5   **Drawing a pictorial representation**   (MP)

❶ **Draw a motion diagram.** The motion diagram develops your intuition for the motion and, especially important, determines whether the signs of v and a are positive or negative.

❷ **Establish a coordinate system.** Select your axes and origin to match the motion. For one-dimensional motion, you want either the x-axis or the y-axis parallel to the motion.

❸ **Sketch the situation.** Not just any sketch. Show the object at the *beginning* of the motion, at the *end,* and at any point where the character of the motion changes. Show the object, not just a dot, but very simple drawings are adequate.

❹ **Define symbols.** Use the sketch to define symbols representing quantities such as position, velocity, acceleration, and time. *Every* variable used later in the mathematical solution should be defined on the sketch. Some will have known values, others are initially unknown, but all should be given symbolic names.

❺ **List known information.** Make a table of the quantities whose values you can determine from the problem statement or that can be found quickly with simple geometry or unit conversions. Some quantities are implied by the problem, rather than explicitly given. Others are determined by your choice of coordinate system.

❻ **Identify the desired unknowns.** What quantity or quantities will allow you to answer the question? These should have been defined as symbols in step 4. Don't list every unknown, only the one or two needed to answer the question.

It's not an overstatement to say that a well-done pictorial representation of the problem will take you halfway to the solution. The following example illustrates how to construct a pictorial representation for a problem that is typical of problems you will see in the next few chapters.

EXAMPLE 1.8 Drawing a pictorial representation

Draw a pictorial representation for the following problem: A rocket sled accelerates at 50 m/s² for 5.0 s, then coasts for 3.0 s. What is the total distance traveled?

VISUALIZE The motion diagram shows an acceleration phase followed by a coasting phase. Because the motion is horizontal, the appropriate coordinate system is an x-axis. We've chosen to place the origin at the starting point. The motion has a beginning, an end, and a point where the nature of the motion changes from accelerating to coasting. These are the three sled positions sketched in FIGURE 1.23. The quantities x, v_x, and t are needed at each of three

points, so these have been defined on the sketch and distinguished by subscripts. Accelerations are associated with *intervals* between the points, so only two accelerations are defined. Values for three quantities are given in the problem statement, although we need to use the motion diagram, where $\vec{a}$ points to the right, to know that $a_{0x} = +50$ m/s² rather than -50 m/s². Other quantities, such as $x_0 = 0$ m and $t_0 = 0$ s, are inferred from our choice of coordinate system. The value $v_{0x} = 0$ m/s is part of our *interpretation* of the problem. Finally, we identify x_2 as the quantity that will answer the question. We now understand quite a bit about the problem and would be ready to start a quantitative analysis.

FIGURE 1.23 A pictorial representation.

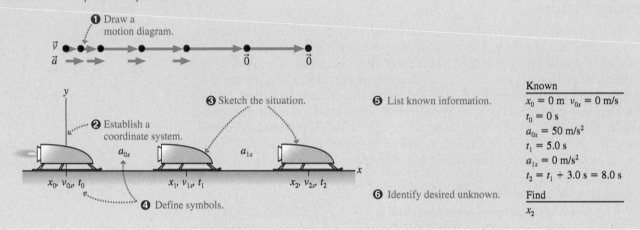

We didn't *solve* the problem; that is not the purpose of the pictorial representation. The pictorial representation is a systematic way to go about interpreting a problem and getting ready for a mathematical solution. Although this is a simple problem, and you probably know how to solve it if you've taken physics before, you will soon be faced with much more challenging problems. Learning good problem-solving skills at the beginning, while the problems are easy, will make them second nature later when you really need them.

Representations

A picture is one way to *represent* your knowledge of a situation. You could also represent your knowledge using words, graphs, or equations. Each **representation of knowledge** gives us a different perspective on the problem. The more tools you have for thinking about a complex problem, the more likely you are to solve it.

There are four representations of knowledge that we will use over and over:

1. The *verbal* representation. A problem statement, in words, is a verbal representation of knowledge. So is an explanation that you write.
2. The *pictorial* representation. The pictorial representation, which we've just presented, is the most literal depiction of the situation.
3. The *graphical* representation. We will make extensive use of graphs.
4. The *mathematical* representation. Equations that can be used to find the numerical values of specific quantities are the mathematical representation.

NOTE ▶ The mathematical representation is only one of many. Much of physics is more about thinking and reasoning than it is about solving equations. ◀

A new building requires careful planning. The architect's visualization and drawings have to be complete before the detailed procedures of construction get under way. The same is true for solving problems in physics.

A Problem-Solving Strategy

One of the goals of this textbook is to help you learn a *strategy* for solving physics problems. The purpose of a strategy is to guide you in the right direction with minimal wasted effort. The four-part problem-solving strategy shown below—**Model, Visualize, Solve, Assess**—is based on using different representations of knowledge. You will see this problem-solving strategy used consistently in the worked examples throughout this textbook, and you should endeavor to apply it to your own problem solving.

Throughout this textbook we will emphasize the first two steps. They are the *physics* of the problem, as opposed to the mathematics of solving the resulting equations. This is not to say that those mathematical operations are always easy—in many cases they are not. But our primary goal is to understand the physics.

General Problem-Solving Strategy   (MP)

MODEL It's impossible to treat every detail of a situation. Simplify the situation with a model that captures the essential features. For example, the object in a mechanics problem is usually represented as a particle.

VISUALIZE This is where expert problem solvers put most of their effort.

- Draw a *pictorial representation*. This helps you visualize important aspects of the physics and assess the information you are given. It starts the process of translating the problem into symbols.
- Use a *graphical representation* if it is appropriate for the problem.
- Go back and forth between these representations; they need not be done in any particular order.

SOLVE Only after modeling and visualizing are complete is it time to develop a *mathematical representation* with specific equations that must be solved. All symbols used here should have been defined in the pictorial representation.

ASSESS Is your result believable? Does it have proper units? Does it make sense?

Textbook illustrations are obviously more sophisticated than what you would draw on your own paper. To show you a figure very much like what you *should* draw, the final example of this section is in a "pencil sketch" style. We will include one or more pencil-sketch examples in nearly every chapter to illustrate exactly what a good problem solver would draw.

EXAMPLE 1.9 Launching a weather rocket
Use the first two steps of the problem-solving strategy to analyze the following problem: A small rocket, such as those used for meteorological measurements of the atmosphere, is launched vertically with an acceleration of 30 m/s². It runs out of fuel after 30 s. What is its maximum altitude?

MODEL We need to do some interpretation. Common sense tells us that the rocket does not stop the instant it runs out of fuel.

Instead, it continues upward, while slowing, until it reaches its maximum altitude. This second half of the motion, after running out of fuel, is like the ball that was tossed upward in the first half of Example 1.6. Because the problem does not ask about the rocket's descent, we conclude that the problem ends at the point of maximum altitude. We'll represent the rocket as a particle.

Continued

VISUALIZE **FIGURE 1.24** shows the pictorial representation in pencil-sketch style. The rocket is speeding up during the first half of the motion, so $\vec{a}_0$ points upward, in the positive y-direction. Thus the initial acceleration is $a_{0y} = 30$ m/s^2. During the second half, as the rocket slows, $\vec{a}_1$ points downward. Thus a_{1y} is a negative number.

This information is included with the known information. Although the velocity v_{2y} wasn't given in the problem statement, we know it must be zero at the very top of the trajectory. Last, we have identified y_2 as the desired unknown. This, of course, is not the only unknown in the problem, but it is the one we are specifically asked to find.

ASSESS If you've had a previous physics class, you may be tempted to assign a_{1y} the value -9.8 m/s^2, the free-fall acceleration. However, that would be true only if there is no air resistance on the rocket. We will need to consider the *forces* acting on the rocket during the second half of its motion before we can determine a value for a_{1y}. For now, all that we can safely conclude is that a_{1y} is negative.

FIGURE 1.24 Pictorial representation for the rocket.

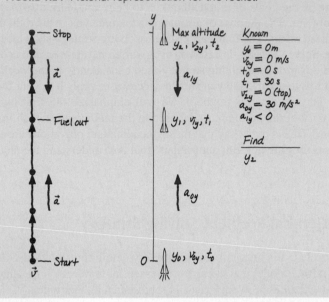

Our task in this section is not to *solve* problems—all that in due time—but to focus on what is happening in a problem. In other words, to make the translation from words to symbols in preparation for subsequent mathematical analysis. Modeling and the pictorial representation will be our most important tools.

1.8 Units and Significant Figures

Science is based upon experimental measurements, and measurements require *units*. The system of units used in science is called *le Système Internationale d'Unités*. These are commonly referred to as **SI units.** Older books often referred to *mks units,* which stands for "meter-kilogram-second," or *cgs units,* which is "centimeter-gram-second." For practical purposes, SI units are the same as mks units. In casual speaking we often refer to *metric units,* although this could mean either mks or cgs units.

All of the quantities needed to understand motion can be expressed in terms of the three basic SI units shown in Table 1.2. Other quantities can be expressed as a combination of these basic units. Velocity, expressed in meters per second or m/s, is a ratio of the length unit to the time unit.

TABLE 1.2 The basic SI units

Quantity	Unit	Abbreviation
time	second	s
length	meter	m
mass	kilogram	kg

Time

The standard of time prior to 1960 was based on the *mean solar day.* As time-keeping accuracy and astronomical observations improved, it became apparent that the earth's rotation is not perfectly steady. Meanwhile, physicists had been developing a device called an *atomic clock.* This instrument is able to measure, with incredibly high precision, the frequency of radio waves absorbed by atoms as they move between two closely spaced energy levels. This frequency can be reproduced with great accuracy at many laboratories around the world. Consequently, the SI unit of time—the second—was redefined in 1967 as follows:

One *second* is the time required for 9,192,631,770 oscillations of the radio wave absorbed by the cesium-133 atom. The abbreviation for second is the letter s.

Several radio stations around the world broadcast a signal whose frequency is linked directly to the atomic clocks. This signal is the time standard, and any time-measuring equipment you use was calibrated from this time standard.

An atomic clock at the National Institute of Standards and Technology is the primary standard of time.

Length

The SI unit of length— the meter—also has a long and interesting history. It was originally defined as one ten-millionth of the distance from the North Pole to the equator along a line passing through Paris. There are obvious practical difficulties with implementing this definition, and it was later abandoned in favor of the distance between two scratches on a platinum-iridium bar stored in a special vault in Paris. The present definition, agreed to in 1983, is as follows:

> One *meter* is the distance traveled by light in vacuum during 1/299,792,458 of a second. The abbreviation for meter is the letter m.

This is equivalent to defining the speed of light to be exactly 299,792,458 m/s. Laser technology is used in various national laboratories to implement this definition and to calibrate secondary standards that are easier to use. These standards ultimately make their way to your ruler or to a meter stick. It is worth keeping in mind that any measuring device you use is only as accurate as the care with which it was calibrated.

Mass

The original unit of mass, the gram, was defined as the mass of 1 cubic centimeter of water. That is why you know the density of water as 1 g/cm³. This definition proved to be impractical when scientists needed to make very accurate measurements. The SI unit of mass—the kilogram—was redefined in 1889 as:

> One *kilogram* is the mass of the international standard kilogram, a polished platinum-iridium cylinder stored in Paris. The abbreviation for kilogram is the symbol kg.

The kilogram is the only SI unit still defined by a manufactured object. Despite the prefix *kilo,* it is the kilogram, not the gram, that is the proper SI unit.

By international agreement, this metal cylinder, stored in Paris, is the definition of the kilogram.

Using Prefixes

We will have many occasions to use lengths, times, and masses that are either much less or much greater than the standards of 1 meter, 1 second, and 1 kilogram. We will do so by using *prefixes* to denote various powers of 10. Table 1.3 lists the common prefixes that will be used frequently throughout this book. Memorize it! Few things in science are learned by rote memory, but this list is one of them. A more extensive list of prefixes is shown inside the cover of the book.

Although prefixes make it easier to talk about quantities, the proper SI units are meters, seconds, and kilograms. Quantities given with prefixed units must be converted to SI units before any calculations are done. Unit conversions are best done at the very beginning of a problem, as part of the pictorial representation.

TABLE 1.3 Common prefixes

Prefix	Power of 10	Abbreviation
mega-	10^6	M
kilo-	10^3	k
centi-	10^{-2}	c
milli-	10^{-3}	m
micro-	10^{-6}	μ
nano-	10^{-9}	n

TABLE 1.4 Useful unit conversions

1 in = 2.54 cm
1 mi = 1.609 km
1 mph = 0.447 m/s
1 m = 39.37 in
1 km = 0.621 mi
1 m/s = 2.24 mph

Unit Conversions

Although SI units are our standard, we cannot entirely forget that the United States still uses English units. Many engineering calculations are done in English units. And even after repeated exposure to metric units in classes, most of us "think" in the English units we grew up with. Thus it remains important to be able to convert back and forth between SI units and English units. Table 1.4 shows several frequently used conversions, and these are worth memorizing if you do not already know them. While the English system was originally based on the length of the king's foot, it is interesting to note that today the conversion 1 in = 2.54 cm is the *definition* of the inch. In other words, the English system for lengths is now based on the meter!

There are various techniques for doing unit conversions. One effective method is to write the conversion factor as a ratio equal to one. For example, using information in Tables 1.3 and 1.4,

$$\frac{10^{-6} \text{ m}}{1 \text{ } \mu\text{m}} = 1 \quad \text{and} \quad \frac{2.54 \text{ cm}}{1 \text{ in}} = 1$$

Because multiplying any expression by 1 does not change its value, these ratios are easily used for conversions. To convert 3.5 μm to meters we would compute

$$3.5 \text{ } \mu\text{m} \times \frac{10^{-6} \text{ m}}{1 \text{ } \mu\text{m}} = 3.5 \times 10^{-6} \text{ m}$$

Similarly, the conversion of 2 feet to meters would be

$$2.00 \text{ ft} \times \frac{12 \text{ in}}{1 \text{ ft}} \times \frac{2.54 \text{ cm}}{1 \text{ in}} \times \frac{10^{-2} \text{ m}}{1 \text{ cm}} = 0.610 \text{ m}$$

Notice how units in the numerator and in the denominator cancel until just the desired units remain at the end. You can continue this process of multiplying by 1 as many times as necessary to complete all the conversions.

Assessment

As we get further into problem solving, we will need to decide whether or not the answer to a problem "makes sense." To determine this, at least until you have more experience with SI units, you may need to convert from SI units back to the English units in which you think. But this conversion does not need to be very accurate. For example, if you are working a problem about automobile speeds and reach an answer of 35 m/s, all you really want to know is whether or not this is a realistic speed for a car. That requires a "quick and dirty" conversion, not a conversion of great accuracy.

Table 1.5 shows several approximate conversion factors that can be used to assess the answer to a problem. Using 1 m/s $\approx$ 2 mph, you find that 35 m/s is roughly 70 mph, a reasonable speed for a car. But an answer of 350 m/s, which you might get after making a calculation error, would be an unreasonable 700 mph. Practice with these will allow you to develop intuition for metric units.

TABLE 1.5 Approximate conversion factors

1 cm $\approx \frac{1}{2}$ in
10 cm $\approx$ 4 in
1 m $\approx$ 1 yard
1 m $\approx$ 3 feet
1 km $\approx$ 0.6 mile
1 m/s $\approx$ 2 mph

NOTE ▶ These approximate conversion factors are accurate only to one significant figure. This is sufficient to assess the answer to a problem, but do *not* use the conversion factors from Table 1.5 for converting English units to SI units at the start of a problem. Use Table 1.4. ◀

Significant Figures

It is necessary to say a few words about a perennial source of difficulty: significant figures. Mathematics is a subject where numbers and relationships can be as precise as desired, but physics deals with a real world of ambiguity. It is important in science and engineering to state clearly what you know about a situation—no less and, especially, no more. Numbers provide one way to specify your knowledge.

If you report that a length has a value of 6.2 m, the implication is that the actual value falls between 6.15 m and 6.25 m and thus rounds to 6.2 m. If that is the case, then reporting a value of simply 6 m is saying less than you know; you are withholding information. On the other hand, to report the number as 6.213 m is wrong. Any person reviewing your work—perhaps a client who hired you—would interpret the number 6.213 m as meaning that the actual length falls between 6.2125 m and 6.2135 m, thus rounding to 6.213 m. In this case, you are claiming to have knowledge and information that you do not really possess.

The way to state your knowledge precisely is through the proper use of **significant figures.** You can think of a significant figure as being a digit that is reliably known. A number such as 6.2 m has *two* significant figures because the next decimal place—the one-hundredths—is not reliably known. As FIGURE 1.25 shows, the best way to determine how many significant figures a number has is to write it in scientific notation.

FIGURE 1.25 Determining significant figures.

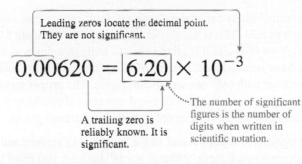

Leading zeros locate the decimal point. They are not significant.

$$0.00620 = \boxed{6.20} \times 10^{-3}$$

A trailing zero is reliably known. It is significant.

The number of significant figures is the number of digits when written in scientific notation.

- The number of significant figures ≠ the number of decimal places.
- Changing units shifts the decimal point but does not change the number of significant figures.

Calculations with numbers follow the "weakest link" rule. The saying, which you probably know, is that "a chain is only as strong as its weakest link." If nine out of ten links in a chain can support a 1000 pound weight, that strength is meaningless if the tenth link can support only 200 pounds. Nine out of the ten numbers used in a calculation might be known with a precision of 0.01%; but if the tenth number is poorly known, with a precision of only 10%, then the result of the calculation cannot possibly be more precise than 10%. The weak link rules!

TACTICS
BOX 1.6   Using significant figures   (MP)

❶ When multiplying or dividing several numbers, or taking roots, the number of significant figures in the answer should match the number of significant figures of the *least* precisely known number used in the calculation.

❷ When adding or subtracting several numbers, the number of decimal places in the answer should match the *smallest* number of decimal places of any number used in the calculation.

❸ It is acceptable to keep one or two extra digits during intermediate steps of a calculation, as long as the final answer is reported with the proper number of significant figures. The goal is to minimize round-off errors in the calculation. But only one or two extra digits, not the seven or eight shown in your calculator display.

Exercises 38–39

EXAMPLE 1.10 Using significant figures
An object consists of two pieces. The mass of one piece has been measured to be 6.47 kg. The volume of the second piece, which is made of aluminum, has been measured to be 4.44×10^{-4} m³. A handbook lists the density of aluminum as 2.7×10^3 kg/m³. What is the total mass of the object?

SOLVE First, calculate the mass of the second piece:

$$m = (4.44 \times 10^{-4} \text{ m}^3)(2.7 \times 10^3 \text{ kg/m}^3)$$

$$= 1.199 \text{ kg} = 1.2 \text{ kg}$$

The number of significant figures of a product must match that of the *least* precisely known number, which is the two-significant-figure density of aluminum. Now add the two masses:

$$\begin{array}{r} 6.47 \text{ kg} \\ + \ 1.2 \ \text{ kg} \\ \hline 7.7 \ \text{ kg} \end{array}$$

The sum is 7.67 kg, but the hundredths place is not reliable because the second mass has no reliable information about this digit. Thus we must round to the one decimal place of the 1.2 kg. The best we can say, with reliability, is that the total mass is 7.7 kg.

TABLE 1.6 Some approximate lengths

	Length (m)
Circumference of the earth	4×10^7
New York to Los Angeles	5×10^6
Distance you can drive in 1 hour	1×10^5
Altitude of jet planes	1×10^4
Distance across a college campus	1000
Length of a football field	100
Length of a classroom	10
Length of your arm	1
Width of a textbook	0.1
Length of your little fingernail	0.01
Diameter of a pencil lead	1×10^{-3}
Thickness of a sheet of paper	1×10^{-4}
Diameter of a dust particle	1×10^{-5}

TABLE 1.7 Some approximate masses

	Mass (kg)
Large airliner	1×10^5
Small car	1000
Large human	100
Medium-size dog	10
Science textbook	1
Apple	0.1
Pencil	0.01
Raisin	1×10^{-3}
Fly	1×10^{-4}

Some quantities can be measured very precisely—three or more significant figures. Others are inherently much less precise—only two significant figures. Examples and problems in this textbook will normally provide data to either two or three significant figures, as is appropriate to the situation. **The appropriate number of significant figures for the answer is determined by the data provided.**

NOTE ▶ Be careful! Many calculators have a default setting that shows two decimal places, such as 5.23. This is dangerous. If you need to calculate 5.23/58.5, your calculator will show 0.09 and it is all too easy to write that down as an answer. By doing so, you have reduced a calculation of two numbers having three significant figures to an answer with only one significant figure. The proper result of this division is 0.0894 or 8.94×10^{-2}. You will avoid this error if you keep your calculator set to display numbers in *scientific notation* with two decimal places. ◀

Proper use of significant figures is part of the "culture" of science and engineering. We will frequently emphasize these "cultural issues" because you must learn to speak the same language as the natives if you wish to communicate effectively. Most students know the rules of significant figures, having learned them in high school, but many fail to apply them. It is important to understand the reasons for significant figures and to get in the habit of using them properly.

Orders of Magnitude and Estimating

Precise calculations are appropriate when we have precise data, but there are many times when a very rough estimate is sufficient. Suppose you see a rock fall off a cliff and would like to know how fast it was going when it hit the ground. By doing a mental comparison with the speeds of familiar objects, such as cars and bicycles, you might judge that the rock was traveling at "about" 20 mph.

This is a one-significant-figure estimate. With some luck, you can distinguish 20 mph from either 10 mph or 30 mph, but you certainly cannot distinguish 20 mph from 21 mph. A one-significant-figure estimate or calculation, such as this, is called an **order-of-magnitude estimate.** An order-of-magnitude estimate is indicated by the symbol ~, which indicates even less precision than the "approximately equal" symbol ≈. You would say that the speed of the rock is $v \sim 20$ mph.

A useful skill is to make reliable estimates on the basis of known information, simple reasoning, and common sense. This is a skill that is acquired by practice. Most chapters in this book will have homework problems that ask you to make order-of-magnitude estimates. The following example is a typical estimation problem.

Tables 1.6 and 1.7 have information that will be useful for doing estimates.

EXAMPLE 1.11 **Estimating a sprinter's speed**
Estimate the speed with which an Olympic sprinter crosses the finish line of the 100 m dash.

SOLVE We do need one piece of information, but it is a widely known piece of sports trivia. That is, world-class sprinters run the 100 m dash in about 10 s. Their *average* speed is $v_{avg} \approx$ (100 m)/(10 s) $\approx$ 10 m/s. But that's only average. They go

slower than average at the beginning, and they cross the finish line at a speed faster than average. How much faster? Twice as fast, 20 m/s, would be ≈40 mph. Sprinters don't seem like they're running as fast as a 40 mph car, so this probably is too fast. Let's *estimate* that their final speed is 50% faster than the average. Thus they cross the finish line at $v \sim 15$ m/s.

STOP TO THINK 1.5 Rank in order, from the most to the least, the number of significant figures in the following numbers. For example, if b has more than c, c has the same number as a, and a has more than d, you could give your answer as b > c = a > d.

a. 82   b. 0.0052   c. 0.430   d. 4.321×10^{-10}

SUMMARY

The goal of Chapter 1 has been to introduce the fundamental concepts of motion.

General Strategy

Motion Diagrams

- Help visualize motion.
- Provide a tool for finding acceleration vectors.

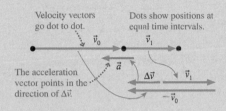

Velocity vectors go dot to dot. Dots show positions at equal time intervals.

The acceleration vector points in the direction of $\Delta \vec{v}$.

▶ These are the average velocity and the average acceleration vectors.

Problem Solving

MODEL Make simplifying assumptions.

VISUALIZE Use:

- **Pictorial representation**
- **Graphical representation**

SOLVE Use a **mathematical representation** to find numerical answers.

ASSESS Does the answer have the proper units? Does it make sense?

Important Concepts

The particle model represents a moving object as if all its mass were concentrated at a single point.

Position locates an object with respect to a chosen coordinate system. Change in position is called displacement.

Velocity is the rate of change of the position vector $\vec{r}$.

Acceleration is the rate of change of the velocity vector $\vec{v}$.

An object has an acceleration if it

- Changes speed and/or
- Changes direction.

Pictorial Representation

❶ Draw a motion diagram.

❷ Establish coordinates.

❸ Sketch the situation.

❹ Define symbols.

❺ List knowns.

❻ Identify desired unknown.

Known
$x_0 = v_{0x} = t_0 = 0$
$a_x = 2.0 \text{ m/s}^2 \quad t_1 = 2.0 \text{ s}$
Find
x_1

Applications

For **motion along a line:**

- Speeding up: $\vec{v}$ and $\vec{a}$ point in the same direction, v_x and a_x have the same sign.
- Slowing down: $\vec{v}$ and $\vec{a}$ point in opposite directions, v_x and a_x have opposite signs.
- Constant speed: $\vec{a} = \vec{0}$, $a_x = 0$.

Acceleration a_x is positive if $\vec{a}$ points right, negative if $\vec{a}$ points left. The sign of a_x does *not* imply speeding up or slowing down.

Significant figures are reliably known digits. The number of significant figures for:

- **Multiplication, division, powers** is set by the value with the fewest significant figures.
- **Addition, subtraction** is set by the value with the smallest number of decimal places.

The appropriate number of significant figures in a calculation is determined by the data provided.

Terms and Notation

motion	particle model	time interval, Δt	representation of knowledge
trajectory	position vector, $\vec{r}$	average speed	SI units
motion diagram	scalar quantity	average velocity, $\vec{v}$	significant figures
operational definition	vector quantity	average acceleration, $\vec{a}$	order-of-magnitude estimate
translational motion	displacement, $\Delta \vec{r}$	position-versus-time graph	
particle	zero vector, $\vec{0}$	pictorial representation	

CONCEPTUAL QUESTIONS

1. How many significant figures does each of the following numbers have?
   a. 6.21   b. 62.1   c. 0.620   d. 0.062
2. How many significant figures does each of the following numbers have?
   a. 6200   b. 0.006200   c. 1.0621   d. 6.21×10^3
3. Is the particle in **FIGURE Q1.3** speeding up? Slowing down? Or can you tell? Explain.

   FIGURE Q1.3   •   •   • ••

4. Does the object represented in **FIGURE Q1.4** have positive or negative value of a_x? Explain.
5. Does the object represented in **FIGURE Q1.5** have a positive or negative value of a_y? Explain.

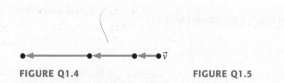

FIGURE Q1.4 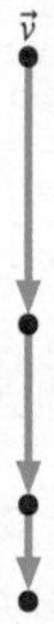   **FIGURE Q1.5**

6. Determine the signs (positive or negative) of the position, velocity, and acceleration for the particle in **FIGURE Q1.6**.

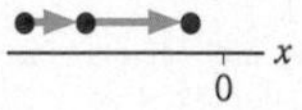

   FIGURE Q1.6

7. Determine the signs (positive or negative) of the position, velocity, and acceleration for the particle in **FIGURE Q1.7**.

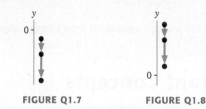

   FIGURE Q1.7   **FIGURE Q1.8**

8. Determine the signs (positive or negative) of the position, velocity, and acceleration for the particle in **FIGURE Q1.8**.

EXERCISES AND PROBLEMS

Exercises

Section 1.1 Motion Diagrams

1. I A car skids to a halt to avoid hitting an object in the road. Draw a basic motion diagram, using the images from the movie, from the time the skid begins until the car is stopped.
2. I You drop a soccer ball from your third-story balcony. Draw a basic motion diagram, using the images from the movie, from the time you release the ball until it touches the ground.
3. I Two bank robbers are driving at a steady speed in their getaway car until they see the police. Then they start to speed up. Draw a basic motion diagram of the getaway car, using images from the movie, from 1 min before the robbers see the police until 1 min afterward.

Section 1.2 The Particle Model

4. I a. Write a paragraph describing the particle model. What is it, and why is it important?

   b. Give two examples of situations, different from those described in the text, for which the particle model is appropriate.
   c. Give an example of a situation, different from those described in the text, for which it would be inappropriate.

Section 1.3 Position and Time

Section 1.4 Velocity

5. I a. What is an *operational definition?*
   b. Give operational definitions of displacement and velocity. Your definition should be given mostly in words and pictures, with a minimum of symbols or mathematics.
6. I A softball player hits the ball and starts running toward first base. Draw a motion diagram, using the particle model, showing her position and her average velocity vectors during the first few seconds of her run.
7. I A softball player slides into second base. Draw a motion diagram, using the particle model, showing his position and his average velocity vectors from the time he begins to slide until he reaches the base.

Section 1.5 Linear Acceleration

8. | Give an operational definition of acceleration. Your definition should be given mostly in words and pictures, with a minimum of symbols or mathematics.

9. | a. Find the average acceleration vector at point 1 of the three-point motion diagram shown in **FIGURE EX1.9**.

   b. Is the object's average speed between points 1 and 2 greater than, less than, or equal to its average speed between points 0 and 1? Explain how you can tell.

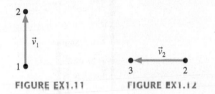

FIGURE EX1.9   FIGURE EX1.10

10. | a. Find the average acceleration vector at point 1 of the three-point motion diagram shown in **FIGURE EX1.10**.

   b. Is the object's average speed between points 1 and 2 greater than, less than, or equal to its average speed between points 0 and 1? Explain how you can tell.

11. | **FIGURE EX1.11** shows two dots of a motion diagram and vector $\vec{v}_1$. Copy this figure and add vector $\vec{v}_2$ and dot 3 if the acceleration vector $\vec{a}$ at dot 2 (a) points up and (b) points down.

FIGURE EX1.11   FIGURE EX1.12

12. | **FIGURE EX1.12** shows two dots of a motion diagram and vector $\vec{v}_2$. Copy this figure and add vector $\vec{v}_1$ and dot 1 if the acceleration vector $\vec{a}$ at dot 2 (a) points to the right and (b) points to the left.

13. | A car travels to the left at a steady speed for a few seconds, then brakes for a stop sign. Draw a complete motion diagram of the car.

14. | A child is sledding on a smooth, level patch of snow. She encounters a rocky patch and slows to a stop. Draw a complete motion diagram of the child and her sled.

15. | A roof tile falls straight down from a two-story building. It lands in a swimming pool and settles gently to the bottom. Draw a complete motion diagram of the tile.

16. | Your roommate drops a tennis ball from a third-story balcony. It hits the sidewalk and bounces as high as the second story. Draw a complete motion diagram of the tennis ball from the time it is released until it reaches the maximum height on its bounce. Be sure to determine and show the acceleration at the lowest point.

17. | A toy car rolls down a ramp, then across a smooth, horizontal floor. Draw a complete motion diagram of the toy car.

Section 1.6 Motion in One Dimension

18. | **FIGURE EX1.18** shows the motion diagram of a drag racer. The camera took one frame every 2 s.

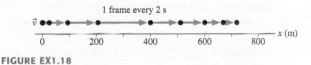

1 frame every 2 s

FIGURE EX1.18

   a. Measure the *x*-value of the racer at each dot. List your data in a table similar to Table 1.1, showing each position and the time at which it occurred.

   b. Make a position-versus-time graph for the drag racer. Because you have data only at certain instants, your graph should consist of dots that are not connected together.

19. | Write a short description of the motion of a real object for which **FIGURE EX 1.19** would be a realistic position-versus-time graph.

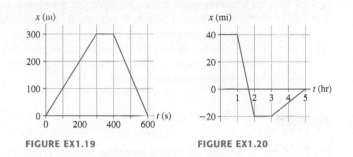

FIGURE EX1.19   FIGURE EX1.20

20. | Write a short description of the motion of a real object for which **FIGURE EX 1.20** would be a realistic position-versus-time graph.

Section 1.7 Solving Problems in Physics

21. | Draw a pictorial representation for the following problem. Do *not* solve the problem. The light turns green, and a bicyclist starts forward with an acceleration of 1.5 m/s². How far must she travel to reach a speed of 7.5 m/s?

22. | Draw a pictorial representation for the following problem. Do *not* solve the problem. What acceleration does a rocket need to reach a speed of 200 m/s at a height of 1.0 km?

Section 1.8 Units and Significant Figures

23. | Convert the following to SI units:
   a. 9.12 μs   b. 3.42 km
   c. 44 cm/ms   d. 80 km/hour

24. | Convert the following to SI units:
   a. 8.0 in   b. 66 ft/s
   c. 60 mph   d. 14 in²

25. | Convert the following to SI units:
   a. 1 hour   b. 1 day
   c. 1 year   d. 32 ft/s²

26. | Using the approximate conversion factors in Table 1.5, convert the following to SI units *without* using your calculator.
   a. 20 ft   b. 60 mi
   c. 60 mph   d. 8 in

27. | Using the approximate conversion factors in Table 1.5, convert the following SI units to English units *without* using your calculator.
   a. 30 cm   b. 25 m/s
   c. 5 km   d. 0.5 cm

28. | Compute the following numbers, applying the significant figure rule adopted in this textbook.
   a. 33.3×25.4 b. $33.3 - 25.4$
   c. $\sqrt{33.3}$ d. $333.3 \div 25.4$

29. | Compute the following numbers, applying the significant figure rule adopted in this textbook.
   a. 33.3^2 b. 33.3×45.1
   c. $\sqrt{22.2} - 1.2$ d. 44.4^{-1}

30. | Estimate (don't measure!) the length of a typical car. Give your answer in both feet and meters. Briefly describe how you arrived at this estimate.

31. | Estimate the height of a telephone pole. Give your answer in both feet and meters. Briefly describe how you arrived at this estimate.

32. | Estimate the average speed with which you go from home to campus via whatever mode of transportation you use most commonly. Give your answer in both mph and m/s. Briefly describe how you arrived at this estimate.

33. | Estimate the average speed with which the hair on your head grows. Give your answer in both m/s and μm/hour. Briefly describe how you arrived at this estimate.

Problems

For Problems 34 through 43, draw a complete pictorial representation. Do *not* solve these problems or do any mathematics.

34. | A Porsche accelerates from a stoplight at 5.0 m/s^2 for five seconds, then coasts for three more seconds. How far has it traveled?

35. | Billy drops a watermelon from the top of a three-story building, 10 m above the sidewalk. How fast is the watermelon going when it hits?

36. | Sam is recklessly driving 60 mph in a 30 mph speed zone when he suddenly sees the police. He steps on the brakes and slows to 30 mph in three seconds, looking nonchalant as he passes the officer. How far does he travel while braking?

37. | A speed skater moving across frictionless ice at 8.0 m/s hits a 5.0-m-wide patch of rough ice. She slows steadily, then continues on at 6.0 m/s. What is her acceleration on the rough ice?

38. | You would like to stick a wet spit wad on the ceiling, so you toss it straight up with a speed of 10 m/s. How long does it take to reach the ceiling, 3.0 m above?

39. | A student standing on the ground throws a ball straight up. The ball leaves the student's hand with a speed of 15 m/s when the hand is 1.5 m above the ground. How long is the ball in the air before it hits the ground? (The student moves her hand out of the way.)

40. | A ball rolls along a smooth horizontal floor at 10 m/s, then starts up a 20° ramp. How high does it go before rolling back down?

41. | A motorist is traveling at 20 m/s. He is 60 m from a stoplight when he sees it turn yellow. His reaction time, before stepping on the brake, is 0.50 s. What steady deceleration while braking will bring him to a stop right at the light?

42. || Ice hockey star Bruce Blades is 5.0 m from the blue line and gliding toward it at a speed of 4.0 m/s. You are 20 m from the blue line, directly behind Bruce. You want to pass the puck to Bruce. With what speed should you shoot the puck down the ice so that it reaches Bruce exactly as he crosses the blue line?

43. || You are standing still as Fred runs past you with the football at a speed of 6.0 yards per second. He has only 30 yards left to go before reaching the goal line to score the winning touchdown. If you begin running at the exact instant he passes you, what acceleration must you maintain to catch him 5.0 yards in front of the goal line?

Problems 44 through 48 show a motion diagram. For each of these problems, write a one or two sentence "story" about a *real object* that has this motion diagram. Your stories should talk about people or objects by name and say what they are doing. Problems 34 through 43 are examples of motion short stories.

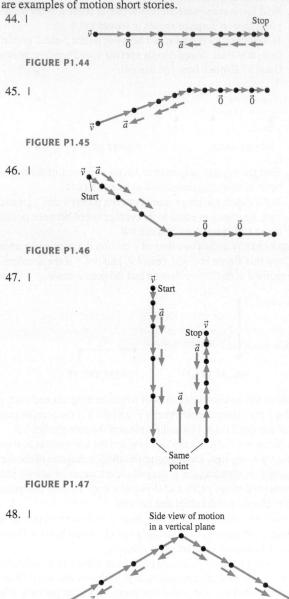

44. |

FIGURE P1.44

45. |

FIGURE P1.45

46. |

FIGURE P1.46

47. |

FIGURE P1.47

48. |

FIGURE P1.48

Problems 49 through 52 show a partial motion diagram. For each:
a. Complete the motion diagram by adding acceleration vectors.
b. Write a physics *problem* for which this is the correct motion diagram. Be imaginative! Don't forget to include enough information to make the problem complete and to state clearly what is to be found.
c. Draw a pictorial representation for your problem.

49. |

FIGURE P1.49

50. |
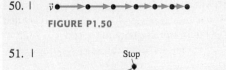
FIGURE P1.50

51. |
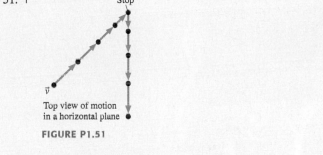

Top view of motion
in a horizontal plane
FIGURE P1.51

52. |
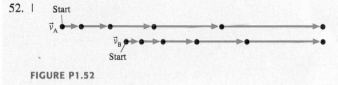

Start
FIGURE P1.52

53. | A regulation soccer field for international play is a rectangle with a length between 100 m and 110 m and a width between 64 m and 75 m. What are the smallest and largest areas that the field could be?

54. || The quantity called *mass density* is the mass per unit volume of a substance. Express the following mass densities in SI units.
   a. Aluminum, 2.7×10^{-3} kg/cm^3
   b. Alcohol, 0.81 g/cm^3

55. | **FIGURE P1.55** shows a motion diagram of a car traveling down a street. The camera took one frame every 10 s. A distance scale is provided.
   a. Measure the *x*-value of the car at each dot. Place your data in a table, similar to Table 1.1, showing each position and the instant of time at which it occurred.
   b. Make a position-versus-time graph for the car. Because you have data only at certain instants of time, your graph should consist of dots that are not connected together.

1 frame every 10 s
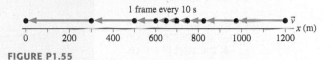
FIGURE P1.55

56. | Write a short description of a real object for which **FIGURE P1.56** would be a realistic position-versus-time graph.

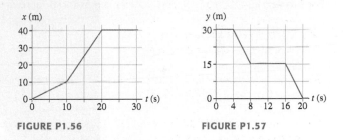

FIGURE P1.56   **FIGURE P1.57**

57. | Write a short description of a real object for which **FIGURE P1.57** would be a realistic position-versus-time graph.

STOP TO THINK ANSWERS

Stop to Think 1.1: B. The images of B are farther apart, so it travels a larger distance than does A during the same intervals of time.

Stop to Think 1.2: a. Dropped ball. **b.** Dust particle. **c.** Descending rocket.

Stop to Think 1.3: e. The average velocity vector is found by connecting one dot in the motion diagram to the next.

Stop to Think 1.4: b. $\vec{v}_2 = \vec{v}_1 + \Delta\vec{v}$, and $\Delta\vec{v}$ points in the direction of $\vec{a}$.

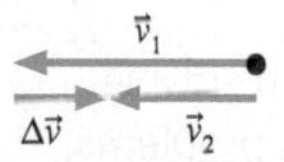

Stop to Think 1.5: d > c > b = a.

2 Kinematics in One Dimension

World-class sprinters have a tremendous acceleration at the start of a race.

► Looking Ahead

The goal of Chapter 2 is to learn how to solve problems about motion in a straight line. In this chapter you will learn to:

- Understand the mathematics of position, velocity, and acceleration for motion along a straight line.
- Use a graphical representation of motion.
- Use an explicit problem-solving strategy for kinematics problems.
- Understand free-fall motion and motion along inclined planes.

◄ Looking Back

Each chapter in this textbook builds on ideas and techniques from previous chapters. The Looking Back feature calls your attention to specific sections that are of major significance to the present chapter. A brief review of these sections will improve your study of this chapter. Please review:

- Sections 1.4–1.5 Velocity and acceleration.
- Section 1.6 Motion in one dimension.
- Section 1.7 Problem solving in physics.

A race, whether between runners, bicyclists, or drag racers, exemplifies the idea of motion. Today, we use electronic stopwatches, video recorders, and other sophisticated instruments to analyze motion, but it hasn't always been so. Galileo, who in the early 1600s was the first scientist to study motion experimentally, used his pulse to measure time!

Galileo made a useful distinction between the *cause* of motion and the *description* of motion. **Kinematics** is the modern name for the mathematical description of motion without regard to causes. The term comes from the Greek word *kinema,* meaning "movement." You know this word through its English variation *cinema*—motion pictures! In this chapter on kinematics we'll develop the mathematical tools for describing motion. Then, in Chapter 5, we'll turn our attention to the *cause* of motion.

We will begin our study of kinematics with motion in one dimension; that is, motion along a straight line. Runners, drag racers, and skiers are just a few examples of motion in one dimension. The kinematics of two-dimensional motion—projectile motion and circular motion—will be considered in Chapter 4.

2.1 Uniform Motion

If you drive your car at a perfectly steady 60 miles per hour (mph), you will cover 60 mi during the first hour, another 60 mi during the second hour, yet another 60 mi during the third hour, and so on. This is an example of what we call *uniform motion.* In this case, 60 mi is not your position, but rather the *change* in your position during each hour; that is, your displacement Δx. Similarly, 1 hour is a time interval Δt rather than a specific instant of time. This suggests the following definition: **Straight-line motion in which equal displacements occur during *any* successive equal-time intervals is called uniform motion.**

The qualifier "any" is important. If during each hour you drive 120 mph for 30 minutes and stop for 30 minutes, you will cover 60 mi during each successive 1 hour interval. But you would *not* have equal displacements during successive 30 minute intervals, so this motion is not uniform. Your constant 60 mph driving is uniform motion because you will find equal displacements no matter how you choose your successive time intervals.

FIGURE 2.1 shows how uniform motion appears in motion diagrams and position-versus-time graphs. Notice that the position-versus-time graph for uniform motion is a straight line. This follows from the requirement that all Δx corresponding to the same Δt be equal. In fact, an alternative definition of uniform motion is: **An object's motion is uniform if and only if its position-versus-time graph is a straight line.**

The slope of a straight-line graph is defined as "rise over run." Because position is graphed on the vertical axis, the "rise" of a position-versus-time graph is the object's displacement Δx. The "run" is the time interval Δt. Consequently, the slope is $\Delta x/\Delta t$. The slope of a straight-line graph is constant, so an object in uniform motion has the *same* value of $\Delta x/\Delta t$ during *any* time interval Δt.

Chapter 1 defined the *average velocity* as $\Delta \vec{r}/\Delta t$. For one-dimensional motion this is simply

$$v_{avg} \equiv \frac{\Delta x}{\Delta t} \text{ or } \frac{\Delta y}{\Delta t} = \text{slope of the position-versus-time graph} \quad (2.1)$$

That is, **the average velocity is the slope of the position-versus-time graph.** Velocity has units of "length per time," such as "miles per hour." The SI units of velocity are meters per second, abbreviated m/s.

NOTE ▶ The symbol $\equiv$ in Equation 2.1 stands for "is defined as" or "is equivalent to." This is a stronger statement than the two sides simply being equal. ◀

Equation 2.1 allows us to associate the slope of the position-versus-time graph, a *geometrical* quantity, with the *physical* quantity that we call the average velocity v_{avg}. This is an extremely important idea. In the case of uniform motion, where the slope $\Delta x/\Delta t$ is the same at all times, it appears that the average velocity is constant and unchanging. Consequently, a final definition of uniform motion is: **An object's motion is uniform if and only if its velocity v_x or v_y is constant and unchanging.** There's no real need to specify "average" for a velocity that doesn't change, so we will drop the subscript and refer to the average velocity as v_x or v_y.

Riding steadily over level ground is a good example of uniform motion.

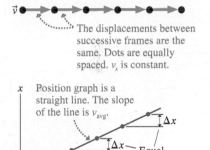

FIGURE 2.1 Motion diagram and position graph for uniform motion.

EXAMPLE 2.1 **Skating with constant velocity**

The position-versus-time graph of FIGURE 2.2 represents the motion of two students on roller blades. Determine their velocities and describe their motion.

MODEL Represent the two students as particles.

VISUALIZE Figure 2.2 is a graphical representation of the students' motion. Both graphs are straight lines, telling us that both skaters are moving uniformly with constant velocities.

SOLVE We can determine the students' velocities by measuring the slopes of the graphs. Skater A undergoes a displacement $\Delta x_A = 2.0$ m during the time interval $\Delta t_A = 0.40$ s. Thus his velocity is

$$(v_x)_A = \frac{\Delta x_A}{\Delta t_A} = \frac{2.0 \text{ m}}{0.40 \text{ s}}$$
$$= 5.0 \text{ m/s}$$

FIGURE 2.2 Graphical representations of two students on roller blades.

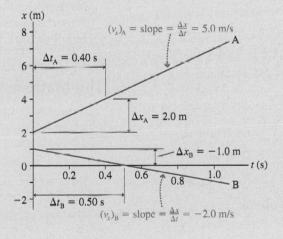

Continued

We need to be more careful with skater B. Although he moves a distance of 1.0 m in 0.50 s, his *displacement* Δx has a very precise definition:

$$\Delta x_B = x_{at\,0.5\,s} - x_{at\,0.0\,s} = 0.0\ m - 1.0\ m = -1.0\ m$$

Careful attention to the signs is very important! This leads to

$$(v_x)_B = \frac{\Delta x_B}{\Delta t_B} = \frac{-1.0\ m}{0.50\ s} = -2.0\ m/s$$

ASSESS The minus sign indicates that skater B is moving to the left. Our interpretation of this graph is that two students on roller blades are moving with constant velocities in opposite directions. Skater A starts at $x = 2.0$ m and moves to the right with a velocity of 5.0 m/s. Skater B starts at $x = 1.0$ m and moves to the left with a velocity of -2.0 m/s. Their speeds, of ≈ 10 mph and ≈ 4 mph, are reasonable for skaters on roller blades.

Example 2.1 brought out several points that are worth emphasizing. These are summarized in Tactics Box 2.1.

TACTICS BOX 2.1   **Interpreting position-versus-time graphs**   (MP)

❶ Steeper slopes correspond to faster speeds.
❷ Negative slopes correspond to negative velocities and, hence, to motion to the left (or down).
❸ The slope is a ratio of intervals, $\Delta x/\Delta t$, not a ratio of coordinates. That is, the slope is *not* simply x/t.
❹ We are distinguishing between the *actual* slope and the *physically meaningful* slope. If you were to use a ruler to measure the rise and the run of the graph, you could compute the actual slope of the line as drawn on the page. That is not the slope to which we are referring when we equate the velocity with the slope of the line. Instead, we find the *physically meaningful* slope by measuring the rise and run using the scales along the axes. The "rise" Δx is some number of meters; the "run" Δt is some number of seconds. The physically meaningful rise and run include units, and the ratio of these units gives the units of the slope.

Exercises 1–3 ✎

An object's **speed** v is how fast it's going, independent of direction. This is simply $v = |v_x|$ or $v = |v_y|$, the magnitude or absolute value of the object's velocity. In Example 2.1, for example, skater B's *velocity* is -2.0 m/s but his *speed* is 2.0 m/s. Speed is a scalar quantity, not a vector.

NOTE ▶ Our mathematical analysis of motion is based on velocity, not speed. The subscript in v_x or v_y is an essential part of the notation, reminding us that, even in one dimension, the velocity is a vector. ◀

The Mathematics of Uniform Motion

We need a mathematical analysis of motion that will be valid regardless of whether an object moves along the x-axis, the y-axis, or any other straight line. Consequently, it will be convenient to write equations for a "generic axis" that we will call the s-axis. The position of an object will be represented by the symbol s and its velocity by v_s.

NOTE ▶ Equations written in terms of s are valid for any one-dimensional motion. In a specific problem, however, you should use either x or y, whichever is appropriate, rather than s. ◀

Consider an object in uniform motion along the s-axis with the linear position-versus-time graph shown in FIGURE 2.3. The object's **initial position** is s_i at time t_i. The term *initial position* refers to the starting point of our analysis or the starting point in a

FIGURE 2.3 The velocity is found from the slope of the position-versus-time graph.

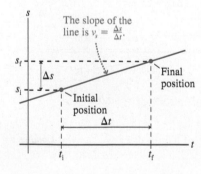

problem; the object may or may not have been in motion prior to t_i. At a later time t_f, the ending point of our analysis or the ending point of a problem, the object's **final position** is s_f.

The object's velocity v_s along the s-axis can be determined by finding the slope of the graph:

$$v_s = \frac{\text{rise}}{\text{run}} = \frac{\Delta s}{\Delta t} = \frac{s_f - s_i}{t_f - t_i} \qquad (2.2)$$

Equation 2.2 is easily rearranged to give

$$s_f = s_i + v_s \, \Delta t \qquad \text{(uniform motion)} \qquad (2.3)$$

Equation 2.3 applies to any time interval Δt during which the velocity is constant.

The velocity of a uniformly moving object tells us the amount by which its position changes during each second. A particle with a velocity of 20 m/s *changes* its position by 20 m during every second of motion: by 20 m during the first second of its motion, by another 20 m during the next second, and so on. If the object starts at $s_i = 10$ m, it will be at $s = 30$ m after 1 second of motion and at $s = 50$ m after 2 seconds of motion. Thinking of velocity like this will help you develop an intuitive understanding of the connection between velocity and position.

EXAMPLE 2.2 Lunch in Cleveland?
Bob leaves home in Chicago at 9:00 A.M. and travels east at a steady 60 mph. Susan, 400 miles to the east in Pittsburgh, leaves at the same time and travels west at a steady 40 mph. Where will they meet for lunch?

MODEL Here is a problem where, for the first time, we can really put all four aspects of our problem-solving strategy into play. To begin, represent Bob and Susan as particles.

VISUALIZE FIGURE 2.4 shows the physical representation (the motion diagram) and the pictorial representation. The equal spacings of the dots in the motion diagram indicate that the motion is uniform. In evaluating the given information, we recognize that the starting time of 9:00 A.M. is not relevant to the problem. Consequently, the initial time is chosen as simply $t_0 = 0$ hr. Bob and Susan are traveling in opposite directions, hence one of the velocities must be a negative number. We have chosen a coordinate system in which Bob starts at the origin and moves to the right (east) while Susan is moving to the left (west). Thus Susan has the negative velocity. Notice how we've assigned position, velocity, and time symbols to each point in the motion. Pay special attention to how subscripts are used to distinguish different points in the problem and to distinguish Bob's symbols from Susan's.

One purpose of the pictorial representation is to establish what we need to find. Bob and Susan meet when they have the same position at the same time t_1. Thus we want to find $(x_1)_B$ at the time when $(x_1)_B = (x_1)_S$. Notice that $(x_1)_B$ and $(x_1)_S$ are Bob's and Susan's *positions*, which are equal when they meet, not the distances they have traveled.

SOLVE The goal of the mathematical representation is to proceed from the pictorial representation to a mathematical solution of the problem. We can begin by using Equation 2.3 to find Bob's and Susan's positions at time t_1 when they meet:

$$(x_1)_B = (x_0)_B + (v_x)_B(t_1 - t_0) = (v_x)_B t_1$$
$$(x_1)_S = (x_0)_S + (v_x)_S(t_1 - t_0) = (x_0)_S + (v_x)_S t_1$$

Notice two things. First, we started by writing the *full* statement of Equation 2.3. Only then did we simplify by dropping those terms known to be zero. You're less likely to make accidental errors if you follow this procedure. Second, we replaced the generic symbol s with the specific horizontal-position symbol x, and we replaced the generic subscripts i and f with the specific symbols 0 and 1 that we defined in the pictorial representation. This is also good problem-solving technique.

FIGURE 2.4 Pictorial representation for Example 2.2.

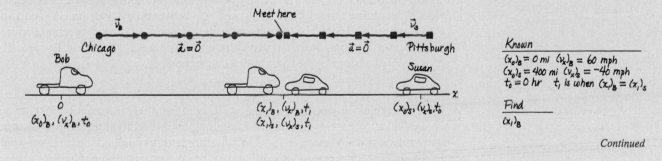

Continued

The condition that Bob and Susan meet is

$$(x_1)_B = (x_1)_S$$

By equating the right-hand sides of the above equations, we get

$$(v_x)_B t_1 = (x_0)_S + (v_x)_S t_1$$

Solving for t_1, we find that they meet at time

$$t_1 = \frac{(x_0)_S}{(v_x)_B - (v_x)_S} = \frac{400 \text{ miles}}{60 \text{ mph} - (-40) \text{ mph}} = 4.0 \text{ hours}$$

Finally, inserting this time back into the equation for $(x_1)_B$ gives

$$(x_1)_B = \left(60 \frac{\text{miles}}{\text{hour}}\right) \times (4.0 \text{ hours}) = 240 \text{ miles}$$

While this is a number, it is not yet the answer to the question. The phrase "240 miles" by itself does not say anything meaningful. Because this is the value of Bob's *position*, and Bob was driving east, the answer to the question is, "They meet 240 miles east of Chicago."

ASSESS Before stopping, we should check whether or not this answer seems reasonable. We certainly expected an answer between 0 miles and 400 miles. We also know that Bob is driving faster than Susan, so we expect that their meeting point will be *more* than halfway from Chicago to Pittsburgh. Our assessment tells us that 240 miles is a reasonable answer.

FIGURE 2.5 Position-versus-time graphs for Bob and Susan.

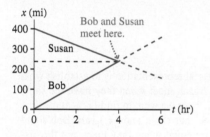

It is instructive to look at this example from a graphical perspective. **FIGURE 2.5** shows position-versus-time graphs for Bob and Susan. Notice the negative slope for Susan's graph, indicating her negative velocity. The point of interest is the intersection of the two lines; this is where Bob and Susan have the same position at the same time. Our method of solution, in which we equated $(x_1)_B$ and $(x_1)_S$, is really just solving the mathematical problem of finding the intersection of two lines.

STOP TO THINK 2.1   Which position-versus-time graph represents the motion shown in the motion diagram?

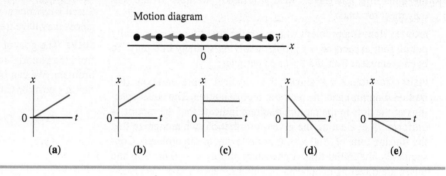

FIGURE 2.6 Motion diagram and position graph of a jet during takeoff.

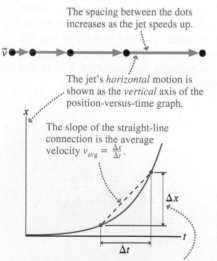

The spacing between the dots increases as the jet speeds up.

The jet's *horizontal* motion is shown as the *vertical* axis of the position-versus-time graph.

The slope of the straight-line connection is the average velocity $v_{avg} = \frac{\Delta x}{\Delta t}$.

The increasing separation of the dots in the motion diagram means that Δx increases and the graph curves upward.

2.2 Instantaneous Velocity

FIGURE 2.6 shows the motion diagram of a jet as it takes off. The increasing length of the velocity vectors tells us that the jet is speeding up, so this is *not* uniform motion. Consequently, the position-versus-time graph is *not* a straight line. The graph curves upward (increasing Δx) as the spacing between the motion-diagram dots increases. We can determine the jet's average speed v_{avg} between any two times t_i and t_f by selecting those two points on the graph, drawing the straight-line connection between them, measuring Δx and Δt, and using these to compute $v_{avg} = \Delta x/\Delta t$. Graphically, v_{avg} is simply the slope of the straight-line connection between the two points.

However, average velocity has only limited usefulness for an object whose velocity isn't constant. Suppose, for example, you drove your car in a straight line for exactly 1 hr, covering exactly 60 mi. All you can discern from this information is that your average velocity was $v_{avg} = 60$ mph. It's quite possible that you got a slow start but later sped up. If you glanced at your car's speedometer 10 min into the trip, you would have seen a speed less than 60 mph. Similar, the speedometer would have read more than 60 mph 10 min before the end of the trip.

In contrast to a velocity averaged over the entire hour, the speedometer reading tells you how fast you're going *at that instant*. We define an object's **instantaneous velocity** to be its velocity—a speed *and* a direction—at a single *instant* of time t.

Such a definition, though, raises some difficult issues. Just what does it mean to have a velocity "at an instant"? Suppose a police officer pulls you over and says, "I just clocked you going 80 miles per hour." You might respond, "But that's impossible. I've only been driving for 20 minutes, so I can't possibly have gone 80 miles." Unfortunately for you, the police officer was a physics major. He replies, "I mean that at the instant I measured your velocity, you were moving at a rate such that you *would* cover a distance of 80 miles *if* you were to continue at that velocity without change for 1 hour. That will be a $200 fine."

Here, again, is the idea that velocity is the *rate* at which an object changes its position. Rates tell us how quickly or how slowly things change, and that idea is conveyed by the word "per." An instantaneous velocity of 80 miles *per* hour means that the rate at which your car's position is changing—at that exact instant—is such that it would travel 80 miles in 1 hour *if* it continued at that rate without change. Whether or not it actually does travel at that velocity for another hour, or even for another millisecond, is not relevant.

The speedometer reading tells you how fast you're going *at that instant.*

Using Motion Diagrams and Graphs

Let's use motion diagrams and position graphs to analyze a rocket as it takes off. We've chosen an object that moves vertically, so that the motion diagram better matches the graph, but our conclusions will apply to motion along any straight line. FIGURE 2.7a shows a motion diagram made using a normal 30-frames-per-second movie camera. We would like to determine the *instantaneous* velocity v_{2y} at point 2. Because the rocket is accelerating, its velocity at 2 is not the same as the average velocity between 1 and 3. How can we measure v_{2y}?

FIGURE 2.7 Motion diagrams and position graphs of an accelerating rocket.

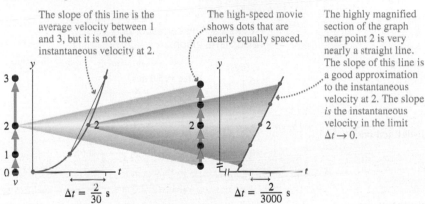

(a) 30 frames per second

The slope of this line is the average velocity between 1 and 3, but it is not the instantaneous velocity at 2.

$\Delta t = \dfrac{2}{30}$ s

(b) 3000 frames per second

The high-speed movie shows dots that are nearly equally spaced.

The highly magnified section of the graph near point 2 is very nearly a straight line. The slope of this line is a good approximation to the instantaneous velocity at 2. The slope *is* the instantaneous velocity in the limit $\Delta t \to 0$.

$\Delta t = \dfrac{2}{3000}$ s

(c) The limiting case

The instantaneous velocity at 2 is the slope of the line tangent to the position graph at that point.

Suppose we use a high-speed camera, one that takes 3000 frames per second, to film just the segment of motion right around point 2. This "magnified" motion diagram is shown in FIGURE 2.7b. At this level of magnification, each velocity vector is *almost* the same length. Further, the greatly magnified section of the curved position graph is *almost* a straight line. That is, the motion appears very nearly uniform on this time scale. If the rocket suddenly changed to *constant*-velocity motion at point 2, it would continue to move with a velocity given by the slope of the graph in Figure 2.7b.

The point of Figure 2.7 is that the average velocity $v_{avg} = \Delta s/\Delta t$ becomes a better and better approximation to the instantaneous velocity v_s as the time interval Δt over which the average is taken gets smaller and smaller. By magnifying the motion diagram, we are using smaller and smaller time intervals Δt. But even 3000 frames per second isn't fast enough. We need to let $\Delta t \to 0$.

We can state this idea mathematically in terms of a limit:

$$v_s \equiv \lim_{\Delta t \to 0} \frac{\Delta s}{\Delta t} = \frac{ds}{dt} \quad \text{(instantaneous velocity)} \quad (2.4)$$

As Δt continues to get smaller, the average velocity $v_{avg} = \Delta s/\Delta t$ reaches a constant or *limiting* value. That is, **the instantaneous velocity at time t is the average velocity during a time interval Δt, centered on t, as Δt approaches zero.** In calculus, this limit is called *the derivative of s with respect to t*, and it is denoted ds/dt. We'll look at derivatives in the next section.

Graphically, $\Delta s/\Delta t$ is the slope of a straight line. As Δt gets smaller (i.e., more and more magnification), the straight line becomes a better and better approximation of the curve *at that one point*. In the limit $\Delta t \to 0$, the straight line is tangent to the curve. As **FIGURE 2.7c** shows, **the instantaneous velocity at time t is the slope of the line that is tangent to the position-versus-time graph at time t.**

EXAMPLE 2.3 Relating a velocity graph to a position graph

FIGURE 2.8 is the position-versus-time graph of a car.

a. Draw the car's velocity-versus-time graph.
b. Describe the car's motion.

FIGURE 2.8 Position-versus-time graph.

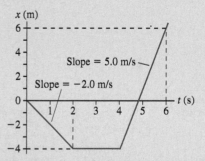

MODEL Represent the car as a particle, with a well-defined position at each instant of time.

VISUALIZE Figure 2.8 is the graphical representation.

SOLVE

a. The car's position-versus-time graph is a sequence of three straight lines. Each of these straight lines represents uniform motion at a constant velocity. We can determine the car's velocity during each interval of time by measuring the slope of the line. From $t = 0$ s to $t = 2$ s ($\Delta t = 2.0$ s) the car's displacement is $\Delta x = -4.0$ m $- 0.0$ m $= -4.0$ m. The velocity during this interval is

$$v_x = \frac{\Delta x}{\Delta t} = \frac{-4.0 \text{ m}}{2.0 \text{ s}} = -2.0 \text{ m/s}$$

The car's position does not change from $t = 2$ s to $t = 4$ s ($\Delta x = 0$), so $v_x = 0$. Finally, the displacement between $t = 4$ s and $t = 6$ s is $\Delta x = 10.0$ m. Thus the velocity during this interval is

$$v_x = \frac{10.0 \text{ m}}{2.0 \text{ s}} = 5.0 \text{ m/s}$$

These velocities are shown on the velocity-versus-time graph of **FIGURE 2.9**.

FIGURE 2.9 The corresponding velocity-versus-time graph.

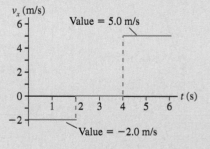

b. The car backs up for 2 s at 2.0 m/s, sits at rest for 2 s, then drives forward at 5.0 m/s for at least 2 s. We can't tell from the graph what happens for $t > 6$ s.

ASSESS The velocity graph and the position graph look completely different. The *value* of the velocity graph at any instant of time equals the *slope* of the position graph.

EXAMPLE 2.4 Finding velocity from position graphically

FIGURE 2.10 shows the position-versus-time graph of an elevator.

a. At which labeled point or points does the elevator have the least speed?
b. At which point or points is the elevator moving the fastest?
c. Sketch an approximate velocity-versus-time graph for the elevator.

FIGURE 2.10 Position-versus-time graph.

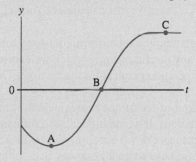

MODEL Represent the elevator as a particle.

VISUALIZE Figure 2.10 is the graphical representation.

SOLVE a. FIGURE 2.11a shows that the elevator has the least speed—no speed at all!—at points A and C. At point A, the speed is only instantaneously zero. At point C, the elevator has actually stopped and remains at rest.
b. The elevator moves the fastest at point B.
c. Although we cannot find an exact velocity-versus-time graph, we can see that the slope, and hence v_y, is initially negative, becomes zero at point A, rises to a maximum value at point B,

FIGURE 2.11 The velocity-versus-time graph is found from the position graph.

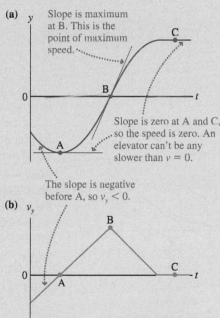

decreases back to zero a little before point C, then remains at zero thereafter. Thus FIGURE 2.11b shows, at least approximately, the elevator's velocity-versus-time graph.

ASSESS Once again, the shape of the velocity graph bears no resemblance to the shape of the position graph. You must transfer *slope* information from the position graph to *value* information on the velocity graph.

A Little Calculus: Derivatives

We have reached the point beyond which Galileo could not proceed because he lacked the mathematical tools. Further progress had to await a new branch of mathematics called *calculus,* invented simultaneously in England by Newton and in Germany by Leibniz. Calculus is designed to deal with instantaneous quantities. In other words, it provides us with the tools for evaluating limits such as the one in Equation 2.4.

The notation ds/dt is called *the derivative of s with respect to t,* and Equation 2.4 defines it as the limiting value of a ratio. As Figure 2.7 showed, ds/dt can be interpreted graphically as the slope of the line that is tangent to the position-versus-time graph at time t.

EXAMPLE 2.5 Finding velocity from position as a derivative

The position of a particle as a function of time is $s = 2t^2$ m, where t is in s. What is the velocity v_s as a function of time?

SOLVE We need to "take the derivative" of s:

$$v_s = \frac{ds}{dt} = \lim_{\Delta t \to 0} \frac{\Delta s}{\Delta t}$$

During the time interval Δt, the particle moves from position $s_{\text{at } t}$ to the new position $s_{\text{at } t+\Delta t}$. Its displacement is

$$\Delta s = s_{\text{at } t+\Delta t} - s_{\text{at } t} = 2(t + \Delta t)^2 - 2t^2$$
$$= 2(t^2 + 2t\Delta t + (\Delta t)^2) - 2t^2$$
$$= 4t\Delta t + 2(\Delta t)^2$$

The average velocity during the time interval Δt is

$$v_{\text{avg}} = \frac{\Delta s}{\Delta t} = \frac{4t\Delta t + 2(\Delta t)^2}{\Delta t} = 4t + 2\Delta t$$

Continued

We can finish by taking the limit $\Delta t \rightarrow 0$ to find

$$v_s = \frac{ds}{dt} = \lim_{\Delta t \to 0} (4t + 2\Delta t) = 4t \text{ m/s}$$

In other words, the function for calculating the velocity at any instant of time is $v_s = 4t$ m/s, where t is in s. At $t = 3$ s, for example, the particle is located at position $s = 18$ m and its instantaneous velocity, at just that instant, is $v_s = 12$ m/s.

FIGURE 2.12 Position-versus-time and velocity-versus-time graphs for Example 2.5.

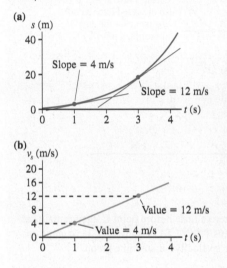

Let's look at this example graphically. FIGURE 2.12a shows the particle's position-versus-time graph $s = 2t^2$ m. FIGURE 2.12b then shows the velocity-versus-time graph, using the velocity function $v = 4t$ m/s that we just calculated. You see that the velocity graph is a straight line.

It is critically important to understand the relationship between these two graphs. The *value* of the velocity graph at any instant of time, which we can read directly off the vertical axis, is the *slope* of the position graph at that same time. This is illustrated at $t = 1$ s and $t = 3$ s.

Example 2.5 showed how the limit of $\Delta s/\Delta t$ can be evaluated to find a derivative, but the procedure is clearly rather tedious. It would hinder us significantly if we had to do this for every new situation. Fortunately, we need only a few basic derivatives in this text. Learn these, and you do not have to go all the way back to the definition in terms of limits.

The only functions we will use in Parts I and II of this book are powers and polynomials. Consider the function $u = ct^n$, where c and n are constants. The following result is proven in calculus:

$$\text{The derivative of } u = ct^n \text{ is } \frac{du}{dt} = nct^{n-1} \qquad (2.5)$$

NOTE ► The symbol u is a "dummy name." Equation 2.5 can be used to take the derivative of *any* function of the form ct^n. ◄

Example 2.5 needed to find the derivative of the function $s = 2t^2$. Using Equation 2.5 with $c = 2$ and $n = 2$, the derivative of $s = 2t^2$ with respect to t is

$$v_s = \frac{ds}{dt} = 2 \cdot 2t^{2-1} = 4t$$

Similarly, the derivative of the function $x = 3/t^2 = 3t^{-2}$ is

$$\frac{dx}{dt} = (-2) \cdot 3t^{-2-1} = -6t^{-3} = -\frac{6}{t^3}$$

A value that doesn't change with time, such as the position of an object at rest, can be represented by the function $u = c = $ constant. That is, the exponent of t^n is $n = 0$. You can see from Equation 2.5 that the derivative of a constant is zero. That is,

$$\frac{du}{dt} = 0 \text{ if } u = c = \text{constant} \qquad (2.6)$$

This makes sense. The graph of the function $u = c$ is simply a horizontal line at height c. The slope of a horizontal line—which is what the derivative du/dt measures—is zero.

The only other information we need about derivatives for now is how to evaluate the derivative of the sum of two or more functions. Let u and w be two separate functions of time. You will learn in calculus that

$$\frac{d}{dt}(u + w) = \frac{du}{dt} + \frac{dw}{dt} \qquad (2.7)$$

That is, the derivative of a sum is the sum of the derivatives.

Scientists and engineers must use calculus to calculate the trajectories of rockets.

NOTE ▶ You may have learned in calculus to take the derivative dy/dx, where y is a function of x. The derivatives we use in physics are the same; only the notation is different. We're interested in how quantities change with time, so our derivatives are with respect to t instead of x. ◀

EXAMPLE 2.6 Using calculus to find the velocity

A particle's position is given by the function $x = (-t^3 + 3t)$ m, where t is in s.

a. What are the particle's position and velocity at $t = 2$ s?
b. Draw graphs of x and v_x during the interval $-3 \text{ s} \leq t \leq 3$ s.
c. Draw a motion diagram to illustrate this motion.

SOLVE

a. We can compute the position at $t = 2$ s directly from the function x:

$$x(\text{at } t = 2 \text{ s}) = -(2)^3 + (3)(2) = -8 + 6 = -2 \text{ m}$$

The velocity is then $v_x = dx/dt$. The function for x is the sum of two polynomials, so

$$v_x = \frac{dx}{dt} = \frac{d}{dt}(-t^3 + 3t) = \frac{d}{dt}(-t^3) + \frac{d}{dt}(3t)$$

The first derivative is a power with $c = -1$ and $n = 3$; the second has $c = 3$ and $n = 1$. Using Equation 2.5,

$$v_x = (-3t^2 + 3) \text{ m/s}$$

where t is in s. Evaluating the velocity at $t = 2$ s gives

$$v_x(\text{at } t = 2 \text{ s}) = -3(2)^2 + 3 = -9 \text{ m/s}$$

The negative sign indicates that the particle, at this instant of time, is moving to the *left* at a speed of 9 m/s.

b. **FIGURE 2.13** shows the position graph and the velocity graph. These were created by computing, and then graphing, the values of x and v_x at several points between -3 s and 3 s. The slope of the position-versus-time graph at $t = 2$ s is 9 m/s; this becomes the *value* that is graphed for the velocity at $t = 2$ s. Similar measurements are shown at $t = -1$ s, where the velocity is instantaneously zero.

c. Finally, we can interpret the graphs in Figure 2.13 to draw the motion diagram shown in **FIGURE 2.14**.

- The particle is initially to the right of the origin ($x > 0$ at $t = -3$ s) but moving to the left ($v_x < 0$). Its *speed* is slowing ($v = |v_x|$ is decreasing), so the velocity vector arrows are getting shorter.
- The particle passes the origin at $t \approx -1.5$ s, but it is still moving to the left.
- The position reaches a minimum at $t = -1$ s; the particle is as far left as it is going. The velocity is *instantaneously* $v_x = 0$ m/s as the particle reverses direction.
- The particle moves back to the right between $t = -1$ s and $t = 1$ s ($v_x > 0$).
- The particle turns around again at $t = 1$ s and begins moving back to the left ($v_x < 0$). It keeps speeding up, then disappears off to the left.

FIGURE 2.13 Position and velocity graphs.

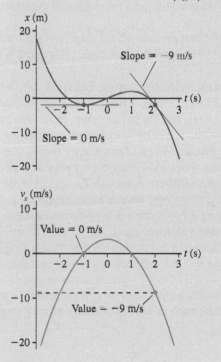

FIGURE 2.14 Motion diagram for Example 2.6.

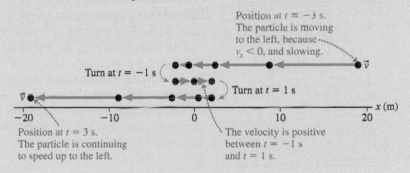

The particle in this example moved out to $x = -2$ m at $t = -1$ s, then returned. The point in its motion where it reversed direction is called a *turning point*. Because the velocity was negative just before reaching the turning point and positive just after, it had to pass through $v_x = 0$ m/s. Thus, a **turning point** is a point where the velocity is instantaneously zero as the particle reverses direction. A second turning point occurs at $t = 1$ s as the particle reaches $x = 2$ m. We will see many future examples of turning points.

STOP TO THINK 2.2   Which velocity-versus-time graph goes with the position-versus-time graph on the left?

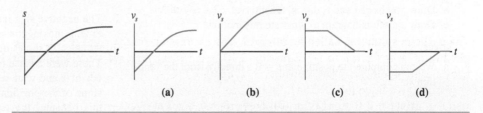

(a)	**(b)**	**(c)**	**(d)**

2.3 Finding Position from Velocity

Equation 2.4 provides a means of finding the instantaneous velocity v_s if we know the position s as a function of time. In mathematical terms, the velocity is the derivative of the position function. Graphically, the velocity is the slope of the position-versus-time graph.

But what about the reverse problem? Can we use the object's velocity to calculate its position at some future time t? Equation 2.3, $s_f = s_i + v_s \Delta t$, does this for the case of uniform motion with a constant velocity. We need to find a more general expression that is valid when v_s is not constant.

FIGURE 2.15a is a velocity-versus-time graph for a particle whose velocity varies with time. Suppose we know the object's position to be s_i at an initial time t_i. Our goal is to find its position s_f at a later time t_f.

Because we know how to handle constant velocities, using Equation 2.3, let's *approximate* the velocity function of Figure 2.15a as a series of constant-velocity steps of width Δt. This is illustrated in **FIGURE 2.15b**. During the first step, from time t_i to time $t_i + \Delta t$, the velocity has the constant value $(v_s)_1$. The velocity is a constant $(v_s)_2$ during the second step from $t_i + \Delta t$ to $t_i + 2\Delta t$, and so on. The velocity during step k has the constant value $(v_s)_k$. Altogether the velocity-versus-time curve has been divided into N constant-velocity steps of equal width Δt. Although the approximation shown in the figure is rather rough, with only nine steps, we can easily imagine that it could be made as accurate as desired by having more and more ever-narrower steps.

The velocity during each step is constant (uniform motion), so we can apply Equation 2.3 to each step. The object's displacement Δs_1 during the first step is simply $\Delta s_1 = (v_s)_1 \Delta t$. The displacement during the second step $\Delta s_2 = (v_s)_2 \Delta t$, and during step k the displacement is $\Delta s_k = (v_s)_k \Delta t$.

The total displacement of the object between t_i and t_f can be approximated as the sum of all the individual displacements during each of the N constant-velocity steps. That is,

$$\Delta s = s_f - s_i \approx \Delta s_1 + \Delta s_2 + \cdots + \Delta s_N = \sum_{k=1}^{N} (v_s)_k \Delta t \qquad (2.8)$$

where Σ (Greek sigma) is the symbol for summation.

FIGURE 2.15 Approximating a velocity-versus-time graph with a series of constant-velocity steps.

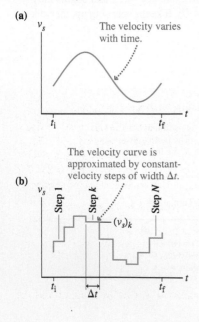

(a)

The velocity varies with time.

(b)

The velocity curve is approximated by constant-velocity steps of width Δt.

With a simple rearrangement, the particle's final position is

$$s_f \approx s_i + \sum_{k=1}^{N} (v_s)_k \Delta t \qquad (2.9)$$

Our goal was to use the velocity to find the final position s_f. Equation 2.9 nearly reaches that goal, but Equation 2.9 is only approximate because the constant-velocity steps are only an approximation of the true velocity graph. But if we now let $\Delta t \rightarrow 0$, each step's width approaches zero while the total number of steps N approaches infinity. In this limit, the series of steps becomes a perfect replica of the velocity-versus-time graph and Equation 2.9 becomes exact. Thus

$$s_f = s_i + \lim_{\Delta t \rightarrow 0} \sum_{k=1}^{N} (v_s)_k \Delta t = s_i + \int_{t_i}^{t_f} v_s \, dt \qquad (2.10)$$

The curlicue symbol is called an *integral*. The expression on the right is read, "the integral of $v_s \, dt$ from t_i to t_f." Equation 2.10 is the result that we were seeking. It allows us to predict an object's position s_f at a future time t_f.

We can give Equation 2.10 an important geometric interpretation. **FIGURE 2.16** shows step k in the approximation of the velocity graph as a long, thin rectangle of height $(v_s)_k$ and width Δt. The product $\Delta s_k = (v_s)_k \, \Delta t$ is the area (base × height) of this small rectangle. The sum in Equation 2.10 adds up all of these rectangular areas to give the total area enclosed between the t-axis and the tops of the steps. The limit of this sum as $\Delta t \rightarrow 0$ is the total area enclosed between the t-axis and the velocity curve. This is called the "area under the curve." Thus a graphical interpretation of Equation 2.10 is:

$$s_f = s_i + \text{area under the velocity curve } v_s \text{ between } t_i \text{ and } t_f \qquad (2.11)$$

NOTE ▶ Wait a minute! The displacement $\Delta s = s_f - s_i$ is a length. How can a length equal an area? Recall earlier, when we found that the velocity is the slope of the position graph, we made a distinction between the *actual* slope and the *physically meaningful* slope? The same distinction applies here. The velocity graph does indeed bound a certain area on the page. That is the actual area, but it is *not* the area to which we are referring. Once again, we need to measure the quantities we are using, v_s and Δt, by referring to the scales on the axes. Δt is some number of seconds while v_s is some number of meters per second. When these are multiplied together, the *physically meaningful* area has units of meters, appropriate for a displacement. The following examples will help make this clear. ◀

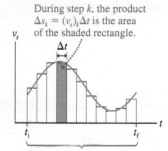

FIGURE 2.16 The total displacement Δs is the "area under the curve."

During step k, the product $\Delta s_k = (v_s)_k \Delta t$ is the area of the shaded rectangle.

During the interval t_i to t_f, the total displacement Δs is the "area under the curve."

EXAMPLE 2.7 The displacement during a drag race
FIGURE 2.17 shows the velocity-versus-time graph of a drag racer. How far does the racer move during the first 3.0 s?

FIGURE 2.17 Velocity-versus-time graph for Example 2.7.

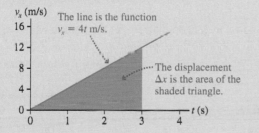

MODEL Represent the drag racer as a particle with a well-defined position at all times.

VISUALIZE Figure 2.17 is the graphical representation.

SOLVE The question "how far" indicates that we need to find a displacement Δx rather than a position x. According to Equation 2.11, the car's displacement $\Delta x = x_f - x_i$ between $t = 0$ s and $t = 3$ s is the area under the curve from $t = 0$ s to $t = 3$ s. The curve in this case is an angled line, so the area is that of a triangle:

$$\Delta x = \text{area of triangle between } t = 0 \text{ s and } t = 3 \text{ s}$$

$$= \tfrac{1}{2} \times \text{base} \times \text{height}$$

$$= \tfrac{1}{2} \times 3 \text{ s} \times 12 \text{ m/s} = 18 \text{ m}$$

The drag racer moves 18 m during the first 3 seconds.

ASSESS The "area" is a product of s with m/s, so Δx has the proper units of m.

EXAMPLE 2.8   Finding an expression for the racer's position

a. Find an algebraic expression for the position x as a function of time t for the drag racer whose velocity-versus-time graph was shown in Figure 2.17. Assume the car's initial position is $x_i = 0$ m at $t_i = 0$ s.

b. Draw the car's position-versus-time graph.

SOLVE

a. Let $x_i = 0$ at $t_i = 0$ and let x be the position at later time t. The straight line for v_x in Figure 2.17 is described by the linear function $v_x = 4t$ m/s, where t is in s. Then

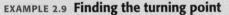

$$x = x_i + \int_0^t v_x \, dt = 0 + \text{area under the triangle between 0 and } t$$

$$= 0 + \tfrac{1}{2}(t - 0)(4t - 0) = 2t^2 \text{ m, where } t \text{ is in s}$$

b. **FIGURE 2.18** shows the drag racer's position-versus-time graph. It's simply a graph of the function $x = 2t^2$ m, where t is in s. Notice that the *linear* velocity graph of Figure 2.17 is associated with a *parabolic* position graph. This is a general result that we will see again.

FIGURE 2.18 The position-versus-time graph for the drag racer whose velocity graph was shown in Figure 2.17.

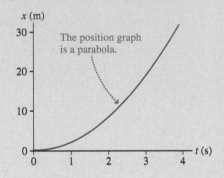

ASSESS This is exactly Example 2.5 in reverse! There we found, by taking the derivative, that a particle whose position is $x = 2t^2$ m has a velocity described by $v_x = 4t$ m/s. Here we have found, by integration, that a drag racer whose velocity is given by $v_x = 4t$ m/s has a position described by $x = 2t^2$ m.

EXAMPLE 2.9   Finding the turning point

FIGURE 2.19 is the velocity graph for a particle that starts at $x_i = 30$ m at time $t_i = 0$ s.

a. Draw a motion diagram for the particle.
b. Where is the particle's turning point?
c. At what time does the particle reach the origin?

FIGURE 2.19 Velocity-versus-time graph for the particle of Example 2.9.

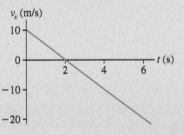

VISUALIZE The particle is initially 30 m to the right of the origin and moving *to the right* ($v_x > 0$) with a speed of 10 m/s. But v_x is decreasing, so the particle is slowing down. At $t = 2$ s the velocity, just for an instant, is zero before becoming negative. This is the turning point. The velocity is negative for $t > 2$ s, so the particle has reversed direction and moves back toward the origin. At some later time, which we want to find, the particle will pass $x = 0$ m.

SOLVE a. **FIGURE 2.20** shows the motion diagram. The distance scale will be established in parts b and c but is shown here for convenience.

b. The particle reaches the turning point at $t = 2$ s. To learn *where* it is at that time we need to find the displacement during the first two seconds. We can do this by finding the area under the curve between $t = 0$ s and $t = 2$ s:

$$x(\text{at } t = 2 \text{ s}) = x_i + \int_{0s}^{2s} v_x \, dt$$

$$= x_i + \text{area under the curve between 0 s and 2 s}$$

$$= 30 \text{ m} + \tfrac{1}{2}(2 \text{ s} - 0 \text{ s})(10 \text{ m/s} - 0 \text{ m/s})$$

$$= 40 \text{ m}$$

The turning point is at $x = 40$ m.

c. The particle needs to move $\Delta x = -40$ m to get from the turning point to the origin. That is, the area under the curve from $t = 2$ s to the desired time t needs to be -40 m. Because the curve is below the axis, with negative values of v_x, the area to the right of $t = 2$ s is a *negative* area. With a bit of geometry, you will find that the triangle with a base extending from $t = 2$ s to $t = 6$ s has an area of -40 m. Thus the particle reaches the origin at $t = 6$ s.

FIGURE 2.20 Motion diagram for the particle whose velocity graph was shown in Figure 2.19.

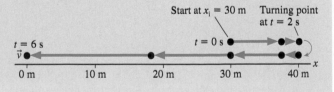

A Little More Calculus: Integrals

Taking the derivative of a function is equivalent to finding the slope of a graph of the function. Similarly, evaluating an integral is equivalent to finding the area under a graph of the function. The graphical method is very important for building intuition about motion but is limited in its practical application. Just as derivatives of standard functions can be evaluated and tabulated, so can integrals.

The integral in Equation 2.10 is called a *definite integral* because there are two definite boundaries to the area we want to find. These boundaries are called the lower (t_i) and upper (t_f) *limits of integration*. For the important function $u = ct^n$, the essential result from calculus is that

$$\int_{t_i}^{t_f} u\, dt = \int_{t_i}^{t_f} ct^n\, dt = \left. \frac{ct^{n+1}}{n+1} \right|_{t_i}^{t_f} = \frac{ct_f^{n+1}}{n+1} - \frac{ct_i^{n+1}}{n+1} \qquad (n \neq -1) \qquad (2.12)$$

The vertical bar in the third step with subscript t_i and superscript t_f is a shorthand notation from calculus that means—as seen in the last step—the integral evaluated at the upper limit t_f *minus* the integral evaluated at the lower limit t_i. You also need to know that for two functions u and w,

$$\int_{t_i}^{t_f} (u + w)\, dt = \int_{t_i}^{t_f} u\, dt + \int_{t_i}^{t_f} w\, dt \qquad (2.13)$$

That is, the integral of a sum is equal to the sum of the integrals.

EXAMPLE 2.10 Using calculus to find the position
Use calculus to solve Example 2.9.

SOLVE Figure 2.19 is a linear graph. Its "y-intercept" is seen to be 10 m/s and its slope is -5 (m/s)/s. Thus the velocity graphed here can be described by the equation

$$v_x = (10 - 5t) \text{ m/s}$$

where t is in s. We can find the position x at time t by using Equation 2.10:

$$x = x_i + \int_0^t v_x\, dt = 30 \text{ m} + \int_0^t (10 - 5t)\, dt$$

$$= 30 \text{ m} + \int_0^t 10\, dt - \int_0^t 5t\, dt$$

We used Equation 2.13 for the integral of a sum to get the final expression. The first integral is a function of the form $u = ct^n$ with $c = 10$ and $n = 0$; the second is of the form $u = ct^n$ with $c = 5$ and $n = 1$. Using Equation 2.12,

$$\int_0^t 10\, dt = \left. 10t \right|_0^t = 10 \cdot t - 10 \cdot 0 = 10t \text{ m}$$

and

$$\int_0^t 5t\, dt = \left. \tfrac{5}{2}t^2 \right|_0^t = \tfrac{5}{2} \cdot t^2 - \tfrac{5}{2} \cdot 0^2 = \tfrac{5}{2}t^2 \text{ m}$$

Combining the pieces gives

$$x = (30 + 10t - \tfrac{5}{2}t^2) \text{ m}$$

where t is in s. The particle's turning point occurs at $t = 2$ s, and its position at that time is

$$x(\text{at } t = 2 \text{ s}) = 30 + (10)(2) - \tfrac{5}{2}(2)^2 = 40 \text{ m}$$

The time at which the particle reaches the origin is found by setting $x = 0$ m:

$$30 + 10t - \tfrac{5}{2}t^2 = 0$$

This quadratic equation has two solutions: $t = -2$ s or $t = 6$ s.

When we solve a quadratic equation, we cannot just arbitrarily select the root we want. Instead, we must decide which is the *meaningful* root. Here the negative root refers to a time before the problem began, so the meaningful one is the positive root, $t = 6$ s.

ASSESS The results agree with the answers we found previously from a graphical solution.

These examples make the point that there are often many ways to solve a problem. The graphical procedures for finding derivatives and integrals are simple, but they work only for a limited range of problems—those where the geometry is simple. The techniques of calculus are more demanding, but these techniques allow us to deal with functions whose graphs are quite complex.

Summing Up

As you work on building intuition about motion, you need to be able to move back and forth between four different representations of the motion:

- The motion diagram;
- The position-versus-time graph;
- The velocity-versus-time graph;
- The description in words.

Given a description of a certain motion, you should be able to sketch the motion diagram and the position and velocity graphs. Given one graph, you should be able to generate the other. And given position and velocity graphs, you should be able to "interpret" them by describing the motion in words or in a motion diagram.

STOP TO THINK 2.3 Which position-versus-time graph goes with the velocity-versus-time graph on the left? The particle's position at $t_i = 0$ s is $x_i = -10$ m.

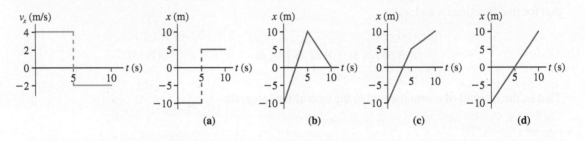

(a)   (b)   (c)   (d)

2.4 Motion with Constant Acceleration

We need one more major concept to describe one-dimensional motion: acceleration. Acceleration, as we noted in Chapter 1, is a rather abstract concept. You cannot "see" the value of acceleration, as you can that of position, nor can you judge it by looking to see if an object is moving quickly or slowly. Nonetheless, acceleration is the linchpin of mechanics. We will see very shortly that Newton's laws relate the acceleration of an object to the forces that are exerted on it.

Let's conduct a race between a Volkswagen Beetle and a Porsche to see which can achieve a velocity of 30 m/s ($\approx$60 mph) in the shortest time. Both cars are equipped with computers that will record the speedometer reading 10 times each second. This gives a nearly continuous record of the *instantaneous* velocity of each car. Table 2.1 shows some of the data. The velocity-versus-time graphs, based on these data, are shown in **FIGURE 2.21**.

How can we describe the difference in performance of the two cars? It is not that one has a different velocity from the other; both achieve every velocity between 0 and 30 m/s. The distinction is how long it took each to *change* its velocity from 0 to 30 m/s. The Porsche changed velocity quickly, in 6.0 s, while the VW needed 15 s to make the same velocity change.

As we compare the two cars, we are looking at the *rate* at which their velocities change. Because the Porsche had a velocity change $\Delta v_s = 30$ m/s during a time interval $\Delta t = 6.0$ s, the *rate* at which its velocity changed was

$$\text{rate of velocity change} = \frac{\Delta v_s}{\Delta t} = \frac{30 \text{ m/s}}{6.0 \text{ s}} = 5.0 \text{ (m/s)/s} \qquad (2.14)$$

Notice the units. They are units of "velocity per second." A rate of velocity change of 5.0 "meters per second per second" means that the velocity increases by 5.0 m/s

TABLE 2.1 Velocities of a Porsche and a Volkswagen Beetle

t(s)	$v_{Porsche}$ (m/s)	v_{VW} (m/s)
0.0	0.0	0.0
0.1	0.5	0.2
0.2	1.0	0.4
0.3	1.5	0.6
0.4	2.0	0.8
⋮	⋮	⋮

FIGURE 2.21 Velocity-versus-time graphs for the Porsche and the VW Beetle.

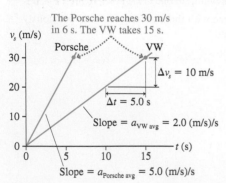

during the first second, by another 5.0 m/s during the next second, and so on. In fact, the velocity will increase by 5.0 m/s during any second in which it is changing at the rate of 5.0 (m/s)/s.

Chapter 1 introduced *acceleration* as "the rate of change of velocity." That is, acceleration measures how quickly or slowly an object's velocity changes. The Porsche's velocity changed quickly, so it had a large acceleration. The VW's velocity changed more slowly, so its acceleration was less. In parallel with our treatment of velocity, let's define the **average acceleration** a_{avg} during the time interval Δt to be

$$a_{avg} = \frac{\Delta v_s}{\Delta t} \qquad \text{(average acceleration)} \qquad (2.15)$$

Because Δv_s and Δt are the "rise" and "run" of a velocity-versus-time graph, we see that a_{avg} can be interpreted graphically as the *slope* of a straight-line velocity-versus-time graph. Figure 2.21 uses this idea to show that the VW's average acceleration is

$$a_{\text{VW avg}} = \frac{\Delta v_s}{\Delta t} = \frac{10 \text{ m/s}}{5.0 \text{ s}} = 2.0 \text{ (m/s)/s} \qquad (2.16)$$

This is less than the acceleration of the Porsche, as expected.

An object whose velocity-versus-time graph is a straight-line graph has a steady and unchanging acceleration. Such a graph represents motion with *constant acceleration*, which we call **uniformly accelerated motion: An object has uniformly accelerated motion if and only if its acceleration a_s is constant and unchanging. The object's velocity-versus-time graph is a straight line, and a_s is the slope of the line.** There's no need to specify "average" if the acceleration is constant, so we'll use the symbol a_s as we discuss motion along the s-axis with constant acceleration.

Act|v
Physics   1.2, 1.3

NOTE ► An important aspect of acceleration is its *sign*. Acceleration $\vec{a}$, like position $\vec{r}$ and velocity $\vec{v}$, is a vector. For motion in one dimension the sign of a_x (or a_y) is positive if the vector $\vec{a}$ points to the right (or up), negative if it points to the left (or down). This was illustrated in Figure 1.19 and the very important Tactics Box 1.4, which you may wish to review. It's particularly important to emphasize that positive and negative values of a_s do *not* correspond to "speeding up" and "slowing down." ◄

EXAMPLE 2.11 Relating acceleration to velocity

a. A particle has a velocity of 10 m/s and a constant acceleration of 2 (m/s)/s. What is its velocity 1 s later? 2 s later?

b. A particle has a velocity of −10 m/s and a constant acceleration of 2 (m/s)/s. What is its velocity 1 s later? 2 s later?

SOLVE

a. An acceleration of 2 (m/s)/s *means* that the velocity increases by 2 m/s every 1 s. If the particle's initial velocity is 10 m/s, then 1 s later its velocity will be 12 m/s. After 2 s, which is 1

additional second later, it will increase by another 2 m/s to 14 m/s. After 3 s it will be 16 m/s. Here a positive a_s is causing the particle to speed up.

b. If the particle's initial velocity is a *negative* −10 m/s but the acceleration is a positive +2 (m/s)/s, then 1 s later the velocity will be −8 m/s. After 2 s it will be −6 m/s, and so on. In this case, a positive a_s is causing the object to *slow down* (decreasing speed v). This agrees with the rule from Tactics Box 1.4: An object is slowing down if and only if v_s and a_s have opposite signs.

NOTE ► It is customary to abbreviate the acceleration units (m/s)/s as m/s². For example, the particles in Example 2.11 had an acceleration of 2 m/s². We will use this notation, but keep in mind the *meaning* of the notation as "(meters per second) per second." ◄

EXAMPLE 2.12 **Running the court**

A basketball player starts at the left end of the court and moves with the velocity shown in FIGURE 2.22. Draw a motion diagram and an acceleration-versus-time graph for the basketball player.

FIGURE 2.22 Velocity-versus-time graph for the basketball player of Example 2.12.

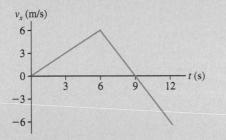

VISUALIZE The velocity is positive (motion to the right) and increasing for the first 6 s, so the velocity arrows in the motion diagram are to the right and getting longer. From $t = 6$ s to 9 s the motion is still to the right (v_x is still positive), but the arrows are getting shorter because v_x is decreasing. There's a turning point at $t = 9$ s, when $v_x = 0$, and after that the motion is to the left (v_x is negative) and getting faster. The motion diagram of FIGURE 2.23a shows the velocity and the acceleration vectors.

SOLVE Acceleration is the slope of the velocity graph. For the first 6 s, the slope has the constant value

$$a_x = \frac{\Delta v_x}{\Delta t} = \frac{6.0 \text{ m/s}}{6.0 \text{ s}} = 1.0 \text{ m/s}^2$$

The velocity decreases by 12 m/s during the 6 s interval from $t = 6$ s to $t = 12$ s, so

$$a_x = \frac{\Delta v_x}{\Delta t} = \frac{-12 \text{ m/s}}{6.0 \text{ s}} = -2.0 \text{ m/s}^2$$

The acceleration graph for these 12 s is shown in FIGURE 2.23b. Notice that there is no change in the acceleration at $t = 9$ s, the turning point.

FIGURE 2.23 Motion diagram and acceleration graph for Example 2.12.

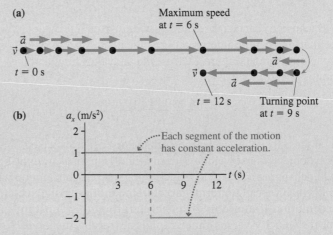

ASSESS The *sign* of a_x does *not* tell us whether the object is speeding up or slowing down. The basketball player is slowing down from $t = 6$ s to $t = 9$ s, then speeding up from $t = 9$ s to $t = 12$ s. Nonetheless, his acceleration is negative during this entire interval because his acceleration vector, as seen in the motion diagram, always points to the left.

FIGURE 2.24 Acceleration and velocity graphs for motion with constant acceleration.

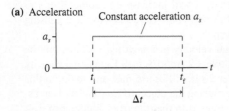

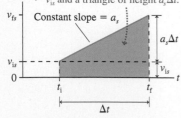

The Kinematic Equations of Constant Acceleration

Consider an object whose acceleration a_s remains constant during the time interval $\Delta t = t_f - t_i$. At the beginning of this interval, at time t_i, the object has initial velocity v_{is} and initial position s_i. Note that t_i is often zero, but it does not have to be. We would like to predict the object's final position s_f and final velocity v_{fs} at time t_f.

The object's velocity is changing because the object is accelerating. FIGURE 2.24a shows the acceleration-versus-time graph, a horizontal line between t_i and t_f. It is not hard to find the object's velocity v_{fs} at a later time t_f. By definition,

$$a_s = \frac{\Delta v_s}{\Delta t} = \frac{v_{fs} - v_{is}}{\Delta t} \tag{2.17}$$

which is easily rearranged to give

$$v_{fs} = v_{is} + a_s \Delta t \tag{2.18}$$

The velocity-versus-time graph, shown in FIGURE 2.24b, is a straight line that starts at v_{is} and has slope a_s.

As you learned in the last section, the object's final position is

$$s_f = s_i + \text{ area under the velocity curve } v_s \text{ between } t_i \text{ and } t_f \tag{2.19}$$

The shaded area in Figure 2.24b can be subdivided into a rectangle of area $v_{is} \Delta t$ and a triangle of area $\frac{1}{2}(a_s \Delta t)(\Delta t) = \frac{1}{2}a_s(\Delta t)^2$. Adding these gives

$$s_f = s_i + v_{is}\Delta t + \tfrac{1}{2}a_s(\Delta t)^2 \tag{2.20}$$

where $\Delta t = t_f - t_i$ is the elapsed time. The quadratic dependence on Δt causes the position-versus-time graph for constant-acceleration motion to have a parabolic shape. You saw this earlier in Figure 2.18, and it will appear below in Figure 2.25.

Equations 2.18 and 2.20 are two of the basic kinematic equations for motion with *constant* acceleration. They allow us to predict an object's position and velocity at a future instant of time. We need one more equation to complete our set, a direct relation between position and velocity. First use Equation 2.18 to write $\Delta t = (v_{fs} - v_{is})/a_s$. Substitute this into Equation 2.20, giving

$$
\begin{aligned}
s_f &= s_i + v_{is}\left(\frac{v_{fs} - v_{is}}{a_s}\right) + \tfrac{1}{2}a_s\left(\frac{v_{fs} - v_{is}}{a_s}\right)^2 \\
&= s_i + \left(\frac{v_{is}v_{fs}}{a_s} - \frac{v_{is}^2}{a_s}\right) + \left(\frac{v_{fs}^2}{2a_s} - \frac{v_{is}v_{fs}}{a_s} + \frac{v_{is}^2}{2a_s}\right) \\
&= s_i + \frac{v_{fs}^2 - v_{is}^2}{2a_s}
\end{aligned}
\tag{2.21}
$$

This is easily rearranged to read

$$v_{fs}^2 = v_{is}^2 + 2a_s\Delta s \tag{2.22}$$

where $\Delta s = s_f - s_i$ is the *displacement* (not the distance!).

Equations 2.18, 2.20, and 2.22, which are summarized in Table 2.2, are the key results for motion with constant acceleration.

FIGURE 2.25 is a comparison of motion with constant velocity (uniform motion) and motion with constant acceleration (uniformly accelerated motion). Notice that uniform motion is really a special case of uniformly accelerated motion in which the constant acceleration happens to be zero. The graphs for a negative acceleration are left as an exercise.

TABLE 2.2 The kinematic equations for motion with constant acceleration

$$v_{fs} = v_{is} + a_s \Delta t$$
$$s_f = s_i + v_{is} \Delta t + \tfrac{1}{2}a_s(\Delta t)^2$$
$$v_{fs}^2 = v_{is}^2 + 2a_s \Delta s$$

FIGURE 2.25 Motion with constant velocity and constant acceleration. These graphs assume $s_i = 0$, $v_{is} > 0$, and (for constant acceleration) $a_s > 0$.

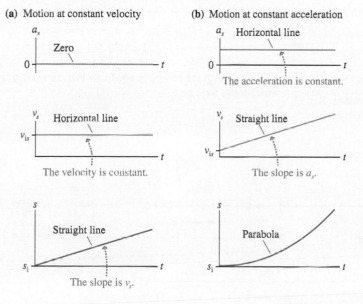

(a) Motion at constant velocity

(b) Motion at constant acceleration

A Problem-Solving Strategy

1.4, 1.5, 1.6, 1.8, 1.9,
1.11, 1.12, 1.13, 1.14

This information can be assembled into a problem-solving strategy for kinematics with constant acceleration.

> **PROBLEM-SOLVING STRATEGY 2.1 Kinematics with constant acceleration** (MP)
>
> **MODEL** Use the particle model. Make simplifying assumptions.
>
> **VISUALIZE** Use different representations of the information in the problem.
>
> - Draw a *pictorial representation*. This helps you assess the information you are given and starts the process of translating the problem into symbols.
> - Use a *graphical representation* if it is appropriate for the problem.
> - Go back and forth between these two representations as needed.
>
> **SOLVE** The mathematical representation is based on the three kinematic equations
>
> $$v_{fs} = v_{is} + a_s \Delta t$$
> $$s_f = s_i + v_{is}\Delta t + \tfrac{1}{2}a_s(\Delta t)^2$$
> $$v_{fs}^2 = v_{is}^2 + 2a_s\Delta s$$
>
> - Use x or y, as appropriate to the problem, rather than the generic s.
> - Replace i and f with numerical subscripts defined in the pictorial representation.
> - Uniform motion with constant velocity has $a_s = 0$.
>
> **ASSESS** Is your result believable? Does it have proper units? Does it make sense?

NOTE ▶ You are strongly encouraged to solve problems on the Dynamics Worksheets found at the back of the *Student Workbook*. These worksheets will help you use the Problem-Solving Strategy and develop good problem-solving skills. End-of-chapter Exercises and Problems suitable for solution on a worksheet are marked with the icon 🖉 . ◀

EXAMPLE 2.13 The motion of a rocket sled

A rocket sled accelerates at 50 m/s^2 for 5.0 s, coasts for 3.0 s, then deploys a braking parachute and decelerates at 3.0 m/s^2 until coming to a halt.

a. What is the maximum velocity of the rocket sled?
b. What is the total distance traveled?

MODEL Represent the rocket sled as a particle.

VISUALIZE FIGURE 2.26 shows the pictorial representation. Recall that we discussed the first two-thirds of this problem as Example 1.8 in Chapter 1.

SOLVE a. The maximum velocity is identified in the pictorial representation as v_{1x}, the velocity at time t_1 when the acceleration phase ends. The first kinematic equation in Table 2.2 gives

$$v_{1x} = v_{0x} + a_{0x}(t_1 - t_0) = a_{0x}t_1$$
$$= (50 \text{ m/s}^2)(5.0 \text{ s}) = 250 \text{ m/s}$$

We started with the complete equation, then simplified by noting which terms were zero.

FIGURE 2.26 Pictorial representation of the rocket sled.

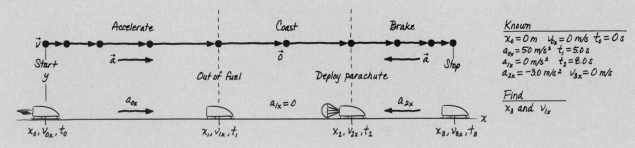

b. Finding the total distance requires several steps. First, the sled's position when the acceleration ends at t_1 is found from the second equation in Table 2.2:

$$x_1 = x_0 + v_{0x}(t_1 - t_0) + \tfrac{1}{2}a_{0x}(t_1 - t_0)^2 = \tfrac{1}{2}a_{0x}t_1^2$$

$$= \tfrac{1}{2}(50 \text{ m/s}^2)(5.0 \text{ s})^2 = 625 \text{ m}$$

During the coasting phase, which is uniform motion with no acceleration ($a_{1x} = 0$),

$$x_2 = x_1 + v_{1x}\Delta t = x_1 + v_{1x}(t_2 - t_1)$$

$$= 625 \text{ m} + (250 \text{ m/s})(3.0 \text{ s}) = 1375 \text{ m}$$

Notice that, in this case, Δt is not simply t. The braking phase is a little different because we don't know how long it lasts.

But we do know that the sled ends with $v_{3x} = 0$ m/s, so we can use the third equation in Table 2.2:

$$v_{3x}^2 = v_{2x}^2 + 2a_{2x}\Delta x = v_{2x}^2 + 2a_{2x}(x_3 - x_2)$$

This can be solved for x_3:

$$x_3 = x_2 + \frac{v_{3x}^2 - v_{2x}^2}{2a_{2x}}$$

$$= 1375 \text{ m} + \frac{0 - (250 \text{ m/s})^2}{2(-3.0 \text{ m/s}^2)} = 11{,}800 \text{ m}$$

ASSESS Using the approximate conversion factor 1 m/s ≈ 2 mph from Table 1.5, we see that the top speed is ≈ 500 mph. The total distance traveled is ≈ 12 km ≈ 7 mi. This is reasonable because it takes a very long distance to stop from a top speed of 500 mph!

NOTE ▶ We used explicit numerical subscripts throughout the mathematical representation, each referring to a symbol that was defined in the pictorial representation. The subscripts i and f in the Table 2.2 equations are just generic "place holders" and don't have unique values. During the acceleration phase we had i = 0 and f = 1. Later, during the coasting phase, these became i = 1 and f = 2. The numerical subscripts have a clear meaning and are less likely to lead to confusion. ◀

EXAMPLE 2.14 **Friday night football**
Fred catches the football while standing directly on the goal line. He immediately starts running forward with an acceleration of 6 ft/s². At the moment the catch is made, Tommy is 20 yards away and heading directly toward Fred with a steady speed of 15 ft/s. If neither deviates from a straight-ahead path, where will Tommy tackle Fred?

MODEL Represent Fred and Tommy as particles.

VISUALIZE The pictorial representation is shown again in FIGURE 2.27. With two moving objects we need the additional subscripts F and T to distinguish Fred's symbols and Tommy's symbols.

SOLVE We want to find *where* Fred and Tommy have the same position. The pictorial representation designates time t_1 as *when* they meet. The axes have been chosen so that Fred starts at $(x_0)_F = 0$ ft and moves to the right while Tommy starts at $(x_0)_T = 60$ ft and runs to the left with a *negative* velocity. The second equation of Table 2.2 allows us to find their positions at time t_1. These are:

$$(x_1)_F = (x_0)_F + (v_{0x})_F(t_1 - t_0) + \tfrac{1}{2}(a_x)_F(t_1 - t_0)^2$$
$$= \tfrac{1}{2}(a_x)_F t_1^2$$
$$(x_1)_T = (x_0)_T + (v_{0x})_T(t_1 - t_0) + \tfrac{1}{2}(a_x)_T(t_1 - t_0)^2$$
$$= (x_0)_T + (v_{0x})_T t_1$$

FIGURE 2.27 Pictorial representation for Example 2.14.

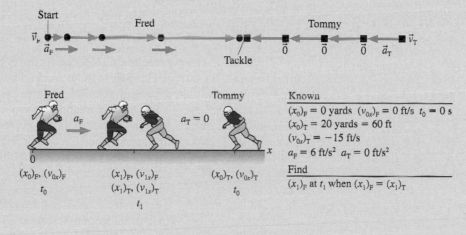

Continued

Notice that Tommy's position equation contains the term $(v_{0x})_T t_1$, not $-(v_{0x})_T t_1$. The fact that he is moving to the left has already been considered in assigning a *negative value* to $(v_{0x})_T$, hence we don't want to add any additional negative signs in the equation. If we now set $(x_1)_F$ and $(x_1)_T$ equal to each other, indicating the point of the tackle, we can solve for t_1:

$$\tfrac{1}{2}(a_x)_F t_1^2 = (x_0)_T + (v_{0x})_T t_1$$

$$\tfrac{1}{2}(a_x)_F t_1^2 - (v_{0x})_T t_1 - (x_0)_T = 0$$

$$3t_1^2 + 15t_1 - 60 = 0$$

The solutions of this quadratic equation for t_1 are $t_1 = (-7.62\text{ s}, +2.62\text{ s})$. The negative time is not meaningful in this problem, so the time of the tackle is $t_1 = 2.62$ s. We've kept an extra significant digit in the solution to minimize round-off error in the next step. Using this value to compute $(x_1)_F$ gives

$$(x_1)_F = \tfrac{1}{2}(a_x)_F t_1^2 = 20.6 \text{ feet} = 6.9 \text{ yards}$$

Tommy makes the tackle at just about the 7-yard line!

ASSESS The answer had to be between 0 yards and 20 yards. Because Tommy was already running, whereas Fred started from rest, it is reasonable that Fred will cover less than half the 20-yard separation before meeting Tommy. Thus 6.9 yards is a reasonable answer.

FIGURE 2.28 Position-versus-time graphs for Fred and Tommy.

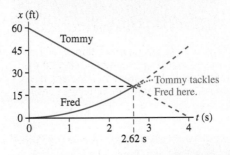

NOTE ▶ The purpose of the assessment step is not to prove that an answer must be right but to rule out answers that, with a little thought, are clearly wrong. ◀

It is worth exploring Example 2.14 graphically. **FIGURE 2.28** shows position-versus-time graphs for Fred and Tommy. The curves intersect at $t = 2.62$ s, and that is where the tackle occurs. You should compare this problem to Example 2.2 and Figure 2.5 for Bob and Susan to notice the similarities and the differences.

STOP TO THINK 2.4 Which velocity-versus-time graph or graphs go with this acceleration-versus-time graph? The particle is initially moving to the right.

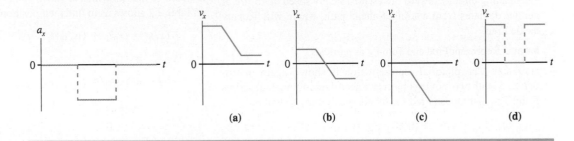

2.5 Free Fall

The motion of an object moving under the influence of gravity only, and no other forces, is called **free fall.** Strictly speaking, free fall occurs only in a vacuum, where there is no air resistance. Fortunately, the effect of air resistance is small for "heavy objects," so we'll make only a very slight error in treating these objects *as if* they were in free fall. For very light objects, such as a feather, or for objects that fall through very large distances and gain very high speeds, the effect of air resistance is *not* negligible. Motion with air resistance is a problem we will study in Chapter 6. Until then, we will restrict our attention to "heavy objects" and will make the reasonable assumption that falling objects are in free fall.

The motion of falling objects has interested scientists since antiquity, but Galileo, in the 17th century, was the first to make detailed measurements. The story of Galileo dropping different weights from the leaning bell tower at the cathedral in Pisa is well known, although historians cannot confirm its truth. But bell towers were common in the Italy of Galileo's day, so he had ample opportunity to make the measurements and observations that he describes in his writings.

Careful observations show that falling objects *don't* "hit the ground" at the same time. There are slight differences in the arrival times, but Galileo correctly identified these differences as due to air resistance. He then imagined an idealized situation of motion in a vacuum. In doing so, Galileo developed a *model* of motion—motion in the absence of air resistance—that could only be approximated by any real object. It was Galileo's innovative use of experiments, models, and mathematics that made him the first "modern" scientist.

Galileo's discovery can be summarized as follows:

- Two objects dropped from the same height will, if air resistance can be neglected, hit the ground at the same time and with the same speed.
- Consequently, **any two objects in free fall, regardless of their mass, have the same acceleration** $\vec{a}_{\text{free fall}}$. This is an especially important conclusion.

FIGURE 2.29a shows the motion diagram of an object that was released from rest and falls freely. **FIGURE 2.29b** shows the object's velocity graph. The motion diagram and graph are identical for a falling pebble and a falling boulder. The fact that the velocity graph is a straight line tells us the motion is one of uniform acceleration, and $a_{\text{free fall}}$ is easily found from the slope of the graph. Careful measurements show that the value of $\vec{a}_{\text{free fall}}$ varies ever so slightly at different places on the earth, due to the slightly non-spherical shape of the earth and to the fact that the earth is rotating. A global average, at sea level, is

$$\vec{a}_{\text{free fall}} = (9.80 \text{ m/s}^2, \text{ vertically downward}) \tag{2.23}$$

For practical purposes, *vertically downward* means along a line toward the center of the earth. However, we'll learn in Chapter 13 that the rotation of the earth has a small effect on both the size and direction of $\vec{a}_{\text{free fall}}$.

The length, or magnitude, of $\vec{a}_{\text{free fall}}$ is known as the **free-fall acceleration,** and it has the special symbol g:

$$g = 9.80 \text{ m/s}^2 \text{ (free-fall acceleration)}$$

Several points about free fall are worthy of note:

- g, by definition, is *always* positive. **There will never be a problem that will use a negative value for g.** But, you say, objects fall when you release them rather than rise, so how can g be positive?
- g is *not* the acceleration $a_{\text{free fall}}$, but simply its magnitude. Because we've chosen the y-axis to point vertically up, the downward acceleration vector $\vec{a}_{\text{free fall}}$ has the one-dimensional acceleration

$$a_y = a_{\text{free fall}} = -g \tag{2.24}$$

It is a_y that is negative, not g.
- Because free fall is motion with constant acceleration, we can use the kinematic equations of Table 2.2 with the acceleration being that of free fall, $a_y = -g$.
- g is not called "gravity." Gravity is a force, not an acceleration. The symbol g recognizes the influence of gravity, but g is *the free-fall acceleration.*
- $g = 9.80 \text{ m/s}^2$ only on earth. Other planets have different values of g. You will learn in Chapter 13 how to determine g for other planets.

NOTE ▶ Despite the name, free fall is not restricted to objects that are literally falling. Any object moving under the influence of gravity only, and no other forces, is in free fall. This includes objects falling straight down, objects that have been tossed or shot straight up, and projectile motion. This chapter considers only objects that move up and down along a vertical line; projectile motion will be studied in Chapter 4. ◀

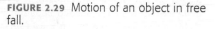
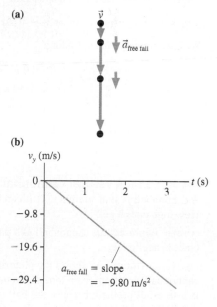

In the absence of air resistance, any two objects fall at the same rate and hit the ground at the same time. The apple and feather seen here are falling in a vacuum.

FIGURE 2.29 Motion of an object in free fall.

(a)

$\vec{v}$

$\vec{a}_{\text{free fall}}$

(b)

v_y (m/s)

$a_{\text{free fall}} = \text{slope}$
$= -9.80 \text{ m/s}^2$

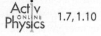

Activ Physics   1.7, 1.10

EXAMPLE 2.15 **A falling rock**

A rock is released from rest at the top of a 100-m-tall building. How long does the rock take to fall to the ground, and what is its impact velocity?

MODEL Represent the rock as a particle. Assume air resistance is negligible.

VISUALIZE **FIGURE 2.30** shows the pictorial representation. We have placed the origin at the ground, which makes $y_0 = 100$ m. Although the rock falls 100 m, it is important to notice that the *displacement* is $\Delta y = y_1 - y_0 = -100$ m.

FIGURE 2.30 Pictorial representation of a falling rock.

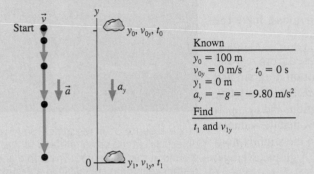

Known
$y_0 = 100$ m
$v_{0y} = 0$ m/s $t_0 = 0$ s
$y_1 = 0$ m
$a_y = -g = -9.80$ m/s^2

Find
t_1 and v_{1y}

SOLVE Free fall is motion with the specific constant acceleration $a_y = -g$. The first question involves a relation between time and distance, so only the second equation in Table 2.2 is relevant. Using $v_{0y} = 0$ m/s and $t_0 = 0$ s, we find

$$y_1 = y_0 + v_{0y}\Delta t + \tfrac{1}{2}a_y\Delta t^2 = y_0 + v_{0y}\Delta t - \tfrac{1}{2}g\Delta t^2 = y_0 - \tfrac{1}{2}gt_1^2$$

We can now solve for t_1, finding:

$$t_1 = \sqrt{\frac{2(y_0 - y_1)}{g}} = \sqrt{\frac{2(100\text{ m} - 0\text{ m})}{9.80\text{ m/s}^2}} = \pm 4.52\text{ s}$$

The $\pm$ sign indicates that there are two mathematical solutions; therefore we have to use physical reasoning to choose between them. A negative t_1 would refer to a time before we dropped the rock, so we select the positive root: $t_1 = 4.52$ s.

Now that we know the fall time, we can use the first kinematic equation to find v_{1y}:

$$v_{1y} = v_{0y} - g\,\Delta t = -gt_1 = -(9.80\text{ m/s}^2)(4.52\text{ s})$$
$$= -44.3\text{ m/s}$$

Alternatively, we could work directly from the third kinematic equation:

$$v_{1y} = \sqrt{v_{0y}{}^2 - 2g\,\Delta y} = \sqrt{-2g(y_1 - y_0)}$$
$$= \sqrt{-2(9.80\text{ m/s}^2)(0\text{ m} - 100\text{ m})} = \pm 44.3\text{ m/s}$$

This method is useful if you don't know Δt. However, we must again choose the correct sign of the square root. Because the velocity vector points downward, the sign of v_y has to be negative. Thus $v_{1y} = -44.3$ m/s. The importance of careful attention to the signs cannot be overemphasized!

A common error would be to say "The rock fell 100 m, so $\Delta y = 100$ m." This would have you trying to take the square root of a negative number. As noted above, Δy is not a distance. It is a *displacement*, with a carefully defined meaning of $y_f - y_i$. In this case, $\Delta y = y_1 - y_0 = -100$ m.

ASSESS Are the answers reasonable? Well, 100 m is about 300 feet, which is about the height of a 30-floor building. How long does it take something to fall 30 floors? Four or five seconds seems pretty reasonable. How fast would it be going at the bottom? Using 1 m/s $\approx$ 2 mph, we find that 44.3 m/s $\approx$ 90 mph. That also seems pretty reasonable after falling 30 floors. Had we misplaced a decimal point, though, and found 443 m/s, we would be suspicious when we converted this to $\approx$ 900 mph! The answers all seem reasonable.

EXAMPLE 2.16 **A vertical cannonball**

A cannonball is shot straight up with an initial speed of 100 m/s. How high does it go?

MODEL Represent the cannonball as a particle. Assume air resistance is negligible.

VISUALIZE **FIGURE 2.31** shows the pictorial representation for the cannonball's motion. Even though the ball was shot upward, this is a free-fall problem because the ball (after being launched) is moving under the influence of gravity *only*. A critical aspect of the problem is knowing where it ends. How do we put "how high" into symbols? The clue is that the very top point of the trajectory is a *turning point*. Recall that the instantaneous velocity at a turning point is $v = 0$. Thus we can characterize the "top" of the trajectory as the point where $v_{1y} = 0$ m/s. This was not explicitly stated but is part of our interpretation of the problem.

FIGURE 2.31 Pictorial representation for Example 2.16.

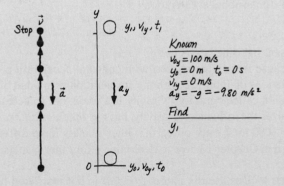

Known
$v_{0y} = 100$ m/s
$y_0 = 0$ m $t_0 = 0$ s
$v_{1y} = 0$ m/s
$a_y = -g = -9.80$ m/s^2

Find
y_1

SOLVE We are looking for a relationship between distance and velocity, without knowing the time interval. This relationship is described mathematically by the third kinematic equation in Table 2.2. Using $y_0 = 0$ m and $v_{1y} = 0$ m/s, we have

$$v_{1y}^2 = 0 = v_{0y}^2 - 2g\Delta y = v_{0y}^2 - 2gy_1$$

Solving for y_1, we find that the cannonball reaches a height

$$y_1 = \frac{v_{0y}^2}{2g} = \frac{(100 \text{ m/s})^2}{2(9.80 \text{ m/s}^2)} = 510 \text{ m}$$

ASSESS Is this answer reasonable? A speed of 100 m/s is $\approx$ 200 mph—that's pretty fast! The calculated height is 510 m $\approx$ 1500 ft. In Example 2.15 we found that an object dropped from 100 m is going 44 m/s when it hits the ground, so it seems reasonable that an object shot upward at 100 m/s will go significantly higher than 100 m. While we cannot say that 510 m is necessarily better than 400 m or 600 m, we can say that it is not unreasonable. The point of the assessment is not to prove that the answer *has* to be right, but to find answers that are obviously wrong.

2.6 Motion on an Inclined Plane

A problem closely related to free fall is that of motion down a straight, but frictionless, inclined plane, such as a skier going down a slope on frictionless snow. **FIGURE 2.32a** shows an object sliding down a frictionless, inclined plane tilted at angle θ. The object's motion is constrained to be parallel to the surface. What is the object's acceleration? Although we're not yet prepared to give a rigorous derivation, we can deduce the acceleration with a plausibility argument.

FIGURE 2.32b shows the free-fall acceleration $\vec{a}_{\text{free fall}}$ the object would have if the incline suddenly vanished. The free-fall acceleration points straight down. This vector can be broken into two pieces: a vector $\vec{a}_\parallel$ that is parallel to the incline and a vector $\vec{a}_\perp$ that is perpendicular to the incline. The vector addition rules of Chapter 1 tell us that $\vec{a}_{\text{free fall}} = \vec{a}_\parallel + \vec{a}_\perp$.

The motion diagram shows that the object's actual acceleration is parallel to the incline. The surface of the incline somehow "blocks" $\vec{a}_\perp$, through a process we will examine in Chapter 6, but $\vec{a}_\parallel$ is unhindered. It is this piece of $\vec{a}_{\text{free fall}}$, parallel to the incline, that accelerates the object.

Figure 2.32b shows that the three vectors form a right triangle with angle θ at the bottom. By definition, the length, or magnitude, of $\vec{a}_{\text{free fall}}$ is g. Vector $\vec{a}_\parallel$ is opposite angle θ, so the length, or magnitude, of $\vec{a}_\parallel$ must be $g\sin\theta$. Consequently, the one-dimensional acceleration along the incline is

$$a_s = \pm g\sin\theta \tag{2.25}$$

The correct sign depends on the direction in which the ramp is tilted, as the following examples will illustrate. We'll use Newton's laws of motion in Chapter 6 to verify Equation 2.25.

Equation 2.25 makes sense. Suppose the plane is perfectly horizontal. If you place an object on a horizontal surface, you expect it to stay at rest with no acceleration. Equation 2.25 gives $a_s = 0$ when $\theta = 0°$, in agreement with our expectations. Now suppose you tilt the plane until it becomes vertical, at $\theta = 90°$. Without friction, an object would simply fall, in free fall, parallel to the vertical surface. Equation 2.25 gives $a_s = -g = a_{\text{free fall}}$ when $\theta = 90°$, again in agreement with our expectations. We see that Equation 2.25 gives the correct result in these *limiting cases*.

FIGURE 2.32 Acceleration on an inclined plane.

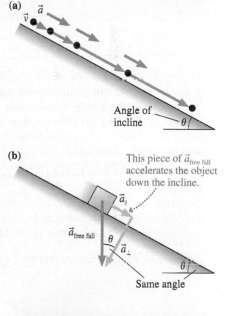

Skiing is an example of motion on an inclined plane.

EXAMPLE 2.17 Skiing down an incline
A skier's speed at the bottom of a 100-m-long, frictionless, snow-covered slope is 20 m/s. What is the angle of the slope?

MODEL Represent the skier as a particle. Assume that air resistance is negligible. Assume that the slope is a straight line.

VISUALIZE FIGURE 2.33 on the next page shows the pictorial representation of the skier. Notice that we've chosen the x-axis to be parallel to the motion. Straight-line motion is almost always easier to analyze if the motion is parallel to a coordinate axis.

Continued

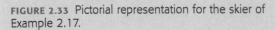

FIGURE 2.33 Pictorial representation for the skier of Example 2.17.

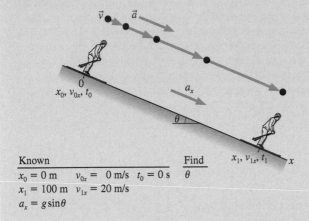

Known			Find
$x_0 = 0$ m	$v_{0x} = 0$ m/s	$t_0 = 0$ s	θ
$x_1 = 100$ m	$v_{1x} = 20$ m/s		
$a_x = g \sin\theta$			

SOLVE The motion diagram shows that the acceleration vector points in the positive x-direction. Thus the one-dimensional acceleration is $a_x = +g \sin\theta$. This is constant-acceleration motion. The third kinematic equation from Table 2.2 is

$$v_{1x}^2 = v_{0x}^2 + 2a_x\Delta x = 2g \sin\theta\Delta x$$

where we used $v_{0x} = 0$ m/s. Solving for $\sin\theta$, we find

$$\sin\theta = \frac{v_{1x}^2}{2g\Delta x} = \frac{(20 \text{ m/s})^2}{2(9.80 \text{ m/s}^2)(100 \text{ m})} = 0.204$$

Thus

$$\theta = \sin^{-1}(0.204) = 12°$$

ASSESS A 100-m-long slope and a speed of 20 m/s ≈ 40 mph are fairly typical parameters for skiing. A 1° angle or an 80° angle would be unrealistic, but 12° seems plausible.

EXAMPLE 2.18 **At the amusement park**

An amusement park ride shoots a car up a frictionless track inclined at 30°. The car rolls up, then rolls back down. If the height of the track is 20 m, what is the maximum allowable speed with which the car can start?

MODEL Represent the car as a particle. Assume air resistance is negligible.

VISUALIZE FIGURE 2.34 shows the pictorial representation of the car. We've chosen the x-axis to be parallel to the motion. The problem starts as the car is shot up the incline, and it ends when

FIGURE 2.34 Pictorial representation for the car of Example 2.18.

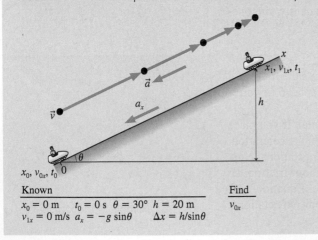

Known			Find
$x_0 = 0$ m	$t_0 = 0$ s	$\theta = 30°$ $h = 20$ m	v_{0x}
$v_{1x} = 0$ m/s	$a_x = -g \sin\theta$	$\Delta x = h/\sin\theta$	

the car reaches its highest point. The highest point is a turning point, so $v_{1x} = 0$ m/s. The motion diagram shows that the acceleration vector points in the negative x-direction, so we need the minus sign: $a_x = -g \sin\theta$. The *maximum* starting speed is that at which the car goes to the very top of the ramp, a height of 20 m.

SOLVE The maximum possible displacement Δx_{max} is related to the height h by

$$\Delta x_{max} = x_1 - x_0 = \frac{h}{\sin 30°} = \frac{20 \text{ m}}{\sin 30°} = 40 \text{ m}$$

The initial speed v_{0x} that allows the car to travel this distance is found from

$$v_{1x}^2 = 0 = v_{0x}^2 + 2a_x\Delta x = v_{0x}^2 - 2g \sin\theta\Delta x$$

$$v_{0x} = \sqrt{2g \sin 30°\Delta x} = \sqrt{2(9.80 \text{ m/s}^2)(0.500)(40 \text{ m})}$$

$$= 20 \text{ m/s}$$

This is the maximum speed, because a car starting any faster will run off the top.

ASSESS 20 m ≈ 60 feet and 20 m/s ≈ 40 mph. It seems plausible that a car would need to be going this fast to gain 60 feet of elevation rolling up a ramp. Be sure you understand why the sign of a_x is negative here but positive in Example 2.17.

Thinking Graphically

Kinematics is the language of motion. We will spend the entire rest of this course studying moving objects, from baseballs to electrons, and the concepts we have developed in this chapter will be used extensively. One of the most important ideas, summarized in Tactics Box 2.2, has been that the relationships between position, velocity, and acceleration can be expressed graphically.

Interpreting graphical representations of motion   (MP)

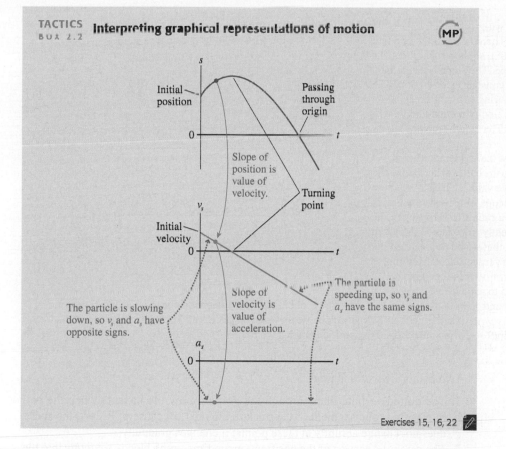

Initial position

Passing through origin

Slope of position is value of velocity.

Turning point

Initial velocity

The particle is slowing down, so v_s and a_s have opposite signs.

Slope of velocity is value of acceleration.

The particle is speeding up, so v_s and a_s have the same signs.

Exercises 15, 16, 22

A good way to solidify your understanding of motion graphs is to consider the problem of a hard, smooth ball rolling on a smooth track. The track is made up of several straight segments connected together. Each segment may be either horizontal or inclined. Your task is to analyze the ball's motion graphically. This will require you to reason about, rather than calculate, the relationships between s, v_s, and a_s.

There are two variations to this type of problem. In the first, you are given a picture of a track and the initial condition of the ball. The problem is then to draw graphs of s, v_s, and a_s. In the second, you are given the graphs, and the problem is to deduce the shape of the track on which the ball is rolling.

There are a small number of rules to follow in each of these problems:

1. Assume that the ball passes smoothly from one segment of the track to the next, with no loss of speed and without ever leaving the track.
2. The position, velocity, and acceleration graphs should be stacked vertically. They should each have the same horizontal scale so that a vertical line drawn through all three connects points describing the same instant of time.
3. The graphs have no numbers, but they should show the correct *relationships*. For example, if the velocity is greater during the first part of the motion than during the second part, then the position graph should be steeper in the first part than in the second.
4. The position s is the position measured *along* the track. Similarly, v_s and a_s are the velocity and acceleration parallel to the track.

EXAMPLE 2.19 From track to graphs
Draw position, velocity, and acceleration graphs for the ball on the frictionless track of **FIGURE 2.35**.

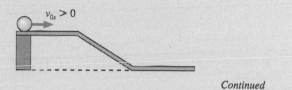

$v_{0s} > 0$

FIGURE 2.35 A ball rolling along a track.

Continued

VISUALIZE It is often easiest to begin with the velocity. Here the ball starts with an initial velocity v_{0s}. There is no acceleration on the horizontal surface ($a_s = 0$ if $\theta = 0°$), so the velocity remains constant until the ball reaches the slope. The slope is an inclined plane that, as we have learned, has constant acceleration. The velocity increases linearly with time during constant-acceleration motion. The ball returns to constant-velocity motion after reaching the bottom horizontal segment. The middle graph of **FIGURE 2.36** shows the velocity.

We have enough information to draw the acceleration graph. We noted that the acceleration is zero while the ball is on the horizontal segments, and a_s has a constant positive value on the slope. These accelerations are consistent with the slope of the velocity graph: zero slope, then positive slope, then a return to zero slope. The acceleration cannot *really* change instantly from zero to a nonzero value, but the change can be so quick that we do not see it on the time scale of the graph. That is what the vertical dotted lines imply.

Finally, we need to find the position-versus-time graph. You might want to refer back to Figure 2.35 to review how the position graph looks for constant-velocity and constant-acceleration motion. The position increases linearly with time during the first segment at constant velocity. It also does so during the third seg-

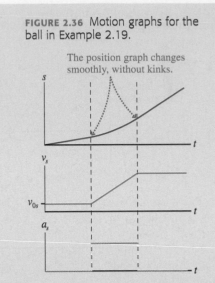

FIGURE 2.36 Motion graphs for the ball in Example 2.19.

ment of motion, but with a steeper slope to indicate a faster velocity. In between, while the acceleration is nonzero but constant, the position graph has a *parabolic* shape.

Two points are worth noting:

1. The dotted vertical lines through the graphs show the instants when the ball moves from one segment of the track to the next. Because of Rule 1, the speed does not change abruptly at these points; it changes gradually.
2. The parabolic section of the position-versus-time graph blends *smoothly* into the straight lines on either side. This is a consequence of Rule 1. An abrupt change of slope (a "kink") would indicate an abrupt change in velocity and would violate Rule 1.

EXAMPLE 2.20 From graphs to track

FIGURE 2.37 shows a set of motion graphs for a ball moving on a track. Draw a picture of the track and describe the ball's initial condition. Each segment of the track is *straight,* but the segments may be tilted.

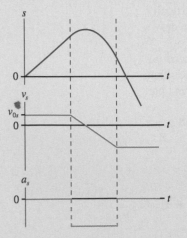

FIGURE 2.37 Motion graphs of a ball rolling on a track of unknown shape.

VISUALIZE Let's begin by examining the velocity graph. The ball starts with initial velocity $v_{0s} > 0$ and maintains this velocity for

awhile; there's no acceleration. Thus the ball must start out rolling to the right on a horizontal track. At the end of the motion, the ball is again rolling on a horizontal track (no acceleration, constant velocity), but it's rolling to the *left* because v_s is negative. Further, the final speed ($|v_s|$) is greater than the initial speed. The middle section of the graph shows us what happens. The ball starts slowing with constant acceleration (rolling uphill), reaches a turning point (s is maximum, $v_s = 0$), then speeds up in the opposite direction (rolling downhill). This is still a negative acceleration because the ball is speeding up in the negative s-direction. It must roll farther downhill than it had rolled uphill before reaching a horizontal section of track. **FIGURE 2.38** shows the track and the initial conditions that are responsible for the graphs of Figure 2.37.

FIGURE 2.38 Track responsible for the motion graphs of Figure 2.37.

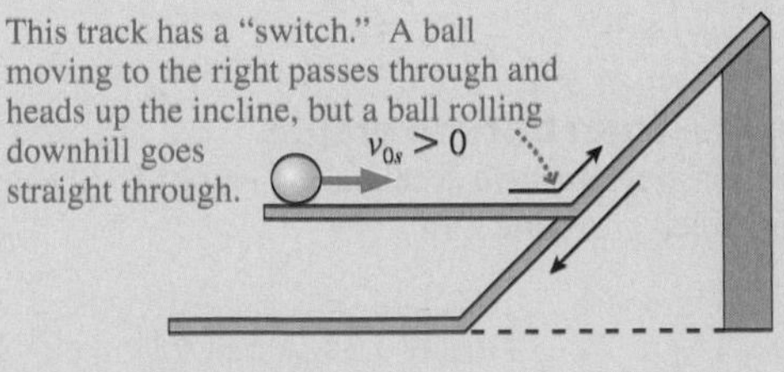

This track has a "switch." A ball moving to the right passes through and heads up the incline, but a ball rolling downhill goes straight through. $v_{0s} > 0$

The ball rolls up the ramp, then back down. Which is the correct acceleration graph?

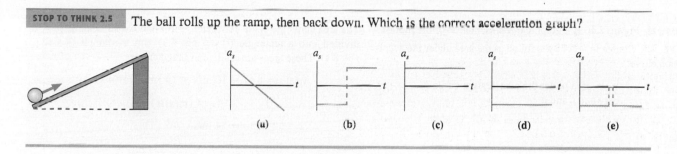

(a)   (b)   (c)   (d)   (e)

2.7 Instantaneous Acceleration

FIGURE 2.39 shows a velocity that increases with time, reaches a maximum, then decreases. This is *not* uniformly accelerated motion. Instead, the acceleration is changing with time.

We can define an instantaneous acceleration in much the same way that we defined the instantaneous velocity. The instantaneous velocity was found to be the limit of the average velocity as the time interval $\Delta t \rightarrow 0$. Graphically, the instantaneous velocity at time t is the slope of the position-versus-time graph at that time. By analogy: The **instantaneous acceleration** a_s at a specific instant of time t is the slope of the line that is tangent to the velocity-versus-time curve at time t. Mathematically, this is

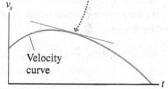

FIGURE 2.39 Motion with nonuniform acceleration.

The instantaneous acceleration at time t is the slope of the line tangent to the velocity curve.

$$a_s \equiv \lim_{\Delta t \rightarrow 0} \frac{\Delta v_s}{\Delta t} = \frac{dv_s}{dt} \qquad \text{(instantaneous acceleration)} \qquad (2.26)$$

The instantaneous acceleration is the derivative (i.e., the rate of change) of the velocity.

The reverse problem—to find the velocity v_s if we know the acceleration a_s at all instants of time—is also important. When we wanted to find the position from the velocity, we took a velocity curve, divided it into N steps, found that the displacement Δs_k during step k was the area $(v_s)_k \Delta t$ of a small rectangle, then added all the steps (i.e., integrated) to find s_f.

We can do the same with acceleration. An acceleration curve can be divided into N very narrow steps so that during each step the acceleration is essentially constant. During step k, the velocity changes by $\Delta(v_s)_k = (a_s)_k \Delta t$. This is the area of the small rectangle under the step. The total velocity change between t_i and t_f is found by adding all the small $\Delta(v_s)_k$. In the limit $\Delta t \rightarrow 0$, we have

$$v_{fs} = v_{is} + \lim_{\Delta t \rightarrow 0} \sum_{k=1}^{N} (a_s)_k \Delta t = v_{is} + \int_{t_i}^{t_f} a_s \, dt \qquad (2.27)$$

This mathematical statement has a graphical interpretation analogous to Equation 2.11. In this case:

$$v_{fs} = v_{is} + \text{area under the acceleration curve } a_s \text{ between } t_i \text{ and } t_f \qquad (2.28)$$

The constant-acceleration equation $v_{fs} = v_{is} + a_s\Delta t$ is a special example of Equation 2.28. If you look back at Figure 2.24a you will see that the quantity $a_s\Delta t$ is the rectangular area under the horizontal acceleration curve.

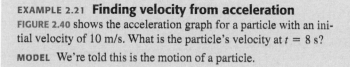

EXAMPLE 2.21 Finding velocity from acceleration
FIGURE 2.40 shows the acceleration graph for a particle with an initial velocity of 10 m/s. What is the particle's velocity at $t = 8$ s?

MODEL We're told this is the motion of a particle.

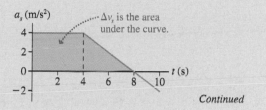

FIGURE 2.40 Acceleration graph for Example 2.21.

Continued

VISUALIZE Figure 2.40 is a graphical representation of the motion.

SOLVE The change in velocity is found as the area under the acceleration curve:

$$v_{fs} = v_{is} + \text{area under the acceleration curve } a_s$$
$$\text{between } t_i \text{ and } t_f$$

The area under the curve between $t_i = 0$ s and $t_f = 8$ s can be subdivided into a rectangle ($0\,\text{s} \leq t \leq 4\,\text{s}$) and a triangle ($4\,\text{s} \leq t \leq 8\,\text{s}$). These areas are easily computed. Thus

$$v_s(\text{at } t = 8\,\text{s}) = 10\,\text{m/s} + (4\,\text{(m/s)/s})(4\,\text{s})$$
$$+ \tfrac{1}{2}(4\,\text{(m/s)/s})(4\,\text{s})$$
$$= 34\,\text{m/s}$$

EXAMPLE 2.22 A nonuniform acceleration

FIGURE 2.41a shows the velocity-versus-time graph for a particle whose velocity is given by $v_s = [10 - (t - 5)^2]$ m/s, where t is in s.

a. Find an expression for the particle's acceleration a_s and draw the acceleration-versus-time graph.

b. Describe the motion.

MODEL We're told that this is a particle.

VISUALIZE The figure shows the velocity graph. It is a parabola centered at $t = 5$ s with an apex $v_{\text{max}} = 10$ m/s. The slope of v_s is positive but decreasing in magnitude for $t < 5$ s. The slope is zero at $t = 5$ s, and it is negative and increasing in magnitude for $t > 5$ s. Thus the acceleration graph should start positive, decrease steadily, pass through zero at $t = 5$ s, then become increasingly negative.

SOLVE a. We can find an expression for a_s by taking the derivative of v_s. First, expand the square to give

$$v_s = (-t^2 + 10t - 15) \text{ m/s}$$

Then use the derivative rule (Equation 2.5) to find

$$a_s = \frac{dv_s}{dt} = (-2t + 10) \text{ m/s}^2$$

where t is in s. This is a linear equation that is graphed in **FIGURE 2.41b**. The graph meets our expectations.

b. This is a complex motion. The particle starts out moving to the left ($v_s < 0$) at 15 m/s. The positive acceleration causes the

FIGURE 2.41 Velocity and acceleration graphs for Example 2.22.

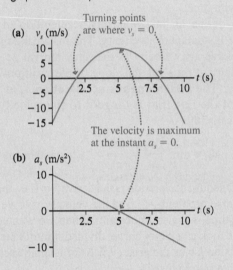

(a) Turning points are where $v_s = 0$.

The velocity is maximum at the instant $a_s = 0$.

speed to decrease (slowing down because v_s and a_s have opposite signs) until the particle reaches a turning point ($v_s = 0$) just before $t = 2$ s. The particle then moves to the right ($v_s > 0$) and speeds up until reaching maximum speed at $t = 5$ s. From $t = 5$ s to just after $t = 8$ s, the particle is still moving to the right ($v_s > 0$) but slowing down. Another turning point occurs just after $t = 8$ s. Then the particle moves back to the left and gains speed as the negative a_s makes the velocity ever more negative.

STOP TO THINK 2.6   Rank in order, from most positive to least positive, the accelerations at points A to C.

a. $a_A > a_B > a_C$
b. $a_C > a_A > a_B$
c. $a_C > a_B > a_A$
d. $a_B > a_A > a_C$

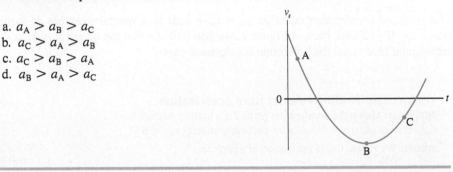

SUMMARY

The goal of Chapter 2 has been to learn how to solve problems about motion in a straight line.

General Principles

Kinematics describes motion in terms of position, velocity, and acceleration.

General kinematic relationships are given **mathematically** by:

Instantaneous velocity $v_s = ds/dt$ = slope of position graph

Instantaneous acceleration $a_s = dv_s/dt$ = slope of velocity graph

Final position $s_f = s_i + \displaystyle\int_{t_i}^{t_f} v_s\, dt = s_i + \begin{cases} \text{area under the velocity} \\ \text{curve from } t_i \text{ to } t_f \end{cases}$

Final velocity $v_{fs} = v_{is} + \displaystyle\int_{t_i}^{t_f} a_s\, dt = v_{is} + \begin{cases} \text{area under the acceleration} \\ \text{curve from } t_i \text{ to } t_f \end{cases}$

Motion with constant acceleration is uniformly accelerated motion. The kinematic equations are:

$$v_{fs} = v_{is} + a_s \Delta t$$
$$s_f = s_i + v_{is}\Delta t + \tfrac{1}{2} a_s (\Delta t)^2$$
$$v_{fs}^2 = v_{is}^2 + 2 a_s \Delta s$$

Uniform motion is motion with constant velocity and zero acceleration:

$$s_f = s_i + v_s \Delta t$$

Important Concepts

Position, velocity, and acceleration are related **graphically.**

- The slope of the position-versus-time graph is the value on the velocity graph.

- The slope of the velocity graph is the value on the acceleration graph.

- s is a maximum or minimum at a turning point, and $v_s = 0$.

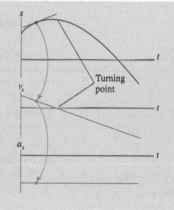

- Displacement is the area under the velocity curve.

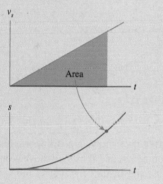

Applications

The **sign of** v_s indicates the direction of motion.

- $v_s > 0$ is motion to the right or up.

- $v_s < 0$ is motion to the left or down.

The **sign of** a_s indicates which way $\vec{a}$ points, *not* whether the object is speeding up or slowing down.

- $a_s > 0$ if $\vec{a}$ points to the right or up.

- $a_s < 0$ if $\vec{a}$ points to the left or down.

- The direction of $\vec{a}$ is found with a motion diagram.

An object is **speeding up** if and only if v_s and a_s have the same sign. An object is **slowing down** if and only if v_s and a_s have opposite signs.

Free fall is constant-acceleration motion with

$$a_y = -g = -9.80 \text{ m/s}^2$$

Motion on an inclined plane has $a_s = \pm g \sin\theta$. The sign depends on the direction of the tilt.

Terms and Notation

kinematics	initial position, s_i	turning point	free fall
uniform motion	final position, s_f	average acceleration, a_{avg}	free-fall acceleration, g
speed, v	instantaneous velocity, v_s	uniformly accelerated motion	instantaneous acceleration, a_s

MP For homework assigned on MasteringPhysics, go to www.masteringphysics.com

Problem difficulty is labeled as | (straightforward) to ||| (challenging).

Problems labeled ✎ can be done on a Dynamics Worksheet.

Problems labeled ▪ integrate significant material from earlier chapters.

CONCEPTUAL QUESTIONS

For Questions 1 through 3, interpret the position graph given in each figure by writing a very short "story" of what is happening. Be creative! Have characters and situations! Simply saying that "a car moves 100 meters to the right" doesn't qualify as a story. Your stories should make *specific reference* to information you obtain from the graph, such as distance moved or time elapsed.

1.

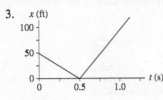

FIGURE Q2.1

2.

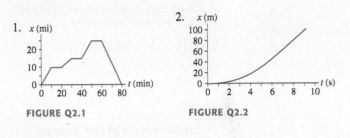

FIGURE Q2.2

3.

FIGURE Q2.3

4. FIGURE Q2.4 shows a position-versus-time graph for the motion of objects A and B as they move along the same axis.
   a. At the instant $t = 1$ s, is the speed of A greater than, less than, or equal to the speed of B? Explain.
   b. Do objects A and B ever have the *same* speed? If so, at what time or times? Explain.

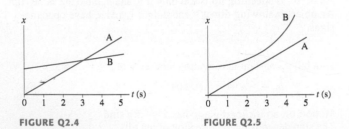

FIGURE Q2.4

FIGURE Q2.5

5. FIGURE Q2.5 shows a position-versus-time graph for the motion of objects A and B as they move along the same axis.
   a. At the instant $t = 1$ s, is the speed of A greater than, less than, or equal to the speed of B? Explain.
   b. Do objects A and B ever have the *same* speed? If so, at what time or times? Explain.

6. FIGURE Q2.6 shows the position-versus-time graph for a moving object. At which lettered point or points:
   a. Is the object *moving* the slowest?
   b. Is the object moving the fastest?
   c. Is the object at rest?
   d. Is the object moving to the left?

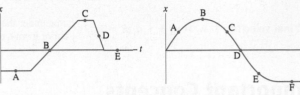

FIGURE Q2.6

FIGURE Q2.7

7. FIGURE Q2.7 shows the position-versus-time graph for a moving object. At which lettered point or points:
   a. Is the object moving the fastest?
   b. Is the object moving to the left?
   c. Is the object speeding up?
   d. Is the object turning around?
8. FIGURE Q2.8 shows six frames from the motion diagrams of two moving cars, A and B.
   a. Do the two cars ever have the same position at one instant of time? If so, in which frame number (or numbers)?
   b. Do the two cars ever have the same velocity at one instant of time? If so, between which two frames?

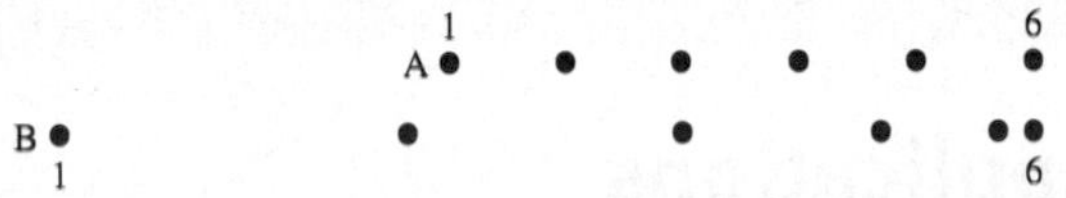

FIGURE Q2.8

9. You're driving along the highway at a steady speed of 60 mph when another car decides to pass you. At the moment when the front of his car is exactly even with the front of your car, and you turn your head to smile at him, do the two cars have equal velocities? Explain.
10. A car is traveling north. Can its acceleration vector ever point south? Explain.
11. (a) Give an example of a vertical motion with a positive velocity and a negative acceleration. (b) Give an example of a vertical motion with a negative velocity and a negative acceleration.
12. A ball is thrown straight up into the air. At each of the following instants, is the magnitude of the ball's acceleration greater than g, equal to g, less than g, or 0? Explain.
    a. Just after leaving your hand.
    b. At the very top (maximum height).
    c. Just before hitting the ground.

13. A rock is *thrown* (not dropped) straight down from a bridge into the river below. At each of the following instants, is the magnitude of the rock's acceleration greater than g, equal to g, less than g, or 0? Explain.
    a. Immediately after being released.
    b. Immediately before hitting the water.

14. Drop a rubber ball or a tennis ball from a height of about 25 cm ($\approx$ 1 ft) and watch carefully as it bounces. Draw a position graph, a velocity graph, and an acceleration graph showing the ball's motion from the instant you drop it until it returns to its maximum height. Stack your three graphs vertically so that the time axes are aligned with each other. Pay particular attention to the time when the ball is in contact with the ground. This is a short interval of time, but it's not zero.

EXERCISES AND PROBLEMS

Exercises

Section 2.1 Uniform Motion

1. | A car starts at the origin and moves with velocity $\vec{v} =$ (10 m/s, northeast). How far from the origin will the car be after traveling for 45 s?

2. || Larry leaves home at 9:05 and runs at constant speed to the lamppost. He reaches the lamppost at 9:07, immediately turns, and runs to the tree. Larry arrives at the tree at 9:10.
    a. What is Larry's average velocity, in yards/min, during each of these two intervals.
    b. What is Larry's average velocity for the entire run?

FIGURE EX2.2

3. || Alan leaves Los Angeles at 8:00 a.m. to drive to San Francisco, 400 mi away. He travels at a steady 50 mph. Beth leaves Los Angeles at 9:00 a.m. and drives a steady 60 mph.
    a. Who gets to San Francisco first?
    b. How long does the first to arrive have to wait for the second?

4. || Julie drives 100 mi to Grandmother's house. On the way to Grandmother's, Julie drives half the distance at 40 mph and half the distance at 60 mph. On her return trip, she drives half the time at 40 mph and half the time at 60 mph.
    a. What is Julie's average speed on the way to Grandmother's house?
    b. What is her average speed on the return trip?

5. | A bicyclist has the position-versus-time graph shown. What is the bicyclist's velocity at $t = 10$ s, at $t = 25$ s, and at $t = 35$ s?

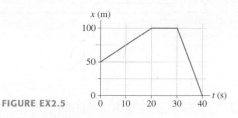

FIGURE EX2.5

Section 2.2 Instantaneous Velocity

Section 2.3 Finding Position from Velocity

6. | FIGURE EX2.6 shows the position graph of a particle.
    a. Draw the particle's velocity graph for the interval $0\text{ s} \le t \le 4\text{ s}$.
    b. Does this particle have a turning point or points? If so, at what time or times?

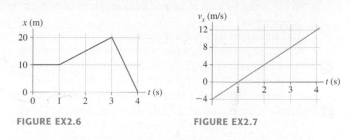

FIGURE EX2.6   FIGURE EX2.7

7. | A particle starts from $x_0 = 10$ m at $t_0 = 0$ s and moves with the velocity graph shown in FIGURE EX2.7.
    a. Does this particle have a turning point? If so, at what time?
    b. What is the object's position at $t = 2$ s, 3 s, and 4 s?

Section 2.4 Motion with Constant Acceleration

8. | FIGURE EX2.8 shows the velocity graph of a particle. Draw the particle's acceleration graph for the interval $0\text{ s} \le t \le 4\text{ s}$. Give both axes an appropriate numerical scale.

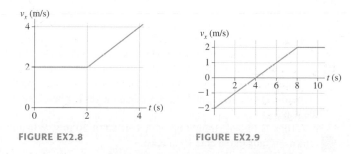

FIGURE EX2.8   FIGURE EX2.9

9. | FIGURE EX2.9 shows the velocity graph of a train that starts from the origin at $t = 0$ s.
    a. Find the acceleration of the train at $t = 3.0$ s.
    b. Draw position and acceleration graphs for the train.

10. | FIGURE EX2.10 shows the velocity graph of a particle moving along the x-axis. Its initial position is $x_0 = 2.0$ m at $t_0 = 0$ s. At $t = 2.0$ s, what are the particle's (a) position, (b) velocity, and (c) acceleration?

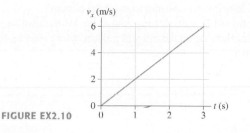

FIGURE EX2.10

11. | **FIGURE EX2.11** shows the velocity-versus-time graph is shown for a particle moving along the x-axis. Its initial position is $x_0 = 2.0$ m at $t_0 = 0$ s.

    a. What are the particle's position, velocity, and acceleration at $t = 1.0$ s?

    b. What are the particle's position, velocity, and acceleration at $t = 3.0$ s?

    FIGURE EX2.11

12. || A jet plane is cruising at 300 m/s when suddenly the pilot turns the engines up to full throttle. After traveling 4.0 km, the jet is moving with a speed of 400 m/s.

    a. What is the jet's acceleration, assuming it to be a constant acceleration?

    b. Is your answer reasonable? Explain.

13. || A speed skater moving across frictionless ice at 8.0 m/s hits a 5.0-m-wide patch of rough ice. She slows steadily, then continues on at 6.0 m/s. What is her acceleration on the rough ice?

14. || A Porsche challenges a Honda to a 400 m race. Because the Porsche's acceleration of 3.5 m/s² is larger than the Honda's 3.0 m/s², the Honda gets a 50 m head start. Both cars start accelerating at the same instant. Who wins?

Section 2.5 Free Fall

15. | Ball bearings are made by letting spherical drops of molten metal fall inside a tall tower—called a *shot tower*—and solidify as they fall.

    a. If a bearing needs 4.0 s to solidify enough for impact, how high must the tower be?

    b. What is the bearing's impact velocity?

16. | A ball is thrown vertically upward with a speed of 19.6 m/s.

    a. What is the ball's velocity and its height after 1.0, 2.0, 3.0, and 4.0 s?

    b. Draw the ball's velocity-versus-time graph. Give both axes an appropriate numerical scale.

17. || A student standing on the ground throws a ball straight up. The ball leaves the student's hand with a speed of 15 m/s when the hand is 2.0 m above the ground. How long is the ball in the air before it hits the ground? (The student moves her hand out of the way.)

18. || A rock is tossed straight up with a speed of 20 m/s. When it returns, it falls into a hole 10 m deep.

    a. What is the rock's velocity as it hits the bottom of the hole?

    b. How long is the rock in the air, from the instant it is released until it hits the bottom of the hole?

Section 2.6 Motion on an Inclined Plane

19. || A skier is gliding along at 3.0 m/s on horizontal, frictionless snow. He suddenly starts down a 10° incline. His speed at the bottom is 15 m/s.

    a. What is the length of the incline?

    b. How long does it take him to reach the bottom?

20. || A car traveling at 30 m/s runs out of gas while traveling up a 20° slope. How far up the hill will it coast before starting to roll back down?

Section 2.7 Instantaneous Acceleration

21. | A particle moving along the x-axis has its position described by the function $x = (2t^2 - t + 1)$ m, where t is in s. At $t = 2$ s what are the particle's (a) position, (b) velocity, and (c) acceleration?

22. || A particle moving along the x-axis has its velocity described by the function $v_x = 2t^2$ m/s, where t is in s. Its initial position is $x_0 = 1$ m at $t_0 = 0$ s. At $t = 1$ s what are the particle's (a) position, (b) velocity, and (c) acceleration?

23. || **FIGURE EX2.23** shows the acceleration-versus-time graph of a particle moving along the x-axis. Its initial velocity is $v_{0x} = 8.0$ m/s at $t_0 = 0$ s. What is the particle's velocity at $t = 4.0$ s?

    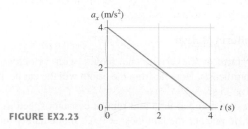

    FIGURE EX2.23

Problems

24. | **FIGURE P2.24** shows the motion diagram, made at two frames of film per second, of a ball rolling along a track. The track has a 3.0-m-long sticky section.

    a. Use the meter stick to measure the positions of the center of the ball. Place your data in a table, similar to Table 1.1, showing each position and the instant of time at which it occurred.

    b. Make a position-versus-time graph for the ball. Because you have data only at certain instants of time, your graph should consist of dots that are not connected together.

    c. What is the *change* in the ball's position from $t = 0$ s to $t = 1.0$ s?

    d. What is the *change* in the ball's position from $t = 2.0$ s to $t = 4.0$ s?

    e. What is the ball's velocity before reaching the sticky section?

    f. What is the ball's velocity after passing the sticky section?

    g. Determine the ball's acceleration on the sticky section of the track.

    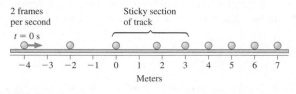

    FIGURE P2.24

25. || A particle's position on the x-axis is given by the function $x = (t^2 - 4t + 2)$ m where t is in s.

    a. Make a position-versus-time graph for the interval 0 s $\leq t \leq 5$ s. Do this by calculating and plotting x every 0.5 s from 0 s to 5 s, then drawing a smooth curve through the points.

b. Determine the particle's velocity at $t = 1.0$ s by drawing the tangent line on your graph and measuring its slope.

c. Determine the particle's velocity at $t = 1.0$ s by evaluating the derivative at that instant. Compare this to your result from part b.

d. Are there any turning points in the particle's motion? If so, at what position or positions?

e. Where is the particle when $v_x = 4.0$ m/s?

f. Draw a motion diagram for the particle.

26. ‖ Three particles move along the x-axis, each starting with $v_{0x} = 10$ m/s at $t_0 = 0$ s. The graph for A is a position-versus-time graph; the graph for B is a velocity-versus-time graph; the graph for C is an acceleration-versus-time graph. Find each particle's velocity at $t = 7.0$ s. Work with the geometry of the graphs, not with kinematic equations.

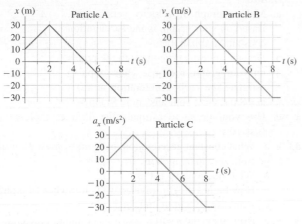

FIGURE P2.26

27. ‖ **FIGURE P2.27** shows the velocity graph for a particle having initial position $x_0 = 0$ m at $t_0 = 0$ s.

a. At what time or times is the particle found at $x = 35$ m? Work with the geometry of the graph, not with kinematic equations.

b. Draw a motion diagram for the particle.

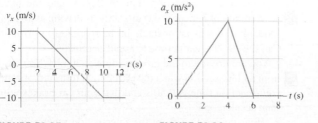

FIGURE P2.27   **FIGURE P2.28**

28. ‖ **FIGURE P2.28** shows the acceleration graph for a particle that starts from rest at $t = 0$ s. Determine the object's velocity at times $t = 0$ s, 2 s, 4 s, 6 s, and 8 s.

29. ‖ A block is suspended from a spring, pulled down, and released. The block's position-versus-time graph is shown in **FIGURE P2.29**.

a. At what times is the velocity zero? At what times is the velocity most positive? Most negative?

b. Draw a reasonable velocity-versus-time graph.

FIGURE P2.29

30. ‖ **FIGURE P2.30** shows the acceleration graph for a particle that starts from rest at $t = 0$ s.

a. Draw the particle's velocity graph over the interval 0 s $\leq t \leq 10$ s. Include an appropriate numerical scale on both axes.

b. Describe, in words, how the velocity graph would differ if the particle had an initial velocity of 2.0 m/s.

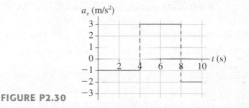

FIGURE P2.30

31. ‖ The position of a particle is given by the function $x = (2t^3 - 9t^2 + 12)$ m, where t is in s.

a. At what time or times is $v_x = 0$ m/s?

b. What are the particle's position and its acceleration at this time(s)?

32. ‖ An object starts from rest at $x = 0$ m at time $t = 0$ s. Five seconds later, at $t = 5.0$ s, the object is observed to be at $x = 40.0$ m and to have velocity $v_x = 11$ m/s.

a. Was the object's acceleration uniform or nonuniform? Explain your reasoning.

b. Sketch the velocity-versus-time graph implied by these data. Is the graph a straight line or curved? If curved, is it concave upward or downward?

33. ‖ A particle's velocity is described by the function $v_x = kt^2$ m/s, where k is a constant and t is in s. The particle's position at $t_0 = 0$ s is $x_0 = -9.0$ m. At $t_1 = 3.0$ s, the particle is at $x_1 = 9.0$ m. Determine the value of the constant k. Be sure to include the proper units.

34. ‖ A particle's acceleration is described by the function $a_x = (10 - t)$ m/s², where t is in s. Its initial conditions are $x_0 = 0$ m and $v_{0x} = 0$ m/s at $t = 0$ s.

a. At what time is the velocity again zero?

b. What is the particle's position at that time?

35. ‖ A ball rolls along the frictionless track shown in **FIGURE P2.35**. Each segment of the track is straight, and the ball passes smoothly from one segment to the next without changing speed or leaving the track. Draw three vertically stacked graphs showing position, velocity, and acceleration versus time. Each graph should have the same time axis, and the proportions of the graph should be qualitatively correct. Assume that the ball has enough speed to reach the top.

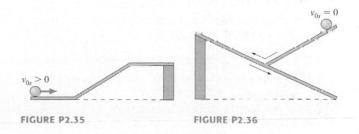

FIGURE P2.35   **FIGURE P2.36**

36. ‖ Draw position, velocity, and acceleration graphs for the ball shown in **FIGURE P2.36**. See Problem 35 for more information.

37. ‖ Draw position, velocity, and acceleration graphs for the ball shown in **FIGURE P2.37**. See Problem 35 for more information. The ball changes direction but not speed as it bounces from the reflecting wall.

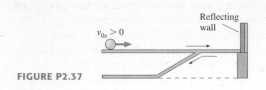

FIGURE P2.37

38. ‖ **FIGURE P2.38** shows a set of kinematic graphs for a ball rolling on a track. All segments of the track are straight lines, but some may be tilted. Draw a picture of the track and also indicate the ball's initial condition.

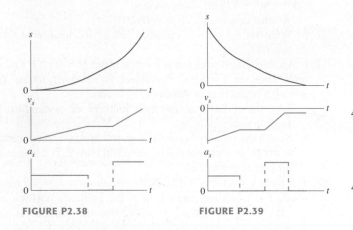

FIGURE P2.38   **FIGURE P2.39**

39. ‖ **FIGURE P2.39** shows a set of kinematic graphs for a ball rolling on a track. All segments of the track are straight lines, but some may be tilted. Draw a picture of the track and also indicate the ball's initial condition.

40. ‖ **FIGURE P2.40** shows a set of kinematic graphs for a ball rolling on a track. All segments of the track are straight lines, but some may be tilted. Draw a picture of the track and also indicate the ball's initial condition.

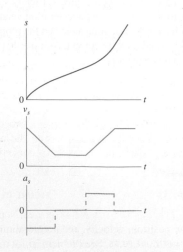

FIGURE P2.40

41. ‖ The takeoff speed for an Airbus A320 jetliner is 80 m/s. Velocity data measured during takeoff are as shown.

t (s)	v_s (m/s)
0	0
10	23
20	46
30	69

  a. What is the takeoff speed in miles per hour?
  b. Is the jetliner's acceleration constant during takeoff? Explain.
  c. At what time do the wheels leave the ground?
  d. For safety reasons, in case of an aborted takeoff, the runway must be three times the takeoff distance. Can an A320 take off safely on a 2.5-mi-long runway?

42. ‖ Does a real automobile have constant acceleration? Measured data for a Porsche 944 Turbo at maximum acceleration are as shown.

t (s)	v_s (mph)
0	0
2	28
4	46
6	60
8	70
10	78

  a. Make a graph of velocity versus time. Based on your graph, is the acceleration constant? Explain.
  b. Draw a smooth curve through the points on your graph, then use your graph to estimate the car's acceleration at 2.0 s and 8.0 s. Give your answer in SI units.
  c. Use your graph to estimate the distance traveled in the first 10 s.

43. ‖ a. What constant acceleration, in SI units, must a car have to go from zero to 60 mph in 10 s?
  b. What fraction of g is this?
  c. How far has the car traveled when it reaches 60 mph? Give your answer both in SI units and in feet.

44. ‖ a. How many days will it take a spaceship to accelerate to the speed of light (3.0×10^8 m/s) with the acceleration g?
  b. How far will it travel during this interval?
  c. What fraction of a light year is your answer to part b? A *light year* is the distance light travels in one year.

  NOTE ▶ We know, from Einstein's theory of relativity, that no object can travel at the speed of light. So this problem, while interesting and instructive, is not realistic. ◀

45. ‖ A driver has a reaction time of 0.50 s, and the maximum deceleration of her car is 6.0 m/s². She is driving at 20 m/s when suddenly she sees an obstacle in the road 50 m in front of her. Can she stop the car in time to avoid a collision?

46. ‖ You are driving to the grocery store at 20 m/s. You are 110 m from an intersection when the traffic light turns red. Assume that your reaction time is 0.50 s and that your car brakes with constant acceleration.
  a. How far are you from the intersection when you begin to apply the brakes?
  b. What acceleration will bring you to rest right at the intersection?
  c. How long does it take you to stop after the light turns red?

47. ‖ You're driving down the highway late one night at 20 m/s when a deer steps onto the road 35 m in front of you. Your reaction time before stepping on the brakes is 0.50 s, and the maximum deceleration of your car is 10 m/s².
  a. How much distance is between you and the deer when you come to a stop?
  b. What is the maximum speed you could have and still not hit the deer?

48. ||| The minimum stopping distance for a car traveling at a speed of 30 m/s is 60 m, including the distance traveled during the driver's reaction time of 0.50 s.
   a. What is the minimum stopping distance for the same car traveling at a speed of 40 m/s?
   b. Draw a position-versus-time graph for the motion of the car in part a. Assume the car is at $x_0 = 0$ m when the driver first sees the emergency situation ahead that calls for a rapid halt.

49. ||| A 200 kg weather rocket is loaded with 100 kg of fuel and fired straight up. It accelerates upward at 30 m/s² for 30 s, then runs out of fuel. Ignore any air resistance effects.
   a. What is the rocket's maximum altitude?
   b. How long is the rocket in the air before hitting the ground?
   c. Draw a velocity-versus-time graph for the rocket from liftoff until it hits the ground.

50. || A 1000 kg weather rocket is launched straight up. The rocket motor provides a constant acceleration for 16 s, then the motor stops. The rocket altitude 20 s after launch is 5100 m. You can ignore any effects of air resistance.
   a. What was the rocket's acceleration during the first 16 s?
   b. What is the rocket's speed as it passes through a cloud 5100 m above the ground?

51. || A lead ball is dropped into a lake from a diving board 5.0 m above the water. After entering the water, it sinks to the bottom with a constant velocity equal to the velocity with which it hit the water. The ball reaches the bottom 3.0 s after it is released. How deep is the lake?

52. || A hotel elevator ascends 200 m with a maximum speed of 5.0 m/s. Its acceleration and deceleration both have a magnitude of 1.0 m/s².
   a. How far does the elevator move while accelerating to full speed from rest?
   b. How long does it take to make the complete trip from bottom to top?

53. || A car starts from rest at a stop sign. It accelerates at 4.0 m/s² for 6.0 s, coasts for 2.0 s, and then slows down at a rate of 3.0 m/s² for the next stop sign. How far apart are the stop signs?

54. || A car accelerates at 2.0 m/s² along a straight road. It passes two marks that are 30 m apart at times $t = 4.0$ s and $t = 5.0$ s. What was the car's velocity at $t = 0$ s?

55. || Santa loses his footing and slides down a frictionless, snowy roof that is tilted at an angle of 30°. If Santa slides 10 m before reaching the edge, what is his speed as he leaves the roof?

56. || Ann and Carol are driving their cars along the same straight road. Carol is located at $x = 2.4$ mi at $t = 0$ hours and drives at a steady 36 mph. Ann, who is traveling in the same direction, is located at $x = 0.0$ mi at $t = 0.50$ hours and drives at a steady 50 mph.
   a. At what time does Ann overtake Carol?
   b. What is their position at this instant?
   c. Draw a position-versus-time graph showing the motion of both Ann and Carol.

57. || A puck slides along the frictionless track shown in FIGURE P2.57 with an initial speed of 5.0 m/s. Assume the puck turns all the corners smoothly, with no loss of speed.

   a. What is the puck's speed as it goes over the top?
   b. What is its speed when it reaches the level track on the right side?
   c. By what percentage does the puck's final speed differ from its initial speed?

58. || A toy train is pushed forward and released at $x_0 = 2.0$ m with a speed of 2.0 m/s. It rolls at a steady speed for 2.0 s, then one wheel begins to stick. The train comes to a stop 6.0 m from the point at which it was released. What is the magnitude of the train's acceleration after its wheel begins to stick?

59. || Bob is driving the getaway car after the big bank robbery. He's going 50 m/s when his headlights suddenly reveal a nail strip that the cops have placed across the road 150 m in front of him. If Bob can stop in time, he can throw the car into reverse and escape. But if he crosses the nail strip, all his tires will go flat and he will be caught. Bob's reaction time before he can hit the brakes is 0.60 s, and his car's maximum deceleration is 10 m/s². Is Bob in jail?

60. || One game at the amusement park has you push a puck up a long, frictionless ramp. You win a stuffed animal if the puck, at its highest point, comes to within 10 cm of the end of the ramp without going off. You give the puck a push, releasing it with a speed of 5.0 m/s when it is 8.5 m from the end of the ramp. The puck's speed after traveling 3.0 m is 4.0 m/s. Are you a winner?

61. || A professional skier's *initial* acceleration on fresh snow is 90% of the acceleration expected on a frictionless, inclined plane, the loss being due to friction. Due to air resistance, his acceleration slowly decreases as he picks up speed. The speed record on a mountain in Oregon is 180 kilometers per hour at the bottom of a 25° slope that drops 200 m.
   a. What exit speed could a skier reach in the absence of air resistance?
   b. What percentage of this ideal speed is lost to air resistance?

62. || Heather and Jerry are standing on a bridge 50 m above a river. Heather throws a rock straight down with a speed of 20 m/s. Jerry, at exactly the same instant of time, throws a rock straight up with the same speed. Ignore air resistance.
   a. How much time elapses between the first splash and the second splash?
   b. Which rock has the faster speed as it hits the water?

63. || Nicole throws a ball straight up. Chad watches the ball from a window 5.0 m above the point where Nicole released it. The ball passes Chad on the way up, and it has a speed of 10 m/s as it passes him on the way back down. How fast did Nicole throw the ball?

64. || A motorist is driving at 20 m/s when she sees that a traffic light 200 m ahead has just turned red. She knows that this light stays red for 15 s, and she wants to reach the light just as it turns green again. It takes her 1.0 s to step on the brakes and begin slowing. What is her speed as she reaches the light at the instant it turns green?

65. || When a 1984 Alfa Romeo Spider sports car accelerates at the maximum possible rate, its motion during the first 20 s is extremely well modeled by the simple equation

$$v_x^2 = \frac{2P}{m}t$$

   where $P = 3.6 \times 10^4$ watts is the car's power output, $m = 1200$ kg is its mass, and v_x is in m/s. That is, the square of the car's velocity increases linearly with time.
   a. What is the car's speed at $t = 10$ s and at $t = 20$ s?

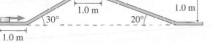

FIGURE P2.57

b. Find a *symbolic expression,* in terms of P, m, and t, for the car's acceleration at time t.

c. Evaluate the acceleration at $t = 1$ s and $t = 10$ s.

d. This simple model fails for t less than about 0.5 s. Explain how you can recognize the failure.

e. Find a *symbolic expression* for the distance the car has traveled at time t.

f. One-quarter mile is 402 m. What is the Spider's best time in a quarter-mile race? (The model's failure in the first 0.5 s has very little effect on your answer because the car travels almost no distance during that time.)

66. ‖ David is driving a steady 30 m/s when he passes Tina, who is sitting in her car at rest. Tina begins to accelerate at a steady 2.0 m/s^2 at the instant when David passes.

a. How far does Tina drive before passing David?

b. What is her speed as she passes him?

67. ‖ A cat is sleeping on the floor in the middle of a 3.0-m-wide room when a barking dog enters with a speed of 1.50 m/s. As the dog enters, the cat (as only cats can do) immediately accelerates at 0.85 m/s^2 toward an open window on the opposite side of the room. The dog (all bark and no bite) is a bit startled by the cat and begins to slow down at 0.10 m/s^2 as soon as it enters the room. Does the dog catch the cat before the cat is able to leap through the window?

68. ‖ You want to visit your friend in Seattle during spring break. To save money, you decide to travel there by train. Unfortunately, your physics final exam took the full 3 hours, so you are late in arriving at the train station. You run as fast as you can, but just as you reach the platform you see your train, 30 m ahead of you down the platform, begin to accelerate at 1.0 m/s^2. You chase after the train at your maximum speed of 8.0 m/s, but there's a barrier 50 m ahead. Will you be able to leap onto the back step of the train before you crash into the barrier?

69. ‖ Jill has just gotten out of her car in the grocery store parking lot. The parking lot is on a hill and is tilted 3°. Fifty meters downhill from Jill, a little old lady lets go of a fully loaded shopping cart. The cart, with frictionless wheels, starts to roll straight downhill. Jill immediately starts to sprint after the cart with her top acceleration of 2.0 m/s^2. How far has the cart rolled before Jill catches it?

70. ‖ As a science project, you drop a watermelon off the top of the Empire State Building, 320 m above the sidewalk. It so happens that Superman flies by at the instant you release the watermelon. Superman is headed straight down with a speed of 35 m/s. How fast is the watermelon going when it passes Superman?

71. ‖ I was driving along at 20 m/s, trying to change a CD and not watching where I was going. When I looked up, I found myself 45 m from a railroad crossing. And wouldn't you know it, a train moving at 30 m/s was only 60 m from the crossing. In a split second, I realized that the train was going to beat me to the crossing and that I didn't have enough distance to stop. My only hope was to accelerate enough to cross the tracks before the train arrived. If my reaction time before starting to accelerate was 0.50 s, what minimum acceleration did my car need for me to be here today writing these words?

In Problems 72 through 75, you are given the kinematic equation or equations that are used to solve a problem. For each of these, you are to:

a. Write a *realistic* problem for which this is the correct equation(s). Be sure that the answer your problem requests is consistent with the equation(s) given.

b. Draw the pictorial representation for your problem.

c. Finish the solution of the problem.

72. $64 \text{ m} = 0 \text{ m} + (32 \text{ m/s})(4 \text{ s} - 0 \text{ s}) + \frac{1}{2}a_x(4 \text{ s} - 0 \text{ s})^2$

73. $(10 \text{ m/s})^2 = v_{0y}^2 - 2(9.8 \text{ m/s}^2)(10 \text{ m} - 0 \text{ m})$

74. $(0 \text{ m/s})^2 = (5 \text{ m/s})^2 - 2(9.8 \text{ m/s}^2)(\sin 10°)(x_1 - 0 \text{ m})$

75. $v_{1x} = 0 \text{ m/s} + (20 \text{ m/s}^2)(5 \text{ s} - 0 \text{ s})$
$x_1 = 0 \text{ m} + (0 \text{ m/s})(5 \text{ s} - 0 \text{ s}) + \frac{1}{2}(20 \text{ m/s}^2)(5 \text{ s} - 0 \text{ s})^2$
$x_2 = x_1 + v_{1x}(10 \text{ s} - 5 \text{ s})$

Challenge Problems

76. The two masses in the figure slide on frictionless wires. They are connected by a pivoting rigid rod of length L. Prove that $v_{2x} = -v_{1y} \tan\theta$.

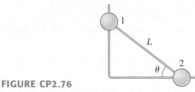

FIGURE CP2.76

77. A rocket is launched straight up with constant acceleration. Four seconds after liftoff, a bolt falls off the side of the rocket. The bolt hits the ground 6.0 s later. What was the rocket's acceleration?

78. Your school science club has devised a special event for homecoming. You've attached a rocket to the rear of a small car that has been decorated in the blue-and-gold school colors. The rocket provides a constant acceleration for 9.0 s. As the rocket shuts off, a parachute opens and slows the car at a rate of 5.0 m/s^2. The car passes the judges' box in the center of the grandstand, 990 m from the starting line, exactly 12 s after you fire the rocket. What is the car's speed as it passes the judges?

79. Careful measurements have been made of Olympic sprinters in the 100-meter dash. A simple but reasonably accurate model is that a sprinter accelerates at 3.6 m/s^2 for $3\frac{1}{3}$ s, then runs at constant velocity to the finish line.

a. What is the race time for a sprinter who follows this model?

b. A sprinter could run a faster race by accelerating faster at the beginning, thus reaching top speed sooner. If a sprinter's top speed is the same as in part a, what acceleration would he need to run the 100-meter dash in 9.9 s?

c. By what percent did the sprinter need to increase his acceleration in order to decrease his time by 1%?

80. Careful measurements have been made of Olympic sprinters in the 100-meter dash. A quite realistic model is that the sprinter's velocity is given by

$$v_x = a(1 - e^{-bt})$$

where t is in s, v_x is in m/s, and the constants a and b are characteristic of the sprinter. Sprinter Carl Lewis's run at the 1987 World Championships is modeled with $a = 11.81$ m/s and $b = 0.6887$ s^{-1}.

a. What was Lewis's acceleration at $t = 0$ s, 2.00 s, and 4.00 s?

b. Find an expression for the distance traveled at time t.

c. Your expression from part b is a transcendental equation, meaning that you can't solve it for t. However, it's not hard to use trial and error to find the time needed to travel a specific distance. To the nearest 0.01 s, find the time Lewis needed to sprint 100.0 m. His official time was 0.01 s more than your answer, showing that this model is very good, but not perfect.

81. A sprinter can accelerate with constant acceleration for 4.0 s before reaching top speed. He can run the 100-meter dash in 10 s. What is his speed as he crosses the finish line?

82. A rubber ball is shot straight up from the ground with speed v_0. Simultaneously, a second rubber ball at height h directly above the first ball is dropped from rest.

a. At what height above the ground do the balls collide? Your answer will be a *symbolic expression* in terms of v_0 and g.

b. What is the maximum value of h for which a collision occurs before the first ball falls back to the ground?

c. For what value of h does the collision occur at the instant when the first ball is at its highest point?

83. The Starship Enterprise returns from warp drive to ordinary space with a forward speed of 50 km/s. To the crew's great surprise, a Klingon ship is 100 km directly ahead, traveling in the same direction at a mere 20 km/s. Without evasive action, the Enterprise will overtake and collide with the Klingons in just slightly over 3.0 s. The Enterprise's computers react instantly to brake the ship. What magnitude acceleration does the Enterprise need to just barely avoid a collision with the Klingon ship? Assume the acceleration is constant.

Hint: Draw a position-versus-time graph showing the motions of both the Enterprise and the Klingon ship. Let $x_0 = 0$ km be the location of the Enterprise as it returns from warp drive. How do you show graphically the situation in which the collision is "barely avoided"? Once you decide what it looks like graphically, express that situation mathematically.

STOP TO THINK ANSWERS

Stop to Think 2.1: d. The particle starts with positive x and moves to negative x.

Stop to Think 2.2: c. The velocity is the slope of the position graph. The slope is positive and constant until the position graph crosses the axis, then positive but decreasing, and finally zero when the position graph is horizontal.

Stop to Think 2.3: b. A constant positive v_x corresponds to a linearly increasing x, starting from $x_i = -10$ m. The constant negative v_x then corresponds to a linearly decreasing x.

Stop to Think 2.4: a and **b.** The velocity is constant while $a = 0$, it decreases linearly while a is negative. Graphs a, b, and c all have the same acceleration, but only graphs a and b have a positive initial velocity that represents a particle moving to the right.

Stop to Think 2.5: d. The acceleration vector points downhill (negative s-direction) and has the constant value $-g\sin\theta$ throughout the motion.

Stop to Think 2.6: c. Acceleration is the slope of the graph. The slope is zero at B. Although the graph is steepest at A, the slope at that point is negative, and so $a_A < a_B$. Only C has a positive slope, so $a_C > a_B$.

3 Vectors and Coordinate Systems

Wind has both a speed and a direction; hence the motion of the wind is described by a vector.

▶ **Looking Ahead**

The goals of Chapter 3 are to learn how vectors are represented and used. In this chapter you will learn to:

- Understand and use the basic properties of vectors.
- Decompose a vector into its components and reassemble vector components into a magnitude and direction.
- Add and subtract vectors both graphically and using components.

◀ **Looking Back**

This chapter continues the development of vectors that was begun in Chapter 1. Please review:

- Section 1.3 Vector addition and subtraction.

Many of the quantities that we use to describe the physical world are simply numbers. For example, the mass of an object is 2 kg, its temperature is 21°C, and it occupies a volume of 250 cm^3. A quantity that is fully described by a single number (with units) is called a **scalar quantity.** Mass, temperature, and volume are all scalars. Other scalar quantities include pressure, density, energy, charge, and voltage. We will often use an algebraic symbol to represent a scalar quantity. Thus m will represent mass, T temperature, V volume, E energy, and so on. Notice that scalars, in printed text, are shown in italics.

Our universe has three dimensions, so some quantities also need a direction for a full description. If you ask someone for directions to the post office, the reply "Go three blocks" will not be very helpful. A full description might be, "Go three blocks south." A quantity having both a size and a direction is called a **vector quantity.**

You met examples of vector quantities in Chapter 1: position, displacement, velocity, and acceleration. You will soon make the acquaintance of others, such as force, momentum, and the electric field. Now, before we begin a study of forces, it's worth spending a little time to look more closely at vectors.

3.1 Vectors

Suppose you are assigned the task of measuring the temperature at various points throughout a building and then showing the information on a building floor plan. To do this, you could put little dots on the floor plan, to show the points at which you made measurements, then write the temperature at that point beside the dot. In other words, as **FIGURE 3.1a** shows, you can represent the temperature at each point with a simple number (with units). Temperature is a scalar quantity.

Having done such a good job on your first assignment, you are next assigned the task of measuring the velocities of several employees as they move about in their work. Recall from Chapter 1 that velocity is a vector; it has both a size and a direction. Simply writing each employee's speed is not sufficient because speed doesn't take into account the direction in which the person moved. After some thought, you conclude that a good way to represent the velocity is by drawing an arrow whose length is proportional to the speed and that points in the direction of motion. Further, as **FIGURE 3.1b** shows, you decide to place the *tail* of an arrow at the point where you measured the velocity.

As this example illustrates, the *geometric representation* of a vector is an arrow, with the tail of the arrow (not its tip!) placed at the point where the measurement is made. The vector then seems to radiate outward from the point to which it is attached. An arrow makes a natural representation of a vector because it inherently has both a length and a direction. As you've already seen, we label vectors by drawing a small arrow over the letter that represents the vector: $\vec{r}$ for position, $\vec{v}$ for velocity, $\vec{a}$ for acceleration, and so on.

The mathematical term for the length, or size, of a vector is **magnitude,** so we can say that **a vector is a quantity having a magnitude and a direction.** As an example, **FIGURE 3.2** shows the geometric representation of a particle's velocity vector $\vec{v}$. The particle's speed at this point is 5 m/s, *and* it is moving in the direction indicated by the arrow. The arrow is drawn with its tail at the point where the velocity was measured.

> **NOTE** ▶ Although the vector arrow is drawn across the page, from its tail to its tip, this does *not* indicate that the vector "stretches" across this distance. Instead, the vector arrow tells us the value of the vector quantity only at the one point where the tail of the vector is placed. ◀

The *magnitude* of a vector is sometimes shown using absolute value signs, but more frequently indicated by the letter without the arrow. For example, the magnitude of the velocity vector in Figure 3.2 is $v = |\vec{v}| = 5$ m/s. This is the object's *speed*. The magnitude of the acceleration vector $\vec{a}$ is written a. **The magnitude of a vector is a scalar quantity.**

> **NOTE** ▶ The magnitude of a vector cannot be a negative number; it must be positive or zero, with appropriate units. ◀

It is important to get in the habit of using the arrow symbol for vectors. If you omit the vector arrow from the velocity vector $\vec{v}$ and write only v, then you're referring only to the object's speed, not its velocity. The symbols $\vec{r}$ and r, or $\vec{v}$ and v, do *not* represent the same thing, so if you omit the vector arrow from vector symbols you will soon have confusion and mistakes.

3.2 Properties of Vectors

Recall from Chapter 1 that the *displacement* is a vector drawn from an object's initial position to its position at some later time. Because displacement is an easy concept to think about, we can use it to introduce some of the properties of vectors. However, these properties apply to *all* vectors, not just to displacement.

Suppose Sam starts from his front door, walks across the street, and ends up 200 ft to the northeast of where he started. Sam's displacement, which we will label $\vec{S}$, is shown in **FIGURE 3.3a** on the next page. The displacement vector is a *straight-line connection* from his initial to his final position, not necessarily his actual path. The dashed line indicates a possible route Sam might have taken, but his displacement is the vector $\vec{S}$.

To describe a vector we must specify both its magnitude and its direction. We can write Sam's displacement as

$$\vec{S} = (200 \text{ ft, northeast})$$

where the first piece of information specifies the magnitude and the second is the direction. The magnitude of Sam's displacement is $S = |\vec{S}| = 200$ ft, the distance between his initial and final points.

FIGURE 3.1 Measurements of scalar and vector quantities.

(a) Temperature, in °C

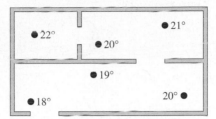

(b) Velocities, in m/s

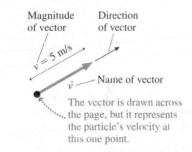

FIGURE 3.2 The velocity vector $\vec{v}$ has both a magnitude and a direction.

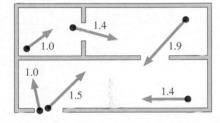

The boat's displacement is the straight-line connection from its initial to its final position.

Sam's next-door neighbor Bill also walks 200 ft to the northeast, starting from his own front door. Bill's displacement $\vec{B}$ = (200 ft, northeast) has the same magnitude and direction as Sam's displacement $\vec{S}$. Because vectors are defined by their magnitude and direction, **two vectors are equal if they have the same magnitude and direction.** This is true regardless of the starting points of the vectors. Thus the two displacements in FIGURE 3.3b are equal to each other, and we can write $\vec{B} = \vec{S}$.

FIGURE 3.3 Displacement vectors.

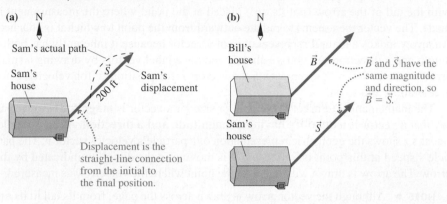

(a) N

Sam's actual path

Sam's house

$\vec{S}$

200 ft

Sam's displacement

Displacement is the straight-line connection from the initial to the final position.

(b) N

Bill's house

$\vec{B}$

$\vec{B}$ and $\vec{S}$ have the same magnitude and direction, so $\vec{B} = \vec{S}$.

Sam's house

$\vec{S}$

NOTE ▶ A vector is unchanged if you move it to a different point on the page as long as you don't change its length or the direction it points. We used this idea in Chapter 1 when we moved velocity vectors around in order to find the average acceleration vector $\vec{a}$. ◀

Vector Addition

FIGURE 3.4 shows the displacement of a hiker who starts at point P and ends at point S. She first hikes 4 miles to the east, then 3 miles to the north. The first leg of the hike is described by the displacement $\vec{A}$ = (4 mi, east). The second leg of the hike has displacement $\vec{B}$ = (3 mi, north). Now, by definition, a vector from the initial position P to the final position S is also a displacement. This is vector $\vec{C}$ on the figure. $\vec{C}$ is the *net displacement* because it describes the net result of the hiker's first having displacement $\vec{A}$, then displacement $\vec{B}$.

If you earn $50 on Saturday and $60 on Sunday, your *net* income for the weekend is the sum of $50 and $60. With scalars, the word *net* implies addition. The same is true with vectors. The net displacement $\vec{C}$ is an initial displacement $\vec{A}$ *plus* a second displacement $\vec{B}$, or

$$\vec{C} = \vec{A} + \vec{B} \tag{3.1}$$

The sum of two vectors is called the **resultant vector.** It's not hard to show that vector addition is commutative: $\vec{A} + \vec{B} = \vec{B} + \vec{A}$. That is, you can add vectors in any order you wish.

Look back at Tactics Box 1.1 on page 8 to see the three-step procedure for adding two vectors. This tip-to-tail method for adding vectors, which is used to find $\vec{C} = \vec{A} + \vec{B}$ in Figure 3.4, is called **graphical addition.** Any two vectors of the same type—two velocity vectors or two force vectors—can be added in exactly the same way.

The graphical method for adding vectors is straightforward, but we need to do a little geometry to come up with a complete description of the resultant vector $\vec{C}$. Vector $\vec{C}$ of Figure 3.4 is defined by its magnitude C and by its direction. Because the three vectors $\vec{A}$, $\vec{B}$, and $\vec{C}$ form a right triangle, the magnitude, or length, of $\vec{C}$ is given by the Pythagorean theorem:

$$C = \sqrt{A^2 + B^2} = \sqrt{(4 \text{ mi})^2 + (3 \text{ mi})^2} = 5 \text{ mi} \tag{3.2}$$

FIGURE 3.4 The net displacement $\vec{C}$ resulting from two displacements $\vec{A}$ and $\vec{B}$.

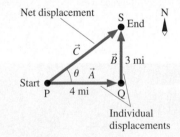

Net displacement

S End

N

$\vec{C}$

$\vec{B}$ 3 mi

θ $\vec{A}$

Start

P 4 mi Q

Individual displacements

Notice that Equation 3.2 uses the magnitudes A and B of the vectors $\vec{A}$ and $\vec{B}$. The angle θ, which is used in Figure 3.4 to describe the direction of $\vec{C}$, is easily found for a right triangle:

$$\theta = \tan^{-1}\left(\frac{B}{A}\right) = \tan^{-1}\left(\frac{3 \text{ mi}}{4 \text{ mi}}\right) = 37° \tag{3.3}$$

Altogether, the hiker's net displacement is

$$\vec{C} = \vec{A} + \vec{B} = (5 \text{ mi}, 37° \text{ north of east}) \tag{3.4}$$

NOTE ▶ Vector mathematics makes extensive use of geometry and trigonometry. Appendix A, at the end of this book, contains a brief review of these topics. ◀

EXAMPLE 3.1 Using graphical addition to find a displacement

A bird flies 100 m due east from a tree, then 200 m northwest (that is, 45° north of west). What is the bird's net displacement?

VISUALIZE FIGURE 3.5 shows the two individual displacements, which we've called $\vec{A}$ and $\vec{B}$. The net displacement is the vector sum $\vec{C} = \vec{A} + \vec{B}$, which is found graphically.

FIGURE 3.5 The bird's net displacement is $\vec{C} = \vec{A} + \vec{B}$.

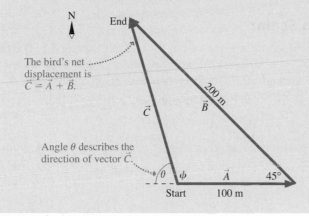

SOLVE The two displacements are $\vec{A} = (100 \text{ m}, \text{east})$ and $\vec{B} = (200 \text{ m}, \text{northwest})$. The net displacement $\vec{C} = \vec{A} + \vec{B}$ is found by drawing a vector from the initial to the final position. But describing $\vec{C}$ is a bit trickier than the example of the hiker because $\vec{A}$ and $\vec{B}$ are not at right angles. First, we can find the magnitude of $\vec{C}$ by using the law of cosines from trigonometry:

$$C^2 = A^2 + B^2 - 2AB\cos(45°)$$
$$= (100 \text{ m})^2 + (200 \text{ m})^2 - 2(100 \text{ m})(200 \text{ m})\cos(45°)$$
$$= 21{,}720 \text{ m}^2$$

Thus $C = \sqrt{21{,}720 \text{ m}^2} = 147$ m. Then a second use of the law of cosines can determine angle ϕ (the Greek letter phi):

$$B^2 = A^2 + C^2 - 2AC\cos\phi$$
$$\phi = \cos^{-1}\left[\frac{A^2 + C^2 - B^2}{2AC}\right] = 106°$$

It is easier to describe $\vec{C}$ with the angle $\theta = 180° - \phi = 74°$. The bird's net displacement is

$$\vec{C} = (147 \text{ m}, 74° \text{ north of west})$$

When two vectors are to be added, it is often convenient to draw them with their tails together, as shown in **FIGURE 3.6a**. To evaluate $\vec{D} + \vec{E}$, you could move vector $\vec{E}$ over to where its tail is on the tip of $\vec{D}$, then use the tip-to-tail rule of graphical addition. That gives vector $\vec{F} = \vec{D} + \vec{E}$ in **FIGURE 3.6b**. Alternatively, **FIGURE 3.6c** shows that the vector sum $\vec{D} + \vec{E}$ can be found as the diagonal of the parallelogram defined by $\vec{D}$ and $\vec{E}$. This method for vector addition, which some of you may have learned, is called the *parallelogram rule* of vector addition.

FIGURE 3.6 Two vectors can be added using the tip-to-tail rule or the parallelogram rule.

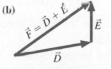

(a)
$\vec{E}$ $\vec{D}$
What is $\vec{D} + \vec{E}$?

(b)
$\vec{F} = \vec{D} + \vec{E}$ $\vec{E}$ $\vec{D}$
Tip-to-tail rule:
Slide the tail of $\vec{E}$ to the tip of $\vec{D}$.

(c)
$\vec{E}$ $\vec{F} = \vec{D} + \vec{E}$ $\vec{D}$
Parallelogram rule:
Find the diagonal of the parallelogram formed by $\vec{D}$ and $\vec{E}$.

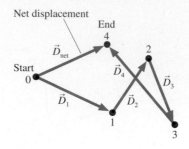

FIGURE 3.7 The net displacement after four individual displacements.

Vector addition is easily extended to more than two vectors. **FIGURE 3.7** shows a hiker moving from initial position 0 to position 1, then position 2, then position 3, and finally arriving at position 4. These four segments are described by displacement vectors $\vec{D}_1$, $\vec{D}_2$, $\vec{D}_3$, and $\vec{D}_4$. The hiker's *net* displacement, an arrow from position 0 to position 4, is the vector $\vec{D}_{net}$. In this case,

$$\vec{D}_{net} = \vec{D}_1 + \vec{D}_2 + \vec{D}_3 + \vec{D}_4 \tag{3.5}$$

The vector sum is found by using the tip-to-tail method three times in succession.

STOP TO THINK 3.1   Which figure shows $\vec{A}_1 + \vec{A}_2 + \vec{A}_3$?

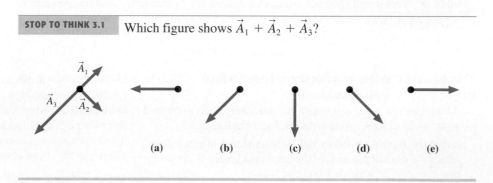

(a)   (b)   (c)   (d)   (e)

Multiplication by a Scalar

Suppose a second bird flies twice as far to the east as the bird in Example 3.1. The first bird's displacement was $\vec{A}_1 = (100 \text{ m, east})$, where a subscript has been added to denote the first bird. The second bird's displacement will then certainly be $\vec{A}_2 = (200 \text{ m, east})$. The words "twice as" indicate a multiplication, so we can say

$$\vec{A}_2 = 2\vec{A}_1$$

Multiplying a vector by a positive scalar gives another vector of *different magnitude* but pointing in the *same direction*.

Let the vector $\vec{A}$ be

$$\vec{A} = (A, \theta_A) \tag{3.6}$$

Now let $\vec{B} = c\vec{A}$, where c is a positive scalar constant. We define the multiplication of a vector by a scalar such that

$$\vec{B} = c\vec{A} \text{ means that } (B, \theta_B) = (cA, \theta_A) \tag{3.7}$$

In other words, the vector is stretched or compressed by the factor c (i.e., vector $\vec{B}$ has magnitude $B = cA$), but $\vec{B}$ points in the same direction as $\vec{A}$. This is illustrated in **FIGURE 3.8**.

We used this property of vectors in Chapter 1 when we asserted that vector $\vec{a}$ points in the same direction as $\Delta\vec{v}$. From the definition

$$\vec{a} = \frac{\Delta\vec{v}}{\Delta t} = \left(\frac{1}{\Delta t}\right)\Delta\vec{v} \tag{3.8}$$

where $(1/\Delta t)$ is a scalar constant, we see that $\vec{a}$ points in the same direction as $\Delta\vec{v}$ but differs in length by the factor $(1/\Delta t)$.

Suppose we multiply $\vec{A}$ by zero. Using Equation 3.7,

$$0 \cdot \vec{A} = \vec{0} = (0 \text{ m, direction undefined}) \tag{3.9}$$

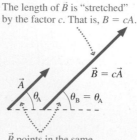

FIGURE 3.8 Multiplication of a vector by a scalar.

The length of $\vec{B}$ is "stretched" by the factor c. That is, $B = cA$.

$\vec{B} = c\vec{A}$

$\vec{A}$

θ_A $\theta_B = \theta_A$

$\vec{B}$ points in the same direction as $\vec{A}$.

The product is a vector having zero length or magnitude. This vector is known as the **zero vector,** denoted $\vec{0}$. The direction of the zero vector is irrelevant; you cannot describe the direction of an arrow of zero length!

What happens if we multiply a vector by a negative number? Equation 3.7 does not apply if $c < 0$ because vector $\vec{B}$ cannot have a negative magnitude. Consider the vector $-\vec{A}$, which is equivalent to multiplying $\vec{A}$ by -1. Because

$$\vec{A} + (-\vec{A}) = \vec{0} \tag{3.10}$$

the vector $-\vec{A}$ must be such that, when it is added to $\vec{A}$, the resultant is the zero vector $\vec{0}$. In other words, the *tip* of $-\vec{A}$ must return to the *tail* of $\vec{A}$, as shown in **FIGURE 3.9**. This will be true only if $-\vec{A}$ is equal in magnitude to $\vec{A}$, but opposite in direction. Thus we can conclude that

$$-\vec{A} = (A, \text{ direction opposite } \vec{A}) \tag{3.11}$$

That is, **multiplying a vector by -1 reverses its direction without changing its length.**

As an example, **FIGURE 3.10** shows vectors $\vec{A}$, $2\vec{A}$, and $-3\vec{A}$. Multiplication by 2 doubles the length of the vector but does not change its direction. Multiplication by -3 stretches the length by a factor of 3 *and* reverses the direction.

FIGURE 3.9 Vector $-\vec{A}$.

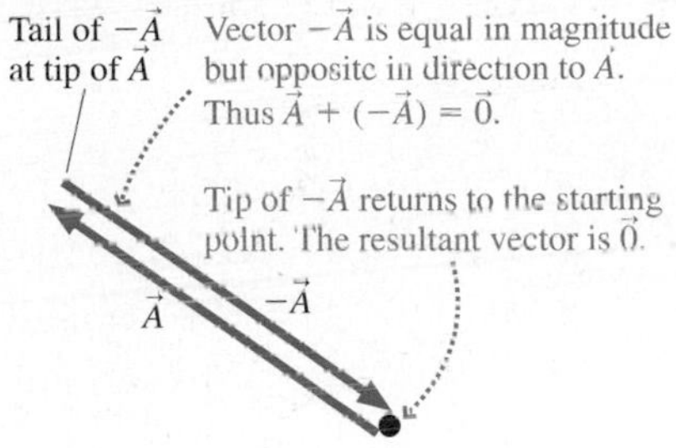

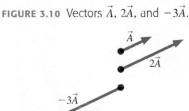

Tail of $-\vec{A}$ at tip of $\vec{A}$ Vector $-\vec{A}$ is equal in magnitude but opposite in direction to $\vec{A}$. Thus $\vec{A} + (-\vec{A}) = \vec{0}$.

Tip of $-\vec{A}$ returns to the starting point. The resultant vector is $\vec{0}$.

FIGURE 3.10 Vectors $\vec{A}$, $2\vec{A}$, and $-3\vec{A}$.

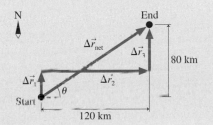

EXAMPLE 3.2 **Velocity and displacement**

Carolyn drives her car north at 30 km/hr for 1 hour, east at 60 km/hr for 2 hours, then north at 50 km/hr for 1 hour. What is Carolyn's net displacement?

SOLVE Chapter 1 defined velocity as

$$\vec{v} = \frac{\Delta \vec{r}}{\Delta t}$$

so the displacement $\Delta \vec{r}$ during the time interval Δt is $\Delta \vec{r} = (\Delta t)\vec{v}$. This is multiplication of the vector $\vec{v}$ by the scalar Δt. Carolyn's velocity during the first hour is $\vec{v}_1 = (30 \text{ km/hr, north})$, so her displacement during this interval is

$$\Delta \vec{r}_1 = (1 \text{ hour})(30 \text{ km/hr, north}) = (30 \text{ km, north})$$

Similarly,

$$\Delta \vec{r}_2 = (2 \text{ hours})(60 \text{ km/hr, east}) = (120 \text{ km, east})$$

$$\Delta \vec{r}_3 = (1 \text{ hour})(50 \text{ km/hr, north}) = (50 \text{ km, north})$$

In this case, multiplication by a scalar changes not only the length of the vector but also its units, from km/hr to km. The direction, however, is unchanged. Carolyn's net displacement is

$$\Delta \vec{r}_{net} = \Delta \vec{r}_1 + \Delta \vec{r}_2 + \Delta \vec{r}_3$$

This addition of the three vectors is shown in **FIGURE 3.11**, using the tip-to-tail method. $\Delta \vec{r}_{net}$ stretches from Carolyn's initial position to her final position. The magnitude of her net displacement is found using the Pythagorean theorem:

$$r_{net} = \sqrt{(120 \text{ km})^2 + (80 \text{ km})^2} = 144 \text{ km}$$

The direction of $\Delta \vec{r}_{net}$ is described by angle θ, which is

$$\theta = \tan^{-1}\left(\frac{80 \text{ km}}{120 \text{ km}}\right) = 34°$$

Thus Carolyn's net displacement is $\Delta \vec{r}_{net} = (144 \text{ km}, 34° \text{ north of east})$.

FIGURE 3.11 The net displacement is the vector sum $\Delta \vec{r}_{net} = \Delta \vec{r}_1 + \Delta \vec{r}_2 + \Delta \vec{r}_3$.

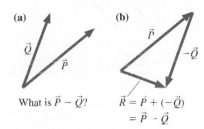

Vector Subtraction

FIGURE 3.12a shows two vectors, $\vec{P}$ and $\vec{Q}$. What is $\vec{R} = \vec{P} - \vec{Q}$? Look back at Tactics Box 1.2 on page 9, which showed how to perform vector subtraction graphically. **FIGURE 3.12b** finds $\vec{P} - \vec{Q}$ by writing $\vec{R} = \vec{P} + (-\vec{Q})$, then using the rules of vector addition.

FIGURE 3.12 Vector subtraction.

(a)

$\vec{Q}$ $\vec{P}$

What is $\vec{P} - \vec{Q}$?

(b)

$\vec{P}$ $-\vec{Q}$

$\vec{R} = \vec{P} + (-\vec{Q})$
$= \vec{P} - \vec{Q}$

Which figure shows $2\vec{A} - \vec{B}$?

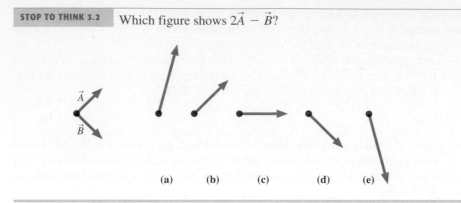

(a)   (b)   (c)   (d)   (e)

3.3 Coordinate Systems and Vector Components

Vectors do not require a coordinate system. We can add and subtract vectors graphically, and we will do so frequently to clarify our understanding of a situation. But the graphical addition of vectors is not an especially good way to find quantitative results. In this section we will introduce a *coordinate representation* of vectors that will be the basis of an easier method for doing vector calculations.

Coordinate Systems

As we noted in the first chapter, the world does not come with a coordinate system attached to it. A coordinate system is an artificially imposed grid that you place on a problem in order to make quantitative measurements. It may be helpful to think of drawing a grid on a piece of transparent plastic that you can then overlay on top of the problem. This conveys the idea that *you* choose:

- Where to place the origin, and
- How to orient the axes.

Different problem solvers may choose to use different coordinate systems; that is perfectly acceptable. However, some coordinate systems will make a problem easier to solve. Part of our goal is to learn how to choose an appropriate coordinate system for each problem.

We will generally use **Cartesian coordinates.** This is a coordinate system with the axes perpendicular to each other, forming a rectangular grid. The standard *xy*-coordinate system with which you are familiar is a Cartesian coordinate system. An *xyz*-coordinate system is a Cartesian coordinate system in three dimensions. There are other possible coordinate systems, such as polar coordinates, but we will not be concerned with those for now.

The placement of the axes is not entirely arbitrary. By convention, the positive *y*-axis is located 90° *counterclockwise* (ccw) from the positive *x*-axis, as illustrated in **FIGURE 3.13**. Figure 3.13 also identifies the four **quadrants** of the coordinate system, I through IV. Notice that the quadrants are counted ccw from the positive *x*-axis.

Coordinate axes have a positive end and a negative end, separated by zero at the origin where the two axes cross. When you draw a coordinate system, it is important to label the axes. This is done by placing *x* and *y* labels at the *positive* ends of the axes, as in Figure 3.13. The purpose of the labels is twofold:

- To identify which axis is which, and
- To identify the positive ends of the axes.

This will be important when you need to determine whether the quantities in a problem should be assigned positive or negative values.

The navigator had better know which way to go, and how far, if she and the crew are to make landfall at the expected location.

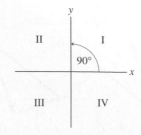

FIGURE 3.13 A conventional Cartesian coordinate system and the quadrants of the *xy*-plane.

Component Vectors

FIGURE 3.14 shows a vector $\vec{A}$ and an xy-coordinate system that we've chosen. Once the directions of the axes are known, we can define two new vectors *parallel to the axes* that we call the **component vectors** of $\vec{A}$. Vector $\vec{A}_x$, called the *x-component vector*, is the projection of $\vec{A}$ along the x-axis. Vector $\vec{A}_y$, the *y-component vector*, is the projection of $\vec{A}$ along the y-axis. Notice that the component vectors are perpendicular to each other.

You can see, using the parallelogram rule, that $\vec{A}$ is the vector sum of the two component vectors:

$$\vec{A} = \vec{A}_x + \vec{A}_y \tag{3.12}$$

In essence, we have broken vector $\vec{A}$ into two perpendicular vectors that are parallel to the coordinate axes. This process is called the **decomposition** of vector $\vec{A}$ into its component vectors.

> **NOTE** ▶ It is not necessary for the tail of $\vec{A}$ to be at the origin. All we need to know is the *orientation* of the coordinate system so that we can draw $\vec{A}_x$ and $\vec{A}_y$ parallel to the axes. ◀

FIGURE 3.14 Component vectors $\vec{A}_x$ and $\vec{A}_y$ are drawn parallel to the coordinate axes such that $\vec{A} = \vec{A}_x + \vec{A}_y$.

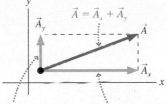

The y-component vector is parallel to the y-axis.   The x-component vector is parallel to the x-axis.

Components

You learned in Chapter 1 to give the one-dimensional kinematic variable v_x a positive sign if the velocity vector $\vec{v}$ points toward the positive end of the x-axis, a negative sign if $\vec{v}$ points in the negative x-direction. The basis of that rule is that v_x is what we call the *x-component* of the velocity vector. We need to extend this idea to vectors in general.

Suppose vector $\vec{A}$ has been decomposed into component vectors $\vec{A}_x$ and $\vec{A}_y$ parallel to the coordinate axes. We can describe each component vector with a single number called the **component**. The *x-component* and *y-component* of vector $\vec{A}$, denoted A_x and A_y, are determined as follows:

TACTICS
BOX 3.1   **Determining the components of a vector**

❶ The absolute value $|A_x|$ of the x-component A_x is the magnitude of the component vector $\vec{A}_x$.

❷ The *sign* of A_x is positive if $\vec{A}_x$ points in the positive x-direction, negative if $\vec{A}_x$ points in the negative x-direction.

❸ The y-component A_y is determined similarly.

Exercises 10–18

In other words, the component A_x tells us two things: how big $\vec{A}_x$ is and, with its sign, which end of the axis $\vec{A}_x$ points toward. **FIGURE 3.15** shows three examples of determining the components of a vector.

FIGURE 3.15 Determining the components of a vector.

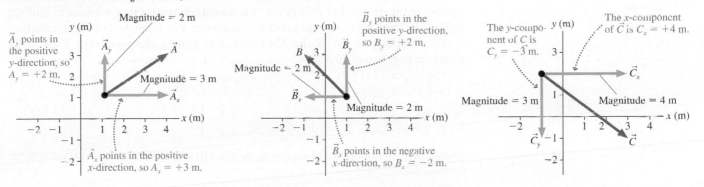

NOTE ▶ Beware of the somewhat confusing terminology. $\vec{A}_x$ and $\vec{A}_y$ are called *component vectors,* whereas A_x and A_y are simply called *components.* The components A_x and A_y are just numbers (with units), so make sure you do *not* put arrow symbols over the components. ◀

Much of physics is expressed in the language of vectors. We will frequently need to decompose a vector into its components. We will also need to "reassemble" a vector from its components. In other words, we need to move back and forth between the geometric and the component representations of a vector.

Consider first the problem of decomposing a vector into its *x*- and *y*-components. FIGURE 3.16a shows a vector $\vec{A}$ at angle θ from the *x*-axis. It is *essential* to use a picture or diagram such as this to *define the angle* you are using to describe the vector's direction.

$\vec{A}$ points to the right and up, so Tactics Box 3.1 tells us that the components A_x and A_y are both positive. We can use trigonometry to find

$$A_x = A\cos\theta$$
$$A_y = A\sin\theta \tag{3.13}$$

where A is the magnitude, or length, of $\vec{A}$. These equations convert the length and angle description of vector $\vec{A}$ into the vector's components, but they are correct *only* if angle θ is measured from the positive *x*-axis.

FIGURE 3.16b shows a vector $\vec{C}$ whose direction is specified by the angle ϕ, measured from the negative *y*-axis. In this case, the components of $\vec{C}$ are

$$C_x = C\sin\phi$$
$$C_y = -C\cos\phi \tag{3.14}$$

The role of sine and cosine is reversed from that in Equations 3.13 because we are using a different angle.

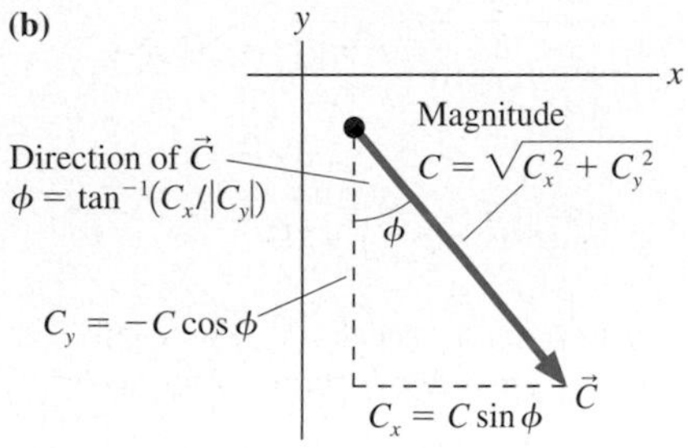

NOTE ▶ Each decomposition requires that you pay close attention to the direction in which the vector points and the angles that are defined. The minus sign, when needed, must be inserted manually. ◀

We can also go in the opposite direction and determine the length and angle of a vector from its *x*- and *y*-components. Because A in Figure 3.16a is the hypotenuse of a right triangle, its length is given by the Pythagorean theorem:

$$A = \sqrt{A_x^2 + A_y^2} \tag{3.15}$$

Similarly, the tangent of angle θ is the ratio of the far side to the adjacent side, so

$$\theta = \tan^{-1}\left(\frac{A_y}{A_x}\right) \tag{3.16}$$

where $\tan^{-1}$ is the inverse tangent function. Equations 3.15 and 3.16 can be thought of as the "reverse" of Equations 3.13.

Equation 3.15 always works for finding the length or magnitude of a vector because the squares eliminate any concerns over the signs of the components. But finding the angle, just like finding the components, requires close attention to how the angle is defined and to the signs of the components. For example, finding the angle of vector $\vec{C}$ in Figure 3.16b requires the length of C_y *without* the minus sign. Thus vector $\vec{C}$ has magnitude and direction

$$C = \sqrt{C_x^2 + C_y^2}$$
$$\phi = \tan^{-1}\left(\frac{C_x}{|C_y|}\right) \tag{3.17}$$

Notice that the roles of *x* and *y* differ from those in Equation 3.16.

FIGURE 3.16 Moving between the geometric representation and the component representation.

(a)

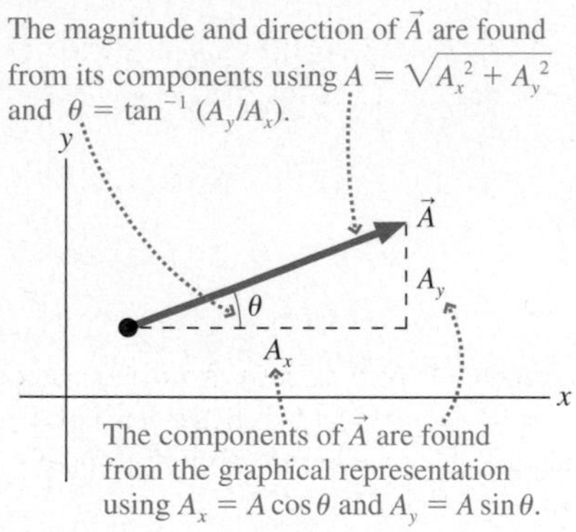

The magnitude and direction of $\vec{A}$ are found from its components using $A = \sqrt{A_x^2 + A_y^2}$ and $\theta = \tan^{-1}(A_y/A_x)$.

The components of $\vec{A}$ are found from the graphical representation using $A_x = A\cos\theta$ and $A_y = A\sin\theta$.

(b)

Direction of $\vec{C}$
$\phi = \tan^{-1}(C_x/|C_y|)$

$C = \sqrt{C_x^2 + C_y^2}$

Magnitude

$C_y = -C\cos\phi$

$C_x = C\sin\phi$

EXAMPLE 3.3 **Finding the components of an acceleration vector**

Find the *x*- and *y*-components of the acceleration vector $\vec{a}$ shown in **FIGURE 3.17**.

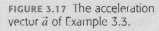

FIGURE 3.17 The acceleration vector $\vec{a}$ of Example 3.3.

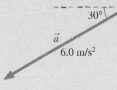

VISUALIZE It's important to *draw* vectors. **FIGURE 3.18** shows the original vector $\vec{a}$ decomposed into components parallel to the axes. Notice that the axes are "acceleration axes" because we're measuring an acceleration vector.

SOLVE The acceleration vector $\vec{a} = (6.0 \text{ m/s}^2, 30°$ below the negative *x*-axis) points to the left (negative *x*-direction) and down (negative *y*-direction), so the components a_x and a_y are both negative:

$$a_x = -a\cos 30° = -(6.0 \text{ m/s}^2)\cos 30° = -5.2 \text{ m/s}^2$$
$$a_y = -a\sin 30° = -(6.0 \text{ m/s}^2)\sin 30° = -3.0 \text{ m/s}^2$$

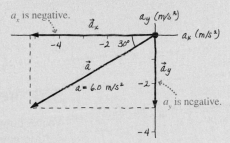

FIGURE 3.18 Decomposition of $\vec{a}$.

ASSESS The units of a_x and a_y are the same as the units of vector $\vec{a}$. Notice that we had to insert the minus signs manually by observing that the vector points left and down.

EXAMPLE 3.4 **Finding the direction of motion**

FIGURE 3.19 shows a car's velocity vector $\vec{v}$. Determine the car's speed and direction of motion.

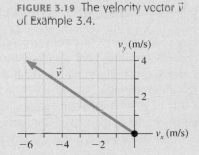

FIGURE 3.19 The velocity vector $\vec{v}$ of Example 3.4.

VISUALIZE **FIGURE 3.20** shows the components v_x and v_y and defines an angle θ with which we can specify the direction of motion.

FIGURE 3.20 Decomposition of $\vec{v}$.

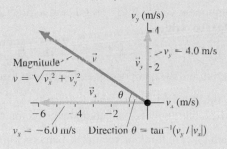

SOLVE We can read the components of $\vec{v}$ directly from the axes: $v_x = -6.0$ m/s and $v_y = 4.0$ m/s. Notice that v_x is negative. This is enough information to find the car's speed v, which is the magnitude of $\vec{v}$:

$$v = \sqrt{v_x^2 + v_y^2} = \sqrt{(-6.0 \text{ m/s})^2 + (4.0 \text{ m/s})^2} = 7.2 \text{ m/s}$$

From trigonometry, angle θ is

$$\theta = \tan^{-1}\left(\frac{v_y}{|v_x|}\right) = \tan^{-1}\left(\frac{4.0 \text{ m/s}}{6.0 \text{ m/s}}\right) = 34°$$

The absolute value signs are necessary because v_x is a negative number. The velocity vector $\vec{v}$ can be written in terms of the speed and the direction of motion as

$$\vec{v} = (7.2 \text{ m/s}, 34° \text{ above the negative } x\text{-axis})$$

or, if the axes are aligned to north,

$$\vec{v} = (7.2 \text{ m/s}, 34° \text{ north of west})$$

What are the x- and y-components C_x and C_y of vector $\vec{C}$?

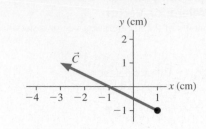

3.4 Vector Algebra

Vector components are a powerful tool for doing mathematics with vectors. In this section you'll learn how to use components to add and subtract vectors. First, we'll introduce an efficient way to write a vector in terms of its components.

Unit Vectors

FIGURE 3.21 The unit vectors $\hat{\imath}$ and $\hat{\jmath}$.

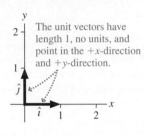

The unit vectors have length 1, no units, and point in the +x-direction and +y-direction.

The vectors $(1, +x\text{-direction})$ and $(1, +y\text{-direction})$, shown in **FIGURE 3.21**, have some interesting and useful properties. Each has a magnitude of 1, no units, and is parallel to a coordinate axis. A vector with these properties is called a **unit vector.** These unit vectors have the special symbols

$$\hat{\imath} \equiv (1, \text{positive } x\text{-direction})$$

$$\hat{\jmath} \equiv (1, \text{positive } y\text{-direction})$$

The notation $\hat{\imath}$ (read "i hat") and $\hat{\jmath}$ (read "j hat") indicates a unit vector with a magnitude of 1.

Unit vectors establish the directions of the positive axes of the coordinate system. Our choice of a coordinate system may be arbitrary, but once we decide to place a coordinate system on a problem we need something to tell us "That direction is the positive x-direction." This is what the unit vectors do.

The unit vectors provide a useful way to write component vectors. The component vector $\vec{A}_x$ is the piece of vector $\vec{A}$ that is parallel to the x-axis. Similarly, $\vec{A}_y$ is parallel to the y-axis. Because, by definition, the vector $\hat{\imath}$ points along the x-axis and $\hat{\jmath}$ points along the y-axis, we can write

$$\vec{A}_x = A_x \hat{\imath}$$
$$\vec{A}_y = A_y \hat{\jmath} \tag{3.18}$$

FIGURE 3.22 The decomposition of vector $\vec{A}$ is $A_x\hat{\imath} + A_y\hat{\jmath}$.

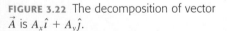

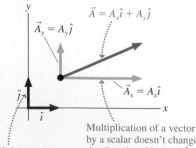

Unit vectors identify the x- and y-directions.

Multiplication of a vector by a scalar doesn't change the direction. Vector $A_x\hat{\imath}$ has length A_x and points in the direction of $\hat{\imath}$.

Equations 3.18 separate each component vector into a length and a direction. The full decomposition of vector $\vec{A}$ can then be written

$$\vec{A} = \vec{A}_x + \vec{A}_y = A_x\hat{\imath} + A_y\hat{\jmath} \tag{3.19}$$

FIGURE 3.22 shows how the unit vectors and the components fit together to form vector $\vec{A}$.

NOTE ▶ In three dimensions, the unit vector along the +z-direction is called $\hat{k}$, and to describe vector $\vec{A}$ we would include an additional component vector $\vec{A}_z = A_z\hat{k}$. ◀

You may have learned in a math class to think of vectors as pairs or triplets of numbers, such as $(4, -2, 5)$. This is another, and completely equivalent, way to write the components of a vector. Thus we could write

$$\vec{B} = 4\hat{\imath} - 2\hat{\jmath} + 5\hat{k} = (4, -2, 5)$$

You will find the notation using unit vectors to be more convenient for the equations we will use in physics, but rest assured that you already know a lot about vectors if you learned about them as pairs or triplets of numbers.

EXAMPLE 3.5 Run rabbit run!
A rabbit, escaping a fox, runs 40.0° north of west at 10.0 m/s. A coordinate system is established with the positive x-axis to the east and the positive y-axis to the north. Write the rabbit's velocity in terms of components and unit vectors.

VISUALIZE FIGURE 3.23 shows the rabbit's velocity vector and the coordinate axes. We're showing a velocity vector, so the axes are labeled v_x and v_y rather than x and y.

FIGURE 3.23 The velocity vector $\vec{v}$ is decomposed into components v_x and v_y.

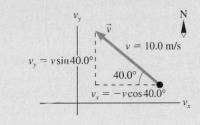

SOLVE 10.0 m/s is the rabbit's *speed,* not its velocity. The velocity, which includes directional information, is

$$\vec{v} = (10.0 \text{ m/s, } 40.0° \text{ north of west})$$

Vector $\vec{v}$ points to the left and up, so the components v_x and v_y are negative and positive, respectively. The components are

$$v_x = -(10.0 \text{ m/s}) \cos 40.0° = -7.66 \text{ m/s}$$

$$v_y = +(10.0 \text{ m/s}) \sin 40.0° = 6.43 \text{ m/s}$$

With v_x and v_y now known, the rabbit's velocity vector is

$$\vec{v} = v_x \hat{\imath} + v_y \hat{\jmath} = (-7.66\hat{\imath} + 6.43\hat{\jmath}) \text{ m/s}$$

Notice that we've pulled the units to the end, rather than writing them with each component.

ASSESS Notice that the minus sign for v_x was inserted manually. **Signs don't occur automatically; you have to set them after checking the vector's direction.**

Working with Vectors

You learned in Section 3.2 how to add vectors graphically, but it is a tedious problem in geometry and trigonometry to find precise values for the magnitude and direction of the resultant. The addition and subtraction of vectors become much easier if we use components and unit vectors.

To see this, let's evaluate the vector sum $\vec{D} = \vec{A} + \vec{B} + \vec{C}$. To begin, write this sum in terms of the components of each vector:

$$\vec{D} = D_x\hat{\imath} + D_y\hat{\jmath} = \vec{A} + \vec{B} + \vec{C}$$
$$= (A_x\hat{\imath} + A_y\hat{\jmath}) + (B_x\hat{\imath} + B_y\hat{\jmath}) + (C_x\hat{\imath} + C_y\hat{\jmath}) \tag{3.20}$$

We can group together all the x-components and all the y-components on the right side, in which case Equation 3.20 is

$$(D_x)\hat{\imath} + (D_y)\hat{\jmath} = (A_x + B_x + C_x)\hat{\imath} + (A_y + B_y + C_y)\hat{\jmath} \tag{3.21}$$

Comparing the x- and y-components on the left and right sides of Equation 3.21, we find:

$$D_x = A_x + B_x + C_x$$
$$D_y = A_y + B_y + C_y \tag{3.22}$$

Stated in words, Equation 3.22 says that we can perform vector addition by adding the x-components of the individual vectors to give the x-component of the resultant and by adding the y-components of the individual vectors to give the y-component of the resultant. This method of vector addition is called **algebraic addition.**

EXAMPLE 3.6 Using algebraic addition to find a displacement

Example 3.1 was about a bird that flew 100 m to the east, then 200 m to the northwest. Use the algebraic addition of vectors to find the bird's net displacement.

VISUALIZE FIGURE 3.24 shows displacement vectors $\vec{A} = (100$ m, east) and $\vec{B} = (200$ m, northwest). We draw vectors tip-to-tail to add them graphically, but it's usually easier to draw them all from the origin if we are going to use algebraic addition.

FIGURE 3.24 The net displacement is $\vec{C} = \vec{A} + \vec{B}$.

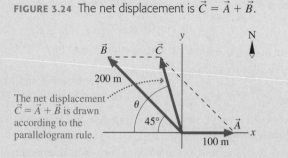

SOLVE To add the vectors algebraically we must know their components. From the figure these are seen to be

$$\vec{A} = 100\,\hat{\imath}\,\text{m}$$

$$\vec{B} = (-200\cos 45°\,\hat{\imath} + 200\sin 45°\,\hat{\jmath})\,\text{m}$$

$$= (-141\hat{\imath} + 141\hat{\jmath})\,\text{m}$$

Notice that vector quantities must include units. Also notice, as you would expect from the figure, that $\vec{B}$ has a negative x-component. Adding $\vec{A}$ and $\vec{B}$ by components gives

$$\vec{C} = \vec{A} + \vec{B} = 100\hat{\imath}\,\text{m} + (-141\hat{\imath} + 141\hat{\jmath})\,\text{m}$$

$$= (100\text{ m} - 141\text{ m})\hat{\imath} + (141\text{ m})\hat{\jmath} = (-41\hat{\imath} + 141\hat{\jmath})\,\text{m}$$

This would be a perfectly acceptable answer for many purposes. However, we need to calculate the magnitude and direction of $\vec{C}$ if we want to compare this result to our earlier answer. The magnitude of $\vec{C}$ is

$$C = \sqrt{C_x^2 + C_y^2} = \sqrt{(-41\text{ m})^2 + (141\text{ m})^2} = 147\text{ m}$$

The angle θ, as defined in Figure 3.24, is

$$\theta = \tan^{-1}\left(\frac{C_y}{|C_x|}\right) = \tan^{-1}\left(\frac{141\text{ m}}{41\text{ m}}\right) = 74°$$

Thus $\vec{C} = (147$ m, $74°$ north of west), in perfect agreement with Example 3.1.

Vector subtraction and the multiplication of a vector by a scalar, using components, are very much like vector addition. To find $\vec{R} = \vec{P} - \vec{Q}$ we would compute

$$R_x = P_x - Q_x$$
$$R_y = P_y - Q_y$$

(3.23)

Similarly, $\vec{T} = c\vec{S}$ would be

$$T_x = cS_x$$
$$T_y = cS_y$$

(3.24)

The next few chapters will make frequent use of *vector equations*. For example, you will learn that the equation to calculate the force on a car skidding to a stop is

$$\vec{F} = \vec{n} + \vec{w} + \mu\vec{f}$$

(3.25)

The following general rule is used to evaluate such an equation:

The x-component of the left-hand side of a vector equation is found by doing arithmetic calculations (addition, subtraction, multiplication) with just the x-components of all the vectors on the right-hand side. A separate set of calculations uses just the y-components and, if needed, the z-components.

Thus Equation 3.25 is really just a shorthand way of writing three simultaneous equations:

$$F_x = n_x + w_x + \mu f_x$$
$$F_y = n_y + w_y + \mu f_y$$
$$F_z = n_z + w_z + \mu f_z$$

(3.26)

In other words, a vector equation is interpreted as meaning: Equate the x-components on both sides of the equals sign, then equate the y-components, and then the z-components. Vector notation allows us to write these three equations in a much more compact form.

Tilted Axes and Arbitrary Directions

As we've noted, the coordinate system is entirely your choice. It is a grid that you impose on the problem in a manner that will make the problem easiest to solve. We will soon meet problems where it will be convenient to tilt the axes of the coordinate system, such as those shown in FIGURE 3.25. The axes are perpendicular, and the y-axis is oriented correctly with respect to the x-axis, so this is a legitimate coordinate system. There is no requirement that the x-axis has to be horizontal.

Finding components with tilted axes is no harder than what we have done so far. Vector $\vec{C}$ in Figure 3.25 can be decomposed into $\vec{C} = C_x\hat{i} + C_y\hat{j}$, where $C_x = C\cos\theta$ and $C_y = C\sin\theta$. Note that the unit vectors $\hat{i}$ and $\hat{j}$ correspond to the *axes*, not to "horizontal" and "vertical," so they are also tilted.

Tilted axes are useful if you need to determine component vectors "parallel to" and "perpendicular to" an arbitrary line or surface. For example, FIGURE 3.26a shows a vector $\vec{A}$ and a tilted line. To find the component vectors of $\vec{A}$ parallel and perpendicular to the line, establish a tilted coordinate system with the x-axis parallel to the line and the y-axis perpendicular to the line, as shown in FIGURE 3.26b. Then $\vec{A}_x$ is equivalent to vector $\vec{A}_\parallel$, the component of $\vec{A}$ parallel to the line, and $\vec{A}_y$ is equivalent to the perpendicular component vector $\vec{A}_\perp$. Notice that $\vec{A} = \vec{A}_\parallel + \vec{A}_\perp$.

If ϕ is the angle between $\vec{A}$ and the line, we can easily calculate the parallel and perpendicular components of $\vec{A}$:

$$A_\parallel = A_x = A\cos\phi$$
$$A_\perp = A_y = A\sin\phi \tag{3.27}$$

It was not necessary to have the tail of $\vec{A}$ on the line in order to find a component of $\vec{A}$ parallel to the line. The line simply indicates a direction, and the component vector $\vec{A}_\parallel$ points in that direction.

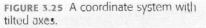
FIGURE 3.25 A coordinate system with tilted axes.

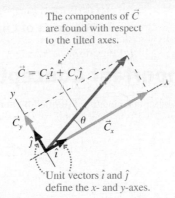

The components of $\vec{C}$ are found with respect to the tilted axes.

$\vec{C} = C_x\hat{i} + C_y\hat{j}$

Unit vectors $\hat{i}$ and $\hat{j}$ define the x- and y-axes.

FIGURE 3.26 Finding the components of $\vec{A}$ parallel to and perpendicular to the line.

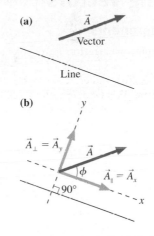

(a) Vector / Line

(b)

EXAMPLE 3.7 **Finding the force perpendicular to a surface**

A horizontal force $\vec{F}$ with a strength of 10 N is applied to a surface. (You'll learn in Chapter 5 that force is a vector quantity measured in units of *newtons*, abbreviated N.) The surface is tilted at a 20° angle. Find the component of the force vector perpendicular to the surface.

VISUALIZE FIGURE 3.27 shows a horizontal force $\vec{F}$ applied to the surface. A tilted coordinate system has its y-axis perpendicular to the surface, so the perpendicular component is $F_\perp = F_y$.

FIGURE 3.27 Finding the component of a force vector perpendicular to a surface.

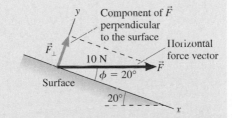

SOLVE From geometry, the force vector $\vec{F}$ makes an angle $\phi = 20°$ with the tilted x-axis. The perpendicular component of $\vec{F}$ is thus

$$F_\perp = F\sin 20° = (10\text{ N})\sin 20° = 3.4\text{ N}$$

STOP TO THINK 3.4 Angle ϕ that specifies the direction of $\vec{C}$ is given by

a. $\tan^{-1}(|C_x|/C_y)$.
b. $\tan^{-1}(C_x/|C_y|)$.
c. $\tan^{-1}(|C_x|/|C_y|)$.
d. $\tan^{-1}(|C_y|/C_x)$.
e. $\tan^{-1}(C_y/|C_x|)$.
f. $\tan^{-1}(|C_y|/|C_x|)$.

SUMMARY

The goals of Chapter 3 have been to learn how vectors are represented and used.

Important Concepts

A **vector** is a quantity described by both a magnitude and a direction.

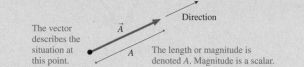

The vector describes the situation at this point.

$\vec{A}$

Direction

The length or magnitude is denoted A. Magnitude is a scalar.

Unit Vectors

Unit vectors have magnitude 1 and no units. Unit vectors $\hat{i}$ and $\hat{j}$ define the directions of the x- and y-axes.

Using Vectors

Components

The component vectors are parallel to the x- and y-axes:

$$\vec{A} = \vec{A}_x + \vec{A}_y = A_x\hat{i} + A_y\hat{j}$$

In the figure at the right, for example:

$$A_x = A\cos\theta \qquad A = \sqrt{A_x^2 + A_y^2}$$
$$A_y = A\sin\theta \qquad \theta = \tan^{-1}(A_y/A_x)$$

▶ Minus signs need to be included if the vector points down or left.

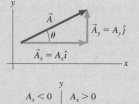

$A_x < 0$	$A_x > 0$
$A_y > 0$	$A_y > 0$
$A_x < 0$	$A_x > 0$
$A_y < 0$	$A_y < 0$

The components A_x and A_y are the magnitudes of the component vectors $\vec{A}_x$ and $\vec{A}_y$ *and* a plus or minus sign to show whether the component vector points toward the positive end or the negative end of the axis.

Working Graphically

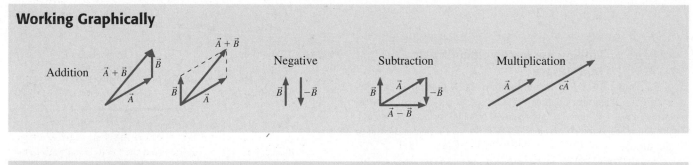

Addition $\vec{A} + \vec{B}$

Negative

Subtraction

Multiplication

Working Algebraically

Vector calculations are done component by component:

$$\vec{C} = 2\vec{A} + \vec{B} \qquad \text{means} \qquad \begin{cases} C_x = 2A_x + B_x \\ C_y = 2A_y + B_y \end{cases}$$

The magnitude of $\vec{C}$ is then $C = \sqrt{C_x^2 + C_y^2}$ and its direction is found using $\tan^{-1}$.

Terms and Notation

scalar quantity	graphical addition	quadrants	component
vector quantity	zero vector, $\vec{0}$	component vector	unit vector, $\hat{i}$ or $\hat{j}$
magnitude	Cartesian coordinates	decomposition	algebraic addition
resultant vector			

MP For homework assigned on MasteringPhysics, go to www.masteringphysics.com

Problem difficulty is labeled as | (straightforward) to ||| (challenging).

CONCEPTUAL QUESTIONS

1. Can the magnitude of the displacement vector be more than the distance traveled? Less than the distance traveled? Explain.
2. If $\vec{C} = \vec{A} + \vec{B}$, can $C = A + B$? Can $C > A + B$? For each, show how or explain why not.
3. If $\vec{C} = \vec{A} + \vec{B}$, can $C = 0$? Can $C < 0$? For each, show how or explain why not.
4. Is it possible to add a scalar to a vector? If so, demonstrate. If not, explain why not.
5. How would you define the *zero vector* $\vec{0}$?
6. Can a vector have a component equal to zero and still have nonzero magnitude? Explain.
7. Can a vector have zero magnitude if one of its components is nonzero? Explain.
8. Suppose two vectors have unequal magnitudes. Can their sum be zero? Explain.

EXERCISES AND PROBLEMS

Exercises

Section 3.1 Vectors

Section 3.2 Properties of Vectors

1. | Trace the vectors in FIGURE EX3.1 onto your paper. Then find (a) $\vec{A} + \vec{B}$ and (b) $\vec{A} - \vec{B}$.

FIGURE EX3.1   FIGURE EX3.2

2. | Trace the vectors in FIGURE EX3.2 onto your paper. Then find (a) $\vec{A} + \vec{B}$ and (b) $\vec{A} - \vec{B}$.

Section 3.3 Coordinate Systems and Vector Components

3. | a. What are the x- and y-components of vector $\vec{E}$ in terms of the angle θ and the magnitude E shown in FIGURE EX3.3?
   b. For the same vector, what are the x- and y-components in terms of the angle ϕ and the magnitude E?

FIGURE EX3.3

4. | A position vector in the first quadrant has an x-component of 6 m and a magnitude of 10 m. What is the value of its y-component?
5. || A velocity vector 40° below the positive x-axis has a y-component of -10 m/s. What is the value of its x-component?
6. | Draw each of the following vectors, then find its x- and y-components.
   a. $\vec{r} = (100 \text{ m}, 45° \text{ below positive } x\text{-axis})$
   b. $\vec{v} = (300 \text{ m/s}, 20° \text{ above positive } x\text{-axis})$
   c. $\vec{a} = (5.0 \text{ m/s}^2, \text{ negative } y\text{-direction})$

7. | Draw each of the following vectors, then find its x- and y-components.
   a. $\vec{v} = (5.0 \text{ cm/s}, \text{ negative } x\text{-direction})$
   b. $\vec{a} = (10 \text{ m/s}^2, 40° \text{ left of negative } y\text{-axis})$
   c. $\vec{F} = (50 \text{ N}, 36.9° \text{ right of positive } y\text{-axis})$
8. | Let $\vec{C} = (3.15 \text{ m}, 15° \text{ above the negative } x\text{-axis})$ and $\vec{D} = (25.6 \text{ m}, 30° \text{ to the right of the negative } y\text{-axis})$. Find the magnitude, the x-component, and the y-component of each vector.
9. | The quantity called the *electric field* is a vector. The electric field inside a scientific instrument is $\vec{E} = (125\hat{\imath} - 250\hat{\jmath})$ V/m, where V/m stands for volts per meter. What are the magnitude and direction of the electric field?

Section 3.4 Vector Algebra

10. | Draw each of the following vectors, label an angle that specifies the vector's direction, then find its magnitude and direction.
    a. $\vec{B} = -4\hat{\imath} + 4\hat{\jmath}$ b. $\vec{r} = (-2.0\hat{\imath} - 1.0\hat{\jmath})$ cm
    c. $\vec{v} = (-10\hat{\imath} - 100\hat{\jmath})$ m/s   d. $\vec{a} = (20\hat{\imath} + 10\hat{\jmath})$ m/s²
11. | Draw each of the following vectors, label an angle that specifies the vector's direction, then find the vector's magnitude and direction.
    a. $\vec{A} = 4\hat{\imath} - 6\hat{\jmath}$ b. $\vec{r} = (50\hat{\imath} + 80\hat{\jmath})$ m
    c. $\vec{v} = (-20\hat{\imath} + 40\hat{\jmath})$ m/s   d. $\vec{a} = (2.0\hat{\imath} - 6.0\hat{\jmath})$ m/s²
12. | Let $\vec{A} = 2\hat{\imath} + 3\hat{\jmath}$ and $\vec{B} = 4\hat{\imath} - 2\hat{\jmath}$.
    a. Draw a coordinate system and on it show vectors $\vec{A}$ and $\vec{B}$.
    b. Use graphical vector subtraction to find $\vec{C} = \vec{A} - \vec{B}$.
13. | Let $\vec{A} = 5\hat{\imath} + 2\hat{\jmath}$, $\vec{B} = -3\hat{\imath} - 5\hat{\jmath}$, and $\vec{C} = \vec{A} + \vec{B}$.
    a. Write vector $\vec{C}$ in component form.
    b. Draw a coordinate system and on it show vectors $\vec{A}$, $\vec{B}$, and $\vec{C}$.
    c. What are the magnitude and direction of vector $\vec{C}$?
14. | Let $\vec{A} = 5\hat{\imath} + 2\hat{\jmath}$, $\vec{B} = -3\hat{\imath} - 5\hat{\jmath}$, and $\vec{D} = \vec{A} - \vec{B}$.
    a. Write vector $\vec{D}$ in component form.
    b. Draw a coordinate system and on it show vectors $\vec{A}$, $\vec{B}$, and $\vec{D}$.
    c. What are the magnitude and direction of vector $\vec{D}$?

15. | Let $\vec{A} = 5\hat{i} + 2\hat{j}$, $\vec{B} = -3\hat{i} - 5\hat{j}$, and $\vec{E} = 2\vec{A} + 3\vec{B}$.

    a. Write vector $\vec{E}$ in component form.

    b. Draw a coordinate system and on it show vectors $\vec{A}$, $\vec{B}$, and $\vec{E}$.

    c. What are the magnitude and direction of vector $\vec{E}$?

16. | Let $\vec{A} = 5\hat{i} + 2\hat{j}$, $\vec{B} = -3\hat{i} - 5\hat{j}$, and $\vec{F} = \vec{A} - 4\vec{B}$.

    a. Write vector $\vec{F}$ in component form.

    b. Draw a coordinate system and on it show vectors $\vec{A}$, $\vec{B}$, and $\vec{F}$.

    c. What are the magnitude and direction of vector $\vec{F}$?

17. | Are the following statements true or false? Explain your answer.

    a. The magnitude of a vector can be different in different coordinate systems.

    b. The direction of a vector can be different in different coordinate systems.

    c. The components of a vector can be different in different coordinate systems.

18. | Let $\vec{B} = (5.0 \text{ m}, 60° \text{ counterclockwise from vertical})$. Find the x- and y-components of $\vec{B}$ in each of the two coordinate systems shown in FIGURE EX3.18.

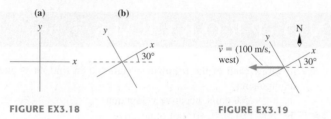

FIGURE EX3.18   FIGURE EX3.19

19. | What are the x- and y-components of the velocity vector shown in FIGURE EX3.19?

Problems

20. | Let $\vec{A} = (3.0 \text{ m}, 20° \text{ south of east})$, $\vec{B} = (2.0 \text{ m}, \text{north})$, and $\vec{C} = (5.0 \text{ m}, 70° \text{ south of west})$.

    a. Draw and label $\vec{A}$, $\vec{B}$, and $\vec{C}$ with their tails at the origin. Use a coordinate system with the x-axis to the east.

    b. Write $\vec{A}$, $\vec{B}$, and $\vec{C}$ in component form, using unit vectors.

    c. Find the magnitude and the direction of $\vec{D} = \vec{A} + \vec{B} + \vec{C}$.

21. | Trace the vectors in FIGURE P3.21 onto your paper. Use the graphical method of vector addition and subtraction to find the following.

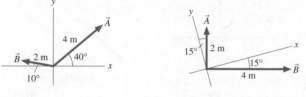

FIGURE P3.21

    a. $\vec{D} + \vec{E} + \vec{F}$ b. $\vec{D} + 2\vec{E}$ c. $\vec{D} - 2\vec{E} + \vec{F}$

22. | Let $\vec{E} = 2\hat{i} + 3\hat{j}$ and $\vec{F} = 2\hat{i} - 2\hat{j}$. Find the magnitude of

    a. $\vec{E}$ and $\vec{F}$ b. $\vec{E} + \vec{F}$ c. $-\vec{E} - 2\vec{F}$

23. | The position of a particle as a function of time is given by $\vec{r} = (5.0\hat{i} + 4.0\hat{j})t^2$ m, where t is in seconds.

    a. What is the particle's distance from the origin at $t = 0, 2$, and 5 s?

    b. Find an expression for the particle's velocity $\vec{v}$ as a function of time.

    c. What is the particle's speed at $t = 0, 2$, and 5 s?

24. || FIGURE P3.24 shows vectors $\vec{A}$ and $\vec{B}$. Let $\vec{C} = \vec{A} + \vec{B}$.

    a. Reproduce the figure on your page as accurately as possible, using a ruler and protractor. Draw vector $\vec{C}$ on your figure, using the graphical addition of $\vec{A}$ and $\vec{B}$. Then determine the magnitude and direction of $\vec{C}$ by *measuring* it with a ruler and protractor.

    b. Based on your figure of part a, use geometry and trigonometry to *calculate* the magnitude and direction of $\vec{C}$.

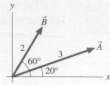

FIGURE P3.24

    c. Decompose vectors $\vec{A}$ and $\vec{B}$ into components, then use these to calculate algebraically the magnitude and direction of $\vec{C}$.

25. || For the three vectors shown in FIGURE P3.25, $\vec{A} + \vec{B} + \vec{C} = -2\hat{i}$. What is vector $\vec{B}$?

    a. Write $\vec{B}$ in component form.

    b. Write $\vec{B}$ as a magnitude and a direction.

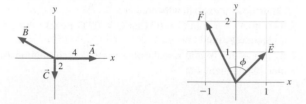

FIGURE P3.25   FIGURE P3.26

26. || a. What is the angle ϕ between vectors $\vec{E}$ and $\vec{F}$ in FIGURE P3.26?

    b. Use geometry and trigonometry to determine the magnitude and direction of $\vec{G} = \vec{E} + \vec{F}$.

    c. Use components to determine the magnitude and direction of $\vec{G} = \vec{E} + \vec{F}$.

27. || FIGURE P3.27 shows vectors $\vec{A}$ and $\vec{B}$. Find vector $\vec{C}$ such that $\vec{A} + \vec{B} + \vec{C} = \vec{0}$. Write your answer in component form.

FIGURE P3.27   FIGURE P3.28

28. ||| FIGURE P3.28 shows vectors $\vec{A}$ and $\vec{B}$. Find $\vec{D} = 2\vec{A} + \vec{B}$. Write your answer in component form.

29. || Find a vector that points in the same direction as the vector $(\hat{i} + \hat{j})$ and whose magnitude is 1.

30. | Carlos runs with velocity $\vec{v} = (5.0 \text{ m/s}, 25° \text{ north of east})$ for 10 minutes. How far to the north of his starting position does Carlos end up?

31. || While vacationing in the mountains you do some hiking. In the morning, your displacement is $\vec{S}_{\text{morning}} = (2000 \text{ m}, \text{east}) + (3000 \text{ m}, \text{north}) + (200 \text{ m}, \text{vertical})$. After lunch, your displacement is $\vec{S}_{\text{afternoon}} = (1500 \text{ m}, \text{west}) + (2000 \text{ m}, \text{north}) - (300 \text{ m}, \text{vertical})$.

    a. At the end of the hike, how much higher or lower are you compared to your starting point?

    b. What is the magnitude of your net displacement for the day?

32. || The minute hand on a watch is 2.0 cm in length. What is the displacement vector of the tip of the minute hand

    a. From 8:00 to 8:20 A.M.?

    b. From 8:00 to 9:00 A.M.?

33. || Bob walks 200 m south, then jogs 400 m southwest, then walks 200 m in a direction 30° east of north.

    a. Draw an accurate graphical representation of Bob's motion. Use a ruler and a protractor!

b. Use either trigonometry or components to find the displacement that will return Bob to his starting point by the most direct route. Give your answer as a distance and a direction.

c. Does your answer to part b agree with what you can measure on your diagram of part a?

34. ‖ Jim's dog Sparky runs 50 m northeast to a tree, then 70 m west to a second tree, and finally 20 m south to a third tree.

a. Draw a picture and establish a coordinate system.

b. Calculate Sparky's net displacement in component form.

c. Calculate Sparky's net displacement as a magnitude and an angle.

35. ‖ A field mouse trying to escape a hawk runs east for 5.0 m, darts southeast for 3.0 m, then drops 1.0 m straight down a hole into its burrow. What is the magnitude of the net displacement of the mouse?

36. | A cannon tilted upward at 30° fires a cannonball with a speed of 100 m/s. What is the component of the cannonball's velocity parallel to the ground?

37. | Jack and Jill ran up the hill at 3.0 m/s. The horizontal component of Jill's velocity vector was 2.5 m/s.

a. What was the angle of the hill?

b. What was the vertical component of Jill's velocity?

38. | A pine cone falls straight down from a pine tree growing on a 20° slope. The pine cone hits the ground with a speed of 10 m/s. What is the component of the pine cone's impact velocity (a) parallel to the ground and (b) perpendicular to the ground?

39. | Mary needs to row her boat across a 100-m-wide river that is flowing to the east at a speed of 1.0 m/s. Mary can row the boat with a speed of 2.0 m/s relative to the water.

a. If Mary rows straight north, how far downstream will she land?

b. Draw a picture showing Mary's displacement due to rowing, her displacement due to the river's motion, and her net displacement.

40. ‖ The treasure map in FIGURE P3.40 gives the following directions to the buried treasure: "Start at the old oak tree, walk due north for 500 paces, then due east for 100 paces. Dig." But when you arrive, you find an angry dragon just north of the tree. To avoid the dragon, you set off along the yellow brick road at an angle 60° east of north. After walking 300 paces you see an opening through the woods. Which direction should you go, and how far, to reach the treasure?

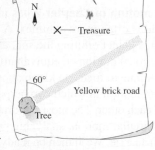

FIGURE P3.40

41. ‖ A jet plane is flying horizontally with a speed of 500 m/s over a hill that slopes upward with a 3% grade (i.e., the "rise" is 3%

of the "run"). What is the component of the plane's velocity perpendicular to the ground?

42. ‖ A flock of ducks is trying to migrate south for the winter, but they keep being blown off course by a wind blowing from the west at 6.0 m/s. A wise elder duck finally realizes that the solution is to fly at an angle to the wind. If the ducks can fly at 8.0 m/s relative to the air, what direction should they head in order to move directly south?

43. ‖ The car in FIGURE P3.43 speeds up as it turns a quarter-circle curve from north to east. When exactly halfway around the curve, the car's acceleration is $\vec{a} = (2.0 \text{ m/s}^2, 15°$ south of east). At this point, what is the component of $\vec{a}$ (a) tangent to the circle and (b) perpendicular to the circle?

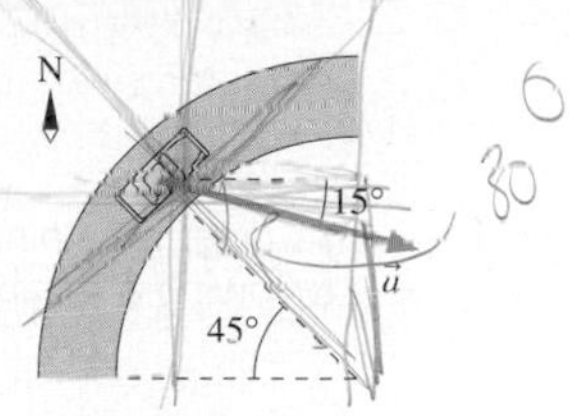

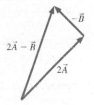

FIGURE P3.43

44. ‖ FIGURE P3.44 shows three ropes tied together in a knot. One of your friends pulls on a rope with 3.0 units of force and another pulls on a second rope with 5.0 units of force. How hard and in what direction must you pull on the third rope to keep the knot from moving?

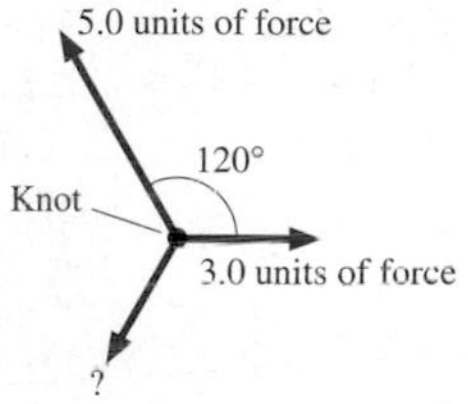

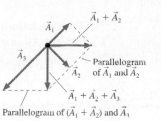

5.0 units of force

120°

Knot

3.0 units of force

?

FIGURE P3.44

45. ‖ Three forces are exerted on an object placed on a tilted floor in FIGURE P3.45. The forces are measured in newtons (N). Assuming that forces are vectors,

a. What is the component of the *net force* $\vec{F}_{\text{net}} = \vec{F}_1 + \vec{F}_2 + \vec{F}_3$ parallel to the floor?

b. What is the component of $\vec{F}_{\text{net}}$ perpendicular to the floor?

c. What are the magnitude and direction of $\vec{F}_{\text{net}}$?

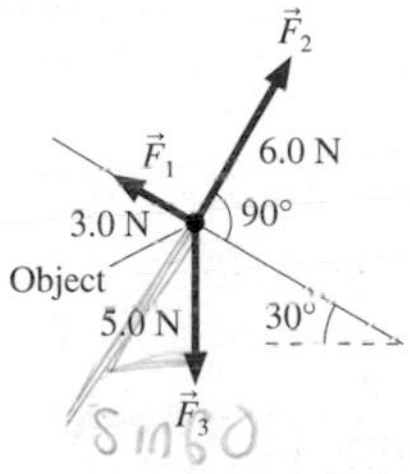

$\vec{F}_2$

6.0 N

$\vec{F}_1$ 90°

3.0 N

Object

5.0 N   30°

$\vec{F}_3$

FIGURE P3.45

46. ‖ FIGURE P3.46 shows four electric charges located at the corners of a rectangle. Like charges, you will recall, repel each other while opposite charges attract. Charge B exerts a repulsive force (directly *away from* B) on charge A of 3.0 N. Charge C exerts an attractive force (directly *toward* C) on charge A of 6.0 N. Finally, charge D exerts an attractive force of 2.0 N on charge A. Assuming that forces are vectors, what are the magnitude and direction of the net force $\vec{F}_{\text{net}}$ exerted on charge A?

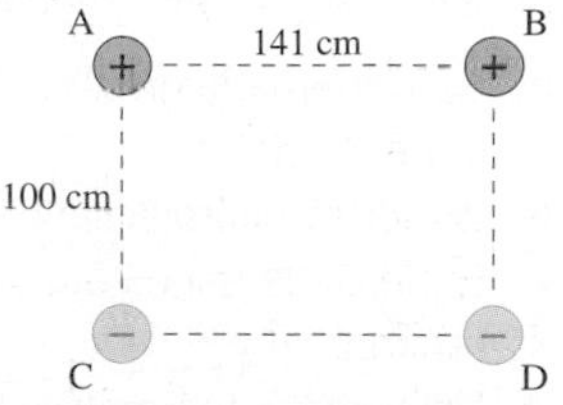

A   141 cm   B

(+)   (+)

100 cm

(−)   (−)

C   D

FIGURE P3.46

STOP TO THINK ANSWERS

Stop to Think 3.1: c. The graphical construction of $\vec{A}_1 + \vec{A}_2 + \vec{A}_3$ is shown at right.

Stop to Think 3.2: a. The graphical construction of $2\vec{A} - \vec{B}$ is shown at right.

Stop to Think 3.3: $C_x = -4$ cm, $C_y = 2$ cm.

Stop to Think 3.4: c. Vector $\vec{C}$ points to the left and down, so both C_x and C_y are negative. C_x is in the numerator because it is the side opposite ϕ.

STOP TO THINK 3.1

$\vec{A}_1$ $\vec{A}_1 + \vec{A}_2$

$\vec{A}_3$

$\vec{A}_2$ Parallelogram of $\vec{A}_1$ and $\vec{A}_2$

$\vec{A}_1 + \vec{A}_2 + \vec{A}_3$

Parallelogram of $(\vec{A}_1 + \vec{A}_2)$ and $\vec{A}_3$

STOP TO THINK 3.2

$-\vec{B}$

$2\vec{A} - \vec{B}$

$2\vec{A}$

Kinematics in Two Dimensions

This diver is a spinning projectile following a parabolic trajectory.

▶ **Looking Ahead**

The goal of Chapter 4 is to learn to solve problems about motion in a plane. In this chapter you will learn to:

- Use kinematics in two dimensions.
- Understand projectile motion.
- Explore the issues of relative motion.
- Understand the mathematics of circular kinematics.

◀ **Looking Back**

This chapter uses vectors to extend kinematics to two dimensions. Please review:

- Section 1.5 Finding acceleration vectors on a motion diagram.
- Sections 2.5 and 2.6 Constant-acceleration kinematics and free fall.
- Sections 3.3 and 3.4 Decomposing vectors into components.

The one-dimensional motion of Chapter 2 has many interesting applications, but motion in the real world is often more complex. A car turning a corner, a basketball sailing toward the hoop, a planet orbiting the sun, and the diver in the photograph are examples of two-dimensional motion or, equivalently, motion in a plane.

This chapter will continue to focus on kinematics, the mathematical description of motion. We'll begin with motion in which two perpendicular components of acceleration are independent of each other. The most important such motion is that of a projectile. Then we'll turn to circular motion, analyzing particles in circular trajectories and rigid objects rotating on an axle. We'll then be ready, in the next chapter, to take up the *cause* of motion.

4.1 Acceleration

In Chapter 1 we defined the *average acceleration* $\vec{a}_{avg}$ of a moving object to be the vector

$$\vec{a}_{avg} = \frac{\Delta \vec{v}}{\Delta t} \qquad (4.1)$$

From its definition, we see that $\vec{a}$ **points in the same direction as** $\Delta\vec{v}$, the change of velocity. As an object moves, its velocity vector can change in two possible ways:

1. The magnitude of $\vec{v}$ can change, indicating a change in speed, or
2. The direction of $\vec{v}$ can change, indicating that the object has changed direction.

The one-dimensional kinematics of Chapter 2 considered only the acceleration of changing speed. Now it's time to look at the acceleration associated with changing direction.

Tactics Box 4.1 shows how we can use the velocity vectors on a motion diagram to find $\Delta \vec{v}$ and thus determine the direction of the average acceleration vector. This is an extension of the ideas of Tactics Box 1.3, which showed how to find $\vec{a}$ for one-dimensional motion.

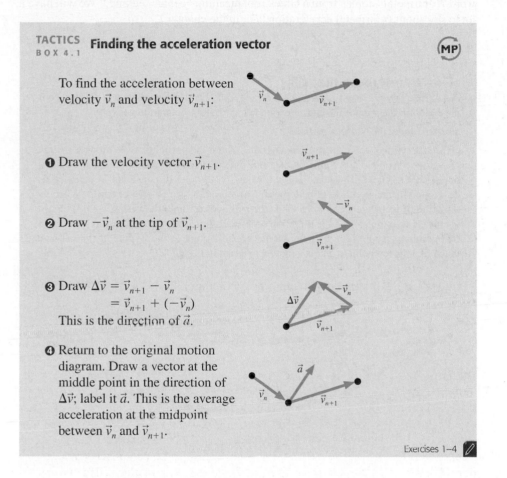

TACTICS BOX 4.1 **Finding the acceleration vector** (MP)

To find the acceleration between velocity $\vec{v}_n$ and velocity $\vec{v}_{n+1}$:

❶ Draw the velocity vector $\vec{v}_{n+1}$.

❷ Draw $-\vec{v}_n$ at the tip of $\vec{v}_{n+1}$.

❸ Draw $\Delta \vec{v} = \vec{v}_{n+1} - \vec{v}_n$
$\quad\quad = \vec{v}_{n+1} + (-\vec{v}_n)$
This is the direction of $\vec{a}$.

❹ Return to the original motion diagram. Draw a vector at the middle point in the direction of $\Delta \vec{v}$; label it $\vec{a}$. This is the average acceleration at the midpoint between $\vec{v}_n$ and $\vec{v}_{n+1}$.

Exercises 1–4

As an example, **FIGURE 4.1** is the motion diagram of Maria riding a Ferris wheel at the amusement park. Although Maria moves at constant speed, as we see from the fact that all the velocity vectors are the same length, she does *not* move with constant velocity. Each velocity vector points a different *direction*, making it a different vector, and that means Maria is accelerating. This is not a "speeding up" or "slowing down" acceleration, but it is still a change of velocity with time.

NOTE ▶ Our everyday use of the word "accelerate" means "speed up." The technical definition of acceleration—the rate of change of velocity—also includes slowing down, as you learned in Chapter 2, as well as changing direction. All these are motions that change the velocity. ◀

The inset to **FIGURE 4.2** on the next page uses the procedure of Tactics Box 4.1 to find the acceleration at the top of the circle. Vector $\vec{v}_n$ is the velocity vector that leads into this dot, while $\vec{v}_{n+1}$ moves away from it. From the circular geometry of the main figure, the two angles marked α are equal. Thus vectors $\vec{v}_{n+1}$ and $-\vec{v}_n$ form an isosceles

FIGURE 4.1 Maria's motion diagram on the Ferris wheel.

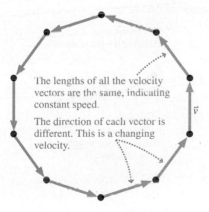

The lengths of all the velocity vectors are the same, indicating constant speed.

The direction of each vector is different. This is a changing velocity.

FIGURE 4.2 Finding Maria's acceleration.

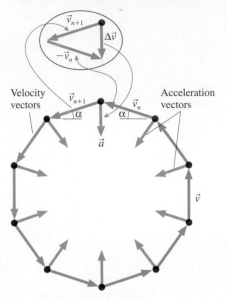

Velocity vectors

Acceleration vectors

triangle and vector $\Delta\vec{v}$ is exactly vertical. When $\vec{a}$ is drawn on the motion diagram, in the same direction as $\Delta\vec{v}$, we see that Maria's acceleration vector points directly to the center of the circle.

No matter which dot you select on the motion diagram in Figure 4.2, the velocity vectors leading toward and away from that dot change in such a way as to cause the acceleration to point to the center of the circle. You should convince yourself of this by finding $\vec{a}$ at several other points around the circle. An acceleration that always points directly toward the center of a circle is called a *centripetal acceleration*. The word "centripetal" comes from a Greek root meaning "center seeking." We will have a lot to say about centripetal acceleration later in the chapter.

EXAMPLE 4.1 Through the valley

A ball rolls down a long hill, through the valley, and back up the other side. Draw a complete motion diagram of the ball, showing velocity and acceleration vectors.

MODEL Model the ball as a particle.

VISUALIZE FIGURE 4.3 is the motion diagram. Where the particle moves along a *straight line,* it speeds up if $\vec{a}$ and $\vec{v}$ point in the same direction and slows down if $\vec{a}$ and $\vec{v}$ point in opposite directions. This idea was the basis for the one-dimensional kinematics we developed in Chapter 2. For linear motion, acceleration is a change of speed. When the direction of $\vec{v}$ changes, as it does when the ball goes through the valley, we need to use vector subtraction to find the direction of $\Delta\vec{v}$ and thus of $\vec{a}$. The procedure is shown at two points in the motion diagram. Notice that the point at the bottom of the valley is much like the top point of Maria's motion diagram in Figure 4.2.

FIGURE 4.3 The motion diagram of the ball of Example 4.1.

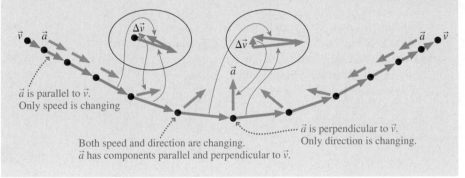

$\vec{a}$ is parallel to $\vec{v}$.
Only speed is changing

Both speed and direction are changing.
$\vec{a}$ has components parallel and perpendicular to $\vec{v}$.

$\vec{a}$ is perpendicular to $\vec{v}$.
Only direction is changing.

FIGURE 4.4 Decomposing the acceleration vector.

This component of $\vec{a}$ is changing the direction of $\vec{v}$.

This component of $\vec{a}$ is changing the length of $\vec{v}$ (i.e., the speed).

Chapter 3 showed how to decompose a vector into two components perpendicular and parallel to a line. In **FIGURE 4.4**, the acceleration vector $\vec{a}$ at one point in the motion diagram of Figure 4.3 has been decomposed into a piece $\vec{a}_{\parallel}$ parallel to $\vec{v}$ and a piece $\vec{a}_{\perp}$ perpendicular to $\vec{v}$. $\vec{a}_{\parallel}$ **is the piece of the acceleration vector that changes the speed.** In this case, the ball is speeding up because $\vec{a}_{\parallel}$ is parallel to the motion. **The component $\vec{a}_{\perp}$ is the piece of the acceleration that causes the velocity to change direction.** Notice that $\vec{a}$ *always* has a perpendicular component at points where the ball is changing directions.

On the straight sections of the hill, where only the speed is changing, the perpendicular component vanishes and $\vec{a}$ is parallel to $\vec{v}$. At the very bottom of the hill, where only the direction is changing, not the speed, the parallel component vanishes and $\vec{a}$ is perpendicular to $\vec{v}$. The important point to remember is that either changing speed *or* changing direction requires an acceleration.

This acceleration will cause the particle to

a. Speed up and curve upward.   b. Speed up and curve downward.
c. Slow down and curve upward.   d. Slow down and curve downward.
e. Move to the right and down.   f. Reverse direction.

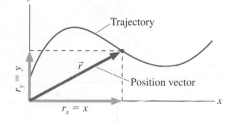

4.2 Two-Dimensional Kinematics

Motion diagrams are an important tool for visualizing motion, but we also need to develop a mathematical description of motion in two dimensions. We're going to begin with motion in which the horizontal and vertical components of acceleration are independent of each other. It will be easier to use x- and y-components of vectors, rather than components parallel and perpendicular to the motion. We'll point out, as we go along, the connection between these two points of view. For convenience, we'll say that the motion is in the xy-plane regardless of whether the plane of motion is horizontal or vertical.

FIGURE 4.5 shows a particle moving along a curved path—its *trajectory*—in the xy-plane. We can locate the particle in terms of its position vector

$$\vec{r} = r_x\hat{i} + r_y\hat{j}$$

where, as you'll recall, $\hat{i}$ and $\hat{j}$ are unit vectors along the x- and y-axes and r_x and r_y are, respectively, the x- and y-components of $\vec{r}$. But r_x is simply x, the x-coordinate of the point. Similarly, r_y is the y-coordinate y. Hence the position vector is

$$\vec{r} = x\hat{i} + y\hat{j} \qquad (4.2)$$

NOTE ▶ In Chapter 2 we made extensive use of position-versus-time graphs, either x versus t or y versus t. Figure 4.5, like many of the graphs we'll use in this chapter, is a graph of y versus x. In other words, it's an actual *picture* of the trajectory, not an abstract representation of the motion. ◀

As the particle in FIGURE 4.6 moves from position $\vec{r}_1$ at time t_1 to position $\vec{r}_2$ at time t_2, its *displacement*, the vector from point 1 to point 2, is

$$\Delta\vec{r} = \vec{r}_2 - \vec{r}_1$$

We can write the displacement vector in component form as

$$\Delta\vec{r} = \Delta x\hat{i} + \Delta y\hat{j} \qquad (4.3)$$

where $\Delta x = x_2 - x_1$ and $\Delta y = y_2 - y_1$ are the horizontal and vertical changes of position.

Chapter 1 defined the *average velocity* of a particle moving through a displacement $\Delta\vec{r}$ in a time interval Δt as

$$\vec{v}_{avg} = \frac{\Delta\vec{r}}{\Delta t} = \frac{\Delta x}{\Delta t}\hat{i} + \frac{\Delta y}{\Delta t}\hat{j} \qquad (4.4)$$

You learned in Chapter 2 that the *instantaneous velocity* is the limit of $\vec{v}_{avg}$ as $\Delta t \to 0$. Taking the limit of Equation 4.4 gives the instantaneous velocity in two dimensions:

$$\vec{v} = \lim_{\Delta t \to 0} \frac{\Delta\vec{r}}{\Delta t} = \frac{d\vec{r}}{dt} = \frac{dx}{dt}\hat{i} + \frac{dy}{dt}\hat{j} \qquad (4.5)$$

But we can also write the velocity vector in terms of its x- and y-components as

$$\vec{v} = v_x\hat{i} + v_y\hat{j} \qquad (4.6)$$

FIGURE 4.5 A particle moving along a trajectory in the xy-plane.

FIGURE 4.6 The particle undergoes displacement $\Delta\vec{r}$.

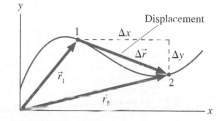

FIGURE 4.7 The instantaneous velocity vector $\vec{v}$ is tangent to the trajectory.

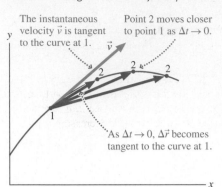

Comparing Equations 4.5 and 4.6, you can see that the velocity vector $\vec{v}$ has x- and y-components

$$v_x = \frac{dx}{dt} \quad \text{and} \quad v_y = \frac{dy}{dt} \tag{4.7}$$

That is, the x-component v_x of the velocity vector is the rate dx/dt at which the particle's x-coordinate is changing. The y-component is similar.

The average velocity $\vec{v}_{avg}$ points in the direction of $\Delta\vec{r}$, a fact we used in Chapter 1 to draw the velocity vectors on motion diagrams. **FIGURE 4.7** shows that $\Delta\vec{r}$ becomes tangent to the trajectory as $\Delta t \to 0$. Consequently, **the instantaneous velocity vector $\vec{v}$ is tangent to the trajectory.**

FIGURE 4.8 illustrates another important feature of the velocity vector. If the vector's angle θ is measured from the positive x-axis, the velocity vector components are

$$v_x = v\cos\theta$$
$$v_y = v\sin\theta \tag{4.8}$$

where

$$v = \sqrt{v_x^2 + v_y^2} \tag{4.9}$$

FIGURE 4.8 Relating the components of $\vec{v}$ to the speed and direction.

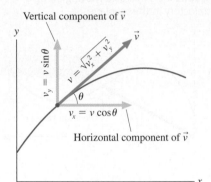

is the particle's *speed* at that point. Speed is always a positive number (or zero), whereas the components are *signed* quantities (i.e., they can be positive or negative) to convey information about the direction of the velocity vector. Conversely, we can use the two velocity components to determine the direction of motion:

$$\tan\theta = \frac{v_y}{v_x} \tag{4.10}$$

NOTE ▶ In Chapter 2, you learned that the *value* of the velocity component v_s at time t is given by the *slope* of the position-versus-time graph at time t. Now we see that the *direction* of the velocity vector $\vec{v}$ is given by the *tangent* to the y-versus-x graph of the trajectory. **FIGURE 4.9** reminds you that these two graphs use different interpretations of the tangent lines. The tangent to the trajectory does not tell us anything about how fast the particle is moving, only its direction. ◀

FIGURE 4.9 Two different uses of tangent lines.

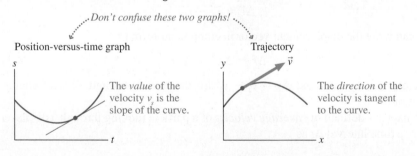

EXAMPLE 4.2 Describing the motion with graphs

A particle's motion is described by the two equations

$$x = 2t^2 \text{ m/s}$$
$$y = (5t + 5) \text{ m/s}$$

where the time t is in s.

a. Draw a graph of the particle's trajectory.
b. Draw a graph of the particle's speed as a function of time.

MODEL These are *parametric equations* that give the particle's coordinates x and y separately in terms of the parameter t.

SOLVE a. The trajectory is a curve in the xy-plane. The easiest way to proceed is to calculate x and y at several instants of time.

t (s)	x (m)	y (m)	v (m/s)
0	0	5	5.0
1	2	10	6.4
2	8	15	9.4
3	18	20	13.0
4	32	25	16.8

These points are plotted in FIGURE 4.10a, then a smooth curve is drawn through them to show the trajectory.

b. The particle's speed is given by Equation 4.9. We first need to use Equation 4.7 to find the components of the velocity vector:

$$v_x = \frac{dx}{dt} = 4t \text{ m/s} \quad \text{and} \quad v_y = \frac{dy}{dt} = 5 \text{ m/s}$$

Using these gives the particle's speed at time t:

$$v = \sqrt{v_x^2 + v_y^2} = \sqrt{16t^2 + 25} \text{ m/s}$$

The speed was computed in the table and is graphed in FIGURE 4.10b.

ASSESS The y-versus-x graph of Figure 4.10a is a trajectory, not a position-versus-time graph. Thus the slope is *not* the particle's speed. The particle is speeding up, as you can see in the second graph, even though the slope of the trajectory is decreasing.

FIGURE 4.10 Two motion graphs for the particle of Example 4.2.

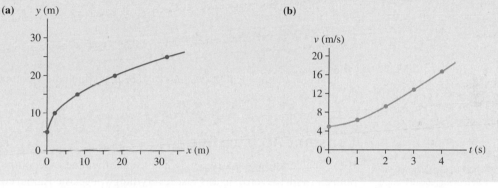

Acceleration

Let's return to the particle moving along a trajectory in the xy-plane. FIGURE 4.11a shows the instantaneous velocity $\vec{v}_1$ at point 1 and, a short time later, velocity $\vec{v}_2$ at point 2. These two vectors are tangent to the trajectory. We can use the vector-subtraction technique, shown in the inset, to find $\vec{a}_{avg}$ on this segment of the trajectory.

If we now take the limit $\Delta t \to 0$, the *instantaneous acceleration* is

$$\vec{a} = \lim_{\Delta t \to 0} \frac{\Delta \vec{v}}{\Delta t} = \frac{d\vec{v}}{dt} \tag{4.11}$$

As $\Delta t \to 0$, points 1 and 2 in Figure 4.11a merge, and the instantaneous acceleration $\vec{a}$ is found at the same point on the trajectory (and the same instant of time) as the instantaneous velocity $\vec{v}$. This is shown in FIGURE 4.11b.

FIGURE 4.11 The average and instantaneous acceleration vectors on a curved trajectory.

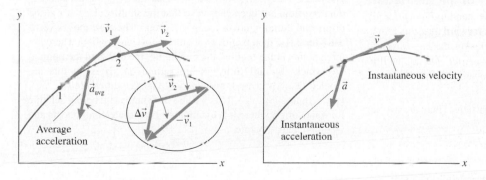

FIGURE 4.12 Decomposition of the instantaneous acceleration $\vec{a}$.

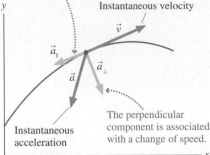

(a) The parallel component is associated with a change of speed.

Instantaneous velocity

The perpendicular component is associated with a change of speed.

Instantaneous acceleration

(b)

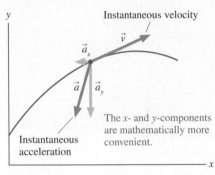

Instantaneous velocity

The x- and y-components are mathematically more convenient.

Instantaneous acceleration

By definition, the acceleration vector $\vec{a}$ is the rate at which the velocity $\vec{v}$ is changing at that instant. To show this, **FIGURE 4.12a** decomposes $\vec{a}$ into components $\vec{a}_\parallel$ and $\vec{a}_\perp$ that are parallel and perpendicular to the trajectory. $\vec{a}_\parallel$ is associated with a change of speed, and $\vec{a}_\perp$ is associated with a change of direction. Both kinds of changes are accelerations. Notice that $\vec{a}_\perp$ always points toward the "inside" of the curve because that is the direction in which $\vec{v}$ is changing.

The parallel and perpendicular components of $\vec{a}$ convey important ideas about acceleration, but it's usually more practical to write $\vec{a}$ in terms of the x- and y-components shown in **FIGURE 4.12b**. Because $\vec{v} = v_x\hat{i} + v_y\hat{j}$, we find

$$\vec{a} = a_x\hat{i} + a_y\hat{j} = \frac{d\vec{v}}{dt} = \frac{dv_x}{dt}\hat{i} + \frac{dv_y}{dt}\hat{j} \tag{4.12}$$

from which we see that

$$a_x = \frac{dv_x}{dt} \quad \text{and} \quad a_y = \frac{dv_y}{dt} \tag{4.13}$$

That is, the x-component of $\vec{a}$ is the rate dv_x/dt at which the x-component of velocity is changing.

Constant Acceleration

If the acceleration $\vec{a} = a_x\hat{i} + a_y\hat{j}$ is constant, then the two components a_x and a_y are both constant (or zero). In this case, everything you learned about constant-acceleration kinematics in Chapter 2 carries over to the x- and y-components of two-dimensional motion.

Consider a particle that moves with constant acceleration from an initial position $\vec{r}_i = x_i\hat{i} + y_i\hat{j}$, starting with initial velocity $\vec{v}_i = v_{ix}\hat{i} + v_{iy}\hat{j}$. Its position and velocity at a final point f are

$$x_f = x_i + v_{ix}\,\Delta t + \tfrac{1}{2}a_x(\Delta t)^2 \qquad y_f = y_i + v_{iy}\,\Delta t + \tfrac{1}{2}a_y(\Delta t)^2$$
$$v_{fx} = v_{ix} + a_x\,\Delta t \qquad\qquad v_{fy} = v_{iy} + a_y\,\Delta t \tag{4.14}$$

There are *many* quantities to keep track of in two-dimensional kinematics, making the pictorial representation all the more important as a problem-solving tool.

NOTE ▶ For constant acceleration, the x-component of the motion and the y-component of the motion are independent of each other. However, they remain connected through the fact that Δt must be the same for both. ◀

EXAMPLE 4.3 Plotting the trajectory of the shuttlecraft
The up thrusters on the shuttlecraft of the starship *Enterprise* give it an upward acceleration of 5.0 m/s². Its forward thrusters provide a forward acceleration of 20 m/s². As it leaves the *Enterprise,* the shuttlecraft turns on only the up thrusters. After clearing the flight deck, 3.0 s later, it adds the forward thrusters. Plot a trajectory of the shuttlecraft for its first 6 s.

MODEL Represent the shuttlecraft as a particle. There are two segments of constant-acceleration motion.

VISUALIZE FIGURE 4.13 shows a pictorial representation. The coordinate system has been chosen so that the shuttlecraft starts at the origin and initially moves along the y-axis. The craft moves vertically for 3.0 s, then begins to acquire a forward motion. There are three points in the motion: the beginning, the end, and the point at the which forward thrusters are turned on. These points are labeled (x_0, y_0), (x_1, y_1), and (x_2, y_2). The velocities are (v_{0x}, v_{0y}), (v_{1x}, v_{1y}), and (v_{2x}, v_{2y}). This will be our standard labeling scheme for trajectories, where it is essential to keep the x-components and y-components separate.

FIGURE 4.13 Pictorial representation of the motion of the shuttlecraft.

FIGURE 4.14 The shuttlecraft trajectory.

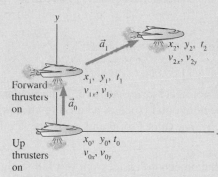

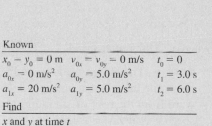

Known
$x_0 = y_0 = 0$ m $v_{0x} = v_{0y} = 0$ m/s $t_0 = 0$
$a_{0x} = 0$ m/s^2 $a_{0y} = 5.0$ m/s^2 $t_1 = 3.0$ s
$a_{1x} = 20$ m/s^2 $a_{1y} = 5.0$ m/s^2 $t_2 = 6.0$ s

Find
x and y at time t

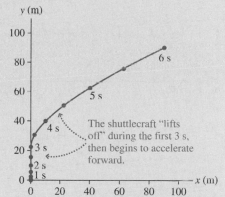

The shuttlecraft "lifts off" during the first 3 s, then begins to accelerate forward.

SOLVE During the first phase of the acceleration, when $a_{0x} = 0$ m/s^2 and $a_{0y} = 5.0$ m/s^2, the motion is described by

$$y = y_0 + v_{0y}(t - t_0) + \tfrac{1}{2}a_{0y}(t - t_0)^2 = 2.5t^2 \text{ m}$$

$$v_y = v_{0y} + a_{0y}(t - t_0) = 5.0t \text{ m/s}$$

where the time t is in s. These equations allow us to calculate the position and velocity at any time t. At $t_1 = 3.0$ s, when the first phase of the motion ends, we find that

$$x_1 = 0 \text{ m} \qquad v_{1x} = 0 \text{ m/s}$$
$$y_1 = 22.5 \text{ m} \qquad v_{1y} = 15 \text{ m/s}$$

During the next 3 s, when $a_{1x} = 20$ m/s^2 and $a_{1y} = 5.0$ m/s^2, the x- and y-coordinates are

$$x = x_1 + v_{1x}(t - t_1) + \tfrac{1}{2}a_{1x}(t - t_1)^2$$
$$= 10(t - 3.0)^2 \text{ m}$$

$$y = y_1 + v_{1y}(t - t_1) + \tfrac{1}{2}a_{1y}(t - t_1)^2$$
$$= \left(22.5 + 15(t - 3.0) + 2.5(t - 3.0)^2\right) \text{ m}$$

where, again, t is in s. To show the trajectory, we've calculated x and y every 0.5 s, plotted the points in **FIGURE 4.14**, and drawn a smooth curve through the points.

STOP TO THINK 4.2   During which time interval or intervals is the particle described by these position graphs at rest? More than one may be correct.

a. 0–1 s
b. 1–2 s
c. 2–3 s
d. 3–4 s

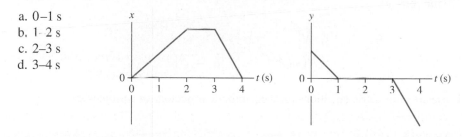

4.3 Projectile Motion

Baseballs and tennis balls flying through the air, Olympic divers, and daredevils shot from cannons all exhibit what we call *projectile motion*. A **projectile** is an object that moves in two dimensions under the influence of only gravity. Projectile motion is an extension of the free-fall motion we studied in Chapter 2. We will continue to neglect the influence of air resistance, leading to results that are a good approximation of reality for relatively heavy objects moving relatively slowly over relatively short distances. As we'll see, projectiles in two dimensions follow a *parabolic trajectory* like the one seen in **FIGURE 4.15**.

FIGURE 4.15 The parabolic trajectory of a bouncing ball.

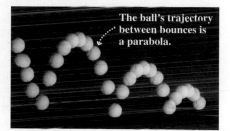

The ball's trajectory between bounces is a parabola.

FIGURE 4.16 A projectile launched with initial velocity $\vec{v}_i$.

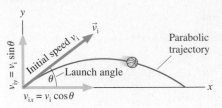

3.1–3.7 Activ Physics ONLINE

The start of a projectile's motion, be it thrown by hand or shot from a gun, is called the *launch,* and the angle θ of the initial velocity $\vec{v}_i$ above the horizontal (i.e., above the *x*-axis) is called the **launch angle**. **FIGURE 4.16** illustrates the relationship between the initial velocity vector $\vec{v}_i$ and the initial values of the components v_{ix} and v_{iy}. You can see that

$$v_{ix} = v_i \cos\theta$$
$$v_{iy} = v_i \sin\theta \qquad (4.15)$$

where v_i is the initial speed.

NOTE ▶ The components v_{ix} and v_{iy} are not necessarily positive. In particular, a projectile launched at an angle *below* the horizontal (such as a ball thrown downward from the roof of a building) has *negative* values for θ and v_{iy}. However, the speed v_i is always positive. ◀

Gravity acts downward, and we know that objects released from rest fall straight down, not sideways. Hence it's reasonable to assume—and we will justify this assumption in Chapter 8—that a projectile has no horizontal acceleration. Its vertical acceleration is simply that of free fall; thus

$$a_x = 0$$
$$a_y = -g \quad \text{(projectile motion)} \qquad (4.16)$$

In other words, **the vertical component of acceleration a_y is just the familiar $-g$ of free fall, while the horizontal component a_x is zero. Projectiles are in free fall.**

To see how these conditions influence the motion, **FIGURE 4.17** shows a projectile launched from $(x_i, y_i) = (0 \text{ m}, 0 \text{ m})$ with an initial velocity $\vec{v}_i = (9.8\hat{i} + 19.6\hat{j})$ m/s. The velocity and acceleration vectors are then shown every 1.0 s. The value of v_x never changes because there's no horizontal acceleration, but v_y decreases by 9.8 m/s every second. This is what it *means* to accelerate at $a_y = -9.8$ m/s^2 = $(-9.8$ m/s$)$ per second.

You can see from Figure 4.17 that **projectile motion is made up of two independent motions:** uniform motion at constant velocity in the horizontal direction and free-fall motion in the vertical direction. The kinematic equations that describe these two motions are

$$x_f = x_i + v_{ix}\,\Delta t \qquad\qquad y_f = y_i + v_{iy}\,\Delta t - \tfrac{1}{2}g(\Delta t)^2$$
$$v_{fx} = v_{ix} = \text{constant} \qquad\qquad v_{fy} = v_{iy} - g\,\Delta t \qquad (4.17)$$

These are parametric equations for the parabolic trajectory of a projectile.

FIGURE 4.17 The velocity and acceleration vectors of a projectile moving along a parabolic trajectory.

The vertical component of velocity decreases by 9.8 m/s every second.

The horizontal component of velocity is constant throughout the motion.

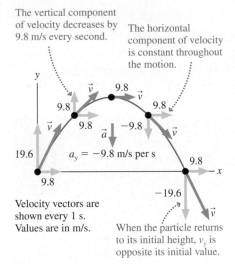

Velocity vectors are shown every 1 s. Values are in m/s.

When the particle returns to its initial height, v_y is opposite its initial value.

EXAMPLE 4.4 Don't try this at home!
A stunt man drives a car off a 10.0-m-high cliff at a speed of 20.0 m/s. How far does the car land from the base of the cliff?

MODEL Represent the car as a particle in free fall. Assume that the car is moving horizontally as it leaves the cliff.

VISUALIZE The pictorial representation, shown in **FIGURE 4.18**, is *very* important because the number of quantities to keep track of in projectile motion problems is quite large. We have chosen to put the origin at the base of the cliff. The assumption that the car is moving horizontally as it leaves the cliff leads to $v_{0x} = v_0$ and $v_{0y} = 0$ m/s. A motion diagram is not essential in projectile motion problems because we already know that the projectile follows a parabolic trajectory with $\vec{a} = -g\hat{j}$.

SOLVE Each point on the trajectory has *x*- and *y*-components of position, velocity, and acceleration but only *one* value of time.

FIGURE 4.18 Pictorial representation for the car of Example 4.4.

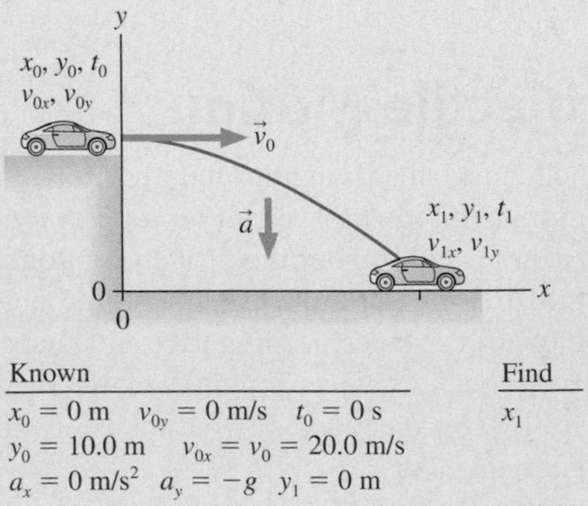

x_0, y_0, t_0
v_{0x}, v_{0y}

$\vec{v}_0$

x_1, y_1, t_1
v_{1x}, v_{1y}

$\vec{a}$

Known		Find
$x_0 = 0$ m $\quad v_{0y} = 0$ m/s $\quad t_0 = 0$ s		x_1
$y_0 = 10.0$ m $\quad v_{0x} = v_0 = 20.0$ m/s		
$a_x = 0$ m/s^2 $\quad a_y = -g$ $\quad y_1 = 0$ m		

4.3 · Projectile Motion   **99**

The time needed to move horizontally to x_1 is the *same* time needed to fall vertically through distance y_0. **Although the horizontal and vertical motions are independent, they are connected through the time t.** This is a critical observation for solving projectile motion problems. The kinematics equations are

$$x_1 = x_0 + v_{0x}(t_1 - t_0) = v_0 t_1$$

$$y_1 = 0 = y_0 + v_{0y}(t_1 - t_0) - \tfrac{1}{2}g(t_1 - t_0)^2 = y_0 - \tfrac{1}{2}g t_1^2$$

We can use the vertical equation to determine the time t_1 needed to fall distance y_0:

$$t_1 = \sqrt{\frac{2y_0}{g}} = \sqrt{\frac{2(10.0 \text{ m})}{9.80 \text{ m/s}^2}} = 1.43 \text{ s}$$

We then insert this expression for t into the horizontal equation to find the distance traveled:

$$x_1 = v_0 t_1 = (20.0 \text{ m/s})(1.43 \text{ s}) = 28.6 \text{ m}$$

ASSESS The cliff height is ≈ 33 ft and the initial speed is $v_0 \approx 40$ mph. Traveling $x_1 = 29$ m ≈ 95 ft before hitting the ground seems reasonable.

The x- and y-equations of Example 4.4 are parametric equations. It's not hard to eliminate t and write an expression for y as a function of x. From the x_1 equation, $t_1 = x_1/v_0$. Substituting this into the y_1 equation, we find

$$y = y_0 - \frac{g}{2v_0^2}x^2 \qquad (4.18)$$

The graph of $y = ax^2$ is a parabola, so Equation 4.18 represents an inverted parabola that starts from height y_0. This proves, as we asserted above, that a projectile follows a parabolic trajectory.

Reasoning About Projectile Motion

Think about the following question:

A heavy ball is thrown exactly horizontally at height h above a horizontal field. At the exact instant that the ball is thrown, a second ball is simply dropped from height h. Which ball hits the ground first?

It may seem hard to believe, but—if air resistance is neglected—the balls hit the ground *simultaneously.* They do so because the horizontal and vertical components of projectile motion are independent of each other. The initial horizontal velocity of the first ball has *no* influence over its vertical motion. Neither ball has any initial motion in the vertical direction, so both fall distance h in the same amount of time. You can see this in **FIGURE 4.19**. The *vertical* motions of the two balls are identical, and they hit the floor simultaneously.

FIGURE 4.20a shows a useful way to think about the trajectory of a projectile. Without gravity, a projectile would follow a straight line. Because of gravity, the particle at time t has "fallen" a distance $\tfrac{1}{2}gt^2$ below this line. The separation grows as $\tfrac{1}{2}gt^2$, giving the trajectory its parabolic shape.

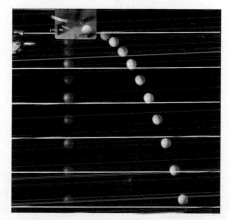

FIGURE 4.19 A projectile launched horizontally falls in the same time as a projectile that is released from rest.

FIGURE 4.20 A projectile follows a parabolic trajectory because it "falls" a distance $\tfrac{1}{2}gt^2$ below a straight-line trajectory.

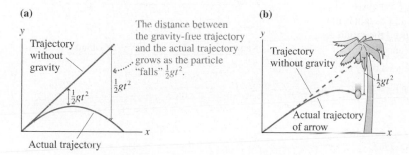

Use this idea to think about the following "classic" problem in physics:

A hungry bow-and-arrow hunter in the jungle wants to shoot down a coconut that is hanging from the branch of a tree. He points his arrow directly at the coconut, but as luck would have it, the coconut falls from the branch at the *exact* instant the hunter releases the string. Does the arrow hit the coconut?

You might think that the arrow will miss the falling coconut, but it doesn't. Although the arrow travels very fast, it follows a slightly curved parabolic trajectory, not a straight line. Had the coconut stayed on the tree, the arrow would have curved under its target as gravity causes it to fall a distance $\frac{1}{2}gt^2$ below the straight line. But $\frac{1}{2}gt^2$ is also the distance the coconut falls while the arrow is in flight. Thus, as FIGURE 4.20b shows, the arrow and the coconut fall the same distance and meet at the same point!

Solving Projectile Motion Problems

This information about projectiles is the basis of a problem-solving strategy.

PROBLEM-SOLVING
STRATEGY 4.1 **Projectile motion problems**   (MP)

MODEL Make simplifying assumptions, such as treating the object as a particle. Is it reasonable to ignore air resistance?

VISUALIZE Use a pictorial representation. Establish a coordinate system with the x-axis horizontal and the y-axis vertical. Show important points in the motion on a sketch. Define symbols and identify what the problem is trying to find.

SOLVE The acceleration is known: $a_x = 0$ and $a_y = -g$. Thus the problem is one of two-dimensional kinematics. The kinematic equations are

$$x_f = x_i + v_{ix}\,\Delta t \qquad\qquad y_f = y_i + v_{iy}\,\Delta t - \tfrac{1}{2}g(\Delta t)^2$$

$$v_{fx} = v_{ix} = \text{constant} \qquad v_{fy} = v_{iy} - g\,\Delta t$$

Δt is the same for the horizontal and vertical components of the motion. Find Δt from one component, then use that value for the other component.

ASSESS Check that your result has the correct units, is reasonable, and answers the question.

EXAMPLE 4.5 The distance of a fly ball
A baseball is hit at angle θ and is caught at the height from which it was hit. If the ball is hit at a 30.0° angle, with what speed must it leave the bat to travel 100 m?

MODEL Represent the ball as a particle. A baseball is fairly heavy and dense, so ignore air resistance.

VISUALIZE FIGURE 4.21 shows the pictorial representation. The height above the ground at which the ball was hit and caught is not relevant because it stays the same, so we have placed the origin at the point where the ball is hit. The ball travels distance x_1.

SOLVE The initial x- and y-components of the ball's velocity are

$$v_{0x} = v_0\cos\theta$$

$$v_{0y} = v_0\sin\theta$$

where v_0 is the initial speed that we need to find.

FIGURE 4.21 Pictorial representation for the baseball of Example 4.5.

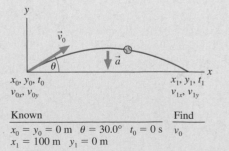

Known		Find
$x_0 = y_0 = 0$ m $\theta = 30.0°$ $t_0 = 0$ s		v_0
$x_1 = 100$ m $y_1 = 0$ m		

The kinematic equations of projectile motion are

$$x_1 = x_0 + v_{0x}(t_1 - t_0)$$
$$= (v_0\cos\theta)t_1$$
$$y_1 = 0 = y_0 + v_{0y}(t_1 - t_0) - \tfrac{1}{2}g(t_1 - t_0)^2$$
$$= (v_0\sin\theta)t_1 - \tfrac{1}{2}gt_1^2$$

We can use the vertical equation to find the time of flight:

$$0 = (v_0\sin\theta)t_1 - \tfrac{1}{2}gt_1^2 = (v_0\sin\theta - \tfrac{1}{2}gt_1)t_1$$

and thus

$$t_1 = 0 \quad \text{or} \quad \frac{2v_0\sin\theta}{g}$$

Both values are legitimate solutions. The first corresponds to the instant when $y = 0$ at the beginning of the trajectory and the second to when $y = 0$ at the end. Clearly, though, we want the sec-ond solution. Substituting this expression for t_1 into the equation for x_1 gives

$$x_1 = (v_0\cos\theta)\frac{2v_0\sin\theta}{g} = \frac{2v_0^2\sin\theta\cos\theta}{g}$$

We can simplify this result by using the trigonometric identity $2\sin\theta\cos\theta = \sin(2\theta)$. The distance traveled by the ball when hit at angle θ is

$$x_1 = \frac{v_0^2\sin(2\theta)}{g}$$

Setting $x_1 = 100$ m and solving for the speed v_0 give

$$v_0 = \sqrt{\frac{gx_1}{\sin(2\theta)}} = \sqrt{\frac{(9.80 \text{ m/s}^2)(100 \text{ m})}{\sin 60.0°}} = 33.6 \text{ m/s}$$

ASSESS A speed of 33.6 m/s $\approx$ 70 mph seems quite reasonable for a batted ball.

As Example 4.5 found, a projectile that lands at the same elevation from which it was fired travels distance

$$\text{distance} = \frac{v_0^2\sin(2\theta)}{g} \tag{4.19}$$

The maximum distance occurs for $\theta = 45°$, where $\sin(2\theta) = 1$. But there's more that we can learn from this equation. Because $\sin(180° - x) = \sin x$, it follows that $\sin(2(90° - \theta)) = \sin(2\theta)$. Consequently, a projectile launched either at angle θ or at angle $(90° - \theta)$ will travel the same distance. FIGURE 4.22 shows the trajectories of projectiles launched with the same initial speed in 15° increments of angle.

NOTE ▶ Equation 4.19 is *not* a general result. It applies *only* in situations where the projectile lands at the same elevation from which it was fired. ◀

FIGURE 4.22 Trajectories of a projectile launched at different angles with a speed of 99 m/s.

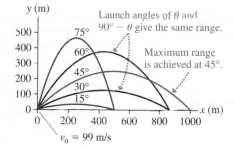

EXAMPLE 4.6 **Hit the box**
Students at an engineering contest use a compressed-air cannon to shoot a softball at a box being hoisted straight up at 10 m/s by a crane. The cannon, tilted upward at a 30° angle, is 100 m from the box and fires by remote control the instant the box leaves the ground. Students can control the launch speed of the softball by setting the air pressure. What launch speed should the students use to hit the box?

MODEL Represent both the softball and the box as particles. Ignore air resistance.

VISUALIZE FIGURE 4.23 shows the pictorial representation. There's a *large* amount of information to keep track of in a problem like this, making the pictorial representation essential for success.

FIGURE 4.23 The pictorial representation of the softball and the box.

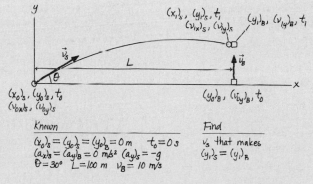

Continued

SOLVE The softball collides with the box if they have the same vertical position at exactly the same instant they have equal horizontal positions. Because the box moves vertically, the two will have the same horizontal position when the ball has traveled distance L to the right. This happens at time

$$t_1 = \frac{L}{(v_{0x})_S} = \frac{L}{v_S \cos\theta}$$

Equating the vertical positions at this instant, $(y_1)_S = (y_1)_B$, gives

$$(v_{0y})_S t_1 - \tfrac{1}{2}g t_1^2 = (v_{0y})_B t_1$$

One factor of t_1 cancels from each term. We can then use $(v_{0y})_S = v_S \sin\theta$, $(v_{0y})_B = v_B$, and the above expression for t_1 to write

$$(v_{0y})_S - \tfrac{1}{2}g t_1 - (v_{0y})_B = v_S \sin\theta - \tfrac{1}{2}g\frac{L}{v_S \cos\theta} - v_B = 0$$

Multiplying through by $2v_S \cos\theta$ gives a quadratic equation for v_S:

$$2\sin\theta\cos\theta\, v_S^2 - 2v_B \cos\theta\, v_S - gL = 0$$

It's important to learn to work problems with symbols rather than numbers. It you had plugged in numbers immediately, you wouldn't have recognized that t_1 cancels in the vertical equation and you would have done a lot of unnecessary calculations. Even so, writing the quadratic-equation solution symbolically is going to produce an ungainly mess. This is a reasonable time to insert numeric values—as long as all values are in SI units! With known values for θ, L, and v_B, the quadratic equation becomes

$$0.866v_S^2 - 17.3v_S - 980 = 0$$

The solutions to this equation are

$$v_S = \frac{17.3 \pm \sqrt{(17.3)^2 + 4(0.866)(980)}}{2(0.866)} = 45 \text{ m/s and } -25 \text{ m/s}$$

Speed must be positive, so the negative answer is not physically meaningful. The ball needs to be launched at a speed of 45 m/s.

ASSESS A speed of 45 m/s ≈ 90 mph. That seems quite reasonable for a ball shot at a target 100 m away.

STOP TO THINK 4.3   A 50 g marble rolls off a table and lands 2 m from the base of the table. A 100 g marble rolls off the same table with the same speed. It lands at distance

 a. Less than 1 m.   b. 1 m.   c. Between 1 m and 2 m.
 d. 2 m.   e. Between 2 m and 4 m.   f. 4 m.

4.4 Relative Motion

You've now dealt many times with problems that say something like "A car travels at 30 m/s" or "A plane travels at 300 m/s." But just what do these statements really mean?

In **FIGURE 4.24**, Amy, Bill, and Carlos are watching a runner. According to Amy, the runner's velocity is $v_x = 5$ m/s. But to Bill, who's riding alongside, the runner is lifting his legs up and down but going neither forward nor backward relative to Bill. As far as Bill is concerned, the runner's velocity is $v_x = 0$ m/s. Carlos sees the runner receding in his rearview mirror, in the *negative x*-direction, getting 10 m farther away from him every second. According to Carlos, the runner's velocity is $v_x = -10$ m/s. Which is the runner's *true* velocity?

Velocity is not a concept that can be true or false. The runner's velocity *relative to Amy* is 5 m/s. That is, his velocity is 5 m/s in a coordinate system attached to Amy and in which Amy is at rest. The runner's velocity relative to Bill is 0 m/s, and the velocity relative to Carlos is -10 m/s. These are all valid descriptions of the runner's motion.

FIGURE 4.24 Amy, Bill, and Carlos each measure the velocity of the runner. The velocities shown are in Amy's reference frame.

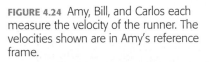
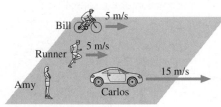

Relative Position

Suppose that Amy and Bill each have a coordinate system attached to their bodies. As Bill bicycles past Amy, he carries his coordinate system with him. Each is at rest in his or her coordinate system. Further, let's imagine that Amy and Bill each have helpers with meter sticks and stopwatches in their coordinate systems. Amy and Bill, with their helpers, are able to measure the position at which a physical event takes place and the time at which it occurs. A coordinate system in which an experimenter (possibly with the assistance of helpers) makes position and time measurements of physical events is called a **reference frame.** Amy and Bill each have their own reference frame.

Let's define two reference frames, shown in FIGURE 4.25, that we'll call frame S and frame S'. (The symbol ' is called a *prime*, and S' is pronounced "S prime.") The coordinate axes in frame S are x and y, while those in S' are x' and y'. Frame S' is moving with velocity $\vec{V}$ relative to frame S. That is, if an experimenter at rest in S measures the motion of the origin of S' as it goes past, she finds that the origin of S' has velocity $\vec{V}$. Of course, an experimenter at rest in S' would say that frame S has velocity $-\vec{V}$. We'll use an uppercase V for the velocity of reference frames, reserving lowercase v for the velocity of objects that move in the reference frames.

> **NOTE** ▶ There's no implication that either reference frame is "at rest." All we know is that the two frames are moving *relative* to each other with velocity $\vec{V}$. ◀

We will stipulate four conditions for reference frames:

1. The frames are oriented the same, with the x- and x'-axes parallel to each other.
2. The origins of frame S and frame S' coincide at $t = 0$.
3. All motion is in the xy-plane, so we don't need to consider the z-axis.
4. The relative velocity $\vec{V}$ is *constant.*

The first three are a matter of how we define the coordinate systems. Item 4, by contrast, is a choice with consequences. It says that we will consider only reference frames that move with constant speed in a straight line. These are called **inertial reference frames,** and we'll find in Chapter 5 that these are the reference frames in which the laws of motion are valid.

Suppose a light bulb flashes at time t. Experimenters in both reference frames see the flash and measure its position. Observers in S place the flash at position $\vec{r}$, as measured with respect to the coordinate system of frame S. Similarly, experimenters in S' determine that the flash occurred at position $\vec{r}'$, relative to the origin of S'. (We'll use primes to indicate positions and velocities measured in frame S'.)

What is the relationship between the position vectors $\vec{r}$ and $\vec{r}'$? It's not hard to see, from FIGURE 4.26, that

$$\vec{r} = \vec{r}' + \vec{R}$$

where $\vec{R}$ is the position vector of the origin of frame S' as measured in frame S.

Frame S' is traveling with velocity $\vec{V}$ relative to frame S, and their origins coincided at $t = 0$. At time t, when the light flashes, the origin of S' has moved to position $\vec{R} = t\vec{V}$. (We've written $t\vec{V}$ rather than $\vec{V}t$ because it is customary to write the scalar first.) Thus

$$\vec{r} = \vec{r}' + t\vec{V} \qquad \text{or} \qquad \vec{r}' = \vec{r} - t\vec{V} \tag{4.20}$$

Equation 4.20 is called the **Galilean transformation of position.** It will be easiest for most purposes to write this in terms of components:

$$
\begin{array}{ll}
x = x' + V_x t & x' = x - V_x t \\
& \text{or} \\
y = y' + V_y t & y' = y - V_y t
\end{array}
\tag{4.21}
$$

If we know *where* and *when* an event occurred in one reference frame, we can *transform* that position into any other reference frame that moves relative to the first with constant velocity $\vec{V}$.

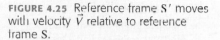

FIGURE 4.25 Reference frame S' moves with velocity $\vec{V}$ relative to reference frame S.

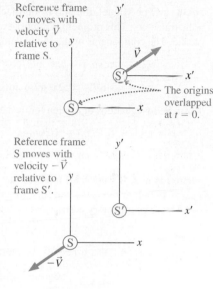

Reference frame S' moves with velocity $\vec{V}$ relative to frame S.

The origins overlapped at $t = 0$.

Reference frame S moves with velocity $-\vec{V}$ relative to frame S'.

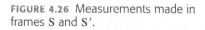

FIGURE 4.26 Measurements made in frames S and S'.

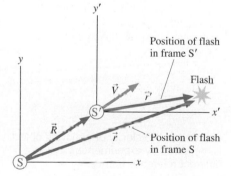

Position of flash in frame S'

Flash

Position of flash in frame S

EXAMPLE 4.7 **Watching a ball toss**

Miguel throws a ball upward at a 63.0° angle with a speed of 22.0 m/s. Nancy rides past Miguel on her bicycle at 10.0 m/s at the instant he releases the ball.

a. Find and graph the ball's trajectory as seen by Miguel.
b. Find and graph the ball's trajectory as seen by Nancy.

SOLVE a. For Miguel, the ball is a projectile that follows a parabolic trajectory. This problem is almost exactly the same as Example 4.5. The components of the initial velocity are

$$v_{0x} = v_0\cos\theta = (22.0 \text{ m/s})\cos 63.0° = 10.0 \text{ m/s}$$

$$v_{0y} = v_0\sin\theta = (22.0 \text{ m/s})\sin 63.0° = 19.6 \text{ m/s}$$

The x- and y-equations of motion for the ball's position at time t are

$$x = x_0 + v_{0x}(t - t_0) = 10.0t \text{ m}$$

$$y = y_0 + v_{0y}(t - t_0) - \tfrac{1}{2}g(t - t_0)^2 = (19.6t - 4.90t^2) \text{ m}$$

where t is in s. It's not hard to show that the ball reaches height $y_{\text{max}} = 19.6$ m at $t = 2.0$ s and hits the ground at $x_{\text{max}} = 40$ m at $t = 4.0$ s. The trajectory is shown in FIGURE 4.27a.

b. We can determine the trajectory Nancy sees by using Equations 4.21 to transform the ball's position from Miguel's reference frame into Nancy's reference frame. Let Miguel be in frame S and Nancy in frame S'. Nancy moves with velocity $\vec{V} = 10.0\hat{i}$ m/s relative to S. In terms of components, $V_x = 10.0$ m/s and $V_y = 0$ m/s. When Miguel, at time t, measures the ball at position (x, y) in frame S, Nancy finds the ball at

$$x' = x - V_x t = 10.0t - 10.0t = 0$$

$$y' = y - V_y t = y$$

Because Nancy's horizontal motion is the same as the ball's ($V_x = v_x = 10.0$ m/s in Miguel's frame), she doesn't see the ball moving either right or left. Nancy's experience is like that of Bill riding beside the runner in Figure 4.24. The ball moves *vertically* up and down in frame S'. Further, the vertical position y' in S' is the same as the vertical position y in S. According to Nancy, the ball goes straight up, reaches a height of 19.6 m, and falls straight back down. It hits the ground right beside her bicycle at $t = 4.0$ s. This is seen in FIGURE 4.27b.

FIGURE 4.27 A ball's trajectory as seen by Miguel and Nancy.

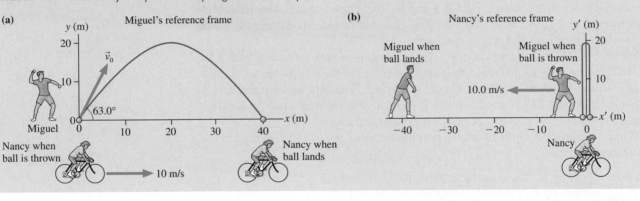

(a) Miguel's reference frame

(b) Nancy's reference frame

In Chapter 2 we studied *free fall,* vertical motion straight up and down. In Section 4.3 we studied the parabolic trajectories of *projectile motion.* Now, from Example 4.7 we see that **free-fall motion and projectile motion are really the same motion, simply seen from two different reference frames.** The motion is vertical in the *one* reference frame whose horizontal motion is the same as the ball's. The trajectory is a parabola in any other reference frame.

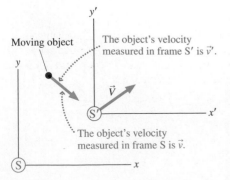

FIGURE 4.28 A velocity of a moving object is measured by experimenters in two different reference frames.

Relative Velocity

Let's think a bit more about Example 4.7. According to an observer in Miguel's reference frame, Miguel throws the ball with velocity $\vec{v}_0 = (10.0\hat{i} + 19.6\hat{j})$ m/s. The ball's initial speed is $v_0 = 22.0$ m/s. But in frame S', where Nancy sees the ball go straight up and down, Miguel throws the ball with velocity $\vec{v}_0' = 19.6\hat{j}$ m/s. An object's velocity measured in frame S is *not* the same as its velocity measured in frame S'.

FIGURE 4.28 shows a *moving object* that is observed from reference frames S and S'. Experimenters in frame S locate the object at position $\vec{r}$ and measure its velocity to be $\vec{v}$. Simultaneously, experimenters in S' measure position $\vec{r}'$ and velocity $\vec{v}'$. The position vectors, which are related by $\vec{r} = \vec{r}' + \vec{R}$, change as the object moves. In addition, $\vec{R}$ changes as the reference frames move relative to each other. The *rate* of change is

$$\frac{d\vec{r}}{dt} = \frac{d\vec{r}'}{dt} + \frac{d\vec{R}}{dt} \qquad (4.22)$$

The derivative $d\vec{r}/dt$, by definition, is the object's velocity $\vec{v}$ measured in frame S. Similarly, $d\vec{r}'/dt$ is the object's velocity $\vec{v}'$ measured in frame S', and $d\vec{R}/dt$ is the velocity $\vec{V}$ of frame S' relative to frame S. Consequently, Equation 4.22 tells us that

$$\vec{v} = \vec{v}' + \vec{V} \qquad \text{or} \qquad \vec{v}' = \vec{v} - \vec{V} \qquad (4.23)$$

Equation 4.23 is the **Galilean transformation of velocity.** If we know an object's velocity measured in one reference frame, we can transform it into the velocity that would be measured by an experimenter in a different reference frame. As FIGURE 4.29 shows, doing so is an exercise in vector addition.

We will often find it convenient, as we did with position, to write Equation 4.23 in terms of components:

$$
\begin{array}{ccc}
v_x = v_x' + V_x & & v_x' = v_x - V_x \\
& \text{or} & \\
v_y = v_y' + V_y & & v_y' = v_y - V_y
\end{array}
\qquad (4.24)
$$

This relationship between velocities measured by experimenters in different frames of reference was recognized by Galileo in his pioneering studies of motion, hence its name.

Let's apply Equation 4.24 to Miguel and Nancy. We've already noted that the ball's initial velocity in Miguel's frame, frame S, is $\vec{v}_0 = (10.0\hat{i} + 19.6\hat{j})$ m/s. Nancy was moving relative to Miguel at velocity $\vec{V} = 10.0\hat{i}$ m/s. We can use Equation 4.24 to transform the velocity to Nancy's frame, frame S', finding

$$v_x' = v_x - V_x = 10.0 \text{ m/s} - 10.0 \text{ m/s} = 0 \text{ m/s}$$

$$v_y' = v_y - V_y = 19.6 \text{ m/s} - 0 \text{ m/s} = 19.6 \text{ m/s}$$

Thus $\vec{v}_0' = 19.6\hat{j}$ m/s. This agrees with our conclusion from Example 4.7.

It's important to understand the distinction between the three velocities $\vec{v}$, $\vec{v}'$, and $\vec{V}$. $\vec{v}$ and $\vec{v}'$ are the velocities of an *object* that is observed from two different reference frames. Experimenters in S use their meter sticks and stopwatches to measure the object's velocity $\vec{v}$ in their reference frame. At the same time, experimenters in S' measure the velocity of the same object to be $\vec{v}'$. $\vec{V}$ is the relative velocity between two *reference frames;* the velocity of S' as measured by an experimenter in S. $\vec{V}$ has nothing to do with the object. It may happen that either $\vec{v}$ or $\vec{v}'$ is zero, meaning that the object is at rest in one reference frame, but we still must distinguish between the object and the reference frame.

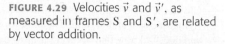

FIGURE 4.29 Velocities $\vec{v}$ and $\vec{v}'$, as measured in frames S and S', are related by vector addition.

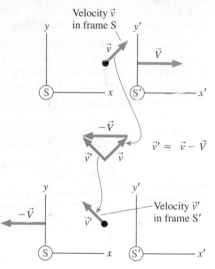

EXAMPLE 4.8 A speeding bullet

The police are chasing a bank robber. While driving at 50 m/s, they fire a bullet to shoot out a tire of his car. The police gun shoots bullets at 300 m/s. What is the bullet's speed as measured by a TV camera crew parked beside the road?

MODEL Assume that all motion is along the *x*-axis. Let the earth be frame S and a frame attached to the police car be S'. Frame S' moves relative to frame S with $V_x = 50$ m/s.

SOLVE The bullet is the moving object that will be observed from both frames. The gun is in frame S', so the bullet travels in this frame with $v_x' = 300$ m/s. We can use Equation 4.24 to transform the bullet's velocity into the earth reference frame:

$$v_x = v_x' + V_x = 300 \text{ m/s} + 50 \text{ m/s} = 350 \text{ m/s}$$

The Galilean velocity transformations are pretty much common sense for one-dimensional motion. Their real usefulness appears when an object travels in a *medium* that moves with respect to the earth. For example, a boat moves relative to the water. What is the boat's net motion if the water is a flowing river? Airplanes fly relative to the air, but the air at high altitudes often flows at high speed. Navigation of boats and planes requires knowing both the motion of the vessel in the medium and the motion of the medium relative to the earth.

EXAMPLE 4.9 **Flying to Cleveland I**

Cleveland is 300 miles east of Chicago. A plane leaves Chicago flying due east at 500 mph. The pilot forgot to check the weather and doesn't know that the wind is blowing to the south at 50 mph. What is the plane's ground speed? Where is the plane 0.60 hour later, when the pilot expects to land in Cleveland?

MODEL Let the earth be reference frame S. Chicago and Cleveland are at rest in the earth's frame. Let the air be frame S'. If the x-axis points east and the y-axis north, then the air is moving with respect to the earth at $\vec{V} = -50\hat{j}$ mph. The plane flies in the air, so its velocity in frame S' is $\vec{v}' = 500\hat{i}$ mph.

FIGURE 4.30 The wind causes a plane flying due east in the air to move to the southeast relative to the earth.

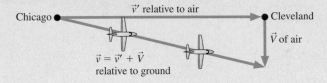

SOLVE The velocity transformation equation $\vec{v} = \vec{v}' + \vec{V}$ is a vector-addition equation. **FIGURE 4.30** shows graphically what happens. Although the nose of the plane points east, the wind carries the plane in a direction somewhat south of east. The plane's velocity relative to the ground is

$$\vec{v} = \vec{v}' + \vec{V} = (500\hat{i} - 50\hat{j}) \text{ mph}$$

The plane's ground speed, its speed in frame S, is

$$v = \sqrt{v_x^2 + v_y^2} = 502 \text{ mph}$$

After flying for 0.60 hour at this velocity, the plane's location (relative to Chicago) is

$$x = v_x t = (500 \text{ mph})(0.60 \text{ hr}) = 300 \text{ mi}$$
$$y = v_y t = (-50 \text{ mph})(0.60 \text{ hr}) = -30 \text{ mi}$$

The plane is 30 mi due south of Cleveland! Although the pilot thought he was flying to the east, his actual heading has been $\tan^{-1}(V/v) = \tan^{-1}(0.10) = 5.72°$ south of east.

EXAMPLE 4.10 **Flying to Cleveland II**

A wiser pilot flying from Chicago to Cleveland on the same day plots a course that will take her directly to Cleveland. In which direction does she fly the plane? How long does it take to reach Cleveland?

MODEL Let the earth be reference frame S. Let the air be frame S'. If the x-axis points east and the y-axis north, then the air is moving with respect to the earth at $\vec{V} = -50\hat{j}$ mph.

SOLVE The objective of navigation is to move between two points on the earth's surface, in frame S. The wiser pilot, who knows that the wind will affect her plane, draws the vector picture of **FIGURE 4.31**. The plane's velocity in frame S is

$$v_x = v_x' + V_x = (500 \text{ mph}) \cos\theta$$
$$v_y = v_y' + V_y = (500 \text{ mph}) \sin\theta - 50 \text{ mph}$$

In plotting her course, the pilot knows that she wants $v_y = 0$ in order to fly due east to Cleveland in the earth's frame. To achieve this, she'll actually have to point the nose of the plane somewhat north of east. The proper heading, found from $v_y = 0$, is

$$\theta = \sin^{-1}\left(\frac{50 \text{ mph}}{500 \text{ mph}}\right) = 5.74°$$

FIGURE 4.31 To travel due east in a south wind, a pilot has to point the plane somewhat to the northeast.

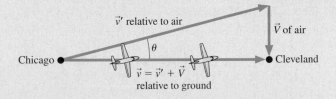

The plane's velocity in frame S is then $\vec{v} = (500 \text{ mph}) \times \cos 5.74\hat{i} = 497\hat{i}$ mph. You can see from Figure 4.31 that the plane's speed v in the earth's frame is slower than its speed v' in the air's reference frame. The time needed to fly to Cleveland at this speed is

$$t = \frac{300 \text{ mi}}{497 \text{ mph}} = 0.604 \text{ hr}$$

It takes 0.004 hr = 14 s longer to reach Cleveland than it would on a day without wind.

ASSESS A boat crossing a river or an ocean current faces the same difficulties. These are exactly the kinds of calculations performed by pilots of boats and planes as part of navigation.

A plane traveling horizontally to the right at 100 m/s flies past a helicopter that is going straight up at 20 m/s. From the helicopter's perspective, the plane's direction and speed are

a. Right and up, less than 100 m/s.
c. Right and up, more than 100 m/s.
e. Right and down, 100 m/s.

b. Right and up, 100 m/s.
d. Right and down, less than 100 m/s.
f. Right and down, more than 100 m/s.

4.5 Uniform Circular Motion

FIGURE 4.32 shows a particle moving around a circle of radius r. The particle might be a satellite in an orbit, a ball on the end of a string, or even just a dot painted on the side of a rotating wheel. Circular motion is another example of motion in a plane, but it is quite different from projectile motion.

To begin the study of circular motion, consider a particle that moves at *constant speed* around a circle of radius r. This is called **uniform circular motion.** Regardless of what the particle represents, its velocity vector $\vec{v}$ is always tangent to the circle. The particle's speed v is constant, so vector $\vec{v}$ is always the same length.

The time interval it takes the particle to go around the circle once, completing one revolution (abbreviated rev), is called the **period** of the motion. Period is represented by the symbol T. It's easy to relate the particle's period T to its speed v. For a particle moving with constant speed, speed is simply distance/time. In one period, the particle moves once around a circle of radius r and travels the circumference $2\pi r$. Thus

$$v = \frac{1 \text{ circumference}}{1 \text{ period}} = \frac{2\pi r}{T} \qquad (4.25)$$

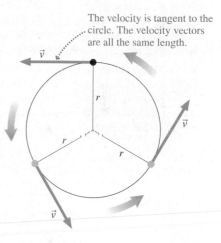

FIGURE 4.32 A particle in uniform circular motion.

The velocity is tangent to the circle. The velocity vectors are all the same length.

EXAMPLE 4.11 A rotating crankshaft

A 4.0-cm-diameter crankshaft turns at 2400 rpm (revolutions per minute). What is the speed of a point on the surface of the crankshaft?

SOLVE We need to determine the time it takes the crankshaft to make 1 rev. First, we convert 2400 rpm to revolutions per second:

$$\frac{2400 \text{ rev}}{1 \text{ min}} \times \frac{1 \text{ min}}{60 \text{ s}} = 40 \text{ rev/s}$$

If the crankshaft turns 40 times in 1 s, the time for 1 rev is

$$T = \frac{1}{40} \text{ s} = 0.025 \text{ s}$$

Thus the speed of a point on the surface, where $r = 2.0 \text{ cm} = 0.020 \text{ m}$, is

$$v = \frac{2\pi r}{T} = \frac{2\pi(0.020 \text{ m})}{0.025 \text{ s}} = 5.0 \text{ m/s}$$

Circular motion is one of the most important types of motion.

Angular Position

Rather than using xy-coordinates, it will be more convenient to describe the position of a particle in circular motion by its distance r from the center of the circle (labeled O) and its angle θ from the positive x-axis. This is shown in **FIGURE 4.33** on the next page. The angle θ is the **angular position** of the particle.

We can distinguish a position above the *x*-axis from a position that is an equal angle below the *x*-axis by *defining* θ to be positive when measured *counterclockwise* (ccw) from the positive *x*-axis. An angle measured clockwise (cw) from the positive *x*-axis has a negative value. "Clockwise" and "counterclockwise" in circular motion are analogous, respectively, to "left of the origin" and "right of the origin" in linear motion, which we associated with negative and positive values of *x*. A particle 30° below the positive *x*-axis is equally well described by either $\theta = -30°$ or $\theta = +330°$. We could also describe this particle by $\theta = \frac{11}{12}$ rev, where *revolutions* are another way to measure the angle.

Although degrees and revolutions are widely used measures of angle, mathematicians and scientists usually find it more useful to measure the angle θ in Figure 4.33 by using the **arc length** *s* that the particle travels along the edge of a circle of radius *r*. We define the angular unit of **radians** such that

$$\theta(\text{radians}) \equiv \frac{s}{r} \tag{4.26}$$

The radian, which is abbreviated rad, is the SI unit of an angle. An angle of 1 rad has an arc length *s* exactly equal to the radius *r*.

The arc length completely around a circle is the circle's circumference $2\pi r$. Thus the angle of a full circle is

$$\theta_{\text{full circle}} = \frac{2\pi r}{r} = 2\pi \text{ rad}$$

This relationship is the basis for the well-known conversion factors

$$1 \text{ rev} = 360° = 2\pi \text{ rad}$$

As a simple example of converting between radians and degrees, let's convert an angle of 1 rad to degrees:

$$1 \text{ rad} = 1 \text{ rad} \times \frac{360°}{2\pi \text{ rad}} = 57.3°$$

Thus a rough approximation is 1 rad $\approx$ 60°. We will often specify angles in degrees, but keep in mind that the SI unit is the radian.

An important consequence of Equation 4.26 is that the arc length spanning angle θ is

$$s = r\theta \qquad (\text{with } \theta \text{ in rad}) \tag{4.27}$$

This is a result that we will use often, but it is valid *only* if θ is measured in radians and not in degrees. This very simple relationship between angle and arc length is one of the primary motivations for using radians.

NOTE ▶ Units of angle are often troublesome. Unlike the kilogram or the second, for which we have standards, the radian is a *defined* unit. Further, its definition as a ratio of two lengths makes it a *pure number* without dimensions. Thus the unit of angle, be it radians or degrees or revolutions, is really just a *name* to remind us that we're dealing with an angle. Consequently, the radian unit sometimes appears or disappears without warning. This seems rather mysterious until you get used to it. This textbook will call your attention to such behavior the first few times it occurs. With a little practice, you'll soon learn when the rad unit is needed and when it's not. ◀

Angular Velocity

FIGURE 4.34 shows a particle moving in a circle from an initial angular position θ_i at time t_i to a final angular position θ_f at a later time t_f. The change $\Delta\theta = \theta_f - \theta_i$ is called the **angular displacement.** We can measure the particle's circular motion in terms of the

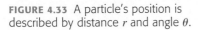
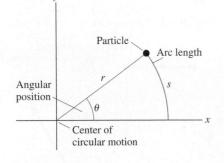

FIGURE 4.33 A particle's position is described by distance *r* and angle θ.

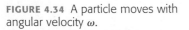
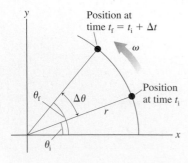

FIGURE 4.34 A particle moves with angular velocity ω.

rate of change of θ, just as we measured the particle's linear motion in terms of the rate of change of its position s.

In analogy with linear motion, let's define the *average angular velocity* to be

$$\text{average angular velocity} \equiv \frac{\Delta\theta}{\Delta t} \qquad (4.28)$$

As the time interval Δt becomes very small, $\Delta t \to 0$, we arrive at the definition of the instantaneous **angular velocity**

$$\omega \equiv \lim_{\Delta t \to 0} \frac{\Delta\theta}{\Delta t} = \frac{d\theta}{dt} \qquad \text{(angular velocity)} \qquad (4.29)$$

The symbol ω is a lowercase Greek omega, *not* an ordinary w. The SI unit of angular velocity is rad/s, but °/s, rev/s, and rev/min are also common units. Revolutions per minute is abbreviated rpm.

Angular velocity is the *rate* at which a particle's angular position is changing as it moves around a circle. A particle that starts from $\theta = 0$ rad with an angular velocity of 0.5 rad/s will be at angle $\theta = 0.5$ rad after 1 s, at $\theta = 1.0$ rad after 2 s, at $\theta = 1.5$ rad after 3 s, and so on. Its angular position is increasing at the *rate* of 0.5 radian per second. In analogy with uniform linear motion, which you studied in Chapter 2, uniform circular motion is motion in which the angle increases at a *constant* rate: **A particle moves with uniform circular motion if and only if its angular velocity ω is constant and unchanging.**

Angular velocity, like the velocity v_s of one-dimensional motion, can be positive or negative. The signs shown in FIGURE 4.35 are based on the fact that θ was defined to be positive for a counterclockwise rotation. Because the definition $\omega = d\theta/dt$ for circular motion parallels the definition $v_s = ds/dt$ for linear motion, the graphical relationships we found between v_s and s in Chapter 2 apply equally well to ω and θ:

- $\omega =$ slope of the θ-versus-t graph at time t
- $\theta_f = \theta_i +$ area under the ω-versus-t graph between t_i and t_f

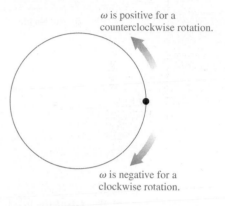

FIGURE 4.35 Positive and negative angular velocities.

ω is positive for a counterclockwise rotation.

ω is negative for a clockwise rotation.

EXAMPLE 4.12 A graphical representation of circular motion

FIGURE 4.36 shows the angular position of a particle moving around a circle of radius r. Describe the particle's motion and draw an ω-versus-t graph.

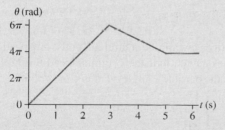

FIGURE 4.36 Angular position graph for the particle of Example 4.12.

SOLVE Although circular motion seems to "start over" every revolution (every 2π rad), the angular position θ continues to increase. $\theta = 6\pi$ rad corresponds to three revolutions. This particle makes 3 ccw rev (because θ is getting more positive) in 3 s, immediately reverses direction and makes 1 cw rev in 2 s, then stops at $t = 5$ s

and holds the position $\theta = 4\pi$ rad. The angular velocity is found by measuring the slope of the graph:

$t = 0\text{–}3$ s   slope $= \Delta\theta/\Delta t = 6\pi$ rad/3 s $= 2\pi$ rad/s

$t = 3\text{–}5$ s   slope $= \Delta\theta/\Delta t = -2\pi$ rad/2 s $= -\pi$ rad/s

$t > 5$ s   slope $= \Delta\theta/\Delta t = 0$ rad/s

These results are shown as an ω-versus-t graph in FIGURE 4.37. For the first 3 s, the motion is uniform circular motion with $\omega = 2\pi$ rad/s. The particle then changes to a different uniform circular motion with $\omega = -\pi$ rad/s for 2 s, then stops.

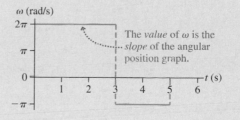

FIGURE 4.37 ω-versus-t graph for the particle of Example 4.12.

The *value* of ω is the *slope* of the angular position graph.

FIGURE 4.38 The ω-versus-t graph for uniform circular motion is a horizontal line.

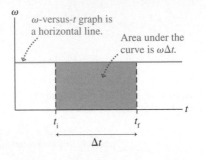

NOTE ▶ In physics, we nearly always want to give results as numerical values. Example 4.11 had a π in the equation, but we used its numerical value to compute $v = 5.0$ m/s. However, angles in radians are an exception to this rule. It's okay to leave a π in the value of θ or ω, and we have done so in Example 4.12. ◀

The angular velocity is constant during uniform circular motion, so the ω-versus-t graph is a horizontal line. It's easy to see from **FIGURE 4.38** that the area under the curve from t_i to t_f is simply $\omega \Delta t$. Consequently,

$$\theta_f = \theta_i + \omega \Delta t \qquad \text{(uniform circular motion)} \qquad (4.30)$$

Equation 4.30 is equivalent, with different variables, to the result $s_f = s_i + v_s \Delta t$ for uniform linear motion. You will see many more instances where circular motion is analogous to linear motion with angular variables replacing linear variables. Thus much of what you learned about linear kinematics carries over to circular motion.

Not surprisingly, the angular velocity ω is closely related to the *period T* of the motion. As a particle goes around a circle one time, its angular displacement is $\Delta\theta = 2\pi$ rad during the interval $\Delta t = T$. Thus, using the definition of angular velocity, we find

$$|\omega| = \frac{2\pi \text{ rad}}{T} \qquad \text{or} \qquad T = \frac{2\pi \text{ rad}}{|\omega|} \qquad (4.31)$$

The period alone gives only the absolute value of $|\omega|$. You need to know the direction of motion to determine the sign of ω.

EXAMPLE 4.13 At the roulette wheel
A small steel roulette ball rolls ccw around the inside of a 30-cm-diameter roulette wheel. The ball completes 2.0 rev in 1.20 s.

a. What is the ball's angular velocity?
b. What is the ball's position at $t = 2.0$ s? Assume $\theta_i = 0$.

MODEL Model the ball as a particle in uniform circular motion.

SOLVE a. The period of the ball's motion, the time for 1 rev, is $T = 0.60$ s. Angular velocity is positive for ccw motion, so

$$\omega = \frac{2\pi \text{ rad}}{T} = \frac{2\pi \text{ rad}}{0.60 \text{ s}} = 10.47 \text{ rad/s}$$

b. The ball starts at $\theta_i = 0$ rad. After $\Delta t = 2.0$ s, its position is given by Equation 4.30:

$$\theta_f = 0 \text{ rad} + (10.47 \text{ rad/s})(2.0 \text{ s}) = 20.94 \text{ rad}$$

where we've kept an extra significant figure to avoid round-off error. Although this is a mathematically acceptable answer, an observer would say that the ball is always located somewhere between 0° and 360°. Thus it is common practice to subtract an integer number of 2π rad, representing the completed revolutions. Because $20.94/2\pi = 3.333$, we can write

$$\theta_f = 20.94 \text{ rad} = 3.333 \times 2\pi \text{ rad}$$
$$= 3 \times 2\pi \text{ rad} + 0.333 \times 2\pi \text{ rad}$$
$$= 3 \times 2\pi \text{ rad} + 2.09 \text{ rad}$$

In other words, at $t = 2.0$ s the ball has completed 3 rev and is 2.09 rad = 120° into its fourth revolution. An observer would say that the ball's position is $\theta_f = 120°$.

STOP TO THINK 4.5 A particle moves cw around a circle at constant speed for 2.0 s. It then reverses direction and moves ccw at half the original speed until it has traveled through the same angle. Which is the particle's angle-versus-time graph?

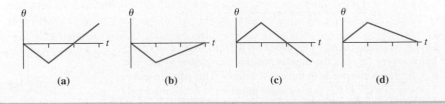

(a)   (b)   (c)   (d)

4.6 Velocity and Acceleration in Uniform Circular Motion

For a particle in circular motion, such as the one in **FIGURE 4.39**, the velocity vector $\vec{v}$ is always tangent to the circle. In other words, the velocity vector has only a *tangential component,* which we will designate v_t.

The tangential velocity component v_t is the rate ds/dt at which the particle moves *around* the circle, where s is the arc length measured from the positive x-axis. From Equation 4.27, the arc length is $s = r\theta$. Taking the derivative, we find

$$v_t = \frac{ds}{dt} = r\frac{d\theta}{dt}$$

But $d\theta/dt$ is the angular velocity ω. Thus the tangential velocity and the angular velocity are related by

$$v_t = \omega r \qquad \text{(with } \omega \text{ in rad/s)} \tag{4.32}$$

NOTE ▶ ω is restricted to rad/s because the relationship $s = r\theta$ is the definition of radians. While it may be convenient in some problems to measure ω in rev/s or rpm, you must convert to SI units of rad/s before using Equation 4.32. ◀

The tangential velocity v_t is positive for ccw motion, negative for cw motion. Because v_t is the only nonzero component of $\vec{v}$, the particle's speed is $v = |v_t| = |\omega| r$. We'll sometimes write this as $v = \omega r$ if there's no ambiguity about the sign of ω. Because a particle in uniform circular motion has constant speed, you can see that it must also rotate with constant angular velocity.

As a simple example, a particle moving cw at 2.0 m/s in a circle of radius 40 cm has angular velocity

$$\omega = \frac{v_t}{r} = \frac{-2.0 \text{ m/s}}{0.40 \text{ m}} = -5.0 \text{ rad/s}$$

where v_t and ω are negative because the motion is clockwise. Notice the units. Velocity divided by distance has units of s^{-1}. But because the division, in this case, gives us an angular quantity, we've inserted the *dimensionless* unit rad to give ω the appropriate units of rad/s.

Acceleration

Figures 4.1 and 4.2 at the beginning of this chapter looked at the uniform circular motion of a Ferris wheel. You are strongly encouraged to review those figures. There we found that a particle in uniform circular motion, although moving with constant speed, has an acceleration because the *direction* of the velocity vector $\vec{v}$ is always changing. The motion-diagram analysis showed that the **acceleration $\vec{a}$ points toward the center of the circle.** The instantaneous velocity is tangent to the circle, so $\vec{v}$ and $\vec{a}$ are perpendicular to each other at all points on the circle, as **FIGURE 4.40** shows.

The acceleration of uniform circular motion is called **centripetal acceleration,** a term from a Greek root meaning "center seeking." Centripetal acceleration is not a new type of acceleration; all we are doing is *naming* an acceleration that corresponds to a particular type of motion. The magnitude of the centripetal acceleration is constant because each successive $\Delta\vec{v}$ in the motion diagram has the same length.

The motion diagram tells us the direction of $\vec{a}$, but it doesn't give us a value for a. To complete our description of uniform circular motion, we need to find a quantitative

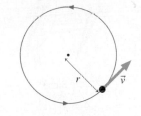

FIGURE 4.39 The velocity vector $\vec{v}$ has only a tangential component v_t.

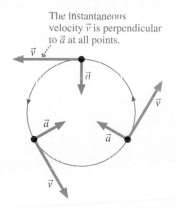

FIGURE 4.40 For uniform circular motion, the acceleration $\vec{a}$ always points to the center.

The instantaneous velocity $\vec{v}$ is perpendicular to $\vec{a}$ at all points.

FIGURE 4.41 Finding the acceleration of circular motion.

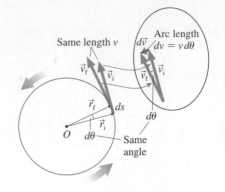

Same length v

Arc length $dv = v\,d\theta$

relationship between a and the particle's speed v. **FIGURE 4.41** shows the position $\vec{r}_i$ and velocity $\vec{v}_i$ at one instant of motion and the position $\vec{r}_f$ and velocity $\vec{v}_f$ an infinitesimal amount of time dt later. During this small interval of time, the particle turned through the infinitesimal angle $d\theta$ and traveled distance $ds = r\,d\theta$.

By definition, the acceleration is $\vec{a} = d\vec{v}/dt$. We can see from the inset to Figure 4.41 that $d\vec{v}$ points toward the center of the circle—that is, $\vec{a}$ is a centripetal acceleration. To find the magnitude of $\vec{a}$, we can see from the isosceles triangle of velocity vectors that, if $d\theta$ is in radians,

$$dv = |d\vec{v}| = v\,d\theta \qquad (4.33)$$

For uniform circular motion at constant speed, $v = ds/dt = r\,d\theta/dt$ and thus the time to turn through angle $d\theta$ is

$$dt = \frac{r\,d\theta}{v} \qquad (4.34)$$

Combining Equations 4.33 and 4.44, we see that the acceleration has magnitude

$$a = |\vec{a}| = \frac{|d\vec{v}|}{dt} = \frac{v\,d\theta}{r\,d\theta/v} = \frac{v^2}{r}$$

4.1 **Activ Physics** ONLINE

In vector notation, utilizing our knowledge that $\vec{a}$ points toward the center, we can write

$$\vec{a} = \left(\frac{v^2}{r},\text{ toward center of circle}\right) \qquad \text{(centripetal acceleration)} \qquad (4.35)$$

Using Equation 4.32, $v = \omega r$, we can also express the magnitude of the centripetal acceleration in terms of the angular velocity ω as

$$a = \omega^2 r \qquad (4.36)$$

NOTE ▶ Centripetal acceleration is not a constant acceleration. The magnitude of the centripetal acceleration is constant during uniform circular motion, but the direction of $\vec{a}$ is constantly changing. Thus the constant-acceleration kinematics equations of Chapter 2 do *not* apply to circular motion. ◀

EXAMPLE 4.14 The acceleration of a Ferris wheel
A typical carnival Ferris wheel has a radius of 9.0 m and rotates 4.0 times per minute. What magnitude acceleration do the riders experience?

MODEL Model the rider as a particle in uniform circular motion.

SOLVE The period is $T = \frac{1}{4}$ min = 15 s. From Equation 4.25, a rider's speed is

$$v = \frac{2\pi r}{T} = \frac{2\pi(9.0\text{ m})}{15\text{ s}} = 3.77\text{ m/s}$$

Consequently, the centripetal acceleration is

$$a = \frac{v^2}{r} = \frac{(3.77\text{ m/s})^2}{9.0\text{ m}} = 1.6\text{ m/s}^2$$

ASSESS This was not intended to be a profound problem, merely to illustrate how centripetal acceleration is computed. The acceleration is enough to be noticed and make the ride interesting, but not enough to be scary.

STOP TO THINK 4.6   Rank in order, from largest to smallest, the centripetal accelerations a_a to a_e of particles a to e.

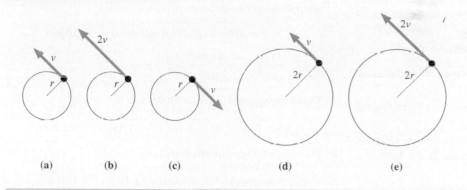

(a)   (b)   (c)   (d)   (e)

4.7 Nonuniform Circular Motion and Angular Acceleration

A roller coaster car doing a loop-the-loop slows down as it goes up one side, speeds up as it comes back down the other. The ball in a roulette wheel gradually slows until it stops. Circular motion with a changing speed is called **nonuniform circular motion.**

Figure 4.12 showed that the acceleration vector for motion in a plane can be decomposed into components $\vec{a}_\parallel$ (parallel to the trajectory) associated with a change of speed and $\vec{a}_\perp$ (perpendicular to the trajectory) associated with a change of direction. Centripetal acceleration is $\vec{a}_\perp$; it is always perpendicular to $\vec{v}$, and it is responsible for the particle constantly changing directions as it moves around the circle. For a particle to speed up or slow down as it moves around a circle, it needs—in addition to the centripetal acceleration—an acceleration parallel to the trajectory or, equivalently, parallel to $\vec{v}$. We'll call this the **tangential acceleration** a_t because, like the velocity v_t, it is always tangent to the circle.

FIGURE 4.42 shows a particle in nonuniform circular motion. *Any* circular motion, whether uniform or nonuniform, has a centripetal acceleration because the particle is changing direction. The centripetal acceleration, which points radially in toward the center of the circle, will now be called the **radial acceleration** a_r. Because of the tangential acceleration, **the acceleration vector $\vec{a}$ of a particle in nonuniform circular motion does *not* point toward the center of the circle.** It points "ahead" of center for a particle that is speeding up, as in Figure 4.42, but it would point "behind" center for a particle slowing down. You can see from Figure 4.42 that the magnitude of the acceleration is

$$a = \sqrt{a_r^2 + a_t^2} \tag{4.37}$$

As the particle speeds up or slows down, the tangential acceleration is simply the rate at which the tangential velocity changes:

$$a_t = \frac{dv_t}{dt} \tag{4.38}$$

If a_t is constant, then the arc length s traveled by the particle around the circle and the tangential velocity v_t are found from constant-acceleration kinematics:

$$s_f = s_i + v_{it}\,\Delta t + \tfrac{1}{2}a_t(\Delta t)^2$$
$$v_{ft} = v_{it} + a_t\,\Delta t \tag{4.39}$$

The roller coaster is in nonuniform circular motion as it goes around the loop.

FIGURE 4.42 Nonuniform circular motion.

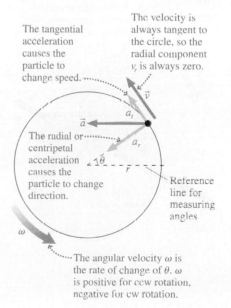

The tangential acceleration causes the particle to change speed.

The velocity is always tangent to the circle, so the radial component v_r is always zero.

The radial or centripetal acceleration causes the particle to change direction.

Reference line for measuring angles

The angular velocity ω is the rate of change of θ. ω is positive for ccw rotation, negative for cw rotation.

EXAMPLE 4.15 Circular rocket motion

A model rocket is attached to the end of a 2.0-m-long rigid rod. The other end of the rod rotates on a frictionless pivot, causing the rocket to move in a horizontal circle. The rocket accelerates at 1.0 m/s² for 10 s, starting from rest, then runs out of fuel.

a. What is the magnitude of $\vec{a}$ at $t = 2.0$ s?

b. What is the rocket's angular velocity, in rpm, when it runs out of fuel?

MODEL Model the rocket as a particle in nonuniform circular motion. Assume that the rocket starts from rest.

VISUALIZE **FIGURE 4.43** is a pictorial representation of the situation. The acceleration caused by the rocket motor is the tangential acceleration, $a_t = 1.0$ m/s².

FIGURE 4.43 The nonuniform circular motion of a model rocket.

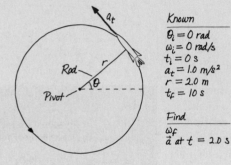

SOLVE a. The rocket motor creates the tangential acceleration $a_t = 1.0$ m/s². As the rocket speeds up, it acquires a radial, or centripetal, acceleration $a_r = v_t^2/r$. At $t = 2.0$ s,

$$v_{2\,s} = v_i + a_t\,\Delta t = 0 + (1.0 \text{ m/s}^2)(2.0 \text{ s}) = 2.0 \text{ m/s}$$

$$a_r = \frac{v_{2\,s}^2}{r} = \frac{(2.0 \text{ m/s})^2}{2.0 \text{ m}} = 2.0 \text{ m/s}^2$$

Thus the magnitude of the acceleration at this instant is

$$a = \sqrt{a_r^2 + a_t^2} = \sqrt{(2.0 \text{ m/s}^2)^2 + (1.0 \text{ m/s}^2)^2} = 2.2 \text{ m/s}^2$$

b. The tangential velocity after 10 s is

$$v_{10\,s} = v_i + a_t\,\Delta t = 0 + (1.0 \text{ m/s}^2)(10.0 \text{ s}) = 10.0 \text{ m/s}$$

and thus the angular velocity is

$$\omega_f = \frac{v_{10s}}{r} = \frac{10.0 \text{ m/s}}{2.0 \text{ m}} = 5.0 \text{ rad/s}$$

This is another situation in which we explicitly inserted the rad unit. Converting to rpm:

$$\omega_f = \frac{5.0 \text{ rad}}{1 \text{ s}} \times \frac{1 \text{ rev}}{2\pi \text{ rad}} \times \frac{60 \text{ s}}{1 \text{ min}} = 48 \text{ rpm}$$

Angular Acceleration

FIGURE 4.44 The two points on the wheel rotate with the same angular velocity.

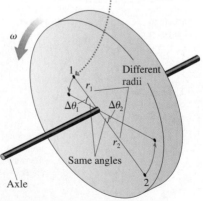

The kinematics of circular motion applies not only to particles but also to rotating solid objects. **FIGURE 4.44** shows a wheel rotating on an axle. Notice that two points on the wheel, marked with dots, turn through the *same angle* as the wheel rotates, even though their radii may be different. That is, $\Delta\theta_1 = \Delta\theta_2$ during some time interval Δt. As a consequence, the two points have equal angular velocities: $\omega_1 = \omega_2$. Thus we can refer to the angular velocity ω *of the wheel*.

Two points in a rotating object may have the same angular velocity, but they have *different* tangential velocities v_t if they have different distances from the point of rotation. Consequently, angular velocity is more useful than tangential velocity for describing a rotating object.

Suppose an object's rotation speeds up or slows down; that is, points on the object have a tangential acceleration a_t. We've seen that $a_t = dv_t/dt$ and that $v_t = r\omega$. Combining these two equations, we find

$$a_t = \frac{d(r\omega)}{dt} = r\frac{d\omega}{dt} \tag{4.40}$$

In taking the derivative, we used the fact that r is a constant for circular motion.

We originally defined acceleration as $a = dv/dt$, the rate of change of the velocity. The derivative in Equation 4.40 is the rate of change of the *angular* velocity. By analogy, let's define the **angular acceleration** α (Greek alpha) to be

$$\alpha \equiv \frac{d\omega}{dt} \qquad \text{(angular acceleration)} \tag{4.41}$$

SUMMARY

The goal of Chapter 4 has been to learn to solve problems about motion in a plane.

General Principles

The instantaneous velocity

$$\vec{v} = d\vec{r}/dt$$

is a vector tangent to the trajectory.

The instantaneous acceleration is

$$\vec{a} = d\vec{v}/dt$$

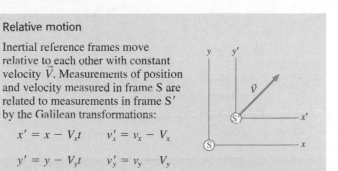

$\vec{a}_\parallel$, the component of $\vec{a}$ parallel to $\vec{v}$, is responsible for change of *speed*. $\vec{a}_\perp$, the component of $\vec{a}$ perpendicular to $\vec{v}$, is responsible for change of *direction*.

Relative motion

Inertial reference frames move relative to each other with constant velocity $\vec{V}$. Measurements of position and velocity measured in frame S are related to measurements in frame S′ by the Galilean transformations:

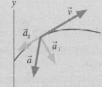

$$x' = x - V_x t \qquad v'_x = v_x - V_x$$
$$y' = y - V_y t \qquad v'_y = v_y - V_y$$

Important Concepts

Uniform Circular Motion

Angular velocity $\omega = d\theta/dt$.
v_t and ω are constant:

$$v_t = \omega r$$

The centripetal acceleration points toward the center of the circle:

$$a = \frac{v^2}{r} = \omega^2 r$$

It changes the particle's direction but not its speed.

Nonuniform Circular Motion

Angular acceleration $\alpha = d\omega/dt$.
The radial acceleration

$$a_r = \frac{v^2}{r} = \omega^2 r$$

changes the particle's direction. The tangential component

$$a_t = \alpha r$$

changes the particle's speed.

Applications

Kinematics in two dimensions

If $\vec{a}$ is constant, then the x- and y-components of motion are independent of each other.

$$x_f = x_i + v_{ix}\Delta t + \tfrac{1}{2}a_x(\Delta t)^2$$
$$y_f = y_i + v_{iy}\Delta t + \tfrac{1}{2}a_y(\Delta t)^2$$
$$v_{fx} = v_{ix} + a_x\Delta t$$
$$v_{fy} = v_{iy} + a_y\Delta t$$

Projectile motion

Projectile motion occurs if the object moves under the influence of only gravity. The motion is a parabola.

- Uniform motion in the horizontal direction with $v_{0x} = v_0\cos\theta$.
- Free-fall motion in the vertical direction with $a_y = -g$ and $v_{0y} = v_0\sin\theta$.
- The x and y kinematic equations have the *same* value for Δt.

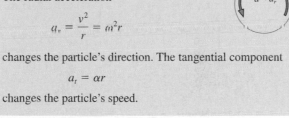

Circular motion kinematics

Period $T = \dfrac{2\pi r}{v} = \dfrac{2\pi}{\omega}$

Angular position $\theta = \dfrac{s}{r}$

$$\omega_f = \omega_i + \alpha\Delta t$$
$$\theta_f = \theta_i + \omega_i\Delta t + \tfrac{1}{2}\alpha(\Delta t)^2$$
$$\omega_f^2 = \omega_i^2 + 2\alpha\Delta\theta$$

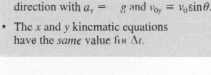

Angle, angular velocity, and angular acceleration are related graphically.

- The angular velocity is the slope of the angular position graph.
- The angular acceleration is the slope of the angular velocity graph.

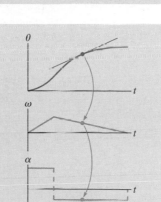

The units of angular acceleration are rad/s². Angular acceleration is the *rate* at which the angular velocity ω changes, just as linear acceleration is the rate at which the linear velocity v changes. FIGURE 4.45 illustrates the idea.

NOTE ▶ Be careful with the sign of α. You learned in Chapter 2 that positive and negative values of the acceleration can't be interpreted as simply "speeding up" and "slowing down." ◀

Because linear acceleration $\vec{a}$ is a vector, positive a_x means that v_x is increasing to the right or decreasing to the left. Negative a_x means that v_x is increasing to the left or decreasing to the right. For rotational motion, α is positive if ω is increasing ccw or decreasing cw, negative if ω is increasing cw or decreasing ccw. These cases are illustrated in FIGURE 4.46.

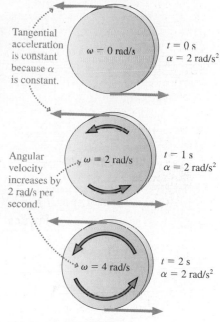

FIGURE 4.45 A wheel with angular acceleration $\alpha = 2$ rad/s².

FIGURE 4.46 The signs of angular velocity and acceleration.

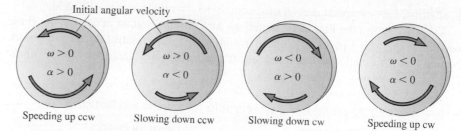

Initial angular velocity

$\omega > 0$ $\alpha > 0$ Speeding up ccw

$\omega > 0$ $\alpha < 0$ Slowing down ccw

$\omega < 0$ $\alpha > 0$ Slowing down cw

$\omega < 0$ $\alpha < 0$ Speeding up cw

Comparing Equations 4.40 and 4.41, we see that the tangential and angular accelerations are related by

$$a_t = r\alpha \qquad (4.42)$$

Two points on a rotating object have the *same* angular acceleration α, but in general they have *different* tangential accelerations because they are moving in circles of different radii. Notice the analogy between Equation 4.42 and the similar equation $v_t = r\omega$ for tangential and angular velocity.

Because α is the time derivative of ω, we can use exactly the same graphical relationships that we found for linear motion:

- α = slope of the ω-versus-t graph at time t
- $\omega_f = \omega_i$ + area under the α-versus-t graph between t_i and t_f

These relationships involving slopes and areas are illustrated in FIGURE 4.47.

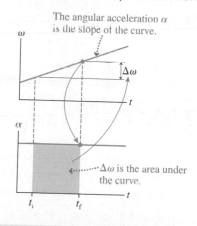

FIGURE 4.47 The graphical relationships between angular velocity and acceleration.

The angular acceleration α is the slope of the curve.

$\Delta\omega$ is the area under the curve.

EXAMPLE 4.16 A rotating wheel

FIGURE 4.48a is a graph of angular velocity versus time for a rotating wheel. Describe the motion and draw a graph of angular acceleration versus time.

SOLVE This is a wheel that starts from rest, gradually speeds up *counterclockwise* until reaching top speed at t_1, maintains a constant angular velocity until t_2, then gradually slows down until stopping at t_3. The motion is always ccw because ω is always positive. The angular acceleration graph of FIGURE 4.48b is based on the fact that α is the slope of the ω-versus-t graph.

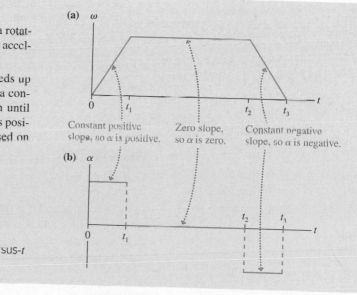

Constant positive slope, so α is positive.   Zero slope, so α is zero.   Constant negative slope, so α is negative.

FIGURE 4.48 ω-versus-t graph and the corresponding α-versus-t graph for a rotating wheel.

The circular kinematic equations, Equation 4.39, can be written in terms of angular quantities if we divide both sides by the radius r:

$$\frac{s_f}{r} = \frac{s_i}{r} + \frac{v_{it}}{r}\Delta t + \frac{1}{2}\frac{a_t}{r}(\Delta t)^2$$

$$\frac{v_{ft}}{r} = \frac{v_{it}}{r} + \frac{a_t}{r}\Delta t$$

You'll recognize that s/r is the angular position θ, v_t/r is the angular velocity ω, and a_t/r is the angular acceleration α. Thus the angular position and velocity after undergoing angular acceleration α are

$$\theta_f = \theta_i + \omega_i\Delta t + \frac{1}{2}\alpha(\Delta t)^2$$
$$\omega_f = \omega_i + \alpha t \qquad \text{(nonuniform circular motion)} \qquad (4.43)$$

7.7 **Activ Physics**

In addition, the centripetal acceleration equation $a_r = v^2/r = \omega^2 r$ is still valid.

Table 4.1 shows the kinematic equations for constant angular acceleration. These equations apply to a particle in circular motion or to the rotation of a rigid object. Notice that the rotational kinematic equations are exactly analogous to the linear kinematic equations.

TABLE 4.1 Rotational and linear kinematics for constant acceleration

Rotational kinematics	Linear kinematics
$\omega_f = \omega_i + \alpha\Delta t$	$v_{fs} = v_{is} + a_s\Delta t$
$\theta_f = \theta_i + \omega_i\Delta t + \frac{1}{2}\alpha(\Delta t)^2$	$s_f = s_i + v_{is}\Delta t + \frac{1}{2}a_s(\Delta t)^2$
$\omega_f^2 = \omega_i^2 + 2\alpha\Delta\theta$	$v_{fs}^2 = v_{is}^2 + 2a_s\Delta s$

EXAMPLE 4.17 Back to the roulette wheel

A small steel roulette ball rolls around the inside of a 30-cm-diameter roulette wheel. It is spun at 150 rpm, but it slows to 60 rpm over an interval of 5.0 s. How many revolutions does the ball make during these 5.0 s?

MODEL The ball is a particle in nonuniform circular motion. Assume constant angular acceleration as it slows.

SOLVE During these 5.0 s the ball rotates through angle

$$\Delta\theta = \theta_f - \theta_i = \omega_i\Delta t + \frac{1}{2}\alpha(\Delta t)^2$$

where $\Delta t = 5.0$ s. We can find the angular acceleration from the initial and final angular velocities, but first they must be converted to SI units:

$$\omega_i = 150\,\frac{\text{rev}}{\text{min}} \times \frac{1\,\text{min}}{60\,\text{s}} \times \frac{2\pi\,\text{rad}}{1\,\text{rev}} = 15.71\,\text{rad/s}$$

$$\omega_f = 60\,\frac{\text{rev}}{\text{min}} = 0.40\omega_i = 6.28\,\text{rad/s}$$

The angular acceleration α is

$$\alpha = \frac{\Delta\omega}{\Delta t} = \frac{6.28\,\text{rad/s} - 15.71\,\text{rad/s}}{5.0\,\text{s}} = -1.89\,\text{rad/s}^2$$

Thus the ball rotates through angle

$$\Delta\theta = (15.71\,\text{rad/s})(5.0\,\text{s}) + \frac{1}{2}(-1.89\,\text{rad/s}^2)(5.0\,\text{s})^2 = 54.9\,\text{rad}$$

Because $54.9/2\pi = 8.75$, the ball completes $8\frac{3}{4}$ revolutions as it slows to 60 rpm.

ASSESS This problem is solved just like the linear kinematics problems you learned to solve in Chapter 2.

STOP TO THINK 4.7 The fan blade is slowing down. What are the signs of ω and α?

a. ω is positive and α is positive.
b. ω is positive and α is negative.
c. ω is negative and α is positive.
d. ω is negative and α is negative.

Terms and Notation

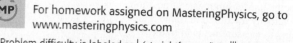

projectile	Galilean transformation of velocity	radians	radial acceleration, a_r
launch angle, θ	uniform circular motion	angular displacement, $\Delta\theta$	angular acceleration, α
reference frame	period, T	angular velocity, ω	
inertial reference frame	angular position, θ	centripetal acceleration, a	
Galilean transformation of position	arc length, s	nonuniform circular motion	
		tangential acceleration, a_t	

(MP) For homework assigned on MasteringPhysics, go to www.masteringphysics.com

Problem difficulty is labeled as | (straightforward) to ||| (challenging).

Problems labeled 🖉 can be done on a Dynamics Worksheet.

Problems labeled ▨ integrate significant material from earlier chapters.

CONCEPTUAL QUESTIONS

1. a. Is the particle in **FIGURE Q4.1** speeding up, slowing down, or traveling at constant speed?
   b. Is this particle curving to the right, curving to the left, or traveling straight?

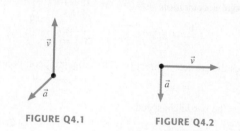

FIGURE Q4.1   **FIGURE Q4.2**

2. Is the particle in **FIGURE Q4.2** following a straight trajectory, a parabolic trajectory, or a circular trajectory? Or is not possible to tell? Explain.

3. Tarzan swings through the jungle by hanging from a vine.
   a. Immediately after stepping off a branch to swing over to another tree, is Tarzan's acceleration $\vec{a}$ zero or not zero? If not zero, which way does it point? Explain.
   b. Answer the same question at the lowest point in Tarzan's swing.

4. A projectile is launched over horizontal ground at an angle between 0° and 90°.
   a. Is there any point on the trajectory where $\vec{v}$ and $\vec{a}$ are parallel to each other? If so, where?
   b. Is there any point where $\vec{v}$ and $\vec{a}$ are perpendicular to each other? If so, where?

5. For a projectile, which of the following quantities are constant during the flight: x, y, r, v_x, v_y, v, a_x, a_y? Which of these quantities are zero throughout the flight?

6. A cart that is rolling at constant velocity on a level table fires a ball straight up.
   a. When the ball comes back down, will it land in front of the launching tube, behind the launching tube, or directly in the tube? Explain.
   b. Will your answer change if the cart is accelerating in the forward direction? If so, how?

7. A rock is thrown from a bridge at an angle 30° below horizontal.
   a. Immediately after the rock is released, is the magnitude of its acceleration greater than, less than, or equal to g? Explain.
   b. At the instant of impact, is the rock's speed greater than, less than, or equal to the speed with which it was thrown? Explain.

8. Rank in order, from shortest to longest (some may be simultaneous), the amount of time it takes each of the projectiles in **FIGURE Q4.8** to hit the ground. Ignore air resistance.

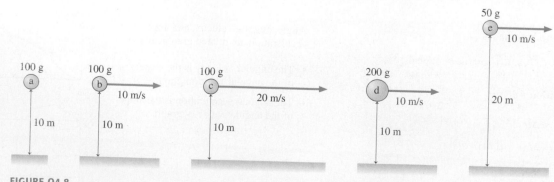

FIGURE Q4.8

9. Anita is running to the right at 5 m/s in **FIGURE Q4.9**. Balls 1 and 2 are thrown toward her by friends standing on the ground. According to Anita, both balls are approaching her at 10 m/s. Which ball was thrown at a faster speed? Or were they thrown with the same speed? Explain.

FIGURE Q4.9

10. An electromagnet on the ceiling of an airplane holds a steel ball. When a button is pushed, the magnet releases the ball. The experiment is first done while the plane is parked on the ground, and the point where the ball hits the floor is marked with an X. Then the experiment is repeated while the plane is flying level at a steady 500 mph. Does the ball land slightly in front of the X (toward the nose of the plane), on the X, or slightly behind the X (toward the tail of the plane)? Explain.

11. Zack is driving past his house in **FIGURE Q4.11**. He wants to toss his physics book out the window and have it land in his driveway. If he lets go of the book exactly as he passes the end of the driveway, should he direct his throw outward and toward the front of the car (throw 1), straight outward (throw 2), or outward and toward the back of the car (throw 3)? Explain.

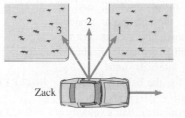

FIGURE Q4.11

12. In **FIGURE Q4.12**, Yvette and Zack are driving down the freeway side by side with their windows down. Zack wants to toss his physics book out the window and have it land in Yvette's front seat. Ignoring air resistance, should he direct his throw outward and toward the front of the car (throw 1), straight outward (throw 2), or outward and toward the back of the car (throw 3)? Explain.

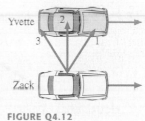

FIGURE Q4.12

13. In uniform circular motion, which of the following quantities are constant: speed, instantaneous velocity, tangential velocity, radial acceleration, tangential acceleration? Which of these quantities are zero throughout the motion?

14. **FIGURE Q4.14** shows three points on a steadily rotating wheel.
    a. Rank in order, from largest to smallest, the angular velocities ω_1, ω_2, and ω_3 of these points. Explain.
    b. Rank in order, from largest to smallest, the speeds v_1, v_2, and v_3 of these points. Explain.

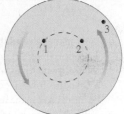

FIGURE Q4.14

15. **FIGURE Q14.15** shows four rotating wheels. For each, determine the signs (+ or −) of ω and α.

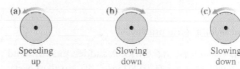

FIGURE Q4.15

16. **FIGURE Q4.16** shows a pendulum at one end point of its arc.
    a. At this point, is ω positive, negative, or zero? Explain.
    b. At this point, is α positive, negative, or zero? Explain.

FIGURE Q4.16

EXERCISES AND PROBLEMS

Exercises

Section 4.1 Acceleration

Problems 1 through 3 show a partial motion diagram. For each:
  a. Complete the motion diagram by adding acceleration vectors.
  b. Write a physics *problem* for which this is the correct motion diagram. Be imaginative! Don't forget to include enough information to make the problem complete and to state clearly what is to be found.

1. |

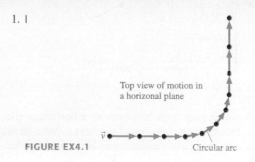

Top view of motion in a horizonal plane

$\vec{v}$

FIGURE EX4.1

Circular arc

2. |

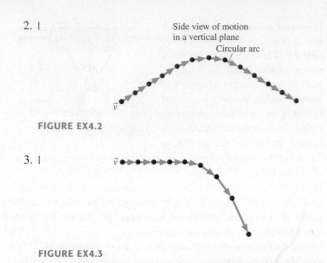

Side view of motion
in a vertical plane
Circular arc

$\vec{v}$

FIGURE EX4.2

3. |

$\vec{v}$

FIGURE EX4.3

4. || Consider a pendulum swinging back and forth on a string. Use a motion diagram analysis and a written explanation to answer the following questions.
   a. At the lowest point in the motion, is the velocity zero or nonzero? Is the acceleration zero or nonzero? If these vectors aren't zero, which way do they point?
   b. At the end of its arc, when the pendulum is at the highest point on the right or left side, is the velocity zero or nonzero? Is the acceleration zero or nonzero? If these vectors aren't zero, which way do they point?

Section 4.2 Two-Dimensional Kinematics

5. || A sailboat is traveling east at 5.0 m/s. A sudden gust of wind gives the boat an acceleration $\vec{a} = (0.80 \text{ m/s}^2, 40° \text{ north of east})$. What are the boat's speed and direction 6.0 s later when the gust subsides?

6. || A particle's trajectory is described by $x = \left(\frac{1}{2}t^3 - 2t^2\right)$ m and $y = \left(\frac{1}{2}t^2 - 2t\right)$ m, where t is in s.
   a. What are the particle's position and speed at $t = 0$ s and $t = 4$ s?
   b. What is the particle's direction of motion, measured as an angle from the x-axis, at $t = 0$ s and $t = 4$ s?

7. || A flying saucer maneuvering with constant acceleration is observed with the positions and velocities shown in **FIGURE EX4.7**. What is the saucer's acceleration $\vec{a}$?

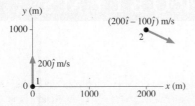

y (m)

1000

$(200\hat{i} - 100\hat{j})$ m/s

2

$200\hat{j}$ m/s

1

x (m)

0   1000   2000

FIGURE EX4.7

8. || A rocket-powered hockey puck moves on a horizontal frictionless table. **FIGURE EX4.8** at the top of the next column shows graphs of v_x and v_y, the x- and y-components of the puck's velocity. The puck starts at the origin.
   a. In which direction is the puck moving at $t = 2$ s? Give your answer as an angle from the x-axis.
   b. How far from the origin is the puck at $t = 5$ s?

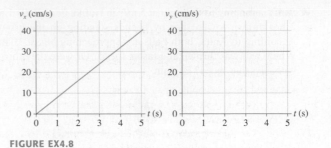

v_x (cm/s)

v_y (cm/s)

FIGURE EX4.8

9. || A rocket-powered hockey puck moves on a horizontal frictionless table. **FIGURE EX4.9** shows graphs of v_x and v_y, the x- and y-components of the puck's velocity. The puck starts at the origin.
   a. What is the magnitude of the puck's acceleration?
   b. How far from the origin is the puck at $t = 0$ s, 5 s, and 10 s?

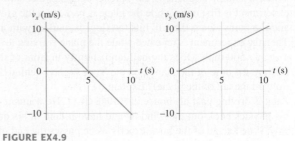

v_x (m/s)

v_y (m/s)

FIGURE EX4.9

Section 4.3 Projectile Motion

10. | A physics student on Planet Exidor throws a ball, and it follows the parabolic trajectory shown in **FIGURE EX4.10**. The ball's position is shown at 1 s intervals until $t = 3$ s. At $t = 1$ s, the ball's velocity is $\vec{v} = (2.0\hat{i} + 2.0\hat{j})$ m/s.
    a. Determine the ball's velocity at $t = 0$ s, 2 s, and 3 s.
    b. What is the value of g on Planet Exidor?
    c. What was the ball's launch angle?

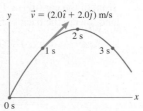

y $\vec{v} = (2.0\hat{i} + 2.0\hat{j})$ m/s

2 s

1 s   3 s

0 s x

FIGURE EX4.10

11. | A ball thrown horizontally at 25 m/s travels a horizontal distance of 50 m before hitting the ground. From what height was the ball thrown?

12. || A rifle is aimed horizontally at a target 50 m away. The bullet hits the target 2.0 cm below the aim point.
    a. What was the bullet's flight time?
    b. What was the bullet's speed as it left the barrel?

13. | A supply plane needs to drop a package of food to scientists working on a glacier in Greenland. The plane flies 100 m above the glacier at a speed of 150 m/s. How far short of the target should it drop the package?

14. | A sailor climbs to the top of the mast, 15 m above the deck, to look for land while his ship moves steadily forward through calm waters at 4.0 m/s. Unfortunately, he drops his spyglass to the deck below.
    a. Where does it land with respect to the base of the mast below him?
    b. Where does it land with respect to a fisherman sitting at rest in his dinghy as the ship goes past? Assume that the fisherman is even with the mast at the instant the spyglass is dropped.

Section 4.4 Relative Motion

15. | Ted is sitting in his lawn chair when Stella flies directly over-head, going southeast at 100 m/s. Five seconds later, a fire-cracker explodes 200 m east of Ted. What are the coordinates of the explosion in Stella's reference frame? Let Stella be at the origin, with her x-axis pointing to the east.

16. ‖ A boat takes 3.0 hours to travel 30 km down a river, then 5.0 hours to return. How fast is the river flowing?

17. ‖ When the moving sidewalk at the airport is broken, as it often seems to be, it takes you 50 s to walk from your gate to baggage claim. When it is working and you stand on the moving sidewalk the entire way, without walking, it takes 75 s to travel the same distance. How long will it take you to travel from the gate to baggage claim if you walk while riding on the moving sidewalk?

18. | Mary needs to row her boat across a 100-m-wide river that is flowing to the east at a speed of 3.0 m/s. Mary can row with a speed of 2.0 m/s.
    a. If Mary rows straight north, where will she land?
    b. Draw a picture showing her displacement due to rowing, her displacement due to the river's motion, and her net displacement.

19. | Susan, driving north at 60 mph, and Shawn, driving east at 45 mph, are approaching an intersection. What is Shawn's speed relative to Susan's reference frame?

Section 4.5 Uniform Circular Motion

20. | FIGURE EX4.20 shows the angular-position-versus-time graph for a particle moving in a circle.
    a. Write a description of the particle's motion.
    b. Draw the angular-velocity-versus-time graph.

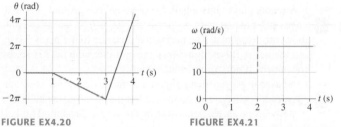

FIGURE EX4.20   FIGURE EX4.21

21. ‖ FIGURE EX4.21 shows the angular-velocity-versus-time graph for a particle moving in a circle. How many revolutions does the object make during the first 4 s?

22. ‖ FIGURE EX4.22 shows the angular-velocity-versus-time graph for a particle moving in a circle, starting from $\theta_0 = 0$ rad at $t = 0$ s. Draw the angular-position-versus-time graph. Include an appropriate scale on both axes.

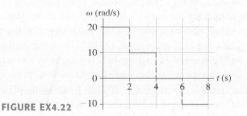

FIGURE EX4.22

23. | An old-fashioned single-play vinyl record rotates on a turntable at 45 rpm. What are (a) the angular velocity in rad/s and (b) the period of the motion?

24. ‖ The earth's radius is about 4000 miles. Kampala, the capital of Uganda, and Singapore are both nearly on the equator. The distance between them is 5000 miles.
    a. Through what angle do you turn, relative to the earth, if you fly from Kampala to Singapore? Give your answer in both radians and degrees.
    b. The flight from Kampala to Singapore takes 9 hours. What is the plane's angular velocity relative to the earth?

Section 4.6 Velocity and Acceleration in Uniform Circular Motion

25. ‖ A 300-m-tall tower is built on the equator. How much faster does a point at the top of the tower move than a point at the bottom? The earth's radius is 6400 km.

26. | How fast must a plane fly along the earth's equator so that the sun stands still relative to the passengers? In which direction must the plane fly, east to west or west to east? Give your answer in both km/hr and mph. The earth's radius is 6400 km.

27. | To withstand "g-forces" of up to 10 g's, caused by suddenly pulling out of a steep dive, fighter jet pilots train on a "human centrifuge." 10 g's is an acceleration of 98 m/s². If the length of the centrifuge arm is 12 m, at what speed is the rider moving when she experiences 10 g's?

28. | The radius of the earth's very nearly circular orbit around the sun is 1.5×10^{11} m. Find the magnitude of the earth's (a) velocity, (b) angular velocity, and (c) centripetal acceleration as it travels around the sun. Assume a year of 365 days.

29. ‖ Your roommate is working on his bicycle and has the bike upside down. He spins the 60-cm-diameter wheel, and you notice that a pebble stuck in the tread goes by three times every second. What are the pebble's speed and acceleration?

Section 4.7 Nonuniform Circular Motion and Angular Acceleration

30. | FIGURE EX4.30 shows the angular velocity graph of the crank-shaft in a car. Draw a graph of the angular acceleration versus time. Include appropriate numerical scales on both axes.

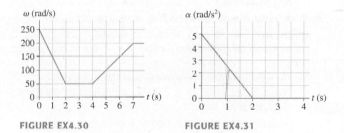

FIGURE EX4.30   FIGURE EX4.31

31. | FIGURE EX4.31 shows the angular acceleration graph of a turntable that starts from rest. Draw a graph of the angular veloc-ity versus time. Include appropriate numerical scales on both axes.

32. | FIGURE EX4.32 shows the angular-velocity-versus-time graph for a particle moving in a circle. How many revolu-tions does the object make during the first 4 s?

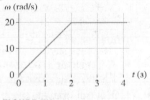

FIGURE EX4.32

33. ‖ a. **FIGURE EX4.33a** shows angular velocity versus time. Draw the corresponding graph of angular acceleration versus time.
    b. **FIGURE EX4.33b** shows angular acceleration versus time. Draw the corresponding graph of angular velocity versus time. Assume $\omega_0 = 0$.

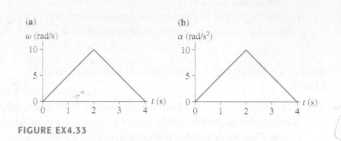

FIGURE EX4.33

34. ‖ A car speeds up as it turns from traveling due south to heading due east. When exactly halfway around the curve, the car's acceleration is 3.0 m/s², 20° north of east. What are the radial and tangential components of the acceleration at that point?

35. ‖ A 5.0-m-diameter merry-go-round is initially turning with a 4.0 s period. It slows down and stops in 20 s.
    a. Before slowing, what is the speed of a child on the rim?
    b. How many revolutions does the merry-go-round make as it stops?

36. ‖ A 3.0-cm-diameter crankshaft that is rotating at 2500 rpm comes to a halt in 1.5 s.
    a. What is the tangential acceleration of a point on the surface?
    b. How many revolutions does the crankshaft make as it stops?

37. | An electric fan goes from rest to 1800 rpm in 4.0 s. What is its angular acceleration?

38. | A bicycle wheel is rotating at 50 rpm when the cyclist begins to pedal harder, giving the wheel a constant angular acceleration of 0.50 rad/s².
    a. What is the wheel's angular velocity, in rpm, 10 s later?
    b. How many revolutions does the wheel make during this time?

Problems

39. ‖ A particle starts from rest at $\vec{r}_0 = 9.0\hat{j}$ m and moves in the xy-plane with the velocity shown in **FIGURE P4.39**. The particle passes through a wire hoop located at $\vec{r}_1 = 20\hat{i}$ m, then continues onward.
    a. At what time does the particle pass through the hoop?
    b. What is the value of v_{4y}, the y-component of the particle's velocity at $t = 4$ s?
    c. Calculate and plot the particle's trajectory.

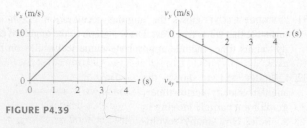

FIGURE P4.39

40. ‖ A projectile's horizontal range on level ground is $R = v_0^2 \sin 2\theta/g$. At what launch angle or angles will the projectile land at half of its maximum possible range?

41. ‖ a. A projectile is launched with speed v_0 and angle θ. Derive an expression for the projectile's maximum height h.
    b. A baseball is hit with a speed of 33.6 m/s. Calculate its height and the distance traveled if it is hit at angles of 30.0°, 45.0°, and 60.0°.

42. ‖ A projectile is fired with an initial speed of 30 m/s at an angle of 60° above the horizontal. The object hits the ground 7.5 s later.
    a. How much higher or lower is the launch point relative to the point where the projectile hits the ground?
    b. To what maximum height above the launch point does the projectile rise?
    c. What are the magnitude and direction of the projectile's velocity at the instant it hits the ground?

43. ‖ In the Olympic shotput event, an athlete throws the shot with an initial speed of 12.0 m/s at a 40.0° angle from the horizontal. The shot leaves her hand at a height of 1.80 m above the ground.
    a. How far does the shot travel?
    b. Repeat the calculation of part (a) for angles 42.5°, 45.0°, and 47.5°. Put all your results, including 40.0°, in a table. At what angle of release does she throw the farthest?

44. ‖ On the Apollo 14 mission to the moon, astronaut Alan Shepard hit a golf ball with a 6 iron. The free-fall acceleration on the moon is 1/6 of its value on earth. Suppose he hit the ball with a speed of 25 m/s at an angle 30° above the horizontal.
    a. How much farther did the ball travel on the moon than it would have on earth?
    b. For how much more time was the ball in flight?

45. ‖ A ball is thrown toward a cliff of height h with a speed of 30 m/s and an angle of 60° above horizontal. It lands on the edge of the cliff 4.0 s later.
    a. How high is the cliff?
    b. What was the maximum height of the ball?
    c. What is the ball's impact speed?

46. ‖ A tennis player hits a ball 2.0 m above the ground. The ball leaves his racquet with a speed of 20.0 m/s at an angle 5.0° above the horizontal. The horizontal distance to the net is 7.0 m, and the net is 1.0 m high. Does the ball clear the net? If so, by how much? If not, by how much does it miss?

47. ‖ A baseball player friend of yours wants to determine his pitching speed. You have him stand on a ledge and throw the ball horizontally from an elevation 4.0 m above the ground. The ball lands 25 m away.
    a. What is his pitching speed?
    b. As you think about it, you're not sure he threw the ball exactly horizontally. As you watch him throw, the pitches seem to vary from 5° below horizontal to 5° above horizontal. What is the *range* of speeds with which the ball might have left his hand?

48. ‖ You are playing right field for the baseball team. Your team is up by one run in the bottom of the last inning of the game when a ground ball slips through the infield and comes straight toward you. As you pick up the ball 65 m from home plate, you see a runner rounding third base and heading for home with the tying run. You throw the ball at an angle of 30° above the horizontal with just the right speed so that the ball is caught by the catcher, standing on home plate, at the same height as you threw it. As you release the ball, the runner is 20.0 m from home plate and running full speed at 8.0 m/s. Will the ball arrive in time for your team's catcher to make the tag and win the game?

49. || You're 6.0 m from one wall of a house. You want to toss a ball to your friend who is 6.0 m from the opposite wall. The throw and catch each occur 1.0 m above the ground.
    a. What minimum speed will allow the ball to clear the roof?
    b. At what angle should you toss the ball?

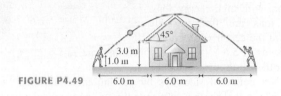

FIGURE P4.49   6.0 m   6.0 m   6.0 m

50. || Sand moves without slipping at 6.0 m/s down a conveyer that is tilted at 15°. The sand enters a pipe 3.0 m below the end of the conveyer belt, as shown in FIGURE P4.50. What is the horizontal distance d between the conveyer belt and the pipe?

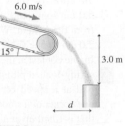

FIGURE P4.50

51. || King Arthur's knights fire a cannon from the top of the castle wall. The cannonball is fired at a speed of 50 m/s and an angle of 30°. A cannonball that was accidentally dropped hits the moat below in 1.5 s.
    a. How far from the castle wall does the cannonball hit the ground?
    b. What is the ball's maximum height above the ground?

52. || A stunt man drives a car at a speed of 20 m/s off a 30-m-high cliff. The road leading to the cliff is inclined upward at an angle of 20°.
    a. How far from the base of the cliff does the car land?
    b. What is the car's impact speed?

53. || A cat is chasing a mouse. The mouse runs in a straight line at a speed of 1.5 m/s. If the cat leaps off the floor at a 30° angle and a speed of 4.0 m/s, at what distance behind the mouse should the cat leap in order to land on the poor mouse?

54. || An assembly line has a staple gun that rolls to the left at 1.0 m/s while parts to be stapled roll past it to the right at 3.0 m/s. The staple gun fires 10 staples per second. How far apart are the staples in the finished part?

55. || Ships A and B leave port together. For the next two hours, ship A travels at 20 mph in a direction 30° west of north while the ship B travels 20° east of north at 25 mph.
    a. What is the distance between the two ships two hours after they depart?
    b. What is the speed of ship A as seen by ship B?

56. || A kayaker needs to paddle north across a 100-m-wide harbor. The tide is going out, creating a tidal current that flows to the east at 2.0 m/s. The kayaker can paddle with a speed of 3.0 m/s.
    a. In which direction should he paddle in order to travel straight across the harbor?
    b. How long will it take him to cross?

57. || Mike throws a ball upward and toward the east at a 63° angle with a speed of 22 m/s. Nancy drives east past Mike at 30 m/s at the instant he releases the ball.
    a. What is the ball's initial angle in Nancy's reference frame?
    b. Find and graph the ball's trajectory as seen by Nancy.

58. || A sailboat is sailing due east at 8.0 mph. The wind appears to blow from the southwest at 12.0 mph.
    a. What are the true wind speed and direction?
    b. What are the true wind speed and direction if the wind appears to blow from the northeast at 12.0 mph?

59. || While driving north at 25 m/s during a rainstorm you notice that the rain makes an angle of 38° with the vertical. While driving back home moments later at the same speed but in the opposite direction, you see that the rain is falling straight down. From these observations, determine the speed and angle of the raindrops relative to the ground.

60. || A plane has an airspeed of 200 mph. The pilot wishes to reach a destination 600 mi due east, but a wind is blowing at 50 mph in the direction 30° north of east.
    a. In what direction must the pilot head the plane in order to reach her destination?
    b. How long will the trip take?

61. || A typical laboratory centrifuge rotates at 4000 rpm. Test tubes have to be placed into a centrifuge very carefully because of the very large accelerations.
    a. What is the acceleration at the end of a test tube that is 10 cm from the axis of rotation?
    b. For comparison, what is the magnitude of the acceleration a test tube would experience if dropped from a height of 1.0 m and stopped in a 1.0-ms-long encounter with a hard floor?

62. || Astronauts use a centrifuge to simulate the acceleration of a rocket launch. The centrifuge takes 30 s to speed up from rest to its top speed of 1 rotation every 1.3 s. The astronaut is strapped into a seat 6.0 m from the axis.
    a. What is the astronaut's tangential acceleration during the first 30 s?
    b. How many g's of acceleration does the astronaut experience when the device is rotating at top speed? Each 9.8 m/s² of acceleration is 1 g.

63. ||| A car starts from rest on a curve with a radius of 120 m and accelerates at 1.0 m/s². Through what angle will the car have traveled when the magnitude of its total acceleration is 2.0 m/s²?

64. || As the earth rotates, what is the speed of (a) a physics student in Miami, Florida, at latitude 26°, and (b) a physics student in Fairbanks, Alaska, at latitude 65°? Ignore the revolution of the earth around the sun. The radius of the earth is 6400 km.

65. || Communications satellites are placed in a circular orbit where they stay directly over a fixed point on the equator as the earth rotates. These are called *geosynchronous orbits*. The radius of the earth is 6.37×10^6 m, and the altitude of a geosynchronous orbit is 3.58×10^7 m ($\approx 22{,}000$ miles). What are (a) the speed and (b) the magnitude of the acceleration of a satellite in a geosynchronous orbit?

66. || A magnetic computer disk 8.0 cm in diameter is initially at rest. A small dot is painted on the edge of the disk. The disk accelerates at 600 rad/s² for $\frac{1}{2}$ s, then coasts at a steady angular velocity for another $\frac{1}{2}$ s. What is the speed of the dot at $t = 1.0$ s? Through how many revolutions has the disk turned?

67. || A high-speed drill rotating ccw at 2400 rpm comes to a halt in 2.5 s.
    a. What is the drill's angular acceleration?
    b. How many revolutions does it make as it stops?

68. || An electric-generator turbine spins at 3600 rpm. Friction is so small that it takes the turbine 10 min to coast to a stop. How many revolutions does it make while stopping?

69. ‖ A wheel initially rotating at 60 rpm experiences the angular acceleration shown in **FIGURE P4.69**. What is the wheel's angular velocity, in rpm, at $t = 3.0$ s?

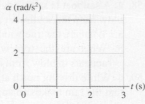

FIGURE P4.69

70. ‖ If you step on your car's brakes hard, the wheels stop turning (i.e., the wheels "lock") after 1.0 revolution. At the same constant acceleration, how many revolutions do the wheels make before stopping if your initial speed is twice as high?

71. ‖ A well-lubricated bicycle wheel spins a long time before stopping. Suppose a wheel initially rotating at 100 rpm takes 60 s to stop. If the angular acceleration is constant, how many revolutions does the wheel make while stopping?

72. ‖ A rock stuck in the tread of a 60.0-cm-diameter bicycle wheel has a tangential speed of 3.00 m/s. When the brakes are applied, the rock's tangential deceleration is 1.00 m/s².

   a. What are the magnitudes of the rock's angular velocity and angular acceleration at $t = 1.50$ s?

   b. At what time is the magnitude of the rock's acceleration equal to g?

73. ‖ A long string is wrapped around a 6.0-cm-diameter cylinder, initially at rest, that is free to rotate on an axle. The string is then pulled with a constant acceleration of 1.5 m/s² until 1.0 m of string has been unwound. If the string unwinds without slipping, what is the cylinder's angular speed, in rpm, at this time?

In Problems 74 through 76 you are given the equations that are used to solve a problem. For each of these, you are to

 a. Write a realistic problem for which these are the correct equations. Be sure that the answer your problem requests is consistent with the equations given.

 b. Finish the solution of the problem, including a pictorial representation.

74. $100 \text{ m} = 0 \text{ m} + (50\cos\theta \text{ m/s})t_1$

   $0 \text{ m} = 0 \text{ m} + (50\sin\theta \text{ m/s})t_1 - \frac{1}{2}(9.80 \text{ m/s}^2)t_1^2$

75. $v_x = -(6.0\cos 45°) \text{ m/s} + 3.0 \text{ m/s}$

   $v_y = (6.0\sin 45°) \text{ m/s} + 0 \text{ m/s}$,

   $100 \text{ m} = v_y t_1, \quad x_1 = v_x t_1$

76. $2.5 \text{ rad} = 0 \text{ rad} + \omega_i(10 \text{ s}) + \big((1.5 \text{ m/s}^2)/2(50 \text{ m})\big)(10 \text{ s})^2$

   $\omega_f = \omega_i + \big((1.5 \text{ m/s}^2)/(50 \text{ m})\big)(10 \text{ s})$

77. Write a realistic problem for which the x-versus-t and y-versus-t graphs shown in **FIGURE P4.77** represent the motion of an object. Be sure the answer your problem requests is consistent with the graphs. Then finish the solution of the problem.

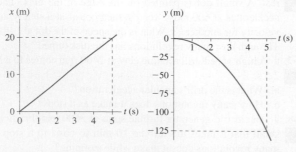

FIGURE P4.77

Challenge Problems

78. You are asked to consult for the city's research hospital, where a group of doctors is investigating the bombardment of cancer tumors with high-energy ions. The ions are fired directly toward the center of the tumor at speeds of 5.0×10^6 m/s. To cover the entire tumor area, the

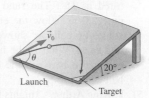

FIGURE CP4.78

ions are deflected sideways by passing them between two charged metal plates that accelerate the ions perpendicular to the direction of their initial motion. The acceleration region is 5.0 cm long, and the ends of the acceleration plates are 1.5 m from the patient. What acceleration is required to deflect an ion 2.0 cm to one side?

79. In one contest at the county fair, a spring-loaded plunger launches a ball at a speed of 3.0 m/s from one corner of a smooth, flat board that is tilted up at a 20° angle. To win, you must make the ball hit a small target at the adjacent corner, 2.50 m away. At what angle θ should you tilt the ball launcher?

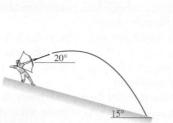

FIGURE CP4.79

80. You are watching an archery tournament when you start wondering how fast an arrow is shot from the bow. Remembering your physics, you ask one of the archers to shoot an arrow parallel to the ground. You find the arrow stuck in the ground 60 m away, making a 3° angle with the ground. How fast was the arrow shot?

81. An archer standing on a 15° slope shoots an arrow 20° above the horizontal, as shown in **FIGURE CP4.81**. How far down the slope does the arrow hit if it is shot with a speed of 50 m/s from 1.75 m above the ground?

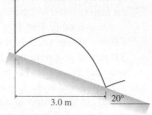

FIGURE CP4.81   **FIGURE CP4.82**

82. A rubber ball is dropped onto a ramp that is tilted at 20°, as shown in **FIGURE CP4.82**. A bouncing ball obeys the "law of reflection," which says that the ball leaves the surface at the same angle it approached the surface. The ball's next bounce is 3.0 m to the right of its first bounce. What is the ball's rebound speed on its first bounce?

83. A skateboarder starts up a 1.0-m-high, 30° ramp at a speed of 7.0 m/s. The skateboard wheels roll without friction. How far from the end of the ramp does the skateboarder touch down?

84. A motorcycle daredevil wants to set a record for jumping over burning school buses. He has hired you to help with the design. He intends to ride off a horizontal platform at 40 m/s, cross the burning buses in a pit below him, then land on a ramp sloping down at 20°. It's very important that he not bounce when he hits

the landing ramp because that could cause him to lose control and crash. You immediately recognize that he won't bounce if his velocity is parallel to the ramp as he touches down. This can be accomplished if the ramp is tangent to his trajectory *and* if he lands right on the front edge of the ramp. There's no room for error! Your task is to determine where to place the landing ramp. That is, how far from the edge of the launching platform should the front edge of the landing ramp be horizontally and how far below it? There's a clause in your contract that requires you to test your design before the hero goes on national television to set the record.

85. A cannon on a train car fires a projectile to the right with speed v_0, relative to the train, from a barrel elevated at angle θ. The cannon fires just as the train, which had been cruising to the right along a level track with speed v_{train}, begins to accelerate with acceleration a. Find an expression for the angle at which the projectile should be fired so that it lands as far as possible from the cannon. You can ignore the small height of the cannon above the track.

86. A child in danger of drowning in a river is being carried downstream by a current that flows uniformly with a speed of 2.0 m/s. The child is 200 m from the shore and 1500 m upstream of the boat dock from which the rescue team sets out. If their boat speed is 8.0 m/s with respect to the water, at what angle from the shore should the pilot leave the shore to go directly to the child?

87. Uri is on a flight from Boston to Los Angeles. His plane is traveling 20° south of west at 500 mph. Val is on a flight from Miami to Seattle. Her plane is traveling 30° north of west at 500 mph. Somewhere over Kansas, Uri's plane passes 1000 ft directly over Val's plane. Uri is sitting on the right side and can see Val's plane below him after they pass. Uri notices that the fuselage of Val's plane doesn't point in the direction that her plane is moving. What is the angle between the fuselage and the direction of motion?

88. An amusement park game, shown in **FIGURE CP4.88**, launches a marble toward a small cup. The marble is placed directly on top of a spring-loaded wheel and held with a clamp. When released, the wheel spins around clockwise at constant angular acceleration, opening the clamp and releasing the marble after making $\frac{11}{12}$ revolution. What angular acceleration is needed for the ball to land in the cup?

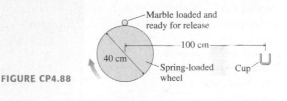

FIGURE CP4.88

STOP TO THINK ANSWERS

Stop to Think 4.1: d. The parallel component of $\vec{a}$ is opposite $\vec{v}$ and will cause the particle to slow down. The perpendicular component of $\vec{a}$ will cause the particle to change direction downward.

Stop to Think 4.2: c. $v = 0$ requires both $v_x = 0$ and $v_y = 0$. Neither x nor y can be changing.

Stop to Think 4.3: d. A projectile's acceleration $\vec{a} = -g\hat{j}$ does not depend on its mass. The second marble has the same initial velocity and the same acceleration, so it follows the same trajectory and lands at the same position.

Stop to Think 4.4: f. The helicopter frame S′ moves with $\vec{V} = 20\hat{j}$ m/s relative to the earth frame S. The plane moves with $\vec{V} = 100\hat{i}$ m/s in the earth's frame. The vector addition in the figure shows that $\vec{v}'$ is longer than $\vec{v}$.

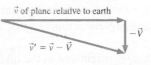

Stop to Think 4.5: b. An initial cw rotation causes the particle's angular position to become increasingly negative. The speed drops to half after reversing direction, so the slope becomes positive and is half as steep as the initial slope. Turning through the same angle returns the particle to $\theta = 0°$.

Stop to Think 4.6: $a_b > a_e > a_a = a_c > a_d$. Centripetal acceleration is v^2/r. Doubling r decreases a_r by a factor of 2. Doubling v increases a_r by a factor of 4. Reversing direction doesn't change a_r.

Stop to Think 4.7: c. ω is negative because the rotation is cw. Because ω is negative but becoming *less* negative, the change $\Delta\omega$ is *positive*. So α is positive.

5 Force and Motion

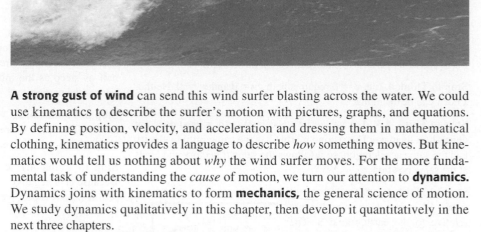

Wind surfing is a memorable example of the connection between force and motion.

▶ **Looking Ahead**

The goal of Chapter 5 is to establish a connection between force and motion. In this chapter you will learn to:

- Recognize what a force is and is not.
- Identify the specific forces acting on an object.
- Draw free-body diagrams.
- Understand the connection between force and motion.

◀ **Looking Back**

To master the material introduced in this chapter, you must understand how acceleration is determined and how vectors are used. Please review:

- Section 1.5 Acceleration.
- Section 3.2 Properties of vectors.

A strong gust of wind can send this wind surfer blasting across the water. We could use kinematics to describe the surfer's motion with pictures, graphs, and equations. By defining position, velocity, and acceleration and dressing them in mathematical clothing, kinematics provides a language to describe *how* something moves. But kinematics would tell us nothing about *why* the wind surfer moves. For the more fundamental task of understanding the *cause* of motion, we turn our attention to **dynamics.** Dynamics joins with kinematics to form **mechanics,** the general science of motion. We study dynamics qualitatively in this chapter, then develop it quantitatively in the next three chapters.

The theory of mechanics originated in the mid-1600s when Sir Isaac Newton formulated his laws of motion. These fundamental principles of mechanics explain how motion occurs as a consequence of forces. Newton's laws are more than 300 years old, but they still form the basis for our contemporary understanding of motion.

A challenge in learning physics is that a textbook is not an experiment. The book can assert that an experiment will have a certain outcome, but you may not be convinced unless you see or do the experiment yourself. Newton's laws are frequently contrary to our intuition, and a lack of familiarity with the evidence for Newton's laws is a source of difficulty for many people. You will have an opportunity through lecture demonstrations and in the laboratory to see for yourself the evidence supporting Newton's laws. Physics is not an arbitrary collection of definitions and formulas, but a consistent theory as to how the universe really works. It is only with experience and evidence that we learn to separate physical fact from fantasy.

5.1 Force

If you kick a ball, it rolls across the floor. If you pull on a door handle, the door opens. You know, from many years of experience, that some sort of *force* is required to move these objects. Our goal is to understand *why* motion occurs, and the observation that force and motion are related is a good place to start.

The two major issues that this chapter will examine are:

- What is a force?
- What is the connection between force and motion?

We begin with the first of these questions in the table below.

What is a force?

A force is a push or a pull.

Our commonsense idea of a **force** is that it is a *push* or a *pull*. We will refine this idea as we go along, but it is an adequate starting point. Notice our careful choice of words: We refer to "*a force*," rather than simply "force." We want to think of a force as a very specific *action*, so that we can talk about a single force or perhaps about two or three individual forces that we can clearly distinguish. Hence the concrete idea of "a force" acting on an object.

A force acts on an object.

Implicit in our concept of force is that a **force acts on an object.** In other words, pushes and pulls are applied *to* something—an object. From the object's perspective, it has a force *exerted* on it. Forces do not exist in isolation from the object that experiences them.

A force requires an agent.

Every force has an **agent,** something that acts or exerts power. That is, a force has a specific, identifiable *cause.* As you throw a ball, it is your hand, while in contact with the ball, that is the agent or the cause of the force exerted on the ball. *If* a force is being exerted on an object, you must be able to identify a specific cause (i.e., the agent) of that force. Conversely, a force is not exerted on an object *unless* you can identify a specific cause or agent. Although this idea may seem to be stating the obvious, you will find it to be a powerful tool for avoiding some common misconceptions about what is and is not a force.

A force is a vector.

If you push an object, you can push either gently or very hard. Similarly, you can push either left or right, up or down. To quantify a push, we need to specify both a magnitude *and* a direction. It should thus come as no surprise that a force is a vector quantity. The general symbol for a force is the vector symbol $\vec{F}$. The size or strength of a force is its magnitude F.

A force can be either a contact force . . .

There are two basic classes of forces, depending on whether the agent touches the object or not. **Contact forces** are forces that act on an object by touching it at a point of contact. The bat must touch the ball to hit it. A string must be tied to an object to pull it. The majority of forces that we will examine are contact forces.

. . . or a long-range force.

Long-range forces are forces that act on an object without physical contact. Magnetism is an example of a long-range force. You have undoubtedly held a magnet over a paper clip and seen the paper clip leap up to the magnet. A coffee cup released from your hand is pulled to the earth by the long-range force of gravity.

Let's summarize these ideas as our definition of force:

- A force is a push or a pull on an object.
- A force is a vector. It has both a magnitude and a direction.
- A force requires an agent. Something does the pushing or pulling.
- A force is either a contact force or a long-range force. Gravity is the only long-range force we will deal with until much later in the book.

NOTE ▶ In the particle model, objects cannot exert forces on themselves. A force on an object will always have an agent or cause external to the object. Now, there are certainly objects that have internal forces (think of all the forces inside the engine of your car!), but the particle model is not valid if you need to consider those internal forces. If you are going to treat your car as a particle and look only at the overall motion of the car as a whole, that motion will be a consequence of external forces acting on the car. ◀

Force Vectors

We can use a simple diagram to visualize how forces are exerted on objects. Because we are using the particle model, in which objects are treated as points, the process of drawing a force vector is straightforward. Here is how it goes:

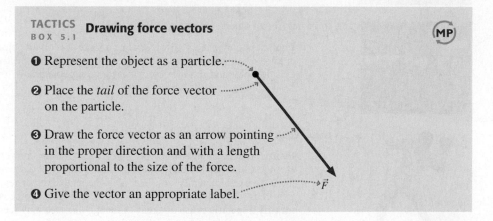

TACTICS BOX 5.1 **Drawing force vectors** (MP)

❶ Represent the object as a particle.

❷ Place the *tail* of the force vector on the particle.

❸ Draw the force vector as an arrow pointing in the proper direction and with a length proportional to the size of the force.

❹ Give the vector an appropriate label. $\vec{F}$

Step 2 may seem contrary to what a "push" should do, but recall that moving a vector does not change it as long as the length and angle do not change. The vector $\vec{F}$ is the same regardless of whether the tail or the tip is placed on the particle. Our reason for using the tail will become clear when we consider how to combine several forces.

FIGURE 5.1 shows three examples of force vectors. One is a push, one a pull, and one a long-range force, but in all three the *tail* of the force vector is placed on the particle representing the object.

FIGURE 5.1 Three examples of forces and their vector representations

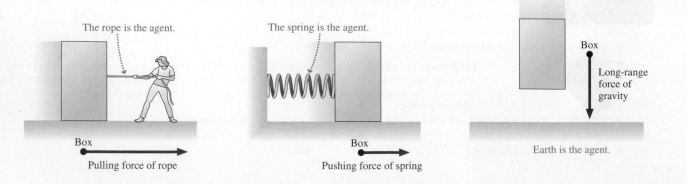

The rope is the agent.

Box
Pulling force of rope

The spring is the agent.

Box
Pushing force of spring

Box
Long-range force of gravity

Earth is the agent.

Combining Forces

FIGURE 5.2 Two forces applied to a box.

FIGURE 5.2a shows a box being pulled by two ropes, each exerting a force on the box. How will the box respond? Experimentally, we find that when several forces $\vec{F}_1$, $\vec{F}_2$, $\vec{F}_3$, . . . are exerted on an object, they combine to form a **net force** given by the *vector sum* of *all* the forces:

$$\vec{F}_{net} \equiv \sum_{i=1}^{N} \vec{F}_i = \vec{F}_1 + \vec{F}_2 + \cdots + \vec{F}_N \qquad (5.1)$$

Recall that $\equiv$ is the symbol meaning "is defined as." Mathematically, this summation is called a **superposition of forces**. The net force is sometimes called the *resultant force*. **FIGURE 5.2b** shows the net force on the box.

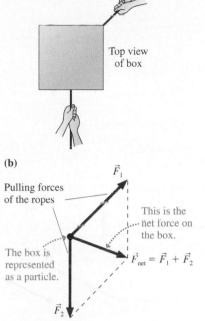

(a)

Top view of box

STOP TO THINK 5.1   Two of the three forces exerted on an object are shown. The net force points to the left. Which is the missing third force?

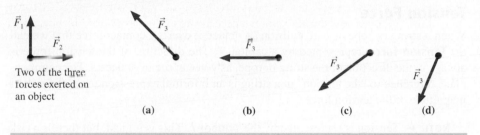

$\vec{F}_1$

$\vec{F}_2$

Two of the three forces exerted on an object

$\vec{F}_3$

$\vec{F}_3$

$\vec{F}_3$

$\vec{F}_3$

(a)   (b)   (c)   (d)

(b)

Pulling forces of the ropes

$\vec{F}_1$

This is the net force on the box.

The box is represented as a particle.

$\vec{F}_{net} = \vec{F}_1 + \vec{F}_2$

$\vec{F}_2$

5.2 A Short Catalog of Forces

There are many forces we will deal with over and over. This section will introduce you to some of them. Many of these forces have special symbols. As you learn the major forces, be sure to learn the symbol for each.

FIGURE 5.3 Gravity.

Gravity

A falling rock is pulled toward the earth by the long-range force of gravity. Gravity—the only long-range force we will encounter in the next few chapters—keeps you in your chair, keeps the planets in their orbits around the sun, and shapes the large-scale structure of the universe. We'll have a thorough look at gravity in Chapter 13. For now we'll concentrate on objects on or near the surface of the earth (or other planet).

The gravitational pull of a planet on an object on or near the surface is called the **gravitational force.** The agent for the gravitational force is the *entire planet* pulling on the object. Gravity acts on *all* objects, whether moving or at rest. The symbol for gravitational force is $\vec{F}_G$. The gravitational force vector always points vertically downward, as shown in **FIGURE 5.3**.

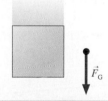

The gravitational force pulls the box down.

$\vec{F}_G$

Ground

> **NOTE** ▶ We often refer to "the weight" of an object. For an object at rest on the surface of a planet, its weight is simply the magnitude F_G of the gravitational force. However, weight and gravitational force are not the same thing, nor is weight the same as mass. We will briefly examine mass later in the chapter, and we'll explore the rather subtle connections among gravity, weight, and mass in Chapter 6. ◀

Spring Force

Springs exert one of the most common contact forces. A spring can either push (when compressed) or pull (when stretched). **FIGURE 5.4** on the next page shows the **spring force,** for which we use the symbol $\vec{F}_{sp}$. In both cases, pushing and pulling, the tail of the force vector is placed on the particle in the force diagram.

A stretched spring exerts a force on an object.

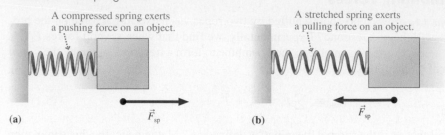

FIGURE 5.4 The spring force.

A compressed spring exerts a pushing force on an object.

A stretched spring exerts a pulling force on an object.

(a) $\vec{F}_{sp}$ (b) $\vec{F}_{sp}$

Although you may think of a spring as a metal coil that can be stretched or compressed, this is only one type of spring. Hold a ruler, or any other thin piece of wood or metal, by the ends and bend it slightly. It flexes. When you let go, it "springs" back to its original shape. This is just as much a spring as is a metal coil.

Tension Force

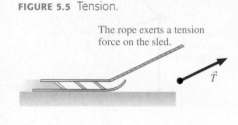

FIGURE 5.5 Tension.

The rope exerts a tension force on the sled.

$\vec{T}$

When a string or rope or wire pulls on an object, it exerts a contact force that we call the **tension force,** represented by a capital $\vec{T}$. The direction of the tension force is always in the direction of the string or rope, as you can see in FIGURE 5.5. The commonplace reference to "the tension" in a string is an informal expression for T, the size or magnitude of the tension force.

NOTE ▶ Tension is represented by the symbol T. This is logical, but there's a risk of confusing the tension T with the identical symbol T for the period of a particle in circular motion. The number of symbols used in science and engineering far exceeds the number of letters in the English alphabet. Even after borrowing from the Greek alphabet, scientists inevitably use some letters several times to represent entirely different quantities. The use of T is the first time we've run into this problem, but it won't be the last. You must be alert to the *context* of a symbol's use to deduce its meaning. ◀

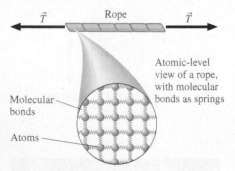

FIGURE 5.6 An atomic model of tension.

$\vec{T}$ Rope $\vec{T}$

Atomic-level view of a rope, with molecular bonds as springs

Molecular bonds

Atoms

If you were to use a very powerful microscope to look inside a rope, you would "see" that it is made of *atoms* joined together by *molecular bonds*. Molecular bonds are not rigid connections between the atoms. They are more accurately thought of as tiny *springs* holding the atoms together, as in FIGURE 5.6. Pulling on the ends of a string or rope stretches the molecular springs ever so slightly. The tension within a rope and the tension force experienced by an object at the end of the rope are really the net spring force being exerted by billions and billions of microscopic springs.

This atomic-level view of tension introduces a new idea: a microscopic **atomic model** for understanding the behavior and properties of macroscopic objects. It is a *model* because atoms and molecular bonds aren't really little balls and springs. We're using macroscopic concepts—balls and springs—to understand atomic-scale phenomena that we cannot directly see or sense. This is a good model for explaining the elastic properties of materials, but it would not necessarily be a good model for explaining other phenomena. We will frequently use atomic models to obtain a deeper understanding of our observations.

Normal Force

If you sit on a bed, the springs in the mattress compress and, as a consequence of the compression, exert an upward force on you. Stiffer springs would show less compression but still exert an upward force. The compression of extremely stiff springs might be measurable only by sensitive instruments. Nonetheless, the springs would compress ever so slightly and exert an upward spring force on you.

FIGURE 5.7 shows an object resting on top of a sturdy table. The table may not visibly flex or sag, but—just as you do to the bed—the object compresses the molecular springs in the table. The size of the compression is very small, but it is not zero. As a consequence, the compressed molecular springs *push upward* on the object. We say that "the table" exerts the upward force, but it is important to understand that the pushing is *really* done by molecular springs. Similarly, an object resting on the ground compresses the molecular springs holding the ground together and, as a consequence, the ground pushes up on the object.

We can extend this idea. Suppose you place your hand on a wall and lean against it, as shown in **FIGURE 5.8** . Does the wall exert a force on your hand? As you lean, you compress the molecular springs in the wall and, as a consequence, they push outward against your hand. So the answer is yes, the wall does exert a force on you.

The force the table surface exerts is vertical; the force the wall exerts is horizontal. In all cases, the force exerted on an object that is pressing against a surface is in a direction *perpendicular* to the surface. Mathematicians refer to a line that is perpendicular to a surface as being *normal* to the surface. In keeping with this terminology, we define the **normal force** as the force exerted by a surface (the agent) against an object that is pressing against the surface. The symbol for the normal force is $\vec{n}$.

We're not using the word *normal* to imply that the force is an "ordinary" force or to distinguish it from an "abnormal force." A surface exerts a force *perpendicular* (i.e., normal) to itself as the molecular springs press *outward*. **FIGURE 5.9** shows an object on an inclined surface, a common situation. Notice how the normal force $\vec{n}$ is perpendicular to the surface.

We have spent a lot of time describing the normal force because many people have a difficult time understanding it. The normal force is a very real force arising from the very real compression of molecular bonds. It is in essence just a spring force, but one exerted by a vast number of microscopic springs acting at once. The normal force is responsible for the "solidness" of solids. It is what prevents you from passing right through the chair you are sitting in and what causes the pain and the lump if you bang your head into a door. Your head can then tell you that the force exerted on it by the door was very real!

Friction

You've certainly observed that a rolling or sliding object, if not pushed or propelled, slows down and eventually stops. You've probably discovered that you can slide better across a sheet of ice than across asphalt. And you also know that most objects stay in place on a table without sliding off even if the table isn't absolutely level. The force responsible for these sorts of behavior is **friction.** The symbol for friction is a lowercase $\vec{f}$.

Friction, like the normal force, is exerted by a surface. But whereas the normal force is perpendicular to the surface, the friction force is always *tangent* to the surface. On a microscopic level, friction arises as atoms from the object and atoms on the surface run into each other. The rougher the surface is, the more these atoms are forced into close proximity and, as a result, the larger the friction force. We will develop a simple model of friction in the next chapter that will be sufficient for our needs. For now, it is useful to distinguish between two kinds of friction:

- *Kinetic friction*, denoted $\vec{f}_k$, appears as an object slides across a surface. This is a force that "opposes the motion," meaning that the friction force vector $\vec{f}_k$ points in a direction opposite the velocity vector $\vec{v}$ (i.e., "the motion").
- *Static friction*, denoted $\vec{f}_s$, is the force that keeps an object "stuck" on a surface and prevents its motion. Finding the direction of $\vec{f}_s$ is a little trickier than finding it for $\vec{f}_k$. Static friction points opposite the direction in which the object *would* move if there were no friction. That is, it points in the direction necessary to *prevent* motion.

FIGURE 5.10 on the next page shows examples of kinetic and static friction.

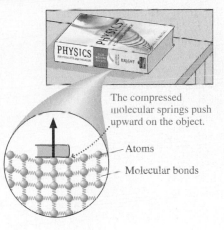

FIGURE 5.7 An atomic model of the force exerted by a table.

The compressed molecular springs push upward on the object.

Atoms

Molecular bonds

FIGURE 5.8 The wall pushes outward.

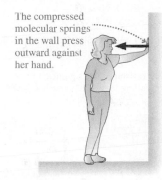

The compressed molecular springs in the wall press outward against her hand.

FIGURE 5.9 The normal force.

$\vec{n}$

The surface pushes outward against the bottom of the frog. The push is perpendicular to the surface.

FIGURE 5.10 Kinetic and static friction.

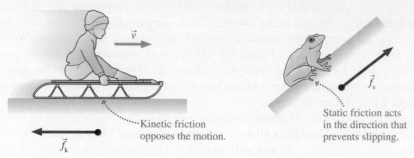

Kinetic friction opposes the motion.

Static friction acts in the direction that prevents slipping.

NOTE ▶ A surface exerts a kinetic friction force when an object moves *relative to* the surface. A package on a conveyor belt is in motion, but it does not experience a kinetic friction force because it is not moving relative to the belt. So to be precise, we should say that the kinetic friction force points opposite to an object's motion *relative to* a surface. ◀

Drag

FIGURE 5.11 Air resistance is an example of drag.

Air resistance is a significant force on falling leaves. It points opposite the direction of motion.

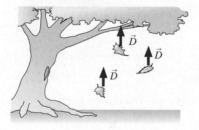

Friction at a surface is one example of a *resistive force,* a force that opposes or resists motion. Resistive forces are also experienced by objects moving through fluids—gases and liquids. The resistive force of a fluid is called **drag** and is symbolized as $\vec{D}$. Drag, like kinetic friction, points opposite the direction of motion. **FIGURE 5.11** shows an example of drag.

Drag can be a large force for objects moving at high speeds or in dense fluids. Hold your arm out the window as you ride in a car and feel how the air resistance against it increases rapidly as the car's speed increases. Drop a lightweight object into a beaker of water and watch how slowly it settles to the bottom. In both cases the drag force is very significant.

For objects that are heavy and compact, that move in air, and whose speed is not too great, the drag force of air resistance is fairly small. To keep things as simple as possible, **you can neglect air resistance in all problems unless a problem explicitly asks you to include it.** The error introduced into calculations by this approximation is generally pretty small. This textbook will not consider objects moving in liquids.

Thrust

FIGURE 5.12 Thrust force on a rocket.

Thrust force is exerted on a rocket by exhaust gases.

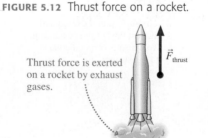

A jet airplane obviously has a force that propels it forward during takeoff. Likewise for the rocket being launched in **FIGURE 5.12**. This force, called **thrust,** occurs when a jet or rocket engine expels gas molecules at high speed. Thrust is a contact force, with the exhaust gas being the agent that pushes on the engine. The process by which thrust is generated is rather subtle, and we will postpone a full discussion until we study Newton's third law in Chapter 7. For now, we will treat thrust as a force opposite the direction in which the exhaust gas is expelled. There's no special symbol for thrust, so we will call it $\vec{F}_{\text{thrust}}$.

Electric and Magnetic Forces

Electricity and magnetism, like gravity, exert long-range forces. The forces of electricity and magnetism act on charged particles. We will study electric and magnetic forces in detail in Part VI of this textbook. For now, it is worth noting that the forces holding molecules together—the molecular bonds—are not actually tiny springs. Atoms and molecules are made of charged particles—electrons and protons—and what we call a molecular bond is really an electric force between these particles. So when we say that the normal force and the tension force are due to "molecular springs," or that friction is due to atoms running into each other, what we're really saying is that these forces, at the most fundamental level, are actually electric forces between the charged particles in the atoms.

5.3 Identifying Forces

Force and motion problems generally have two basic steps:

1. Identify all of the forces acting on an object.
2. Use Newton's laws and kinematics to determine the motion.

Understanding the first step is the primary goal of this chapter. We'll turn our attention to step 2 in the next chapter.

A typical physics problem describes an object that is being pushed and pulled in various directions. Some forces are given explicitly; others are only implied. In order to proceed, it is necessary to determine all the forces that act on the object. It is also necessary to avoid including forces that do not really exist. Now that you have learned the properties of forces and seen a catalog of typical forces, we can develop a step-by-step method for identifying each force in a problem. This procedure for identifying forces will become part of the *pictorial representation* of the problem.

Force	Notation
General force	$\vec{F}$
Gravitational force	$\vec{F}_G$
Spring force	$\vec{F}_{sp}$
Tension	$\vec{T}$
Normal force	$\vec{n}$
Static friction	$\vec{f}_s$
Kinetic friction	$\vec{f}_k$
Drag	$\vec{D}$
Thrust	$\vec{F}_{thrust}$

TACTICS
BOX 5.2 **Identifying forces** (MP)

❶ **Identify the object of interest.** This is the object whose motion you wish to study.
❷ **Draw a picture of the situation.** Show the object of interest and all other objects—such as ropes, springs, or surfaces—that touch it.
❸ **Draw a closed curve around the object.** Only the object of interest is inside the curve; everything else is outside.
❹ **Locate every point on the boundary of this curve where other objects touch the object of interest.** These are the points where *contact forces* are exerted on the object.
❺ **Name and label each contact force acting on the object.** There is at least one force at each point of contact; there may be more than one. When necessary, use subscripts to distinguish forces of the same type.
❻ **Name and label each long-range force acting on the object.** For now, the only long-range force is the gravitational force.

Exercises 3–8 ✐

EXAMPLE 5.1 Forces on a bungee jumper
A bungee jumper has leapt off a bridge and is nearing the bottom of her fall. What forces are being exerted on the bungee jumper?

VISUALIZE

FIGURE 5.13 Forces on a bungee jumper.

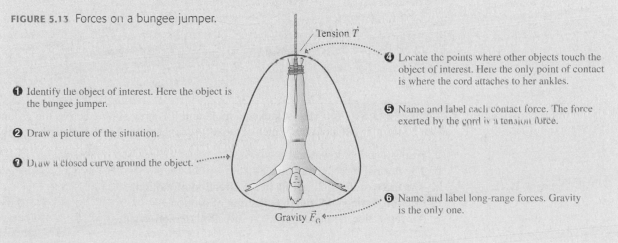

Tension $\vec{T}$

❶ Identify the object of interest. Here the object is the bungee jumper.

❷ Draw a picture of the situation.

❸ Draw a closed curve around the object.

❹ Locate the points where other objects touch the object of interest. Here the only point of contact is where the cord attaches to her ankles.

❺ Name and label each contact force. The force exerted by the cord is a tension force.

❻ Name and label long-range forces. Gravity is the only one.

Gravity $\vec{F}_G$

EXAMPLE 5.2 Forces on a skier

A skier is being towed up a snow-covered hill by a tow rope. What forces are being exerted on the skier?

VISUALIZE

FIGURE 5.14 Forces on a skier.

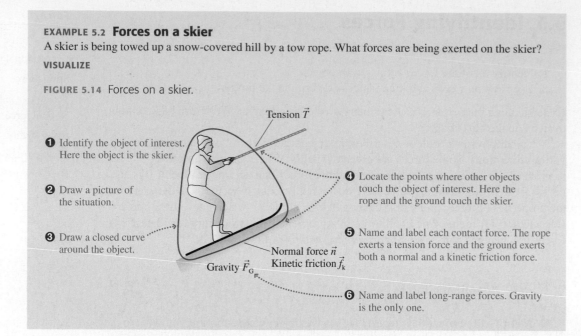

❶ Identify the object of interest. Here the object is the skier.

❷ Draw a picture of the situation.

❸ Draw a closed curve around the object.

Tension $\vec{T}$

❹ Locate the points where other objects touch the object of interest. Here the rope and the ground touch the skier.

❺ Name and label each contact force. The rope exerts a tension force and the ground exerts both a normal and a kinetic friction force.

Normal force $\vec{n}$
Kinetic friction $\vec{f}_k$
Gravity $\vec{F}_G$

❻ Name and label long-range forces. Gravity is the only one.

NOTE ▶ You might have expected two friction forces and two normal forces in Example 5.2, one on each ski. Keep in mind, however, that we're working within the particle model, which represents the skier by a single point. A particle has only one contact with the ground, so there is a single normal force and a single friction force. The particle model is valid if we want to analyze the translational motion of the skier as a whole, but we would have to go beyond the particle model to find out what happens to each ski. ◀

Now that you're getting the hang of this, the next example is meant to look much more like a sketch you should make when asked to identify forces in a homework problem.

EXAMPLE 5.3 Forces on a rocket

A rocket is being launched to place a new satellite in orbit. Air resistance is not negligible. What forces are being exerted on the rocket?

VISUALIZE

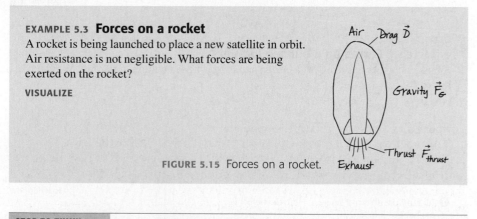

FIGURE 5.15 Forces on a rocket.

STOP TO THINK 5.2 You've just kicked a rock, and it is now sliding across the ground about 2 meters in front of you. Which of these forces act on the rock? List all that apply.

a. Gravity, acting downward.
b. The normal force, acting upward.
c. The force of the kick, acting in the direction of motion.
d. Friction, acting opposite the direction of motion.
e. Air resistance, acting opposite the direction of motion.

5.4 What Do Forces Do? A Virtual Experiment

The fundamental question is: How does an object move when a force is exerted on it? The only way to answer this question is to do experiments. To do experiments, however, we need a way to reproduce the same amount of force again and again.

Let's conduct a "virtual experiment," one you can easily visualize. Imagine using your fingers to stretch a rubber band to a certain length—say 10 centimeters—that you can measure with a ruler. We'll call this the *standard length*. FIGURE 5.16 shows the idea. You know that a stretched rubber band exerts a force because your fingers *feel* the pull. Furthermore, this is a reproducible force. The rubber band exerts the same force every time you stretch it to the standard length. We'll call this the *standard force F*.

Not surprisingly, two identical rubber bands, each stretched to the standard length, exert twice the pull of one rubber band: $F_{net} = 2F$. N side-by-side rubber bands, each pulled to the standard length, will exert N times the standard force: $F_{net} = NF$.

Now we're ready to start the virtual experiment. Imagine an object to which you can attach rubber bands, such as a block of wood with a hook. If you attach a rubber band and stretch it to the standard length, the object experiences the same force F as did your finger. N rubber bands attached to the object will exert N times the force of one rubber band. The rubber bands give us a way of applying a known and reproducible force to an object.

Our task is to measure the object's motion in response to these forces. Imagine using the rubber bands to pull the object across a horizontal table. Friction between the object and the surface might affect our results, so let's just eliminate friction. This is, after all, a virtual experiment! (In practice you could nearly eliminate friction by pulling a smooth block over a smooth sheet of ice or by supporting the object on a cushion of air.)

If you stretch the rubber band and then release the object, it moves toward your hand. But as it does so, the rubber band gets shorter and the pulling force decreases. To keep the pulling force constant, you must *move your hand* at just the right speed to keep the length of the rubber band from changing! FIGURE 5.17 shows the experiment being carried out. Once the motion is complete, you can use motion diagrams (made from movie frames from a camera) and kinematics to analyze the object's motion.

FIGURE 5.16 A reproducible force.

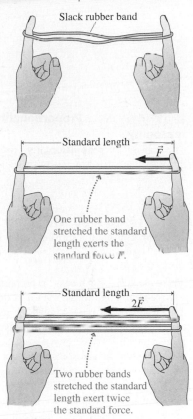

Slack rubber band

Standard length — $\vec{F}$

One rubber band stretched the standard length exerts the standard force F.

Standard length — $2\vec{F}$

Two rubber bands stretched the standard length exert twice the standard force.

FIGURE 5.17 Measuring the motion of an object that is pulled with a constant force.

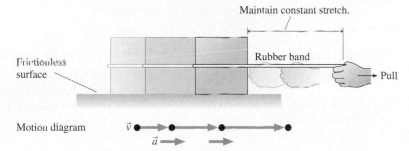

Maintain constant stretch.

Frictionless surface

Rubber band

→ Pull

Motion diagram $\vec{v}$

$\vec{a}$

TABLE 5.1 Acceleration due to an increasing force

Rubber bands	Force	Acceleration
1	F	a_1
2	$2F$	$a_2 = 2a_1$
3	$3F$	$a_3 = 3a_1$
⋮	⋮	⋮
N	NF	$a_N = Na_1$

The first important finding of this experiment is that **an object pulled with a constant force moves with a constant acceleration.** This finding could not have been anticipated in advance. It's conceivable that the object would speed up for a while, then move with a steady speed. Or that it would continue to speed up, but that the *rate* of increase, the acceleration, would steadily decline. These are conceivable motions, but they're not what happens. Instead, the object accelerates *with a constant acceleration* for as long as you pull it with a constant force.

What happens if you increase the force by using several rubber bands? To find out, use 2 rubber bands. Stretch both to the standard length to double the force, then measure the acceleration. Then measure the acceleration due to 3 rubber bands, then 4, and so on. Table 5.1 shows the results of this experiment. You can see that doubling the force causes twice the acceleration, tripling the force causes three times the acceleration, and so on.

FIGURE 5.18 is a graph of the data. Force is the independent variable, the one you can control, so we've placed force on the horizontal axis to make an acceleration-versus-

FIGURE 5.18 Graph of acceleration versus force.

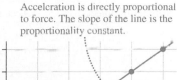

Acceleration is directly proportional to force. The slope of the line is the proportionality constant.

Acceleration (in multiples of a_1)

$5a_1$
$4a_1$
$3a_1$
$2a_1$
$1a_1$
0

0 1 2 3 4 5
Force (number of rubber bands)

force graph. The graph reveals our second important finding, that **the acceleration is directly proportional to the force.** This result can be written

$$a = cF \qquad (5.2)$$

where c, called the *proportionality constant,* is the slope of the graph.

MATHEMATICAL ASIDE **Proportionality and proportional reasoning**

The concept of **proportionality** arises frequently in physics. A quantity symbolized by u is *proportional* to another quantity symbolized by v if

$$u = cv$$

where c (which might have units) is called the **proportionality constant.** This relationship between u and v is often written

$$u \propto v$$

where the symbol $\propto$ means "is proportional to."

If v is doubled to $2v$, then u is doubled to $c(2v) = 2(cv) = 2u$. In general, if v is changed by any factor f, then u changes by the same factor. This is the essence of what we *mean* by proportionality.

A graph of u versus v is a straight line *passing through the origin* (i.e., the y-intercept is zero) with slope $= c$. Notice that proportionality is a much more specific relationship between u and v than mere linearity. The linear equation $u = cv + b$ has a straight-line graph, but it doesn't pass through the origin (unless b happens to be zero) and doubling v does not double u.

The slope is c.
The graph passes through the origin.
u is proportional to v.

If $u \propto v$, then $u_1 = cv_1$ and $u_2 = cv_2$. Dividing the second equation by the first, we find

$$\frac{u_2}{u_1} = \frac{v_2}{v_1}$$

By working with *ratios*, we can deduce information about u without needing to know the value of c. (This would not be true if

the relationship were merely linear.) This is called **proportional reasoning.**

Proportionality is not limited to being linearly proportional. The graph on the left below shows that u is clearly not proportional to w. But a graph of u versus $1/w^2$ is a straight line passing through the origin, thus, in this case, u is proportional to $1/w^2$, or $u \propto 1/w^2$. We would say that "u is proportional to the inverse square of w."

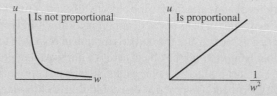

Is not proportional   *Is proportional*

u is proportional to the inverse square of w.

EXAMPLE u is proportional to the inverse square of w. By what factor does u change if w is tripled?

SOLUTION This is an opportunity for proportional reasoning; we don't need to know the proportionality constant. If u is proportional to $1/w^2$, then

$$\frac{u_2}{u_1} = \frac{1/w_2^2}{1/w_1^2} = \frac{1}{w_2^2/w_1^2} = \left(\frac{1}{w_2/w_1}\right)^2$$

Tripling w, for which $w_2/w_1 = 3$, changes u to

$$u_2 = \left(\frac{1}{w_2/w_1}\right)^2 u_1 = \left(\frac{1}{3}\right)^2 u_1 = \frac{1}{9} u_1$$

Tripling w causes u to become $\frac{1}{9}$ of its original value.

Many *Student Workbook* and end-of-chapter homework questions will require proportional reasoning. It's an important skill to learn.

TABLE 5.2 Acceleration with different numbers of objects

Number of objects	Acceleration
1	a_1
2	$a_2 = \frac{1}{2} a_1$
3	$a_3 = \frac{1}{3} a_1$
⋮	⋮
N	$a_N = \frac{1}{N} a_1$

The final question for our virtual experiment is: How does the acceleration depend on the size of the object? (The "size" of an object is somewhat ambiguous. We'll be more precise below.) To find out, glue the original object and an identical copy together, and then, applying the *same force* as you applied to the original, single object, measure the acceleration of this new object. Doing several such experiments, applying the same force to each object, would give you the results shown in Table 5.2. An object twice the size of the original has only half the acceleration of the original object when both are subjected to the same force.

FIGURE 5.19 adds these results to the graph of Figure 5.18. You can see that the proportionality constant c between acceleration and force—the slope of the line—changes with the size of the object. The graph for an object twice the size of the original is a line with half the slope. It may seem surprising that larger objects have smaller slopes, so you'll want to think about this carefully.

Mass

Now, "twice the size" is a little vague; we could mean the object's external dimensions or some other measure. Although *mass* is a common word, we've avoided the term so far because we first need to define what mass is. Because we made the larger objects in our experiment from the same material as the original object, an object twice the size has twice as many atoms—twice the amount of matter— as the original. Thus it should come as no surprise that it has twice the mass as the original. Loosely speaking, **an object's mass is a measure of the amount of matter it contains.** This is certainly our everyday meaning of *mass,* but it is not yet a precise definition.

Figure 5.19 shows that an object with twice the amount of matter as the original accelerates only half as quickly if both experience the same force. An object with N times as much matter has only $\frac{1}{N}$ of the original acceleration. The more matter an object has, the more it *resists* accelerating in response to a force. You're familiar with this idea: Your car is much harder to push than your bicycle. The tendency of an object to resist a *change* in its velocity (i.e., to resist acceleration) is called **inertia.** Figure 5.19 tells us that larger objects have more inertia than smaller objects of the same material.

We can make this idea precise by defining the **inertial mass** m of an object to be

$$m \equiv \frac{1}{\text{slope of the acceleration-versus-force graph}} = \frac{F}{a}$$

(Notice that this is another *operational definition.*) We usually refer to the inertial mass as simply "the mass." Mass is an *intrinsic* property of an object. It is the property that determines how an object accelerates in response to an applied force.

We can now answer the question with which we started: How does an object move when a force is exerted on it? Figure 5.18 showed that the acceleration is directly proportional to the force, a conclusion that we wrote in Equation 5.2 with the unspecified proportionality constant c. Now we see that c, the slope of the acceleration-versus-force graph, is the inverse of the inertial mass m. Thus we've found that a force of magnitude F causes an object of mass m to accelerate with

$$a = \frac{F}{m} \tag{5.3}$$

A force causes an object to *accelerate!* Furthermore, the size of the acceleration is directly proportional to the size of the force and inversely proportional to the object's mass.

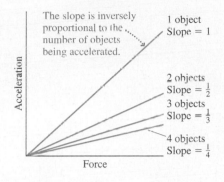

FIGURE 5.19 Acceleration-versus-force graphs for objects of different sizes.

STOP TO THINK 5.3   Two rubber bands stretched to the standard length cause an object to accelerate at 2 m/s². Suppose another object with twice the mass is pulled by four rubber bands stretched to the standard length. The acceleration of this second object is

a. 1 m/s²   b. 2 m/s²   c. 4 m/s'   d. 8 m/s²   e. 16 m/s²

Hint: Use proportional reasoning.

5.5 Newton's Second Law

Equation 5.3 is an important finding, but our experiment was limited to looking at an object's response to a single applied force. Realistically, an object is likely to be subjected to several distinct forces $\vec{F}_1, \vec{F}_2, \vec{F}_3, \ldots$ that may point in different directions. What happens then? In that case, it is found experimentally that the acceleration is determined by the *net* force.

Newton was the first to recognize the connection between force and motion. This relationship is known today as Newton's second law.

> **Newton's second law** An object of mass m subjected to forces $\vec{F}_1$, $\vec{F}_2$, $\vec{F}_3$, . . . will undergo an acceleration $\vec{a}$ given by
>
> $$\vec{a} = \frac{\vec{F}_{net}}{m} \tag{5.4}$$
>
> where the net force $\vec{F}_{net} = \vec{F}_1 + \vec{F}_2 + \vec{F}_3 + \cdots$ is the vector sum of all forces acting on the object. The acceleration vector $\vec{a}$ points in the same direction as the net force vector $\vec{F}_{net}$.

The significance of Newton's second law cannot be overstated. There was no reason to suspect that there should be any simple relationship between force and acceleration. Yet there it is, a simple but exceedingly powerful equation relating the two.

The critical idea is that **an object accelerates in the direction of the net force vector $\vec{F}_{net}$**. It's also worth noting that the object responds only to the forces it feels *at this instant*. The object has no will or intent to act on its own, nor does it have any memory of forces that may have been exerted at earlier times.

We can rewrite Newton's second law in the form

$$\vec{F}_{net} = m\vec{a} \tag{5.5}$$

which is how you'll see it presented in many textbooks. Equations 5.3 and 5.4 are mathematically equivalent, but Equation 5.4 better describes the central idea of Newtonian mechanics: A force applied to an object causes the object to accelerate.

NOTE ▶ Be careful not to think that one force "overcomes" the others to determine the motion. Forces are not in competition with each other! It is $\vec{F}_{net}$, the sum of *all* the forces, that determines the acceleration $\vec{a}$. ◀

As an example, **FIGURE 5.20a** shows a box being pulled by two ropes. The ropes exert tension forces $\vec{T}_1$ and $\vec{T}_2$ on the box. **FIGURE 5.20b** represents the box as a particle, shows the forces acting on the box, and adds them graphically to find the net force $\vec{F}_{net}$. The box will accelerate in the direction of $\vec{F}_{net}$ with an acceleration of magnitude

$$\vec{a} = \frac{\vec{F}_{net}}{m} = \frac{\vec{T}_1 + \vec{T}_2}{m}$$

NOTE ▶ The acceleration is *not* $(T_1 + T_2)/m$. You must add the forces as *vectors*, not merely add their magnitudes as scalars. ◀

Units of Force

Because $\vec{F}_{net} = m\vec{a}$, the units of force must be mass units multiplied by acceleration units. We've previously specified the SI unit of mass as the kilogram. We can now define the basic unit of force as "the force that causes a 1 kg mass to accelerate at 1 m/s²." From the second law, this force is

$$1 \text{ basic unit of force} \equiv 1 \text{ kg} \times 1 \frac{m}{s^2} = 1 \frac{\text{kg m}}{s^2}$$

This basic unit of force is called a newton:

One **newton** is the force that causes a 1 kg mass to accelerate at 1 m/s². The abbreviation for newton is N. Mathematically, 1 N = 1 kg m/s².

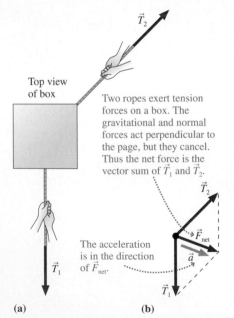

FIGURE 5.20 Acceleration of a pulled box.

$\vec{T}_2$

Top view of box

Two ropes exert tension forces on a box. The gravitational and normal forces act perpendicular to the page, but they cancel. Thus the net force is the vector sum of $\vec{T}_1$ and $\vec{T}_2$.

$\vec{T}_2$

$\vec{F}_{net}$

$\vec{a}$

The acceleration is in the direction of $\vec{F}_{net}$.

$\vec{T}_1$

$\vec{T}_1$

(a)   **(b)**

The newton is a *secondary unit,* meaning that it is defined in terms of the *primary units* of kilograms, meters, and seconds. We will introduce other secondary units as needed.

It is important to develop a feeling for what the sizes of forces should be. Table 5.3 shows some typical forces. As you can see, "typical" forces on "typical" objects are likely to be in the range 0.01–10,000 N. Forces less than 0.01 N are too small to consider unless you are dealing with very small objects. Forces greater than 10,000 N would make sense only if applied to very massive objects.

Forces Are Interactions

There's one more important aspect of forces. If you push against a door (the object) to close it, the door pushes back against your hand (the agent). If a tow rope pulls on a car (the object), the car pulls back on the rope (the agent). In general, if an agent exerts a force on an object, the object exerts a force on the agent. We really need to think of a force as an *interaction* between two objects. This idea is captured in Newton's third law—that for every action there is an equal but opposite reaction.

Although the interaction perspective is a more exact way to view forces, it adds complications that we would like to avoid for now. Our approach will be to start by focusing on how a single object responds to forces exerted on it. Then, in Chapter 7, we'll return to Newton's third law and the larger issue of how two or more objects interact with each other.

TABLE 5.3 Approximate magnitude of some typical forces

Force	Approximate magnitude (newtons)
Weight of a U.S. quarter	0.05
Weight of a 1 pound object	5
Weight of a 110 pound person	500
Propulsion force of a car	5,000
Thrust force of a rocket motor	5,000,000

STOP TO THINK 5.4   Three forces act on an object. In which direction does the object accelerate?

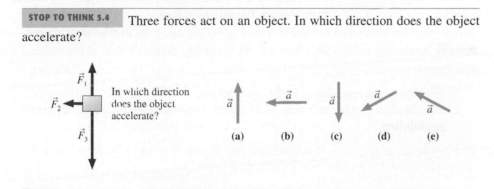

5.6 Newton's First Law

As we remarked earlier, Aristotle and his contemporaries in the world of ancient Greece were very interested in motion. One question they asked was: What is the "natural state" of an object if left to itself? It does not take an expensive research program to see that every moving object on earth, if left to itself, eventually comes to rest. Aristotle concluded that the natural state of an earthly object is to be at rest. An object at rest requires no explanation; it is doing precisely what comes naturally to it. A moving object, though, is not in its natural state and thus requires an explanation: Why is this object moving? What keeps it going and prevents it from being in its natural state?

Galileo reopened the question of the "natural state" of objects. He suggested focusing on the *limiting case* in which resistance to the motion (e.g., friction or air resistance) is zero. Many careful experiments in which he minimized the influence of friction led Galileo to a conclusion that was in sharp contrast to Aristotle's belief that rest is an object's natural state.

Galileo found that an external influence (i.e., a force) is needed to make an object accelerate—to *change* its velocity. In particular, a force is needed to put an object in motion. But, in the absence of friction or air resistance, a moving object continues to move along a straight line forever with no loss of speed. In other words, the natural state of an object—its behavior if free of external influences—is *uniform motion* with constant velocity! This does not happen in practice because friction or air resistance prevents the object from being left alone. "At rest" has no special significance in Galileo's view of motion; it is simply uniform motion that happens to have $\vec{v} = \vec{0}$.

It was left to Newton to generalize this result, and today we call it Newton's first law of motion.

> **Newton's first law** An object that is at rest will remain at rest, or an object that is moving will continue to move in a straight line with constant velocity, if and only if the net force acting on the object is zero.

Newton's first law is also known as the *law of inertia*. If an object is at rest, it has a tendency to stay at rest. If it is moving, it has a tendency to continue moving with the *same velocity*.

NOTE ▶ The first law refers to *net* force. An object can remain at rest, or can move in a straight line with constant velocity, even though forces are exerted on it as long as the *net* force is zero. ◀

Notice the "if and only if" aspect of Newton's first law. If an object is at rest or moves with constant velocity, then we can conclude that there is no net force acting on it. Conversely, if no net force is acting on it, we can conclude that the object will have constant velocity, not just constant speed. The direction remains constant, too!

An object on which the net force is zero, $\vec{F}_{net} = \vec{0}$, is said to be in **mechanical equilibrium**. According to Newton's first law, there are two distinct forms of mechanical equilibrium:

1. The object is at rest. This is **static equilibrium**.
2. The object is moving in a straight line with constant velocity. This is **dynamic equilibrium**.

Two examples of mechanical equilibrium are shown in **FIGURE 5.21**. Both share the common feature that the acceleration is zero: $\vec{a} = \vec{0}$.

What Good Is Newton's First Law?

The first law completes our definition of force. It answers the question: What is a force? If an "influence" on an object causes the object's velocity to change, the influence is a force.

Newton's first law changes the question the ancient Greeks were trying to answer: What causes an object to move? Newton's first law says **no cause is needed for an object to move!** Uniform motion is the object's natural state. Nothing at all is required for it to remain in that state. The proper question, according to Newton, is: What causes an object to *change* its velocity? Newton, with Galileo's help, also gave us the answer. **A *force* is what causes an object to change its velocity.**

The preceding paragraph contains the essence of Newtonian mechanics. This new perspective on motion, however, is often contrary to our common experience. We all know perfectly well that you must keep pushing an object—exerting a force on it—to keep it moving. Newton is asking us to change our point of view and to consider motion *from the object's perspective* rather than from our personal perspective. As far as the object is concerned, our push is just one of several forces acting on it. Others might include friction, air resistance, or gravity. Only by knowing the *net* force can we determine the object's motion.

Newton's first law may seem to be merely a special case of Newton's second law. After all, the equation $\vec{F}_{net} = m\vec{a}$ tells us that an object moving with constant velocity ($\vec{a} = \vec{0}$) has $\vec{F}_{net} = \vec{0}$. The difficulty is that the second law assumes that we already

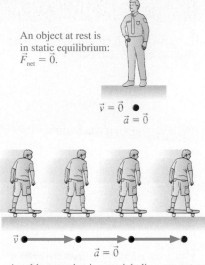

FIGURE 5.21 Two examples of mechanical equilibrium.

An object at rest is in static equilibrium: $\vec{F}_{net} = \vec{0}$.

$\vec{v} = \vec{0}$
$\vec{a} = \vec{0}$

$\vec{v}$
$\vec{a} = \vec{0}$

An object moving in a straight line at constant velocity is in dynamic equilibrium: $\vec{F}_{net} = \vec{0}$.

know what force is. The purpose of the first law is to *identify* a force as something that disturbs a state of equilibrium. The second law then describes how the object responds to this force. Thus from a *logical* perspective, the first law really is a separate statement that must precede the second law. But this is a rather formal distinction. From a pedagogical perspective it is better—as we have done—to use a commonsense understanding of force and start with Newton's second law.

Inertial Reference Frames

If a car stops suddenly, you may be "thrown" into the windshield if you're not wearing your seat belt. You have a very real forward acceleration *relative to the car,* but is there a force pushing you forward? A force is a push or a pull caused by an identifiable agent in contact with the object. Although you *seem* to be pushed forward, there's no agent to do the pushing.

The difficulty—an acceleration without an apparent force—comes from using an inappropriate reference frame. Your acceleration measured in a reference frame attached to the car is not the same as your acceleration measured in a reference frame attached to the ground. Newton's second law says $\vec{F}_{net} = m\vec{a}$. But which $\vec{a}$? Measured in which reference frame?

We define an **inertial reference frame** as a reference frame in which Newton's laws are valid. The first law provides a convenient way to test whether a reference frame is inertial. If $\vec{a} = \vec{0}$ (an object is at rest or moving with constant velocity) only when $\vec{F}_{net} = \vec{0}$, then the reference frame in which $\vec{a}$ is measured is an inertial reference frame.

Not all reference frames are inertial reference frames. **FIGURE 5.22a** shows a physics student cruising at constant velocity in an airplane. If the student places a ball on the floor, it stays there. There are no horizontal forces, and the ball remains at rest relative to the airplane. That is, $\vec{a} = \vec{0}$ in the airplane's reference frame when $\vec{F}_{net} = \vec{0}$. Newton's first law is satisfied, so this airplane is an inertial reference frame.

The physics student in **FIGURE 5.22b** conducts the same experiment during takeoff. She carefully places the ball on the floor just as the airplane starts to accelerate down the runway. You can imagine what happens. The ball rolls to the back of the plane as the passengers are being pressed back into their seats. Nothing exerts a horizontal contact force on the ball, yet the ball accelerates *in the plane's reference frame.* This violates Newton's first law, so the plane is *not* an inertial reference frame during takeoff.

In the first example, the plane is traveling with constant velocity. In the second, the plane is accelerating. **Accelerating reference frames are not inertial reference frames.** Consequently, Newton's laws are not valid in a reference frame attached to an accelerating object.

The earth is not exactly an inertial reference frame because the earth rotates on its axis and orbits the sun. However, the earth's acceleration is so small that violations of Newton's laws can be measured only in high-precision experiments. We will treat the earth and laboratories attached to the earth as inertial reference frames, an approximation that is exceedingly well justified.

In Chapter 4 we defined inertial reference frames to be those reference frames moving with constant velocity. These are the reference frames in which Newton's laws are valid. Because the earth is (very nearly) an inertial reference frame, the airplane of Figure 5.22a, which is moving at constant velocity relative to the earth, is also an inertial reference frame. But a car braking to a stop is not, so you *cannot* use Newton's laws in the car's reference frame.

To understand the motion of objects in the car, such as the passengers, you need to measure velocities and accelerations *relative to the ground.* From the perspective of an observer on the ground, the body of a passenger in a braking car tries to continue moving forward with constant velocity, exactly as we would expect on the basis of Newton's first law, while his immediate surroundings are decelerating. The passenger is not "thrown" into the windshield. Instead, the windshield runs into the passenger!

This guy thinks there's a force hurling him into the windshield. What a dummy!

FIGURE 5.22 Reference frames.

(a)

$$\vec{a} = \vec{0}$$

The ball stays in place.

A ball with no horizontal forces stays at rest in an airplane cruising at constant velocity. The airplane is an inertial reference frame.

(b)

Accelerating

The ball rolls to the back.

The ball rolls to the back of the plane during takeoff. An accelerating plane is not an inertial reference frame.

Common Misconceptions About Force

It is important to identify correctly all the forces acting on an object. It is equally important not to include forces that do not really exist. We have established a number of criteria for identifying forces; the two critical ones are:

- A force has an agent. Something tangible and identifiable causes the force.
- Forces exist at the point of contact between the agent and the object experiencing the force (except for the few special cases of long-range forces).

We all have had many experiences suggesting that a force is necessary to keep something moving. Consider a bowling ball rolling along on a smooth floor. It is very tempting to think that a horizontal "force of motion" keeps it moving in the forward direction. But if we draw a closed curve around the ball, *nothing contacts it* except the floor. No agent is giving the ball a forward push. According to our definition, then, there is *no* forward "force of motion" acting on the ball. So what keeps it going? Recall our discussion of the first law: *No* cause is needed to keep an object moving at constant velocity. It continues to move forward simply because of its inertia.

There's no "force of motion" or any other forward force on this arrow. It continues to move because of inertia.

One reason for wanting to include a "force of motion" is that we tend to view the problem from our perspective as one of the agents of force. You certainly have to keep pushing to shove a box across the floor at constant velocity. If you stop, it stops. Newton's laws, though, require that we adopt the object's perspective. The box experiences your pushing force in one direction *and* a friction force in the opposite direction. The box moves at constant velocity if the *net* force is zero. This will be true as long as your pushing force exactly balances the friction force. When you stop pushing, the friction force causes an acceleration that slows and stops the box.

A related problem occurs if you throw a ball. A pushing force was indeed required to accelerate the ball *as it was thrown.* But that force disappears the instant the ball loses contact with your hand. The force does not stick with the ball as the ball travels through the air. Once the ball has acquired a velocity, *nothing* is needed to keep it moving with that velocity.

A final difficulty worth noting is the force due to air pressure. You may have learned in an earlier science class that air, like any fluid, exerts forces on objects. Perhaps you learned this idea as "the air presses down with a weight of 15 pounds on every square inch." There is only one error here, but it is a serious one: the word *down.* Air pressure, at sea level, does indeed exert a force of 15 pounds per square inch, but in *all* directions. It presses down on the top of an object, but also inward on the sides and upward on the bottom. For most purposes, the *net* force due to air pressure is zero! The only way to experience an air pressure force is to form a seal around one side of the object and then remove the air, creating a *vacuum.* When you press a suction cup against the wall, you press the air out and the rubber forms a seal that prevents the air from returning. Now the air pressure does hold the suction cup in place! We do not need to be concerned with air pressure until Part III of this book.

5.7 Free-Body Diagrams

Having discussed at length what is and is not a force, we are ready to assemble our knowledge about force and motion into a single diagram called a *free-body diagram.* You will learn in the next chapter how to write the equations of motion directly from the free-body diagram. Solution of the equations is a mathematical exercise—possibly a difficult one, but nonetheless an exercise that could be done by a computer. The *physics* of the problem, as distinct from the purely calculational aspects, are the steps that lead to the free-body diagram.

A **free-body diagram,** part of the *pictorial representation* of a problem, represents the object as a particle and shows *all* of the forces acting on the object.

TACTICS
BOX 5.3   **Drawing a free-body diagram**   (MP)

❶ **Identify all forces acting on the object.** This step was described in Tactics Box 5.2.

❷ **Draw a coordinate system.** Use the axes defined in your pictorial representation. If those axes are tilted, for motion along an incline, then the axes of the free-body diagram should be similarly tilted.

❸ **Represent the object as a dot at the origin of the coordinate axes.** This is the particle model.

❹ **Draw vectors representing each of the identified forces.** This was described in Tactics Box 5.1. Be sure to label each force vector.

❺ **Draw and label the *net force* vector $\vec{F}_{net}$.** Draw this vector beside the diagram, not on the particle. Or, if appropriate, write $\vec{F}_{net} = \vec{0}$. Then check that $\vec{F}_{net}$ points in the same direction as the acceleration vector $\vec{a}$ on your motion diagram.

Exercises 24–29 🖉

EXAMPLE 5.4 **An elevator accelerates upward**

An elevator, suspended by a cable, speeds up as it moves upward from the ground floor. Identify the forces and draw a free-body diagram of the elevator.

MODEL Treat the elevator as a particle.

VISUALIZE

FIGURE 5.23 Free-body diagram of an elevator accelerating upward.

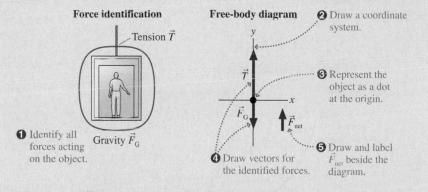

Force identification

Tension $\vec{T}$

Gravity $\vec{F}_G$

❶ Identify all forces acting on the object.

Free-body diagram

❷ Draw a coordinate system.

❸ Represent the object as a dot at the origin.

❹ Draw vectors for the identified forces.

❺ Draw and label $\vec{F}_{net}$ beside the diagram.

ASSESS The coordinate axes, with a vertical *y*-axis, are the ones we would use in a pictorial representation of the motion. The elevator is accelerating upward, so $\vec{F}_{net}$ must point upward. For this to be true, the magnitude of $\vec{T}$ must be larger than the magnitude of $\vec{F}_G$. The diagram has been drawn accordingly.

EXAMPLE 5.5 **An ice block shoots across a frozen lake**

Bobby straps a small model rocket to a block of ice and shoots it across the smooth surface of a frozen lake. Friction is negligible. Draw a pictorial representation of the block of ice.

MODEL Treat the block of ice as a particle. The pictorial representation consists of a motion diagram to determine $\vec{a}$, a force-identification picture, and a free-body diagram. The statement of the situation implies that friction is negligible.

Continued

VISUALIZE

FIGURE 5.24 Pictorial representation for a block of ice shooting across a frictionless frozen lake.

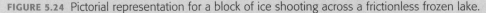

Motion diagram   Force identification   Free-body diagram

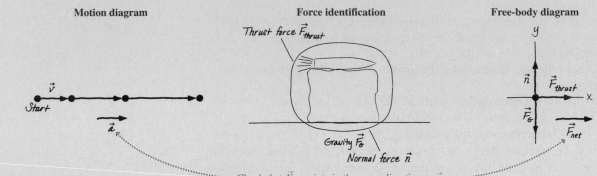

ASSESS The motion diagram tells us that the acceleration is in the positive x-direction. According to the rules of vector addition, this can be true only if the upward-pointing $\vec{n}$ and the downward-pointing $\vec{F}_G$ are equal in magnitude and thus cancel each other $((F_G)_y = -n_y)$. The vectors have been drawn accordingly, and this leaves the net force vector pointing toward the right, in agreement with $\vec{a}$ from the motion diagram.

EXAMPLE 5.6 A skier is pulled up a hill

A tow rope pulls a skier up a snow-covered hill at a constant speed. Draw a pictorial representation of the skier.

MODEL This is Example 5.2 again with the additional information that the skier is moving at constant speed. The skier will be treated as a particle in *dynamic equilibrium*. If we were doing a kinematics problem, the pictorial representation would use a tilted coordinate system with the x-axis parallel to the slope, so we use these same tilted coordinate axes for the free-body diagram.

VISUALIZE

FIGURE 5.25 Pictorial representation for a skier being towed at a constant speed.

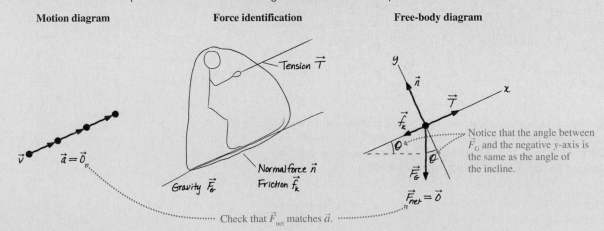

Motion diagram   Force identification   Free-body diagram

ASSESS We have shown $\vec{T}$ pulling parallel to the slope and $\vec{f}_k$, which opposes the direction of motion, pointing down the slope. $\vec{n}$ is perpendicular to the surface and thus along the y-axis. Finally, and this is important, the gravitational force $\vec{F}_G$ is vertically downward, not along the negative y-axis. In fact, you should convince yourself from the geometry that the angle θ between the $\vec{F}_G$ vector and the negative y-axis is the same as the angle θ of the incline above the horizontal. The skier moves in a straight line with constant speed, so $\vec{a} = \vec{0}$ and, from Newton's first law, $\vec{F}_{net} = \vec{0}$. Thus we have drawn the vectors such that the y-component of $\vec{F}_G$ is equal in magnitude to $\vec{n}$. Similarly, $\vec{T}$ must be large enough to match the negative x-components of both $\vec{f}_k$ and $\vec{F}_G$.

Free-body diagrams will be our major tool for the next several chapters. Careful practice with the workbook exercises and homework in this chapter will pay immediate benefits in the next chapter. Indeed, it is not too much to assert that a problem is half solved, or even more, when you complete the free-body diagram.

STOP TO THINK 5.5   An elevator suspended by a cable is moving upward and slowing to a stop. Which free-body diagram is correct?

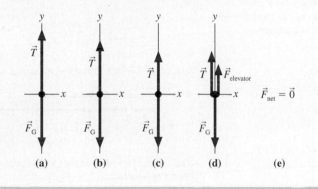

(a)   (b)   (c)   (d)   (e)

SUMMARY

The goal of Chapter 5 has been to learn how force and motion are connected.

General Principles

Newton's First Law

An object at rest will remain at rest, or an object that is moving will continue to move in a straight line with constant velocity, if and only if the net force on the object is zero.

$$\vec{F}_{net} = \vec{0}$$

$$\vec{a} = \vec{0}$$

The first law tells us that no "cause" is needed for motion. Uniform motion is the "natural state" of an object.

Newton's laws are valid only in inertial reference frames.

Newton's Second Law

An object with mass m will undergo acceleration

$$\vec{a} = \frac{1}{m}\vec{F}_{net}$$

where $\vec{F}_{net} = \vec{F}_1 + \vec{F}_2 + \vec{F}_3 + \cdots$ is the vector sum of all the individual forces acting on the object.

$$\vec{F}_{net}$$

The second law tells us that a net force causes an object to accelerate. This is the connection between force and motion that we are seeking.

Important Concepts

Acceleration is the link to kinematics.

From $\vec{F}_{net}$, find $\vec{a}$.
From a, find v and x.

$\vec{a} = \vec{0}$ is the condition for **equilibrium**.

Static equilibrium if $\vec{v} = \vec{0}$.
Dynamic equilibrium if $\vec{v}$ = constant.

Equilibrium occurs if and only if $\vec{F}_{net} = \vec{0}$.

Mass is the resistance of an object to acceleration. It is an intrinsic property of an object.

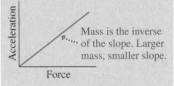

Mass is the inverse of the slope. Larger mass, smaller slope.

Force is a push or a pull on an object.

- Force is a vector, with a magnitude and a direction.
- Force requires an agent.
- Force is either a contact force or a long-range force.

Key Skills

Identifying Forces

Forces are identified by locating the points where other objects touch the object of interest. These are points where contact forces are exerted. In addition, objects with mass feel a long-range gravitational force.

Thrust force $\vec{F}_{thrust}$

Gravity $\vec{F}_G$ Normal force $\vec{n}$

Free-Body Diagrams

A free-body diagram represents the object as a particle at the origin of a coordinate system. Force vectors are drawn with their tails on the particle. The net force vector is drawn beside the diagram.

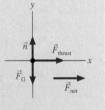

Terms and Notation

dynamics	gravitational force, $\vec{F}_G$	proportionality	mechanical equilibrium
mechanics	spring force, $\vec{F}_{sp}$	proportionality constant	static equilibrium
force, $\vec{F}$	tension force, $\vec{T}$	proportional reasoning	dynamic equilibrium
agent	atomic model	inertia	inertial reference frame
contact force	normal force, $\vec{n}$	inertial mass, m	free-body diagram
long-range force	friction, $\vec{f}_k$ or $\vec{f}_s$	Newton's second law	
net force, $\vec{F}_{net}$	drag, $\vec{D}$	newton, N	
superposition of forces	thrust, $\vec{F}_{thrust}$	Newton's first law	

| (MP) | For homework assigned on MasteringPhysics, go to www.masteringphysics.com | Problem difficulty is labeled as I (straightforward) to III (challenging). |

CONCEPTUAL QUESTIONS

1. An elevator suspended by a cable is descending at constant velocity. How many force vectors would be shown on a free-body diagram? List them.

2. A compressed spring is pushing a block across a rough horizontal table. How many force vectors would be shown on a free-body diagram? List them.

3. A brick is falling from the roof of a three-story building. How many force vectors would be shown on a free-body diagram? List them.

4. In **FIGURE Q5.4**, block B is falling and dragging block A across a table. How many force vectors would be shown on a free-body diagram of block A? List them.

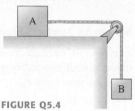

FIGURE Q5.4

5. You toss a ball straight up in the air. Immediately after you let go of it, what forces are acting on the ball? For each force you list, (a) state whether it is a contact force or a long-range force and (b) identify the agent of the force.

6. A constant force applied to A causes A to accelerate at 5 m/s². The same force applied to B causes an acceleration of 3 m/s². Applied to C, it causes an acceleration of 8 m/s².
   a. Which object has the largest mass? Explain.
   b. Which object has the smallest mass?
   c. What is the ratio m_A/m_B of the mass of A to the mass of B?

7. An object experiencing a constant force accelerates at 10 m/s². What will the acceleration of this object be if
   a. The force is doubled? Explain.
   b. The mass is doubled?
   c. The force is doubled *and* the mass is doubled?

8. An object experiencing a constant force accelerates at 8 m/s². What will the acceleration of this object be if
   a. The force is halved? Explain.
   b. The mass is halved?
   c. The force is halved *and* the mass is halved?

9. If an object is at rest, can you conclude that there are no forces acting on it? Explain.

10. If a force is exerted on an object, is it possible for that object to be moving with constant velocity? Explain.

11. Is the statement "An object always moves in the direction of the net force acting on it" true or false? Explain.

12. Newton's second law says $\vec{F}_{net} = m\vec{a}$. So is $m\vec{a}$ a force? Explain.

13. Is it possible for the friction force on an object to be in the direction of motion? If so, give an example. If not, why not?

14. Suppose you press your physics book against a wall hard enough to keep it from moving. Does the friction force on the book point (a) into the wall, (b) out of the wall, (c) up, (d) down, or (e) is there no friction force? Explain.

15. **FIGURE Q5.15** shows a hollow tube forming three-quarters of a circle. It is lying flat on a table. A ball is shot through the tube at high speed. As the ball emerges from the other end, does it follow path A, path B, or path C? Explain.

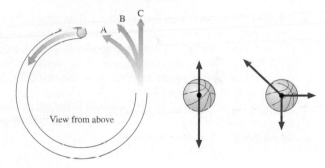

FIGURE Q5.15   **FIGURE Q5.16**

16. Which, if either, of the basketballs in **FIGURE Q5.16** are in equilibrium? Explain.

17. Which of the following are inertial reference frames? Explain.
    a. A car driving at steady speed on a straight and level road.
    b. A car driving at steady speed up a 10° incline.
    c. A car speeding up after leaving a stop sign.
    d. A car driving at steady speed around a curve.

EXERCISES AND PROBLEMS

Exercises

Section 5.3 Identifying Forces

1. I A mountain climber is hanging from a rope in the middle of a crevasse. The rope is vertical. Identify the forces on the mountain climber.

2. I A car is parked on a steep hill. Identify the forces on the car.

3. I A baseball player is sliding into second base. Identify the forces on the baseball player.

4. II A jet plane is speeding down the runway during takeoff. Air resistance is not negligible. Identify the forces on the jet.

5. II An arrow has just been shot from a bow and is now traveling horizontally. Air resistance is not negligible. Identify the forces on the arrow.

Section 5.4 What Do Forces Do? A Virtual Experiment

6. | Two rubber bands pulling on an object cause it to accelerate at 1.2 m/s².
    a. What will be the object's acceleration if it is pulled by four rubber bands?
    b. What will be the acceleration of two of these objects glued together if they are pulled by two rubber bands?

7. | Two rubber bands cause an object to accelerate with acceleration a. How many rubber bands are needed to cause an object with half the mass to accelerate three times as quickly?

8. || FIGURE EX5.8 shows an acceleration-versus-force graph for three objects pulled by rubber bands. The mass of object 2 is 0.20 kg. What are the masses of objects 1 and 3? Explain your reasoning.

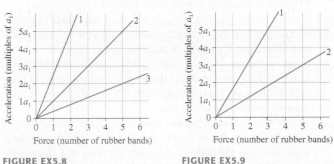

FIGURE EX5.8   **FIGURE EX5.9**

9. || FIGURE EX5.9 shows acceleration-versus-force graphs for two objects pulled by rubber bands. What is the mass ratio m_1/m_2?

10. | For an object starting from rest and accelerating with constant acceleration, distance traveled is proportional to the square of the time. If an object travels 2.0 furlongs in the first 2.0 s, how far will it travel in the first 4.0 s?

11. || The period of a pendulum is proportional to the square root of its length. A 2.0-m-long pendulum has a period of 3.0 s. What is the period of a 3.0-m-long pendulum?

Section 5.5 Newton's Second Law

12. | Write a one-paragraph essay on the topic "Force and Motion." Explain in your own words the connection between force and motion. Where possible, cite *evidence* supporting your statements.

13. | FIGURE EX5.13 shows an acceleration-versus-force graph for a 500 g object. What acceleration values go in the blanks on the vertical scale?

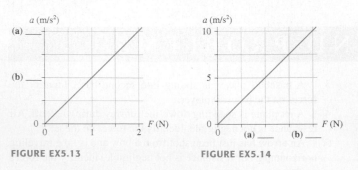

FIGURE EX5.13   **FIGURE EX5.14**

14. | FIGURE EX5.14 shows an acceleration-versus-force graph for a 200 g object. What force values go in the blanks on the horizontal scale?

15. | FIGURE EX5.15 shows an object's acceleration-versus-force graph. What is the object's mass?

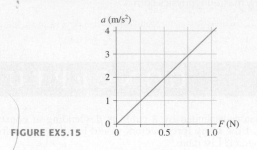

FIGURE EX5.15

16. | Based on the information in Table 5.3, estimate
    a. The weight of a laptop computer.
    b. The propulsion force of a bicycle.

17. | Based on the information in Table 5.3, estimate
    a. The weight of a pencil.
    b. The propulsion force of a sprinter.

Section 5.6 Newton's First Law

Exercises 18 through 20 show two of the three forces acting on an object in equilibrium. Redraw the diagram, showing all three forces. Label the third force $\vec{F}_3$.

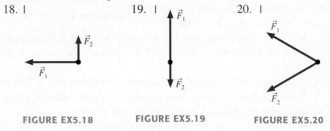

FIGURE EX5.18   **FIGURE EX5.19**   **FIGURE EX5.20**

Section 5.7 Free-Body Diagrams

Exercises 21 through 23 show a free-body diagram. For each:
    a. Redraw the free-body diagram.
    b. Write a short description of a real object for which this is the correct free-body diagram. Use Examples 5.4, 5.5, and 5.6 as models of what a description should be like.

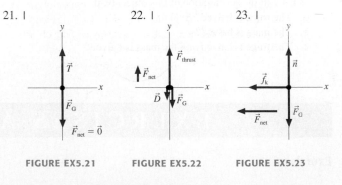

FIGURE EX5.21   **FIGURE EX5.22**   **FIGURE EX5.23**

Exercises 24 through 27 describe a situation. For each, identify all forces acting on the object and draw a free-body diagram of the object.

24. | You are sitting on a bench in the park.
25. | An ice hockey puck glides across frictionless ice.
26. | A steel beam is being lifted straight up at steady speed by a crane.
27. | Your physics textbook is sliding across the table.

Problems

28. | Redraw the two motion diagrams shown in FIGURE P5.28, then draw a vector beside each one to show the direction of the net force acting on the object. Explain your reasoning.

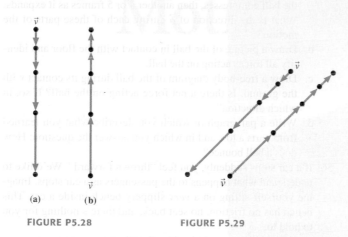

(a)   (b)

FIGURE P5.28   **FIGURE P5.29**

29. | Redraw the two motion diagrams shown in FIGURE P5.29, then draw a vector beside each one to show the direction of the net force acting on the object. Explain your reasoning.

30. | A single force with x-component F_x acts on a 2.0 kg object as it moves along the x-axis. The object's acceleration graph (a_x versus t) is shown in FIGURE P5.30. Draw a graph of F_x versus t.

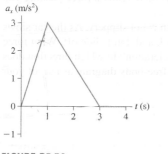

FIGURE P5.30 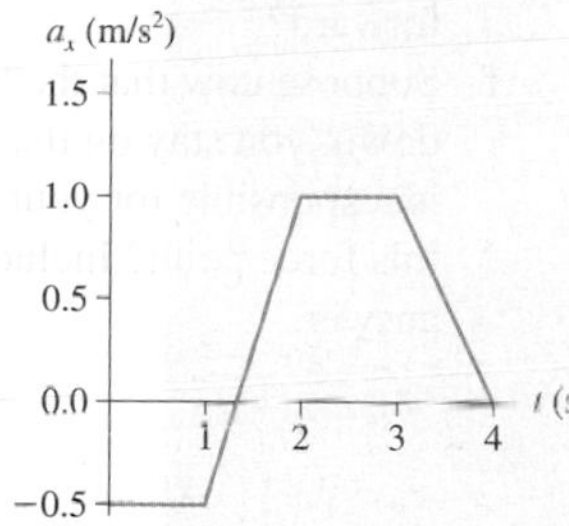   **FIGURE P5.31**

31. | A single force with x-component F_x acts on a 500 g object as it moves along the x-axis. The object's acceleration graph (a_x versus t) is shown in FIGURE P5.31. Draw a graph of F_x versus t.

32. | A single force with x-component F_x acts on a 2.0 kg object as it moves along the x-axis. A graph of F_x versus t is shown in FIGURE P5.32. Draw an acceleration graph (a_x versus t) for this object.

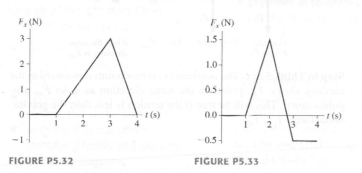

FIGURE P5.32   **FIGURE P5.33**

33. | A single force with x-component F_x acts on a 500 g object as it moves along the x-axis. A graph of F_x versus t is shown in FIGURE P5.33. Draw an acceleration graph (a_x versus t) for this object.

34. | A constant force is applied to an object, causing the object to accelerate at 10 m/s². What will the acceleration be if
   a. The force is halved?
   b. The object's mass is halved?
   c. The force and the object's mass are both halved?
   d. The force is halved and the object's mass is doubled?

35. | A constant force is applied to an object, causing the object to accelerate at 8.0 m/s². What will the acceleration be if
   a. The force is doubled?
   b. The object's mass is doubled?
   c. The force and the object's mass are both doubled?
   d. The force is doubled and the object's mass is halved?

Problems 36 through 42 show a free-body diagram. For each:
   a. Redraw the diagram.
   b. Identify the direction of the acceleration vector $\vec{a}$ and show it as a vector next to your diagram. Or, if appropriate, write $\vec{a} = \vec{0}$.
   c. If possible, identify the direction of the velocity vector $\vec{v}$ and show it as a labeled vector.
   d. Write a short description of a real object for which this is the correct free-body diagram. Use Examples 5.4, 5.5, and 5.6 as models of what a description should be like.

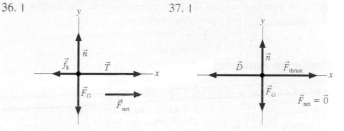

FIGURE P5.36   **FIGURE P5.37**

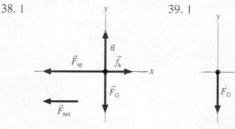

FIGURE P5.38   **FIGURE P5.39**

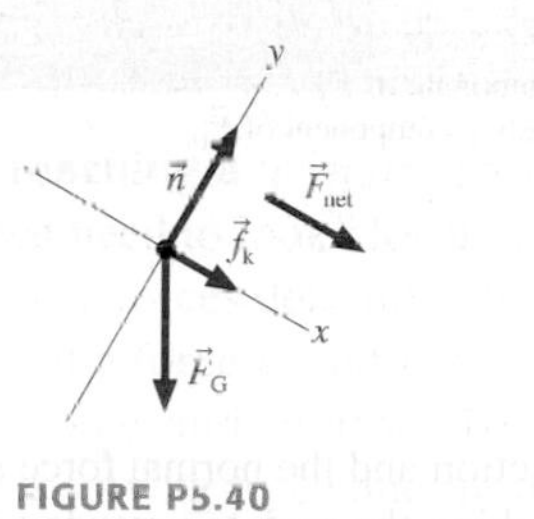

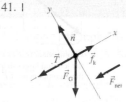

FIGURE P5.40   **FIGURE P5.41**

42. |

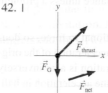

FIGURE P5.42

The concept of equilibrium is essential for the engineering analysis of stationary objects such as bridges.

6.1 Equilibrium

An object on which the net force is zero is said to be in *equilibrium*. The object might be at rest in *static equilibrium,* or it might be moving along a straight line with constant velocity in *dynamic equilibrium*. Both are identical from a Newtonian perspective because $\vec{F}_{net} = \vec{0}$ and $\vec{a} = \vec{0}$.

Newton's first law is the basis for a four-step *strategy* for solving equilibrium problems.

PROBLEM-SOLVING
STRATEGY 6.1   **Equilibrium problems**   (MP)

MODEL   Make simplifying assumptions. When appropriate, represent the object as a particle.

VISUALIZE

- Establish a coordinate system, define symbols, and identify what the problem is asking you to find. This is the process of translating words into symbols.
- Identify all forces acting on the object and show them on a free-body diagram.
- These elements form the **pictorial representation** of the problem.

SOLVE   The mathematical representation is based on Newton's first law:

$$\vec{F}_{net} = \sum_i \vec{F}_i = \vec{0}$$

The vector sum of the forces is found directly from the free-body diagram.

ASSESS   Check that your result has the correct units, is reasonable, and answers the question.

Newton's laws are *vector equations*. Recall from Chapter 3 that the vector equation in the step labeled Solve is a shorthand way of writing two simultaneous equations:

$$(F_{net})_x = \sum_i (F_i)_x = 0$$

$$(F_{net})_y = \sum_i (F_i)_y = 0$$

(6.1)

In other words, each component of $\vec{F}_{net}$ must simultaneously be zero. Although real-world situations often have forces pointing in three dimensions, thus requiring a third equation for the *z*-component of $\vec{F}_{net}$, we will restrict ourselves for now to problems that can be analyzed in two dimensions.

NOTE ▶ The equilibrium condition of Equations 6.1 applies only to particles, which cannot rotate. Equilibrium of an extended object, which can rotate, requres an additional condition. We will study the equilibrium of extended objects in Chapter 12.◄

Equilibrium problems occur frequently, especially in engineering applications. Let's look at a couple of examples.

Static Equilibrium

EXAMPLE 6.1 **Three-way tug-of-war**

You and two friends find three ropes tied together with a single knot and decide to have a three-way tug-of-war. Avery pulls to the west with 100 N of force, while Brandon pulls to the south with 200 N. How hard, and in which direction, should you pull to keep the knot from moving?

MODEL We'll treat the *knot* in the rope as a particle in static equilibrium.

FIGURE 6.1 Pictorial representation for a knot in static equilibrium.

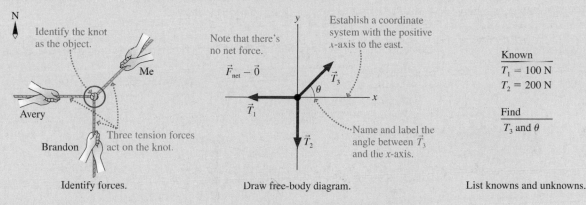

Identify the knot as the object.

Three tension forces act on the knot.

Identify forces.

Note that there's no net force.

$\vec{F}_{net} = \vec{0}$

Establish a coordinate system with the positive *x*-axis to the east.

Name and label the angle between $\vec{T}_3$ and the *x*-axis.

Draw free-body diagram.

Known
$T_1 = 100$ N
$T_2 = 200$ N

Find
T_3 and θ

List knowns and unknowns.

VISUALIZE FIGURE 6.1 shows how to draw a pictorial representation. We've chosen the *y*-axis to point north, and we've labeled the three forces $\vec{T}_1$, $\vec{T}_2$, and $\vec{T}_3$. Notice that we've *defined* angle θ to indicate the direction of your pull.

SOLVE The free-body diagram shows the tension forces $\vec{T}_1$, $\vec{T}_2$, and $\vec{T}_3$ acting on the knot. Newton's first law, written in component form, is

$$(F_{net})_x = \sum_i (F_i)_x = T_{1x} + T_{2x} + T_{3x} = 0$$

$$(F_{net})_y = \sum_i (F_i)_y = T_{1y} + T_{2y} + T_{3y} = 0$$

NOTE ► You might have been tempted to write $-T_{1x}$ in the first equation because $\vec{T}_1$ points in the negative *x*-direction. But the net force, by definition, is the *sum* of all the individual forces. The fact that $\vec{T}_1$ points to the left will be taken into account when we *evaluate* the components. ◄

The components of the force vectors can be evaluated directly from the free-body diagram:

$$T_{1x} = -T_1 \qquad T_{1y} = 0$$
$$T_{2x} = 0 \qquad T_{2y} = -T_2$$
$$T_{3x} = +T_3\cos\theta \qquad T_{3y} = +T_3\sin\theta$$

This is where the signs enter, with T_{1x} being assigned a negative value because $\vec{T}_1$ points to the left. Similarly, $T_{2y} = -T_2$. With these components, Newton's first law becomes

$$-T_1 + T_3\cos\theta = 0$$
$$-T_2 + T_3\sin\theta = 0$$

These are two simultaneous equations for the two unknowns T_3 and θ. We will encounter equations of this form on many occasions, so make a note of the method of solution. First, rewrite the two equations as

$$T_1 = T_3\cos\theta$$
$$T_2 = T_3\sin\theta$$

Next, divide the second equation by the first to eliminate T_3:

$$\frac{T_2}{T_1} = \frac{T_3\sin\theta}{T_3\cos\theta} = \tan\theta$$

Then solve for θ:

$$\theta = \tan^{-1}\left(\frac{T_2}{T_1}\right) = \tan^{-1}\left(\frac{200\text{ N}}{100\text{ N}}\right) = 63.4°$$

Finally, use θ to find T_3:

$$T_3 = \frac{T_1}{\cos\theta} = \frac{100\text{ N}}{\cos 63.4°} = 224\text{ N}$$

The force that maintains equilibrium and prevents the knot from moving is thus

$$\vec{T}_3 = (224\text{ N}, 63.4° \text{ north of east})$$

ASSESS Is this result reasonable? Because your friends pulled west and south, you expected to pull in a generally northeast direction. You also expected to pull harder than either of them but, because they didn't pull in the same direction, less than the sum of their pulls. The result for $\vec{T}_3$ meets these expectations.

Dynamic Equilibrium

A car with a weight of 15,000 N is being towed up a 20° slope at constant velocity. Friction is negligible. The tow rope is rated at 6000 N maximum tension. Will it break?

MODEL We'll treat the car as a particle in dynamic equilibrium. We'll ignore friction.

VISUALIZE This problem asks for a yes or no answer, not a number, but we still need a quantitative analysis. Part of our analysis of the problem statement is to determine which quantity or quantities allow us to answer the question. In this case the answer is clear: We need to calculate the tension in the rope. **FIGURE 6.2** shows the pictorial representation. Note the similarities to Examples 5.2 and 5.6 in Chapter 5, which you may want to review.

We noted in Chapter 5 that the weight of an object at rest is the magnitude F_G of the gravitational force acting on it, and that information has been listed as known. We'll examine weight more closely later in the chapter.

FIGURE 6.2 Pictorial representation of a car being towed up a hill.

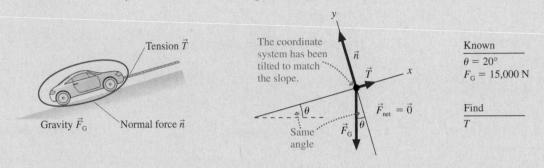

SOLVE The free-body diagram shows forces $\vec{T}$, $\vec{n}$, and $\vec{F}_G$ acting on the car. Newton's first law is

$$(F_{net})_x = \sum F_x = T_x + n_x + (F_G)_x = 0$$

$$(F_{net})_y = \sum F_y = T_y + n_y + (F_G)_y = 0$$

Notice that we dropped the label i from the sum. From here on, we'll use $\sum F_x$ and $\sum F_y$ as a simple shorthand notation to indicate that we're adding all the x-components and all the y-components of the forces.

We can deduce the components directly from the free-body diagram:

$$T_x = T \qquad\qquad T_y = 0$$
$$n_x = 0 \qquad\qquad n_y = n$$
$$(F_G)_x = -F_G\sin\theta \qquad (F_G)_y = -F_G\cos\theta$$

NOTE ▶ The gravitational force has both x- and y-components in this coordinate system, both of which are negative due to the direction of the vector $\vec{F}_G$. You'll see this situation often, so be sure you understand where $(F_G)_x$ and $(F_G)_y$ come from. ◀

With these components, the first law becomes

$$T - F_G\sin\theta = 0$$
$$n - F_G\cos\theta = 0$$

The first of these can be rewritten as

$$T = F_G\sin\theta$$
$$= (15,000\text{ N})\sin 20° = 5100\text{ N}$$

Because $T < 6000$ N, we conclude that the rope will *not* break. It turned out that we did not need the y-component equation in this problem.

ASSESS Because there's no friction, it would not take *any* tension force to keep the car rolling along a horizontal surface ($\theta = 0°$). At the other extreme, $\theta = 90°$, the tension force would need to equal the car's weight ($T = 15,000$ N) to lift the car straight up at constant velocity. The tension force for a 20° slope should be somewhere in between, and 5100 N is a little less than half the weight of the car. That our result is reasonable doesn't prove it's right, but we have at least ruled out careless errors that give unreasonable results.

6.2 Using Newton's Second Law

2.1, 2.2, 2.3, 2.4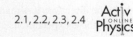

Equilibrium is important, but it is a special case of motion. Newton's second law is a more general link between force and motion. We now need a strategy for using Newton's second law to solve dynamics problems.

The essence of Newtonian mechanics can be expressed in two steps:

- The forces on an object determine its acceleration $\vec{a} = \vec{F}_{net}/m$.
- The object's trajectory can be determined by using $\vec{a}$ in the equations of kinematics.

These two ideas are the basis of a strategy for solving dynamics problems.

PROBLEM SOLVING
STRATEGY 6.2 Dynamics problems   (MP)

MODEL Make simplifying assumptions.

VISUALIZE Draw a **pictorial representation**.

- Show important points in the motion with a sketch, establish a coordinate system, define symbols, and identify what the problem is trying to find. This is the process of translating words into symbols.
- Use a motion diagram to determine the object's acceleration vector $\vec{a}$.
- Identify all forces acting on the object and show them on a free-body diagram.
- It's OK to go back and forth between these steps as you visualize the situation.

SOLVE The mathematical representation is based on Newton's second law:

$$\vec{F}_{net} = \sum_i \vec{F}_i = m\vec{a}$$

The vector sum of the forces is found directly from the free-body diagram. Depending on the problem, either

- Solve for the acceleration, then use kinematics to find velocities and positions; or
- Use kinematics to determine the acceleration, then solve for unknown forces.

ASSESS Check that your result has the correct units, is reasonable, and answers the question.

Newton's second law is a vector equation. To apply the step labeled Solve, you must write the second law as two simultaneous equations:

$$(F_{net})_x = \sum F_x = ma_x$$
$$(F_{net})_y = \sum F_y = ma_y$$

(6.2)

The primary goal of this chapter is to illustrate the use of this strategy. Let's start with some examples.

EXAMPLE 6.3 Speed of a towed car

A 1500 kg car is pulled by a tow truck. The tension in the tow rope is 2500 N, and a 200 N friction force opposes the motion. If the car starts from rest, what is its speed after 5.0 seconds?

MODEL We'll treat the car as an accelerating particle. We'll assume, as part of our *interpretation* of the problem, that the road is horizontal and that the direction of motion is to the right.

VISUALIZE FIGURE 6.3 on the next page shows the pictorial representation. We've established a coordinate system and defined symbols to represent kinematic quantities. We've identified the speed v_1, rather than the velocity v_{1x}, as what we're trying to find.

SOLVE We begin with Newton's second law:

$$(F_{net})_x = \sum F_x = T_x + f_x + n_x + (F_G)_x = ma_x$$
$$(F_{net})_y = \sum F_y = T_y + f_y + n_y + (F_G)_y = ma_y$$

All four forces acting on the car have been included in the vector sum. The equations are perfectly general, with $+$ signs everywhere, because the four vectors are *added* to give $\vec{F}_{net}$. We can now "read" the vector components from the free-body diagram:

$$T_x = +T \qquad T_y = 0$$
$$n_x = 0 \qquad n_y = +n$$
$$f_x = -f \qquad f_y = 0$$
$$(F_G)_x = 0 \qquad (F_G)_y = -F_G$$

Continued

FIGURE 6.3 Pictorial representation of a car being towed.

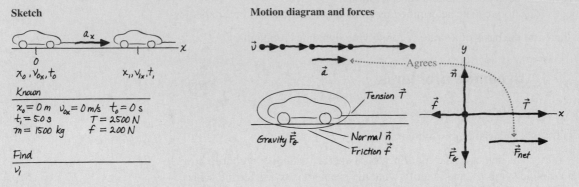

The signs of the components depend on which way the vectors point. Substituting these into the second-law equations and dividing by m give

$$a_x = \frac{1}{m}(T - f)$$

$$= \frac{1}{1500 \text{ kg}}(2500 \text{ N} - 200 \text{ N}) = 1.53 \text{ m/s}^2$$

$$a_y = \frac{1}{m}(n - F_G)$$

NOTE ▶ Newton's second law has allowed us to determine a_x exactly but has given only an algebraic expression for a_y. However, we know *from the motion diagram* that $a_y = 0$! That is, the motion is purely along the x-axis, so there is *no* acceleration along

the y-axis. The requirement $a_y = 0$ allows us to conclude that $n = F_G$. Although we do not need n for this problem, it will be important in many future problems. ◀

We can finish by using constant-acceleration kinematics to find the velocity:

$$v_{1x} = v_{0x} + a_x \Delta t$$

$$= 0 + (1.53 \text{ m/s}^2)(5.0 \text{ s})$$

$$= 7.7 \text{ m/s}$$

The problem asked for the *speed* after 5.0 s, which is $v_1 = 7.7$ m/s.

ASSESS 7.7 m/s ≈ 15 mph, a reasonable speed after 5 s of acceleration.

EXAMPLE 6.4 **Altitude of a rocket**

A 500 g model rocket with a gravitational force of 4.90 N is launched straight up. The small rocket motor burns for 5.00 s and has a steady thrust of 20.0 N. What maximum altitude does the rocket reach? Assume that the mass loss of the burned fuel is negligible.

MODEL We'll treat the rocket as an accelerating particle. Air resistance will be neglected.

VISUALIZE The pictorial representation of **FIGURE 6.4** finds that this is a two-part problem. First, the rocket accelerates straight up. Second, the rocket continues going up as it slows down, a free-fall situation. The maximum altitude is at the end of the second part of the motion.

SOLVE We now know what the problem is asking, have established relevant symbols and coordinates, and know what the forces are. We begin the mathematical representation by writing Newton's second law, in component form, as the rocket accelerates upward. The free-body diagram shows two forces, so

$$(F_{net})_x = \sum F_x = (F_{thrust})_x + (F_G)_x = ma_{0x}$$

$$(F_{net})_y = \sum F_y = (F_{thrust})_y + (F_G)_y = ma_{0y}$$

The fact that vector $\vec{F}_G$ points downward—and which might have tempted you to use a minus sign in the y-equation—will be taken into account when we *evaluate* the components. None of the vectors in this problem has an x-component, so only the y-component of the second law is needed. We can use the free-body diagram to see that

$$(F_{thrust})_y = +F_{thrust}$$

$$(F_G)_y = -F_G$$

This is the point at which the directional information about the force vectors enters. The y-component of the second law is then

$$a_{0y} = \frac{1}{m}(F_{thrust} - F_G)$$

$$= \frac{20.0 \text{ N} - 4.90 \text{ N}}{0.500 \text{ kg}} = 30.2 \text{ m/s}^2$$

Notice that we converted the mass to SI units of kilograms before doing any calculations and that, because of the definition of the newton, the division of newtons by kilograms automatically gives the correct SI units of acceleration.

FIGURE 6.4 Pictorial representation of a rocket launch.

Sketch

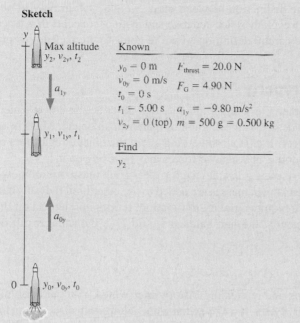

Known

$y_0 = 0$ m $F_{thrust} = 20.0$ N
$v_{0y} = 0$ m/s $F_G = 4.90$ N
$t_0 = 0$ s
$t_1 = 5.00$ s $a_{1y} = -9.80$ m/s^2
$v_{2y} = 0$ (top) $m = 500$ g $= 0.500$ kg

Find

y_2

Motion diagram and forces

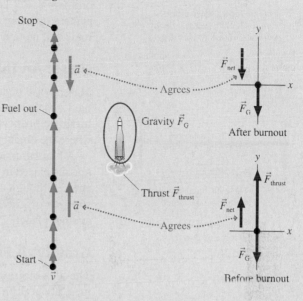

The acceleration of the rocket is constant until it runs out of fuel, so we can use constant-acceleration kinematics to find the altitude and velocity at burnout ($\Delta t = t_1 = 5.00$ s):

$$y_1 = y_0 + v_{0y}\Delta t + \tfrac{1}{2}a_{0y}(\Delta t)^2$$
$$= \tfrac{1}{2}a_{0y}(\Delta t)^2 = 377 \text{ m}$$
$$v_{1y} = v_{0y} + a_{0y}\Delta t = a_{0y}\Delta t = 151 \text{ m/s}$$

The only force on the rocket after burnout is gravity, so the second part of the motion is free fall with $a_{1y} = -g$. We do not know how long it takes to reach the top, but we do know that the final velocity is $v_{2y} = 0$.

We can use free-fall kinematics to find the maximum altitude:

$$v_{2y}^2 = 0 = v_{1y}^2 - 2g\Delta y = v_{1y}^2 - 2g(y_2 - y_1)$$

which we can solve to find

$$y_2 = y_1 + \frac{v_{1y}^2}{2g} = 377 \text{ m} + \frac{(151 \text{ m/s})^2}{2(9.80 \text{ m/s}^2)}$$
$$= 1540 \text{ m} = 1.54 \text{ km}$$

ASSESS The maximum altitude reached by this rocket is 1.54 km, or just slightly under one mile. While this does not seem unreasonable for a high-acceleration rocket, the neglect of air resistance was probably not a terribly realistic assumption.

These first examples have shown all the details. Our purpose has been to show how the problem-solving strategy is put into practice. Future examples will be briefer, but the basic *procedure* will remain the same.

STOP TO THINK 6.1 A Martian lander is approaching the surface. It is slowing its descent by firing its rocket motor. Which is the correct free-body diagram for the lander?

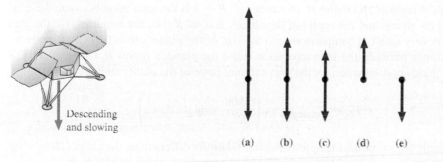

FIGURE 6.5 A pan balance measures mass.

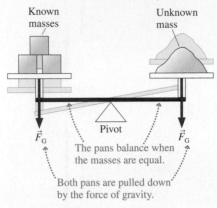

If the unknown mass differs from the known masses, the beam will rotate about the pivot.

Known masses

Unknown mass

$\vec{F}_G$

Pivot

The pans balance when the masses are equal.

$\vec{F}_G$

Both pans are pulled down by the force of gravity.

FIGURE 6.6 Newton's law of gravity.

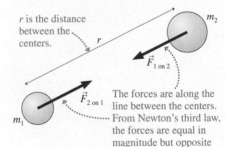

r is the distance between the centers.

r

m_2

$\vec{F}_{1\ on\ 2}$

$\vec{F}_{2\ on\ 1}$

m_1

The forces are along the line between the centers. From Newton's third law, the forces are equal in magnitude but opposite in direction.

FIGURE 6.7 Gravity near the surface of a planet.

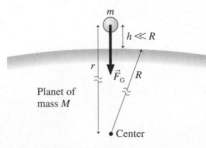

m

$h \ll R$

r

$\vec{F}_G$

R

Planet of mass M

Center

6.3 Mass, Weight, and Gravity

We often do not make a large distinction between mass, weight, and gravity in our ordinary use of language. However, these are separate and distinct concepts in science and engineering, and we need careful definitions if we're going to think clearly about force and motion.

Mass: An Intrinsic Property

Mass, you'll recall from Chapter 5, is a scalar quantity that describes an object's inertia. Loosely speaking, it also describes the amount of matter in an object. **Mass is an intrinsic property of an object.** It tells us something about the object, regardless of where the object is, what it's doing, or whatever forces may be acting on it.

A *pan balance,* shown in **FIGURE 6.5**, is a device for measuring mass. An unknown mass is placed in one pan, then known masses are added to the other until the pans balance. Although a pan balance requires gravity to function, it does not depend on the strength of gravity. Consequently, the pan balance would give the same result on another planet.

Gravity: A Force

The idea of gravity has a long and interesting history intertwined with our evolving ideas about earth and the solar system. It was Newton who—along with discovering his three laws of motion—first recognized that **gravity is an attractive, long-range force between *any* two objects.** Somewhat more loosely, gravity is a force that acts on mass.

FIGURE 6.6 shows two objects with masses m_1 and m_2 separated by distance r. Each object pulls on the other with a force given by *Newton's law of gravity:*

$$F_{1\ on\ 2} = F_{2\ on\ 1} = \frac{Gm_1m_2}{r^2} \qquad \text{(Newton's law of gravity)} \qquad (6.3)$$

where $G = 6.67 \times 10^{-11}\ \mathrm{N\,m^2/kg^2}$, called the *gravitational constant,* is one of the basic constants of nature. You can see from the units of G that the force will be in newtons if the masses are in kilograms and the distance is in meters, all standard SI units. Note that the gravitational force is a vector, with a direction; Equation 6.3 gives only the magnitude of the force. The force gets weaker as the distance between the objects increases.

Because G is a very small number, the force between two human-sized objects is minuscule, completely insignificant in comparison with other forces. That's why you're not aware of being tugged toward everything around you. Only when one or both objects is planet-size or larger does gravity become an important force. Indeed, Chapter 13 will explore in detail the application of Newton's law of gravity to the orbits of satellites and planets.

Newton's law of gravity, with its inverse-square dependence on distance, is a rather complicated force. It would be very useful to have a simpler version of the gravitational force for objects on or very near the surface of a planet, things like balls and cars and planes. **FIGURE 6.7** shows an object of mass m at height h above the surface of a planet of mass M and radius R. Distance $r = R + h$ is the separation between the center of the planet and the center of the object. If $h \ll R$ (i.e., the height above the surface is very small in comparison with the size of the planet), then there's virtually no difference between the true separation r and the planet's radius R. Consequently, a very good approximation for the gravitational force of the planet on mass m is simply

$$\vec{F}_G = \vec{F}_{\text{planet on } m} = \left(\frac{GMm}{R^2},\ \text{straight down} \right) \qquad (6.4)$$

On earth, for example, the approximation GMm/R^2 differs from the exact GMm/r^2 by only 0.3% at a height of 10 km (33,000 ft), the height at which jet planes fly.

For motions whose vertical and horizontal extents are less than roughly 10 km, we can approximate the earth as a flat surface (i.e., the earth's curvature is irrelevant over these distances) that pulls on objects with a gravitational force given by Equation 6.4. This **flat-earth approximation** is another model, but one we've shown is well justified for small-scale motions on or near the surface of the earth, the types of motion we'll be studying in the next few chapters.

Notice that the gravitational force of Equation 6.4 is directly proportional to the object's mass m. We can write the gravitational force even more simply as

$$\vec{F}_G = (mg, \text{ straight down}) \qquad \text{(gravitational force)} \qquad (6.5)$$

where the quantity g is defined to be

$$g = \frac{GM}{R^2} \qquad (6.6)$$

In fact, the direction of the gravitational force defines what we *mean* by "straight down."

The quantity g—sometimes called the *gravitational field* of a planet—is a property of the planet, depending only on the planet's mass and size. Once we've calculated g, we can use it to find the gravitational force on any object near the planet. (We will develop the *field model* of long-range forces when we study electricity and magnetism in Part VI.)

But why did we choose to call it g, a symbol we've already used as the free-fall acceleration? To see the connection, FIGURE 6.8 shows the free-body diagram of an object in free fall near the surface of a planet. With $\vec{F}_{net} = \vec{F}_G$, Newton's second law predicts that the acceleration of an object in free fall is

$$\vec{a}_{\text{free fall}} = \frac{\vec{F}_{net}}{m} = \frac{\vec{F}_G}{m} = (g, \text{ straight down}) \qquad (6.7)$$

Interestingly, the magnitude $a_{\text{free fall}}$ of the free-fall acceleration is simply g, the magnitude of the gravitational field. Because g is a property of the planet, independent of the object, **all objects on the same planet, regardless of mass, have the same free-fall acceleration.** We introduced this idea in Chapter 2 as an experimental discovery of Galileo, but now we see that the mass independence of $\vec{a}_{\text{free fall}}$ is a theoretical prediction of Newton's law of gravity.

The last thing to check is whether Newton's law predicts the correct value, which we know from experiment (at least at midlatitudes on the earth's surface) to be $g = |a_{\text{free fall}}| = 9.80 \text{ m/s}^2$. Things are a bit complicated by the fact that the earth isn't a perfect sphere, but we can use the average radius ($R_{\text{earth}} = 6.37 \times 10^6$ m) and mass ($M_{\text{earth}} = 5.98 \times 10^{24}$ kg) of the earth to calculate

$$g_{\text{earth}} = \frac{GM_{\text{earth}}}{(R_{\text{earth}})^2} = \frac{(6.67 \times 10^{-11} \text{ N m}^2/\text{kg}^2)(5.98 \times 10^{24} \text{ kg})}{(6.37 \times 10^6 \text{ m})^2} = 9.83 \text{ N/kg}$$

You should convince yourself that N/kg is equivalent to m/s^2, so $g_{\text{earth}} = 9.83 \text{ m/s}^2$. (Data for other astronomical objects, which you may need for homework, are located inside the back cover of the book.)

Newton's prediction is very close, but it's not quite right. The free-fall acceleration *would* be 9.83 m/s^2 on a stationary earth, but, in reality, the earth is rotating on its axis. The "missing" 0.03 m/s^2 is due to the earth's rotation, a claim we'll justify when we study circular motion in Chapter 8. Because we're on the outside of a rotating sphere, rather like being on the outside edge of a merry-go-round, the effect of rotation is to "weaken" gravity.

Our goal is to analyze motion from within our own reference frame, a reference frame attached to the earth. Strictly speaking, Newton's laws of motion are not valid in our reference frame because it is rotating and thus is not an inertial reference frame.

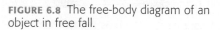

FIGURE 6.8 The free-body diagram of an object in free fall.

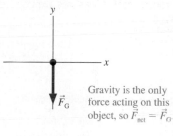

Gravity is the only force acting on this object, so $\vec{F}_{net} = \vec{F}_G$.

Fortunately, we can use Newton's laws to analyze motion near the earth's surface, and we can use $F_G = mg$ for the gravitational force *if* we use $g = |a_{\text{free fall}}| = 9.80 \text{ m/s}^2$ rather than $g = g_{\text{earth}}$. (This assertion is proved in more advanced classes.) In our rotating reference frame, $\vec{F}_G$ is the *effective gravitational force*, the true gravitational force given by Newton's law of gravity plus a small correction due to our rotation. This is the force to show on free-body diagrams and use in calculations.

NOTE ▶ You may be familiar with the idea that future space stations will generate "artificial gravity" by rotating. From *within* a rotating reference frame, the effects of rotation can't be distinguished from the effects of gravity. On our rotating earth, we can measure only the combined influence of gravity and rotation, hence the idea of the *effective* gravitational force. Because the rotational correction is very small, the term "gravitational force" will, unless noted otherwise, mean the effective gravitational force we actually experience on our rotating planet. ◀

Weight: A Measurement

When you weigh yourself, you stand on a *spring scale* and compress a spring. You weigh apples in the grocery store by placing them in a spring scale and stretching a spring. The reading of a spring scale, such as the two shown in FIGURE 6.9, is F_{sp}, the magnitude of the force the spring is exerting.

With that in mind, let's define the **weight** of an object as the reading F_{sp} of a calibrated spring scale on which the object is stationary. That is, **weight is a measurement, the result of "weighing" an object.** Because F_{sp} is a force, weight is measured in newtons.

Suppose the scales in Figure 6.9 are at rest relative to the earth. Then the object being weighed is in static equilibrium, with $\vec{F}_{\text{net}} = \vec{0}$. The stretched spring *pulls* up, the compressed spring *pushes* up, but in both cases $\vec{F}_{\text{net}} = \vec{0}$ only if the upward spring force exactly balances the downward gravitational force:

$$F_{\text{sp}} = F_G = mg$$

Because we defined weight as the reading F_{sp} of a spring scale, the weight of a stationary object is

$$w = mg \qquad \text{(weight of a stationary object)} \qquad (6.8)$$

The scale does not "know" the weight of the object. All it can do is to measure how much its spring is stretched or compressed. On earth, a student with a mass of 70 kg has weight $w = (70 \text{ kg})(9.80 \text{ m/s}^2) = 686 \text{ N}$ *because* he compresses a spring until the spring pushes upward with 686 N. On a different planet, with a different value for g, the expansion or compression of the spring would be different and the student's weight would be different.

NOTE ▶ **Mass and weight are not the same thing.** Mass, in kg, is an intrinsic property of an object; its value is unique and always the same. Weight, in N, does depend on the object's mass, but it also depends on the situation—the strength of gravity and, as we will see, whether or not the object is accelerating. Weight is *not* a property of the object, and thus weight does not have a unique value. ◀

The unit of force in the English system is the *pound*, which is defined as $1 \text{ lb} \equiv 4.45 \text{ N}$. An object whose weight (on earth) is $w = mg = 4.45 \text{ N}$ has mass

$$m = \frac{w}{g} = \frac{4.45 \text{ N}}{9.80 \text{ m/s}^2} = 0.454 \text{ kg} = 454 \text{ g}$$

You may have learned in previous science classes that "1 pound = 454 grams" or, equivalently, that "1 kg = 2.2 lb." Strictly speaking, these well-known "conversion factors" are not true. They are comparing a weight (pounds) to a mass (kilograms). The correct statement is: "A mass of 1 kg has a weight *on earth* of 2.2 pounds." On another planet, the weight of a 1 kg mass would be something other than 2.2 pounds.

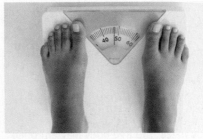

A spring scale, such as the familiar bathroom scale, measures weight, not mass.

FIGURE 6.9 A spring scale measures weight.

(a)

The scale reading is the magnitude of $\vec{F}_{\text{sp}}$.

Cutaway detail showing the spring

The object is stretching the spring.

$\vec{F}_{\text{sp}}$

$\vec{F}_G$

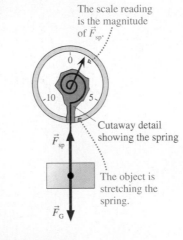

(b)

The object is compressing the spring.

$\vec{F}_{\text{sp}}$

$\vec{F}_G$

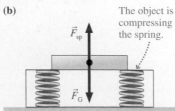

EXAMPLE 6.5 Mass and weight on Jupiter
What is the kilograms-to-pounds conversion factor on Jupiter, where the free-fall acceleration is 25.9 m/s²?

SOLVE Consider an object with a mass of 1 kg. Its weight on Jupiter is

$$w_{Jupiter} = mg_{Jupiter} = (1 \text{ kg})(25.9 \text{ m/s})^2$$

$$= 25.9 \text{ N} \times \frac{1 \text{ lb}}{4.45 \text{ N}} = 5.82 \text{ lb}$$

If you had gone to school on Jupiter, you would have learned that 1 kg = 5.82 lb.

You may never have thought about it, but you cannot directly feel or sense gravity. Your *sensation*—how heavy you feel—is due to contact forces pressing against you, forces that touch you and activate nerve endings in your skin. As you read this, your sensation of weight is due to the normal force exerted on you by the chair in which you are sitting. When you stand, you feel the contact force of the floor pushing against your feet.

But recall the sensations you feel while accelerating. You feel "heavy" when an elevator suddenly accelerates upward, but this sensation vanishes as soon as the elevator reaches a steady speed. Your stomach seems to rise a little and you feel lighter than normal as the upward-moving elevator brakes to a halt or a roller coaster goes over the top. Has your weight actually changed?

To answer this question, **FIGURE 6.10** shows a man weighing himself on a spring scale in an accelerating elevator. The only forces acting on the man are the upward spring force of the scale and the downward gravitational force. This seems to be the same situation as Figure 6.9b, but there's one big difference: The man is accelerating, hence there must be a net force on the man in the direction of $\vec{a}$.

For the net force $\vec{F}_{net}$ to point upward, the magnitude of the spring force must be *greater* than the magnitude of the gravitational force. That is, $F_{sp} > mg$. Looking at the free-body diagram in Figure 6.10, we see that the y-component of Newton's second law is

$$(F_{net})_y = (F_{sp})_y + (F_G)_y = F_{sp} - mg = ma_y \qquad (6.9)$$

where m is the man's mass.

We defined weight as the reading F_{sp} of a calibrated spring scale *on which the object is stationary*. That is the case here as the scale and man accelerate upward together. Thus the man's weight as he accelerates vertically is

$$w = \text{scale reading } F_{sp} = mg + ma_y = mg\left(1 + \frac{a_y}{g}\right) \qquad (6.10)$$

If an object is either at rest or moving with constant velocity, then $a_y = 0$ and $w = mg$. That is, the weight of an object at rest is the magnitude of the (effective) gravitational force acting on it. But its weight differs if it has a vertical acceleration.

You *do* weigh more as an elevator accelerates upward ($a_y > 0$) because the reading of a scale—a weighing—increases. Similarly, your weight is less when the acceleration vector $\vec{a}$ points downward ($a_y < 0$) because the scale reading goes down. Weight, as we've defined it, corresponds to your sensation of heaviness or lightness.*

We found Equation 6.10 by considering a person in an accelerating elevator, but it applies to any object with a vertical acceleration. Further, an object doesn't really have

FIGURE 6.10 A man weighing himself in an accelerating elevator.

The man feels heavier than normal while accelerating upward.

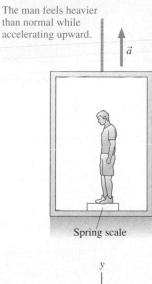

Spring scale

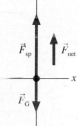

*Surprisingly, there is no universally agreed-upon definition of *weight*. Some textbooks define weight as the gravitational force on an object, $\vec{w} = (mg, \text{down})$. In that case, the scale reading of an accelerating object, and your sensation of weight, is often called *apparent weight*. This textbook prefers the operational definition of *weight* as being what a scale reads, the result of a weighing measurement. You should be aware of these differences if you refer to other textbooks.

to be on a scale to have a weight; an object's weight is the magnitude of the contact force supporting it. It makes no difference whether this is the spring force of the scale or simply the normal force of the floor.

> **NOTE** ▶ Informally, we sometimes say "This object weighs such and such" or "The weight of this object is. . . ." Strictly speaking, we should use the term "mass" because we're talking about a property of the object. Nonetheless, these expressions are widely used, and we'll interpret them as meaning mg, the weight of an object of mass m at rest ($a_y = 0$) on the surface of the earth or some other astronomical body. ◀

Weightlessness

Suppose the elevator cable breaks and the elevator, along with the man and his scale, plunges straight down in free fall! What will the scale read? When the free-fall acceleration $a_y = -g$ is used in Equation 6.10, we find $w = 0$. In other words, *the man has no weight!*

Think about this carefully. Suppose, as the elevator falls, the man inside releases a ball from his hand. In the absence of air resistance, as Galileo discovered, both the man and the ball would fall at the same rate. From the man's perspective, the ball would appear to "float" beside him. Similarly, the scale would float beneath him and not press against his feet. He is what we call *weightless*. Gravity is still pulling down on him—that's why he's falling—but he has no *sensation* of weight as everything floats around him in free fall.

But isn't this exactly what happens to astronauts orbiting the earth? You've seen films of astronauts and various objects floating inside the space shuttle. If an astronaut tries to stand on a scale, it does not exert any force against her feet and reads zero. She is said to be weightless. But if the criterion to be weightless is to be in free fall, and if astronauts orbiting the earth are weightless, does this mean that they are in free fall? This is a very interesting question to which we shall return in Chapter 8.

Astronauts are weightless as they orbit the earth.

STOP TO THINK 6.2   An elevator that has descended from the 50th floor is coming to a halt at the 1st floor. As it does, your weight is

  a. More than mg.   b. Less than mg.   c. Equal to mg.   d. Zero.

6.4 Friction

Friction is absolutely essential for many things we do. Without friction you could not walk, drive, or even sit down (you would slide right off the chair!). It is sometimes useful to think about idealized frictionless situations, but it is equally necessary to understand a real world where friction is present. Although friction is a complicated force, many aspects of friction can be described with a simple model.

Static Friction

Chapter 5 defined *static friction* $\vec{f}_s$ as the force on an object that keeps it from slipping. **FIGURE 6.11** shows a person pushing on a box with horizontal force $\vec{F}_{push}$. If the box remains at rest, "stuck" to the floor, it must be because of a static friction force pushing back to the left. The box is in static equilibrium, so the static friction must exactly balance the pushing force:

$$f_s = F_{push} \tag{6.11}$$

To determine the direction of $\vec{f}_s$, decide which way the object would move if there were no friction. The static friction force $\vec{f}_s$ points in the *opposite* direction to prevent the motion.

FIGURE 6.11 Static friction keeps an object from slipping.

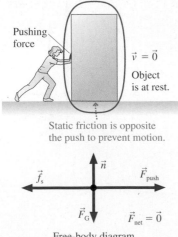

Pushing force

$\vec{v} = \vec{0}$

Object is at rest.

Static friction is opposite the push to prevent motion.

$\vec{f}_s$ $\vec{n}$ $\vec{F}_{push}$

$\vec{F}_G$ $\vec{F}_{net} = \vec{0}$

Free-body diagram

Unlike the gravitational force, which has the precise and unambiguous magnitude $F_G = mg$, the size of the static friction force depends on how hard you push. The harder the person in Figure 6.11 pushes, the harder the floor pushes back. Reduce the pushing force, and the static friction force will automatically be reduced to match. Static friction acts in *response* to an applied force. **FIGURE 6.12** illustrates this idea.

But there's clearly a limit to how big f_s can get. If you push hard enough, the object slips and starts to move. In other words, the static friction force has a *maximum* possible size $f_{s\,max}$.

- An object remains at rest as long as $f_s < f_{s\,max}$.
- The object slips when $f_s = f_{s\,max}$.
- A static friction force $f_s > f_{s\,max}$ is not physically possible.

Experiments with friction (first done by Leonardo da Vinci) show that $f_{s\,max}$ is proportional to the magnitude of the normal force. That is,

$$f_{s\,max} = \mu_s n \qquad (6.12)$$

where the proportionality constant μ_s is called the **coefficient of static friction.** The coefficient is a dimensionless number that depends on the materials of which the object and the surface are made. Table 6.1 shows some typical coefficients of friction. It is to be emphasized that these are only approximate. The exact value of the coefficient depends on the roughness, cleanliness, and dryness of the surfaces.

> **NOTE** ▶ Equation 6.12 does *not* say $f_s = \mu_s n$. The value of f_s depends on the force or forces that static friction has to balance to keep the object from moving. It can have any value from 0 up to, but not exceeding, $\mu_s n$. ◀

Kinetic Friction

Once the box starts to slide, in **FIGURE 6.13**, the static friction force is replaced by a kinetic friction force $\vec{f}_k$. Experiments show that kinetic friction, unlike static friction, has a nearly *constant* magnitude. Furthermore, the size of the kinetic friction force is *less* than the maximum static friction, $f_k < f_{s\,max}$, which explains why it is easier to keep the box moving than it was to start it moving. The direction of $\vec{f}_k$ is always opposite to the direction in which an object slides across the surface.

The kinetic friction force is also proportional to the magnitude of the normal force:

$$f_k = \mu_k n \qquad (6.13)$$

where μ_k is called the **coefficient of kinetic friction.** Table 6.1 includes typical values of μ_k. You can see that $\mu_k < \mu_s$, causing the kinetic friction to be less than the maximum static friction.

Rolling Friction

If you slam on the brakes hard enough, your car tires slide against the road surface and leave skid marks. This is kinetic friction. A wheel *rolling* on a surface also experiences friction, but not kinetic friction. The portion of the wheel that contacts the surface is stationary with respect to the surface, not sliding. To see this, roll a wheel slowly and watch how it touches the ground.

Textbooks draw wheels as circles, but no wheel is perfectly round. The weight of the wheel, and of any object supported by the wheel, causes the bottom of the wheel to flatten where it touches the surface, as **FIGURE 6.14** on the next page shows. The contact area between a car tire and the road is fairly large. The contact area between a steel locomotive wheel and a steel rail is much less, but it's not zero.

Molecular bonds are quickly established where the wheel presses against the surface. These bonds have to be broken as the wheel rolls forward, and the effort needed to break them causes **rolling friction.** (Think how it is to walk with a wad of chewing

FIGURE 6.12 Static friction acts in *response* to an applied force.

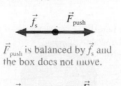

$\vec{F}_{push}$ is balanced by $\vec{f}_s$ and the box does not move.

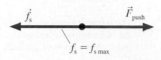

As $\vec{F}_{push}$ increases, $\vec{f}_s$ grows . . .

. . . until f_s reaches $f_{s\,max}$. Now, if $\vec{F}_{push}$ gets any bigger, the object will start to move.

TABLE 6.1 Coefficients of friction

Materials	Static μ_s	Kinetic μ_k	Rolling μ_r
Rubber on concrete	1.00	0.80	0.02
Steel on steel (dry)	0.80	0.60	0.002
Steel on steel (lubricated)	0.10	0.05	
Wood on wood	0.50	0.20	
Wood on snow	0.12	0.06	
Ice on ice	0.10	0.03	

FIGURE 6.13 The kinetic friction force is opposite the direction of motion.

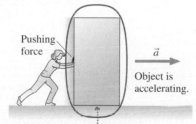

Pushing force

$\vec{a}$

Object is accelerating.

Kinetic friction is opposite the motion.

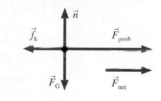

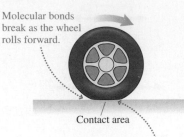

Molecular bonds break as the wheel rolls forward.

Contact area

The wheel flattens where it touches the surface, giving a contact area rather than a point of contact.

2.5, 2.6

gum stuck to the sole of your shoe!) The force of rolling friction can be calculated in terms of a **coefficient of rolling friction** μ_r:

$$f_r = \mu_r n \qquad (6.14)$$

Rolling friction acts very much like kinetic friction, but values of μ_r (see Table 6.1) are much lower than values of μ_k. This is why it is easier to roll an object on wheels than to slide it.

A Model of Friction

These ideas can be summarized in a *model* of friction:

Static: $\vec{f_s} \leq (\mu_s n$, direction as necessary to prevent motion)
Kinetic: $\vec{f_k} = (\mu_k n$, direction opposite the motion) $\qquad (6.15)$
Rolling: $\vec{f_r} = (\mu_r n$, direction opposite the motion)

Here "motion" means "motion relative to the surface." The maximum value of static friction $f_{s\,max} = \mu_s n$ occurs at the point where the object slips and begins to move.

NOTE ▶ Equations 6.15 are a "model" of friction, not a "law" of friction. These equations provide a reasonably accurate, but not perfect, description of how friction forces act. For example, we've ignored the surface area of the object because surface area has little effect. Likewise, our model assumes that the kinetic friction force is independent of the object's speed. This is a fairly good, but not perfect, approximation. Equations 6.15 are a simplification of reality that works reasonably well, which is what we mean by a "model." They are not a "law of nature" on a level with Newton's laws. ◀

FIGURE 6.15 summarizes these ideas graphically by showing how the friction force changes as the magnitude of an applied force $\vec{F}_{push}$ increases.

FIGURE 6.15 The friction force response to an increasing applied force.

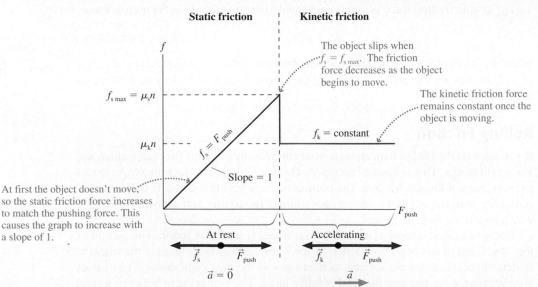

Rank in order, from largest to smallest, the sizes of the friction forces $\vec{f}_a$ to $\vec{f}_e$ in these 5 different situations. The box and the floor are made of the same materials in all situations.

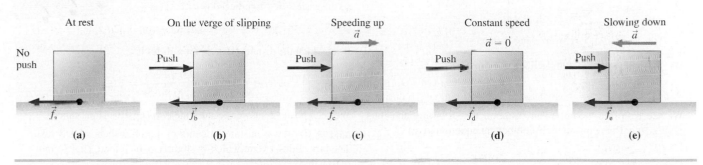

At rest	On the verge of slipping	Speeding up	Constant speed	Slowing down
No push	Push	Push	Push	Push
$\vec{f}_a$	$\vec{f}_b$	$\vec{f}_c$	$\vec{f}_d$	$\vec{f}_e$
(a)	(b)	(c)	(d)	(e)

EXAMPLE 6.6 **How far does a box slide?**

Carol pushes a 50 kg wood box across a wood floor at a steady speed of 2.0 m/s. How much force does Carol exert on the box? If she stops pushing, how far will the box slide before coming to rest?

MODEL We model the box as a particle and we describe the friction forces with the model of static and kinetic friction. This is a two-part problem: first while Carol is pushing the box, then as it slides after she releases it.

VISUALIZE This is a fairly complex situation, one that calls for careful visualization. **FIGURE 6.16** shows the pictorial representation both while Carol pushes, when $\vec{a} = \vec{0}$, and after she stops. We've placed $x = 0$ at the point where she stops pushing because this is the point where the kinematics calculation for "How far?" will begin. Notice that each part of the motion needs its own free-body diagram. The box is moving until the very instant that the problem ends, so only kinetic friction is relevant.

SOLVE We'll start by finding how hard Carol has to push to keep the box moving at a steady speed. The box is in dynamic equilibrium ($\vec{a} = \vec{0}$), and Newton's first law is

$$\sum F_x = F_{push} - f_k = 0$$

$$\sum F_y = n - F_G = n - mg = 0$$

where we've used $F_G = mg$ for the gravitational force. The negative sign occurs in the first equation because $\vec{f}_k$ points to the left and thus the *component* is negative: $(f_k)_x = -f_k$. Similarly, $(F_G)_y = -F_G$ because the gravitational force vector points down. In addition to Newton's laws, we also have our model of kinetic friction:

$$f_k = \mu_k n$$

Altogether we have three simultaneous equations in the three unknowns F_{push}, f_k, and n. Fortunately, these equations are easy to solve. The y-component of Newton's law tells us that $n = mg$. We can then find the friction force to be

$$f_k = \mu_k mg$$

We substitute this into the x-component of the first law, giving

$$F_{push} = f_k = \mu_k mg$$

$$= (0.20)(50 \text{ kg})(9.80 \text{ m/s}^2) = 98 \text{ N}$$

where μ_k for wood on wood was taken from Table 6.1. This is how hard Carol pushes to keep the box moving at a steady speed.

The box is not in equilibrium after Carol stops pushing it. Our strategy for the second half of the problem is to use Newton's second law to find the acceleration, then use kinematics to find how far the box moves before stopping. We know from the

FIGURE 6.16 Pictorial representation of a box sliding across a floor.

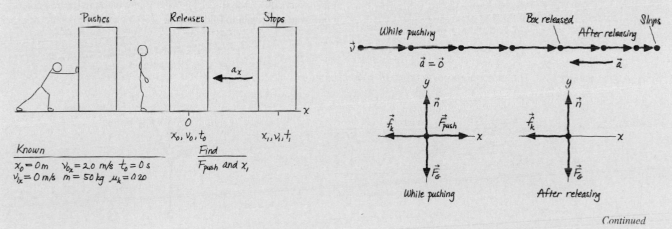

Continued

motion diagram that $a_y = 0$. Newton's second law, applied to the second free-body diagram of Figure 6.16, is

$$\sum F_x = -f_k = ma_x$$
$$\sum F_y = n - mg = ma_y = 0$$

We also have our model of friction,

$$f_k = \mu_k n$$

We see from the y-component equation that $n = mg$, and thus $f_k = \mu_k mg$. Using this in the x-component equation gives

$$ma_x = -f_k = -\mu_k mg$$

This is easily solved to find the box's acceleration:

$$a_x = -\mu_k g = -(0.20)(9.80 \text{ m/s}^2) = -1.96 \text{ m/s}^2$$

The acceleration component a_x is negative because the acceleration vector $\vec{a}$ points to the left, as we see from the motion diagram.

Now we are left with a problem of constant-acceleration kinematics. We are interested in a distance, rather than a time interval, so the easiest way to proceed is

$$v_{1x}^2 = 0 = v_{0x}^2 + 2a_x \Delta x = v_{0x}^2 + 2a_x x_1$$

from which the distance that the box slides is

$$x_1 = \frac{-v_{0x}^2}{2a_x} = \frac{-(2.0 \text{ m/s})^2}{2(-1.96 \text{ m/s}^2)} = 1.0 \text{ m}$$

We get a positive answer because the two negative signs cancel.

ASSESS Carol was pushing at 2 m/s ≈ 4 mph, which is fairly fast. The box slides 1.0 m, which is slightly over 3 feet. That sounds reasonable.

NOTE ▶ We needed both the horizontal and the vertical components of the second law even though the motion was entirely horizontal. This need is typical when friction is involved because we must find the normal force before we can evaluate the friction force. ◀

EXAMPLE 6.7 **Dumping a file cabinet**

A 50 kg steel file cabinet is in the back of a dump truck. The truck's bed, also made of steel, is slowly tilted. What is the size of the static friction force on the cabinet when the bed is tilted 20°? At what angle will the file cabinet begin to slide?

MODEL We'll model the file cabinet as a particle. We'll also use the model of static friction. The file cabinet will slip when the static friction force reaches its maximum value $f_{s\,max}$.

VISUALIZE FIGURE 6.17 shows the pictorial representation when the truck bed is tilted at angle θ. We can make the analysis easier if we tilt the coordinate system to match the bed of the truck. To prevent the file cabinet from slipping, the static friction force must point *up* the slope.

SOLVE The file cabinet is in static equilibrium. Newton's first law is

$$(F_{net})_x = \sum F_x = n_x + (F_G)_x + (f_s)_x = 0$$
$$(F_{net})_y = \sum F_y = n_y + (F_G)_y + (f_s)_y = 0$$

From the free-body diagram we see that f_s has only a *negative x*-component and that n has only a positive y-component. The gravitational force vector can be written $\vec{F}_G = +F_G \sin\theta \hat{i} - F_G \cos\theta \hat{j}$, so $\vec{F}_G$ has both x- and y-components in this coordinate system. Thus the first law becomes

$$\sum F_x = F_G \sin\theta - f_s = mg\sin\theta - f_s = 0$$
$$\sum F_y = n - F_G \cos\theta = n - mg\cos\theta = 0$$

where we've used $F_G = mg$. The x-component equation allows us to determine the size of the static friction force when $\theta = 20°$:

$$f_s = mg\sin\theta = (50 \text{ kg})(9.80 \text{ m/s}^2)\sin 20°$$
$$= 170 \text{ N}$$

This value does not require knowing μ_s. We simply have to find the size of the friction force that will balance the component of $\vec{F}_G$ that points down the slope. The coefficient of static friction enters only when we want to find the angle at which the file cabinet slips.

FIGURE 6.17 The pictorial representation of a file cabinet in a tilted dump truck.

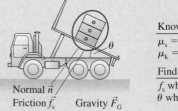

Known
$\mu_s = 0.80$ $m = 50$ kg
$\mu_k = 0.60$

Find
f_s where $\theta = 20°$
θ where cabinet slips

Normal $\vec{n}$
Friction $\vec{f}_s$ Gravity $\vec{F}_G$

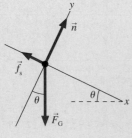

Slipping occurs when the static friction reaches its maximum value

$$f_s = f_{s\,max} = \mu_s n$$

From the y-component of Newton's law we see that $n = mg\cos\theta$. Consequently,

$$f_{s\,max} = \mu_s mg\cos\theta$$

Substituting this into the x-component of the first law gives

$$mg\sin\theta - \mu_s mg\cos\theta = 0$$

The mg in both terms cancels, and we find

$$\frac{\sin\theta}{\cos\theta} = \tan\theta = \mu_s$$

$$\theta = \tan^{-1}\mu_s = \tan^{-1}(0.80) = 39°$$

ASSESS Steel doesn't slide all that well on unlubricated steel, so a fairly large angle is not surprising. The answer seems reasonable. It is worth noting that $n = mg\cos\theta$ in this example. A common error is to use simply $n = mg$. Be sure to evaluate the normal force within the context of each specific problem.

The angle at which slipping begins is called the *angle of repose*. FIGURE 6.18 shows that knowing the angle of repose can be very important because it is the angle at which loose materials (gravel, sand, snow, etc.) begin to slide on a mountainside, leading to landslides and avalanches.

FIGURE 6.18 The angle of repose is the angle at which loose materials, such as gravel or snow, begin to slide.

Causes of Friction

It is worth a brief pause to look at the *causes* of friction. All surfaces, even those quite smooth to the touch, are very rough on a microscopic scale. When two objects are placed in contact, they do not make a smooth fit. Instead, as FIGURE 6.19 shows, the high points on one surface become jammed against the high points on the other surface, while the low points are not in contact at all. Only a very small fraction (typically 10^{-4}) of the surface area is in actual contact. The amount of contact depends on how hard the surfaces are pushed together, which is why friction forces are proportional to n.

At the points of actual contact, the atoms in the two materials are pressed closely together and molecular bonds are established between them. These bonds are the "cause" of the static friction force. For an object to slip, you must push it hard enough to break these molecular bonds between the surfaces. Once they are broken, and the two surfaces are sliding against each other, there are still attractive forces between the atoms on the opposing surfaces as the high points of the materials push past each other. However, the atoms move past each other so quickly that they do not have time to establish the tight bonds of static friction. That is why the kinetic friction force is smaller.

Occasionally, in the course of sliding, two high points will be forced together so closely that they do form a tight bond. As the motion continues, it is not this surface bond that breaks but weaker bonds at the *base* of one of the high points. When this happens, a small piece of the object is left behind "embedded" in the surface. This is what we call *abrasion*. Abrasion causes materials to wear out as a result of friction, be they the piston rings in your car or the seat of your pants. In machines, abrasion is minimized with lubrication, a very thin film of liquid between the surfaces that allows them to "float" past each other with many fewer points in actual contact.

Friction, at the atomic level, is a very complex phenomenon. A detailed understanding of friction is at the forefront of engineering research today, where it is especially important for designing highly miniaturized machines and nanostructures.

6.5 Drag

The air exerts a drag force on objects as they move through the air. You experience drag forces every day as you jog, bicycle, ski, or drive your car. The drag force is especially important for the skydiver at the beginning of the chapter.

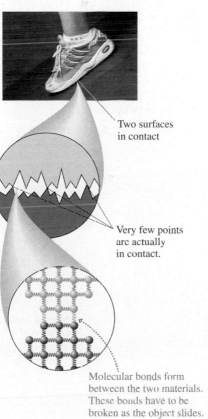

FIGURE 6.19 An atomic-level view of friction.

Two surfaces in contact

Very few points are actually in contact.

Molecular bonds form between the two materials. These bonds have to be broken as the object slides.

FIGURE 6.20 The drag force on a high-speed motorcyclist is significant.

The drag force $\vec{D}$

- Is opposite in direction to $\vec{v}$.
- Increases in magnitude as the object's speed increases.

FIGURE 6.20 illustrates the drag force.

Drag is a more complex force than ordinary friction because drag depends on the object's speed. Drag also depends on the object's shape and on the density of the medium through which it moves. Fortunately, we can use a fairly simple *model* of drag if the following three conditions are met:

- The object's size (diameter) is between a few millimeters and a few meters.
- The object's speed is less than a few hundred meters per second.
- The object is moving through the air near the earth's surface.

These conditions are usually satisfied for balls, people, cars, and many other objects of the everyday world. Under these conditions, the drag force can be written

$$\vec{D} \approx (\tfrac{1}{4}Av^2, \text{ direction opposite the motion}) \qquad (6.16)$$

where A is the cross-section area of the object. The size of the drag force is proportional to the *square* of the object's speed. This model of drag fails for objects that are very small (such as dust particles), very fast (such as jet planes), or that move in other media (such as water). We'll leave those situations to more advanced textbooks.

NOTE ▶ Let's look at this model more closely. You may have noticed that an area multiplied by a speed squared does not give units of force. Unlike the $\tfrac{1}{2}$ in $\Delta x = \tfrac{1}{2}a(\Delta t)^2$, which is a "pure" number, the $\tfrac{1}{4}$ in the expression for $\vec{D}$ has units. This number depends on the air's density, and it's actually $\tfrac{1}{4}$ kg/m^3. We've suppressed the units in Equation 6.16, but doing so gives us an expression that works *only* if A is in m^2 and v is in m/s. Equation 6.16 cannot be converted to other units. And the number is not exactly $\tfrac{1}{4}$, which is why Equation 6.16 has an $\approx$ sign rather than an $=$ sign, but it's close enough to allow Equation 6.16 to be a reasonable yet simple model of drag. ◀

The area in Equation 6.16 is the cross section of the object as it "faces into the wind." **FIGURE 6.21** shows how to calculate the cross-section area for objects of different shape. It's interesting to note that the magnitude of the drag force, $\tfrac{1}{4}Av^2$, depends on the object's *size and shape* but not on its *mass*. We will see shortly that this mass independence has important consequences.

FIGURE 6.21 Cross-section areas for objects of different shape.

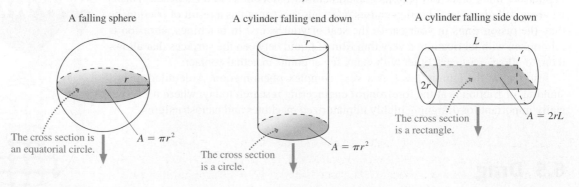

A falling sphere — The cross section is an equatorial circle. $A = \pi r^2$

A cylinder falling end down — The cross section is a circle. $A = \pi r^2$

A cylinder falling side down — The cross section is a rectangle. $A = 2rL$

EXAMPLE 6.8 Air resistance compared to rolling friction

The profile of a typical 1500 kg passenger car, as seen from the front, is 1.6 m wide and 1.4 m high. At what speed does the magnitude of the drag equal the magnitude of the rolling friction?

MODEL Treat the car as a particle. Use the models of rolling friction and drag.

VISUALIZE FIGURE 6.22 shows the car and a free-body diagram. A full pictorial representation is not needed because we won't be doing any kinematics calculations.

FIGURE 6.22 A car experiences both rolling friction and drag.

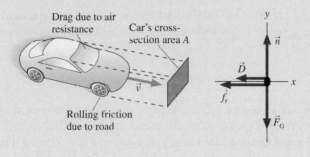

SOLVE Drag is less than friction at low speeds, where air resistance is negligible. But drag increases as v increases, so there will be a speed at which the two forces are equal in size. Above this speed, drag is more important than rolling friction.

The magnitudes of the forces are $D = \frac{1}{4}Av^2$ and $f_r = \mu_r n$. There's no motion and no acceleration in the vertical direction, so we can see from the free-body diagram that $n = F_G = mg$. Thus $f_r = \mu_r mg$. Equating friction and drag, we have

$$\frac{1}{4}Av^2 = \mu_r mg$$

Solving for v, we find

$$v = \sqrt{\frac{4\mu_r mg}{A}} = \sqrt{\frac{4(0.02)(1500 \text{ kg})(9.8 \text{ m/s}^2)}{(1.4 \text{ m})(1.6 \text{ m})}} = 23 \text{ m/s}$$

where the value of μ_r for rubber on concrete was taken from Table 6.1.

ASSESS 23 m/s is approximately 50 mph, a reasonable result. This calculation shows that our assumption that we can ignore air resistance is really quite good for car speeds less than 30 or 40 mph. Calculations that neglect drag will be increasingly inaccurate as speeds go above 50 mph.

FIGURE 6.23 shows a ball moving up and down vertically. If there were no air resistance, the ball would be in free fall with $a_{\text{free fall}} = -g$ throughout its flight. Let's see how drag changes this.

Referring to Figure 6.23:

1. The drag force $\vec{D}$ points down as the ball rises. This *increases* the net force on the ball and causes the ball to slow down *more quickly* than it would in a vacuum. The magnitude of the acceleration, which we'll calculate below, is $|a| > g$.
2. The drag force decreases as the ball slows.
3. $\vec{v} = \vec{0}$ at the highest point in the ball's motion, so there's no drag and the acceleration is simply $a_{\text{free fall}} = -g$.
4. The drag force increases as the ball speeds up.
5. The drag force $\vec{D}$ points up as the ball falls. This *decreases* the net force on the ball and causes the ball to speed up *less quickly* than it would in a vacuum. The magnitude of the acceleration is $|a| < g$.

FIGURE 6.23 Drag force on a ball moving vertically.

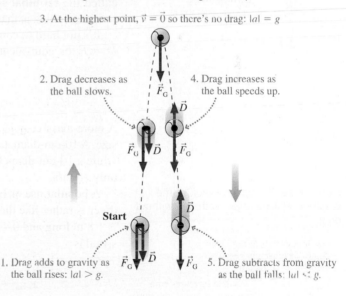

We can use Newton's second law to find the ball's acceleration $a_\uparrow$ as it rises. You can see from the forces in Figure 6.23 that

$$a_\uparrow = \frac{(F_{\text{net}})_y}{m} = \frac{mg - D}{m} = -\left(g + \frac{D}{m}\right) \qquad (6.17)$$

The magnitude of $a_\uparrow$, which is the ball's deceleration as it rises, is $g + D/m$. Air resistance causes the ball to slow down *more quickly* than it would in a vacuum. But Equation 6.17 tells us more. Because D depends on the object's size but not on its mass, drag has a larger *effect* (larger acceleration) on a less massive ball than on a more massive ball of the same size.

A Ping-Pong ball and a golf ball are about the same size, but it's harder to throw the Ping-Pong ball than the golf ball. We can now give an *explanation:*

- The drag force has the same magnitude for two objects of equal size.
- According to Newton's second law, the acceleration (the *effect* of the force) depends inversely on the mass.
- Therefore, the effect of the drag force is larger on a less massive ball than on a more massive ball of equal size.

As the ball in Figure 6.23 falls, its acceleration $a_\downarrow$ is

$$a_\downarrow = \frac{(F_{net})_y}{m} = \frac{-mg + D}{m} = -\left(g - \frac{D}{m}\right) \tag{6.18}$$

The magnitude of $a_\downarrow$ is $g - D/m$, so the ball speeds up *less quickly* than it would in a vacuum. Once again, the effect is larger for a less massive ball than for a more massive ball of equal size.

Terminal Speed

FIGURE 6.24 An object falling at terminal speed.

Terminal speed is reached when the drag force exactly balances the gravitational force: $\vec{a} = \vec{0}$.

The drag force increases as an object falls and gains speed. If the object falls far enough, it will eventually reach a speed, shown in **FIGURE 6.24**, at which $D = F_G$. That is, the drag force will be equal and opposite to the gravitational force. The net force at this speed is $\vec{F}_{net} = \vec{0}$, so there is no further acceleration and the object falls with a *constant* speed. The speed at which the exact balance between the upward drag force and the downward gravitational force causes an object to fall without acceleration is called the **terminal speed** v_{term}. Once an object has reached terminal speed, it will continue falling at that speed until it hits the ground.

It's not hard to compute the terminal speed. It is the speed, by definition, at which $D = F_G$ or, equivalently, $\frac{1}{4}Av^2 \approx mg$. This speed is

$$v_{term} \approx \sqrt{\frac{4mg}{A}} \tag{6.19}$$

A more massive object has a larger terminal speed than a less massive object of equal size. A 10-cm-diameter lead ball, with a mass of 6 kg, has a terminal speed of 170 m/s, while a 10-cm-diameter Styrofoam ball, with a mass of 50 g, has a terminal speed of only 15 m/s.

A popular use of Equation 6.19 is to find the terminal speed of a skydiver. A skydiver is rather like the cylinder of Figure 6.21 falling "side down." A typical skydiver is 1.8 m long and 0.40 m wide ($A = 0.72$ m^2) and has a mass of 75 kg. His terminal speed is

$$v_{term} \approx \sqrt{\frac{4mg}{A}} = \sqrt{\frac{4(75 \text{ kg})(9.8 \text{ m/s}^2)}{0.72 \text{ m}^2}} = 64 \text{ m/s}$$

This is roughly 140 mph. A higher speed can be reached by falling feet first or head first, which reduces the area A.

FIGURE 6.25 shows the results of a more detailed calculation for a falling object. Without drag, the velocity graph is a straight line with slope $= a_y = -g$. When drag is included, the slope steadily decreases in magnitude and approaches zero (no further acceleration) as the object reaches terminal speed.

Although we've focused our analysis on objects moving vertically, the same ideas apply to objects moving horizontally. If an object is thrown or shot horizontally, $\vec{D}$ causes the object to slow down. An airplane reaches its maximum speed, which is analogous to the terminal speed, when the drag is equal and opposite to the thrust: $D = F_{thrust}$. The net force is then zero and the plane cannot go any faster. The maximum speed of a passenger jet is about 550 mph.

FIGURE 6.25 The velocity-versus-time graph of a falling object with and without drag.

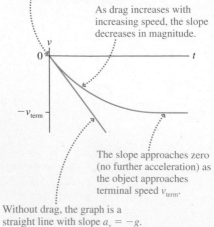

The velocity starts at zero, then becomes increasingly negative (motion in −y-direction).

As drag increases with increasing speed, the slope decreases in magnitude.

The slope approaches zero (no further acceleration) as the object approaches terminal speed v_{term}.

Without drag, the graph is a straight line with slope $a_y = -g$.

STOP TO THINK 6.4   The terminal speed of a Styrofoam ball is 15 m/s. Suppose a Styrofoam ball is shot straight down with an initial speed of 30 m/s. Which velocity graph is correct?

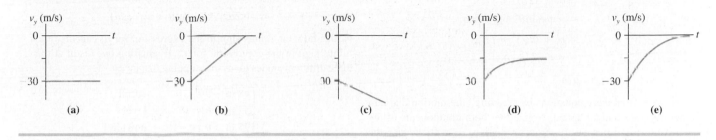

(a)   (b)   (c)   (d)   (e)

6.6 More Examples of Newton's Second Law

We will finish this chapter with three additional examples in which we use the problem-solving strategy in more complex scenarios.

Activ ONLINE Physics   2.7, 2.8, 2.9

EXAMPLE 6.9 **Stopping distances**

A 1500 kg car is traveling at a speed of 30 m/s when the driver slams on the brakes and skids to a halt. Determine the stopping distance if the car is traveling up a 10° slope, down a 10° slope, or on a level road.

MODEL We'll represent the car as a particle and we'll use the model of kinetic friction. We want to solve the problem only once, not three separate times, so we'll leave the slope angle θ unspecified until the end.

VISUALIZE **FIGURE 6.26** shows the pictorial representation. We've shown the car sliding uphill, but these representations work equally well for a level or downhill slide if we let θ be zero or negative, respectively. We've used a tilted coordinate system so that the motion is along one of the axes. We've *assumed* that the car is traveling to the right, although the problem didn't state this. You could equally well make the opposite assumption, but you would have to be careful with negative values of x and v_x. The car *skids* to a halt, so we've taken the coefficient of *kinetic* friction for rubber on concrete from Table 6.1.

FIGURE 6.26 Pictorial representation of a skidding car.

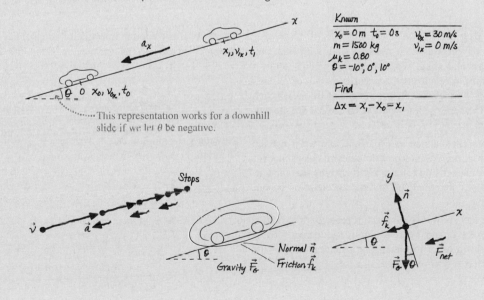

Continued

SOLVE Newton's second law and the model of kinetic friction are

$$\sum F_x = n_x + (F_G)_x + (f_k)_x$$
$$= -mg\sin\theta - f_k = ma_x$$

$$\sum F_y = n_y + (F_G)_y + (f_k)_y$$
$$= n - mg\cos\theta = ma_y = 0$$

$$f_k = \mu_k n$$

We've written these equations by "reading" the motion diagram and the free-body diagram. Notice that both components of the gravitational force vector $\vec{F}_G$ are negative. $a_y = 0$ because the motion is entirely along the x-axis.

The second equation gives $n = mg\cos\theta$. Using this in the friction model, we find $f_k = \mu_k mg\cos\theta$. Inserting this result back into the first equation then gives

$$ma_x = -mg\sin\theta - \mu_k mg\cos\theta$$
$$= -mg(\sin\theta + \mu_k\cos\theta)$$
$$a_x = -g(\sin\theta + \mu_k\cos\theta)$$

This is a constant acceleration. Constant-acceleration kinematics gives

$$v_{1x}^2 = 0 = v_{0x}^2 + 2a_x(x_1 - x_0) = v_{0x}^2 + 2a_x x_1$$

which we can solve for the stopping distance x_1:

$$x_1 = -\frac{v_{0x}^2}{2a_x} = \frac{v_{0x}^2}{2g(\sin\theta + \mu_k\cos\theta)}$$

Notice how the minus sign in the expression for a_x canceled the minus sign in the expression for x_1. Evaluating our result at the three different angles gives the stopping distances:

$$x_1 = \begin{cases} 48 \text{ m} & \theta = 10° & \text{uphill} \\ 57 \text{ m} & \theta = 0° & \text{level} \\ 75 \text{ m} & \theta = -10° & \text{downhill} \end{cases}$$

The implications are clear about the danger of driving downhill too fast!

ASSESS 30 m/s ≈ 60 mph and 57 m ≈ 180 feet on a level surface. This is similar to the stopping distances you learned when you got your driver's license, so the results seem reasonable. Additional confirmation comes from noting that the expression for a_x becomes $-g\sin\theta$ if $\mu_k = 0$. This is what you learned in Chapter 2 for the acceleration on a frictionless inclined plane.

This is a good example for pointing out the advantages of working problems *algebraically*. If you had started plugging in numbers early, you would not have found that the mass eventually cancels out and you would have done several needless calculations. In addition, it is now easy to calculate the stopping distance for different angles. Had you been computing numbers, rather than algebraic expressions, you would have had to go all the way back to the beginning for each angle.

EXAMPLE 6.10 **A dog sled race**

It's dog sled race day in Alaska! A wooden sled, with rider and supplies, has a mass of 200 kg. When the starting gun sounds, it takes the dogs 15 m to reach their "cruising speed" of 5.0 m/s across the snow. Two ropes are attached to the sled, one on each side of the dogs. The ropes pull upward at 10°. What are the tensions in the ropes at the start of the race?

MODEL We'll represent the sled as a particle and we'll use the model of kinetic friction. We interpret the question as asking for the *magnitude T* of the tension forces. We'll assume that the tensions in the two ropes are equal and that the acceleration is constant during the first 15 m.

VISUALIZE FIGURE 6.27 shows the pictorial representation. Notice that the tension forces $\vec{T}_1$ and $\vec{T}_2$ are tilted up, but the net force is directly to the right in order to match the acceleration $\vec{a}$ of the motion diagram.

SOLVE We have enough information to calculate the acceleration. We can then use $\vec{a}$ to find the tension. From kinematics,

$$v_{1x}^2 = v_{0x}^2 + 2a_x(x_1 - x_0) = 2a_x x_1$$

$$a_x = \frac{v_{1x}^2}{2x_1} = \frac{(5.0 \text{ m/s})^2}{2(15 \text{ m})} = 0.833 \text{ m/s}^2$$

Newton's second law can be written by "reading" the free-body diagram:

$$\sum F_x = n_x + T_{1x} + T_{2x} + (F_G)_x + (f_k)_x$$
$$= 2T\cos\theta - f_k = ma_x$$

$$\sum F_y = n_y + T_{1y} + T_{2y} + (F_G)_y + (f_k)_y$$
$$= n + 2T\sin\theta - mg = ma_y = 0$$

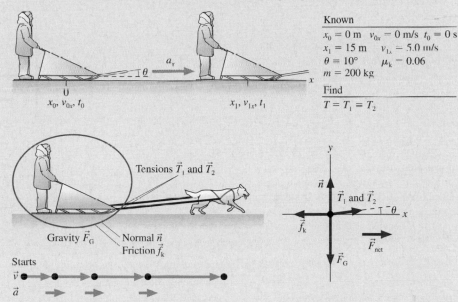

FIGURE 6.27 Pictorial representation of an accelerating dog sled.

Make sure you understand where all the terms come from, including their signs. We've used $F_G = mg$ and our knowledge that $\vec{a}$ has only an x-component. The tensions $\vec{T}_1$ and $\vec{T}_2$ have both x- and y-components. The assumption of equal tensions allows us to write $T_1 = T_2 = T$, and this introduces the factors of 2.

In addition, we have the model of kinetic friction

$$f_k = \mu_k n$$

From the y-equation and the friction equation,

$$n = mg - 2T\sin\theta$$

$$f_k = \mu_k n = \mu_k mg - 2\mu_k T\sin\theta$$

Notice that n is *not* equal to mg. The y-components of the tension forces support part of the weight, so the ground does not press against the bottom of the sled as hard as it would otherwise.

Substituting the friction back into the x-equation gives

$$2T\cos\theta - (\mu_k mg - 2\mu_k T\sin\theta)$$
$$= 2T(\cos\theta + \mu_k\sin\theta) - \mu_k mg = ma_x$$
$$T = \frac{1}{2}\frac{m(a_x + \mu_k g)}{\cos\theta + \mu_k\sin\theta}$$

Using $a_x = 0.833$ m/s^2 from above with $m = 200$ kg and $\theta = 10°$, we find that the tension is

$$T = 140 \text{ N}$$

ASSESS It's a bit hard to assess this result. We do know that the weight of the sled is $mg \approx 2000$ N. We also know that the dogs can drag a sled over snow (small μ_k) but probably can't lift the sled straight up, so we anticipate that $T \ll 2000$ N. Our calculation agrees.

EXAMPLE 6.11 **Make sure the cargo doesn't slide**

A 100 kg box of dimensions 50 cm × 50 cm × 50 cm is in the back of a flatbed truck. The coefficients of friction between the box and the bed of the truck are $\mu_s = 0.40$ and $\mu_k = 0.20$. What is the maximum acceleration the truck can have without the box slipping?

MODEL This is a somewhat different problem from any we have looked at thus far. Let the box, which we'll model as a particle, be the object of interest. It contacts other objects only where it touches the truck bed, so only the truck can exert contact forces on

the box. If the box does *not* slip, then there is no motion of the box *relative to the truck* and the box must accelerate *with the truck*: $a_{box} = a_{truck}$. As the box accelerates, it must, according to Newton's second law, have a net force acting on it. But from what?

Imagine, for a moment, that the truck bed is frictionless. The box would slide backward (as seen in the truck's reference frame) as the truck accelerates. The force that prevents sliding is *static friction*, so the truck must exert a static friction force on the box to "pull" the box along with it and prevent the box from sliding *relative to the truck.*

Continued

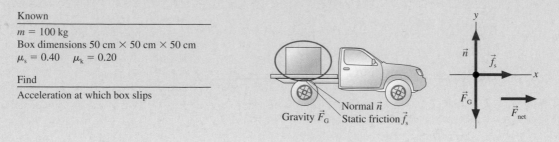

FIGURE 6.28 Pictorial representation for the box in a flatbed truck.

Known

$m = 100$ kg
Box dimensions 50 cm × 50 cm × 50 cm
$\mu_s = 0.40$ $\mu_k = 0.20$

Find

Acceleration at which box slips

Gravity $\vec{F}_G$ Normal $\vec{n}$
Static friction $\vec{f}_s$

VISUALIZE This situation is shown in **FIGURE 6.28**. There is only one horizontal force on the box, $\vec{f}_s$, and it points in the *forward* direction to accelerate the box. Notice that we're solving the problem with the ground as our reference frame. Newton's laws are not valid in the accelerating truck because it is not an inertial reference frame.

SOLVE Newton's second law, which we can "read" from the free-body diagram, is

$$\sum F_x = f_s = ma_x$$
$$\sum F_y = n - F_G = n - mg = ma_y = 0$$

Now, static friction, you will recall, can be *any* value between 0 and $f_{s\,max}$. If the truck accelerates slowly, so that the box doesn't slip, then $f_s < f_{s\,max}$. However, we're interested in the acceleration a_{max} at which the box begins to slip. This is the acceleration at which f_s reaches its maximum possible value

$$f_s = f_{s\,max} = \mu_s n$$

The y-equation of the second law and the friction model combine to give $f_{s\,max} = \mu_s mg$. Substituting this into the x-equation, and noting that a_x is now a_{max}, we find

$$a_{max} = \frac{f_{s\,max}}{m} = \mu_s g = 3.9 \text{ m/s}^2$$

The truck must keep its acceleration less than 3.9 m/s² if slipping is to be avoided.

ASSESS 3.9 m/s² is about one-third of g. You may have noticed that items in a car or truck are likely to *tip over* when you start or stop, but they slide only if you really floor it and accelerate very quickly. So this answer seems reasonable. Notice that the dimensions of the crate were not needed. Real-world situations rarely have exactly the information you need, no more and no less. Many problems in this textbook will require you to assess the information in the problem statement in order to learn which is relevant to the solution.

The mathematical representation of this last example was quite straightforward. The challenge was in the analysis that preceded the mathematics—that is, in the *physics* of the problem rather than the mathematics. It is here that our analysis tools— motion diagrams, force identification, and free-body diagrams—prove their value.

SUMMARY

The goal of Chapter 6 has been to learn how to solve problems about motion in a straight line.

General Strategy

All examples in this chapter follow a four-part strategy. You'll become a better problem solver if you adhere to it as you do the homework problems. The *Dynamics Worksheets* in the *Student Workbook* will help you structure your work in this way.

Equilibrium Problems

Object at rest or moving with constant velocity.

MODEL   Make simplifying assumptions.

VISUALIZE

- Translate words into symbols.
- Identify forces.
- Draw a free-body diagram.

SOLVE   Use Newton's first law:

$$\vec{F}_{net} = \sum_i \vec{F}_i = \vec{0}$$

"Read" the vectors from the free-body diagram.

ASSESS   Is the result reasonable?

Go back and forth between these steps as needed.

Dynamics Problems

Object accelerating.

MODEL   Make simplifying assumptions.

VISUALIZE

- Translate words into symbols.
- Draw a sketch to define the situation.
- Draw a motion diagram.
- Identify forces.
- Draw a free-body diagram.

SOLVE   Use Newton's second law:

$$\vec{F}_{net} = \sum_i \vec{F}_i = m\vec{a}$$

"Read" the vectors from the free-body diagram. Use kinematics to find velocities and positions.

ASSESS   Is the result reasonable?

Important Concepts

Specific information about three important forces:

Gravity $\vec{F}_G = (mg, \text{downward})$

Friction $f_s = (0 \text{ to } \mu_s n, \text{ direction as necessary to prevent motion})$

$\vec{f}_k = (\mu_k n, \text{ direction opposite the motion})$

$\vec{f}_r = (\mu_r n, \text{ direction opposite the motion})$

Drag $\vec{D} \approx (\frac{1}{4}Av^2, \text{ direction opposite the motion})$

Newton's laws are vector expressions. You must write them out by **components**:

$$(F_{net})_x = \sum F_x = ma_x \text{ or } 0$$

$$(F_{net})_y = \sum F_y = ma_y \text{ or } 0$$

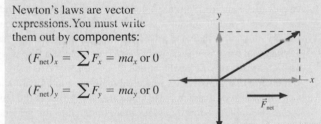

Applications

The **weight** of an object is the reading of a calibrated spring scale on which the object is stationary. Weight is the result of weighing. The weight of an object with vertical acceleration a_y is

$$w = mg\left(1 + \frac{a_y}{g}\right)$$

A falling object reaches **terminal speed**

$$v_{term} \approx \sqrt{\frac{4mg}{A}}$$

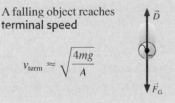

Terminal speed is reached when the drag force exactly balances the gravitational force: $\vec{a} = 0$.

Terms and Notation

flat-earth approximation
weight
coefficient of static friction, μ_s

coefficient of kinetic friction, μ_k
rolling friction

coefficient of rolling friction, μ_r
terminal speed, v_{term}

MP   For homework assigned on MasteringPhysics, go to www.masteringphysics.com

Problem difficulty is labeled as | (straightforward) to ||| (challenging).

Problems labeled ✏ can be done on a Dynamics Worksheet.
Problems labeled ▨ integrate significant material from earlier chapters.

CONCEPTUAL QUESTIONS

1. Are the objects described here in static equilibrium, dynamic equilibrium, or not in equilibrium at all? Explain.
   a. A 200 pound barbell is held over your head.
   b. A girder is lifted at constant speed by a crane.
   c. A girder is being lowered into place. It is slowing down.
   d. A jet plane has reached its cruising speed and altitude.
   e. A box in the back of a truck doesn't slide as the truck stops.

2. A ball tossed straight up has $v = 0$ at its highest point. Is it in equilibrium? Explain.

3. Kat, Matt, and Nat are arguing about why a physics book on a table doesn't fall. According to Kat, "Gravity pulls down on it, but the table is in the way so it can't fall." "Nonsense," says Matt. "There are all kinds of forces acting on the book, but the upward forces overcome the downward forces to prevent it from falling." "But what about Newton's first law?" counters Nat. "It's not moving, so there can't be any forces acting on it." None of the statements is exactly correct. Who comes closest, and how would you change his or her statement to make it correct?

4. "Forces cause an object to move." Do you agree or disagree with this statement? Explain.

5. If you know all of the forces acting on a moving object, can you tell the direction the object is moving? If yes, explain how. If no, give an example.

6. An elevator, hanging from a single cable, moves upward at constant speed. Friction and air resistance are negligible. Is the tension in the cable greater than, less than, or equal to the gravitational force on the elevator? Explain. Include a free-body diagram as part of your explanation.

7. An elevator, hanging from a single cable, moves downward and is slowing. Friction and air resistance are negligible. Is the tension in the cable greater than, less than, or equal to the gravitational force on the elevator? Explain. Include a free-body diagram as part of your explanation.

8. The three arrows in **FIGURE Q6.8** have left the bow and are traveling parallel to the ground. Air resistance is negligible. Rank in order, from largest to smallest, the magnitudes F_a, F_b, and F_c of the *horizontal* forces acting on the arrows. Some may be equal. Give your answer in the form a > b = c and explain your ranking.

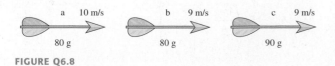

FIGURE Q6.8

9. Are the following statements true or false? Explain.
   a. The mass of an object depends on its location.
   b. The weight of an object depends on its location.
   c. Mass and weight describe the same thing in different units.

10. An astronaut takes his bathroom scale to the moon and then stands on it. Is the reading of the scale his weight? Explain.

11. The four balls in **FIGURE Q6.11** have been thrown straight up. They have the same size, but different masses. Air resistance is negligible. Rank in order, from largest to smallest, the magnitude of the net force acting on each ball. Some may be equal. Give your answer in the form a > b = c > d and explain your ranking.

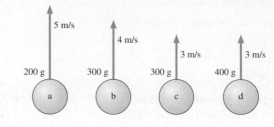

FIGURE Q6.11

12. The terms "vertical" and "horizontal" are frequently used in physics. Give *operational definitions* for these two terms. An operational definition defines a term by how it is measured or determined. Your definition should apply equally well in a laboratory or on a steep mountainside.

13. Suppose you attempt to pour out 100 g of salt, using a pan balance for measurements, while in a rocket accelerating upward. Will the quantity of salt be too much, too little, or the correct amount? Explain.

14. A box with a passenger inside is launched straight up into the air by a giant rubber band. Before launch, the passenger stood on a scale and weighed 750 N. Once the box has left the rubber band but is still moving upward, is the passenger's weight more than 750 N, 750 N, less than 750 N but not zero, or zero? Explain.

15. An astronaut orbiting the earth is handed two balls that have identical outward appearances. However, one is hollow while the other is filled with lead. How can the astronaut determine which is which? Cutting or altering the balls is not allowed.

16. A hand presses down on the book in **FIGURE Q6.16**. Is the normal force of the table on the book larger than, smaller than, or equal to mg?

FIGURE Q6.16   Book of mass m

17. Suppose you push a hockey puck of mass m across frictionless ice for a time Δt, starting from rest, giving the puck speed v after traveling distance d. If you repeat the experiment with a puck of mass $2m$,
    a. How long will you have to push for the puck to reach the same speed v?
    b. How long will you have to push for the puck to travel the same distance d?

18. A block pushed along the floor with velocity v_{0x} slides a distance d after the pushing force is removed.
    a. If the mass of the block is doubled but its initial velocity is not changed, what distance does the block slide before stopping?
    b. If the initial velocity is doubled to $2v_{0x}$ but the mass is not changed, what distance does the block slide before stopping?

19. Can the friction force on an object ever point in the direction of the object's motion? If yes, give an example. If no, why not?

20. A crate of fragile dishes is in the back of a pickup truck. The truck accelerates north from a stop sign, and the crate moves without slipping. Does the friction force on the crate point north or south? Or is the friction force zero? Explain.

21. The three boxes in **FIGURE Q6.21** move through the air as shown. Rank in order, from largest to smallest, the magnitudes of the three drag forces D_a, D_b, and D_c acting on the boxes. Some may be equal. Give your answer in the form a > b = c and explain your ranking.

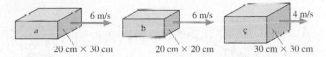

FIGURE Q6.21

22. Five balls move through the air as shown in **FIGURE Q6.22**. All five have the same size and shape. Air resistance is not negligible. Rank in order, from largest to smallest, the magnitudes of the accelerations a_a to a_e. Some may be equal. Give your answer in the form a > b = c > d > e and explain your ranking.

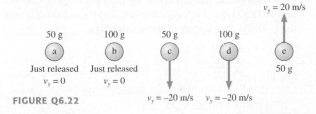

FIGURE Q6.22

EXERCISES AND PROBLEMS

Exercises

Section 6.1 Equilibrium

1. | The three ropes in **FIGURE EX6.1** are tied to a small, very light ring. Two of the ropes are anchored to walls at right angles, and the third rope pulls as shown. What are T_1 and T_2, the magnitudes of the tension forces in the first two ropes?

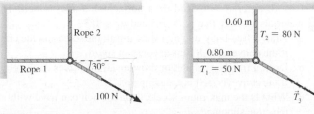

FIGURE EX6.1   **FIGURE EX6.2**

2. | The three ropes in **FIGURE EX6.2** are tied to a small, very light ring. Two of these ropes are anchored to walls at right angles with the tensions shown in the figure. What are the magnitude and direction of the tension $\vec{T}_3$ in the third rope?

3. || A 20 kg loudspeaker is suspended 2.0 m below the ceiling by two 3.0-m-long cables that angle outward at equal angles. What is the tension in the cables?

4. || A football coach sits on a sled while two of his players build their strength by dragging the sled across the field with ropes. The friction force on the sled is 1000 N and the angle between the two ropes is 20°. How hard must each player pull to drag the coach at a steady 2.0 m/s?

Section 6.2 Using Newton's Second Law

5. | In each of the two free-body diagrams, the forces are acting on a 2.0 kg object. For each diagram, find the values of a_x and a_y, the x- and y-components of the acceleration.

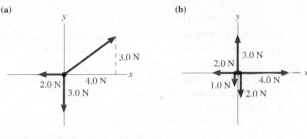

FIGURE EX6.5

6. ‖ In each of the two free-body diagrams, the forces are acting on a 2.0 kg object. For each diagram, find the values of a_x and a_y, the x- and y-components of the acceleration.

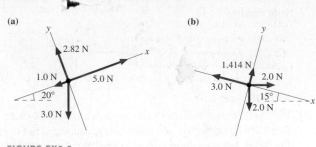

FIGURE EX6.6

7. ‖ In each of the two free-body diagrams, the forces are acting on a 5.0 kg object. For each diagram, find the values of a_x and a_y, the x- and y-components of the acceleration.

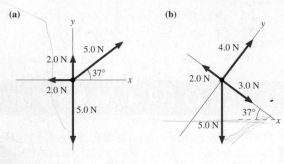

FIGURE EX6.7

8. ‖ FIGURE EX6.8 shows the velocity graph of a 2.0 kg object as it moves along the x-axis. What is the net force acting on this object at $t = 1$ s? At 4 s? At 7 s?

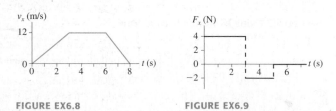

FIGURE EX6.8   **FIGURE EX6.9**

9. ‖ FIGURE EX6.9 shows the force acting on a 2.0 kg object as it moves along the x-axis. The object is at rest at the origin at $t = 0$ s. What are its acceleration and velocity at $t = 6$ s?

10. | A horizontal rope is tied to a 50 kg box on frictionless ice. What is the tension in the rope if:
    a. The box is at rest?
    b. The box moves at a steady 5.0 m/s?
    c. The box has $v_x = 5.0$ m/s and $a_x = 5.0$ m/s²?

11. | A 50 kg box hangs from a rope. What is the tension in the rope if:
    a. The box is at rest?
    b. The box moves up at a steady 5.0 m/s?
    c. The box has $v_y = 5.0$ m/s and is speeding up at 5.0 m/s²?
    d. The box has $v_y = 5.0$ m/s and is slowing down at 5.0 m/s²?

12. | What thrust does a 200 g model rocket need in order to have a vertical acceleration of 10 m/s²
    a. On Earth?
    b. On the moon, where $g = 1.62$ m/s²?

Section 6.3 Mass, Weight, and Gravity

13. | An astronaut's weight while standing on earth is 800 N. What is his weight on Mars, where $g = 3.76$ m/s²?

14. | A woman has a mass of 55 kg.
    a. What is her weight while standing on earth?
    b. What are her mass and her weight on the moon, where $g = 1.62$ m/s²?

15. | It takes the elevator in a skyscraper 4.0 s to reach its cruising speed of 10 m/s. A 60 kg passenger gets aboard on the ground floor. What is the passenger's weight
    a. Before the elevator starts moving?
    b. While the elevator is speeding up?
    c. After the elevator reaches its cruising speed?

16. | FIGURE EX6.16 shows the velocity graph of a 75 kg passenger in an elevator. What is the passenger's weight at $t = 1$ s? At 5 s? At 9 s?

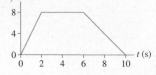

FIGURE EX6.16

Section 6.4 Friction

17. | Bonnie and Clyde are sliding a 300 kg bank safe across the floor to their getaway car. The safe slides with a constant speed if Clyde pushes from behind with 385 N of force while Bonnie pulls forward on a rope with 350 N of force. What is the safe's coefficient of kinetic friction on the bank floor?

18. | A stubborn, 120 kg mule sits down and refuses to move. To drag the mule to the barn, the exasperated farmer ties a rope around the mule and pulls with his maximum force of 800 N. The coefficients of friction between the mule and the ground are $\mu_s = 0.8$ and $\mu_k = 0.5$. Is the farmer able to move the mule?

19. | A 10 kg crate is placed on a horizontal conveyor belt. The materials are such that $\mu_s = 0.5$ and $\mu_k = 0.3$.
    a. Draw a free-body diagram showing all the forces on the crate if the conveyer belt runs at constant speed.
    b. Draw a free-body diagram showing all the forces on the crate if the conveyer belt is speeding up.
    c. What is the maximum acceleration the belt can have without the crate slipping?

20. ‖ A 4000 kg truck is parked on a 15° slope. How big is the friction force on the truck?

21. ‖ A 1500 kg car skids to a halt on a wet road where $\mu_k = 0.50$. How fast was the car traveling if it leaves 65-m-long skid marks?

22. ‖ An Airbus A320 jetliner has a takeoff mass of 75,000 kg. It reaches its takeoff speed of 82 m/s (180 mph) in 35 s. What is the thrust of the engines? You can neglect air resistance but not rolling friction.

23. ‖ A 50,000 kg locomotive is traveling at 10 m/s when its engine and brakes both fail. How far will the locomotive roll before it comes to a stop?

24. ‖ Estimate the size of the friction force on a baseball player sliding into second base.

Section 6.5 Drag

25. || A 75 kg skydiver can be modeled as a rectangular "box" with dimensions $20 \text{ cm} \times 40 \text{ cm} \times 180 \text{ cm}$. What is his terminal speed if he falls feet first?

26. || A 6.5-cm-diameter tennis ball has a terminal speed of 26 m/s. What is the ball's mass?

Problems

27. || A 5.0 kg object initially at rest at the origin is subjected to the time-varying force shown in FIGURE P6.27. What is the object's velocity at $t = 6$ s?

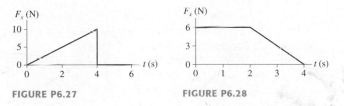

FIGURE P6.27   FIGURE P6.28

28. || A 2.0 kg object initially at rest at the origin is subjected to the time-varying force shown in FIGURE P6.28. What is the object's velocity at $t = 4$ s?

29. || A 1000 kg steel beam is supported by two ropes. What is the tension in each?

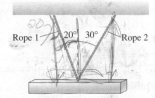

Rope 1 20° 30° Rope 2

FIGURE P6.29

30. || In an electricity experiment, a 1.0 g plastic ball is suspended on a 60-cm-long string and given an electric charge. A charged rod brought near the ball exerts a horizontal electrical force $\vec{F}_{\text{elec}}$ on it, causing the ball to swing out to a 20° angle and remain there.
    a. What is the magnitude of $\vec{F}_{\text{elec}}$?
    b. What is the tension in the string?

31. || A 500 kg piano is being lowered into position by a crane while two people steady it with ropes pulling to the sides. Bob's rope pulls to the left, 15° below horizontal, with 500 N of tension. Ellen's rope pulls toward the right, 25° below horizontal.
    a. What tension must Ellen maintain in her rope to keep the piano descending at a steady speed?
    b. What is the tension in the main cable supporting the piano?

32. Henry gets into an elevator on the 50th floor of a building and it begins moving at $t = 0$ s. The figure shows his weight over the next 12 s.

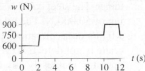

FIGURE P6.32

    a. Is the elevator's initial direction up or down? Explain how you can tell.
    b. What is Henry's mass?
    c. How far has Henry traveled at $t = 12$ s?

33. || Zach, whose mass is 80 kg, is in an elevator descending at 10 m/s. The elevator takes 3.0 s to brake to a stop at the first floor.
    a. What is Zach's weight before the elevator starts braking?
    b. What is Zach's weight while the elevator is braking?

34. || You've always wondered about the acceleration of the elevators in the 101-story-tall Empire State Building. One day, while visiting New York, you take your bathroom scale into the elevator and stand on it. The scale reads 150 lb as the door closes. The reading varies between 120 lb and 170 lb as the elevator travels 101 floors. What conclusions can you draw?

35. || An accident victim with a broken leg is being placed in traction. The patient wears a special boot with a pulley attached to the sole. The foot and boot together have a mass of 4.0 kg, and the doctor has decided to hang a 6.0 kg mass from the rope. The boot is held suspended by the ropes and does not touch the bed.

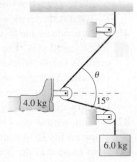

FIGURE P6.35

    a. Determine the amount of tension in the rope by using Newton's laws to analyze the hanging mass.
    b. The net traction force needs to pull straight out on the leg. What is the proper angle θ for the upper rope?
    c. What is the net traction force pulling on the leg?
    Hint: If the pulleys are frictionless, which we will assume, the tension in the rope is constant from one end to the other.

36. || Seat belts and air bags save lives by reducing the forces exerted on the driver and passengers in an automobile collision. Cars are designed with a "crumple zone" in the front of the car. In the event of an impact, the passenger compartment decelerates over a distance of about 1 m as the front of the car crumples. An occupant restrained by seat belts and air bags decelerates with the car. By contrast, an unrestrained occupant keeps moving forward with no loss of speed (Newton's first law!) until hitting the dashboard or windshield. These are unyielding surfaces, and the unfortunate occupant then decelerates over a distance of only about 5 mm.
    a. A 60 kg person is in a head-on collision. The car's speed at impact is 15 m/s. Estimate the net force on the person if he or she is wearing a seat belt and if the air bag deploys.
    b. Estimate the net force that ultimately stops the person if he or she is not restrained by a seat belt or air bag.
    c. How do these two forces compare to the person's weight?

37. || Compressed air is used to fire a 50 g ball vertically upward from a 1.0-m-tall tube. The air exerts an upward force of 2.0 N on the ball as long as it is in the tube. How high does the ball go above the top of the tube?

38. || A rifle with a barrel length of 60 cm fires a 10 g bullet with a horizontal speed of 400 m/s. The bullet strikes a block of wood and penetrates to a depth of 12 cm.
    a. What resistive force (assumed to be constant) does the wood exert on the bullet?
    b. How long does it take the bullet to come to rest?
    c. Draw a velocity-versus-time graph for the bullet in the wood.

39. || A 20,000 kg rocket has a rocket motor that generates 3.0×10^5 N of thrust.
    a. What is the rocket's initial upward acceleration?
    b. At an altitude of 5000 m the rocket's acceleration has increased to 6.0 m/s². What mass of fuel has it burned?

40. ‖ A 2.0 kg steel block is at rest on a steel table. A horizontal string pulls on the block.
    a. What is the minimum string tension needed to move the block?
    b. If the string tension is 20 N, what is the block's speed after moving 1.0 m?
    c. If the string tension is 20 N and the table is coated with oil, what is the block's speed after moving 1.0 m?

41. ‖ Sam, whose mass is 75 kg, takes off across level snow on his jet-powered skis. The skis have a thrust of 200 N and a coefficient of kinetic friction on snow of 0.10. Unfortunately, the skis run out of fuel after only 10 s.
    a. What is Sam's top speed?
    b. How far has Sam traveled when he finally coasts to a stop?

42. ‖‖ Sam, whose mass is 75 kg, takes off down a 50-m-high, 10° slope on his jet-powered skis. The skis have a thrust of 200 N. Sam's speed at the bottom is 40 m/s. What is the coefficient of kinetic friction of his skis on snow?

43. ‖ A baggage handler drops your 10 kg suitcase onto a conveyor belt running at 2.0 m/s. The materials are such that $\mu_s = 0.50$ and $\mu_k = 0.30$. How far is your suitcase dragged before it is riding smoothly on the belt?

44. ‖ You and your friend Peter are putting new shingles on a roof pitched at 25°. You're sitting on the very top of the roof when Peter, who is at the edge of the roof directly below you, 5.0 m away, asks you for the box of nails. Rather than carry the 2.5 kg box of nails down to Peter, you decide to give the box a push and have it slide down to him. If the coefficient of kinetic friction between the box and the roof is 0.55, with what speed should you push the box to have it gently come to rest right at the edge of the roof?

45. ‖ It's moving day, and you need to push a 100 kg box up a 20° ramp into the truck. The coefficients of friction for the box on the ramp are $\mu_s = 0.90$ and $\mu_k = 0.60$. Your largest pushing force is 1000 N. Can you get the box into the truck without assistance if you get a running start at the ramp? If you stop on the ramp, will you be able to get the box moving again?

46. ‖ A 2.0 kg wood block is launched up a wooden ramp that is inclined at a 30° angle. The block's initial speed is 10 m/s.
    a. What vertical height does the block reach above its starting point?
    b. What speed does it have when it slides back down to its starting point?

47. ‖‖ It's a snowy day and you're pulling a friend along a level road on a sled. You've both been taking physics, so she asks what you think the coefficient of friction between the sled and the snow is. You've been walking at a steady 1.5 m/s, and the rope pulls up on the sled at a 30° angle. You estimate that the mass of the sled, with your friend on it, is 60 kg and that you're pulling with a force of 75 N. What answer will you give?

48. ‖ A horizontal rope pulls a 10 kg wood sled across frictionless snow. A 5.0 kg wood box rides on the sled. What is the largest tension force for which the box doesn't slip?

49. ‖ A pickup truck with a steel bed is carrying a steel file cabinet. If the truck's speed is 15 m/s, what is shortest distance in which it can stop without the file cabinet sliding?

50. ‖ You're driving along at 25 m/s with your aunt's valuable antiques in the back of your pickup truck when suddenly you see a giant hole in the road 55 m ahead of you. Fortunately, your foot is right beside the brake and your reaction time is zero! Will the antiques be as fortunate?
    a. Can you stop the truck before it falls into the hole?
    b. If your answer to part a is yes, can you stop without the antiques sliding and being damaged? Their coefficients of friction are $\mu_s = 0.60$ and $\mu_k = 0.30$.
    Hint: You're not trying to stop in the shortest possible distance. What's your best strategy for avoiding damage to the antiques?

51. ‖ The 2.0 kg wood box in **FIGURE P6.51** slides down a vertical wood wall while you push on it at a 45° angle. What magnitude of force should you apply to cause the box to slide down at a constant speed?

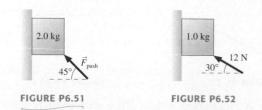

FIGURE P6.51   **FIGURE P6.52**

52. ‖ A 1.0 kg wood block is pressed against a vertical wood wall by the 12 N force shown in **FIGURE P6.52**. If the block is initially at rest, will it move upward, move downward, or stay at rest?

53. ‖ What is the terminal speed for an 80 kg skier going down a 40° snow-covered slope on wooden skis? Assume that the skier is 1.8 m tall and 0.40 m wide.

54. ‖‖ A ball is shot from a compressed-air gun at twice its terminal speed.
    a. What is the ball's initial acceleration, as a multiple of g, if it is shot straight up?
    b. What is the ball's initial acceleration, as a multiple of g, if it is shot straight down?
    c. Draw a plausible velocity-versus-time graph for the ball that is shot straight down.

55. ‖ An artist friend of yours needs help hanging a 500 lb sculpture from the ceiling. For artistic reasons, she wants to use just two ropes. One will be 30° from vertical, the other 60°. She needs you to determine the smallest diameter rope that can safely support this expensive piece of art. On a visit to the hardware store you find that rope is sold in increments of $\frac{1}{8}$-inch diameter and that the safety rating is 4000 pounds per square inch of cross section. What diameter rope should you buy?

56. ‖ You've been called in to investigate a construction accident in which the cable broke while a crane was lifting a 4500 kg container. The steel cable is 2.0 cm in diameter and has a safety rating of 50,000 N. The crane is designed not to exceed speeds of 3.0 m/s or accelerations of 1.0 m/s², and your tests find that the crane is not defective. What is your conclusion? Did the crane operator recklessly lift too heavy a load? Or was the cable defective?

57. ‖ You've entered a "slow ski race" where the winner is the skier who takes the *longest* time to go down a 15° slope without ever stopping. You need to choose the best wax to apply to your skis. Red wax has a coefficient of kinetic friction 0.25, yellow is 0.20, green is 0.15, and blue is 0.10. Having just finished taking physics, you realize that a wax too slippery will cause you to accelerate down the slope and lose the race. But a wax that's too

sticky will cause you to stop and be disqualified. You know that a strong headwind will apply a 50 N horizontal force against you as you ski, and you know that your mass is 82 kg. Which wax do you choose?

58. ‖ A 1.0 kg ball hangs from the ceiling of a truck by a 1.0-m-long string. The back of the truck, where you are riding with the ball, has no windows and has been completely soundproofed. The truck travels along an exceedingly smooth test track, and you feel no bumps or bounces as it moves. Your only instruments are a meter stick, a protractor, and a stopwatch.

   a. The driver tells you, over a loudspeaker, that the truck is either at rest, or it is moving forward at a steady speed of 5 m/s. Can you determine which it is? If so, how? If not, why not?

   b. Next, the driver tells you that the truck is either moving forward with a steady speed of 5 m/s, or it is accelerating at 5 m/s². Can you determine which it is? If so, how? If not, why not?

   c. Suppose the truck has been accelerating forward at 5 m/s² long enough for the ball to achieve a steady position. Does the ball have an acceleration? If so, what are the magnitude and direction of the ball's acceleration?

   d. Draw a free-body diagram that shows all forces acting on the ball as the truck accelerates.

   e. Suppose the ball makes a 10° angle with the vertical. If possible, determine the truck's velocity. If possible, determine the truck's acceleration.

59. ‖ Imagine *hanging* from a big spring scale as it moves vertically with acceleration a_y. Show that Equation 6.10 is the correct expression for your weight.

60. ‖ A particle of mass m moving along the x-axis experiences the net force $F_x = ct$, where c is a constant. The particle has velocity v_{0x} at $t = 0$. Find an algebraic expression for the particle's velocity v_x at a later time t.

61. ‖ Astronauts in space "weigh" themselves by oscillating on a spring. Suppose the position of an oscillating 75 kg astronaut is given by $x = (0.30 \text{ m}) \sin((\pi \text{ rad/s}) \cdot t)$, where t is in s. What force does the spring exert on the astronaut at (a) $t = 1.0$ s and (b) 1.5 s. Note that the angle of the sine function is in radians.

62. ‖‖ An object moving in a liquid experiences a *linear* drag force: $\vec{D} = (bv, \text{ direction opposite the motion})$, where b is a constant called the *drag coefficient*. For a sphere of radius R, the drag constant can be computed as $b = 6\pi\eta R$, where η is the *viscosity* of the liquid.

   a. Find an algebraic expression for the terminal speed v_{term} of a spherical particle of radius R and mass m falling through a liquid of viscosity η.

   b. Water at 20°C has viscosity $\eta = 1.0 \times 10^{-3}$ Ns/m². Sand grains have density 2400 kg/m³. Suppose a 1.0-mm-diameter sand grain is dropped into a 50-m-deep lake whose water is a constant 20°C. If the sand grain reaches terminal speed almost instantly (a quite good approximation), how long will it take the sand grain to settle to the bottom of the lake?

Problems 63 through 65 show a free-body diagram. For each:

   a. Write a realistic dynamics problem for which this is the correct free-body diagram. Your problem should ask a question that can be answered with a value of position or velocity (such as "How

far?" or "How fast?"), and should give sufficient information to allow a solution.

   b. Solve your problem!

63.
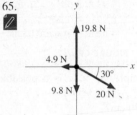
FIGURE P6.63

64.
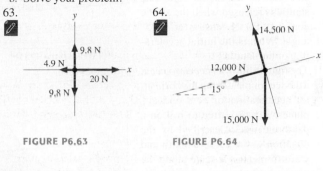
FIGURE P6.64

65.

FIGURE P6.65

In Problems 66 through 68 you are given the dynamics equations that are used to solve a problem. For each of these, you are to

   a. Write a realistic problem for which these are the correct equations.

   b. Draw the free-body diagram and the pictorial representation for your problem.

   c. Finish the solution of the problem.

66. $-0.80n = (1500 \text{ kg})a_x$
    $n - (1500 \text{ kg})(9.80 \text{ m/s}^2) = 0$

67. $T - 0.20n - (20 \text{ kg})(9.80 \text{ m/s}^2) \sin 20°$
    $\quad = (20 \text{ kg})(2.0 \text{ m/s}^2)$
    $n - (20 \text{ kg})(9.80 \text{ m/s}^2) \cos 20° = 0$

68. $(100 \text{ N}) \cos 30° - f_k = (20 \text{ kg})a_x$
    $n + (100 \text{ N}) \sin 30° - (20 \text{ kg})(9.80 \text{ m/s}^2) = 0$
    $f_k = 0.20n$

Challenge Problems

69. Try this! Hold your right hand out with your palm perpendicular to the ground, as if you were getting ready to shake hands. You can't hold anything in your palm this way because it would fall straight down. Use your left hand to hold a small object, such as a ball or a coin, against your outstretched palm, then let go as you quickly swing your hand to the left across your body, parallel to the ground. You'll find that the object stays against your palm; it doesn't slip or fall.

   a. Is the condition for keeping the object against your palm one of maintaining a certain minimum velocity v_{min}? Or one of maintaining a certain minimum acceleration a_{min}? Explain.

   b. Suppose the object's mass is 50 g, with $\mu_s = 0.80$ and $\mu_k = 0.40$. Determine either v_{min} or a_{min}, whichever you answered in part a.

70. A machine has an 800 g steel shuttle that is pulled along a square steel rail by an elastic cord. The shuttle is released when the elastic cord has 20 N tension at a 45° angle. What is the initial acceleration of the shuttle?

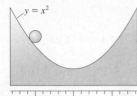

FIGURE CP6.70

71. The figure shows an *accelerometer,* a device for measuring the horizontal acceleration of cars and airplanes. A ball is free to roll on a parabolic track described by the equation $y = x^2$, where both x and y are in meters. A scale along the bottom is used to measure the ball's horizontal position x.

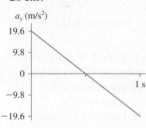

FIGURE CP6.71

   a. Find an expression that allows you to use a measured position x (in m) to compute the acceleration a_x (in m/s²). (For example, $a_x = 3x$ is a possible expression.)
   b. What is the acceleration if $x = 20$ cm?

72. A testing laboratory wants to determine if a new widget can withstand large accelerations and decelerations. To find out, they glue a 5.0 kg widget to a test stand that will drive it vertically up and down. The graph shows its acceleration during the first second, starting from rest.

FIGURE CP6.72

   a. Identify the forces acting on the widget and draw a free-body diagram.
   b. Determine the value of n_y, the y-component of the normal force acting on the widget, during the first second of motion. Give your answer as a graph of n_y versus t.
   c. Your answer to part b should show an interval of time during which n_y is negative. How can this be? Explain what it means physically for n_y to be negative.
   d. At what time is the weight of the widget a maximum? What is the acceleration at this time?
   e. Is the weight of the widget ever zero? If so, at what time does this happen? What is the acceleration at that time?
   f. Suppose the technician forgets to glue the widget to the test stand. Will the widget remain on the test stand throughout the

first second, or will it fly off the stand at some instant of time? If so, at what time will this occur?

73. An object moving in a liquid experiences a *linear* drag force: $\vec{D} = (bv$, direction opposite the motion), where b is a constant called the *drag coefficient*. For a sphere of radius R, the drag constant can be computed as $b = 6\pi\eta R$, where η is the *viscosity* of the liquid.

   a. Find an algebraic expression for $v_x(t)$, the x-component of velocity as a function of time, for a spherical particle of radius R and mass m that is shot horizontally with initial speed v_0 through a liquid of viscosity η.
   b. Water at 20°C has viscosity $\eta = 1.0 \times 10^{-3}$ Ns/m². Suppose a 4.0-cm-diameter, 33 g ball is shot horizontally into a tank of 20°C water. How long will it take for the horizontal speed to decrease to 50% of its initial value?

74. An object moving in a liquid experiences a *linear* drag force: $\vec{D} = (bv$, direction opposite the motion), where b is a constant called the *drag coefficient*. For a sphere of radius R, the drag constant can be computed as $b = 6\pi\eta R$, where η is the *viscosity* of the liquid.

   a. Use what you've learned in calculus to prove that
$$a_x = v_x \frac{dv_x}{dx}$$

   b. Find an algebraic expression for $v_x(x)$, the x-component of velocity as a function of distance traveled, for a spherical particle of radius R and mass m that is shot horizontally with initial speed v_0 through a liquid of viscosity η.
   c. Water at 20°C has viscosity $\eta = 1.0 \times 10^{-3}$ Ns/m². Suppose a 1.0-cm-diameter, 1.0 g marble is shot horizontally into a tank of 20°C water at 10 cm/s. How far will it travel before stopping?

75. An object with cross section A is shot horizontally across frictionless ice. Its initial velocity is v_{0x} at $t_0 = 0$ s. Air resistance is not negligible.

   a. Show that the velocity at time t is given by the expression
$$v_x = \frac{v_{0x}}{1 + Av_{0x}t/4m}$$

   b. A 1.6-m-wide, 1.4-m-high, 1500 kg car hits a very slick patch of ice while going 20 m/s. If friction is neglected, how long will it take until the car's speed drops to 10 m/s? To 5 m/s?
   c. Assess whether or not it is reasonable to neglect kinetic friction.

STOP TO THINK ANSWERS

Stop to Think 6.1: a. The lander is descending and slowing. The acceleration vector points upward, and so $\vec{F}_{net}$ points upward. This can be true only if the thrust has a larger magnitude than the weight.

Stop to Think 6.2: a. You are descending and slowing, so your acceleration vector points upward and there is a net upward force on you. The floor pushes up against your feet harder than gravity pulls down.

Stop to Think 6.3: $f_b > f_c = f_d = f_e > f_a$. Situations c, d, and e are all kinetic friction, which does not depend on either velocity or accel-

eration. Kinetic friction is smaller than the maximum static friction that is exerted in b. $f_a = 0$ because no friction is needed to keep the object at rest.

Stop to Think 6.4: d. The ball is shot *down* at 30 m/s, so $v_{0y} = -30$ m/s. This exceeds the terminal speed, so the upward drag force is *larger* than the downward weight force. Thus the ball *slows down* even though it is "falling." It will slow until $v_y = -15$ m/s, the terminal velocity, then maintain that velocity.

These two sumo wrestlers are *interacting* with each other.

7 Newton's Third Law

▶ **Looking Ahead**

The goal of Chapter 7 is to use Newton's third law to understand interacting objects. In this chapter you will learn to:

- Identify action/reaction pairs of forces in interacting objects.
- Understand and use Newton's third law.
- Use an expanded problem-solving strategy for dynamics problems.
- Understand the role of strings, ropes, and pulleys.

◀ **Looking Back**

This chapter further develops the concept of force. Please review:

- Sections 5.1–5.3 The basic concept of force and the atomic-level view of tension.
- Section 6.2 The basic problem-solving strategy for dynamics.

Rather than a single particle responding to a well-defined force, these sumo wrestlers are *interacting* with each other. The harder one sumo wrestler pushes, the harder the other pushes back. A hammer and a nail, your foot and a soccer ball, and the earth-moon system are other examples of interacting objects.

Newton's second law is not sufficient to explain what happens when two or more objects interact. Newton's second law, the essence of single-particle dynamics, treats an object as an isolated entity acted upon by external forces. Chapter 7 will introduce a new law of physics, Newton's *third* law, that describes how two objects interact with each other.

Newton's third law brings us to the pinnacle of Newton's theory of forces and motion. The tools you will have learned when you finish this chapter can be used to solve complex but realistic dynamics problems.

7.1 Interacting Objects

Our goal is to understand how two objects interact. Think about the hammer and nail in FIGURE 7.1 on the next page. The hammer certainly exerts a force on the nail as it drives the nail forward. At the same time, the nail exerts a force on the hammer. If you are not sure that it does, imagine hitting the nail with a glass hammer. It's the force of the nail on the hammer that causes the glass to shatter.

If you stop to think about it, any time that object A pushes or pulls on object B, object B pushes or pulls back on object A. As sumo wrestler A pushes on sumo wrestler B, B pushes back on A. (If A pushed forward without B pushing back, A would fall over in the same way you do if someone suddenly opens a door you're

FIGURE 7.1 The hammer and nail are interacting with each other.

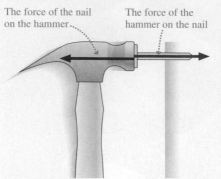

The force of the nail on the hammer...

The force of the hammer on the nail

FIGURE 7.2 An action/reaction pair of forces.

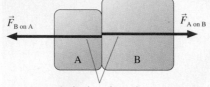

$\vec{F}_{\text{B on A}}$

$\vec{F}_{\text{A on B}}$

A

B

Action/reaction pair

leaning against.) Your chair pushes upward on you (a normal force) while, at the same time, you push down on the chair. These are examples of what we call an *interaction*. An **interaction** is the mutual influence of two objects on each other.

To be more specific, if object A exerts a force $\vec{F}_{\text{A on B}}$ on object B, then object B exerts a force $\vec{F}_{\text{B on A}}$ on object A. This pair of forces, shown in **FIGURE 7.2**, is called an **action/reaction pair.** Two objects interact by exerting an action/reaction pair of forces on each other. Notice the very explicit subscripts on the force vectors. The first letter is the *agent,* the second letter is the object on which the force acts. $\vec{F}_{\text{A on B}}$ is a force exerted *by* A *on* B. The distinction is important, and we will use this explicit notation for much of this chapter.

> **NOTE** ▶ The name "action/reaction pair" is somewhat misleading. The forces occur simultaneously, and we cannot say which is the "action" and which the "reaction." Neither is there any implication about cause and effect; the action does not *cause* the reaction. **An action/reaction pair of forces exists as a pair, or not at all.** In identifying action/reaction pairs, the labels are the key. Force $\vec{F}_{\text{A on B}}$ is paired with force $\vec{F}_{\text{B on A}}$. ◀

The sumo wrestlers and the hammer and nail interact through contact forces. The same idea holds true for long-range forces. You probably have played with kitchen magnets or bar magnets. As you hold two magnets, you can feel with your fingertips that *both* have forces pulling on them.

But what about gravity? If you release a ball, it falls because the earth's gravity exerts a downward force $\vec{F}_{\text{earth on ball}}$ on it. But does the ball also pull upward on the earth? That is, is there a force $\vec{F}_{\text{ball on earth}}$?

Newton was the first to recognize that, indeed, the ball *does* pull upward on the earth. Likewise, the moon pulls on the earth in response to the earth's gravity pulling on the moon. Newton's evidence was the tides. Scientists and astronomers had studied and timed the ocean's tides since antiquity. It was known that the tides depend on the phase of the moon, but Newton was the first to understand that the tides are the ocean's response to the gravitational pull of the moon on the earth. As **FIGURE 7.3** shows, the flexible water bulges toward the moon while the relatively inflexible crust of the earth remains stationary.

FIGURE 7.3 The ocean tides are an indication of the long-range gravitational interaction of the earth and the moon.

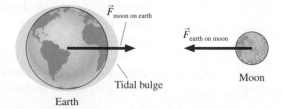

$\vec{F}_{\text{moon on earth}}$

$\vec{F}_{\text{earth on moon}}$

Moon

Tidal bulge

Earth

Objects, Systems, and the Environment

Chapters 5 and 6 considered forces acting on a single object that we modeled as a particle. **FIGURE 7.4a** shows a diagrammatic representation of single-particle dynamics. If all the forces acting on the particle are known, we can use Newton's second law, $\vec{a} = \vec{F}_{\text{net}}/m$, to determine the particle's acceleration.

We now want to extend the particle model to situations in which two or more objects, each represented as a particle, interact with each other. For example, **FIGURE 7.4b** shows three objects interacting via action/reaction pairs of forces. The forces can be given labels such as $\vec{F}_{\text{1 on 2}}$ and $\vec{F}_{\text{2 on 1}}$. How do these particles move?

FIGURE 7.4 Single-particle dynamics and a model of interacting objects.

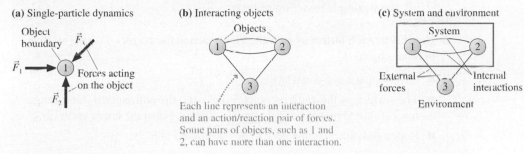

(a) Single-particle dynamics

Object boundary

$\vec{F}_3$

$\vec{F}_1$

1

Forces acting on the object

$\vec{F}_2$

(b) Interacting objects

Objects

1

2

3

Each line represents an interaction and an action/reaction pair of forces. Some pairs of objects, such as 1 and 2, can have more than one interaction.

(c) System and environment

System

1

2

External forces

3

Internal interactions

Environment

We will often be interested in the motion of some of the objects, say objects 1 and 2, but not of others. For example, objects 1 and 2 might be the hammer and the nail, while object 3 is the earth. The earth interacts with both the hammer and the nail via gravity, but in a practical sense the earth remains "at rest" while the hammer and nail move. Let's define the **system** as those objects whose motion we want to analyze and the **environment** as objects external to the system.

FIGURE 7.4c is a new kind of diagram, an **interaction diagram,** in which we've enclosed the objects of the system in a box and represented interactions as lines connecting objects. This is a rather abstract, schematic diagram, but it captures the essence of the interactions. Notice that interactions with objects in the environment are called **external forces.** For the hammer and nail, the gravitational force on each—an interaction with the earth—is an external force.

NOTE ▶ The system–environment distinction is a practical matter, not a fundamental distinction. If object A pushes or pulls on object B, then B pushes or pulls on A. *Every* force is one member of an action/reaction pair, and there is no such thing as a true "external force." What we call an external force is an interaction between an object of interest, one we've chosen to place inside the system, and an object whose motion is not of interest. ◀

Newton's second law, $\vec{a} = \vec{F}_{net}/m$, applies *separately* to objects 1 and 2 in Figure 7.4c:

$$\text{Object 1:} \qquad \vec{a}_1 = \frac{\vec{F}_{1\,net}}{m_1} = \frac{1}{m_1} \sum \vec{F}_{on\,1}$$

$$\text{Object 2:} \qquad \vec{a}_2 = \frac{\vec{F}_{2\,net}}{m_2} = \frac{1}{m_2} \sum \vec{F}_{on\,2}$$

(7.1)

The net force on object 1, denoted $\sum \vec{F}_{on\,1}$, is the sum of *all* forces acting *on* object 1. The sum includes both forces due to object 2 ($\vec{F}_{2\,on\,1}$) and any external forces originating in the environment.

NOTE ▶ Forces exerted *by* object 1, such as $\vec{F}_{1\,on\,2}$, do *not* appear in the equation for object 1. Objects change their motion in response to forces exerted *on* them, not to forces exerted *by* them. ◀

The bat and the ball are interacting with each other.

7.2 Analyzing Interacting Objects

The key steps for analyzing interacting objects are (1) the identification of the action/reaction pairs of forces and (2) the drawing of free-body diagrams. The interaction diagram will be our primary tool.

TACTICS
BOX 7.1   Analyzing interacting objects

(MP)

❶ Represent each object as a circle. Place each in the correct position relative to other objects.

- Give each a name and a label.
- The surface of the earth (contact forces) and the entire earth (long-range forces) should be considered separate objects. Label the entire earth EE.
- Ropes and pulleys often need to be considered objects.

❷ Identify interactions. Draw connecting lines between the circles to represent interactions.

- Draw *one* line for each interaction. Label it with the type of force.
- Every interaction line connects two and only two objects.
- There can be at most two interactions at a surface: a force parallel to the surface (e.g., friction) and a force perpendicular to the surface (e.g., a normal force).
- The entire earth interacts only by the long-range gravitational force.

❸ Identify the system. Identify the objects of interest; draw and label a box enclosing them. This completes the interaction diagram.

❹ Draw a free-body diagram for each object in the system. Include only the forces acting *on* each object, not forces exerted by the object.

- Every interaction line crossing the system boundary is one external force acting on the object. The usual force symbols, such as $\vec{n}$ and $\vec{T}$, can be used.
- Every interaction line within the system represents an action/reaction pair of forces. There is one force vector on *each* of the objects, and these forces always point in opposite directions. Use labels like $\vec{F}_{1\text{ on }2}$ and $\vec{F}_{2\text{ on }1}$.
- Connect the two action/reaction forces—which must be on *different* free-body diagrams—with a dashed line.

Exercises 1–7 ✐

We'll illustrate these ideas with two concrete examples. The first example will be much longer than usual because we'll go carefully through all the steps in the reasoning.

EXAMPLE 7.1 Pushing a crate

FIGURE 7.5 shows a person pushing a large crate across a rough surface. Identify all interactions, show them on an interaction diagram, then draw free-body diagrams of the person and the crate.

VISUALIZE The interaction diagram of **FIGURE 7.6** starts by representing every object as a circle in the correct position but separated from all other objects. The person and the crate are obvious objects. The earth is also an object that both exerts and experiences forces, but it's necessary to distinguish between the surface, which exerts contact forces, and the entire earth, which exerts the long-range gravitational force.

Figure 7.6 also identifies the various interactions. Some, like the pushing interaction between the person and the crate, are

FIGURE 7.5 A person pushes a crate across a rough floor.

FIGURE 7.6 The interaction diagram.

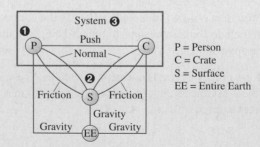

P = Person
C = Crate
S = Surface
EE = Entire Earth

fairly obvious. The interactions with the earth are a little trickier. Gravity, a long-range force, is an interaction between each object (including the surface!) and the earth as a whole. Friction forces and normal forces are contact interactions between each object and the earth's surface. These are two different interac-

tions, so two interaction lines connect the crate to the surface and the person to the surface. Altogether, there are eight interactions. Finally, we've enclosed the person and crate in a box labeled System. These are the objects whose motion we wish to analyze.

NOTE ▶ Interactions are between two *different* objects. None of the interactions are between an object and itself. ◀

We can now draw free-body diagrams for the objects in the system, the crate and the person. **FIGURE 7.7** correctly locates the crate's free-body diagram to the right of the person's free-body diagram. For each, three interaction lines cross the system boundary and thus represent external forces. These are the gravitational force from the entire earth, the upward normal force from the surface, and a friction force from the surface. We can use familiar labels such as $\vec{n}_P$ and $\vec{f}_C$, but **it's very important to distinguish different forces with subscripts.** There's now more than one normal force. If you

call both simply $\vec{n}$, you're almost certain to make mistakes when you start writing out the second-law equations.

The directions of the normal forces and the gravitational forces are clear, but we have to be careful with friction. Friction force $\vec{f}_C$ is kinetic friction of the crate sliding across the surface, so it points left, opposite the motion. But what about friction between the person and the surface? It is tempting to draw force $\vec{f}_P$ pointing to the left. After all, friction forces are supposed to be in the direction opposite the motion. But if we did so, the person would have two forces to the left, $\vec{F}_{C\,on\,P}$ and $\vec{f}_P$, and none to the right, causing the person to accelerate *backward!* That is clearly not what happens, so what is wrong?

Imagine pushing a crate to the right across loose sand. Each time you take a step, you tend to kick the sand to the *left*, behind you. Thus friction force $\vec{f}_{P\,on\,S}$, the force of the person pushing against the earth's surface, is to the *left*. In reaction, the force of the earth's surface against the person is a friction force to the *right*. It is force $\vec{f}_{S\,on\,P}$, which we've shortened to $\vec{f}_P$, that causes the person to accelerate in the forward direction. Further, as we'll discuss more below, this is a *static* friction force; your foot is planted on the ground, not sliding across the surface.

Finally, we have one internal interaction. The crate is pushed with force $\vec{F}_{P\,on\,C}$. If A pushes or pulls on B, then B pushes or pulls back on A. The reaction to force $\vec{F}_{P\,on\,C}$ is $\vec{F}_{C\,on\,P}$, the crate pushing back against the person's hands. Force $\vec{F}_{P\,on\,C}$ is a force exerted on the crate, so it's shown on the crate's free-body diagram. Force $\vec{F}_{C\,on\,P}$ is exerted on the person, so it is drawn on the person's free-body diagram. **The two forces of an action/reaction pair never occur on the same object.** Notice that forces $\vec{F}_{P\,on\,C}$ and $\vec{F}_{C\,on\,P}$ are pointing in opposite directions. We've connected them with a dashed line to show that they are an action/reaction pair.

ASSESS The completed free-body diagrams of Figure 7.7 could now be the basis for a quantitative analysis.

FIGURE 7.7 Free-body diagrams of the person and the crate.

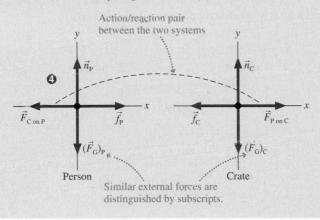

Propulsion

The friction force $\vec{f}_P$ (force of surface on person) is an example of **propulsion.** It is the force that a system with an internal source of energy uses to drive itself forward. Propulsion is an important feature not only of walking or running but also of the forward motion of cars, jets, and rockets. Propulsion is somewhat counterintuitive, so it is worth a closer look.

If you try to walk across a frictionless floor, your foot slips and slides *backward.* In order for you to walk, the floor needs to have friction so that your foot *sticks* to the floor as you straighten your leg, moving your body forward. The friction that prevents slipping is *static* friction. Static friction, you will recall, acts in the direction that prevents slipping. The static friction force $\vec{f}_P$ has to point in the *forward* direction to prevent your foot from slipping backward. It is this forward-directed static friction force that propels you forward! The force of your foot on the floor, the other half of the action/reaction pair, is in the opposite direction.

The distinction between you and the crate is that you have an *internal source of energy* that allows you to straighten your leg by pushing backward against the surface. In essence, you walk by pushing the earth away from you. The earth's surface responds by pushing you forward. These are static friction forces. In contrast, all the crate can do is slide, so *kinetic* friction opposes the motion of the crate.

What force causes this sprinter to accelerate?

FIGURE 7.8 shows how propulsion works. A car uses its motor to spin the tires, causing the tires to push backward against the ground. This is why dirt and gravel are kicked backward, not forward. The earth's surface responds by pushing the car forward. These are also *static* friction forces. The tire is rolling, but the bottom of the tire, where it contacts the road, is instantaneously at rest. If it weren't, you would leave one giant skid mark as you drove and would burn off the tread within a few miles.

FIGURE 7.8 Examples of propulsion.

The person pushes backward against the earth. The earth pushes forward on the person. Static friction.

The car pushes backward against the earth. The earth pushes forward on the car. Static friction.

The rocket pushes the hot gases backward. The gases push the rocket forward. Thrust force.

Rocket motors are somewhat different because they are not pushing *against* anything. That's why rocket propulsion works in the vacuum of space. Instead, the rocket engine pushes hot, expanding gases out of the back of the rocket. In response, the exhaust gases push the rocket forward with the force we've called *thrust*.

EXAMPLE 7.2 Towing a car

A tow truck uses a rope to pull a car along a horizontal road, as shown in **FIGURE 7.9**. Identify all interactions, show them on an interaction diagram, then draw free-body diagrams of each object in the system.

FIGURE 7.9 A truck towing a car.

VISUALIZE The interaction diagram of **FIGURE 7.10** represents the objects as separate circles, but with the correct relative positions. The rope is shown as a separate object. Many of the interactions are identical to those in Example 7.1. The system—the objects in motion—consists of the truck, the rope, and the car.

The three objects in the system require three free-body diagrams, shown in **FIGURE 7.11**. Gravity, friction, and normal forces at the surface are all interactions that cross the system boundary and are shown as external forces. The car is an inert object rolling along. It would slow and stop if the rope were cut, so the surface

FIGURE 7.10 The interaction diagram.

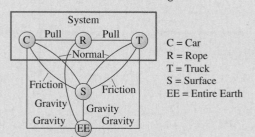

C = Car
R = Rope
T = Truck
S = Surface
EE = Entire Earth

must exert a rolling friction force $\vec{f}_C$ to the left. The truck, however, has an internal source of energy. The truck's drive wheels push the ground to the left with force $\vec{f}_{T \text{ on } S}$. In reaction, the ground propels the truck forward, to the right, with force $\vec{f}_T$.

We next need to identify the horizontal forces between the car, the truck, and the rope. The rope pulls on the car with a tension force $\vec{T}_{R \text{ on } C}$. You might be tempted to put the reaction force on the truck because we say that "the truck pulls the car," but the truck is not in contact with the car. The truck pulls on the rope, then the rope pulls on the car. Thus the reaction to $\vec{T}_{R \text{ on } C}$ is a force on the *rope:* $\vec{T}_{C \text{ on } R}$. These are an action/reaction pair. At the other end, $\vec{T}_{T \text{ on } R}$ and $\vec{T}_{R \text{ on } T}$ are also an action/reaction pair.

FIGURE 7.11 Free-body diagrams of Example 7.2.

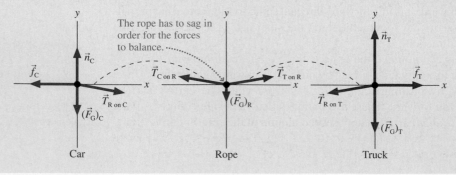

NOTE ▶ Drawing an interaction diagram helps you avoid making mistakes because it shows very clearly what is interacting with what. ◀

Notice that the tension forces of the rope *cannot* be horizontal. If they were, the rope's free-body diagram would show a net downward force and the rope would accelerate downward. The tension forces $\vec{T}_{\text{T on R}}$ and $\vec{T}_{\text{C on R}}$ have to angle slightly upward to balance the gravitational force, so any real rope has to sag at least a little in the center.

ASSESS Make sure you avoid the common error of considering $\vec{n}$ and $\vec{F}_{\text{G}}$ to be an action/reaction pair. These are both forces on the *same* object, whereas the two forces of an action/reaction pair are always on two *different* objects that are interacting with each other. The normal and gravitational forces are often equal in magnitude, as they are in this example, but that doesn't make them an action/reaction pair of forces.

STOP TO THINK 7.1 A fishing line of negligible mass lifts a fish upward at constant speed. The line and the fish are the system, the fishing pole is part of the environment. What, if anything, is wrong with the free-body diagrams?

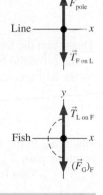

7.3 Newton's Third Law

Newton was the first to recognize how the two members of an action/reaction pair of forces are related to each other. Today we know this as Newton's third law:

Newton's third law Every force occurs as one member of an action/reaction pair of forces.

- The two members of an action/reaction pair act on two *different* objects.
- The two members of an action/reaction pair are equal in magnitude but opposite in direction: $\vec{F}_{\text{A on B}} = -\vec{F}_{\text{B on A}}$.

We deduced most of the third law in Section 7.2. There we found that the two members of an action/reaction pair are always opposite in direction (see Figures 7.7 and 7.11). According to the third law, this will always be true. But the most significant portion of the third law, which is by no means obvious, is that the two members of an action/reaction pair have *equal* magnitudes. That is, $F_{\text{A on B}} = F_{\text{B on A}}$. This is the quantitative relationship that will allow you to solve problems of interacting objects.

Newton's third law is frequently stated as "For every action there is an equal but opposite reaction." While this is indeed a catchy phrase, it lacks the preciseness of our preferred version. In particular, it fails to capture an essential feature of action/reaction pairs—that they each act on a *different* object.

NOTE ▶ Newton's third law extends and completes our concept of *force*. We can now recognize force as an *interaction* between objects rather than as some "thing" with an independent existence of its own. The concept of an interaction will become increasingly important as we begin to study the laws of momentum and energy. ◀

Reasoning with Newton's Third Law

Newton's third law is easy to state but harder to grasp. For example, consider what happens when you release a ball. Not surprisingly, it falls down. But if the ball and the earth exert equal and opposite forces on each other, as Newton's third law alleges, why don't you see the earth "fall up" to meet the ball?

The key to understanding this and many similar puzzles is that **the forces are equal but the accelerations are not.** Equal causes can produce very unequal effects. **FIGURE 7.12** shows equal-magnitude forces on the ball and the earth. The force on ball B is simply the gravitational force of Chapter 6:

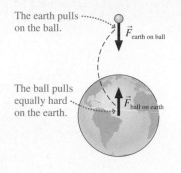

FIGURE 7.12 The action/reaction forces of a ball and the earth are equal in magnitude.

The earth pulls on the ball.

$\vec{F}_{\text{earth on ball}}$

The ball pulls equally hard on the earth.

$\vec{F}_{\text{ball on earth}}$

$$\vec{F}_{\text{earth on ball}} = (\vec{F}_{\text{G}})_{\text{B}} = -m_{\text{B}}g\hat{j} \qquad (7.2)$$

where m_{B} is the mass of the ball. According to Newton's second law, this force gives the ball an acceleration

$$\vec{a}_{\text{B}} = \frac{(\vec{F}_{\text{G}})_{\text{B}}}{m_{\text{B}}} = -g\hat{j} \qquad (7.3)$$

This is just the familiar free-fall acceleration.

According to Newton's third law, the ball pulls up on the earth with force $\vec{F}_{\text{ball on earth}}$. As the ball accelerates down, the earth as a whole has an upward acceleration

$$\vec{a}_{\text{E}} = \frac{\vec{F}_{\text{ball on earth}}}{m_{\text{E}}} \qquad (7.4)$$

where m_{E} is the mass of the earth. Because $\vec{F}_{\text{earth on ball}}$ and $\vec{F}_{\text{ball on earth}}$ are an action/reaction pair, $\vec{F}_{\text{ball on earth}}$ must be equal in magnitude and opposite in direction to $\vec{F}_{\text{earth on ball}}$. That is,

$$\vec{F}_{\text{ball on earth}} = -\vec{F}_{\text{earth on ball}} = -(\vec{F}_{\text{G}})_{\text{B}} = +m_{\text{B}}g\hat{j} \qquad (7.5)$$

Using this result in Equation 7.4, we find the upward acceleration of the earth as a whole is

$$\vec{a}_{\text{E}} = \frac{\vec{F}_{\text{ball on earth}}}{m_{\text{E}}} = \frac{m_{\text{B}}g\hat{j}}{m_{\text{E}}} = \left(\frac{m_{\text{B}}}{m_{\text{E}}}\right)g\hat{j} \qquad (7.6)$$

The upward acceleration of the earth is less than the downward acceleration of the ball by the factor $m_{\text{B}}/m_{\text{E}}$. If we assume a 1 kg ball, we can estimate the magnitude of $\vec{a}_{\text{E}}$:

$$a_{\text{E}} = \frac{1 \text{ kg}}{6 \times 10^{24} \text{ kg}}g \approx 2 \times 10^{-24} \text{ m/s}^2$$

With this incredibly small acceleration, it would take the earth 8×10^{15} years, approximately 500,000 times the age of the universe, to reach a speed of 1 mph! So we certainly would not expect to see or feel the earth "fall up" after dropping a ball.

NOTE ▶ Newton's third law equates the size of two forces, not two accelerations. The acceleration continues to depend on the mass, as Newton's second law states. **In an interaction between two objects of different mass, the lighter mass will do essentially all of the accelerating even though the forces exerted on the two objects are equal.** ◀

EXAMPLE 7.3 The forces on accelerating boxes

The hand shown in **FIGURE 7.13** pushes boxes A and B to the right across a frictionless table. The mass of B is larger than the mass of A.

a. Draw free-body diagrams of A, B, and the hand H, showing only the *horizontal* forces. Connect action/reaction pairs with dashed lines.

b. Rank in order, from largest to smallest, the horizontal forces shown on your free-body diagrams.

FIGURE 7.13 Hand H pushes boxes A and B.

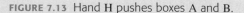
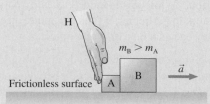

H

$m_{\text{B}} > m_{\text{A}}$

$\vec{a}$

Frictionless surface   A   B

VISUALIZE a. The hand H pushes on box A, and A pushes back on H. Thus $\vec{F}_{H\ on\ A}$ and $\vec{F}_{A\ on\ H}$ are an action/reaction pair. Similarly, A pushes on B and B pushes back on A. The hand H does not touch box B, so there is no interaction between them. There is no friction. **FIGURE 7.14** shows the four horizontal forces and identifies two action/reaction pairs. (We've chosen to ignore forces of the wrist or arm on the hand because our objects of interest are the boxes A and B.) Notice that each force is shown on the free-body diagram of the object that it acts *on*.

b. According to Newton's third law, $F_{A\ on\ H} = F_{H\ on\ A}$ and $F_{A\ on\ B} = F_{B\ on\ A}$. But the third law is not our only tool. Because the boxes are accelerating to the right, Newton's *second* law tells us that box A must have a net force to the right. Consequently, $F_{H\ on\ A} > F_{B\ on\ A}$. Thus

$$F_{A\ on\ H} = F_{H\ on\ A} > F_{B\ on\ A} = F_{A\ on\ B}$$

ASSESS You might have expected $F_{A\ on\ B}$ to be larger than $F_{H\ on\ A}$ because $m_B > m_A$. It's true that the *net* force on B is larger than the *net* force on A, but we have to reason more closely to judge the individual forces. Notice how we used both the second and the third laws to answer this question.

FIGURE 7.14 The free-body diagrams, showing only the horizontal forces.

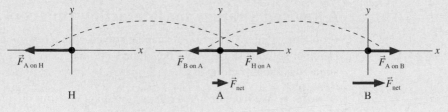

STOP TO THINK 7.2   Car B is stopped for a red light. Car A, which has the same mass as car B, doesn't see the red light and runs into the back of B. Which of the following statements is true?

a. B exerts a force on A, but A doesn't exert a force on B.
b. B exerts a larger force on A than A exerts on B.
c. B exerts the same amount of force on A as A exerts on B.
d. A exerts a larger force on B than B exerts on A.
e. A exerts a force on B, but B doesn't exert a force on A.

Acceleration Constraints

Newton's third law is one quantitative relationship you can use to solve problems of interacting objects. In addition, we frequently have other information about the motion in a problem. For example, think about the two boxes in Example 7.3. As long as they're touching, box A *has* to have exactly the same acceleration as box B. If they were to accelerate differently, either box B would take off on its own or it would suddenly slow down and box A would run over it! Our problem implicitly assumes that neither of these is happening. Thus the two accelerations are *constrained* to be equal: $\vec{a}_A = \vec{a}_B$. A well-defined relationship between the accelerations of two or more objects is called an **acceleration constraint.** It is an independent piece of information that can help solve a problem.

In practice, we'll express acceleration constraints in terms of the *x*- and *y*-components of $\vec{a}$. Consider the car being towed in **FIGURE 7.15**. As long as the rope is under tension, the accelerations are constrained to be equal: $\vec{a}_C = \vec{a}_T$. This is one-dimensional motion, so for problem solving we would use just the *x*-components a_{Cx} and a_{Tx}. In terms of these components, the acceleration constraint is

$$a_{Cx} = a_{Tx} = a_x$$

Because the accelerations of both objects are equal, we can drop the subscripts C and T and call both of them a_x.

FIGURE 7.15 The car and the truck have the same acceleration.

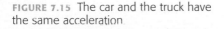

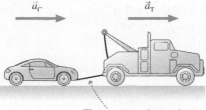

The rope is under tension.

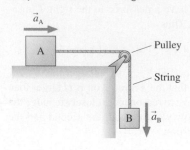

FIGURE 7.16 The string constrains the two objects to accelerate together.

Don't assume the accelerations of A and B will always have the same sign. Consider blocks A and B in **FIGURE 7.16**. The blocks are connected by a string, so they are constrained to move together and their accelerations have equal magnitudes. But A has a positive acceleration (to the right) in the x-direction while B has a negative acceleration (downward) in the y-direction. Thus the acceleration constraint is

$$a_{Ax} = -a_{By}$$

This relationship does *not* say that a_{Ax} is a negative number. It is simply a relational statement, saying that a_{Ax} is (-1) times whatever a_{By} happens to be. The acceleration a_{By} in Figure 7.16 is a negative number, so a_{Ax} is positive. In some problems, the signs of a_{Ax} and a_{By} may not be known until the problem is solved, but the *relationship* is known from the beginning.

A Revised Strategy for Interacting-Objects Problems

Problems of interacting objects can be solved with a few modifications to the basic problem-solving strategy we developed in Chapter 6. A revised problem-solving strategy is shown below.

NOTE ▶ We have dropped the motion diagram from the pictorial representation. Motion diagrams served a useful function in the early chapters, but by now you should be able to determine the directions of the acceleration vectors without the need for an explicit diagram. But if you are uncertain—use one! ◀

PROBLEM-SOLVING
STRATEGY 7.1 **Interacting-objects problems** (MP)

MODEL Identify which objects are part of the system and which are part of the environment. Make simplifying assumptions.

VISUALIZE Draw a pictorial representation.

- Show important points in the motion with a sketch. You may want to give each object a separate coordinate system. Define symbols and identify what the problem is trying to find.
- Identify acceleration constraints.
- Draw an interaction diagram to identify the forces on each object and all action/reaction pairs.
- Draw a *separate* free-body diagram for each object.
- Connect the force vectors of action/reaction pairs with dashed lines. Use subscript labels to distinguish forces that act independently on more than one object.

SOLVE Use Newton's second and third laws.

- Write the equations of Newton's second law for *each* object, using the force information from the free-body diagrams.
- Equate the magnitudes of action/reaction pairs.
- Include the acceleration constraints, the friction model, and other quantitative information relevant to the problem.
- Solve for the acceleration, then use kinematics to find velocities and positions.

ASSESS Check that your result has the correct units, is reasonable, and answers the question.

You might be puzzled that the Solve step calls for the use of the third law to equate just the *magnitudes* of action/reaction forces. What about the "opposite in direction" part of the third law? You have already used it! Your free-body diagrams should show the two members of an action/reaction pair to be opposite in direction, and that information will have been utilized in writing the second-law equations. Because the directional information has already been used, all that is left is the magnitude information.

NOTE ▶ Two steps are especially important when drawing the free-body diagrams. First, draw a *separate* diagram for each object. The diagrams need not have the same coordinate system. Second, show only the forces acting *on* that object. The force $\vec{F}_{A \text{ on } B}$ goes on the free-body diagram of object B, but $\vec{F}_{B \text{ on } A}$ goes on the diagram of object A. The two members of an action/reaction pair *always* appear on two different free-body diagrams—*never* on the same diagram. ◀

EXAMPLE 7.4 **Keep the crate from sliding**

You and a friend have just loaded a 200 kg crate filled with priceless art objects into the back of a 2000 kg truck. As you press down on the accelerator, force $\vec{F}_{\text{surface on truck}}$ propels the truck forward. To keep things simple, call this just $\vec{F}_T$. What is the maximum magnitude $\vec{F}_T$ can have without the crate sliding? The static and kinetic coefficients of friction between the crate and the bed of the truck are 0.80 and 0.30. Rolling friction of the truck is negligible.

MODEL The crate and the truck are separate objects that form the system. We'll model them as particles. The earth and the road surface are part of the environment.

VISUALIZE The sketch in **FIGURE 7.17** establishes a coordinate system, lists the known information, and—new to problems of interacting objects—identifies the acceleration constraint. As long as the crate doesn't slip, it must accelerate *with* the truck. Both accelerations are in the positive x-direction, so the acceleration constraint in this problem is

$$a_{Cx} = a_{Tx} = a_x$$

The interaction diagram of Figure 7.17 shows the crate interacting twice with the truck—a friction force parallel to the surface of the truck bed and a normal force perpendicular to this surface. The truck interacts similarly with the road surface, but notice that the crate does not interact with the ground; there's no contact between them. The two interactions within the system are each an action/reaction pair, so this is a total of four forces. You can also see four external forces crossing the system boundary, so the free-body diagrams should show a total of eight forces.

Finally, the interaction information is transferred to the free-body diagrams, where we see friction between the crate and truck as an action/reaction pair and the normal forces (the truck pushes up on the crate, the crate pushes down on the truck) as another action/reaction pair. It's easy to overlook forces such as $\vec{f}_{C \text{ on } T}$, but you won't make this mistake if you first identify action/reaction pairs on an interaction diagram. Note that $\vec{f}_{C \text{ on } T}$ and $\vec{f}_{T \text{ on } C}$ are *static* friction forces because they are forces that prevent slipping; force $\vec{f}_{T \text{ on } C}$ must point forward to prevent the crate from sliding out the back of the truck.

SOLVE Now we're ready to write Newton's second law. For the crate:

$$\sum (F_{\text{on crate}})_x = f_{T \text{ on } C} = m_C a_{Cx} = m_C a_x$$

$$\sum (F_{\text{on crate}})_y = n_{T \text{ on } C} - (F_G)_C = n_{T \text{ on } C} - m_C g = 0$$

For the truck:

$$\sum (F_{\text{on truck}})_x = F_T - f_{C \text{ on } T} = m_T a_{Tx} = m_T a_x$$

$$\sum (F_{\text{on truck}})_y = n_T - (F_G)_T - n_{C \text{ on } T}$$
$$= n_T - m_T g - n_{C \text{ on } T} = 0$$

Be sure you agree with all the signs, which are based on the free-body diagrams. The net force in the y-direction is zero because there's no motion in the y-direction. It may seem like a lot of effort to write all the subscripts, but it is very important in problems with more than one object.

FIGURE 7.17 Pictorial representation of the crate and truck in Example 7.4.

Sketch

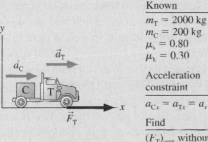

Known
$m_T = 2000 \text{ kg}$
$m_C = 200 \text{ kg}$
$\mu_s = 0.80$
$\mu_k = 0.30$

Acceleration constraint

$a_{Cx} = a_{Tx} = a_x$

Find

$(F_T)_{\text{max}}$ without slipping

Interaction diagram

Free-body diagrams

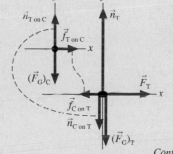

Continued

Notice that we've already used the acceleration constraint $a_{Cx} = a_{Tx} = a_x$. Another important piece of information is Newton's third law, which tells us that $f_{C\,on\,T} = f_{T\,on\,C}$ and $n_{C\,on\,T} = n_{T\,on\,C}$. Finally, we know that the maximum value of F_T will occur when the static friction on the crate reaches its maximum value:

$$f_{T\,on\,C} = f_{s\,max} = \mu_s n_{T\,on\,C}$$

The friction depends on the normal force on the crate, not the normal force on the truck.

Now we can assemble all the pieces. From the y-equation of the crate, $n_{T\,on\,C} = m_C g$. Thus

$$f_{T\,on\,C} = \mu_s n_{T\,on\,C} = \mu_s m_C g$$

Using this in the x-equation of the crate, we find that the acceleration is

$$a_x = \frac{f_{T\,on\,C}}{m_C} = \mu_s g$$

This is the crate's maximum acceleration without slipping. Now use this acceleration *and* the fact that $f_{C\,on\,T} = f_{T\,on\,C} = \mu_s m_C g$ in the x-equation of the truck to find

$$F_T - f_{C\,on\,T} = F_T - \mu_s m_C g = m_T a_x = m_T \mu_s g$$

Solving for F_T, we find the maximum propulsion without the crate sliding is

$$(F_T)_{max} = \mu_s (m_T + m_C) g$$
$$= (0.80)(2200 \text{ kg})(9.80 \text{ m/s}^2) = 17,000 \text{ N}$$

ASSESS This is a hard result to assess. Few of us have any intuition about the size of forces that propel cars and trucks. Even so, the fact that the forward force on the truck is a significant fraction (80%) of the combined weight of the truck and the crate seems plausible. We might have been suspicious if F_T had been only a tiny fraction of the weight or much greater than the weight.

As you can see, there are many equations and many pieces of information to keep track of when solving a problem of interacting objects. These problems are not inherently harder than the problems you learned to solve in Chapter 6, but they do require a high level of organization. Using the systematic approach of the problem-solving strategy will help you solve similar problems successfully.

STOP TO THINK 7.3   Boxes A and B are sliding to the right across a frictionless table. The hand H is slowing them down. The mass of A is larger than the mass of B. Rank in order, from largest to smallest, the *horizontal* forces on A, B, and H.

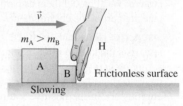

a. $F_{B\,on\,H} = F_{H\,on\,B} = F_{A\,on\,B} = F_{B\,on\,A}$

b. $F_{B\,on\,H} = F_{H\,on\,B} > F_{A\,on\,B} = F_{B\,on\,A}$

c. $F_{B\,on\,H} = F_{H\,on\,B} < F_{A\,on\,B} = F_{B\,on\,A}$

d. $F_{H\,on\,B} = F_{H\,on\,A} > F_{A\,on\,B}$

7.4 Ropes and Pulleys

Many objects are connected by strings, ropes, cables, and so on. In single-particle dynamics, we defined *tension* as the force exerted on an object by a rope or string. Now we need to think more carefully about the string itself. Just what do we mean when we talk about the tension "in" a string?

Tension Revisited

FIGURE 7.18 Tension forces within the rope are due to stretching the spring-like molecular bonds.

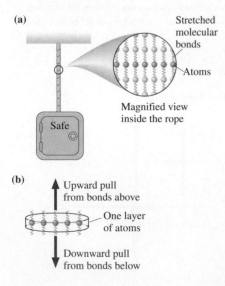

FIGURE 7.18a shows a heavy safe hanging from a rope, placing the rope under tension. If you cut the rope, the safe and the lower portion of the rope will fall. Thus there must be a force *within* the rope by which the upper portion of the rope pulls upward on the lower portion to prevent it from falling.

Chapter 5 introduced an atomic-level model in which tension is due to the stretching of spring-like molecular bonds within the rope. Stretched springs exert pulling forces, and the combined pulling force of billions of stretched molecular springs in a string or rope is what we call *tension*.

An important aspect of tension is that it pulls equally *in both directions*. **FIGURE 7.18b** is a very thin cross section through the rope. This small piece of rope is in equilibrium, so it must be pulled equally from both sides. To gain a mental picture, imagine holding your arms outstretched and having two friends pull on them. You'll remain at rest—but "in tension"—as long as they pull with equal strength in opposite directions. But if one lets go, analogous to the breaking of molecular bonds if a rope breaks or is cut, you'll fly off in the other direction!

EXAMPLE 7.5 **Pulling a rope**

FIGURE 7.19a shows a student pulling horizontally with a 100 N force on a rope that is attached to a wall. In **FIGURE 7.19b**, two students in a tug-of-war pull on opposite ends of a rope with 100 N each. Is the tension in the second rope larger than, smaller than, or the same as that in the first rope?

FIGURE 7.19 Pulling on a rope. Which produces a larger tension?

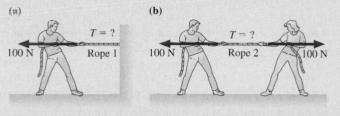

SOLVE Surely pulling on a rope from both ends causes more tension than pulling on one end. Right? Before jumping to conclusions, let's analyze the situation carefully.

Suppose we make an imaginary slice through the rope, as shown in **FIGURE 7.20a**. The right half of the rope pulls on the left half with $\vec{T}_{\text{R on L}}$ while the left half pulls back on the right half with $\vec{T}_{\text{L on R}}$. These two forces are an action/reaction pair, and their magnitude is what we mean by "the tension in the rope." The left half of the rope is in equilibrium, so force $\vec{T}_{\text{R on L}}$ has to balance exactly the 100 N force with which the student is pulling. Thus

$$T_{\text{L on R}} = T_{\text{R on L}} = F_{\text{S on L}} = 100 \text{ N}$$

The first equality is based on Newton's third law (action/reaction pair). The second equality follows from Newton's first law (left half is in equilibrium). This reasoning leads us to the conclusion that the tension in the first rope is 100 N.

Now make an imaginary slice through the rope in **FIGURE 7.20b**. The left half of the rope is pulled by forces $\vec{T}_{\text{R on L}}$ and $\vec{F}_{\text{S1 on L}}$. This half of the rope is again in equilibrium because the rope is at rest, so from Newton's first law

$$T_{\text{R on L}} = F_{\text{S1 on L}} = 100 \text{ N}$$

Similarly, the right half of the rope is pulled by forces $\vec{T}_{\text{L on R}}$ and $\vec{F}_{\text{S2 on R}}$. This piece of the rope is also in equilibrium, so

$$T_{\text{L on R}} = F_{\text{S2 on R}} = 100 \text{ N}$$

The tension in the rope has not changed! It is still 100 N.

You may have *assumed* that the student on the right in Figure 7.20b is doing something to the rope that the wall in Figure 7.20a does not do. But let's look more closely. **FIGURE 7.21** shows a detailed view of the point at which the rope of Figure 7.20a is tied to the wall. Because the rope pulls on the wall with force $\vec{F}_{\text{R on W}}$, the wall must pull back on the rope (action/reaction pair) with force $\vec{F}_{\text{W on R}}$. And because the rope as a whole is in equilibrium, the wall's pull to the right must balance the student's pull to the left: $F_{\text{W on R}} = F_{\text{S on R}} = 100 \text{ N}$.

FIGURE 7.21 A closer look at the forces on the rope.

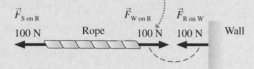

In other words, the wall in Figure 7.20a pulls the right end of the rope with a force of 100 N. The student in Figure 7.20b pulls the right end of the rope with a force of 100 N. The rope does not care whether it is pulled by a wall or by a hand. It experiences the same forces in both cases, so the rope's tension is the same 100 N in both.

FIGURE 7.20 Analysis of tension forces.

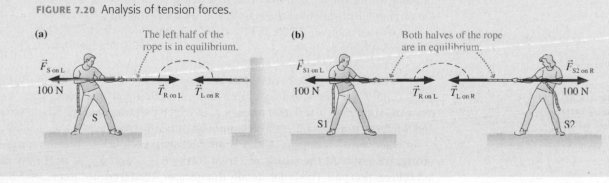

STOP TO THINK 7.4   All three 50 kg blocks are at rest. Is the tension in rope 2 greater than, less than, or equal to the tension in rope 1?

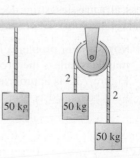

The Massless String Approximation

The tension is constant throughout a rope that is in equilibrium, but what happens if the rope is accelerating? For example, FIGURE 7.22a shows two connected blocks being pulled by force $\vec{F}$. Is the string's tension at the right end, where it pulls back on B, the same as the tension at the left end, where it pulls on A?

FIGURE 7.22   The string's tension pulls forward on block A, backward on block B.

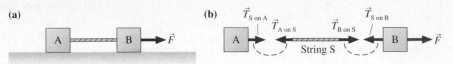

FIGURE 7.22b shows the horizontal forces acting on the blocks and the string. If the string is accelerating, then it must have a net force applied to it. The only forces acting on the string are $\vec{T}_{\text{A on S}}$ and $\vec{T}_{\text{B on S}}$, so Newton's second law *for the string* is

$$(F_{\text{net}})_x = T_{\text{B on S}} - T_{\text{A on S}} = m_s a_x \tag{7.7}$$

where m_s is the mass of the string.

If the string is accelerating, then the tensions at the two ends can *not* be the same. In fact, you can see that

$$T_{\text{B on S}} = T_{\text{A on S}} + m_s a_x \tag{7.8}$$

The tension at the "front" of the string is higher than the tension at the "back." This difference in the tensions is necessary to accelerate the string! On the other hand, the tension is constant throughout a string in equilibrium ($a_x = 0$). This was the situation in Example 7.5.

Often in physics and engineering problems the mass of the string or rope is much less than the masses of the objects that it connects. In such cases, we can adopt the **massless string approximation.** In the limit $m_s \rightarrow 0$, Equation 7.8 becomes

$$T_{\text{B on S}} = T_{\text{A on S}} \qquad \text{(massless string approximation)} \tag{7.9}$$

In other words, **the tension in a massless string is constant.** This is nice, but it isn't the primary justification for the massless string approximation.

Look again at Figure 7.22b. If $T_{\text{B on S}} = T_{\text{A on S}}$, then

$$\vec{T}_{\text{S on A}} = -\vec{T}_{\text{S on B}} \tag{7.10}$$

That is, the force on block A is equal and opposite to the force on block B. Forces $\vec{T}_{\text{S on A}}$ and $\vec{T}_{\text{S on B}}$ act *as if* they are an action/reaction pair of forces. Thus we can draw the simplified diagram of FIGURE 7.23 in which the string is missing and blocks A and B interact directly with each other through forces that we can call $\vec{T}_{\text{A on B}}$ and $\vec{T}_{\text{B on A}}$.

In other words, **if objects A and B interact with each other through a massless string, we can omit the string and treat forces $\vec{F}_{\text{A on B}}$ and $\vec{F}_{\text{B on A}}$ as if they are an action/reaction pair.** This is not literally true because A and B are not in contact. Nonetheless, all a massless string does is transmit a force from A to B without changing the magnitude of that force. This is the real significance of the massless string approximation.

NOTE ▶ For problems in this book, you can assume that any strings or ropes are massless unless the problem explicitly states otherwise. The simplified view of Figure 7.23 is appropriate under these conditions. But if the string has a mass, it must be treated as a separate object. ◀

The tension in the cable pulls upward on the seat and, simultaneously, pulls downward on the motor and supports at the top of the lift.

FIGURE 7.23   The massless string approximation allows objects A and B to act *as if* they are directly interacting.

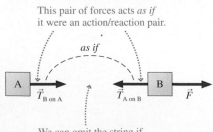

This pair of forces acts *as if* it were an action/reaction pair.

We can omit the string if we assume it is massless.

EXAMPLE 7.6 Comparing two tensions

Blocks A and B in **FIGURE 7.24** are connected by massless string 2 and pulled across a frictionless table by massless string 1. B has a larger mass than A. Is the tension in string 2 larger than, smaller than, or equal to the tension in string 1?

FIGURE 7.24 Blocks A and B are pulled across a frictionless table by massless strings.

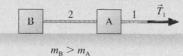

$$m_B > m_A$$

MODEL The massless string approximation allows us to treat A and B *as if* they interact directly with each other. The blocks are accelerating because there's a force to the right and no friction.

SOLVE B has a larger mass, so it may be tempting to conclude that string 2, which pulls B, has a greater tension than string 1, which pulls A. The flaw in this reasoning is that Newton's second law tells us only about the *net* force. The net force on B *is* larger than the net force on A, but the net force on A is *not* just the tension $\vec{T}_1$ in the forward direction. The tension in string 2 also pulls *backward* on A!

FIGURE 7.25 shows the horizontal forces in this frictionless situation. Forces $\vec{T}_{A \text{ on } B}$ and $\vec{T}_{B \text{ on } A}$ act *as if* they are an action/reaction pair.

FIGURE 7.25 The horizontal forces on blocks A and B.

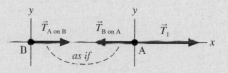

From Newton's third law,

$$T_{A \text{ on } B} = T_{B \text{ on } A} = T_2$$

where T_2 is the tension in string 2. From Newton's second law, the net force on A is

$$(F_{A \text{ net}})_x = T_1 - T_{B \text{ on } A} = T_1 - T_2 = m_A a_{Ax}$$

The net force on A is the *difference* in tensions. The blocks are accelerating to the right, making $a_{Ax} > 0$, so

$$T_1 > T_2$$

The tension in string 2 is *smaller* than the tension in string 1.

ASSESS This is not an intuitively obvious result. A careful study of the reasoning in this example is worthwhile. An alternative analysis would note that $\vec{T}_1$ pulls *both* blocks, of combined mass $(m_A + m_B)$, whereas $\vec{T}_2$ pulls only block B. Thus string 1 must have the larger tension.

Pulleys

Strings and ropes often pass over pulleys. The application might be as simple as lifting a heavy weight or as complex as the internal cable-and-pulley arrangement that precisely moves a robot arm.

FIGURE 7.26a shows a simple situation in which block B drags block A across a frictionless table as it falls. **FIGURE 7.26b** shows the objects separately as well as the forces. As the string moves, static friction between the string and pulley causes the pulley to turn. If we assume that

- The string *and* the pulley are both massless, and
- There is no friction where the pulley turns on its axle,

FIGURE 7.26 Blocks A and B are connected by a string that passes over a pulley.

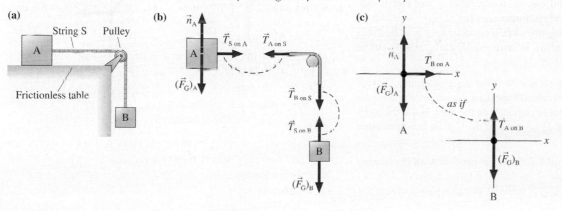

then no net force is needed to accelerate the string or turn the pulley. In this case,

$$T_{\text{A on S}} = T_{\text{B on S}}$$

In other words, **the tension in a massless string remains constant as it passes over a massless, frictionless pulley.**

Because of this, we can draw the simplified free-body diagram of FIGURE 7.26c on the previous page, in which the string and pulley are omitted. Forces $\vec{T}_{\text{A on B}}$ and $\vec{T}_{\text{B on A}}$ act *as if* they are an action/reaction pair, even though they are not opposite in direction. We can again say that A and B are objects that interact with each other *through the string,* and thus the force of A on B is paired with the force of B on A. The tension force gets "turned" by the pulley, which is why the two forces are not opposite each other but we can still equate their magnitudes.

> **STOP TO THINK 7.5** In Figure 7.26 on the previous page, is the tension in the string greater than, less than, or equal to the gravitational force acting on block B?

7.5 Examples of Interacting-Objects Problems

We will conclude this chapter with four extended examples. Although the mathematics will be more involved than in any of our work up to this point, we will continue to emphasize the *reasoning* one uses in approaching problems such as these. The solutions will be based on Problem-Solving Strategy 7.1. In fact, these problems are now reaching such a level of complexity that, for all practical purposes, it becomes impossible to work them unless you are following a well-planned strategy. Our earlier emphasis on identifying forces and using free-body diagrams will now really begin to pay off!

EXAMPLE 7.7 Mountain climbing

A 90 kg mountain climber is suspended from the ropes shown in FIGURE 7.27a. The maximum tension that rope 3 can withstand before breaking is 1500 N. What is the smallest that angle θ can become before the rope breaks and the climber falls into the gorge?

MODEL Climber C, who can be modeled as a particle, is one object. The other point where forces are exerted is the knot, where the three ropes are tied together. We'll consider knot K to be a second object. Both objects are in static equilibrium. We'll assume massless ropes.

VISUALIZE FIGURE 7.27b shows two free-body diagrams. Forces $\vec{T}_{\text{C on K}}$ and $\vec{T}_{\text{K on C}}$ are not, strictly speaking, an action/reaction pair because the climber is not in contact with the knot. But if the ropes are massless, $\vec{T}_{\text{C on K}}$ and $\vec{T}_{\text{K on C}}$ act *as if* they are an action/reaction pair.

SOLVE This is static equilibrium, so the net forces on the climber and on the knot are zero.

FIGURE 7.27 A mountain climber hanging from ropes.

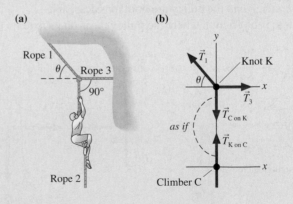

For the climber:

$$\sum (F_{on\,C})_y = T_{K\,on\,C} - mg = 0$$

And for the knot:

$$\sum (F_{on\,K})_x = T_3 - T_1 \cos\theta = 0$$

$$\sum (F_{on\,K})_y = T_1 \sin\theta - T_{C\,on\,K} = 0$$

From Newton's third law,

$$T_{C\,on\,K} = T_{K\,on\,C}$$

But $T_{K\,on\,C} = mg$ from the climber's equation, so $T_{C\,on\,K} = mg$. Using this gives us the knot's equations:

$$T_1 \cos\theta = T_3$$

$$T_1 \sin\theta = mg$$

Dividing the second of these by the first gives

$$\frac{T_1 \sin\theta}{T_1 \cos\theta} = \tan\theta = \frac{mg}{T_3}$$

If angle θ is too small, tension T_3 will exceed 1500 N. The smallest possible θ, at which T_3 reaches 1500 N, is

$$\theta_{min} = \tan^{-1}\left(\frac{mg}{T_{3\,max}}\right) = \tan^{-1}\left(\frac{(90\text{ kg})(9.80\text{ m/s}^2)}{1500\text{ N}}\right) = 30°$$

EXAMPLE 7.8 **The show must go on!**

A 200 kg set used in a play is stored in the loft above the stage. The rope holding the set passes up and over a pulley, then is tied backstage. The director tells a 100 kg stagehand to lower the set. When he unties the rope, the set falls and the unfortunate man is hoisted into the loft. What is the stagehand's acceleration?

MODEL The system is the stagehand M and the set S, which we will model as particles. Assume a massless rope and a massless, frictionless pulley.

VISUALIZE FIGURE 7.28 shows the pictorial representation. The man's acceleration a_{My} is positive, while the set's acceleration a_{Sy} is negative. These two accelerations have the same magnitude because the two objects are connected by a rope, but they have opposite signs. Thus the acceleration constraint is $a_{Sy} = -a_{My}$. Forces $\vec{T}_{M\,on\,S}$ and $\vec{T}_{S\,on\,M}$ are not literally an action/reaction pair, but they act *as if* they are because the rope is massless and the pulley is massless and frictionless. Notice that the pulley has "turned" the tension force so that $\vec{T}_{M\,on\,S}$ and $\vec{T}_{S\,on\,M}$ are *parallel* to each other rather than opposite, as members of a true action/reaction pair would have to be.

SOLVE Newton's second law for the man and the set are

$$\sum (F_{on\,M})_y = T_{S\,on\,M} - m_M g = m_M a_{My}$$

$$\sum (F_{on\,S})_y = T_{M\,on\,S} - m_S g = m_S a_{Sy} = -m_S a_{My}$$

Only the y-equations are needed. Notice that we used the acceleration constraint in the last step. Newton's third law is

$$T_{M\,on\,S} = T_{S\,on\,M} = T$$

where we can drop the subscripts and call the tension simply T. With this substitution, the two second-law equations can be written

$$T - m_M g = m_M a_{My}$$

$$T - m_S g = -m_S a_{My}$$

These are simultaneous equations in the two unknowns T and a_{My}. We can eliminate T by subtracting the second equation from the first to give

$$(m_S - m_M)g = (m_S + m_M)a_{My}$$

Finally, we can solve for the hapless stagehand's acceleration:

$$a_{My} = \frac{m_S - m_M}{m_S + m_M}g = \frac{100\text{ kg}}{300\text{ kg}}9.80\text{ m/s}^2 = 3.27\text{ m/s}^2$$

This is also the acceleration with which the set falls. If the rope's tension was needed, we could now find it from $T = m_M a_{My} + m_M g$.

ASSESS If the stagehand weren't holding on, the set would fall with free-fall acceleration g. The stagehand acts as a *counterweight* to reduce the acceleration.

FIGURE 7.28 Pictorial representation for Example 7.8.

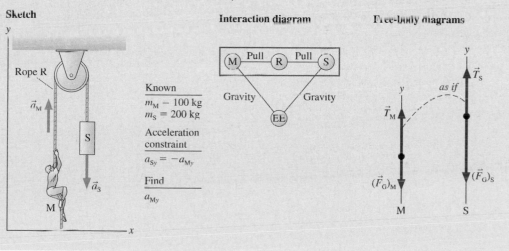

Sketch

Rope R

Known
$m_M = 100$ kg
$m_S = 200$ kg

Acceleration constraint
$a_{Sy} = -a_{My}$

Find
a_{My}

Interaction diagram

Pull   Pull
M — R — S
Gravity   Gravity
EE

Free-body diagrams

as if

$\vec{T}_M$ $\vec{T}_S$

$(\vec{F}_G)_M$ $(\vec{F}_G)_S$

M   S

EXAMPLE 7.9 A not-so-clever bank robbery

Bank robbers have pushed a 1000 kg safe to a second-story floor-to-ceiling window. They plan to break the window, then lower the safe 3.0 m to their truck. Not being too clever, they stack up 500 kg of furniture, tie a rope between the safe and the furniture, and place the rope over a pulley. Then they push the safe out the window. What is the safe's speed when it hits the truck? The coefficient of kinetic friction between the furniture and the floor is 0.50.

MODEL This is a continuation of the situation that we analyzed in Figures 7.16 and 7.26, which are worth reviewing. The system is the safe S and the furniture F, which we will model as particles. We will assume a massless rope and a massless, frictionless pulley.

VISUALIZE The safe and the furniture are tied together, so their accelerations have the same magnitude. The safe has a y-component of acceleration a_{Sy} that is negative because the safe accelerates in the negative y-direction. The furniture has an x-component a_F that is positive. Thus the acceleration constraint is

$$a_{Fx} = -a_{Sy}$$

The free-body diagrams of **FIGURE 7.29** are modeled after Figure 7.26 but now include a kinetic friction force on the furniture. Forces $\vec{T}_{\text{F on S}}$ and $\vec{T}_{\text{S on F}}$ act *as if* they are an action/reaction pair, so they have been connected with a dashed line.

SOLVE We can write Newton's second law directly from the free-body diagrams. For the furniture,

$$\sum (F_{\text{on F}})_x = T_{\text{S on F}} - f_k = T - f_k = m_F a_{Fx} = -m_F a_{Sy}$$

$$\sum (F_{\text{on F}})_y = n - m_F g = 0$$

And for the safe,

$$\sum (F_{\text{on S}})_y = T - m_S g = m_S a_{Sy}$$

Notice how we used the acceleration constraint in the first equation. We also went ahead and made use of Newton's third law:

$T_{\text{F on S}} = T_{\text{S on F}} = T$. We have one additional piece of information, the model of kinetic friction:

$$f_k = \mu_k n = \mu_k m_F g$$

where we used the y-equation of the furniture to deduce that $n = m_F g$. Substitute this result for f_k into the x-equation of the furniture, then rewrite the furniture's x-equation and the safe's y-equation:

$$T - \mu_k m_F g = -m_F a_{Sy}$$

$$T - m_S g = m_S a_{Sy}$$

We have succeeded in reducing our knowledge to two simultaneous equations in the two unknowns a_{Sy} and T. Subtract the second equation from the first to eliminate T:

$$(m_S - \mu_k m_F)g = -(m_S + m_F)a_{Sy}$$

Finally, solve for the safe's acceleration:

$$a_{Sy} = -\left(\frac{m_S - \mu_k m_F}{m_S + m_F}\right)g$$

$$= -\frac{1000 \text{ kg} - 0.5(500 \text{ kg})}{1000 \text{ kg} + 500 \text{ kg}} 9.80 \text{ m/s}^2 = -4.9 \text{ m/s}^2$$

Now we need to calculate the kinematics of the falling safe. Because the time of the fall is not known or needed, we can use

$$v_{1y}^2 = v_{0y}^2 + 2a_{Sy}\,\Delta y = 0 + 2a_{Sy}(y_1 - y_0) = -2a_{Sy}y_0$$

$$v_1 = \sqrt{-2a_{Sy}y_0} = \sqrt{-2(-4.9 \text{ m/s}^2)(3.0 \text{ m})} = 5.4 \text{ m/s}$$

The value of v_{1y} is negative, but we only needed to find the speed so we took the absolute value. It seems unlikely that the truck will survive the impact of the 1000 kg safe!

FIGURE 7.29 Pictorial representation for Example 7.9.

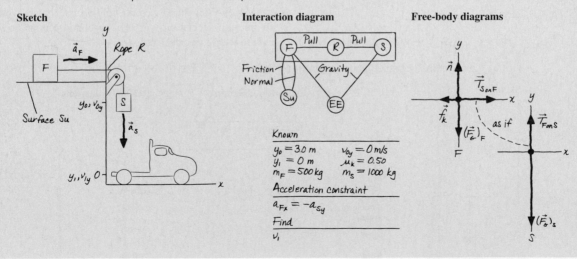

EXAMPLE 7.10 Pushing a package

A 40 kg boy works at his dad's hardware store. One of the boy's jobs is to unload the delivery truck. He places each package on a 30° ramp and shoves it up the ramp into the storeroom. He needs to shove the package with an acceleration of at least 1.0 m/s² in order for the package to make it to the top of the ramp. One day the ground is wet with rain and he's wearing slick leather-soled shoes. The coefficient of static friction between his shoes and the ground is only 0.25. The largest package of the day is 15 kg, and its coefficient of kinetic friction on the ramp is 0.40. Can he give the package a big enough shove to reach the top of the ramp without his feet slipping?

MODEL The system is the boy B and the package P, which we will model as particles.

VISUALIZE There's a lot of information in this problem, so the pictorial representation of **FIGURE 7.30** is essential. The package is moving up an incline, whereas the boy, if he slips, will move horizontally. Consequently, it is useful to give them different coordinate systems. The free-body diagrams show that the boy pushes the package with force $\vec{F}_{\text{B on P}}$ and the package pushes back with force $\vec{F}_{\text{P on B}}$. If static friction does its job, it must point *forward* to prevent the boy's feet from slipping backward. To answer the question, we'll first calculate how much static friction is needed for the boy to push the package with an acceleration of 1.0 m/s². Then we'll compare that to the maximum possible static friction $f_{s\,\text{max}}$.

SOLVE Now we're ready to write Newton's second law. The boy is in static equilibrium, with $\vec{F}_{\text{net}} = \vec{0}$, so his equations are

$$\sum (F_{\text{on B}})_x = f_s - F_{\text{P on B}} \cos\theta = f_s - F\cos\theta = 0$$

$$\sum (F_{\text{on B}})_y = n_B - m_B g - F\sin\theta = 0$$

The package is accelerating up the ramp as he pushes it, so the package's equations are

$$\sum (F_{\text{on P}})_x = F - f_k - m_P g \sin\theta = m_P a_x$$

$$\sum (F_{\text{on P}})_y = n_P - m_P g \cos\theta = 0$$

We went ahead and made use of Newton's third law: $F_{\text{P on B}} = F_{\text{B on P}} = F$. The package's y-equation tells us that $n_P = m_P g \cos\theta$, so the kinetic friction on the package is

$$f_k = \mu_k n_P = \mu_k m_P g \cos\theta$$

If we substitute this into the package's x-equation, we can solve for force F:

$$F - \mu_k m_P g \cos\theta - m_P g \sin\theta = m_P a_x$$

$$F = m_P(a_x + g\sin\theta + \mu_k g\cos\theta) = 139\ \text{N}$$

This is the size of the force that will accelerate the package up the ramp at 1.0 m/s². If we now use this in the boy's x-equation, we find

$$f_s = F\cos\theta = 120\ \text{N}$$

The boy *needs* this much static friction to push the package without slipping. But needing 120 N of friction doesn't mean that 120 N is available. The maximum possible static friction is $f_{s\,\text{max}} = \mu_s n_B$. In this situation, the normal force acting on the boy is not simply F_G but is affected by the vertical component of $\vec{F}_{\text{P on B}}$. From his y-equation we find

$$n_B = m_B g + F\sin\theta = 462\ \text{N}$$

Thus the maximum static friction without slipping is

$$f_{s\,\text{max}} = \mu_s n_B = 115\ \text{N}$$

Consequently, the boy *cannot* shove hard enough without slipping.

ASSESS This is an excellent illustration of how crucial it is to focus on clarifying information, identifying forces, and drawing free-body diagrams. The rest of the problem was not trivial, but we could work our way through it with confidence after having identified the interactions and found the free-body diagrams. It would be hopeless, even for an experienced physicist, to try to go directly to Newton's laws without this analysis.

FIGURE 7.30 Pictorial representation for Example 7.10.

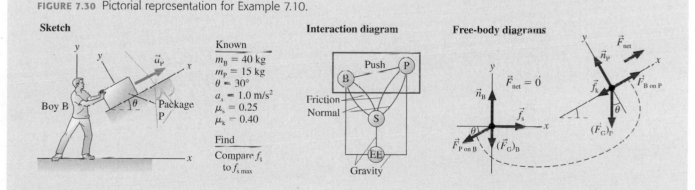

STOP TO THINK 7.6 A small car is pushing a larger truck that has a dead battery. The mass of the truck is larger than the mass of the car. Which of the following statements is true?

a. The car exerts a force on the truck, but the truck doesn't exert a force on the car.

b. The car exerts a larger force on the truck than the truck exerts on the car.

c. The car exerts the same amount of force on the truck as the truck exerts on the car.

d. The truck exerts a larger force on the car than the car exerts on the truck.

e. The truck exerts a force on the car, but the car doesn't exert a force on the truck.

SUMMARY

The goal of Chapter 7 has been to learn to use Newton's third law to understand interacting objects.

General Principles

Newton's Third Law

Every force occurs as one member of an **action/reaction pair** of forces. The two members of an action/reaction pair:

- Act on two *different* objects.

- Are equal in magnitude but opposite in direction:

$$\vec{F}_{\text{A on B}} = -\vec{F}_{\text{B on A}}$$

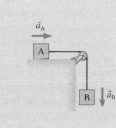

Solving Interacting-Objects Problems

MODEL Choose the objects of interest.

VISUALIZE
Draw a pictorial representation.
    Sketch and define coordinates.
    Identify acceleration constraints.
    Draw an interaction diagram.
    Draw a separate free-body diagram for each object.
    Connect action/reaction pairs with dashed lines.

SOLVE Write Newton's second law for each object.
    Include *all* forces acting *on* each object.
    Use Newton's third law to equate the magnitudes of
    action/reaction pairs.
    Include acceleration constraints and friction.

ASSESS Is the result reasonable?

Important Concepts

Objects, systems, and the environment

Objects whose motion is of interest are the system.
Objects whose motion is not of interest form the environment.
The objects of interest interact with the environment, but those interactions can be considered external forces.

Interaction diagram

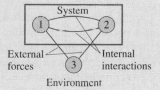

Applications

Acceleration constraints

Objects that are constrained to move together must have accelerations of equal magnitude: $a_A = a_B$. This must be expressed in terms of components, such as $a_{Ax} = -a_{By}$.

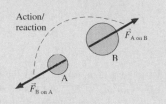

Strings and pulleys

The tension in a string or rope pulls in both directions. The tension is constant in a string if the string is:

- Massless, or

- In equilibrium

Objects connected by massless strings passing over massless, frictionless pulleys act *as if* they interact via an action/reaction pair of forces.

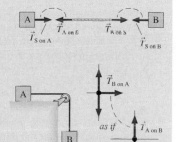

Terms and Notation

interaction	environment	propulsion	acceleration constraint
action/reaction pair	interaction diagram	Newton's third law	massless string approximation
system	external force		

CONCEPTUAL QUESTIONS

1. You find yourself in the middle of a frozen lake with a surface so slippery ($\mu_s = \mu_k = 0$) you cannot walk. However, you happen to have several rocks in your pocket. The ice is extremely hard. It cannot be chipped, and the rocks slip on it just as much as your feet do. Can you think of a way to get to shore? Use pictures, forces, and Newton's laws to explain your reasoning.

2. How do you paddle a canoe in the forward direction? Explain. Your explanation should include diagrams showing forces on the water and forces on the paddle.

3. How does a rocket take off? What is the upward force on it? Your explanation should include diagrams showing forces on the rocket and forces on the parcel of hot gas that was just expelled from the rocket's exhaust.

4. How do basketball players jump straight up into the air? Your explanation should include pictures showing forces on the player and forces on the ground.

5. A mosquito collides head-on with a car traveling 60 mph. Is the force of the mosquito on the car larger than, smaller than, or equal to the force of the car on the mosquito? Explain.

6. A mosquito collides head-on with a car traveling 60 mph. Is the magnitude of the mosquito's acceleration larger than, smaller than, or equal to the magnitude of the car's acceleration? Explain.

7. A small car is pushing a large truck. They are speeding up. Is the force of the truck on the car larger than, smaller than, or equal to the force of the car on the truck?

8. A very smart 3-year-old child is given a wagon for her birthday. She refuses to use it. "After all," she says, "Newton's third law says that no matter how hard I pull, the wagon will exert an equal but opposite force on me. So I will never be able to get it to move forward." What would you say to her in reply?

9. Teams red and blue are having a tug-of-war. According to Newton's third law, the force with which the red team pulls on the blue team exactly equals the force with which the blue team pulls on the red team. How can one team ever win? Explain.

10. Will hanging a magnet in front of the iron cart in **FIGURE Q7.10** make it go? Explain.

FIGURE Q7.10

11. **FIGURE Q7.11** shows two masses at rest. The string is massless and the pulley is frictionless. The spring scale reads in kg. What is the reading of the scale?

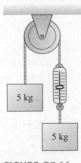

FIGURE Q7.11

12. **FIGURE Q7.12** shows two masses at rest. The string is massless and the pulley is frictionless. The spring scale reads in kg. What is the reading of the scale?

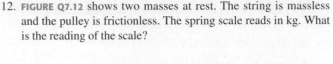

FIGURE Q7.12

13. The hand in **FIGURE Q7.13** is pushing on the back of block A. Blocks A and B, with $m_B > m_A$, are connected by a massless string and slide on a frictionless surface. Is the force of the string on B larger than, smaller than, or equal to the force of the hand on A? Explain.

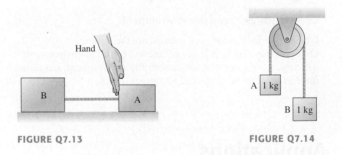

FIGURE Q7.13   **FIGURE Q7.14**

14. Blocks A and B in **FIGURE Q7.14** are connected by a massless string over a massless, frictionless pulley. The blocks have just been released from rest. Will the pulley rotate clockwise, counterclockwise, or not at all? Explain.

15. In case a in **FIGURE Q7.15**, block A is accelerated across a frictionless table by a hanging a 10 N weight (1.02 kg). In case b, block A is accelerated across a frictionless table by a steady 10 N tension in the string. The string is massless, and the pulley is massless and frictionless. Is A's acceleration in case b greater than, less than, or equal to its acceleration in case a? Explain.

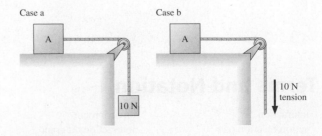

FIGURE Q7.15

EXERCISES AND PROBLEMS

Exercises

Section 7.2 Analyzing Interacting Objects

Exercises 1 through 6 describe a situation. For each:
  a. Draw an interaction diagram, following the steps of Tactics Box 7.1.
  b. Identify the "system" on your interaction diagram.
  c. Draw a free-body diagram for each object in the system. Use dashed lines to connect the members of an action/reaction pair.

1. | A weightlifter stands up from a squatting position while holding a heavy barbell across his shoulders.
2. | A soccer ball and a bowling ball have a head-on collision. Rolling friction is negligible.
3. | A mountain climber is using a rope to pull a bag of supplies up a 45° slope. The rope is not massless.
4. | A battery-powered toy car pushes a stuffed rabbit across the floor.
5. || Block A in FIGURE EX7.5 is heavier than block B and is sliding down the incline. All surfaces have friction. The rope is massless, and the massless pulley turns on frictionless bearings. The rope and the pulley are among the interacting objects, but you'll have to decide if they're part of the system.

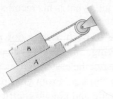

FIGURE EX7.5   **FIGURE EX7.6**

6. || Block A in FIGURE EX7.6 is sliding down the incline. The rope is massless, and the massless pulley turns on frictionless bearings, but the surface is not frictionless. The rope and the pulley are among the interacting objects, but you'll have to decide if they're part of the system.

Section 7.3 Newton's Third Law

7. | a. How much force does an 80 kg astronaut exert on his chair while sitting at rest on the launch pad?
     b. How much force does the astronaut exert on his chair while accelerating straight up at 10 m/s²?
8. || FIGURE EX7.8 shows two strong magnets on opposite sides of a small table. The long-range attractive force between the magnets keeps the lower magnet in place.

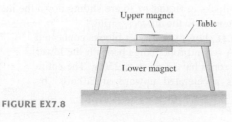

FIGURE EX7.8

  a. Draw an interaction diagram and draw free-body diagrams for both magnets and the table. Use dashed lines to connect the members of an action/reaction pair.
  b. Suppose the weight of the table is 20 N, the weight of each magnet is 2.0 N, and the magnetic force on the lower magnet is three times its weight. Find the magnitude of each of the forces shown on your free-body diagrams.
9. || A 1000 kg car pushes a 2000 kg truck that has a dead battery. When the driver steps on the accelerator, the drive wheels of the car push against the ground with a force of 4500 N. Rolling friction can be neglected.
  a. What is the magnitude of the force of the car on the truck?
  b. What is the magnitude of the force of the truck on the car?
10. || Blocks with masses of 1 kg, 2 kg, and 3 kg are lined up in a row on a frictionless table. All three are pushed forward by a 12 N force applied to the 1 kg block.
  a. How much force does the 2 kg block exert on the 3 kg block?
  b. How much force does the 2 kg block exert on the 1 kg block?
11. || A massive steel cable drags a 20 kg block across a horizontal, frictionless surface. A 100 N force applied to the cable causes the block to reach a speed of 4.0 m/s in a distance of 2.0 m. What is the mass of the cable?

Section 7.4 Ropes and Pulleys

12. | What is the tension in the rope of FIGURE EX7.12?

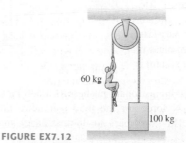

60 kg

100 kg

FIGURE EX7.12

13. | Jimmy has caught two fish in Yellow Creek. He has tied the line holding the 3.0 kg steelhead trout to the tail of the 1.5 kg carp. To show the fish to a friend, he lifts upward on the carp with a force of 60 N.
  a. Draw separate free-body diagrams for the trout and the carp. Label all forces, then use dashed lines to connect action/reaction pairs or forces that act as if they are a pair.
  b. Rank in order, from largest to smallest, the magnitudes of all the forces shown on your free-body diagrams. Explain your reasoning.
14. | A 2-m-long, 500 g rope pulls a 10 kg block of ice across a horizontal, frictionless surface. The block accelerates at 2.0 m/s². How much force pulls forward on (a) the ice, (b) the rope?

15. | The cable cars in San Francisco are pulled along their tracks by an underground steel cable that moves along at 9.5 mph. The cable is driven by large motors at a central power station and extends, via an intricate pulley arrangement, for several miles beneath the city streets. The length of a cable stretches by up to 100 ft during its lifetime. To keep the tension constant, the cable passes around a 1.5-m-diameter "tensioning pulley" that rolls back and forth on rails, as shown in **FIGURE EX7.15**. A 2000 kg block is attached to the tensioning pulley's cart, via a rope and pulley, and is suspended in a deep hole. What is the tension in the cable car's cable?

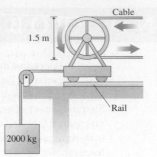

FIGURE EX7.15

16. | A 2.0 kg rope hangs from the ceiling. What is the tension at the midpoint of the rope?

17. || A mobile at the art museum has a 2.0 kg steel cat and a 4.0 kg steel dog suspended from a lightweight cable, as shown in **FIGURE EX7.17**. It is found that $\theta_1 = 20°$ when the center rope is adjusted to be perfectly horizontal. What are the tension and the angle of rope 3?

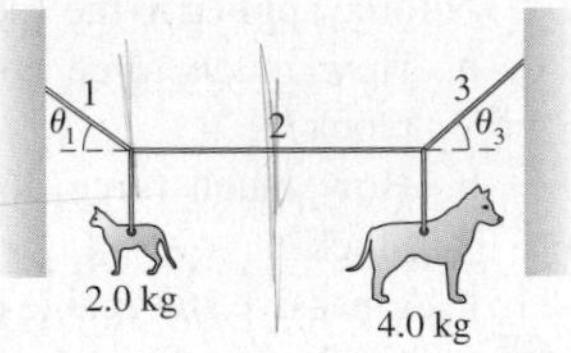

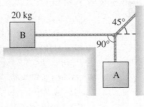

FIGURE EX7.17

Problems

18. || Block B in **FIGURE P7.18** rests on a surface for which the static and kinetic coefficients of friction are 0.60 and 0.40, respectively. The ropes are massless. What is the maximum mass of block A for which the system is in equilibrium?

FIGURE P7.18

19. || An 80 kg spacewalking astronaut pushes off a 640 kg satellite, exerting a 100 N force for the 0.50 s it takes him to straighten his arms. How far apart are the astronaut and the satellite after 1.0 min?

20. || A massive steel cable drags a 20 kg block across a horizontal, frictionless surface. A 100 N force applied to the cable causes the block to reach a speed of 4.0 m/s in 2.0 s. What is the difference in tension between the two ends of the cable?

21. || A 1.0-m-long massive steel cable drags a 20 kg block across a horizontal, frictionless surface. A 100 N force applied to the cable causes the block to travel 4.0 m in 2.0 s. Graph the tension in the cable as a function of position along the cable, starting at the point where the cable is attached to the block.

22. || A 3.0-m-long, 2.2 kg rope is suspended from the ceiling. Graph the tension in the rope as a function of position along the rope, starting from the bottom.

23. || The sled dog in **FIGURE P7.23** drags sleds A and B across the snow. The coefficient of friction between the sleds and the snow is 0.10. If the tension in rope 1 is 150 N, what is the tension in rope 2?

FIGURE P7.23

24. || While driving to work last year, I was holding my coffee mug in my left hand while changing the CD with my right hand. Then the cell phone rang, so I placed the mug on the flat part of my dashboard. Then, believe it or not, a deer ran out of the woods and on to the road right in front of me. Fortunately, my reaction time was zero, and I was able to stop from a speed of 20 m/s in a mere 50 m, just barely avoiding the deer. Later tests revealed that the static and kinetic coefficients of friction of the coffee mug on the dash are 0.50 and 0.30, respectively; the coffee and mug had a mass of 0.50 kg; and the mass of the deer was 120 kg. Did my coffee mug slide?

25. || a. Why can a car accelerate but a house cannot? Your explanation should be in terms of forces and their properties.
    b. Two-thirds of the weight of a 1500 kg car rests on the drive wheels. What is the maximum acceleration of this car on a concrete surface?

26. || A Federation starship $(2.0 \times 10^6 \text{ kg})$ uses its tractor beam to pull a shuttlecraft $(2.0 \times 10^4 \text{ kg})$ aboard from a distance of 10 km away. The tractor beam exerts a constant force of $4.0 \times 10^4 \text{ N}$ on the shuttlecraft. Both spacecraft are initially at rest. How far does the starship move as it pulls the shuttlecraft aboard?

27. || Bob, who has a mass of 75 kg, can throw a 500 g rock with a speed of 30 m/s. The distance through which his hand moves as he accelerates the rock from rest until he releases it is 1.0 m.
    a. What constant force must Bob exert on the rock to throw it with this speed?
    b. If Bob is standing on frictionless ice, what is his recoil speed after releasing the rock?

28. || You see the boy next door trying to push a crate down the sidewalk. He can barely keep it moving, and his feet occasionally slip. You start to wonder how heavy the crate is. You call to ask the boy his mass, and he replies "50 kg." From your recent physics class you estimate that the static and kinetic coefficients of friction are 0.8 and 0.4 for the boy's shoes, and 0.5 and 0.2 for the crate. Estimate the mass of the crate.

29. || Two packages at UPS start sliding down the 20° ramp shown in **FIGURE P7.29**. Package A has a mass of 5.0 kg and a coefficient of friction of 0.20. Package B has a mass of 10 kg and a coefficient of friction of 0.15. How long does it take package A to reach the bottom?

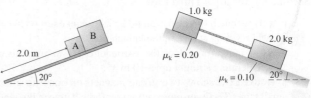

FIGURE P7.29   **FIGURE P7.30**

30. || The two blocks in **FIGURE P7.30** are sliding down the incline. What is the tension in the massless string?

31. || **FIGURE P7.31** shows two 1.0 kg blocks connected by a rope. A second rope hangs beneath the lower block. Both ropes have a mass of 250 g. The entire assembly is accelerated upward at 3.0 m/s² by force $\vec{F}$.
    a. What is F?
    b. What is the tension at the top end of rope 1?
    c. What is the tension at the bottom end of rope 1?
    d. What is the tension at the top end of rope 2?

FIGURE P7.31

32. ‖ The 1.0 kg block in **FIGURE P7.32** is tied to the wall with a rope. It sits on top of the 2.0 kg block. The lower block is pulled to the right with a tension force of 20 N. The coefficient of kinetic friction at both the lower and upper surfaces of the 2.0 kg block is $\mu_k = 0.40$.
    a. What is the tension in the rope holding the 1.0 kg block to the wall?
    b. What is the acceleration of the 2.0 kg block?

FIGURE P7.32   **FIGURE P7.33**

33. ‖ The coefficient of static friction is 0.60 between the two blocks in **FIGURE P7.33**. The coefficient of kinetic friction between the lower block and the floor is 0.20. Force $\vec{F}$ causes both blocks to cross a distance of 5.0 m, starting from rest. What is the least amount of time in which this motion can be completed without the top block sliding on the lower block?

34. ‖‖ The lower block in **FIGURE P7.34** is pulled on by a rope with a tension force of 20 N. The coefficient of kinetic friction between the lower block and the surface is 0.30. The coefficient of kinetic friction between the lower block and the upper block is also 0.30. What is the acceleration of the 2.0 kg block?

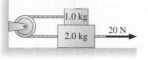

FIGURE P7.34

35. ‖‖ A rope attached to a 20 kg wood sled pulls the sled up a 20° snow-covered hill. A 10 kg wood box rides on top of the sled. If the tension in the rope steadily increases, at what value of the tension does the box slip?

36. ‖ The 100 kg block in **FIGURE P7.36** takes 6.0 s to reach the floor after being released from rest. What is the mass of the block on the left?

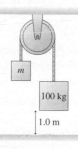

FIGURE P7.36   **FIGURE P7.37**

37. ‖ The 10.2 kg block in **FIGURE P7.37** is held in place by the massless rope passing over two massless, frictionless pulleys. Find the tensions T_1 to T_5 and the magnitude of force $\vec{F}$.

38. ‖ The coefficient of kinetic friction between the 2.0 kg block in **FIGURE P7.38** and the table is 0.30. What is the acceleration of the 2.0 kg block?

FIGURE P7.38   **FIGURE P7.39**

39. ‖ **FIGURE P7.39** shows a block of mass m resting on a 20° slope. The block has coefficients of friction $\mu_s = 0.80$ and $\mu_k = 0.50$ with the surface. It is connected via a massless string over a massless, frictionless pulley to a hanging block of mass 2.0 kg.
    a. What is the minimum mass m that will stick and not slip?
    b. If this minimum mass is nudged ever so slightly, it will start being pulled up the incline. What acceleration will it have?

40. ‖ A 4.0 kg box is on a frictionless 35° slope and is connected via a massless string over a massless, frictionless pulley to a hanging 2.0 kg weight. The picture for this situation is similar to Figure P7.39.
    a. What is the tension in the string if the 4.0 kg box is *held* in place, so that it cannot move?
    b. If the box is then released, which way will it move on the slope?
    c. What is the tension in the string once the box begins to move?

41. ‖ The 1.0 kg physics book in **FIGURE P7.41** is connected by a string to a 500 g coffee cup. The book is given a push up the slope and released with a speed of 3.0 m/s. The coefficients of friction are $\mu_s = 0.50$ and $\mu_k = 0.20$.
    a. How far does the book slide?
    b. At the highest point, does the book stick to the slope, or does it slide back down?

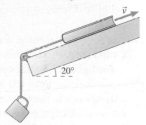

FIGURE P7.41

42. ‖ The 2000 kg cable car shown in **FIGURE P7.42** descends a 200-m-high hill. In addition to its brakes, the cable car controls its speed by pulling an 1800 kg counterweight up the other side of the hill. The rolling friction of both the cable car and the counterweight are negligible.

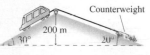

FIGURE P7.42

    a. How much braking force does the cable car need to descend at constant speed?
    b. One day the brakes fail just as the cable car leaves the top on its downward journey. What is the runaway car's speed at the bottom of the hill?

43. ‖ The century-old *ascensores* in Valparaiso, Chile, are small cable cars that go up and down the steep hillsides. As **FIGURE P7.43** shows, one car ascends as the other descends. The cars use a two-cable arrangement to compensate for friction; one cable passing around a large pulley connects the cars, the second is pulled by a small motor. Suppose the mass of both cars (with passengers) is 1500 kg, the coefficient of rolling friction is 0.020, and the cars move at constant speed. What is the tension in the (a) the connecting cable and (b) the cable to the motor?

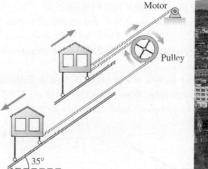

FIGURE P7.43

44. ‖ A house painter uses the chair and pulley arrangement of FIGURE P7.44 to lift himself up the side of a house. The painter's mass is 70 kg and the chair's mass is 10 kg. With what force must he pull down on the rope in order to accelerate upward at 0.20 m/s^2?

FIGURE P7.44

45. ‖‖ A 70 kg tightrope walker stands at the center of a rope. The rope supports are 10 m apart and the rope sags 10° at each end. The tightrope walker crouches down, then leaps straight up with an acceleration of 8.0 m/s^2 to catch a passing trapeze. What is the tension in the rope as he jumps?

46. ‖ Find an expression for the magnitude of the horizontal force F in FIGURE P7.46 for which m_1 does not slip either up or down along the wedge. All surfaces are frictionless.

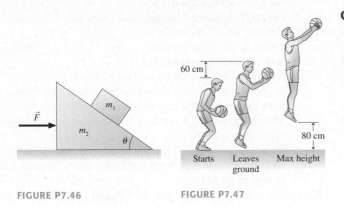

FIGURE P7.46   **FIGURE P7.47**

47. ‖ A 100 kg basketball player can leap straight up in the air to a height of 80 cm, as shown in FIGURE P7.47. You can understand how by analyzing the situation as follows:
    a. The player bends his legs until the upper part of his body has dropped by 60 cm, then he begins his jump. Draw separate free-body diagrams for the player and for the floor *as* he is jumping, but before his feet leave the ground.
    b. Is there a net force on the player as he jumps (before his feet leave the ground)? How can that be? Explain.
    c. With what speed must the player leave the ground to reach a height of 80 cm?
    d. What was his acceleration, assumed to be constant, as he jumped?
    e. Suppose the player jumps while standing on a bathroom scale that reads in newtons. What does the scale read before he jumps, as he is jumping, and after his feet leave the ground?

Problems 48 and 49 show the free-body diagrams of two interacting systems. For each of these, you are to
    a. Write a realistic problem for which these are the correct free-body diagrams. Be sure that the answer your problem requests is consistent with the diagrams shown.
    b. Finish the solution of the problem.

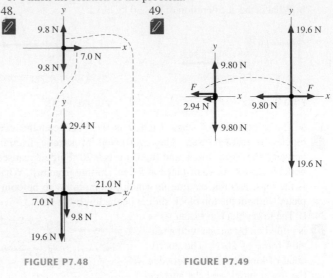

FIGURE P7.48   **FIGURE P7.49**

Challenge Problems

50. A 100 g ball of clay is thrown horizontally with a speed of 10 m/s toward a 900 g block resting on a frictionless surface. It hits the block and sticks. The clay exerts a constant force on the block during the 10 ms it takes the clay to come to rest relative to the block. After 10 ms, the block and the clay are sliding along the surface as a single system.
    a. What is their speed after the collision?
    b. What is the force of the clay on the block during the collision?
    c. What is the force of the block on the clay?

    NOTE ▶ This problem can be worked using the conservation laws you will be learning in the next few chapters. However, here you're asked to solve the problem using Newton's laws. ◄

51. In FIGURE CP7.51, find an expression for the acceleration of m_1. Assume the table is frictionless.
    Hint: Think carefully about the acceleration constraint.

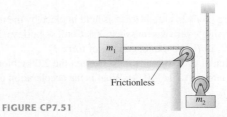

FIGURE CP7.51

52. What is the acceleration of the 2.0 kg block in FIGURE CP7.52 across the frictionless table?

    Hint: Think carefully about the acceleration constraint.

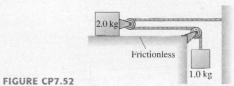

FIGURE CP7.52

53. FIGURE CP7.53 shows a 200 g hamster sitting on an 800 g wedge-shaped block. The block, in turn, rests on a spring scale.

    a. Initially, static friction is sufficient to keep the hamster from moving. In this case, the hamster and the block are effectively a single 1000 g mass and the scale should read 9.8 N. Show that this is the case by treating the hamster and the block as *separate* objects and analyzing the forces.

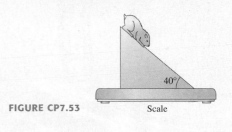

FIGURE CP7.53   Scale

b. An extra-fine lubricating oil having $\mu_s = \mu_k = 0$ is sprayed on the top surface of the block, causing the hamster to slide down. Friction between the block and the scale is large enough that the block does *not* slip on the scale. What does the scale read as the hamster slides down?

54. FIGURE CP7.54 shows three hanging masses connected by massless strings over two massless, frictionless pulleys.

    a. Find the acceleration constraint for this system. It is a single equation relating a_{1y}, a_{2y}, and a_{3y}.

    Hint: y_A isn't constant.

    b. Find an expression for the tension in string A.

    Hint: You should be able to write four second-law equations. These, plus the acceleration constraint, are five equations in five unknowns.

    c. Suppose: $m_1 = 2.5$ kg, $m_2 = 1.5$ kg, and $m_3 = 4.0$ kg. Find the acceleration of each.

    d. The 4.0 kg mass would appear to be in equilibrium. Explain why it accelerates.

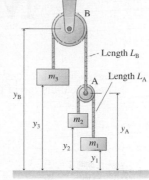

FIGURE CP7.54

STOP TO THINK ANSWERS

Stop to Think 7.1: The gravitational force and the tension force are incorrectly identified as an action/reaction pair. Force $\vec{T}_{\text{L on F}}$ should be paired with force $\vec{T}_{\text{F on L}}$. Gravity is the pull of the entire earth, so $(\vec{F}_G)_F$ should be paired with a force pulling up on the entire earth.

Stop to Think 7.2: c. Newton's third law says that the force of A on B is *equal* and opposite to the force of B on A. This is always true. The speed of the objects isn't relevant.

Stop to Think 7.3: b. $F_{\text{B on H}} = F_{\text{H on B}}$ and $F_{\text{A on B}} = F_{\text{B on A}}$ because these are action/reaction pairs. Box B is slowing down and therefore must have a net force to the left. So from Newton's second law we also know that $F_{\text{H on B}} > F_{\text{A on B}}$.

Stop to Think 7.4: Equal to. Each block is hanging in equilibrium, with no net force, so the upward tension force is mg.

Stop to Think 7.5: Less than. Block B is *accelerating* downward, so the net force on B must point down. The only forces acting on B are the tension and gravity, so $T_{\text{S on B}} < (F_G)_B$.

Stop to Think 7.6: c. Newton's third law says that the force of A on B is *equal* and opposite to the force of B on A. This is always true. The mass of the objects isn't relevant.

Dynamics II: Motion in a Plane

Why doesn't the roller coaster fall off the track at the top of the loop?

▶ **Looking Ahead**

The goal of Chapter 8 is to learn to solve problems about motion in a plane. In this chapter you will learn to:

■ Understand dynamics in two dimensions.

■ Use Newton's laws to analyze circular motion.

■ Understand circular orbits of satellites and planets.

■ Think about weight and fictitious forces for objects in circular motion.

◀ **Looking Back**

This chapter extends ideas of one-dimensional dynamics into two dimensions. Please review:

■ Chapter 4 Kinematics of planar and circular motion.

■ Sections 6.1 and 6.2 Using Newton's first and second laws.

■ Section 6.3 Gravity and weight.

A roller coaster doing a loop-the-loop is a dramatic example of circular motion. But why doesn't the car fall off the track when it's upside down at the top of the loop? To answer this question, we must study how objects move in circles. We have limited ourselves in Chapters 6 and 7 to motion along a straight line, but motion in the real world is often in two or three dimensions. A car turning a corner, a planet orbiting the sun, and the roller coaster in the photograph are examples of two-dimensional motion in a plane. Restricting ourselves to one dimension has allowed us to concentrate on basic physics principles, but the time has come to broaden our horizons.

Newton's laws are "laws of nature." They describe all motion, not just motion along a straight line. This chapter will extend the application of Newton's laws to new situations. We'll begin with motion in which the x- and y-components of the acceleration are independent of each other. Projectile motion is an important example. We'll then turn to circular motion, where the components are *not* independent.

8.1 Dynamics in Two Dimensions

Newton's second law, $\vec{a} = \vec{F}_{net}/m$, determines an object's acceleration. It makes no distinction between linear motion and planar motion. In general, the x- and y-components of the acceleration vector are given by

$$a_x = \frac{(F_{net})_x}{m} \quad \text{and} \quad a_y = \frac{(F_{net})_y}{m} \tag{8.1}$$

For the straight-line motion of Chapters 6 and 7, we were able to choose a coordinate system where either a_x or a_y was zero. This simplified the analysis, but such a choice is not always possible.

Suppose the x- and y-components of acceleration are *independent* of each other. That is, a_x does not depend on either y or v_y, and similarly a_y does not depend on x or v_x. Then Problem-Solving Strategy 6.2 for dynamics problems, on page 155, is still valid. As a quick review, you should

1. Draw a pictorial representation—a motion diagram (if needed) and a free-body diagram.
2. Use Newton's second law in component form:

$$(F_{net})_x = \sum F_x = ma_x \quad \text{and} \quad (F_{net})_y = \sum F_y = ma_y$$

The force components (including proper signs) are found from the free-body diagram.
3. Solve for the acceleration. If the acceleration is constant, use the two-dimensional kinematic equations of Chapter 4 to find velocities and positions:

$$x_f = x_i + v_{ix}\Delta t + \tfrac{1}{2}a_x(\Delta t)^2 \qquad y_f = y_i + v_{iy}\Delta t + \tfrac{1}{2}a_y(\Delta t)^2$$

$$v_{fx} = v_{ix} + a_x\Delta t \qquad v_{fy} = v_{iy} + a_y\Delta t$$

EXAMPLE 8.1 Rocketing in the wind

A small rocket for gathering weather data has a mass of 30 kg and generates 1500 N of thrust. On a windy day, the wind exerts a 20 N horizontal force on the rocket. If the rocket is launched straight up, what is the shape of its trajectory, and by how much has it been deflected sideways when it reaches a height of 1.0 km? Because the rocket goes much higher than this, assume there's no significant mass loss during the first 1.0 km of flight.

MODEL Model the rocket as a particle. We need to find the *function $y(x)$* describing the curve the rocket follows. Because rockets have pointy, aerodynamic shapes, we'll assume no vertical air resistance.

VISUALIZE FIGURE 8.1 shows a pictorial representation. We've chosen a coordinate system with a vertical y-axis. Three forces act on the rocket: two vertical (we'll assume the wind doesn't cause the rocket to rotate, which would change the thrust angle) and one horizontal. The wind force is essentially drag (the rocket is moving sideways relative to the wind), so we've labeled it $\vec{D}$.

FIGURE 8.1 Pictorial representation of the rocket launch.

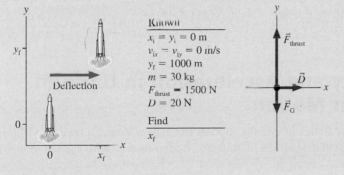

Known
$x_i = y_i = 0$ m
$v_{ix} = v_{iy} = 0$ m/s
$y_f = 1000$ m
$m = 30$ kg
$F_{thrust} = 1500$ N
$D = 20$ N

Find
x_f

SOLVE The vertical and horizontal forces are independent of each other, so we can follow the problem-solving strategy summarized above. Newton's second law is

$$a_x = \frac{(F_{net})_x}{m} = \frac{D}{m}$$

$$a_y = \frac{(F_{net})_y}{m} = \frac{F_{thrust} - mg}{m}$$

Both accelerations are constant, so we can use the kinematic equations to find

$$x = \tfrac{1}{2}a_x(\Delta t)^2 = \frac{D}{2m}(\Delta t)^2$$

$$y = \tfrac{1}{2}a_y(\Delta t)^2 = \frac{F_{thrust} - mg}{2m}(\Delta t)^2$$

where we used the fact that all initial positions and velocities are zero. From the x-equation, $(\Delta t)^2 = 2mx/D$. Substituting this into the y-equation, we find

$$y(x) = \frac{F_{thrust} - mg}{D}x$$

This is the equation of the rocket's trajectory. It is a linear equation. Somewhat surprisingly, given that the rocket has both vertical and horizontal accelerations, its trajectory is a *straight line*. We can rearrange this result to find the deflection at height y:

$$x = \frac{D}{F_{thrust} - mg}y$$

From the data provided, we can calculate a deflection of 17 m at a height of 1000 m.

ASSESS The solution depended on the fact that the time parameter Δt is the *same* for both components of the motion.

When drag is included, the angle for maximum range of a projectile depends both on its size and mass and on the initial speed. The optimum angle is roughly 35° for baseballs. The flight of a golf ball is even more complex because the dimples and the high rate of spin greatly affect its aerodynamics. Professional golfers achieve their maximum distance at launch angles of barely 15°.

FIGURE 8.2 Motion of a projectile with drag.

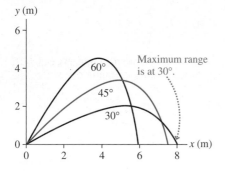

Projectile Motion

Chapter 4 developed the kinematics of projectile motion. The important result is that—in the absence of air resistance—a projectile follows a parabolic trajectory. We arrived at that conclusion simply by asserting a downward acceleration $a_y = -g$ with no horizontal acceleration. Now we can use Newton's laws to justify that assertion.

We found in Chapter 6 that the gravitational force on an object near the surface of a planet is $\vec{F}_G = (mg, \text{down})$. If we choose a coordinate system with a vertical y-axis, then

$$\vec{F}_G = -mg\hat{\jmath} \tag{8.2}$$

Consequently, from Newton's second law, the acceleration is

$$a_x = \frac{(F_G)_x}{m} = 0$$
$$a_y = \frac{(F_G)_y}{m} = -g \tag{8.3}$$

These were the accelerations of Chapter 4 that led to the parabolic motion of a drag-free projectile. The vertical motion is free fall, while the horizontal motion is one of constant velocity.

However, the situation is quite different for a low-mass projectile, where the effects of drag are too large to ignore. From Chapter 6, the drag on a projectile is $\vec{D} \approx (\frac{1}{4}Av^2$, direction opposite the motion), where A is the cross-section area. We'll leave it as a homework problem for you to show that the acceleration of a projectile subject to drag is

$$a_x = -\frac{A}{4m}v_x\sqrt{v_x^2 + v_y^2}$$
$$a_y = -g - \frac{A}{4m}v_y\sqrt{v_x^2 + v_y^2} \tag{8.4}$$

Here the components of acceleration are *not* independent of each other because a_x depends on v_y and vice versa. It turns out that these two equations cannot be solved exactly for the trajectory, but they can be solved numerically. **FIGURE 8.2** shows the numerical solution for the motion of a 5 g plastic ball that's been hit with an initial speed of 25 m/s. It doesn't travel very far (the maximum distance would be more than 60 m in a vacuum), and the maximum range is no longer reached for a launch angle of 45°. In this case, maximum distance is achieved by hitting the ball at a 30° angle. A 60° launch angle, which gives the same distance as 30° in vacuum, travels only ≈75% as far. Notice that the trajectories are not at all parabolic.

STOP TO THINK 8.1   This acceleration will cause the particle to

a. Speed up and curve upward.   b. Speed up and curve downward.
c. Slow down and curve upward.   d. Slow down and curve downward.
e. Move to the right and down.   f. Reverse direction.

8.2 Velocity and Acceleration in Uniform Circular Motion

We studied the mathematics of circular motion in Chapter 4, and a review is *highly* recommended. Recall that a particle in uniform circular motion with angular velocity ω has speed $v = \omega r$ and centripetal acceleration

$$\vec{a} = \left(\frac{v^2}{r}, \text{toward center of circle}\right) = (\omega^2 r, \text{toward center of circle}) \tag{8.5}$$

Now we're ready to study *dynamics*—how forces *cause* circular motion.

The *xy*-coordinate system we've been using for linear motion and projectile motion is not the best coordinate system for circular dynamics. FIGURE 8.3 shows a circular trajectory and the plane in which the circle lies. Let's establish a coordinate system with its origin at the point where the particle is located. The axes are defined as follows:

- The *r*-axis (radial axis) points *from* the particle *toward* the center of the circle.
- The *t*-axis (tangential axis) is tangent to the circle, pointing in the ccw direction.
- The *z*-axis is perpendicular to the plane of motion.

The three axes of this *rtz*-coordinate system are mutually perpendicular, just like the axes of the familiar *xyz*-coordinate system. Notice how the axes move with the particle so that the *r*-axis always points to the center of the circle. It will take a little getting used to, but you will soon see that circular-motion problems are most easily described in these coordinates.

FIGURE 8.4 shows a vector $\vec{A}$ in the plane of motion. We can decompose $\vec{A}$ into its radial and tangential components:

$$A_r = A \cos\phi$$

$$A_t = A \sin\phi$$

where ϕ is the angle with the *r*-axis. The positive *r*-direction, by definition, is toward the center of the circle, so the radial component A_r has a positive value. $\vec{A}$ lies in the plane of motion, so its perpendicular component is $A_z = 0$.

> **NOTE** ▶ In Chapter 4, we noted that the acceleration vector $\vec{a}$ can be decomposed into a component $\vec{a}_\parallel$ parallel to the motion and a component $\vec{a}_\perp$ perpendicular to the motion. That idea is the basis for the *rtz*-coordinate system. Because the velocity vector $\vec{v}$ is tangent to the circle, the tangential component A_t of vector $\vec{A}$ is the component of $\vec{A}$ parallel to the motion. The radial component A_r is the component perpendicular to the motion. ◀

For a particle in uniform circular motion, such as the one in FIGURE 8.5, the velocity vector $\vec{v}$ is tangent to the circle. In other words, **the velocity vector has only a tangential component v_t.** The radial and perpendicular components of $\vec{v}$ are always zero.

The tangential velocity component v_t is the rate ds/dt at which the particle moves *around* the circle, where *s* is the arc length measured from the positive *x*-axis. From Chapter 4, the arc length is $s = r\theta$. Taking the derivative, we find

$$v_t = \frac{ds}{dt} = r\frac{d\theta}{dt}$$

But $d\theta/dt$ is the angular velocity ω. Thus the velocity in *rtz*-coordinates is

$$v_r = 0$$
$$v_t = \omega r \quad \text{(with } \omega \text{ in rad/s)} \tag{8.6}$$
$$v_z = 0$$

> **NOTE** ▶ ω is restricted to rad/s because the relationship $s = r\theta$ is the definition of radians. While it may be convenient in some problems to measure ω in rev/s or rpm, you must convert to SI units of rad/s before using Equation 8.6. ◀

We defined ω to be positive for a counterclockwise (ccw) rotation; hence the tangential velocity v_t is positive for ccw motion, negative for cw motion. Because v_t is the only nonzero component of $\vec{v}$, the particle's speed is $v = |v_t| = |\omega|r$. We'll sometimes write this as $v = \omega r$ if there's no ambiguity about the sign of ω.

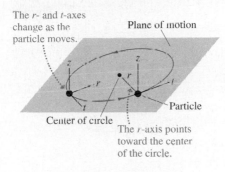

FIGURE 8.3 The *rtz*-coordinate system.

The *r*- and *t*-axes change as the particle moves.

Plane of motion

Particle

Center of circle

The *r*-axis points toward the center of the circle.

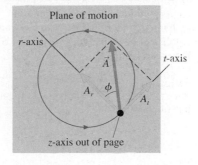

FIGURE 8.4 Vector $\vec{A}$ can be decomposed into radial and tangential components.

Plane of motion

r-axis

t-axis

$\vec{A}$

A_r ϕ A_t

z-axis out of page

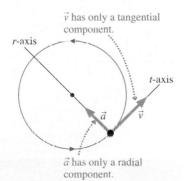

FIGURE 8.5 The velocity and acceleration vectors in the *rtz*-coordinate system.

$\vec{v}$ has only a tangential component.

r-axis

t-axis

$\vec{a}$ $\vec{v}$

$\vec{a}$ has only a radial component.

4.1 Act|v Physics

The acceleration of uniform circular motion, seen in Figure 8.5 and given by Equation 8.5, points to the center of the circle. Thus **the acceleration vector has only a radial component** a_r. This acceleration is conveniently written in the *rtz*-coordinate system as

$$a_r = \frac{v^2}{r} = \omega^2 r$$

$$a_t = 0 \qquad\qquad (8.7)$$

$$a_z = 0$$

With $\vec{v}$ and $\vec{a}$ each having only one nonzero component, you can begin to see the advantages of the *rtz*-coordinate system. For convenience, we'll often refer to the component a_r as "the centripetal acceleration."

EXAMPLE 8.2 The acceleration of an atomic electron

We will later study the Bohr atom. This is a simple model of the hydrogen atom in which an electron orbits a proton at a radius of 5.29×10^{-11} m with a period of 1.52×10^{-16} s. What is the electron's centripetal acceleration?

SOLVE From Chapter 4, the electron's speed is

$$v = \frac{2\pi r}{T} = \frac{2\pi(5.29 \times 10^{-11} \text{ m})}{1.52 \times 10^{-16} \text{ s}} = 2.19 \times 10^6 \text{ m/s}$$

Then from Equations 8.7,

$$a_r = \frac{v^2}{r} = \frac{(2.19 \times 10^6 \text{ m/s})^2}{5.29 \times 10^{-11} \text{ m}} = 9.07 \times 10^{22} \text{ m/s}^2$$

ASSESS This example demonstrates the unbelievably enormous accelerations that take place at the atomic level. It should then come as no surprise that atomic particles may behave in ways that our intuition, trained by accelerations of only a few m/s², cannot easily grasp.

STOP TO THINK 8.2 Rank in order, from largest to smallest, the centripetal accelerations $(a_r)_a$ to $(a_r)_e$ of particles a to e.

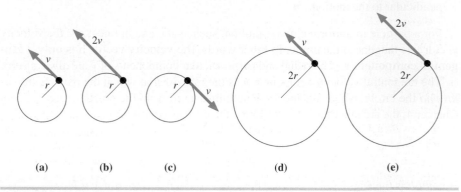

(a) (b) (c) (d) (e)

Highway and racetrack curves are banked to allow the normal force of the road to provide the centripetal acceleration of the turn.

8.3 Dynamics of Uniform Circular Motion

A particle in uniform circular motion is clearly not traveling at constant velocity in a straight line. Consequently, according to Newton's first law, the particle *must* have a net force acting on it. We've already determined the acceleration of a particle in uniform circular motion—the centripetal acceleration of Equation 8.5. Newton's second law tells us exactly how much net force is needed to cause this acceleration:

$$\vec{F}_{net} = m\vec{a} = \left(\frac{mv^2}{r}, \text{ toward center of circle}\right) \qquad (8.8)$$

In other words, a particle of mass m moving at constant speed v around a circle of radius r must have a net force of magnitude mv^2/r pointing toward the center of the circle. Without such a force, the particle would move off in a straight line tangent to the circle.

FIGURE 8.6 shows the net force $\vec{F}_{net}$ acting on a particle as it undergoes uniform circular motion. You can see that $\vec{F}_{net}$ **points along the radial axis of the** rtz-**coordinate system, toward the center of the circle.** The tangential and perpendicular components of $\vec{F}_{net}$ are zero.

NOTE ▶ The force described by Equation 8.8 is not a *new* force. Our rules for identifying forces have not changed. What we are saying is that a particle moves with uniform circular motion *if and only if* a net force always points toward the center of the circle. The force itself must have an identifiable agent and will be one of our familiar forces, such as tension, friction, or the normal force. Equation 8.8 simply tells us how the force needs to act—how strongly and in which direction—to cause the particle to move with speed v in a circle of radius r. ◀

The usefulness of the rtz-coordinate system becomes apparent when we write Newton's second law, Equation 8.8, in terms of the r-, t-, and z-components:

$$(F_{net})_r = \sum F_r = ma_r = \frac{mv^2}{r} = m\omega^2 r$$

$$(F_{net})_t = \sum F_t = ma_t = 0 \qquad (8.9)$$

$$(F_{net})_z = \sum F_z = ma_z = 0$$

Notice that we've used our explicit knowledge of the acceleration, as given in Equation 8.7, to write the right-hand sides of these equations. **For uniform circular motion, the sum of the forces along the t-axis and along the z-axis *must* equal zero, and the sum of the forces along the r-axis *must* equal ma_r where a_r is the centripetal acceleration.**

A few examples will clarify these ideas and show how some of the forces you've come to know can be involved in circular motion.

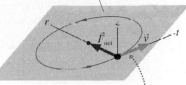

FIGURE 8.6 The net force points in the radial direction, toward the center of the circle.

Plane of motion

Without the force, the particle would continue moving in the direction of $\vec{v}$.

EXAMPLE 8.3 Spinning in a circle

An energetic father places his 20 kg child on a 5.0 kg cart to which a 2.0-m-long rope is attached. He then holds the end of the rope and spins the cart and child around in a circle, keeping the rope parallel to the ground. If the tension in the rope is 100 N, how many revolutions per minute (rpm) does the cart make? Rolling friction between the cart's wheels and the ground is negligible.

MODEL Model the child in the cart as a particle in uniform circular motion.

VISUALIZE FIGURE 8.7 shows the pictorial representation. A circular-motion problem usually does not have starting and ending points like a projectile problem, so numerical subscripts such as x_1 or y_2

are usually not needed. Here we need to define the cart's speed v and the radius r of the circle. Further, a motion diagram is not needed for uniform circular motion because we already know the acceleration $\vec{a}$ points to the center of the circle.

The essential part of the pictorial representation is the free-body diagram. **For uniform circular motion we'll draw the free-body diagram in the rz-plane, looking at the edge of the circle, because this is the plane of the forces.** The contact forces acting on the cart are the normal force of the ground and the tension force of the rope. The normal force is perpendicular to the plane of the motion and thus in the z-direction. The direction of $\vec{T}$ is determined by the statement that the rope is parallel

FIGURE 8.7 Pictorial representation of a cart spinning in a circle.

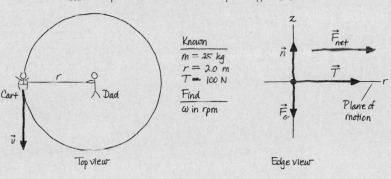

Known
$m = 25 \text{ kg}$
$r = 2.0 \text{ m}$
$T = 100 \text{ N}$

Find
ω in rpm

Top view

Edge view

Continued

to the ground. In addition, there is the long-range gravitational force $\vec{F}_G$.

SOLVE We defined the r-axis to point toward the center of the circle, so $\vec{T}$ points in the positive r-direction and has r-component $T_r = T$. Newton's second law, using the rtz-components of Equations 8.9, is

$$\sum F_r = T = \frac{mv^2}{r}$$

$$\sum F_z = n - mg = 0$$

We've taken the r- and z-components of the forces directly from the free-body diagram, as you learned to do in Chapter 6. Then we've *explicitly* equated the sums to $a_r = v^2/r$ and $a_z = 0$. This is the basic strategy for all uniform circular-motion problems. From the z-equation we can find that $n = mg$. This would be useful if we needed to determine a friction force, but it's not needed in this problem. From the r-equation, the speed of the cart is

$$v = \sqrt{\frac{rT}{m}} = \sqrt{\frac{(2.0 \text{ m})(100 \text{ N})}{25 \text{ kg}}} = 2.83 \text{ m/s}$$

The cart's angular velocity is then found from Equation 8.6:

$$\omega = \frac{v_t}{r} = \frac{v}{r} = \frac{2.83 \text{ m/s}}{2.0 \text{ m}} = 1.41 \text{ rad/s}$$

This is another case where we inserted the radian unit because ω is specifically an *angular* velocity. Finally, we need to convert ω to rpm:

$$\omega = \frac{1.41 \text{ rad}}{1 \text{ s}} \times \frac{1 \text{ rev}}{2\pi \text{ rad}} \times \frac{60 \text{ s}}{1 \text{ min}} = 14 \text{ rpm}$$

ASSESS 14 rpm corresponds to a period $T = 4.3$ s. This result is reasonable.

This has been a fairly typical circular-motion problem. You might want to think about how the solution would change if the rope was *not* parallel to the ground.

EXAMPLE 8.4 **Turning the corner I**

What is the maximum speed with which a 1500 kg car can make a left turn around a curve of radius 50 m on a level (unbanked) road without sliding?

MODEL Although the car turns only a quarter of a circle, we can model the car as a particle in uniform circular motion as it goes around the turn. Assume that rolling friction is negligible.

VISUALIZE FIGURE 8.8 shows the pictorial representation. The car moves along a circular arc at constant speed for the quarter-circle necessary to complete the turn. The motion before and after the turn is not relevant to the problem. The more interesting issue is *how* a car turns a corner. What force or forces cause the direction of the velocity vector to change? Imagine you are driving a car on a completely frictionless road, such as a very icy road. You would not be able to turn a corner. Turning the steering wheel would be of no use; the car would slide straight ahead, in accordance with both Newton's first law and the experience of anyone who has ever driven on ice! So it must be *friction* that somehow allows the car to turn.

Figure 8.8 shows the top view of a tire as it turns a corner. If the road surface were frictionless, the tire would slide straight ahead. The force that prevents an object from sliding across a surface is *static friction*. Static friction $\vec{f}_s$ pushes *sideways* on the tire,

toward the center of the circle. How do we know the direction is sideways? If $\vec{f}_s$ had a component either parallel to $\vec{v}$ or opposite to $\vec{v}$, it would cause the car to speed up or slow down. Because the car changes direction but not speed, static friction must be perpendicular to $\vec{v}$. $\vec{f}_s$ causes the centripetal acceleration of circular motion around the curve, and thus the free-body diagram, drawn from behind the car, shows the static friction force pointing toward the center of the circle.

SOLVE Because the static friction force has a maximum value, there will be a maximum speed with which a car can turn without sliding. The maximum speed is reached when the static friction force reaches its maximum $f_{s\,max} = \mu_s n$. If the car enters the curve at a speed higher than the maximum, static friction will not be large enough to provide the necessary centripetal acceleration and the car will slide.

The static friction force points in the positive r-direction, so its radial component is simply the magnitude of the vector: $(f_s)_r = f_s$. Newton's second law in the rtz-coordinate system is

$$\sum F_r = f_s = \frac{mv^2}{r}$$

$$\sum F_z = n - mg = 0$$

FIGURE 8.8 Pictorial representation of a car turning a corner.

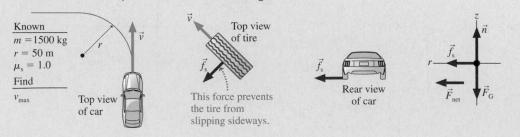

Known
$m = 1500$ kg
$r = 50$ m
$\mu_s = 1.0$
Find
v_{max}

Top view of car

$\vec{v}$

Top view of tire

$\vec{f}_s$

This force prevents the tire from slipping sideways.

$\vec{f}_s$

Rear view of car

$\vec{n}$

$\vec{f}_s$

$\vec{F}_{net}$ $\vec{F}_G$

The only difference from Example 8.3 is that the tension force toward the center has been replaced by a static friction force toward the center. From the radial equation, the speed is

$$v = \sqrt{\frac{rf_s}{m}}$$

The speed will be a maximum when f_s reaches its maximum value:

$$f_s = f_{s\,max} = \mu_s n = \mu_s mg$$

where we used $n = mg$ from the z-equation. At that point,

$$v_{max} = \sqrt{\frac{rf_{s\,max}}{m}} = \sqrt{\mu_s rg}$$

$$= \sqrt{(1.0)(50\text{ m})(9.80\text{ m/s}^2)} = 22\text{ m/s}$$

where we found $\mu_s = 1.0$ in Table 6.1.

ASSESS 22 m/s $\approx$ 45 mph, a reasonable answer for how fast a car can take an unbanked curve. Notice that the car's mass canceled out and that the final equation for v_{max} is quite simple. This is another example of why it pays to work algebraically until the very end.

Because μ_s depends on road conditions, the maximum safe speed through turns can vary dramatically. Wet roads, in particular, lower the value of μ_s and thus lower the speed of turns. A car that handles normally while driving straight ahead on a wet road can suddenly slide out of control when turning a corner. Icy conditions are even worse. The corner you turn every day at 45 mph will require a speed of no more than 15 mph if the coefficient of static friction drops to 0.1.

Activ Physics 4.5

EXAMPLE 8.5 Turning the corner II

A highway curve of radius 70 m is banked at a 15° angle. At what speed v_0 can a car take this curve without assistance from friction?

MODEL The car is a particle in uniform circular motion.

VISUALIZE Having just discussed the role of friction in turning corners, it is perhaps surprising to suggest that the same turn can also be accomplished without friction. Example 8.4 considered a level roadway, but real highway curves are *banked* by being tilted up at the outside edge of the curve. The angle is modest on ordinary highways, but it can be quite large on high-speed racetracks. The purpose of banking becomes clear if you look at the free-body diagram in FIGURE 8.9. The normal force $\vec{n}$ is perpendicular to the road, so tilting the road causes $\vec{n}$ to have a component toward the center of the circle. The radial component n_r is the inward force that causes the centripetal acceleration needed to turn the car. Notice that we are *not* using a tilted coordinate system, although this looks rather like an inclined-plane problem. The center of the circle is in the same horizontal plane as the car, and for circular-motion problems we need the r-axis to pass through the center. Tilted axes are for *linear* motion along an incline.

SOLVE Without friction, $n_r = n \sin\theta$ is the only component of force in the radial direction. It is this inward component of the normal force on the car that causes it to turn the corner. Newton's second law is

$$\sum F_r = n \sin\theta = \frac{mv_0^2}{r}$$

$$\sum F_z = n \cos\theta - mg = 0$$

where θ is the angle at which the road is banked and we've assumed that the car is traveling at the correct speed v_0. From the z-equation,

$$n = \frac{mg}{\cos\theta}$$

Substituting this into the r-equation and solving for v_0 give

$$\frac{mg}{\cos\theta}\sin\theta = mg\tan\theta = \frac{mv_0^2}{r}$$

$$v_0 = \sqrt{rg\tan\theta} = 14\text{ m/s}$$

ASSESS This is $\approx$ 28 mph, a reasonable speed. Only at this very specific speed can the turn be negotiated without reliance on friction forces.

FIGURE 8.9 Pictorial representation of a car on a banked curve.

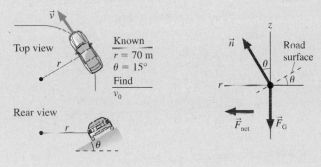

FIGURE 8.10 Free-body diagrams showing the static friction force when $v > v_0$ and when $v < v_0$.

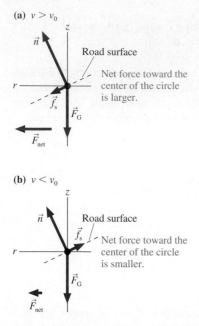

(a) $v > v_0$

Road surface

Net force toward the center of the circle is larger.

(b) $v < v_0$

Road surface

Net force toward the center of the circle is smaller.

It's interesting to explore what happens at other speeds. The car will need to rely on both the banking *and* friction if it takes the curve at a speed higher or lower than v_0. **FIGURE 8.10a** has modified the free-body diagram to include a static friction force. Remember that $\vec{f_s}$ must be parallel to the surface, so it is tilted downward at angle θ. Because $\vec{f_s}$ has a component in the positive r-direction, the *net* radial force is larger than that provided by $\vec{n}$ alone. This will allow the car to take the curve at $v > v_0$. We could use a quantitative analysis similar to Example 8.5 to determine the maximum speed on a banked curve by analyzing Figure 8.10a when $f_s = f_{s\,max}$.

But what about taking the curve at a speed $v < v_0$? In this situation, the r-component of the normal force is too big; not that much center-directed force is needed. As **FIGURE 8.10b** shows, the net force can be reduced by having $\vec{f_s}$ point *up* the slope! This seems very strange at first, but consider the limiting case in which the car is parked on the banked curve, with $v = 0$. Were it not for a static friction force pointing *up* the slope, the car would slide sideways down the incline. In fact, for any speed less than v_0 the car will slip to the inside of the curve unless it is prevented from doing so by a static friction force pointing up the slope.

Our analysis thus finds three divisions of speed. At v_0, the car turns the corner with no assistance from friction. At greater speeds, the car will slide out of the curve unless an inward-directed friction force increases the size of the net force. And last, at lesser speeds, the car will slip down the incline unless an outward-directed friction force prevents it from doing so.

EXAMPLE 8.6 **A rock in a sling**

A Stone Age hunter places a 1.0 kg rock in a sling and swings it in a horizontal circle around his head on a 1.0-m-long vine. If the vine breaks at a tension of 200 N, what is the maximum angular speed, in rpm, with which he can swing the rock?

MODEL Model the rock as a particle in uniform circular motion.

VISUALIZE This problem appears, at first, to be essentially the same as Example 8.3, where the father spun his child around on a rope. However, the lack of a normal force from a supporting surface makes a *big* difference. In this case, the *only* contact force on the rock is the tension in the vine. Because the rock moves in a horizontal circle, you may be tempted to draw a free-body diagram like **FIGURE 8.11a**, where $\vec{T}$ is directed along the r-axis. You will quickly run into trouble, however, because this diagram has a net force in the z-direction and it is impossible to satisfy $\sum F_z = 0$. The gravitational force $\vec{F_G}$ certainly points vertically downward, so the difficulty must be with $\vec{T}$.

As an experiment, tie a small weight to a string, swing it over your head, and check the *angle* of the string. You will quickly discover that the string is *not* horizontal but, instead, is angled downward. The sketch of **FIGURE 8.11b** labels the angle θ. Notice that the

rock moves in a *horizontal* circle, so the center of the circle is *not* at his hand. The r-axis points to the center of the circle, but the tension force is directed along the vine. Thus the correct free-body diagram is the one in Figure 8.11b.

SOLVE The free-body diagram shows that the downward gravitational force is balanced by an upward component of the tension, leaving the radial component of the tension to cause the centripetal acceleration. Newton's second law is

$$\sum F_r = T\cos\theta = \frac{mv^2}{r}$$

$$\sum F_z = T\sin\theta - mg = 0$$

where θ is the angle of the vine below horizontal. From the z-equation we find

$$\sin\theta = \frac{mg}{T}$$

$$\theta = \sin^{-1}\left(\frac{(1.0\text{ kg})(9.8\text{ m/s}^2)}{200\text{ N}}\right) = 2.81°$$

where we've evaluated the angle at the maximum tension of 200 N. The vine's angle of inclination is small but not zero.

FIGURE 8.11 Pictorial representation of a rock in a sling.

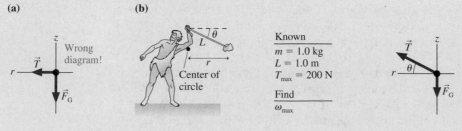

(a)

Wrong diagram!

(b)

Center of circle

Known
$m = 1.0$ kg
$L = 1.0$ m
$T_{max} = 200$ N

Find
ω_{max}

Turning now to the r-equation, we find the rock's speed is

$$v = \sqrt{\frac{rT\cos\theta}{m}}$$

$$v = \sqrt{\frac{LT\cos^2\theta}{m}} = \sqrt{\frac{(1.0\text{ m})(200\text{ N})(\cos 2.81°)^2}{1.0\text{ kg}}} = 14.1\text{ m/s}$$

We can now find the maximum angular speed, the value of ω that brings the tension to the breaking point.

Careful! The radius r of the circle is *not* the length L of the vine. You can see in Figure 8.11b that $r = L\cos\theta$. Thus

$$\omega_{max} = \frac{v}{r} = \frac{v}{L\cos\theta} = \frac{14.1\text{ rad}}{1\text{ s}} \times \frac{1\text{ rev}}{2\pi\text{ rad}} \times \frac{60\text{ s}}{1\text{ min}} = 135\text{ rpm}$$

STOP TO THINK 8.3 A block on a string spins in a horizontal circle on a frictionless table. Rank order, from largest to smallest, the tensions T_a to T_e acting on blocks a to e.

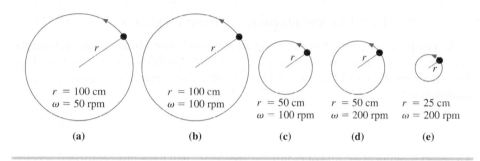

| (a) | (b) | (c) | (d) | (e) |

$r = 100$ cm $\omega = 50$ rpm — (a)
$r = 100$ cm $\omega = 100$ rpm — (b)
$r = 50$ cm $\omega = 100$ rpm — (c)
$r = 50$ cm $\omega = 200$ rpm — (d)
$r = 25$ cm $\omega = 200$ rpm — (e)

8.4 Circular Orbits

Satellites orbit the earth, the earth orbits the sun, and our entire solar system orbits the center of the Milky Way galaxy. Not all orbits are circular, but in this section we'll limit our analysis to circular orbits. We'll look at the elliptical orbits of satellites and planets in Chapter 13.

How does a satellite orbit the earth? What forces act on it? Why does it move in a circle? To answer these important questions, let's return, for a moment, to projectile motion. Projectile motion occurs when the only force on an object is gravity. Our analysis of projectiles assumed that the earth is flat and that the acceleration due to gravity is everywhere straight down. This is an acceptable approximation for projectiles of limited range, such as baseballs or cannon balls, but there comes a point where we can no longer ignore the curvature of the earth.

FIGURE 8.12 shows a perfectly smooth, spherical, airless planet with one tower of height h. A projectile is launched from this tower parallel to the ground ($\theta = 0°$) with speed v_0. If v_0 is very small, as in trajectory A, the "flat-earth approximation" is valid and the problem is identical to Example 4.4 in which a car drove off a cliff. The projectile simply falls to the ground along a parabolic trajectory.

As the initial speed v_0 is increased, the projectile begins to notice that the ground is curving out from beneath it. It is falling the entire time, always getting closer to the ground, but the distance that the projectile travels before finally reaching the ground—that is, its range—increases because the projectile must "catch up" with the ground that is curving away from it. Trajectories B and C are of this type. The actual calculation of these trajectories is beyond the scope of this textbook, but you should be able to understand the factors that influence the trajectory.

If the launch speed v_0 is sufficiently large, there comes a point where the curve of the trajectory and the curve of the earth are parallel. In this case, the projectile "falls" but it never gets any closer to the ground! This is the situation for trajectory D. A closed trajectory around a planet or star, such as trajectory D, is called an **orbit.**

FIGURE 8.12 Projectiles being launched at increasing speeds from height h on a smooth, airless planet.

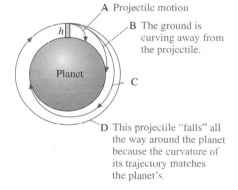

A Projectile motion

B The ground is curving away from the projectile.

C

D This projectile "falls" all the way around the planet because the curvature of its trajectory matches the planet's.

For homework assigned on MasteringPhysics, go to www.masteringphysics.com

Problem difficulty is labeled as | (straightforward) to ||| (challenging).

Problems labeled ✎ can be done on a Dynamics Worksheet.
Problems labeled ▨ integrate significant material from earlier chapters.

CONCEPTUAL QUESTIONS

1. Tarzan swings through the jungle on a vine. At the lowest point of his swing, is the tension in the vine greater than, less than, or equal to the gravitational force on Tarzan? Explain.

2. A car runs out of gas while driving down a hill. It rolls through the valley and starts up the other side. At the very bottom of the valley, which of the free-body diagrams in FIGURE Q8.2 is correct? The car is moving to the right, and drag and rolling friction are negligible.

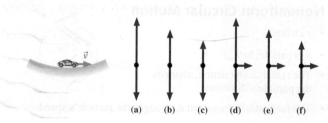

FIGURE Q8.2

3. FIGURE Q8.3 is a bird's-eye view of particles moving in horizontal circles on a tabletop. All are moving at the same speed. Rank in order, from largest to smallest, the tensions T_a to T_d. Give your answer in the form a > b = c > d and explain your ranking.

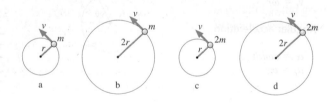

FIGURE Q8.3

4. A ball on a string moves in a vertical circle. When the ball is at its lowest point, is the tension in the string greater than, less than, or equal to the gravitational force on the ball? Explain.

5. FIGURE Q8.5 shows two balls of equal mass moving in vertical circles. Is the tension in string A greater than, less than, or equal to the tension in string B if the balls travel over the top of the circle (a) with equal speed and (b) with equal angular velocity?

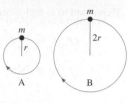

FIGURE Q8.5

6. Ramon and Sally are observing a toy car speed up as it goes around a circular track. Ramon says, "The car's speeding up, so there must be a net force parallel to the track." "I don't think so," replies Sally. "It's moving in a circle, and that requires centripetal acceleration. The net force has to point to the center of the circle." Do you agree with Ramon, Sally, or neither? Explain.

7. A jet plane is flying on a level course at constant speed. The engines are at full throttle.
   a. What is the net force on the plane? Explain.
   b. Draw a free-body diagram of the plane as seen from the side with the plane flying to the right. Name (don't just label) any and all forces shown on your diagram.
   c. Airplanes bank when they turn. Draw a free-body diagram of the plane as seen from behind as it makes a right turn.
   d. *Why* do planes bank as they turn? Explain.

8. A small projectile is launched parallel to the ground at height $h = 1$ m with sufficient speed to orbit a completely smooth, airless planet. A bug rides inside a small hole inside the projectile. Is the bug weightless? Explain.

9. You can swing a ball on a string in a vertical circle if you swing it fast enough. But if you swing too slowly, the string goes slack as the ball nears the top. Explain *why* there's a minimum speed to keep the ball moving in a circle.

10. A golfer starts with the club over her head and swings it to reach maximum speed as it contacts the ball. Halfway through her swing, when the golf club is parallel to the ground, does the acceleration vector of the club head point (a) straight down, (b) parallel to the ground, approximately toward the golfer's shoulders, (c) approximately toward the golfer's feet, or (d) toward a point above the golfer's head? Explain.

EXERCISES AND PROBLEMS

Exercises

Section 8.1 Dynamics in Two Dimensions

1. || As a science fair project, you want to launch an 800 g model rocket straight up and hit a horizontally moving target as it passes 30 m above the launch point. The rocket engine provides a constant thrust of 15.0 N. The target is approaching at a speed of 15 m/s. At what horizontal distance between the target and the rocket should you launch?

2. || A 500 g model rocket is on a cart that is rolling to the right at a speed of 3.0 m/s. The rocket engine, when it is fired, exerts an 8.0 N thrust on the rocket. Your goal is to have the rocket pass through a small horizontal hoop that is 20 m above the launch point. At what horizontal distance left of the hoop should you launch?

3. ‖ A 4.0×10^{10} kg asteroid is heading directly toward the center of the earth at a steady 20 km/s. To save the planet, astronauts strap a giant rocket to the asteroid perpendicular to its direction of travel. The rocket generates 5.0×10^9 N of thrust. The rocket is fired when the asteroid is 4.0×10^6 km away from earth. You can ignore the earth's gravitational force on the asteroid and their rotation about the sun.

    a. If the mission fails, how many hours is it until the asteroid impacts the earth?

    b. The radius of the earth is 6400 km. By what minimum angle must the asteroid be deflected to just miss the earth?

    c. The rocket fires at full thrust for 300 s before running out of fuel. Is the earth saved?

Section 8.2 Velocity and Acceleration in Uniform Circular Motion

Section 8.3 Dynamics of Uniform Circular Motion

4. | A 1500 kg car drives around a flat 200-m-diameter circular track at 25 m/s. What are the magnitude and direction of the net force on the car? What causes this force?

5. | A 1500 kg car takes a 50-m-radius unbanked curve at 15 m/s. What is the size of the friction force on the car?

6. ‖ A 200 g block on a 50-cm-long string swings in a circle on a horizontal, frictionless table at 75 rpm.

    a. What is the speed of the block?

    b. What is the tension in the string?

7. ‖ In the Bohr model of the hydrogen atom, an electron (mass $m = 9.1 \times 10^{-31}$ kg) orbits a proton at a distance of 5.3×10^{-11} m. The proton pulls on the electron with an electric force of 8.2×10^{-8} N. How many revolutions per second does the electron make?

8. ‖ A highway curve of radius 500 m is designed for traffic moving at a speed of 90 km/hr. What is the correct banking angle of the road?

9. ‖ Suppose the moon were held in its orbit not by gravity but by a massless cable attached to the center of the earth. What would be the tension in the cable? Use the table of astronomical data inside the back cover of the book.

10. ‖ A 30 g ball rolls around a 40-cm-diameter L-shaped track, shown in FIGURE EX8.10, at 60 rpm. What is the magnitude of the net force that the track exerts on the ball? Rolling friction can be neglected.

FIGURE EX8.10

Section 8.4 Circular Orbits

11. ‖ A satellite orbiting the moon very near the surface has a period of 110 min. What is the moon's acceleration due to gravity? Astronomical data are inside the back cover of the book.

12. ‖ What is the acceleration due to gravity of the sun at the distance of the earth's orbit? Astronomical data are inside the back cover of the book.

Section 8.5 Fictitious Forces

Section 8.6 Why Does the Water Stay in the Bucket?

13. | A car drives over the top of a hill that has a radius of 50 m. What maximum speed can the car have without flying off the road at the top of the hill?

14. ‖ The weight of passengers on a roller coaster increases by 50% as the car goes through a dip with a 30 m radius of curvature. What is the car's speed at the bottom of the dip?

15. ‖ A roller coaster car crosses the top of a circular loop-the-loop at twice the critical speed. What is the ratio of the normal force to the gravitational force?

16. ‖ The normal force equals the magnitude of the gravitational force as a roller coaster car crosses the top of a 40-m-diameter loop-the-loop. What is the car's speed at the top?

17. ‖ A student has 65-cm-long arms. What is the minimum angular velocity (in rpm) for swinging a bucket of water in a vertical circle without spilling any? The distance from the handle to the bottom of the bucket is 35 cm.

Section 8.7 Nonuniform Circular Motion

18. | A new car is tested on a 200-m-diameter track. If the car speeds up at a steady 1.5 m/s², how long after starting is the magnitude of its centripetal acceleration equal to the tangential acceleration?

19. ‖ A toy train rolls around a horizontal 1.0-m-diameter track. The coefficient of rolling friction is 0.10.

    a. What is the magnitude of the train's angular acceleration after it is released?

    b. How long does it take the train to stop if it's released with an angular speed of 30 rpm?

Problems

20. ‖ A popular pastime is to see who can push an object closest to the edge of a table without its going off. You push the 100 g object and release it 2.0 m from the table edge. Unfortunately, you push a little too hard. The object slides across, sails off the edge, falls 1.0 m to the floor, and lands 30 cm from the edge of the table. If the coefficient of kinetic friction is 0.50, what was the object's speed as you released it?

21. ‖ Alice tapes a small, 200 g model rocket to a 400 g ice hockey puck. The rocket generates 8.0 N of thrust. Alice orients the puck so that the rocket's nose points in the positive y-direction, then pushes the puck across frictionless ice in the positive x-direction with a speed of 2.0 m/s. The rocket fires at the exact instant the puck crosses the origin. Find an equation $y(x)$ for the puck's trajectory, then graph it.

22. ‖ Sam (75 kg) takes off up a 50-m-high, 10° frictionless slope on his jet-powered skis. The skis have a thrust of 200 N. He keeps his skis tilted at 10° after becoming airborne, as shown in FIGURE P8.22. How far does Sam land from the base of the cliff?

FIGURE P8.22

23. ‖ A motorcycle daredevil plans to ride up a 2.0-m-high, 20° ramp, sail across a 10-m-wide pool filled with hungry crocodiles, and land at ground level on the other side. He has done this stunt many times and approaches it with confidence. Unfortunately, the motorcycle engine dies just as he starts up the ramp. He is going 11 m/s at that instant, and the rolling friction of his rubber tires is not negligible. Does he survive, or does he become crocodile food?

24. || A 5000 kg interceptor rocket is launched at an angle of 44.7°. The thrust of the rocket motor is 140,700 N.
    a. Find an equation $y(x)$ that describes the rocket's trajectory.
    b. What is the shape of the trajectory?
    c. At what elevation does the rocket reach the speed of sound, 330 m/s?

25. || A rocket-powered hockey puck has a thrust of 2.0 N and a total mass of 1.0 kg. It is released from rest on a frictionless table, 4.0 m from the edge of a 2.0 m drop. The front of the rocket is pointed directly toward the edge. How far does the puck land from the base of the table?

26. || A 500 g model rocket is resting horizontally at the top edge of a 40-m-high wall when it is accidentally bumped. The bump pushes it off the edge with a horizontal speed of 0.5 m/s and at the same time causes the engine to ignite. When the engine fires, it exerts a constant 20 N horizontal thrust away from the wall.
    a. How far from the base of the wall does the rocket land?
    b. Describe the trajectory of the rocket while it travels to the ground.

27. || Communications satellites are placed in circular orbits where they stay directly over a fixed point on the equator as the earth rotates. These are called *geosynchronous orbits*. The altitude of a geosynchronous orbit is 3.58×10^7 m ($\approx 22{,}000$ miles).
    a. What is the period of a satellite in a geosynchronous orbit?
    b. Find the value of g at this altitude.
    c. What is the weight of a 2000 kg satellite in a geosynchronous orbit?

28. || A 75 kg man weighs himself at the north pole and at the equator. Which scale reading is higher? By how much?

29. || The father of Example 8.3 stands at the summit of a conical hill as he spins his 20 kg child around on a 5.0 kg cart with a 2.0-m-long rope. The sides of the hill are inclined at 20°. He again keeps the rope parallel to the ground, and friction is negligible. What rope tension will allow the cart to spin with the same 14 rpm it had in the example?

30. || A 500 g ball swings in a vertical circle at the end of a 1.5-m-long string. When the ball is at the bottom of the circle, the tension in the string is 15 N. What is the speed of the ball at that point?

31. ||| A concrete highway curve of radius 70 m is banked at a 15° angle. What is the maximum speed with which a 1500 kg rubber-tired car can take this curve without sliding?

32. || A student ties a 500 g rock to a 1.0-m-long string and swings it around her head in a horizontal circle. At what angular speed, in rpm, does the string tilt down at a 10° angle?

33. || A 5.0 g coin is placed 15 cm from the center of a turntable. The coin has static and kinetic coefficients of friction with the turntable surface of $\mu_s = 0.80$ and $\mu_k = 0.50$. The turntable very slowly speeds up to 60 rpm. Does the coin slide off?

34. || You've taken your neighbor's young child to the carnival to ride the rides. She wants to ride The Rocket. Eight rocket-shaped cars hang by chains from the outside edge of a large steel disk. A vertical axle through the center of the ride turns the disk, causing the cars to revolve in a circle. You've just finished taking physics, so you decide to figure out the speed of the cars while you wait. You estimate that the disk is 5 m in diameter and the chains are 6 m long. The ride takes 10 s to reach full speed, then the cars swing out until the chains are 20° from vertical. What is the car's speed?

35. || A *conical pendulum* is formed by attaching a 500 g ball to a 1.0-m-long string, then allowing the mass to move in a horizontal circle of radius 20 cm. **FIGURE P8.35** shows that the string traces out the surface of a cone, hence the name.

a. What is the tension in the string?
b. What is the ball's angular speed, in rpm?

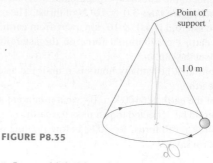

Point of support

1.0 m

FIGURE P8.35

36. || In an old-fashioned amusement park ride, passengers stand inside a 5.0-m-diameter hollow steel cylinder with their backs against the wall. The cylinder begins to rotate about a vertical axis. Then the floor on which the passengers are standing suddenly drops away! If all goes well, the passengers will "stick" to the wall and not slide. Clothing has a static coefficient of friction against steel in the range 0.60 to 1.0 and a kinetic coefficient in the range 0.40 to 0.70. A sign next to the entrance says "No children under 30 kg allowed." What is the minimum angular speed, in rpm, for which the ride is safe?

37. || A 10 g steel marble is spun so that it rolls at 150 rpm around the *inside* of a vertically oriented steel tube. The tube, shown in **FIGURE P8.37**, is 12 cm in diameter. Assume that the rolling resistance is small enough for the marble to maintain 150 rpm for several seconds. During this time, will the marble spin in a horizontal circle, at constant height, or will it spiral down the inside of the tube?

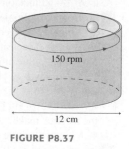

150 rpm

12 cm

FIGURE P8.37

38. || Three cars are driving at 25 m/s along the road shown in **FIGURE P8.38**. Car B is at the bottom of a hill and car C is at the top. Both hills have a 200 m radius of curvature. Suppose each car suddenly brakes hard and starts to skid. What is the tangential acceleration (i.e., the acceleration parallel to the road) of each car? Assume $\mu_k = 1.0$.

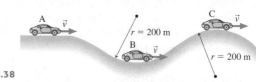

A $\vec{v}$ C $\vec{v}$

$r = 200$ m

B $\vec{v}$

$r = 200$ m

FIGURE P8.38

39. || A 500 g ball moves in a vertical circle on a 102-cm-long string. If the speed at the top is 4.0 m/s, then the speed at the bottom will be 7.5 m/s. (You'll learn how to show this in Chapter 10.)
    a. What is the gravitational force acting on the ball?
    b. What is the tension in the string when the ball is at the top?
    c. What is the tension in the string when the ball is at the bottom?

40. || While at the county fair, you decide to ride the Ferris wheel. Having eaten too many candy apples and elephant ears, you find the motion somewhat unpleasant. To take your mind off your stomach, you wonder about the motion of the ride. You estimate the radius of the big wheel to be 15 m, and you use your watch to find that each loop around takes 25 s.
    a. What are your speed and magnitude of your acceleration?

b. What is the ratio of your weight at the top of the ride to your weight while standing on the ground?

c. What is the ratio of your weight at the bottom of the ride to your weight while standing on the ground?

41. || In an amusement park ride called The Roundup, passengers stand inside a 16-m-diameter rotating ring. After the ring has acquired sufficient speed, it tilts into a vertical plane, as shown in **FIGURE P8.41**.

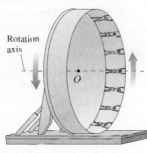

a. Suppose the ring rotates once every 4.5 s. If a rider's mass is 55 kg, with how much force does the ring push on her at the top of the ride? At the bottom?

FIGURE P8.41

b. What is the longest rotation period of the wheel that will prevent the riders from falling off at the top?

42. || You have a new job designing rides for an amusement park. In one ride, the rider's chair is attached by a 9.0-m-long chain to the top of a tall rotating tower. The tower spins the chair and rider around at the rate of 1.0 rev every 4.0 s. In your design, you've assumed that the maximum possible combined weight of the chair and rider is 150 kg. You've found a great price for chain at the local discount store, but your supervisor wonders if the chain is strong enough. You contact the manufacturer and learn that the chain is rated to withstand a tension of 3000 N. Will this chain be strong enough for the ride?

43. || Suppose you swing a ball in a vertical circle on a 1.0-m-long string. As you probably know from experience, there is a *minimum* angular velocity ω_{min} you must maintain if you want the ball to complete the full circle. If you swing the ball at $\omega < \omega_{min}$, then the string goes slack before the ball reaches the top of the circle. What is ω_{min}? Give your answer in rpm.

44. || A heavy ball with a weight of 100 N ($m = 10.2$ kg) is hung from the ceiling of a lecture hall on a 4.5-m-long rope. The ball is pulled to one side and released to swing as a pendulum, reaching a speed of 5.5 m/s as it passes through the lowest point. What is the tension in the rope at that point?

45. || It is proposed that future space stations create an artificial gravity by rotating. Suppose a space station is constructed as a 1000-m-diameter cylinder that rotates about its axis. The inside surface is the deck of the space station. What rotation period will provide "normal" gravity?

46. || Mass m_1 on the frictionless table of **FIGURE P8.46** is connected by a string through a hole in the table to a hanging mass m_2. With what speed must m_1 rotate in a circle of radius r if m_2 is to remain hanging at rest?

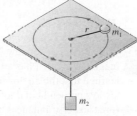

FIGURE P8.46

47. || A 100 g ball on a 60 cm-long string is swung in a vertical circle about a point 200 cm above the floor. The tension in the string when the ball is at the very bottom of the circle is 5.0 N. A very sharp knife is suddenly inserted, as shown in **FIGURE P8.47**, to cut the string directly below the point of support. How far to the right of where the string was cut does the ball hit the floor?

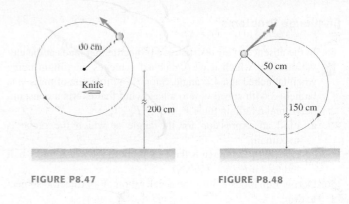

FIGURE P8.47   **FIGURE P8.48**

48. || A 60 g ball is tied to the end of a 50-cm-long string and swung in a vertical circle. The center of the circle, as shown in **FIGURE P8.48**, is 150 cm above the floor. The ball is swung at the minimum speed necessary to make it over the top without the string going slack. If the string is released at the instant the ball is at the top of the loop, how far to the right does the ball hit the ground?

49. || A 100 g ball on a 60-cm-long string is swung in a vertical circle about a point 200 cm above the floor. The string suddenly breaks when it is parallel to the ground and the ball is moving upward. The ball reaches a height 600 cm above the floor. What was the tension in the string an instant before it broke?

50. || A 1500 kg car starts from rest and drives around a flat 50-m-diameter circular track. The forward force provided by the car's drive wheels is a constant 1000 N.

a. What are the magnitude and direction of the car's acceleration at $t = 10$ s? Give the direction as an angle from the r-axis.

b. If the car has rubber tires and the track is concrete, at what time does the car begin to slide out of the circle?

51. || A 500 g steel block rotates on a steel table while attached to a 2.0-m-long massless rod. Compressed air fed through the rod is ejected from a nozzle on the back of the block, exerting a thrust force of 3.5 N. The nozzle is 70° from the radial line, as shown in **FIGURE P8.51**. The block starts from rest.

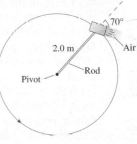

a. What is the block's angular velocity after 10 rev?

FIGURE P8.51

b. What is the tension in the rod after 10 rev?

52. || A 2.0 kg ball swings in a vertical circle on the end of an 80-cm-long string. The tension in the string is 20 N when its angle from the highest point on the circle is $\theta = 30°$.

a. What is the ball's speed when $\theta = 30°$?

b. What are the magnitude and direction of the ball's acceleration when $\theta = 30°$?

In Problems 53 and 54 you are given the equation (or equations) used to solve a problem. For each of these, you are to

a. Write a realistic problem for which this is the correct equation. Be sure that the answer your problem requests is consistent with the equation given.

b. Finish the solution of the problem.

53. $60\ N = (0.30\ kg)\omega^2(0.50\ m)$

54. $(1500\ kg)(9.8\ m/s^2) - 11,760\ N = (1500\ kg)\ v^2/(200\ m)$

Challenge Problems

55. In the absence of air resistance, a projectile that lands at the elevation from which it was launched achieves maximum range when launched at a 45° angle. Suppose a projectile of mass m is launched with speed v_0 into a headwind that exerts a constant, horizontal retarding force $\vec{F}_{\text{wind}} = -F_{\text{wind}}\hat{\imath}$.

   a. Find an expression for the angle at which the range is maximum.

   b. By what percentage is the maximum range of a 0.50 kg ball reduced if $F_{\text{wind}} = 0.60$ N?

56. Derive Equations 8.4 for the acceleration of a projectile subject to drag.

57. Driving a spaceship isn't as easy as it looks in the movies. Imagine you're a physics student in the 31st century. You live in a remote space colony where the gravitational force from any stars or planets is negligible. You're on your way home from school, coasting along in your 20,000 kg personal spacecraft at 2.0 km/s, when the computer alerts you to the fact that the entrance to your pod is 500 km away along a line 30° from your present heading, as shown in FIGURE CP8.57. You need to make a left turn so that you can enter the pod going straight ahead at 1.0 km/s. You could do this with a series of small rocket burns, but you want to impress the girls in the spacecraft behind

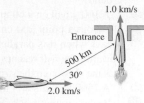

FIGURE CP8.57

you by getting through the entrance with a single rocket burn. You can use small thrusters to quickly rotate your spacecraft to a different orientation before and after the main rocket burn.

   a. You need to determine three things: How to orient your spacecraft for the main rocket burn, the magnitude F_{thrust} of the rocket burn, and the length of the burn. Use a coordinate system in which you start at the origin and are initially moving along the x-axis. Measure the orientation of your spacecraft by the angle it makes with the positive x-axis. Your initial orientation is 0°. You can end the burn before you reach the entrance, but you're not allowed to have the engine on as you pass through the entrance. Mass loss during the burn is negligible.

   b. Calculate your position coordinates every 50 s until you reach the entrance, then plot a graph of your trajectory. Be sure to label the position of the entrance.

58. A small ball rolls around a horizontal circle at height y inside the cone shown in FIGURE CP8.58. Find an expression of the ball's speed in terms of a, h, y, and g.

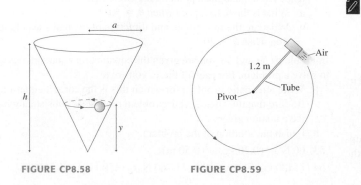

FIGURE CP8.58   FIGURE CP8.59

59. A 500 g steel block rotates on a steel table while attached to a 1.2-m-long hollow tube as shown in FIGURE CP8.59. Compressed air fed through the tube and ejected from a nozzle on the back of the block exerts a thrust force of 4.0 N perpendicular to the tube. The maximum tension the tube can withstand without breaking is 50 N. If the block starts from rest, how many revolutions does it make before the tube breaks?

60. Two wires are tied to the 2.0 kg sphere shown in FIGURE CP8.60. The sphere revolves in a horizontal circle at constant speed.

   a. For what speed is the tension the same in both wires?

   b. What is the tension?

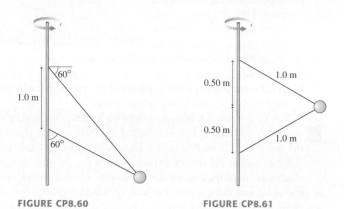

FIGURE CP8.60   FIGURE CP8.61

61. Two wires are tied to the 300 g sphere shown in FIGURE CP8.61. The sphere revolves in a horizontal circle at a constant speed of 7.5 m/s. What is the tension in each of the wires?

62. A small ball rolls around a horizontal circle at height y inside a frictionless hemispherical bowl of radius R, as shown in FIGURE CP8.62.

   a. Find an expression for the ball's angular velocity in terms of R, y, and g.

   b. What is the minimum value of ω for which the ball can move in a circle?

   c. What is ω in rpm if $R = 20$ cm and the ball is halfway up?

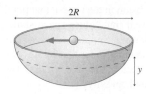

FIGURE CP8.62

63. You are flying to New York. You've been reading the in-flight magazine, which has an article about the physics of flying. You learned that the airflow over the wings creates a *lift force* that is always perpendicular to the wings. In level flight, the upward lift force exactly balances the downward gravitational force. The pilot comes on to say that, because of heavy traffic, the plane is going to circle the airport for a while. She says that you'll maintain a speed of 400 mph at an altitude of 20,000 ft. You start to wonder what the diameter of the plane's circle around the airport is. You notice that the pilot has banked the plane so that the wings are 10° from horizontal. The safety card in the seatback pocket informs you that the plane's wing span is 250 ft. What can you learn about the diameter?

64. If a vertical cylinder of water (or any other liquid) rotates about its axis, as shown in **FIGURE CP8.64**, the surface forms a smooth curve. Assuming that the water rotates as a unit (i.e., all the water rotates with the same angular velocity), show that the shape of the surface is a parabola described by the equation $z = (\omega^2/2\,g)r^2$.

Hint: Each particle of water on the surface is subject to only two forces: gravity and the normal force due to the water underneath it. The normal force, as always, acts perpendicular to the surface.

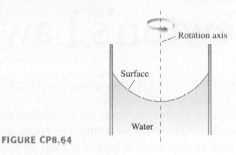

FIGURE CP8.64

STOP TO THINK ANSWERS

Stop to Think 8.1: d. The parallel component of $\vec{a}$ is opposite $\vec{v}$ and will cause the particle to slow down. The perpendicular component of $\vec{a}$ will cause the particle to change directions in a downward direction.

Stop to Think 8.2: $(a_r)_b > (a_r)_e > (a_r)_a = (a_r)_c > (a_r)_d$. Centripetal acceleration is v^2/r. Doubling r decreases a_r by a factor of 2. Doubling v increases a_r by a factor of 4. Reversing direction doesn't change a_r.

Stop to Think 8.3: $T_d > T_b = T_e > T_c > T_a$. The center-directed force is $m\omega^2 r$. Changing r by a factor of 2 changes the tension by a factor of 2, but changing ω by a factor of 2 changes the tension by a factor of 4.

Stop to Think 8.4: b. The car is moving in a circle, so there must be a net force toward the center of the circle. The circle is below the car, so the net force must point downward. This can be true only if $F_G > n$.

Stop to Think 8.5: c. The ball does not have a "memory" of its previous motion. The velocity $\vec{v}$ is straight up at the instant the string breaks. The only force on the ball after the string breaks is the gravitational force, straight down. This is just like tossing a ball straight up.

Newton's Laws

The goal of Part I has been to discover the connection between force and motion. We started with *kinematics,* which is the mathematical description of motion; then we proceeded to *dynamics,* which is the explanation of motion in terms of forces. Newton's three laws of motion form the basis of our explanation. All of the examples we have studied so far are applications of Newton's laws.

The table below is called a *knowledge structure* for Newton's laws. A knowledge structure summarizes the essential concepts, the general principles, and the primary applications of a theory. The first section of the table tells us that Newtonian mechanics is concerned with how *particles* respond to *forces.* The second section indicates that we have introduced only three general principles, Newton's three laws of motion.

You use this knowledge structure by working your way through it, from top to bottom. Once you recognize a problem

as a dynamics problem, you immediately know to start with Newton's laws. You can then determine the category of motion and apply Newton's second law in the appropriate form. Newton's third law will help you identify the forces acting on particles as they interact. Finally, the kinematic equations for that category of motion allow you to reach the solution you seek.

The knowledge structure provides the *procedural knowledge* for solving dynamics problems, but it does not represent the total knowledge required. You must add to it knowledge about what position and velocity are, about how forces are identified, about action/reaction pairs, about drawing and using free-body diagrams, and so on. These are specific *tools* for problem solving. The problem-solving strategies of Chapters 5 through 8 combine the procedures and the tools into a powerful method for thinking about and solving problems.

KNOWLEDGE STRUCTURE I Newton's Laws

ESSENTIAL CONCEPTS	Particle, acceleration, force, interaction
BASIC GOALS	How does a particle respond to a force? How do objects interact?

GENERAL PRINCIPLES	**Newton's first law**	An object will remain at rest or will continue to move with constant velocity (equilibrium) if and only if $\vec{F}_{net} = \vec{0}$.
	Newton's second law	$\vec{F}_{net} = m\vec{a}$
	Newton's third law	$\vec{F}_{A \text{ on } B} = -\vec{F}_{B \text{ on } A}$

BASIC PROBLEM-SOLVING STRATEGY Use Newton's second law for each particle or object. Use Newton's third law to equate the magnitudes of the two members of an action/reaction pair.

Linear motion

$$\sum F_x = ma_x \quad \text{or} \quad \sum F_x = 0$$

$$\sum F_y = 0 \qquad\qquad \sum F_y = ma_y$$

Trajectory motion

$$\sum F_x = ma_x$$

$$\sum F_y = ma_y$$

Circular motion

$$\sum F_r = mv^2/r = m\omega^2 r$$

$$\sum F_t = 0 \text{ or } ma_t$$

$$\sum F_z = 0$$

Linear and trajectory kinematics

Uniform acceleration: $v_{fs} = v_{is} + a_s\Delta t$

(a_s = constant) $s_f = s_i + v_{is}\Delta t + \frac{1}{2}a_s(\Delta t)^2$

$v_{fs}^2 = v_{is}^2 + 2a_s\Delta s$

Trajectories: The same equations are used for both x and y.

Uniform motion: $s_f = s_i + v_s\Delta t$

($a = 0, v_s$ = constant)

General case $v_s = ds/dt$ = slope of the position graph

$a_s = dv_s/dt$ = slope of the velocity graph

$v_{fs} = v_{is} + \int_{t_i}^{t_f} a_s\, dt = v_{is} + $ area under the acceleration curve

$s_f = s_i + \int_{t_i}^{t_f} v_s\, dt = s_i + $ area under the velocity curve

Circular kinematics

Uniform circular motion:

$T = 2\pi r/v = 2\pi/\omega$

$\theta_f = \theta_i + \omega\Delta t$

$a_r = v^2/r = \omega^2 r$

$v_t = \omega r$

Nonuniform circular motion:

$\omega_f = \omega_i + \alpha\Delta t$

$\theta_f = \theta_i + \omega_i\Delta t + \frac{1}{2}\alpha(\Delta t)^2$

The Forces of Nature

What are the fundamental forces of nature? That is, what set of distinct, irreducible forces can explain everything we know about nature? This is a question that has long intrigued physicists. For example, friction is not a fundamental force because it can be reduced to electric forces between atoms. What about other forces?

Physicists have long recognized three basic forces: the gravitational force, the electric force, and the magnetic force. The gravitational force is an inherent attraction between two masses. The electric force is a force between charges. The magnetic force, which is a bit more mysterious, causes compass needles to point north and holds your shopping list on the refrigerator door.

In the 1860s, the Scottish physicist James Clerk Maxwell developed a theory that *unified* the electric and magnetic forces into a single *electromagnetic force*. Where there had appeared to be two separate forces, Maxwell found there to be a single force that, under appropriate conditions, exhibits "electric behavior" or "magnetic behavior." Maxwell used his theory to predict the existence of *electromagnetic waves,* including light. Our entire telecommunications industry is testimony to Maxwell's genius.

Maxwell's electromagnetic force was soon found to be the "glue" holding atoms, molecules, and solids together. With the exception of gravity, *every* force we have considered so far can be traced to electromagnetic forces between atoms.

The discovery of the atomic nucleus, about 1910, presented difficulties that could not be explained by either gravitational or electromagnetic forces. The atomic nucleus is an unimaginably dense ball of protons and neutrons. But what holds it together against the repulsive electric forces between the protons? There must be an attractive force inside the nucleus that is stronger than the repulsive electric force. This force, called the *strong force,* is the force that holds atomic nuclei together. The strong force is a *short-range* force, extending only about 10^{-14} m. It is completely negligible outside the nucleus. The subatomic particles called *quarks,* of which you have likely heard, are part of our understanding of how the strong force works.

In the 1930s, physicists found that the nuclear radioactivity called *beta decay* could not be explained by either the electromagnetic or the strong force. Careful experiments established that the decay is due to a previously undiscovered force within the nucleus. The strength of this force is less than either the strong force or the electromagnetic force, so this new force was named the *weak force*. Although discovered in conjunction with radioactivity, it is now known to play an important role in the fusion reactions that power the stars.

By 1940, the recognized forces of nature were four: the gravitational force, the electromagnetic force, the strong force, and the weak force. Physicists were understandably curious whether all four of these were truly fundamental or if some of them could be further unified. Indeed, innovative work in the 1960s and 1970s produced a theory that unified the electromagnetic force and the weak force.

Predictions of this new theory were confirmed during the 1980s at some of the world's largest particle accelerators, and we now speak of the *electroweak force.* Under appropriate conditions, the electroweak force exhibits either "electromagnetic behavior" or "weak behavior." But under other conditions, new phenomena appear that are consequences of the full electroweak force. These conditions appear on earth only in the largest and most energetic particle accelerators, which is why we were not previously aware of the unified nature of the these two forces. However, the earliest moments of the Big Bang provided the right conditions for the electroweak force to play a significant role. Thus a theory developed to help us understand the workings of nature on the smallest subatomic scale has unexpectedly given us powerful new insights into the origin of the universe.

The success of the electroweak theory has prompted efforts to unify the electroweak force and the strong force into a *grand unified theory*. Only time will tell if the strong force and the electroweak force are really just two different aspects of a single force, or if they are truly distinct. Some physicists even envision a day when all the forces of nature will be unified in a single theory, the so-called *Theory of Everything!* For today, however, our understanding of the forces of nature is in terms of three fundamental forces: the gravitational force, the electroweak force, and the strong force.

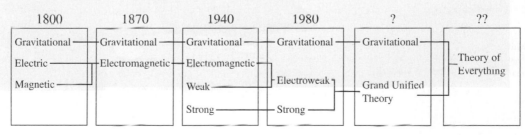

FIGURE I.1 An historical progression of our understanding of the fundamental forces of nature.

9 Impulse and Momentum

An exploding firework is a
dramatic event. Nonetheless,
the explosion must obey
some simple laws of physics.

▶ **Looking Ahead**

The goals of Chapter 9 are to
introduce the ideas of impulse and
momentum and to learn a new
problem-solving strategy based on
conservation laws. In this chapter you
will learn to:

- Understand and use the concepts
  of impulse and momentum.
- Use a new before-and-after
  pictorial representation.
- Use momentum bar charts.
- Solve problems using the law of
  conservation of momentum.
- Apply these ideas to explosions
  and collisions.

◀ **Looking Back**

The law of conservation of
momentum is based on Newton's
third law. Please review:

- Sections 7.2–7.3 Action/reaction
  force pairs and Newton's third law.

An *explosion* is a complex interaction pushing two or more objects apart. Using
Newton's second law to predict the outcome of an explosion would be a daunting
challenge. Nevertheless, some explosions have very simple outcomes. For example,
consider a 75 kg archer on ice skates. If the archer shoots a 75 g arrow forward, the
archer recoils backward. This may lack the drama of fireworks, but nonetheless it is an
explosion into two parts. The interaction between the archer, the bow, and the arrow is
very complex, yet the archer's recoil speed is always 1/1000 the speed of the arrow.
How can such a complex interaction give rise to such a simple outcome?

The opposite of an explosion is a *collision*. Imagine a train car rolling along the
tracks toward an identical car at rest. The two cars couple together upon impact and
then roll down the tracks together. The forces between the train cars during the collision are unimaginably complex, but the two coupled cars roll away with exactly half
the speed of the single car before impact. Another simple outcome.

Our goal in this chapter is to learn how to predict these simple outcomes without
having to know all the details of the interaction forces. The new idea that will make
this possible is *momentum*, a concept we will use to relate the situation "before" an
interaction to the situation "after" the interaction. This before-and-after perspective
will be a powerful new problem-solving tool.

9.1 Momentum and Impulse

Wham! The collision of a tennis ball with a racket is a dramatic, complex interaction
in which the ball suddenly changes direction. Trying to analyze the collision with
Newton's second law would be a daunting task. Nonetheless, our goal in this chapter

is to find a simple relationship between the velocities of the objects before the interaction and their velocities after the interaction. We'll start by looking at collisions; later in the chapter we'll examine explosions.

A **collision** is a short-duration interaction between two objects. The collision between a tennis ball and a racket, or a baseball and a bat, may seem instantaneous to your eye, but that is a limitation of your perception. A careful look at the photograph reveals that the right side of the ball is flattened and pressed up against the strings of the racket. It takes time to compress the ball, and more time for the ball to re-expand as it leaves the racket.

The duration of a collision depends on the materials from which the objects are made, but 1 to 10 ms (0.001 to 0.010 s) is fairly typical. This is the time during which the two objects are in contact with each other. The harder the objects, the shorter the contact time. A collision between two steel balls lasts less than 1 ms.

FIGURE 9.1 shows a microscopic view of a collision in which object A bounces off object B. The spring-like molecular bonds—the same bonds that cause normal forces and tension forces—compress during the collision, then re-expand as A bounces back. The forces $\vec{F}_{\text{A on B}}$ and $\vec{F}_{\text{B on A}}$ are an action/reaction pair and, according to Newton's third law, have equal magnitudes: $F_{\text{A on B}} = F_{\text{B on A}}$. The force increases rapidly as the bonds compress, reaches a maximum at the instant A is at rest (point of maximum compression), then decreases as the bonds re-expand.

A tennis ball collides with a racket. Notice that the right side of the ball is flattened.

FIGURE 9.1 Atomic model of a collision.

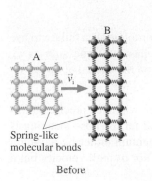
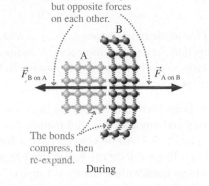
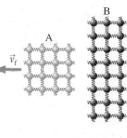

Spring-like molecular bonds

A and B exert equal but opposite forces on each other.

$\vec{F}_{\text{B on A}}$ $\vec{F}_{\text{A on B}}$

The bonds compress, then re-expand.

Before   During   After

A large force exerted during a small interval of time is called an **impulsive force.** The force of a tennis racket on a ball, which would look much like FIGURE 9.2, is a good example of an impulsive force. Notice that an impulsive force has a well-defined duration.

NOTE ▶ Until now, we have not dealt with forces that change with time. Because an impulsive force is a function of time, we will write it as $F(t)$. ◀

To explore the implications of a collision, FIGURE 9.3 on the next page shows a particle traveling in a straight line along the x-axis with initial velocity v_{ix}. The particle suddenly collides with another object and experiences an impulsive force $F_x(t)$ that begins at time t_i and ends at time t_f. After the collision, the particle has final velocity v_{fx}.

NOTE ▶ Both v_x and F_x are components of vectors and thus have *signs* indicating which way the vectors point. ◀

We can analyze the collision with Newton's second law to find the final velocity. Acceleration in one dimension is $a_x = dv_x/dt$, so the second law is

$$ma_x = m\frac{dv_x}{dt} = F_x(t)$$

FIGURE 9.2 The rapidly changing magnitude of the force during a collision.

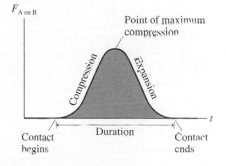

$F_{\text{A on B}}$

Point of maximum compression

Compression   Expansion

Contact begins   Duration   Contact ends

FIGURE 9.3 A particle undergoes a collision.

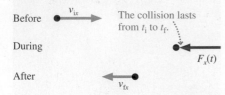

Before

During

After

The collision lasts from t_i to t_f.

v_{ix}

$F_x(t)$

v_{fx}

After multiplying both sides by dt, we can write the second law as

$$m \, dv_x = F_x(t) \, dt \qquad (9.1)$$

The force is nonzero only during the interval of time from t_i to t_f, so let's integrate Equation 9.1 over this interval. The velocity changes from v_{ix} to v_{fx} during the collision; thus

$$m \int_{v_i}^{v_f} dv_x = mv_{fx} - mv_{ix} = \int_{t_i}^{t_f} F_x(t) \, dt \qquad (9.2)$$

We need some new tools to help us make sense of Equation 9.2.

Momentum

The product of a particle's mass and velocity is called the *momentum* of the particle:

$$\text{momentum} = \vec{p} = m\vec{v} \qquad (9.3)$$

Momentum, like velocity, is a vector. The units of momentum are kg m/s.

NOTE ▶ The plural of "momentum" is "momenta," from its Latin origin. ◀

The momentum vector $\vec{p}$ is parallel to the velocity vector $\vec{v}$. **FIGURE 9.4** shows that $\vec{p}$, like any vector, can be decomposed into x- and y-components. Equation 9.3, which is a vector equation, is a shorthand way to write the simultaneous equations

$$p_x = mv_x$$
$$p_y = mv_y$$

NOTE ▶ One of the most common errors in momentum problems is a failure to use the appropriate signs. The momentum component p_x has the same sign as v_x. Momentum is *negative* for a particle moving to the left (on the x-axis) or down (on the y-axis). ◀

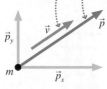

Momentum is a vector pointing in the same direction as the object's velocity.

$\vec{p}_y$

$\vec{v}$

$\vec{p}$

m

$\vec{p}_x$

Momentum is another term that we use in everyday speech without a precise definition. In physics and engineering, momentum is a technical term whose meaning is defined in Equation 9.3. An object can have a large momentum either by having a small mass but a large velocity (a bullet fired from a rifle) or a small velocity but a large mass (a large truck rolling at a slow 1 mph).

Newton actually formulated his second law in terms of momentum rather than acceleration:

$$\vec{F} = m\vec{a} = m\frac{d\vec{v}}{dt} = \frac{d(m\vec{v})}{dt} = \frac{d\vec{p}}{dt} \qquad (9.4)$$

This statement of the second law, saying that **force is the rate of change of momentum,** is more general than our earlier version $\vec{F} = m\vec{a}$. It allows for the possibility that the mass of the object might change, such as a rocket that is losing mass as it burns fuel.

Returning to Equation 9.2, you can see that mv_{ix} and mv_{fx} are p_{ix} and p_{fx}, the x-component of the particle's momentum before and after the collision. Further, $p_{fx} - p_{ix}$ is Δp_x, the *change* in the particle's momentum. In terms of momentum, Equation 9.2 is

$$\Delta p_x = p_{fx} - p_{ix} = \int_{t_i}^{t_f} F_x(t) \, dt \qquad (9.5)$$

Now we need to examine the right-hand side of Equation 9.5.

Impulse

Equation 9.5 tells us that the particle's change in momentum is related to the time integral of the force. Let's define a quantity J_x called the *impulse* to be

$$\text{impulse} = J_x = \int_{t_i}^{t_f} F_x(t)\, dt \qquad (9.6)$$

$$= \text{area under the } F_x(t) \text{ curve between } t_i \text{ and } t_f$$

Strictly speaking, impulse has units of N s, but you should be able to show that N s are equivalent to kg m/s, the units of momentum.

The interpretation of the integral in Equation 9.6 as an area under a curve is especially important. **FIGURE 9.5a** portrays the impulse graphically. Because the force changes in a complicated way during a collision, it is often useful to describe the collision in terms of an *average* force F_{avg}. As **FIGURE 9.5b** shows, F_{avg} is the height of a rectangle that has the same area, and thus the same impulse, as the real force curve. The impulse exerted during the collision is

$$J_x = F_{avg}\,\Delta t \qquad (9.7)$$

Equation 9.2, which we found by integrating Newton's second law, can now be rewritten in terms of impulse and momentum as

$$\Delta p_x = J_x \qquad \text{(impulse-momentum theorem)} \qquad (9.8)$$

This result is called the **impulse-momentum theorem.** The name is rather unusual, but it's not the name that is important. The important new *idea* is that **an impulse delivered to a particle changes the particle's momentum.** The momentum p_{fx} "after" an interaction, such as a collision or an explosion, is equal to the momentum p_{ix} "before" the interaction *plus* the impulse that arises from the interaction:

$$p_{fx} = p_{ix} + J_x \qquad (9.9)$$

The impulse-momentum theorem tells us that we do *not* need to know all the details of the force function $F_x(t)$ to learn how the particle rebounds. No matter how complicated the force, only the integral of the force—the area under the force curve—is needed to find p_{fx}.

FIGURE 9.6 illustrates the impulse-momentum theorem for a rubber ball bouncing off a wall. Notice the signs; they are very important. The ball is initially traveling toward the right, so v_{ix} and p_{ix} are positive. After the bounce, v_{fx} and p_{fx} are negative. The force *on the ball* is toward the left, so F_x is also negative. The graphs show how the force and the momentum change with time.

Although the interaction is very complex, the impulse—the area under the force graph—is all we need to know to find the ball's velocity as it rebounds from the wall. The final momentum is

$$p_{fx} = p_{ix} + J_x = p_{ix} + \text{area under the force curve}$$

Thus the final velocity is

$$v_{fx} = \frac{p_{fx}}{m} = v_{ix} + \frac{\text{area under the force curve}}{m}$$

In this example, the area has a negative value.

Momentum Bar Charts

The impulse-momentum theorem tells us that **impulse transfers momentum to an object.** If an object has 2 kg m/s of momentum, a 1 kg m/s impulse exerted on the object increases its momentum to 3 kg m/s. That is, $p_{fx} = p_{ix} + J_x$.

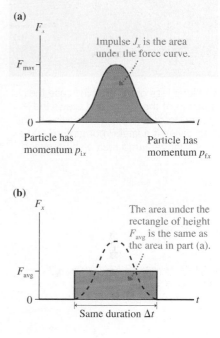

FIGURE 9.5 Looking at the impulse graphically.

(a) Impulse J_x is the area under the force curve.

Particle has momentum p_{ix} Particle has momentum p_{fx}

(b) The area under the rectangle of height F_{avg} is the same as the area in part (a).

Same duration Δt

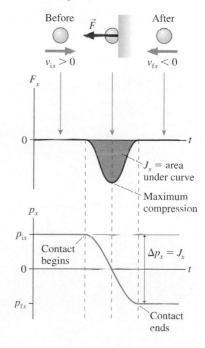

FIGURE 9.6 The impulse-momentum theorem helps us understand a rubber ball bouncing off a wall.

Before   After

$v_{ix} > 0$ $v_{fx} < 0$

$J_x = $ area under curve

Maximum compression

Contact begins $\Delta p_x = J_x$

Contact ends

The long legs of this frog increase the duration of the jump. This allows the ground to deliver a larger impulse to the frog, giving it a larger momentum and thus a longer jump than a short-legged animal.

We can represent this "momentum accounting" with a **momentum bar chart.** FIGURE 9.7a shows a bar chart in which one unit of impulse adds to an initial two units of momentum to give three units of momentum. The bar chart of FIGURE 9.7b represents the ball colliding with a wall in Figure 9.6. Momentum bar charts are a tool for visualizing an interaction.

FIGURE 9.7 Two examples of momentum bar charts.

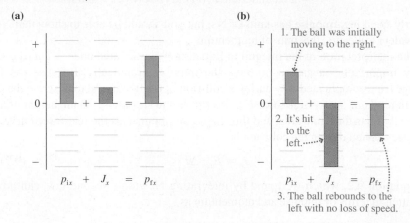

NOTE ▶ The vertical scale of a momentum bar chart has no numbers; it can be adjusted to match any problem. However, be sure that all bars in a given problem use a consistent scale. ◀

STOP TO THINK 9.1 The cart's change of momentum is

a. -30 kg m/s
b. -20 kg m/s
c. 0 kg m/s
d. 10 kg m/s
e. 20 kg m/s
f. 30 kg m/s

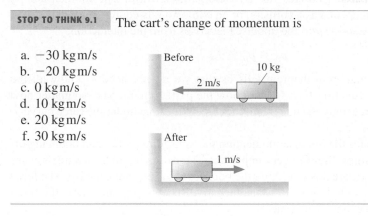

9.2 Solving Impulse and Momentum Problems

Pictorial representations have become an important problem-solving tool. The pictorial representations you learned to draw in Part I were oriented toward the use of Newton's laws and a subsequent kinematic analysis. Now we are interested in making a connection between "before" and "after."

Drawing a before-and-after pictorial representation   (MP)

❶ **Sketch the situation.** Use two drawings, labeled "Before" and "After," to show the objects *before* they interact and again *after* they interact.
❷ **Establish a coordinate system.** Select your axes to match the motion.
❸ **Define symbols.** Define symbols for the masses and for the velocities before and after the interaction. Position and time are not needed.
❹ **List known information.** Give the values of quantities that are known from the problem statement or that can be found quickly with simple geometry or unit conversions. Before-and-after pictures are simpler than the pictures for dynamics problems, so listing known information on the sketch is adequate.
❺ **Identify the desired unknowns.** What quantity or quantities will allow you to answer the question? These should have been defined in step 3.
❻ If appropriate, **draw a momentum bar chart** to clarify the situation and establish appropriate signs.

Exercises 16–18

NOTE ▶ The generic subscripts i and f, for *initial* and *final*, are adequate in equations for a simple problem, but using numerical subscripts, such as v_{1x} and v_{2x}, will help keep all the symbols straight in more complex problems. ◀

EXAMPLE 9.1 Hitting a baseball
A 150 g baseball is thrown with a speed of 20 m/s. It is hit straight back toward the pitcher at a speed of 40 m/s. The interaction force between the ball and the bat is shown in **FIGURE 9.8**. What *maximum* force F_{max} does the bat exert on the ball? What is the *average* force of the bat on the ball?

FIGURE 9.8 The interaction force between the baseball and the bat.

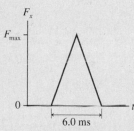

MODEL Model the baseball as a particle and the interaction as a collision.

VISUALIZE FIGURE 9.9 is a before-and-after pictorial representation. The steps from Tactics Box 9.1 are explicitly noted. Because F_x is positive (a force to the right), we know the ball was initially moving toward the left and is hit back toward the right. Thus we converted the statements about *speeds* into information about *velocities*, with v_{ix} negative.

SOLVE Until now we've consistently started the mathematical representation with Newton's second law. Now we want to use the impulse-momentum theorem:

$$\Delta p_x = J_x = \text{area under the force curve}$$

We know the velocities before and after the collision, so we can calculate the ball's momentum:

$$p_{ix} = mv_{ix} = (0.15 \text{ kg})(-20 \text{ m/s}) = -3.0 \text{ kg m/s}$$
$$p_{fx} = mv_{fx} = (0.15 \text{ kg})(40 \text{ m/s}) = 6.0 \text{ kg m/s}$$

FIGURE 9.9 A before-and-after pictorial representation.

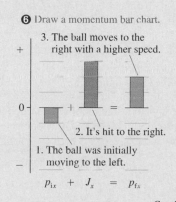

Continued

Thus the *change* in momentum is

$$\Delta p_x = p_{fx} - p_{ix} = 9.0 \text{ kg m/s}$$

The force curve is a triangle with height F_{max} and width 6.0 ms. The area under the curve is

$$J_x = \text{area} = \frac{1}{2} \times F_{max} \times (0.0060 \text{ s}) = (F_{max})(0.0030 \text{ s})$$

According to the impulse-momentum theorem,

$$9.0 \text{ kg m/s} = (F_{max})(0.0030 \text{ s})$$

Thus the *maximum* force is

$$F_{max} = \frac{9.0 \text{ kg m/s}}{0.0030 \text{ s}} = 3000 \text{ N}$$

The *average* force, which depends on the collision duration $\Delta t = 0.0060$ s, has the smaller value:

$$F_{avg} = \frac{J_x}{\Delta t} = \frac{\Delta p_x}{\Delta t} = \frac{9.0 \text{ kg m/s}}{0.0060 \text{ s}} = 1500 \text{ N}$$

ASSESS F_{max} is a large force, but quite typical of the impulsive forces during collisions. The main thing to focus on is our new perspective: an impulse changes the momentum of an object.

Other forces often act on an object during a collision or other brief interaction. In Example 9.1, for instance, the baseball is also acted on by gravity. Usually these other forces are *much* smaller than the interaction forces. The 1.5 N weight of the ball is vastly less than the 3000 N force of the bat on the ball. We can reasonably neglect these small forces *during* the brief time of the impulsive force by using what is called the **impulse approximation.**

When we use the impulse approximation, p_{ix} and p_{fx} (and v_{ix} and v_{fx}) are then the momenta (and velocities) *immediately* before and *immediately* after the collision. For example, the velocities in Example 9.1 are those of the ball just before and after it collides with the bat. We could then do a follow-up problem, including gravity and drag, to find the ball's speed a second later as the second baseman catches it. We'll look at some two-part examples later in the chapter.

EXAMPLE 9.2 **A bouncing ball**

A 100 g rubber ball is dropped from a height of 2.00 m onto a hard floor. FIGURE 9.10 shows the force that the floor exerts on the ball. How high does the ball bounce?

MODEL Model the ball as a particle subjected to an impulsive force while in contact with the floor. Using the impulse approximation, we'll neglect gravity during these 8.00 ms. The fall and subsequent rise are free-fall motion.

FIGURE 9.10 The force of the floor on a bouncing rubber ball.

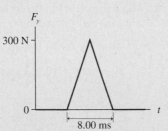

VISUALIZE FIGURE 9.11 is a pictorial representation. Here we have a three-part problem (downward free fall, impulsive collision, upward free fall), so the pictorial motion includes both the before and after of the collision (v_{1y} changing to v_{2y}) and the beginning and end of the free-fall motion. The bar chart shows the momentum change during the brief collision. Note that p is negative for downward motion.

FIGURE 9.11 Pictorial representation of the ball and a momentum bar chart of the collision with the floor.

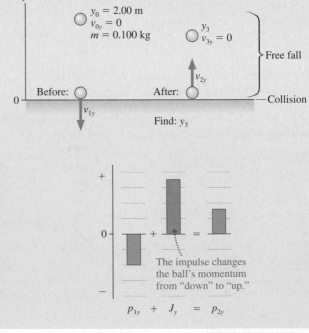

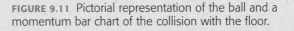

SOLVE Velocity v_{1y}, the ball's velocity *immediately* before the collision, is found using free-fall kinematics with $\Delta y = -2.0$ m:

$$v_{1y}^2 = v_{0y}^2 - 2g\Delta y = 0 - 2g\Delta y$$

$$v_{1y} = \sqrt{-2g\Delta y} = \sqrt{-2(9.80 \text{ m/s}^2)(-2.00 \text{ m})} = -6.26 \text{ m/s}$$

We've chosen the negative root because the ball is moving in the negative y-direction.

The impulse-momentum theorem is $p_{2y} = p_{1y} + J_y$. The initial momentum, just before the collision, is $p_{1y} = mv_{1y} = -0.626$ kg m/s. The force of the floor is upward, so J_y is positive. From Figure 9.10, the impulse J_y is

$$J_y = \text{area under the force curve} = \frac{1}{2} \times (300 \text{ N}) \times (0.0080 \text{ s})$$

$$= 1.200 \text{ N s}$$

Thus

$$p_{2y} = p_{1y} + J_y = (-0.626 \text{ kg m/s}) + 1.200 \text{ N s} = 0.574 \text{ kg m/s}$$

and the post-collision velocity is

$$v_{2y} = \frac{p_{2y}}{m} = \frac{0.574 \text{ kg m/s}}{0.100 \text{ kg}} = 5.74 \text{ m/s}$$

The rebound speed is less than the impact speed, as expected. Finally a second use of free-fall kinematics yields

$$v_{3y}^2 = 0 = v_{2y}^2 - 2g\Delta y = v_{2y}^2 - 2gy_3$$

$$y_3 = \frac{v_{2y}^2}{2g} = \frac{(5.74 \text{ m/s})^2}{2(9.80 \text{ m/s}^2)} = 1.68 \text{ m}$$

The ball bounces back to a height of 1.68 m.

ASSESS The ball bounces back to less than its initial height, which is realistic.

NOTE ▶ Example 9.2 illustrates an important point: The impulse-momentum theorem applies *only* during the brief interval in which an impulsive force is applied. Many problems will have segments of the motion that must be analyzed with kinematics or Newton's laws. The impulse-momentum theorem is a new and useful tool, but it doesn't replace all that you've learned up until now. ◀

STOP TO THINK 9.2   A 10 g rubber ball and a 10 g clay ball are thrown at a wall with equal speeds. The rubber ball bounces, the clay ball sticks. Which ball exerts a larger impulse on the wall?

a. The clay ball exerts a larger impulse because it sticks.
b. The rubber ball exerts a larger impulse because it bounces.
c. They exert equal impulses because they have equal momenta.
d. Neither exerts an impulse on the wall because the wall doesn't move.

9.3 Conservation of Momentum

The impulse-momentum theorem was derived from Newton's second law and is really just an alternative way of looking at that law. It is used in the context of single-particle dynamics, much as we used Newton's law in Chapters 5–8.

This chapter opened by noting that very complex interactions, such as two train cars coupling together, sometimes have very simple outcomes. To predict the outcomes, we need to see how Newton's *third* law looks in the language of impulse and momentum. Newton's third law will lead us to one of the most important conservation laws in physics.

FIGURE 9.12 shows two objects with initial velocities $(v_{ix})_1$ and $(v_{ix})_2$. The objects collide, then bounce apart with final velocities $(v_{fx})_1$ and $(v_{fx})_2$. The forces during the collision, as the objects are interacting, are the action/reaction pair $\vec{F}_{1 \text{ on } 2}$ and $\vec{F}_{2 \text{ on } 1}$. For now, we'll continue to assume that the motion is one dimensional along the x-axis.

NOTE ▶ The notation, with all the subscripts, may seem excessive. But there are two objects, and each has an initial and a final velocity, so we need to distinguish among four different velocities. ◀

FIGURE 9.12 A collision between two objects.

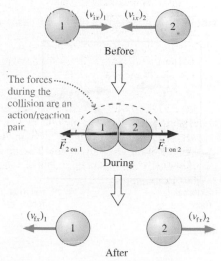

The forces during the collision are an action/reaction pair.

Newton's second law for each object *during* the collision is

$$\frac{d(p_x)_1}{dt} = (F_x)_{2 \text{ on } 1}$$

$$\frac{d(p_x)_2}{dt} = (F_x)_{1 \text{ on } 2} = -(F_x)_{2 \text{ on } 1} \tag{9.10}$$

We made explicit use of Newton's third law in the second equation.

Although Equations 9.10 are for two different objects, suppose—just to see what happens—we were to *add* these two equations. If we do, we find that

$$\frac{d(p_x)_1}{dt} + \frac{d(p_x)_2}{dt} = \frac{d}{dt}((p_x)_1 + (p_x)_2) = (F_x)_{2 \text{ on } 1} + (-(F_x)_{2 \text{ on } 1}) = 0 \quad (9.11)$$

If the time derivative of the quantity $(p_x)_1 + (p_x)_2$ is zero, it must be the case that

$$(p_x)_1 + (p_x)_2 = \text{constant} \tag{9.12}$$

Equation 9.12 is a conservation law! If $(p_x)_1 + (p_x)_2$ is a constant, then the sum of the momenta *after* the collision equals the sum of the momenta *before* the collision. That is,

$$(p_{fx})_1 + (p_{fx})_2 = (p_{ix})_1 + (p_{ix})_2 \tag{9.13}$$

Furthermore, this equality is independent of the interaction force. We don't need to know anything about $\vec{F}_{1 \text{ on } 2}$ and $\vec{F}_{2 \text{ on } 1}$ to make use of Equation 9.13.

As an example, **FIGURE 9.13** is a before-and-after pictorial representation of two equal-mass train cars colliding and coupling. Equation 9.13 relates the momenta of the cars after the collision to their momenta before the collision:

$$m_1(v_{fx})_1 + m_2(v_{fx})_2 = m_1(v_{ix})_1 + m_2(v_{ix})_2$$

Initially, car 1 is moving with velocity $(v_{ix})_1 = v_i$ while car 2 is at rest. Afterward, they roll together with the common final velocity v_f. Furthermore, $m_1 = m_2 = m$. With this information, the sum of the momenta is

$$mv_f + mv_f = 2mv_f = mv_i + 0$$

The mass cancels, and we find that the train cars' final velocity is $v_f = \frac{1}{2}v_i$. That is, we can make the very simple prediction that the final speed is exactly half the initial speed of car 1 without knowing anything at all about the very complex interaction between the two cars as they collide.

Law of Conservation of Momentum

Equation 9.13 illustrates the idea of a conservation law for momentum, but it was derived for the specific case of two particles colliding in one dimension. Our goal is to develop a more general law of conservation of momentum, a law that will be valid in three dimensions and that will work for any type of interaction. The next few paragraphs are fairly mathematical, so you might want to begin by looking ahead to Equations 9.21 and the statement of the law of conservation of momentum to see where we're heading.

Consider a system consisting of N particles. **FIGURE 9.14** shows a simple case where $N = 3$. The particles might be large entities (cars, baseballs, etc.), or they might be the microscopic atoms in a gas. We can identify each particle by an identification number k. Every particle in the system *interacts* with every other particle via action/reaction pairs of forces $\vec{F}_{j \text{ on } k}$ and $\vec{F}_{k \text{ on } j}$. In addition, every particle is subjected to possible *external forces* $\vec{F}_{\text{ext on } k}$ from agents outside the system.

FIGURE 9.13 Two colliding train cars.

Before:

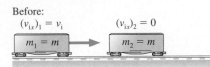

After:

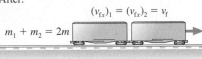

FIGURE 9.14 A system of particles.

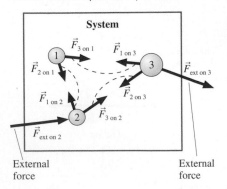

External force

External force

If particle k has velocity $\vec{v}_k$, its momentum is $\vec{p}_k = m_k\vec{v}_k$. We define the **total momentum** $\vec{P}$ of the system as the vector sum

$$\vec{P} = \text{total momentum} = \vec{p}_1 + \vec{p}_2 + \vec{p}_3 + \cdots + \vec{p}_N = \sum_{k=1}^{N} \vec{p}_k \qquad (9.14)$$

In other words, the total momentum *of the system* is the sum of all the individual momenta.

The time derivative of $\vec{P}$ tells us how the total momentum of the system changes with time:

$$\frac{d\vec{P}}{dt} = \sum_k \frac{d\vec{p}_k}{dt} = \sum_k \vec{F}_k \qquad (9.15)$$

where we used Newton's second law for each particle in the form $\vec{F}_k = d\vec{p}_k/dt$, which was Equation 9.4.

The net force acting on particle k can be divided into *external forces,* from outside the system, and *interaction forces* due to the other particles in the system:

$$\vec{F}_k = \sum_{j \neq k} \vec{F}_{j \text{ on } k} + \vec{F}_{\text{ext on } k} \qquad (9.16)$$

The restriction $j \neq k$ expresses the fact that particle k does not exert a force on itself. Using this in Equation 9.15 gives the rate of change of the total momentum P of the system:

$$\frac{d\vec{P}}{dt} = \sum_k \sum_{j \neq k} \vec{F}_{j \text{ on } k} + \sum_k \vec{F}_{\text{ext on } k} \qquad (9.17)$$

The double sum on $\vec{F}_{j \text{ on } k}$ adds *every* interaction force within the system. But the interaction forces come in action/reaction pairs, with $\vec{F}_{k \text{ on } j} = -\vec{F}_{j \text{ on } k}$, so $\vec{F}_{k \text{ on } j} + \vec{F}_{j \text{ on } k} = \vec{0}$. Consequently, **the sum of all the interaction forces is zero.** As a result, Equation 9.17 becomes

$$\frac{d\vec{P}}{dt} = \sum_k \vec{F}_{\text{ext on } k} = \vec{F}_{\text{net}} \qquad (9.18)$$

where $\vec{F}_{\text{net}}$ is the net force exerted on the system by agents outside the system. But this is just Newton's second law written for the system as a whole! That is, **the rate of change of the total momentum of the system is equal to the net force applied to the system.**

Equation 9.18 has two very important implications. First, we can analyze the motion of the system as a whole without needing to consider interaction forces between the particles that make up the system. In fact, we have been using this idea all along as an *assumption* of the particle model. When we treat cars and rocks and baseballs as particles, we assume that the internal forces between the atoms—the forces that hold the object together—do not affect the motion of the object as a whole. Now we have *justified* that assumption.

The second implication of Equation 9.18, and the more important one from the perspective of this chapter, applies to what we call an *isolated system.* An **isolated system** is a system for which the *net* external force is zero: $\vec{F}_{\text{net}} = \vec{0}$. That is, an isolated system is one on which there are *no* external forces or for which the external forces are balanced and add to zero.

For an isolated system, Equation 9.18 is simply

$$\frac{d\vec{P}}{dt} = \vec{0} \qquad \text{(isolated system)} \qquad (9.19)$$

The total momentum of the rocket + gases system is conserved, so the rocket accelerates forward as the gases are expelled backward.

In other words, **the *total* momentum of an isolated system does not change.** The total momentum $\vec{P}$ remains constant, *regardless* of whatever interactions are going on *inside* the system. The importance of this result is sufficient to elevate it to a law of nature, alongside Newton's laws.

> **Law of conservation of momentum**   The total momentum $\vec{P}$ of an isolated system is a constant. Interactions within the system do not change the system's total momentum.

NOTE ▶ It is worth emphasizing the critical role of Newton's third law in the derivation of Equation 9.19. The law of conservation of momentum is a direct consequence of the fact that interactions within an isolated system are action/reaction pairs. ◀

Mathematically, the law of conservation of momentum for an isolated system is

$$\vec{P}_f = \vec{P}_i \tag{9.20}$$

The total momentum after an interaction is equal to the total momentum before the interaction. Because Equation 9.20 is a vector equation, the equality is true for each of the components of the momentum vector. That is,

$$(p_{fx})_1 + (p_{fx})_2 + (p_{fx})_3 + \cdots = (p_{ix})_1 + (p_{ix})_2 + (p_{ix})_3 + \cdots$$
$$(p_{fy})_1 + (p_{fy})_2 + (p_{fy})_3 + \cdots = (p_{iy})_1 + (p_{iy})_2 + (p_{iy})_3 + \cdots \tag{9.21}$$

The x-equation is an extension of Equation 9.13 to N interacting particles.

EXAMPLE 9.3   Two balls shot from a tube

A 10 g ball and a 30 g ball are placed in a tube with a massless compressed spring between them. When the spring is released, the 10 g ball flies out of the tube at a speed of 6.0 m/s. With what speed does the 30 g ball emerge from the other end?

MODEL The two balls are the system. The balls interact with each other, but they form an isolated system because, for each ball, the upward normal force of the tube balances the downward gravitational force to make $\vec{F}_{net} = \vec{0}$. Thus the total momentum of the system is conserved.

FIGURE 9.15 Before-and-after pictorial representation for two balls shot out of a tube.

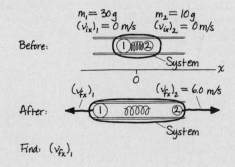

Find: $(v_{fx})_1$

VISUALIZE FIGURE 9.15 shows a before-and-after pictorial representation for the two balls. The total momentum before the spring is released is $\vec{P}_i = \vec{0}$ because both balls are at rest. Consequently, the *total* momentum will be $\vec{0}$ after the spring is released. The mathematical statement of momentum conservation, Equation 9.21, is

$$m_1(v_{fx})_1 + m_2(v_{fx})_2 = m_1(v_{ix})_1 + m_2(v_{ix})_2 = 0$$

where we've written the x-component of the momenta in terms of v_x and used the fact that the initial velocities are both zero.

SOLVE Solving for $(v_{fx})_1$, we find

$$(v_{fx})_1 = -\frac{m_2}{m_1}(v_{fx})_2 = -\frac{1}{3}(v_{fx})_2 = -2.0 \text{ m/s}$$

The 30 g ball emerges with a *speed* of 2.0 m/s, one-third the speed of the 10 g ball.

ASSESS The *total* momentum of the system is zero, but the individual momenta are not. Because the balls must have momenta of equal magnitude (but opposite signs) a ball with 3 times the mass must have $\frac{1}{3}$ the speed. We didn't need to know any details about the spring to arrive at this result.

A Strategy for Conservation of Momentum Problems

Our derivation of the law of conservation of momentum and the conditions under which it holds suggests a problem-solving strategy.

Activ ONLINE Physics   6.3, 6.4, 6.6, 6.7, 6.10

PROBLEM-SOLVING STRATEGY 9.1 **Conservation of momentum**   (MP)

MODEL Clearly define *the system*.

- If possible, choose a system that is isolated ($\vec{F}_{net} = \vec{0}$) or within which the interactions are sufficiently short and intense that you can ignore external forces for the duration of the interaction (the impulse approximation). Momentum is conserved.
- If it's not possible to choose an isolated system, try to divide the problem into parts such that momentum is conserved during one segment of the motion. Other segments of the motion can be analyzed using Newton's laws or, as you'll learn in Chapters 10 and 11, conservation of energy.

VISUALIZE Draw a before-and-after pictorial representation. Define symbols that will be used in the problem, list known values, and identify what you're trying to find.

SOLVE The mathematical representation is based on the law of conservation of momentum: $\vec{P}_f = \vec{P}_i$. In component form, this is

$$(p_{fx})_1 + (p_{fx})_2 + (p_{fx})_3 + \cdots = (p_{ix})_1 + (p_{ix})_2 + (p_{ix})_3 + \cdots$$

$$(p_{fy})_1 + (p_{fy})_2 + (p_{fy})_3 + \cdots = (p_{iy})_1 + (p_{iy})_2 + (p_{iy})_3 + \cdots$$

ASSESS Check that your result has the correct units, is reasonable, and answers the question.

EXAMPLE 9.4 **Rolling away**

Bob sees a stationary cart 8.0 m in front of him. He decides to run to the cart as fast as he can, jump on, and roll down the street. Bob has a mass of 75 kg and the cart's mass is 25 kg. If Bob accelerates at a steady 1.0 m/s², what is the cart's speed just after Bob jumps on?

MODEL This is a two-part problem. First Bob accelerates across the ground. Then Bob lands on and sticks to the cart, a "collision" between Bob and the cart. The interaction forces between Bob and the cart (i.e., friction) act only over the fraction of a second it takes Bob's feet to become stuck to the cart. Using the impulse approxi-

mation allows the system Bob + cart to be treated as an isolated system during the brief interval of the "collision," and thus the total momentum of Bob + cart is conserved during this interaction. But the system Bob + cart is *not* an isolated system for the entire problem because Bob's initial acceleration has nothing to do with the cart.

VISUALIZE Our strategy is to divide the problem into an *acceleration* part, which we can analyze using kinematics, and a *collision* part, which we can analyze with momentum conservation. The pictorial representation of **FIGURE 9.16** includes information

---

FIGURE 9.16 Pictorial representation of Bob and the cart.

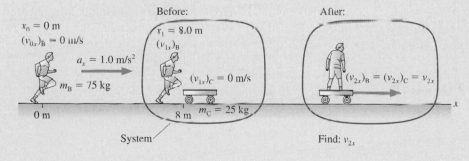

Continued

about both parts. Notice two important points. First, Bob's velocity $(v_{1x})_B$ at the end of his run is his "before" velocity for the collision. Second, Bob and the cart move together at the end, so v_{2x} is their common final velocity.

SOLVE The first part of the mathematical representation is kinematics. We don't know how long Bob accelerates, but we do know his acceleration and the distance. Thus

$$(v_{1x})_B{}^2 = (v_{0x})_B{}^2 + 2a_x(x_1 - x_0) = 2a_x x_1$$

His velocity after accelerating for 8.0 m is

$$(v_{1x})_B = \sqrt{2a_x x_1} = 4.0 \text{ m/s}$$

The second part of the problem, the collision, uses conservation of momentum: $P_{2x} = P_{1x}$. Written in terms of the individual momenta, this is

$$m_B(v_{2x})_B + m_C(v_{2x})_C = (m_B + m_C)v_{2x}$$
$$= m_B(v_{1x})_B + m_C(v_{1x})_C = m_B(v_{1x})_B$$

where we've used $(v_{1x})_C = 0$ m/s because the cart starts at rest. Solving for v_{2x}, we find

$$v_{2x} = \frac{m_B}{m_B + m_C}(v_{1x})_B = \frac{75 \text{ kg}}{100 \text{ kg}} \times 4.0 \text{ m/s} = 3.0 \text{ m/s}$$

The cart's speed is 3.0 m/s immediately after Bob jumps on.

Notice how easy this was! No forces, no acceleration constraints, no simultaneous equations. Why didn't we think of this before? Conservation laws are indeed powerful, but they can answer only certain questions. Had we wanted to know how far Bob slid across the cart before sticking to it, how long the slide took, or what the cart's acceleration was during the collision, we would not have been able to answer such questions on the basis of the conservation law. There is a price to pay for finding a simple connection between before and after, and that price is the loss of information about the details of the interaction. If we are satisfied with knowing only about before and after, then conservation laws are a simple and straightforward way to proceed. But many problems *do* require us to understand the interaction, and for these there is no avoiding Newton's laws.

It Depends on the System

The first step in the problem-solving strategy asks you to clearly define *the system*. This is worth emphasizing because many problem-solving errors arise from trying to apply momentum conservation to an inappropriate system. **The goal is to choose a system whose momentum will be conserved.** Even then, it is the *total* momentum of the system that is conserved, not the momenta of the individual particles within the system.

As an example, consider what happens if you drop a rubber ball and let it bounce off a hard floor. Is momentum conserved during the collision of the ball with the floor? You might be tempted to answer yes because the ball's rebound speed is very nearly equal to its impact speed. But there are two errors in this reasoning.

First, momentum depends on *velocity,* not speed. The ball's velocity and momentum just before the collision are negative. They are positive after the collision. Even if their magnitudes are equal, the ball's momentum after the collision is *not* equal to its momentum before the collision.

But more important, we haven't defined the system. The momentum of what? Whether or not momentum is conserved depends on the system. **FIGURE 9.17** shows two different choices of systems. In **FIGURE 9.17a**, where the ball itself is chosen as the system, the gravitational force of the earth on the ball is an external force. This force causes the ball to accelerate toward the earth, changing the ball's momentum. The force of the floor on the ball is also an external force. The impulse of $\vec{F}_{\text{floor on ball}}$ changes the ball's momentum from "down" to "up" as the ball bounces. The momentum of this system is most definitely *not* conserved.

FIGURE 9.17b shows a different choice. Here the system is ball + earth. Now the gravitational forces and the impulsive forces of the collision are interactions *within* the system. This is an isolated system, so the *total* momentum $\vec{P} = \vec{p}_{\text{ball}} + \vec{p}_{\text{earth}}$ is conserved.

FIGURE 9.17 Whether or not momentum is conserved as a ball falls to earth depends on your choice of the system.

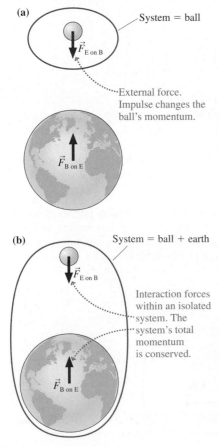

(a)

System = ball

$\vec{F}_{\text{E on B}}$

External force. Impulse changes the ball's momentum.

$\vec{F}_{\text{B on E}}$

(b)

System = ball + earth

$\vec{F}_{\text{E on B}}$

Interaction forces within an isolated system. The system's total momentum is conserved.

$\vec{F}_{\text{B on E}}$

In fact, the total momentum is $\vec{P} = \vec{0}$. Before you release the ball, both the ball and the earth are at rest (in the earth's reference frame). The total momentum is zero before you release the ball, so it will *always* be zero. Consider the situation just before the ball hits the floor. If the ball's velocity is v_{By}, it must be the case that

$$m_B v_{By} + m_E v_{Ey} = 0$$

and thus

$$v_{Ey} = -\frac{m_B}{m_E} v_{By}$$

In other words, as the ball is pulled down toward the earth, the ball pulls up on the earth (action/reaction pair of forces) until the entire earth reaches velocity v_{Ey}. The earth's momentum is equal and opposite to the ball's momentum.

Why don't we notice the earth "leaping up" toward us each time we drop something? Because of the earth's enormous mass relative to everyday objects. A typical rubber ball has a mass of 60 g and hits the ground with a velocity of about -5 m/s. The earth's upward velocity is thus

$$v_{Ey} \approx -\frac{6 \times 10^{-2}\ \text{kg}}{6 \times 10^{24}\ \text{kg}}(-5\ \text{m/s}) = 5 \times 10^{-26}\ \text{m/s}$$

The earth does, indeed, have a momentum equal and opposite to that of the ball, but the earth is so massive that it needs only an infinitesimal velocity to match the ball's momentum. At this speed, it would take the earth 300 million years to move the diameter of an atom!

STOP TO THINK 9.3 Objects A and C are made of different materials, with different "springiness," but they have the same mass and are initially at rest. When ball B collides with object A, the ball ends up at rest. When ball B is thrown with the same speed and collides with object C, the ball rebounds to the left. Compare the velocities of A and C after the collisions. Is v_A greater than, equal to, or less than v_C?

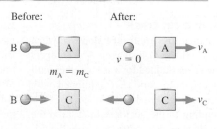

9.4 Inelastic Collisions

Collisions can have different possible outcomes. A rubber ball dropped on the floor bounces, but a ball of clay sticks to the floor without bouncing. A golf club hitting a golf ball causes the ball to rebound away from the club, but a bullet striking a block of wood embeds itself in the block.

A collision in which the two objects stick together and move with a common final velocity is called a **perfectly inelastic collision.** The clay hitting the floor and the bullet embedding itself in the wood are examples of perfectly inelastic collisions. Other examples include railroad cars coupling together upon impact and darts hitting a dart board. FIGURE 9.18 emphasizes the fact that the two objects have a common final velocity after they collide.

In an *elastic collision*, by contrast, the two objects bounce apart. We've looked at some examples of elastic collisions, but a full analysis requires ideas about energy. We will return to elastic collisions in Chapter 10.

FIGURE 9.18 An inelastic collision.

Two objects approach and collide.

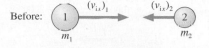

They stick and move together.

EXAMPLE 9.5 **An inelastic glider collision**

In a laboratory experiment, a 200 g air-track glider and a 400 g air-track glider are pushed toward each other from opposite ends of the track. The gliders have Velcro tabs on the front and will stick together when they collide. The 200 g glider is pushed with an initial speed of 3.0 m/s. The collision causes it to reverse direction at 0.40 m/s. What was the initial speed of the 400 g glider?

FIGURE 9.19 The before-and-after pictorial representation of an inelastic collision.

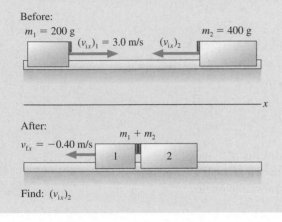

Before:

$m_1 = 200$ g

$(v_{ix})_1 = 3.0$ m/s

$(v_{ix})_2$

$m_2 = 400$ g

After:

$v_{fx} = -0.40$ m/s

$m_1 + m_2$

Find: $(v_{ix})_2$

MODEL Model the gliders as particles. Define the two gliders together as the system. This is an isolated system, so its total momentum is conserved in the collision. The gliders stick together, so this is a perfectly inelastic collision.

VISUALIZE FIGURE 9.19 shows a pictorial representation. We've chosen to let the 200 g glider (glider 1) start out moving to the right, so $(v_{ix})_1$ is a positive 3.0 m/s. The gliders move to the left after the collision, so their common final velocity is $v_{fx} = -0.40$ m/s. Velocity $(v_{ix})_2$ will be negative.

SOLVE The law of conservation of momentum, $P_{fx} = P_{ix}$, is

$$(m_1 + m_2)v_{fx} = m_1(v_{ix})_1 + m_2(v_{ix})_2$$

where we made use of the fact that the combined mass $m_1 + m_2$ moves together after the collision. We can easily solve for the initial velocity of the 400 g glider:

$$(v_{ix})_2 = \frac{(m_1 + m_2)v_{fx} - m_1(v_{ix})_1}{m_2}$$

$$= \frac{(0.60 \text{ kg})(-0.40 \text{ m/s}) - (0.20 \text{ kg})(3.0 \text{ m/s})}{0.40 \text{ kg}}$$

$$= -2.1 \text{ m/s}$$

The negative sign, which we anticipated, indicates that the 400 g glider started out moving to the left. The initial *speed* of the glider, which we were asked to find, is 2.1 m/s.

EXAMPLE 9.6 **Momentum in a car crash**

A 2000 kg Cadillac had just started forward from a stop sign when it was struck from behind by a 1000 kg Volkswagen. The bumpers became entangled, and the two cars skidded forward together until they came to rest. Fortunately, both cars were equipped with airbags and the drivers were using seat belts, so no one was injured. Officer Tom, responding to the accident, measured the skid marks to be 3.0 m long. He also took testimony from the driver that the Cadillac's speed just before the impact was 5.0 m/s. Officer Tom charged the Volkswagen driver with reckless driving. Should the Volkswagen driver also be charged with exceeding the 50 km/hr speed limit? The judge calls you as an "expert witness" to analyze the evidence. What is your conclusion?

MODEL This is really *two* problems. First, there is an inelastic collision. The two cars are not an isolated system because of external friction forces, but friction is not going to be significant during the brief collision. Within the impulse approximation, the momentum of the Volkswagen + Cadillac system will be conserved in the collision. Then we have a second problem, a dynamics problem of the two cars sliding.

VISUALIZE FIGURE 9.20a is a pictorial representation showing both the before and after of the collision and the more familiar picture for the dynamics of the skidding. We do not need to consider forces during the collision because we will use the law of conservation of momentum, but we do need a free-body diagram of the cars during the subsequent skid. This is shown in FIGURE 9.20b.

FIGURE 9.20 Pictorial representation and a free-body diagram of the cars as they skid.

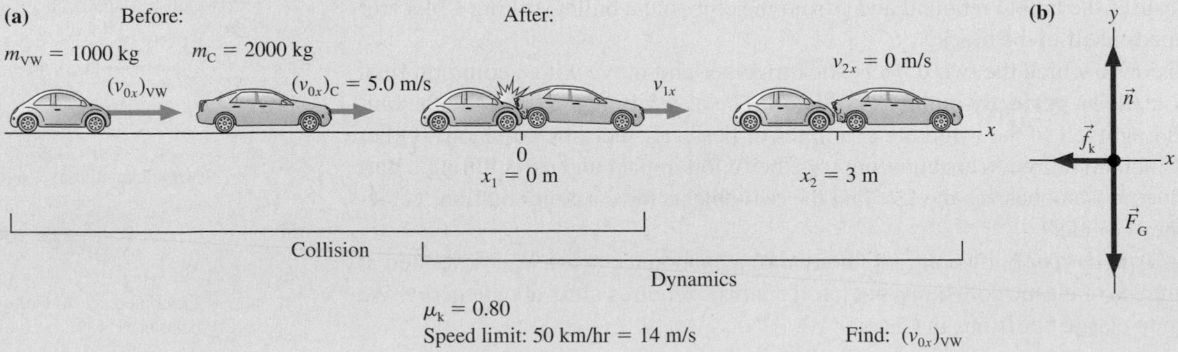

(a) Before:

$m_{VW} = 1000$ kg $m_C = 2000$ kg

$(v_{0x})_{VW}$ $(v_{0x})_C = 5.0$ m/s

After:

v_{1x}

$v_{2x} = 0$ m/s

$x_1 = 0$ m

$x_2 = 3$ m

Collision

Dynamics

$\mu_k = 0.80$

Speed limit: 50 km/hr = 14 m/s

(b)

$\vec{n}$

$\vec{f}_k$

$\vec{F}_G$

Find: $(v_{0x})_{VW}$

The cars have a common velocity v_{1x} just after the collision. This is the *initial velocity* for the dynamics problem. Our goal is to find $(v_{0x})_{VW}$, the Volkswagen's velocity at the moment of impact. The 50 km/hr speed limit has been converted to 14 m/s.

SOLVE First, the inelastic collision. The law of conservation of momentum is

$$(m_{VW} + m_C)v_{1x} = m_{VW}(v_{0x})_{VW} + m_C(v_{0x})_C$$

Solving for the initial velocity of the Volkswagen, we find

$$(v_{0x})_{VW} = \frac{(m_{VW} + m_C)v_{1x} - m_C(v_{0x})_C}{m_{VW}}$$

To evaluate $(v_{0x})_{VW}$, we need to know v_{1x}, the velocity *immediately* after the collision as the cars begin to skid. This information will come out of the dynamics of the skid. Newton's second law, based on the free-body diagram, and the model of kinetic friction are

$$\sum F_x = -f_k = (m_{VW} + m_C)a_x$$
$$\sum F_y = n - (m_{VW} + m_C)g = 0$$
$$f_k - \mu_k n$$

where we have noted that $\vec{f}_k$ points to the left (negative x-component) and that the total mass is $m_{VW} + m_C$. From the y-equation and the friction equation,

$$f_k - \mu_k(m_{VW} + m_C)g$$

Using this in the x-equation gives us the acceleration during the skid:

$$a_x = \frac{-f_k}{m_{VW} + m_C} = -\mu_k g = -7.84 \text{ m/s}^2$$

where the coefficient of kinetic friction for rubber on concrete is taken from Table 6.1. With the acceleration determined, we can move on to the kinematics. This is constant acceleration, so

$$v_{2x}^2 = 0 = v_{1x}^2 + 2a_x(x_2 - x_1) = v_{1x}^2 + 2a_x x_2$$

Hence the skid starts with velocity

$$v_{1x} = \sqrt{-2a_x x_2} = \sqrt{-2(-7.84 \text{ m/s}^2)(3.0 \text{ m})} = 6.9 \text{ m/s}$$

As we have noted, this is the final velocity of the collision. Inserting v_{1x} back into the momentum conservation equation, we finally determine that

$$(v_{0x})_{VW} = \frac{(3000 \text{ kg})(6.9 \text{ m/s}) - (2000 \text{ kg})(5.0 \text{ m/s})}{1000 \text{ kg}}$$
$$= 11 \text{ m/s}$$

On the basis of your testimony, the Volkswagen driver is *not* charged with speeding!

NOTE ▶ Momentum is conserved only for an isolated system. In this example, momentum was conserved during the collision (isolated system) but *not* during the skid (not an isolated system). In practice, it is not unusual for momentum to be conserved in one part or one aspect of a problem but not in others. ◀

STOP TO THINK 9.4 The two particles are both moving to the right. Particle 1 catches up with particle 2 and collides with it. The particles stick together and continue on with velocity v_f. Which of these statements is true?

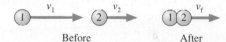

Before   After

a. v_f is greater than v_1. b. $v_f = v_1$. c. v_f is greater than v_2 but less than v_1.
d. $v_f = v_2$. e. v_f is less than v_2. f. Can't tell without knowing the masses.

9.5 Explosions

An **explosion**, where the particles of the system move apart from each other after a brief, intense interaction, is the opposite of a collision. The explosive forces, which could be from an expanding spring or from expanding hot gases, are *internal* forces. If the system is isolated, its total momentum during the explosion will be conserved.

EXAMPLE 9.7 **Recoil**

A 10 g bullet is fired from a 3.0 kg rifle with a speed of 500 m/s. What is the recoil speed of the rifle?

MODEL A simple analysis would say that the rifle exerts a force on the bullet and the bullet, by Newton's third law, exerts a force on the rifle, causing the rifle to recoil. However, this is a little *too* simple. After all, the rifle has no means by which to exert a force on the bullet. Instead, the rifle causes a small mass of gunpowder to explode. The expanding gas then exerts forces on *both* the bullet and the rifle.

Let's define the system to be bullet + gas + rifle. The forces due to the expanding gas during the explosion are internal forces, within the system. Any friction forces between the bullet and the rifle as the bullet travels down the barrel are also internal forces. Gravity, the only external force, is balanced by the normal forces of the barrel on the bullet and the person holding the rifle, so $\vec{F}_{net} = \vec{0}$. This is an isolated system and the law of conservation of momentum applies.

VISUALIZE FIGURE 9.21 shows a pictorial representation before and after the bullet is fired.

SOLVE The x-component of the total momentum is $P_x = (p_x)_B + (p_x)_R + (p_x)_{gas}$. Everything is at rest before the trigger is pulled, so the initial momentum is zero. After the trigger is pulled, the momentum of the expanding gas is the sum of the momenta of all the molecules in the gas. For every molecule moving in the forward direction with velocity v and momentum mv there is, on average, another molecule moving in the opposite direction with velocity $-v$ and thus momentum $-mv$. When summed over the enormous

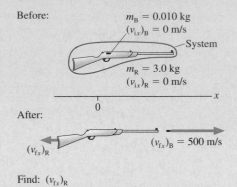

FIGURE 9.21 Before-and-after pictorial representation of a rifle firing a bullet.

Before:
$m_B = 0.010$ kg
$(v_{ix})_B = 0$ m/s
System
$m_R = 3.0$ kg
$(v_{ix})_R = 0$ m/s
x
0

After:
$(v_{fx})_R$
$(v_{fx})_B = 500$ m/s

Find: $(v_{fx})_R$

number of molecules in the gas, we will be left with $p_{gas} \approx 0$. In addition, the mass of the gas is much less than that of the rifle or bullet. For both reasons, we can reasonably neglect the momentum of the gas. The law of conservation of momentum is thus

$$P_{fx} = m_B(v_{fx})_B + m_R(v_{fx})_R = P_{ix} = 0$$

Solving for the rifle's velocity, we find

$$(v_{fx})_R = -\frac{m_B}{m_R}(v_{fx})_B = -\frac{0.010 \text{ kg}}{3.0 \text{ kg}} \times 500 \text{ m/s} = -1.7 \text{ m/s}$$

The minus sign indicates that the rifle's recoil is to the left. The recoil *speed* is 1.7 m/s.

We would not know where to begin to solve a problem such as this using Newton's laws. But Example 9.7 is a simple problem when approached from the before-and-after perspective of a conservation law. The selection of bullet + gas + rifle as "the system" was the critical step. For momentum conservation to be a useful principle, we had to select a system in which the complicated forces due to expanding gas and friction were all internal forces. The rifle by itself is *not* an isolated system, so its momentum is *not* conserved.

EXAMPLE 9.8 **Radioactivity**

A ^{238}U uranium nucleus is radioactive. It spontaneously disintegrates into a small fragment that is ejected with a measured speed of 1.50×10^7 m/s and a "daughter nucleus" that recoils with a measured speed of 2.56×10^5 m/s. What are the atomic masses of the ejected fragment and the daughter nucleus?

MODEL The notation ^{238}U indicates the isotope of uranium with an atomic mass of 238 u, where u is the abbreviation for the *atomic mass unit*. The nucleus contains 92 protons (uranium is atomic number 92) and 146 neutrons. The disintegration of a nucleus is, in essence, an explosion. Only *internal* nuclear forces are involved, so the total momentum is conserved in the decay.

VISUALIZE FIGURE 9.22 shows the pictorial representation. The mass of the daughter nucleus is m_1 and that of the ejected fragment is m_2. Notice that we converted the speed information to velocity information, giving $(v_{fx})_1$ and $(v_{fx})_2$ opposite signs.

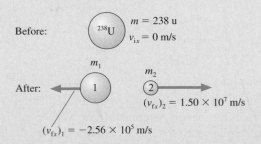

FIGURE 9.22 Before-and-after pictorial representation of the decay of a ^{238}U nucleus.

Before:
^{238}U
$m = 238$ u
$v_{ix} = 0$ m/s

m_1
m_2

After:
1
2
$(v_{fx})_2 = 1.50 \times 10^7$ m/s
$(v_{fx})_1 = -2.56 \times 10^5$ m/s

Find: m_1 and m_2

SOLVE The nucleus was initially at rest, hence the total momentum is zero. The momentum after the decay is still zero if the two pieces fly apart in opposite directions with momenta equal in magnitude but opposite in sign. That is,

$$P_{fx} = m_1(v_{fx})_1 + m_2(v_{fx})_2 = P_{ix} = 0$$

Although we know both final velocities, this is not enough information to find the two unknown masses. However, we also have another conservation law, conservation of mass, that requires

$$m_1 + m_2 = 238 \text{ u}$$

Combining these two conservation laws gives

$$m_1(v_{fx})_1 + (238 \text{ u} - m_1)(v_{fx})_2 = 0$$

The mass of the daughter nucleus is

$$m_1 = \frac{(v_{fx})_2}{(v_{fx})_2 - (v_{fx})_1} \times 238 \text{ u}$$

$$= \frac{1.50 \times 10^7 \text{ m/s}}{(1.50 \times 10^7 - (-2.56 \times 10^5)) \text{ m/s}} \times 238 \text{ u} = 234 \text{ u}$$

With m_1 known, the mass of the ejected fragment is $m_2 = 238 - m_1 = 4$ u.

ASSESS All we learn from a momentum analysis is the masses. Chemical analysis shows that the daughter nucleus is the element thorium, atomic number 90, with two fewer protons than uranium. The ejected fragment carried away two protons as part of its mass of 4 u, so it must be a particle with two protons and two neutrons. This is the nucleus of a helium atom, ^{4}He, which in nuclear physics is called an *alpha particle* α. Thus the radioactive decay of ^{238}U can be written as ^{238}U $\rightarrow$ ^{234}Th $+$ α.

Much the same reasoning explains how a rocket or jet aircraft accelerates. **FIGURE 9.23** shows a rocket with a parcel of fuel on board. Burning converts the fuel to hot gases that are expelled from the rocket motor. If we choose rocket + gases to be the system, the burning and expulsion are both internal forces. There are no other forces, so the total momentum of the rocket + gases system must be conserved. The rocket gains forward velocity and momentum as the exhaust gases are shot out the back, but the *total* momentum of the system remains zero.

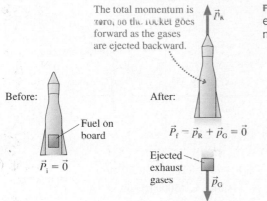

The total momentum is zero, so the rocket goes forward as the gases are ejected backward.

FIGURE 9.23 Rocket propulsion is an example of conservation of momentum.

Many people find it hard to understand how a rocket can accelerate in the vacuum of space because there is nothing to "push against." Thinking in terms of momentum, you can see that the rocket does not push against anything *external*, but only against the gases that it pushes out the back. In return, in accordance with Newton's third law, the gases push forward on the rocket. The details of rocket propulsion are more complex than we want to handle, because the mass of the rocket is changing, but you should be able to use the law of conservation of momentum to understand the basic principle by which rocket propulsion occurs.

STOP TO THINK 9.5 An explosion in a rigid pipe shoots out three pieces. A 6 g piece comes out the right end. A 4 g piece comes out the left end with twice the speed of the 6 g piece. From which end, left or right, does the third piece emerge?

Collisions and explosions often involve motion in two dimensions.

9.6 Momentum in Two Dimensions

Our examples thus far have been confined to motion along a one-dimensional axis. Many practical examples of momentum conservation involve motion in a plane. The total momentum $\vec{P}$ is a *vector* sum of the momenta $\vec{p} = m\vec{v}$ of the individual particles. Consequently, as we found in Section 9.3, momentum is conserved only if each component of $\vec{P}$ is conserved:

$$(p_{fx})_1 + (p_{fx})_2 + (p_{fx})_3 + \cdots = (p_{ix})_1 + (p_{ix})_2 + (p_{ix})_3 + \cdots$$
$$(p_{fy})_1 + (p_{fy})_2 + (p_{fy})_3 + \cdots = (p_{iy})_1 + (p_{iy})_2 + (p_{iy})_3 + \cdots \qquad (9.22)$$

In this section we'll apply momentum conservation to motion in two dimensions.

EXAMPLE 9.9 Momentum in a 2D car crash

The 2000 kg Cadillac and the 1000 kg Volkswagen of Example 9.6 meet again the following week, just after leaving the auto body shop where they had been repaired. The stoplight has just turned green, and the Cadillac, heading north, drives forward into the intersection. The Volkswagen, traveling east, fails to stop. The Volkswagen crashes into the left front fender of the Cadillac, then the cars stick together and slide to a halt. Officer Tom, responding to the accident, sees that the skid marks go 35° northeast from the point of impact. The Cadillac driver, who keeps a close eye on the speedometer, reports that he was traveling at 3.0 m/s when the accident occurred. How fast was the Volkswagen going just before the impact?

MODEL This is an inelastic collision. The total momentum of the Volkswagen + Cadillac system is conserved.

VISUALIZE FIGURE 9.24 is a before-and-after pictorial representation. The Volkswagen travels on the x-axis and the Cadillac on the y-axis; hence $(v_{0y})_{VW} = 0$ and $(v_{0x})_C = 0$.

SOLVE After the collision, the two cars move with the common velocity $\vec{v}_1$. The velocity components, as in a projectile motion problem, are $v_{1x} = v_1 \cos\theta$ and $v_{1y} = v_1 \sin\theta$. Thus the simultaneous x- and y-momentum equations are

$$(m_C + m_{VW})v_{1x} = (m_C + m_{VW})v_1\cos\theta$$
$$= m_C(v_{0x})_C + m_{VW}(v_{0x})_{VW} = m_{VW}(v_{0x})_{VW}$$
$$(m_C + m_{VW})v_{1y} = (m_C + m_{VW})v_1\sin\theta$$
$$= m_C(v_{0y})_C + m_{VW}(v_{0y})_{VW} = m_C(v_{0y})_C$$

We can use the y-equation to find the speed immediately after impact:

FIGURE 9.24 Pictorial representation of the collision between the Cadillac and the Volkswagen.

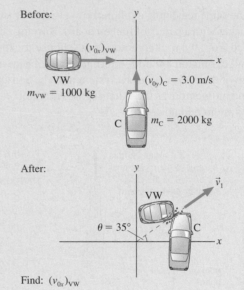

$$v_1 = \frac{m_C(v_{0y})_C}{(m_C + m_{VW})\sin\theta} = \frac{(2000 \text{ kg})(3.0 \text{ m/s})}{(3000 \text{ kg})\sin 35°} = 3.49 \text{ m/s}$$

Using this value for v_1 in the x-equation, we find that the Volkswagen's velocity was

$$(v_{0x})_{VW} = \frac{(m_C + m_{VW})v_1\cos\theta}{m_{VW}} = 8.6 \text{ m/s}$$

FIGURE 9.25 The momentum vectors of the car crash.

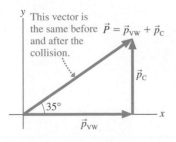

It's instructive to examine this collision with a picture of the momentum vectors. Before the collision, $\vec{p}_{VW} = (1000 \text{ kg})(8.6 \text{ m/s})\hat{\imath} = 8600\hat{\imath}$ kg m/s and $\vec{p}_C = (2000 \text{ kg})(3.0 \text{ m/s})\hat{\jmath} = 6000\hat{\jmath}$ kg m/s. These vectors, and their sum $\vec{P} = \vec{p}_{VW} + \vec{p}_C$ are shown in FIGURE 9.25. You can see that the total momentum vector makes a 35° angle with the x-axis. The individual momenta change in the collision, *but the total momentum does not.* That is why the skid marks are 35° north of east.

EXAMPLE 9.10 **A three-piece explosion**
A 10 g projectile is traveling east at 2.0 m/s when it suddenly explodes into three pieces. A 3.0 g fragment is shot due west at 10 m/s while another 3.0 g fragment travels 40° north of east at 12 m/s. What are the speed and direction of the third fragment?

MODEL Although many complex forces are involved in the explosion, they are all internal to the system. There are no external forces, so this is an isolated system and its total momentum is conserved.

VISUALIZE FIGURE 9.26 shows a before-and-after pictorial representation. We'll use uppercase M and V to distinguish the initial object from the three pieces into which it explodes.

FIGURE 9.26 Before-and-after pictorial representation of the three-piece explosion.

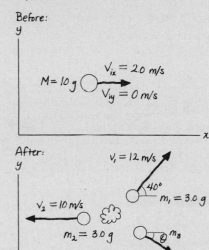

Find: v_3 and θ

SOLVE The system is the initial object and the subsequent three pieces. Conservation of momentum requires

$$m_1(v_{fx})_1 + m_2(v_{fx})_2 + m_3(v_{fx})_3 = MV_{ix}$$
$$m_1(v_{fy})_1 + m_2(v_{fy})_2 + m_3(v_{fy})_3 = MV_{iy}$$

Conservation of mass implies that

$$m_3 = M - m_1 - m_2 = 4.0 \text{ g}$$

Neither the original object nor m_2 has any momentum along the y-axis. We can use Figure 9.26 to write out the x- and y-components of $\vec{v}_1$ and $\vec{v}_3$, leading to

$$m_1 v_1 \cos 40° - m_2 v_2 + m_3 v_3 \cos\theta = MV$$
$$m_1 v_1 \sin 40° - m_3 v_3 \sin\theta = 0$$

where we used $(v_{fx})_2 = -v_2$ because m_2 is moving in the negative x-direction. Inserting known values in these equations gives us

$$-2.42 + 4v_3\cos\theta = 20$$
$$23.14 - 4v_3\sin\theta = 0$$

We can leave the masses in grams in this situation because the conversion factor to kilograms appears on both sides of the equation and thus cancels out. To solve, first use the second equation to write $v_3 = 5.79/\sin\theta$. Substitute this result into the first equation, noting that $\cos\theta/\sin\theta = 1/\tan\theta$, to get

$$-2.42 + 4\left(\frac{5.79}{\sin\theta}\right)\cos\theta = -2.42 + \frac{23.14}{\tan\theta} = 20$$

Now solve for θ:

$$\tan\theta = \frac{23.14}{20 + 2.42} = 1.03$$
$$\theta = \tan^{-1}(1.03) = 45.8°$$

Finally, use this result in the earlier expression for v_3 to find

$$v_3 = \frac{5.79}{\sin 45.8°} = 8.1 \text{ m/s}$$

The third fragment, with a mass of 4.0 g, is shot 46° south of east at a speed of 8.1 m/s.

SUMMARY

The goals of Chapter 9 have been to introduce the ideas of impulse and momentum and to learn a new problem-solving strategy based on conservation laws.

General Principles

Law of Conservation of Momentum

The total momentum $\vec{P} = \vec{p}_1 + \vec{p}_2 + \cdots$ of an isolated system is a constant. Thus

$$\vec{P}_f = \vec{P}_i$$

Newton's Second Law

In terms of momentum, Newton's second law is

$$\vec{F} = \frac{d\vec{p}}{dt}$$

Solving Momentum Conservation Problems

MODEL Choose an isolated system or a system that is isolated during at least part of the problem.

VISUALIZE Draw a pictorial representation of the system before and after the interaction.

SOLVE Write the law of conservation of momentum in terms of vector components:

$$(p_{fx})_1 + (p_{fx})_2 + \cdots = (p_{ix})_1 + (p_{ix})_2 + \cdots$$

$$(p_{fy})_1 + (p_{fy})_2 + \cdots = (p_{iy})_1 + (p_{iy})_2 + \cdots$$

ASSESS Is the result reasonable?

Important Concepts

Momentum $\vec{p} = m\vec{v}$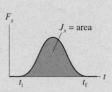

Impulse $J_x = \int_{t_i}^{t_f} F_x(t)\, dt$ = area under force curve

Impulse and momentum are related by the impulse-momentum theorem

$$\Delta p_x = J_x$$

This is an alternative statement of Newton's second law.

System A group of interacting particles.

Isolated system A system on which there are no external forces or the net external force is zero.

Before-and-after pictorial representation

- Define the system.
- Use two drawings to show the system *before* and *after* the interaction.
- List known information and identify what you are trying to find.

Applications

Collisions Two or more particles come together. In a perfectly inelastic collision, they stick together and move with a common final velocity.

Explosions Two or more particles move away from each other.

Two dimensions No new ideas, but both the x- and y-components of P must be conserved, giving two simultaneous equations.

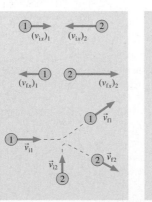

Momentum bar charts display the impulse-momentum theorem $p_{fx} = p_{ix} + J_x$ in graphical form.

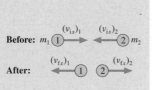

Terms and Notation

collision	impulse-momentum theorem	isolated system	perfectly inelastic collision
impulsive force	momentum bar chart	law of conservation of	explosion
momentum, $\vec{p}$	impulse approximation	momentum	
impulse, J_x	total momentum, $\vec{P}$		

MP For homework assigned on MasteringPhysics, go to www.masteringphysics.com Problem difficulty is labeled as | (straightforward) to ||| (challenging).	Problems labeled can be done on a Momentum Worksheet. Problems labeled integrate significant material from earlier chapters.

CONCEPTUAL QUESTIONS

1. Rank in order, from largest to smallest, the momenta $(p_x)_a$ to $(p_x)_e$ of the objects in **FIGURE Q9.1**.

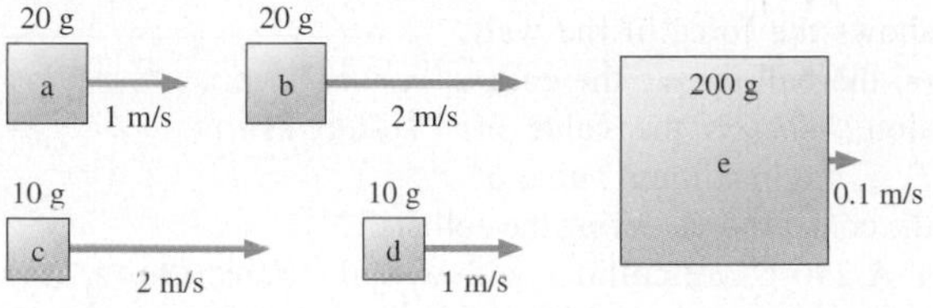

FIGURE Q9.1

2. Explain the concept of *impulse* in nonmathematical language. That is, don't simply put the equation in words to say that "impulse is the time integral of force." Explain it in terms that would make sense to an educated person who had never heard of it.
3. Explain the concept of *isolated system* in nonmathematical language that would make sense to an educated person who had never heard of it.
4. A 0.2 kg plastic cart and a 20 kg lead cart can both roll without friction on a horizontal surface. Equal forces are used to push both carts forward for a time of 1 s, starting from rest. After the force is removed at $t = 1$ s, is the momentum of the plastic cart greater than, less than, or equal to the momentum of the lead cart? Explain.
5. A 0.2 kg plastic cart and a 20 kg lead cart can both roll without friction on a horizontal surface. Equal forces are used to push both carts forward for a distance of 1 m, starting from rest. After traveling 1 m, is the momentum of the plastic cart greater than, less than, or equal to the momentum of the lead cart? Explain.
6. Angie, Brad, and Carlos are discussing a physics problem in which two identical bullets are fired with equal speeds at equal-mass wood and steel blocks resting on a frictionless table. One bullet bounces off the steel block while the second becomes embedded in the wood block. "All the masses and speeds are the same," says Angie, "so I think the blocks will have equal speeds after the collisions." "But what about momentum?" asks Brad. "The bullet hitting the wood block transfers all its momentum and energy to the block, so the wood block should end up going faster than the steel block." "I think the bounce is an important factor," replies Carlos. "The steel block will be faster because the bullet bounces off it and goes back the other direction." Which of these three do you agree with, and why?
7. It feels better to catch a hard ball while wearing a padded glove than to catch it bare handed. Use the ideas of this chapter to explain why.
8. Automobiles are designed with "crumple zones" intended to collapse in a collision. Use the ideas of this chapter to explain why.
9. A 2 kg object is moving to the right with a speed of 1 m/s when it experiences an impulse of 4 Ns. What are the object's speed and direction after the impulse?
10. A 2 kg object is moving to the right with a speed of 1 m/s when it experiences an impulse of -4 Ns. What are the object's speed and direction after the impulse?
11. A golf club continues forward after hitting the golf ball. Is momentum conserved in the collision? Explain, making sure you are careful to identify "the system."
12. Suppose a rubber ball collides head-on with a steel ball of equal mass traveling in the opposite direction with equal speed. Which ball, if either, receives the larger impulse? Explain.
13. Two particles collide, one of which was initially moving and the other initially at rest.
    a. Is it possible for *both* particles to be at rest after the collision? Give an example in which this happens, or explain why it can't happen.
    b. Is it possible for *one* particle to be at rest after the collision? Give an example in which this happens, or explain why it can't happen.
14. Two ice skaters, Paula and Ricardo, push off from each other. Ricardo weighs more than Paula.
    a. Which skater, if either, has the greater momentum after the push-off? Explain.
    b. Which skater, if either, has the greater speed after the push-off? Explain.
15. An object at rest explodes into three fragments. **FIGURE Q9.15** shows the momentum vectors of two of the fragments. What are p_x and p_y of the third fragment?

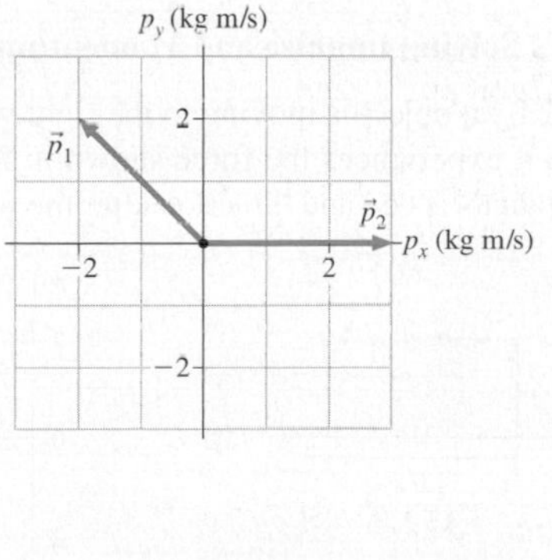

FIGURE Q9.15

EXERCISES AND PROBLEMS

Exercises

Section 9.1 Momentum and Impulse

1. | What is the magnitude of the momentum of
   a. A 1500 kg car traveling at 10 m/s?
   b. A 200 g baseball thrown at 40 m/s?

2. | At what speed do a bicycle and its rider, with a combined mass of 100 kg, have the same momentum as a 1500 kg car traveling at 5.0 m/s?

3. | What impulse does the force shown in FIGURE EX9.3 exert on a 250 g particle?

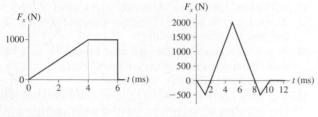

FIGURE EX9.3   FIGURE EX9.4

4. || What is the impulse on a 3.0 kg particle that experiences the force shown in FIGURE EX9.4?

5. || In FIGURE EX9.5, what value of F_{max} gives an impulse of 6.0 N s?

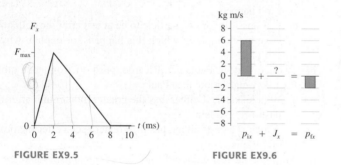

FIGURE EX9.5   FIGURE EX9.6

$$p_{ix} + J_x = p_{fx}$$

6. || FIGURE EX9.6 is an incomplete momentum bar chart for a collision that lasts 10 ms. What are the magnitude and direction of the average collision force exerted on the object?

Section 9.2 Solving Impulse and Momentum Problems

7. | A 2.0 kg object is moving to the right with a speed of 1.0 m/s when it experiences the force shown in FIGURE EX9.7. What are the object's speed and direction after the force ends?

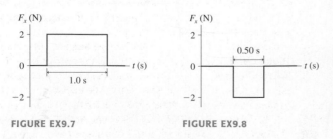

FIGURE EX9.7   FIGURE EX9.8

8. | A 2.0 kg object is moving to the right with a speed of 1.0 m/s when it experiences the force shown in FIGURE EX9.8. What are the object's speed and direction after the force ends?

9. | A sled slides along a horizontal surface on which the coefficient of kinetic friction is 0.25. Its velocity at point A is 8.0 m/s and at point B is 5.0 m/s. Use the impulse-momentum theorem to find how long the sled takes to travel from A to B.

10. | Use the impulse-momentum theorem to find how long a falling object takes to increase its speed from 5.5 m/s to 10.4 m/s.

11. || A 60 g tennis ball with an initial speed of 32 m/s hits a wall and rebounds with the same speed. FIGURE EX9.11 shows the force of the wall on the ball during the collision. What is the value of F_{max}, the maximum value of the contact force during the collision?

FIGURE EX9.11

12. || A 250 g ball collides with a wall. FIGURE EX9.12 shows the ball's velocity and the force exerted on the ball by the wall. What is v_{fx}, the ball's rebound velocity?

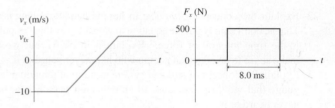

FIGURE EX9.12

13. || A 600 g air-track glider collides with a spring at one end of the track. FIGURE EX9.13 shows the glider's velocity and the force exerted on the glider by the spring. How long is the glider in contact with the spring?

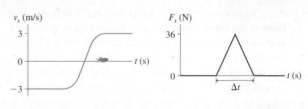

FIGURE EX9.13

Section 9.3 Conservation of Momentum

14. | A 10,000 kg railroad car is rolling at 2.0 m/s when a 4000 kg load of gravel is suddenly dropped in. What is the car's speed just after the gravel is loaded?

15. | A 5000 kg open train car is rolling on frictionless rails at 22 m/s when it starts pouring rain. A few minutes later, the car's speed is 20 m/s. What mass of water has collected in the car?

16. || A 10-m-long glider with a mass of 680 kg (including the passengers) is gliding horizontally through the air at 30 m/s when a 60 kg skydiver drops out by releasing his grip on the glider. What is the glider's velocity just after the skydiver lets go?

Section 9.4 Inelastic Collisions

17. | A 300 g bird flying along at 6.0 m/s sees a 10 g insect heading straight toward it with a speed of 30 m/s. The bird opens its mouth wide and enjoys a nice lunch. What is the bird's speed immediately after swallowing?

18. | The parking brake on a 2000 kg Cadillac has failed, and it is rolling slowly, at 1 mph, toward a group of small children. Seeing the situation, you realize you have just enough time to drive your 1000 kg Volkswagen head-on into the Cadillac and save the children. With what speed should you impact the Cadillac to bring it to a halt?

19. | A 1500 kg car is rolling at 2.0 m/s. You would like to stop the car by firing a 10 kg blob of sticky clay at it. How fast should you fire the clay?

Section 9.5 Explosions

20. | A 50 kg archer, standing on frictionless ice, shoots a 100 g arrow at a speed of 100 m/s. What is the recoil speed of the archer?

21. | In Problem 27 of Chapter 7 you found the recoil speed of Bob as he throws a rock while standing on frictionless ice. Bob has a mass of 75 kg and can throw a 500 g rock with a speed of 30 m/s. Find Bob's recoil speed again, this time using momentum.

22. || Dan is gliding on his skateboard at 4.0 m/s. He suddenly jumps backward off the skateboard, kicking the skateboard forward at 8.0 m/s. How fast is Dan going as his feet hit the ground? Dan's mass is 50 kg and the skateboard's mass is 5.0 kg.

Section 9.6 Momentum in Two Dimensions

23. | Two particles collide and bounce apart. **FIGURE EX9.23** shows the initial momenta of both and the final momentum of particle 2. What is the final momentum of particle 1? Write your answer in component form.

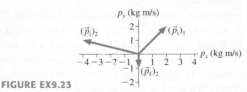

FIGURE EX9.23

24. || A 20 g ball of clay traveling east at 3.0 m/s collides with a 30 g ball of clay traveling north at 2.0 m/s. What are the speed and the direction of the resulting 50 g ball of clay?

Problems

25. || A 50 g ball is launched from ground level at an angle 30° above the horizon. Its initial speed is 25 m/s.
    a. What are the values of p_x and p_y an instant after the ball is launched, at the point of maximum altitude, and an instant before the ball hits the ground?
    b. Why is one component of $\vec{p}$ constant? Explain.
    c. For the component of $\vec{p}$ that changes, show that the change in momentum is equal to the gravitational force on the ball multiplied by the time of flight. Explain why this is so.

26. || Far in space, where gravity is negligible, a 425 kg rocket traveling at 75 m/s fires its engines. **FIGURE P9.26** shows the thrust force as a function of time. The mass lost by the rocket during these 30 s is negligible.
    a. What impulse does the engine impart to the rocket?
    b. At what time does the rocket reach its maximum speed? What is the maximum speed?

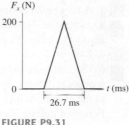

FIGURE P9.26

27. || Force $F_x = (10\ \text{N})\sin(2\pi t/4.0\ \text{s})$ is exerted on a 250 g particle during the interval $0\ \text{s} \le t \le 2.0\ \text{s}$. If the particle starts from rest, what is its speed at $t = 2.0\ \text{s}$?

28. || A tennis player swings her 1000 g racket with a speed of 10 m/s. She hits a 60 g tennis ball that was approaching her at a speed of 20 m/s. The ball rebounds at 40 m/s.
    a. How fast is her racket moving immediately after the impact? You can ignore the interaction of the racket with her hand for the brief duration of the collision.
    b. If the tennis ball and racket are in contact for 10 ms, what is the average force that the racket exerts on the ball? How does this compare to the gravitational force on the ball?

29. || A 200 g ball is dropped from a height of 2.0 m, bounces on a hard floor, and rebounds to a height of 1.5 m. **FIGURE P9.29** shows the impulse received from the floor. What maximum force does the floor exert on the ball?

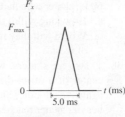

FIGURE P9.29

30. || A 40 g rubber ball is dropped from a height of 1.8 m and rebounds to two-thirds of its initial height.
    a. What are the magnitude and direction of the impulse that the floor exerts on the ball?
    b. Using simple observations of an ordinary rubber ball, sketch a physically plausible graph of the force of the floor on the ball as a function of time.
    c. Make a plausible estimate of how long the ball is in contact with the floor, then use this quantity to calculate the approximate average force of the floor on the ball.

31. || A 500 g cart is released from rest 1.00 m from the bottom of a frictionless, 30.0° ramp. The cart rolls down the ramp and bounces off a rubber block at the bottom. **FIGURE P9.31** shows the force during the collision. After the cart bounces, how far does it roll back up the ramp?

FIGURE P9.31

32. || A particle of mass m is at rest at $t = 0$. Its momentum for $t > 0$ is given by $p_x = 6t^2$ kg m/s, where t is in s. Find an expression for $F_x(t)$, the force exerted on the particle as a function of time.

33. || A small rocket to gather weather data is launched straight up. Several seconds into the flight, its velocity is 120 m/s and it is accelerating at 18 m/s². At this instant, the rocket's mass is 48 kg and it is losing mass at the rate of 0.50 kg/s as it burns fuel. What is the net force on the rocket? **Hint:** Newton's second law was presented in a new form in this chapter.

34. | Three identical train cars, coupled together, are rolling east at 2.0 m/s. A fourth car traveling east at 4.0 m/s catches up with the three and couples to make a four-car train. A moment later, the train cars hit a fifth car that was at rest on the tracks, and it couples to make a five-car train. What is the speed of the five-car train?

35. || A 30 g dart is shot straight up at 9.0 m/s. At the same instant, a 20 g ball of cork is dropped from 3.0 m above the dart. What are the speed and direction of the cork ball immediately after it is hit by the dart? Assume the collision is exactly head-on and the dart sticks in the cork.

36. ‖ Most geologists believe that the dinosaurs became extinct 65 million years ago when a large comet or asteroid struck the earth, throwing up so much dust that the sun was blocked out for a period of many months. Suppose an asteroid with a diameter of 2.0 km and a mass of 1.0×10^{13} kg hits the earth with an impact speed of 4.0×10^4 m/s.
    a. What is the earth's recoil speed after such a collision? (Use a reference frame in which the earth was initially at rest.)
    b. What percentage is this of the earth's speed around the sun? (Use the astronomical data inside the back cover.)

37. ‖ At the center of a 50-m-diameter circular ice rink, a 75 kg skater traveling north at 2.5 m/s collides with and holds onto a 60 kg skater who had been heading west at 3.5 m/s.
    a. How long will it take them to glide to the edge of the rink?
    b. Where will they reach it? Give your answer as an angle north of west.

38. ‖ Two ice skaters, with masses of 50 kg and 75 kg, are at the center of a 60-m-diameter circular rink. The skaters push off against each other and glide to opposite edges of the rink. If the heavier skater reaches the edge in 20 s, how long does the lighter skater take to reach the edge?

39. ‖ A firecracker in a coconut blows the coconut into three pieces. Two pieces of equal mass fly off south and west, perpendicular to each other, at 20 m/s. The third piece has twice the mass as the other two. What are the speed and direction of the third piece? Give the direction as an angle east of north.

40. ‖ One billiard ball is shot east at 2.0 m/s. A second, identical billiard ball is shot west at 1.0 m/s. The balls have a glancing collision, not a head-on collision, deflecting the second ball by 90° and sending it north at 1.41 m/s. What are the speed and direction of the first ball after the collision? Give the direction as an angle south of east.

41. ‖ A 10 g bullet is fired into a 10 kg wood block that is at rest on a wood table. The block, with the bullet embedded, slides 5.0 cm across the table. What was the speed of the bullet?

42. ‖ Fred (mass 60 kg) is running with the football at a speed of 6.0 m/s when he is met head-on by Brutus (mass 120 kg), who is moving at 4.0 m/s. Brutus grabs Fred in a tight grip, and they fall to the ground. Which way do they slide, and how far? The coefficient of kinetic friction between football uniforms and Astro-turf is 0.30.

43. ‖ You are part of a search-and-rescue mission that has been called out to look for a lost explorer. You've found the missing explorer, but you're separated from him by a 200-m-high cliff and a 30-m-wide raging river. To save his life, you need to get a 5.0 kg package of emergency supplies across the river. Unfortunately, you can't throw the package hard enough to make it across. Fortunately, you happen to have a 1.0 kg rocket intended for launching flares. Improvising quickly, you attach a sharpened stick to the front of the rocket, so that it will impale itself into the package of supplies, then fire the rocket at ground level toward the supplies. What minimum speed must the rocket have just before impact in order to save the explorer's life?

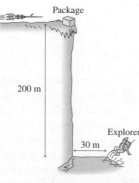

Package

200 m

30 m

Explorer

FIGURE P9.43

44. ‖ A 20 g ball of clay is shot to the right (in the positive x-direction) at 12 m/s toward a 40 g ball of clay at rest. The two balls of clay collide and stick together. Call this reference frame S.
    a. What is the total momentum in frame S?
    b. What is the velocity $\vec{V}$ of a reference frame S′ in which the total momentum is zero?
    c. After the collision, what is the velocity in frame S′ of the resulting 60 g ball of clay? Answering this question requires only thought, no calculations.
    d. Use your answer to part c and the Galilean transformation of velocity to find the post-collision velocity of the 60 g ball of clay in reference frame S.

45. ‖ An object at rest on a flat, horizontal surface explodes into two fragments, one seven times as massive as the other. The heavier fragment slides 8.2 m before stopping. How far does the lighter fragment slide? Assume that both fragments have the same coefficient of kinetic friction.

46. ‖ A 1500 kg weather rocket accelerates upward at 10 m/s². It explodes 2.0 s after liftoff and breaks into two fragments, one twice as massive as the other. Photos reveal that the lighter fragment traveled straight up and reached a maximum height of 530 m. What were the speed and direction of the heavier fragment just after the explosion?

47. ‖ In a ballistics test, a 25 g bullet traveling horizontally at 1200 m/s goes through a 30-cm-thick 350 kg stationary target and emerges with a speed of 900 m/s. The target is free to slide on a smooth horizontal surface.
    a. How long is the bullet in the target? What average force does it exert on the target?
    b. What is the target's speed just after the bullet emerges?

48. | Two 500 g blocks of wood are 2.0 m apart on a frictionless table. A 10 g bullet is fired at 400 m/s toward the blocks. It passes all the way through the first block, then embeds itself in the second block. The speed of the first block immediately afterward is 6.0 m/s. What is the speed of the second block after the bullet stops in it?

49. ‖ The skiing duo of Brian (80 kg) and Ashley (50 kg) is always a crowd pleaser. In one routine, Brian, wearing wood skis, starts at the top of a 200-m-long, 20° slope. Ashley waits for him halfway down. As he skis past, she leaps into his arms and he carries her the rest of the way down. What is their speed at the bottom of the slope?

50. ‖ In a military test, a 575 kg unmanned spy plane is traveling north at an altitude of 2700 m and a speed of 450 m/s. It is intercepted by a 1280 kg rocket traveling east at 725 m/s. If the rocket and the spy plane become enmeshed in a tangled mess, where, relative to the point of impact, do they hit the ground? Give the direction as an angle east of north.

51. ‖ A spaceship of mass 2.0×10^6 kg is cruising at a speed of 5.0×10^6 m/s when the antimatter reactor fails, blowing the ship into three pieces. One section, having a mass of 5.0×10^5 kg, is blown straight backward with a speed of 2.0×10^6 m/s. A second piece, with mass 8.0×10^5 kg, continues forward at 1.0×10^6 m/s. What are the direction and speed of the third piece?

52. ‖ A 30 ton rail car and a 90 ton rail car, initially at rest, are connected together with a giant but massless compressed spring between them. When released, the 30 ton car is pushed away at a speed of 4.0 m/s relative to the 90 ton car. What is the speed of the 30 ton car relative to the ground?

53. || A 75 kg shell is fired with an initial speed of 125 m/s at an angle 55° above horizontal. Air resistance is negligible. At its highest point, the shell explodes into two fragments, one four times more massive than the other. The heavier fragment lands directly below the point of the explosion. If the explosion exerts forces only in the horizontal direction, how far from the launch point does the lighter fragment land?

54. || A proton (mass 1 u) is shot at a speed of 5.0×10^7 m/s toward a gold target. The nucleus of a gold atom (mass 197 u) repels the proton and deflects it straight back toward the source with 90% of its initial speed. What is the recoil speed of the gold nucleus?

55. || A proton (mass 1 u) is shot toward an unknown target nucleus at a speed of 2.50×10^6 m/s. The proton rebounds with its speed reduced by 25% while the target nucleus acquires a speed of 3.12×10^5 m/s. What is the mass, in atomic mass units, of the target nucleus?

56. | The nucleus of the polonium isotope ^{214}Po (mass 214 u) is radioactive and decays by emitting an alpha particle (a helium nucleus with mass 4 u). Laboratory experiments measure the speed of the alpha particle to be 1.92×10^7 m/s. Assuming the polonium nucleus was initially at rest, what is the recoil speed of the nucleus that remains after the decay?

57. || A neutron is an electrically neutral subatomic particle with a mass just slightly greater than that of a proton. A free neutron is radioactive and decays after a few minutes into other subatomic particles. In one experiment, a neutron at rest was observed to decay into a proton (mass 1.67×10^{-27} kg) and an electron (mass 9.11×10^{-31} kg). The proton and electron were shot out back-to-back. The proton speed was measured to be 1.0×10^5 m/s and the electron speed was 3.0×10^7 m/s. No other decay products were detected.
    a. Was momentum conserved in the decay of this neutron?

    NOTE ▶ Experiments such as this were first performed in the 1930s and seemed to indicate a failure of the law of conservation of momentum. In 1933, Wolfgang Pauli postulated that the neutron might have a *third* decay product that is virtually impossible to detect. Even so, it can carry away just enough momentum to keep the total momentum conserved. This proposed particle was named the *neutrino*, meaning "little neutral one." Neutrinos were, indeed, discovered nearly 20 years later. ◀

    b. If a neutrino was emitted in the above neutron decay, in which direction did it travel? Explain your reasoning.
    c. How much momentum did this neutrino "carry away" with it?

58. || A 20 g ball of clay traveling east at 2.0 m/s collides with a 30 g ball of clay traveling 30° south of west at 1.0 m/s. What are the speed and direction of the resulting 50 g blob of clay?

59. || FIGURE P9.59 shows a collision between three balls of clay. The three hit simultaneously and stick together. What are the speed and direction of the resulting blob of clay?

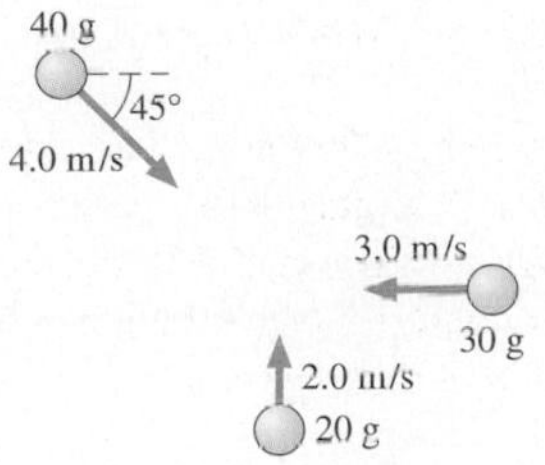

FIGURE P9.59

60. || A 2100 kg truck is traveling east through an intersection at 2.0 m/s when it is hit simultaneously from the side and the rear. (Some people have all the luck!) One car is a 1200 kg compact traveling north at 5.0 m/s. The other is a 1500 kg midsize traveling east at 10 m/s. The three vehicles become entangled and slide as one body. What are their speed and direction just after the collision?

61. || The carbon isotope ^{14}C is used for carbon dating of archeological artifacts. ^{14}C (mass 2.34×10^{-26} kg) decays by the process known as *beta decay* in which the nucleus emits an electron (the beta particle) and a subatomic particle called a neutrino. In one such decay, the electron and the neutrino are emitted at right angles to each other. The electron (mass 9.11×10^{-31} kg) has a speed of 5.0×10^7 m/s and the neutrino has a momentum of 8.0×10^{-24} kg m/s. What is the recoil speed of the nucleus?

In Problems 62 through 65 you are given the equation used to solve a problem. For each of these, you are to
  a. Write a realistic problem for which this is the correct equation.
  b. Finish the solution of the problem, including a pictorial representation.

62. $(0.10 \text{ kg})(40 \text{ m/s}) - (0.10 \text{ kg})(-30 \text{ m/s}) = \frac{1}{2}(1400 \text{ N}) \Delta t$

63. $(600 \text{ g})(4.0 \text{ m/s}) = (400 \text{ g})(3.0 \text{ m/s}) + (200 \text{ g})(v_{ix})_2$

64. $(3000 \text{ kg})v_{fx} = (2000 \text{ kg})(5.0 \text{ m/s}) + (1000 \text{ kg})(-4.0 \text{ m/s})$

65. $(50 \text{ g})(v_{fx})_1 + (100 \text{ g})(7.5 \text{ m/s}) = (150 \text{ g})(1.0 \text{ m/s})$

Challenge Problems

66. A 1000 kg cart is rolling to the right at 5.0 m/s. A 70 kg man is standing on the right end of the cart. What is the speed of the cart if the man suddenly starts running to the left with a speed of 10 m/s relative to the cart?

67. Ann (mass 50 kg) is standing at the left end of a 15-m-long, 500 kg cart that has frictionless wheels and rolls on a frictionless track. Initially both Ann and the cart are at rest. Suddenly, Ann starts running along the cart at a speed of 5.0 m/s relative to the cart. How far will Ann have run *relative to the ground* when she reaches the right end of the cart?

68. A 20 kg wood ball hangs from a 2.0 m-long wire. The maximum tension the wire can withstand without breaking is 400 N. A 1.0 kg projectile traveling horizontally hits and embeds itself in the wood ball. What is the largest speed this projectile can have without causing the cable to break?

69. A two-stage rocket is traveling at 1200 m/s with respect to the earth when the first stage runs out of fuel. Explosive bolts release the first stage and push it backward with a speed of 35 m/s relative to the second stage. The first stage is three times as massive as the second stage. What is the speed of the second stage after the separation?

70. The Army of the Nation of Whynot has a plan to propel small vehicles across the battlefield by shooting them, from behind, with a machine gun. They've hired you as a consultant to help with an upcoming test. A 100 kg test vehicle will roll along frictionless rails. The vehicle has a tall "sail" made of ultrahard steel. Previous tests have shown that a 20 g bullet traveling at 400 m/s rebounds from the sail at 200 m/s. The design objective is for the cart to reach a speed of 12 m/s in 20 s. You need to tell them how many bullets to fire per second. A five-star general will watch the test, so your ability to get future consulting jobs will depend on the outcome.

71. You are the ground-control commander of a 2000 kg scientific rocket that is approaching Mars at a speed of 25,000 km/hr. It needs to quickly slow to 15,000 km/hr to begin a controlled descent to the surface. If the rocket enters the Martian atmosphere too fast it will burn up, and if it enters too slowly, it will use up its maneuvering fuel before reaching the surface and will crash. The rocket has a new braking system: Several 5.0 kg "bullets" on the front of the rocket can be fired straight ahead. Each has a high-explosive charge that fires it at a speed of 139,000 m/s relative to the rocket. You need to send the rocket an instruction to tell it how many bullets to fire. Success will bring you fame and glory, but failure of this $500,000,000 mission will ruin your career.

72. You are a world-famous physicist-lawyer defending a client who has been charged with murder. It is alleged that your client, Mr. Smith, shot the victim, Mr. Wesson. The detective who investigated the scene of the crime found a second bullet, from a shot that missed Mr. Wesson, that had embedded itself into a chair. You arise to cross-examine the detective.

You: In what type of chair did you find the bullet?
Det: A wooden chair.
You: How massive was this chair?
Det: It had a mass of 20 kg.

You: How did the chair respond to being struck with a bullet?
Det: It slid across the floor.
You: How far?
Det: A good three centimeters. The slide marks on the dusty floor are quite distinct.
You: What kind of floor was it?
Det: A wood floor, very nice oak planks.
You: What was the mass of the bullet you retrieved from the chair?
Det: Its mass was 10 g.
You: And how far had it penetrated into the chair?
Det: A distance of 1.5 cm.
You: Have you tested the gun you found in Mr. Smith's possession?
Det: I have.
You: What is the muzzle velocity of bullets fired from that gun?
Det: The muzzle velocity is 450 m/s.
You: And the barrel length?
Det: The gun has a barrel length of 16 cm.

With only a slight hesitation, you turn confidently to the jury and proclaim, "My client's gun did not fire these shots!" How are you going to convince the jury and the judge?

STOP TO THINK ANSWERS

Stop to Think 9.1: f. The cart is initially moving in the negative x-direction, so $p_{ix} = -20$ kg m/s. After it bounces, $p_{fx} = 10$ kg m/s. Thus $\Delta p = (10 \text{ kg m/s}) - (-20 \text{ kg m/s}) = 30$ kg m/s.

Stop to Think 9.2: b. The clay ball goes from $v_{ix} = v$ to $v_{fx} = 0$, so $J_{clay} = \Delta p_x = -mv$. The rubber ball rebounds, going from $v_{ix} = v$ to $v_{fx} = -v$ (same speed, opposite direction). Thus $J_{rubber} = \Delta p_x = -2mv$. The rubber ball has a larger momentum change, and this requires a larger impulse.

Stop to Think 9.3: Less than. The ball's momentum $m_B v_B$ is the same in both cases. Momentum is conserved, so the *total* momentum is the same after both collisions. The ball that rebounds from C has *negative* momentum, so C must have a larger momentum than A.

Stop to Think 9.4: c. Momentum conservation requires $(m_1 + m_2) \times v_f = m_1 v_1 + m_2 v_2$. Because $v_1 > v_2$, it must be that $(m_1 + m_2) \times v_f = m_1 v_1 + m_2 v_2 > m_1 v_2 + m_2 v_2 = (m_1 + m_2) v_2$. Thus $v_f > v_2$. Similarly, $v_2 < v_1$ so $(m_1 + m_2) v_f = m_1 v_1 + m_2 v_2 < m_1 v_1 + m_2 v_1 = (m_1 + m_2) v_1$. Thus $v_f < v_1$. The collision causes m_1 to slow down and m_2 to speed up.

Stop to Think 9.5: Right end. The pieces started at rest, so the total momentum of the system is zero. It's an isolated system, so the total momentum after the explosion is still zero. The 6 g piece has momentum $6v$. The 4 g piece, with velocity $-2v$, has momentum $-8v$. The combined momentum of these two pieces is $-2v$. In order for P to be zero, the third piece must have a *positive* momentum $(+2v)$ and thus a positive velocity.

10 Energy

This pole vaulter can lift herself nearly 6 m (20 ft) off the ground by transforming the kinetic energy of her run into gravitational potential energy.

► **Looking Ahead**

The goals of Chapter 10 are to introduce the ideas of kinetic and potential energy and to learn a new problem-solving strategy based on conservation of energy. In this chapter you will learn to:

- Understand and use the concepts of kinetic and potential energy.
- Use energy bar graphs.
- Use and interpret energy diagrams.
- Solve problems using the law of conservation of mechanical energy.
- Apply these ideas to elastic collisions.

◄ **Looking Back**

Our introduction to energy will be based on free fall. We will also use the before-and-after pictorial representation developed for impulse and momentum problems. Please review

- Section 2.6 Free-fall kinematics.
- Sections 9.2–9.3 Before-and-after pictorial representations and conservation of momentum.

Energy. It's a word you hear all the time. We use chemical energy to heat our homes and bodies, electrical energy to power our lights and computers, and solar energy to grow our crops and forests. We're told to use energy wisely and not to waste it. Athletes and weary students consume "energy bars" and "energy drinks" to gain quick energy.

But just what is energy? The concept of energy has grown and changed with time, and it is not easy to define in a general way just what energy is. Rather than starting with a formal definition, we're going to let the concept of energy expand slowly over the course of several chapters. The purpose of this chapter is to introduce the two most fundamental forms of energy, kinetic energy and potential energy. Our goal is to understand the characteristics of energy, how energy is used, and, especially important, how energy is transformed from one form to another. For example, this pole vaulter, after years of training, has become extraordinarily proficient at transforming kinetic energy into gravitational potential energy.

Ultimately we will discover a very powerful conservation law for energy. Some scientists consider the law of conservation of energy to be the most important of all the laws of nature. But all that in due time; first we have to start with the basic ideas.

10.1 A "Natural Money" Called Energy

We will start by discussing what seems to be a completely unrelated topic: money. As you will discover, monetary systems have much in common with energy. Let's begin with a short story.

The Parable of the Lost Penny

John was a hard worker. His only source of income was the paycheck he received each month. Even though most of each paycheck had to be spent on basic necessities, John managed to keep a respectable balance in his checking account. He even saved enough to occasionally buy a few stocks and bonds, his investment in the future.

John never cared much for pennies, so he kept a jar by the door and dropped all his pennies into it at the end of each day. Eventually, he reasoned, his saved pennies would be worth taking to the bank and converting into crisp new dollar bills.

John found it fascinating to keep track of these various forms of money. He noticed, to his dismay, that the amount of money in his checking account did not spontaneously increase overnight. Furthermore, there seemed to be a definite correlation between the size of his paycheck and the amount of money he had in the bank. So John decided to embark on a systematic study of money.

He began, as would any good scientist, by using his initial observations to formulate a hypothesis. John called this hypothesis a *model* of the monetary system. He found that he could represent his monetary model with the flowchart shown in FIGURE 10.1.

FIGURE 10.1 John's model of the monetary system.

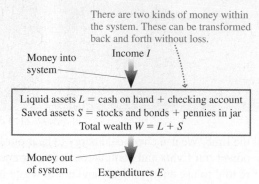

As the chart shows, John divided his money into two basic types, liquid assets and saved assets. The *liquid assets L*, which included his checking account and the cash in his pockets, were moneys available for immediate use. His *saved assets S*, which included his stocks and bonds as well as the jar of pennies, had the *potential* to be converted into liquid assets, but they were not available for immediate use. John decided to call the sum total of assets his *wealth:* $W = L + S$.

John's assets were, more or less, simply definitions. The more interesting question, he thought, was how his wealth depended on his *income I* and *expenditures E*. These represented money transferred *to* him by his employer and money transferred *by* him to stores and bill collectors. After painstakingly collecting and analyzing his data, John finally determined that the relationship between monetary transfers and wealth is

$$\Delta W = I - E$$

John interpreted this equation to mean that the *change* in his wealth, ΔW, was numerically equal to the *net* monetary transfer $I - E$.

During a week-long period when John stayed home sick, isolated from the rest of the world, he had neither income nor expenses. In grand confirmation of his hypothesis, he found that his wealth W_f at the end of the week was identical to his wealth W_i at the week's beginning. That is, $W_f = W_i$. This occurred despite the fact that he had moved pennies from his pocket to the jar and also, by telephone, had sold some stocks and transferred the money to his checking account. In other words, John found that he could make all of the *internal* conversions of assets from one form to another that he wanted, but his total wealth remained constant (W = constant) as long as he was isolated from the world. This seemed such a remarkable rule that John named it the *law of conservation of wealth*.

One day, however, John added up his income and expenditures for the week and the changes in his various assets, and he was 1¢ off! Inexplicably, some money seemed to have vanished. He was devastated. All those years of careful research, and now it seemed that his monetary hypothesis might not be true. Under some circumstances, yet to be discovered, it looked like $\Delta W \neq I - E$. Off by a measly penny. A wasted scientific life. . . .

But wait! In a flash of inspiration, John realized that perhaps there were other types of assets, yet to be discovered, and that his monetary hypothesis would still be valid if *all* assets were included. Weeks went by as John, in frantic activity, searched fruitlessly for previously *hidden* assets. Then one day, as John lifted the cushion off the sofa to vacuum out the potato chip crumbs—lo and behold, there it was!—the missing penny!

John raced to complete his theory, now including the sofa (as well as the washing machine) as a previously unknown form of saved assets that needed to be included in S. Other researchers soon discovered other types of assets, such as the remarkable find of the "cash in the mattress." To this day, when *all* known assets are included, monetary scientists have never found a violation of John's simple hypothesis that $\Delta W = I - E$. John was last seen sailing for Stockholm to collect the Nobel Prize for his Theory of Wealth.

Energy

John, despite his diligent efforts, did not discover a law of nature. The monetary system is a human construction that, by design, obeys John's "laws." Monetary system laws, such as that you cannot print money in your basement, are enforced by society, not by nature. But suppose that physical objects possessed a "natural money" that was governed by a theory, or model, similar to John's. An object might have several different forms of natural money that could be converted back and forth, but the total amount of an object's natural money would *change* only if natural money were *transferred* to or from the object. Two key words here, as in John's model, are *transfer* and *change*.

One of the greatest and most significant discoveries of science is that there is such a "natural money" called **energy.** You have heard of some of the many forms of energy, such as solar energy or nuclear energy, but others may be new to you. These forms of energy can differ as much as a checking account differs from loose change in the sofa. Much of our study is going to be focused on the *transformation* of energy from one form to another. Much of modern technology is concerned with transforming energy, such as changing the chemical energy of oil molecules to electrical energy or to the kinetic energy of your car.

As we use energy concepts, we will be "accounting" for energy that is transferred into or out of a system or that is transformed from one form to another within a system. **FIGURE 10.2** shows a simple model of energy that is based on John's model of the monetary system. There are many details that must be added to this model, but it's a good starting point. The fact that nature "balances the books" for energy is one of the most profound discoveries of science.

A major goal is to discover the conditions under which energy is conserved. Surprisingly, the *law of conservation of energy* was not recognized until the mid-19th century, long after Newton. The reason, similar to John's lost penny, was that it took scientists a long time to realize how many types of energy there are and the various ways that energy can be converted from one form to another. As you'll soon learn, energy ideas go well beyond Newtonian mechanics to include new concepts about heat, about chemical energy, and about the energy of the individual atoms and molecules that make up a system. All of these forms of energy will ultimately have to be included in our accounting scheme for energy.

There's a lot to say about energy, and energy is an abstract idea, so we'll take it one step at a time. Much of the "theory" will be postponed until Chapter 11, after you've had some practice using the basic concepts of energy introduced in this chapter. We will extend these ideas in Part IV when we reach the study of thermodynamics.

10.2 Kinetic Energy and Gravitational Potential Energy

To begin, consider an object in vertical free fall. It can only move up or down, and the only force acting on it is the gravitational force $\vec{F}_G$. The object's position and velocity are given by the free-fall kinematics of Chapter 2, with $a_y = -g$.

FIGURE 10.3 is a before-and-after pictorial representation of an object in free fall, as you learned to draw in Chapter 9. We didn't call attention to it in Chapter 2, but one of the free-fall equations also relates "before" and "after." In particular, the kinematic equation

$$v_{fy}^2 = v_{iy}^2 + 2a_y\Delta y = v_{iy}^2 - 2g(y_f - y_i) \tag{10.1}$$

can easily be rewritten as

$$v_{fy}^2 + 2gy_f = v_{iy}^2 + 2gy_i \tag{10.2}$$

Equation 10.2 is a conservation law for free-fall motion. It tells us that the quantity $v_y^2 + 2gy$ has the same value *after* free fall (regardless of whether the motion is upward or downward) that it had *before* free fall. But free fall is a very specific type of motion, so it's not clear if this "law" has any wider validity. Let's introduce a more general technique to arrive at the same result, but a technique that can be extended to other types of motion.

Newton's second law for one-dimensional motion along the *y*-axis is

$$(F_{net})_y = ma_y = m\frac{dv_y}{dt} \tag{10.3}$$

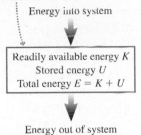

FIGURE 10.2 An initial model of energy. Compare this model to Figure 10.1.

There are two kinds of energy within the system. These can be transformed back and forth without loss.

Energy into system

Readily available energy K
Stored energy U
Total energy $E = K + U$

Energy out of system

This photovoltaic panel is transforming solar energy into electrical energy.

FIGURE 10.3 The before-and-after representation of an object in free fall.

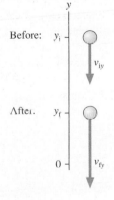

The net force on an object in free fall is $(F_{net})_y = -mg$, so Equation 10.3 is

$$m\frac{dv_y}{dt} = -mg \tag{10.4}$$

Recall, from calculus, that we can use the chain rule to write

$$\frac{dv_y}{dt} = \frac{dv_y}{dy}\frac{dy}{dt} = v_y\frac{dv_y}{dy} \tag{10.5}$$

where we used $v_y = dy/dt$. Substituting this into Equation 10.4 gives

$$mv_y\frac{dv_y}{dy} = -mg \tag{10.6}$$

The chain rule has allowed us to change from a derivative of v_y with respect to time to a derivative of v_y with respect to position. This simple change will be the key step on the road to energy.

We can rewrite Equation 10.6 as

$$mv_y\, dv_y = -mg\, dy \tag{10.7}$$

Now we can integrate both sides of the equation. However, we have to be careful to make sure the limits of integration match. We want to integrate from "before," when the object is at position y_i and has velocity v_{iy}, to "after," when the object is at position y_f and has velocity v_{fy}. Figure 10.3 shows these points in the motion. With these limits, the integrals are

$$\int_{v_{iy}}^{v_{fy}} mv_y\, dv_y = -\int_{y_i}^{y_f} mg\, dy \tag{10.8}$$

Carrying out the integrations, with m and g as constants, we find

$$\frac{1}{2}mv_y^2\Big|_{v_{iy}}^{v_{fy}} = \frac{1}{2}mv_{fy}^2 - \frac{1}{2}mv_{iy}^2 = -mgy\Big|_{y_i}^{y_f} = -mgy_f + mgy_i \tag{10.9}$$

Because v_y is squared wherever it appears in Equation 10.9, the sign of v_y is not relevant. All we need to know are the initial and final *speeds* v_i and v_f. With this, Equation 10.9 can be written

$$\frac{1}{2}mv_f^2 + mgy_f = \frac{1}{2}mv_i^2 + mgy_i \tag{10.10}$$

You should recognize that Equation 10.10, other than a constant factor of $\frac{1}{2}m$, is the same as Equation 10.2. This seems like a lot of effort to get to a result we already knew. However, our purpose was not to get the answer but to introduce a *procedure* that will turn out to have other valuable applications.

Kinetic and Potential Energy

6.1 Activ Physics ONLINE

The quantity

$$K = \frac{1}{2}mv^2 \quad \text{(kinetic energy)} \tag{10.11}$$

is called the **kinetic energy** of the object. The quantity

$$U_g = mgy \quad \text{(gravitational potential energy)} \tag{10.12}$$

is the object's **gravitational potential energy.** These are the two basic forms of energy. **Kinetic energy is an energy of motion.** It depends on the object's speed but not its location. **Potential energy is an energy of position.** It depends on the object's position but not its speed.

One of the most important characteristics of energy is that it is a scalar, not a vector. Kinetic energy depends on an object's speed v but *not* on the direction of motion. The kinetic energy of a particle is the same whether it moves up or down or left or right. Consequently, the mathematics of using energy is often much easier than the vector mathematics required by force and acceleration.

NOTE ▶ By its definition, kinetic energy can never be a negative number. If you find, in the course of solving a problem, that K is negative –stop! You have made an error somewhere. Don't just "lose" the minus sign and hope that everything turns out OK. ◀

The unit of kinetic energy is mass multiplied by velocity squared. In the SI system of units, this is $kg \, m^2/s^2$. The unit of energy is so important that is has been given its own name, the **joule.** We define:

$$1 \text{ joule} = 1 \text{ J} = 1 \text{ kg} \, m^2/s^2$$

The unit of potential energy, $kg \times m/s^2 \times m = kg \, m^2/s^2$, is also the joule.

To give you an idea about the size of a joule, consider a 0.5 kg mass (weight on earth $\approx$ 1 lb) moving at 4 m/s ($\approx$10 mph). Its kinetic energy is

$$K = \frac{1}{2}mv^2 = \frac{1}{2}(0.5 \text{ kg})(4 \text{ m/s})^2 = 4 \text{ J}$$

Its gravitational potential energy at a height of 1 m ($\approx$ 3 ft) is

$$U_g = mgy = (0.5 \text{ kg})(9.8 \text{ m/s}^2)(1 \text{ m}) \approx 5 \text{ J}$$

This suggests that ordinary-sized objects moving at ordinary speeds will have energies of a fraction of a joule up to, perhaps, a few thousand joules (a running person has $K \approx 1000$ J). A high-speed truck might have $K \approx 10^6$ J.

NOTE ▶ You *must* have masses in kg and velocities in m/s before doing energy calculations. ◀

In terms of energy, Equation 10.10 says that for an object in free fall,

$$K_f + U_{gf} = K_i + U_{gi} \tag{10.13}$$

In other words, the sum $K + U_g$ of kinetic energy and gravitational potential energy is not changed by free fall. Its value *after* free fall (regardless of whether the motion is upward or downward) is the same as *before* free fall. **FIGURE 10.4** illustrates this important idea.

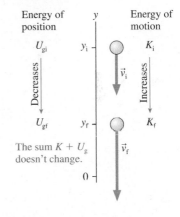

FIGURE 10.4 Kinetic energy and gravitational potential energy.

EXAMPLE 10.1 **Launching a pebble**

Bob uses a slingshot to shoot a 20 g pebble straight up with a speed of 25 m/s. How high does the pebble go?

MODEL This is free-fall motion, so the sum of the kinetic and gravitational potential energy does not change as the pebble rises.

VISUALIZE FIGURE 10.5 shows a before-and-after pictorial representation. The pictorial representation for energy problems is essentially the same as the pictorial representation you learned in Chapter 9 for momentum problems. We'll use numerical subscripts 0 and 1 for the initial and final points.

SOLVE Equation 10.13,

$$K_1 + U_{g1} = K_0 + U_{g0}$$

tells us that the sum $K + U_g$ is not changed by the motion.

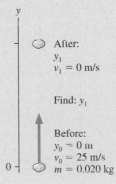

FIGURE 10.5 Pictorial representation of a pebble shot upward from a slingshot.

Continued

Using the definitions of K and U_g,

$$\frac{1}{2}mv_1^2 + mgy_1 = \frac{1}{2}mv_0^2 + mgy_0$$

Here $y_0 = 0$ m and $v_1 = 0$ m/s, so the equation simplifies to

$$mgy_1 = \frac{1}{2}mv_0^2$$

This is easily solved for the height y_1:

$$y_1 = \frac{v_0^2}{2g} = \frac{(25 \text{ m/s})^2}{2(9.80 \text{ m/s}^2)} = 32 \text{ m}$$

ASSESS Notice that the mass canceled and wasn't needed, a fact about free fall that you should remember from Chapter 2.

Energy Bar Charts

The pebble of Example 10.1 started with all kinetic energy, an energy of motion. As the pebble ascends, kinetic energy is converted into gravitational potential energy, *but the sum of the two doesn't change*. At the top, the pebble's energy is entirely potential energy. The simple bar chart in FIGURE 10.6 shows graphically how kinetic energy is transformed into gravitational potential energy as a pebble rises. The potential energy is then transformed back into kinetic energy as the pebble falls. The sum $K + U_g$ remains constant throughout the motion.

FIGURE 10.6 Simple energy bar chart for a pebble tossed into the air.

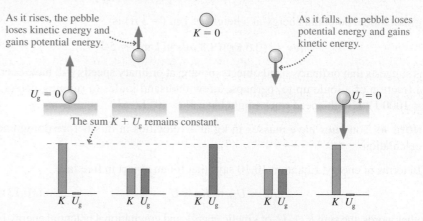

FIGURE 10.7a is an energy bar chart more suitable to problem solving. The chart is a graphical representation of the energy equation $K_f + U_{gf} = K_i + U_{gi}$. FIGURE 10.7b applies this to the pebble of Example 10.1. The initial kinetic energy is transformed entirely into potential energy as the pebble reaches its highest point. There are no numerical scales on a bar chart, but you should draw the bar heights proportional to the amount of each type of energy.

FIGURE 10.7 An energy bar chart suitable for problem solving.

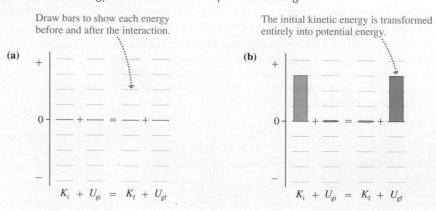

STOP TO THINK 10.1 Rank in order, from largest to smallest, the gravitational potential energies of balls a to d.

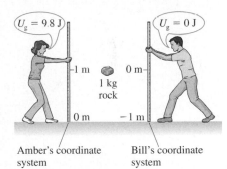

The Zero of Potential Energy

Our expression for the gravitational potential energy $U_g = mgy$ seems straightforward. But you might notice, on further reflection, that the value of U_g depends on where you choose to put the origin of your coordinate system. Consider FIGURE 10.8, where Amber and Bill are attempting to determine the potential energy of a 1 kg rock that is 1 m above the ground. Amber chooses to put the origin of her coordinate system on the ground, measures $y_{rock} = 1$ m, and quickly computes $U_g = mgy = 9.8$ J. Bill, on the other hand, read Chapter 1 very carefully and recalls that it is entirely up to him where to locate the origin of his coordinate system. So he places his origin next to the rock, measures $y_{rock} = 0$ m, and declares that $U_g = mgy = 0$ J!

How can the potential energy of one rock at one position in space have two different values? The source of this apparent difficulty comes from our interpretation of Equation 10.9. The integral of $-mgdy$ resulted in the expression $-mg(y_f - y_i)$, and this led us to propose that $U_g = mgy$. But all we are *really* justified in concluding is that the potential energy *changes* by $\Delta U = -mg(y_f - y_i)$. To go beyond this and claim $U_g = mgy$ is consistent with $\Delta U = -mg(y_f - y_i)$, but so also would be a claim that $U_g = mgy + C$, where C is any constant.

No matter where the rock is located, Amber's value of y will always equal Bill's value plus 1 m. Consequently, her value of the potential energy will always equal Bill's value plus 9.8 J. That is, their values of U_g differ by a constant. Nonetheless, both will calculate exactly the *same* value for ΔU if the rock changes position.

FIGURE 10.8 Amber and Bill use coordinate systems with different origins to determine the potential energy of a rock.

EXAMPLE 10.2 The speed of a falling rock

The 1.0 kg rock shown in Figure 10.8 is released from rest. Use both Amber's and Bill's perspectives to calculate its speed just before it hits the ground.

MODEL This is free-fall motion, so the sum of the kinetic and gravitational potential energy does not change as the rock falls.

VISUALIZE FIGURE 10.9 shows a before-and-after pictorial representation using both Amber's and Bill's coordinate systems.

FIGURE 10.9 The before-and-after pictorial representation of a falling rock.

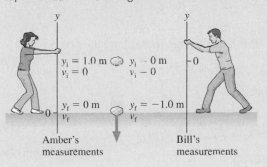

Amber's measurements   Bill's measurements

SOLVE The energy equation is $K_f + U_{gf} = K_i + U_{gi}$. Bill and Amber both agree that $K_i = 0$ because the rock was released from rest, so we have

$$K_f = \frac{1}{2}mv_f^2 = -(U_{gf} - U_{gi}) = -\Delta U$$

According to Amber, $U_{gi} = mgy_i = 9.8$ J and $U_{gf} = mgy_f = 0$ J. Thus

$$\Delta U_{Amber} = U_{gf} - U_{gi} = -9.8 \text{ J}$$

The rock *loses* potential energy as it falls. According to Bill, $U_{gi} = mgy_i = 0$ J and $U_{gf} = mgy_f = -9.8$ J. Thus

$$\Delta U_{Bill} = U_{gf} - U_{gi} = -9.8 \text{ J}$$

Bill has different values for U_{gi} and U_{gf} but the *same* value for ΔU. Thus they both agree that the rock hits the ground with speed

$$v_f = \sqrt{\frac{-2\Delta U}{m}} = \sqrt{\frac{-2(-9.8 \text{ J})}{1.0 \text{ kg}}} = 4.4 \text{ m/s}$$

FIGURE 10.10 shows energy bar charts for Amber and Bill. Despite their disagreement over the value of U_g, Amber and Bill arrive at the same value for v_f and their K_f bars are the same height. The reason is that only ΔU has physical significance, not U_g itself, and Amber and Bill found the same value for ΔU. **You can place the origin of your coordinate system, and thus the "zero of potential energy," wherever you choose and be assured of getting the correct answer to a problem.**

FIGURE 10.10 Amber's and Bill's energy bar charts for the falling rock.

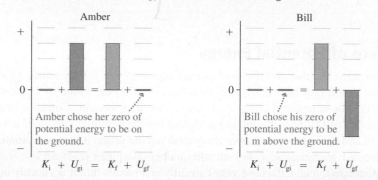

Amber chose her zero of potential energy to be on the ground.

Bill chose his zero of potential energy to be 1 m above the ground.

$$K_i + U_{gi} = K_f + U_{gf}$$

$$K_i + U_{gi} = K_f + U_{gf}$$

NOTE ▶ Gravitational potential energy can be negative, as U_{gf} is for Bill. **A negative value for U_g means that the particle has *less* potential for motion at that point than it does at $y = 0$.** But there's nothing wrong with that. Contrast this with kinetic energy, which *cannot* be negative. ◀

10.3 A Closer Look at Gravitational Potential Energy

FIGURE 10.11 A particle moving along a frictionless surface of arbitrary shape.

(a)

(b)

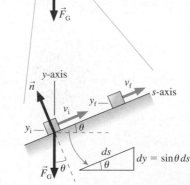

The concept of energy would be of little interest or use if it applied only to free fall. Let's begin to expand the idea. FIGURE 10.11a shows an object of mass m sliding along a frictionless surface. The only forces acting on the object are gravity and the normal force from the surface. If the surface is curved, you know from calculus that we can subdivide the surface into many small (perhaps infinitesimal) straight-line segments. FIGURE 10.11b shows a magnified segment of the surface that, over some small distance, is a straight line at angle θ.

We can analyze the motion along this small segment using the procedure of Equations 10.3 through 10.10. We define an s-axis parallel to the direction of motion. Newton's second law along this axis is

$$(F_{net})_s = ma_s = m\frac{dv_s}{dt} \tag{10.14}$$

Using the chain rule, we can write Equation 10.14 as

$$(F_{net})_s = m\frac{dv_s}{dt} = m\frac{dv_s}{ds}\frac{ds}{dt} = mv_s\frac{dv_s}{ds} \tag{10.15}$$

where, in the last step, we used $ds/dt = v_s$.

You can see from Figure 10.11b that the net force along the s-axis is

$$(F_{net})_s = -F_G\sin\theta = -mg\sin\theta \tag{10.16}$$

Thus Newton's second law becomes

$$-mg\sin\theta = mv_s\frac{dv_s}{ds} \tag{10.17}$$

Multiplying both sides by ds gives

$$mv_s dv_s = -mg\sin\theta\, ds \tag{10.18}$$

You can see from the figure that $\sin\theta\, ds$ is dy, so Equation 10.18 becomes

$$mv_s\, dv_s = -mg\, dy \qquad (10.19)$$

This is *identical* to Equation 10.7, which we found for free fall. Consequently, integrating this equation from "before" to "after" leads again to Equation 10.10:

$$\frac{1}{2}mv_f^2 + mgy_f = \frac{1}{2}mv_i^2 + mgy_i \qquad (10.20)$$

where v_i^2 and v_f^2 are the squares of the *speeds* at the beginning and end of this segment of the motion.

We previously defined the kinetic energy $K = \frac{1}{2}mv^2$ and the gravitational potential energy $U_g = mgy$. Equation 10.20 shows that

$$K_f + U_{gf} = K_i + U_{gi} \qquad (10.21)$$

for a particle moving along *any* frictionless surface, regardless of the shape.

NOTE ▶ For energy calculations, the y-axis is specifically a *vertical* axis. Gravitational potential energy depends on the *height* above the earth's surface. A tilted coordinate system, such as we often used in dynamics problems, doesn't work for problems with gravitational potential energy. ◀

The roller coaster's potential energy is converted to kinetic energy as it speeds toward the bottom of the hill.

STOP TO THINK 10.2 A small child slides down the four frictionless slides a–d. Each has the same height. Rank in order, from largest to smallest, her speeds v_a to v_d at the bottom.

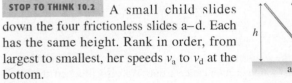
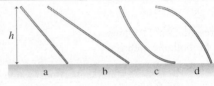

EXAMPLE 10.3 The speed of a sled

Christine runs forward with her sled at 2.0 m/s. She hops onto the sled at the top of a 5.0-m-high, very slippery slope. What is her speed at the bottom?

MODEL Model Christine and the sled as a particle. Assume the slope is frictionless. In that case, the sum of her kinetic and gravitational potential energy does not change as she slides down.

VISUALIZE FIGURE 10.12a shows a before-and-after pictorial representation. We are not told the angle of the slope, or even if it is a straight slope, but the *change* in potential energy depends only on the height Christine descends and *not* on the shape of the hill. FIGURE 10.12b shows an energy bar chart in which we see an initial kinetic *and* potential energy being transformed into entirely

kinetic energy as she goes down the slope. The purpose of the bar chart is to visualize how the energy changes, and we can show that without knowing any numerical values.

SOLVE The quantity $K + U_g$ is the same at the bottom of the hill as it was at the top. Thus

$$\frac{1}{2}mv_1^2 + mgy_1 = \frac{1}{2}mv_0^2 + mgy_0$$

This is easily solved for Christine's speed at the bottom:

$$v_1 = \sqrt{v_0^2 + 2g(y_0 - y_1)} = \sqrt{v_0^2 + 2gh} = 10 \text{ m/s}$$

ASSESS We did not need the mass of either Christine or the sled,

FIGURE 10.12 Pictorial representation and energy bar chart of Christine sliding down the hill.

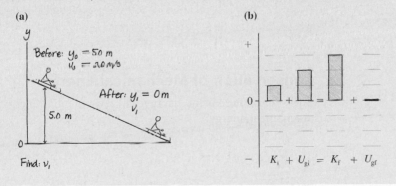

(a)

Before: $y_0 = 5.0$ m
$u_0 = 2.0$ m/s
After: $y_1 = 0$ m
v_1
5.0 m
Find: v_1

(b)

$K_i + U_{gi} = K_f + U_{gf}$

Notice that the normal force $\vec{n}$ doesn't enter an energy analysis. The equation $K_f + U_{gf} = K_i + U_{gi}$ is a statement about how the particle's speed changes as it changes position. $\vec{n}$ does not have a component in the direction of motion, so it cannot change the particle's speed.

The same is true for an object tied to a string and moving in a circle. The tension in the string causes the direction to change, but $\vec{T}$ does not have a component in the direction of motion and does not change the speed of the object. Hence Equation 10.21 also applies to a *pendulum*.

EXAMPLE 10.4 A ballistic pendulum

A 10 g bullet is fired into a 1200 g wood block hanging from a 150-cm-long string. The bullet embeds itself into the block, and the block then swings out to an angle of 40°. What was the speed of the bullet? (This is called a *ballistic pendulum*.)

MODEL This is a two-part problem. The impact of the bullet with the block is an inelastic collision. We haven't done any analysis to let us know what happens to energy during a collision, but you learned in Chapter 9 that *momentum* is conserved in an inelastic collision. After the collision is over, the block swings out as a pendulum. The sum of the kinetic and gravitational potential energy does not change as the block swings to its largest angle.

VISUALIZE FIGURE 10.13 is a pictorial representation in which we've identified before-and-after quantities for both the collision and the swing.

FIGURE 10.13 A ballistic pendulum is used to measure the speed of a bullet.

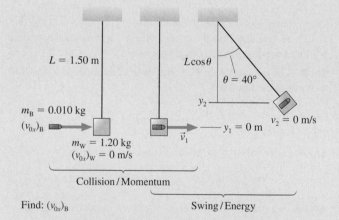

Find: $(v_{0x})_B$

SOLVE The momentum conservation equation $P_f = P_i$ applied to the inelastic collision gives

$$(m_W + m_B)v_{1x} = m_W(v_{0x})_W + m_B(v_{0x})_B$$

The wood block is initially at rest, with $(v_{0x})_W = 0$, so the bullet's velocity is

$$(v_{0x})_B = \frac{m_W + m_B}{m_B}v_{1x}$$

where v_{1x} is the velocity of the block + bullet *immediately* after the collision, as the pendulum begins to swing. If we can determine v_{1x} from an analysis of the swing, then we will be able to calculate the speed of the bullet. Turning our attention to the swing, the energy equation $K_f + U_{gf} = K_i + U_{gi}$ is

$$\frac{1}{2}(m_W + m_B)v_2^2 + (m_W + m_B)gy_2$$

$$= \frac{1}{2}(m_W + m_B)v_1^2 + (m_W + m_B)gy_1$$

We used the *total* mass $(m_W + m_B)$ of the block and embedded bullet, but notice that it cancels out. We also dropped the x-subscript on v_1 because for energy calculations we need only speed, not velocity. The speed is zero at the top of the swing $(v_2 = 0)$, and we've defined the y-axis such that $y_1 = 0$ m. Thus

$$v_1 = \sqrt{2gy_2}$$

The initial speed is found simply from the maximum height of the swing. You can see from the geometry of Figure 10.13 that

$$y_2 = L - L\cos\theta = L(1 - \cos\theta) = 0.351 \text{ m}$$

With this, the initial velocity of the pendulum, immediately after the collision, is

$$v_{1x} = v_1 = \sqrt{2gy_2} = \sqrt{2(9.80 \text{ m/s}^2)(0.351 \text{ m})} = 2.62 \text{ m/s}$$

Having found v_{1x} from an energy analysis of the swing, we can now calculate that the speed of the bullet was

$$(v_{0x})_B = \frac{m_W + m_B}{m_B}v_{1x} = \frac{1.210 \text{ kg}}{0.010 \text{ kg}} \times 2.62 \text{ m/s} = 320 \text{ m/s}$$

ASSESS It would have been very difficult to solve this problem using Newton's laws, but it yielded to a straightforward analysis based on the concepts of momentum and energy.

Conservation of Mechanical Energy

The sum of the kinetic energy and the potential energy of a system is called the **mechanical energy:**

$$E_{mech} = K + U \tag{10.22}$$

Here K is the total kinetic energy of all the particles in the system and U is the potential energy stored in the system. Our examples thus far suggest that a particle's mechanical energy does not change as it moves under the influence of gravity. The kinetic energy and the potential energy can change, as they are transformed back and forth into each other, but their sum remains constant. We can express the unchanging value of E_{mech} as

$$\Delta E_{mech} = \Delta K + \Delta U = 0 \qquad (10.23)$$

This statement is called the **law of conservation of mechanical energy.**

> **NOTE** ▶ The law of conservation of mechanical energy does *not* say $\Delta K = \Delta U$. One of the changes has to be positive while the other is negative if energy is to be conserved. ◀

But is this really a law of nature? Consider a box that is given a shove and then slides along the floor until it stops. The box loses kinetic energy as it slows down, but $\Delta U_g = 0$ because y doesn't change. Thus ΔE_{mech} is *not* zero for the box; its mechanical energy is not conserved.

In Chapter 9 you learned that momentum is conserved only for an isolated system. One of the important goals of this chapter and the next is to learn the conditions under which mechanical energy is conserved. We've seen thus far that mechanical energy *is* conserved for a particle that moves along a frictionless trajectory under the influence of gravity, but mechanical energy is *not* conserved when there is friction.

You know, of course, that after the box slides across the floor, both the box and the floor are slightly warmer than before. The kinetic energy has not been transformed into potential energy, but *something* has happened. We've already noted that there are different kinds of energy. Perhaps friction causes the kinetic energy to be transformed into a form of energy other than potential energy. This is a very important issue, one that we'll begin to explore in the next chapter.

The Basic Energy Model

We're beginning to develop what we'll call the *basic energy model*. This is a model of energy as a form of "natural money." It is based on three hypotheses:

1. Kinetic energy is associated with the motion of a particle, and potential energy is associated with its position.
2. Kinetic energy can be transformed into potential energy, and potential energy can be transformed into kinetic energy.
3. Under some circumstances the mechanical energy $E_{mech} = K + U$ is conserved. Its value at the end of a process equals its value at the beginning.

Our task, if the basic energy model is to be useful, is to answer three crucial questions:

1. Under what conditions is E_{mech} conserved?
2. What happens to the energy when E_{mech} isn't conserved?
3. How do you calculate the potential energy U for forces other than gravity?

There are many parts to the energy puzzle, and we must put them together piece by piece. This chapter is focused on how to use energy in situations where E_{mech} is conserved. We will turn our attention to answering these three important questions in the next chapter. For now, we can begin to develop a strategy for using energy to solve problems.

STOP TO THINK 10.3   A box slides along the frictionless surface shown in the figure. It is released from rest at the position shown. Is the highest point the box reaches on the other side at level a, level b, or level c?

10.4 Restoring Forces and Hooke's Law

If you stretch a rubber band, a force appears that tries to pull the rubber band back to its equilibrium, or unstretched, length. A force that restores a system to an equilibrium position is called a **restoring force.** Systems that exhibit restoring forces are called **elastic.** The most basic examples of elasticity are things like springs and rubber bands. If you stretch a spring, a tension-like force pulls back. Similarly, a compressed spring tries to re-expand to its equilibrium length. Other examples of elasticity and restoring forces abound. The steel beams bend slightly as you drive your car over a bridge, but they are restored to equilibrium after your car passes by. Nearly everything that stretches, compresses, flexes, bends, or twists exhibits a restoring force and can be called elastic.

We're going to use a simple spring as a prototype of elasticity. Suppose you have a spring whose **equilibrium length** is L_0. This is the length of the spring when it is neither pushing nor pulling. If you now stretch the spring to length L, how hard does it pull back? One way to find out is to attach the spring to a bar, as shown in **FIGURE 10.14**, then to hang a mass m from the spring. The mass stretches the spring to length L. Lengths L_0 and L are easily measured with a meter stick.

The mass hangs in static equilibrium, so the upward spring force $\vec{F}_{sp}$ exactly balances the downward gravitational force $\vec{F}_G$ to give $\vec{F}_{net} = \vec{0}$. That is,

$$F_{sp} = F_G = mg \tag{10.24}$$

By using different masses to stretch the spring to different lengths, we can determine how F_{sp}, the magnitude of the spring's restoring force, depends on the length L.

FIGURE 10.15 shows measured data for the restoring force of a real spring. Notice that the quantity graphed along the horizontal axis is $\Delta s = L - L_0$. This is the distance that the end of the spring has moved, which we call the **displacement from equilibrium.** The graph shows that the restoring force is proportional to the displacement. That is, the data fall along the straight line

$$F_{sp} = k\,\Delta s \tag{10.25}$$

The proportionality constant k, the slope of the force-versus-displacement graph, is called the **spring constant.** The units of the spring constant are N/m.

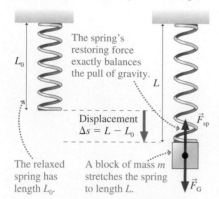

Springs and rubber bands store energy—potential energy—that can be transformed into kinetic energy.

FIGURE 10.14 A hanging mass stretches a spring of equilibrium length L_0 to length L.

The spring's restoring force exactly balances the pull of gravity.

L_0

L

Displacement $\Delta s = L - L_0$

$\vec{F}_{sp}$

The relaxed spring has length L_0.

A block of mass m stretches the spring to length L.

$\vec{F}_G$

NOTE ▶ The force does not depend on the spring's physical length L but, instead, on the *displacement* Δs of the end of the spring. ◀

The spring constant k is a property that characterizes a spring, just as mass m characterizes a particle. If k is large, it takes a large pull to cause a significant stretch, and we call the spring a "stiff" spring. A spring with small k can be stretched with very little force, and we call it a "soft" spring. The spring constant for the spring in Figure 10.15 can be determined from the slope of the straight line to be $k = 3.5$ N/m.

NOTE ▶ Just as we used massless strings, we will adopt the idealization of a *massless spring*. While not a perfect description, it is a good approximation if the mass attached to a spring is much larger than the mass of the spring itself. ◀

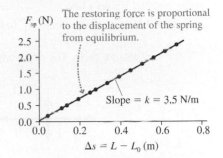

FIGURE 10.15 Measured data for the restoring force of a real spring.

Hooke's Law

FIGURE 10.16 shows a spring along a generic s-axis. The equilibrium position of the end of the spring is denoted s_e. This is the *position*, or coordinate, of the free end of the spring, *not* the spring's equilibrium length L_0.

When the spring is stretched, the displacement from equilibrium $\Delta s = s - s_e$ is *positive* while $(F_{sp})_s$, the s-component of the restoring force pointing to the left, is *negative*. If the spring is compressed, the displacement from equilibrium Δs is negative while the s-component of $\vec{F}_{sp}$, which now points to the right, is positive. Either way, the sign of the force component $(F_{sp})_s$ is always opposite to the sign of the displacement Δs. We can write this mathematically as

$$(F_{sp})_s = -k\Delta s \qquad \text{(Hooke's law)} \qquad (10.26)$$

where $\Delta s = s - s_e$ is the displacement of the end of the spring from equilibrium. The minus sign is the mathematical indication of a *restoring* force.

Equation 10.26 for the restoring force of a spring is called **Hooke's law.** This "law" was first suggested by Robert Hooke, a contemporary (and sometimes bitter rival) of Newton. Hooke's law is not a true "law of nature," in the sense that Newton's laws are, but is actually just a *model* of a restoring force. It works extremely well for some springs, as in Figure 10.15, but less well for others. Hooke's law will fail for any spring that is compressed or stretched too far.

NOTE ▶ Some of you, in an earlier physics course, may have learned Hooke's law as $F_{sp} = -kx$ (for a spring along the x-axis), rather than as $-k\Delta x$. This can be misleading, and it is a common source of errors. The restoring force will be $-kx$ *only* if the coordinate system in the problem is chosen such that the origin is at the equilibrium position of the free end of the spring. That is, $\Delta x = x$ only if $x_e = 0$. This is often done, but in some problems it will be more convenient to locate the origin of the coordinate system elsewhere. If you try to use $F_{sp} = -kx$ after the origin has moved elsewhere—big trouble! So make sure you learn Hooke's law as $(F_{sp})_s = -k\Delta s$. ◀

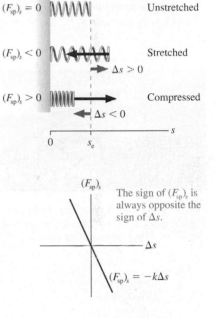

FIGURE 10.16 The direction of $\vec{F}_{sp}$ is always opposite the displacement $\Delta \vec{s}$.

EXAMPLE 10.5   Pull until it slips

FIGURE 10.17 shows a spring attached to a 2.0 kg block. The other end of the spring is pulled by a motorized toy train that moves forward at 5.0 cm/s. The spring constant is 50 N/m, and the coefficient of static friction between the block and the surface is 0.60. The spring is at its equilibrium length at $t = 0$ s when the train starts to move. When does the block slip?

FIGURE 10.17 A toy train stretches the spring until the block slips.

Continued

MODEL Model the block as a particle and the spring as an ideal spring obeying Hooke's law.

VISUALIZE FIGURE 10.18 is a free-body diagram for the block.

FIGURE 10.18 The free-body diagram.

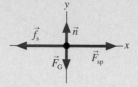

SOLVE Recall that the tension in a massless string pulls equally at *both* ends of the string. The same is true for the spring force: It pulls (or pushes) equally at *both* ends. This is the key to solving the problem. As the right end of the spring moves, stretching the spring, the spring pulls backward on the train *and* forward on the block with equal strength. As the spring stretches, the static fric-

tion force on the block increases in magnitude to keep the block at rest. The block is in static equilibrium, so

$$\sum (F_{net})_x = (F_{sp})_x + (f_s)_x = F_{sp} - f_s = 0$$

where F_{sp} is the *magnitude* of the spring force. The magnitude is $F_{sp} = k\Delta x$, where $\Delta x = v_x t$ is the distance the train has moved. Thus

$$f_s = F_{sp} = k\Delta x$$

The block slips when the static friction force reaches its maximum value $f_{s\,max} = \mu_s n = \mu_s mg$. This occurs when the train has moved

$$\Delta x = \frac{f_{s\,max}}{k} = \frac{\mu_s mg}{k} = \frac{(0.60)(2.0\ \text{kg})(9.80\ \text{m/s}^2)}{50\ \text{N/m}}$$

$$= 0.235\ \text{m} = 23.5\ \text{cm}$$

The time at which the block slips is

$$t = \frac{\Delta x}{v_x} = \frac{23.5\ \text{cm}}{5.0\ \text{cm/s}} = 4.7\ \text{s}$$

The slip can range from a few centimeters in a relatively small earthquake to several meters in a very large earthquake.

This example illustrates a class of motion called *stick-slip motion*. Once the block slips, it will shoot forward some distance, then stop and stick again. If the train continues to move forward, there will be a recurring sequence of stick, slip, stick, slip, stick.... Calculating the period of this stick-slip motion is not hard, although it's a bit beyond where we are right now.

Earthquakes are an important example of stick-slip motion. The large tectonic plates making up the earth's crust are attempting to slide past each other, but friction causes the edges of the plates to stick together. The continued motion of the plates bends and deforms the rocks along the boundary. You may think of rocks as rigid and brittle, but large masses of rock, especially under the immense pressures within the earth, are somewhat elastic and can be "stretched." Eventually the elastic force of the deformed rocks exceeds the friction force between the plates. An earthquake occurs as the plates slip and lurch forward. Once the tension is released, the plates stick together again and the process starts all over.

STOP TO THINK 10.4 The graph shows force versus displacement for three springs. Rank in order, from largest to smallest, the spring constants k_a, k_b, and k_c.

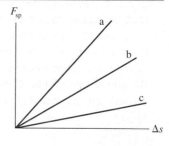

10.5 Elastic Potential Energy

The forces we have worked with thus far—gravity, friction, tension—have been constant forces. That is, their magnitudes do not change as an object moves. That feature has been important because the kinematic equations we developed in Chapter 2 are for motion with constant acceleration. But a spring force exerts a *variable* force. The force is zero if $\Delta s = 0$ (no displacement), and it steadily increases as the stretching increases. The "natural motion" of a mass on a spring—think of pulling down on a spring and then releasing it—is an *oscillation*. This is *not* constant-acceleration motion, and we haven't yet developed the kinematics to handle oscillatory motion.

But suppose we're interested not in the time dependence of motion, only in before-and-after situations. For example, FIGURE 10.19 shows a before-and-after situation in which a spring launches a ball. Asking how the compression of the spring (the "before") affects the speed of the ball (the "after") is very different from wanting to know the ball's position as a function of time as the spring expands.

You certainly have a sense that a compressed spring has "stored energy," and Figure 10.19 shows clearly that the stored energy is transferred to the kinetic energy of the ball. Let's analyze this process with the same method we developed for motion under the influence of gravity. Newton's second law for the ball is

$$(F_{net})_s = ma_s = m\frac{dv_s}{dt} \tag{10.27}$$

The net force on the ball is given by Hooke's law, $(F_{net})_s = -k(s - s_e)$. Thus

$$m\frac{dv_s}{dt} = -k(s - s_e) \tag{10.28}$$

We'll use a generic s-axis, although it is better in actual problem solving to use x or y, depending on whether the motion is horizontal or vertical.

As we did before, use the chain rule to write

$$\frac{dv_s}{dt} = \frac{dv_s}{ds}\frac{ds}{dt} = v_s\frac{dv_s}{ds} \tag{10.29}$$

We substitute this into Equation 10.28 and then multiply both sides by ds to get

$$mv_s\, dv_s = -k(s - s_e)\, ds \tag{10.30}$$

We can integrate both sides of the equation from the initial conditions i to the final conditions f—that is, integrate "from before to after"—to give

$$\int_{v_i}^{v_f} mv_s\, dv_s = \frac{1}{2}mv_f^2 - \frac{1}{2}mv_i^2 = -k\int_{s_i}^{s_f} (s - s_e)\, ds \tag{10.31}$$

The integral on the right is not difficult, but many of you are new to calculus so we'll proceed step by step. The easiest way to get the answer in the most useful form is to make a change of variables. Define $u = (s - s_e)$, in which case $ds = du$. This changes the integrand from $(s - s_e)\, ds$ to $u\, du$.

When we change variables, we also must change the limits of integration. In particular, $s = s_i$ at the lower integration limit makes $u = s_i - s_e = \Delta s_i$, where Δs_i is the initial displacement of the spring from equilibrium. Likewise, $s = s_f$ makes $u = s_f - s_e = \Delta s_f$ at the upper limit. FIGURE 10.20 clarifies the meanings of Δs_i and Δs_f.

With this change of variables, the integral is

$$-k\int_{s_i}^{s_f} (s - s_e)\, ds = -k\int_{\Delta s_i}^{\Delta s_f} u\, du = -\frac{1}{2}ku^2\Big|_{\Delta s_i}^{\Delta s_f} \tag{10.32}$$

$$= -\frac{1}{2}k(\Delta s_f)^2 + \frac{1}{2}k(\Delta s_i)^2$$

Using this result makes Equation 10.31 become

$$\frac{1}{2}mv_f^2 - \frac{1}{2}mv_i^2 = -\frac{1}{2}k(\Delta s_f)^2 + \frac{1}{2}k(\Delta s_i)^2 \tag{10.33}$$

which can be rewritten as

$$\frac{1}{2}mv_f^2 + \frac{1}{2}k(\Delta s_f)^2 = \frac{1}{2}mv_i^2 + \frac{1}{2}k(\Delta s_i)^2 \tag{10.34}$$

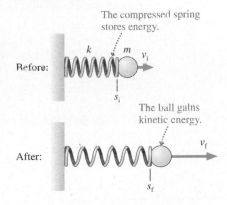

FIGURE 10.19 Before and after a spring launches a ball.

The compressed spring stores energy.

Before:

The ball gains kinetic energy.

After:

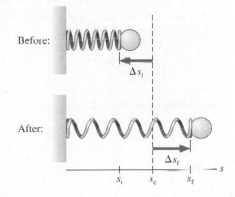

FIGURE 10.20 The initial and final displacements of the spring.

Before:

After:

We've succeeded in our goal of relating before and after. In particular, the quantity

$$\frac{1}{2}mv^2 + \frac{1}{2}k(\Delta s)^2 \qquad (10.35)$$

does not change as the spring compresses or expands. You recognize $\frac{1}{2}mv^2$ as the kinetic energy K. Let's define the **elastic potential energy** U_s of a spring to be

$$U_s = \frac{1}{2}k(\Delta s)^2 \qquad \text{(elastic potential energy)} \qquad (10.36)$$

Then Equation 10.34 tells us that an object moving on a spring obeys

$$K_f + U_{sf} = K_i + U_{si} \qquad (10.37)$$

In other words, the mechanical energy $E_{mech} = K + U_s$ is conserved for an object moving *without friction* on an ideal spring.

NOTE ▶ Because Δs is squared, the elastic potential energy is positive for a spring that is either stretched or compressed. U_s is zero when the spring is at its equilibrium length L_0 and $\Delta s = 0$. ◀

EXAMPLE 10.6 A spring-launched plastic ball

A spring-loaded toy gun launches a 10 g plastic ball. The spring, with spring constant 10 N/m, is compressed by 10 cm as the ball is pushed into the barrel. When the trigger is pulled, the spring is released and shoots the ball back out. What is the ball's speed as it leaves the barrel? Assume friction is negligible.

MODEL Assume an ideal spring that obeys Hooke's law. Also assume that the gun is held firmly enough to prevent recoil. There's no friction; hence the mechanical energy $K + U_s$ is conserved.

VISUALIZE FIGURE 10.21a shows a before-and-after pictorial representation. The compressed spring will push on the ball until the spring has returned to its equilibrium length. We have chosen to put the origin of the coordinate system at the equilibrium position of the free end of the spring, making $x_1 = -10$ cm and $x_2 = x_e = 0$ cm. It's also useful to look at an energy bar chart. The bar chart of FIGURE 10.21b shows the potential energy stored in the compressed spring being entirely transformed into the kinetic energy of the ball.

SOLVE The energy conservation equation is $K_2 + U_{s2} = K_1 + U_{s1}$. We can use the elastic potential energy of the spring, Equation 10.36, to write this as

$$\frac{1}{2}mv_2^2 + \frac{1}{2}k(x_2 - x_e)^2 = \frac{1}{2}mv_1^2 + \frac{1}{2}k(x_1 - x_e)^2$$

Notice that we used x, rather than the generic s, and that we explicitly wrote out the meaning of Δx_1 and Δx_2. Using $x_2 = x_e = 0$ m and $v_1 = 0$ m/s simplifies this to

$$\frac{1}{2}mv_2^2 = \frac{1}{2}kx_1^2$$

It is now straightforward to solve for the ball's speed:

$$v_2 = \sqrt{\frac{kx_1^2}{m}} = \sqrt{\frac{(10 \text{ N/m})(-0.10 \text{ m})^2}{0.010 \text{ kg}}} = 3.2 \text{ m/s}$$

FIGURE 10.21 Pictorial representation and energy bar chart of a ball being shot from a spring-loaded toy gun.

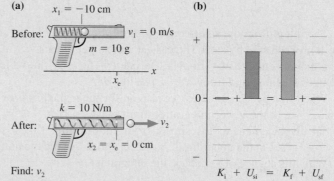

ASSESS This is a problem that we could *not* have solved with Newton's laws. The acceleration is not constant, and we have not learned how to handle the kinematics of nonconstant acceleration. But with conservation of energy—it's easy!

If an object attached to a spring moves vertically, the system has both elastic *and* gravitational potential energy. The mechanical energy then contains *two* potential energy terms:

$$E_{mech} = K + U_g + U_s \qquad (10.38)$$

In other words, there are now two distinct ways of storing energy inside the system. The following example demonstrates this idea.

EXAMPLE 10.7 A spring-launched satellite

Prince Harry the Horrible wanted to be the first to launch a satellite. He placed a 2.0 kg payload on top of a very stiff 2.0-m-long spring with a spring constant of 50,000 N/m. Then the prince had his strongest men use a winch to crank the spring down to a length of 80 cm. When released, the spring shot the payload straight up. How high did it go?

MODEL Assume an ideal spring that obeys Hooke's law. There's no friction, and we'll assume no drag; hence the mechanical energy $K + U_g + U_s$ is conserved.

VISUALIZE FIGURE 10.22a shows the satellite ready for launch. We have chosen to place the origin of the coordinate system on the ground, which means that the equilibrium position of the end of the unstretched spring is *not* $y_e = 0$ m but, instead, $y_e = 2.0$ m. The payload reaches height y_2, where $v_2 = 0$ m/s.

SOLVE The energy conservation equation $K_2 + U_{s2} + U_{g2} = K_1 + U_{s1} + U_{g1}$ is

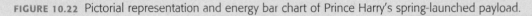

$$\frac{1}{2}mv_2^2 + \frac{1}{2}k(y_e - y_e)^2 + mgy_2 = \frac{1}{2}mv_1^2 + \frac{1}{2}k(y_1 - y_e)^2 + mgy_1$$

Notice that the elastic potential energy term on the left has $(y_e - y_e)^2$, not $(y_2 - y_e)^2$. The payload moves to position y_2, *but the spring does not!* The end of the spring stops at y_e. Both the initial and final speeds v_1 and v_2 are zero. Solving for the height:

$$y_2 = y_1 + \frac{k(y_1 - y_e)^2}{2mg} = 1800 \text{ m}$$

ASSESS FIGURE 10.22b shows an energy bar chart. The net effect of the launch is to transform the potential energy stored in the spring entirely into gravitational potential energy. The kinetic energy is zero at the beginning and zero again at the highest point. The payload does have kinetic energy as it comes off the spring, but we did not need to know this energy to solve the problem.

FIGURE 10.22 Pictorial representation and energy bar chart of Prince Harry's spring-launched payload.

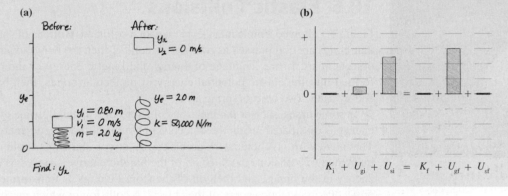

EXAMPLE 10.8 Pushing apart

A spring with spring constant 2000 N/m is sandwiched between a 1.0 kg block and a 2.0 kg block on a frictionless table. The blocks are pushed together to compress the spring by 10 cm, then released. What are the velocities of the blocks as they fly apart?

MODEL Assume an ideal spring that obeys Hooke's law. There's no friction; hence the mechanical energy $K + U_s$ is conserved. In addition, because the blocks and spring form an isolated system, their total momentum is conserved.

VISUALIZE FIGURE 10.23 is a pictorial representation.

FIGURE 10.23 Pictorial representation of the blocks and spring.

SOLVE The initial energy, with the spring compressed, is entirely potential. The final energy is entirely kinetic. The energy conservation equation $K_f + U_{sf} = K_i + U_{si}$ is

$$\frac{1}{2}m_1(v_f)_1^2 + \frac{1}{2}m_2(v_f)_2^2 + 0 = 0 + 0 + \frac{1}{2}k(\Delta x_i)^2$$

Notice that *both* blocks contribute to the kinetic energy. The energy equation has two unknowns, $(v_f)_1$ and $(v_f)_2$, and one equation is not enough to solve the problem. Fortunately, momentum is also conserved. The initial momentum is zero because both blocks are at rest, so the momentum equation is

$$m_1(v_{fx})_1 + m_2(v_{fx})_2 = 0$$

which can be solved to give

$$(v_{fx})_1 = -\frac{m_2}{m_1}(v_{fx})_2$$

The minus sign indicates that the blocks move in opposite directions. The speed $(v_f)_1 = (m_2/m_1)(v_f)_2$ is all we need to calculate the kinetic energy. Substituting $(v_f)_1$ into the energy equation gives

$$\frac{1}{2}m_1\left(\frac{m_2}{m_1}(v_f)_2\right)^2 + \frac{1}{2}m_2(v_f)_2^2 = \frac{1}{2}k(\Delta x_i)^2$$

Continued

which simplifies to

$$m_2\left(1 + \frac{m_2}{m_1}\right)(v_f)_2^2 = k(\Delta x_i)^2$$

Solving for $(v_f)_2$, we find

$$(v_f)_2 = \sqrt{\frac{k(\Delta x_i)^2}{m_2(1 + m_2/m_1)}} = 1.8 \text{ m/s}$$

Finally, we can go back to find

$$(v_{fx})_1 = -\frac{m_2}{m_1}(v_{fx})_2 = -3.6 \text{ m/s}$$

The 2.0 kg block moves to the right at 1.8 m/s while the 1.0 kg block goes left at 3.6 m/s.

ASSESS This example shows just how powerful a problem-solving tool the conservation laws are.

STOP TO THINK 10.5 A spring-loaded gun shoots a plastic ball with a speed of 4 m/s. If the spring is compressed twice as far, the ball's speed will be

a. 2 m/s.   b. 4 m/s.
c. 8 m/s.   d. 16 m/s.

10.6 Elastic Collisions

Figure 9.1 showed a molecular-level view of a collision. Billions of spring-like molecular bonds are compressed as two objects collide, then the bonds expand and push the objects apart. In the language of energy, the kinetic energy of the objects is transformed into the elastic potential energy of molecular bonds, then back into kinetic energy as the two objects spring apart.

In some cases, such as the inelastic collisions of Chapter 9, some of the mechanical energy is dissipated inside the objects and not all of the kinetic energy is recovered. That is, $K_f < K_i$. (A homework problem will let you show this explicitly.) We're now interested in collisions in which *all* of the kinetic energy is stored as elastic potential energy in the bonds, and then *all* of the stored energy is transformed back into the post-collision kinetic energy of the objects. A collision in which mechanical energy is conserved is called a **perfectly elastic collision.**

Needless to say, most real collisions fall somewhere between perfectly elastic and perfectly inelastic. A rubber ball bouncing on the floor might "lose" 20% of its kinetic energy on each bounce and return to only 80% of the height of the previous bounce. Perfectly elastic and perfectly inelastic collisions are limiting cases rarely seen in the real world, but they are nonetheless instructive for demonstrating the major ideas without making the mathematics too complex. Collisions between two very hard objects, such as two billiard balls or two steel balls, come close to being perfectly elastic.

FIGURE 10.24 shows a head-on, perfectly elastic collision of a ball of mass m_1, having initial velocity $(v_{ix})_1$, with a ball of mass m_2 that is initially at rest. The balls' velocities after the collision are $(v_{fx})_1$ and $(v_{fx})_2$. These are velocities, not speeds, and have signs. Ball 1, in particular, might bounce backward and have a negative value for $(v_{fx})_1$.

The collision must obey two conservation laws: conservation of momentum (obeyed in any collision) and conservation of mechanical energy (because the collision is perfectly elastic). Although the energy is transformed into potential energy during the collision, the mechanical energy before and after the collision is purely kinetic energy. Thus

A perfectly elastic collision conserves both momentum and mechanical energy.

6.2 Activ ONLINE Physics

FIGURE 10.24 A perfectly elastic collision.

Before: ①$\xrightarrow{(v_{ix})_1}$ ② K_i

During: ①② Energy is stored in compressed molecular bonds, then released as the bonds re-expand.

After: ①→ ②→ $K_f = K_i$
        $(v_{fx})_1$ $(v_{fx})_2$

momentum conservation: $m_1(v_{fx})_1 + m_2(v_{fx})_2 = m_1(v_{ix})_1$ (10.39)

energy conservation: $\frac{1}{2}m_1(v_{fx})_1^2 + \frac{1}{2}m_2(v_{fx})_2^2 = \frac{1}{2}m_1(v_{ix})_1^2$ (10.40) ·

Momentum conservation alone is not sufficient to analyze the collision because there are two unknowns: the two final velocities. That is why we did not consider perfectly elastic collisions in Chapter 9. Energy conservation gives us another condition. Isolating $(v_{fx})_1$ in Equation 10.39 gives

$$(v_{fx})_1 = (v_{ix})_1 - \frac{m_2}{m_1}(v_{fx})_2 \qquad (10.41)$$

We substitute this into Equation 10.40:

$$\frac{1}{2}m_1\left((v_{ix})_1 - \frac{m_2}{m_1}(v_{fx})_2\right)^2 + \frac{1}{2}m_2(v_{fx})_2^2$$

$$= \frac{1}{2}\left(m_1(v_{ix})_1^2 - 2m_2(v_{ix})_1(v_{fx})_2 + \frac{m_2^2}{m_1}(v_{fx})_2^2 + m_2(v_{fx})_2^2\right)$$

$$= \frac{1}{2}m_1(v_{ix})_1^2$$

This looks rather gruesome, but the first terms on each side cancel and the resulting equation can be rearranged to give

$$(v_{fx})_2\left[\left(1 + \frac{m_2}{m_1}\right)(v_{fx})_2 - 2(v_{ix})_1\right] = 0 \qquad (10.42)$$

One possible solution to this equation is seen to be $(v_{fx})_2 = 0$. However, this solution is of no interest; it is the case where ball 1 misses ball 2. The other solution is

$$(v_{fx})_2 = \frac{2}{1 + m_2/m_1}(v_{ix})_1 = \frac{2m_1}{m_1 + m_2}(v_{ix})_1$$

which, finally, can be substituted back into to Equation 10.41 to yield $(v_{fx})_1$. The complete solution is

$$(v_{fx})_1 = \frac{m_1 - m_2}{m_1 + m_2}(v_{ix})_1$$

(perfectly elastic collision with ball 2 initially at rest)

$$(v_{fx})_2 = \frac{2m_1}{m_1 + m_2}(v_{ix})_1 \qquad (10.43)$$

Equations 10.43 allow us to compute the final velocity of each ball. These equations are a little difficult to interpret, so let us look at the three special cases shown in **FIGURE 10.25**.

Case 1: $m_1 = m_2$. This is the case of one billiard ball striking another of equal mass. For this case, Equations 10.43 give

$$v_{1f} = 0$$
$$v_{2f} = v_{1i}$$

Case 2: $m_1 \gg m_2$. This is the case of a bowling ball running into a Ping-Pong ball. We do not want an exact solution here, but an approximate solution for the limiting case that $m_1 \to \infty$. Equations 10.43 in this limit give

$$v_{1f} \approx v_{1i}$$
$$v_{2f} \approx 2v_{1i}$$

Case 3: $m_1 \ll m_2$. Now we have the reverse case of a Ping-Pong ball colliding with a bowling ball. Here we are interested in the limit $m_1 \to 0$, in which case Equations 10.43 become

$$v_{1f} \approx -v_{1i}$$
$$v_{2f} \approx 0$$

These cases agree well with our expectations and give us confidence that Equations 10.43 accurately describe a perfectly elastic collision.

FIGURE 10.25 Three special elastic collisions.

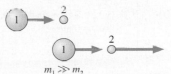

$m_1 = m_2$

Ball 1 stops. Ball 2 goes forward with $v_2 = v_1$.

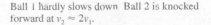

$m_1 \gg m_2$

Ball 1 hardly slows down. Ball 2 is knocked forward at $v_2 \approx 2v_1$.

$m_1 \ll m_2$

Ball 1 bounces off ball 2 with almost no loss of speed. Ball 2 hardly moves.

EXAMPLE 10.9 A rebounding pendulum

A 200 g steel ball hangs on a 1.0-m-long string. The ball is pulled sideways so that the string is at a 45° angle, then released. At the very bottom of its swing the ball strikes a 500 g steel paperweight that is resting on a frictionless table. To what angle does the ball rebound?

MODEL This is a challenging problem. We can divide it into three parts. First the ball swings down as a pendulum. Second, the ball and paperweight have a collision. Steel balls bounce off each other very well, so we will assume that the collision is perfectly elastic. Third, the ball, after it bounces off the paperweight, swings back up as a pendulum.

VISUALIZE FIGURE 10.26 shows four distinct moments of time: as the ball is released, an instant before the collision, an instant after the collision but before the ball and paperweight have had time to move, and as the ball reaches its highest point on the rebound. Call the ball A and the paperweight B, so $m_A = 0.20$ kg and $m_B = 0.50$ kg.

SOLVE Part 1: The first part involves the ball only. Its initial height is

$$(y_0)_A = L - L\cos\theta_0 = L(1 - \cos\theta_0) = 0.293 \text{ m}$$

We can use conservation of mechanical energy to find the ball's velocity at the bottom, just before impact on the paperweight:

$$\frac{1}{2}m_A(v_1)_A^2 + m_A g(y_1)_A = \frac{1}{2}m_A(v_0)_A^2 + m_A g(y_0)_A$$

We know $(v_0)_A = 0$. Solving for the velocity at the bottom, where $(y_1)_A = 0$, gives

$$(v_1)_A = \sqrt{2g(y_0)_A} = 2.40 \text{ m/s}$$

Part 2: The ball and paperweight undergo a perfectly elastic collision in which the paperweight is initially at rest. These are the conditions for which Equations 10.43 were derived. The velocities *immediately* after the collision, prior to any further motion, are

$$(v_{2x})_A = \frac{m_A - m_B}{m_A + m_B}(v_{1x})_A = -1.03 \text{ m/s}$$

$$(v_{2x})_B = \frac{2m_A}{m_A + m_B}(v_{1x})_A = +1.37 \text{ m/s}$$

The ball rebounds toward the left with a speed of 1.03 m/s while the paperweight moves to the right at 1.37 m/s. Kinetic energy has been conserved (you might want to check this), but it is now shared between the ball and the paperweight.

Part 3: Now the ball is a pendulum with an initial speed of 1.03 m/s. Mechanical energy is again conserved, so we can find its maximum height at the point where $(v_3)_A = 0$:

$$\frac{1}{2}m_A(v_3)_A^2 + m_A g(y_3)_A = \frac{1}{2}m_A(v_2)_A^2 + m_A g(y_2)_A$$

Solving for the maximum height gives

$$(y_3)_A = \frac{(v_2)_A^2}{2g} = 0.0541 \text{ m}$$

The height $(y_3)_A$ is related to angle θ_3 by $(y_3)_A = L(1 - \cos\theta_3)$. This can be solved to find the angle of rebound:

$$\theta_3 = \cos^{-1}\left(1 - \frac{(y_3)_A}{L}\right) = 19°$$

The paperweight speeds away at 1.37 m/s and the ball rebounds to an angle of 19°.

FIGURE 10.26 Four moments in the collision of a pendulum with a paperweight.

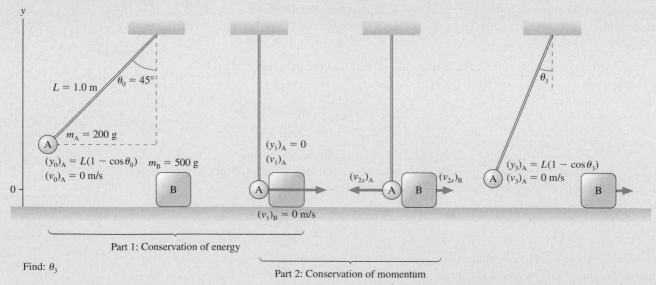

Using Reference Frames

Equations 10.43 assumed that ball 2 was at rest prior to the collision. Suppose, however, you need to analyze the perfectly elastic collision that is just about to take place in FIGURE 10.27. What are the direction and speed of each ball after the collision? You could solve the simultaneous momentum and energy equations, but the mathematics becomes quite messy when both balls have an initial velocity. Fortunately, there's an easier way.

You already know the answer—Equations 10.43—when ball 2 is initially at rest. And in Chapter 4 you learned the Galilean transformation of velocity. This transformation relates an object's velocity v as measured in reference frame S to its velocity v' in a different reference frame S′ that moves with velocity V relative to S. The Galilean transformation provides an elegant and straightforward way to analyze the collision of Figure 10.27.

FIGURE 10.27 A perfectly elastic collision in which both balls have an initial velocity.

TACTICS
BOX 10.1

Analyzing elastic collisions   (MP)

❶ Use the Galilean transformation to transform the initial velocities of balls 1 and 2 from the "lab frame" S to a reference frame S′ in which ball 2 is at rest.
❷ Use Equations 10.43 to determine the outcome of the collision in frame S′.
❸ Transform the final velocities back to the "lab frame" S.

FIGURE 10.28a shows the "before" situation in reference frame S, which we can think of as the lab frame. Notice, compared to Figure 10.27, that we've given $(v_{ix})_2$ as a *velocity* with an appropriate sign. The frame S′ in which ball 2 is at rest is a frame that is traveling alongside ball 2 with the same velocity: $V = -3.0$ m/s.

FIGURE 10.28 The collision seen in two reference frames, S and S′.

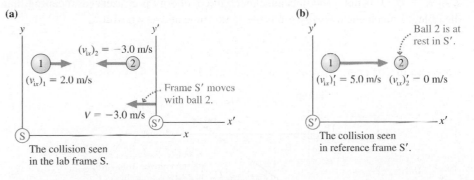

(a)

The collision seen in the lab frame S.

(b)

The collision seen in reference frame S′.

The Galilean transformation of velocities is

$$v' = v - V \qquad (10.44)$$

where a prime represents a velocity measured in frame S′. We can apply this to find the initial velocities of the two balls in S′:

$$(v_{ix})'_1 = (v_{ix})_1 - V = 2.0 \text{ m/s} - (-3.0 \text{ m/s}) = 5.0 \text{ m/s}$$
$$(v_{ix})'_2 = (v_{ix})_2 - V = -3.0 \text{ m/s} - (-3.0 \text{ m/s}) = 0 \text{ m/s} \qquad (10.45)$$

FIGURE 10.28b shows the "before" situation in reference frame S′, where ball 2 is at rest.

Now we can use Equations 10.43 to find the post-collision velocities in frame S′:

$$(v_{fx})'_1 = \frac{m_1 - m_2}{m_1 + m_2}(v_{ix})'_1 = 1.7 \text{ m/s}$$

$$(v_{fx})'_2 = \frac{2m_1}{m_1 + m_2}(v_{ix})'_1 = 6.7 \text{ m/s}$$

(10.46)

Frame S′ hasn't changed—it is still moving at $V = -3.0$ m/s—but the collision has caused both balls to have a velocity in S′.

Finally, we need to apply the reverse transformation $v = v' + V$, with the same V, to transform the post-collision velocities back to the lab frame:

$$(v_{fx})_1 = (v_{fx})'_1 + V = 1.7 \text{ m/s} + (-3.0 \text{ m/s}) = -1.3 \text{ m/s}$$

$$(v_{fx})_2 = (v_{fx})'_2 + V = 6.7 \text{ m/s} + (-3.0 \text{ m/s}) = 3.7 \text{ m/s}$$

(10.47)

FIGURE 10.29 shows the situation after the collision. It's not hard to check that these final velocities do, indeed, conserve both momentum and energy.

FIGURE 10.29 The post-collision velocities in the lab frame.

$(v_{fx})_1 = -1.3$ m/s $(v_{fx})_2 = 3.7$ m/s

10.7 Energy Diagrams

Potential energy is an energy of position. The gravitational potential energy depends on the height of an object, and the elastic potential energy depends on a spring's displacement. Other potential energies you will meet in the future will depend in some way on position. Functions of position are easy to represent as graphs. A graph showing a system's potential energy and total energy as a function of position is called an **energy diagram.** Energy diagrams allow you to visualize motion based on energy considerations. They can also be useful problem-solving tools, and they will play an important role when we get to quantum physics in Part VII.

FIGURE 10.30 is the energy diagram of a particle in free fall. The gravitational potential energy $U_g = mgy$ is graphed as a line through the origin with slope mg. The *potential-energy curve* is labeled PE. The line labeled TE is the *total energy line*, $E = K + U_g$. It is horizontal because mechanical energy is conserved, meaning that the object's mechanical energy E has the same value at every position.

FIGURE 10.30 The energy diagram of a particle in free fall.

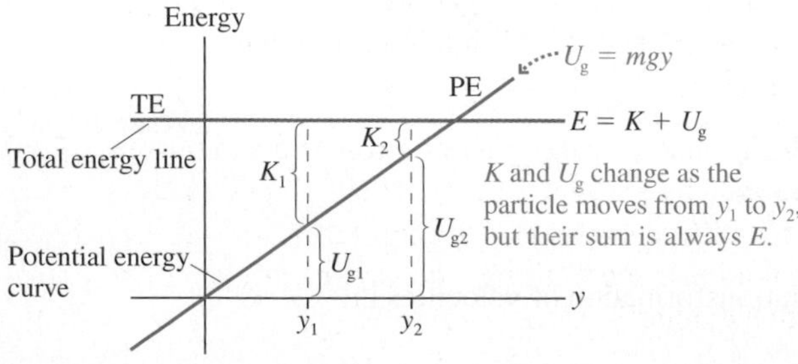

Suppose the particle is at position y_1. By definition, the distance from the axis to the potential-energy curve is the particle's potential energy U_{g1} at that position. Because $K_1 = E - U_{g1}$, the distance between the potential-energy curve and the total energy line is the particle's kinetic energy.

The four-frame "movie" of **FIGURE 10.31** illustrates how an energy diagram is used to visualize motion. The first frame shows a particle projected upward from $y_a = 0$ with kinetic energy K_a. Initially the energy is entirely kinetic, with $U_{ga} = 0$. A pictorial representation and an energy bar chart help to illustrate what the energy diagram is showing.

FIGURE 10.31 A four-frame "movie" of a particle in free fall.

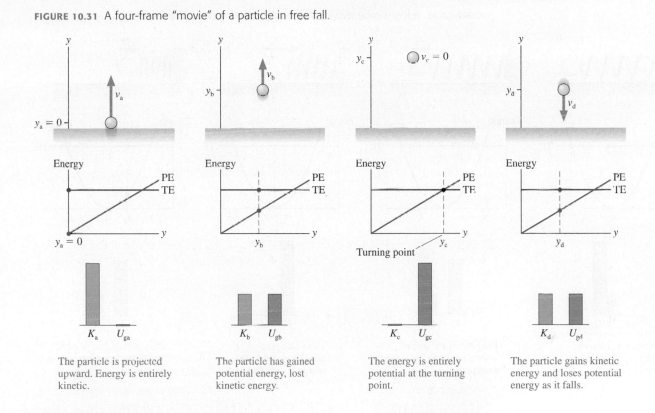

The particle is projected upward. Energy is entirely kinetic.

The particle has gained potential energy, lost kinetic energy.

The energy is entirely potential at the turning point.

The particle gains kinetic energy and loses potential energy as it falls.

In the second frame, the particle has gained height but lost speed. The potential-energy curve U_{gb} is higher, and the distance K_b between the potential-energy curve and the total energy line is less. The particle continues rising and slowing until, in the third frame, it reaches the y-value where the total energy line crosses the potential-energy curve. This point, where $K = 0$ and the energy is entirely potential, is a *turning point* where the particle reverses direction. Finally, we see the particle speeding up as it falls.

A particle with this amount of total energy would need negative kinetic energy to be to the right of the point, at y_c, where the total energy line crosses the potential-energy curve. Negative K is not physically possible, so **the particle cannot be at positions with $U > E$.** Now, it's certainly true that you could make the particle reach a larger value of y simply by throwing it harder. But that would increase E and move the total energy line higher.

NOTE ▶ The TE line is under your control. You can move the TE line as far up or down as you wish by changing the initial conditions, such as projecting the particle upward with a different speed or dropping it from a different height. Once you've determined the initial conditions, you can use the energy diagram to analyze the motion for that amount of total energy. ◀

FIGURE 10.32 shows the energy diagram of a mass on a horizontal spring. The potential-energy curve $U_s = \frac{1}{2}k(x - x_e)^2$ is a parabola centered at the equilibrium position x_e. The PE curve is determined by the spring constant; you can't change it. But you can set the TE to any height you wish simply by stretching the spring to the proper length. The figure shows one possible TE line.

Suppose you pull the mass out to position x_R and release it. **FIGURE 10.33** on the next page is a four-frame movie of the subsequent motion. Initially, the energy is entirely potential. The restoring force of the spring pulls the mass toward x_e, increasing the kinetic energy as the potential energy decreases. The mass has maximum speed at position x_e, where $U_s = 0$, and then it slows down as the spring starts to compress.

FIGURE 10.32 The energy diagram of a mass on a horizontal spring.

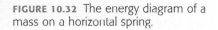

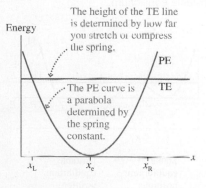

The height of the TE line is determined by how far you stretch or compress the spring.

The PE curve is a parabola determined by the spring constant.

FIGURE 10.33 A four-frame movie of a mass oscillating on a spring.

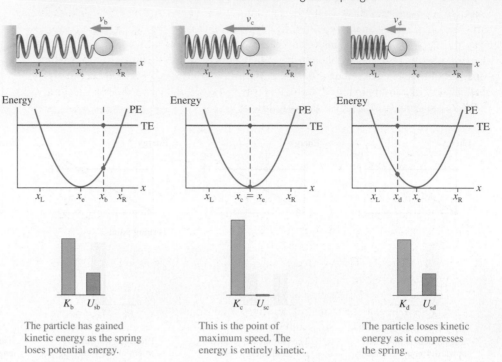

The mass is released from rest. The energy is entirely potential.

The particle has gained kinetic energy as the spring loses potential energy.

This is the point of maximum speed. The energy is entirely kinetic.

The particle loses kinetic energy as it compresses the spring.

If the movie were to continue, you should be able to visualize that position x_L is a turning point. The mass will instantaneously have $v_L = 0$ and $K_L = 0$, then reverse direction as the spring starts to expand. The mass will speed up until x_e, then slow down until reaching x_R, where it started. This is another turning point. It will reverse direction again and start the process over. In other words, the mass will *oscillate* back and forth between the left and right turning points at x_L and x_R where the TE line crosses the PE curve.

FIGURE 10.34 applies these ideas to a more general energy diagram. We don't know how this potential energy was created, but we can visualize the motion of a particle that has this potential energy. Suppose the particle is released from rest at position x_1. How will it then move?

The particle's kinetic energy at x_1 is zero; hence the TE line must cross the PE curve at this point. The particle cannot move to the left because $U > E$, so it begins to move toward the right. The particle speeds up from x_1 to x_2 as U decreases and K increases, then slows down from x_2 to x_3 as it goes up the "potential-energy hill." The particle doesn't stop at x_3 because it still has kinetic energy. It speeds up from x_3 to x_4, reaching its maximum speed at x_4, then slows down between x_4 and x_5. Position x_5 is a turning point, a point where the TE line crosses the PE curve. The particle is instantaneously at rest, then reverses direction. The particle will oscillate back and forth between x_1 and x_5, following the pattern of slowing down and speeding up that we've outlined.

Equilibrium Positions

Positions x_2, x_3, and x_4, where the potential energy has a local minimum or maximum, are special positions. Consider a particle with the total energy E_2 shown in **FIGURE 10.35**. The particle can be at rest at x_2, with $K = 0$, but it cannot move away from x_2. In other words, a particle with energy E_2 is in *static equilibrium* at x_2. If you disturb the particle, giving it a small kinetic energy and a total energy just *slightly* larger than E_2, the particle will undergo a very small oscillation centered on x_2, like a marble in the bottom of a bowl. An equilibrium for which small disturbances cause small oscillations is called a point of **stable equilibrium.** You should recognize that *any* minimum in the PE curve is a point of stable equilibrium. Position x_4 is also a point of stable equilibrium, in this case for a particle with $E = 0$.

FIGURE 10.34 A more general energy diagram.

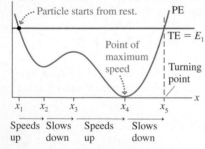

FIGURE 10.35 Points of stable and unstable equilibrium.

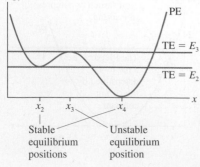

Figure 10.35 also shows a particle with energy E_3 that is tangent to the curve at x_3. If a particle is placed *exactly* at x_3, it will stay there at rest ($K = 0$). But if you disturb the particle at x_3, giving it an energy only slightly more than E_3, it will speed up as it moves away from x_3. This is like trying to balance a marble on top of a hill. The slightest displacement will cause the marble to roll down the hill. A point of equilibrium for which a small disturbance causes the particle to move away is called a point of **unstable equilibrium.** Any maximum in the PE curve, such as x_3, is a point of unstable equilibrium.

We can summarize these lessons as follows:

TACTICS
BOX 10.2 **Interpreting an energy diagram** (MP)

❶ The distance from the axis to the PE curve is the particle's potential energy. The distance from the PE curve to the TE line is its kinetic energy. These are transformed as the position changes, causing the particle to speed up or slow down, but the sum $K + U$ doesn't change.

❷ A point where the TE line crosses the PE curve is a turning point. The particle reverses direction.

❸ The particle cannot be at a point where the PE curve is above the TE line.

❹ The PE curve is determined by the properties of the system—mass, spring constant, and the like. You cannot change the PE curve. However, you can raise or lower the TE line simply by changing the initial conditions to give the particle more or less total energy.

❺ A minimum in the PE curve is a point of stable equilibrium. A maximum in the PE curve is a point of unstable equilibrium.

Exercises 18–20 ✎

EXAMPLE 10.10 **Balancing a mass on a spring**
A spring of length L_0 and spring constant k is standing on one end. A block of mass m is placed on the spring, compressing it. What is the length of the compressed spring?

MODEL Assume an ideal spring obeying Hooke's law. The block + spring system has both gravitational potential energy U_g *and* elastic potential energy U_s. The block sitting on top of the spring is at a point of stable equilibrium (small disturbances cause the block to oscillate slightly around the equilibrium position), so we can solve this problem by looking at the energy diagram.

VISUALIZE FIGURE 10.36a is a pictorial representation. We've used a coordinate system with the origin at ground level, so the equilibrium position of the uncompressed spring is $y_e = L_0$.

SOLVE FIGURE 10.36b shows the two potential energies separately and also shows the total potential energy:

$$U_{tot} = U_g + U_s = mgy + \frac{1}{2}k(y - L_0)^2$$

The equilibrium position (the minimum of U_{tot}) has shifted from L_0 to a smaller value of y, closer to the ground. We can find the

FIGURE 10.36 The block + spring system has both gravitational and elastic potential energy.

Continued

equilibrium by locating the position of the minimum in the PE curve. You know from calculus that the minimum of a function is at the point where the derivative (or slope) is zero. The derivative of U_{tot} is

$$\frac{dU_{tot}}{dy} = mg + k(y - L_0)$$

The derivative is zero at the point y_{eq}, so we can easily find

$$mg + k(y_{eq} - L_0) = 0$$

$$y_{eq} = L_0 - \frac{mg}{k}$$

The block compresses the spring by the length mg/k from its original length L_0, giving it a new equilibrium length $L_0 - mg/k$.

STOP TO THINK 10.6   A particle with the potential energy shown in the graph is moving to the right. It has 1 J of kinetic energy at $x = 1$ m. Where is the particle's turning point?

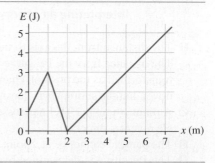

Molecular Bonds

Let's end this chapter by seeing how energy diagrams can allow us to understand something about molecular bonds. A *molecular bond* that holds two atoms together is an electric interaction between the charged electrons and nuclei. **FIGURE 10.37** shows the potential-energy diagram for the diatomic molecule HCl (hydrogen chloride) as it has been experimentally determined. Distance x is the *atomic separation*, the distance between the hydrogen and the chlorine atoms. Note the very tiny distances: 1 nm = 10^{-9} m.

FIGURE 10.37 The energy diagram of the diatomic molecule HCl.

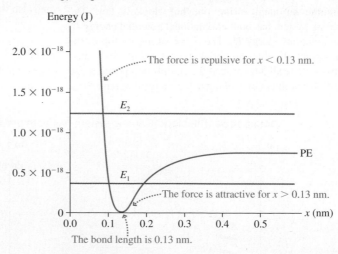

Although the potential energy is an electric energy, we can *interpret* the diagram using the steps in Tactics Box 10.2. The first thing you might notice is that this potential-energy diagram has some similarities to a spring, with a deep potential-energy valley, but also some significant differences.

The molecule has a stable equilibrium at an atomic separation of $x_{eq} = 0.13$ nm. This is the *bond length* of HCl, and you can find this value listed in chemistry books. If we try to push the atoms closer together (smaller x), the potential energy rises very rapidly. Physically, this is the repulsive electric force between the electrons orbiting each atom, preventing the atoms from getting too close.

There is also an attractive force between the atoms, called the *polarization force*. It is similar to the static electricity force by which a comb that has been brushed through your hair attracts small pieces of paper. If you try to pull the atoms apart (larger x), the attractive polarization force resists and is responsible for the increasing potential energy for $x > x_{eq}$. The equilibrium position is where the repulsive force between the electrons and the attractive polarization force are exactly balanced.

The repulsive force keeps getting stronger as you push the atoms together, and thus the potential-energy curve keeps getting steeper on the left. But the attractive polarization force gets *weaker* as the atoms get farther apart. This is why the potential-energy curve becomes *less* steep as the atomic separation increases. Ultimately, at very large x, the potential energy no longer changes. This is not surprising because two distant atoms do not interact with each other. This difference between the repulsive and attractive forces leads to an *asymmetric* curve.

It turns out that, for quantum physics reasons, a molecule cannot have $E = 0$ and thus cannot simply rest at the equilibrium position. By requiring the molecule to have some energy, such as E_1, we see that the atoms oscillate back and forth between two turning points. This is a *molecular vibration,* and atoms held together by molecular bonds are constantly vibrating. For a molecule having an energy $E_1 = 0.35 \times 10^{-18}$ J, as illustrated in Figure 10.37, the bond oscillates in length between roughly 0.10 nm and 0.18 nm.

Suppose we increase the molecule's energy to $E_2 = 1.25 \times 10^{-18}$ J. This could happen if the molecule absorbs some light. You can see from the energy diagram that atoms with this energy are not bound together at large values of x. There is no turning point on the right, so the atoms will keep moving apart. By raising the molecule's energy to E_2 we have *broken the molecular bond*. If the atoms happen to be moving together at the time the energy changes, they will "bounce" one last time (there is still a *left* turning point), then move away from each other and not return. The breaking of molecular bonds through the absorption of light is called *photodissociation*. It is an important process in making integrated circuits.

EXERCISES AND PROBLEMS

Exercises

Section 10.2 Kinetic Energy and Gravitational Potential Energy

1. | Which has the larger kinetic energy, a 10 g bullet fired at 500 m/s or a 75 kg student running at 5.5 m/s?

2. | The lowest point in Death Valley is 85 m below sea level. The summit of nearby Mt. Whitney has an elevation of 4420 m. What is the change in potential energy of an energetic 65 kg hiker who makes it from the floor of Death Valley to the top of Mt. Whitney?

3. | At what speed does a 1000 kg compact car have the same kinetic energy as a 20,000 kg truck going 25 km/hr?

4. | a. What is the kinetic energy of a 1500 kg car traveling at a speed of 30 m/s (≈ 65 mph)?
   b. From what height would the car have to be dropped to have this same amount of kinetic energy just before impact?
   c. Does your answer to part b depend on the car's mass?

5. | A boy reaches out of a window and tosses a ball straight up with a speed of 10 m/s. The ball is 20 m above the ground as he releases it. Use energy to find
   a. The ball's maximum height above the ground.
   b. The ball's speed as it passes the window on its way down.
   c. The speed of impact on the ground.

6. || a. With what minimum speed must you toss a 100 g ball straight up to hit the 10-m-high roof of the gymnasium if you release the ball 1.5 m above the ground? Solve this problem using energy.
   b. With what speed does the ball hit the ground?

7. || An oxygen atom is four times as massive as a helium atom. In an experiment, a helium atom and an oxygen atom have the same kinetic energy. What is the ratio v_{He}/v_O of their speeds?

Section 10.3 A Closer Look at Gravitational Potential Energy

8. | A 50 g ball is released from rest 1.0 m above the bottom of the track shown in FIGURE EX10.8. It rolls down a straight 30° segment, then back up a parabolic segment whose shape is given by $y = \frac{1}{4}x^2$, where x and y are in m. How high will the ball go on the right before reversing direction and rolling back down?

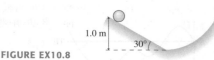

FIGURE EX10.8

1.0 m   30°

9. | A 55 kg skateboarder wants to just make it to the upper edge of a "quarter pipe," a track that is one-quarter of a circle with a radius of 3.0 m. What speed does he need at the bottom?

10. || What minimum speed does a 100 g puck need to make it to the top of a 3.0-m-long, 20° frictionless ramp?

11. || A pendulum is made by tying a 500 g ball to a 75-cm-long string. The pendulum is pulled 30° to one side, then released.
   a. What is the ball's speed at the lowest point of its trajectory?
   b. To what angle does the pendulum swing on the other side?

12. | A 20 kg child is on a swing that hangs from 3.0-m-long chains. What is her maximum speed if she swings out to a 45°angle?

13. | A 1500 kg car traveling at 10 m/s suddenly runs out of gas while approaching the valley shown in FIGURE EX10.13. What will be the car's speed as it coasts into the gas station on the other side of the valley?

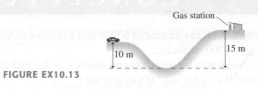

Gas station

10 m   15 m

FIGURE EX10.13

Section 10.4 Restoring Forces and Hooke's Law

14. | A runner wearing spiked shoes pulls a 20 kg sled across frictionless ice using a horizontal spring with spring constant 150 N/m. The spring is stretched 20 cm from its equilibrium length. What is the acceleration of the sled?

15. | You need to make a spring scale for measuring mass. You want each 1.0 cm length along the scale to correspond to a mass difference of 100 g. What should be the value of the spring constant?

16. || A 10-cm-long spring is attached to the ceiling. When a 2.0 kg mass is hung from it, the spring stretches to a length of 15 cm.
   a. What is the spring constant k?
   b. How long is the spring when a 3.0 kg mass is suspended from it?

17. || A 5.0 kg mass hanging from a spring scale is slowly lowered onto a vertical spring, as shown in FIGURE EX10.17. The scale reads in newtons.
   a. What does the spring scale read just before the mass touches the lower spring?
   b. The scale reads 20 N when the lower spring has been compressed by 2.0 cm. What is the value of the spring constant for the lower spring?
   c. At what compression length will the scale read zero?

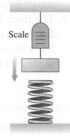

Scale

FIGURE EX10.17

18. || A 60 kg student is standing atop a spring in an elevator as it accelerates upward at 3.0 m/s². The spring constant is 2500 N/m. By how much is the spring compressed?

Section 10.5 Elastic Potential Energy

19. | How much energy can be stored in a spring with $k = 500$ N/m if the maximum possible stretch is 20 cm?

20. | How far must you stretch a spring with $k = 1000$ N/m to store 200 J of energy?

21. || A student places her 500 g physics book on a frictionless table. She pushes the book against a spring, compressing the spring by 4.0 cm, then releases the book. What is the book's speed as it slides away? The spring constant is 1250 N/m.

22. | A block sliding along a horizontal frictionless surface with speed v collides with a spring and compresses it by 2.0 cm. What will be the compression if the same block collides with the spring at a speed of $2v$?

23. || A 10 kg runaway grocery cart runs into a spring with spring constant 250 N/m and compresses it by 60 cm. What was the speed of the cart just before it hit the spring?

24. ‖ As a 15,000 kg jet plane lands on an aircraft carrier, its tail hook snags a cable to slow it down. The cable is attached to a spring with spring constant 60,000 N/m. If the spring stretches 30 m to stop the plane, what was the plane's landing speed?

Section 10.6 Elastic Collisions

25. | A 50 g marble moving at 2.0 m/s strikes a 20 g marble at rest. What is the speed of each marble immediately after the collision?

26. | A proton is traveling to the right at 2.0×10^7 m/s. It has a head-on perfectly elastic collision with a carbon atom. The mass of the carbon atom is 12 times the mass of the proton. What are the speed and direction of each after the collision?

27. ‖ A 50 g ball of clay traveling at speed v_0 hits and sticks to a 1.0 kg brick sitting at rest on a frictionless surface.
   a. What is the speed of the brick after the collision?
   b. What percentage of the ball's initial energy is lost in this collision?

28. ‖ Ball 1, with a mass of 100 g and traveling at 10 m/s, collides head-on with ball 2, which has a mass of 300 g and is initially at rest. What is the final velocity of each ball if the collision is (a) perfectly elastic? (b) perfectly inelastic?

Section 10.7 Energy Diagrams

29. | FIGURE EX10.29 is the potential-energy diagram for a 20 g particle that is released from rest at $x = 1.0$ m.
   a. Will the particle move to the right or to the left? How can you tell?
   b. What is the particle's maximum speed? At what position does it have this speed?
   c. Where are the turning points of the motion?

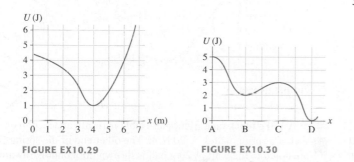

FIGURE EX10.29   FIGURE EX10.30

30. | FIGURE EX10.30 is the potential-energy diagram for a 500 g particle that is released from rest at A. What are the particle's speeds at B, C, and D?

31. ‖ What is the maximum speed of a 2.0 g particle that oscillates between $x = 2.0$ mm and $x = 8.0$ mm in FIGURE EX10.31?

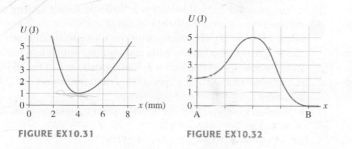

FIGURE EX10.31   FIGURE EX10.32

32. ‖ a. In FIGURE EX10.32, what minimum speed does a 100 g particle need at point A to reach point B?
   b. What minimum speed does a 100 g particle need at point B to reach point A?

Problems

33. | You're driving at 35 km/hr when the road suddenly descends 15 m into a valley. You take your foot off the accelerator and coast down the hill. Just as you reach the bottom you see the policeman hiding behind the speed limit sign that reads "70 km/hr." Are you going to get a speeding ticket?

34. ‖ A cannon tilted up at a 30° angle fires a cannon ball at 80 m/s from atop a 10-m-high fortress wall. What is the ball's impact speed on the ground below?

35. ‖ Your friend's Frisbee has become stuck 16 m above the ground in a tree. You want to dislodge the Frisbee by throwing a rock at it. The Frisbee is stuck pretty tight, so you figure the rock needs to be traveling at least 5.0 m/s when it hits the Frisbee.
   a. Does the speed with which you throw the rock depend on the angle at which you throw it? Explain.
   b. If you release the rock 2.0 m above the ground, with what minimum speed must you throw it?

36. ‖ A very slippery ice cube slides in a *vertical* plane around the inside of a smooth, 20-cm-diameter horizontal pipe. The ice cube's speed at the bottom of the circle is 3.0 m/s.
   a. What is the ice cube's speed at the top?
   b. Find an algebraic expression for the ice cube's speed when it is at angle θ, where the angle is measured counterclockwise from the bottom of the circle. Your expression should give 3.0 m/s for $\theta = 0°$ and your answer to part a for $\theta = 180°$.
   c. Make a graph of v versus θ for one complete revolution.

37. ‖ A 50 g rock is placed in a slingshot and the rubber band is stretched. The force of the rubber band on the rock is shown by the graph in FIGURE P10.37.
   a. Is the rubber band stretched to the right or to the left? How can you tell?
   b. Does this rubber band obey Hooke's law? Explain.
   c. What is the rubber band's spring constant k?
   d. The rubber band is stretched 30 cm and then released. What is the speed of the rock?

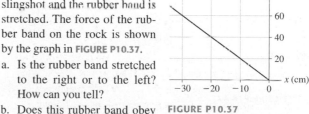

FIGURE P10.37

38. ‖ The spring in FIGURE P10.38a is compressed by Δx. It launches the block across a frictionless surface with speed v_0. The two springs in FIGURE P10.38b are identical to the spring of Figure P10.38a. They are compressed by the same Δx and used to launch the same block. What is the block's speed now?

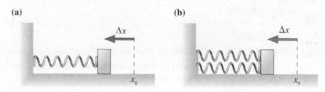

FIGURE P10.38

39. || The spring in FIGURE P10.39a is compressed by   It launches the block across a frictionless surface with speed v_0. The two springs in FIGURE P10.39b are identical to the spring of Figure P10.39a. They are compressed the same *total* Δx and used to launch the same block. What is the block's speed now?

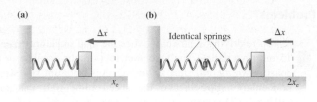

FIGURE P10.39

40. || A 500 g rubber ball is dropped from a height of 10 m and undergoes a perfectly elastic collision with the earth.
    a. What is the earth's velocity after the collision? Assume the earth was at rest just before the collision.
    b. How many years would it take the earth to move 1.0 mm at this speed?

41. || A 50 g ice cube can slide without friction up and down a 30° slope. The ice cube is pressed against a spring at the bottom of the slope, compressing the spring 10 cm. The spring constant is 25 N/m. When the ice cube is released, what distance will it travel up the slope before reversing direction?

42. || A package of mass m is released from rest at a warehouse loading dock and slides down a 3.0-m-high frictionless chute to a waiting truck. Unfortunately, the truck driver went on a break without having removed the previous package, of mass $2m$, from the bottom of the chute.
    a. Suppose the packages stick together. What is their common speed after the collision?
    b. Suppose the collision between the packages is perfectly elastic. To what height does the package of mass m rebound?

FIGURE P10.42

43. || A 100 g granite cube slides down a 40° frictionless ramp. At the bottom, just as it exits onto a horizontal table, it collides with a 200 g steel cube at rest. How high above the table should the granite cube be released to give the steel cube a speed of 150 cm/s?

44. ||| A 1000 kg safe is 2.0 m above a heavy-duty spring when the rope holding the safe breaks. The safe hits the spring and compresses it 50 cm. What is the spring constant of the spring?

45. || A vertical spring with $k = 490$ N/m is standing on the ground. You are holding a 5.0 kg block just above the spring, not quite touching it.
    a. How far does the spring compress if you let go of the block suddenly?
    b. How far does the spring compress if you slowly lower the block to the point where you can remove your hand without disturbing it?
    c. Why are your two answers different?

46. || The desperate contestants on a TV survival show are very hungry. The only food they can see is some fruit hanging on a branch high in a tree. Fortunately, they have a spring they can use to launch a rock. The spring constant is 1000 N/m, and they can compress the spring a maximum of 30 cm. All the rocks on the island seem to have a mass of 400 g.
    a. With what speed does the rock leave the spring?
    b. If the fruit hangs 15 m above the ground, will they feast or go hungry?

47. || A massless pan hangs from a spring that is suspended from the ceiling. When empty, the pan is 50 cm below the ceiling. If a 100 g clay ball is placed gently on the pan, the pan hangs 60 cm below the ceiling. Suppose the clay ball is dropped from the ceiling onto an empty pan. What is the pan's distance from the ceiling when the spring reaches its maximum length?

48. || You have been hired to design a spring-launched roller coaster that will carry two passengers per car. The car goes up a 10-m-high hill, then descends 15 m to the track's lowest point. You've determined that the spring can be compressed a maximum of 2.0 m and that a loaded car will have a maximum mass of 400 kg. For safety reasons, the spring constant should be 10% larger than the minimum needed for the car to just make it over the top.
    a. What spring constant should you specify?
    b. What is the maximum speed of a 350 kg car if the spring is compressed the full amount?

49. || It's been a great day of new, frictionless snow. Julie starts at the top of the 60° slope shown in FIGURE P10.49. At the bottom, a circular arc carries her through a 90° turn, and she then launches off a 3.0-m-high ramp. How far horizontally is her touchdown point from the end of the ramp?

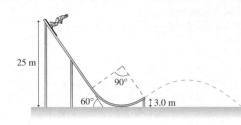

FIGURE P10.49

50. || A 100 g block on a frictionless table is firmly attached to one end of a spring with $k = 20$ N/m. The other end of the spring is anchored to the wall. A 20 g ball is thrown horizontally toward the block with a speed of 5.0 m/s.
    a. If the collision is perfectly elastic, what is the ball's speed immediately after the collision?
    b. What is the maximum compression of the spring?
    c. Repeat parts a and b for the case of a perfectly inelastic collision.

51. || You have been asked to design a "ballistic spring system" to measure the speed of bullets. A bullet of mass m is fired into a block of mass M. The block, with the embedded bullet, then slides across a frictionless table and collides with a horizontal spring whose spring constant is k. The opposite end of the spring is anchored to a wall. The spring's maximum compression d is measured.
    a. Find an expression for the bullet's speed v_B in terms of m, M, k, and d.

b. What was the speed of a 5.0 g bullet if the block's mass is 2.0 kg and if the spring, with $k = 50$ N/m, was compressed by 10 cm?

c. What fraction of the bullet's energy is "lost"? Where did it go?

52. ‖ You have been asked to design a "ballistic spring system" to measure the speed of bullets. A spring whose spring constant is k is suspended from the ceiling. A block of mass M hangs from the spring. A bullet of mass m is fired vertically upward into the bottom of the block. The spring's maximum compression d is measured.

a. Find an expression for the bullet's speed v_B in terms of m, M, k, and d.

b. What was the speed of a 10 g bullet if the block's mass is 2.0 kg and if the spring, with $k = 50$ N/m, was compressed by 45 cm?

53. ‖ A roller coaster car on the frictionless track shown in **FIGURE P10.53** starts from rest at height h. The track's valley and hill consist of circular-shaped segments of radius R.

a. What is the *maximum* height h_{max} from which the car can start so as not to fly off the track when going over the hill? Give your answer as a multiple of R.
   Hint: First find the maximum speed for going over the hill.

b. Evaluate h_{max} for a roller coaster that has $R = 10$ m.

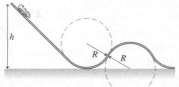

FIGURE P10.53

54. ‖ A block of mass m slides down a frictionless track, then around the inside of a circular loop-the-loop of radius R. From what minimum height h must the block start to make it around the loop without falling off? Give your answer as a multiple of R.

55. ‖ A new event has been proposed for the Winter Olympics. An athlete will sprint 100 m, starting from rest, then leap onto a 20 kg bobsled. The person and bobsled will then slide down a 50-m-long ice-covered ramp, sloped at 20°, and into a spring with a carefully calibrated spring constant of 2000 N/m. The athlete who compresses the spring the farthest wins the gold medal. Lisa, whose mass is 40 kg, has been training for this event. She can reach a maximum speed of 12 m/s in the 100 m dash.

a. How far will Lisa compress the spring?

b. The Olympic committee has very exact specifications about the shape and angle of the ramp. Is this necessary? What factors about the ramp are important?

FIGURE P10.55

56. ‖‖ A 20 g ball is fired horizontally with speed v_0 toward a 100 g ball hanging motionless from a 1.0-m-long string. The balls undergo a head-on, perfectly elastic collision, after which the 100 g ball swings out to a maximum angle $\theta_{max} = 50°$. What was v_0?

57. ‖ A 100 g ball moving to the right at 4.0 m/s collides head-on with a 200 g ball that is moving to the left at 3.0 m/s.

a. If the collision is perfectly elastic, what are the speed and direction of each ball after the collision?

b. If the collision is perfectly inelastic, what are the speed and direction of the combined balls after the collision?

58. ‖ A 100 g ball moving to the right at 4.0 m/s catches up and collides with a 400 g ball that is moving to the right at 1.0 m/s. If the collision is perfectly elastic, what are the speed and direction of each ball after the collision?

59. ‖ **FIGURE P10.59** shows the potential energy of a 500 g particle as it moves along the x-axis. Suppose the particle's mechanical energy is 12 J.

a. Where are the particle's turning points?

b. What is the particle's speed when it is at $x = 2.0$ m?

c. What is the particle's maximum speed? At what position or positions does this occur?

d. Write a description of the motion of the particle as it moves from the left turning point to the right turning point.

e. Suppose the particle's energy is lowered to 4.0 J. Describe the possible motions.

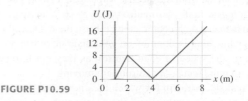

FIGURE P10.59

60. ‖ The ammonia molecule NH_3 has the tetrahedral structure shown in **FIGURE P10.60a**. The three hydrogen atoms form a triangle in the xy-plane at $z = 0$. The nitrogen atom is the apex of the pyramid. **FIGURE P10.60b** shows the potential energy of the nitrogen atom along a z-axis that is perpendicular to the H_3 triangle.

a. At room temperature, the nitrogen atom has $\approx 0.4 \times 10^{-20}$ J of mechanical energy. Describe the position and motion of the nitrogen atom.

b. The nitrogen atom can gain energy if the molecule absorbs energy from a light wave. Describe the motion of the nitrogen atom if its energy is 2×10^{-20} J.

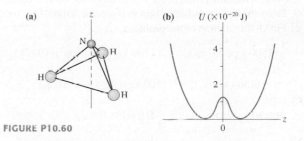

FIGURE P10.60

61. ‖ A particle has potential energy

$$U(x) = x + \sin((2 \text{ rad/m})x)$$

over the range $0 \text{ m} \leq x \leq \pi$ m.

a. Where are the equilibrium positions in this range?

b. For each, is it a point of stable or unstable equilibrium?

62. ‖ Protons and neutrons (together called *nucleons*) are held together in the nucleus of an atom by a force called the *strong force*. At very small separations, the strong force between two nucleons is larger than the repulsive electrical force between two protons—hence its name. But the strong force quickly weakens as the distance between the protons increases. A well-established model for the potential energy of two nucleons interacting via the strong force is

$$U = U_0[1 - e^{-x/x_0}]$$

where x is the distance between the centers of the two nucleons, x_0 is a constant having the value $x_0 = 2.0 \times 10^{-15}$ m, and $U_0 = 6.0 \times 10^{-11}$ J.

   a. Calculate and draw an accurate potential-energy curve from $x = 0$ m to $x = 10 \times 10^{-15}$ m. Either calculate about 10 points by hand or use computer software.
   b. Quantum effects are essential for a proper understanding of how nucleons behave. Nonetheless, let us innocently consider two neutrons *as if* they were small, hard, electrically neutral spheres of mass 1.67×10^{-27} kg and diameter 1.0×10^{-15} m. (We will consider neutrons rather than protons so as to avoid complications from the electric forces between protons.) You are going to hold two neutrons 5.0×10^{-15} m apart, measured between their centers, then release them. Draw the total energy line for this situation on your diagram of part a.
   c. What is the speed of each neutron as they crash together? Keep in mind that *both* neutrons are moving.

63. Write a realistic problem for which the energy bar chart shown in **FIGURE P10.63** correctly shows the energy at the beginning and end of the problem.

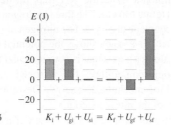

FIGURE P10.63 $K_i + U_{gi} + U_{si} = K_f + U_{gf} + U_{sf}$

In Problems 64 through 67 you are given the equation used to solve a problem. For each of these, you are to
   a. Write a realistic problem for which this is the correct equation.
   b. Draw the before-and-after pictorial representation.
   c. Finish the solution of the problem.

64. $\frac{1}{2}(1500 \text{ kg})(5.0 \text{ m/s})^2 + (1500 \text{ kg})(9.80 \text{ m/s}^2)(10 \text{ m})$

$= \frac{1}{2}(1500 \text{ kg})(v_i)^2 + (1500 \text{ kg})(9.80 \text{ m/s}^2)(0 \text{ m})$

65. $\frac{1}{2}(0.20 \text{ kg})(2.0 \text{ m/s})^2 + \frac{1}{2}k(0 \text{ m})^2$

$= \frac{1}{2}(0.20 \text{ kg})(0 \text{ m/s})^2 + \frac{1}{2}k(-0.15 \text{ m})^2$

66. $(0.10 \text{ kg} + 0.20 \text{ kg})v_{1x} = (0.10 \text{ kg})(3.0 \text{ m/s})$

$\frac{1}{2}(0.30 \text{ kg})(0 \text{ m/s})^2 + \frac{1}{2}(3.0 \text{ N/m})(\Delta x_2)^2$

$= \frac{1}{2}(0.30 \text{ kg})(v_{1x})^2 + \frac{1}{2}(3.0 \text{ N/m})(0 \text{ m})^2$

67. $\frac{1}{2}(0.50 \text{ kg})(v_f)^2 + (0.50 \text{ kg})(9.80 \text{ m/s}^2)(0 \text{ m})$

$+ \frac{1}{2}(400 \text{ N/m})(0 \text{ m})^2$

$= \frac{1}{2}(0.50 \text{ kg})(0 \text{ m/s})^2$

$+ (0.50 \text{ kg})(9.80 \text{ m/s}^2)((-0.10 \text{ m})\sin 30°)$

$+ \frac{1}{2}(400 \text{ N/m})(-0.10 \text{ m})^2$

Challenge Problems

68. In a physics lab experiment, a compressed spring launches a 20 g metal ball at a 30° angle. Compressing the spring 20 cm causes the ball to hit the floor 1.5 m below the point at which it leaves the spring after traveling 5.0 m horizontally. What is the spring constant?

69. A pendulum is formed from a small ball of mass m on a string of length L. As **FIGURE CP10.69** shows, a peg is height $h = L/3$ above the pendulum's lowest point. From what minimum angle θ must the pendulum be released in order for the ball to go over the top of the peg without the string going slack?

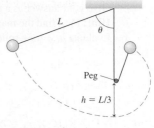

FIGURE CP10.69

70. It's your birthday, and to celebrate you're going to make your first bungee jump. You stand on a bridge 100 m above a raging river and attach a 30-m-long bungee cord to your harness. A bungee cord, for practical purposes, is just a long spring, and this cord has a spring constant of 40 N/m. Assume that your mass is 80 kg. After a long hesitation, you dive off the bridge. How far are you above the water when the cord reaches its maximum elongation?

71. A 10 kg box slides 4.0 m down the frictionless ramp shown in **FIGURE CP10.71**, then collides with a spring whose spring constant is 250 N/m.
   a. What is the maximum compression of the spring?
   b. At what compression of the spring does the box have its maximum speed?

FIGURE CP10.71

72. Old naval ships fired 10 kg cannon balls from a 200 kg cannon. It was very important to stop the recoil of the cannon, since otherwise the heavy cannon would go careening across the deck of the ship. In one design, a large spring with spring constant 20,000 N/m was placed behind the cannon. The other end of the spring braced against a post that was firmly anchored to the ship's frame. What was the speed of the cannon ball if the spring compressed 50 cm when the cannon was fired?

73. A 2.0 kg cart has a spring with $k = 5000$ N/m attached to its front, parallel to the ground. This cart rolls at 4.0 m/s toward a stationary 1.0 kg cart.
   a. What is the maximum compression of the spring during the collision?
   b. What is the speed of each cart after the collision?

74. The air-track carts in **FIGURE CP10.74** are sliding to the right at 1.0 m/s. The spring between them has a spring constant of 120 N/m and is compressed 4.0 cm. The carts slide past a flame that burns through the string holding them together. Afterward, what are the speed and direction of each cart?

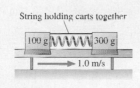

String holding carts together

100 g ⌇WWWWW⌇ 300 g

→ 1.0 m/s

FIGURE CP10.74

75. A 100 g steel ball and a 200 g steel ball each hang from 1.0-m-long strings. At rest, the balls hang side by side, barely touching. The 100 g ball is pulled to the left until the angle between its string and vertical is 45°. The 200 g ball is pulled to a 45° angle on the right. The balls are released so as to collide at the very bottom of their swings. To what angle does each ball rebound?

76. A sled starts from rest at the top of the frictionless, hemispherical, snow-covered hill shown in **FIGURE CP10.76**.
   a. Find an expression for the sled's speed when it is at angle ϕ.
   b. Use Newton's laws to find the maximum speed the sled can have at angle ϕ without leaving the surface.
   c. At what angle ϕ_{max} does the sled "fly off" the hill?

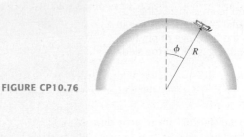

ϕ R

FIGURE CP10.76

STOP TO THINK ANSWERS

Stop to Think 10.1: $(U_g)_c > (U_g)_b = (U_g)_d > (U_g)_a$. Gravitational potential energy depends only on height, not on speed.

Stop to Think 10.2: $v_a = v_b = v_c = v_d$. Her increase in kinetic energy depends only on the vertical height through which she falls, not the shape of the slide.

Stop to Think 10.3: b. Mechanical energy is conserved on a frictionless surface. Because $K_i = 0$ and $K_f = 0$, it must be true that $U_f = U_i$ and thus $y_f = y_i$. The final height matches the initial height.

Stop to Think 10.4: $k_a > k_b > k_c$. The spring constant is the slope of the force-versus-displacement graph.

Stop to Think 10.5: c. U_s depends on $(\Delta s)^2$, so doubling the compression increases U_s by a factor of 4. All the potential energy is converted to kinetic energy, so K increases by a factor of 4. But K depends on v^2, so v increases by only a factor of $(4)^{1/2} = 2$.

Stop to Think 10.6: $x = 6$ m. From the graph, the particle's potential energy at $x = 1$ m is $U = 3$ J. Its total energy is thus $E = K + U = 4$ J. A TE line at 4 J crosses the PE curve at $x = 6$ m.

11 Work

This bobsled team is increasing the sled's kinetic energy by pushing it forward. In the language of physics, they are doing *work* on the sled.

▶ **Looking Ahead**

The goal of Chapter 11 is to develop a more complete understanding of energy and its conservation. In this chapter you will learn to:

- Understand and apply the basic energy model.
- Calculate the work done on a system.
- Understand and use a more complete statement of conservation of energy.
- Use a general strategy for solving energy problems.
- Calculate the power supplied to or dissipated by a system.

◀ **Looking Back**

This chapter continues to develop energy ideas that were introduced in Chapter 10. Please review:

- Sections 10.2–10.3 Gravitational potential energy.
- Sections 10.4–10.5 Hooke's law and elastic potential energy.

Chapter 10 introduced the concept of energy. Although energy appears to be a useful idea, three major questions remain unanswered:

- How many kinds of energy are there?
- Under what conditions is energy conserved?
- How does a system gain or lose energy?

For example, this bobsled is gaining kinetic energy, but it's not doing so by losing potential energy. Instead, the runners are giving it kinetic energy by pushing it faster and faster. One of our goals in this chapter is to relate the energy gained by the sled to the strength of their push. Energy transferred by pushes and pulls is called *work*.

We will also explore how energy is *dissipated*. Because of friction, a bobsled sliding across a horizontal surface gradually slows and stops. What happens to its kinetic energy? By addressing these issues, we will put the concept of energy on a firmer foundation.

Many of the ideas of this chapter will be new and, in some cases, rather abstract. Because of this, we will begin with an overview of where the chapter will take us, then come back to fill in the details.

11.1 The Basic Energy Model

Consider a system of interacting objects. For example:

- A car skids to a halt (car + earth).
- A ball oscillates on a spring (ball + spring + earth).

The system can be characterized by two quantities: the *kinetic energy* and the *potential energy*. Kinetic energy K is an energy due to the *motion* of the objects. The potential energy U, which is often thought of as "stored energy," is due to *interactions* between the objects. For example, two balls connected by a stretched spring have a potential energy.

The sum of kinetic and potential energy is the system's *mechanical energy:* $E_{mech} = K + U$. The term *mechanical* designates this form of energy as being due to motion and mechanical effects, such as stretching springs, rather than chemical effects or heat effects.

But mechanical energy is not the only energy. If you peered inside a ball at rest, with zero mechanical energy, you would see the atoms inside the ball vibrating back and forth on their spring-like molecular bonds. This microscopic motion of the atoms and molecules *within* an object is a form of energy distinct from the object's mechanical energy. The total energy of the moving atoms and stretched bonds inside the object is called the system's **thermal energy E_{th}.**

Thermal energy is associated with the system's *temperature*. A higher temperature means more microscopic motion and thus more thermal energy. Friction raises the temperature—think of rubbing your hands together briskly—so a system with friction "runs down" as its mechanical energy is transformed into thermal energy. We'll say more about thermal energy in Section 11.7.

> **NOTE** ▶ A particle has no internal structure and can't have any thermal energy. A consideration of thermal energy is our first step *beyond* the particle model. ◀

We can define the **system energy E_{sys}** as the sum of the mechanical energy *of* the objects plus the thermal energy of the atoms *inside* the objects. That is,

$$E_{sys} = E_{mech} + E_{th} = K + U + E_{th} \qquad (11.1)$$

As **FIGURE 11.1** shows, kinetic and potential energy can be changed back and forth into each other. You studied these processes in Chapter 10. Kinetic and potential energy can also be changed into thermal energy, but, as we'll discuss later, thermal energy is not normally changed into kinetic or potential energy. Energy exchanges within the system are called **energy transformations.** Energy transformations within the system do not change the value of E_{sys}.

> **NOTE** ▶ We will use an arrow → as a shorthand way to indicate an energy transformation. If the kinetic energy of a car is transformed into thermal energy as it skids to a halt, we will indicate this by $K \rightarrow E_{th}$. ◀

A system is always surrounded by a larger *environment*. Unless the system is completely isolated, it has the possibility of exchanging energy with the environment. An energy exchange between the system and the environment is called an **energy transfer.** There are two primary energy-transfer processes. The first, and the only one we will be concerned with for now, is due to forces—pushes and pulls—exerted on the system by the environment. For example, you give a ball kinetic energy by pushing on it. This *mechanical* transfer of energy to or from the system is called **work.** The symbol for work is W.

The second means of transferring energy between the system and its environment is a *nonmechanical* process called *heat*. Heat is a crucial idea that we will add to the energy model when we study thermodynamics, but for now we want to concentrate on the mechanical transfer of energy via work.

FIGURE 11.2 shows a **basic energy model** in which energy can be *transferred* to or from the system and energy can be *transformed* within the system. Notice how similar Figure 11.2 is to John's model of the monetary system in Chapter 10. As a *basic* model, Figure 11.2 is certainly not complete, and we will add new features to the model as needed. Nonetheless, it is a good starting point.

FIGURE 11.1 Energy can be transformed within the system.

$$
\boxed{
\begin{array}{c}
\textbf{System} \\[4pt]
E_{mech} = K + U \\[6pt]
K \leftrightarrow U \\[4pt]
\downarrow \quad \downarrow \\[4pt]
E_{th} \\[6pt]
E_{sys} = K + U + E_{th}
\end{array}
}
$$

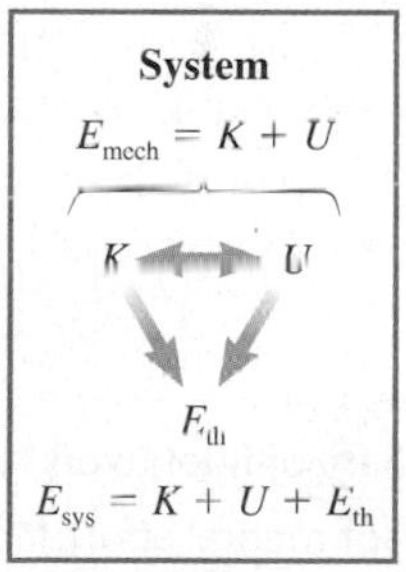

FIGURE 11.2 The basic energy model of a system interacting with its environment.

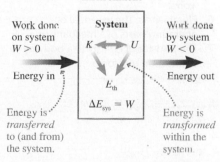

Work done on system $W > 0$

Energy in

Work done by system $W < 0$

Energy out

Environment

System
$K \leftrightarrow U$
E_{th}
$\Delta E_{sys} = W$

Energy is *transferred* to (and from) the system.

Energy is *transformed* within the system.

As the arrows in Figure 11.2 show, energy can both enter and leave the system. We'll distinguish between the two directions of energy flow by allowing the work W to be either positive or negative. The sign of W is interpreted as follows:

$W > 0$ **The environment does work on the system and the system's energy increases.**

$W < 0$ **The system does work on the environment and the system's energy decreases.**

This is equivalent to considering expenditures (i.e., money out) to be negative income. In fact, this is how accountants really do handle expenditures.

What is the relationship among the quantities of the basic energy model? Our hypothesis, which is confirmed by experiment, is that

$$\Delta E_{sys} = \Delta K + \Delta U + \Delta E_{th} = W \qquad (11.2)$$

The two essential ideas of the basic energy model and Equation 11.2 are:

1. Energy can be *transferred* to a system by doing work on the system. This process changes the energy of the system: $\Delta E_{sys} = W$.
2. Energy can be *transformed* within the system among K, U, and E_{th}. These processes don't change the energy of the system: $\Delta E_{sys} = 0$.

This is the essence of the basic energy model. The rest of Chapter 11 will substantiate Equation 11.2 and look at its many implications.

STOP TO THINK 11.1   A child slides down a playground slide at constant speed. The energy transformation is

a. $U \rightarrow K$ b. $K \rightarrow U$
c. There is no transformation because energy is conserved.
d. $U \rightarrow E_{th}$ e. $K \rightarrow E_{th}$

11.2 Work and Kinetic Energy

"Work" is a common word in the English language, with many meanings. When you first think of work, you probably think of the first two definitions in this list. After all, we talk about "working out," or we say, "I just got home from work." But that is *not* what work means in physics.

The basic energy model uses "work" in the sense of definition 7: energy transferred to or from a body or system by the application of force. The critical question we must answer is: *How much energy* does a force transfer?

We can answer this question by following the procedure we used in Chapter 10 to find the potential energy of gravity and of a spring. We'll begin, in **FIGURE 11.3**, with a force $\vec{F}$ acting on a particle of mass m as the particle moves along an s-axis from an initial position s_i, with kinetic energy K_i, to a final position s_f where the kinetic energy is K_f.

NOTE ▶ $\vec{F}$ may not be the only force acting on the particle. However, for now we'll assume that $\vec{F}$ is the only force with a component parallel to the s-axis and hence is the only force capable of changing the particle's speed. ◀

The force component F_s parallel to the s-axis causes the particle to speed up or slow down, thus transferring energy to or from the particle. We say that force $\vec{F}$ *does work*

One dictionary defines "work" as:

1. Physical or mental effort; labor.
2. The activity by which one makes a living.
3. A task or duty.
4. Something produced as a result of effort, such as a *work of art*.
5. Plural *works:* A factory or plant where industry is carried on, such as *steel works.*
6. Plural *works:* The essential or operating parts of a mechanism.
7. The transfer of energy to a body by application of a force.

on the particle. Our goal is to find a relationship between F_s and ΔK. The s-component of Newton's second law is

$$F_s = ma_s = m\frac{dv_s}{dt} \tag{11.3}$$

where the v_s is the s-component of $\vec{v}$. As we did in Chapter 10, we can use the chain rule to write

$$m\frac{dv_s}{dt} = m\frac{dv_s}{ds}\frac{ds}{dt} = mv_s\frac{dv_s}{ds} \tag{11.4}$$

where $ds/dt = v_s$. Substituting Equation 11.4 into Equation 11.3 gives

$$F_s = mv_s\frac{dv_s}{ds} \tag{11.5}$$

The crucial step here, as it was in Chapter 10, was changing from a derivative with respect to time to a derivative with respect to position. We're going to want to integrate, so we first multiply through by ds to get

$$mv_s\,dv_s = F_s\,ds \tag{11.6}$$

Now we can integrate both sides from "before," where the position is s_i and the speed is v_i, to "after," giving

$$\int_{v_i}^{v_f} mv_s\,dv_s = \frac{1}{2}mv_s^2\Big|_{v_i}^{v_f} = \frac{1}{2}mv_f^2 - \frac{1}{2}mv_i^2 = \int_{s_i}^{s_f} F_s\,ds \tag{11.7}$$

The left side of Equation 11.7 is ΔK, the change in the particle's kinetic energy as it moves from s_i to s_f. The integral on the right apparently specifies the extent to which the applied force changes the particle's kinetic energy. We define the *work* done by force $\vec{F}$ as the particle moves from s_i to s_f as

$$W = \int_{s_i}^{s_f} F_s\,ds \tag{11.8}$$

The unit of work, that of force multiplied by distance, is the Nm. Using the definition of the newton gives

$$1\,\text{Nm} = 1\,(\text{kgm/s}^2)\,\text{m} = 1\,\text{kgm}^2/\text{s}^2 = 1\,\text{J}$$

Thus the unit of work is really the unit of energy. This is consistent with the idea that work is a transfer of energy. Rather than use Nm, we will measure work, just as we do energy, in joules.

Using Equation 11.8 as the definition of work, we can write Equation 11.7 as

$$\Delta K = W \tag{11.9}$$

Equation 11.9 is the quantitative statement that a force transfers kinetic energy to a particle, and thus *changes* the particle's kinetic energy, by pushing or pulling on it. Furthermore, **Equation 11.8 gives us a specific method to calculate *how much energy is transferred by the push or pull.*** This energy transfer, by mechanical means, is what we mean by the term "work."

Notice that *no* work is done if there is no displacement ($s_f - s_i$) because an integral that spans no interval is zero. **To change a particle's energy, a force must be applied as the particle undergoes a displacement.** If you were to hold a 200 lb weight over your head, you might break out in a sweat and your arms would tire. You might "feel" that you had done a lot of work, but you would have done *zero* work in the physics sense because the weight was not displaced while you were holding it and thus you transferred no energy to it.

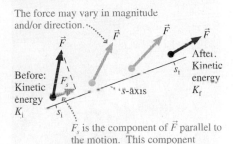

FIGURE 11.3 Force $\vec{F}$ does work as the particle moves from s_i to s_f.

The force may vary in magnitude and/or direction.

Before: Kinetic energy K_i

After: Kinetic energy K_f

s-axis

F_s is the component of $\vec{F}$ parallel to the motion. This component changes the particle's speed and thus its kinetic energy.

This pitcher is increasing the ball's kinetic energy by doing work on it.

The Work-Kinetic Energy Theorem

Equation 11.8 is the work done by one force. Because $\vec{F}_{net} = \sum \vec{F}_i$, it's easy to see that the net work done on a particle by several forces is $W_{net} = \sum W_i$, where W_i is the work done by force $\vec{F}_i$. In that case, Equation 11.9 becomes

$$\Delta K = W_{net} \qquad (11.10)$$

This basic idea—that the net work done on a particle causes the particle's kinetic energy to change—is a general principle, one worth giving a name:

> **The work-kinetic energy theorem** When one or more forces act on a particle as it is displaced from an initial position to a final position, the net work done on the particle by these forces causes the particle's kinetic energy to *change* by $\Delta K = W_{net}$.

One of the questions that opened this chapter was "How does a system gain or lose energy?" The work-kinetic energy theorem begins to answer that question by saying that **a system gains or loses kinetic energy when work transfers energy between the environment and the system.**

An Analogy with the Impulse-Momentum Theorem

You might have noticed that there is a similarity between the work-kinetic energy theorem and the impulse-momentum theorem of Chapter 9:

Work-kinetic energy theorem: $\quad \Delta K = W = \displaystyle\int_{s_i}^{s_f} F_s \, ds$

$$(11.11)$$

Impulse-momentum theorem: $\quad \Delta p_s = J_s = \displaystyle\int_{t_i}^{t_f} F_s \, dt$

FIGURE 11.4 Impulse and work are both the area under a force graph, but it's very important to know what the horizontal axis is.

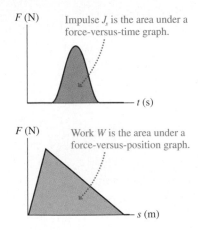

In both cases, a force acting on a particle changes the state of the system. If the force acts over a time interval from t_i to t_f, it creates an *impulse* that changes the particle's momentum. If the force acts over the spatial interval from s_i to s_f, it does *work* that changes the particle's kinetic energy. **FIGURE 11.4** shows that the geometric interpretation of impulse as the area under the F-versus-t graph applies equally well to an interpretation of work as the area under the F-versus-s graph.

This does not mean that a force *either* creates an impulse *or* does work but does not do both. Quite the contrary. A force acting on a particle *both* creates an impulse *and* does work, changing both the momentum and the kinetic energy of the particle. Whether you use the work-kinetic energy theorem or the impulse-momentum theorem depends on the question you are trying to answer.

We can, in fact, express the kinetic energy in terms of the momentum as

$$K = \frac{1}{2}mv^2 = \frac{(mv)^2}{2m} = \frac{p^2}{2m} \qquad (11.12)$$

You cannot change a particle's kinetic energy without also changing its momentum.

STOP TO THINK 11.2 A particle moving along the x-axis experiences the force shown in the graph. If the particle has 2.0 J of kinetic energy as it passes $x = 0$ m, what is its kinetic energy when it reaches $x = 4$ m?

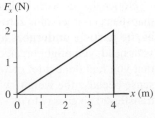

11.3 Calculating and Using Work

The work-kinetic energy theorem is a formal statement about the energy transferred to or from a particle by pushes and pulls. For it to be useful, we must be able to calculate the work. In this section we'll practice calculating work and using the work-kinetic energy theorem. We'll also introduce a new mathematical idea, the *dot product* of two vectors, that will allow us to write the work in a compact notation.

Constant Force

We'll begin by calculating the work done by a force $\vec{F}$ that acts with a *constant* strength and in a *constant* direction as a particle moves along a straight line through a displacement $\Delta\vec{r}$. As FIGURE 11.5a shows, we'll define the s-axis to point in the direction of motion.

FIGURE 11.5b shows the force acting on the particle as it moves along the line. The force vector $\vec{F}$ makes an angle θ with respect to the displacement $\Delta\vec{r}$, so the component of the force vector along the direction of motion is $F_s = F\cos\theta$. According to Equation 11.8, the work done on the particle by this force is

$$W = \int_{s_i}^{s_f} F_s \, ds = \int_{s_i}^{s_f} F\cos\theta \, ds$$

Both F and θ are constant, so they can be taken outside the integral. Thus

$$W = F\cos\theta \int_{s_i}^{s_f} ds = F\cos\theta(s_f - s_i) = F(\Delta r)\cos\theta \qquad (11.13)$$

where we used $s_f - s_i = \Delta r$, the magnitude of the particle's displacement. We can use Equation 11.13 to calculate the work done by a constant force if we know the magnitude F of the force, the angle θ of the force from the line of motion, and the distance Δr through which the particle is displaced.

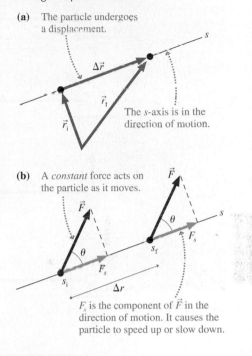

FIGURE 11.5 Work being done by a *constant* force as a particle moves through displacement $\Delta\vec{r}$.

(a) The particle undergoes a displacement.

The s-axis is in the direction of motion.

(b) A *constant* force acts on the particle as it moves.

F_s is the component of $\vec{F}$ in the direction of motion. It causes the particle to speed up or slow down.

Activ Physics ONLINE 5.1

EXAMPLE 11.1 Pulling a suitcase

A rope inclined upward at a 45° angle pulls a suitcase through the airport. The tension in the rope is 20 N. How much work does the tension do if the suitcase is pulled 100 m?

MODEL Model the suitcase as a particle.

VISUALIZE FIGURE 11.6 shows a pictorial representation.

SOLVE The motion is along the x-axis, so in this case $\Delta r = \Delta x$. We can use Equation 11.13 to find that the tension does work:

$$W = T(\Delta x)\cos\theta = (20 \text{ N})(100 \text{ m})\cos 45° = 1400 \text{ J}$$

FIGURE 11.6 Pictorial representation of a suitcase pulled by a rope.

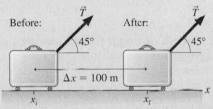

Before: $\vec{T}$ 45°

After: $\vec{T}$ 45°

$\Delta x = 100$ m

ASSESS Because a person pulls the rope, we would say informally that the person does 1400 J of work on the suitcase.

According to the basic energy model, work can be either positive or negative to indicate energy transfer into or out of the system. The quantities F and Δr are always positive, so the sign of W is determined entirely by the angle θ between the force $\vec{F}$ and the displacement $\Delta\vec{r}$.

TACTICS BOX 11.1 Calculating the work done by a constant force

(MP)

Force and displacement	θ	Work W	Sign	Energy transfer
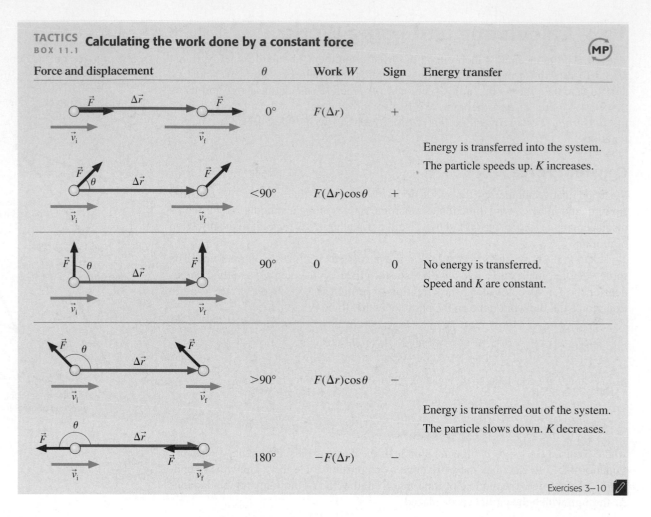	0°	$F(\Delta r)$	+	
	<90°	$F(\Delta r)\cos\theta$	+	Energy is transferred into the system. The particle speeds up. K increases.
	90°	0	0	No energy is transferred. Speed and K are constant.
	>90°	$F(\Delta r)\cos\theta$	−	Energy is transferred out of the system. The particle slows down. K decreases.
	180°	$-F(\Delta r)$	−	

Exercises 3–10

NOTE ▶ You may have learned in an earlier physics course that work is "force times distance." This is *not* the definition of work, merely a special case. Work is "force times distance" only if the force is constant *and* parallel to the displacement (i.e., $\theta = 0°$). ◀

EXAMPLE 11.2 Work during a rocket launch

A 150,000 kg rocket is launched straight up. The rocket motor generates a thrust of 4.0×10^6 N. What is the rocket's speed at a height of 500 m? Ignore air resistance and any slight mass loss.

MODEL Model the rocket as a particle. Thrust and gravity are constant forces that do work on the rocket.

VISUALIZE FIGURE 11.7 shows a pictorial representation and a free-body diagram.

SOLVE We can solve this problem with the work-kinetic energy theorem $\Delta K = W_{net}$. Both forces do work on the rocket. The thrust is in the direction of motion, with $\theta = 0°$, and thus

$$W_{thrust} = F_{thrust}(\Delta r) = (4.0 \times 10^6 \text{ N})(500 \text{ m}) = 2.00 \times 10^9 \text{ J}$$

The gravitational force points downward, opposite the displacement $\Delta \vec{r}$, so $\theta = 180°$. Thus the work done by gravity is

$$W_{grav} = -F_G(\Delta r) = -mg(\Delta r)$$
$$= -(1.5 \times 10^5 \text{ kg})(9.8 \text{ m/s}^2)(500 \text{ m}) = -0.74 \times 10^9 \text{ J}$$

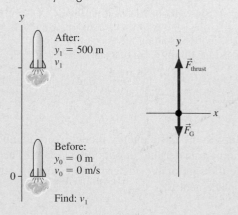

FIGURE 11.7 Pictorial representation and free-body diagram of a rocket launch.

The work done by the thrust is positive. By itself, the thrust would cause the rocket to speed up. The work done by gravity is negative. By itself, gravity would cause the rocket to slow down. The work-kinetic energy theorem, using $v_0 = 0$ m/s, is

$$\Delta K = \frac{1}{2}mv_1^2 - 0 = W_{net} = W_{thrust} + W_{grav} - 1.26 \times 10^9 \text{ J}$$

This is easily solved for the speed:

$$v_1 = \sqrt{\frac{2W_{net}}{m}} = 130 \text{ m/s}$$

ASSESS The net work is positive, meaning that energy is transferred *to* the rocket. In response, the rocket speeds up.

NOTE ▶ The work done by a force depends on the angle θ between the force $\vec{F}$ and the displacement $\Delta\vec{r}$, *not* on the direction the particle is moving. The work done on all four particles in FIGURE 11.8 is the same, despite the fact that they are moving in four different directions. ◀

Force Perpendicular to the Direction of Motion

FIGURE 11.9a shows a bird's-eye view of a car turning a corner. As you learned in Chapter 8, a friction force points toward the center of the circle. How much work does friction do on the car?

Zero! In FIGURE 11.9b we've "bent" the s-axis to follow the curve. You can see that the friction force is everywhere perpendicular to the small displacement $d\vec{s}$. F_s, the component of the force parallel to the displacement, is everywhere zero. Thus static friction does *no* work on the car. This shouldn't be surprising. You know that the car's speed, and hence its kinetic energy, doesn't change as it rounds the curve. Thus, according to the work-kinetic energy theorem, $W = \Delta K = 0$.

FIGURE 11.9 The friction force does no work.

FIGURE 11.8 The same amount of work is done on each of these particles.

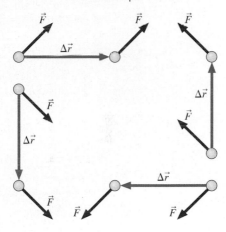

(a)
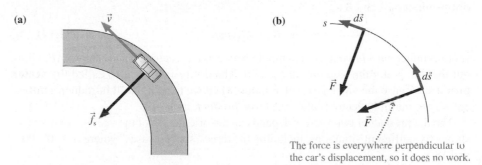

(b)

The force is everywhere perpendicular to the car's displacement, so it does no work.

We used a car on a curve as a concrete example, but this is a general result: **A force everywhere perpendicular to the motion does no work.** A perpendicular force changes the *direction* of motion but not the particle's speed.

EXAMPLE 11.3 Pushing a puck
A 500 g ice hockey puck slides across frictionless ice with an initial speed of 2.0 m/s. A compressed-air gun can be used to exert a 1.0 N force on the puck. The air gun is aimed at the front edge of the puck with the compressed-air flow 30° below the horizontal. This force is applied continuously as the puck moves 50 cm. What is the puck's final speed?

MODEL Model the puck as a particle. Use the work-kinetic energy theorem to find its final speed.

VISUALIZE FIGURE 11.10 shows a pictorial representation. The angle between the compressed-air force $\vec{F}$ and the displacement $\Delta\vec{r}$ is $\theta = 150°$.

FIGURE 11.10 Pictorial representation of the puck.

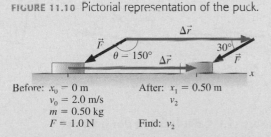

Before: $x_0 = 0$ m
$v_0 = 2.0$ m/s
$m = 0.50$ kg
$F = 1.0$ N

After: $x_1 = 0.50$ m
v_2

Find: v_2

SOLVE Three forces act on the puck: gravity, the normal force, and the force of the compressed air. Gravity and the normal force are perpendicular to the direction of motion ($\theta = 90°$), hence they do

Continued

no work on the puck. The only work W is done by the compressed-air force $\vec{F}$. The work is

$$W = F(\Delta r)\cos\theta = (1.0 \text{ N})(0.50 \text{ m})\cos 150° = -0.433 \text{ J}$$

Now we can use the work-kinetic energy theorem to compute the final speed:

$$\Delta K = \frac{1}{2}mv_1^2 - \frac{1}{2}mv_0^2 = W$$

and thus

$$v_1 = \sqrt{v_0^2 + \frac{2W}{m}} = \sqrt{(2.0 \text{ m/s})^2 + \frac{2(-0.433 \text{ J})}{0.50 \text{ kg}}}$$

$$= 1.5 \text{ m/s}$$

ASSESS The work is negative, meaning that energy is transferred *from* the puck. In response, the puck slows down.

STOP TO THINK 11.3 A crane lowers a steel girder into place. The girder moves with constant speed. Consider the work W_G done by gravity and the work W_T done by the tension in the cable. Which of the following is correct?

a. W_G is positive and W_T is positive.
b. W_G is positive and W_T is negative.
c. W_G is negative and W_T is positive.

d. W_G is negative and W_T is negative.
e. W_G and W_T are both zero.

The Dot Product of Two Vectors

There's something different about the quantity $F(\Delta r)\cos\theta$ in Equation 11.13. We've spent many chapters adding vectors, but this is the first time we've *multiplied* two vectors. Multiplying vectors is not like multiplying scalars. In fact, there is more than one way to multiply vectors. We will introduce one way now, the *dot product*.

FIGURE 11.11 shows two vectors, $\vec{A}$ and $\vec{B}$, with angle α between them. We define the **dot product** of $\vec{A}$ and $\vec{B}$ as

$$\vec{A} \cdot \vec{B} = AB\cos\alpha \qquad (11.14)$$

A dot product *must have* the dot symbol · between the vectors. The notation $\vec{A}\vec{B}$, without the dot, is *not* the same thing as $\vec{A} \cdot \vec{B}$. The dot product is also called the **scalar product** because the value is a scalar. Later, when we need it, we'll introduce a different way to multiply vectors called the *cross product*.

The dot product of two vectors depends on the orientation of the vectors. **FIGURE 11.12** shows five different situations, including the three "special cases" where $\alpha = 0°$, $90°$, and $180°$.

> **NOTE** ▶ The dot product of a vector with itself is well defined. If $\vec{B} = \vec{A}$ (i.e., $\vec{B}$ is a copy of $\vec{A}$), then $\alpha = 0°$. Thus $\vec{A} \cdot \vec{A} = A^2$. ◀

FIGURE 11.11 Vectors $\vec{A}$ and $\vec{B}$, with angle α between them.

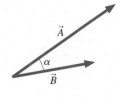

FIGURE 11.12 The dot product $\vec{A} \cdot \vec{B}$ as α ranges from 0° to 180°.

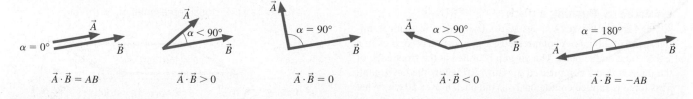

$\alpha = 0°$ $\quad \vec{A} \cdot \vec{B} = AB$

$\alpha < 90°$ $\quad \vec{A} \cdot \vec{B} > 0$

$\alpha = 90°$ $\quad \vec{A} \cdot \vec{B} = 0$

$\alpha > 90°$ $\quad \vec{A} \cdot \vec{B} < 0$

$\alpha = 180°$ $\quad \vec{A} \cdot \vec{B} = -AB$

EXAMPLE 11.4 Calculating a dot product

Compute the dot product of the two vectors in **FIGURE 11.13**.

SOLVE The angle between the vectors is $\alpha = 30°$, so

$$\vec{A} \cdot \vec{B} = AB\cos\alpha = (3)(4)\cos 30° = 10.4$$

FIGURE 11.13 Vectors $\vec{A}$ and $\vec{B}$ of Example 11.4.

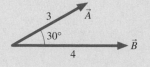

Like vector addition and subtraction, calculating the dot product of two vectors is often performed most easily using vector components. FIGURE 11.14 reminds you of the unit vectors $\hat{i}$ and $\hat{j}$ that point in the positive x-direction and positive y-direction. The two unit vectors are perpendicular to each other, so their dot product is $\hat{i} \cdot \hat{j} = 0$. Furthermore, because the magnitudes of $\hat{i}$ and $\hat{j}$ are 1, $\hat{i} \cdot \hat{i} = 1$ and $\hat{j} \cdot \hat{j} = 1$.

In terms of components, we can write the dot product of vectors $\vec{A}$ and $\vec{B}$ as

$$\vec{A} \cdot \vec{B} = (A_x\hat{i} + A_y\hat{j}) \cdot (B_x\hat{i} + B_y\hat{j})$$

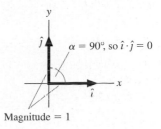

FIGURE 11.14 The unit vectors $\hat{i}$ and $\hat{j}$.

$\alpha = 90°$, so $\hat{i} \cdot \hat{j} = 0$

Magnitude = 1

Multiplying this out, and using the results for the dot products of the unit vectors:

$$\vec{A} \cdot \vec{B} = A_xB_x\hat{i} \cdot \hat{i} + (A_xB_y + A_yB_x)\hat{i} \cdot \hat{j} + A_yB_y\hat{j} \cdot \hat{j}$$
$$= A_xB_x + A_yB_y \tag{11.15}$$

That is, the **dot product is the sum of the products of the components.**

EXAMPLE 11.5 Calculating a dot product using components

Compute the dot product of $\vec{A} = 3\hat{i} + 3\hat{j}$ and $\vec{B} = 4\hat{i} - \hat{j}$.

SOLVE FIGURE 11.15 shows vectors $\vec{A}$ and $\vec{B}$. We could calculate the dot product by first doing the geometry needed to find the angle between the vectors and then using Equation 11.14. But calculating the dot product from the vector components is much easier. It is

$$\vec{A} \cdot \vec{B} = A_xB_x + A_yB_y = (3)(4) + (3)(-1) = 9$$

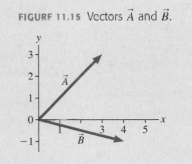

FIGURE 11.15 Vectors $\vec{A}$ and $\vec{B}$.

Looking at Equation 11.13, the work done by a constant force, you should recognize that it is the dot product of the force vector and the displacement vector:

$$W = \vec{F} \cdot \Delta\vec{r} \quad \text{(work done by a constant force)} \tag{11.16}$$

This definition of work is valid for a constant force.

EXAMPLE 11.6 Calculating work using the dot product

A 70 kg skier is gliding at 2.0 m/s when he starts down a very slippery 50-m-long, 10° slope. What is his speed at the bottom?

MODEL Model the skier as a particle and interpret "very slippery" to mean frictionless. Use the work-kinetic energy theorem to find his final speed.

VISUALIZE FIGURE 11.16 shows a pictorial representation.

FIGURE 11.16 Pictorial representation of the skier.

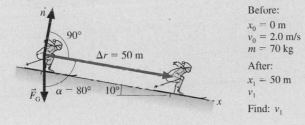

90°

$\Delta r = 50$ m

$\vec{F}_G$ $\alpha = 80°$ 10°

Before:
$x_0 = 0$ m
$v_0 = 2.0$ m/s
$m = 70$ kg

After:
$x_1 = 50$ m
v_1

Find: v_1

SOLVE The only forces on the skier are $\vec{F}_G$ and $\vec{n}$. The normal force is perpendicular to the motion and thus does no work. The work done by gravity is easily calculated as a dot product:

$$W = \vec{F}_G \cdot \Delta\vec{r} = mg(\Delta r)\cos\alpha$$
$$= (70\text{ kg})(9.8\text{ m/s}^2)(50\text{ m})\cos 80° = 5960\text{ J}$$

Notice that the angle *between* the vectors is 80°, not 10°. Then, from the work-kinetic energy theorem, we find

$$\Delta K = \frac{1}{2}mv_1^2 - \frac{1}{2}mv_0^2 = W$$
$$v_1 = \sqrt{v_0^2 + \frac{2W}{m}} = \sqrt{(2.0\text{ m/s})^2 + \frac{2(5960\text{ J})}{70\text{ kg}}} = 13\text{ m/s}$$

NOTE ▶ While in the midst of the mathematics of calculating work, do not lose sight of what the work-kinetic energy theorem is all about. It is a statement about *energy transfer*, saying that work is the energy transferred to or from the system due to forces exerted on the system. Work causes the system's kinetic energy to either increase or decrease. ◀

STOP TO THINK 11.4   Which force does the most work?

a. The 10 N force.
b. The 8 N force.
c. The 6 N force.
d. They all do the same amount of work.

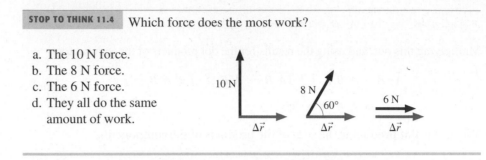

11.4 The Work Done by a Variable Force

We've learned how to calculate the work done on an object by a constant force, but what about a force that changes in either magnitude or direction as the object moves? Equation 11.8, the definition of work, is all we need:

$$W = \int_{s_i}^{s_f} F_s \, ds = \text{area under the force-versus-position graph} \quad (11.17)$$

The integral sums up the small amounts of work $F_s \, ds$ done in each step along the trajectory. The only new feature, because F_s now varies with position, is that we cannot take F_s outside the integral. We must evaluate the integral either geometrically, by finding the area under the curve, or by actually doing the integration.

EXAMPLE 11.7 Using work to find the speed of a car

A 1500 kg car accelerates from rest. **FIGURE 11.17** shows the net force on the car (propulsion force minus any drag forces) as it travels from $x = 0$ m to $x = 200$ m. What is the car's speed after traveling 200 m?

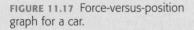

FIGURE 11.17 Force-versus-position graph for a car.

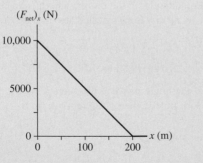

SOLVE The acceleration $a_x = (F_{net})_x / m$ is high as the car starts but decreases as the car picks up speed because of increasing drag. Figure 11.17 is a more realistic portrayal of the net force on a car than was our earlier model of a constant force. But a variable force means that we cannot use the familiar constant-acceleration kinematics.

Instead, we can use the work-kinetic energy theorem. Because $v_i = 0$ m/s, we have

$$\Delta K = \frac{1}{2} m v_f^2 - 0 = W_{net}$$

Starting from $x_i = 0$ m, the work is

$$W_{net} = \int_{0\,m}^{x_f} (F_{net})_x \, dx$$

$$= \text{area under the } (F_{net})_x\text{-versus-}x \text{ graph from 0 m to } x_f$$

The area under the curve of Figure 11.17 is that of a triangle of width 200 m. Thus

$$W_{net} = \text{area} = \frac{1}{2}(10{,}000 \text{ N})(200 \text{ m}) = 1{,}000{,}000 \text{ J}$$

The work-kinetic energy theorem then gives

$$v_f = \sqrt{\frac{2W_{net}}{m}} = \sqrt{\frac{2(1{,}000{,}000 \text{ J})}{1500 \text{ kg}}} = 37 \text{ m/s}$$

ASSESS Because $1 \text{ J} = 1 \text{ kg m}^2/\text{s}^2$, the quantity W/m has units m^2/s^2. Thus the units of v_f are m/s, as expected.

EXAMPLE 11.8 Using the work-kinetic energy theorem for a spring

The "pincube machine" was an ill-fated predecessor of the pinball machine. A 100 g cube is launched by pulling a spring back 20 cm and releasing it. What is the cube's launch speed, as it leaves the spring, if the spring constant is 20 N/m and the coefficient of kinetic friction is 0.10?

MODEL Model the spring as an ideal spring obeying Hooke's law. Use the work-kinetic energy theorem to find the launch speed.

VISUALIZE FIGURE 11.18 shows a before-and-after pictorial representation and a free-body diagram. We've placed the origin of the x-axis at the equilibrium position of the spring.

FIGURE 11.18 Pictorial representation and free-body diagram for Example 11.8.

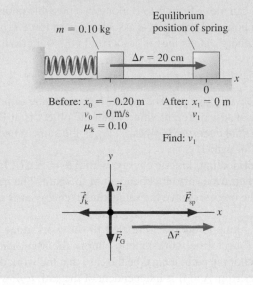

SOLVE The normal force and gravity are perpendicular to the motion and do no work. We can use the work-kinetic energy theorem, with $v_0 = 0$ m/s, to find the launch speed:

$$\Delta K = \frac{1}{2}mv_1^2 - 0 = W_{net} = W_{fric} + W_{sp}$$

Friction is a constant force $f_k = \mu_k mg$ in the direction *opposite* the motion, with $\theta = 180°$, so the work done by friction is

$$W_{fric} = \vec{f}_k \cdot \Delta\vec{r} = f_k(\Delta r)\cos 180° = -\mu_k mg\Delta x = -0.020 \text{ J}$$

The negative work of friction would, by itself, slow the block down.

The spring force is a variable force: $(F_{sp})_x = -k\Delta x = -kx$, where $\Delta x = x - x_e = x$ because we chose a coordinate system with $x_e = 0$ m. Despite the minus sign, $(F_{sp})_x$ is a positive quantity (force pointing to the right) because x is negative throughout the motion. The spring force points in the direction of motion, so W_{sp} is positive. We can use Equation 11.17 to evaluate W_{sp}:

$$W_{sp} = \int_{x_0}^{x_1} (F_{sp})_x \, dx = -k\int_{x_0}^{x_1} x \, dx = -\frac{1}{2}kx^2 \Big|_{x_0}^{x_1}$$

$$= -\left(\frac{1}{2}kx_1^2 - \frac{1}{2}kx_0^2\right)$$

Evaluating W_{sp} for $x_0 = -0.20$ m and $x_1 = 0$ m gives

$$W_{sp} = \frac{1}{2}(20 \text{ N/m})(-0.20 \text{ m})^2 = 0.400 \text{ J}$$

The net work is $W_{net} = W_{fric} + W_{sp} = 0.380$ J, with which we can now find

$$v_1 = \sqrt{\frac{2W_{net}}{m}} = \sqrt{\frac{2(0.380 \text{ J})}{0.100 \text{ kg}}} = 2.8 \text{ m/s}$$

You might have noticed that the work done by the spring looks a lot like the spring's potential energy $U_{sp} = \frac{1}{2}k\Delta x^2$. The next section will find a connection between work and potential energy.

11.5 Force, Work, and Potential Energy

Now that we've related force to work, it's time to look more closely at the connections among force, work, and potential energy. As a starting point, let's calculate the work done by gravity on an object sliding along a frictionless path of arbitrary shape. FIGURE 11.19 shows the object moving from an initial position at height y_i to a final position at height y_f. The displacement ds is essentially a straight line during the very small segment of the motion shown in the inset. The small amount of work dW_{grav} done by gravity as the object moves through ds is

$$dW_{grav} = \vec{F}_G \cdot \Delta\vec{r} = mg\cos\theta \, ds \qquad (11.18)$$

It's easy to see that $\cos\theta \, ds$ is the vertical displacement, but we need to be careful with signs. The small displacement ds is positive because we earlier chose the s-axis to be positive in the direction of motion. But the y-axis points upward, so dy in Figure 11.19 is negative. In particular, $dy = -\cos\theta \, ds$. Thus the work done by gravity is

$$dW_{grav} = -mg \, dy \qquad (11.19)$$

FIGURE 11.19 An object moves along an arbitrarily shaped path.

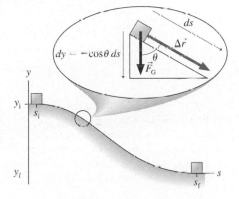

FIGURE 11.20 The work done by gravity is the same in all four cases.

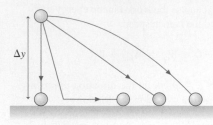

FIGURE 11.21 An object can move from A to B along either path 1 or path 2.

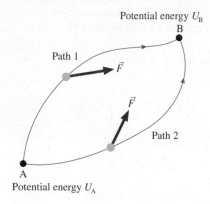

The main feature of Equation 11.19 is that dW_{grav} is independent of θ. It depends on the vertical displacement dy but *not* on the slope of the surface. The total work done by gravity is found by adding the work done in each segment of the motion (i.e., by integrating Equation 11.19). The result is

$$W_{grav} = -mg(y_f - y_i) = -mg\Delta y \qquad (11.20)$$

Notice that **the work done by gravity is independent of the path followed by the object.** It depends on the initial and final heights, but not at all on how the object gets from height y_i to height y_f. For example, **FIGURE 11.20** shows a particle moving along four different paths that have the same vertical displacement Δy. Despite the very different trajectories, the work done by gravity is the same in all four cases.

Conservative and Nonconservative Forces

The path independence of the work is perhaps surprising, but it turns out to be an essential ingredient of any force for which there is a potential energy. To see this, **FIGURE 11.21** shows an object that can move from A to B along two possible paths while force $\vec{F}$ acts on it. Assume that a potential energy U is associated with force $\vec{F}$ in much the same way that the potential energy $U_g = mgy$ is associated with the gravitational force $\vec{F}_G = -mg\hat{j}$.

There are three steps in the logic:

1. Potential energy is an energy of position. The system has one value of potential energy when the object is at A, a different value when the object is at B. Thus the overall change in potential energy $\Delta U = U_B - U_A$ is the same whether the object moves along path 1 or path 2.
2. Potential energy is transformed into kinetic energy, with $\Delta K = -\Delta U$. If ΔU is independent of the path, then ΔK is also independent of the path. The transformation of energy causes the object to have the same kinetic energy at B no matter which path it follows.
3. The change in an object's kinetic energy is related to the work done on the object by force $\vec{F}$. According to the work-kinetic energy theorem, $\Delta K = W$. Because ΔK is independent of the path, it *must* be the case that the work done by force $\vec{F}$ as the object moves from A to B is independent of the path followed.

A force for which the work done on an object as it moves from an initial to a final position is independent of the path followed is called a **conservative force.** (The name, as you'll soon see, is related to the conditions under which mechanical energy is conserved.) The importance of conservative forces is that **a potential energy can be associated with any conservative force.** For example, our analysis of Figure 11.19 showed that gravity is a conservative force. Consequently, we can establish a gravitational potential energy.

To establish a general connection between work and potential energy, suppose an object moves from initial position i to final position f under the influence of a conservative force $\vec{F}$. We'll denote the work done by the force as $W_c(i \rightarrow f)$, where the notation $i \rightarrow f$ means "as the object moves from position i to position f." Because $\Delta K = W$ and $\Delta K = -\Delta U$, the potential energy difference between these two points must be

$$\Delta U = U_f - U_i = -W_c(i \rightarrow f) \qquad (11.21)$$

Equation 11.21 is a general definition of the potential energy associated with a conservative force.

For example, in Equation 11.20 we found that the work due to gravity is independent of the path and is $W_{grav}(i \rightarrow f) = -mg(y_f - y_i)$. The gravitational potential energy is defined by

$$U_f - U_i = -W_{grav}(i \rightarrow f) = mgy_f - mgy_i$$

and thus $U_g = mgy$. This agrees with the gravitational potential energy of Chapter 10. That's not unexpected. The analysis of Chapter 10 that led to $U_g = mgy$ was really a calculation of work, although we didn't call it that at the time. What we've now done is to generalize that analysis to apply to *any* conservative force.

> **NOTE** ▶ Equation 11.21 defines only the *change* in potential energy ΔU. We can add a constant to both U_f and U_i without changing ΔU. This was the basis for our discussion in Chapter 10 about the zero of potential energy. ◀

What about springs? A homework problem will let you show that Hooke's law is also a conservative force. In Example 11.8 we showed that the work done by a spring is

$$W_{sp}(i \rightarrow f) = \int_{x_i}^{x_f} F_{sp}\, dx = -\left(\frac{1}{2}kx_f^2 - \frac{1}{2}kx_i^2\right)$$

from which it follows that $U_s = \frac{1}{2}kx^2$. Example 11.8 was a "special case" in that we defined the coordinate system to make $x_e = 0$. A more general analysis would give $U_s = \frac{1}{2}k(\Delta s)^2$, as you learned in Chapter 10.

Not all forces are conservative forces. For example, Figure 11.22 is a bird's-eye view of two particles sliding across a surface. The friction force always points opposite the direction of motion, 180° from $d\vec{s}$, hence the small amount of work done during displacement $d\vec{s}$ is $dW_{fric} = \vec{f}_k \cdot d\vec{s} = -\mu_k mg\, ds$. Summed over the entire path, the work done by friction as a particle travels total distance Δs is $W_{fric} = -\mu_k mg\Delta s$. We see that the work done by friction depends on Δs, the distance traveled. More work is done on the particle traveling the longer path, so the work done by friction is *not* independent of the path followed.

> **NOTE** ▶ This analysis applies only to the motion of a particle, which has no internal structure and cannot heat up. These ideas will be extended to more realistic situations—such as a car skidding to a halt—in Section 11.7 on thermal energy. The particle equation $W_{fric} = -\mu_k mg\Delta s$ should *not* be used in problem solving. ◀

A force for which the work is *not* independent of the path is called a **nonconservative force.** It is not possible to define a potential energy for a nonconservative force. Friction is a nonconservative force, so we cannot define a potential energy of friction.

This makes sense. If you toss a ball straight up, kinetic energy is transformed into gravitational potential energy. The ball has the potential to transform this energy back into kinetic energy, and it does so as the ball falls. But you cannot recover the kinetic energy lost to friction as a box slides to a halt. There's no "potential" that can be transformed back into kinetic energy.

FIGURE 11.22 Top view of two particles sliding across a surface.

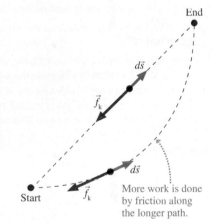

Mechanical Energy

Consider a system of objects interacting via both conservative forces and nonconservative forces. The conservative forces do work W_c as the particles move from initial positions i to final positions f. The nonconservative forces do work W_{nc}. The total work done by *all* forces is $W_{net} = W_c + W_{nc}$. The change in the system's kinetic energy ΔK, as determined by the work-kinetic energy theorem, is

$$\Delta K = W_{net} = W_c(i \rightarrow f) + W_{nc}(i \rightarrow f) \qquad (11.22)$$

The work done by the conservative forces can now be associated with a potential energy U. According to Equation 11.21, $W_c(i \rightarrow f) = -\Delta U$. With this definition, Equation 11.22 becomes

$$\Delta K + \Delta U = \Delta E_{mech} = W_{nc} \qquad (11.23)$$

where, as in Chapter 10, the *mechanical energy* is $E_{mech} = K + U$.

Now we can see that **mechanical energy is conserved if there are no nonconservative forces.** That is

$$\Delta E_{mech} = 0 \text{ if } W_{nc} = 0 \qquad (11.24)$$

Mechanical energy isn't always conserved. Here, mechanical energy is being transferred into thermal energy.

This important conclusion is what we called the law of conservation of mechanical energy in Chapter 10. There we saw that friction prevents E_{mech} from being conserved, but we really didn't know why. Equation 11.23 tells us that any nonconservative force causes the mechanical energy to change. Friction and other "dissipative forces" lead to a loss of mechanical energy. Other outside forces, such as the pull of a rope, might increase the mechanical energy.

Equally important, Equation 11.23 tells us what to do if the mechanical energy isn't conserved. You can still use energy concepts to analyze the motion if you compute the work done by the nonconservative forces.

EXAMPLE 11.9 Using work and potential energy together

The skier from Example 11.6 repeats his run after the wind comes up. Recall that the 70 kg skier was gliding at 2.0 m/s when he started down a 50-m-long, 10°, frictionless slope. What is his speed at the bottom if the wind exerts a steady 50 N retarding force opposite his motion?

MODEL This time let the system be the skier and the earth.

VISUALIZE Figure 11.16 showed the pictorial representation and free-body diagram.

SOLVE In solving this problem with the work-kinetic energy theorem, we had to explicitly calculate the work done by the gravity. Now let's use Equation 11.23. Gravity is a conservative force that we can associate with the gravitational potential energy U_g. The retarding force of the wind is nonconservative. Thus

$$\Delta K + \Delta U_g = W_{nc} = W_{wind}$$

The gravitational potential energy is $U_g = mgy$. Because the wind force is opposite the skier's motion, with $\theta = 180°$ it does work $W_{wind} = \vec{F}_{wind} \cdot \Delta \vec{r} = -F_{wind}\Delta r$. Thus the energy equation becomes

$$\frac{1}{2}mv_1^2 - \frac{1}{2}mv_0^2 + mgy_1 - mgy_0 = -F_{wind}\Delta r$$

Using $v_0 = 2.0$ m/s, $y_0 = (50 \text{ m})\sin 10° = 8.68$ m, and $y_1 = 0$ m, we find

$$v_1 = \sqrt{v_0^2 + 2gy_0 - 2F_{wind}\Delta r/m} = 10 \text{ m/s}$$

ASSESS What appeared to be a difficult problem, with both gravity and a retarding force, turned out to be straightforward when analyzed with energy and work. The skier's final speed is about 25% less when the wind is blowing.

Example 11.6 illustrates an important idea. When we associate a potential energy with a conservative force, we

- Enlarge the system to include all objects that interact via conservative forces.
- "Precompute" the work. We can do this because we don't need to know what paths the objects are going to follow. This precomputed work becomes a potential energy and moves from the right side of $\Delta K = W$ to the left side of Equation 11.23.

In Example 11.6, the system consisted of just the skier. We treated the gravitational force as a force from the environment doing work on the system. In Example 11.9, where we revisited the same problem, we brought the earth into the system and represented the conservative earth-skier interaction with a potential energy.

NOTE ▶ When you use a potential energy, you've already taken the work of that force into account. Don't compute the work explicitly, or you'll be double counting it! ◀

To analyze a problem using work and energy, you can either

1. Use the work-kinetic energy theorem $\Delta K = W$ and explicitly compute the work done by *every* force. This was the method of Example 11.6. Or
2. Represent the work done by conservative forces as potential energies, then use $\Delta K + \Delta U = W_{nc}$. The only work that must be computed is the work of any nonconservative forces. This was the method of Example 11.9.

It's important to recognize that **these two methods yield the same result!** It's simply that method 2 "precomputes" some of the work and represents it as a potential energy. In practice, **method 2 is always easier and is the preferred method.**

11.6 Finding Force from Potential Energy

We know how to find the potential energy due to a conservative force. Now we need to learn how to go in reverse. That is, if we know an object's potential energy, how do we find the force acting on it?

FIGURE 11.23a shows an object moving through a *small* displacement Δs while being acted on by a conservative force $\vec{F}$. If Δs is sufficiently small, the force component F_s in the direction of motion is essentially constant during the displacement. The work done on the object as it moves from s to $s + \Delta s$ is

$$W(s \rightarrow s + \Delta s) = F_s \Delta s \qquad (11.25)$$

This work is shown in **FIGURE 11.23b** as the area under the force curve in the narrow rectangle of width Δs.

Because $\vec{F}$ is a conservative force, the object's potential energy as it moves through Δs changes by

$$\Delta U = -W(s \rightarrow s + \Delta s) = -F_s \Delta s$$

which we can rewrite as

$$F_s = -\frac{\Delta U}{\Delta s} \qquad (11.26)$$

In the limit $\Delta s \rightarrow 0$, we find that the force at position s is

$$F_s = \lim_{\Delta s \rightarrow 0}\left(-\frac{\Delta U}{\Delta s}\right) = -\frac{dU}{ds} \qquad (11.27)$$

We see that the force on the object is the *negative* of the derivative of the potential energy with respect to position. **FIGURE 11.23c** shows that we can interpret this result graphically by saying

$$F_s = \text{the negative of the slope of the } U\text{-versus-}s \text{ graph at } s \qquad (11.28)$$

In practice, of course, we will usually use either $F_x = -dU/dx$ or $F_y = -dU/dy$.

As an example, consider the gravitational potential energy $U_g = mgy$. **FIGURE 11.24a** shows the potential-energy diagram U_g versus y. It is simply a straight-line graph passing through the origin. The force on the object at position y, according to Equations 11.27 and 11.28, is simply

$$(F_G)_y = -\frac{dU_g}{dy} = -(\text{slope of } U_g) = -mg$$

The negative sign, as always, indicates that the force points in the negative y-direction. **FIGURE 11.24b** shows the corresponding F-versus-y graph. At each point, the *value* of F is equal to the negative of the *slope* of the U-versus-y graph. This is similar to position and velocity graphs, where the value of v_x at any time t is equal to the slope of the x-versus-t graph.

We already knew that $(F_G)_y = -mg$, of course, so the point of this particular example was to illustrate the meaning of Equation 11.28 rather than to find out anything new. Had we *not* known the gravitational force, we see is that it is possible to find it from the potential energy.

FIGURE 11.25 on the next page is a more interesting example. The slope of the potential-energy graph is negative between x_1 and x_2. This means that the force on the object, which is the negative of the slope of U, is *positive*. An object between x_1 and x_2 experiences a force toward the right. The force decreases as the magnitude of the slope decreases until, at x_2, $F_x = 0$. This is consistent with our prior identification of x_2 as a point of stable *equilibrium*. The slope is positive (force negative and thus to the left)

FIGURE 11.23 Relating force and potential energy.

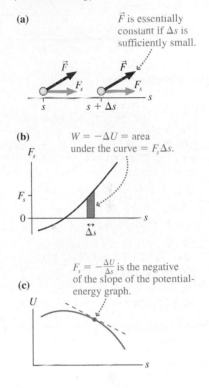

(a) $\vec{F}$ is essentially constant if Δs is sufficiently small.

(b) $W = -\Delta U =$ area under the curve $= F_s \Delta s$.

(c) $F_s = -\frac{\Delta U}{\Delta s}$ is the negative of the slope of the potential-energy graph.

FIGURE 11.24 Gravitational potential energy and force diagrams.

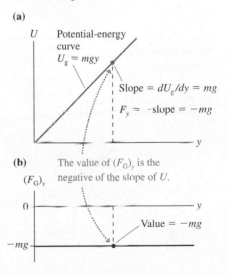

(a) U Potential-energy curve $U_g = mgy$

Slope $= dU_g/dy = mg$

$F_y = -\text{slope} = -mg$

(b) The value of $(F_G)_y$ is the negative of the slope of U.

$(F_G)_y$

Value $= -mg$

FIGURE 11.25 A potential-energy diagram and the corresponding force diagram.

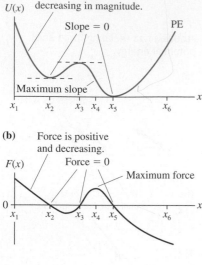

(a) Slope is negative and decreasing in magnitude.

$U(x)$

Slope = 0

PE

Maximum slope

x_1 x_2 x_3 x_4 x_5 x_6 x

(b) Force is positive and decreasing.

$F(x)$ Force = 0

Maximum force

0

x_1 x_2 x_3 x_4 x_5 x_6 x

between x_2 and x_3, zero (zero force) at the unstable equilibrium point x_3, and so on. Point x_4, where the slope is most negative, is the point of maximum force.

FIGURE 11.25b is a plausible graph of F versus x. We don't know the exact shape because we don't have an exact expression for U, but the force graph must look very much like this.

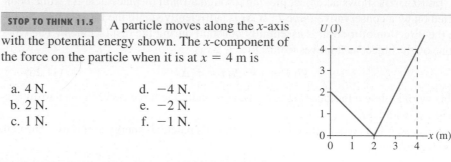

STOP TO THINK 11.5 A particle moves along the x-axis with the potential energy shown. The x-component of the force on the particle when it is at $x = 4$ m is

a. 4 N.   d. −4 N.
b. 2 N.   e. −2 N.
c. 1 N.   f. −1 N.

11.7 Thermal Energy

All of the objects we handle and use every day consist of vast numbers of particle-like atoms. We will use the terms **macrophysics** to refer to the motion and dynamics of the object as a whole and **microphysics** to refer to the motion of atoms. You recognize the prefix *micro,* meaning "small." You may not be familiar with *macro,* which means "large" or "large-scale."

Kinetic and Potential Energy at the Microscopic Level

FIGURE 11.26 Two perspectives of motion and energy.

(a) The macroscopic motion of the system as a whole

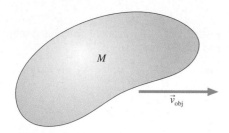

M

$\vec{v}_{obj}$

(b) The microscopic motion of the atoms inside

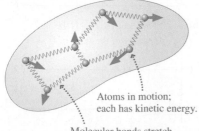

Atoms in motion; each has kinetic energy.

Molecular bonds stretch and compress; each has potential energy.

Figure 11.26 shows two different perspectives of an object. In the macrophysics perspective of **FIGURE 11.26a** you see an object of mass M moving as a whole with velocity v_{obj}. As a consequence of its motion, the object has macroscopic kinetic energy $K_{macro} = \frac{1}{2}Mv_{obj}^2$.

FIGURE 11.26b is a microphysics view of the same object, where now we see a *system of particles.* Each of these atoms is moving about, and in doing so they stretch and compress the spring-like bonds between them. Consequently, there is a *microscopic* kinetic and potential energy associated with the motion of atoms and bonds.

The kinetic energy of one atom is exceedingly small, but there are enormous numbers of atoms in a macroscopic object. The total kinetic energy of all the atoms is what we call the *microscopic kinetic energy* K_{micro}. The total potential energy of all the bonds is the *microscopic potential energy* U_{micro}. These microscopic energies are quite distinct from the energies K_{macro} and U_{macro} of the object as a whole.

Is the microscopic energy worth worrying about? To see, consider a 500 g (≈ 1 lb) iron ball moving at the respectable speed of 20 m/s (≈ 45 mph). Its macroscopic kinetic energy is

$$K_{macro} = \frac{1}{2}Mv_{obj}^2 = 100 \text{ J}$$

A periodic table of the elements shows that iron has atomic mass 56. Recall from chemistry that 56 g of iron is 1 gram-molecular weight and has Avogadro's number ($N_A = 6.02 \times 10^{23}$) of atoms. Thus 500 g of iron is ≈ 9 gram-molecular weights and contains $N \approx 9N_A \approx 5.4 \times 10^{24}$ iron atoms. The mass of each atom is

$$m = \frac{M}{N} \approx \frac{0.50 \text{ kg}}{5.4 \times 10^{24}} \approx 9 \times 10^{-26} \text{ kg}$$

How fast do atoms move? In Part IV you'll learn that the speed of sound in air at room temperature is ≈ 340 m/s. Sound travels by atoms bumping into each other, so the atoms in the air must have a speed of at least 340 m/s. The speed of sound in solids is even higher, usually ≈1000 m/s. As a rough estimate, $v \approx 500$ m/s is a reasonable guess. The kinetic energy of one iron atom at this speed is

$$K_{atom} = \frac{1}{2}mv^2 \approx 1.1 \times 10^{-20}\,J$$

This is very tiny, but there are a great many atoms. If we assume, for our estimate, that all atoms move at this speed, the microscopic kinetic energy is

$$K_{micro} \approx NK_{atom} \approx 60,000\,J$$

We'll later see that, on average, U_{micro} for a solid is equal to K_{micro}, so the total microscopic energy is ≈120,000 J. The microscopic energy is much larger than the macroscopic kinetic energy of the object as a whole!

The combined microscopic kinetic and potential energy of the atoms is called the *thermal energy* of the system:

$$E_{th} = K_{micro} + U_{micro} \qquad (11.29)$$

This energy is usually hidden from view in our macrophysics perspective, but it is quite real. We will discover later, when we reach thermodynamics, that the thermal energy is proportional to the *temperature* of the system. Raising the temperature causes the atoms to move faster and the bonds to stretch more, giving the system more thermal energy.

NOTE ▶ The microscopic energy of atoms is *not* called "heat." The word "heat," like the word "work," has a narrow and precise meaning in physics that is much more restricted than its use in everyday language. We will introduce the concept of heat later, when we need it. For the time being we want to use the correct term "thermal energy" to describe the random, thermal motion of the particles in a system. If the temperature of a system goes up (i.e., it gets hotter), it is because the system's thermal energy has increased. ◀

Dissipative Forces

At the beginning of the chapter we asked: "What happens to the energy?" when a system "runs down" because of friction. If you shove a book across the table, it gradually slows down and stops. Where did the energy go? The common answer "It went into heat" isn't quite right.

FIGURE 11.27, the atomic model of friction from Chapter 6, shows why. Molecular bonds get stretched on *both* sides of the boundary as two objects slide against each other. When these temporary bonds break, the atoms snap back into position and start vibrating with microscopic kinetic energy. (Imagine having several balls connected by springs. If you pull one ball and release it, you cause the whole system to jiggle and vibrate.) In other words, atomic interactions at the boundary transform the kinetic energy K_{macro} of the moving object— it's slowing down—into microscopic kinetic and potential energy of vibrating atoms and stretched bonds. The energy transformation is $K \rightarrow E_{th}$, and we perceive this as an increased temperature of *both* objects. Thus the correct answer to "What happens to the energy?" is "It is transformed into thermal energy."

Forces such as friction and drag cause the macroscopic kinetic energy of a system to be "dissipated" as thermal energy. Hence these are called **dissipative forces.** Dissipative forces are always nonconservative forces. The energy analysis of dissipative forces is a bit subtle. Because friction causes *both* objects to get warmer, we must define the system to include both objects—both the book *and* the table, or both the car *and* the road.

FIGURE 11.28 on the next page shows a box being pulled at constant speed across a horizontal surface with friction. As you can imagine, both the surface and the box are getting warmer—increasing thermal energy. But neither the kinetic nor the potential

FIGURE 11.27 The atomic-level view of friction.

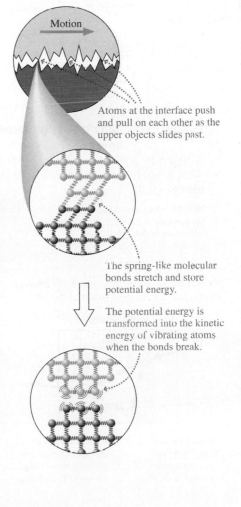

Atoms at the interface push and pull on each other as the upper objects slides past.

The spring-like molecular bonds stretch and store potential energy.

The potential energy is transformed into the kinetic energy of vibrating atoms when the bonds break.

FIGURE 11.28 Work done by tension is dissipated as increased thermal energy.

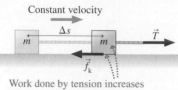

Constant velocity

Work done by tension increases the thermal energy of the box *and* the surface.

The ballplayer's kinetic energy is being transformed into thermal energy.

energy of the box is changing, so where is the thermal energy coming from? Recall, from the basic energy model, that work is energy transferred to a system by forces from the environment. If we define the system to be box + surface, then the increasing thermal energy of the system is entirely due to the work being done on the system by tension in the rope: $\Delta E_{th} = W_{tension}$.

The work done by tension in pulling the box a distance Δs is simply $W_{tension} = T\Delta s$; thus $\Delta E_{th} = T\Delta s$. Because the box is moving with constant velocity, Newton's first law $\vec{F}_{net} = \vec{0}$ requires the tension to exactly balance the friction force: $T = f_k$. Consequently, the increase in thermal energy due to the dissipative force of friction is

$$\Delta E_{th} = f_k\Delta s \quad \text{(increased thermal energy due to friction)} \quad (11.30)$$

Notice that the increase in thermal energy is directly proportional to the total distance of sliding. **Dissipative forces always increase the thermal energy; they never decrease it.**

You might wonder why we didn't simply calculate the work done by friction. The rather subtle reason is that work is defined only for forces acting on a *particle* or on a completely rigid object that can be modeled as a particle. A particle has no internal structure and thus cannot have thermal energy. Thermal energy requires us to deal with extended objects, nonrigid systems of many particle-like atoms. That's why the brief introduction of thermal energy at the beginning of the chapter noted the need to start moving beyond the particle model.

There is work being done on individual atoms at the boundary as they are pulled this way and that, but we would need a detailed knowledge of atomic-level friction forces to calculate this work. The friction force $\vec{f}_k$ is an average force on the object as a whole; it is not a force on any particular particle, so we cannot use it to calculate work. Further, increasing thermal energy is not an energy transfer from the book to the surface or from the surface to the book. Both book *and* surface are gaining thermal energy at the expense of the macroscopic kinetic energy.

NOTE ▶ The analysis of thermal energy is rather subtle, as we noted above. The considerations that led to Equation 11.30 do allow us to calculate the total increase in thermal energy of the entire system, but we cannot determine what fraction of ΔE_{th} goes to the book and what fraction goes to the surface. ◀

EXAMPLE 11.10 Calculating the increase in thermal energy

A rope pulls a 10 kg wooden crate 3.0 m across a wood floor. What is the change in thermal energy? The coefficient of kinetic friction is 0.20.

MODEL Let the system be crate + floor. Assume the floor is horizontal.

SOLVE The friction force on an object moving on a horizontal surface is $F_k = \mu_k n = \mu_k mg$. Thus the change in thermal energy, given by Equation 11.30, is

$$\Delta E_{th} = f_k\Delta s = \mu_k mg\Delta s$$
$$= (0.20)(10 \text{ kg})(9.80 \text{ m/s}^2)(3.0 \text{ m}) = 59 \text{ J}$$

ASSESS The thermal energy of the crate *and* floor increases by 59 J. We cannot determine ΔE_{th} for the crate (or floor) alone.

FIGURE 11.29 A system with both internal interaction forces and external forces.

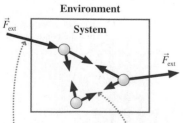

Environment

System

$\vec{F}_{ext}$

$\vec{F}_{ext}$

Work done by forces from the environment is external work W_{ext}.

Interaction forces can be either conservative or dissipative. These do work W_c and W_{diss}.

11.8 Conservation of Energy

Let's return to the basic energy model and start pulling together the many ideas introduced in this chapter. **FIGURE 11.29** shows a general system consisting of several macroscopic objects. These objects interact with each other, and they may be acted on by external forces from the environment. Both the interaction forces and the external forces do work on the objects. The change in the system's kinetic energy is given by the work-kinetic energy theorem, $\Delta K = W_{net}$.

We previously divided W_{net} into the work W_c done by conservative forces and the work W_{nc} done by nonconservative forces. The work done by the conservative forces can be represented by a potential energy U. Let's now make a further distinction by dividing the nonconservative forces into *dissipative forces* and *external forces*. That is,

$$W_{nc} = W_{diss} + W_{ext} \quad (11.31)$$

To illustrate what we mean by an external force, suppose you pick up a box at rest on the floor and place it at rest on a table. The box gains gravitational potential energy, but $\Delta K = 0$. Or consider pulling the box across the table with a string. The box gains kinetic energy, but not by transforming potential energy. The force of your hand and the tension of the string are forces that "reach in" from the environment to change the system. Thus they are *external forces*.

We have to be careful choosing the system if we want this distinction to be valid. As you can imagine, we're going to associate W_{diss} with ΔE_{th}. We want the thermal energy E_{th} to be an energy *of the system*. Otherwise, it wouldn't make sense to talk about transforming kinetic energy into thermal energy. But for E_{th} to be an energy of the system, *both* objects involved in a dissipative interaction must be part of the system. The book sliding across the table raises the temperature of both the book *and the table*. Consequently, we must include both the book *and the table* in the system. The dissipative forces, like the conservative forces, are atomic-level interaction forces *inside* the system.

With this distinction, the work-kinetic energy theorem is

$$\Delta K = W_c + W_{diss} + W_{ext} \tag{11.32}$$

As before, we define the potential energy U such that $\Delta U = -W_c$. Remember that potential energy is really just the precomputed work of a conservative force. We've also seen that the work done by dissipative forces—the forces stretching the bonds at the boundary—increases the system's thermal energy: $\Delta E_{th} = -W_{diss}$. With these substitutions, the work-kinetic energy theorem becomes

$$\Delta K = -\Delta U + -\Delta E_{th} + W_{ext}$$

We can write this more profitably as

$$\Delta K + \Delta U + \Delta E_{th} = \Delta E_{mech} + \Delta E_{th} = \Delta E_{sys} = W_{ext} \tag{11.33}$$

where $E_{sys} = E_{mech} + E_{th}$ is the total energy of the system. Equation 11.33 is the **energy equation** of the system.

Equation 11.33 is our most general statement about how the energy of a system changes, but we still need to give a clear interpretation as to what it says. In Chapter 9 we defined an *isolated system* as a system for which the *net* external force is zero. It follows that no external work is done on an isolated system: $W_{ext} = 0$. Thus one conclusion from Equation 11.33 is that **the total energy E_{sys} of an isolated system is conserved.** That is, $\Delta E_{sys} = 0$ for an isolated system. If, in addition, the system is also nondissipative (i.e., no friction forces), then $\Delta E_{th} = 0$. In that case, the mechanical energy E_{mech} is conserved.

These conclusions about energy can be summarized as the *law of conservation of energy:*

> **Law of conservation of energy** The total energy $E_{sys} = E_{mech} + E_{th}$ of an isolated system is a constant. The kinetic, potential, and thermal energy within the system can be transformed into each other, but their sum cannot change. Further, the mechanical energy $E_{mech} = K + U$ is conserved if the system is both isolated and nondissipative.

The law of conservation of energy is one of the most powerful statements in physics.

FIGURE 11.30a redraws the basic energy model of Figure 11.2. Now you can see that this is a pictorial representation of Equation 11.33. E_{sys}, the total energy of the system, changes only if external forces transfer energy into or out of the system by doing work on the system. The kinetic, potential, and thermal energy within the system can be transformed into each other by interaction forces within the system. As **FIGURE 11.30b** shows, $E_{sys} = K + U + E_{th}$ remains constant if the system is isolated. The *transfer* and *transformation* of energy are what the basic energy model is all about.

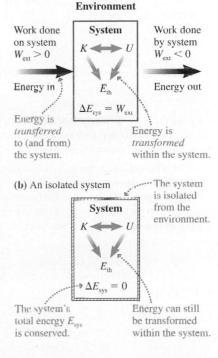

FIGURE 11.30 The basic energy model is a pictorial representation of the energy equation.

(a) A system interacting with its environment

Environment

Work done on system $W_{ext} > 0$

System $K \leftrightarrow U$

Work done by system $W_{ext} < 0$

Energy in

E_{th}

Energy out

$\Delta E_{sys} = W_{ext}$

Energy is *transferred* to (and from) the system.

Energy is *transformed* within the system.

(b) An isolated system

The system is isolated from the environment.

System $K \leftrightarrow U$

E_{th}

$\Delta E_{sys} = 0$

The system's total energy E_{sys} is conserved.

Energy can still be transformed within the system.

Energy Bar Charts

The energy bar charts of Chapter 10 can now be expanded to include the thermal energy and the work done by external forces. The energy equation, Equation 11.33, can be written

$$K_i + U_i + W_{ext} = K_f + U_f + \Delta E_{th} \qquad (11.34)$$

The left side is the "before" condition ($K_i + U_i$) plus any energy that is added to or removed from the system. The right side is the "after" situation. The "energy accounting" of Equation 11.34 can be represented by the bar chart of FIGURE 11.31.

FIGURE 11.31 An energy bar chart shows how all the energy is accounted for.

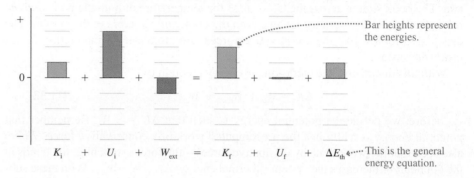

NOTE ▶ We don't have any way to determine $(E_{th})_i$ or $(E_{th})_f$, but ΔE_{th} is always positive whenever the system contains dissipative forces. ◀

Let's look at a few examples.

EXAMPLE 11.11 Energy bar chart I

A speeding car skids to a halt. Show the energy transfers and transformations on an energy bar chart.

SOLVE The car has an initial kinetic energy K_i. That energy is transformed into the thermal energy of the car and the road. The potential energy doesn't change and no work is done by external forces, so the process is an energy transformation $K_i \rightarrow E_{th}$. This is shown in FIGURE 11.32. E_{sys} is conserved but E_{mech} is not.

FIGURE 11.32 Energy bar chart for Example 11.11.

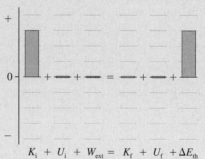

EXAMPLE 11.12 Energy bar chart II

A rope lifts a box at constant speed. Show the energy transfers and transformations on an energy bar chart.

SOLVE The tension in the rope is an external force that does work on the box, increasing the potential energy of the box. The kinetic energy is unchanged because the speed is constant. The process is an energy transfer $W_{ext} \rightarrow U_f$, as FIGURE 11.33 shows. This is not an isolated system, so E_{sys} is not conserved.

FIGURE 11.33 Energy bar chart for Example 11.12.

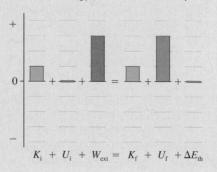

EXAMPLE 11.13 Energy bar chart III

The box that was lifted in Example 11.12 falls at a steady speed as the rope spins a generator and causes a lightbulb to glow. Air resistance is negligible. Show the energy transfers and transformations on an energy bar chart.

SOLVE The initial potential energy decreases, but K does not change and $\Delta E_{th} = 0$. The tension in the rope is an external force that does work, but W_{ext} is negative in this case because $\vec{T}$ points up while the displacement $\Delta \vec{r}$ is down. Negative work means that energy is transferred from the system to the environment or, in more informal terms, that the *system does work on the environment*. The falling box does work on the generator to spin it and light the bulb. Energy is transferred out of the system and eventually ends up in the lightbulb as electrical energy. The process is $U_i \rightarrow W_{ext}$. This is shown in **FIGURE 11.34**.

FIGURE 11.34 Energy bar chart for Example 11.13.

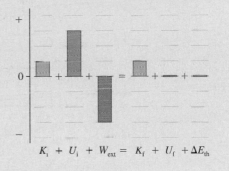

$$K_i + U_i + W_{ext} = K_f + U_f + \Delta E_{th}$$

Strategy for Energy Problems

This is a good place to summarize the strategy we have been developing for using the concept of energy.

Act|v
Physics   5.2–5.7, 6.5, 6.8, 6.9

PROBLEM-SOLVING STRATEGY 11.1 Solving energy problems (MP)

MODEL Identify which objects are part of the system and which are in the environment. If possible, choose a system without friction or other dissipative forces. Some problems may need to be subdivided into two or more parts.

VISUALIZE Draw a before-and-after pictorial representation and an energy bar chart. A free-body diagram can be helpful if you're going to calculate work, although often the forces are simple enough to show on the pictorial representation.

SOLVE If the system is both isolated and nondissipative, then the mechanical energy is conserved:

$$K_f + U_f = K_i + U_i$$

If there are external or dissipative forces, calculate W_{ext} and ΔE_{th}. Then use the more general energy equation

$$K_f + U_f + \Delta E_{th} = K_i + U_i + W_{ext}$$

Kinematics and/or other conservation laws may be needed for some problems.

ASSESS Check that your result has the correct units, is reasonable, and answers the question.

EXAMPLE 11.14 Stretching a spring

The 5.0 kg box is attached to one end of a spring with spring constant 80 N/m. The other end of the spring is anchored to a wall. Initially the box is at rest at the spring's equilibrium position. A rope with a constant tension of 100 N then pulls the box away from the wall. What is the speed of the box after it has moved 50 cm? The coefficient of friction between the box and the floor is 0.30.

MODEL This is a complex situation, but one that we can analyze. First, identify the box, the spring, and the floor as the system. We need the floor inside the system because friction increases the temperature of the box *and* the floor. The tension in the rope is an external force. The work W_{ext} done by the rope's tension transfers energy into the system, causing K, U_s, and E_{th} all to increase.

Continued

FIGURE 11.35 Pictorial representation and energy bar chart for Example 11.14.

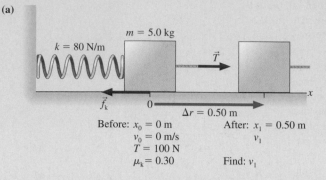

(a)

$k = 80$ N/m

$m = 5.0$ kg

$\vec{T}$

$\vec{f_k}$ 0 $\Delta r = 0.50$ m x

Before: $x_0 = 0$ m   After: $x_1 = 0.50$ m
$v_0 = 0$ m/s v_1
$T = 100$ N
$\mu_k = 0.30$ Find: v_1

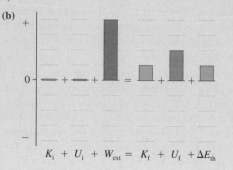

(b)

$K_i + U_i + W_{ext} = K_f + U_f + \Delta E_{th}$

VISUALIZE FIGURE 11.35a is a before-and-after pictorial representation. The energy transfers and transformations are shown in the energy bar chart of FIGURE 11.35b.

SOLVE The external work done by the rope's tension is

$$W_{ext} = \vec{T} \cdot \Delta\vec{r} = T(\Delta x)\cos 0° = (100 \text{ N})(0.50 \text{ m}) = 50.0 \text{ J}$$

The increase in thermal energy is given by Equation 11.30:

$$\Delta E_{th} = f_k \Delta x = \mu_k mg \Delta x$$

$$= (0.30)(5.0 \text{ kg})(9.80 \text{ m/s}^2)(0.50 \text{ m}) = 7.4 \text{ J}$$

The energy equation $K_f + U_f + \Delta E_{th} = K_i + U_i + W_{ext}$ is

$$\frac{1}{2}mv_1^2 + \frac{1}{2}kx_1^2 + \Delta E_{th} = \frac{1}{2}mv_0^2 + \frac{1}{2}kx_0^2 + W_{ext}$$

We know that $x_0 = 0$ m and $v_0 = 0$ m/s, so the energy equation simplifies to

$$\frac{1}{2}mv_1^2 = W_{ext} - \Delta E_{th} - \frac{1}{2}kx_1^2$$

Solving for the final speed v_1 gives

$$v_1 = \sqrt{\frac{2(W_{ext} - \Delta E_{th} - \frac{1}{2}kx_1^2)}{m}} = 3.6 \text{ m/s}$$

ASSESS The work done by the rope's tension is energy transferred to the system. Part of the energy increases the speed of the box, part increases the potential energy stored in the spring, and part is transformed into increased thermal energy, increasing the temperature. We had to bring all the energy ideas together to solve this problem.

A Good Start, But . . .

We've made a good start at understanding energy, but there's still much to do. First, work is not the only way to transfer energy to a system. Suppose you put a pan of water on the stove and turn on the burner. The water temperature goes up, meaning that E_{th} is increasing, but no work is done. Instead, energy is transferred to the water by a *nonmechanical* means that we will call *heat*. Heat, which has the symbol Q, is the transfer of energy when there is a temperature difference between the system and the environment.

If we include heat as a second means of transferring energy, Equation 11.33, the energy equation, becomes

$$\Delta E_{sys} = W_{ext} + Q \tag{11.35}$$

This more general statement about energy is called the *first law of thermodynamics*. We will expand our basic energy model to include heat when we reach the study of thermodynamics in Part IV. Equation 11.35 will become essential for understanding thermal processes. The important point to notice for now is that we have developed a quite general model of energy that can later be expanded to include additional types of energy and energy transfers. Thermodynamics will be an extension of the ideas that we've established in Chapters 10 and 11, not an entirely new subject.

Second, there's something unusual about thermal energy. If you toss a block straight up, the kinetic energy is transformed into gravitational potential energy. After the block reaches the turning point, where $K = 0$, the potential energy is transformed back into kinetic energy as the block falls. If, instead, you push the block across a table, the block's kinetic energy is transformed (via friction) into thermal energy. But once the block stops ($K = 0$), you *never* see the thermal energy transformed back into macroscopic kinetic energy.

Why not? The law of conservation of energy would not be violated if E_{th} decreased and K increased. Think how practical this could be. The brakes of your car get very hot when you stop. You would hardly need your car engine if you could transform that thermal energy back into kinetic energy when the light turns green. But no one has ever done so.

There appears to be a one-way nature to the microscopic thermal energy that isn't true for an object's macroscopic kinetic or potential energy. It's easy to transform kinetic energy into thermal energy, difficult or impossible to transform it back. It seems as if some other law of physics is acting to prevent this. And indeed there is: a very important statement about energy transformation called the *second law of thermodynamics*.

So our basic energy model is a good start, but there's still much to do in Part IV as we expand these ideas into the full science of thermodynamics.

STOP TO THINK 11.6   A child at the playground slides down a pole at constant speed. This is a situation in which

a. $U \rightarrow K$. E_{mech} is not conserved but E_{sys} is.
b. $U \rightarrow E_{th}$. E_{mech} is conserved.
c. $U \rightarrow E_{th}$. E_{mech} is not conserved but E_{sys} is.
d. $K \rightarrow E_{th}$. E_{mech} is not conserved but E_{sys} is.
e. $U \rightarrow W_{ext}$. Neither E_{mech} nor E_{sys} is conserved.

11.9 Power

Work is a transfer of energy between the environment and a system. In many situations we would like to know *how quickly* the energy is transferred. Does the force act quickly and transfer the energy very rapidly, or is it a slow and lazy transfer of energy? If you need to buy a motor to lift 2000 lb of bricks up 50 ft, it makes a *big* difference whether the motor has to do this in 30 s or 30 min!

The question "How quickly?" implies that we are talking about a *rate*. For example, the velocity of an object—how quickly it is moving—is the *rate of change* of position. So when we raise the issue of how quickly the energy is transferred, we are talking about the *rate of transfer* of energy. The rate at which energy is transferred or transformed is called the **power** P, and it is defined as

$$P \equiv \frac{dE_{sys}}{dt} \tag{11.36}$$

The unit of power is the **watt**, which is defined as 1 watt = 1 W = 1 J/s.

A force that is doing work (i.e., transferring energy) at a rate of 3 J/s has an "output power" of 3 W. The system gaining energy at the rate of 3 J/s is said to "consume" 3 W of power. Common prefixes used with power are mW (milliwatts), kW (kilowatts), and MW (megawatts).

The English unit of power is the *horsepower*. The conversion factor to watts is

1 horsepower = 1 hp = 746 W

Many common appliances, such as motors, are rated in hp.

EXAMPLE 11.15 Choosing a motor

What power motor is needed to lift a 2000 kg elevator at a steady 3.0 m/s?

SOLVE The tension in the cable does work on the elevator to lift it. Because the cable is pulled by the motor, we say that the motor does the work of lifting the elevator. The net force is zero because the elevator moves at constant velocity, so the tension is simply $T = mg = 19,600$ N. The energy gained by the elevator is

$$\Delta E_{sys} = W_{ext} = T(\Delta y)$$

The power required to give the system this much energy in a time interval Δt is

$$P = \frac{\Delta E_{sys}}{\Delta t} = \frac{T(\Delta y)}{\Delta t}$$

But $\Delta y = v\Delta t$, so $P = Tv = (19,600 \text{ N})(3.0 \text{ m/s}) = 58,800 \text{ W} = 79$ hp.

Highly trained athletes have a tremendous power output.

The idea of power as a *rate* of energy transfer applies no matter what the form of energy. **FIGURE 11.36** shows three examples of the idea of power. For now, we want to focus primarily on *work* as the source of energy transfer. Within this more limited scope, power is simply the **rate of doing work:** $P = dW/dt$. If a particle moves through a small displacement $d\vec{r}$ while acted on by force $\vec{F}$, the force does a small amount of work dW given by

$$dW = \vec{F} \cdot d\vec{r}$$

Dividing both sides by dt, to give a rate of change, yields

$$\frac{dW}{dt} = \vec{F} \cdot \frac{d\vec{r}}{dt}$$

But $d\vec{r}/dt$ is the velocity $\vec{v}$, so we can write the power as

$$P = \vec{F} \cdot \vec{v} = Fv\cos\theta \qquad (11.37)$$

In other words, the power delivered to a particle by a force acting on it is the dot product of the force and the particle's velocity. These ideas will become clearer with some examples.

FIGURE 11.36 Examples of power.

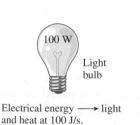

Electrical energy ⟶ light and heat at 100 J/s.

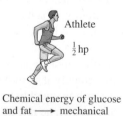

Athlete $\frac{1}{2}$ hp

Chemical energy of glucose and fat ⟶ mechanical energy at ≈350 J/s ≈ $\frac{1}{2}$ hp.

Gas furnace 20 kW

Chemical energy of gas ⟶ thermal energy at 20,000 J/s.

EXAMPLE 11.16 Power output of a motor

A factory uses a motor and a cable to drag a 300 kg machine to the proper place on the factory floor. What power must the motor supply to drag the machine at a speed of 0.50 m/s? The coefficient of friction between the machine and the floor is 0.60.

SOLVE The force applied by the motor, through the cable, is the tension force $\vec{T}$. This force does work on the machine with power $P = Tv$. The machine is in dynamic equilibrium because the

motion is at constant velocity, hence the tension in the rope balances the friction and is

$$T = f_k = \mu_k mg$$

The motor's power output is

$$P = Tv = \mu_k mgv = 882 \text{ W}$$

EXAMPLE 11.17 Power output of a car engine

A 1500 kg car has a front profile that is 1.6 m wide and 1.4 m high. The coefficient of rolling friction is 0.02. What power must the engine provide to drive at a steady 30 m/s ($\approx$65 mph) if 25% of the power is "lost" before reaching the drive wheels?

SOLVE The net force on a car moving at a steady speed is zero. The motion is opposed both by rolling friction and by air resistance. The forward force on the car $\vec{F}_{car}$ (recall that this is really $\vec{F}_{ground\ on\ car}$, a reaction to the drive wheels pushing backward on the ground with $\vec{F}_{car\ on\ ground}$) exactly balances the two opposing forces:

$$F_{car} = f_r + D$$

where $\vec{D}$ is the drag due to the air. Using the results of Chapter 6, where both rolling friction and drag were introduced, this becomes

$$F_{car} = \mu_r mg + \frac{1}{4}Av^2 = 294\ N + 504\ N = 798\ N$$

$A = (1.6\ m) \times (1.4\ m)$ is the front cross-section area of the car. The power required to push the car forward at this speed is

$$P_{car} = F_{car}v = (798\ N)(30\ m/s) = 23,900\ W = 32\ hp$$

This is the power *needed* at the drive wheels to push the car against the dissipative forces of friction and air resistance. The power output of the engine is larger because some energy is used to run the water pump, the power steering, and other accessories. In addition, energy is lost to friction in the drive train. If 25% of the power is lost (a typical value), leading to $P_{car} = 0.75P_{engine}$, the engine's power output is

$$P_{engine} = \frac{P_{car}}{0.75} = 31,900\ W = 43\ hp$$

ASSESS Automobile engines are typically rated at $\approx$200 hp. Most of that power is reserved for fast acceleration and climbing hills.

STOP TO THINK 11.7 Four students run up the stairs in the time shown. Rank in order, from largest to smallest, their power outputs P_a to P_d.

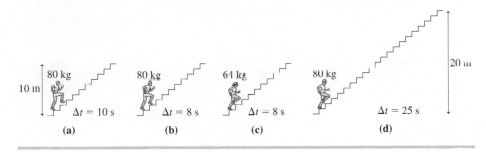

SUMMARY

The goal of Chapter 11 has been to develop a more complete understanding of energy and its conservation.

General Principles

Basic Energy Model

- Energy is *transferred* to or from the system by work.

- Energy is *transformed* within the system.

Two versions of the energy equation are

$$\Delta E_{sys} = \Delta K + \Delta U + \Delta E_{th} = W_{ext}$$

$$K_f + U_f + \Delta E_{th} = K_i + U_i + W_{ext}$$

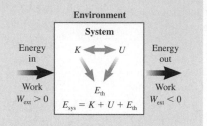

Environment
System

Energy in

$K \longleftrightarrow U$

Energy out

Work $W_{ext} > 0$

E_{th}

Work $W_{ext} < 0$

$E_{sys} = K + U + E_{th}$

Solving Energy Problems

MODEL Identify objects in the system.

VISUALIZE Draw a before-and-after pictorial representation and an energy bar chart.

SOLVE Use the energy equation

$$K_f + U_f + \Delta E_{th} = K_i + U_i + W_{ext}$$

ASSESS Is the result reasonable?

Law of Conservation of Energy

- **Isolated system:** $W_{ext} = 0$. The total energy $E_{sys} = E_{mech} + E_{th}$ is conserved. $\Delta E_{sys} = 0$.

- **Isolated, nondissipative system:** $W_{ext} = 0$ and $W_{diss} = 0$. The mechanical energy E_{mech} is conserved.

$$\Delta E_{mech} = 0 \text{ or } K_f + U_f = K_i + U_i$$

Important Concepts

The work-kinetic energy theorem is

$$\Delta K = W_{net} = W_c + W_{diss} + W_{ext}$$

With $W_c = -\Delta U$ for conservative forces and $W_{diss} = -\Delta E_{th}$ for dissipative forces, this becomes the energy equation.

The work done by a force on a particle as it moves from s_i to s_f is

$$W = \int_{s_i}^{s_f} F_s\, ds = \text{area under the force curve}$$

$$= \vec{F} \cdot \Delta \vec{r} \text{ if } \vec{F} \text{ is a constant force}$$

Conservative forces are forces for which the work is independent of the path followed. The work done by a conservative force can be represented as a **potential energy:**

$$\Delta U = U_f - U_i = -W_c(i \rightarrow f)$$

A conservative force is found from the potential energy by

$$F_s = -dU/ds = \text{negative of the slope of the PE curve}$$

Dissipative forces transform **macroscopic energy** into thermal energy, which is the **microscopic energy** of the atoms and molecules. For friction:

$$\Delta E_{th} = f_k \Delta s$$

Applications

Power is the rate at which energy is transferred or transformed:

$$P = \frac{dE_{sys}}{dt}$$

For a particle moving with velocity $\vec{v}$, the power delivered to the particle by force $\vec{F}$ is $P = \vec{F} \cdot \vec{v} = Fv\cos\theta$.

Energy bar charts display the energy equation $K_f + U_f + \Delta E_{th} = K_i + U_i + W_{ext}$ in graphical form.

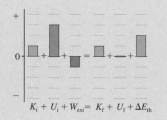

$K_i + U_i + W_{ext} = K_f + U_f + \Delta E_{th}$

Dot product

$$\vec{A} \cdot \vec{B} = AB\cos\alpha = A_x B_x + A_y B_y$$

Terms and Notation

thermal energy, E_{th}	work-kinetic energy theorem	microphysics
system energy, E_{sys}	dot product	dissipative force
energy transformation	scalar product	energy equation
energy transfer	conservative force	law of conservation of energy
work, W	nonconservative force	power, P
basic energy model	macrophysics	watt, W

(MP) For homework assigned on MasteringPhysics, go to www.masteringphysics.com

Problem difficulty is labeled as | (straightforward) to ||| (challenging).

Problems labeled ✎ can be done on an Energy Worksheet.

Problems labeled ▨ integrate significant material from earlier chapters.

CONCEPTUAL QUESTIONS

1. What are the two primary processes by which energy can be transferred from the environment to a system?

2. A process occurs in which a system's potential energy decreases while the system does work on the environment. Does the system's kinetic energy increase, decrease, or stay the same? Or is there not enough information to tell? Explain.

3. A process occurs in which a system's potential energy increases while the environment does work on the system. Does the system's kinetic energy increase, decrease, or stay the same? Or is there not enough information to tell? Explain.

4. The kinetic energy of a system decreases while its potential energy and thermal energy are unchanged. Does the environment do work on the system, or does the system do work on the environment? Explain.

5. You drop a ball from a high balcony and it falls freely. Does the ball's kinetic energy increase by equal amounts in equal time intervals, or by equal amounts in equal distances? Explain.

6. A particle moves in a vertical plane along the *closed* path seen in **FIGURE Q11.6**, starting at A and eventually returning to its starting point. How much work is done on the particle by gravity? Explain.

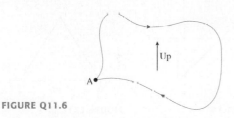

FIGURE Q11.6

7. A 0.2 kg plastic cart and a 20 kg lead cart both roll without friction on a horizontal surface. Equal forces are used to push both carts forward a distance of 1 m, starting from rest. After traveling 1 m, is the kinetic energy of the plastic cart greater than, less than, or equal to the kinetic energy of the lead cart? Explain.

8. You need to raise a heavy block by pulling it with a massless rope. You can either (a) pull the block straight up height h, or (b) pull it up a long, frictionless plane inclined at a 15° angle until its height has increased by h. Assume you will move the block at constant speed either way. Will you do more work in case a or case b? Or is the work the same in both cases? Explain.

9. a. If the force on a particle at some point in space is zero, must its potential energy also be zero at that point? Explain.
   b. If the potential energy of a particle at some point in space is zero, must the force on it also be zero at that point? Explain.

10. What is meant by an *isolated system*?

11. A car traveling at 60 mph slams on its brakes and skids to a halt. What happened to the kinetic energy the car had just before stopping?

12. What energy transformations occur as a skier glides down a gentle slope at constant speed?

13. Give a *specific* example of a situation in which
    a. $W_{ext} \rightarrow K$ with $\Delta U = 0$ and $\Delta E_{th} = 0$.
    b. $W_{ext} \rightarrow E_{th}$ with $\Delta K = 0$ and $\Delta U = 0$.

14. The motor of a crane uses power P to lift a steel beam. By what factor must the motor's power increase to lift the beam twice as high in half the time?

EXERCISES AND PROBLEMS

Exercises

Section 11.2 Work and Kinetic Energy

Section 11.3 Calculating and Using Work

1. | Evaluate the dot product of the three pairs of vectors in FIGURE EX11.1.

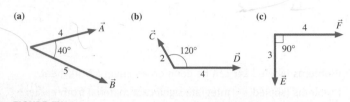

(a)   **(b)**   **(c)**

FIGURE EX11.1

2. | Evaluate the dot product of the three pairs of vectors in FIGURE EX11.2.

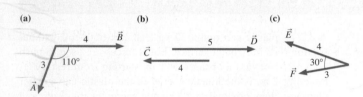

(a)   **(b)**   **(c)**

FIGURE EX11.2

3. | Evaluate the dot product $\vec{A} \cdot \vec{B}$ if
   a. $\vec{A} = 3\hat{i} - 4\hat{j}$ and $\vec{B} = -2\hat{i} + 6\hat{j}$.
   b. $\vec{A} = 2\hat{i} + 3\hat{j}$ and $\vec{B} = 6\hat{i} - 4\hat{j}$.
4. | Evaluate the dot product $\vec{A} \cdot \vec{B}$ if
   a. $\vec{A} = 4\hat{i} + 2\hat{j}$ and $\vec{B} = -3\hat{i} - 2\hat{j}$.
   b. $\vec{A} = -4\hat{i} + 2\hat{j}$ and $\vec{B} = -\hat{i} - 2\hat{j}$.
5. ‖ What is the angle θ between vectors $\vec{A}$ and $\vec{B}$ in each part of Exercise 3?
6. ‖ What is the angle θ between vectors $\vec{A}$ and $\vec{B}$ in each part of Exercise 4?
7. | How much work is done by the force $\vec{F} = (6.0\hat{i} - 3.0\hat{j})$ N on a particle that moves through displacement (a) $\Delta\vec{r} = 2.0\hat{i}$ m and (b) $\Delta\vec{r} = 2.0\hat{j}$ m?
8. | How much work is done by the force $\vec{F} = (-4.0\hat{i} - 6.0\hat{j})$ N on a particle that moves through displacement (a) $\Delta\vec{r} = 3.0\hat{i}$ m and (b) $\Delta\vec{r} = (-3.0\hat{i} + 2.0\hat{j})$ m?
9. ‖ A 20 g particle is moving to the left at 30 m/s. How much net work must be done on the particle to cause it to move to the right at 30 m/s?
10. | A 2.0 kg book is lying on a 0.75-m-high table. You pick it up and place it on a bookshelf 2.25 m above the floor.
    a. How much work does gravity do on the book?
    b. How much work does your hand do on the book?
11. ‖ The two ropes seen in FIGURE EX11.11 are used to lower a 255 kg piano 5.00 m from a second-story window to the ground. How much work is done by each of the three forces?

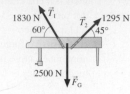

FIGURE EX11.11

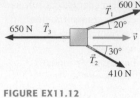

FIGURE EX11.12

12. | The three ropes shown in the bird's-eye view of FIGURE EX11.12 are used to drag a crate 3.0 m across the floor. How much work is done by each of the three forces?

13. | FIGURE EX11.13 is the velocity-versus-time graph for a 2.0 kg object moving along the x-axis. Determine the work done on the object during each of the five intervals AB, BC, CD, DE, and EF.

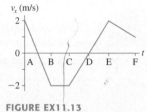

FIGURE EX11.13

Section 11.4 The Work Done by a Variable Force

14. | FIGURE EX11.14 is the force-versus-position graph for a particle moving along the x-axis. Determine the work done on the particle during each of the three intervals 0–1 m, 1–2 m, and 2–3 m.

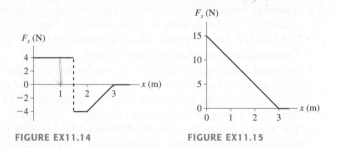

FIGURE EX11.14   **FIGURE EX11.15**

15. ‖ A 500 g particle moving along the x-axis experiences the force shown in FIGURE EX11.15. The particle's velocity is 2.0 m/s at $x = 0$ m. What is its velocity at $x = 1$ m, 2 m, and 3 m?
16. ‖ A 2.0 kg particle moving along the x-axis experiences the force shown in FIGURE EX11.16. The particle's velocity is 4.0 m/s at $x = 0$ m. What is its velocity at $x = 2$ m and 4 m?

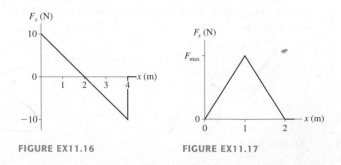

FIGURE EX11.16   **FIGURE EX11.17**

17. ‖ A 500 g particle moving along the x-axis experiences the force shown in FIGURE EX11.17. The particle goes from $v_x = 2.0$ m/s at $x = 0$ m to $v_x = 6.0$ m/s at $x = 2$ m. What is F_{max}?

Section 11.5 Force, Work, and Potential Energy

Section 11.6 Finding Force from Potential Energy

18. ‖ A particle has the potential energy shown in FIGURE EX11.18. What is the x-component of the force on the particle at $x = 5$, 15, 25, and 35 cm?

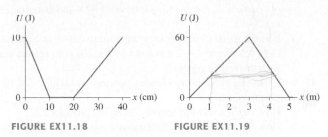

FIGURE EX11.18   FIGURE EX11.19

19. ‖ A particle has the potential energy shown in FIGURE EX11.19. What is the x-component of the force on the particle at $x = 1$ m and 4 m?

20. ‖ A particle moving along the y-axis has the potential energy $U = 4y^3$ J, where y is in m.
    a. Graph the potential energy from $y = 0$ m to $y = 2$ m.
    b. What is the y-component of the force on the particle at $y = 0$ m, 1 m, and 2 m?

21. ‖ A particle moving along the x-axis has the potential energy $U = 10/x$ J, where x is in m.
    a. Graph the potential energy from $x = 1$ m to $x = 10$ m.
    b. What is the x-component of the force on the particle at $x = 2$ m, 5 m, and 8 m?

Section 11.7 Thermal Energy

22. ‖ The mass of a carbon atom is 2.0×10^{-26} kg.
    a. What is the kinetic energy of a carbon atom moving with a speed of 500 m/s?
    b. Two carbon atoms are joined by a spring-like carbon-carbon bond. The potential energy stored in the bond has the value you calculated in part a if the bond is stretched 0.050 nm. What is the bond's spring constant?

23. ‖ In Part IV you'll learn to calculate that 1 mole (6.02×10^{23} atoms) of helium atoms in the gas phase has 3700 J of microscopic kinetic energy at room temperature. If we assume that all atoms move with the same speed, what is that speed? The mass of a helium atom is 6.68×10^{-27} kg.

24. ‖ A 1500 kg car traveling at 20 m/s skids to a halt.
    a. Describe the energy transfers and transformations occurring during the skid.
    b. What is the change in the combined thermal energy of the car and the road surface?

25. ‖ A 20 kg child slides down a 3.0-m-high playground slide. She starts from rest, and her speed at the bottom is 2.0 m/s.
    a. Describe the energy transfers and transformations occurring during the slide.
    b. What is the change in the combined thermal energy of the slide and the seat of her pants?

Section 11.8 Conservation of Energy

26. ‖ A system loses 400 J of potential energy. In the process, it does 400 J of work on the environment and the thermal energy increases by 100 J. Show this process on an energy bar chart.

27. ‖ A system gains 500 J of kinetic energy while losing 200 J of potential energy. The thermal energy increases 100 J. Show this process on an energy bar chart.

28. ‖ How much work is done by the environment in the process shown in FIGURE EX11.28? Is energy transferred from the environment to the system or from the system to the environment?

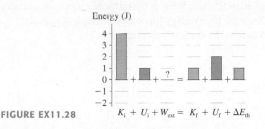

FIGURE EX11.28 $K_i + U_i + W_{ext} = K_f + U_f + \Delta E_{th}$

29. ‖ A cable with 20.0 N of tension pulls straight up on a 1.02 kg block that is initially at rest. What is the block's speed after being lifted 2.00 m? Solve this problem using work and energy.

Section 11.9 Power

30. ‖ a. How much work does an elevator motor do to lift a 1000 kg elevator a height of 100 m?
    b. How much power must the motor supply to do this in 50 s at constant speed?

31. ‖ a. How much work must you do to push a 10 kg block of steel across a steel table at a steady speed of 1.0 m/s for 3.0 s?
    b. What is your power output while doing so?

32. ‖ At midday, solar energy strikes the earth with an intensity of about 1 kW/m². What is the area of a solar collector that could collect 150 MJ of energy in 1 hr? This is roughly the energy content of 1 gallon of gasoline.

33. ‖ Which consumes more energy, a 1.2 kW hair dryer used for 10 min or a 10 W night light left on for 24 hr?

34. ‖ The electric company bills you in "kilowatt hours," abbreviated kWh.
    a. Is this energy, power, or force? Explain.
    b. Monthly electric use for a typical household is 500 kWh. What is this in basic SI units?

35. ‖ A 50 kg sprinter, starting from rest, runs 50 m in 7.0 s at constant acceleration.
    a. What is the magnitude of the horizontal force acting on the sprinter?
    b. What is the sprinter's power output at 2.0 s, 4.0 s, and 6.0 s?

Problems

36. ‖ A particle moves from A to D in FIGURE P11.36 while experiencing force $\vec{F} = (6\hat{i} + 8\hat{j})$ N. How much work does the force do if the particle follows path (a) ABD, (b) ACD, and (c) AD? Is this a conservative force? Explain.

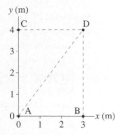

FIGURE P11.36

37. ‖ A 100 g particle experiences the one-dimensional, conservative force F_x shown in FIGURE P11.37.
   a. Draw a graph of the potential energy U from $x = 0$ m to $x = 5$ m. Let the zero of the potential energy be at $x = 0$ m.
   Hint: Think about the definition of potential energy *and* the geometric interpretation of the work done by a varying force.
   b. The particle is shot toward the right from $x = 1.0$ m with a speed of 25 m/s. What is the particle's mechanical energy?
   c. Draw the total energy line on your graph of part a.
   d. Where is the particle's turning point?

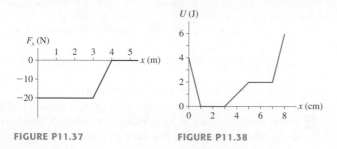

FIGURE P11.37   FIGURE P11.38

38. ‖ A 10 g particle has the potential energy shown in FIGURE P11.38.
   a. Draw a force-versus-position graph from $x = 0$ cm to $x = 8$ cm.
   b. How much work does the force do as the particle moves from $x = 2$ cm to $x = 6$ cm?
   c. What speed does the particle need at $x = 2$ cm to arrive at $x = 6$ cm with a speed of 10 m/s?

39. ‖ a. FIGURE P11.39a shows the force F_x exerted on a particle that moves along the x-axis. Draw a graph of the particle's potential energy as a function of position x. Let U be zero at $x = 0$ m.
   b. FIGURE P11.39b shows the potential energy U of a particle that moves along the x-axis. Draw a graph of the force F_x as a function of position x.

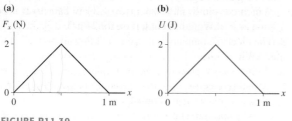

FIGURE P11.39

40. ‖ FIGURE P11.40 is the velocity-versus-time graph of a 500 g particle that starts at $x = 0$ m and moves along the x-axis. Draw graphs of the following by calculating and plotting numerical values at $t = 0, 1, 2, 3,$ and 4 s. Then sketch lines or curves of the appropriate shape between the points. Make sure you include appropriate scales on both axes of each graph.
   a. Acceleration versus time.
   b. Position versus time.
   c. Kinetic energy versus time.
   d. Force versus time.
   e. Use your F_x-versus-t graph to determine the *impulse* delivered to the particle during the time interval 0−2 s and also the interval 2−4 s.
   f. Use the impulse-momentum theorem to determine the parti-

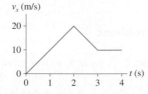

FIGURE P11.40

cle's velocity at $t = 2$ s and at $t = 4$ s. Do your results agree with the velocity graph?
   g. Now draw a graph of force versus *position*. This requires no calculations; just think carefully about what you learned in parts a to d.
   h. Use your F_x-versus-x graph to determine the *work* done on the particle during the time interval 0−2 s and also the interval 2−4 s.
   i. Use the work-kinetic energy theorem to determine the particle's velocity at $t = 2$ s and at $t = 4$ s. Do your results agree with the velocity graph?

41. ‖ A 1000 kg elevator accelerates upward at 1.0 m/s² for 10 m, starting from rest.
   a. How much work does gravity do on the elevator?
   b. How much work does the tension in the elevator cable do on the elevator?
   c. Use the work-kinetic energy theorem to find the kinetic energy of the elevator as it reaches 10 m.
   d. What is the speed of the elevator as it reaches 10 m?

42. ‖ Bob can throw a 500 g rock with a speed of 30 m/s. He moves his hand forward 1.0 m while doing so.
   a. How much work does Bob do on the rock?
   b. How much force, assumed to be constant, does Bob apply to the rock?
   c. What is Bob's maximum power output as he throws the rock?

43. ‖ Doug pushes a 5.0 kg crate up a 2.0-m-high 20° frictionless slope by pushing it with a constant *horizontal* force of 25 N. What is the speed of the crate as it reaches the top of the slope?
   a. Solve this problem using work and energy.
   b. Solve this problem using Newton's laws.

44. ‖ Sam, whose mass is 75 kg, straps on his skis and starts down a 50-m-high, 20° frictionless slope. A strong headwind exerts a *horizontal* force of 200 N on him as he skies. Find Sam's speed at the bottom (a) using work and energy, (b) using Newton's laws.

45. ‖‖ Susan's 10 kg baby brother Paul sits on a mat. Susan pulls the mat across the floor using a rope that is angled 30° above the floor. The tension is a constant 30 N and the coefficient of friction is 0.20. Use work and energy to find Paul's speed after being pulled 3.0 m.

46. ‖ A horizontal spring with spring constant 100 N/m is compressed 20 cm and used to launch a 2.5 kg box across a frictionless, horizontal surface. After the box travels some distance, the surface becomes rough. The coefficient of kinetic friction of the box on the surface is 0.15. Use work and energy to find how far the box slides across the rough surface before stopping.

47. ‖ A baggage handler throws a 15 kg suitcase horizontally along the floor of an airplane luggage compartment with an initial speed of 1.2 m/s. The suitcase slides 2.0 m before stopping. Use work and energy to find the suitcase's coefficient of kinetic friction on the floor.

48. ‖ Truck brakes can fail if they get too hot. In some mountainous areas, ramps of loose gravel are constructed to stop runaway trucks that have lost their brakes. The combination of a slight upward slope and a large coefficient of rolling resistance as the truck tires sink into the gravel brings the truck safely to a halt. Suppose a gravel ramp slopes upward at 6.0° and the coefficient of rolling friction is 0.40. Use work and energy to find the length of a ramp that will stop a 15,000 kg truck that enters the ramp at 35 m/s ($\approx$75 mph).

49. ‖ A freight company uses a compressed spring to shoot 2.0 kg packages up a 1.0-m-high frictionless ramp into a truck, as **FIGURE P11.49** shows. The spring constant is 500 N/m and the spring is compressed 30 cm.
   a. What is the speed of the package when it reaches the truck?
   b. A careless worker spills his soda on the ramp. This creates a 50-cm-long sticky spot with a coefficient of kinetic friction 0.30. Will the next package make it into the truck?

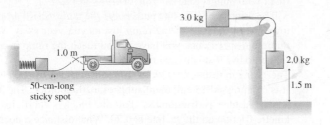

FIGURE P11.49   FIGURE P11.50

50. ‖ Use work and energy to find the speed of the 2.0 kg block in **FIGURE P11.50** just before it hits the floor if (a) the table is frictionless and if (b) the coefficient of kinetic friction of the 3.0 kg block is 0.15.

51. ‖ An 8.0 kg crate is pulled 5.0 m up a 30° incline by a rope angled 18° above the incline. The tension in the rope is 120 N, and the crate's coefficient of kinetic friction on the incline is 0.25.
   a. How much work is done by tension, by gravity, and by the normal force?
   b. What is the increase in thermal energy of the crate and incline?

52. ‖ A 10.2 kg weather rocket generates a thrust of 200 N. The rocket, pointing upward, is clamped to the top of a vertical spring. The bottom of the spring, whose spring constant is 500 N/m, is anchored to the ground.
   a. Initially, before the engine is ignited, the rocket sits at rest on top of the spring. How much is the spring compressed?
   b. After the engine is ignited, what is the rocket's speed when the spring has stretched 40 cm? For comparison, what would be the rocket's speed after traveling this distance if it weren't attached to the spring?

53. ‖ A 50 kg ice skater is gliding along the ice, heading due north at 4.0 m/s. The ice has a small coefficient of static friction, to prevent the skater from slipping sideways, but $\mu_k = 0$. Suddenly, a wind from the northeast exerts a force of 4.0 N on the skater.
   a. Use work and energy to find the skater's speed after gliding 100 m in this wind.
   b. What is the minimum value of μ_s that allows her to continue moving straight north?

54. ‖ a. A 50 g ice cube can slide without friction up and down a 30° slope. The ice cube is pressed against a spring at the bottom of the slope, compressing the spring 10 cm. The spring constant is 25 N/m. When the ice cube is released, what total distance will it travel up the slope before reversing direction?
   b. The ice cube is replaced by a 50 g plastic cube whose coefficient of kinetic friction is 0.20. How far will the plastic cube travel up the slope?

55. ‖ A 5.0 kg box slides down a 5.0-m-high frictionless hill, starting from rest, across a 2.0-m-wide horizontal surface, then hits a horizontal spring with spring constant 500 N/m. The other end of the spring is anchored against a wall. The ground under the

spring is frictionless, but the 2.0-m-wide horizontal surface is rough. The coefficient of kinetic friction of the box on this surface is 0.25.
   a. What is the speed of the box just before reaching the rough surface?
   b. What is the speed of the box just before hitting the spring?
   c. How far is the spring compressed?
   d. Including the first crossing, how many *complete* trips will the box make across the rough surface before coming to rest?

56. ‖ The spring shown in **FIGURE P11.56** is compressed 50 cm and used to launch a 100 kg physics student. The track is frictionless until it starts up the incline. The student's coefficient of kinetic friction on the 30° incline is 0.15.
   a. What is the student's speed just after losing contact with the spring?
   b. How far up the incline does the student go?

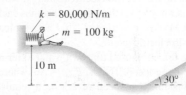

$k = 80,000$ N/m
$m = 100$ kg
10 m
30°

FIGURE P11.56

57. ‖ A block of mass m starts from rest at height h. It slides down a frictionless incline, across a rough horizontal surface of length L, then up a frictionless incline. The coefficient of kinetic friction on the rough surface is μ_k.
   a. What is the block's speed at the bottom of the first incline?
   b. How high does the block go on the second incline?
   Give your answers in terms of m, h, L, μ_k, and g.

58. ‖ Show that Hooke's law for an ideal spring is a conservative force. To do so, first calculate the work done by the spring as it expands from A to B. Then calculate the work done by the spring as it expands from A to point C, which is beyond B, then returns from C to B.

59. ‖ A clever engineer designs a "sprong" that obeys the force law $F_x = -q(x - x_e)^3$, where x_e is the equilibrium position of the end of the sprong and q is the sprong constant. For simplicity, we'll let $x_e = 0$ m. Then $F_x = -qx^3$.
   a. What are the units of q?
   b. Draw a graph of F_x versus x.
   c. Find an expression for the potential energy of a stretched or compressed sprong.
   d. A sprong-loaded toy gun shoots a 20 g plastic ball. What is the launch speed if the sprong constant is 40,000, with the units you found in part a, and the sprong is compressed 10 cm? Assume the barrel is frictionless.

60. ‖ A particle of mass m starts from $x_0 = 0$ m with $v_0 > 0$ m/s. The particle experiences the variable force $F_x = F_0 \sin(cx)$ as it moves to the right along the x-axis, where F_0 and c are constants.
   a. What are the units of F_0?
   b. What are the units of c?
   c. At what position x_{max} does the force first reach a maximum value? Your answer will be in terms of the constants F_0 and c and perhaps other numerical constants.
   d. Sketch a graph of F versus x from x_0 to x_{max}.
   e. What is the particle's velocity as it reaches x_{max}? Give your answer in terms of m, v_0, F_0, and c.

61. ‖ a. Estimate the height in meters of the two flights of stairs that go from the first to the third floor of a building.
    b. Estimate how long it takes you to *run* up these two flights of stairs.
    c. Estimate your power output in both watts and horsepower while running up the stairs.

62. ‖ A 5.0 kg cat leaps from the floor to the top of a 95-cm-high table. If the cat pushes against the floor for 0.20 s to accomplish this feat, what was her average power output during the pushoff period?

63. ‖ A 2.0 hp electric motor on a water well pumps water from 10 m below the surface. The density of water is 1.0 kg per liter. How many liters of water does the motor pump in 1 hr?

64. ‖ In a hydroelectric dam, water falls 25 m and then spins a turbine to generate electricity.
    a. What is ΔU of 1.0 kg of water?
    b. Suppose the dam is 80% efficient at converting the water's potential energy to electrical energy. How many kilograms of water must pass through the turbines each second to generate 50 MW of electricity? This is a typical value for a small hydroelectric dam.

65. ‖ The force required to tow a water skier at speed v is proportional to the speed. That is, $F_{tow} = Av$, where A is a proportionality constant. If a speed of 2.5 mph requires 2 hp, how much power is required to tow a water skier at 7.5 mph?

66. ‖ Estimate the maximum speed of a horse. Assume that a horse is 1.8 m tall and 0.5 m wide.

67. ‖ The engine in a 1500 kg car has a maximum power output of 200 hp, but 25% of the power is lost before reaching the drive wheels. The car has a front profile that is 1.6 m wide and 1.4 m high. The coefficient of rolling friction is 0.02. What is the car's top speed? Is this answer reasonable?

68. ‖ A Porsche 944 Turbo has a rated engine power of 217 hp. 30% of the power is lost in the drive train, and 70% reaches the wheels. The total mass of the car and driver is 1480 kg, and two-thirds of the weight is over the drive wheels.
    a. What is the maximum acceleration of the Porsche on a concrete surface where $\mu_s = 1.00$?
    Hint: What force pushes the car forward?
    b. If the Porsche accelerates at a_{max}, what is its speed when it reaches maximum power output?
    c. How long does it take the Porsche to reach the maximum power output?

In Problems 69 through 72 you are given the equation(s) used to solve a problem. For each of these, you are to
  a. Write a realistic problem for which this is the correct equation(s).
  b. Draw a pictorial representation.
  c. Finish the solution of the problem.

69. $\frac{1}{2}(2.0 \text{ kg})(4.0 \text{ m/s})^2 + 0$

    $+ (0.15)(2.0 \text{ kg})(9.8 \text{ m/s}^2)(2.0 \text{ m}) = 0 + 0 + T(2.0 \text{ m})$

70. $\frac{1}{2}(20 \text{ kg})v_1^2 + 0$

    $+ (0.15)(20 \text{ kg})(9.8 \text{ m/s}^2)\cos 40°((2.5 \text{ m})/\sin 40°)$

    $= 0 + (20 \text{ kg})(9.8 \text{ m/s}^2)(2.5 \text{ m}) + 0$

71. $F_{push} - (0.20)(30 \text{ kg})(9.8 \text{ m/s}^2) = 0$

    $75 \text{ W} = F_{push}v$

72. $T - (1500 \text{ kg})(9.8 \text{ m/s}^2) = (1500 \text{ kg})(1.0 \text{ m/s}^2)$

    $P = T(2.0 \text{ m/s})$

Challenge Problems

73. You've taken a summer job at a water park. In one stunt, a water skier is going to glide up the 2.0-m-high frictionless ramp shown in FIGURE CP11.73, then sail over a 5.0-m-wide tank filled with hungry sharks. You will be driving the boat that pulls her to the ramp. She'll drop the tow rope at the base of the ramp just as you veer away. What minimum speed must you have as you reach the ramp in order for her to live to do this again tomorrow?

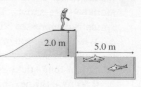

FIGURE CP11.73

74. The spring in FIGURE CP11.74 has a spring constant of 1000 N/m. It is compressed 15 cm, then launches a 200 g block. The horizontal surface is frictionless, but the block's coefficient of kinetic friction on the incline is 0.20. What distance d does the block sail through the air?

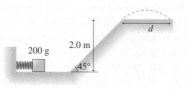

FIGURE CP11.74

75. As a hobby, you like to participate in reenactments of Civil War battles. Civil War cannons were "muzzle loaded," meaning that the gunpowder and the cannonball were inserted into the output end of the muzzle, then tamped into place with a long plunger. To recreate the authenticity of muzzle-loaded cannons, but without the danger of real cannons, Civil War buffs have invented a spring-powered cannon that fires a 1.0 kg plastic ball. A spring, with spring constant 3000 N/m, is mounted at the back of the barrel. You place a ball in the barrel, then use a long plunger to press the ball against the spring and lock the spring into place, ready for firing. In order for the latch to catch, the ball has to be moving at a speed of at least 2.0 m/s when the spring has been compressed 30 cm. The coefficient of friction of the ball in the barrel is 0.30. The plunger doesn't touch the sides of the barrel.
    a. If you push the plunger with a constant force, what is the minimum force that you must use to compress and latch the spring? You can assume that no effort was required to push the ball down the barrel to where it first contacts the spring.
    b. What is the cannon's muzzle velocity if the ball travels a total distance of 1.5 m to the end of the barrel?

76. The equation mgy for gravitational potential energy is valid only for objects near the surface of a planet. Consider two very large objects of mass m_1 and m_2, such as stars or planets, whose centers are separated by the large distance r. These two large objects exert gravitational forces on each other. You'll learn in Chapter 13 that the gravitational potential energy is

$$U = -\frac{Gm_1m_2}{r}$$

where $G = 6.67 \times 10^{-11} \text{ Nm}^2/\text{kg}^2$ is called the *gravitational constant*.
    a. Sketch a graph of U versus r. The mathematical difficulty at $r = 0$ is not a physically significant problem because the masses will collide before they get that close together.

b. What separation r has been chosen as the point of zero potential energy? Does this make sense? Explain.

c. Two stars are at rest 1.0×10^{14} m apart. This is about 10 times the diameter of the solar system. The first star is the size of our sun, with a mass of 2.0×10^{30} kg and a radius of 7.0×10^8 m. The second star has mass 8.0×10^{30} kg and radius of 11.0×10^8 m. Gravitational forces pull the two stars together. What is the speed of each star at the moment of impact?

77. A gardener pushes a 12 kg lawnmower whose handle is tilted up $37°$ above horizontal. The lawnmower's coefficient of rolling friction is 0.15. How much power does the gardener have to supply to push the lawnmower at a constant speed of 1.2 m/s? Assume his push is parallel to the handle.

STOP TO THINK ANSWERS

Stop to Think 11.1: d. Constant speed means $\Delta K = 0$. Gravitational potential energy is lost, and friction heats up the slide and the child's pants.

Stop to Think 11.2: 6.0 J. $K_f = K_i + W$. W is the area under the curve, which is 4.0 J.

Stop to Think 11.3: b. The gravitational force $\vec{F}_G$ is in the same direction as the displacement. It does positive work. The tension force $\vec{T}$ is opposite the displacement. It does negative work.

Stop to Think 11.4: c. $W = F(\Delta r)\cos\theta$. The 10 N force at $90°$ does no work at all. $\cos 60° = \frac{1}{2}$, so the 8 N force does less work than the 6 N force.

Stop to Think 11.5: e. Force is the negative of the slope of the potential energy diagram. At $x = 4$ m the potential energy has risen by 4 J over a distance of 2 m, so the slope is 2 J/m = 2 N.

Stop to Think 11.6: c. Constant speed means $\Delta K = 0$. Gravitational potential energy is lost, and friction heats up the pole and the child's hands.

Stop to Think 11.7: $P_b > P_a = P_c > P_d$. The work done is $mg\Delta y$, so the power is $mg\Delta y/\Delta t$. Runner b does the same work as a but in less time. The ratio $m/\Delta t$ is the same for a and c. Runner d does twice the work of a but takes more than twice as long.

Conservation Laws

In Part II we have discovered that we don't need to know all the details of an interaction to relate the properties of a system "before" an interaction to the system's properties "after" the interaction. Along the way, we found two important quantities, momentum and energy, that characterize a system of particles.

Momentum and energy have specific conditions under which they are conserved. In particular, the total momentum $\vec{P}$ and the total energy E_{sys} are conserved for an *isolated system*, one on which the net external force is zero. Further, the system's mechanical energy is conserved if the system is both isolated and nondissipative (i.e., no friction forces). These ideas are captured in the two most important conservation laws, the law of conservation of momentum and the law of conservation of energy.

Of course, not all systems are isolated. For both momentum and energy, it was useful to develop a *model* of a system interacting with its environment. Interactions between the system and the environment change the system's momentum and energy. In particular,

- Impulse is the transfer of momentum to or from the system: $\Delta p_s = J_s$.
- Work is the transfer of energy to or from the system: $\Delta E_{sys} = W_{ext}$.

Interactions within the system do not change $\vec{P}$ or E_{sys}. The kinetic, potential, and thermal energy within the system can be transformed without changing E_{sys}. The basic energy model is built around the twin ideas of the transfer and the transformation of energy.

The table below is a knowledge structure of conservation laws. You should compare this with the knowledge structure of Newtonian mechanics in the Part I Summary. Add the problem-solving strategies, and you now have a very powerful set of tools for understanding motion.

KNOWLEDGE STRUCTURE II **Conservation Laws**

ESSENTIAL CONCEPTS	Impulse, momentum, work, energy
BASIC GOALS	How is the system "after" an interaction related to the system "before"?
	What quantities are conserved, and under what conditions?

GENERAL PRINCIPLES	**Impulse-momentum theorem**	$\Delta p_s = J_s$
	Work-kinetic energy theorem	$\Delta K = W_{net} = W_c + W_{diss} + W_{ext}$
	Energy equation	$\Delta E_{sys} = \Delta K + \Delta U + \Delta E_{th} = W_{ext}$

CONSERVATION LAWS

For an isolated system, with $\vec{F}_{net} = \vec{0}$ and $W_{net} = 0$
- The total momentum $\vec{P}$ is conserved.
- The total energy $E_{sys} = E_{mech} + E_{th}$ is conserved.

For an isolated and nondissipative system, with $W_{diss} = 0$
- The mechanical energy $E_{mech} = K + U$ is conserved.

BASIC PROBLEM-SOLVING STRATEGY Draw a before-and-after pictorial representation, then use the momentum or energy equations to relate "before" to "after." Where possible, choose a system for which momentum and/or energy are conserved. If necessary, calculate impulse and/or work.

Basic model of momentum and energy

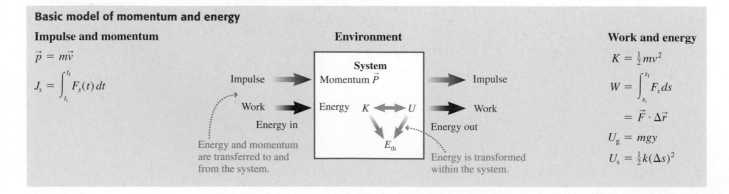

Impulse and momentum

$\vec{p} = m\vec{v}$

$J_s = \int_{t_i}^{t_f} F_s(t)\, dt$

Environment

Impulse → **System** Momentum $\vec{P}$ → Impulse

Work → Energy $K \leftrightarrow U$ → Work

Energy in $\searrow E_{th} \swarrow$ Energy out

Energy and momentum are transferred to and from the system.

Energy is transformed within the system.

Work and energy

$K = \frac{1}{2}mv^2$

$W = \int_{s_i}^{s_f} F_s\, ds$

$= \vec{F} \cdot \Delta\vec{r}$

$U_g = mgy$

$U_s = \frac{1}{2}k(\Delta s)^2$

Energy Conservation

You hear it all the time. Turn off lights. Buy a more fuel-efficient car. Conserve energy. But why conserve energy if energy is already conserved? Consider the earth as a whole. No work is done on the earth. And while heat energy flows from the sun to the earth, the earth radiates an equal amount of heat back into space. With no work and no net heat flow, the earth's total energy E_{earth} is conserved.

Pumping oil, driving your car, running a nuclear reactor, and turning on the lights are all interactions *within* the earth system. They transform energy from one type to another, but they don't affect the value of E_{earth}. Consider some examples.

- Crude oil, stored in the earth, has chemical energy E_{chem}. Chemical energy, a form of microscopic potential energy, is released when chemical reactions rearrange the bonds. As you burn gasoline in your car engine, the chemical energy is transformed into the kinetic energy of the moving pistons. This kinetic energy, in turn, is transformed into the car's kinetic energy. The car's kinetic energy is ultimately dissipated as thermal energy in the brakes, air, tires, and road because of friction and drag. Overall, the energy process of driving looks like

$$E_{chem} \rightarrow K_{piston} \rightarrow K_{car} \rightarrow E_{th}$$

- Water stored behind a dam has gravitational potential energy U_g. Potential energy is transformed into kinetic energy as the water falls, then into the spinning turbine's kinetic energy. The turbine converts mechanical energy into electric energy E_{elec}. The electric energy reaches a lightbulb where it is transformed partly into thermal energy (lightbulbs are hot!) and partly into light energy. The light is absorbed by surfaces, heating them slightly and thus transforming the light energy into thermal energy. The overall energy process is

$$U_g \rightarrow K_{water} \rightarrow K_{turbine} \rightarrow E_{elec} \rightarrow E_{light} \rightarrow E_{th}$$

Do you notice a trend? Stored energy (fossil fuel, water behind a dam) is transformed through a series of steps, some of which are considered "useful," until the energy is ultimately dissipated as thermal energy. **The total energy has not changed, but its "usefulness" has.**

Thermal energy is rarely "useful" energy. A room full of moving air molecules has a huge thermal energy, but you can't run your lights or your air conditioner with it. You can't turn the thermal energy of your hot brakes back into the kinetic energy of the car. Energy may be conserved, but there's a one-way characteristic of the transformations.

The energy stored in fuels and the energy of the sun are "high-quality energy" because of their potential to be transformed into such useful forms of energy as moving your car and heating your house. But as **FIGURE II.1** shows, high-quality energy becomes "degraded" into thermal energy, where it is no longer useful. Thus the phrase "conserve energy" isn't used literally. Instead, it means to conserve or preserve the earth's sources of high-quality energy.

Conserving high-quality energy is important because fossil fuels are a finite resource. Experts may disagree as to how long fossil fuels will last, but all agree that it won't be forever. Oil and natural gas will likely become scarce during your lifetime. In addition, burning fossil fuel generates carbon dioxide, a major contributor to global warming. Energy conservation helps fuels last longer and minimizes their side effects.

There are two paths to conserving energy. One is to use less high-quality energy. Turning off lights and bicycling rather than driving are actions that preserve high-quality energy. A second path is to use energy more efficiently. That is, get more of the useful activity (miles driven, rooms lit) for the same amount of high-quality energy.

Lightbulbs offer a good example. A 100 W incandescent lightbulb actually produces only about 10 W of light energy. Ninety watts of the high-quality electric energy is immediately degraded as thermal energy without doing anything useful. By contrast, a 25 W compact fluorescent bulb generates the same 10 W of light but only 15 W of thermal energy. The same amount of high-quality energy can light four times as many rooms if 100 W incandescent bulbs are replaced by 25 W compact fluorescent bulbs.

So why conserve energy if energy is already conserved? Because technological society needs a dependable and sustainable supply of high-quality energy. Both technology improvement and lifestyle choices will help us achieve a sustainable energy future.

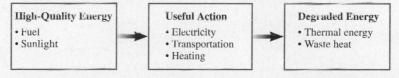

FIGURE PSII.1 "Using" energy transforms high-quality energy into thermal energy.

SOLVE a. We can use Equations 12.4 to calculate that the center of mass is

$$x_{cm} = \frac{m_1 x_1 + m_2 x_2}{m_1 + m_2}$$

$$= \frac{(2.0 \text{ kg})(0.0 \text{ m}) + (0.50 \text{ kg})(0.50 \text{ m})}{2.0 \text{ kg} + 0.50 \text{ kg}} = 0.10 \text{ m}$$

$y_{cm} = 0$ because all the masses are on the x-axis. The center of mass is 20% of the way from the 2.0 kg ball to the 0.50 kg ball.

b. Each ball rotates about the center of mass. The radii of the circles are $r_1 = 0.10$ m and $r_2 = 0.40$ m. The tangential velocities are $(v_i)_t = r_i \omega$, but this equation requires ω to be in rad/s. The conversion is

$$\omega = 40 \frac{\text{rev}}{\text{min}} \times \frac{1 \text{ min}}{60 \text{ s}} \times \frac{2\pi \text{ rad}}{1 \text{ rev}} = 4.19 \text{ rad/s}$$

Consequently,

$$(v_1)_t = r_1 \omega = (0.10 \text{ m})(4.19 \text{ rad/s}) = 0.42 \text{ m/s}$$

$$(v_2)_t = r_2 \omega = (0.40 \text{ m})(4.19 \text{ rad/s}) = 1.68 \text{ m/s}$$

ASSESS The center of mass is closer to the heavier ball than to the lighter ball. We expected this because x_{cm} is a mass-weighted average of the positions. But the lighter mass moves faster because it is farther from the rotation axis.

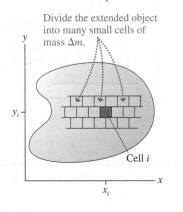

FIGURE 12.7 Calculating the center of mass of an extended object.

Divide the extended object into many small cells of mass Δm.

Cell i

For any realistic object, carrying out the summations of Equations 12.4 over all the atoms in the object is not practical. Instead, as **FIGURE 12.7** shows, we can divide an extended object into many small cells or boxes, each with the very small mass Δm. We will number the cells 1, 2, 3, . . . , just as we did the particles. Cell i has coordinates (x_i, y_i) and mass $m_i = \Delta m$. The center-of-mass coordinates are then

$$x_{cm} = \frac{1}{M} \sum_i x_i \, \Delta m \quad \text{and} \quad y_{cm} = \frac{1}{M} \sum_i y_i \, \Delta m$$

Now, as you might expect, we'll let the cells become smaller and smaller, with the total number increasing. As each cell becomes infinitesimally small, we can replace Δm with dm and the sum by an integral. Then

$$x_{cm} = \frac{1}{M} \int x \, dm \quad \text{and} \quad y_{cm} = \frac{1}{M} \int y \, dm \qquad (12.5)$$

Equations 12.5 are a formal definition of the center of mass, but they are *not* ready to integrate in this form. First, integrals are carried out over *coordinates*, not over masses. Before we can integrate, we must replace dm by an equivalent expression involving a coordinate differential such as dx or dy. Second, no limits of integration have been specified. The procedure for using Equations 12.5 is best shown with an example.

EXAMPLE 12.3 The center of mass of a rod

Find the center of mass of a thin, uniform rod of length L and mass M. Use this result to find the tangential acceleration of one tip of a 1.60-m-long rod that rotates about its center of mass with an angular acceleration of 6.0 rad/s².

VISUALIZE **FIGURE 12.8** shows the rod. We've chosen a coordinate system such that the rod lies along the x-axis from 0 to L. Because the rod is "thin," we'll assume that $y_{cm} = 0$.

FIGURE 12.8 Finding the center of mass of a long, thin rod.

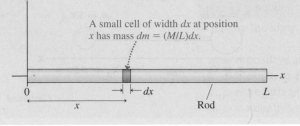

A small cell of width dx at position x has mass $dm = (M/L)dx$.

0        $\vdash dx$ L

x Rod

SOLVE Our first task is to find x_{cm}, which lies somewhere on the x-axis. To do this, we divide the rod into many small cells of mass dm. One such cell, at position x, is shown. The cell's width is dx. Because the rod is *uniform,* the mass of this little cell is the *same fraction* of the total mass M that dx is of the total length L. That is,

$$\frac{dm}{M} = \frac{dx}{L}$$

Consequently, we can express dm in terms of the coordinate differential dx as

$$dm = \frac{M}{L} dx$$

NOTE ▶ The change of variables from dm to the differential of a coordinate is *the* key step in calculating the center of mass. ◀

With this expression for dm, Equation 12.5 for x_{cm} becomes

$$x_{cm} = \frac{1}{M} \left(\frac{M}{L} \int x \, dx \right) = \frac{1}{L} \int_0^L x \, dx$$

where in the last step we've noted that summing "all the mass in the rod" means integrating from $x = 0$ to $x = L$. This is a straightforward integral to carry out, giving

$$x_{cm} = \frac{1}{L}\left[\frac{x^2}{2}\right]_0^L = \frac{1}{L}\left[\frac{L^2}{2} - 0\right] = \frac{1}{2}L$$

The center of mass is at the center of the rod. For a 1.60-m-long rod, each tip of the rod rotates in a circle with $r = \frac{1}{2}L = 0.80$ m.

The tangential acceleration, the rate at which the tip is speeding up, is

$$a_t = r\alpha = (0.80\text{ m})(6.0\text{ rad/s}^2) = 4.8\text{ m/s}^2$$

ASSESS You could have guessed that the center of mass is at the center of the rod, but now we've shown it rigorously.

NOTE ▶ For any symmetrical object of uniform density, the center of mass is at the physical center of the object. ◀

To see where the center-of-mass equations come from, **FIGURE 12.9** shows an object rotating about its center of mass. Particle i is moving in a circle, so it *must* have a centripetal acceleration. Acceleration requires a force, and this force is due to tension in the molecular bonds that hold the object together. Force $\vec{T}_i$ on particle i has magnitude

$$T_i = m_i(a_i)_r = m_i r_i \omega^2 \tag{12.6}$$

where r_i is the distance of particle i from the center of mass and we used Equation 12.3 for a_r. All points in a rigid rotating object have the *same* angular velocity, so ω doesn't need a subscript.

The internal tension forces are all paired as action/reaction forces, equal in magnitude but opposite in direction, so the sum of all the tension forces must be zero. That is, $\sum \vec{T}_i = \vec{0}$. The x-component of this sum is

$$\sum_i (T_i)_x = \sum_i T_i \cos\theta_i = \sum_i (m_i r_i \omega^2)\cos\theta_i = 0 \tag{12.7}$$

You can see from Figure 12.9 that $\cos\theta_i = (x_{cm} - x_i)/r_i$. Thus

$$\sum_i (T_i)_x = \sum_i (m_i r_i \omega^2)\frac{x_{cm} - x_i}{r_i} = \left(\sum_i m_i x_{cm} - \sum_i m_i x_i\right)\omega^2 = 0 \tag{12.8}$$

This equation will be true if the term in parentheses is zero. x_{cm} is a constant, so we can bring it outside the summation to write

$$\sum_i m_i x_{cm} - \sum_i m_i x_i = \left(\sum_i m_i\right)x_{cm} - \sum_i m_i x_i = M x_{cm} - \sum_i m_i x_i = 0 \tag{12.9}$$

where we used the fact that $\sum m_i$ is simply the object's total mass M. Solving for x_{cm}, we find the x-coordinate of the object's center of mass to be

$$x_{cm} = \frac{1}{M}\sum_i m_i x_i = \frac{m_1 x_1 + m_2 x_2 + m_3 x_3 + \cdots}{m_1 + m_2 + m_3 + \cdots} \tag{12.10}$$

This was Equation 12.4. The y-equation is found similarly.

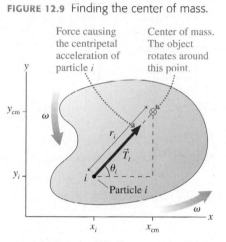

FIGURE 12.9 Finding the center of mass.

Force causing the centripetal acceleration of particle i

Center of mass. The object rotates around this point.

12.3 Rotational Energy

A rotating rigid body has kinetic energy because all atoms in the object are in motion. The kinetic energy due to rotation is called **rotational kinetic energy.**

FIGURE 12.10 on the next page shows a few of the particles making up a solid object that rotates with angular velocity ω. Particle i, which rotates in a circle of radius r_i,

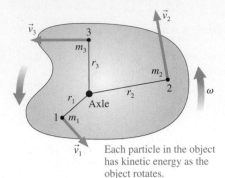

Each particle in the object has kinetic energy as the object rotates.

moves with speed $v_i = r_i \omega$. The object's rotational kinetic energy is the sum of the kinetic energies of each of the particles:

$$K_{rot} = \frac{1}{2}m_1 v_1^2 + \frac{1}{2}m_2 v_2^2 + \cdots$$

$$= \frac{1}{2}m_1 r_1^2 \omega^2 + \frac{1}{2}m_2 r_2^2 \omega^2 + \cdots = \frac{1}{2}\left(\sum_i m_i r_i^2\right)\omega^2 \quad (12.11)$$

The quantity $\sum m_i r_i^2$ is called the object's **moment of inertia** I:

$$I = m_1 r_1^2 + m_2 r_2^2 + m_3 r_3^2 + \cdots = \sum_i m_i r_i^2 \quad (12.12)$$

The units of moment of inertia are kg m^2. **An object's moment of inertia depends on the axis of rotation.** Once the axis is specified, allowing the values of r_i to be determined, the moment of inertia *about that axis* can be calculated from Equation 12.12.

> **NOTE ▶** The "moment" in *moment of inertia* has nothing to do with time. The term stems from the Latin *momentum,* meaning "motion." ◀

Written using the moment of inertia I, the rotational kinetic energy is

$$K_{rot} = \frac{1}{2}I\omega^2 \quad (12.13)$$

Rotational kinetic energy is *not* a new form of energy. This is the familiar kinetic energy of motion, only now expressed in a form that is especially convenient for rotational motion. Notice the analogy with the familiar $\frac{1}{2}mv^2$.

EXAMPLE 12.4 A rotating widget

Students participating in an engineering project design the triangular widget seen in **FIGURE 12.11**. The three masses, held together by lightweight plastic rods, rotate in the plane of the page about an axle passing through the right-angle corner. At what angular velocity does the widget have 100 mJ of rotational energy?

FIGURE 12.11 The rotating widget.

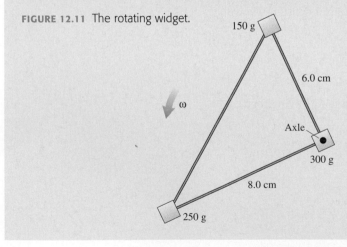

MODEL The widget can be modeled as three particles connected by massless rods.

SOLVE Rotational energy is $K = \frac{1}{2}I\omega^2$. The moment of inertia is measured about the rotation axis, thus

$$I = \sum_i m_i r_i^2 = (0.25\ \text{kg})(0.080\ \text{m})^2 + (0.15\ \text{kg})(0.060\ \text{m})^2$$
$$+ (0.30\ \text{kg})(0\ \text{m})^2$$
$$= 2.14 \times 10^{-3}\ \text{kg m}^2$$

The largest mass makes no contribution to I because it doesn't rotate. With I known, the desired angular velocity is

$$\omega = \sqrt{\frac{2K}{I}} = \sqrt{\frac{2(0.10\ \text{J})}{2.14 \times 10^{-3}\ \text{kg m}^2}}$$

$$= 9.67\ \text{rad/s} \times \frac{1\ \text{rev}}{2\pi\ \text{rad}} = 1.54\ \text{rev/s} = 92\ \text{rpm}$$

ASSESS The moment of inertia depends on the distance of each mass from the rotation axis. The moment of inertia would be different for an axle passing through either of the other two masses, and thus the required angular velocity would be different.

Before rushing to calculate moments of inertia, let's get a better understanding of the meaning. First, notice that **moment of inertia is the rotational equivalent of mass.** It plays the same role in Equation 12.13 as mass m in the now-familiar $K = \frac{1}{2}mv^2$. Recall that the quantity we call *mass* was actually defined as the *inertial mass*. Objects with larger mass have a larger inertia, meaning that they're harder to accelerate. Similarly, an object with a larger moment of inertia is harder to rotate. The fact that *moment of inertia* retains the word "inertia" reminds us of this.

But why does the moment of inertia depend on the distances r_i from the rotation axis? Think about the two wheels shown in **FIGURE 12.12**. They have the same total mass M and the same radius R. As you probably know from experience, it's much easier to spin the wheel whose mass is concentrated at the center than to spin the one whose mass is concentrated around the rim. This is because having the mass near the center (smaller values of r_i) lowers the moment of inertia.

Thus an object's moment of inertia depends not only on the object's mass but also on *how the mass is distributed* around the rotation axis. This is well known to bicycle racers. Every time a cyclist accelerates, she has to "spin up" the wheels and tires. The larger the moment of inertia, the more effort it takes and the slower her acceleration. For this reason, racers use the lightest possible tires, and they put those tires on wheels that have been designed to keep the mass as close as possible to the center without sacrificing the necessary strength and rigidity.

Moments of inertia for many solid objects are tabulated and found in various science and engineering handbooks. You would need to compute I yourself only for an object of unusual shape. Table 12.2 is a short list of common moments of inertia. We'll see in the next section where these come from, but do notice how I depends on the rotation axis.

If the rotation axis is not through the center of mass, then rotation may cause the center of mass to move up or down. In that case, the object's gravitational potential energy $U_g = Mgy_{cm}$ will change. If there are no dissipative forces (i.e., if the axle is frictionless) and if no work is done by external forces, then the object's mechanical energy

$$E_{mech} = K_{rot} + U_g = \frac{1}{2}I\omega^2 + Mgy_{cm} \qquad (12.14)$$

is a conserved quantity.

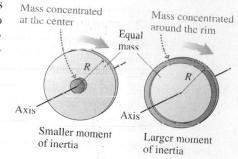

FIGURE 12.12 Moment of inertia depends on both the mass and how the mass is distributed.

 7.12, 7.13

TABLE 12.2 Moments of inertia of objects with uniform density

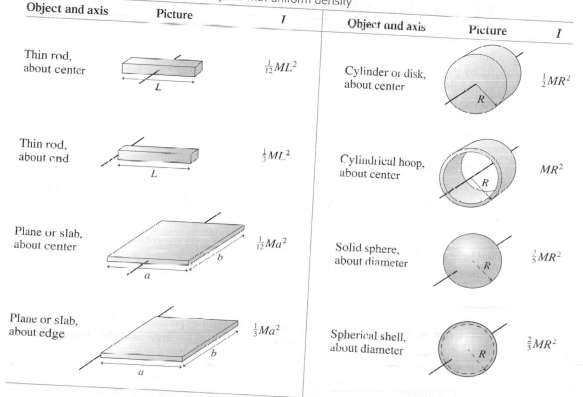

Object and axis	Picture	I	Object and axis	Picture	I
Thin rod, about center		$\frac{1}{12}ML^2$	Cylinder or disk, about center		$\frac{1}{2}MR^2$
Thin rod, about end		$\frac{1}{3}ML^2$	Cylindrical hoop, about center		MR^2
Plane or slab, about center		$\frac{1}{12}Ma^2$	Solid sphere, about diameter		$\frac{2}{5}MR^2$
Plane or slab, about edge		$\frac{1}{3}Ma^2$	Spherical shell, about diameter		$\frac{2}{3}MR^2$

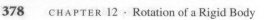

EXAMPLE 12.5   Th
A 1.0-m-long, 20(
wall. It is held out
the tip of the rod a

MODEL The mec
hinge is frictionl
transformed into

VISUALIZE FIGURI
resentation of th
system at the piv

FIGURE 12.13 A

12. The solid cylinder and cylindrical shell in **FIGURE Q12.12** have the same mass, same radius, and turn on frictionless, horizontal axles. (The cylindrical shell has light-weight spokes connccting the shell to the axle.) A rope is wrap-ped around each cylinder and tied to a block. The blocks have the same mass and are held the same height above the ground. Both blocks are released simultane-ously. Which hits the ground first? Or is it a tie? Explain.

13. A diver in the pike position (legs straight, hands on ankles) usu-ally makes only one or one-and-a-half rotations. To make two

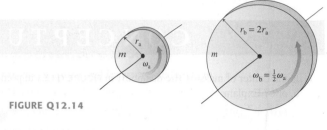

FIGURE Q12.12

or three rotations, the diver goes into a tuck position (knees bent, body curled up tight). Why?

14. Is the angular momentum of disk a in **FIGURE Q12.14** larger than, smaller than, or equal to the angular momentum of disk b? Explain.

FIGURE Q12.14

EXERCISES AND PROBLEMS

Exercises

Section 12.1 Rotational Motion

1. | A skater holds her arms outstretched as she spins at 180 rpm. What is the speed of her hands if they are 140 cm apart?

2. ‖ A high-speed drill reaches 2000 rpm in 0.50 s.
   a. What is the drill's angular acceleration?
   b. Through how many revolutions does it turn during this first 0.50 s?

3. ‖ An 18-cm-long bicycle crank arm, with a pedal at one end is attached to a 20-cm-diameter sprocket, the toothed disk around which the chain moves. A cyclist riding this bike increases her pedaling rate from 60 rpm to 90 rpm in 10 s.
   a. What is the tangential acceleration of the pedal?
   b. What length of chain passes over the top of the sprocket dur-ing this interval?

4. ‖ A ceiling fan with 80-cm-diameter blades is turning at 60 rpm. Suppose the fan coasts to a stop 25 s after being turned off.
   a. What is the speed of the tip of a blade 10 s after the fan is turned off?
   b. Through how many revolutions does the fan turn while stopping?

Section 12.2 Rotation About the Center of Mass

5. | How far from the center of the earth is the center of mass of the earth + moon system? Data for the earth and moon can be found inside the back cover of the book.

6. | The three masses shown in **FIGURE EX12.6** are connected by mass-less, rigid rods. What are the coordinates of the center of mass?

7. | The three masses shown in **FIGURE EX12.7** are connected by mass-less, rigid rods. What are the coordinates of the center of mass?

8. ‖ A 100 g ball and a 200 g ball are connected by a 30-cm-long, massless, rigid rod. The balls rotate about their center of mass at 120 rpm. What is the speed of the 100 g ball?

Section 12.3 Rotational Energy

9. ‖ What is the rotational kinetic energy of the earth? Assume the earth is a uniform sphere. Data for the earth can be found inside the back cover of the book.

10. ‖ The three 200 g masses in **FIG-URE EX12.10** are connected by mass-less, rigid rods to form a triangle. What is the triangle's rotational kin-etic energy if it rotates at 5.0 rev/s about an axis through the center?

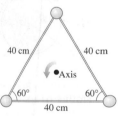

FIGURE EX12.10

11. ‖ A thin, 100 g disk with a diameter of 8.0 cm rotates about an axis through its center with 0.15 J of kinetic energy. What is the speed of a point on the rim?

12. ‖ A drum major twirls a 96-cm-long, 400 g baton about its center of mass at 100 rpm. What is the baton's rotational kinetic energy?

13. ‖ A 300 g ball and a 600 g ball are connected by a 40-cm-long massless, rigid rod. The structure rotates about its center of mass at 100 rpm. What is its rotational kinetic energy?

Section 12.4 Calculating Moment of Inertia

14. | The four masses shown in **FIGURE EX12.14** are connected by massless, rigid rods.
   a. Find the coordinates of the center of mass.
   b. Find the moment of inertia about an axis that passes through mass A and is perpen-dicular to the page.

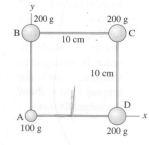

FIGURE EX12.14

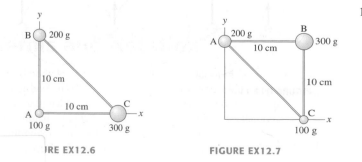

RE EX12.6

FIGURE EX12.7

15. | The four masses shown in **FIGURE EX12.14** are connected by massless, rigid rods.
   a. Find the coordinates of the center of mass.
   b. Find the moment of inertia about a diagonal axis that passes through masses B and D.

16. | The three masses shown in **FIGURE EX12.16** are connected by massless, rigid rods
   a. Find the coordinates of the center of mass.
   b. Find the moment of inertia about an axis that passes through mass A and is perpendicular to the page.
   c. Find the moment of inertia about an axis that passes through masses B and C.

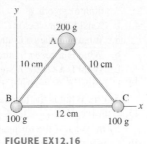

FIGURE EX12.16

17. || A 25 kg solid door is 220 cm tall, 91 cm wide. What is the door's moment of inertia for (a) rotation on its hinges and (b) rotation about a vertical axis inside the door, 15 cm from one edge?

18. || A 12-cm-diameter CD has a mass of 21 g. What is the CD's moment of inertia for rotation about a perpendicular axis (a) through its center and (b) through the edge of the disk?

Section 12.5 Torque

19. | In **FIGURE EX12.19**, what is the net torque about the axle?

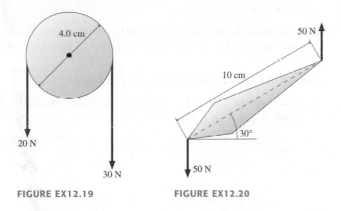

FIGURE EX12.19   **FIGURE EX12.20**

20. || In **FIGURE EX12.20**, what is the net torque about the center of mass?

21. | The tune-up specifications of a car call for the spark plugs to be tightened to a torque of 38 N m. You plan to tighten the plugs by pulling on the end of a 25-cm-long wrench. Because of the cramped space under the hood, you'll need to pull at an angle of 120° with respect to the wrench shaft. With what force must you pull?

22. || The 20-cm-diameter disk in **FIGURE EX12.22** can rotate on an axle through its center. What is the net torque about the axle?

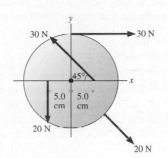

FIGURE EX12.22

23. || A 4.0-m-long, 500 kg steel beam extends horizontally from the point where it has been bolted to the framework of a new building under construction. A 70 kg construction worker stands at the far end of the beam. What is the magnitude of the torque about the point where the beam is bolted into place?

24. || An athlete at the gym holds a 3.0 kg steel ball in his hand. His arm is 70 cm long and has a mass of 4.0 kg. What is the magnitude of the torque about his shoulder if he holds his arm
   a. Straight out to his side, parallel to the floor?
   b. Straight, but 45° below horizontal?

Section 12.6 Rotational Dynamics

Section 12.7 Rotation About a Fixed Axis

25. | An object's moment of inertia is 2.0 kg m². Its angular velocity is increasing at the rate of 4.0 rad/s per second. What is the torque on the object?

26. || An object whose moment of inertia is 4.0 kg m² experiences the torque shown in **FIGURE EX12.26**. What is the object's angular velocity at $t = 3.0$ s? Assume it starts from rest.

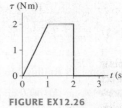

FIGURE EX12.26

27. || A 1.0 kg ball and a 2.0 kg ball are connected by a 1.0-m-long rigid, massless rod. The rod is rotating cw about its center of mass at 20 rpm. What torque will bring the balls to a halt in 5.0 s?

28. || A 200 g, 20-cm-diameter plastic disk is spun on an axle through its center by an electric motor. What torque must the motor supply to take the disk from 0 to 1800 rpm in 4.0 s?

29. || Starting from rest, a 12-cm-diameter compact disk takes 3.0 s to reach its operating angular velocity of 2000 rpm. Assume that the angular acceleration is constant. The disk's moment of inertia is 2.5×10^{-5} kg m².
   a. How much torque is applied to the disk?
   b. How many revolutions does it make before reaching full speed?

30. || The 200 g model rocket shown in **FIGURE EX12.30** generates 4.0 N of thrust. It spins in a horizontal circle at the end of a 100 g rigid rod. What is its angular acceleration?

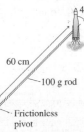

FIGURE EX12.30

Section 12.8 Static Equilibrium

31. || How much torque must the pin exert to keep the rod in **FIGURE EX12.31** from rotating?

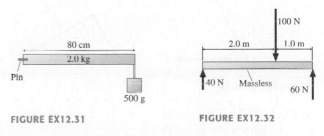

FIGURE EX12.31   **FIGURE EX12.32**

32. || Is the object in **FIGURE EX12.32** in equilibrium? Explain.

33. ‖ The two objects in FIGURE EX12.33 are balanced on the pivot. What is distance d?

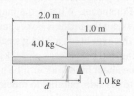

FIGURE EX12.33

34. ‖ A 5.0 kg cat and a 2.0 kg bowl of tuna fish are at opposite ends of a 4.0-m-long seesaw. How far to the left of the pivot must a 4.0 kg cat stand to keep the seesaw balanced?

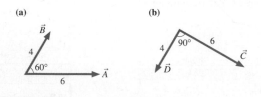

FIGURE EX12.34

Section 12.9 Rolling Motion

35. ‖ A car tire is 60 cm in diameter. The car is traveling at a speed of 20 m/s.
    a. What is the tire's rotation frequency, in rpm?
    b. What is the speed of a point at the top edge of the tire?
    c. What is the speed of a point at the bottom edge of the tire?

36. ‖ A 500 g, 8.0-cm-diameter can rolls across the floor at 1.0 m/s. What is the can's kinetic energy?

37. ‖ An 8.0-cm-diameter, 400 g sphere is released from rest at the top of a 2.1-m-long, 25° incline. It rolls, without slipping, to the bottom.
    a. What is the sphere's angular velocity at the bottom of the incline?
    b. What fraction of its kinetic energy is rotational?

Section 12.10 The Vector Description of Rotational Motion

38. ⏐ Evaluate the cross products $\vec{A} \times \vec{B}$ and $\vec{C} \times \vec{D}$.

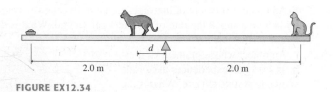

(a)   **(b)**

FIGURE EX12.38

39. ⏐ Evaluate the cross products $\vec{A} \times \vec{B}$ and $\vec{C} \times \vec{D}$.

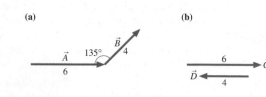

(a)   **(b)**

FIGURE EX12.39

40. ⏐ a. What is $(\hat{\imath} \times \hat{\jmath}) \times \hat{\imath}$?
    b. What is $\hat{\imath} \times (\hat{\jmath} \times \hat{\imath})$?

41. ⏐ a. What is $\hat{\imath} \times (\hat{\imath} \times \hat{\jmath})$?
    b. What is $(\hat{\imath} \times \hat{\jmath}) \times \hat{k}$?

42. ⏐ Vector $\vec{A} = 3\hat{\imath} + \hat{\jmath}$ and vector $\vec{B} = 3\hat{\imath} - 2\hat{\jmath} + 2\hat{k}$.
    a. What is the cross product $\vec{A} \times \vec{B}$?
    b. Show vectors $\vec{A}$, $\vec{B}$, and $\vec{A} \times \vec{B}$ on a three-dimensional coordinate system.

43. ⏐ Consider the vector $\vec{C} = 3\hat{\imath}$.
    a. What is a vector $\vec{D}$ such that $\vec{C} \times \vec{D} = \vec{0}$?
    b. What is a vector $\vec{E}$ such that $\vec{C} \times \vec{E} = 6\hat{k}$?
    c. What is a vector $\vec{F}$ such that $\vec{C} \times \vec{F} = -3\hat{\jmath}$?

44. ⏐ Force $\vec{F} = -10\hat{\jmath}$ N is exerted on a particle at $\vec{r} = (5\hat{\imath} + 5\hat{\jmath})$ m. What is the torque on the particle about the origin?

45. ⏐ Force $\vec{F} = (-10\hat{\imath} + 10\hat{\jmath})$ N is exerted on a particle at $\vec{r} = 5\hat{\jmath}$ m. What is the torque on the particle about the origin?

46. ‖ What are the magnitude and direction of the angular momentum relative to the origin of the 200 g particle in FIGURE EX12.46?

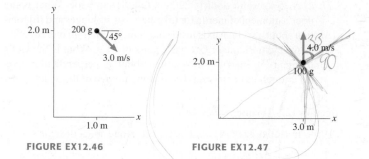

FIGURE EX12.46   FIGURE EX12.47

47. ‖ What are the magnitude and direction of the angular momentum relative to the origin of the 100 g particle in FIGURE EX12.47?

Section 12.11 Angular Momentum of a Rigid Body

48. ‖ What is the angular momentum of the 500 g rotating bar in FIGURE EX12.48?

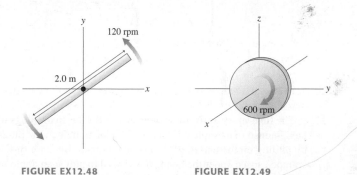

FIGURE EX12.48   FIGURE EX12.49

49. ‖ What is the angular momentum of the 2.0 kg, 4.0-cm-diameter rotating disk in FIGURE EX12.49?

50. ‖ How fast, in rpm, would a 100 g, 50-cm-diameter beach ball have to spin to have an angular momentum of 0.10 kg m²/s?

Problems

51. ‖‖ A 60-cm-diameter wheel is rolling along at 20 m/s. What is the speed of a point at the front edge of the wheel?

52. ‖‖ An equilateral triangle 5.0 cm on a side rotates about its center of mass at 120 rpm. What is the speed of one tip of the triangle?

15. | The four masses shown in **FIGURE EX12.14** are connected by massless, rigid rods.
   a. Find the coordinates of the center of mass.
   b. Find the moment of inertia about a diagonal axis that passes through masses B and D.

16. | The three masses shown in **FIGURE EX12.16** are connected by massless, rigid rods.
   a. Find the coordinates of the center of mass.
   b. Find the moment of inertia about an axis that passes through mass A and is perpendicular to the page.
   c. Find the moment of inertia about an axis that passes through masses B and C.

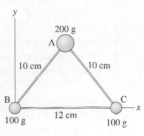

FIGURE EX12.16

17. || A 25 kg solid door is 220 cm tall, 91 cm wide. What is the door's moment of inertia for (a) rotation on its hinges and (b) rotation about a vertical axis inside the door, 15 cm from one edge?

18. || A 12-cm-diameter CD has a mass of 21 g. What is the CD's moment of inertia for rotation about a perpendicular axis (a) through its center and (b) through the edge of the disk?

Section 12.5 Torque

19. | In **FIGURE EX12.19**, what is the net torque about the axle?

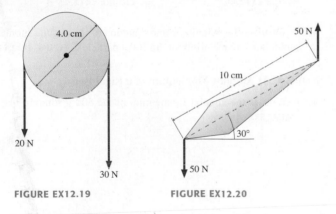

FIGURE EX12.19   **FIGURE EX12.20**

20. || In **FIGURE EX12.20**, what is the net torque about the center of mass?

21. | The tune-up specifications of a car call for the spark plugs to be tightened to a torque of 38 N m. You plan to tighten the plugs by pulling on the end of a 25-cm-long wrench. Because of the cramped space under the hood, you'll need to pull at an angle of 120° with respect to the wrench shaft. With what force must you pull?

22. || The 20-cm-diameter disk in **FIGURE EX12.22** can rotate on an axle through its center. What is the net torque about the axle?

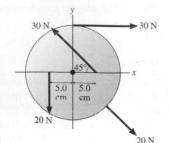

FIGURE EX12.22

23. || A 4.0-m-long, 500 kg steel beam extends horizontally from the point where it has been bolted to the framework of a new building under construction. A 70 kg construction worker stands at the far end of the beam. What is the magnitude of the torque about the point where the beam is bolted into place?

24. || An athlete at the gym holds a 3.0 kg steel ball in his hand. His arm is 70 cm long and has a mass of 4.0 kg. What is the magnitude of the torque about his shoulder if he holds his arm
   a. Straight out to his side, parallel to the floor?
   b. Straight, but 45° below horizontal?

Section 12.6 Rotational Dynamics

Section 12.7 Rotation About a Fixed Axis

25. | An object's moment of inertia is 2.0 kg m^2. Its angular velocity is increasing at the rate of 4.0 rad/s per second. What is the torque on the object?

26. || An object whose moment of inertia is 4.0 kg m^2 experiences the torque shown in **FIGURE EX12.26**. What is the object's angular velocity at $t = 3.0$ s? Assume it starts from rest.

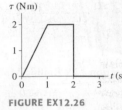

FIGURE EX12.26

27. || A 1.0 kg ball and a 2.0 kg ball are connected by a 1.0-m-long rigid, massless rod. The rod is rotating cw about its center of mass at 20 rpm. What torque will bring the balls to a halt in 5.0 s?

28. || A 200 g, 20-cm-diameter plastic disk is spun on an axle through its center by an electric motor. What torque must the motor supply to take the disk from 0 to 1800 rpm in 4.0 s?

29. || Starting from rest, a 12-cm-diameter compact disk takes 3.0 s to reach its operating angular velocity of 2000 rpm. Assume that the angular acceleration is constant. The disk's moment of inertia is 2.5×10^{-5} kg m^2.
   a. How much torque is applied to the disk?
   b. How many revolutions does it make before reaching full speed?

30. || The 200 g model rocket shown in **FIGURE EX12.30** generates 4.0 N of thrust. It spins in a horizontal circle at the end of a 100 g rigid rod. What is its angular acceleration?

FIGURE EX12.30

Section 12.8 Static Equilibrium

31. || How much torque must the pin exert to keep the rod in **FIGURE EX12.31** from rotating?

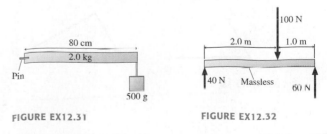

FIGURE EX12.31   **FIGURE EX12.32**

32. || Is the object in **FIGURE EX12.32** in equilibrium? Explain.

33. || The two objects in FIGURE EX12.33 are balanced on the pivot. What is distance d?

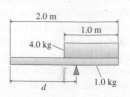

FIGURE EX12.33

34. || A 5.0 kg cat and a 2.0 kg bowl of tuna fish are at opposite ends of a 4.0-m-long seesaw. How far to the left of the pivot must a 4.0 kg cat stand to keep the seesaw balanced?

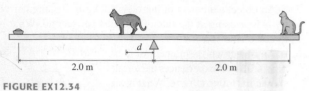

FIGURE EX12.34

Section 12.9 Rolling Motion

35. || A car tire is 60 cm in diameter. The car is traveling at a speed of 20 m/s.
    a. What is the tire's rotation frequency, in rpm?
    b. What is the speed of a point at the top edge of the tire?
    c. What is the speed of a point at the bottom edge of the tire?

36. || A 500 g, 8.0-cm-diameter can rolls across the floor at 1.0 m/s. What is the can's kinetic energy?

37. || An 8.0-cm-diameter, 400 g sphere is released from rest at the top of a 2.1-m-long, 25° incline. It rolls, without slipping, to the bottom.
    a. What is the sphere's angular velocity at the bottom of the incline?
    b. What fraction of its kinetic energy is rotational?

Section 12.10 The Vector Description of Rotational Motion

38. | Evaluate the cross products $\vec{A} \times \vec{B}$ and $\vec{C} \times \vec{D}$.

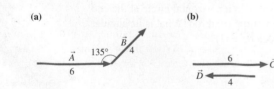

FIGURE EX12.38

39. | Evaluate the cross products $\vec{A} \times \vec{B}$ and $\vec{C} \times \vec{D}$.

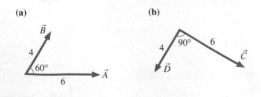

FIGURE EX12.39

40. | a. What is $(\hat{i} \times \hat{j}) \times \hat{i}$?
    b. What is $\hat{i} \times (\hat{j} \times \hat{i})$?

41. | a. What is $\hat{i} \times (\hat{i} \times \hat{j})$?
    b. What is $(\hat{i} \times \hat{j}) \times \hat{k}$?

42. | Vector $\vec{A} = 3\hat{i} + \hat{j}$ and vector $\vec{B} = 3\hat{i} - 2\hat{j} + 2\hat{k}$.
    a. What is the cross product $\vec{A} \times \vec{B}$?
    b. Show vectors $\vec{A}$, $\vec{B}$, and $\vec{A} \times \vec{B}$ on a three-dimensional coordinate system.

43. | Consider the vector $\vec{C} = 3\hat{i}$.
    a. What is a vector $\vec{D}$ such that $\vec{C} \times \vec{D} = \vec{0}$?
    b. What is a vector $\vec{E}$ such that $\vec{C} \times \vec{E} = 6\hat{k}$?
    c. What is a vector $\vec{F}$ such that $\vec{C} \times \vec{F} = -3\hat{j}$?

44. | Force $\vec{F} = -10\hat{j}$ N is exerted on a particle at $\vec{r} = (5\hat{i} + 5\hat{j})$ m. What is the torque on the particle about the origin?

45. | Force $\vec{F} = (-10\hat{i} + 10\hat{j})$ N is exerted on a particle at $\vec{r} = 5\hat{j}$ m. What is the torque on the particle about the origin?

46. || What are the magnitude and direction of the angular momentum relative to the origin of the 200 g particle in FIGURE EX12.46?

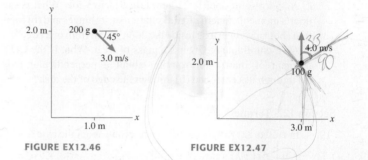

FIGURE EX12.46   **FIGURE EX12.47**

47. || What are the magnitude and direction of the angular momentum relative to the origin of the 100 g particle in FIGURE EX12.47?

Section 12.11 Angular Momentum of a Rigid Body

48. || What is the angular momentum of the 500 g rotating bar in FIGURE EX12.48?

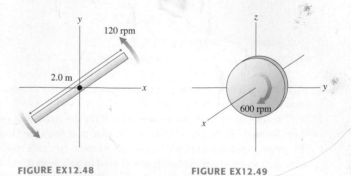

FIGURE EX12.48   **FIGURE EX12.49**

49. || What is the angular momentum of the 2.0 kg, 4.0-cm-diameter rotating disk in FIGURE EX12.49?

50. || How fast, in rpm, would a 100 g, 50-cm-diameter beach ball have to spin to have an angular momentum of 0.10 kg m^2/s?

Problems

51. ||| A 60-cm-diameter wheel is rolling along at 20 m/s. What is the speed of a point at the front edge of the wheel?

52. ||| An equilateral triangle 5.0 cm on a side rotates about its center of mass at 120 rpm. What is the speed of one tip of the triangle?

53. || An 800 g steel plate has the shape of the isosceles triangle shown in FIGURE P12.53. What are the x- and y-coordinates of the center of mass?
    Hint: Divide the triangle into vertical strips of width dx, then relate the mass dm of a strip at position x to the values of x and dx.

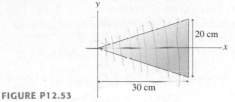

FIGURE P12.53

54. || What are the x- and y-coordinates of the center of mass for the uniform steel plate shown in FIGURE P12.54?

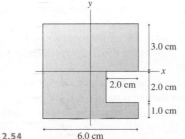

FIGURE P12.54   6.0 cm

55. || What is the moment of inertia of a 2.0 kg, 20-cm-diameter disk for rotation about an axis (a) through the center, and (b) through the edge of the disk?

56. || Determine the moment of inertia about the axis of the object shown in FIGURE P12.56.

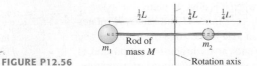

FIGURE P12.56

57. || Calculate by direct integration the moment of inertia for a thin rod of mass M and length L about an axis located distance d from one end. Confirm that your answer agrees with Table 12.2 when $d = 0$ and when $d = L/2$.

58. || a. A disk of mass M and radius R has a hole of radius r centered on the axis. Calculate the moment of inertia of the disk.
    b. Confirm that your answer agrees with Table 12.2 when $r = 0$ and when $r = R$.
    c. A 4.0-cm-diameter disk with a 3.0-cm-diameter hole rolls down a 50-cm-long, 20° ramp. What is its speed at the bottom? What percent is this of the speed of a particle sliding down a frictionless ramp?

59. || Calculate the moment of inertia of a rectangular plate for rotation about a perpendicular axis through the center.

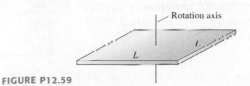

FIGURE P12.59

60. || Calculate the moment of inertia of the steel plate in FIGURE P12.53 for rotation about a perpendicular axis passing through the origin.

61. | A 3.0-m-long ladder, as shown in Figure 12.39, leans against a frictionless wall. The coefficient of static friction between the ladder and the floor is 0.40. What is the minimum angle the ladder can make with the floor without slipping?

62. || A 3.0-m-long rigid beam with a mass of 100 kg is supported at each end. An 80 kg student stands 2.0 m from support 1. How much upward force does each support exert on the beam?

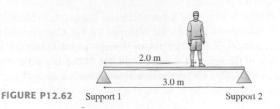

FIGURE P12.62   Support 1   Support 2

63. || An 80 kg construction worker sits down 2.0 m from the end of a 1450 kg steel beam to eat his lunch. The cable supporting the beam is rated at 15,000 N. Should the worker be worried?

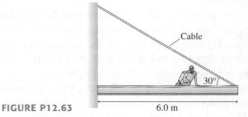

FIGURE P12.63   6.0 m

64. || A 40 kg, 5.0-m-long beam is supported, but not attached to, the two posts in FIGURE P12.64. A 20 kg boy starts walking along the beam. How close can he get to the right end of the beam without it falling over?

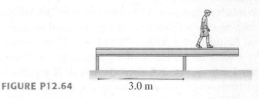

FIGURE P12.64   3.0 m

65. || Your task in a science contest is to stack four identical uniform bricks, each of length L, so that the top brick is as far to the right as possible without the stack falling over. Is it possible, as FIGURE P12.65 shows, to stack the bricks such that no part of the top brick is over the table? Answer this question by determining the maximum possible value of d.

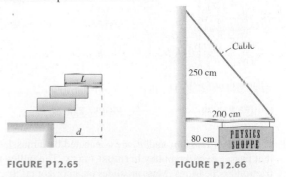

FIGURE P12.65   **FIGURE P12.66**

66. || A 120-cm-wide sign hangs from a 5.0 kg, 200-cm-long pole. A cable of negligible mass supports the end of the rod as shown in FIGURE P12.66. What is the maximum mass of the sign if the maximum tension in the cable without breaking is 300 N?

67. ‖ A 3.0 kg block is attached to a string that is wrapped around a 2.0 kg, 4.0-cm-diameter *hollow* cylinder that is free to rotate. (Use Figure 12.34 but treat the cylinder as hollow.) The block is released 1.0 m above the ground.
    a. Use Newton's second law to find the speed of the block as it hits the ground.
    b. Use conservation of energy to find the speed of the block as it hits the ground.

68. ‖ A 60-cm-long, 500 g bar rotates in a horizontal plane on an axle that passes through the center of the bar. Compressed air is fed in through the axle, passes through a small hole down the length of the bar, and escapes as air jets from holes at the ends of the bar. The jets are perpendicular to the bar's axis. Starting from rest, the bar spins up to an angular velocity of 150 rpm at the end of 10 s.
    a. How much force does each jet of escaping air exert on the bar?
    b. If the axle is moved to one end of the bar while the air jets are unchanged, what will be the bar's angular velocity at the end of 10 seconds?

69. ‖ Flywheels are large, massive wheels used to store energy. They can be spun up slowly, then the wheel's energy can be released quickly to accomplish a task that demands high power. An industrial flywheel has a 1.5 m diameter and a mass of 250 kg. Its maximum angular velocity is 1200 rpm.
    a. A motor spins up the flywheel with a constant torque of 50 Nm. How long does it take the flywheel to reach top speed?
    b. How much energy is stored in the flywheel?
    c. The flywheel is disconnected from the motor and connected to a machine to which it will deliver energy. Half the energy stored in the flywheel is delivered in 2.0 s. What is the average power delivered to the machine?
    d. How much torque does the flywheel exert on the machine?

70. ‖ The two blocks in **FIGURE P12.70** are connected by a massless rope that passes over a pulley. The pulley is 12 cm in diameter and has a mass of 2.0 kg. As the pulley turns, friction at the axle exerts a torque of magnitude 0.50 Nm. If the blocks are released from rest, how long does it take the 4.0 kg block to reach the floor?

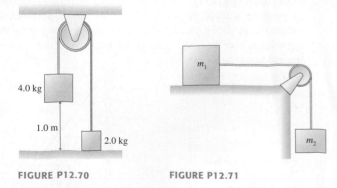

FIGURE P12.70   FIGURE P12.71

71. ‖ Blocks of mass m_1 and m_2 are connected by a massless string that passes over the pulley in **FIGURE P12.71**. The pulley turns on frictionless bearings. Mass m_1 slides on a horizontal, frictionless surface. Mass m_2 is released while the blocks are at rest.
    a. Assume the pulley is massless. Find the acceleration of m_1 and the tension in the string. This is a Chapter 7 review problem.

    b. Suppose the pulley has mass m_p and radius R. Find the acceleration of m_1 and the tensions in the upper and lower portions of the string. Verify that your answers agree with part a if you set $m_p = 0$.

72. ‖ The 2.0 kg, 30-cm-diameter disk in **FIGURE P12.72** is spinning at 300 rpm. How much friction force must the brake apply to the rim to bring the disk to a halt in 3.0 s?

FIGURE P12.72

73. ‖ Suppose the connecting tunnel in Example 12.11 has a mass of 50,000 kg.
    a. How far from the 100,000 kg rocket is the center of mass of the entire structure?
    b. What is the structure's angular velocity after 30 s?

74. ‖‖ A hollow sphere is rolling along a horizontal floor at 5.0 m/s when it comes to a 30° incline. How far up the incline does it roll before reversing direction?

75. ‖ Masses M and m are joined together by a massless, rigid rod of length L. They rotate about a perpendicular axis at distance x from mass M.
    a. For rotation at angular velocity ω, for what x does this rotating barbell have minimum rotational energy?
    b. What is the physical significance of this value of x?

76. ‖ A 5.0 kg, 60-cm-diameter disk rotates on an axle passing through one edge. The axle is parallel to the floor. The cylinder is held with the center of mass at the same height as the axle, then released.
    a. What is the cylinder's initial angular acceleration?
    b. What is the cylinder's angular velocity when it is directly below the axle?

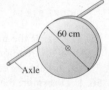

FIGURE P12.76

77. ‖ A hoop of mass M and radius R rotates about an axle at the edge of the hoop. The hoop starts at its highest position and is given a very small push to start it rotating. At its lowest position, what are (a) the angular velocity and (b) the speed of the lowest point on the hoop?

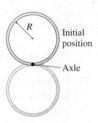

FIGURE P12.77

78. ‖ A long, thin rod of mass M and length L is standing straight up on a table. Its lower end rotates on a frictionless pivot. A very slight push causes the rod to fall over. As it hits the table, what are (a) the angular velocity and (b) the speed of the tip of the rod?

79. ‖ A sphere of mass M and radius R is rigidly attached to a thin rod of radius r that passes through the sphere at distance $\frac{1}{2}R$ from the center. A string wrapped around the rod pulls with tension T. Find an expression for the sphere's angular acceleration. The rod's moment of inertia is negligible.

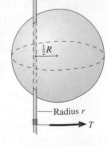

FIGURE P12.79

80. ‖ You've been given a pulley for your birthday. It's a fairly big pulley, 12 cm in diameter and with a mass of 2.0 kg. You get to

wondering whether the pulley is uniform. That is, is the mass evenly distributed, or is it concentrated toward the center or near the rim? To find out, you hang the pulley on a hook, wrap a string around it several times, and suspend your 1.0 kg physics book 1.0 m above the floor. With your stopwatch, you find that it takes 0.71 s for your book to hit the floor. What can you conclude about the pulley?

81. ‖ A satellite follows the elliptical orbit shown. The only force on the satellite is the gravitational attraction of the planet. The satellite's speed at point a is 8000 m/s.
    a. Is there any torque on the satellite? Explain.
    b. What is the satellite's speed at point b?
    c. What is the satellite's speed at point c?

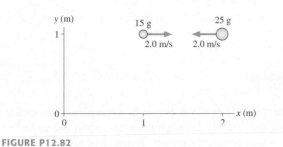

FIGURE P12.81

82. ‖ **FIGURE P12.82** shows two balls of clay approaching each other.
    a. Calculate the total angular momentum relative to the origin at this instant.
    b. Calculate the total angular momentum an instant before they collide.
    c. Calculate the total angular momentum an instant after the collision.

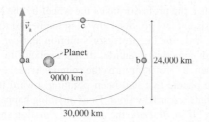

FIGURE P12.82

83. ‖ A 2.0 kg wood block hangs from the bottom of a 1.0 kg, 1.0-m-long rod. The block and rod form a pendulum that swings on a frictionless pivot at the top end of the rod. A 10 g bullet is fired into the block, where it sticks, causing the pendulum to swing out to a 30° angle. What was the speed of the bullet? You can treat the wood block as a particle.

84. ‖ A 10 g bullet traveling at 400 m/s strikes a 10 kg, 1.0-m-wide door at the edge opposite the hinge. The bullet embeds itself in the door, causing the door to swing open. What is the angular velocity of the door just after impact?

85. ‖ A solid sphere of radius R is placed at a height of 30 cm on a 15° slope. It is released and rolls, without slipping, to the bottom.
    a. From what height should a circular hoop of radius R be released on the same slope in order to equal the sphere's speed at the bottom?
    b. Can a circular hoop of different diameter be released from a height of 30 cm and match the sphere's speed at the bottom? If so, what is the diameter? If not, why not?

86. ‖ A 2.0 kg, 20-cm-diameter turntable rotates at 100 rpm on frictionless bearings. Two 500 g blocks fall from above, hit the turntable simultaneously at opposite ends of a diagonal, and stick. What is the turntable's angular velocity, in rpm, just after this event?

87. ‖‖ A 200 g, 40-cm-diameter turntable rotates on frictionless bearings at 60 rpm. A 20 g block sits at the center of the turntable. A compressed spring shoots the block radially outward along a frictionless groove in the surface of the turntable. What is the turntable's rotation angular velocity when the block reaches the outer edge?

88. ‖ A merry-go-round is a common piece of playground equipment. A 3.0-m-diameter merry-go-round with a mass of 250 kg is spinning at 20 rpm. John runs tangent to the merry-go-round at 5.0 m/s, in the same direction that it is turning, and jumps onto the outer edge. John's mass is 30 kg. What is the merry-go-round's angular velocity, in rpm, after John jumps on?

89. ‖ A 200 g toy car is placed on a narrow 60-cm-diameter track with wheel grooves that keep the car going in a circle. The 1.0 kg track is free to turn on a frictionless, vertical axis. The spokes have negligible mass. After the car's switch is turned on, it soon reaches a steady speed of 0.75 m/s relative to the track. What then is the track's angular velocity, in rpm?

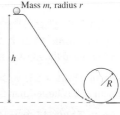

FIGURE P12.89

90. ‖ A 45 kg figure skater is spinning on the toes of her skates at 1.0 rev/s. Her arms are outstretched as far as they will go. In this orientation, the skater can be modeled as a cylindrical torso (40 kg, 20 cm average diameter, 160 cm tall) plus two rod-like arms (2.5 kg each, 66 cm long) attached to the outside of the torso. The skater then raises her arms straight above her head, where she appears to be a 45 kg, 20-cm-diameter, 200-cm-tall cylinder. What is her new rotation frequency, in revolutions per second?

Challenge Problems

91. The marble rolls down a track and around a loop-the-loop of radius R. The marble has mass m and radius r. What minimum height h must the track have for the marble to make it around the loop-the-loop without falling off?

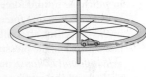

FIGURE CP12.91

92. **FIGURE CP12.92** shows a triangular block of Swiss cheese sitting on a cheese board. You and your friends start to wonder what will happen if you slowly tilt the board, increasing angle θ. Emily thinks the cheese will start to slide before it topples over. Fred thinks it will topple before starting to slide. Some quick Internet research on your part reveals that the coefficient of static friction of Swiss cheese on wood is 0.90. Who is right?

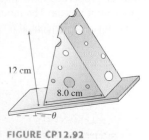

FIGURE CP12.92

93. ‖ A cube of mass m slides without friction at speed v_0. It undergoes a perfectly elastic collision with the bottom tip of a rod of length d and mass $M = 2m$. The rod is pivoted about a frictionless axle through its center, and initially it hangs straight down and is at rest. What is the cube's velocity—both speed and direction—after the collision?

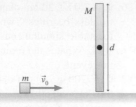

FIGURE CP12.93

94. A 75 g, 30-cm-long rod hangs vertically on a frictionless, horizontal axle passing through its center. A 10 g ball of clay traveling horizontally at 2.5 m/s hits and sticks to the very bottom tip of the rod. To what maximum angle, measured from vertical, does the rod (with the attached ball of clay) rotate?

95. During most of its lifetime, a star maintains an equilibrium size in which the inward force of gravity on each atom is balanced by an outward pressure force due to the heat of the nuclear reactions in the core. But after all the hydrogen "fuel" is consumed by nuclear fusion, the pressure force drops and the star undergoes a *gravitational collapse* until it becomes a *neutron star*. In a neutron star, the electrons and protons of the atoms are squeezed together by gravity until they fuse into neutrons. Neutron stars spin very rapidly and emit intense pulses of radio and light waves, one pulse per rotation. These "pulsing stars" were discovered in the 1960s and are called *pulsars*.

    a. A star with the mass ($M = 2.0 \times 10^{30}$ kg) and size ($R = 7.0 \times 10^8$ m) of our sun rotates once every 30 days. After undergoing gravitational collapse, the star forms a pulsar that is observed by astronomers to emit radio pulses every 0.10 s. By treating the neutron star as a solid sphere, deduce its radius.

    b. What is the speed of a point on the equator of the neutron star? Your answer will be somewhat too large because a star cannot be accurately modeled as a solid sphere. Even so, you will be able to show that a star, whose mass is 10^6 larger than the earth's, can be compressed by gravitational forces to a size smaller than a typical state in the United States!

96. A physics professor stands at rest on a 5.0 kg, 50-cm-diameter frictionless turntable. His assistant has a 64-cm-diameter bicycle wheel to which 4.0 kg of lead weights have been added around the rim. Handles extend outward from the axis so that the wheel can be held as it spins. The assistant spins the wheel to 180 rpm and holds it in a horizontal plane (the rotation axis is vertical) such that the rotation is ccw as seen from the ceiling. He then hands the spinning wheel to the professor.

    a. When the professor takes the wheel by the handles and the assistant lets go, does anything happen to the professor? If so, *describe* the professor's motion and *calculate* any relevant numerical quantities. If not, explain why not.

    b. Then the professor turns the spinning wheel over 180° so that the handle that had been pointing toward the ceiling now points toward the floor. Does anything happen to the professor? If so, *describe* the professor's motion and *calculate* any relevant numerical quantities. If not, explain why not.

    Hint: You'll need to *model* both the professor and the wheel. The professor has a total mass of 75 kg. His legs and torso are 70 kg. They have an average diameter of 25 cm and a height of 180 cm. His arms are 2.5 kg each, and he holds the handles of the wheel 45 cm from the center of his body. Don't forget that the wheel both spins *and* moves with the professor.

STOP TO THINK ANSWERS

Stop to Think 12.1: d. ω is negative because the rotation is cw. Because ω is negative and becoming *more* negative, the change $\Delta\omega$ is also negative. So α is negative.

Stop to Think 12.2: $I_a > I_d > I_b > I_c$. The moment of inertia is smaller when the mass is more concentrated near the rotation axis.

Stop to Think 12.3: $\tau_e > \tau_a = \tau_d > \tau_b > \tau_c$. The tangential component in e is larger than 2 N.

Stop to Think 12.4: $\alpha_b > \alpha_a > \alpha_c = \alpha_d = \alpha_e$. Angular acceleration is proportional to torque and inversely proportional to the moment of inertia. The moment of inertia depends on the *square* of the radius. The tangential force component in e is the same as in d.

Stop to Think 12.5: c > d > a = b. To keep the meter stick in equilibrium, the student must supply a torque equal and opposite to the torque due to the hanging masses. Torque depends on the mass *and* on how far the mass is from the pivot point.

Stop to Think 12.6: d. There is no net torque on the bucket + rain system, so the angular momentum is conserved. The addition of mass on the outer edge of the circle increases I, so ω must decrease. Mechanical energy is not conserved because the raindrop collisions are inelastic.

13 Newton's Theory of Gravity

The beautiful rings of Saturn consist of countless centimeter-sized ice crystals, all orbiting the planet under the influence of gravity.

▶ **Looking Ahead**

The goal of Chapter 13 is to use Newton's theory of gravity to understand the motion of satellites and planets. In this chapter you will learn to:

- Place Newton's discovery of the law of gravity in historical context.
- Use Newton's theory of gravity to solve problems about orbital motion.
- Understand Kepler's laws of planetary orbits.
- Understand and use gravitational potential energy.

◀ **Looking Back**

Newton's theory of gravity depends on uniform circular motion. Please review:

- Section 6.3 Gravity and weight.
- Sections 8.3 and 8.4 Uniform circular motion and circular orbits.
- Section 10.2 Gravitational potential energy.
- Section 12.10 Angular momentum.

Every ancient culture was fascinated with the motion of the heavens above. Without city lights or urban haze, the nighttime sky and the daytime sun were ever-present, powerful experiences. The unknown people who built Stonehenge clearly used it as a solar observatory, and the ancient Babylonians learned to predict the occurrence of solar eclipses.

Our fascination with the sky and the stars has not diminished in the 21st century. Today our interest may be in galaxies, black holes, and the Big Bang, but we're still exploring the heavens. One of the most important discoveries of science is that one pervasive force is dominant throughout the universe. This force is responsible for phenomena ranging from the orbiting space shuttle and solar eclipses to the dynamics of galaxies and the expansion of the universe. It is the force of gravity.

Newton's formulation of his theory of gravity was a pivotal event in the history of science. It was the first scientific theory to have broad explanatory and predictive power. Although Newton's theory is now over three centuries old, its importance has not diminished with time.

13.1 A Little History

The study of the structure of the universe is called **cosmology.** The ancient Greeks developed a cosmological model, illustrated in **FIGURE 13.1** on the next page, with the earth at the center of the universe while the moon, the sun, the planets, and the stars were points of light turning about the earth on large "celestial spheres." This viewpoint was further expanded by the second-century Egyptian astronomer Ptolemy (the

FIGURE 13.1 The earth-centered cosmology of the ancient Greek and medieval periods.

Sphere of Mars
Sphere of the sun
Sphere of Venus

Earth

P is silent). He developed an elaborate mathematical model of the solar system that quite accurately predicted the complex planetary motions.

Then, in 1543, the medieval world was turned on its head with the publication of Nicholas Copernicus's *De Revolutionibus*. Copernicus argued that it is not the earth at rest in the center of the universe—it is the sun! Furthermore, Copernicus asserted that all of the planets, including the earth, revolve about the sun (hence his title) in circular orbits. But not until many decades later, when Galileo used a telescope to study the heavens, did the Copernican view become widely accepted.

Tycho and Kepler

The greatest medieval astronomer was Tycho Brahe, a Dane born just three years after Copernicus's death. For 30 years, from 1570 to 1600, Tycho compiled the most accurate astronomical observations the world had known. The invention of the telescope was still to come, but Tycho developed ingenious mechanical sighting devices that allowed him to determine the positions of stars and planets in the sky with unprecedented accuracy.

Tycho had a young mathematical assistant named Johannes Kepler. Kepler had become one of the first outspoken defenders of Copernicus, and his goal was to find evidence for circular planetary orbits in Tycho's records. To appreciate the difficulty of this task, keep in mind that Kepler was working before the development of graphs or of calculus—and certainly before calculators! His mathematical tools were algebra, geometry, and trigonometry, and he was faced with thousands upon thousands of individual observations of planetary positions measured as angles above the horizon.

Many years of work led Kepler to discover that the orbits are not circles, as Copernicus claimed, but *ellipses.* Furthermore, the speed of a planet is not constant but varies as it moves around the ellipse.

Kepler's laws, as we call them today, state that

1. Planets move in elliptical orbits, with the sun at one focus of the ellipse.
2. A line drawn between the sun and a planet sweeps out equal areas during equal intervals of time.
3. The square of a planet's orbital period is proportional to the cube of the semimajor-axis length.

FIGURE 13.2a shows that an ellipse has two *foci* (plural of *focus*), and the sun occupies one of these. The long axis of the ellipse is the *major axis,* and half the length of this axis is called the *semimajor-axis length.* As the planet moves, a line drawn from the sun to the planet "sweeps out" an area. **FIGURE 13.2b** shows two such areas. Kepler's discovery that the areas are equal for equal Δt implies that the planet moves faster when near the sun, slower when farther away.

FIGURE 13.2 The elliptical orbit of a planet about the sun.

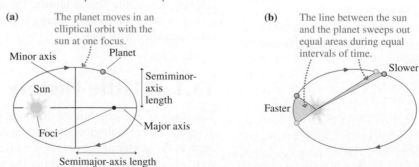

(a) The planet moves in an elliptical orbit with the sun at one focus.

Minor axis
Planet
Sun
Semiminor-axis length
Foci
Major axis
Semimajor-axis length

(b) The line between the sun and the planet sweeps out equal areas during equal intervals of time.

Slower
Faster

All the planets except Mercury and Pluto have elliptical orbits that are only very slightly distorted circles. As FIGURE 13.3 shows, a circle is an ellipse in which the two foci move to the center, effectively making one focus, and the semimajor-axis length becomes the radius. Because the mathematics of ellipses is difficult, this chapter will focus on circular orbits.

Kepler made an additional contribution that is less widely recognized but was essential to prepare the way for Newton. For Ptolemy and, later, Copernicus, the role of the sun was merely to light and warm the earth and planets. Kepler was the first to suggest that the sun was a center of force that somehow *caused* the planetary motions. Now, Kepler was working before Galileo and Newton, so he did not speak in terms of forces and centripetal accelerations. He thought that some type of rays or spirit emanated from the sun and pushed the planets around their orbits. The value of his contribution was not the specific mechanism he proposed but his introduction of the idea that the sun somehow exerts forces on the planets to determine their motion.

Kepler published the first two of his laws in 1609, the same year in which Galileo first turned a telescope to the heavens. Through his telescope Galileo could *see* moons orbiting Jupiter, just as Copernicus had suggested the planets orbit the sun. He could *see* that Venus has phases, like the moon, which implied its orbital motion about the sun. By the time of Galileo's death in 1642, the Copernican revolution was complete.

In hindsight, we can see that Kepler's analysis and Galileo's observations had set the stage for a major theoretical leap. All that was needed was a great intellect to recognize and pull together these ideas. Enter Isaac Newton, one of the most brilliant scientists ever to live.

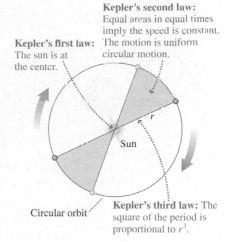

FIGURE 13.3 A circular orbit is a special case of an elliptical orbit.

Kepler's second law: Equal areas in equal times imply the speed is constant. The motion is uniform circular motion.

Kepler's first law: The sun is at the center.

Sun

Circular orbit

Kepler's third law: The square of the period is proportional to r^3.

13.2 Isaac Newton

Isaac Newton was born to a poor farming family in 1642, the year of Galileo's death. He entered Trinity College at Cambridge University at age 19 as a "subsizar," a poor student who had to work his way through school. Newton graduated in 1665, at age 23, just as an outbreak of the plague in England forced the universities to close for two years. He returned to his family farm for that period, during which he made important experimental discoveries in optics, laid the foundations for his theories of mechanics and gravitation, and made major progress toward his invention of calculus as a whole new branch of mathematics.

A popular image has Newton thinking of the idea of gravity after an apple fell on his head. This amusing story is at least close to the truth. Newton himself said that the "notion of gravitation" came to him as he "sat in a contemplative mood" and "was occasioned by the fall of an apple." It occurred to him that, perhaps, the apple was attracted to the *center* of the earth but was prevented from getting there by the earth's surface. And if the apple was so attracted, why not the moon?

Robert Hooke, discoverer of Hooke's law, had already suggested that the planets might be attracted to the sun with a strength proportional to the inverse square of the distance between the sun and the planet. This seems to have been a hunch rather than being based on any particular evidence, and Hooke failed to follow up on the idea. Newton's genius was not just his successful application of Hooke's suggestion, but his sudden realization that **the force of the sun on the planets was identical to the force of the earth on the apple.** In other words, gravitation is a *universal* force between all objects in the universe! This is not shocking today, but no one before Newton had ever thought that the mundane motion of objects on earth had any connection at all with the stately motion of the planets through the heavens.

Newton reasoned along the following lines. Suppose the moon's circular motion around the earth is due to the pull of the earth's gravity. Then, as you learned in Chapter 8 and is shown in FIGURE 13.4, the moon must be in *free fall* with the free-fall acceleration $g_{\text{at moon}}$.

Isaac Newton, 1642–1727.

FIGURE 13.4 The moon is in free fall around the earth.

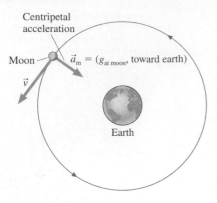

NOTE ▶ We need to be careful with notation. The symbol g_{moon} is the free-fall acceleration caused by the *moon's* gravity—that is, the acceleration of a falling object on the moon. Here we're interested in the acceleration *of* the moon by the earth's gravity, which we'll call $g_{at\ moon}$. ◀

The centripetal acceleration of an object in uniform circular motion is

$$a_r = g_{at\ moon} = \frac{v_m^2}{r_m} \tag{13.1}$$

The moon's speed is related to the radius r_m and period T_m of its orbit by $v_m =$ circumference/period $= 2\pi r_m/T_m$. Combining these, Newton found

$$g_{at\ moon} = \frac{4\pi^2 r_m}{T_m^2} = \frac{4\pi^2 (3.84 \times 10^8 \text{ m})}{(2.36 \times 10^6 \text{ s})^2} = 0.00272 \text{ m/s}^2$$

Astronomical measurements had established a reasonably good value for r_{moon} by the time of Newton, and the period $T_m = 27.3$ days was quite well known.

The moon's centripetal acceleration is significantly less than the free-fall acceleration on the earth's surface. In fact,

$$\frac{g_{at\ moon}}{g_{on\ earth}} = \frac{0.00272 \text{ m/s}^2}{9.80 \text{ m/s}^2} = \frac{1}{3600}$$

This is an interesting result, but it was Newton's next step that was critical. He compared the radius of the moon's orbit to the radius of the earth:

$$\frac{r_m}{R_e} = \frac{3.84 \times 10^8 \text{ m}}{6.37 \times 10^6 \text{ m}} = 60.2$$

NOTE ▶ We'll use a lowercase r, as in r_m, to indicate the radius of an orbit. We'll use an uppercase R, as in R_e, to indicate the radius of a star or planet. ◀

Newton recognized that $(60.2)^2$ is almost exactly 3600. Thus, he reasoned:

- If g has the value 9.80 at the earth's surface, and
- If the force of gravity and g decrease in size depending inversely on the square of the distance from the center of the earth,
- Then g will have exactly the value it needs at the distance of the moon to cause the moon to orbit the earth with a period of 27.3 days.

I deduced that the forces which keep the planets in their orbs must be reciprocally as the squares of their distances from the centers about which they revolve; and thereby compared the force requisite to keep the Moon in her orb with the force of gravity at the surface of the Earth; and found them answer pretty nearly.

Isaac Newton

His two ratios were not identical (because the earth isn't a perfect sphere and the moon's orbit isn't a perfect circle), but he found them to "answer pretty nearly" and knew that he had to be on the right track.

This flash of insight changed our most basic understanding of the universe. Copernicus displaced the earth from the center of the universe, and now Newton had shown that the laws of the heavens and the laws of earth are the same. Nonetheless, Newton did not publish his results for a long 22 years. The issue that troubled him was treating the sun, the earth, and the other planets as if they were single particles with all their mass at the center. If his idea about a universal force was correct, then *every atom* in the earth exerts a force on *every atom* in the moon. Newton had to show that all of these forces add up to give a result that is identical with treating the bodies as single particles. This is a problem in integral calculus, and Newton had first to develop the necessary mathematics. He did eventually succeed, and his theory of gravitation was published in 1687 along with his theory of mechanics (which we know as Newton's laws) in his great work *Philosophia Naturalis Principia Mathematica* (Mathematical Principles of Natural Philosophy). The rest is history.

A satellite orbits the earth with constant speed at a height above the surface equal to the earth's radius. The magnitude of the satellite's acceleration is

a. $4g_{\text{on earth}}$ b. $2g_{\text{on earth}}$ c. $g_{\text{on earth}}$

d. $\frac{1}{2}g_{\text{on earth}}$ e. $\frac{1}{4}g_{\text{on earth}}$ f. 0

13.3 Newton's Law of Gravity

Newton proposed that *every* object in the universe attracts *every other* object with a force that is

1. Inversely proportional to the square of the distance between the objects.
2. Directly proportional to the product of the masses of the two objects.

To make these ideas more specific, **FIGURE 13.5** shows masses m_1 and m_2 separated by distance r. Each mass exerts an attractive force on the other, a force that we call the **gravitational force.** These two forces form an action/reaction pair, so $\vec{F}_{1 \text{ on } 2}$ is equal and opposite to $\vec{F}_{2 \text{ on } 1}$. The magnitude of the forces is given by Newton's law of gravity.

FIGURE 13.5 The gravitational forces on masses m_1 and m_2.

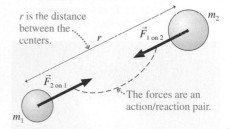

> **Newton's law of gravity** If two objects with masses m_1 and m_2 are a distance r apart, the objects exert attractive forces on each other of magnitude
>
> $$F_{1 \text{ on } 2} = F_{2 \text{ on } 1} = \frac{Gm_1m_2}{r^2} \qquad (13.2)$$
>
> The forces are directed along the straight line joining the two objects.

The constant G, called the **gravitational constant,** is a proportionality constant necessary to relate the masses, measured in kilograms, to the force, measured in newtons. In the SI system of units, G has the value

$$G = 6.67 \times 10^{-11} \, \text{N m}^2/\text{kg}^2$$

FIGURE 13.6 is a graph of the gravitational force as a function of the distance between the two masses. As you can see, an inverse-square force decreases rapidly.

Strictly speaking, Equation 13.2 is valid only for particles. As we noted, however, Newton was able to show that this equation also applies to spherical objects, such as planets, if r is the distance between their centers. Our intuition and common sense suggest this to us, as they did to Newton. The rather difficult proof is not essential, so we will omit it.

FIGURE 13.6 The gravitational force is an inverse-square force.

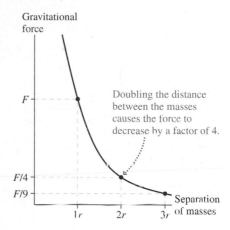

Gravitational Force and Weight

Knowing G, we can calculate the size of the gravitational force. Consider two 1.0 kg masses that are 1.0 m apart. According to Newton's law of gravity, these two masses exert an attractive gravitational force on each other of magnitude

$$F_{1 \text{ on } 2} = F_{2 \text{ on } 1} = \frac{Gm_1m_2}{r^2}$$

$$= \frac{(6.67 \times 10^{-11} \, \text{N m}^2/\text{kg}^2)(1.0 \, \text{kg})(1.0 \, \text{kg})}{(1.0 \, \text{m})^2} = 6.67 \times 10^{-11} \, \text{N}$$

This is an exceptionally tiny force, especially when compared to the gravitational force of the entire earth on each mass: $F_G = mg = 9.8$ N.

The fact that the gravitational force between two ordinary-size objects is so small is the reason we are not aware of it. As you sit there reading, you are being attracted to this book, to the person sitting next to you, and to every object around you, but the forces are so tiny in comparison to the normal forces and friction forces acting on you that they are completely undetectable. Only when one (or both) of the masses is exceptionally large—planet-size—does the force of gravity become important.

We find a more respectable result if we calculate the force *of the earth* on a 1.0 kg mass at the earth's surface:

$$F_{\text{earth on 1 kg}} = \frac{GM_e m_{1\,\text{kg}}}{R_e^2}$$

$$= \frac{(6.67 \times 10^{-11}\,\text{N}\,\text{m}^2/\text{kg}^2)(5.98 \times 10^{24}\,\text{kg})(1.0\,\text{kg})}{(6.37 \times 10^6\,\text{m})^2} = 9.8\,\text{N}$$

where the distance between the mass and the center of the earth is the earth's radius. The earth's mass M_e and radius R_e were taken from Table 13.2 in Section 13.6. This table, which is also printed inside the back cover of the book, contains astronomical data that will be used for examples and homework.

The force $F_{\text{earth on 1 kg}} = 9.8$ N is exactly the weight of a stationary 1.0 kg mass: $F_G = mg = 9.8$ N. Is this a coincidence? Of course not. Weight—the upward force of a spring scale—exactly balances the downward gravitational force, so numerically they must be equal.

Although weak, gravity is a *long-range* force. No matter how far apart two objects may be, there is a gravitational attraction between them given by Equation 13.2. Consequently, gravity is the most ubiquitous force in the universe. It not only keeps your feet on the ground, it also keeps the earth orbiting the sun, the solar system orbiting the center of the Milky Way galaxy, and the entire Milky Way galaxy performing an intricate orbital dance with other galaxies making up what is called the "local cluster" of galaxies.

The dynamics of stellar motions, spanning many thousands of light years, are governed by Newton's law of gravity.

A galaxy of $\approx 10^{11}$ stars spanning a distance greater than 100,000 light years.

The Principle of Equivalence

Newton's law of gravity depends on a rather curious assumption. The concept of *mass* was introduced in Chapter 4 by considering the relationship between force and acceleration. The *inertial mass* of an object, which is the mass that appears in Newton's second law, is found by measuring the object's acceleration a in response to force F:

$$m_{\text{inert}} = \text{inertial mass} = \frac{F}{a} \tag{13.3}$$

Gravity plays no role in this definition of mass.

The quantities m_1 and m_2 in Newton's law of gravity are being used in a very different way. Masses m_1 and m_2 govern the strength of the gravitational attraction between two objects. The mass used in Newton's law of gravity is called the **gravitational mass.** The gravitational mass of an object can be determined by measuring the attractive force exerted on it by another mass M a distance r away:

$$m_{\text{grav}} = \text{gravitational mass} = \frac{r^2 F_{M\,\text{on}\,m}}{GM} \tag{13.4}$$

Acceleration does not enter into the definition of the gravitational mass.

These are two very different concepts of mass. Yet Newton, in his theory of gravity, asserts that the inertial mass in his second law is the very same mass that governs the strength of the gravitational attraction between two objects. The assertion that $m_{\text{grav}} = m_{\text{inert}}$ is called the **principle of equivalence.** It says that inertial mass is *equivalent to* gravitational mass.

As a hypothesis about nature, the principle of equivalence is subject to experimental verification or disproof. Many exceptionally clever experiments have looked for any difference between the gravitational mass and the inertial mass, and they have shown that any difference, if it exists at all, is less than 10 parts in a trillion! As far as we know today, the gravitational mass and the inertial mass are exactly the same thing.

But why should a quantity associated with the dynamics of motion, relating force to acceleration, have anything at all to do with the gravitational attraction? This is a question that intrigued Einstein and eventually led to his general theory of relativity, the theory about curved space-time and black holes. General relativity is beyond the scope of this textbook, but it explains the principle of equivalence as a property of space itself.

Newton's Theory of Gravity

Newton's theory of gravity is more than just Equation 13.2. The *theory* of gravity consists of:

1. A specific force law for gravity, given by Equation 13.2, *and*
2. The principle of equivalence, *and*
3. An assertion that Newton's three laws of motion are universally applicable. These laws are as valid for heavenly bodies, the planets and stars, as for earthly objects.

Consequently, everything we have learned about forces, motion, and energy is relevant to the dynamics of satellites, planets, and galaxies.

STOP TO THINK 13.2   The figure shows a binary star system. The mass of star 2 is twice the mass of star 1. Compared to $\vec{F}_{1 \text{ on } 2}$, the magnitude of the force $\vec{F}_{2 \text{ on } 1}$ is

a. Four times as big.
b. Twice as big.
c. The same size.
d. Half as big.
e. One-quarter as big.

m_1

$\vec{F}_{2 \text{ on } 1}$

m_2

13.4 Little *g* and Big *G*

The familiar equation $F_G = mg$ works well when an object is on the surface of a planet, but mg will not help us find the force exerted on the same object if it is in orbit around the planet. Neither can we use mg to find the force of attraction between the earth and the moon. Newton's law of gravity provides a more fundamental starting point because it describes a *universal* force that exists between all objects.

To illustrate the connection between Newton's law of gravity and the familiar $F_G = mg$, **FIGURE 13.7** shows an object of mass m on the surface of Planet X. Planet X inhabitant Mr. Xhzt, standing on the surface, finds that the downward gravitational force is $F_G = mg_X$, where g_X is the free-fall acceleration on Planet X.

We, taking a more cosmic perspective, reply, "Yes, that is the force *because* of a universal force of attraction between your planet and the object. The size of the force is determined by Newton's law of gravity."

We and Mr. Xhzt are both correct. Whether you think locally or globally, we and Mr. Xhzt must arrive at the *same numerical value* for the magnitude of the force. Suppose an object of mass m is on the surface of a planet of mass M and radius R. The local gravitational force is

$$F_G = mg_{\text{surface}} \tag{13.5}$$

where g_{surface} is the acceleration due to gravity at the planet's surface. The force of gravitational attraction for an object on the surface ($r = R$), as given by Newton's law of gravity, is

$$F_{M \text{ on } m} = \frac{GMm}{R^2} \tag{13.6}$$

FIGURE 13.7 Weighing an object of mass m on Planet X.

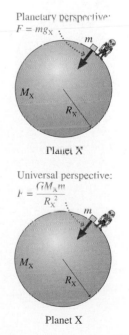

Planetary perspective:
$F = mg_X$

M_X

R_X

Planet X

Universal perspective:
$F = \dfrac{GM_X m}{R_X^2}$

M_X

R_X

Planet X

Because these are two names and two expressions for the same force, we can equate the right-hand sides to find that

$$g_{\text{surface}} = \frac{GM}{R^2} \qquad (13.7)$$

We have used Newton's law of gravity to *predict* the value of g at the surface of a planet. The value depends on the mass and radius of the planet as well as on the value of G, which establishes the overall strength of the gravitational force.

The expression for g_{surface} in Equation 13.7 is valid for any planet or star. Using the mass and radius of Mars (planetary data are found later in this chapter, in Table 13.2, and inside the back cover of the book), we can predict the Martian value of g:

$$g_{\text{Mars}} = \frac{GM_{\text{Mars}}}{R_{\text{Mars}}^2} = \frac{(6.67 \times 10^{-11} \, \text{Nm}^2/\text{kg}^2)(6.42 \times 10^{23} \, \text{kg})}{(3.37 \times 10^6 \, \text{m})^2} = 3.8 \, \text{m/s}^2$$

NOTE ▶ We noted in Chapter 6 that measured values of g are very slightly smaller on a rotating planet. We'll ignore rotation in this chapter. ◀

Decrease of *g* with Distance

Equation 13.7 gives g_{surface} at the surface of a planet. More generally, imagine an object of mass m at distance $r > R$ from the center of a planet. Further, suppose that gravity from the planet is the only force acting on the object. Then its acceleration, the free-fall acceleration, is given by Newton's second law:

$$g = \frac{F_{M \, \text{on} \, m}}{m} = \frac{GM}{r^2} \qquad (13.8)$$

This more general result agrees with Equation 13.7 if $r = R$, but it allows us to determine the "local" free-fall acceleration at distances $r > R$. Equation 13.8 expresses Newton's discovery, with regard to the moon, that g decreases inversely with the square of the distance.

FIGURE 13.8 shows a satellite orbiting at height h above the earth's surface. Its distance from the center of the earth is $r = R_e + h$. Most people have a mental image that satellites orbit "far" from the earth, but in reality h is typically 200 miles $\approx$ 3×10^5 m, while $R_e = 6.37 \times 10^6$ m. Thus the satellite is barely "skimming" the earth at a height only about 5% of the earth's radius!

The value of g at height h above the earth is

$$g = \frac{GM_e}{(R_e + h)^2} = \frac{GM_e}{R_e^2(1 + h/R_e)^2} = \frac{g_{\text{earth}}}{(1 + h/R_e)^2} \qquad (13.9)$$

where $g_{\text{earth}} = 9.83 \, \text{m/s}^2$ is the value calculated from Equation 13.7 for $h = 0$ on a nonrotating earth. Table 13.1 shows the value of g evaluated at several values of h.

FIGURE 13.8 A satellite orbits the earth at height h.

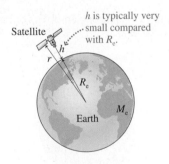

Satellite

h is typically very small compared with R_e.

r
h
R_e
Earth
M_e

TABLE 13.1 Variation of g with height above the ground

Height h	Example	g (m/s²)
0 m	ground	9.83
4500 m	Mt. Whitney	9.82
10,000 m	jet airplane	9.80
300,000 m	space shuttle	8.90
35,900,000 m	communications satellite	0.22

NOTE ▶ The free-fall acceleration of a satellite such as the space shuttle is only slightly less than the ground-level value. An object in orbit is not "weightless" because there is no gravity in space but because it is in free fall, as you learned in Chapter 8. ◀

Weighing the Earth

We can predict g if we know the earth's mass. But how do we know the value of M_e? We cannot place the earth on a giant pan balance, so how is its mass known? Furthermore, how do we know the value of G? These are interesting and important questions.

Newton did not know the value of G. He could say that the gravitational force is proportional to the product m_1m_2 and inversely proportional to r^2, but he had no means of knowing the value of the proportionality constant.

Determining G requires a *direct* measurement of the gravitational force between two known masses at a known separation. The small size of the gravitational force between ordinary-size objects makes this quite a feat. Yet the English scientist Henry Cavendish came up with an ingenious way of doing so with a device called a *torsion balance*. Two fairly small masses m, typically about 10 g, are placed on the ends of a lightweight rod. The rod is hung from a thin fiber, as shown in FIGURE 13.9a, and allowed to reach equilibrium.

If the rod is then rotated slightly and released, a *restoring force* will return it to equilibrium. This is analogous to displacing a spring from equilibrium, and in fact the restoring force and the angle of displacement obey a version of Hooke's law: $F_{restore} = k\Delta\theta$. The "torsion constant" k can be determined by timing the period of oscillations. Once k is known, a force that twists the rod slightly away from equilibrium can be measured by the product $k\Delta\theta$. It is possible to measure very small angular deflections, so this device can be used to determine very small forces.

Two larger masses M (typically lead spheres with $M \approx 10$ kg) are then brought close to the torsion balance, as shown in FIGURE 13.9b. The gravitational attraction that they exert on the smaller hanging masses causes a very small but measurable twisting of the balance, enough to measure $F_{M \text{ on } m}$. Because m, M, and r are all known, Cavendish was able to determine G from

$$G = \frac{F_{M \text{ on } m} r^2}{Mm} \qquad (13.10)$$

His first results were not highly accurate, but improvements over the years in this and similar experiments have produced the value of G accepted today.

With an independently determined value of G, we can return to Equation 13.7 to find

$$M_e = \frac{g_{earth} R_e^2}{G} \qquad (13.11)$$

We have weighed the earth! The value of g_{earth} at the earth's surface is known with great accuracy from kinematics experiments. The earth's radius R_e is determined by surveying techniques. Combining our knowledge from these very different measurements has given us a way to determine the mass of the earth.

The free-fall acceleration g is nearly constant on the surface of any given planet, but is different for each planet. The gravitational constant G is a constant of a different nature. It is what we call a *universal constant*. Its value establishes the strength of one of the fundamental forces of nature. As far as we know, the gravitational force between two masses would be the same anywhere in the universe. Universal constants tell us something about the most basic and fundamental properties of nature. You will soon meet other universal constants.

FIGURE 13.9 Cavendish's experiment to measure G.

(a)
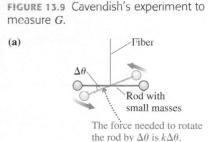

The force needed to rotate the rod by $\Delta\theta$ is $k\Delta\theta$.

(b)
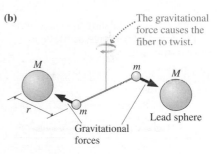

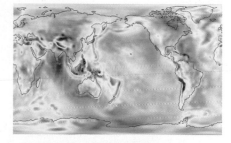

The free-fall acceleration varies slightly due to mountains and to variation in the density of the earth's crust. This map shows the *gravitational anomaly*, with red regions of slightly stronger gravity and blue regions of slightly weaker gravity. The variation is tiny, less than 0.001 m/s².

STOP TO THINK 13.3 A planet has four times the mass of the earth, but the acceleration due to gravity on the planet's surface is the same as on the earth's surface. The planet's radius is

a. $4R_e$ b. $2R_e$ c. R_e d. $\frac{1}{2}R_e$ e. $\frac{1}{4}R_e$

13.5 Gravitational Potential Energy

Gravitational problems are ideal for the conservation-law tools we developed in Chapters 9 through 11. Because gravity is the only force, and it is a conservative force, both the momentum and the mechanical energy of the system $m_1 + m_2$ are conserved. To employ conservation of energy, however, we need to determine an appropriate form for the gravitational potential energy for two particles interacting via Newton's law of gravity.

The definition of potential energy that we developed in Chapter 11 is

$$\Delta U = U_f - U_i = -W_c(i \rightarrow f) \tag{13.12}$$

where $W_c(i \rightarrow f)$ is the work done by a conservative force as a particle moves from position i to position f. Strictly speaking, this defines only ΔU, the *change* in potential energy. To find an explicit expression for U, we must choose a zero point of the potential energy.

For a flat earth, we used $F = -mg$ and the choice that $U = 0$ at the surface ($y = 0$) to arrive at the now-familiar $U_g = mgy$. This result for U_g is valid only for $y \ll R_e$, when the earth's curvature and size are not apparent. We now need to find an expression for the gravitational potential energy of masses that interact over *large* distances.

FIGURE 13.10 shows two particles of mass m_1 and m_2. Let's calculate the work done on mass m_2 by the conservative force $\vec{F}_{1 \text{ on } 2}$ as m_2 moves from an initial position at distance r to a final position very far away. The force, which points to the left, is opposite the displacement; hence this force does *negative* work. Consequently, due to the minus sign in Equation 13.12, ΔU is *positive*. A pair of masses *gains* potential energy as the masses move farther apart, just as a particle near the earth's surface gains potential energy as it moves to a higher altitude.

We can establish a coordinate system with m_1 at the origin and m_2 moving along the x-axis. The gravitational force is a variable force, so we need the full definition of work:

$$W(i \rightarrow f) = \int_{x_i}^{x_f} F_x \, dx \tag{13.13}$$

$\vec{F}_{1 \text{ on } 2}$ points toward the left, so its x-component is $(F_{1 \text{ on } 2})_x = -Gm_1m_2/x^2$. As mass m_2 moves from $x_i = r$ to $x_f = \infty$, the potential energy changes by

$$\Delta U = U_{\text{at }\infty} - U_{\text{at }r} = -\int_r^\infty (F_{1 \text{ on } 2})_x \, dx = -\int_r^\infty \left(\frac{-Gm_1m_2}{x^2} \right) dx$$

$$= +Gm_1m_2 \int_r^\infty \frac{dx}{x^2} = -\left. \frac{Gm_1m_2}{x} \right|_r^\infty = \frac{Gm_1m_2}{r} \tag{13.14}$$

NOTE ▶ We chose to integrate along the x-axis, but the fact that gravity is a conservative force means that ΔU will have this value if m_2 moves from r to ∞ along *any* path. ◀

To proceed further, we need to choose the point where $U = 0$. We would like our choice to be valid for any star or planet, regardless of its mass and radius. This will be the case if we set $U = 0$ at the point where the interaction between the masses vanishes. According to Newton's law of gravity, the strength of the interaction is zero only when $r = \infty$. Two masses infinitely far apart will have no tendency, or potential, to move together, so we will *choose* to place the zero point of potential energy at $r = \infty$. That is, $U_{\text{at }\infty} = 0$.

This choice gives us the gravitational potential energy of masses m_1 and m_2:

$$U_g = -\frac{Gm_1m_2}{r} \tag{13.15}$$

This is the potential energy of masses m_1 and m_2 when their *centers* are separated by distance r. **FIGURE 13.11** is a graph of U_g as a function of the distance r between the masses. Notice that it asymptotically approaches 0 as $r \rightarrow \infty$.

FIGURE 13.10 Calculating the work done by the gravitational force as mass m_2 moves from r to ∞.

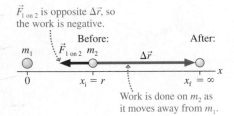

$\vec{F}_{1 \text{ on } 2}$ is opposite $\Delta \vec{r}$, so the work is negative.

Before: After:

m_1 $\vec{F}_{1 \text{ on } 2}$ m_2 $\Delta \vec{r}$

0 $x_i = r$ $x_f = \infty$

Work is done on m_2 as it moves away from m_1.

FIGURE 13.11 The gravitational potential-energy curve.

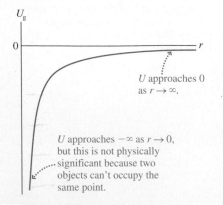

U_g

0 r

U approaches 0 as $r \rightarrow \infty$.

U approaches $-\infty$ as $r \rightarrow 0$, but this is not physically significant because two objects can't occupy the same point.

NOTE ▶ Although Equation 13.15 looks rather similar to Newton's law of gravity, it depends only on $1/r$, *not* on $1/r^2$. ◀

It may seem disturbing that the potential energy is negative, but we encountered similar situations in Chapter 10. All a negative potential energy means is that the potential energy of the two masses at separation r is *less* than their potential energy at infinite separation. It is only the *change* in U that has physical significance, and the change will be the same no matter where we place the zero of potential energy.

Suppose two masses a distance r_1 apart are released from rest. How will they move? From a force perspective, you would note that each mass experiences an attractive force and accelerates toward the other. The energy perspective of **FIGURE 13.12** tells us the same thing. By moving toward smaller r (that is, $r_1 \rightarrow r_2$), the system *loses* potential energy and *gains* kinetic energy while conserving E_{mech}. The system is "falling downhill," although in a more general sense than we think about on a flat earth.

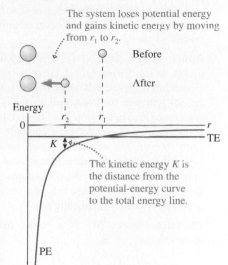

The system loses potential energy and gains kinetic energy by moving from r_1 to r_2.

The kinetic energy K is the distance from the potential-energy curve to the total energy line.

EXAMPLE 13.1 Crashing into the sun

Suppose the earth were suddenly to cease revolving around the sun. The gravitational force would then pull it directly into the sun. What would be the earth's speed as it crashed?

MODEL Model the earth and the sun as spherical masses. This is an isolated system, so its mechanical energy is conserved.

VISUALIZE **FIGURE 13.13** is a before-and-after pictorial representation for this gruesome cosmic event. The "crash" occurs as the earth touches the sun, at which point the distance between their centers is $r_2 = R_s + R_e$. The initial separation r_1 is the radius of the earth's *orbit* about the sun, not the radius of the earth.

FIGURE 13.13 Before-and-after pictorial representation of the earth crashing into the sun (not to scale).

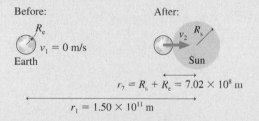

Before:

R_e

$v_1 = 0$ m/s

Earth

After:

v_2 R_s

Sun

$r_2 = R_s + R_e = 7.02 \times 10^8$ m

$r_1 = 1.50 \times 10^{11}$ m

SOLVE Strictly speaking, the kinetic energy is the sum $K = K_{\text{earth}} + K_{\text{sun}}$. However, the sun is so much more massive than the earth that the lightweight earth does almost all of the moving. It is a reasonable approximation to consider the sun as remaining at rest. In that case, the energy conservation equation $K_2 + U_2 = K_1 + U_1$ is

$$\frac{1}{2}M_e v_2^2 - \frac{GM_s M_e}{R_s + R_e} = 0 - \frac{GM_s M_e}{r_1}$$

This is easily solved for the earth's speed at impact. Using data from Table 13.2, we find

$$v_2 = \sqrt{2GM_s\left(\frac{1}{R_s + R_e} - \frac{1}{r_1}\right)} = 6.13 \times 10^5 \text{ m/s}$$

ASSESS The earth would be really flying along at over 1 million miles per hour as it crashed into the sun! It is worth noting that we do not have the mathematical tools to solve this problem using Newton's second law because the acceleration is not constant. But the solution is straightforward when we use energy conservation.

EXAMPLE 13.2 Escape speed

A 1000 kg rocket is fired straight away from the surface of the earth. What speed does the rocket need to "escape" from the gravitational pull of the earth and never return? Assume a nonrotating earth.

MODEL In a simple universe, consisting of only the earth and the rocket, an insufficient launch speed will cause the rocket eventually to fall back to earth. Once the rocket finally slows to a halt, gravity will ever so slowly pull it back. The only way the rocket can escape is to never stop ($v = 0$) and thus never have a turning point! That is, the rocket must continue moving away from the earth forever. The *minimum* launch speed for escape, which is called the **escape speed,** will cause the rocket to stop ($v = 0$) only as it reaches $r = \infty$. Now ∞, of course, is not a "place," so a statement like this means that we want the rocket's speed to approach $v = 0$ asymptotically as $r \rightarrow \infty$.

VISUALIZE FIGURE 13.14 is a before-and-after pictorial representation.

SOLVE Energy conservation $K_2 + U_2 = K_1 + U_1$ is

$$0 + 0 = \frac{1}{2}mv_1^2 - \frac{GM_em}{R_e}$$

where we used the fact that both the kinetic and potential energy are zero at $r = \infty$. Thus the escape speed is

$$v_{escape} = v_1 = \sqrt{\frac{2GM_e}{R_e}} = 11{,}200 \text{ m/s} \approx 25{,}000 \text{ mph}$$

ASSESS The problem was mathematically easy; the difficulty was deciding how to interpret it. That is why—as you have now seen many times—the "physics" of a problem consists of thinking, interpreting, and modeling. We will see variations on this problem in the future, with both gravity and electricity, so you might want to review the *reasoning* involved. Notice that the answer does *not* depend on the rocket's mass, so this is the escape speed for any object.

FIGURE 13.14 Pictorial representation of a rocket launched with sufficient speed to escape the earth's gravity.

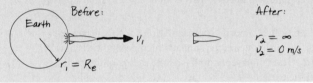

The Flat-Earth Approximation

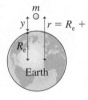

FIGURE 13.15 We can treat the earth as flat if $y \ll R_e$.

For a spherical earth:

$$U_g = -\frac{GM_em}{R_e + y}$$

We can treat the earth as flat if $y \ll R_e$:

$$U_g = mgy$$

How does Equation 13.15 for the gravitational potential energy relate to our previous use of $U_g = mgy$ on a flat earth? **FIGURE 13.15** shows an object of mass m located at height y above the surface of the earth. The object's distance from the earth's center is $r = R_e + y$ and its gravitational potential energy is

$$U_g = -\frac{GM_em}{r} = -\frac{GM_em}{R_e + y} = -\frac{GM_em}{R_e(1 + y/R_e)} \qquad (13.16)$$

where, in the last step, we factored R_e out of the denominator.

Suppose the object is very close to the earth's surface ($y \ll R_e$). In that case, the ratio $y/R_e \ll 1$. There is an approximation you will learn about in calculus, called the *binomial approximation,* that says

$$(1 + x)^n \approx 1 + nx \qquad \text{if } x \ll 1 \qquad (13.17)$$

As an illustration, you can easily use your calculator to find that $1/1.01 = 0.9901$, to four significant figures. But suppose you wrote $1.01 = 1 + 0.01$. You could then use the binomial approximation to calculate

$$\frac{1}{1.01} = \frac{1}{1 + 0.01} = (1 + 0.01)^{-1} \approx 1 + (-1)(0.01) = 0.9900$$

You can see that the approximate answer is off by only 0.01%.

If we call $y/R_e = x$ in Equation 13.16 and use the binomial approximation, with $n = -1$, we find

$$U_g(\text{if } y \ll R_e) \approx -\frac{GM_em}{R_e}\left(1 - \frac{y}{R_e}\right) = -\frac{GM_em}{R_e} + m\left(\frac{GM_e}{R_e^2}\right)y \qquad (13.18)$$

Now the first term is just the gravitational potential energy U_0 when the object is at ground level ($y = 0$). In the second term, you can recognize $GM_e/R_e^2 = g_{earth}$ from the definition of g in Equation 13.7. Thus we can write Equation 13.18 as

$$U_g(\text{if } y \ll R_e) = U_0 + mg_{earth}y \qquad (13.19)$$

Although we chose U_g to be zero when $r = \infty$, we are always free to change our minds. If we change the zero point of potential energy to be $U_0 = 0$ at the surface, which is the choice we made in Chapter 10, then Equation 13.19 becomes

$$U_g(\text{if } y \ll R_e) = mg_{earth}y \qquad (13.20)$$

We can sleep easier knowing that Equation 13.15 for the gravitational potential energy is consistent with our earlier "flat-earth" expression for the potential energy when $y \ll R_e$.

EXAMPLE 13.3 The speed of a satellite

A less-than-successful inventor wants to launch small satellites into orbit by launching them straight up from the surface of the earth at very high speed.

a. With what speed should he launch the satellite if it is to have a speed of 500 m/s at a height of 400 km? Ignore air resistance.
b. By what percentage would your answer be in error if you used a flat-earth approximation?

MODEL Mechanical energy is conserved if we ignore drag.

VISUALIZE FIGURE 13.16 shows a pictorial representation.

FIGURE 13.16 Pictorial representation of a satellite launched straight up.

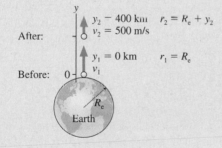

SOLVE a. Although the height is exaggerated in the figure, 400 km = 400,000 m is high enough that we cannot ignore the earth's spherical shape. The energy conservation equation $K_2 + U_2 = K_1 + U_1$ is

$$\frac{1}{2}mv_2^2 - \frac{GM_em}{R_e + y_2} = \frac{1}{2}mv_1^2 - \frac{GM_em}{R_e + y_1}$$

where we've written the distance between the satellite and the earth's center as $r = R_e + y$. The initial height is $y_1 = 0$. Notice that the satellite mass m cancels and is not needed. Solving for the launch speed, we have

$$v_1 = \sqrt{v_2^2 + 2GM_e\left(\frac{1}{R_e} - \frac{1}{R_e + y_2}\right)} = 2770 \text{ m/s}$$

This is about 6000 mph, much less than the escape speed.

b. The calculation is the same in the flat-earth approximation except that we use $U_g = mgy$. Thus

$$\frac{1}{2}mv_2^2 + mgy_2 = \frac{1}{2}mv_1^2 + mgy_1$$

$$v_1 = \sqrt{v_2^2 + 2gy_2} = 2840 \text{ m/s}$$

The flat-earth value of 2840 m/s is 70 m/s too big. The error, as a percentage of the correct 2770 m/s, is

$$\text{error} = \frac{70}{2770} \times 100 = 2.5\%$$

ASSESS The true speed is less than the flat-earth approximation because the force of gravity decreases with height. Launching a rocket against a decreasing force takes less effort than it would with the flat-earth force of mg at all heights.

STOP TO THINK 13.4   Rank in order, from largest to smallest, the absolute values of the gravitational potential energies of these pairs of masses. The numbers give the relative masses and distances.

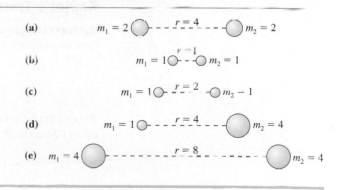

13.6 Satellite Orbits and Energies

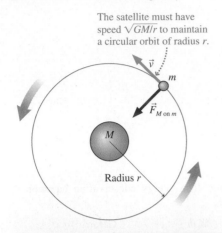

The satellite must have speed $\sqrt{GM/r}$ to maintain a circular orbit of radius r.

$\vec{v}$

m

$\vec{F}_{M \text{ on } m}$

M

Radius r

The International Space Station appears to be floating, but it's actually traveling at nearly 8000 m/s as it orbits the earth.

Solving Newton's second law to find the trajectory of a mass moving under the influence of gravity is mathematically beyond this textbook. It turns out that the solution is a set of elliptical orbits. This is Kepler's first law, which he discovered empirically by analyzing Tycho Brahe's observations. Kepler had no *reason* why orbits should be ellipses rather than some other shape. Newton was able to show that ellipses are a *consequence* of his theory of gravity.

The mathematics of ellipses is rather difficult, so we will restrict most of our analysis to the limiting case in which an ellipse becomes a circle. Most planetary orbits differ only very slightly from being circular. The earth's orbit, for example has a (semiminor axis/semimajor axis) ratio of 0.99986—very close to a true circle!

FIGURE 13.17 shows a massive body M, such as the earth or the sun, with a lighter body m orbiting it. The lighter body is called a **satellite,** even though it may be a planet orbiting the sun. Newton's second law for the satellite is

$$F_{M \text{ on } m} = \frac{GMm}{r^2} = ma_r = \frac{mv^2}{r} \tag{13.21}$$

Thus the speed of a satellite in a circular orbit is

$$v = \sqrt{\frac{GM}{r}} \tag{13.22}$$

A satellite must have this specific speed in order to have a circular orbit of radius r about the larger mass M. If the velocity differs from this value, the orbit will become elliptical rather than circular. Notice that the orbital speed does *not* depend on the satellite's mass m. This is consistent with our previous discovery, for motion on a flat earth, that motion due to gravity is independent of the mass.

EXAMPLE 13.4 The speed of the space shuttle
The space shuttle in a 300-km-high orbit ($\approx$ 180 mi) wants to capture a smaller satellite for repairs. What are the speeds of the shuttle and the satellite in this orbit?

SOLVE Despite their different masses, the shuttle, the satellite, and the astronaut working in space to make the repairs all travel side by side with the same speed. They are simply in free fall together. Using $r = R_e + h$ with $h = 300$ km $= 3.00 \times 10^5$ m, we find the speed

$$v = \sqrt{\frac{(6.67 \times 10^{-11}\, \text{N m}^2/\text{kg}^2)(5.98 \times 10^{24}\, \text{kg})}{6.67 \times 10^6\, \text{m}}}$$

$$= 7730\, \text{m/s} \approx 17,000\, \text{mph}$$

ASSESS The answer depends on the mass of the earth but *not* on the mass of the satellite.

Kepler's Third Law

4.6

An important parameter of circular motion is the *period*. Recall that the period T is the time to complete one full orbit. The relationship among speed, radius, and period is

$$v = \frac{\text{circumference}}{\text{period}} = \frac{2\pi r}{T} \tag{13.23}$$

We can find a relationship between a satellite's period and the radius of its orbit by using Equation 13.22 for v:

$$v = \frac{2\pi r}{T} = \sqrt{\frac{GM}{r}} \tag{13.24}$$

Squaring both sides and solving for T give

$$T^2 = \left(\frac{4\pi^2}{GM}\right)r^3 \tag{13.25}$$

In other words, the *square* of the period is proportional to the *cube* of the radius. This is Kepler's third law. You can see that Kepler's third law is a direct consequence of Newton's law of gravity.

Table 13.2 contains astronomical information about the sun, the earth, the moon, and other planets of the solar system. We can use these data to check the validity of Equation 13.25. FIGURE 13.18 is a graph of $\log T$ versus $\log r$ for all the planets in Table 13.2 except Mercury. Notice that the scales on each axis are increasing logarithmically—by *factors* of 10—rather than linearly. (Also, the vertical axis has converted T to the SI units of s.) As you can see, the graph is a straight line with a statistical "best fit" equation

$$\log T = 1.500 \log r - 9.264$$

As a homework problem, you can show that the slope of 1.500 for this "log-log graph" confirms the prediction of Equation 13.25. You'll also use the y-intercept value of this line to determine the mass of the sun.

A particularly interesting application of Equation 13.25 is to communication satellites that are in **geosynchronous orbits** above the earth. These satellites have a period of 24 hours, making their orbital motion synchronous with the earth's rotation. As a result, a satellite in such an orbit appears to remain stationary over one point on the earth's equator. Equation 13.25 allows us to compute the radius of an orbit with this period:

$$r_{geo} = R_e + h_{geo} = \left[\left(\frac{GM}{4\pi^2}\right)T^2\right]^{1/3}$$
$$= \left[\left(\frac{(6.67 \times 10^{-11}\,\text{N m}^2/\text{kg}^2)(5.98 \times 10^{24}\,\text{kg})}{4\pi^2}\right)(86,400\,\text{s})^2\right]^{1/3}$$
$$= 4.225 \times 10^7\,\text{m}$$

The height of the orbit is

$$h_{geo} = r_{geo} - R_e = 3.59 \times 10^7\,\text{m} = 35,900\,\text{km} \approx 22,300\,\text{mi}$$

NOTE ▶ When using Equation 13.25, the period *must* be in SI units of s. ◀

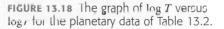

FIGURE 13.18 The graph of $\log T$ versus $\log r$ for the planetary data of Table 13.2.

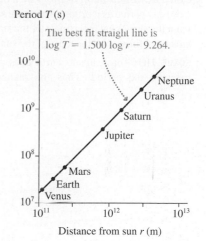

TABLE 13.2 Useful astronomical data

Planetary body	Mean distance from sun (m)	Period (years)	Mass (kg)	Mean radius (m)
Sun	–	–	1.99×10^{30}	6.96×10^8
Moon	3.84×10^8*	27.3 days	7.36×10^{22}	1.74×10^6
Mercury	5.79×10^{10}	0.241	3.18×10^{23}	2.43×10^6
Venus	1.08×10^{11}	0.615	4.88×10^{24}	6.06×10^6
Earth	1.50×10^{11}	1.00	5.98×10^{24}	6.37×10^6
Mars	2.28×10^{11}	1.88	6.42×10^{23}	3.37×10^6
Jupiter	7.78×10^{11}	11.9	1.90×10^{27}	6.99×10^7
Saturn	1.43×10^{12}	29.5	5.68×10^{26}	5.85×10^7
Uranus	2.87×10^{12}	84.0	8.68×10^{25}	2.33×10^7
Neptune	4.50×10^{12}	165	1.03×10^{26}	2.21×10^7

*Distance from earth.

Geosynchronous orbits are much higher than the low-earth orbits used by the space shuttle and remote-sensing satellites, where $h \approx 300$ km. Communications satellites in geosynchronous orbits were first proposed in 1948 by science fiction writer Arthur C. Clarke, 10 years before the first artificial satellite of any type!

EXAMPLE 13.5 Extrasolar planets

Astronomers using the most advanced telescopes have only recently seen evidence of planets orbiting nearby stars. These are called *extrasolar planets*. Suppose a planet is observed to have a 1200 day period as it orbits a star at the same distance that Jupiter is from the sun. What is the mass of the star in solar masses? (1 *solar mass* is defined to be the mass of the sun.)

SOLVE Here "day" means earth days, as used by astronomers to measure the period. Thus the planet's period in SI units is

$T = 1200$ days $= 1.037 \times 10^8$ s. The orbital radius is that of Jupiter, which we can find in Table 13.2 to be $r = 7.78 \times 10^{11}$ m. Solving Equation 13.25 for the mass of the star gives

$$M = \frac{4\pi^2 r^3}{GT^2} = 2.59 \times 10^{31} \text{ kg} \times \frac{1 \text{ solar mass}}{1.99 \times 10^{30} \text{ kg}}$$

$$= 13 \text{ solar masses}$$

ASSESS This is a large, but not extraordinary, star.

STOP TO THINK 13.5 Two planets orbit a star. Planet 1 has orbital radius r_1 and planet 2 has $r_2 = 4r_1$. Planet 1 orbits with period T_1. Planet 2 orbits with period

a. $T_2 = 8T_1$ b. $T_2 = 4T_1$ c. $T_2 = 2T_1$

d. $T_2 = \frac{1}{2}T_1$ e. $T_2 = \frac{1}{4}T_1$ f. $T_2 = \frac{1}{8}T_1$

Kepler's Second Law

FIGURE 13.19 Angular momentum is conserved for a planet in an elliptical orbit.

(a)

The gravitational force points straight at the sun and exerts no torque.

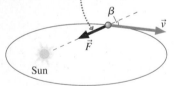

(b)

Area ΔA is swept out during Δt.

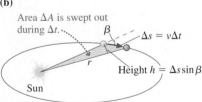

FIGURE 13.19a shows a satellite moving in an elliptical orbit. In Chapter 12 we defined a particle's *angular momentum* to be

$$L = mrv\sin\beta \qquad (13.26)$$

where β is the angle between $\vec{r}$ and $\vec{v}$. For a circular orbit, where β is always 90°, this reduces to simply $L = mrv$.

The only force on the satellite, the gravitational force, points directly toward the star or planet that the satellite is orbiting and exerts no torque; thus **the satellite's angular momentum is conserved as it orbits.**

The satellite moves forward a small distance $\Delta s = v\Delta t$ during the small interval of time Δt. This motion defines the triangle of area ΔA shown in **FIGURE 13.19b**. ΔA is the area "swept out" by the satellite during Δt. You can see that the height of the triangle is $h = \Delta s\sin\beta$, so the triangle's area is

$$\Delta A = \frac{1}{2} \times \text{base} \times \text{height} = \frac{1}{2} \times r \times \Delta s\sin\beta = \frac{1}{2}rv\sin\beta \, \Delta t \quad (13.27)$$

The *rate* at which the area is swept out by the satellite as it moves is

$$\frac{\Delta A}{\Delta t} = \frac{1}{2}rv\sin\beta = \frac{mrv\sin\beta}{2m} = \frac{L}{2m} \qquad (13.28)$$

The angular momentum L is conserved, so it has the same value at every point in the orbit. Consequently, the rate at which the area is swept out by the satellite is constant. This is Kepler's second law, which says that a line drawn between the sun and a planet sweeps out equal areas during equal intervals of time. We see that Kepler's second law is really a consequence of the conservation of angular momentum.

Kepler and Newton

Kepler's laws summarize observational data about the motions of the planets. They were an outstanding achievement, but they did not form a theory. Newton put forward a *theory*, a specific set of relationships between force and motion that allows *any* motion to be understood and calculated. Newton's theory of gravity has allowed us to *deduce* Kepler's laws and, thus, to understand them at a more fundamental level.

Furthermore, Kepler's laws are not perfectly accurate. The planets, in addition to being attracted to the sun, are also attracted toward each other and toward their orbiting moons. The consequences of these additional forces are small, but over time they provide measurable effects not contained in Kepler's laws. With Newton's theory we can use the inverse-square law to calculate the net force acting on each planet due to the sun and all other planets, then solve Newton's second law to determine the dynamics. The mathematics of the solution can be exceedingly difficult, and today is all done with computers, but even with hand calculations this procedure in the mid-19th century predicted the existence of an undiscovered planet that was having minor effects on the orbital motion of Uranus. The planet Neptune was discovered in 1846, just where the calculations predicted.

Orbital Energetics

Let us conclude this chapter by thinking about the energetics of orbital motion. We found, with Equation 13.24, that a satellite in a circular orbit must have $v^2 = GM/r$. A satellite's speed is determined entirely by the size of its orbit. The satellite's kinetic energy is thus

$$K = \frac{1}{2}mv^2 = \frac{GMm}{2r} \tag{13.29}$$

But $-GMm/r$ is the potential energy, U_g, so

$$K = -\frac{1}{2}U_g \tag{13.30}$$

This is an interesting result. In all our earlier examples, the kinetic and potential energy were two independent parameters. In contrast, a satellite can move in a circular orbit *only* if there is a very specific relationship between K and U. It is not that K and U *have* to have this relationship, but if they do not, the trajectory will be elliptical rather than circular.

Equation 13.30 gives us the mechanical energy of a satellite in a circular orbit:

$$E_{\text{mech}} = K + U_g = \frac{1}{2}U_g \tag{13.31}$$

The gravitational potential energy is negative, hence the *total* mechanical energy is also negative. Negative total energy is characteristic of a **bound system,** a system in which the satellite is bound to the central mass by the gravitational force and cannot get away. In an unbound system, the satellite can move infinitely far away to where $U = 0$. Because the kinetic energy K must be >0, the total energy of an unbound system must be ≥ 0. A negative value of E_{mech} tells us that the satellite is unable to escape the central mass.

FIGURE 13.20 shows the energies of a satellite in a circular orbit as a function of the orbit's radius. Notice how $E_{\text{mech}} = \frac{1}{2}U_g$. This figure can help us understand the energetics of transferring a satellite from one orbit to another. Suppose a satellite is in an orbit of radius r_1 and we'd like it to be in a larger orbit of radius r_2. The kinetic energy at r_2 is less than at r_1 (the satellite moves more slowly in the larger orbit), but you can see that the total energy *increases* as r increases. Consequently, transferring a satellite to a larger orbit requires a net energy increase $\Delta E > 0$. Where does this increase of energy come from?

FIGURE 13.20 The kinetic, potential, and total energy of a satellite in a circular orbit.

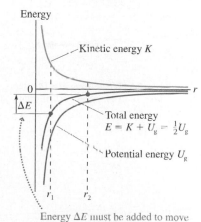

Energy ΔE must be added to move a satellite from an orbit with radius r_1 to radius r_2.

Artificial satellites are raised to higher orbits by firing their rocket motors to create a forward thrust. This force does work on the satellite, and the energy equation of Chapter 11 tells us that this work increases the satellite's energy by $\Delta E_{mech} = W_{ext}$. Thus the energy to "lift" a satellite into a higher orbit comes from the chemical energy stored in the rocket fuel.

EXAMPLE 13.6 **Raising a satellite**

How much work must be done to boost a 1000 kg communications satellite from a low earth orbit with $h = 300$ km, where it is released by the space shuttle, to a geosynchronous orbit?

SOLVE The required work is $W_{ext} = \Delta E_{mech}$, and from Equation 13.31 we see that $\Delta E_{mech} = \frac{1}{2} \Delta U_g$. The initial orbit has radius $r_{shuttle} = R_e + h = 6.67 \times 10^6$ m. We earlier found the radius of a geosynchronous orbit to be 4.22×10^7 m. Thus

$$W_{ext} = \Delta E_{mech} = \frac{1}{2} \Delta U_g = \frac{1}{2}(-GM_e m)\left(\frac{1}{r_{geo}} - \frac{1}{r_{shuttle}}\right) = 2.52 \times 10^{10} \text{ J}$$

ASSESS It takes a lot of energy to boost satellites to high orbits!

You might think that the way to get a satellite into a larger orbit would be to point the thrusters toward the earth and blast outward. That would work fine *if* the satellite were initially at rest and moved straight out along a linear trajectory. But an orbiting satellite is already moving and has significant inertia. A force directed straight outward would *change* the satellite's velocity vector in that direction but would not cause it to *move* along that line. (Remember all those earlier motion diagrams for motion along curved trajectories.) In addition, a force directed outward would be almost at right angles to the motion and would do essentially zero work. Navigating in space is not as easy as it appears in *Star Wars!*

To move the satellite in **FIGURE 13.21** from the orbit with radius r_1 to the larger circular orbit of radius r_2, the thrusters are turned on at point 1 to apply a brief *forward* thrust force in the direction of motion, *tangent* to the circle. This force does a significant amount of work because the force is parallel to the displacement, so the satellite quickly gains kinetic energy ($\Delta K > 0$). But $\Delta U_g = 0$ because the satellite does not have time to change its distance from the earth during a thrust of short duration. With the kinetic energy increased, but not the potential energy, the satellite no longer meets the requirement $K = -\frac{1}{2} U_g$ for a circular orbit. Instead, it goes into an elliptical orbit.

In the elliptical orbit, the satellite moves "uphill" toward point 2 by transforming kinetic energy into potential energy. At point 2, the satellite has arrived at the desired distance from earth and has the "right" value of the potential energy, but its kinetic energy is now *less* than needed for a circular orbit. (The analysis is more complex than we want to pursue here. It will be left for a homework Challenge Problem.) If no action is taken, the satellite will continue on its elliptical orbit and "fall" back to point 1. But another *forward* thrust at point 2 increases its kinetic energy, without changing U_g, until the kinetic energy reaches the value $K = -\frac{1}{2} U_g$ required for a circular orbit. Presto! The second burn kicks the satellite into the desired circular orbit of radius r_2. The work $W_{ext} = \Delta E_{mech}$ is the *total* work done in both burns. It takes a more extended analysis to see how the work has to be divided between the two burns, but even without those details you now have enough knowledge about orbits and energy to understand the ideas that are involved.

FIGURE 13.21 Transferring a satellite to a larger circular orbit.

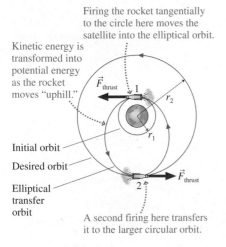

Firing the rocket tangentially to the circle here moves the satellite into the elliptical orbit.

Kinetic energy is transformed into potential energy as the rocket moves "uphill."

$\vec{F}_{thrust}$

Initial orbit

Desired orbit

Elliptical transfer orbit

$\vec{F}_{thrust}$

A second firing here transfers it to the larger circular orbit.

SUMMARY

**The goal of Chapter 13 has been to use Newton's theory of gravity
to understand the motion of satellites and planets.**

General Principles

Newton's Theory of Gravity

1. Two objects with masses M and m a distance r apart exert attractive
   gravitational forces on each other of magnitude

$$F_{M \text{ on } m} = F_{m \text{ on } M} = \frac{GMm}{r^2}$$

where the **gravitational constant** is $G = 6.67 \times 10^{-11} \, \text{N m}^2/\text{kg}^2$.

2. Gravitational mass and inertial mass are equivalent.

3. Newton's three laws of motion apply to satellites, planets, and stars.

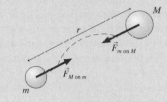

Important Concepts

Orbital motion of a planet (or satellite) is described by **Kepler's laws:**

1. Orbits are ellipses with the sun (or planet) at one focus.

2. A line between the sun and the planet sweeps out equal areas during equal intervals of time.

3. The square of the planet's period T is proportional to the cube of the orbit's semimajor axis.

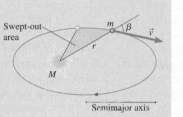

Circular orbits are a special case of an ellipse. For a circular orbit around a mass M,

$$v = \sqrt{\frac{GM}{r}} \quad \text{and} \quad T^2 = \left(\frac{4\pi^2}{GM}\right)r^3$$

Conservation of angular momentum

The angular momentum $L = mrv\sin\beta$ remains constant throughout the orbit. Kepler's second law is a consequence of this law.

Orbital energetics

A satellite's mechanical energy $E_{\text{mech}} = K + U_g$ is conserved, where the gravitational potential energy is

$$U_g = -\frac{GMm}{r}$$

For circular orbits, $K = -\frac{1}{2}U_g$ and $E_{\text{mech}} = \frac{1}{2}U_g$. Negative total energy is characteristic of a **bound system.**

Applications

For a planet of mass M and radius R,

- The free-fall acceleration on the surface is $g_{\text{surface}} = \dfrac{GM}{R^2}$

- The escape speed is $v_{\text{escape}} = \sqrt{\dfrac{2GM}{R}}$

- The radius of a geosynchronous orbit is $r_{\text{geo}} = \left(\dfrac{GM}{4\pi^2}T^2\right)^{1/3}$

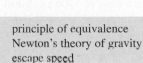

Terms and Notation

cosmology	Newton's law of gravity	principle of equivalence	satellite
Kepler's laws	gravitational constant, G	Newton's theory of gravity	geosynchronous orbit
gravitational force	gravitational mass	escape speed	bound system

(MP) For homework assigned on MasteringPhysics, go to
www.masteringphysics.com

Problem difficulty is labeled as | (straightforward) to ||| (challenging).

Problems labeled ■ integrate significant material from earlier chapters.

CONCEPTUAL QUESTIONS

1. Is the earth's gravitational force on the sun larger than, smaller than, or equal to the sun's gravitational force on the earth? Explain.

2. The gravitational force of a star on orbiting planet 1 is F_1. Planet 2, which is twice as massive as planet 1 and orbits at twice the distance from the star, experiences gravitational force F_2. What is the ratio F_1/F_2?

3. A 1000 kg satellite and a 2000 kg satellite follow exactly the same orbit around the earth.
   a. What is the ratio F_1/F_2 of the force on the first satellite to that on the second satellite?
   b. What is the ratio a_1/a_2 of the acceleration of the first satellite to that of the second satellite?

4. How far away from the earth must an orbiting spacecraft be for the astronauts inside to be weightless? Explain.

5. A space shuttle astronaut is working outside the shuttle as it orbits the earth. If he drops a hammer, will it fall to earth? Explain why or why not.

6. The free-fall acceleration at the surface of planet 1 is 20 m/s^2. The radius and the mass of planet 2 are twice those of planet 1. What is g on planet 2?

7. *Why* is the gravitational potential energy of two masses negative? Note that saying "because that's what the equation gives" is *not* an explanation.

8. The escape speed from Planet X is 10,000 m/s. Planet Y has the same radius as Planet X but is twice as dense. What is the escape speed from Planet Y?

9. Planet X orbits the star Omega with a "year" that is 200 earth days long. Planet Y circles Omega at four times the distance of Planet X. How long is a year on Planet Y?

10. The mass of Jupiter is 300 times the mass of the earth. Jupiter orbits the sun with $T_{Jupiter} = 11.9$ yr in an orbit with $r_{Jupiter} = 5.2r_{earth}$. Suppose the earth could be moved to the distance of Jupiter and placed in a circular orbit around the sun. Which of the following describes the earth's new period? Explain.
    a. 1 yr
    b. Between 1 yr and 11.9 yr
    c. 11.9 yr
    d. More than 11.9 yr
    e. It would depend on the earth's speed.
    f. It's impossible for a planet of earth's mass to orbit at the distance of Jupiter.

11. Satellites in near-earth orbit experience a very slight drag due to the extremely thin upper atmosphere. These satellites slowly but surely spiral inward, where they finally burn up as they reach the thicker lower levels of the atmosphere. The radius decreases so slowly that you can consider the satellite to have a circular orbit at all times. As a satellite spirals inward, does it speed up, slow down, or maintain the same speed? Explain.

EXERCISES AND PROBLEMS

Exercises

Section 13.3 Newton's Law of Gravity

1. || What is the ratio of the sun's gravitational force on you to the earth's gravitational force on you?

2. || The centers of a 10 kg lead ball and a 100 g lead ball are separated by 10 cm.
   a. What gravitational force does each exert on the other?
   b. What is the ratio of this gravitational force to the gravitational force of the earth on the 100 g ball?

3. || What is the ratio of the sun's gravitational force on the moon to the earth's gravitational force on the moon?

4. || A 1.0-m-diameter lead sphere has a mass of 5900 kg. A dust particle rests on the surface. What is the ratio of the gravitational force of the sphere on the dust particle to the gravitational force of the earth on the dust particle?

5. || Estimate the force of attraction between a 50 kg woman and a 70 kg man sitting 1.0 m apart.

6. || The space shuttle orbits 300 km above the surface of the earth.
   a. What is the gravitational force on a 1.0 kg sphere inside the space shuttle?
   b. The sphere floats around inside the space shuttle, apparently "weightless." How is this possible?

Section 13.4 Little g and Big G

7. | a. What is the free-fall acceleration at the surface of the sun?
   b. What is the sun's free-fall acceleration at the distance of the earth?

8. | What is the free-fall acceleration at the surface of (a) the moon and (b) Jupiter?

9. || A sensitive gravimeter at a mountain observatory finds that the free-fall acceleration is 0.0075 m/s^2 less than that at sea level. What is the observatory's altitude?

10. ‖ Suppose we could shrink the earth without changing its mass. At what fraction of its current radius would the free-fall acceleration at the surface be three times its present value?

11. ‖ Planet Z is 10,000 km in diameter. The free-fall acceleration on Planet Z is 8.0 m/s².
    a. What is the mass of Planet Z?
    b. What is the free-fall acceleration 10,000 km above Planet Z's north pole?

Section 13.5 Gravitational Potential Energy

12. | An astronaut on earth can throw a ball straight up to a height of 15 m. How high can he throw the ball on Mars?

13. | What is the escape speed from Jupiter?

14. ‖ A rocket is launched straight up from the earth's surface at a speed of 15,000 m/s. What is its speed when it is very far away from the earth?

15. ‖ A space station orbits the sun at the same distance as the earth but on the opposite side of the sun. A small probe is fired away from the station. What minimum speed does the probe need to escape the solar system?

16. ‖ You have been visiting a distant planet. Your measurements have determined that the planet's mass is twice that of earth but the free-fall acceleration at the surface is only one-fourth as large.
    a. What is the planet's radius?
    b. To get back to earth, you need to escape the planet. What minimum speed does your rocket need?

Section 13.6 Satellite Orbits and Energies

17. | The *asteroid belt* circles the sun between the orbits of Mars and Jupiter. One asteroid has a period of 5.0 earth years. What are the asteroid's orbital radius and speed?

18. | Use information about the earth and its orbit to determine the mass of the sun.

19. | You are the science officer on a visit to a distant solar system. Prior to landing on a planet you measure its diameter to be 1.8×10^7 m and its rotation period to be 22.3 hours. You have previously determined that the planet orbits 2.2×10^{11} m from its star with a period of 402 earth days. Once on the surface you find that the free-fall acceleration is 12.2 m/s². What are the mass of (a) the planet and (b) the star?

20. ‖ Three satellites orbit a planet of radius R, as shown in **FIGURE EX13.20**. Satellites S_1 and S_3 have mass m. Satellite S_2 has mass $2m$. Satellite S_1 orbits in 250 minutes and the force on S_1 is 10,000 N.
    a. What are the periods of S_2 and S_3?
    b. What are the forces on S_2 and S_3?
    c. What is the kinetic-energy ratio K_1/K_3 for S_1 and S_3?

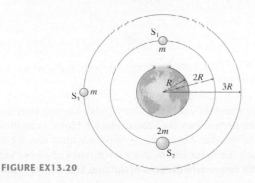

FIGURE EX13.20

21. ‖ A satellite orbits the sun with a period of 1.0 day. What is the radius of its orbit?

22. ‖ The space shuttle is in a 350-km-high orbit. What are the shuttle's orbital period, in minutes, and its speed?

23. ‖ An earth satellite moves in a circular orbit at a speed of 5500 m/s. What is its orbital period?

24. ‖ What are the speed and altitude of a geosynchronous satellite orbiting Mars? Mars rotates on its axis once every 24.8 hours.

Problems

25. ‖ Two spherical objects have a combined mass of 150 kg. The gravitational attraction between them is 8.00×10^{-6} N when their centers are 20 cm apart. What is the mass of each?

26. ‖ Two 100 kg lead spheres are suspended from 100-m-long massless cables. The tops of the cables have been carefully anchored *exactly* 1 m apart. What is the distance between the centers of the spheres?

27. ‖ A 20 kg sphere is at the origin and a 10 kg sphere is at $(x, y) = (20 \text{ cm}, 0 \text{ cm})$. At what point or points could you place a small mass such that the net gravitational force on it due to the spheres is zero?

28. ‖ **FIGURE P13.28** shows three masses. What are the magnitude and the direction of the net gravitational force on (a) the 20.0 kg mass and (b) the 5.0 kg mass? Give the direction as an angle cw or ccw from the y-axis.

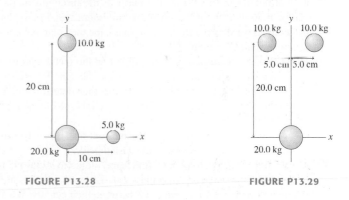

FIGURE P13.28   **FIGURE P13.29**

29. ‖ What are the magnitude and direction of the net gravitational force on the 20.0 kg mass in **FIGURE P13.29**?

30. ‖ What is the total gravitational potential energy of the three masses in **FIGURE P13.28**?

31. ‖ What is the total gravitational potential energy of the three masses in **FIGURE P13.29**?

32. ‖ a. At what height above the earth is the acceleration due to gravity 10% of its value at the surface?
    b. What is the speed of a satellite orbiting at that height?

33. ‖ A 1.0 kg object is released from rest 500 km (≈300 miles) above the earth.
    a. What is its impact speed as it hits the ground? Ignore air resistance.
    b. What would the impact speed be if the earth were flat?
    c. By what percentage is the flat-earth calculation in error?

34. ‖ A projectile is shot straight up from the earth's surface at a speed of 10,000 km/hr. How high does it go?

35. ‖ A huge cannon is assembled on an airless planet. The planet has a radius of 5.0×10^6 m and a mass of 2.6×10^{24} kg. The cannon fires a projectile straight up at 5000 m/s.
    a. What height does the projectile reach above the surface?
    b. An observation satellite orbits the planet at a height of 1000 km. What is the projectile's speed as it passes the satellite?

36. ‖ An object of mass m is dropped from height h above a planet of mass M and radius R. Find an expression for the object's speed as it hits the ground.

37. ‖ Two meteoroids are heading for earth. Their speeds as they cross the moon's orbit are 2.0 km/s.
    a. The first meteoroid is heading straight for earth. What is its speed of impact?
    b. The second misses the earth by 5000 km. What is its speed at its closest point?

38. ‖ A binary star system has two stars, each with the same mass as our sun, separated by 1.0×10^{12} m. A comet is very far away and essentially at rest. Slowly but surely, gravity pulls the comet toward the stars. Suppose the comet travels along a straight line that passes through the midpoint between the two stars. What is the comet's speed at the midpoint?

39. ‖ Suppose that on earth you can jump straight up a distance of 50 cm. Can you escape from a 4.0-km-diameter asteroid with a mass of 1.0×10^{14} kg?

40. ‖ A projectile is fired straight away from the moon from a base on the far side of the moon, away from the earth. What is the projectile's escape speed from the earth-moon system?

41. ‖ A projectile is fired from the earth in the direction of the earth's motion around the sun. What minimum speed must the projectile have relative to the earth to escape the solar system? Ignore the earth's rotation.
    Hint: This is a three-part problem. First find the speed a projectile at the earth's distance needs to escape the sun. Transform that speed into the earth's reference frame, then determine how fast the projectile must be launched to have this speed when far from the earth.

42. ‖ Two Jupiter-size planets are released from rest 1.0×10^{11} m apart. What are their speeds as they crash together?

43. ‖‖ Two spherical asteroids have the same radius R. Asteroid 1 has mass M and asteroid 2 has mass $2M$. The two asteroids are released from rest with distance $10R$ between their centers. What is the speed of each asteroid just before they collide?
    Hint: You will need to use two conservation laws.

44. ‖‖ A starship is circling a distant planet of radius R. The astronauts find that the free-fall acceleration at their altitude is half the value at the planet's surface. How far above the surface are they orbiting? Your answer will be a multiple of R.

45. ‖ Three stars, each with the mass and radius of our sun, form an equilateral triangle 5.0×10^9 m on a side. If all three are simultaneously released from rest, what are their speeds as they crash together in the center?

46. ‖ A 4000 kg lunar lander is in orbit 50 km above the surface of the moon. It needs to move out to a 300-km-high orbit in order to link up with the mother ship that will take the astronauts home. How much work must the thrusters do?

47. ‖ The space shuttle is in a 250-km-high circular orbit. It needs to reach a 610-km-high circular orbit to catch the Hubble Space Telescope for repairs. The shuttle's mass is 75,000 kg. How much energy is required to boost it to the new orbit?

48. ‖ a. How much energy must a 50,000 kg space shuttle lose to descend from a 500-km-high circular orbit to a 300-km-high orbit?
    b. Give a *qualitative* description, including a sketch, of how the shuttle would do this.

49. ‖ While visiting Planet Physics, you toss a rock straight up at 11 m/s and catch it 2.5 s later. While you visit the surface, your cruise ship orbits at an altitude equal to the planet's radius every 230 min. What are the (a) mass and (b) radius of Planet Physics?

50. ‖ In 2000, NASA placed a satellite in orbit around an asteroid. Consider a spherical asteroid with a mass of 1.0×10^{16} kg and a radius of 8.8 km.
    a. What is the speed of a satellite orbiting 5.0 km above the surface?
    b. What is the escape speed from the asteroid?

51. ‖ NASA would like to place a satellite in orbit around the moon such that the satellite always remains in the same position over the lunar surface. What is the satellite's altitude?

52. ‖ A satellite orbiting the earth is directly over a point on the equator at 12:00 midnight every two days. It is not over that point at any time in between. What is the radius of the satellite's orbit?

53. ‖ Figure 13.18 showed a graph of log T versus log r for the planetary data given in Table 13.2. Such a graph is called a *log-log graph*. The scales in Figure 13.18 are logarithmic, not linear, meaning that each division along the axis corresponds to a *factor* of 10 increase in the value. Strictly speaking, the "correct" labels on the y-axis should be 7, 8, 9, and 10 because these are the logarithms of $10^7, \ldots, 10^{10}$.
    a. Consider two quantities u and v that are related by the expression $v^p = Cu^q$, where C is a constant. The exponents p and q are not necessarily integers. Define $x = \log u$ and $y = \log v$. Find an expression for y in terms of x.
    b. What *shape* will a graph of y versus x have? Explain.
    c. What *slope* will a graph of y versus x have? Explain.
    d. Figure 13.18 showed that the "best fit" line passing through all the planetary data points has the equation $\log T = 1.500 \log r - 9.264$. This is an *experimentally* determined relationship between $\log T$ and $\log r$, using measured data. Is this experimental result consistent with what you would expect from Newton's theory of gravity? Explain.
    e. Use the experimentally determined "best fit" line to find the mass of the sun.

54. ‖ **FIGURE P13.54** shows two planets of mass m orbiting a star of mass M. The planets are in the same orbit, with radius r, but are always at opposite ends of a diameter. Find an exact expression for the orbital period T.

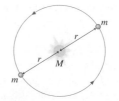

FIGURE P13.54

55. ‖ Large stars can explode as they finish burning their nuclear fuel, causing a *supernova*. The explosion blows away the outer layers of the star. According to Newton's third law, the forces that push the outer layers away have *reaction forces* that are inwardly directed on the core of the star. These forces compress

the core and can cause the core to undergo a *gravitational collapse*. The gravitational forces keep pulling all the matter together tighter and tighter, crushing atoms out of existence. Under these extreme conditions, a proton and an electron can be squeezed together to form a neutron. If the collapse is halted when the neutrons all come into contact with each other, the result is an object called a *neutron star,* an entire star consisting of solid nuclear matter. Many neutron stars rotate about their axis with a period of ≈ 1 s and, as they do so, send out a pulse of electromagnetic waves once a second. These stars were discovered in the 1960s and are called *pulsars.*

  a. Consider a neutron star with a mass equal to the sun, a radius of 10 km, and a rotation period of 1.0 s. What is the speed of a point on the equator of the star?

  b. What is g at the surface of this neutron star?

  c. A stationary 1.0 kg mass has a weight on earth of 9.8 N. What would be its weight on the star?

  d. How many revolutions per minute are made by a satellite orbiting 1.0 km above the surface?

  e. What is the radius of a geosynchronous orbit about the neutron star?

56. ‖ The solar system is 25,000 light years from the center of our Milky Way galaxy. One *light year* is the distance light travels in one year at a speed of 3.0×10^8 m/s. Astronomers have determined that the solar system is orbiting the center of the galaxy at a speed of 230 km/s.

  a. Assuming the orbit is circular, what is the period of the solar system's orbit? Give your answer in years.

  b. Our solar system was formed roughly 5 billion years ago. How many orbits has it completed?

  c. The gravitational force on the solar system is the net force due to all the matter inside our orbit. Most of that matter is concentrated near the center of the galaxy. Assume that the matter has a spherical distribution, like a giant star. What is the approximate mass of the galactic center?

  d. Assume that the sun is a typical star with a typical mass. If galactic matter is made up of stars, approximately how many stars are in the center of the galaxy?

Astronomers have spent many years trying to determine how many stars there are in the Milky Way. The number of stars seems to be only about 10% of what you found in part d. In other words, about 90% of the mass of the galaxy appears to be in some form other than stars. This is called the *dark matter* of the universe. No one knows what the dark matter is. This is one of the outstanding scientific questions of our day.

57. ‖ Astronomers discover a binary star system that has a period of 90 days. The binary star system consists of two equal-mass stars, each with a mass twice that of the sun, that rotate like a dumbbell about the *center of mass* at the midpoint between them. How far apart are the two stars?

58. ‖ Three stars, each with the mass of our sun, form an equilateral triangle with sides 1.0×10^{12} m long. (This triangle would just about fit within the orbit of Jupiter.) The triangle has to rotate, because otherwise the stars would crash together in the center. What is the period of rotation? Give your answer in years.

59. ‖ Pluto moves in a fairly elliptical orbit around the sun. Pluto's speed at its closest approach of 4.43×10^9 km is 6.12 km/s. What is Pluto's speed at the most distant point in its orbit, where it is 7.30×10^9 km from the sun?

60. ‖ Mercury moves in a fairly elliptical orbit around the sun. Mercury's speed is 38.8 km/s when it is at its most distant point, 6.99×10^{10} m from the sun. How far is Mercury from the sun at its closest point, where its speed is 59.0 km/s?

61. ‖ Comets move around the sun in very elliptical orbits. At its closet approach, in 1986, Comet Halley was 8.79×10^7 km from the sun and moving with a speed of 54.6 km/s. What was the comet's speed when it crossed Neptune's orbit in 2006?

62. ‖ A spaceship is in a circular orbit of radius r_0 about a planet of mass M. A brief but intense firing of its engine in the forward direction decreases the spaceship's speed by 50%. This causes the spaceship to move into an elliptical orbit.

  a. What is the spaceship's new speed, just after the rocket burn is complete, in terms of M, G, and r_0?

  b. In terms of r_0, what are the spaceship's maximum and minimum distance from the planet in its new orbit?

63. ‖ A satellite orbiting the earth has a speed of 5.5 km/s when its distance from the center of the earth is 11,000 km.

  a. Is the satellite in a circular orbit?

  b. Is the satellite in a bound orbit?

64. ‖ A planet is orbiting a star when, for no apparent reason, the star's gravity suddenly vanishes. As **FIGURE P13.64** shows, the planet then obeys Newton's first law and heads outward along a straight line. Is Kepler's second law still obeyed? That is, are equal areas swept out in equal intervals of time as the planet moves away?

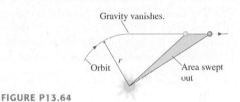

Gravity vanishes.

Orbit r Area swept out

FIGURE P13.64

In Problems 65 through 68 you are given the equation(s) used to solve a problem. For each of these, you are to

  a. Write a realistic problem for which this is the correct equation(s).

  b. Draw a pictorial representation.

  c. Finish the solution of the problem.

65. $\dfrac{(6.67 \times 10^{-11} \, \text{N} \, \text{m}^2/\text{kg}^2)(5.68 \times 10^{26} \, \text{kg})}{r^2}$

$= \dfrac{(6.67 \times 10^{-11} \, \text{N} \, \text{m}^2/\text{kg}^2)(5.98 \times 10^{24} \, \text{kg})}{(6.37 \times 10^6 \, \text{m})^2}$

66. $\dfrac{(6.67 \times 10^{-11} \, \text{N} \, \text{m}^2/\text{kg}^2)(5.98 \times 10^{24} \, \text{kg})(1000 \, \text{kg})}{r^2}$

$= \dfrac{(1000 \, \text{kg})(1997 \, \text{m/s})^2}{r}$

67. $\dfrac{1}{2}(100 \, \text{kg})v_2^2$

$- \dfrac{(6.67 \times 10^{-11} \, \text{N} \, \text{m}^2/\text{kg}^2)(7.36 \times 10^{22} \, \text{kg})(100 \, \text{kg})}{1.74 \times 10^6 \, \text{m}}$

$= 0 - \dfrac{(6.67 \times 10^{-11} \, \text{N} \, \text{m}^2/\text{kg}^2)(7.36 \times 10^{22} \, \text{kg})(100 \, \text{kg})}{3.48 \times 10^6 \, \text{m}}$

68. $(2.0 \times 10^{30} \text{ kg})v_{\text{f1}} + (4.0 \times 10^{30} \text{ kg})v_{\text{f2}} = 0$

$\frac{1}{2}(2.0 \times 10^{30} \text{ kg})v_{\text{f1}}^2 + \frac{1}{2}(4.0 \times 10^{30} \text{ kg})v_{\text{f2}}^2$

$\quad - \dfrac{(6.67 \times 10^{-11} \text{ Nm}^2/\text{kg}^2)(2.0 \times 10^{30} \text{ kg})(4.0 \times 10^{30} \text{ kg})}{1.0 \times 10^9 \text{ m}}$

$= 0 + 0$

$\quad - \dfrac{(6.67 \times 10^{-11} \text{ Nm}^2/\text{kg}^2)(2.0 \times 10^{30} \text{ kg})(4.0 \times 10^{30} \text{ kg})}{1.0 \times 10^{12} \text{ m}}$

Challenge Problems

69. A satellite in a circular orbit of radius r has period T. A satellite in a nearby orbit with radius $r + \Delta r$, where $\Delta r \ll r$, has the very slightly different period $T + \Delta T$.
    a. Show that

$$\frac{\Delta T}{T} = \frac{3}{2}\frac{\Delta r}{r}$$

    b. Two earth satellites are in parallel orbits with radii 6700 km and 6701 km. One day they pass each other, 1 km apart, along a line radially outward from the earth. How long will it be until they are again 1 km apart?

70. In 1996, the Solar and Heliospheric Observatory (SOHO) was "parked" in an orbit slightly inside the earth's orbit, as shown in FIGURE CP13.70. The satellite's period in this orbit is exactly one year, so it remains fixed relative to the earth. At this point, called a *Lagrange point,* the light from the sun is never blocked by the earth, yet the satellite remains "nearby" so that data are easily transmitted to earth. What is SOHO's distance from the earth?

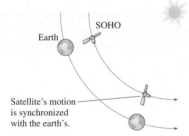

FIGURE CP13.70

Hint: Use the binomial approximation. SOHO's distance from the earth is much less than the earth's distance from the sun.

71. The space shuttle, in a 300-km-high orbit, needs to perform an experiment that has to take place well away from the spacecraft. To do so, a 100 kg payload is "lowered" toward the earth on a 10-km-long massless rope. (We'll overlook the details of how they do this and simply assume they can.) The payload can be hauled back on board the shuttle after the experiment. Assume that any initial motions associated with lowering the payload have damped out and that the shuttle and payload are flying in steady-state conditions.
    a. What is the angle of the rope as measured from a line drawn from the center of the earth through the payload? Explain.
    b. What is the tension in the rope?

72. Your job with NASA is to monitor satellite orbits. One day, during a routine survey, you find that a 400 kg satellite in a 1000-km-high circular orbit is going to collide with a smaller 100 kg satellite traveling in the same orbit but in the opposite direction. Knowing the construction of the two satellites, you expect they will become enmeshed into a single piece of space debris. When you notify your boss of this impending collision, he asks you to quickly determine whether the space debris will continue to orbit or crash into the earth. What will the outcome be?

73. The two stars in a binary star system have masses 2.0×10^{30} kg and 6.0×10^{30} kg. They are separated by 2.0×10^{12} m. What are
    a. The system's rotation period, in years?
    b. The speed of each star?

74. A moon lander is orbiting the moon at an altitude of 1000 km. By what percentage must it decrease its speed so as to just graze the moon's surface one-half period later?

75. Let's look in more detail at how a satellite is moved from one circular orbit to another. FIGURE CP13.75 shows two circular orbits, of radii r_1 and r_2, and an elliptical orbit that connects them. Points 1 and 2 are at the ends of the semimajor axis of the ellipse.

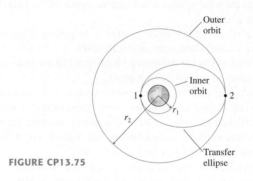

FIGURE CP13.75

    a. A satellite moving along the elliptical orbit has to satisfy two conservation laws. Use these two laws to prove that the velocities at points 1 and 2 are

$$v_1' = \sqrt{\frac{2GM(r_2/r_1)}{r_1 + r_2}} \quad \text{and} \quad v_2' = \sqrt{\frac{2GM(r_1/r_2)}{r_1 + r_2}}$$

    The prime indicates that these are the velocities on the elliptical orbit. Both reduce to Equation 13.22 if $r_1 = r_2 = r$.
    b. Consider a 1000 kg communication satellite that needs to be boosted from an orbit 300 km above the earth to a geosynchronous orbit 35,900 km above the earth. Find the velocity v_1 on the inner circular orbit and the velocity v_1' at the low point on the elliptical orbit that spans the two circular orbits.
    c. How much work must the rocket motor do to transfer the satellite from the circular orbit to the elliptical orbit?
    d. Now find the velocity v_2' at the high point of the elliptical orbit and the velocity v_2 of the outer circular orbit.
    e. How much work must the rocket motor do to transfer the satellite from the elliptical orbit to the outer circular orbit?
    f. Compute the total work done and compare your answer to the result of Example 13.6.

76. **FIGURE CP13.76** shows a particle of mass m at distance x from the center of a very thin cylinder of mass M and length L. The particle is outside the cylinder, so $x > L/2$.
   a. Calculate the gravitational potential energy of these two masses.
   b. Use what you know about the relationship between force and potential energy to find the magnitude of the gravitational force on m when it is at position x.

77. **FIGURE CP13.77** shows a particle of mass m at distance x along the axis of a very thin ring of mass M and radius R.
   a. Calculate the gravitational potential energy of these two masses.
   b. Use what you know about the relationship between force and potential energy to find the magnitude of the gravitational force on m when it is at position x.

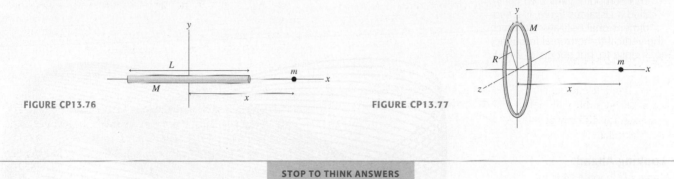

FIGURE CP13.76   FIGURE CP13.77

STOP TO THINK ANSWERS

Stop to Think 13.1: e. The acceleration decreases inversely with the square of the distance. At height R_e, the distance from the center of the earth is $2R_e$.

Stop to Think 13.2: c. Newton's third law requires $F_{1 \text{ on } 2} = F_{2 \text{ on } 1}$.

Stop to Think 13.3: b. $g_{surface} = GM/R^2$. Because of the square, a radius twice as large balances a mass four times as large.

Stop to Think 13.4: In absolute value, $U_e > U_a = U_b = U_d > U_c$. $|U_g|$ is proportional to $m_1 m_2/r$.

Stop to Think 13.5: a. T^2 is proportional to r^3, or T is proportional to $r^{3/2}$. $4^{3/2} = 8$.

14 Oscillations

This computer-generated figure, called a Lissajous figure, is a two-dimensional oscillation in which the vertical-to-horizontal frequency ratio is close to, but not quite, 2-to-1.

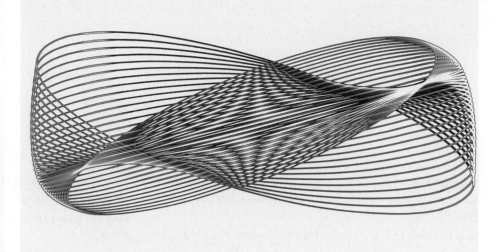

This striking computer-generated image is quite pretty. It is also demonstrating an important type of motion—*oscillatory motion.* Examples of oscillatory motion abound. A marble rolling back and forth in the bottom of a bowl and a car bouncing up and down on its springs are oscillating. So are a piece of vibrating machinery, a ringing bell, and the current in an electric circuit used to drive an antenna. A vibrating guitar string pushes the air molecules back and forth to send out a sound wave, showing that oscillations are closely related to waves.

Oscillatory motion is a repetitive motion back and forth about an equilibrium position. Swinging motions and vibrations of all kinds are oscillatory motions. All oscillatory motion is *periodic.*

Our goal in this chapter is to study the physics of oscillations. Much of our analysis will focus on the most basic form of oscillatory motion, *simple harmonic motion.* We will start with the kinematics of simple harmonic motion—a mathematical description of the motion. Then we will examine oscillatory motion from the twin perspectives of energy and Newton's laws. Finally, we will look at how oscillations are built up by driving forces and how they decay over time.

14.1 Simple Harmonic Motion

Objects or systems of objects that undergo oscillatory motion are called **oscillators.** FIGURE 14.1 shows position-versus-time graphs for three different oscillating systems. Although the shapes of the graphs are different, all these oscillators have two things in common:

1. The oscillation takes place about an equilibrium position, and
2. The motion is periodic.

The time to complete one full cycle, or one oscillation, is called the **period** of the motion. Period is given the symbol T.

A closely related piece of information is the number of cycles, or oscillations, completed per second. If the period is $\frac{1}{10}$ s, then the oscillator can complete 10 cycles in one second. Conversely, an oscillation period of 10 s allows only $\frac{1}{10}$ of a cycle to be completed per second. In general, T seconds per cycle implies that $1/T$ cycles will be completed each second. The number of cycles per second is called the **frequency** f of the oscillation. The relationship between frequency and period is

$$f = \frac{1}{T} \quad \text{or} \quad T = \frac{1}{f} \tag{14.1}$$

The units of frequency are **hertz,** abbreviated Hz, named in honor of the German physicist Heinrich Hertz, who produced the first artificially generated radio waves in 1887. By definition,

$$1 \text{ Hz} \equiv 1 \text{ cycle per second} = 1 \text{ s}^{-1}$$

We will frequently deal with very rapid oscillations and make use of the units shown in Table 14.1.

NOTE ▶ Uppercase and lowercase letters *are* important. 1 MHz is 1 megahertz = 10^6 Hz, but 1 mHz is 1 millihertz = 10^{-3} Hz! ◀

EXAMPLE 14.1 Frequency and period of a radio station

What is the oscillation period for the broadcast of a 100 MHz FM radio station?

SOLVE The frequency of current oscillations in the radio transmitter is 100 MHz = 1.00×10^8 Hz. The period is the inverse of the frequency; hence

$$T = \frac{1}{f} = \frac{1}{1.00 \times 10^8 \text{ Hz}} = 1.00 \times 10^{-8} \text{ s} = 10.0 \text{ ns}$$

A system can oscillate in many ways, but we will be especially interested in the smooth *sinusoidal* oscillation of the third graph in Figure 14.1. This sinusoidal oscillation, the most basic of all oscillatory motions, is called **simple harmonic motion,** often abbreviated SHM. Let's look at a graphical description before we dive into the mathematics of simple harmonic motion.

FIGURE 14.2a shows an air-track glider attached to a spring. If the glider is pulled out a few centimeters and released, it will oscillate back and forth on the nearly frictionless air track. FIGURE 14.2b shows actual results from an experiment in which a computer was used to measure the glider's position 20 times every second. This is a position-versus-time graph that has been rotated 90° from its usual orientation in order for the x-axis to match the motion of the glider.

The object's maximum displacement from equilibrium is called the **amplitude** A of the motion. The object's position oscillates between $x = -A$ and $x = +A$. When using a graph, notice that the amplitude is the distance from the *axis* to the maximum, *not* the distance from the minimum to the maximum.

FIGURE 14.1 Examples of position-versus-time graphs for oscillating systems.

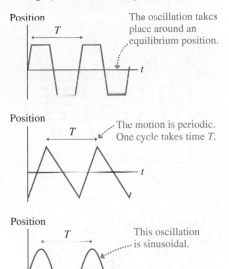

The oscillation takes place around an equilibrium position.

The motion is periodic. One cycle takes time T.

This oscillation is sinusoidal.

TABLE 14.1 Units of frequency

Frequency	Period
10^3 Hz = 1 kilohertz = 1 kHz	1 ms
10^6 Hz = 1 megahertz = 1 MHz	1 μs
10^9 Hz = 1 gigahertz = 1 GHz	1 ns

FIGURE 14.2 A prototype simple-harmonic-motion experiment.

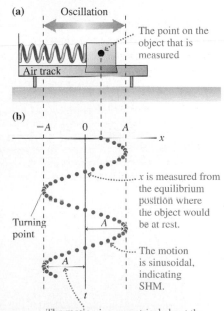

(a) Oscillation

The point on the object that is measured

Air track

(b)

x is measured from the equilibrium position where the object would be at rest.

Turning point

The motion is sinusoidal, indicating SHM.

The motion is symmetrical about the equilibrium position. Maximum distance to the left and to the right is A.

FIGURE 14.3 Position and velocity graphs of the experimental data.

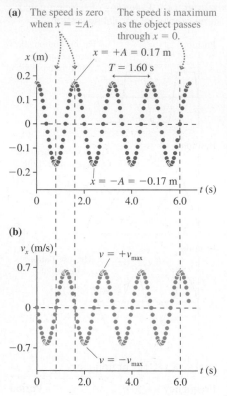

(a) The speed is zero when $x = \pm A$.   The speed is maximum as the object passes through $x = 0$.

x (m)

$x = +A = 0.17$ m

$T = 1.60$ s

$x = -A = -0.17$ m

t (s)

(b)

v_x (m/s)

$v = +v_{max}$

$v = -v_{max}$

t (s)

FIGURE 14.3a shows the data with the graph axes in their "normal" positions. You can see that the amplitude in this experiment was $A = 0.17$ m, or 17 cm. You can also measure the period to be $T = 1.60$ s. Thus the oscillation frequency was $f = 1/T = 0.625$ Hz.

FIGURE 14.3b is a velocity-versus-time graph that the computer produced by using $\Delta x/\Delta t$ to find the slope of the position graph at each point. The velocity graph is also sinusoidal, oscillating between $-v_{max}$ (maximum speed to the left) and $+v_{max}$ (maximum speed to the right). As the figure shows,

- The instantaneous velocity is zero at the points where $x = \pm A$. These are the *turning points* in the motion.
- The maximum speed v_{max} is reached as the object passes through the equilibrium position at $x = 0$ m. The *velocity* is positive as the object moves to the right but *negative* as it moves to the left.

We can ask three important questions about this oscillating system:

1. How is the maximum speed v_{max} related to the amplitude A?
2. How are the period and frequency related to the object's mass m, the spring constant k, and the amplitude A?
3. Is the sinusoidal oscillation a consequence of Newton's laws?

A mass oscillating on a spring is the prototype of simple harmonic motion. Our analysis, in which we answer these questions, will be of a spring-mass system. Even so, most of what we learn will be applicable to other types of SHM.

Kinematics of Simple Harmonic Motion

FIGURE 14.4 redraws the position-versus-time graph of **FIGURE 14.3a** as a smooth curve. Although these are empirical data (we don't yet have any "theory" of oscillation) the position-versus-time graph is clearly a cosine function. We can write the object's position as

$$x(t) = A\cos\left(\frac{2\pi t}{T}\right) \tag{14.2}$$

where the notation $x(t)$ indicates that the position x is a *function* of time t. Because $\cos(2\pi) = \cos(0)$, it's easy to see that the position at time $t = T$ is the same as the position at $t = 0$. In other words, this is a cosine function with period T. Be sure to convince yourself that this function agrees with the five special points shown in Figure 14.4.

FIGURE 14.4 The position-versus-time graph for simple harmonic motion.

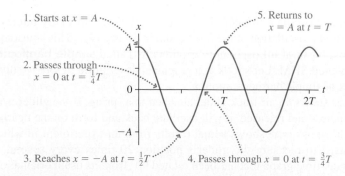

1. Starts at $x = A$

2. Passes through $x = 0$ at $t = \frac{1}{4}T$

3. Reaches $x = -A$ at $t = \frac{1}{2}T$

4. Passes through $x = 0$ at $t = \frac{3}{4}T$

5. Returns to $x = A$ at $t = T$

NOTE ► The argument of the cosine function is in *radians*. That will be true throughout this chapter. It's especially important to remember to set your calculator to radian mode before working oscillation problems. Leaving it in degree mode will lead to major errors. ◄

We can write Equation 14.2 in two alternative forms. Because the oscillation frequency is $f = 1/T$, we can write

$$x(t) = A\cos(2\pi ft) \tag{14.3}$$

Recall from Chapter 4 that a particle in circular motion has an *angular velocity* ω that is related to the period by $\omega = 2\pi/T$, where ω is in rad/s. Now that we've defined the frequency f, you can see that ω and f are related by

$$\omega \text{ (in rad/s)} = \frac{2\pi}{T} = 2\pi f \text{ (in Hz)} \tag{14.4}$$

In this context, ω is called the **angular frequency**. The position can be written in terms of ω as

$$x(t) = A\cos\omega t \tag{14.5}$$

Equations 14.2, 14.3, and 14.5 are equivalent ways to write the position of an object moving in simple harmonic motion.

Just as the position graph was clearly a cosine function, the velocity graph shown in FIGURE 14.5 is clearly an "upside-down" sine function with the same period T. The velocity v_x, which is a function of time, can be written

$$v_x(t) = -v_{max}\sin\left(\frac{2\pi t}{T}\right) = -v_{max}\sin(2\pi ft) = -v_{max}\sin\omega t \tag{14.6}$$

NOTE ▶ v_{max} is the maximum *speed* and thus is a *positive* number. The minus sign in Equation 14.6 is needed to turn the sine function upside down. ◀

We deduced Equation 14.6 from the experimental results, but we could equally well find it from the position function of Equation 14.2. After all, velocity is the time derivative of position. Table 14.2 reminds you of the derivatives of sine and cosine functions. Using the derivative of the cosine function, we find

$$v_x(t) = \frac{dx}{dt} = -\frac{2\pi A}{T}\sin\left(\frac{2\pi t}{T}\right) = -2\pi fA\sin(2\pi ft) = -\omega A\sin\omega t \tag{14.7}$$

We can draw an important conclusion by comparing Equation 14.7, the mathematical definition of velocity, to Equation 14.6, the empirical description of the velocity. Namely, the maximum speed of an oscillation is

$$v_{max} = \frac{2\pi A}{T} = 2\pi fA = \omega A \tag{14.8}$$

Equation 14.8 answers the first question we posed above, which was how the maximum speed v_{max} is related to the amplitude A. Not surprisingly, the object moves faster if you stretch the spring farther and give the oscillation a larger amplitude.

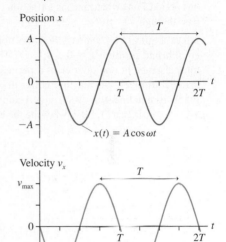

FIGURE 14.5 Position and velocity graphs for simple harmonic motion.

TABLE 14.2 Derivatives of sine and cosine functions

$$\frac{d}{dt}\big(a\sin(bt + c)\big) = +ab\cos(bt + c)$$

$$\frac{d}{dt}\big(a\cos(bt + c)\big) = -ab\sin(bt + c)$$

EXAMPLE 14.2 A system in simple harmonic motion
An air-track glider is attached to a spring, pulled 20.0 cm to the right, and released at $t = 0$ s. It makes 15 oscillations in 10.0 s.

a. What is the period of oscillation?
b. What is the object's maximum speed?
c. What are the position and velocity at $t = 0.800$ s?

MODEL An object oscillating on a spring is in SHM.

SOLVE a. The oscillation frequency is

$$f = \frac{15 \text{ oscillations}}{10.0 \text{ s}} = 1.50 \text{ oscillations/s} = 1.50 \text{ Hz}$$

Thus the period is $T = 1/f = 0.667$ s.

b. The oscillation amplitude is $A = 0.200$ m. Thus

$$v_{max} = \frac{2\pi A}{T} = \frac{2\pi(0.200 \text{ m})}{0.667 \text{ s}} = 1.88 \text{ m/s}$$

c. The object starts at $x = +A$ at $t = 0$ s. This is exactly the oscillation described by Equations 14.2 and 14.6. The position at $t = 0.800$ s is

$$x = A\cos\left(\frac{2\pi t}{T}\right) = (0.200 \text{ m})\cos\left(\frac{2\pi(0.800 \text{ s})}{0.667 \text{ s}}\right)$$

$$= (0.200 \text{ m})\cos(7.54 \text{ rad}) = 0.0625 \text{ m} = 6.25 \text{ cm}$$

Continued

The velocity at this instant of time is

$$v_x = -v_{max} \sin\left(\frac{2\pi t}{T}\right) = -(1.88 \text{ m/s}) \sin\left(\frac{2\pi(0.800 \text{ s})}{0.667 \text{ s}}\right)$$

$$= -(1.88 \text{ m/s}) \sin(7.54 \text{ rad}) = -1.79 \text{ m/s} = -179 \text{ cm/s}$$

At $t = 0.800$ s, which is slightly more than one period, the object is 6.25 cm to the right of equilibrium and moving to the *left* at 179 cm/s. Notice the use of radians in the calculations.

EXAMPLE 14.3 Finding the time

A mass oscillating in simple harmonic motion starts at $x = A$ and has period T. At what time, as a fraction of T, does the object first pass through $x = \frac{1}{2}A$?

SOLVE Figure 14.4 showed that the object passes through the equilibrium position $x = 0$ at $t = \frac{1}{4}T$. This is one-quarter of the total distance in one-quarter of a period. You might expect it to take $\frac{1}{8}T$ to reach $\frac{1}{2}A$, but this is not the case because the SHM graph is not linear between $x = A$ and $x = 0$. We need to use $x(t) = A\cos(2\pi t/T)$. First, we write the equation with $x = \frac{1}{2}A$:

$$x = \frac{A}{2} = A\cos\left(\frac{2\pi t}{T}\right)$$

Then we solve for the time at which this position is reached:

$$t = \frac{T}{2\pi}\cos^{-1}\left(\frac{1}{2}\right) = \frac{T}{2\pi}\frac{\pi}{3} = \frac{1}{6}T$$

ASSESS The motion is slow at the beginning and then speeds up, so it takes longer to move from $x = A$ to $x = \frac{1}{2}A$ than it does to move from $x = \frac{1}{2}A$ to $x = 0$. Notice that the answer is independent of the amplitude A.

STOP TO THINK 14.1 An object moves with simple harmonic motion. If the amplitude and the period are both doubled, the object's maximum speed is

 a. Quadrupled.   b. Doubled.   c. Unchanged.
 d. Halved.   e. Quartered.

14.2 Simple Harmonic Motion and Circular Motion

The graphs of Figure 14.5 and the position function $x(t) = A\cos\omega t$ are for an oscillation in which the object just happened to be at $x_0 = A$ at $t = 0$. But you will recall that $t = 0$ is an arbitrary choice, the instant of time when you or someone else starts a stopwatch. What if you had started the stopwatch when the object was at $x_0 = -A$, or when the object was somewhere in the middle of an oscillation? In other words, what if the oscillator had different *initial conditions*. The position graph would still show an oscillation, but neither Figure 14.5 nor $x(t) = A\cos\omega t$ would describe the motion correctly.

To learn how to describe the oscillation for other initial conditions it will help to turn to a topic you studied in Chapter 4—circular motion. There's a very close connection between simple harmonic motion and circular motion.

Imagine you have a turntable with a small ball glued to the edge. **FIGURE 14.6a** shows how to make a "shadow movie" of the ball by projecting a light past the ball and onto a screen. The ball's shadow oscillates back and forth as the turntable rotates. This is certainly periodic motion, with the same period as the turntable, but is it simple harmonic motion?

To find out, you could place a real object on a real spring directly below the shadow, as shown in **FIGURE 14.6b**. If you did so, and if you adjusted the turntable to have the same period as the spring, you would find that the shadow's motion exactly matches the simple harmonic motion of the object on the spring. **Uniform circular motion projected onto one dimension is simple harmonic motion.**

To understand this, consider the particle in **FIGURE 14.7**. It is in uniform circular motion, moving *counterclockwise* in a circle with radius A. As in Chapter 4, we can locate the particle by the angle ϕ measured ccw from the x-axis. Projecting the ball's shadow onto a screen in Figure 14.6 is equivalent to observing just the x-component

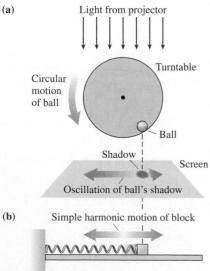

FIGURE 14.6 A projection of the circular motion of a rotating ball matches the simple harmonic motion of an object on a spring.

(a)

Light from projector

Circular motion of ball

Turntable

Ball

Shadow

Screen

Oscillation of ball's shadow

(b) Simple harmonic motion of block

of the particle's motion. Figure 14.7 shows that the x-component, when the particle is at angle ϕ, is

$$x = A\cos\phi \tag{14.9}$$

Recall that the particle's *angular velocity*, in rad/s, is

$$\omega = \frac{d\phi}{dt} \tag{14.10}$$

This is the rate at which the angle ϕ is increasing. If the particle starts from $\phi_0 = 0$ at $t = 0$, its angle at a later time t is simply

$$\phi = \omega t \tag{14.11}$$

As ϕ increases, the particle's x-component is

$$x(t) = A\cos\omega t \tag{14.12}$$

This is identical to Equation 14.5 for the position of a mass on a spring! Thus the x-component of a particle in uniform circular motion is simple harmonic motion.

NOTE ▶ When used to describe oscillatory motion, ω is called the *angular frequency* rather than the angular velocity. The angular frequency of an oscillator has the same numerical value, in rad/s, as the angular velocity of the corresponding particle in circular motion. ◀

The names and units can be a bit confusing until you get used to them. It may help to notice that *cycle* and *oscillation* are not true units. Unlike the "standard meter" or the "standard kilogram," to which you could compare a length or a mass, there is no "standard cycle" to which you can compare an oscillation. Cycles and oscillations are simply counted events. Thus the frequency f has units of hertz, where $1\ \text{Hz} = 1\ \text{s}^{-1}$. We may *say* "cycles per second" just to be clear, but the actual units are only "per second."

The radian is the SI unit of angle. However, the radian is a *defined* unit. Further, its definition as a ratio of two lengths ($\theta = s/r$) makes it a *pure number* without dimensions. As we noted in Chapter 4, the unit of angle, be it radians or degrees, is really just a *name* to remind us that we're dealing with an angle. The 2π in the equation $\omega = 2\pi f$ (and in similar situations), which is stated without units, *means* 2π rad/cycle. When multiplied by the frequency f in cycles/s, it gives the frequency in rad/s. That is why, in this context, ω is called the angular *frequency*.

NOTE ▶ *Hertz* is specifically "cycles per second" or "oscillations per second." It is used for f but *not* for ω. We'll always be careful to use rad/s for ω, but you should be aware that many books give the units of ω as simply s^{-1}. ◀

The Phase Constant

Now we're ready to consider the issue of other initial conditions. The particle in Figure 14.7 started at $\phi_0 = 0$. This was equivalent to an oscillator starting at the far right edge, $x_0 = A$. **FIGURE 14.8** shows a more general situation in which the initial angle ϕ_0 can have any value. The angle at a later time t is then

$$\phi = \omega t + \phi_0 \tag{14.13}$$

In this case, the particle's projection onto the x-axis at time t is

$$x(t) = A\cos(\omega t + \phi_0) \tag{14.14}$$

If Equation 14.14 describes the particle's projection, then it must also be the position of an oscillator in simple harmonic motion. The oscillator's velocity v_x is found by taking the derivative dx/dt. The resulting equations,

$$x(t) = A\cos(\omega t + \phi_0)$$

$$v_x(t) = -\omega A\sin(\omega t + \phi_0) = -v_{max}\sin(\omega t + \phi_0) \tag{14.15}$$

are the two primary kinematic equations of simple harmonic motion.

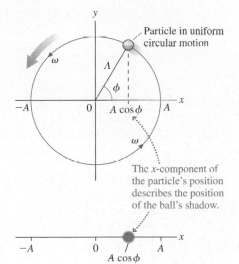

FIGURE 14.7 A particle in uniform circular motion with radius A and angular velocity ω.

Particle in uniform circular motion

The x-component of the particle's position describes the position of the ball's shadow.

A cup on the turntable in a microwave oven moves in a circle. But from the outside, you see the cup sliding back and forth—in simple harmonic motion!

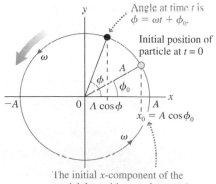

FIGURE 14.8 A particle in uniform circular motion with initial angle ϕ_0.

Angle at time t is $\phi = \omega t + \phi_0$.

Initial position of particle at $t = 0$

$x_0 = A\cos\phi_0$

The initial x-component of the particle's position can be anywhere between $-A$ and A, depending on ϕ_0.

The quantity $\phi = \omega t + \phi_0$, which steadily increases with time, is called the **phase** of the oscillation. The phase is simply the *angle* of the circular-motion particle whose shadow matches the oscillator. The constant ϕ_0 is called the **phase constant.** It specifies the *initial conditions* of the oscillator.

To see what the phase constant means, set $t = 0$ in Equations 14.15:

$$x_0 = A\cos\phi_0$$
$$v_{0x} = -\omega A \sin\phi_0$$

(14.16)

The position x_0 and velocity v_{0x} at $t = 0$ are the initial conditions. **Different values of the phase constant correspond to different starting points on the circle and thus to different initial conditions.**

The perfect cosine function of Figure 14.5 and the equation $x(t) = A\cos\omega t$ are for an oscillation with $\phi_0 = 0$ rad. You can see from Equations 14.16 that $\phi_0 = 0$ rad implies $x_0 = A$ and $v_0 = 0$. That is, the particle starts from rest at the point of maximum displacement.

FIGURE 14.9 illustrates these ideas by looking at three values of the phase constant: $\phi_0 = \pi/3$ rad (60°), $-\pi/3$ rad ($-60°$), and π rad (180°). For each value of ϕ_0 you see the oscillator at its starting position, the starting position shown on a circle, and both position and velocity graphs. All the graphs have the same amplitude and the same period, but they are *shifted* relative to the graphs of Figure 14.5 (which were for $\phi_0 = 0$ rad) so that the maximum displacement $x = A$ occurs at a time other than $t = 0$.

FIGURE 14.9 Oscillations described by the phase constants $\phi_0 = \pi/3$ rad, $-\pi/3$ rad, and π rad.

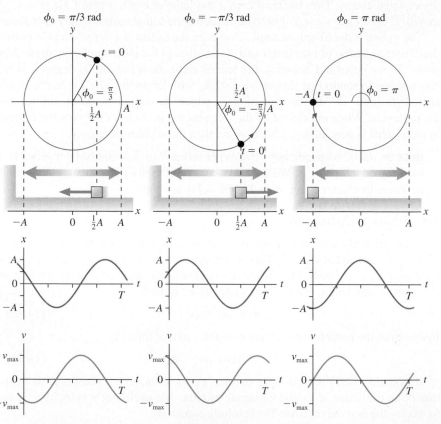

Notice that $\phi_0 = \pi/3$ rad and $\phi_0 = -\pi/3$ rad have the same starting position, $x_0 = \frac{1}{2}A$. This is a property of the cosine function in Equation 14.16. But these are *not* the same initial conditions. In one case the oscillator starts at $\frac{1}{2}A$ while moving to the right, in the other case it starts at $\frac{1}{2}A$ while moving to the left. You can distinguish between the two by visualizing the circular motion.

All values of the phase constant ϕ_0 between 0 and π rad correspond to a particle in the upper half of the circle and *moving to the left*. Thus v_{0x} is negative. All values of the phase constant ϕ_0 between π and 2π rad (or, as they are usually stated, between $-\pi$ and 0 rad) have the particle in the lower half of the circle and *moving to the right*. Thus v_{0x} is positive. If you're told that the oscillator is at $x = \frac{1}{2}A$ and moving to the right at $t = 0$, then the phase constant must be $\phi_0 = -\pi/3$ rad, not $+\pi/3$ rad.

EXAMPLE 14.4 Using the initial conditions

An object on a spring oscillates with a period of 0.80 s and an amplitude of 10 cm. At $t = 0$ s, it is 5.0 cm to the left of equilibrium and moving to the left. What are its position and direction of motion at $t = 2.0$ s?

MODEL An object oscillating on a spring is in simple harmonic motion.

SOLVE We can find the phase constant ϕ_0 from the initial condition $x_0 = -5.0$ cm $= A\cos\phi_0$. This condition gives

$$\phi_0 = \cos^{-1}\left(\frac{x_0}{A}\right) = \cos^{-1}\left(-\frac{1}{2}\right) = \pm\frac{2}{3}\pi \text{ rad} = \pm 120°$$

Because the oscillator is moving to the *left* at $t = 0$, it is in the upper half of the circular-motion diagram and must have a phase constant between 0 and π rad. Thus ϕ_0 is $\frac{2}{3}\pi$ rad. The angular frequency is

$$\omega = \frac{2\pi}{T} = \frac{2\pi}{0.80 \text{ s}} = 7.85 \text{ rad/s}$$

Thus the object's position at time $t = 2.0$ s is

$$x(t) = A\cos(\omega t + \phi_0)$$
$$= (10 \text{ cm})\cos\left((7.85 \text{ rad/s})(2.0 \text{ s}) + \frac{2}{3}\pi\right)$$
$$= (10 \text{ cm})\cos(17.8 \text{ rad}) = 5.0 \text{ cm}$$

The object is now 5.0 cm to the right of equilibrium. But which way is it moving? There are two ways to find out. The direct way is to calculate the velocity at $t = 2.0$ s:

$$v_x = -\omega A\sin(\omega t + \phi_0) = +68 \text{ cm/s}$$

The velocity is positive, so the motion is to the right. Alternatively, we could note that the phase at $t = 2.0$ s is $\phi = 17.8$ rad. Dividing by π, you can see that

$$\phi = 17.8 \text{ rad} = 5.67\pi \text{ rad} = (4\pi + 1.67\pi) \text{ rad}$$

The 4π rad represents two complete revolutions. The "extra" phase of 1.67π rad falls between π and 2π rad, so the particle in the circular-motion diagram is in the lower half of the circle and moving to the right.

NOTE ▶ The inverse-cosine function $\cos^{-1}$ is a *two-valued* function. Your calculator returns a single value, an angle between 0 rad and π rad. But the negative of this angle is also a solution. As Example 14.4 demonstrates, you must use additional information to choose between them. ◀

STOP TO THINK 14.2

The figure shows four oscillators at $t = 0$. Which one has the phase constant $\phi_0 = \pi/4$ rad?

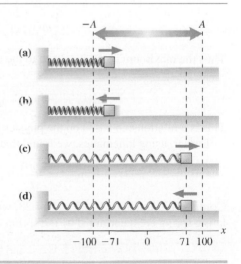

14.3 Energy in Simple Harmonic Motion

We've begun to develop the mathematical language of simple harmonic motion, but thus far we haven't included any physics. We've made no mention of the mass of the object or the spring constant of the spring. An energy analysis, using the tools of Chapters 10 and 11, is a good starting place.

FIGURE 14.10 The energy is transformed between kinetic energy and potential energy as the object oscillates, but the mechanical energy $E = K + U$ doesn't change.

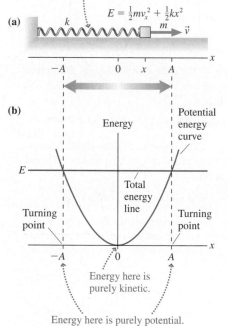

Energy is transformed between kinetic and potential, but the total mechanical energy E doesn't change.

$E = \frac{1}{2}mv_x^2 + \frac{1}{2}kx^2$

(a)

(b)

Energy

Potential energy curve

E

Total energy line

Turning point

Turning point

Energy here is purely kinetic.

Energy here is purely potential.

FIGURE 14.10a shows an object oscillating on a spring, our prototype of simple harmonic motion. Now we'll specify that the object has mass m, the spring has spring constant k, and the motion takes place on a frictionless surface. You learned in Chapter 10 that the elastic potential energy when the object is at position x is $U_s = \frac{1}{2}k(\Delta x)^2$, where $\Delta x = x - x_e$ is the displacement from the equilibrium position x_e. In this chapter we'll always use a coordinate system in which $x_e = 0$, making $\Delta x = x$. There's no chance for confusion with gravitational potential energy, so we can omit the subscript s and write the elastic potential energy as

$$U = \frac{1}{2}kx^2 \qquad (14.17)$$

Thus the mechanical energy of an object oscillating on a spring is

$$E = K + U = \frac{1}{2}mv_x^2 + \frac{1}{2}kx^2 \qquad (14.18)$$

FIGURE 14.10b is an energy diagram, showing the potential-energy curve $U = \frac{1}{2}kx^2$ as a parabola. Recall that a particle oscillates between the *turning points* where the total energy line E crosses the potential-energy curve. The left turning point is at $x = -A$, and the right turning point is at $x = +A$. To go beyond these points would require a negative kinetic energy, which is physically impossible.

You can see that **the particle has purely potential energy at $x = \pm A$ and purely kinetic energy as it passes through the equilibrium point at $x = 0$.** At maximum displacement, with $x = \pm A$ and $v_x = 0$, the energy is

$$E(\text{at } x = \pm A) = U = \frac{1}{2}kA^2 \qquad (14.19)$$

At $x = 0$, where $v_x = \pm v_{max}$, the energy is

$$E(\text{at } x = 0) = K = \frac{1}{2}m(v_{max})^2 \qquad (14.20)$$

The system's mechanical energy is conserved because the surface is frictionless and there are no external forces, so the energy at maximum displacement and the energy at maximum speed, Equations 14.19 and 14.20, must be equal. That is

$$\frac{1}{2}m(v_{max})^2 = \frac{1}{2}kA^2 \qquad (14.21)$$

Thus the maximum speed is related to the amplitude by

$$v_{max} = \sqrt{\frac{k}{m}}A \qquad (14.22)$$

This is a relationship based on the physics of the situation.

Earlier, using kinematics, we found that

$$v_{max} = \frac{2\pi A}{T} = 2\pi f A = \omega A \qquad (14.23)$$

Comparing Equations 14.22 and 14.23, we see that frequency and period of an oscillating spring are determined by the spring constant k and the object's mass m:

$$\omega = \sqrt{\frac{k}{m}} \qquad f = \frac{1}{2\pi}\sqrt{\frac{k}{m}} \qquad T = 2\pi\sqrt{\frac{m}{k}} \qquad (14.24)$$

These three expressions are really only one equation. They say the same thing, but each expresses it in slightly different terms.

Equations 14.24 are the answer to the second question we posed at the beginning of the chapter, where we asked how the period and frequency are related to the object's mass m, the spring constant k, and the amplitude A. It is perhaps surprising, but **the period and frequency do not depend on the amplitude A.** A small oscillation and a large oscillation have the same period.

Because energy is conserved, we can combine Equations 14.18, 14.19, and 14.20 to write

$$E = \frac{1}{2}mv_x^2 + \frac{1}{2}kx^2 = \frac{1}{2}kA^2 = \frac{1}{2}m(v_{max})^2 \quad \text{(conservation of energy)} \quad (14.25)$$

Any pair of these expressions may be useful, depending on the known information. For example, you can use the amplitude A to find the speed at any point x by combining the first and second expressions for E. The speed v at position x is

$$v = \sqrt{\frac{k}{m}(A^2 - x^2)} = \omega\sqrt{A^2 - x^2} \quad (14.26)$$

Similarly, you can use the first and second expressions to find the amplitude from the initial conditions x_0 and v_0:

$$A = \sqrt{x_0^2 + \frac{mv_0^2}{k}} = \sqrt{x_0^2 + \left(\frac{v_0}{\omega}\right)^2} \quad (14.27)$$

FIGURE 14.11 shows graphically how the kinetic and potential energy change with time. They both oscillate but remain *positive* because x and v_x are squared. Energy is continuously being transformed back and forth between the kinetic energy of the moving block and the stored potential energy of the spring, but their sum remains constant. Notice that K and U both oscillate *twice* each period; make sure you understand why.

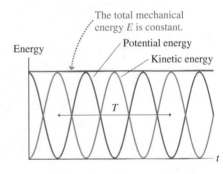

FIGURE 14.11 Kinetic energy, potential energy, and the total mechanical energy for simple harmonic motion.

The total mechanical energy E is constant.

Energy — Potential energy — Kinetic energy

T

t

EXAMPLE 14.5 Using conservation of energy
A 500 g block on a spring is pulled a distance of 20 cm and released. The subsequent oscillations are measured to have a period of 0.80 s. At what position or positions is the block's speed 1.0 m/s?

MODEL The motion is SHM. Energy is conserved.

SOLVE The block starts from the point of maximum displacement, where $E = U = \frac{1}{2}kA^2$. At a later time, when the position is x and the velocity is v_x, energy conservation requires

$$\frac{1}{2}mv_x^2 + \frac{1}{2}kx^2 = \frac{1}{2}kA^2$$

Solving for x, we find

$$x = \sqrt{A^2 - \frac{mv_x^2}{k}} = \sqrt{A^2 - \left(\frac{v}{\omega}\right)^2}$$

where we used $k/m = \omega^2$ from Equation 14.24. The angular frequency is easily found from the period: $\omega = 2\pi/T = 7.85$ rad/s. Thus

$$x = \sqrt{(0.20 \text{ m})^2 - \left(\frac{1.0 \text{ m/s}}{7.85 \text{ rad/s}}\right)^2} = \pm 0.15 \text{ m} = \pm 15 \text{ cm}$$

There are two positions because the block has this speed on either side of equilibrium.

STOP TO THINK 14.3

Four springs have been compressed from their equilibrium position at $x = 0$ cm. When released, they will start to oscillate. Rank in order, from highest to lowest, the maximum speeds of the oscillators.

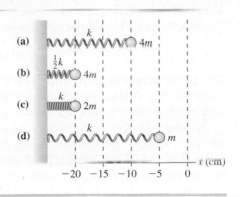

(a) k $4m$

(b) $\frac{1}{2}k$ $4m$

(c) k $2m$

(d) k m

x (cm)

$-20 \quad -15 \quad -10 \quad -5 \quad 0$

14.4 The Dynamics of Simple Harmonic Motion

9.1, 9.2 **Activ Physics**

Our analysis thus far has been based on the experimental observation that the oscillation of a spring "looks" sinusoidal. It's time to show that Newton's second law *predicts* sinusoidal motion.

A motion diagram will help us visualize the object's acceleration. FIGURE 14.12 shows one cycle of the motion, separating motion to the left and motion to the right to make the diagram clear. As you can see, the object's velocity is large as it passes through the equilibrium point at $x = 0$, but $\vec{v}$ is *not changing* at that point. Acceleration measures the *change* of the velocity; hence $\vec{a} = \vec{0}$ at $x = 0$.

FIGURE 14.12 Motion diagram of simple harmonic motion. The left and right motions are separated vertically for clarity but really occur along the same line.

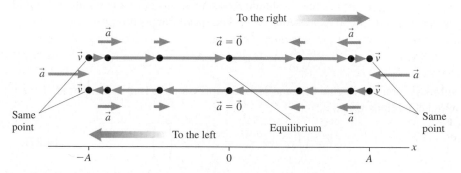

In contrast, the velocity is changing rapidly at the turning points. At the right turning point, $\vec{v}$ changes from a right-pointing vector to a left-pointing vector. Thus the acceleration $\vec{a}$ at the right turning point is large and *to the left*. In one-dimensional motion, the acceleration component a_x has a large *negative* value at the right turning point. Similarly, the acceleration $\vec{a}$ at the left turning point is large and *to the right*. Consequently, a_x has a large positive value at the left turning point.

NOTE ▶ This is the same motion-diagram analysis we used in Chapter 1 to determine the acceleration at the turning point of a ball tossed straight up. ◀

Our motion-diagram analysis suggests that the acceleration a_x is a maximum (most positive) when the displacement is most negative, a minimum (most negative) when the displacement is a maximum, and zero when $x = 0$. This is confirmed by taking the derivative of the velocity:

$$a_x = \frac{dv_x}{dt} = \frac{d}{dt}(-\omega A \sin \omega t) = -\omega^2 A \cos \omega t \qquad (14.28)$$

then graphing it.

FIGURE 14.13 shows the position graph that we started with in Figure 14.4 and the corresponding acceleration graph. Comparing the two, you can see that the acceleration graph looks like an upside-down position graph. In fact, because $x = A \cos \omega t$, Equation 14.28 for the acceleration can be written

$$a_x = -\omega^2 x \qquad (14.29)$$

That is, **the acceleration is proportional to the negative of the displacement.** The acceleration is, indeed, most positive when the displacement is most negative and is most negative when the displacement is most positive.

Our interest in the acceleration is that the acceleration is related to the net force by Newton's second law. Consider again our prototype mass on a spring, shown in FIGURE 14.14. This is the simplest possible oscillation, with no distractions due to friction or gravitational forces. We will assume the spring itself to be massless.

FIGURE 14.13 Position and acceleration graphs for an oscillating spring. We've chosen $\phi_0 = 0$.

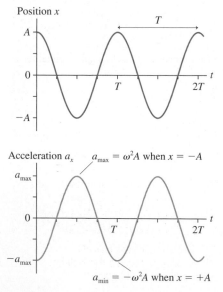

As you learned in Chapter 10, the spring force is given by Hooke's law:

$$(F_{sp})_x = -k\Delta x \qquad (14.30)$$

The minus sign indicates that the spring force is a **restoring force,** a force that always points back toward the equilibrium position. If we place the origin of the coordinate system at the equilibrium position, as we've done throughout this chapter, then $\Delta x = x$ and Hooke's law is simply $(F_{sp})_x = -kx$.

The x-component of Newton's second law for the object attached to the spring is

$$(F_{net})_x = (F_{sp})_x = -kx = ma_x \qquad (14.31)$$

Equation 14.31 is easily rearranged to read

$$a_x = -\frac{k}{m}x \qquad (14.32)$$

You can see that Equation 14.32 is identical to Equation 14.29 if the system oscillates with angular frequency $\omega = \sqrt{k/m}$. We previously found this expression for ω from an energy analysis. Our experimental observation that the acceleration is proportional to the *negative* of the displacement is exactly what Hooke's law would lead us to expect. That's the good news.

The bad news is that a_x is not a constant. As the object's position changes, so does the acceleration. Nearly all of our kinematic tools have been based on constant acceleration. We can't use those tools to analyze oscillations, so we must go back to the very definition of acceleration:

$$a_x = \frac{dv_x}{dt} = \frac{d^2x}{dt^2}$$

Acceleration is the second derivative of position with respect to time. If we use this definition in Equation 14.32, it becomes

$$\frac{d^2x}{dt^2} = -\frac{k}{m}x \qquad \text{(equation of motion for a mass on a spring)} \qquad (14.33)$$

Equation 14.33, which is called the **equation of motion,** is a second-order differential equation. Unlike other equations we've dealt with, Equation 14.33 cannot be solved by direct integration. We'll need to take a different approach.

Solving the Equation of Motion

The solution to an algebraic equation such as $x^2 = 4$ is a number. The solution to a differential equation is a *function.* The x in Equation 14.33 is really $x(t)$, the position as a function of time. The solution to this equation is a function $x(t)$ whose second derivative is the function itself multiplied by $(-k/m)$.

One important property of differential equations that you will learn about in math is that the solutions are *unique.* That is, there is only *one* solution to Equation 14.33. If we were able to *guess* a solution, the uniqueness property would tell us that we had found the *only* solution. That might seem a rather strange way to solve equations, but in fact differential equations are frequently solved by using your knowledge of what the solution needs to look like to guess an appropriate function. Let us give it a try!

We know from experimental evidence that the oscillatory motion of a spring appears to be sinusoidal. Let us *guess* that the solution to Equation 14.33 should have the functional form

$$x(t) = A\cos(\omega t + \phi_0) \qquad (14.34)$$

where A, ω, and ϕ_0 are unspecified constants that we can adjust to any values that might be necessary to satisfy the differential equation.

If you were to guess that a solution to the algebraic equation $x^2 = 4$ is $x = 2$, you would verify your guess by substituting it into the original equation to see if it works.

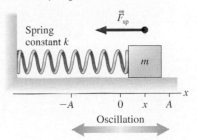

An optical technique called *interferometry* reveals the bell-like vibrations of a wine glass.

We need to do the same thing here: Substitute our guess for $x(t)$ into Equation 14.33 to see if, for an appropriate choice of the three constants, it works. To do so, we need the second derivative of $x(t)$. That is straightforward:

$$x(t) = A\cos(\omega t + \phi_0)$$

$$\frac{dx}{dt} = -\omega A\sin(\omega t + \phi_0) \tag{14.35}$$

$$\frac{d^2x}{dt^2} = -\omega^2 A\cos(\omega t + \phi_0)$$

If we now substitute the first and third of Equations 14.35 into Equation 14.33, we find

$$-\omega^2 A\cos(\omega t + \phi_0) = -\frac{k}{m}A\cos(\omega t + \phi_0) \tag{14.36}$$

Equation 14.36 will be true at all instants of time if and only if $\omega^2 = k/m$. There do not seem to be any restrictions on the two constants A and ϕ_0.

So we have found—by guessing!—that *the* solution to the equation of motion for a mass oscillating on a spring is

$$x(t) = A\cos(\omega t + \phi_0) \tag{14.37}$$

where the angular frequency

$$\omega = 2\pi f = \sqrt{\frac{k}{m}} \tag{14.38}$$

is determined by the mass and the spring constant.

> **NOTE** ▶ Once again we see that the oscillation frequency is independent of the amplitude A. ◀

Equations 14.37 and 14.38 seem somewhat anticlimactic because we've been using these results for the last several pages. But keep in mind that we had been *assuming* $x = A\cos\omega t$ simply because the experimental observations "looked" like a cosine function. We've now justified that assumption by showing that Equation 14.37 really is the solution to Newton's second law for a mass on a spring. **The *theory* of oscillation, based on Hooke's law for a spring and Newton's second law, is in good agreement with the experimental observations.** This conclusion gives an affirmative answer to the last of the three questions that we asked early in the chapter, which was whether the sinusoidal oscillation of SHM is a consequence of Newton's laws.

EXAMPLE 14.6 Analyzing an oscillator

At $t = 0$ s, a 500 g block oscillating on a spring is observed moving to the right at $x = 15$ cm. It reaches a maximum displacement of 25 cm at $t = 0.30$ s.

a. Draw a position-versus-time graph for one cycle of the motion.
b. At what times during the first cycle does the mass pass through $x = 20$ cm?

MODEL The motion is simple harmonic motion.

SOLVE a. The position equation of the block is $x(t) = A\cos(\omega t + \phi_0)$. We know that the amplitude is $A = 0.25$ m and that $x_0 = 0.15$ m. From these two pieces of information we obtain the phase constant:

$$\phi_0 = \cos^{-1}\left(\frac{x_0}{A}\right) = \cos^{-1}(0.60) = \pm 0.927 \text{ rad}$$

The object is initially moving to the right, which tells us that the phase constant must be between $-\pi$ and 0 rad. Thus $\phi_0 = -0.927$ rad. The block reaches its maximum displacement $x_{max} = A$ at time $t = 0.30$ s. At that instant of time

$$x_{max} = A = A\cos(\omega t + \phi_0)$$

This can be true only if $\cos(\omega t + \phi_0) = 1$, which requires $\omega t + \phi_0 = 0$. Thus

$$\omega = \frac{-\phi_0}{t} = \frac{-(-0.927 \text{ rad})}{0.30 \text{ s}} = 3.09 \text{ rad/s}$$

Now that we know ω, it is straightforward to compute the period:

$$T = \frac{2\pi}{\omega} = 2.0 \text{ s}$$

FIGURE 14.15 graphs $x(t) = (25\,\text{cm})\cos(3.09t - 0.927)$, where t is in s, from $t = 0$ s to $t = 2.0$ s.

FIGURE 14.15 Position-versus-time graph for the oscillator of Example 14.6.

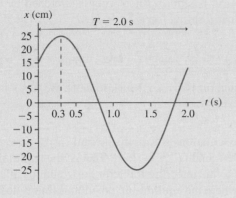

b. From $x = A\cos(\omega t + \phi_0)$, the time at which the mass reaches position $x = 20$ cm is

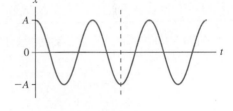

$$t = \frac{1}{\omega}\left(\cos^{-1}\left(\frac{x}{A}\right) - \phi_0\right)$$

$$= \frac{1}{3.09\ \text{rad/s}}\left(\cos^{-1}\left(\frac{20\ \text{cm}}{25\ \text{cm}}\right) + 0.927\ \text{rad}\right) = 0.51\ \text{s}$$

A calculator returns only one value of $\cos^{-1}$, in the range 0 to π rad, but we noted earlier that $\cos^{-1}$ actually has two values. Indeed, you can see in Figure 14.15 that there are two times at which the mass passes $x = 20$ cm. Because they are symmetrical on either side of $t = 0.30$ s, when $x = A$, the first point is $(0.51\ \text{s} - 0.30\ \text{s}) = 0.21$ s *before* the maximum. Thus the mass passes through $x = 20$ cm at $t = 0.09$ s and again at $t = 0.51$ s.

STOP TO THINK 14.4 This is the position graph of a mass on a spring. What can you say about the velocity and the force at the instant indicated by the dashed line?

a. Velocity is positive; force is to the right.
b. Velocity is negative; force is to the right.
c. Velocity is zero; force is to the right.
d. Velocity is positive; force is to the left.
e. Velocity is negative; force is to the left.
f. Velocity is zero; force is to the left.
g. Velocity and force are both zero.

14.5 Vertical Oscillations

We have focused our analysis on a horizontally oscillating spring. But the typical demonstration you'll see in class is a mass bobbing up and down on a spring hung vertically from a support. Is it safe to assume that a vertical oscillation is the same as a horizontal oscillation? Or does the additional force of gravity change the motion? Let us look at this more carefully.

FIGURE 14.16 shows a block of mass m hanging from a spring of spring constant k. An important fact to notice is that the equilibrium position of the block is *not* where the spring is at its unstretched length. At the equilibrium position of the block, where it hangs motionless, the spring has stretched by ΔL.

Finding ΔL is a static-equilibrium problem in which the upward spring force balances the downward gravitational force on the block. The y-component of the spring force is given by Hooke's law:

$$(F_{sp})_y = -k\Delta y = +k\Delta L \tag{14.39}$$

Equation 14.39 makes a distinction between ΔL, which is simply a *distance* and is a positive number, and the displacement Δy. The block is displaced downward, so $\Delta y = -\Delta L$. Newton's first law for the block in equilibrium is

$$(F_{net})_y = (F_{sp})_y + (F_G)_y = k\Delta L - mg = 0 \tag{14.40}$$

from which we can find

$$\Delta L = \frac{mg}{k} \tag{14.41}$$

This is the distance the spring stretches when the block is attached to it.

Activ Physics ONLINE   9.4, 9.5

FIGURE 14.16 Gravity stretches the spring.

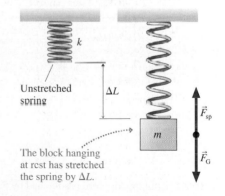

Unstretched spring

The block hanging at rest has stretched the spring by ΔL.

FIGURE 14.17 The block oscillates around the equilibrium position.

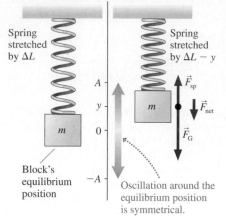

Spring stretched by ΔL

Spring stretched by $\Delta L - y$

Block's equilibrium position

Oscillation around the equilibrium position is symmetrical.

Let the block oscillate around this equilibrium position, as shown in **FIGURE 14.17**. We've now placed the origin of the y-axis at the block's equilibrium position in order to be consistent with our analyses of oscillations throughout this chapter. If the block moves upward, as the figure shows, the spring gets shorter compared to its equilibrium length, but the spring is still *stretched* compared to its unstretched length in Figure 14.16. When the block is at position y, the spring is stretched by an amount $\Delta L - y$ and hence exerts an *upward* spring force $F_{sp} = k(\Delta L - y)$. The net force on the block at this point is

$$(F_{net})_y = (F_{sp})_y + (F_G)_y = k(\Delta L - y) - mg = (k\Delta L - mg) - ky \quad (14.42)$$

But $k\Delta L - mg$ is zero, from Equation 14.41, so the net force on the block is simply

$$(F_{net})_y = -ky \quad (14.43)$$

Equation 14.43 for vertical oscillations is *exactly* the same as Equation 14.31 for horizontal oscillations, where we found $(F_{net})_x = -kx$. That is, the restoring force for vertical oscillations is identical to the restoring force for horizontal oscillations. The role of gravity is to determine where the equilibrium position is, but it doesn't affect the oscillatory motion around the equilibrium position.

Because the net force is the same, Newton's second law has exactly the same oscillatory solution:

$$y(t) = A\cos(\omega t + \phi_0) \quad (14.44)$$

with, again, $\omega = \sqrt{k/m}$. The vertical oscillations of a mass on a spring are the same simple harmonic motion as those of a block on a horizontal spring. This is an important finding because it was not obvious that the motion would still be simple harmonic motion when gravity was included. Because the motions are the same, **everything we have learned about horizontal oscillations is equally valid for vertical oscillations.**

EXAMPLE 14.7 **Bungee oscillations**

An 83 kg student hangs from a bungee cord with spring constant 270 N/m. The student is pulled down to a point where the cord is 5.0 m longer than its unstretched length, then released. Where is the student, and what is his velocity 2.0 s later?

MODEL A bungee cord can be modeled as a spring. Vertical oscillations on the bungee cord are SHM.

VISUALIZE FIGURE 14.18 shows the situation.

FIGURE 14.18 A student on a bungee cord oscillates about the equilibrium position.

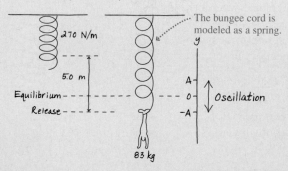

The bungee cord is modeled as a spring.

270 N/m

5.0 m

Equilibrium

Release

Oscillation

83 kg

SOLVE Although the cord is stretched by 5.0 m when the student is released, this is *not* the amplitude of the oscillation. Oscillations occur around the equilibrium position, so we have to begin by

finding the equilibrium point where the student hangs motionless. The cord stretch at equilibrium is given by Equation 14.41:

$$\Delta L = \frac{mg}{k} = 3.0 \text{ m}$$

Stretching the cord 5.0 m pulls the student 2.0 m below the equilibrium point, so $A = 2.0$ m. That is, the student oscillates with amplitude $A = 2.0$ m about a point 3.0 m beneath the bungee cord's original end point. The student's position as a function of time, as measured from the equilibrium position, is

$$y(t) = (2.0 \text{ m})\cos(\omega t + \phi_0)$$

where $\omega = \sqrt{k/m} = 1.80$ rad/s The initial condition

$$y_0 = A\cos\phi_0 = -A$$

requires the phase constant to be $\phi_0 = \pi$ rad. At $t = 2.0$ s the student's position and velocity are

$$y = (2.0 \text{ m})\cos((1.80 \text{ rad/s})(2.0 \text{ s}) + \pi \text{ rad}) = 1.8 \text{ m}$$

$$v_y = -\omega A\sin(\omega t + \phi_0) = -1.6 \text{ m/s}$$

The student is 1.8 m *above* the equilibrium position, or 1.2 m *below* the original end of the cord. Because his velocity is negative, he's passed through the highest point and is heading back down.

14.6 The Pendulum

Now let's look at another very common oscillator: a pendulum. FIGURE 14.19a shows a mass m attached to a string of length L and free to swing back and forth. The pendulum's position can be described by the arc of length s, which is zero when the pendulum hangs straight down. Because angles are measured ccw, s and θ are positive when the pendulum is to the right of center, negative when it is to the left.

Two forces are acting on the mass: the string tension $\vec{T}$ and gravity $\vec{F}_G$. It will be convenient to do what we did in our study of circular motion: Divide the forces into tangential components, parallel to the motion, and radial components parallel to the string. These are shown on the free-body diagram of FIGURE 14.19b.

Newton's second law for the tangential component, parallel to the motion, is

$$(F_{net})_t = \sum F_t = (F_G)_t = -mg\sin\theta = ma_t \qquad (14.45)$$

Using $a_t = d^2s/dt^2$ for acceleration "around" the circle, and noting that the mass cancels, we can write Equation 14.45 as

$$\frac{d^2s}{dt^2} = -g\sin\theta \qquad (14.46)$$

where angle θ is related to the arc length by $\theta = s/L$. This is the equation of motion for an oscillating pendulum. The sine function makes this equation more complicated than the equation of motion for an oscillating spring.

The Small-Angle Approximation

Suppose we restrict the pendulum's oscillations to *small angles* of less than about 10°. This restriction allows us to make use of an interesting and important piece of geometry.

FIGURE 14.20 shows an angle θ and a circular arc of length $s = r\theta$. A right triangle has been constructed by dropping a perpendicular from the top of the arc to the axis. The height of the triangle is $h = r\sin\theta$. Suppose that the angle θ is "small." In that case there is very little difference between h and s. If $h \approx s$, then $r\sin\theta \approx r\theta$. It follows that

$$\sin\theta \approx \theta \qquad (\theta \text{ in radians})$$

The result that $\sin\theta \approx \theta$ for small angles is called the **small-angle approximation.** We can similarly note that $l \approx r$ for small angles. Because $l = r\cos\theta$, it follows that $\cos\theta \approx 1$. Finally, we can take the ratio of sine and cosine to find $\tan\theta \approx \sin\theta \approx \theta$. Table 14.3 summarizes the results of the small-angle approximation. We will have other occasions to use the small-angle approximation throughout the remainder of this text.

NOTE ▶ The small-angle approximation is valid *only* if angle θ is in radians! ◀

How small does θ have to be to justify using the small-angle approximation? It's easy to use your calculator to find that the small-angle approximation is good to three significant figures, an error of $\leq 0.1\%$, up to angles of ≈ 0.10 rad ($\approx 5°$). In practice, we will use the approximation up to about 10°, but for angles any larger it rapidly loses validity and produces unacceptable results.

If we restrict the pendulum to $\theta < 10°$, we can use $\sin\theta \approx \theta = s/L$. In that case, Equation 14.45 for the net force on the mass is

$$(F_{net})_t = -\frac{mg}{L}s$$

FIGURE 14.19 The motion of a pendulum.

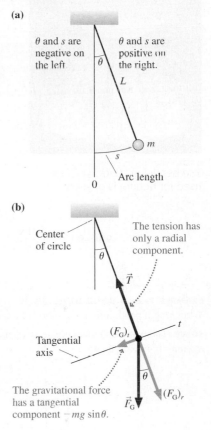

FIGURE 14.20 The geometrical basis of the small-angle approximation.

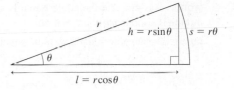

TABLE 14.3 Small-angle approximations. θ must be in radians.

$\sin\theta \approx \theta$
$\cos\theta \approx 1$
$\tan\theta \approx \sin\theta \approx \theta$

The pendulum clock has been used for hundreds of years.

9.10–9.12 Actjv ONLINE Physjcs

and the equation of motion becomes

$$\frac{d^2s}{dt^2} = -\frac{g}{L}s \qquad (14.47)$$

This is *exactly* the same as Equation 14.33 for a mass oscillating on a spring. The names are different, with x replaced by s and k/m by g/L, but that does not make it a different equation.

Because we know the solution to the spring problem, we can immediately write the solution to the pendulum problem just by changing variables and constants:

$$s(t) = A\cos(\omega t + \phi_0) \qquad \text{or} \qquad \theta(t) = \theta_{max}\cos(\omega t + \phi_0) \quad (14.48)$$

The angular frequency

$$\omega = 2\pi f = \sqrt{\frac{g}{L}} \qquad (14.49)$$

is determined by the length of the string. The pendulum is interesting in that **the frequency, and hence the period, is independent of the mass.** It depends only on the length of the pendulum. The amplitude A and the phase constant ϕ_0 are determined by the initial conditions, just as they were for an oscillating spring.

EXAMPLE 14.8 A pendulum clock

What length pendulum has a period of exactly 1 s?

SOLVE The period is independent of the mass and depends only on the length. From Equation 14.49,

$$T = \frac{1}{f} = 2\pi\sqrt{\frac{L}{g}}$$

Solving for L, we find

$$L = g\left(\frac{T}{2\pi}\right)^2 = 0.248 \text{ m}$$

ASSESS This is a convenient length for a practical clock.

EXAMPLE 14.9 The maximum angle of a pendulum

A 300 g mass on a 30-cm-long string oscillates as a pendulum. It has a speed of 0.25 m/s as it passes through the lowest point. What maximum angle does the pendulum reach?

MODEL Assume that the angle remains small, in which case the motion is simple harmonic motion.

SOLVE The angular frequency of the pendulum is

$$\omega = \sqrt{\frac{g}{L}} = \sqrt{\frac{9.8 \text{ m/s}^2}{0.30 \text{ m}}} = 5.72 \text{ rad/s}$$

The speed at the lowest point is $v_{max} = \omega A$, so the amplitude is

$$A = s_{max} = \frac{v_{max}}{\omega} = \frac{0.25 \text{ m/s}}{5.72 \text{ rad/s}} = 0.0437 \text{ m}$$

The maximum angle, at the maximum arc length s_{max}, is

$$\theta_{max} = \frac{s_{max}}{L} = \frac{0.04347 \text{ m}}{0.30 \text{ m}} = 0.145 \text{ rad} = 8.3°$$

ASSESS Because the maximum angle is less than 10°, our analysis based on the small-angle approximation is valid.

The Conditions for Simple Harmonic Motion

You can begin to see how, in a sense, we have solved *all* simple-harmonic-motion problems once we have solved the problem of the horizontal spring. The restoring force of a spring, $F_{sp} = -kx$, is directly proportional to the displacement x from equilibrium. The pendulum's restoring force, in the small-angle approximation, is directly proportional to the displacement s. A restoring force that is directly proportional to the displacement from equilibrium is called a **linear restoring force.** For *any* linear restoring force, the equation of motion is identical to the spring equation (other than perhaps using different symbols). Consequently, **any system with a linear restoring force will undergo simple harmonic motion around the equilibrium position.**

This is why an oscillating spring is the prototype of SHM. Everything that we learn about an oscillating spring can be applied to the oscillations of any other linear restoring force, ranging from the vibration of airplane wings to the motion of electrons in electric circuits. Let's summarize this information with a Tactics Box.

Activ Physics ONLINE 9.6–9.9

TACTICS BOX 14.1 Identifying and analyzing simple harmonic motion (MP)

❶ If the net force acting on a particle is a linear restoring force, the motion will be simple harmonic motion around the equilibrium position.

❷ The position as a function of time is $x(t) = A\cos(\omega t + \phi_0)$. The velocity as a function of time is $v_x(t) = -\omega A\sin(\omega t + \phi_0)$. The maximum speed is $v_{max} = \omega A$. The equations are given here in terms of x, but they can be written in terms of y, θ, or some other parameter if the situation calls for it.

❸ The amplitude A and the phase constant ϕ_0 are determined by the initial conditions through $x_0 = A\cos\phi_0$ and $v_{0x} = -\omega A\sin\phi_0$.

❹ The angular frequency ω (and hence the period $T = 2\pi/\omega$) depends on the physics of the particular situation. But ω does *not* depend on A or ϕ_0.

❺ Mechanical energy is conserved. Thus $\frac{1}{2}mv_x^2 + \frac{1}{2}kx^2 = \frac{1}{2}kA^2 = \frac{1}{2}m(v_{max})^2$. Energy conservation provides a relationship between position and velocity that is independent of time.

Exercises 7–12, 15–19

The Physical Pendulum

A mass on a string is often called a *simple pendulum*. But you can also make a pendulum from any solid object that swings back and forth on a pivot under the influence of gravity. This is called a *physical pendulum*.

FIGURE 14.21 shows a physical pendulum of mass M for which the distance between the pivot and the center of mass is l. The moment arm of the gravitational force acting at the center of mass is $d = l\sin\theta$, so the gravitational torque is

$$\tau = -Mgd = -Mgl\sin\theta$$

The torque is negative because, for positive θ, it's causing a clockwise rotation. If we restrict the angle to being small ($\theta < 10°$), as we did for the simple pendulum, we can use the small-angle approximation to write

$$\tau = -Mgl\theta \tag{14.50}$$

Gravity causes a linear restoring torque on the pendulum—that is, the torque is directly proportional to the angular displacement θ—so we expect the physical pendulum to undergo SHM.

Newton's second law for rotational motion is

$$\alpha = \frac{d^2\theta}{dt^2} = \frac{\tau}{I}$$

where I is the object's moment of inertia about the pivot point. Using Equation 14.50 for the torque, we find

$$\frac{d^2\theta}{dt^2} = \frac{-Mgl}{I}\theta \tag{14.51}$$

Comparison with Equation 14.33 shows that this is again the SHM equation of motion, this time with angular frequency

$$\omega = 2\pi f = \sqrt{\frac{Mgl}{I}} \tag{14.52}$$

It appears that the frequency depends on the mass of the pendulum, but recall that the moment of inertia is directly proportional to M. Thus M cancels and the frequency of a physical pendulum, like that of a simple pendulum, is independent of mass.

FIGURE 14.21 A physical pendulum.

EXAMPLE 14.10 A swinging leg as a pendulum

A student in a biomechanics lab measures the length of his leg, from hip to heel, to be 0.90 m. What is the frequency of the pendulum motion of the student's leg? What is the period?

MODEL We can model a human leg reasonably well as a rod of uniform cross section, pivoted at one end (the hip) to form a physical pendulum. The center of mass of a uniform leg is at the midpoint, so $l = L/2$.

SOLVE The moment of inertia of a rod pivoted about one end is $I = \frac{1}{3}ML^2$, so the pendulum frequency is

$$f = \frac{1}{2\pi}\sqrt{\frac{Mgl}{I}} = \frac{1}{2\pi}\sqrt{\frac{Mg(L/2)}{ML^2/3}} = \frac{1}{2\pi}\sqrt{\frac{3g}{2L}} = 0.64 \text{ Hz}$$

The corresponding period is $T = 1/f = 1.6$ s. Notice that we didn't need to know the mass.

ASSESS As you walk, your legs do swing as physical pendulums as you bring them forward. The frequency is fixed by the length of your legs and their distribution of mass; it doesn't depend on amplitude. Consequently, you don't increase your walking speed by taking more rapid steps—changing the frequency is difficult. You simply take longer strides, changing the amplitude but not the frequency.

STOP TO THINK 14.5   One person swings on a swing and finds that the period is 3.0 s. A second person of equal mass joins him. With two people swinging, the period is

a. 6.0 s	b. >3.0 s but not necessarily 6.0 s
c. 3.0 s	d. <3.0 s but not necessarily 1.5 s
e. 1.5 s	f. Can't tell without knowing the length

14.7 Damped Oscillations

The shock absorbers in cars and trucks are heavily damped springs. The vehicle's vertical motion, after hitting a rock or a pothole, is a damped oscillation.

A pendulum left to itself gradually slows down and stops. The sound of a ringing bell gradually dies away. All real oscillators do run down—some very slowly but others quite quickly—as friction or other dissipative forces transform their mechanical energy into the thermal energy of the oscillator and its environment. An oscillation that runs down and stops is called a **damped oscillation.**

There are many possible reasons for the dissipation of energy: air resistance, friction, internal forces within the metal of the spring as it flexes, and so on. While it would be impractical to account for all of these, a reasonable model is to consider only air resistance because, in many cases, it will be the predominant dissipative force.

The drag force of air resistance is a complex force. There is no "law of air resistance" to tell us exactly how big air-resistance forces are. Chapter 6 introduced a *model* of air resistance in which the drag force was proportional to v^2. That's a good model when velocities are reasonably high, as they are for runners, baseballs, and cars, but a pendulum or an oscillating spring usually moves much more slowly. It is known from experiments that the drag force on *slowly* moving objects is *linearly* proportional to the velocity. Thus a reasonable model of the drag force for a slowly moving object is

$$\vec{D} = -b\vec{v} \qquad \text{(model of the drag force)} \qquad (14.53)$$

where the minus sign is the mathematical statement that the force is always opposite in direction to the velocity in order to slow the object.

The **damping constant** b depends in a complicated way on the shape of the object (long, narrow objects have less air resistance than wide, flat ones) *and* on the viscosity of the air or other medium in which the particle moves. The damping constant plays the same role in our model of air resistance that the coefficient of friction does in our model of friction.

The units of b need to be such that they will give units of force when multiplied by units of velocity. As you can confirm, these units are kg/s. A value $b = 0$ kg/s corresponds to the limiting case of no resistance, in which case the mechanical energy is conserved. A typical value of b for a spring or a pendulum in air is ≤ 0.10 kg/s. Oddly shaped objects or objects moving in a liquid (which is much more viscous than air) can have significantly larger values of b.

FIGURE 14.22 shows a mass oscillating on a spring in the presence of a drag force. With the drag included, Newton's second law is

$$(F_{net})_x = (F_{sp})_x + D_x = -kx - bv_x = ma_x \qquad (14.54)$$

Using $v_x = dx/dt$ and $a_x = d^2x/dt^2$, we can write Equation 14.54 as

$$\frac{d^2x}{dt^2} + \frac{b}{m}\frac{dx}{dt} + \frac{k}{m}x = 0 \qquad (14.55)$$

FIGURE 14.22 An oscillating mass in the presence of a drag force.

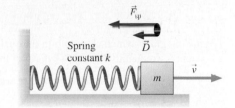

Equation 14.55 is the equation of motion of a damped oscillator. If you compare it to Equation 14.33, the equation of motion for a block on a frictionless surface, you'll see that it differs by the inclusion of the term involving dx/dt.

Equation 14.55 is another second-order differential equation. We will simply assert (and, as a homework problem, you can confirm) that the solution is

$$x(t) = Ae^{-bt/2m}\cos(\omega t + \phi_0) \qquad \text{(damped oscillator)} \qquad (14.56)$$

where the angular frequency is given by

$$\omega = \sqrt{\frac{k}{m} - \frac{b^2}{4m^2}} = \sqrt{\omega_0^2 - \frac{b^2}{4m^2}} \qquad (14.57)$$

Here $\omega_0 = \sqrt{k/m}$ is the angular frequency of an undamped oscillator ($b = 0$). The constant e is the base of natural logarithms, so $e^{-bt/2m}$ is an *exponential function*.

Because $e^0 = 1$, Equation 14.56 reduces to our previous solution, $x(t) = A\cos(\omega t + \phi_0)$, when $b = 0$. This makes sense and gives us confidence in Equation 14.56. A *lightly damped* system, which oscillates many times before stopping, is one for which $b/2m \ll \omega_0$. In that case, $\omega \approx \omega_0$ is a good approximation. That is, light damping does not affect the oscillation frequency. (*Heavy damping*, which stops the motion within a few oscillations, causes the oscillation frequency to be significantly lowered.) We will focus on lightly damped systems for the rest of this section.

FIGURE 14.23 is a graph of the position $x(t)$ for a lightly damped oscillator, as given by Equation 14.56. Notice that the term $Ae^{-bt/2m}$, which is shown by the dashed line, acts as a slowly varying amplitude:

$$x_{max}(t) = Ae^{-bt/2m} \qquad (14.58)$$

where A is the *initial* amplitude, at $t = 0$. The oscillation keeps bumping up against this line, slowly dying out with time.

A slowly changing line that provides a border to a rapid oscillation is called the **envelope** of the oscillations. In this case, the oscillations have an *exponentially decaying envelope*. Make sure you study Figure 14.23 long enough to see how both the oscillations and the decaying amplitude are related to Equation 14.56.

Changing the amount of damping, by changing the value of b, affects how quickly the oscillations decay. **FIGURE 14.24** shows just the envelope $x_{max}(t)$ for several oscillators that are identical except for the value of the damping constant b. (You need to imagine a rapid oscillation within each envelope, as in Figure 14.23). Increasing b causes the oscillations to damp more quickly, while decreasing b makes them last longer.

FIGURE 14.23 Position-versus-time graph for a damped oscillator.

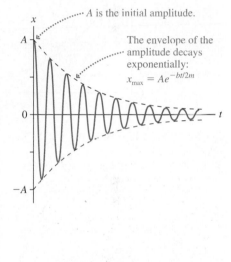

FIGURE 14.24 Several oscillation envelopes, corresponding to different values of the damping constant b.

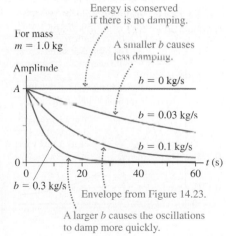

MATHEMATICAL ASIDE **Exponential decay**

Exponential decay occurs in a vast number of physical systems of importance in science and engineering. Mechanical vibrations, electric circuits, and nuclear radioactivity all exhibit exponential decay.

The number $e = 2.71828\ldots$ is the base of natural logarithms in the same way that 10 is the base of ordinary logarithms. It arises naturally in calculus from the integral

$$\int \frac{du}{u} = \ln u$$

This integral—which shows up in the analysis of many physical systems—frequently leads to solutions of the form

$$u = Ae^{-v/v_0} = A\exp(-v/v_0)$$

where exp is the *exponential function*.

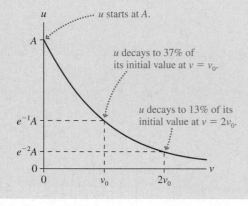

A graph of u illustrates what we mean by *exponential decay*. It starts with $u = A$ at $v = 0$ (because $e^0 = 1$) and then steadily decays, asymptotically approaching zero. The quantity v_0 is called the *decay constant*. When $v = v_0$, $u = e^{-1}A = 0.37A$. When $v = 2v_0$, $u = e^{-2}A = 0.13A$.

Arguments of functions must be pure numbers, without units. That is, we can evaluate e^{-2}, but $e^{-2\,\text{kg}}$ makes no sense. If v/v_0 is a pure number, which it must be, then the decay constant v_0 must have the same units as v. If v represents position, then v_0 is a length; if v represents time, then v_0 is a time interval. In a specific situation, v_0 is often called the *decay length* or the *decay time*. It is the length or time in which the quantity decays to 37% of its initial value.

No matter what the process is or what u represents, **a quantity that decays exponentially decays to 37% of its initial value when one decay constant has passed.** Thus exponential decay is a universal behavior. Every time you meet a new system that exhibits exponential decay, its behavior will be exactly the same as every other exponential decay. The decay curve always looks exactly like the figure shown here. Once you've learned the properties of exponential decay, you'll immediately know how to apply this knowledge to a new situation.

Energy in Damped Systems

When considering the oscillator's mechanical energy, it is useful to define the **time constant** τ (Greek tau) to be

$$\tau = \frac{m}{b} \tag{14.59}$$

Because b has units of kg/s, τ has units of seconds. With this definition, we can write the oscillation amplitude as $x_{\text{max}}(t) = Ae^{-t/2\tau}$.

Because of the drag force, the mechanical energy is no longer conserved. At any particular time we can compute the mechanical energy from

$$E(t) = \frac{1}{2}k(x_{\text{max}})^2 = \frac{1}{2}k(Ae^{-t/2\tau})^2 = \left(\frac{1}{2}kA^2\right)e^{-t/\tau} = E_0 e^{-t/\tau} \tag{14.60}$$

where $E_0 = \frac{1}{2}kA^2$ is the initial energy at $t = 0$ and where we used $(z^m)^2 = z^{2m}$. In other words, **the oscillator's mechanical energy decays exponentially with time constant τ.**

As FIGURE 14.25 shows, the time constant is the amount of time needed for the energy to decay to e^{-1}, or 37%, of its initial value. We say that the time constant τ measures the "characteristic time" during which the energy of the oscillation is dissipated. Roughly two-thirds of the initial energy is gone after one time constant has elapsed, and nearly 90% has dissipated after two time constants have gone by.

For practical purposes, we can speak of the time constant as the *lifetime* of the oscillation—about how long it lasts. An oscillator with $\tau = 3$ s will oscillate for roughly 3 s, while one with $\tau = 30$ s will continue for roughly 30 s. Mathematically,

FIGURE 14.25 Exponential decay of the mechanical energy of an oscillator.

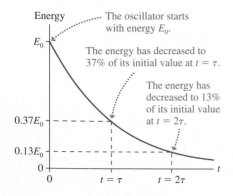

there is never a time when the oscillation is "over." The decay approaches zero asymptotically, but it never gets there in any finite time. The best we can do is define a characteristic time when the motion is "almost over," and that is what the time constant τ does.

EXAMPLE 14.11 A damped pendulum

A 500 g mass swings on a 60-cm-string as a pendulum. The amplitude is observed to decay to half its initial value after 35.0 s.

a. What is the time constant for this oscillator?

b. At what time will the *energy* have decayed to half its initial value?

MODEL The motion is a damped oscillation.

SOLVE a. The initial amplitude at $t = 0$ is $x_{max} = A$. At $t = 35.0$ s the amplitude is $x_{max} = \frac{1}{2}A$. The amplitude of oscillation at time t is given by Equation 14.58:

$$x_{max}(t) = Ae^{-bt/2m} = Ae^{-t/2\tau}$$

In this case,

$$\frac{1}{2}A = Ae^{-(35.0\ s)/2\tau}$$

Notice that we do not need to know A itself because it cancels out. To solve for τ, take the natural logarithm of both sides of the equation:

$$\ln\left(\frac{1}{2}\right) = -\ln 2 = \ln e^{-(35.0\ s)/2\tau} = -\frac{35.0\ s}{2\tau}$$

This is easily rearranged to give

$$\tau = \frac{35.0\ s}{2\ln 2} = 25.2\ s$$

If desired, we could now determine the damping constant to be $b = m/\tau = 0.020$ kg/s.

b. The energy at time t is given by

$$E(t) = E_0 e^{-t/\tau}$$

The time at which an exponential decay is reduced to $\frac{1}{2}E_0$, half its initial value, has a special name. It is called the **half-life** and given the symbol $t_{1/2}$. The concept of the half-life is widely used in applications such as radioactive decay. To relate $t_{1/2}$ to τ, first write

$$E(\text{at } t = t_{1/2}) = \frac{1}{2}E_0 = E_0 e^{-t_{1/2}/\tau}$$

The E_0 cancels, giving

$$\frac{1}{2} = e^{-t_{1/2}/\tau}$$

Again, we take the natural logarithm of both sides:

$$\ln\left(\frac{1}{2}\right) = -\ln 2 = \ln e^{-t_{1/2}/\tau} = -t_{1/2}/\tau$$

Finally, we solve for $t_{1/2}$:

$$t_{1/2} = \tau \ln 2 = 0.693\tau$$

This result that $t_{1/2}$ is 69% of τ is valid for any exponential decay. In this particular problem, half the energy is gone at

$$t_{1/2} = (0.693)(25.2\ s) = 17.5\ s$$

ASSESS The oscillator loses energy faster than it loses amplitude. This is what we should expect because the energy depends on the *square* of the amplitude.

STOP TO THINK 14.6   Rank in order, from largest to smallest, the time constants τ_a to τ_d of the decays shown in the figure. All the graphs have the same scale.

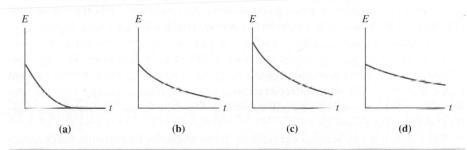

(a)   (b)   (c)   (d)

14.8 Driven Oscillations and Resonance

Thus far we have focused on the free oscillations of an isolated system. Some initial disturbance displaces the system from equilibrium, and it then oscillates freely until its energy is dissipated. These are very important situations, but they do not exhaust the possibilities. Another important situation is an oscillator that is subjected to a periodic external force. Its motion is called a **driven oscillation.**

A simple example of a driven oscillation is pushing a child on a swing, where your push is a periodic external force applied to the swing. A more complex example is a car driving over a series of equally spaced bumps. Each bump causes a periodic upward force on the car's shock absorbers, which are big, heavily damped springs. The electromagnetic coil on the back of a loudspeaker cone provides a periodic magnetic force to drive the cone back and forth, causing it to send out sound waves. Air turbulence moving across the wings of an aircraft can exert periodic forces on the wings and other aerodynamic surfaces, causing them to vibrate if they are not properly designed.

As these examples suggest, driven oscillations have many important applications. However, driven oscillations are a mathematically complex subject. We will simply hint at some of the results, saving the details for more advanced classes.

Consider an oscillating system that, when left to itself, oscillates at a frequency f_0. We will call this the **natural frequency** of the oscillator. The natural frequency for a mass on a spring is $\sqrt{k/m}/2\pi$, but it might be given by some other expression for another type of oscillator. Regardless of the expression, f_0 is simply the frequency of the system if it is displaced from equilibrium and released.

Suppose that this system is subjected to a *periodic* external force of frequency f_{ext}. This frequency, which is called the **driving frequency,** is completely independent of the oscillator's natural frequency f_0. Somebody or something in the environment selects the frequency f_{ext} of the external force, causing the force to push on the system f_{ext} times every second.

Although it is possible to solve Newton's second law with an external driving force, we will be content to look at a graphical representation of the solution. The most important result is that the oscillation amplitude depends very sensitively on the frequency f_{ext} of the driving force. The response to the driving frequency is shown in **FIGURE 14.26** for a system with $m = 1.0$ kg, a natural frequency $f_0 = 2.0$ Hz, and a damping constant $b = 0.20$ kg/s. This graph of amplitude versus driving frequency, called the **response curve,** occurs in many different applications.

When the driving frequency is substantially different from the oscillator's natural frequency, at the right and left edges of Figure 14.26, the system oscillates but the amplitude is very small. The system simply does not respond well to a driving frequency that differs much from f_0. As the driving frequency gets closer and closer to the natural frequency, the amplitude of the oscillation rises dramatically. After all, f_0 is the frequency at which the system "wants" to oscillate, so it is quite happy to respond to a driving frequency near f_0. Hence the amplitude reaches a maximum when the driving frequency exactly matches the system's natural frequency: $f_{ext} = f_0$.

You can understand this if you think about the energy. When f_{ext} matches f_0, the external force always pushes the oscillator at the same point in its cycle. For example, you always push a child on a swing just as the swing reaches its highest point on your side. Such push always *adds energy* to the system, pushing the amplitude higher.

By contrast, suppose you try to push a swing at some frequency other than its natural oscillation frequency. Sometimes you would push it as it goes forward, thus adding energy to the system, but in other cycles you would be trying to push it forward as it comes back. This would decelerate the swing and remove energy from the system. The net result would be a small amplitude. Only the frequency-matching condition builds up the amplitude.

The amplitude can become exceedingly large when the frequencies match, especially if the damping constant is very small. **FIGURE 14.27** shows the same oscillator with three different values of the damping constant. There's very little response if the damping constant is increased to 0.80 kg/s, but the amplitude for $f_{ext} = f_0$ becomes very large when the damping constant is reduced to 0.08 kg/s. This large-amplitude response to a driving force whose frequency matches the natural frequency of the system is a phenomenon called **resonance.** The condition for resonance is

$$f_{ext} = f_0 \qquad \text{(resonance condition)} \qquad (14.61)$$

Within the context of driven oscillations, the natural frequency f_0 is often called the **resonance frequency.**

FIGURE 14.26 The response curve shows the amplitude of a driven oscillator at frequencies near its natural frequency of 2.0 Hz.

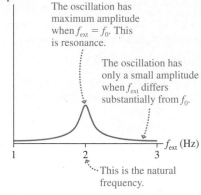

Amplitude

The oscillation has maximum amplitude when $f_{ext} = f_0$. This is resonance.

The oscillation has only a small amplitude when f_{ext} differs substantially from f_0.

f_{ext} (Hz)

This is the natural frequency.

FIGURE 14.27 The resonance amplitude becomes higher and narrower as the damping constant decreases.

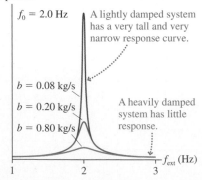

Amplitude

$f_0 = 2.0$ Hz

A lightly damped system has a very tall and very narrow response curve.

$b = 0.08$ kg/s

$b = 0.20$ kg/s

$b = 0.80$ kg/s

A heavily damped system has little response.

f_{ext} (Hz)

There are many examples of resonance. We've seen that pushing a child on a swing is one. "Tuned circuits" in your radio or cell phone are another, one we'll examine in Part VI.

An important feature of Figure 14.27 is how the amplitude and width of the resonance depend on the damping constant. A heavily damped system responds fairly little, even at resonance, but it responds to a wide range of driving frequencies. Very lightly damped systems can reach exceptionally high amplitudes, but notice that the range of frequencies to which the system responds becomes narrower and narrower as b decreases.

This allows us to understand why a few singers can break crystal goblets but not inexpensive, everyday glasses. An inexpensive glass gives a "thud" when tapped, but a fine crystal goblet "rings" for several seconds. In physics terms, the goblet has a much longer time constant than the glass. That, in turn, implies that the goblet is very lightly damped while the ordinary glass is heavily damped (because the internal forces within the glass are not those of a high-quality crystal structure).

The singer causes a sound wave to impinge on the goblet, exerting a small driving force at the frequency of the note she is singing. If the singer's frequency matches the natural frequency of the goblet—resonance! Only the lightly damped goblet, like the top curve in Figure 14.27, can reach amplitudes large enough to shatter. The restriction, though, is that its natural frequency has to be matched very precisely. The sound also has to be very loud.

It is worth noting that there are many mechanical systems, such as the wings on airplanes, for which it is essential that resonances be avoided! It is important to understand the conditions of resonance in order to design structures without them.

A singer or musical instrument can shatter a crystal goblet by matching the goblet's natural oscillation frequency.

SUMMARY

The goal of Chapter 14 has been to understand systems that oscillate with simple harmonic motion.

General Principles

Dynamics

SHM occurs when a **linear restoring force** acts to return a system to an equilibrium position.

Horizontal spring

$(F_{net})_x = -kx$

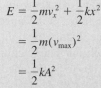

Vertical spring

The origin is at the equilibrium position $\Delta L = mg/k$.

$(F_{net})_y = -ky$

$$\omega = \sqrt{\frac{k}{m}} \qquad T = 2\pi\sqrt{\frac{m}{k}}$$

Pendulum

$$(F_{net})_t = -\left(\frac{mg}{L}\right)s$$

$$\omega = \sqrt{\frac{g}{L}} \qquad T = 2\pi\sqrt{\frac{L}{g}}$$

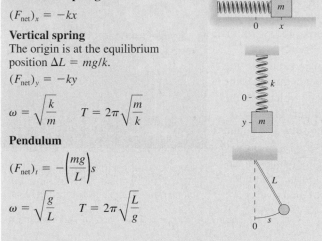

Energy

If there is **no friction** or dissipation, kinetic and potential energy are alternately transformed into each other, but the total mechanical energy $E = K + U$ is conserved.

$$E = \frac{1}{2}mv_x^2 + \frac{1}{2}kx^2$$
$$= \frac{1}{2}m(v_{max})^2$$
$$= \frac{1}{2}kA^2$$

In a **damped system,** the energy decays exponentially

$$E = E_0 e^{-t/\tau}$$

where τ is the **time constant.**

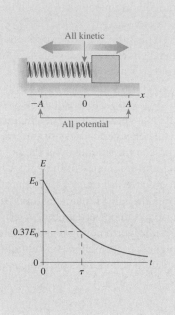

Important Concepts

Simple harmonic motion (SHM) is a sinusoidal oscillation with period T and amplitude A.

Frequency $f = \dfrac{1}{T}$

Angular frequency

$$\omega = 2\pi f = \frac{2\pi}{T}$$

Position $x(t) = A\cos(\omega t + \phi_0)$

$$= A\cos\left(\frac{2\pi t}{T} + \phi_0\right)$$

Velocity $v_x(t) = -v_{max}\sin(\omega t + \phi_0)$ with maximum speed $v_{max} = \omega A$

Acceleration $a_x = -\omega^2 x$

SHM is the projection onto the x-axis of **uniform circular motion.**

$\phi = \omega t + \phi_0$ is the **phase**

The position at time t is

$$x(t) = A\cos\phi$$
$$= A\cos(\omega t + \phi_0)$$

The **phase constant** ϕ_0 determines the initial conditions:

$$x_0 = A\cos\phi_0 \qquad v_{0x} = -\omega A\sin\phi_0$$

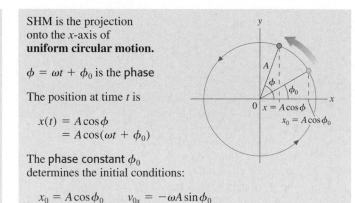

Applications

Resonance

When a system is driven by a periodic external force, it responds with a large-amplitude oscillation if $f_{ext} \approx f_0$, where f_0 is the system's natural oscillation frequency, or **resonant frequency.**

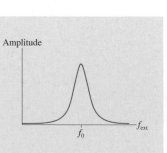

Damping

If there is a drag force $\vec{D} = -b\vec{v}$, where b is the damping constant, then (for lightly damped systems)

$$x(t) = Ae^{-bt/2m}\cos(\omega t + \phi_0)$$

The time constant for energy loss is $\tau = m/b$.

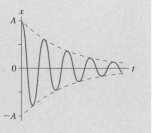

Terms and Notation

oscillatory motion	amplitude, A	linear restoring force	natural frequency, f_0
oscillator	angular frequency, ω	damped oscillation	driving frequency, f_{ext}
period, T	phase, ϕ	damping constant, b	response curve
frequency, f	phase constant, ϕ_0	envelope	resonance
hertz, Hz	restoring force	time constant, τ	resonance frequency, f_0
simple harmonic motion,	equation of motion	half-life, $t_{1/2}$	
SHM	small-angle approximation	driven oscillation	

(MP) For homework assigned on MasteringPhysics, go to www.masteringphysics.com
Problem difficulty is labeled as | (straightforward) to ||| (challenging).

Problems labeled ▮ integrate significant material from earlier chapters.

CONCEPTUAL QUESTIONS

1. A block oscillating on a spring has period $T = 2$ s. What is the period if:
   a. The block's mass is doubled? Explain. Note that you do not know the value of either m or k, so do *not* assume any particular values for them. The required analysis involves thinking about ratios.
   b. The value of the spring constant is quadrupled?
   c. The oscillation amplitude is doubled while m and k are unchanged?

2. A pendulum on Planet X, where the value of g is unknown, oscillates with a period $T = 2$ s. What is the period of this pendulum if:
   a. Its mass is doubled? Explain. Note that you do not know the value of m, L, or g, so do not assume any specific values. The required analysis involves thinking about ratios.
   b. Its length is doubled?
   c. Its oscillation amplitude is doubled?

3. **FIGURE Q14.3** shows a position-versus-time graph for a particle in SHM. What are (a) the amplitude A, (b) the angular frequency ω, and (c) the phase constant ϕ_0? Explain.

FIGURE Q14.3

4. **FIGURE Q14.4** shows a position-versus-time graph for a particle in SHM
   a. What is the phase constant ϕ_0? Explain.
   b. What is the phase of the particle at each of the three numbered points on the graph?

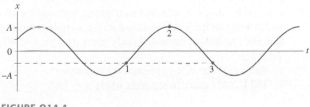

FIGURE Q14.4

5. **FIGURE Q14.5** shows a velocity-versus-time graph for a particle in SHM.
   a. What is the phase constant ϕ_0? Explain.
   b. What is the phase of the particle at each of the three numbered points on the graph?

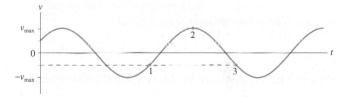

FIGURE Q14.5

6. Equation 14.25 states that $\frac{1}{2}kA^2 = \frac{1}{2}m(v_{max})^2$. What does this mean? Write a couple of sentences explaining how to interpret this equation.

7. **FIGURE Q14.7** shows the potential-energy diagram and the total energy line of a particle oscillating on a spring.
   a. What is the spring's equilibrium length?
   b. Where are the turning points of the motion? Explain.
   c. What is the particle's maximum kinetic energy?
   d. What will be the turning points if the particle's total energy is doubled?

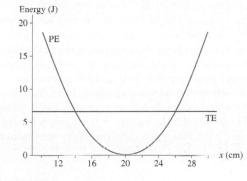

FIGURE Q14.7

8. A block oscillating on a spring has an amplitude of 20 cm. What will the block's amplitude be if its total energy is doubled? Explain.

9. A block oscillating on a spring has a maximum speed of 20 cm/s. What will the block's maximum speed be if its total energy is doubled? Explain.

10. Suppose the damping constant b of an oscillator increases.
    a. Is the medium more resistive or less resistive?
    b. Do the oscillations damp out more quickly or less quickly?
    c. Is the time constant τ increased or decreased?

11. a. Describe the difference between τ and T. Don't just *name* them; say what is different about the physical concepts they represent.
    b. Describe the difference between τ and $t_{1/2}$.

12. What is the difference between the driving frequency and the natural frequency of an oscillator?

EXERCISES AND PROBLEMS

Exercises

Section 14.1 Simple Harmonic Motion

1. | When a guitar string plays the note "A," the string vibrates at 440 Hz. What is the period of the vibration?

2. | An air-track glider attached to a spring oscillates between the 10 cm mark and the 60 cm mark on the track. The glider completes 10 oscillations in 33 s. What are the (a) period, (b) frequency, (c) angular frequency, (d) amplitude, and (e) maximum speed of the glider?

3. || An air-track glider is attached to a spring. The glider is pulled to the right and released from rest at $t = 0$ s. It then oscillates with a period of 2.0 s and a maximum speed of 40 cm/s.
    a. What is the amplitude of the oscillation?
    b. What is the glider's position at $t = 0.25$ s?

Section 14.2 Simple Harmonic Motion and Circular Motion

4. || What are the (a) amplitude, (b) frequency, and (c) phase constant of the oscillation shown in **FIGURE EX14.4**?

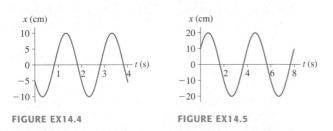

FIGURE EX14.4   **FIGURE EX14.5**

5. || What are the (a) amplitude, (b) frequency, and (c) phase constant of the oscillation shown in **FIGURE EX14.5**?

6. || An object in simple harmonic motion has an amplitude of 4.0 cm, a frequency of 2.0 Hz, and a phase constant of $2\pi/3$ rad. Draw a position graph showing two cycles of the motion.

7. || An object in simple harmonic motion has an amplitude of 8.0 cm, a frequency of 0.25 Hz, and a phase constant of $-\pi/2$ rad. Draw a position graph showing two cycles of the motion.

8. || An object in simple harmonic motion has amplitude 4.0 cm and frequency 4.0 Hz, and at $t = 0$ s it passes through the equilibrium point moving to the right. Write the function $x(t)$ that describes the object's position.

9. || An object in simple harmonic motion has amplitude 8.0 cm and frequency 0.50 Hz. At $t = 0$ s it has its most negative velocity. Write the function $x(t)$ that describes the object's position.

10. || An air-track glider attached to a spring oscillates with a period of 1.5 s. At $t = 0$ s the glider is 5.00 cm left of the equilibrium position and moving to the right at 36.3 cm/s.
    a. What is the phase constant?
    b. What is the phase at $t = 0$ s, 0.5 s, 1.0 s, and 1.5 s?

Section 14.3 Energy in Simple Harmonic Motion

Section 14.4 The Dynamics of Simple Harmonic Motion

11. | A block attached to a spring with unknown spring constant oscillates with a period of 2.0 s. What is the period if
    a. The mass is doubled?
    b. The mass is halved?
    c. The amplitude is doubled?
    d. The spring constant is doubled?
    Parts a to d are independent questions, each referring to the initial situation.

12. || A 200 g air-track glider is attached to a spring. The glider is pushed in 10 cm and released. A student with a stopwatch finds that 10 oscillations take 12.0 s. What is the spring constant?

13. || A 200 g mass attached to a horizontal spring oscillates at a frequency of 2.0 Hz. At $t = 0$ s, the mass is at $x = 5.0$ cm and has $v_x = -30$ cm/s. Determine:
    a. The period.   b. The angular frequency.
    c. The amplitude.   d. The phase constant.
    e. The maximum speed.   f. The maximum acceleration.
    g. The total energy.   h. The position at $t = 0.40$ s.

14. || The position of a 50 g oscillating mass is given by $x(t) = (2.0 \text{ cm})\cos(10t - \pi/4)$, where t is in s. Determine:
    a. The amplitude.   b. The period.
    c. The spring constant.   d. The phase constant.
    e. The initial conditions. f. The maximum speed.
    g. The total energy.   h. The velocity at $t = 0.40$ s.

15. || A 1.0 kg block is attached to a spring with spring constant 16 N/m. While the block is sitting at rest, a student hits it with a hammer and almost instantaneously gives it a speed of 40 cm/s. What are
    a. The amplitude of the subsequent oscillations?
    b. The block's speed at the point where $x = \frac{1}{2}A$?

Section 14.5 Vertical Oscillations

16. | A spring is hanging from the ceiling. Attaching a 500 g physics book to the spring causes it to stretch 20 cm in order to come to equilibrium.
    a. What is the spring constant?
    b. From equilibrium, the book is pulled down 10 cm and released. What is the period of oscillation?
    c. What is the book's maximum speed? At what position or positions does it have this speed?

17. || A spring is hung from the ceiling. When a block is attached to its end, it stretches 2.0 cm before reaching its new equilibrium length. The block is then pulled down slightly and released. What is the frequency of oscillation?

18. || A spring with spring constant 15 N/m hangs from the ceiling. A ball is attached to the spring and allowed to come to rest. It is then pulled down 6.0 cm and released. If the ball makes 30 oscillations in 20 s, what are its (a) mass and (b) maximum speed?

Section 14.6 The Pendulum

19. | A mass on a string of unknown length oscillates as a pendulum with a period of 4.0 s. What is the period if
    a. The mass is doubled?   b. The string length is doubled?
    c. The string length is halved?   d. The amplitude is doubled?
    Parts a to d are independent questions, each referring to the initial situation.

20. | The angle of a pendulum is $\theta(t) = (0.10 \text{ rad})\cos(5t + \pi)$, where t is in s. Determine:
    a. The amplitude.   b. The frequency.
    c. The phase constant.   d. The length of the string.
    e. The initial angle.   f. The angle at $t = 2.0$ s.

21. || A 200 g ball is tied to a string. It is pulled to an angle of 8.0° and released to swing as a pendulum. A student with a stopwatch finds that 10 oscillations take 12 s. How long is the string?

22. | What is the period of a 1.0-m-long pendulum on (a) the earth and (b) Venus?

23. | What is the length of a pendulum whose period on the moon matches the period of a 2.0-m-long pendulum on the earth?

24. | Astronauts on the first trip to Mars take along a pendulum that has a period on earth of 1.50 s. The period on Mars turns out to be 2.45 s. What is the free-fall acceleration on Mars?

25. || The 20-cm-long wrench in FIGURE EX14.25 swings on its hook with a period of 0.90 s. When the wrench hangs from a spring of spring constant 360 N/m, it stretches the spring 3.0 cm. What is the wrench's moment of inertia about the hook?

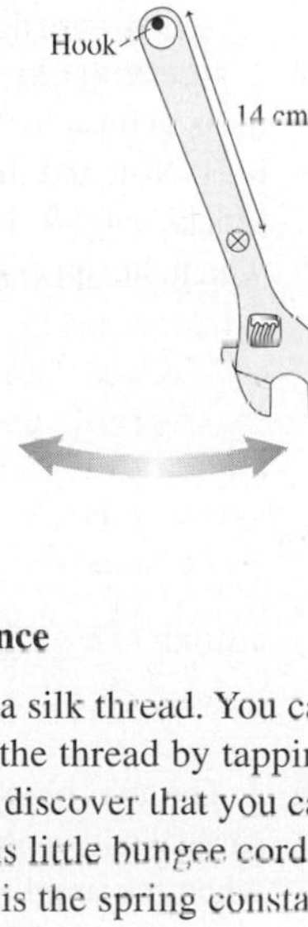

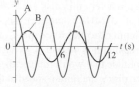

FIGURE EX14.25

Section 14.7 Damped Oscillations

Section 14.8 Driven Oscillations and Resonance

26. | A 2.0 g spider is dangling at the end of a silk thread. You can make the spider bounce up and down on the thread by tapping lightly on his feet with a pencil. You soon discover that you can give the spider the largest amplitude on his little bungee cord if you tap exactly once every second. What is the spring constant of the silk thread?

27. || The amplitude of an oscillator decreases to 36.8% of its initial value in 10.0 s. What is the value of the time constant?

28. || Calculate and draw an accurate position graph from $t = 0$ s to $t = 10$ s of a damped oscillator having a frequency of 1.0 Hz and a time constant of 4.0 s.

29. | In a science museum, a 110 kg brass pendulum bob swings at the end of a 15.0-m-long wire. The pendulum is started at exactly 8:00 A.M. every morning by pulling it 1.5 m to the side and releasing it. Because of its compact shape and smooth surface, the pendulum's damping constant is only 0.010 kg/s. At exactly 12:00 noon, how many oscillations will the pendulum have completed and what is its amplitude?

30. || A spring with spring constant 15.0 N/m hangs from the ceiling. A 500 g ball is attached to the spring and allowed to come to rest. It is then pulled down 6.0 cm and released. What is the time constant if the ball's amplitude has decreased to 3.0 cm after 30 oscillations?

Problems

31. || FIGURE P14.31 is the position-versus-time graph of a particle in simple harmonic motion.
    a. What is the phase constant?
    b. What is the velocity at $t = 0$ s?
    c. What is v_{max}?

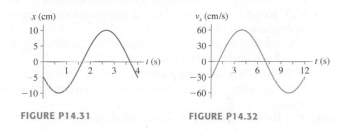

FIGURE P14.31   FIGURE P14.32

32. || FIGURE P14.32 is the velocity-versus-time graph of a particle in simple harmonic motion.
    a. What is the amplitude of the oscillation?
    b. What is the phase constant?
    c. What is the position at $t = 0$ s?

33. || The two graphs in FIGURE P14.33 are for two different vertical mass-spring systems.
    a. What is the frequency of system A? What is the first time at which the mass has maximum speed while traveling in the upward direction?
    b. What is the period of system B? What is the first time at which the energy is all potential?
    c. If both systems have the same mass, what is the ratio k_A/k_B of their spring constants?

FIGURE P14.33

34. || An object in SHM oscillates with a period of 4.0 s and an amplitude of 10 cm. How long does the object take to move from $x = 0.0$ cm to $x = 6.0$ cm?

35. || A 1.0 kg block oscillates on a spring with spring constant 20 N/m. At $t = 0$ s the block is 20 cm to the right of the equilibrium position and moving to the left at a speed of 100 cm/s. Determine the period of oscillation and draw a graph of position versus time.

36. || Astronauts in space cannot weigh themselves by standing on a bathroom scale. Instead, they determine their mass by oscillating on a large spring. Suppose an astronaut attaches one end of a large spring to her belt and the other end to a hook on the wall of the space capsule. A fellow astronaut then pulls her away from the wall and releases her. The spring's length as a function of time is shown in FIGURE P14.36.
   a. What is her mass if the spring constant is 240 N/m?
   b. What is her speed when the spring's length is 1.2 m?

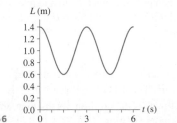

FIGURE P14.36

37. || The motion of a particle is given by $x(t) = (25 \text{ cm})\cos(10t)$, where t is in s. At what time is the kinetic energy twice the potential energy?

38. || a. When the displacement of a mass on a spring is $\frac{1}{2}A$, what fraction of the energy is kinetic energy and what fraction is potential energy?
   b. At what displacement, as a fraction of A, is the energy half kinetic and half potential?

39. || For a particle in simple harmonic motion, show that $v_{max} = (\pi/2)v_{avg}$ where v_{avg} is the average speed during one cycle of the motion.

40. || A 100 g ball attached to a spring with spring constant 2.5 N/m oscillates horizontally on a frictionless table. Its velocity is 20 cm/s when $x = -5.0$ cm.
   a. What is the amplitude of oscillation?
   b. What is the ball's maximum acceleration?
   c. What is the ball's position when the acceleration is maximum?
   d. What is the speed of the ball when $x = 3.0$ cm?

41. || A block on a spring is pulled to the right and released at $t = 0$ s. It passes $x = 3.00$ cm at $t = 0.685$ s, and it passes $x = -3.00$ cm at $t = 0.886$ s.
   a. What is the angular frequency?
   b. What is the amplitude?
   Hint: $\cos(\pi - \theta) = -\cos\theta$.

42. || A 300 g oscillator has a speed of 95.4 cm/s when its displacement is 3.0 cm and 71.4 cm/s when its displacement is 6.0 cm. What is the oscillator's maximum speed?

43. || An ultrasonic transducer, of the type used in medical ultrasound imaging, is a very thin disk ($m = 0.10$ g) driven back and forth in SHM at 1.0 MHz by an electromagnetic coil.
   a. The maximum restoring force that can be applied to the disk without breaking it is 40,000 N. What is the maximum oscillation amplitude that won't rupture the disk?
   b. What is the disk's maximum speed at this amplitude?

44. || A 5.0 kg block hangs from a spring with spring constant 2000 N/m. The block is pulled down 5.0 cm from the equilibrium position and given an initial velocity of 1.0 m/s back toward equilibrium. What are the (a) frequency, (b) amplitude, and (c) total mechanical energy of the motion?

45. || The prongs of a tuning fork each vibrate with an amplitude of 0.50 mm at the tuning fork's frequency of 440 Hz.
   a. What is the maximum speed of the tip of one prong?
   b. A 10 μg flea was sitting on the tip of the prong when the tuning fork was sounded. Surface tension allows a flea's feet to hold onto a smooth surface with a force of up to 1.0 mN. Will the flea be able to hold onto the vibrating prong, or will it be thrown off?

46. ||| A 200 g block hangs from a spring with spring constant 10 N/m. At $t = 0$ s the block is 20 cm below the equilibrium point and moving upward with a speed of 100 cm/s. What are the block's
   a. Oscillation frequency?
   b. Distance from equilibrium when the speed is 50 cm/s?
   c. Position at $t = 1.0$ s?

47. || A spring with spring constant k is suspended vertically from a support and a mass m is attached. The mass is held at the point where the spring is not stretched. Then the mass is released and begins to oscillate. The lowest point in the oscillation is 20 cm below the point where the mass was released. What is the oscillation frequency?

48. || While grocery shopping, you put several apples in the spring scale in the produce department. The scale reads 20 N, and you use your ruler (which you always carry with you) to discover that the pan goes down 9.0 cm when the apples are added. If you tap the bottom of the apple-filled pan to make it bounce up and down a little, what is its oscillation frequency? Ignore the mass of the pan.

49. || A compact car has a mass of 1200 kg. Assume that the car has one spring on each wheel, that the springs are identical, and that the mass is equally distributed over the four springs.
   a. What is the spring constant of each spring if the empty car bounces up and down 2.0 times each second?
   b. What will be the car's oscillation frequency while carrying four 70 kg passengers?

50. || A 500 g block slides along a frictionless surface at a speed of 0.35 m/s. It runs into a horizontal massless spring with spring constant 50 N/m that extends outward from a wall. It compresses the spring, then is pushed back in the opposite direction by the spring, eventually losing contact with the spring.
   a. How long does the block remain in contact with the spring?
   b. How would your answer to part a change if the block's initial speed were doubled?

51. || FIGURE P14.51 shows a 1.0 kg mass riding on top of a 5.0 kg mass as it oscillates on a frictionless surface. The spring constant is 50 N/m and the coefficient of static friction between the two blocks is 0.50. What is the maximum oscillation amplitude for which the upper block does not slip?

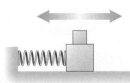

FIGURE P14.51

52. || The two blocks in Figure P14.51 oscillate on a frictionless surface with a period of 1.5 s. The upper block just begins to slip when the amplitude is increased to 40 cm. What is the coefficient of static friction between the two blocks?

53. ‖ It has recently become possible to "weigh" DNA molecules by measuring the influence of their mass on a nano-oscillator. **FIGURE P14.53** shows a thin rectangular cantilever etched out of silicon (density 2300 kg/m³) with a small gold dot at the end. If pulled down and released, the end of the cantilever vibrates with simple harmonic motion, moving up and down like a diving board after a jump. When bathed with DNA molecules whose ends have been modified to bind with gold, one or more molecules may attach to the gold dot. The addition of their mass causes a very slight—but measurable—decrease in the oscillation frequency.

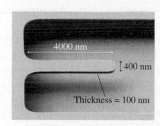

FIGURE P14.53

A vibrating cantilever of mass M can be modeled as a block of mass $\frac{1}{3}M$ attached to a spring. (The factor of $\frac{1}{3}$ arises from the moment of inertia of a bar pivoted at one end.) Neither the mass nor the spring constant can be determined very accurately—perhaps to only two significant figures—but the oscillation frequency can be measured with very high precision simply by counting the oscillations. In one experiment, the cantilever was initially vibrating at exactly 12 MHz. Attachment of a DNA molecule caused the frequency to decrease by 50 Hz. What was the mass of the DNA?

54. ‖ It is said that Galileo discovered a basic principle of the pendulum—that the period is independent of the amplitude by using his pulse to time the period of swinging lamps in the cathedral as they swayed in the breeze. Suppose that one oscillation of a swinging lamp takes 5.5 s.
    a. How long is the lamp chain?
    b. What maximum speed does the lamp have if its maximum angle from vertical is 3.0°?

55. ‖‖ A 100 g mass on a 1.0-m-long string is pulled 8.0° to one side and released. How long does it take for the pendulum to reach 4.0° on the opposite side?

56. ‖ The earth's free-fall acceleration varies from 9.78 m/s² at the equator to 9.83 m/s² at the poles, both because the earth is rotating and it's not a perfect sphere. A pendulum whose length is precisely 1.000 m can be used to measure g. Such a device is called a *gravimeter*.
    a. How long do 100 oscillations take at the equator?
    b. How long do 100 oscillations take at the north pole?
    c. Is the difference between your answers to parts a and b measurable? What kind of instrument could you use to measure the difference?
    d. Suppose you take your gravimeter to the top of a high mountain peak near the equator. There you find that 100 oscillations take 201.0 s. What is g on the mountain top?

57. ‖ Show that Equation 14.52 for the angular frequency of a physical pendulum gives Equation 14.49 when applied to a simple pendulum of a mass on a string.

58. ‖ A 15-cm-long, 200 g rod is pivoted at one end. A 20 g ball of clay is stuck on the other end. What is the period if the rod and clay swing as a pendulum?

59. ‖ A circular hoop of mass M and radius R is pivoted on an axle passing through one edge, as shown in **FIGURE P14.59**. Find an expression for the frequency of small oscillations.

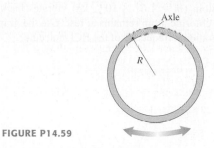

FIGURE P14.59

60. ‖‖‖ A 250 g air-track glider is attached to a spring with spring constant 4.0 N/m. The damping constant due to air resistance is 0.015 kg/s. The glider is pulled out 20 cm from equilibrium and released. How many oscillations will it make during the time in which the amplitude decays to e^{-1} of its initial value?

61. ‖ A 500 g air-track glider attached to a spring with spring constant 10 N/m is sitting at rest on a frictionless air track. A 250 g glider is pushed toward it from the far end of the track at a speed of 120 cm/s. It collides with and sticks to the 500 g glider. What are the amplitude and period of the subsequent oscillations?

62. ‖ A 200 g block attached to a horizontal spring is oscillating with an amplitude of 2.0 cm and a frequency of 2.0 Hz. Just as it passes through the equilibrium point, moving to the right, a sharp blow directed to the left exerts a 20 N force for 1.0 ms. What are the new (a) frequency and (b) amplitude?

63. ‖ A pendulum consists of a massless, rigid rod with a mass at one end. The other end is pivoted on a frictionless pivot so that it can turn through a complete circle. The pendulum is inverted, so the mass is directly above the pivot point, then released. The speed of the mass as it passes through the lowest point is 5.0 m/s. If the pendulum undergoes small-amplitude oscillations at the bottom of the arc, what will the frequency be?

64. ‖ **FIGURE P14.64** is a top view of an object of mass m connected between two stretched rubber bands of length L. The object rests on a frictionless surface. At equilibrium, the tension in each rubber band is T. Find an expression for the frequency of oscillations *perpendicular* to the rubber bands. Assume the amplitude is sufficiently small that the magnitude of the tension in the rubber bands is essentially unchanged as the mass oscillates.

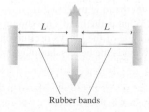

FIGURE P14.64   Rubber bands

65. ‖ A molecular bond can be modeled as a spring between two atoms that vibrate with simple harmonic motion. **FIGURE P14.65** shows an SHM approximation for the potential energy of an HCl molecule. For $E < 4 \times 10^{-19}$ J it is a good approximation to the more accurate HCl potential-energy curve that was shown in Figure 10.37. Because the chlorine atom is so much more massive than the hydrogen atom, it is reasonable to assume that the hydrogen atom ($m = 1.67 \times 10^{-27}$ kg) vibrates back and forth while the chlorine atom remains at rest. Use the graph to estimate the vibrational frequency of the HCl molecule.

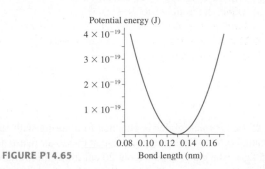

FIGURE P14.65

66. ‖ An ice cube can slide around the inside of a vertical circular hoop of radius R. It undergoes small-amplitude oscillations if displaced slightly from the equilibrium position at the lowest point. Find an expression for the period of these small-amplitude oscillations.

67. ‖ A penny rides on top of a piston as it undergoes vertical simple harmonic motion with an amplitude of 4.0 cm. If the frequency is low, the penny rides up and down without difficulty. If the frequency is steadily increased, there comes a point at which the penny leaves the surface.
    a. At what point in the cycle does the penny first lose contact with the piston?
    b. What is the maximum frequency for which the penny just barely remains in place for the full cycle?

68. ‖ On your first trip to Planet X you happen to take along a 200 g mass, a 40-cm-long spring, a meter stick, and a stopwatch. You're curious about the free-fall acceleration on Planet X, where ordinary tasks seem easier than on earth, but you can't find this information in your Visitor's Guide. One night you suspend the spring from the ceiling in your room and hang the mass from it. You find that the mass stretches the spring by 31.2 cm. You then pull the mass down 10.0 cm and release it. With the stopwatch you find that 10 oscillations take 14.5 s. Can you now satisfy your curiosity?

69. ‖ The 15 g head of a bobble-head doll oscillates in SHM at a frequency of 4.0 Hz.
    a. What is the spring constant of the spring on which the head is mounted?
    b. Suppose the head is pushed 2.0 cm against the spring, then released. What is the head's maximum speed as it oscillates?
    c. The amplitude of the head's oscillations decreases to 0.5 cm in 4.0 s. What is the head's damping constant?

70. ‖ An oscillator with a mass of 500 g and a period of 0.50 s has an amplitude that decreases by 2.0% during each complete oscillation.
    a. If the initial amplitude is 10 cm, what will be the amplitude after 25 oscillations?
    b. At what time will energy be reduced to 60% of its initial value?

71. ‖ A 200 g oscillator in a vacuum chamber has a frequency of 2.0 Hz. When air is admitted, the oscillation decreases to 60% of its initial amplitude in 50 s. How many oscillations will have been completed when the amplitude is 30% of its initial value?

72. ‖ Prove that the expression for $x(t)$ in Equation 14.56 is a solution to the equation of motion for a damped oscillator, Equation 14.55, if and only if the angular frequency ω is given by the expression in Equation 14.57.

73. ‖ A block on a frictionless table is connected as shown in **FIGURE P14.73** to two springs having spring constants k_1 and k_2. Show that the block's oscillation frequency is given by

$$f = \sqrt{f_1^2 + f_2^2}$$

where f_1 and f_2 are the frequencies at which it would oscillate if attached to spring 1 or spring 2 alone.

FIGURE P14.73

74. ‖ A block on a frictionless table is connected as shown in **FIGURE P14.74** to two springs having spring constants k_1 and k_2. Find an expression for the block's oscillation frequency f in terms of the frequencies f_1 and f_2 at which it would oscillate if attached to spring 1 or spring 2 alone.

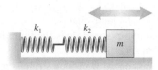

FIGURE P14.74

Challenge Problems

75. A block hangs in equilibrium from a vertical spring. When a second identical block is added, the original block sags by 5.0 cm. What is the oscillation frequency of the two-block system?

76. A 1.00 kg block is attached to a horizontal spring with spring constant 2500 N/m. The block is at rest on a frictionless surface. A 10 g bullet is fired into the block, in the face opposite the spring, and sticks.
    a. What was the bullet's speed if the subsequent oscillations have an amplitude of 10.0 cm?
    b. Could you determine the bullet's speed by measuring the oscillation frequency? If so, how? If not, why not?

77. A spring is standing upright on a table with its bottom end fastened to the table. A block is dropped from a height 3.0 cm above the top of the spring. The block sticks to the top end of the spring and then oscillates with an amplitude of 10 cm. What is the oscillation frequency?

78. Jose, whose mass is 75 kg, has just completed his first bungee jump and is now bouncing up and down at the end of the cord. His oscillations have an initial amplitude of 11.0 m and a period of 4.0 s.
    a. What is the spring constant of the bungee cord?
    b. What is Jose's maximum speed while oscillating?
    c. From what height above the lowest point did Jose jump?
    d. If the damping constant due to air resistance is 6.0 kg/s, how many oscillations will Jose make before his amplitude has decreased to 2.0 m?

    Hint: Although not entirely realistic, treat the bungee cord as an ideal spring that can be compressed to a shorter length as well as stretched to a longer length.

79. A 1000 kg car carrying two 100 kg football players travels over a bumpy "washboard" road with the bumps spaced 3.0 m apart. The driver finds that the car bounces up and down with maximum amplitude when he drives at a speed of 5.0 m/s (≈ 11 mph). The car then stops and picks up three more 100 kg passengers. By how much does the car body sag on its suspension when these three additional passengers get in?

80. **FIGURE CP14.80** shows a 200 g uniform rod pivoted at one end. The other end is attached to a horizontal spring. The spring is neither stretched nor compressed when the rod hangs straight down. What is the rod's oscillation period? You can assume that the rod's angle from vertical is always small.

FIGURE CP14.80

STOP TO THINK ANSWERS

Stop to Think 14.1: c. $v_{max} = 2\pi A/T$. Doubling A and T leaves v_{max} unchanged.

Stop to Think 14.2: d. Think of circular motion. At 45°, the particle is in the first quadrant (positive x) and moving to the left (negative v_x).

Stop to Think 14.3: c > b > a = d. Energy conservation $\frac{1}{2}kA^2 = \frac{1}{2}m(v_{max})^2$ gives $v_{max} = \sqrt{k/m}\,A$. k or m has to be increased or decreased by a factor of 4 to have the same effect as increasing or decreasing A by a factor of 2.

Stop to Think 14.4: c. $v_x = 0$ because the slope of the position graph is zero. The negative value of x shows that the particle is left of the equilibrium position, so the restoring force is to the right.

Stop to Think 14.5: c. The period of a pendulum does not depend on its mass.

Stop to Think 14.6: $\tau_d > \tau_b = \tau_c > \tau_a$. The time constant is the time to decay to 37% of the initial height. The time constant is independent of the initial height.

15 Fluids and Elasticity

Kayaking through the rapids requires an intuitive understanding of fluids.

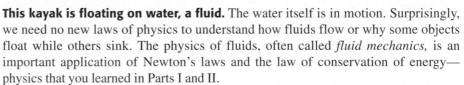

► **Looking Ahead**

The goal of Chapter 15 is to understand macroscopic systems that flow or deform. In this chapter you will learn to:

- Understand and use the concept of mass density.
- Understand pressure in liquids and gases.
- Use a wide variety of units for measuring pressure.
- Use Archimedes' principle to understand buoyancy.
- Use an ideal-fluid model to investigate how fluids flow.
- Calculate the elastic deformation of solids and liquids.

◄ **Looking Back**

The material in this chapter depends on the conditions of equilibrium. Please review:

- Section 5.6 Equilibrium and Newton's first law.
- Section 10.4 Hooke's law and restoring forces.

This kayak is floating on water, a fluid. The water itself is in motion. Surprisingly, we need no new laws of physics to understand how fluids flow or why some objects float while others sink. The physics of fluids, often called *fluid mechanics,* is an important application of Newton's laws and the law of conservation of energy—physics that you learned in Parts I and II.

Fluids are macroscopic systems, and our study of fluids will take us well beyond the particle model. Two new concepts, *density* and *pressure,* will be introduced to describe macroscopic systems. We'll begin with *fluid statics,* situations in which the fluid remains at rest. Suction cups and floating aircraft carriers are just two of the applications we'll explore. Then we'll turn to fluids in motion. Bernoulli's equation, the governing principle of *fluid dynamics,* will explain how water flows through fire hoses, how airplanes stay aloft, and many things in between. We'll then end this chapter with a brief look at a different but related property of macroscopic systems, the *elasticity* of solids.

15.1 Fluids

Quite simply, a **fluid** is a substance that flows. Because they flow, fluids take the shape of their container rather than retaining a shape of their own. You may think that gases and liquids are quite different, but both are fluids, and their similarities are often more important than their differences.

Gases and Liquids

A **gas,** shown in FIGURE 15.1a, is a system in which each molecule moves through space as a free, noninteracting particle until, on occasion, it collides with another molecule or with the wall of the container. The gas you are most familiar with is air, a mixture of mostly nitrogen and oxygen molecules. Gases are fairly simple macroscopic systems, and Part IV of this textbook will delve into the thermal properties of gases. For now, two properties of gases interest us:

1. Gases are *fluids.* They flow, and they exert pressure on the walls of their container.
2. Gases are *compressible.* That is, the volume of a gas is easily increased or decreased, a consequence of the "empty space" between the molecules.

Liquids are more complicated than either gases or solids. Liquids, like solids, are nearly *incompressible.* This property tells us that the molecules in a liquid, as in a solid, are about as close together as they can get without coming into contact with each other. At the same time, a liquid flows and deforms to fit the shape of its container. The fluid nature of a liquid tells us that the molecules are free to move around.

These observations suggest the model of a **liquid** shown in FIGURE 15.1b. Here you see a system in which the molecules are loosely held together by weak molecular bonds. The bonds are strong enough that the molecules never get far apart but not strong enough to prevent the molecules from sliding around each other.

Volume and Density

One important parameter that characterizes a macroscopic system is its volume V, the amount of space the system occupies. The SI unit of volume is m^3. Nonetheless, both cm^3 and, to some extent, liters (L) are widely used metric units of volume. In most cases, you *must* convert these to m^3 before doing calculations.

While it is true that 1 m = 100 cm, it is *not* true that $1 m^3 = 100 cm^3$. FIGURE 15.2 shows that the volume conversion factor is $1 m^3 = 10^6 cm^3$. You can think of this process as cubing the linear conversion factor:

$$1 m^3 = 1 m^3 \times \left(\frac{100 \text{ cm}}{1 \text{ m}}\right)^3 = 10^6 cm^3$$

A liter is $1000 cm^3$, so $1 m^3 = 10^3$ L. A milliliter (1 mL) is the same as $1 cm^3$.

A system is also characterized by its *density.* Suppose you have several blocks of copper, each of different size. Each block has a different mass m and a different volume V. Nonetheless, all the blocks are copper, so there should be some quantity that has the *same* value for all the blocks, telling us, "This is copper, not some other material." The most important such parameter is the *ratio* of mass to volume, which we call the **mass density** ρ (lowercase Greek rho):

$$\rho = \frac{m}{V} \qquad \text{(mass density)} \qquad (15.1)$$

Conversely, an object of density ρ has mass

$$m = \rho V \qquad (15.2)$$

The SI units of mass density are kg/m^3. Nonetheless, units of g/cm^3 are widely used. You need to convert these to SI units before doing most calculations. You must convert both the grams to kilograms and the cubic centimeters to cubic meters. The net result is the conversion factor

$$1 g/cm^3 = 1000 kg/m^3$$

The mass density is usually called simply "the density" if there is no danger of confusion. However, we will meet other types of density as we go along, and sometimes it

FIGURE 15.1 Simple atomic models of gases and liquids.

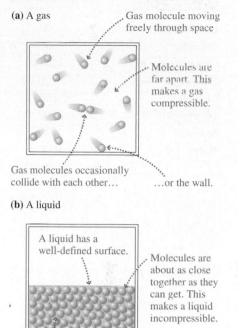

(a) A gas

Gas molecule moving freely through space

Molecules are far apart. This makes a gas compressible.

Gas molecules occasionally collide with each other...

...or the wall.

(b) A liquid

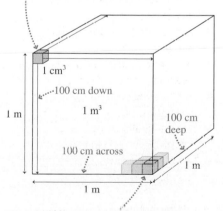

A liquid has a well-defined surface.

Molecules are about as close together as they can get. This makes a liquid incompressible.

Molecules have weak bonds between them, keeping them close together. But the molecules can slide around each other, allowing the liquid to flow and conform to the shape of its container.

FIGURE 15.2 There are $10^6 cm^3$ in $1 m^3$.

Subdivide the 1 m × 1 m × 1 m cube into little cubes 1 cm on a side. You will get 100 subdivisions along each edge.

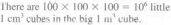

$1 cm^3$

100 cm down

$1 m^3$

100 cm deep

100 cm across

1 m

1 m

1 m

100 cm

There are 100 × 100 × 100 = 10^6 little $1 cm^3$ cubes in the big $1 m^3$ cube.

TABLE 15.1 Densities of fluids at standard temperature (0°C) and pressure (1 atm)

Substance	ρ (kg/m³)
Air	1.28
Ethyl alcohol	790
Gasoline	680
Glycerin	1260
Helium gas	0.18
Mercury	13,600
Oil (typical)	900
Seawater	1030
Water	1000

is important to be explicit about which density you are using. Table 15.1 provides a short list of mass densities of various fluids. Notice the enormous difference between the densities of gases and liquids. Gases have lower densities because the molecules in gases are farther apart than in liquids.

What does it *mean* to say that the density of gasoline is 680 kg/m³ or, equivalently, 0.68 g/cm³? Density is a mass-to-volume ratio. It is often described as the "mass per unit volume," but for this to make sense you have to know what is meant by "unit volume." Regardless of which system of length units you use, a **unit volume** is one of those units cubed. For example, if you measure lengths in meters, a unit volume is 1 m³. But 1 cm³ is a unit volume if you measure lengths in cm, and 1 mi³ is a unit volume if you measure lengths in miles.

Density is the mass of one unit of volume, whatever the units happen to be. To say that the density of gasoline is 680 kg/m³ is to say that the mass of 1 m³ of gasoline is 680 kg. The mass of 1 cm³ of gasoline is 0.68 g, so the density of gasoline in those units is 0.68 g/cm³.

The mass density is independent of the object's size. That is, mass and volume are parameters that characterize a *specific piece* of some substance—say copper—whereas the mass density characterizes the substance itself. All pieces of copper have the same mass density, which differs from the mass density of any other substance. Thus mass density allows us to talk about the properties of copper in general without having to refer to any specific piece of copper.

EXAMPLE 15.1 Weighing the air
What is the mass of air in a living room with dimensions 4.0 m × 6.0 m × 2.5 m?

MODEL Table 15.1 gives air density at a temperature of 0°C. The air density doesn't vary significantly over a small range of temperatures (we'll study this issue in the next chapter), so we'll use this value even though most people keep their living room warmer than 0°C.

SOLVE The room's volume is

$$V = (4.0\,\text{m}) \times (6.0\,\text{m}) \times (2.5\,\text{m}) = 60\,\text{m}^3$$

The mass of the air is

$$m = \rho V = (1.28\,\text{kg/m}^3)(60\,\text{m}^3) = 77\,\text{kg}$$

ASSESS This is perhaps more mass than you might have expected from a substance that hardly seems to be there. For comparison, a swimming pool this size would contain 60,000 kg of water.

STOP TO THINK 15.1   A piece of glass is broken into two pieces of different size. Rank in order, from largest to smallest, the mass densities of pieces a, b, and c.

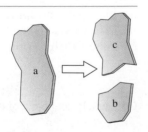

15.2 Pressure

"Pressure" is a word we all know and use. You probably have a commonsense idea of what pressure is. For example, you feel the effects of varying pressure against your eardrums when you swim underwater or take off in an airplane. Cans of whipped cream are "pressurized" to make the contents squirt out when you press the nozzle. It's hard to open a "vacuum sealed" jar of jelly the first time, but easy after the seal is broken.

You've undoubtedly seen water squirting out of a hole in the side of a container, as in FIGURE 15.3. Notice that the water emerges at greater speed from a hole at greater depth. And you've probably felt the air squirting out of a hole in a bicycle tire or inflatable air mattress. These observations suggest that

- "Something" pushes the water or air *sideways*, out of the hole.
- In a liquid, the "something" is larger at greater depths. In a gas, the "something" appears to be the same everywhere.

Our goal is to turn these everyday observations into a precise definition of pressure.

FIGURE 15.4 shows a fluid—either a liquid or a gas—pressing against a small area A with force $\vec{F}$. This is the force that pushes the fluid out of a hole. In the absence of a hole, $\vec{F}$ pushes against the wall of the container. Let's define the **pressure** at this point in the fluid to be the ratio of the force to the area on which the force is exerted:

$$p = \frac{F}{A} \tag{15.3}$$

Notice that pressure is a scalar, not a vector. You can see, from Equation 15.3, that a fluid exerts a force of magnitude

$$F = pA \tag{15.4}$$

on a surface of area A. The force is *perpendicular* to the surface.

NOTE ▶ Pressure itself is *not* a force, even though we sometimes talk informally about "the force exerted by the pressure." The correct statement is that the *fluid* exerts a force on a surface. ◀

From its definition, pressure has units of N/m^2. The SI unit of pressure is the **pascal,** defined as

$$1 \text{ pascal} = 1 \text{ Pa} \equiv 1 \text{ N/m}^2$$

This unit is named for the 17th-century French scientist Blaise Pascal, who was one of the first to study fluids. Large pressures are often given in kilopascals, where $1 \text{ kPa} = 1000 \text{ Pa}$.

Equation 15.3 is the basis for the simple pressure-measuring device shown in FIGURE 15.5a. Because the spring constant k and the area A are known, we can determine the pressure by measuring the compression of the spring. Once we've built such a device, we can place it in various liquids and gases to learn about pressure. FIGURE 15.5b shows what we can learn from a series of simple experiments.

FIGURE 15.3 Water pressure pushes the water *sideways*, out of the holes.

FIGURE 15.4 The fluid presses against area A with force $\vec{F}$.

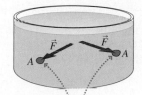

The fluid pushes with force $\vec{F}$ against area A.

FIGURE 15.5 Learning about pressure.

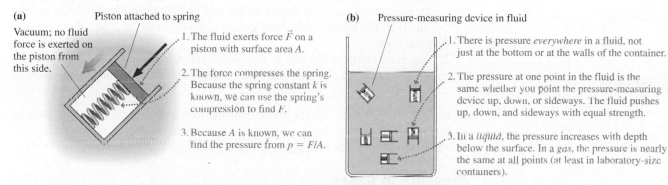

(a) Piston attached to spring

Vacuum; no fluid force is exerted on the piston from this side.

1. The fluid exerts force $\vec{F}$ on a piston with surface area A.

2. The force compresses the spring. Because the spring constant k is known, we can use the spring's compression to find F.

3. Because A is known, we can find the pressure from $p = F/A$.

(b) Pressure-measuring device in fluid

1. There is pressure *everywhere* in a fluid, not just at the bottom or at the walls of the container.

2. The pressure at one point in the fluid is the same whether you point the pressure-measuring device up, down, or sideways. The fluid pushes up, down, and sideways with equal strength.

3. In a *liquid*, the pressure increases with depth below the surface. In a *gas*, the pressure is nearly the same at all points (at least in laboratory-size containers).

The first statement in Figure 15.5b is especially important. Pressure exists at *all* points within a fluid, not just at the walls of the container. You may recall that tension exists at *all* points in a string, not only at its ends where it is tied to an object. We understood tension as the different parts of the string *pulling* against each other. Pressure is an analogous idea, except that the different parts of a fluid are *pushing* against each other.

FIGURE 15.6 A liquid and a gas in a weightless environment.

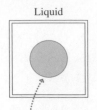

Liquid   Gas

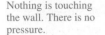

Nothing is touching the wall. There is no pressure.

Molecules are colliding with the wall. There is pressure.

FIGURE 15.7 The pressure in a gas is due to the net force of the molecules colliding with the walls.

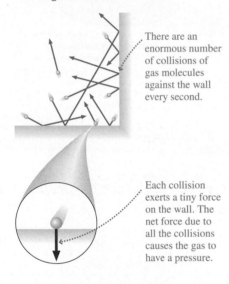

There are an enormous number of collisions of gas molecules against the wall every second.

Each collision exerts a tiny force on the wall. The net force due to all the collisions causes the gas to have a pressure.

FIGURE 15.8 Gravity affects the pressure of the fluids.

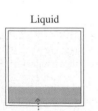

Slightly less density and pressure at the top

Liquid   Gas

As gravity pulls down, the liquid exerts a force on the bottom and sides of its container.

Gravity has little effect on the pressure of the gas.

Causes of Pressure

Gases and liquids are both fluids, but they have some important differences. Liquids are nearly incompressible; gases are highly compressible. The molecules in a liquid attract each other via molecular bonds; the molecules in a gas do not interact other than through occasional collisions. These differences affect how we think about pressure in gases and liquids.

Imagine that you have two sealed jars, each containing a small amount of mercury and nothing else. All the air has been removed from the jars. Suppose you take the two jars into orbit on the space shuttle, where they are weightless. One jar you keep cool, so that the mercury is a liquid. The other you heat until the mercury boils and becomes a gas. What can we say about the pressure in these two jars?

As **FIGURE 15.6** shows, molecular bonds hold the liquid mercury together. It might quiver like Jello, but it remains a cohesive drop floating in the center of the jar. The liquid drop exerts no forces on the walls, so there's *no* pressure in the jar containing the liquid. (If we actually did this experiment, a very small fraction of the mercury would be in the vapor phase and create what is called *vapor pressure*. We can make the vapor pressure negligibly small by keeping the temperature low.)

The gas is different. Figure 15.1 introduced an atomic model of a gas in which a molecule moves freely until it collides with another molecule or with a wall of the container. **FIGURE 15.7** shows some of the gas molecules colliding with a wall. Recall, from our study of collisions in Chapter 9, that each molecule as it bounces exerts a tiny impulse on the wall. The impulse from any one collision is extremely small, but there are an extraordinarily large number of collisions every second. These collisions cause the gas to have a pressure.

The gas pressure can be calculated from the net force the molecules exert on the wall, divided by the area of the wall. We will do that calculation in Chapter 18. For now, we'll simply note that the pressure is proportional to the gas density in the container and to the absolute temperature.

FIGURE 15.8 shows the jars back on earth. Because of gravity, the liquid now fills the bottom of the jar and exerts a force on the bottom and the sides. Liquid mercury is incompressible, so the volume of liquid in Figure 15.8 is the same as in Figure 15.6. There is still no pressure on the top of the jar (other than the very small vapor pressure).

At first glance, the situation in the gas-filled jar seems unchanged from Figure 15.6. However, the earth's gravitational pull causes the gas density to be *slightly* more at the bottom of the jar than at the top. Because the pressure due to collisions is proportional to the density, the pressure is *slightly* larger at the bottom of the jar than at the top.

Thus there appear to be two contributions to the pressure in a container of fluid:

1. A *gravitational contribution* that arises from gravity pulling down on the fluid. Because a fluid can flow, forces are exerted on both the bottom and sides of the container. The gravitational contribution depends on the strength of the gravitational force.

2. A *thermal contribution* due to the collisions of freely moving gas molecules with the walls. The thermal contribution depends on the absolute temperature of the gas.

A detailed analysis finds that these two contributions are not entirely independent of each other, but the distinction is useful for a basic understanding of pressure. Let's see how these two contributions apply to different situations.

Pressure in Gases

The pressure in a laboratory-size container of gas is due almost entirely to the thermal contribution. A container would have to be ≈ 100 m tall for gravity to cause the pressure at the top to be even 1% less than the pressure at the bottom. Laboratory-size containers are much less than 100 m tall, so we can quite reasonably assume that p has the *same* value at all points in a laboratory-size container of gas. A homework problem will let you verify that the gravitational contribution to the pressure in a container of gas is negligible.

Decreasing the number of molecules in a container decreases the gas pressure simply because there are fewer collisions with the walls. If a container is completely empty, with no atoms or molecules, then the pressure is $p = 0$ Pa. This is a *perfect vacuum*. No perfect vacuum exists in nature, not even in the most remote depths of outer space, because it is impossible to completely remove every atom from a region of space. In practice, a **vacuum** is an enclosed space in which $p \ll 1$ atm. Using $p = 0$ Pa is then a very good approximation.

Atmospheric Pressure

The earth's atmosphere is *not* a laboratory-size container. The height of the atmosphere is such that the gravitational contribution to pressure *is* important. As **FIGURE 15.9** shows, the density of air slowly decreases with increasing height until reaching zero in the vacuum of space. Consequently, the pressure of the air, what we call the *atmospheric pressure* p_{atmos}, decreases with height. The air pressure is less in Denver than in Miami.

The atmospheric pressure *at sea level* varies slightly with the weather, but the global average sea-level pressure is 101,300 Pa. Consequently, we define the **standard atmosphere** as

$$1 \text{ standard atmosphere} = 1 \text{ atm} \equiv 101,300 \text{ Pa} = 101.3 \text{ kPa}$$

The standard atmosphere, usually referred to simply as "atmospheres," is a commonly used unit of pressure. But it is not an SI unit, so you must convert atmospheres to pascals before doing most calculations with pressure.

> **NOTE** ▶ Unless you happen to live right at sea level, the atmospheric pressure around you is somewhat less than 1 atm. Pressure experiments use a barometer to determine the actual atmospheric pressure. For simplicity, this textbook will always assume that the pressure of the air is $p_{atmos} = 1$ atm unless stated otherwise. ◀

Given that the pressure of the air at sea level is 101.3 kPa, you might wonder why the weight of the air doesn't crush your forearm when you rest it on a table. Your forearm has a surface area of $\approx 200 \text{ cm}^2 = 0.02 \text{ m}^2$, so the force of the air pressing against it is ≈ 2000 N (≈ 450 pounds). How can you even lift your arm?

The reason, as **FIGURE 15.10** shows, is that a fluid exerts pressure forces in *all* directions. There *is* a downward force of ≈ 2000 N on your forearm, but the air underneath your arm exerts an upward force of the same magnitude. The *net* force is very close to zero. (To be accurate, there is a net *upward* force called the buoyant force. We'll study buoyancy in Section 15.4. For most objects, the buoyant force of the air is too small to notice.)

But, you say, there isn't any air under my arm if I rest it on a table. Actually, there is. There would be a *vacuum* under your arm if there were no air. Imagine placing your arm on the top of a large vacuum cleaner suction tube. What happens? You feel a downward force as the vacuum cleaner "tries to suck your arm in." However, the downward force you feel is not a *pulling* force from the vacuum cleaner. It is the *pushing* force of the air above your arm *when the air beneath your arm is removed and cannot push back*. Air molecules do not have hooks! They have no ability to "pull" on your arm. The air can only push.

Vacuum cleaners, suction cups, and other similar devices are powerful examples of how strong atmospheric pressure forces can be *if* the air is removed from one side of an object so as to produce an unbalanced force. The fact that we are *surrounded* by the fluid allows us to move around in the air, just as we swim underwater, oblivious of these strong forces.

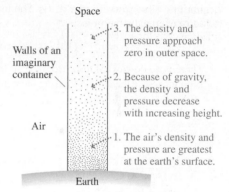

FIGURE 15.9 The pressure and density decrease with increasing height in the atmosphere.

Space

3. The density and pressure approach zero in outer space.

Walls of an imaginary container

2. Because of gravity, the density and pressure decrease with increasing height.

Air

1. The air's density and pressure are greatest at the earth's surface.

Earth

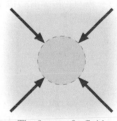

FIGURE 15.10 Pressure forces in a fluid push with equal strength in all directions.

The forces of a fluid push in *all* directions.

Removing the air from a container has very real consequences.

EXAMPLE 15.2 A suction cup

A 10.0-cm-diameter suction cup is pushed against a smooth ceiling. What is the maximum mass of an object that can be suspended from the suction cup without pulling it off the ceiling? The mass of the suction cup is negligible.

MODEL Pushing the suction cup against the ceiling pushes the air out. We'll assume that the volume enclosed between the suction cup and the ceiling is a perfect vacuum with $p = 0$ Pa. We'll also assume that the pressure in the room is 1 atm.

VISUALIZE FIGURE 15.11 shows a free-body diagram of the suction cup stuck to the ceiling. The downward normal force of the ceiling is distributed around the rim of the suction cup, but in the particle model we can show this as a single force vector.

SOLVE The suction cup remains stuck to the ceiling, in static equilibrium, as long as $F_{air} = n + F_G$. The magnitude of the upward force exerted by the air is

$$F_{air} = pA = p\pi r^2 = (101,300 \text{ Pa})\pi(0.050 \text{ m})^2 = 796 \text{ N}$$

There is no downward force from the air in this case because there is no air inside the cup. Increasing the hanging mass decreases the

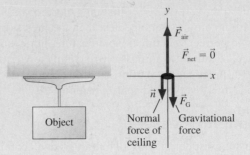

FIGURE 15.11 A suction cup is held to the ceiling by air pressure pushing upward on the bottom.

normal force n by an equal amount. The maximum weight has been reached when n is reduced to zero. Thus

$$(F_G)_{max} = mg = F_{air} = 796 \text{ N}$$

$$m = \frac{796 \text{ N}}{g} = 81 \text{ kg}$$

Hence this suction cup can support a mass of up to 81 kg.

Pressure in Liquids

Gravity causes a liquid to fill the bottom of a container. Thus it's not surprising that the pressure in a liquid is due almost entirely to the gravitational contribution. We'd like to determine the pressure at depth d below the surface of the liquid. We will assume that the liquid is at rest; flowing liquids will be considered later in this chapter.

The shaded cylinder of liquid in **FIGURE 15.12** extends from the surface to depth d. This cylinder, like the rest of the liquid, is in static equilibrium with $\vec{F}_{net} = \vec{0}$. Three forces act on this cylinder: the gravitational force mg, a downward force p_0A due to the pressure p_0 at the surface of the liquid, and an upward force pA due to the liquid beneath the cylinder pushing up on the bottom of the cylinder. This third force is a consequence of our earlier observation that different parts of a fluid push against each other. Pressure p, which is what we're trying to find, is the pressure at the bottom of the cylinder.

The upward force balances the two downward forces, so

$$pA = p_0A + mg \tag{15.5}$$

The liquid is a cylinder of cross-section area A and height d. Its volume is $V = Ad$ and its mass is $m = \rho V = \rho Ad$. Substituting this expression for the mass of the liquid into Equation 15.5, we find that the area A cancels from all terms. The pressure at depth d in a liquid is

$$p = p_0 + \rho gd \qquad \text{(hydrostatic pressure at depth } d) \tag{15.6}$$

where ρ is the liquid's density. Because the fluid is at rest, the pressure given by Equation 15.6 is called the **hydrostatic pressure.** The fact that g appears in Equation 15.6 reminds us that this a gravitational contribution to the pressure.

As expected, $p = p_0$ at the surface, where $d = 0$. Pressure p_0 is often due to the air or other gas above the liquid. $p_0 = 1$ atm $= 101.3$ kPa for a liquid that is open to the air. However, p_0 can also be the pressure due to a piston or a closed surface pushing down on the top of the liquid.

NOTE ▶ Equation 15.6 assumes that the liquid is *incompressible;* that is, its density ρ doesn't increase with depth. This is an excellent assumption for liquids, but not a

FIGURE 15.12 Measuring the pressure at depth d in a liquid.

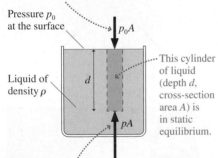

Whatever is above the liquid pushes down on the top of the cylinder.

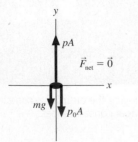

Free-body diagram of the column of liquid

good one for a gas, which *is* compressible. Even so, Equation 15.6 can be used with gases over fairly small distances, a few tens of meters or less, because the density is nearly constant over these distances. Equation 15.6 should not be used for calculating the pressure at different heights in the atmosphere. (A homework problem will let you derive a different equation for the pressure of the atmosphere.) ◄

EXAMPLE 15.3 The pressure on a submarine

A submarine cruises at a depth of 300 m. What is the pressure at this depth? Give the answer in both pascals and atmospheres.

SOLVE The density of seawater, from Table 15.1, is $\rho = 1030 \text{ kg/m}^3$. The pressure at depth $d = 300$ m is found from Equation 15.6 to be

$$p = p_0 + \rho g d = 1.013 \times 10^5 \text{ Pa}$$
$$+ (1030 \text{ kg/m}^3)(9.80 \text{ m/s}^2)(300 \text{ m}) = 3.13 \times 10^6 \text{ Pa}$$

Converting the answer to atmospheres gives

$$p = 3.13 \times 10^6 \text{ Pa} \times \frac{1 \text{ atm}}{1.013 \times 10^5 \text{ Pa}} = 30.9 \text{ atm}$$

ASSESS The pressure deep in the ocean is very large. Windows on submersibles must be very thick to withstand the large forces.

FIGURE 15.13 Some properties of a liquid in hydrostatic equilibrium are not what you might expect.

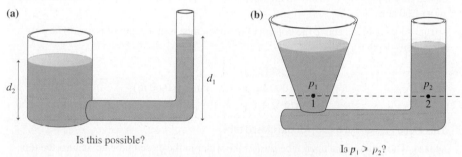

(a) d_2 ... d_1 Is this possible?

(b) p_1 1 ... p_2 2 Is $p_1 > p_2$?

The hydrostatic pressure in a liquid depends only on the depth and the pressure at the surface. This observation has some important implications. **FIGURE 15.13a** shows two connected tubes. It's certainly true that the larger volume of liquid in the wide tube weighs more than the liquid in the narrow tube. You might think that this extra weight would push the liquid in the narrow tube higher than in the wide tube. But it doesn't. If d_1 were larger than d_2, then, according to the hydrostatic pressure equation, the pressure at the bottom of the narrow tube would be higher than the pressure at the bottom of the wide tube. This *pressure difference* would cause the liquid to *flow* from right to left until the heights were equal.

Thus a first conclusion: **A connected liquid in hydrostatic equilibrium rises to the same height in all open regions of the container.**

FIGURE 15.13b shows two connected tubes of different shape. The conical tube holds more liquid above the dotted line, so you might think that $p_1 > p_2$. But it isn't. Both points are at the same depth, thus $p_1 = p_2$. You can arrive at the same conclusion by thinking about the pressure at the bottom of the tubes. If p_1 were larger than p_2, the pressure at the bottom of the left tube would be larger than the pressure at the bottom of the right tube. This would cause the liquid to flow until the pressures were equal.

If $p_1 = p_2$, you might be wondering what's holding up the "extra" liquid in the conical tube. **FIGURE 15.14** shows that the weight of this extra liquid is supported by the wall of the tube. Only the liquid that's *directly above* point 1 needs to be supported by the pressure at point 1.

Thus a second conclusion: **The pressure is the same at all points on a horizontal line through a connected liquid in hydrostatic equilibrium.**

NOTE ► Both of these conclusions are restricted to liquids in hydrostatic equilibrium. The situation is different for flowing fluids, as we'll see later in the chapter. ◄

FIGURE 15.14 The weight of the liquid is supported by the wall of the tube.

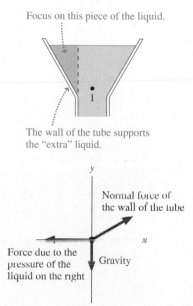

Focus on this piece of the liquid.

1

The wall of the tube supports the "extra" liquid.

Normal force of the wall of the tube

Force due to the pressure of the liquid on the right

Gravity

EXAMPLE 15.4 **Pressure in a closed tube**

Water fills the tube shown in FIGURE 15.15. What is the pressure at the top of the closed tube?

FIGURE 15.15 A water-filled tube.

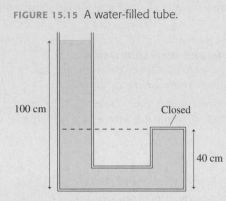

100 cm

Closed

40 cm

MODEL This is a liquid in hydrostatic equilibrium. The closed tube is not an open region of the container, so the water cannot rise to an equal height. Nevertheless, the pressure is still the same at all points on a horizontal line. In particular, the pressure at the top of the closed tube equals the pressure in the open tube at the height of the dashed line. Assume $p_0 = 1.00$ atm.

SOLVE A point 40 cm above the bottom of the open tube is at a depth of 60 cm. The pressure at this depth is

$$p = p_0 + \rho g d = 1.013 \times 10^5 \text{ Pa}$$
$$+ (1000 \text{ kg/m}^3)(9.80 \text{ m/s}^2)(0.60 \text{ m})$$
$$= 1.072 \times 10^5 \text{ Pa} = 1.06 \text{ atm}$$

This is the pressure at the top of the closed tube.

ASSESS The water in the open tube *pushes* the water in the closed tube up against the top of the tube, which is why the pressure is greater than 1 atm.

We can draw one more conclusion from the hydrostatic pressure equation $p = p_0 + \rho g d$. If we change the pressure p_0 at the surface to p_1, the pressure at depth d becomes $p' = p_1 + \rho g d$. The *change* in pressure $\Delta p = p_1 - p_0$ is the same at all points in the fluid, independent of the size or shape of the container. This idea, that **a change in the pressure at one point in an incompressible fluid appears undiminished at all points in the fluid,** was first recognized by Blaise Pascal and is called **Pascal's principle.**

For example, if we compressed the air above the open tube in Example 15.4 to a pressure of 1.5 atm, an increase of 0.5 atm, the pressure at the top of the closed tube would increase to 1.56 atm. Pascal's principle is the basis for hydraulic systems, as we'll see in the next section.

STOP TO THINK 15.2 Water is slowly poured into the container until the water level has risen into tubes A, B, and C. The water doesn't overflow from any of the tubes. How do the water depths in the three columns compare to each other?

a. $d_A > d_B > d_C$
b. $d_A < d_B < d_C$
c. $d_A = d_B = d_C$
d. $d_A = d_C > d_B$
e. $d_A = d_C < d_B$

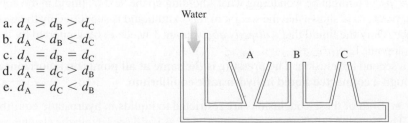

Water

15.3 Measuring and Using Pressure

The pressure in a fluid is measured with a *pressure gauge,* often a device very similar to that in Figure 15.5. The fluid pushes against some sort of spring, usually a diaphragm, and the spring's displacement is registered by a pointer on a dial.

Many pressure gauges, such as tire gauges and the gauges on air tanks, measure not the actual or absolute pressure p but what is called **gauge pressure.** The gauge pressure, denoted p_g, is the pressure *in excess* of 1 atm. That is,

$$p_g = p - 1 \text{ atm} \tag{15.7}$$

You must add 1 atm = 101.3 kPa to the reading of a pressure gauge to find the absolute pressure p that you need for doing most science or engineering calculations: $p = p_g + 1$ atm.

A tire-pressure gauge reads the gauge pressure p_g, not the absolute pressure p. The gauge reads zero when the tire is flat, but this doesn't mean there is a vacuum inside. Zero gauge pressure means the inside pressure is 1 atm.

EXAMPLE 15.5 An underwater pressure gauge

An underwater pressure gauge reads 60 kPa. What is its depth?

MODEL The gauge reads gauge pressure, not absolute pressure.

SOLVE The hydrostatic pressure at depth d, with $p_0 = 1$ atm, is $p = 1$ atm $+ \rho g d$. Thus the gauge pressure is

$$p_g = p - 1 \text{ atm} = (1 \text{ atm} + \rho g d) - 1 \text{ atm} = \rho g d$$

The term $\rho g d$ is the pressure *in excess* of atmospheric pressure and thus *is* the gauge pressure. Solving for d, we find

$$d = \frac{60,000 \text{ Pa}}{(1000 \text{ kg/m}^3)(9.80 \text{ m/s}^2)} = 6.1 \text{ m}$$

Solving Hydrostatic Problems

We now have enough information to formulate a set of rules for thinking about hydrostatic problems.

TACTICS BOX 15.1 Hydrostatics   (MP)

❶ **Draw a picture.** Show open surfaces, pistons, boundaries, and other features that affect pressure. Include height and area measurements and fluid densities. Identify the points at which you need to find the pressure.

❷ **Determine the pressure at surfaces.**

- **Surface open to the air:** $p_0 = p_{atmos}$, usually 1 atm.
- **Surface covered by a gas:** $p_0 = p_{gas}$.
- **Closed surface:** $p = F/A$ where F is the force the surface, such as a piston, exerts on the fluid.

❸ **Use horizontal lines.** Pressure in a connected fluid is the same at any point along a horizontal line.

❹ **Allow for gauge pressure.** Pressure gauges read $p_g = p - 1$ atm.

❺ **Use the hydrostatic pressure equation.** $p = p_0 + \rho g d$.

Exercises 4–13 🖉

FIGURE 15.16 A manometer is used to measure gas pressure.

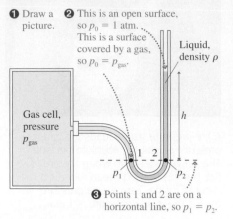

❶ Draw a picture.

❷ This is an open surface, so $p_0 = 1$ atm.
This is a surface covered by a gas, so $p_0 = p_{gas}$.

Liquid, density ρ

Gas cell, pressure p_{gas}

h

p_1 p_2

❸ Points 1 and 2 are on a horizontal line, so $p_1 = p_2$.

Manometers and Barometers

Gas pressure is sometimes measured with a device called a *manometer*. A manometer, shown in **FIGURE 15.16**, is a U-shaped tube connected to the gas at one end and open to the air at the other end. The tube is filled with a liquid—usually mercury—of density ρ. The liquid is in static equilibrium. A scale allows the user to measure the height h of the right side above the left side.

Steps 1–3 from Tactics Box 15.1 lead to the conclusion that the pressures p_1 and p_2 must be equal. Pressure p_1, at the surface on the left, is simply the gas pressure: $p_1 = p_{gas}$. Pressure p_2 is the hydrostatic pressure at depth $d = h$ in the liquid on the right: $p_2 = 1$ atm $+ \rho gh$. Equating these two pressures gives

$$p_{gas} = 1 \text{ atm} + \rho gh \tag{15.8}$$

Figure 15.16 assumed $p_{gas} > 1$ atm, so the right side of the liquid is higher than the left. Equation 15.8 is also valid for $p_{gas} < 1$ atm if the distance of the right side *below* the left side is considered to be a negative value of h.

EXAMPLE 15.6 Using a manometer

The pressure of a gas cell is measured with a mercury manometer. The mercury is 36.2 cm higher in the outside arm than in the arm connected to the gas cell.

a. What is the gas pressure?
b. What is the reading of a pressure gauge attached to the gas cell?

SOLVE a. From Table 15.1, the density of mercury is $\rho = 13,600$ kg/m³. Equation 15.8 with $h = 0.362$ m gives

$$p_{gas} = 1 \text{ atm} + \rho gh = 149.5 \text{ kPa}$$

We had to change 1 atm to 101,300 Pa before adding. Converting the result to atmospheres, $p_{gas} = 1.476$ atm.

b. The pressure gauge reads gauge pressure: $p_g = p - 1$ atm $= 0.476$ atm or 48.2 kPa.

ASSESS Manometers are useful over a pressure range from near vacuum up to ≈2 atm. For higher pressures, the mercury column would be too tall to be practical.

FIGURE 15.17 A barometer.

(a) Seal and invert tube.

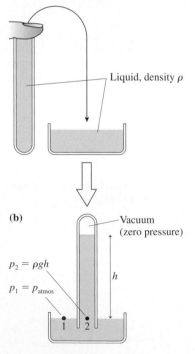

Liquid, density ρ

(b)

Vacuum (zero pressure)

$p_2 = \rho gh$

$p_1 = p_{atmos}$

h

1   2

Another important pressure-measuring instrument is the *barometer,* which is used to measure the atmospheric pressure p_{atmos}. **FIGURE 15.17a** shows a glass tube, sealed at the bottom, that has been completely filled with a liquid. If we temporarily seal the top end, we can invert the tube and place it in a beaker of the same liquid. When the temporary seal is removed, some, but not all, of the liquid runs out, leaving a liquid column in the tube that is a height h above the surface of the liquid in the beaker. This device, shown in **FIGURE 15.17b**, is a barometer. What does it measure? And why doesn't *all* the liquid in the tube run out?

We can analyze the barometer much as we did the manometer. Points 1 and 2 in Figure 15.17b are on a horizontal line drawn even with the surface of the liquid. The liquid is in hydrostatic equilibrium, so the pressure at these two points must be equal. Liquid runs out of the tube only until a balance is reached between the pressure at the base of the tube and the pressure of the air.

You can think of a barometer as rather like a seesaw. If the pressure of the atmosphere increases, it presses down on the liquid in the beaker. This forces liquid up the tube until the pressures at points 1 and 2 are equal. If the atmospheric pressure falls, liquid has to flow out of the tube to keep the pressures equal at these two points.

The pressure at point 2 is the pressure due to the weight of the liquid in the tube plus the pressure of the gas above the liquid. But in this case there is no gas above the liquid! Because the tube had been completely full of liquid when it was inverted, the space left behind when the liquid ran out is a vacuum (ignoring a very slight *vapor pressure* of the liquid, negligible except in extremely precise measurements). Thus pressure p_2 is simply $p_2 = \rho gh$.

Equating p_1 and p_2 gives

$$p_{atmos} = \rho gh \tag{15.9}$$

Thus we can measure the atmosphere's pressure by measuring the height of the liquid column in a barometer.

The average air pressure at sea level causes a column of mercury in a mercury barometer to stand 760 mm above the surface. Knowing that the density of mercury is 13,600 kg/m^3 (at 0°C), we can use Equation 15.9 to find that the average atmospheric pressure is

$$p_{atmos} = \rho_{Hg}gh = (13{,}600 \text{ kg/m}^3)(9.80 \text{ m/s}^2)(0.760 \text{ m})$$

$$= 1.013 \times 10^5 \text{ Pa} = 101.3 \text{ kPa}$$

This is the value given earlier as "one standard atmosphere."

The barometric pressure varies slightly from day to day as the weather changes. Weather systems are called *high-pressure systems* or *low-pressure systems,* depending on whether the local sea-level pressure is higher or lower than one standard atmosphere. Higher pressure is usually associated with fair weather, while lower pressure portends rain.

Pressure Units

In practice, pressure is measured in several different units. This plethora of units and abbreviations has arisen historically as scientists and engineers working on different subjects (liquids, high-pressure gases, low-pressure gases, weather, etc.) developed what seemed to them the most convenient units. These units continue in use through tradition, so it is necessary to become familiar with converting back and forth between them. Table 15.2 gives the basic conversions.

TABLE 15.2 Pressure units

Unit	Abbreviation	Conversion to 1 atm	Uses
pascal	Pa	101.3 kPa	SI unit: 1 Pa = 1 N/m^2
atmosphere	atm	1 atm	general
millimeters of mercury	mm of Hg	760 mm of Hg	gases and barometric pressure
inches of mercury	in	29.92 in	barometric pressure in U.S. weather forecasting
pounds per square inch	psi	14.7 psi	engineering and industry

Blood Pressure

The last time you had a medical checkup, the doctor may have told you something like "Your blood pressure is 120 over 80." What does that mean?

About every 0.8 s, assuming a pulse rate of 75 beats per minute, your heart "beats." The heart muscles contract and push blood out into your aorta. This contraction, like squeezing a balloon, raises the pressure in your heart. The pressure increase, in accordance with Pascal's principle, is transmitted through all your arteries.

FIGURE 15.18 is a pressure graph showing how blood pressure changes during one cycle of the heartbeat. The medical condition of *high blood pressure* usually means that your systolic pressure is higher than necessary for blood circulation. The high pressure causes undue stress and strain on your entire circulatory system, often leading to serious medical problems. Low blood pressure can cause you to get dizzy if you stand up quickly because the pressure isn't adequate to pump the blood up to your brain.

Blood pressure is measured with a cuff that goes around your arm. The doctor or nurse pressurizes the cuff, places a stethoscope over the artery in your arm, then slowly releases the pressure while watching a pressure gauge. Initially, the cuff squeezes the artery shut and cuts off the blood flow. When the cuff pressure drops below the systolic pressure, the pressure pulse during each beat of your heart forces the artery open briefly

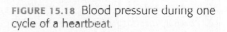
FIGURE 15.18 Blood pressure during one cycle of a heartbeat.

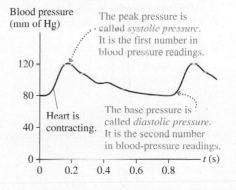

and a squirt of blood goes through. You can feel this, and the doctor or nurse records the pressure when she hears the blood start to flow. This is your systolic pressure.

This pulsing of the blood through your artery lasts until the cuff pressure reaches the diastolic pressure. Then the artery remains open continuously and the blood flows smoothly. This transition is easily heard in the stethoscope, and the doctor or nurse records your diastolic pressure.

Blood pressure is measured in millimeters of mercury. And it is a gauge pressure, the pressure in excess of 1 atm. A fairly typical blood pressure of a healthy young adult is 120/80, meaning that the systolic pressure is $p_g = 120$ mm of Hg (absolute pressure $p = 880$ mm of Hg) and the diastolic pressure is 80 mm of Hg.

The Hydraulic Lift

The use of pressurized liquids to do useful work is a technology known as **hydraulics.** Pascal's principle is the fundamental idea underlying hydraulic devices. If you increase the pressure at one point in a liquid by pushing a piston in, that pressure increase is transmitted to all points in the liquid. A second piston at some other point in the fluid can then push outward and do useful work.

The brake system in your car is a hydraulic system. Stepping on the brake pushes a piston into the *master brake cylinder* and increases the pressure in the *brake fluid.* The fluid itself hardly moves, but the pressure increase is transmitted to the four wheels where it pushes the brake pads against the spinning brake disk. You've used a pressurized liquid to achieve the useful goal of stopping your car.

One advantage of hydraulic systems over simple mechanical linkages is the possibility of *force multiplication.* To see how this works, we'll analyze a *hydraulic lift,* such as the one that lifts your car at the repair shop. **FIGURE 15.19a** shows force $\vec{F}_2$, perhaps due to the weight of mass m, pressing down on a liquid via a piston of area A_2. A much smaller force $\vec{F}_1$ presses down on a piston of area A_1. Can this system possibly be in equilibrium?

As you now know, the hydrostatic pressure is the same at all points along a horizontal line through a fluid. Consider the line passing through the liquid/piston interface on the left in Figure 15.19a. Pressures p_1 and p_2 must be equal, thus

$$p_0 + \frac{F_1}{A_1} = p_0 + \frac{F_2}{A_2} + \rho g h \qquad (15.10)$$

The atmosphere presses equally on both sides, so p_0 cancels. The system is in static equilibrium if

$$F_2 = \frac{A_2}{A_1} F_1 - \rho g h A_2 \qquad (15.11)$$

If the height h is very small, so that the term $\rho g h A_2$ is negligible, then F_2 (the weight of the heavy object) is larger than F_1 by the factor A_2/A_1. In other words, a small force applied to a small piston really can support a large car because both apply the *same pressure* to the fluid. The ratio A_2/A_1 is a force-multiplying factor.

> **NOTE** ▶ Force $\vec{F}_2$ is the force of the heavy object pushing *down* on the liquid. According to Newton's third law, the liquid pushes *up* on the object with a force of equal magnitude. Thus F_2 in Equation 15.11 is the "lifting force." ◀

Suppose we need to lift the car higher. If piston 1 is pushed down distance d_1, as in **FIGURE 15.19b**, it displaces volume $V_1 = A_1 d_1$ of liquid. Because the liquid is incompressible, V_1 must equal the volume $V_2 = A_2 d_2$ added beneath piston 2 as it rises distance d_2. That is,

$$d_2 = \frac{d_1}{A_2/A_1} \qquad (15.12)$$

The distance is *divided* by the same factor as that by which force is multiplied. A small force may be able to support a heavy weight, but you have to push the small piston a large distance to raise the heavy weight by a small amount.

FIGURE 15.19 A hydraulic lift.

(a)

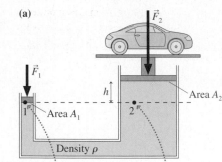

Pressure p_1 is due to atmospheric pressure p_0 *plus* pressure F_1/A_1, due to $\vec{F}_1$.

Pressure p_2 is p_0 *plus* F_2/A_2 *plus* $\rho g h$ from the liquid column of height h.

(b)

Because the fluid is incompressible, $A_1 d_1 = A_2 d_2$.

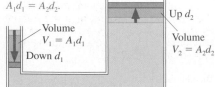

This conclusion is really just a statement of energy conservation. Work is done *on* the liquid by a small force pushing the liquid through a large displacement. Work is done *by* the liquid when it lifts the heavy weight through a small distance. A full analysis must consider the fact that the gravitational potential energy of the liquid is also changing, so we can't simply equate the output work to the input work, but you can see that energy considerations require piston 1 to move farther than piston 2.

Force $\vec{F}_1$ in Equation 15.11 is the force that balances the heavy object at height h. As a homework problem, you can show that force $\vec{F}_1$ must be increased by

$$\Delta F = \rho g (A_1 + A_2)d_2 \qquad (15.13)$$

to lift the heavy object through distance d_2 to a new height $h + d_2$, where ρ is the density of the liquid. Surprisingly, ΔF is independent of the weight you're lifting.

EXAMPLE 15.7 Lifting a car

The hydraulic lift at a car repair shop is filled with oil. The car rests on a 25-cm-diameter piston. To lift the car, compressed air is used to push down on a 6.0-cm-diameter piston.

a. What air-pressure force will support a 1300 kg car level with the compressed-air piston?

b. By how much must the air-pressure force be increased to lift the car 2.0 m?

MODEL Assume that the oil is incompressible. Its density, from Table 15.1, is 900 kg/m³.

SOLVE a. The weight of the car pressing on the piston is $F_2 = mg = 12{,}700$ N. The piston areas are $A_1 = \pi(0.030 \text{ m})^2 = 0.00283 \text{ m}^2$ and $A_2 = \pi(0.125 \text{ m})^2 = 0.0491 \text{ m}^2$. The force

required to hold the car level with the compressed air piston, with $h = 0$ m, is

$$F_1 = \frac{F_2}{A_2/A_1} = \frac{12{,}700 \text{ N}}{(0.0491 \text{ m}^2)/(0.00283 \text{ m}^2)} = 730 \text{ N}$$

b. To raise the car $d_2 = 2.0$ m, the air-pressure force must be increased by

$$\Delta F = \rho g (A_1 + A_2)d_2 = 920 \text{ N}$$

ASSESS 730 N is roughly the weight of an average adult man. The multiplication factor $A_2/A_1 = (25 \text{ cm}/6 \text{ cm})^2 = 17$ makes it quite easy to hold up the car.

STOP TO THINK 15.3   Rank in order, from largest to smallest, the magnitudes of the forces $\vec{F}_a$, $\vec{F}_b$, and $\vec{F}_c$ required to balance the masses. The masses are in kilograms.

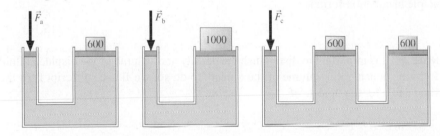

15.4 Buoyancy

A rock, as you know, sinks like a rock. Wood floats on the surface of a lake. A penny with a mass of a few grams sinks, but a massive steel aircraft carrier floats. How can we understand these diverse phenomena?

An air mattress floats effortlessly on the surface of a swimming pool. But if you've ever tried to push an air mattress underwater, you know it is nearly impossible. As you push down, the water pushes up. This net upward force of a fluid is called the **buoyant force.**

The basic reason for the buoyant force is easy to understand. FIGURE 15.20 shows a cylinder submerged in a liquid. The pressure in the liquid increases with depth, so the pressure at the bottom of the cylinder is larger than at the top. Both cylinder ends have

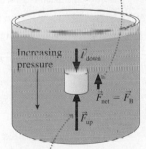

FIGURE 15.20 The buoyant force arises because the fluid pressure at the bottom of the cylinder is larger than at the top.

The net force of the fluid on the cylinder is the buoyant force $\vec{F}_B$.

$F_{up} > F_{down}$ because the pressure is greater at the bottom. Hence the fluid exerts a net upward force.

equal area, so force $\vec{F}_{up}$ is larger than force $\vec{F}_{down}$. (Remember that pressure forces push in *all* directions.) Consequently, the pressure in the liquid exerts a *net upward force* on the cylinder of magnitude $F_{net} = F_{up} - F_{down}$. This is the buoyant force.

The submerged cylinder illustrates the idea in a simple way, but the result is not limited to cylinders or to liquids. Suppose we isolate a parcel of fluid of arbitrary shape and volume by drawing an imaginary boundary around it, as shown in FIGURE 15.21a. This parcel is in static equilibrium. Consequently, the gravitational force pulling down on the parcel must be balanced by an upward force. The upward force, which is exerted on this parcel of fluid by the surrounding fluid, is the buoyant force $\vec{F}_B$. The buoyant force matches the weight of the fluid: $F_B = mg$.

Imagine that we could somehow remove this parcel of fluid and instantaneously replace it with an object of exactly the same shape and size, as shown in FIGURE 15.21b. Because the buoyant force is exerted by the *surrounding* fluid, and the surrounding fluid hasn't changed, the buoyant force on this new object is *exactly the same* as the buoyant force on the parcel of fluid that we removed.

When an object (or a portion of an object) is immersed in a fluid, it *displaces* fluid that would otherwise fill that region of space. This fluid is called the **displaced fluid.** The displaced fluid's volume is exactly the volume of the portion of the object that is immersed in the fluid. Figure 15.21 leads us to conclude that the magnitude of the upward buoyant force matches the weight of this displaced fluid.

This idea was first recognized by the ancient Greek mathematician and scientist Archimedes, perhaps the greatest scientist of antiquity, and today we know it as *Archimedes' principle*.

FIGURE 15.21 The buoyant force on an object is the same as the buoyant force on the fluid it displaces.

(a)   Imaginary boundary around a parcel of fluid

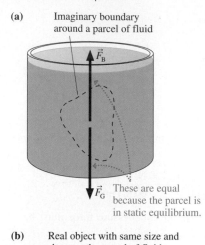

$\vec{F}_G$ These are equal because the parcel is in static equilibrium.

(b)   Real object with same size and shape as the parcel of fluid

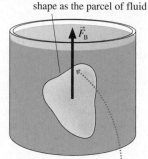

The buoyant force on the object is the same as on the parcel of fluid because the *surrounding* fluid has not changed.

> **Archimedes' principle** A fluid exerts an upward buoyant force $\vec{F}_B$ on an object immersed in or floating on the fluid. The magnitude of the buoyant force equals the weight of the fluid displaced by the object.

Suppose the fluid has density ρ_f and the object displaces volume V_f of fluid. The mass of the displaced fluid is $m_f = \rho_f V_f$ and so its weight is $m_f g = \rho_f V_f g$. Thus Archimedes' principle in equation form is

$$F_B = \rho_f V_f g \qquad (15.14)$$

NOTE ▶ It is important to distinguish the density and volume of the displaced fluid from the density and volume of the object. To do so, we'll use subscript f for the fluid and o for the object. ◀

EXAMPLE 15.8 Holding a block of wood underwater

A 10 cm × 10 cm × 10 cm block of wood with density 700 kg/m³ is held underwater by a string tied to the bottom of the container. What is the tension in the string?

MODEL The buoyant force is given by Archimedes' principle.

VISUALIZE FIGURE 15.22 shows the forces acting on the wood.

SOLVE The block is in static equilibrium, so

$$\sum F_y = F_B - T - m_o g = 0$$

Thus the tension is $T = F_B - m_o g$. The mass of the block is $m_o = \rho_o V_o$, and the buoyant force, given by Equation 15.14, is $F_B = \rho_f V_f g$. Thus

$$T = \rho_f V_f g - \rho_o V_o g = (\rho_f - \rho_o) V_o g$$

FIGURE 15.22 The forces acting on the submerged wood.

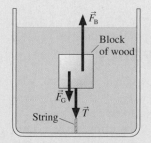

where we've used the fact that $V_f = V_o$ for a completely submerged object. The volume is $V_o = 1000 \text{ cm}^3 = 1.0 \times 10^{-3} \text{ m}^3$, and hence the tension in the string is

$$T = \left((1000 \text{ kg/m}^3) - (700 \text{ kg/m}^3)\right)$$
$$\times (1.0 \times 10^{-3} \text{ m}^3)(9.8 \text{ m/s}^2) = 2.9 \text{ N}$$

ASSESS The tension depends on the *difference* in densities. The tension would vanish if the wood density matched the water density.

Float or Sink?

If you *hold* an object underwater and then release it, it either floats to the surface, sinks, or remains "hanging" in the water. How can we predict which it will do? The net force on the object an instant after you release it is $\vec{F}_{net} = (F_B - m_o g)\hat{k}$. Whether it heads for the surface or the bottom depends on whether the buoyancy force F_B is larger or smaller than the object's weight $m_o g$.

The magnitude of the buoyant force is $\rho_f V_f g$. The weight of a uniform object, such as a block of steel, is simply $\rho_o V_o g$. But a compound object, such as a scuba diver, may have pieces of varying density. If we define the **average density** to be $\rho_{avg} = m_o/V_o$, the weight of a compound object is $\rho_{avg} V_o g$.

Comparing $\rho_f V_f g$ to $\rho_{avg} V_o g$, and noting that $V_f = V_o$ for an object that is fully submerged, we see that an object floats or sinks depending on whether the fluid density ρ_f is larger or smaller than the object's average density ρ_{avg}. If the densities are equal, the object is in static equilibrium and hangs motionless. This is called **neutral buoyancy**. These conditions are summarized in Tactics Box 15.2.

TACTICS
BOX 15.2   **Finding whether an object floats or sinks**   (MP)

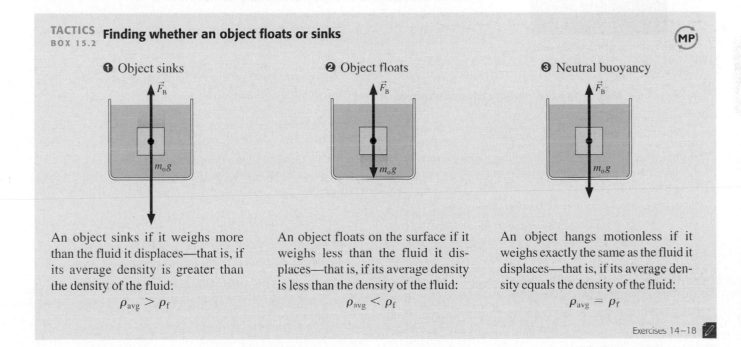

❶ Object sinks

❷ Object floats

❸ Neutral buoyancy

An object sinks if it weighs more than the fluid it displaces—that is, if its average density is greater than the density of the fluid:

$$\rho_{avg} > \rho_f$$

An object floats on the surface if it weighs less than the fluid it displaces—that is, if its average density is less than the density of the fluid:

$$\rho_{avg} < \rho_f$$

An object hangs motionless if it weighs exactly the same as the fluid it displaces—that is, if its average density equals the density of the fluid:

$$\rho_{avg} = \rho_f$$

Exercises 14–18

As an example, steel is denser than water, so a chunk of steel sinks. Oil is less dense than water, so oil floats on water. Fish use *swim bladders* filled with air and scuba divers use weighted belts to adjust their average density to match the water. Both are examples of neutral buoyancy.

FIGURE 15.23 A floating object is in static equilibrium.

An object of density ρ_o and volume V_o is floating on a fluid of density ρ_f.

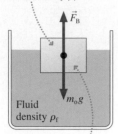

The submerged volume of the object is equal to the volume V_f of displaced fluid.

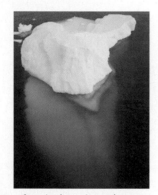

90% of an iceberg is underwater.

If you release a block of wood underwater, the net upward force causes the block to shoot to the surface. Then what? Let's begin with a *uniform* object such as the block shown in **FIGURE 15.23**. This object contains nothing tricky, like indentations or voids. Because it's floating, it must be the case that $\rho_o < \rho_f$.

Now that the object is floating, it's in static equilibrium. The upward buoyant force, given by Archimedes' principle, exactly balances the downward weight of the object. That is,

$$F_B = \rho_f V_f g = m_o g = \rho_o V_o g \qquad (15.15)$$

In this case, the volume of the displaced fluid is *not* the same as the volume of the object. In fact, we can see from Equation 15.15 that the volume of fluid displaced by a floating object of uniform density is

$$V_f = \frac{\rho_o}{\rho_f} V_o < V_o \qquad (15.16)$$

You've often heard it said that "90% of an iceberg is underwater." Equation 15.16 is the basis for that statement. Most icebergs break off glaciers and are fresh-water ice with a density of 917 kg/m³. The density of seawater is 1030 kg/m³. Thus

$$V_f = \frac{917 \text{ kg/m}^3}{1030 \text{ kg/m}^3} V_o = 0.89 V_o$$

V_f, the displaced water, is the volume of the iceberg that is underwater. You can see that, indeed, 89% of the volume of an iceberg is underwater.

> **NOTE ▶** Equation 15.16 applies only to *uniform* objects. It does not apply to boats, hollow spheres, or other objects of nonuniform composition. ◄

EXAMPLE 15.9 Measuring the density of an unknown liquid

You need to determine the density of an unknown liquid. You notice that a block floats in this liquid with 4.6 cm of the side of the block submerged. When the block is placed in water, it also floats but with 5.8 cm submerged. What is the density of the unknown liquid?

MODEL The block is an object of uniform composition.

VISUALIZE **FIGURE 15.24** shows the block and defines the cross-section area A and submerged lengths h_u in the unknown liquid and h_w in water.

FIGURE 15.24 More of the block is submerged in water than in an unknown liquid.

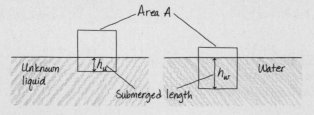

SOLVE The block is floating, so Equation 15.16 applies. The block displaces volume $V_u = Ah_u$ of the unknown liquid. Thus

$$V_u = Ah_u = \frac{\rho_o}{\rho_u} V_o$$

Similarly, the block displaces volume $V_w = Ah_w$ of the water, leading to

$$V_w = Ah_w = \frac{\rho_o}{\rho_w} V_o$$

Because there are two fluids, we've used subscripts w for water and u for the unknown in place of the fluid subscript f. The product $\rho_o V_o$ appears in both equations; hence

$$\rho_u Ah_u = \rho_w Ah_w$$

The unknown area A cancels, and the density of the unknown liquid is

$$\rho_u = \frac{h_w}{h_u} \rho_w = \frac{5.8 \text{ cm}}{4.6 \text{ cm}} 1000 \text{ kg/m}^3 = 1260 \text{ kg/m}^3$$

ASSESS Comparison with Table 15.1 shows that the unknown liquid is likely to be glycerin.

Boats

We'll conclude by designing a boat. FIGURE 15.25 is a physicist's idea of a boat. Four massless but rigid walls are attached to a solid steel plate of mass m_0 and area A. As the steel plate settles down into the water, the sides allow the boat to displace a volume of water much larger than that displaced by the steel alone. The boat will float if the weight of the displaced water equals the weight of the boat.

In terms of density, the boat will float if $\rho_{avg} < \rho_f$. If the sides of the boat are height h, the boat's volume is $V_0 = Ah$ and its average density is $\rho_{avg} = m_0/V_0 = m_0/Ah$. The boat will float if

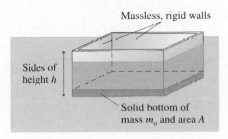

FIGURE 15.25 A physicist's boat.

Massless, rigid walls

Sides of height h

Solid bottom of mass m_0 and area A

$$\rho_{avg} = \frac{m_0}{Ah} < \rho_f \qquad (15.17)$$

Thus the minimum height of the sides, a height that would allow the boat to float (in perfectly still water!) with water right up to the rails, is

$$h_{min} = \frac{m_0}{\rho_f A} \qquad (15.18)$$

As a quick example, a 5 m × 10 m steel "barge" with a 2-cm-thick floor has an area of 50 m² and a mass of 7900 kg. The minimum height of the massless walls, as given by Equation 15.18, is 16 cm.

Real ships and boats are more complicated, but the same idea holds true. Whether it's made of concrete, steel, or lead, **a boat will float if its geometry allows it to displace enough water to equal the weight of the boat.**

STOP TO THINK 15.4 An ice cube is floating in a glass of water that is filled entirely to the brim. When the ice cube melts, the water level will

a. Fall.   b. Stay the same, right at the brim.   c. Rise, causing the water to spill.

15.5 Fluid Dynamics

The wind blowing through your hair, a white-water river, and oil gushing from an oil well are examples of fluids in motion. We've focused thus far on fluid statics, but it's time to turn our attention to fluid dynamics.

Fluid flow is a complex subject. Many aspects, especially turbulence and the formation of eddies, are still not well understood and are areas of current science and engineering research. We will avoid these difficulties by using a simplified *model*. The **ideal-fluid model** provides a good, though not perfect, description of fluid flow in many situations. It captures the essence of fluid flow while eliminating unnecessary details.

The ideal-fluid model can be expressed in three assumptions about a fluid:

1. The fluid is *incompressible*. This is a good assumption for liquids, less so for gases.
2. The fluid is *nonviscous*. Water flows much more easily than pancake syrup because the syrup is a very *viscous* fluid. **Viscosity,** a resistance to flow, is analogous to kinetic friction. Assuming that a fluid is nonviscous is equivalent to assuming there's no friction. This is the weakest assumption for many liquids, but assuming a nonviscous liquid avoids major mathematical difficulties.
3. The flow is *steady*. That is, the fluid velocity at each point in the fluid is constant; it does not fluctuate or change with time. Flow under these conditions is called **laminar flow,** and it is distinguished from *turbulent flow*.

The rising smoke in the photograph of FIGURE 15.26 begins as laminar flow, recognizable by the smooth contours, but at some point undergoes a transition to turbulent

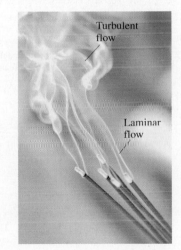

FIGURE 15.26 Rising smoke changes from laminar flow to turbulent flow.

Turbulent flow

Laminar flow

flow. A laminar-to-turbulent transition is not uncommon in fluid flow. The ideal-fluid model can be applied to the laminar flow, but not to the turbulent flow.

The Equation of Continuity

FIGURE 15.27 is another interesting photograph. Here smoke is being used to help engineers visualize the airflow around a car in a wind tunnel. The smoothness of the flow tells us this is laminar flow. But notice also how the individual smoke trails retain their identity. They don't cross or get mixed together. Each smoke trail represents a *streamline* in the fluid.

FIGURE 15.27 The laminar airflow around a car in a wind tunnel is made visible with smoke. Each smoke trail represents a streamline.

Streamline

Imagine that we could inject a colored drop of water into a stream of water flowing as an ideal fluid. Because the flow is steady and frictionless, and the water is incompressible, this colored drop would maintain its identity as it flowed along. Its shape might change, becoming compressed or elongated, but it would not mix with the surrounding water.

The path or trajectory followed by this "particle of fluid" is called a **streamline.** Smoke particles mixed with the air allow you to see the streamlines in the photograph of Figure 15.27. Notice how the individual smoke trails retain their identity. **FIGURE 15.28** illustrates three important properties of streamlines.

A bundle of neighboring streamlines, such as those shown in **FIGURE 15.29a**, form a **flow tube.** Because streamlines never cross, all the streamlines that cross plane 1 within area A_1 later cross plane 2 within area A_2. A flow tube is like an invisible pipe that keeps this portion of the flowing fluid distinct from other portions. Real pipes are also flow tubes.

FIGURE 15.28 Particles in an ideal fluid move along streamlines.

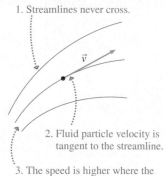

1. Streamlines never cross.

$\vec{v}$

2. Fluid particle velocity is tangent to the streamline.

3. The speed is higher where the streamlines are closer together.

FIGURE 15.29 A flow tube.

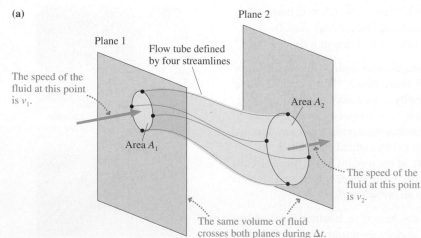

(a)

Plane 1

Plane 2

Flow tube defined by four streamlines

The speed of the fluid at this point is v_1.

Area A_2

Area A_1

The speed of the fluid at this point is v_2.

The same volume of fluid crosses both planes during Δt.

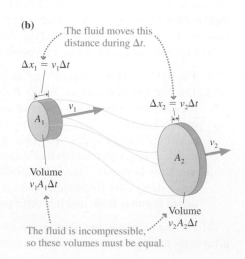

(b)

The fluid moves this distance during Δt.

$\Delta x_1 = v_1 \Delta t$

v_1

A_1

$\Delta x_2 = v_2 \Delta t$

v_2

A_2

Volume $v_1 A_1 \Delta t$

Volume $v_2 A_2 \Delta t$

The fluid is incompressible, so these volumes must be equal.

When you squeeze a toothpaste tube, the volume of toothpaste that emerges matches the amount by which you reduce the volume of the tube. An incompressible fluid in a flow tube acts the same way. Fluid is not created or destroyed within the flow tube, and it cannot be stored. If volume V enters the flow tube through area A_1 during some interval of time Δt, then an equal volume V must leave the flow tube through area A_2.

FIGURE 15.29b shows the flow crossing A_1 during a small interval of time Δt. If the fluid speed at this point is v_1, the fluid moves forward a small distance $\Delta x_1 = v_1 \Delta t$ and fills the volume $V_1 = A_1 \Delta x_1 = v_1 A_1 \Delta t$. The same analysis for the fluid crossing A_2 with fluid speed v_2 would find $V_2 = v_2 A_2 \Delta t$. These two volumes must be equal, leading to the conclusion that

FIGURE 15.30 The flow tube diameter changes as the speed increases. This is a consequence of the equation of continuity.

$$v_1 A_1 = v_2 A_2 \qquad (15.19)$$

Equation 15.19 is called the **equation of continuity,** and it is one of two important equations for the flow of an ideal fluid. The equation of continuity says that **the volume of an incompressible fluid entering one part of a flow tube must be matched by an equal volume leaving downstream.**

An important consequence of the equation of continuity is that **flow is faster in narrower parts of a flow tube, slower in wider parts.** You're familiar with this conclusion from many everyday observations. For example, water flowing from the faucet shown in **FIGURE 15.30** picks up speed as it falls. As a result, the flow tube "necks down" to a smaller diameter.

The quantity

$$Q = vA \qquad (15.20)$$

is called the **volume flow rate.** The SI units of Q are m^3/s, although in practice Q may be measured in cm^3/s, liters per minute, or, in the United States, gallons per minute. Another way to express the meaning of the equation of continuity is to say that **the volume flow rate is constant at all points in a flow tube.**

EXAMPLE 15.10 Gasoline through a pipe

An oil refinery pumps gasoline into a 1000 L holding tank through an 8.0-cm-diameter pipe. The tank can be filled in 2.0 min.

a. What is the speed of the gasoline through the pipe?
b. Farther upstream, the pipe's diameter is 16 cm. What is the flow speed in this section of pipe?

MODEL Treat the gasoline as an ideal fluid. The pipe is a flow tube, so the equation of continuity applies.

SOLVE a. The volume flow rate is $Q = (1000 \text{ L})/(120 \text{ s}) = 8.33 \text{ L/s}$. To convert this to SI units, recall that $1 \text{ L} = 10^{-3} \text{ m}^3$.

Thus $Q = 8.33 \times 10^{-3} \text{ m}^3/\text{s}$. We can find the speed of the gasoline from Equation 15.20:

$$v = \frac{Q}{A} = \frac{Q}{\pi r^2} = \frac{8.33 \times 10^{-3} \text{ m}^3/\text{s}}{\pi (0.040 \text{ m})^2} = 1.66 \text{ m/s}$$

b. $Q = vA$ remains constant. The cross-section area depends on the square of the radius, so the pipe's cross-section area upsteam is a factor of 4 larger. Consequently, the flow speed must be a factor of 4 smaller, or 0.41 m/s.

STOP TO THINK 15.5 The figure shows volume flow rates (in cm^3/s) for all but one tube. What is the volume flow rate through the unmarked tube? Is the flow direction in or out?

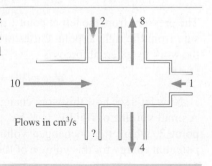

Flows in cm^3/s

Bernoulli's Equation

The equation of continuity is one of two important relationships for ideal fluids. The other is a statement of energy conservation. The general statement of energy conservation that you learned in Chapter 11 is

$$\Delta K + \Delta U = W_{\text{ext}} \qquad (15.21)$$

where W_{ext} is the work done by any external forces.

Let's see how this applies to the flow tube of FIGURE 15.31. Our system for analysis is the volume of fluid within the flow tube. Work is done on this volume of fluid by the pressure forces of the *surrounding* fluid. At point 1, the fluid to the left of the flow tube exerts force $\vec{F}_1$ on the system. This force points to the right. At the other end of the flow tube, at point 2, the fluid to the right of the flow tube exerts force $\vec{F}_2$ to the left. The pressure inside the flow tube is not relevant because those forces are internal to the system. Only external forces change the total energy.

FIGURE 15.31 Energy analysis of a flow tube.

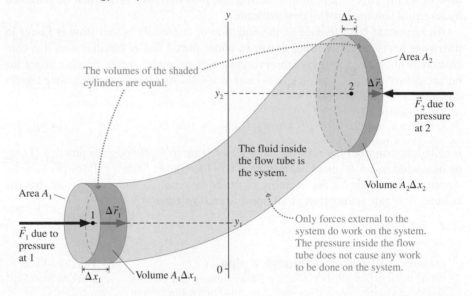

At point 1, force $\vec{F}_1$ pushes the fluid through displacement $\Delta \vec{r}_1$. $\vec{F}_1$ and $\Delta \vec{r}_1$ are parallel, so the work done on the fluid at this point is

$$W_1 = \vec{F}_1 \cdot \Delta \vec{r}_1 = F_1 \Delta r_1 = (p_1 A_1) \Delta x_1 = p_1 V \qquad (15.22)$$

The A_1 and Δx_1 enter the equation from different terms, but they conveniently combine to give the fluid volume V.

The situation is much the same at point 2 except that $\vec{F}_2$ points opposite the displacement $\Delta \vec{r}_2$. This introduces a $\cos(180°) = -1$ into the dot product for the work, giving

$$W_2 = \vec{F}_2 \cdot \Delta \vec{r}_2 = -F_2 \Delta r_2 = -(p_2 A_2) \Delta x_2 = -p_2 V \qquad (15.23)$$

The pressure from the left at point 1 pushes the fluid ahead, a positive work. The pressure from the right at point 2 tries to slow the fluid down, a negative work. Together, the work by external forces is

$$W_{\text{ext}} = W_1 + W_2 = p_1 V - p_2 V \qquad (15.24)$$

Now let's see how this work changes the kinetic and potential energy of the system. A small volume of fluid $V = A_1 \Delta x_1$ passes point 1 and, at some later time, arrives at point 2, where the unchanged volume is $V = A_2 \Delta x_2$. The change in gravitational potential energy for this volume of fluid is

$$\Delta U = mgy_2 - mgy_1 = \rho V g y_2 - \rho V g y_1 \qquad (15.25)$$

where ρ is the fluid density. Similarly, the change in kinetic energy is

$$\Delta K = \frac{1}{2}mv_2^2 - \frac{1}{2}mv_1^2 = \frac{1}{2}\rho V v_2^2 - \frac{1}{2}\rho V v_1^2 \qquad (15.26)$$

Combining Equations 15.24, 15.25, and 15.26 gives us the energy equation for the fluid in the flow tube:

$$\frac{1}{2}\rho V v_2^2 \quad \frac{1}{2}\rho V v_1^2 \; | \; \rho V g y_2 - \rho V g y_1 - p_1 V - p_2 V \qquad (15.27)$$

The volume V cancels out of all the terms. If we regroup the terms, the energy equation becomes

$$p_1 + \frac{1}{2}\rho v_1^2 + \rho g y_1 = p_2 + \frac{1}{2}\rho v_2^2 + \rho g y_2 \qquad (15.28)$$

Equation 15.28 is called **Bernoulli's equation.** It is named for the 18th-century Swiss scientist Daniel Bernoulli, who made some of the earliest studies of fluid dynamics.

Bernoulli's equation is really nothing more than a statement about work and energy. It is sometimes useful to express Bernoulli's equation in the alternative form

$$p + \frac{1}{2}\rho v^2 + \rho g y = \text{constant} \qquad (15.29)$$

This version of Bernoulli's equation tells us that the quantity $p + \frac{1}{2}\rho v^2 + \rho g y$ remains constant along a streamline.

One important implication of Bernoulli's equation is easily demonstrated. Before reading the next paragraph, try the simple experiment illustrated in **FIGURE 15.32**. Really, do try this!

What happened? You probably expected your breath to press the strip of paper down. Instead, the strip *rose*. In fact, the harder you blow, the more nearly the strip becomes parallel to the floor. This counterintuitive result is a consequence of Bernoulli's equation. As the air speed above the strip of paper increases, the pressure has to *decrease* to keep the quantity $p + \frac{1}{2}\rho v^2 + \rho g y$ constant. Consequently, the air pressure above the strip is less than the air pressure beneath the strip, resulting in a net upward force on the paper.

NOTE ▶ Using Bernoulli's equation is very much like using the law of conservation of energy. Rather than identifying a "before" and "after," you want to identify two points on a streamline. As the following examples show, Bernoulli's equation is often used in conjunction with the equation of continuity. ◀

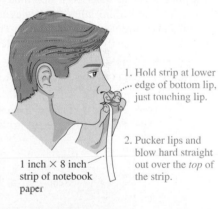

FIGURE 15.32 A simple demonstration of Bernoulli's equation.

1. Hold strip at lower edge of bottom lip, just touching lip.

2. Pucker lips and blow hard straight out over the *top* of the strip.

1 inch × 8 inch strip of notebook paper

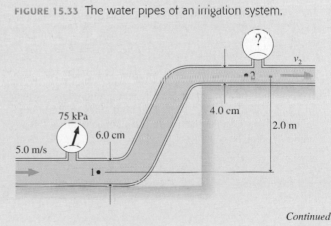

EXAMPLE 15.11 **An irrigation system**
Water flows through the pipes shown in **FIGURE 15.33**. The water's speed through the lower pipe is 5.0 m/s and a pressure gauge reads 75 kPa. What is the reading of the pressure gauge on the upper pipe?

MODEL Treat the water as an ideal fluid obeying Bernoulli's equation. Consider a streamline connecting point 1 in the lower pipe with point 2 in the upper pipe.

FIGURE 15.33 The water pipes of an irrigation system.

?
v_2
2
4.0 cm
75 kPa
6.0 cm
2.0 m
5.0 m/s
1●

Continued

SOLVE Bernoulli's equation, Equation 15.28, relates the pressure, fluid speed, and heights at points 1 and 2. It is easily solved for the pressure p_2 at point 2:

$$p_2 = p_1 + \frac{1}{2}\rho v_1^2 - \frac{1}{2}\rho v_2^2 + \rho g y_1 - \rho g y_2$$

$$= p_1 + \frac{1}{2}\rho(v_1^2 - v_2^2) + \rho g(y_1 - y_2)$$

All quantities on the right are known except v_2, and that is where the equation of continuity will be useful. The cross-section areas and water speeds at points 1 and 2 are related by

$$v_1 A_1 = v_2 A_2$$

from which we find

$$v_2 = \frac{A_1}{A_2}v_1 = \frac{r_1^2}{r_2^2}v_1 = \frac{(0.030\ \text{m})^2}{(0.020\ \text{m})^2}(5.0\ \text{m/s}) = 11.25\ \text{m/s}$$

The pressure at point 1 is $p_1 = 75$ kPa + 1 atm = 176,300 Pa. We can now use the above expression for p_2 to calculate $p_2 = 105,900$ Pa. This is the absolute pressure; the pressure gauge on the upper pipe will read

$$p_2 = 105,900\ \text{Pa} - 1\ \text{atm} = 4.6\ \text{kPa}$$

ASSESS Reducing the pipe size decreases the pressure because it makes $v_2 > v_1$. Gaining elevation also reduces the pressure.

EXAMPLE 15.12 **Hydroelectric power**

Small hydroelectric plants in the mountains sometimes bring the water from a reservoir down to the power plant through enclosed tubes. In one such plant, the 100-cm-diameter intake tube in the base of the dam is 50 m below the reservoir surface. The water drops 200 m through the tube before flowing into the turbine through a 50-cm-diameter nozzle.

a. What is the water speed into the turbine?
b. By how much does the inlet pressure differ from the hydrostatic pressure at that depth?

MODEL Treat the water as an ideal fluid obeying Bernoulli's equation. Consider a streamline that begins at the surface of the reservoir and ends at the exit of the nozzle. The pressure at the surface is $p_1 = p_{\text{atmos}}$ and $v_1 \approx 0$ m/s. The water discharges into air, so $p_3 = p_{\text{atmos}}$ at the exit.

VISUALIZE FIGURE 15.34 is a pictorial representation of the situation.

FIGURE 15.34 Pictorial representation of the water flow to a hydroelectric plant.

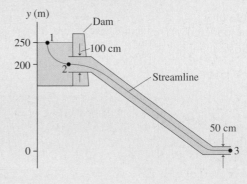

SOLVE a. The power plant is in the mountains, where $p_{\text{atmos}} < 1$ atm, but p_{atmos} occurs on both sides of Bernoulli's equation and cancels. Bernoulli's equation, with $v_1 = 0$ m/s and $y_3 = 0$ m, is

$$p_{\text{atmos}} + \rho g y_1 = p_{\text{atmos}} + \frac{1}{2}\rho v_3^2$$

p_{atmos} cancels, as expected, as does the density ρ. Solving for v_3 gives

$$v_3 = \sqrt{2g y_1} = \sqrt{2(9.80\ \text{m/s}^2)(250\ \text{m})} = 70\ \text{m/s}$$

b. You might expect the pressure p_2 at the intake to be the hydrostatic pressure $p_{\text{atmos}} + \rho g d$ at depth d. But the water is *flowing* into the intake tube, so it's not in static equilibrium. We can find the intake speed v_2 from the equation of continuity:

$$v_2 = \frac{A_3}{A_2}v_3 = \frac{r_3^2}{r_2^2}\sqrt{2g y_1}$$

The intake is along the streamline between points 1 and 3, so we can apply Bernoulli's equation to points 1 and 2:

$$p_{\text{atmos}} + \rho g y_1 = p_2 + \frac{1}{2}\rho v_2^2 + \rho g y_2$$

Solving this equation for p_2, and noting that $y_1 - y_2 = d$, we find

$$p_2 = p_{\text{atmos}} + \rho g(y_1 - y_2) - \frac{1}{2}\rho v_2^2$$

$$= p_{\text{atmos}} + \rho g d - \frac{1}{2}\rho\left(\frac{r_3}{r_2}\right)^4(2g y_1)$$

$$= p_{\text{static}} - \rho g y_1\left(\frac{r_3}{r_2}\right)^4$$

The intake pressure is *less* than hydrostatic pressure by the amount

$$\rho g y_1\left(\frac{r_3}{r_2}\right)^4 = 153,000\ \text{Pa} = 1.5\ \text{atm}$$

ASSESS The water's exit speed from the nozzle is the same as if it fell 250 m from the surface of the reservoir. This isn't surprising because we've assumed a nonviscous (i.e., frictionless) liquid. "Real" water would have less speed but still flow very fast.

Two Applications

The speed of a flowing gas is often measured with a device called a **Venturi tube.** Venturi tubes measure gas speeds in environments as different as chemistry laboratories, wind tunnels, and jet engines.

FIGURE 15.35 shows gas flowing through a tube that changes from cross-section area A_1 to area A_2. A U-shaped glass tube containing liquid of density ρ_{liq} connects the two segments of the flow tube. When gas flows through the horizontal tube, the liquid stands height h higher in the side of the U tube connected to the narrow segment of the flow tube.

Figure 15.35 shows how a Venturi tube works. We can make this analysis quantitative and determine the gas-flow speed from the liquid height h. Two pieces of information we have to work with are Bernoulli's equation

$$p_1 + \frac{1}{2}\rho v_1^2 + \rho g y_1 = p_2 + \frac{1}{2}\rho v_2^2 + \rho g y_2 \qquad (15.30)$$

and the equation of continuity

$$v_2 A_2 = v_1 A_1 \qquad (15.31)$$

In addition, the hydrostatic equation for the liquid tells us that the pressure p_2 above the right tube differs from the pressure p_1 above the left tube by $\rho_{\text{liq}} g h$. That is,

$$p_2 = p_1 - \rho_{\text{liq}} g h \qquad (15.32)$$

First we use Equations 15.31 and 15.32 to eliminate v_2 and p_2 in Bernoulli's equation:

$$p_1 + \frac{1}{2}\rho v_1^2 = (p_1 - \rho_{\text{liq}} g h) + \frac{1}{2}\rho \left(\frac{A_1}{A_2}\right)^2 v_1^2 \qquad (15.33)$$

The potential energy terms have disappeared because $y_1 = y_2$ for a horizontal tube. Equation 15.33 can now be solved for v_1, then v_2 is obtained from Equation 15.31. We'll skip a few algebraic steps and go right to the result:

$$v_1 = A_2 \sqrt{\frac{2\rho_{\text{liq}} g h}{\rho(A_1^2 - A_2^2)}}$$

$$\qquad (15.34)$$

$$v_2 = A_1 \sqrt{\frac{2\rho_{\text{liq}} g h}{\rho(A_1^2 - A_2^2)}}$$

In practice, the equations for the gas-flow speeds have to be corrected for the fact that the gas, which is compressible, is not an ideal liquid. But Equation 15.34 is reasonably accurate even without corrections as long as the flow speeds are much less than the speed of sound, about 340 m/s. For us, the Venturi tube is an example of the power of Bernoulli's equation.

As a final example, we can use Bernoulli's equation to understand, at least qualitatively, how airplane wings generate *lift*. FIGURE 15.36 shows the cross section of an airplane wing. This shape is called an *airfoil*.

Although you usually think of an airplane moving through the air, in the airplane's reference frame it is the air that flows across a stationary wing. As it does, the streamlines must separate. The bottom of the wing does not significantly alter the streamlines going under the wing. But the streamlines going over the top of the wing get bunched together. This bunching reduces the cross-section area of a flow tube of streamlines. Consequently, in accordance with the equation of continuity, the air speed must increase as it flows across the top of the wing.

As you've seen several times, an increased air speed implies a decreased air pressure. This is the lesson of Bernoulli's equation. Because the air pressure above the wing is less than the air pressure below, the air exerts a net upward force on the wing, just as it did on the paper strip you blew across. The upward force of the air due to a pressure difference across the wing is called **lift.**

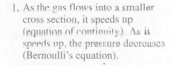

FIGURE 15.35 A Venturi tube measures gas-flow speeds.

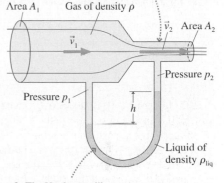

1. As the gas flows into a smaller cross section, it speeds up (equation of continuity). As it speeds up, the pressure decreases (Bernoulli's equation).

Area A_1 Gas of density ρ $\vec{v}_2$ Area A_2

$\vec{v}_1$

Pressure p_2

Pressure p_1

h

Liquid of density ρ_{liq}

2. The U tube acts like a manometer. The liquid level is higher on the side where the pressure is lower.

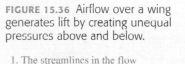

FIGURE 15.36 Airflow over a wing generates lift by creating unequal pressures above and below.

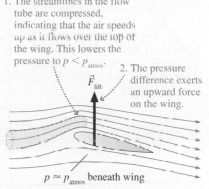

1. The streamlines in the flow tube are compressed, indicating that the air speeds up as it flows over the top of the wing. This lowers the pressure to $p < p_{\text{atmos}}$.

2. The pressure difference exerts an upward force on the wing.

$\vec{F}_{\text{lift}}$

$p \approx p_{\text{atmos}}$ beneath wing

A complete analysis of the lift of a wing is quite complicated and involves many factors in addition to Bernoulli's equation. Nonetheless, you should now be able to understand one of the important physical principles that are involved.

STOP TO THINK 15.6 Rank in order, from highest to lowest, the liquid heights h_a to h_d. The airflow is from left to right.

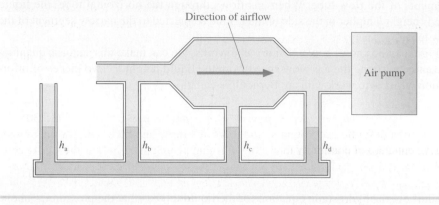

15.6 Elasticity

The final subject to explore in this chapter is elasticity. Although elasticity applies primarily to solids rather than fluids, you will see that similar ideas come into play.

Tensile Stress and Young's Modulus

Suppose you clamp one end of a solid rod while using a strong machine to pull on the other with force $\vec{F}$. **FIGURE 15.37a** shows the experimental arrangement. We usually think of solids as being, well, solid. But any material, be it plastic, concrete, or steel, will stretch as the spring-like molecular bonds expand.

FIGURE 15.37b shows graphically the amount of force needed to stretch the rod by the amount ΔL. This graph contains several regions of interest. First is the *elastic region,* ending at the *elastic limit.* As long as ΔL is less than the elastic limit, the rod will return to its initial length L when the force is removed. Just such a reversible stretch is what we mean when we say a material is *elastic.* A stretch beyond the elastic limit will permanently deform the object; it will not return to its initial length when the force is removed. And, not surprisingly, there comes a point when the rod breaks.

For most materials, the graph begins with a *linear region,* which is where we will focus our attention. If ΔL is within the linear region, the force needed to stretch the rod is

$$F = k\Delta L \tag{15.35}$$

where k is the slope of the graph. You'll recognize Equation 15.35 as none other than Hooke's law.

The difficulty with Equation 15.35 is that the proportionality constant k depends both on the composition of the rod—whether it is, say, plastic or aluminum—and on the rod's length and cross-section area. It would be useful to characterize the elastic properties of plastic in general, or aluminum in general, without needing to know the dimensions of a specific rod.

We can meet this goal by thinking about Hooke's law at the atomic scale. The elasticity of a material is directly related to the spring constant of the molecular bonds between neighboring atoms. As **FIGURE 15.38** shows, the force pulling each bond is proportional to the quantity F/A. This force causes each bond to stretch by an amount proportional to $\Delta L/L$. We don't know what the proportionality constants are, but we don't need to. Hooke's law applied to a molecular bond tells us that the force pulling on a

FIGURE 15.37 Stretching a solid rod.

(a)

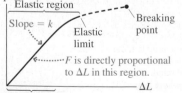

The pulling force stretches the spring-like molecular bonds.

Clamp

Area A

The rod stretches this far.

Solid rod

L ΔL

$\vec{F}$

(b)

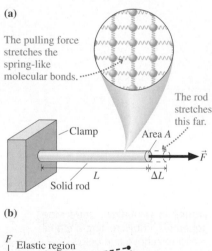

F

Elastic region

Slope = k

Elastic limit

Breaking point

F is directly proportional to ΔL in this region.

ΔL

Linear region

bond is proportional to the amount that the bond stretches. Thus F/A must be proportional to $\Delta L/L$. We can write their proportionality as

$$\frac{F}{A} = Y\frac{\Delta L}{L} \tag{15.36}$$

The proportionality constant Y is called **Young's modulus.** It is directly related to the spring constant of the molecular bonds, so it depends on the material from which the object is made but *not* on the object's geometry.

A comparison of Equations 15.35 and 15.36 shows that Young's modulus can be written as

$$Y = \frac{kL}{A} \tag{15.37}$$

This is not a definition of Young's modulus but simply an expression for making an experimental determination of the value of Young's modulus. This k is the spring constant of the rod seen in Figure 15.37. It is a quantity easily measured in the laboratory.

The quantity F/A, where A is the cross-section area, is called **tensile stress.** Notice that it is essentially the same definition as pressure. Even so, tensile stress differs in that the stress is applied in a particular direction whereas pressure forces are exerted in all directions. Another difference is that stress is measured in N/m^2 rather than pascals. The quantity $\Delta L/L$, the fractional increase in the length, is called **strain.** Strain is dimensionless. The numerical values of strain are always very small because solids cannot be stretched very much before reaching the breaking point.

With these definitions, Equation 15.36 can be written

$$\text{stress} = Y \times \text{strain} \tag{15.38}$$

Because strain is dimensionless, Young's modulus Y has the same dimensions as stress, namely N/m^2. Table 15.3 gives values of Young's modulus for several common materials. Large values of Y characterize materials that are stiff and rigid. "Softer" materials, at least relatively speaking, have smaller values of Y. You can see that steel has a larger Young's modulus than aluminum.

TABLE 15.3 Elastic properties of various materials

Substance	Young's modulus (N/m^2)	Bulk modulus (N/m^2)
Aluminum	7×10^{10}	7×10^{10}
Concrete	3×10^{10}	–
Copper	11×10^{10}	14×10^{10}
Mercury	–	3×10^{10}
Plastic (polystyrene)	0.3×10^{10}	–
Steel	20×10^{10}	16×10^{10}
Water	–	0.2×10^{10}
Wood (Douglas fir)	1×10^{10}	–

We introduced Young's modulus by considering how materials stretch. But Equation 15.38 and Young's modulus also apply to the compression of materials. Compression is particularly important in engineering applications, where beams, columns, and support foundations are compressed by the load they bear. Concrete is often compressed, as in columns that support highway overpasses, but rarely stretched.

NOTE ▶ Whether the rod is stretched or compressed, Equation 15.38 is valid only in the linear region of the graph in Figure 15.37b. The breaking point is usually well outside the linear region, so you can't use Young's modulus to compute the maximum possible stretch or compression. ◀

FIGURE 15.38 A material's elasticity is directly related to the spring constant of the molecular bonds.

The number of bonds is proportional to area A. If the rod is pulled with force F, the force pulling on each bond is proportional to F/A.

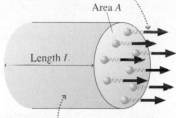

Area A

Length l

The number of bonds along the rod is proportional to length L. If the rod stretches by ΔL, the stretch of each bond is proportional to $\Delta L/L$.

Concrete is a widely used building material because it is relatively inexpensive and, with its large Young's modulus, it has tremendous compressional strength.

EXAMPLE 15.13 Stretching a wire

A 2.0-m-long, 1.0-mm-diameter wire is suspended from the ceiling. Hanging a 4.5 kg mass from the wire stretches the wire's length by 1.0 mm. What is Young's modulus for this wire? Can you identify the material?

MODEL The hanging mass creates tensile stress in the wire.

SOLVE The force pulling on the wire, which is simply the weight of the hanging mass, produces tensile stress

$$\frac{F}{A} = \frac{mg}{\pi r^2} = \frac{(4.5\ \text{kg})(9.80\ \text{m/s}^2)}{\pi(0.0005\ \text{m})^2} = 5.6 \times 10^7\ \text{N/m}^2$$

The resulting stretch of 1.0 mm is a strain of $\Delta L/L = (1.0\ \text{mm})/(2000\ \text{mm}) = 5.0 \times 10^{-4}$. Thus Young's modulus for the wire is

$$Y = \frac{F/A}{\Delta L/L} = 11 \times 10^{10}\ \text{N/m}^2$$

Referring to Table 15.3, we see that the wire is made of copper.

Volume Stress and the Bulk Modulus

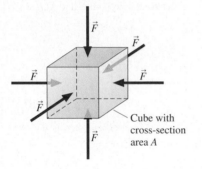

FIGURE 15.39 An object is compressed by pressure forces pushing equally on all sides.

Cube with cross-section area A

Young's modulus characterizes the response of an object to being pulled in one direction. FIGURE 15.39 shows an object being squeezed in all directions. For example, objects under water are squeezed from all sides by the water pressure. The force per unit area F/A applied to *all* surfaces of an object is called the **volume stress.** Because the force pushes equally on all sides, the volume stress (unlike the tensile stress) really is the same as pressure p.

No material is perfectly rigid. A volume stress applied to an object compresses its volume slightly. The **volume strain** is defined as $\Delta V/V$. The volume strain is a *negative* number because the volume stress *decreases* the volume.

Volume stress, or pressure, is linearly proportional to the volume strain, much as the tensile stress is linearly proportional to the strain in a rod. That is,

$$\frac{F}{A} = p = -B\frac{\Delta V}{V} \tag{15.39}$$

where B is called the **bulk modulus.** The negative sign in Equation 15.39 ensures that the pressure is a positive number. Table 15.3 gives values of the bulk modulus for several materials. Smaller values of B correspond to materials that are more easily compressed. Both solids and liquids can be compressed and thus have a bulk modulus, whereas Young's modulus applies only to solids.

EXAMPLE 15.14 Compressing a sphere

A 1.00-m-diameter solid steel sphere is lowered to a depth of 10,000 m in a deep ocean trench. By how much does its diameter shrink?

MODEL The water pressure applies a volume stress to the sphere.

SOLVE The water pressure at $d = 10,000$ m is

$$p = p_0 + \rho g d = 1.01 \times 10^8\ \text{Pa}$$

where we used the density of seawater. The bulk modulus of steel, taken from Table 15.3, is $16 \times 10^{10}\ \text{N/m}^2$. Thus the volume strain is

$$\frac{\Delta V}{V} = -\frac{p}{B} = -\frac{1.01 \times 10^8\ \text{Pa}}{16 \times 10^{10}\ \text{Pa}} = -6.3 \times 10^{-4}$$

The volume of a sphere is $V = \frac{4}{3}\pi r^3$. For a very small change, we can use calculus to relate the volume change to the change in radius:

$$\Delta V = \frac{4\pi}{3}\Delta(r^3) = \frac{4\pi}{3} \cdot 3r^2\Delta r = 4\pi r^2\Delta r$$

Using this expression for ΔV gives the volume strain:

$$\frac{\Delta V}{V} = \frac{4\pi r^2\Delta r}{\frac{4}{3}\pi r^3} = \frac{3\Delta r}{r} = -6.3 \times 10^{-4}$$

Solving for Δr gives $\Delta r = -1.05 \times 10^{-4}\ \text{m} = -0.105$ mm. The diameter changes by twice this, decreasing 0.21 mm.

ASSESS The immense pressure of the deep ocean causes only a tiny change in the sphere's diameter. You can see that treating solids and liquids as incompressible is an excellent approximation under nearly all circumstances.

SUMMARY

The goal of Chapter 15 has been to understand macroscopic systems that flow or deform.

General Principles

Fluid Statics

Gases

- Freely moving particles
- Compressible
- Pressure primarily thermal
- Pressure is constant in a laboratory-size container

Liquids

- Loosely bound particles
- Incompressible
- Pressure primarily gravitational
- Hydrostatic pressure at depth d is $p = p_0 + \rho g d$

Fluid Dynamics

Ideal-fluid model

- Incompressible
- Smooth, laminar flow
- Nonviscous

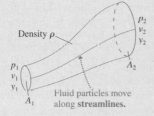

Fluid particles move along **streamlines**.

Equation of continuity

$$v_1 A_1 = v_2 A_2$$

Bernoulli's equation

$$p_1 + \tfrac{1}{2}\rho v_1^2 + \rho g y_1 = p_2 + \tfrac{1}{2}\rho v_2^2 + \rho g y_2$$

Bernoulli's equation is a statement of energy conservation.

Important Concepts

Density $\rho = m/V$, where m is mass and V is volume.

Pressure $p = F/A$, where F is the magnitude of the fluid force and A is the area on which the force acts.

- Pressure exists at all points in a fluid.
- Pressure pushes equally in all directions.
- Pressure is constant along a horizontal line.
- Gauge pressure is $p_g = p - 1$ atm.

Applications

Buoyancy is the upward force of a fluid on an object.

Archimedes' principle

The magnitude of the buoyant force equals the weight of the fluid displaced by the object.

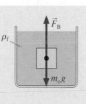

Sink	$\rho_{avg} > \rho_f$	$F_B < m_o g$
Rise to surface	$\rho_{avg} < \rho_f$	$F_B > m_o g$
Neutrally buoyant	$\rho_{avg} = \rho_f$	$F_B = m_o g$

Elasticity describes the deformation of solids and liquids under stress.

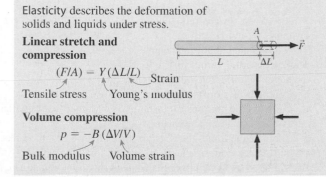

Linear stretch and compression

$$(F/A) = Y(\Delta L/L)$$

Tensile stress   Young's modulus

Volume compression

$$p = -B(\Delta V/V)$$

Bulk modulus   Volume strain

Terms and Notation

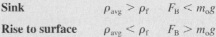

fluid	hydrostatic pressure	ideal-fluid model	Venturi tube
gas	Pascal's principle	viscosity	lift
liquid	gauge pressure, p_g	laminar flow	Young's modulus, Y
mass density, ρ	hydraulics	streamline	tensile stress
unit volume	buoyant force	flow tube	strain
pressure, p	displaced fluid	equation of continuity	volume stress
pascal, Pa	Archimedes' principle	volume flow rate, Q	volume strain
vacuum	average density, ρ_{avg}	Bernoulli's equation	bulk modulus, B
standard atmosphere, atm	neutral buoyancy		

CONCEPTUAL QUESTIONS

1. An object has density ρ.
   a. Suppose each of the object's three dimensions is increased by a factor of 2 without changing the material of which the object is made. Will the density change? If so, by what factor? Explain.
   b. Suppose each of the object's three dimensions is increased by a factor of 2 without changing the object's mass. Will the density change? If so, by what factor? Explain.

2. Rank in order, from largest to smallest, the pressures at a, b, and c in FIGURE Q15.2. Explain.

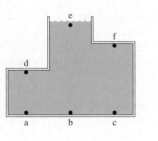

FIGURE Q15.2

3. Rank in order, from largest to smallest, the pressures at d, e, and f in FIGURE Q15.2. Explain.

4. FIGURE Q15.4 shows two rectangular tanks, A and B, full of water. They have equal depths and equal thicknesses (the dimension into the page) but different widths.

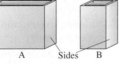

FIGURE Q15.4

   a. Compare the forces the water exerts on the bottoms of the tanks. Is F_A larger than, smaller than, or equal to F_B? Explain.
   b. Compare the forces the water exerts on the sides of the tanks. Is F_A larger than, smaller than, or equal to F_B? Explain.

5. In FIGURE Q15.5, is p_A larger than, smaller than, or equal to p_B? Explain.

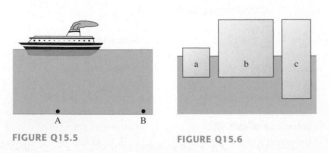

FIGURE Q15.5   **FIGURE Q15.6**

6. Rank in order, from largest to smallest, the densities of blocks a, b, and c in FIGURE Q15.6. Explain.

7. Blocks a, b, and c in FIGURE Q15.7 have the same volume. Rank in order, from largest to smallest, the sizes of the buoyant forces F_a, F_b, and F_c on a, b, and c. Explain.

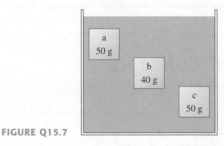

FIGURE Q15.7

8. Blocks a, b, and c in FIGURE Q15.7 have the same density. Rank in order, from largest to smallest, the sizes of the buoyant forces F_a, F_b, and F_c on a, b, and c. Explain.

9. The two identical beakers in FIGURE Q15.9 are filled to the same height with water. Beaker B has a plastic sphere floating in it. Which beaker, with all its contents, weighs more? Or are they equal? Explain.

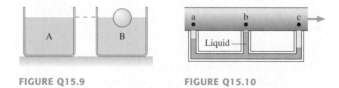

FIGURE Q15.9   **FIGURE Q15.10**

10. Gas flows through the pipe of FIGURE Q15.10. You can't see into the pipe to know how the inner diameter changes. Rank in order, from largest to smallest, the gas speeds v_a, v_b, and v_c at points a, b, and c. Explain.

11. Wind blows over the house in FIGURE Q15.11. A window on the ground floor is open. Is there an airflow through the house? If so, does the air flow in the window and out the chimney, or in the chimney and out the window? Explain.

FIGURE Q15.11

12. A 2000 N force stretches a wire by 1 mm. A second wire of the same material is twice as long and has twice the diameter. How much force is needed to stretch it by 1 mm? Explain.

13. A wire is stretched right to the breaking point by a 5000 N force. A longer wire made of the same material has the same diameter. Is the force that will stretch it right to the breaking point larger than, smaller than, or equal to 5000 N? Explain.

EXERCISES AND PROBLEMS

Exercises

Section 15.1 Fluids

1. || A 250 mL beaker holds 240 g of liquid. What is the liquid's density in SI units?
2. | Containers A and B have equal volumes. Container A holds helium gas at 1.0 atm pressure and 0°C. Container B is completely filled with a liquid whose mass is 7000 times the mass of helium gas in container A. Identify the liquid in container B.
3. | A 6 m × 12 m swimming pool slopes linearly from a 1.0 m depth at one end to a 3.0 m depth at the other. What is the mass of water in the pool?
4. || a. 50 g of gasoline are mixed with 50 g of water. What is the average density of the mixture?
   b. 50 cm³ of gasoline are mixed with 50 cm³ of water. What is the average density of the mixture?

Section 15.2 Pressure

5. | The deepest point in the ocean is 11 km below sea level, deeper than Mt. Everest is tall. What is the pressure in atmospheres at this depth?
6. || a. What volume of water has the same mass as 8.0 m³ of ethyl alcohol?
   b. If this volume of water is in a cubic tank, what is the pressure at the bottom?
7. || A 1.0-m-diameter vat of liquid is 2.0 m deep. The pressure at the bottom of the vat is 1.3 atm. What is the mass of the liquid in the vat?
8. || A 50-cm-thick layer of oil floats on a 120-cm-thick layer of water. What is the pressure at the bottom of the water layer?
9. || A research submarine has a 20-cm-diameter window 8.0 cm thick. The manufacturer says the window can withstand forces up to 1.0×10^6 N. What is the submarine's maximum safe depth? The pressure inside the submarine is maintained at 1.0 atm.
10. || A 20 cm diameter circular cover is placed over a 10-cm-diameter hole that leads into an evacuated chamber. The pressure in the chamber is 20 kPa. How much force is required to pull the cover off?

Section 15.3 Measuring and Using Pressure

11. | What is the height of a water barometer at atmospheric pressure?
12. || How far must a 2.0 cm-diameter piston be pushed down into one cylinder of a hydraulic lift to raise an 8.0-cm-diameter piston by 20 cm?
13. | What is the longest vertical soda straw you could possibly drink from?
14. || What is the minimum hose diameter of an ideal vacuum cleaner that could lift a 10 kg (22 lb) dog off the floor?

Section 15.4 Buoyancy

15. | A 6.0-cm-diameter sphere with a mass of 89.3 g is neutrally buoyant in a liquid. Identify the liquid.

16. | A 6.0-cm-tall cylinder floats in water with its axis perpendicular to the surface. The length of the cylinder above water is 2.0 cm. What is the cylinder's mass density?
17. | A sphere completely submerged in water is tethered to the bottom with a string. The tension in the string is one-third the weight of the sphere. What is the density of the sphere?
18. | A 5.0 kg rock whose density is 4800 kg/m³ is suspended by a string such that half of the rock's volume is under water. What is the tension in the string?
19. | What is the tension in the string?

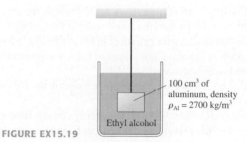

100 cm³ of aluminum, density $\rho_{Al} = 2700$ kg/m³

Ethyl alcohol

FIGURE EX15.19

20. | A 10-cm-diameter, 20-cm-tall steel cylinder ($\rho_{steel} = 7900$ kg/m³) floats in mercury. The axis of the cylinder is perpendicular to the surface. What length of steel is above the surface?
21. | You and your friends are playing in the swimming pool with a 60-cm-diameter beach ball. How much force would be needed to push the ball completely under water?
22. || Styrofoam has a density of 150 kg/m³. What is the maximum mass that can hang without sinking from a 50 cm diameter Styrofoam sphere in water? Assume the volume of the mass is negligible compared to that of the sphere.

Section 15.5 Fluid Dynamics

23. || Water flowing through a 2.0-cm-diameter pipe can fill a 300 L bathtub in 5.0 minutes. What is the speed of the water in the pipe?
24. || A 1.0-cm-diameter pipe widens to 2.0 cm, then narrows to 5.0 mm. Liquid flows through the first segment at a speed of 4.0 m/s.
   a. What is the speed in the second and third segments?
   b. What is the volume flow rate through the pipe?
25. || A long horizontal tube has a square cross section with sides of width L. A fluid moves through the tube with speed v_0. The tube then changes to a circular cross section with diameter L. What is the fluid's speed in the circular part of the tube?
26. || What does the top pressure gauge read?

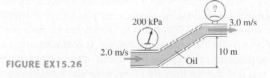

200 kPa   3.0 m/s

2.0 m/s   10 m

Oil

FIGURE EX15.26

Section 15.6 Elasticity

27. | An 80-cm-long, 1.0-mm-diameter steel guitar string must be tightened to a tension of 2000 N by turning the tuning screws. By how much is the string stretched?

28. | A 70 kg mountain climber dangling in a crevasse stretches a 50-m-long, 1.0-cm-diameter rope by 8.0 cm. What is Young's modulus for the rope?

29. || What hanging mass will stretch a 2.0-m-long, 0.50-mm-diameter steel wire by 1.0 mm?

30. || A 3.0-m-tall, 50-cm-diameter concrete column supports a 200,000 kg load. By how much is the column compressed?

31. | a. What is the pressure at a depth of 5000 m in the ocean?
    b. What is the fractional volume change $\Delta V/V$ of seawater at this pressure?
    c. What is the density of seawater at this pressure?

Problems

32. || A gymnasium is 16 m high. By what percent is the air pressure at the floor greater than the air pressure at the ceiling?

33. || The two 60-cm-diameter cylinders in **FIGURE P15.33**, closed at one end, open at the other, are joined to form a single cylinder, then the air inside is removed.
    a. How much force does the atmosphere exert on the flat end of each cylinder?
    b. Suppose one cylinder is bolted to a sturdy ceiling. How many 100 kg football players would need to hang from the lower cylinder to pull the two cylinders apart?

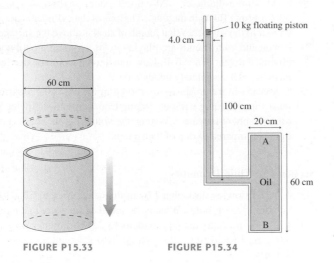

FIGURE P15.33   **FIGURE P15.34**

34. || a. In **FIGURE P15.34**, how much force does the fluid exert on the end of the cylinder at A?
    b. How much force does the fluid exert on the end of the cylinder at B?

35. || A friend asks you how much pressure is in your car tires. You know that the tire manufacturer recommends 30 psi, but it's been a while since you've checked. You can't find a tire gauge in the car, but you do find the owner's manual and a ruler. Fortunately, you've just finished taking physics, so you tell your friend, "I don't know, but I can figure it out." From the owner's manual you find that the car's mass is 1500 kg. It seems reasonable to assume that each tire supports one-fourth of the weight. With the ruler you find that the tires are 15 cm wide and the flattened segment of the tire in contact with the road is 13 cm long. What answer will you give your friend?

36. || A 2.0 mL syringe has an inner diameter of 6.0 mm, a needle inner diameter of 0.25 mm, and a plunger pad diameter (where you place your finger) of 1.2 cm. A nurse uses the syringe to inject medicine into a patient whose blood pressure is 140/100.
    a. What is the minimum force the nurse needs to apply to the syringe?
    b. The nurse empties the syringe in 2.0 s. What is the flow speed of the medicine through the needle?

37. || What is the total mass of the earth's atmosphere?

38. || Suppose the density of the earth's atmosphere were a constant 1.3 kg/m³, independent of height, until reaching the top. How thick would the atmosphere be?

39. || Your science teacher has assigned you the task of building a water barometer. You've learned that the pressure of the atmosphere can vary by as much as 5% from 1 standard atmosphere as the weather changes.
    a. What minimum height must your barometer have?
    b. One stormy day the TV weather person says, "The barometric pressure this afternoon is a low 29.55 inches." What is the height of the water in your barometer?

40. || The container shown in **FIGURE P15.40** is filled with oil. It is open to the atmosphere on the left.
    a. What is the pressure at point A?
    b. What is the pressure difference between points A and B? Between points A and C?

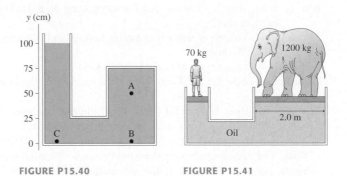

FIGURE P15.40   **FIGURE P15.41**

41. || a. The 70 kg student in **FIGURE P15.41** balances a 1200 kg elephant on a hydraulic lift. What is the diameter of the piston the student is standing on?
    b. A second 70 kg student joins the first student. How high do they lift the elephant?

42. || A 55 kg cheerleader uses an oil-filled hydraulic lift to hold four 110 kg football players at a height of 1.0 m. If her piston is 16 cm in diameter, what is the diameter of the football players' piston?

43. || Figure 15.19 showed a hydraulic lift with force $\vec{F}_1$ balancing force $\vec{F}_2$. Assume that force $\vec{F}_2$ is the unchanging weight mg of an object of mass m. Derive Equation 15.13, which states that the force *increment* needed to lift the weight through distance d_2 is $\Delta F = \rho g(A_1 + A_2)d_2$, where ρ is the density of the liquid.

44. || A U-shaped tube, open to the air on both ends, contains mercury. Water is poured into the left arm until the water column is 10.0 cm deep. How far upward from its initial position does the mercury in the right arm rise?

45. || Glycerin is poured into an open U-shaped tube until the height in both sides is 20 cm. Ethyl alcohol is then poured into one arm until the height of the alcohol column is 20 cm. The two liquids do not mix. What is the difference in height between the top surface of the glycerin and the top surface of the alcohol?

46. || Geologists place *tiltmeters* on the sides of volcanoes to measure the displacement of the surface as magma moves inside the volcano. Although most tiltmeters today are electronic, the traditional tiltmeter, used for decades, consisted of two or more water-filled metal cans placed some distance apart and connected by a hose. FIGURE P15.46 shows two such cans, each having a window to measure the water height. Suppose the cans are placed so that the water level in both is initially at the 5.0 cm mark. A week later, the water level in can 2 is at the 6.5 cm mark.
    a. Did can 2 move up or down relative to can 1? By what distance?
    b. Where is the water level now in can 1?

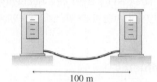

FIGURE P15.46   100 m

47. || Water stands at depth d behind a dam of width w.
    a. Find an expression for the net force of the water on the dam.
    b. Evaluate the net force on a 100-m-wide dam with a 60 m water depth.
    Hint: This problem requires an integration.

48. || An aquarium tank is 100 cm long, 35 cm wide, and 40 cm deep. It is filled to the top.
    a. What is the force of the water on the bottom (100 cm × 35 cm) of the tank?
    b. What is the force of the water on the front window (100 cm × 40 cm) of the tank?
    Hint: This problem requires an integration.

49. || It's possible to use the ideal-gas law to show that the density of the earth's atmosphere decreases exponentially with height. That is, $\rho = \rho_0 \exp(-z/z_0)$, where z is the height above sea level, ρ_0 is the density at sea level (you can use the Table 15.1 value), and z_0 is called the *scale height* of the atmosphere. (See Challenge Problem 76.)
    a. Determine the value of z_0.
    b. What is the density of the air in Denver, at an elevation of 1600 m? What percent of sea-level density is this?
    Hint: This problem requires an integration. What is the weight of a column of air?

50. | You need to determine the density of a ceramic statue. If you suspend it from a spring scale, the scale reads 28.4 N. If you then lower the statue into a tub of water, so that it is completely submerged, the scale reads 17.0 N. What is the statue's density?

51. || A cylinder with cross-section area A floats with its long axis vertical in a liquid of density ρ.
    a. Pressing down on the cylinder pushes it deeper into the liquid. Find an expression for the force needed to push the cylinder distance x deeper into the liquid and hold it there.
    b. A 4.0-cm-diameter cylinder floats in water. How much work must be done to push the cylinder 10 cm deeper into the water?
    Hint: An integration is required.

52. || A less-dense liquid of density ρ_1 floats on top of a more-dense liquid of density ρ_2. A uniform cylinder of length l and density ρ, with $\rho_1 < \rho < \rho_2$, floats at the interface with its long axis vertical. What fraction of the length is in the more-dense liquid?

53. || A 30-cm-tall, 4.0-cm-diameter plastic tube has a sealed bottom. 250 g of lead pellets are poured into the bottom of the tube, whose mass is 30 g, then the tube is lowered into a liquid. The tube floats with 5.0 cm extending above the surface. What is the density of the liquid?

54. || One day when you come into physics lab you find several plastic hemispheres floating like boats in a tank of fresh water. Each lab group is challenged to determine the heaviest rock that can be placed in the bottom of a plastic boat without sinking it. You get one try. Sinking the boat gets you no points, and the maximum number of points goes to the group that can place the heaviest rock without sinking. You begin by measuring one of the hemispheres, finding that it has a mass of 21 g and a diameter of 8.0 cm. What is the mass of the heaviest rock that, in perfectly still water, won't sink the plastic boat?

55. || A spring with spring constant 35 N/m is attached to the ceiling, and a 5.0-cm-diameter, 1.0 kg metal cylinder is attached to its lower end. The cylinder is held so that the spring is neither stretched nor compressed, then a tank of water is placed underneath with the surface of the water just touching the bottom of the cylinder. When released, the cylinder will oscillate a few times but, damped by the water, quickly reach an equilibrium position. When in equilibrium, what length of the cylinder is submerged?

56. || A 1.0 g balloon is filled with helium gas until it becomes a 20-cm-diameter sphere. What maximum mass can be tied to the balloon (with a massless string) without the balloon sinking to the floor?

57. || A 355 mL soda can is 6.2 cm in diameter and has a mass of 20 g. Such a soda can half full of water is floating upright in water. What length of the can is above the water level?

58. ||| The bottom of a steel "boat" is a 5.0 m × 10 m × 2.0 cm piece of steel ($\rho_{steel} = 7900$ kg/m^3). The sides are made of 0.50-cm-thick steel. What minimum height must the sides have for this boat to float in perfectly calm water?

59. || Water flows at 5.0 L/s through a horizontal pipe that narrows smoothly from 10 cm diameter to 5.0 cm diameter. A pressure gauge in the narrow section reads 50 kPa. What is the reading of a pressure gauge in the wide section?

60. || A nuclear power plant draws 3.0×10^6 L/min of cooling water from the ocean. If the water is drawn in through two parallel, 3.0-m-diameter pipes, what is the water speed in each pipe?

61. || Water flows from the pipe shown in the figure with a speed of 4.0 m/s.
    a. What is the water pressure as it exits into the air?
    b. What is the height h of the standing column of water?

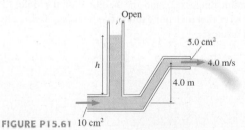

FIGURE P15.61 10 cm^2

62. || Water flowing out of a 16-mm-diameter faucet fills a 2.0 L bottle in 10 s. At what distance below the faucet has the water stream narrowed to 10 mm diameter?

63. || A hurricane wind blows across a 6.0 m × 15.0 m flat roof at a speed of 130 km/hr.
    a. Is the air pressure above the roof higher or lower than the pressure inside the house? Explain.
    b. What is the pressure difference?
    c. How much force is exerted on the roof? If the roof cannot withstand this much force, will it "blow in" or "blow out"?

64. || Air flows through this tube at a rate of 1200 cm³/s. Assume that air is an ideal fluid. What is the height h of mercury in the right side of the U-tube?

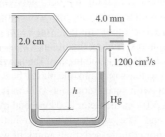

FIGURE P15.64

65. || Air flows through the tube shown in FIGURE P15.65. Assume that air is an ideal fluid.
    a. What are the air speeds v_1 and v_2 at points 1 and 2?
    b. What is the volume flow rate?

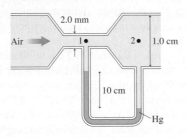

FIGURE P15.65

66. || A water tank of height h has a small hole at height y. The water is replenished to keep h from changing. The water squirting from the hole has range x. The range approaches zero as $y \to 0$ because the water squirts right onto the table. The range also approaches zero as $y \to h$ because the horizontal velocity becomes zero. Thus there must be some height y between 0 and h for which the range is a maximum.
    a. Find an algebraic expression for the flow speed v with which the water exits the hole at height y.
    b. Find an algebraic expression for the range of a particle shot horizontally from height y with speed v.
    c. Combine your expressions from parts a and b. Then find the maximum range x_{max} and the height y of the hole. "Real" water won't achieve quite this range because of viscosity, but it will be close.

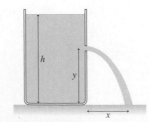

FIGURE P15.66

67. || A 4.0-mm-diameter hole is 1.0 m below the surface of a 2.0-m-diameter tank of water.
    a. What is the volume flow rate through the hole, in L/min?
    b. What is the rate, in mm/min, at which the water level in the tank will drop if the water is not replenished?

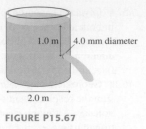

FIGURE P15.67

68. || A large 10,000 L aquarium is supported by four wood posts (Douglas fir) at the corners. Each post has a square 4.0 cm × 4.0 cm cross section and is 80 cm tall. By how much is each post compressed by the weight of the aquarium?

69. || At what ocean depth would the volume of an aluminum sphere be reduced by 0.10%?

70. || A cylindrical steel pressure vessel with volume 1.30 m³ is to be tested. The vessel is entirely filled with water, then a piston at one end of the cylinder is pushed in until the pressure inside the vessel has increased by 2000 kPa. Suddenly, a safety plug on the top bursts. How many liters of water come out?

Challenge Problems

71. The 1.0-m-tall cylinder in FIGURE CP15.71 contains air at a pressure of 1 atm. A very thin, frictionless piston of negligible mass is placed at the top of the cylinder, to prevent any air from escaping, then mercury is slowly poured into the cylinder until no more can be added without the cylinder overflowing. What is the height h of the column of compressed air?

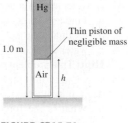

FIGURE CP15.71

    Hint: Boyle's law, which you learned in chemistry, says $p_1 V_1 = p_2 V_2$ for a gas compressed at constant temperature, which we will assume to be the case.

72. In FIGURE CP15.72, a cone of density ρ_o and total height l floats in a liquid of density ρ_f. The height of the cone above the liquid is h. What is the ratio h/l of the exposed height to the total height?

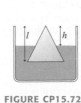

FIGURE CP15.72

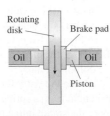

FIGURE CP15.73

73. Disk brakes, such as those in your car, operate by using pressurized oil to push outward on a piston. The piston, in turn, presses brake pads against a spinning rotor or wheel, as seen in FIGURE CP15.73. Consider a 15 kg industrial grinding wheel, 26 cm in diameter, spinning at 900 rpm. The brake pads are actuated by 2.0-cm-diameter pistons, and they contact the wheel an average distance 12 cm from the axis. If the coefficient of kinetic friction between the brake pad and the wheel is 0.60, what oil pressure is needed to stop the wheel in 5.0 s?

74. A cylinder of density ρ_o, length l, and cross-section area A floats in a liquid of density ρ_f with its axis perpendicular to the surface. Length h of the cylinder is submerged when the cylinder floats at rest.
    a. Show that $h = (\rho_o/\rho_f)l$.
    b. Suppose the cylinder is distance y *above* its equilibrium position. Find an expression for $(F_{net})_y$, the y-component of the net force on the cylinder. Use what you know to cancel terms and write this expression as simply as possible.
    c. You should recognize your result of part b as a version of Hooke's law. What is the "spring constant" k?
    d. If you push a floating object down and release it, it bobs up and down. So it is like a spring in the sense that it oscillates if displaced from equilibrium. Use your "spring constant" and what you know about simple harmonic motion to show that the cylinder's oscillation period is

$$T = 2\pi\sqrt{\frac{h}{g}}$$

    e. What is the oscillation period for a 100-m-tall iceberg ($\rho_{ice} = 917 \text{ kg/m}^3$) in seawater?
75. A cylindrical tank of diameter $2R$ contains water to a depth d. A small hole of diameter $2r$ is opened in the bottom of the tank. $r \ll R$, so the tank drains slowly. Find an expression for the time it takes to drain the tank completely.
76. The pressure of the atmosphere decreases with increasing elevation. Let's figure out how.
    a. Establish a z-axis that points up, with $z = 0$ at sea level. Suppose the pressure at height z is known to be p and the air density is ρ. Use the hydrostatic pressure equation to write an expression for the pressure at height $z + dz$, where dz is so small that the density has not changed. Your expression will

be in terms of p, ρ, dz, and perhaps some constants. The pressure *decreases* as you gain elevation, so be careful with signs.
    b. Using your expression from part a, write an expression for dp, the amount by which the pressure *changes* in going from z to $z + dz$. Pressure is decreasing, so your expression should be negative.
    c. You need to integrate your expression from part b, but you can't because the density ρ is not a constant. *If* the temperature remains constant, which we will assume, then the ideal-gas law implies that pressure is directly proportional to density. That is, $p/\rho = p_0/\rho_0$, where p_0 and ρ_0 are the sea-level values of pressure and density. Use this to rewrite your expression for dp in terms of p, dz, and various constants.
    d. Now you have an integrable expression, although you must first divide by p to get all the pressure terms on one side of the equation. Carry out the integration and use the fact that $p = p_0$ at $z = 0$ to determine the integration constant. Then solve for the pressure at height z. Your final result should be in the form $p = p_0\exp(-z/z_0)$.
    e. z_0 is called the *scale height* of the atmosphere. It is the height at which $p = e^{-1}p_0$, or about 37% of the sea-level pressure. Determine the numerical value of z_0.
    f. The lower layer of the atmosphere, called the troposphere, has a height of about 15,000 m. This is the region of the atmosphere where weather occurs. Above it is the stratosphere, where conditions are very different. Draw a graph of pressure versus height up to a height of 15,000 m.

Comment: We assumed a constant-temperature atmosphere. In the real atmosphere, the temperature in the troposphere decreases with increasing height. This alters how the pressure changes, but not enormously. Your result is a reasonably good approximation.

STOP TO THINK ANSWERS

Stop to Think 15.1: $\rho_a = \rho_b = \rho_c$. Density depends only on what the object is made of, not how big the pieces are.

Stop to Think 15.2: c. These are all open tubes, so the liquid rises to the same height in all three despite their different shapes.

Stop to Think 15.3: $F_b > F_a = F_c$. The masses in c do not add. The pressure underneath each of the two large pistons is mg/A_2, and the pressure under the small piston must be the same.

Stop to Think 15.4: b. The weight of the displaced water equals the weight of the ice cube. When the ice cube melts and turns into water, that amount of water will exactly fill the volume that the ice cube is now displacing.

Stop to Think 15.5: 1 cm³/s out. The fluid is incompressible, so the sum of what flows in must match the sum of what flows out. 13 cm³/s is known to be flowing in, while 12 cm³/s flows out. An additional 1 cm³/s must flow out to achieve balance.

Stop to Think 15.6: $h_b > h_d > h_c > h_a$. The liquid level is higher where the pressure is lower. The pressure is lower where the flow speed is higher. The flow speed is highest in the narrowest tube, zero in the open air.

Applications of Newtonian Mechanics

We have developed two parallel perspectives of motion, each with its own concepts and techniques. We focused on the first of these in Part I, where we dealt with the relationship between force and motion. Newton's second law is the principle most central to the force/motion perspective. Then, in Part II, we developed a before-and-after perspective based on the idea of conservation laws. Newton's laws were essential in the development of conservation laws, but they remain hidden in the background when the conservation laws are applied. Together, these two perspectives form the heart of Newtonian mechanics.

Our goal in Part III has been to see how Newtonian mechanics is applied to several diverse but important topics. We added only one new law of physics in Part III, Newton's law of gravity, and we introduced few completely new concepts. Instead, we've broadened our understanding of the

force/motion perspective and the conservation-law perspective through our investigations of rotational motion, gravity, oscillations, and fluids. In reviewing Part III, pay close attention to the interplay between these two perspectives. Recognizing which is the best tool in a particular situation will help you improve your problem-solving ability.

Our knowledge of mechanics is now essentially complete. We will add a few additional ideas as we need them, but our journey into physics will be taking us in entirely new directions as we continue on. Hence this is an opportune moment to step back a bit to take a look at the "big picture." Newtonian mechanics may seem all very factual and straightforward to us today, but keep in mind that these ideas are all human inventions. There was a time when they did not exist and when our concepts of nature were quite different from what they are today.

KNOWLEDGE STRUCTURE III Applications of Newtonian Mechanics

Rotation of a Rigid Body

A rigid body is a system of particles.
Rotational motion is analogous to linear motion.

Rotational motion	Linear motion
Angular acceleration α	Acceleration a
Torque τ	Force F
Moment of inertia I	Mass m
Angular momentum L	Momentum p

- **Newton's second law** $\tau_{net} = I\alpha$
- **Rotational kinetic energy** $K = \frac{1}{2}I\omega^2$

Newton's Theory of Gravity

Any two masses exert attractive gravitational forces on each other.

Newton's law of gravity is

$$F_{m \text{ on } M} = F_{M \text{ on } m} = \frac{GMm}{r^2}$$

- Kepler's laws describe the elliptical orbits of satellites and planets.

- The gravitational potential energy is

$$U_g = -\frac{GMm}{r}$$

NEWTON'S LAWS
+
CONSERVATION LAWS

Oscillations

Systems with a linear restoring force exhibit simple harmonic oscillation.

- The **kinematic equations of SHM** are

$$x(t) = A\cos(\omega t + \phi_0)$$
$$v(t) = -v_{max}\sin(\omega t + \phi_0)$$

where $v_{max} = \omega A$ and the phase constant ϕ_0 describes the initial conditions.

- **Energy is transformed between kinetic and potential** as the system oscillates. In an undamped system, the total mechanical energy

$$E = \frac{1}{2}mv^2 + \frac{1}{2}kx^2 = \frac{1}{2}m(v_{max})^2 = \frac{1}{2}kA^2$$

is conserved.

Fluids and Elasticity

Fluids are systems that flow. Gases and liquids are fluids. Fluids are better characterized by density and pressure than by mass and force.

- **Liquids** Pressure is primarily gravitational. The hydrostatic pressure is

$$p = p_0 + \rho g d$$

- **Gases** Pressure is primarily thermal. Pressure in a container is constant.

- **Archimedes' principle** The buoyant force is equal to the weight of the displaced fluid.

For fluid flow, **Bernoulli's equation**

$$p_1 + \frac{1}{2}\rho v_1^2 + \rho g y_1 = p_2 + \frac{1}{2}\rho v_2^2 + \rho g y_2$$

is really a statement of energy conservation.

The Newtonian Synthesis

Newton's achievements, praised by no less than Einstein as "perhaps the greatest advance in thought that a single individual was ever privileged to make," are often called the *Newtonian synthesis*. "Synthesis" means "the uniting or combining of separate elements to form a coherent whole." It is often said of Newton that he "united the heavens and the earth." In doing so, he changed forever the way we view ourselves and our relationship to the universe.

As we noted in Chapter 13, medieval cosmology considered the heavenly bodies to be perfect, unchanging objects quite unrelated to imperfect and changeable earthly matter. Their perfection and immortality symbolized the perfection of God above, while the material bodies of humans were imperfect and mortal. This cosmology was mirrored in medieval feudal society. The king—ordained by God and whose symbol was the sun—was surrounded by a small circle of nobles and a larger circle of serfs and peasants. Taken together, the ideas and institutions of science, religion, and society of this time form what we call the medieval *worldview*. Their worldview, in its many facets, was hierarchical and authoritarian, reflecting their understanding of "natural order" in the universe.

Copernicus weakened medieval cosmology by questioning the position of the earth in the universe. Galileo, with his telescope, found that the heavens are not perfect and unchanging. Now, at the end of the 17th century, the success of Newton's theories implied that the sun and the planets were merely ordinary matter, obeying the same natural laws as earthly matter. This uniting of earthly motions and heavenly motions—the *synthesis* in the Newtonian synthesis—dealt the final blow to the medieval worldview.

Newton's success changed the way we see and think about the universe. Rather than seeing whirling celestial spheres, people began to think of the universe in terms of the motion of material particles following rigid laws. This Newtonian conception of the cosmos is often called a "clockwork universe." The technology of clocks was progressing rapidly in the 18th century, and people everywhere admired the consistency and predictability of these little machines. The Newtonian universe is a very large machine, but one that is consistent, predictable, and law-abiding. In other words, a perfect clock.

Major thinkers of the 17th and 18th centuries soon concluded that God had created the world by placing all the particles in their original positions, then giving them a push to get them going. God, in this role, was called the "prime mover." But once the universe was started, it went along perfectly well just by obeying Newton's laws. No divine intervention or guidance was needed. This is certainly a very different view of our relationship to God and the universe than was contained in the medieval worldview.

Newton also influenced the way people think about themselves and their society. His theories clearly demonstrated that the universe is not random or capricious but, instead, follows natural laws. Others soon began to apply the concept of natural law to human nature, human behavior, and human institutions. The main protagonist in this school of thought was the English philosopher and political scientist John Locke, a contemporary of Newton. Locke developed a theory of human behavior from the ideas of natural laws and empirical evidence. We cannot go into Locke's theories here, but Newton's success helped to propel Locke's ideas into the mainstream of 18th-century political thought.

Locke's writings had a great influence on a young American named Thomas Jefferson. The concept of natural laws, as they apply to individuals, is very much behind Jefferson's enunciation of "unalienable rights" in the Declaration of Independence. In fact, the first sentence of the Declaration refers explicitly to "the Laws of Nature and of Nature's God." The idea of *checks and balances,* built into the Constitution of the United States, is very much a mechanical and clock-like model of how political institutions function.

Just as medieval feudalism mirrored the medieval understanding of the universe, contemporary constitutional democracy mirrors, in many ways, the Newtonian cosmology. Hierarchy and authority have been replaced by equality and law because they now seem to us the "natural order" of things. Having grown up with this modern worldview, we find it difficult to imagine any other. Nonetheless, it is important to realize that vastly different worldviews have existed at other times and in other cultures.

Science has changed dramatically in the last hundred-odd years. Newton's clockwork universe has been superseded by relativity and quantum physics. Entirely new theories and sciences, such as evolution, ecology, and psychology, have appeared. These new ideas are slowly working their way into other areas of thought and human activity, and bit by bit they are changing the ways in which we see ourselves, our society, and our relationship to nature. A future worldview is in the making.

Mathematics Review

Algebra

Using exponents:
$$a^{-x} = \frac{1}{a^x} \qquad a^x a^y = a^{(x+y)} \qquad \frac{a^x}{a^y} = a^{(x-y)} \qquad (a^x)^y = a^{xy}$$

$$a^0 = 1 \qquad a^1 = a \qquad a^{1/n} = \sqrt[n]{a}$$

Fractions:
$$\left(\frac{a}{b}\right)\left(\frac{c}{d}\right) = \frac{ac}{bd} \qquad \frac{a/b}{c/d} = \frac{ad}{bc} \qquad \frac{1}{1/a} = a$$

Logarithms:
If $a = e^x$, then $\ln(a) = x$ $\qquad\qquad \ln(e^x) = x \qquad\qquad e^{\ln(x)} = x$

$$\ln(ab) = \ln(a) + \ln(b) \qquad \ln\left(\frac{a}{b}\right) = \ln(a) - \ln(b) \qquad \ln(a^n) = n\ln(a)$$

The expression $\ln(a + b)$ cannot be simplified.

Linear equations: The graph of the equation $y = ax + b$ is a straight line. a is the slope of the graph. b is the y-intercept.

Proportionality: To say that y is proportional to x, written $y \propto x$, means that $y = ax$, where a is a constant. Proportionality is a special case of linearity. A graph of a proportional relationship is a straight line that passes through the origin. If $y \propto x$, then

$$\frac{y_1}{y_2} = \frac{x_1}{x_2}$$

Slope $a = \dfrac{\text{rise}}{\text{run}} = \dfrac{\Delta y}{\Delta x}$

Δy

Δx

y-intercept $= b$

Quadratic equation: The quadratic equation $ax^2 + bx + c = 0$ has the two solutions $x = \dfrac{-b \pm \sqrt{b^2 - 4ac}}{2a}$.

Geometry and Trigonometry

Area and volume:

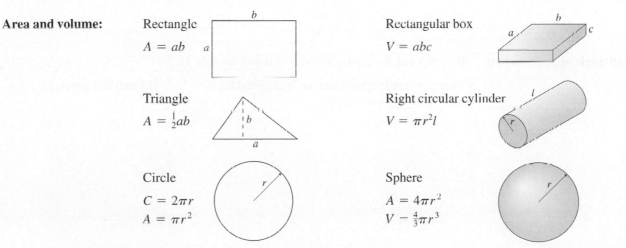

Rectangle
$$A = ab$$

Triangle
$$A = \tfrac{1}{2}ab$$

Circle
$$C = 2\pi r$$
$$A = \pi r^2$$

Rectangular box
$$V = abc$$

Right circular cylinder
$$V = \pi r^2 l$$

Sphere
$$A = 4\pi r^2$$
$$V = \tfrac{4}{3}\pi r^3$$

Arc length and angle: The angle θ in radians is defined as $\theta = s/r$.

The arc length that spans angle θ is $s = r\theta$.

2π rad $= 360°$

Right triangle: Pythagorean theorem $c = \sqrt{a^2 + b^2}$ or $a^2 + b^2 = c^2$

$$\sin\theta = \frac{b}{c} = \frac{\text{far side}}{\text{hypotenuse}} \qquad \theta = \sin^{-1}\left(\frac{b}{c}\right)$$

$$\cos\theta = \frac{a}{c} = \frac{\text{adjacent side}}{\text{hypotenuse}} \qquad \theta = \cos^{-1}\left(\frac{a}{c}\right)$$

$$\tan\theta = \frac{b}{a} = \frac{\text{far side}}{\text{adjacent side}} \qquad \theta = \tan^{-1}\left(\frac{b}{a}\right)$$

General triangle: $\alpha + \beta + \gamma = 180° = \pi$ rad

Law of cosines $c^2 = a^2 + b^2 - 2ab\cos\gamma$

Identities:

$$\tan\alpha = \frac{\sin\alpha}{\cos\alpha} \qquad\qquad\qquad \sin^2\alpha + \cos^2\alpha = 1$$

$$\sin(-\alpha) = -\sin\alpha \qquad\qquad \cos(-\alpha) = \cos\alpha$$

$$\sin(\alpha \pm \beta) = \sin\alpha\cos\beta \pm \cos\alpha\sin\beta \qquad \cos(\alpha \pm \beta) = \cos\alpha\cos\beta \mp \sin\alpha\sin\beta$$

$$\sin(2\alpha) = 2\sin\alpha\cos\alpha \qquad\qquad \cos(2\alpha) = \cos^2\alpha - \sin^2\alpha$$

$$\sin(\alpha \pm \pi/2) = \pm\cos\alpha \qquad\qquad \cos(\alpha \pm \pi/2) = \mp\sin\alpha$$

$$\sin(\alpha \pm \pi) = -\sin\alpha \qquad\qquad \cos(\alpha \pm \pi) = -\cos\alpha$$

Expansions and Approximations

Binomial expansion: $(1 + x)^n = 1 + nx + \dfrac{n(n-1)}{2}x^2 + \cdots$

Binomial approximation: $(1 + x)^n \approx 1 + nx$ if $x \ll 1$

Trigonometric expansions: $\sin\alpha = \alpha - \dfrac{\alpha^3}{3!} + \dfrac{\alpha^5}{5!} - \dfrac{\alpha^7}{7!} + \cdots$ for α in rad

$\cos\alpha = 1 - \dfrac{\alpha^2}{2!} + \dfrac{\alpha^4}{4!} - \dfrac{\alpha^6}{6!} + \cdots$ for α in rad

Small-angle approximation: If $\alpha \ll 1$ rad, then $\sin\alpha \approx \tan\alpha \approx \alpha$ and $\cos\alpha \approx 1$.

The small-angle approximation is excellent for $\alpha < 5°$ (≈ 0.1 rad) and generally acceptable up to $\alpha \approx 10°$.

Calculus

The letters a and n represent constants in the following derivatives and integrals.

Derivatives

$$\frac{d}{dx}(a) = 0$$

$$\frac{d}{dx}(ax) = a$$

$$\frac{d}{dx}\left(\frac{a}{x}\right) = -\frac{a}{x^2}$$

$$\frac{d}{dx}(ax^n) = anx^{n-1}$$

$$\frac{d}{dx}(\ln(ax)) = \frac{1}{x}$$

$$\frac{d}{dx}(e^{ax}) = ae^{ax}$$

$$\frac{d}{dx}(\sin(ax)) = a\cos(ax)$$

$$\frac{d}{dx}(\cos(ax)) = -a\sin(ax)$$

Integrals

$$\int x\,dx = \frac{1}{2}x^2$$

$$\int x^2\,dx = \frac{1}{3}x^3$$

$$\int \frac{1}{x^2}\,dx = -\frac{1}{x}$$

$$\int x^n\,dx = \frac{x^{n+1}}{n+1} \qquad n \neq -1$$

$$\int \frac{dx}{x} = \ln x$$

$$\int \frac{dx}{a+x} = \ln(a+x)$$

$$\int \frac{x\,dx}{a+x} = x - a\ln(a+x)$$

$$\int \frac{dx}{\sqrt{x^2 \pm a^2}} = \ln\left(x + \sqrt{x^2 \pm a^2}\right)$$

$$\int \frac{x\,dx}{\sqrt{x^2 \pm a^2}} = \sqrt{x^2 \pm a^2}$$

$$\int \frac{dx}{x^2 + a^2} = \frac{1}{a}\tan^{-1}\left(\frac{x}{a}\right)$$

$$\int \frac{dx}{(x^2 + a^2)^2} = \frac{1}{2a^3}\tan^{-1}\left(\frac{x}{a}\right) + \frac{x}{2a^2(x^2 + a^2)}$$

$$\int \frac{dx}{(x^2 \pm a^2)^{3/2}} = \frac{\pm x}{a^2\sqrt{x^2 \pm a^2}}$$

$$\int \frac{x\,dx}{(x^2 \pm a^2)^{3/2}} = -\frac{1}{\sqrt{x^2 \pm a^2}}$$

$$\int e^{ax}\,dx = \frac{1}{a}e^{ax}$$

$$\int xe^{ax}\,dx = \frac{1}{a^2}e^{ax}(ax - 1)$$

$$\int \sin(ax)\,dx = -\frac{1}{a}\cos(ax)$$

$$\int \cos(ax)\,dx = \frac{1}{a}\sin(ax)$$

$$\int \sin^2(ax)\,dx = \frac{x}{2} - \frac{\sin(2ax)}{4a}$$

$$\int \cos^2(ax)\,dx = \frac{x}{2} + \frac{\sin(2ax)}{4a}$$

$$\int_0^\infty x^n e^{-ax}\,dx = \frac{n!}{a^{n+1}}$$

$$\int_0^\infty e^{-ax^2}\,dx = \frac{1}{2}\sqrt{\frac{\pi}{a}}$$

Periodic Table of Elements

Atomic number — 27
Co — Symbol
58.9 — Atomic mass

Transition elements

Inner transition elements

Period																		
1	1 H 1.0																	2 He 4.0
2	3 Li 6.9	4 Be 9.0										5 B 10.8	6 C 12.0	7 N 14.0	8 O 16.0	9 F 19.0	10 Ne 20.2
3	11 Na 23.0	12 Mg 24.3										13 Al 27.0	14 Si 28.1	15 P 31.0	16 S 32.1	17 Cl 35.5	18 Ar 39.9
4	19 K 39.1	20 Ca 40.1	21 Sc 45.0	22 Ti 47.9	23 V 50.9	24 Cr 52.0	25 Mn 54.9	26 Fe 55.8	27 Co 58.9	28 Ni 58.7	29 Cu 63.5	30 Zn 65.4	31 Ga 69.7	32 Ge 72.6	33 As 74.9	34 Se 79.0	35 Br 79.9	36 Kr 83.8
5	37 Rb 85.5	38 Sr 87.6	39 Y 88.9	40 Zr 91.2	41 Nb 92.9	42 Mo 95.9	43 Tc 96.9	44 Ru 101.1	45 Rh 102.9	46 Pd 106.4	47 Ag 107.9	48 Cd 112.4	49 In 114.8	50 Sn 118.7	51 Sb 121.8	52 Te 127.6	53 I 126.9	54 Xe 131.3
6	55 Cs 132.9	56 Ba 137.3	57 La 138.9	72 Hf 178.5	73 Ta 180.9	74 W 183.9	75 Re 186.2	76 Os 190.2	77 Ir 192.2	78 Pt 195.1	79 Au 197.0	80 Hg 200.6	81 Tl 204.4	82 Pb 207.2	83 Bi 209.0	84 Po 209.0	85 At 210.0	86 Rn 222.0
7	87 Fr 223.0	88 Ra 226.0	89 Ac 227.0	104 Rf 261	105 Db 262	106 Sg 263	107 Bh 264	108 Hs 269	109 Mt 268	110 Ds 271	111 Rg 272	112 285						

Lanthanides 6	58 Ce 140.1	59 Pr 140.9	60 Nd 144.2	61 Pm 144.9	62 Sm 150.4	63 Eu 152.0	64 Gd 157.3	65 Tb 158.9	66 Dy 162.5	67 Ho 164.9	68 Er 167.3	69 Tm 168.9	70 Yb 173.0	71 Lu 175.0
Actinides 7	90 Th 232.0	91 Pa 231.0	92 U 238.0	93 Np 237.0	94 Pu 239.1	95 Am 241.1	96 Cm 244.1	97 Bk 249.1	98 Cf 252.1	99 Es 257.1	100 Fm 257.1	101 Md 258.1	102 No 259.1	103 Lr 262.1

Answers

Answers to Odd-Numbered Exercises and Problems

Chapter 1

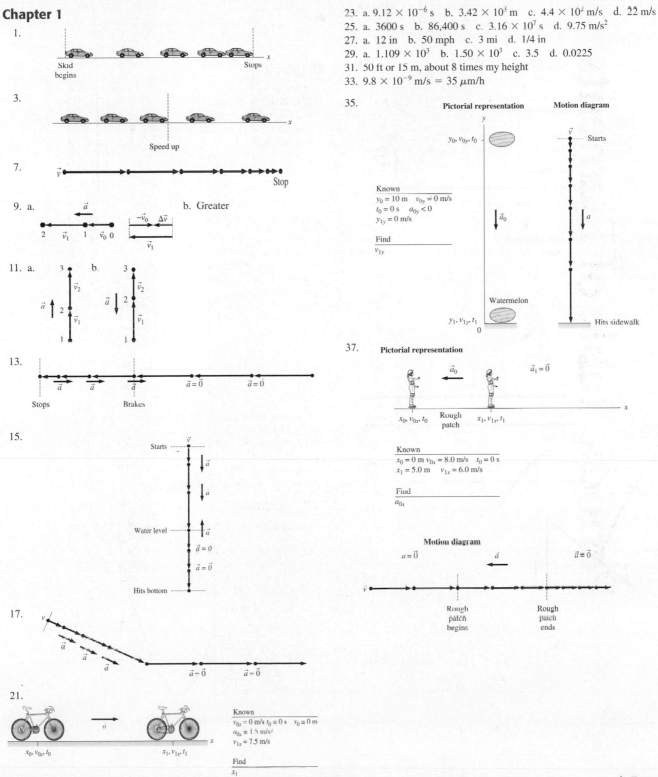

1.

3.

7.

9. a.   b. Greater

11. a.   b.

13.

15.

17.

21.

23. a. 9.12×10^{-6} s   b. 3.42×10^3 m   c. 4.4×10^2 m/s   d. 22 m/s
25. a. 3600 s   b. 86,400 s   c. 3.16×10^7 s   d. 9.75 m/s^2
27. a. 12 in   b. 50 mph   c. 3 mi   d. 1/4 in
29. a. 1.109×10^3 b. 1.50×10^3 c. 3.5   d. 0.0225
31. 50 ft or 15 m, about 8 times my height
33. 9.8×10^{-9} m/s $= 35$ μm/h

35.

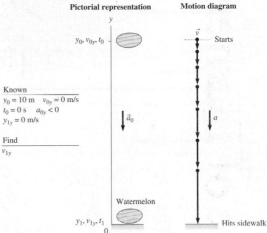

37.

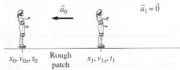

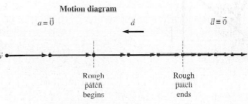

39.

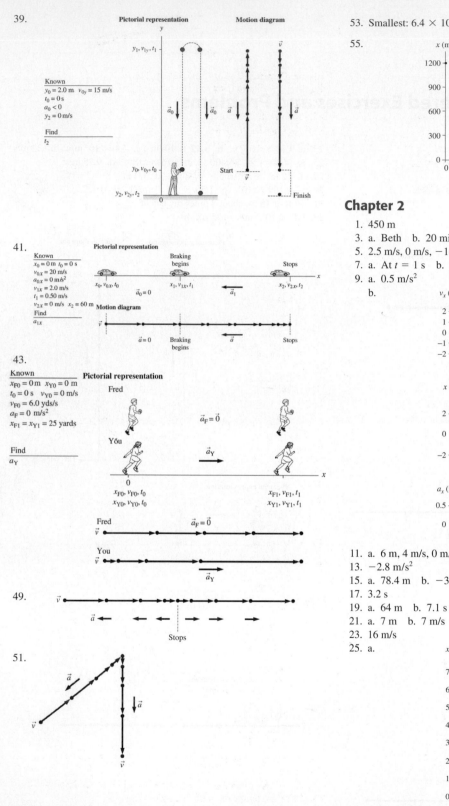

53. Smallest: 6.4×10^3 m², largest: 8.3×10^3 m²

55.

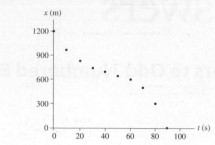

41.

43.

49.

51.

Chapter 2

1. 450 m
3. a. Beth   b. 20 min
5. 2.5 m/s, 0 m/s, −10 m/s
7. a. At $t = 1$ s   b. 10 m, 16 m, 26 m
9. a. 0.5 m/s²

b.

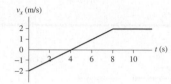

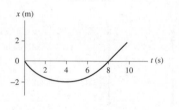

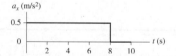

11. a. 6 m, 4 m/s, 0 m/s²   b. 13.0 m, 2 m/s, −2 m/s
13. −2.8 m/s²
15. a. 78.4 m   b. −39.2 m/s
17. 3.2 s
19. a. 64 m   b. 7.1 s
21. a. 7 m   b. 7 m/s   c. 7 m/s²
23. 16 m/s
25. a.

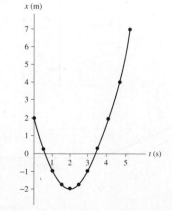

c. −2 m/s   d. −2 m   e. 2 m

f.

Turn
around at
$t = 2.0$ s

$\vec{a} \longrightarrow$

$\vec{v}$

a

$\vec{v}$

27. a. 4 s, 8 s

   b. $\vec{v}$

   Turning point
   at $t = 6$ s

   $\vec{a}$

   $\vec{v}$

29. a. Zero at $t = 0$ s, 1 s, 2 s, 3 s, ...; most positive at
   $t = 0.5$ s, 2.5 s, ...; most negative at $t = 1.5$ s, 3.5 s, ...

   b. v_y

   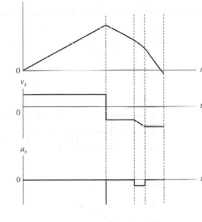

31. a. 0 s and 3 s   b. 12 m and −18 m/s²; −15 m and 18 m/s²
33. 2.0 m/s³
35.

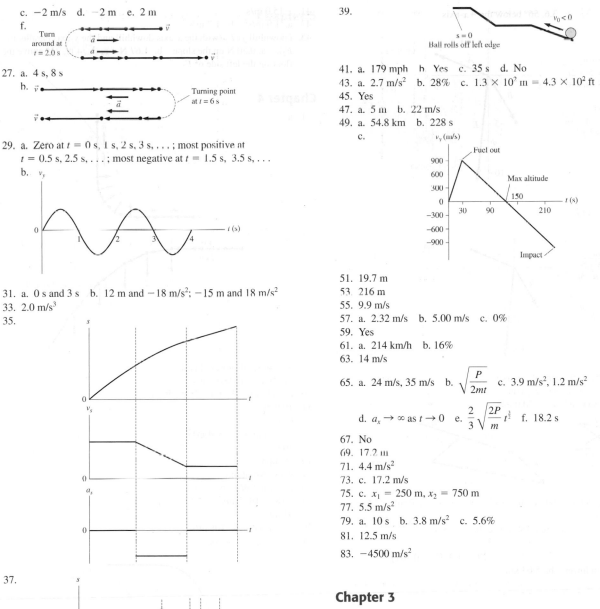

37.

39.
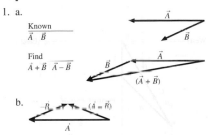

$v_0 < 0$

$s = 0$
Ball rolls off left edge

41. a. 179 mph   b. Yes   c. 35 s   d. No
43. a. 2.7 m/s²   b. 28%   c. 1.3×10^7 m $= 4.3 \times 10^2$ ft
45. Yes
47. a. 5 m   b. 22 m/s
49. a. 54.8 km   b. 228 s

   c. v_y (m/s)

                        Fuel out

   900

   600   Max altitude

   300
                        150
   0   t (s)
              30   90   210
   −300

   −600

   −900
                   Impact

51. 19.7 m
53. 216 m
55. 9.9 m/s
57. a. 2.32 m/s   b. 5.00 m/s   c. 0%
59. Yes
61. a. 214 km/h   b. 16%
63. 14 m/s

65. a. 24 m/s, 35 m/s   b. $\sqrt{\dfrac{P}{2mt}}$ c. 3.9 m/s², 1.2 m/s²

   d. $a_x \to \infty$ as $t \to 0$ e. $\dfrac{2}{3}\sqrt{\dfrac{2P}{m}}\, t^{\frac{3}{2}}$ f. 18.2 s

67. No
69. 17.2 m
71. 4.4 m/s²
73. c. 17.2 m/s
75. c. $x_1 = 250$ m, $x_2 = 750$ m
77. 5.5 m/s²
79. a. 10 s   b. 3.8 m/s²   c. 5.6%
81. 12.5 m/s
83. −4500 m/s²

Chapter 3

1. a.

   Known
   $\vec{A}$ $\vec{B}$

   Find
   $\vec{A} + \vec{B}$ $\vec{A} - \vec{B}$

   $\vec{A}$

   $\vec{B}$

   $\vec{B}$

   $\vec{A}$

   $(\vec{A} + \vec{B})$

   b.

   $-\vec{B}$ $(\vec{A} - \vec{B})$

   $\vec{A}$

3. a. $-E\cos\theta, E\sin\theta$ b. $E_x = E\sin\psi, E_y = E\cos\psi$
5. 12 m/s
7. a. −5 cm/s, 0 cm/s   b. −6.4 m/s², −7.7 m/s²   c. 30 N, 40 N
9. 280 V/m, 63.4° below the +x-axis
11. a. 7.21, 56.3° below the +x-axis
    b. 94.3 m, 58.0° above the +x-axis
    c. 44.7 m/s, 63.4° above the −x-axis
    d. 6.3 m/s², 18.4° right of the −y-axis

31.

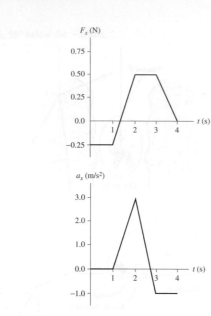

F_x (N)

0.75

0.50

0.25

0.00

t (s)

1 2 3 4

−0.25

33.

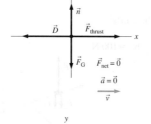

a_x (m/s²)

3.0

2.0

1.0

0.0   t (s)

1 2 3 4

−1.0

35. a. 16 m/s² b. 4 m/s² c. 8 m/s² d. 32 m/s²

37.

y

$\vec{n}$

$\vec{D}$ $\vec{F}_{thrust}$ x

$\vec{F}_G$ $\vec{F}_{net} = \vec{0}$

$\vec{a} = \vec{0}$

$\vec{v}$

39.

y

x

$\vec{F}_G$ $\vec{F}_{net}$ $\vec{a}$

41.

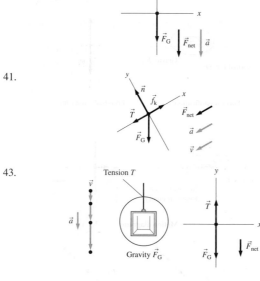

y

$\vec{n}$

$\vec{f}_k$ x

$\vec{T}$ $\vec{F}_{net}$

$\vec{F}_G$ $\vec{a}$

$\vec{v}$

43.

Tension T

$\vec{v}$

$\vec{a}$

y

$\vec{T}$

x

Gravity $\vec{F}_G$ $\vec{F}_G$ $\vec{F}_{net}$

45.

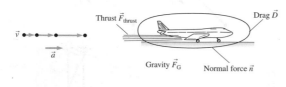

Thrust $\vec{F}_{thrust}$ Drag $\vec{D}$

$\vec{v}$

$\vec{a}$

Gravity $\vec{F}_G$ Normal force $\vec{n}$

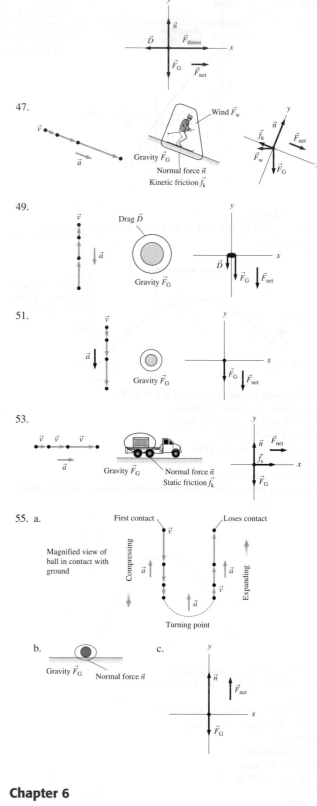

y

$\vec{n}$

$\vec{D}$ $\vec{F}_{thrust}$ x

$\vec{F}_G$ $\vec{F}_{net}$

47.

$\vec{v}$ Wind $\vec{F}_w$ y

$\vec{n}$

$\vec{f}_k$ $\vec{F}_{net}$

$\vec{a}$ Gravity $\vec{F}_G$ $\vec{F}_w$ x

Normal force $\vec{n}$ $\vec{F}_G$

Kinetic friction $\vec{f}_k$

49.

$\vec{v}$ Drag $\vec{D}$ y

$\vec{a}$ x

$\vec{D}$

Gravity $\vec{F}_G$ $\vec{F}_G$ $\vec{F}_{net}$

51.

$\vec{v}$ y

$\vec{a}$ x

Gravity $\vec{F}_G$ $\vec{F}_G$ $\vec{F}_{net}$

53.

$\vec{v}$ $\vec{v}$ $\vec{v}$ y

$\vec{n}$ $\vec{F}_{net}$

$\vec{a}$ $\vec{f}_s$ x

Gravity $\vec{F}_G$ Normal force $\vec{n}$ $\vec{F}_G$

Static friction $\vec{f}_k$

55. a.

First contact   Loses contact

$\vec{v}$

Magnified view of
ball in contact with
ground

Compressing $\vec{a}$ $\vec{a}$ Expanding

$\vec{v}$

$\vec{a}$

Turning point

b.   c.

y

Gravity $\vec{F}_G$ Normal force $\vec{n}$

$\vec{n}$ $\vec{F}_{net}$

x

$\vec{F}_G$

Chapter 6

1. $T_1 = 86.7$ N, $T_2 = 50.0$ N
3. 147 N
5. a. $a_x = 1.0$ m/s², $a_y = 0$ b. $a_x = 1.0$ m/s², $a_y = 0$
7. a. $a_x = 0.40$ m/s², $a_y = 0.0$ m/s²
   b. $a_x = 0.80$ m/s², $a_y = 0.0$ m/s²

9. 4 m/s, 0 m/s²
11. a. 490 N   b. 490 N   c. 740 N   d. 240 N
13. 307 N
15. a. 590 N   b. 740 N   c. 590 N
17. 0.250
19. a.   c. 4.9 m/s²

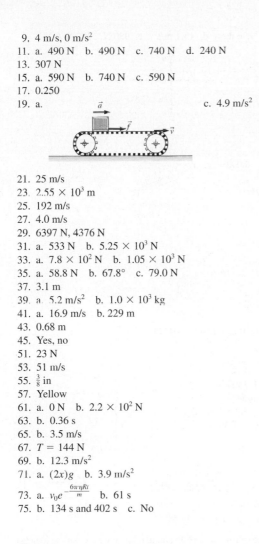

21. 25 m/s
23. 2.55 × 10³ m
25. 192 m/s
27. 4.0 m/s
29. 6397 N, 4376 N
31. a. 533 N   b. 5.25 × 10³ N
33. a. 7.8 × 10² N   b. 1.05 × 10³ N
35. a. 58.8 N   b. 67.8°   c. 79.0 N
37. 3.1 m
39. a. 5.2 m/s²   b. 1.0 × 10³ kg
41. a. 16.9 m/s   b. 229 m
43. 0.68 m
45. Yes, no
51. 23 N
53. 51 m/s
55. $\frac{3}{8}$ in
57. Yellow
61. a. 0 N   b. 2.2 × 10² N
63. b. 0.36 s
65. b. 3.5 m/s
67. $T = 144$ N
69. b. 12.3 m/s²
71. a. $(2x)g$ b. 3.9 m/s²
73. a. $v_0 e^{-\frac{6\pi\eta Rt}{m}}$ b. 61 s
75. b. 134 s and 402 s   c. No

Chapter 7

1. a.

Interaction diagram

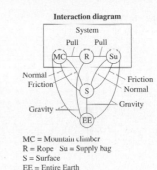

BB – Barbells
WL – Weight lifter
S = Surface   EE = Entire Earth

b. The system is the weightlifter and barbell
c.   **Free-body diagrams**

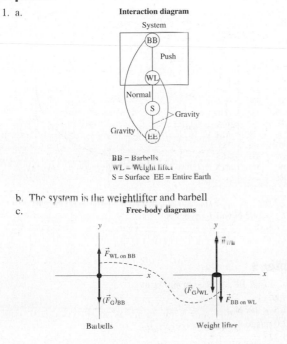

Barbells   Weight lifter

3. a.

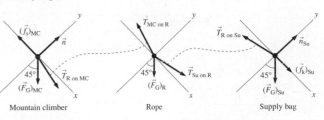

MC = Mountain climber
R = Rope   Su = Supply bag
S = Surface
EE = Entire Earth

b. The system consists of the mountain climber, rope, and bag of supplies
c.

Free-body diagrams

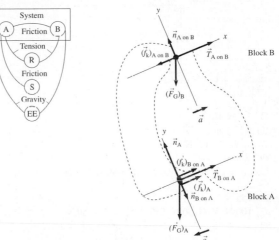

Mountain climber   Rope   Supply bag

5. a.   **Interaction diagram**   **Free-body diagrams**

b. The system consists of the two blocks

c.   **Interaction diagram**   **Free-body diagrams**

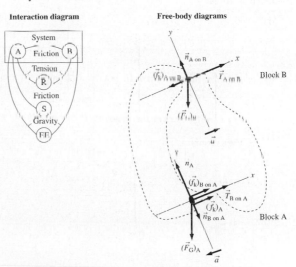

7. a. 7.8×10^2 N   b. 1.6×10^3 N
9. a. 3000 N   b. 3000 N
11. 5 kg
13. a.

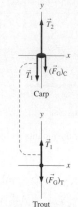

Carp

Trout

b. $T_2 > T_1 > (F_G)_T > (F_G)_C$
15. 9800 N
17. 67 N, 36°
19. 42 m apart
21.

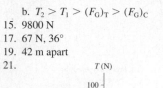

23. 2.7×10^2 N
25. 6.533 m/s^2
27. a. 2.3×10^2 N   b. 0.20 m/s
29. 1.48 s
31. a. 32 N   b. 19.2 N   c. 16.0 N   d. 3.2 N
33. 1.75 s
35. 155 N
37. 100 N, 50 N, 50 N, 150 N, 50 N, $F = 50$ N
39. a. 1.83 kg   b. 1.32 m/s^2
41. a. 0.67 m   b. slides back down
43. a. 8.2×10^3 N   b. 4.8×10^2 N
45. 3.6×10^3 N
47. a.

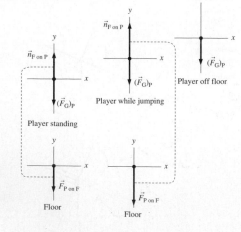

Player standing

Player while jumping

Player off floor

Floor

Floor

b. Yes   c. 3.96 m/s   d. 13.1 m/s^2 e. 980 N, 2290 N, 0 N
49. b. 0.47 m
51. $a_1 = \dfrac{2m_2 g}{4m_1 + m_2}$
53. b. 8.99 N

Chapter 8

1. 39 m
3. a. 56 h   b. 0.092°   c. Yes
5. 6.8 kN
7. 6.6×10^{15} rev/s
9. 2.01×10^{20} N
11. 1.58 m/s^2
13. 22 m/s
15. 3
17. 30 rpm
19. a. 2.0 rad/s^2 b. 1.6 s
21. $1.67x^2$
23. Crocodile food
25. 3.0 m
27. a. 24.0 h   b. 0.223 m/s^2 c. 0 N
29. 179 N
31. 34 m/s
33. No
35. a. 5.00 N   b. 30 rpm
37. Horizontal circle
39. a. 4.9 N   b. 2.9 N   c. 32 N
41. a. 3.2×10^2 N, 1.4 kN   b. 5.7 s
43. 30 rpm
45. 45.0 s
47. 2.6 m
49. 13.1 N
51. a. 6.6 rad/s   b. 43 N
53. b. $\omega = 20$ rad/s
55. a. $\theta = \frac{1}{2} \tan^{-1}(mg/F)$ b. 11.5%

57. a. Rotate the spacecraft 153.4° counterclockwise so that the exhaust is 26.6° below the positive x-axis. Fire with a thrust of 103,300 N for 433 s.
   b.

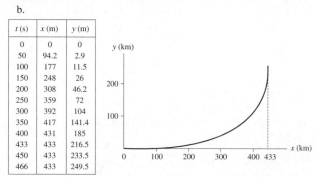

t (s)	x (m)	y (m)
0	0	0
50	94.2	2.9
100	177	11.5
150	248	26
200	308	46.2
250	359	72
300	392	104
350	417	141.4
400	431	185
433	433	216.5
450	433	233.5
466	433	249.5

59. 3.7 rev
61. $T_1 = 14.2$ N and $T_2 = 8.3$ N
63. 37 km

Chapter 9

1. a. 1.5×10^4 kg m/s   b. 8.0 kg m/s
3. 4 N s
5. 1.5×10^3 N
7. 2.0 m/s to the right
9. 1.22 s

11. 9.6×10^2 N
13. 0.20 s
15. 5.0×10^2 kg
17. 4.8 m/s
19. 3.0×10^2 m/s
21. 0.20 m/s
23. $(-2\hat{i} + 4\hat{j})$ kg m/s
25. $(1.08, 0.63)$ kg m/s when thrown, $(1.08, 0)$ kg m/s at the top, $(1.08, -0.63)$ kg m/s just before hitting the ground
27. 51 m/s
29. 9.3×10^2 N
31. 0.50 m
33. 8.0×10^2 N
35. 2.13 m/s, up
37. a. 12.0 s   b. 42° north of west
39. 14.1 m/s, 45° east of north
41. 4.4×10^2 m/s
43. 28 m/s
45. 4.0×10^2 m
47. a. 286 μs, 26 kN   b. 0.021 m/s
49. 27.8 m/s
51. 1.46×10^7 m/s in the forward direction
53. 4.5 km
55. 14.0 u
57. b. and c. 1.40×10^{-22} kg m/s in the direction of the electron
59. 0.85 m/s, 72° below $+x$
61. 1.97×10^3 m/s
63. c. $(v_{ix})_2 = 6.0$ m/s
65. c. $(v_{fx})_1 = -12$ m/s
67. 13.6 m
69. 1226 m/s
71. 8

Chapter 10

1. The bullet
3. 112 km/h
5. a. 25.1 m   b. 10 m/s   c. 22 m/s
7. 2.0
9. 7.7 m/s
11. a. 1.40 m/s   b. 30°
13. 1.41 m/s
15. 98 N/m
17. a. 49 N   b. 1.45×10^3 N/m   c. 3.4 cm
19. 10 J
21. 2.0 m/s
23. 3.0 m/s
25. 0.86 m/s and 2.9 m/s
27. a. $0.048v_0$ b. 95%
29. a. Right   b. 17.3 m/s   c. $x = 1.0$ m and 6.0 m
31. 63 m/s
33. Yes
35. a. No   b. 17.3 m/s
37. c. 2.0×10^2 N/m   d. 19 m/s
39. $v_0/\sqrt{2}$
41. 51 cm
43. 25.8 cm
45. a. 0.20 m   b. 0.10 m
47. 93 cm
49. 43 m
51. a. $\sqrt{\dfrac{(m + M)kd^2}{m^2}}$ b. 2.0×10^2 m/s   c. 0.9975
53. a. $\frac{3}{2}R$ b. 15 m
55. a. 3.5 m   b. No, height
57. a. 100 g ball: -5.3 m/s; the 200 g ball: 1.7 m/s   b. -0.67 m/s

59. a. $x = 1$ m and $x = 7$ m   b. 4.0 m/s   c. 6.9 m/s
61. a. $x_1 = \dfrac{\pi}{3}$ and $x_2 = \dfrac{2\pi}{3}$ b. $\dfrac{\pi}{3}$: unstable, $\dfrac{2\pi}{3}$: stable
65. c. 36 N/m
67. c. 2.6 m/s
69. $\theta = 80.4°$
71. a. 1.46 m   b. 19.6 cm
73. a. 4.6 cm   b. $v_{A3} = 1.33$ m/s and $v_{B3} = 5.3$ m/s
75. 100 g ball rebounds to 79°, 200 g ball rebounds to 14.7°

Chapter 11

1. a. 15.3   b. -4.0 c. 0
3. a. -30 b. 0
5. a. 162°   b. 90°
7. a. 12.0 J   b. 6.0 J
9. 0 J
11. 1.250×10^4 J by the gravity, -7.92×10^3 J by $\vec{T}_1$, -4.58×10^3 J by $\vec{T}_2$
13. AB: 0 J, BC: 0 J, CD: -4.0 J, DE: $+4.0$ J, EF: -3.0 J
15. 7.35 m/s, 9.17 m/s, 9.70 m/s
17. 8.0 N
19. -20 N at $x = 1$ m, 30 N at $x = 4$ m
21. a.
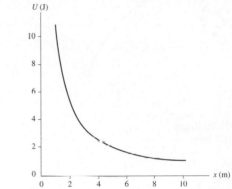
b. 2.5 N, 0.40 N, and 0.156 N
23. 1360 m/s
25. b. 5.5×10^2 J
27.
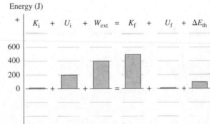
29. 6.26 m/s
31. a. 176 J b. 59 W
33. Night light
35. b. 0.41 kW, 0.83 kW, 1.25 kW
37. a.
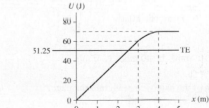

b. 51.25 J   d. 2.56 m

39.

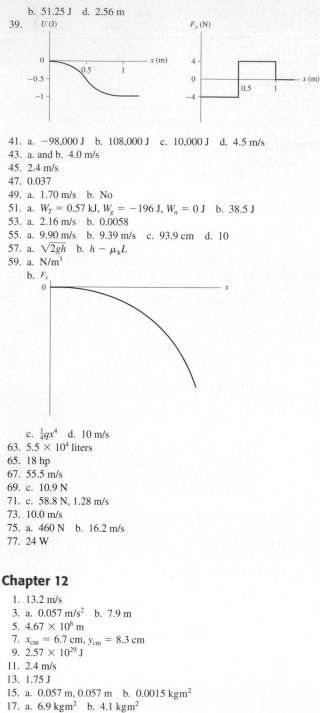

41. a. −98,000 J   b. 108,000 J   c. 10,000 J   d. 4.5 m/s
43. a. and b. 4.0 m/s
45. 2.4 m/s
47. 0.037
49. a. 1.70 m/s   b. No
51. a. $W_T = 0.57$ kJ, $W_g = -196$ J, $W_n = 0$ J   b. 38.5 J
53. a. 2.16 m/s   b. 0.0058
55. a. 9.90 m/s   b. 9.39 m/s   c. 93.9 cm   d. 10
57. a. $\sqrt{2gh}$ b. $h - \mu_k L$
59. a. N/m³
b. F_x

c. $\frac{1}{4}qx^4$ d. 10 m/s
63. 5.5×10^4 liters
65. 18 hp
67. 55.5 m/s
69. c. 10.9 N
71. c. 58.8 N, 1.28 m/s
73. 10.0 m/s
75. a. 460 N   b. 16.2 m/s
77. 24 W

Chapter 12

1. 13.2 m/s
3. a. 0.057 m/s²   b. 7.9 m
5. 4.67×10^6 m
7. $x_{cm} = 6.7$ cm, $y_{cm} = 8.3$ cm
9. 2.57×10^{29} J
11. 2.4 m/s
13. 1.75 J
15. a. 0.057 m, 0.057 m   b. 0.0015 kg m²
17. a. 6.9 kg m²   b. 4.1 kg m²
19. −0.20 N m
21. 176 N
23. 12.5 kN m
25. 8.0 N m
27. 0.28 N m
29. a. 1.75×10^{-3} N m   b. 50 rev
31. 11.76 N m
33. 1.40 m
35. a. 6.4×10^2 rpm   b. 40 m/s   c. 0 m/s
37. a. 88 rad/s   b. $\frac{2}{7}$
39. a. (21, out of the page)   b. (24, into the page)
41. a. $-\hat{j}$ b. $\vec{0}$
43. a. $n\hat{i}$ b. $2\hat{j}$ c. $1\hat{k}$

45. $50\hat{k}$ N m
47. $1.20\hat{k}$ kg m²/s or (1.20 kg m²/s, out of page)
49. (0.025 kg m²/s, into page) (or $-0.025\hat{i}$ kg m²/s)
51. 28 m/s
53. 20 cm, 0 cm
55. a. 0.010 kg m²   b. 0.030 kg m²
59. $\frac{1}{6}ML^2$
61. 51°
63. Yes
65. Yes because $d_{max} = 25L/24$
67. a. 3.4 m/s   b. 3.4 m/s
69. a. 177 s   b. 5.6×10^5 J   c. 1.4×10^5 W   d. 1.30 kN m

71. a. $a = \dfrac{m_2 g}{m_1 + m_2}, T = \dfrac{m_1 m_2 g}{m_1 + m_2}$

b. $a = \dfrac{m_2 g}{m_1 + m_2 + \frac{1}{2}m_p}$ $T_1 = \dfrac{m_1 m_2 g}{m_1 + m_2 + \frac{1}{2}m_p}$

$T_2 = \dfrac{m_2 (m_1 + \frac{1}{2}m_p)g}{m_1 + m_2 + \frac{1}{2}m_p}$

73. a. 57.9 m   b. 0.23 rad/s
75. a. $\dfrac{m}{m + M}L$ b. Center of mass
77. a. $\sqrt{2g/r}$ b. $\sqrt{8gR}$

79. $\dfrac{20Tr}{13MR^2}$

81. a. No   b. 2000 m/s   c. 4000 m/s
83. 3.9×10^2 m/s
85. a. 43 cm
87. 50 rpm
89. 4.0 rpm
91. $2.7(R - r)$
93. $\frac{1}{5}v_0$ to the right
95. a. 137 km   b. 8.6×10^6 m/s

Chapter 13

1. 6.00×10^{-4}
3. 2.18
5. 2.3×10^{-7} N
7. a. 274 m/s²   b. 5.90×10^{-3} m/s²
9. 2.43 km
11. a. 3.0×10^{24} kg   b. 0.89 m/s²
13. 60.2 km/s
15. 4.21×10^4 m/s
17. 4.37×10^{11} m, 1.74×10^4 m/s
19. a. 1.48×10^{25} kg   b. 5.2×10^{30} kg
21. 2.9×10^9 m
23. 4.2 h
25. 46 kg and 104 kg
27. (11.7 cm, 0 cm)
29. $3.0 \times 10^{-7}\hat{j}$ N
31. -1.96×10^{-7} J
33. a. 3.02 km/s   b. 3.13 km/s   c. 3.6%
35. a. 2.8×10^6 m   b. 3.7 km/s
37. a. 11.3 km/s   b. 8.94 km/s
39. Yes
41. 12.2 km/s
43. $0.516(GM/R)^{1/2}$, $1.032(GM/R)^{1/2}$
45. 3.71×10^5 m/s
47. 1.17×10^{11} J
49. a. 5.8×10^{22} kg   b. 1.33×10^6 m
51. 8.67×10^7 m
53. a. $y = (q/p)x + (\log C)/p$ b. Linear   c. q/p e. 1.996×10^{30} kg

55. a. 6.3×10^4 m/s   b. 1.33×10^{12} m/s^2 c. 1.33×10^{12} N
    d. 9.5×10^4 orbits/minute   e. 1.50×10^6 m
57. 9.33×10^{10} m
59. 3.71 km/s
61. 4.49 km/s
63. a. No   b. Yes
65. c. 6.21×10^7 m
67. c. 1680 m/s
69. b. 282 days
71. a. $0°$ b. 4.04 N
73. a. 24 years   b. 12.3 km/s, 4.1 km/s
75. b. 7730 m/s, 10,160 m/s   c. 2.17×10^{10} J   d. 1600 m/s, 3070 m/s
    e. 3.43×10^9 J   f. 2.513×10^{10} J

77. a. $-\dfrac{GmM}{\sqrt{x^2 + R^2}}$ b. $GmM\dfrac{x}{(x^2 + R^2)^{3/2}}$

Chapter 14

1. 2.27 ms
3. a. 12.7 cm   b. 9.0 cm
5. a. 20 cm   b. 0.25 Hz   c. $-60°$
7.

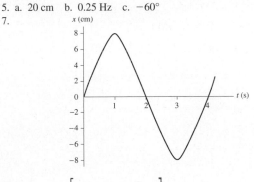

9. $(8.0 \text{ cm})\cos\left[(\pi \text{ rad/s})t + \dfrac{\pi}{2}\text{rad}\right]$

11. a. 2.8 s   b. 1.41 s   c. 2.0 s   d. 1.41 s
13. a. 0.50 s   b. 4π rad/s   c. 5.54 cm   d. 0.45 rad   e. 70 cm/s
    f. 8.8 m/s^2 g. 0.049 J   h. 3.8 cm
15. a. 10.0 cm   b. 35 cm/s
17. 3.5 Hz
19. a. 4.0 s   b. 5.7 s   c. 2.8 s   d. 4.0 s
21. 36 cm
23. 0.330 m
25. 3.1×10^{-2} kg m^2
27. 5.0 s
29. 1853, 0.780 m
31. a. $\frac{2}{3}\pi$ rad   b. -13.6 cm/s   c. 15.7 cm/s
33. a. 0.25 Hz, 3.0 s   b. 6.0 s, 1.5 s   c. 2.25
35. 1.405 s, x (m)

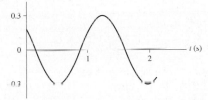

37. 0.096 s
41. a. 2.00 rad/s   b. 15.0 cm
43. a. 10.1 μm   b. 64 m/s

45. a. 1.38 m/s   b. No
47. 1.58 Hz
49. a. 4.7×10^4 N/m   b. 1.80 Hz
51. 0.59 m
53. 1.02×10^{-21} kg
55. 0.67 s

59. $\dfrac{1}{2\pi}\sqrt{\dfrac{g}{2R}}$

61. 0.110 m, 1.72 s
63. 0.62 Hz
65. 7.9×10^{13} Hz
67. a. Highest point   b. 2.5 Hz
69. a. 9.5 N/m   b. 0.50 m/s   c. $b = 0.0104$ kg/s
71. 236 oscillations
75. 1.58 Hz
77. 1.83 Hz
79. 2.23 cm

Chapter 15

1. 960 kg/m^3
3. 1.44×10^5 kg
5. 1.10×10^3 atmospheres
7. 2.4×10^3 kg
9. 3.2 km
11. 10.3 m
13. 10.3 m
15. 7.9×10^2 kg/m^3; ethyl alcohol
17. 750 kg/m^3
19. 1.87 N
21. 1.11 kN
23. 3.2 m/s
27. 1.02 cm
29. 2.0 kg
31. a. 5.057×10^7 Pa   b. -0.025 c. 1056 kg/m^3
33. a. 2.9×10^4 N   b. 30 players
35. 27 psi
37. 5.27×10^{18} kg
39. a. 10.85 m   b. 10.21 m
41. a. 0.48 m   b. 2.3 cm
45. 7.5 cm
47. a. $\frac{1}{2}\rho gwd^2$ b. 1.76×10^9 N
49. a. 8080 m   b. 1.05 kg/m^3, 82%
51. a. $\rho_{\text{liq}}Agx$ b. 0.62 J
53. 8.9×10^2 kg/m^3
55. 18.1 cm
57. 5.2 cm
59. 53 kPa
61. a. p_{atmos} b. 4.6 m
63. a. Lower   b. 0.83 kPa   c. 7.5×10^4 N, out
65. a. $v_1 = 144$ m/s, $v_2 = 5.8$ m/s   b. 4.5×10^{-3} m^3/s
67. a. 3.3 L/min   b. 1.06 mm/min
69. 6.9 km
71. 76 cm
73. 53 kPa

75. $\dfrac{R^2}{r^2}\sqrt{\dfrac{2d}{g}}$

Credits

Index